THE ALLIED
OCCUPATION OF *Japan*
1945–1952

THE ALLIED OCCUPATION

Compiled and edited for the
Joint Committee on Japanese Studies of the
Social Science Research Council–
American Council of Learned Societies
and the Center for Japanese Studies of
the University of Michigan by

Chicago 1974

OF *Japan*

1945–1952

An Annotated Bibliography of Western-Language Materials

ROBERT E. WARD and FRANK JOSEPH SHULMAN
   with the assistance of MASASHI NISHIHARA
   and MARY TOBIN ESPEY

AMERICAN LIBRARY ASSOCIATION

This work has been published as a companion volume to Sakamoto Yoshikazu, et al., comp. *Nihon senryō bunken mokuroku* (A Bibliography on the Allied Occupation of Japan). Tokyo: Nihon Gakujutsu Shinkōkai (Japan Society for the Promotion of Science), 1972. xxiv, 349p.

Library of Congress Cataloging in Publication Data

Ward, Robert Edward.
    The Allied occupation of Japan, 1945–1952.

    1. Japan—History—Allied occupation, 1945–1952—Bibliography. I. Shulman, Frank Joseph, 1943– joint author. II. Joint Committee on Japanese Studies. III. Michigan. University. Center for Japanese Studies. IV. Title.
Z3308.A5W35   016.95204   73-8772
ISBN 0-8389-0127-1

Copyright © 1974 by the American Library Association
    All rights reserved. No part of this publication may be reproduced in any form without permission in writing from the publisher, except by a reviewer who may quote brief passages in a review.

Printed in the United States of America

This volume is dedicated to our Japanese colleagues and friends who compiled the companion volume on Japanese-language sources relating to the Occupation, and to the advancement of the types of collaborative research between Japanese and American scholars that both volumes so well exemplify.

Contents

Foreword, by John Richardson	xi
Introduction	xiii
Abbreviations	xix
Bibliographies	1
Major Newspaper and Periodical Sources	11
Archival Materials	20
Presurrender Planning before 2 September 1945	33
Planning in the United States	34
In Official Quarters	34
In Private Quarters	39
Planning in Japan	62
Planning Elsewhere	71
Major International Conferences and High-Level Diplomacy	81
Biographical Literature	91
Materials Associated with SCAP Headquarters	97
Training Arrangements in the United States for the Military Government of Japan	100
The Decision to Use Atomic Weapons	104
General Collections of Official Documents, Speeches, etc.	108

Contents

The Occupation Period, 2 September 1945–28 April 1952	112
General Materials	113
Supreme Commander for the Allied Powers (SCAP)	
Situation and Progress Reports	113
SCAP Official History of the Occupation	123
SCAP Reports by Subordinate Headquarters	137
SCAP Press Releases and Conferences	141
SCAP Analyses and Translations of the Japanese Press	142
SCAP Administrative Directives to the Japanese Government	145
General Collections of Official Documents	148
Calendar of General Commentaries, 1945–72	152
1945	152
1946	162
1947	178
1948	192
1949	205
1950	215
1951	222
1952	231
1953–72	235
International Aspects	260
Foreign Policies of the United States and Other Nations	260
International Participation	281
Organization, Staff, Functions	296
The Supreme Commander for the Allied Powers	311
Douglas MacArthur	311
Primary Materials	311
Secondary Materials	318
Matthew B. Ridgway	328
Punitive and Precautionary Aspects	329
Territorial Dismemberment of the Japanese Empire	329
The Demilitarization Program	335
The War Crimes Trials	340
Official Documentation	341
Unofficial Commentaries	351
The Purge	374
Reparations Payments	379
The Repatriation Program	391

Contents

Political, Legal, and Administrative Aspects	396
Constitutional Change	397
The Imperial System	414
Changes in the Legal System	424
The Judicial System	435
Local Government and Administration	441
Changes in the Police System	448
Political Parties and Elections	452
Administrative Organization and the Bureaucracy	473
Economic Aspects	480
Calendar of General Commentaries on the Economy and SCAP's Role Within It, 1946–72	481
1946	481
1947	485
1948	490
1949	499
1950	513
1951	518
1952	523
1953–72	527
Taxation	538
Land Reform	544
Labor Unions and Labor Conditions	559
The *Zaibatsu* Deconcentration Program	576
Natural Resources in General	586
Agriculture, Fisheries, and Forestry	591
Textiles, Power, and Other Industries	603
Other Areas of Occupation Participation	611
Japanese Social Organization and National Character	611
Population Problems	632
The Educational System	638
Mass Media and Censorship	678
Public Health, Welfare, and Social Security	687
Religion	694
Miscellaneous	705
Japanese Reactions	716
Termination of the Occupation	727
The Peace Treaty, 1947–72	728

Contents

	1947	728
	1948	735
	1949	738
	1950	740
	1951	746
	1952	772
	1953–72	777
	The Security Treaty, Administrative Agreement, and Japanese Rearmament	781
	Japan's Reentry into the Postwar World	797
Author Index		805
Periodical Index		821
Appendix: List of High-Ranking Occupation Personnel		835
Introduction		835
Abbreviations of Rank Designations		836
Classified List		837
Organizational Charts of SCAP Headquarters		853
	Military Government Section	855
	Staff Functions of SCAP (AG omitted) October 1945	856
	General Headquarters, SCAP, Toyko, Japan, 26 August 1946	857
	General Headquarters, SCAP, Tokyo, Japan, 10 September 1947	858
	General Headquarters, SCAP, Tokyo, Japan, 5 June 1948	859
	General Headquarters, SCAP, Tokyo, Japan, 23 July 1949	860
	General Headquarters, SCAP, Tokyo, Japan, 1950	861
	General Headquarters, SCAP, Tokyo, Japan, 1951	862
Personnel Name Index		863

Foreword

This volume represents the first research project completed under the auspices of the Joint Committee on U.S.–Japan Cultural and Educational Cooperation. This standing committee promotes Japanese and American cooperation in the fields of education, culture, communications, and mutual understanding. It provides a continuing forum for cultural cooperation between the biennial conferences on Educational and Cultural Interchange between the two countries.

The American research for this publication was supported in part by a grant from the U.S. Department of State's Bureau of Educational and Cultural Affairs. A companion volume in Japanese was supported by the Ministry of Education in Japan.

It is appropriate that this first joint research effort should focus on that period when the American and Japanese societies became most closely enmeshed: the Allied Occupation of Japan from 2 September 1945 to 28 April 1952.

It seems strange that there has been so little systematic study of this period by the scholars of any country. The American attempt to introduce quickly and peacefully such far-reaching social, political, economic, and psychological changes into a totally alien and war-torn foreign society, and then to withdraw from the position of authority, must be unique in history. A study of the period reveals much about American social and political methods and motivations. And for an understanding of the new Japanese society—so different, yet derived from the old—it is fascinating to analyze the relative influences exerted by Japanese attitudes of toleration, welcome, suspicion, acceptance, rejection, adaptation, or confirmation of the changes introduced from the outside world.

It is our belief in the Department of State that these materials and their Japanese counterparts will be helpful in shedding new light on this important period of history and our hope that they will further the cooperation and collabo-

Foreword

ration between Japanese and Americans that is both a product of this better mutual understanding and the genesis for this study.

JOHN RICHARDSON, JR.
Assistant Secretary of State

Introduction

As recognition of the accomplishments and capacities of postwar Japan spreads throughout the West, so too does interest in the national history that underlies and explains this remarkable record. No single segment of that history is more seminal or fascinating than the period of the Allied occupation of Japan: 2 September 1945 to 28 April 1952—some six years and eight months long. While it is true that no major episode in a nation's history is ever truly discontinuous with the past, there are periods of extraordinary innovation when change is more salient than continuity, particularly in the consciousness of the population concerned. The occupation years were such a period for Japan.

Not since early Meiji times (1868–90) had the Japanese people been subjected to such a spate of new and profoundly disturbing experiences. Never in recorded history had they been defeated in a major war; never had they been subject to a foreign occupation; and not since the post-Restoration period had they been exposed to so systematic and sweeping an endeavor to bring about fundamental changes in their social institutions, values, attitudes, and behavior. Furthermore, on this occasion the basic initiatives and control lay not with Japanese leaders but with the power that was primarily responsible for Japan's defeat in World War II: the United States of America, operating through an agent known as the Supreme Commander for the Allied Powers (SCAP).

Although legally and technically an Allied occupation, the occupation of Japan was in every meaningful sense almost completely American in genesis and control. With the exception of the postwar territorial dismemberment of the Japanese empire and two largely empty gestures toward international participation in the form of the Far Eastern Commission and the Allied Council for Japan, the United States organized, staffed, and directed all aspects of the postwar military regime in Japan.

Introduction

The most remarkable aspect of this American occupation of postwar Japan was the scope and complexity of its endeavors. Far more than the rewriting of statutes or tinkering with the forms of parliamentary government were involved. The occupation literally set about to remake Japanese society along more peaceable and democratic lines. A new constitution was written and enacted. The nation was disarmed. Women and youth were enfranchised. Labor was encouraged to organize and bargain collectively. The structure and practice of private business were substantially altered. The system of land tenure and ownership in the countryside was drastically revised. The ranks of the country's political and economic leadership were purged and reorganized. Existing legal and social relationships within the Japanese family system and society in general were scrutinized, found wanting, and new dispositions were authorized and supported by law. The public educational system was thoroughly shaken up and redesigned from kindergarten through graduate school. The mass media were subjected simultaneously to both censorship and encouragement to play a freer and more positive role in a new society. Governmentally supported religious organizations were disestablished. In short, very few groups or institutions escaped some degree of occupation attention and intervention during this eighty-month period. As a consequence, the structure and operations of Japanese society were significantly altered.

Not all of these endeavors were successful. Indeed, SCAP itself changed its mind about the desirability of some of them during the course of the occupation. The Japanese successfully modified or subverted some programs well before the conclusion of the peace treaty and substantially revised or eliminated others after 1952. On balance, however, the number of major political, economic, and social changes initiated or stimulated by the occupation that survive today is truly surprising. Their longevity, of course, is due more to the fact that in time they acquired either support or toleration from the Japanese people and government than to the initial role which SCAP played. Some such external catalyst, nonetheless, was essential at the outset. In this sense it may be said that the occupation is seminal to an understanding of the emergence of the New Japan of the 1970s.

Under these circumstances it is an interesting comment on the ways of academics that the occupation period has attracted so little scholarly attention to date. While we do not lack a substantial literature in English, Japanese, and certain other languages about developments in Japan during these early postwar years—as the following pages will make clear—a very small proportion of this is a product of serious, systematic scholarship. The vast bulk is contemporary or soon-after-the-fact description and commentary by journalists, participants, or more casual observers. Much of the writing by professional scholars is not notably different from this in intent or quality. Particularly notable is the paucity of attempts to look systematically at the occupation as a whole or in major part, to relate it organically to previous and subsequent developments, to assess its role and contributions to modern Japanese history, or to analyze it in terms of the larger lessons it may provide with respect to the process of planned social and political change on an intensive and nationwide scale. Viewed in this last context, the occupation of Japan is certainly one of the most promising case studies afforded by modern history.

It is hoped that this annotated bibliography, together with its companion volume of Japanese-language materials on the occupation, will serve both to stimulate and assist scholarly studies along these neglected lines. The undertaking has been a collaborative one—initiated, planned, and carried out jointly by Japanese and American scholars. It originated at a meeting of a subcommittee of the Department of State's Committee on Educational and Cultural Relations with Japan and a counterpart group from the Japan Society for the Promotion of Science (Nihon Gakujutsu Shinkōkai) held in Honolulu in January 1968. Subsequently the management of the American side of the joint endeavor was taken over by the Social Science Research Council–American Council of Learned Societies' Joint Committee on Japanese Studies. The project has been financed on the American side by a grant from the Department of State's Bureau of Educational and Cultural Affairs supplemented by funds from the Ford Foundation and the Center for Japanese Studies at the University of Michigan. This assistance is gratefully acknowledged. The Japanese side of the enterprise has been supported by grants from the Ministry of Education.

At this writing the companion volume produced by a team of Japanese scholars is already in print. It is entitled *Nihon senryō bunken mokuroku* (A Bibliography on the Allied Occupation of Japan. Tokyo: Japan Society for the Promotion of Science, 1972. xxiv, 349p.). Those primarily responsible for its compilation were: Ukai Nobushige (Seikei University), Sakamoto Yoshikazu (Tokyo University), Ōkōchi Kazuo (Tokyo University), Ashibe Nobuyoshi (Tokyo University), Ariizumi Tōru (Sophia University), Ōkita Saburō (Japan Economic Research Center), Tsuru Shigeto (Hitotsubashi University), Nakamura Takafusa (Tokyo University), Uchikawa Yoshimi (Tokyo University), Maeda Yōichi (Tokyo University), Oguchi Iichi (Tokyo University, emeritus), Hiratsuka Masunori (National Institute for Educational Research), and Harada Taneo (National Institute for Educational Research). The volume consists of an introduction and some 3,000 entries relating to the occupation. The items described are all in Japanese, as is the text of the volume.

The present companion to the Japanese volume is intended to treat the literature of the occupation, in the principal Western languages, that appeared through the end of 1972. The endeavor has sought to provide a reasonably complete and annotated guide to at least the more important items involved. While "importance" has in practice been loosely and generously defined, an attempt has been made to restrict coverage to items which relate at least in part to the planning, staffing, structure, operations, or direct consequences of the occupation and Japanese or foreign relations or reactions thereto. In general, but not in all cases, this has led to the exclusion of items that describe or analyze developments in or concerning Japan during this period without reference to the presence or influence of the occupation. The exceptions are works that supply contextual information of substantial relevance and value. The reader should also be informed that a consid-

Introduction

erable number of items that concern Japan during this period but that have been excluded from this bibliography as too tangential in relevance may easily be identified by consulting the bibliographies listed in the first section of this work.

While our attention has focused primarily on the occupation period proper (2 September 1945–28 April 1952), there has been no disposition to view these limits as impermeable. At one extreme a very substantial amount of advance planning for the occupation preceded the actual surrender of Japan. At the other, the occupation really did not terminate abruptly in April 1952. In fact, power was being returned gradually to the Japanese government for some time before that while the problems of Japan's reentry into the international community extended for some distance on either side of the day that the Treaty of San Francisco went into effect. At both of these extremes the relevant literature has been cited without regard to the time limits of the occupation itself.

While these have been our goals, we are painfully aware that our performance has fallen short in several respects. Although it has been possible to examine and provide descriptive—not critical—annotations of varying length for most of the 3,170 items that constitute the bibliography, a number have eluded our best efforts. These items have not been annotated and have been included as bare citations on the implicit promise of their titles or authorship.

All items have been listed alphabetically by author within each section of the bibliography and have been numbered serially from 1 to 2537. One item—the Columbia University Oral History Project, no.43—has some seventeen subentries distinguished as 43a, 43b, etc. For various reasons, many pertinent items came to our attention only after entry numbers were finally allocated. These have been inserted at the appropriate point and bear the number of the preceding entry plus the letter *a*, *b*, or *c*.

When an item refers in significant part to more than a single aspect of the occupation, it has been treated in one of two ways. If its coverage is truly general —defined in practice as treating more than three aspects of the occupation as defined in the table of contents—it has been placed in a general category; for example, the section providing a calendar of general commentaries or the section dealing with the economy in general and SCAP's role within it. If its treatment is more restricted than that, unnumbered cross-reference entries have been inserted in the appropriate sections. These provide the author, short title, and date of publication, and refer the reader to the main or annotated entry for the item in question.

Two types of indexes have also been supplied. The first is a normal author index that also includes the editors of certain publications cited and the names of individuals who have provided recorded interviews about the occupation. The second index is intended to simplify the labor of readers wishing to isolate serial or recurrent accounts of the occupation that share a common editorial viewpoint or at least a common locus of publication. Examples would be the numerous editorials or reports about the occupation appearing in the *Economist*, the *Far Eastern Survey*, the *Nation*, and the *Soviet Press Translations*. Entries within this index are listed under the titles of the serial publications concerned and provide the names of the authors publishing in them, dates of the items in question, and the relevant entry numbers. It is hoped that the table of contents is detailed enough to make a subject index unnecessary.

A further attempt to orient the reader with respect to the literature of any given aspect of the occupation takes the form of brief introductory statements or essays by the compilers on the subject concerned. These are unnumbered and appear at the beginning of most sections and subsections. Organization charts that depict the structure of SCAP headquarters on different occasions during the occupation period are appended to the text.

Needless to say, the quality of our coverage varies appreciably. It is obviously best for materials published in the United States, Canada, Australia, and Great Britain and includes as well the major English-language journals and books that appeared in Japan during the postwar period. A strenuous effort made to identify and describe at least the major publications associated with SCAP headquarters has been reasonably successful. A more thorough job—while desirable—would have required access to the voluminous central files of the occupation itself which are held by the National Archives in large part. Unfortunately—and, in our opinion, unreasonably—only a small portion of these are as yet available to scholars. There also have been linguistic, bibliographical, and other difficulties with relevant materials in other European languages. We undoubtedly have missed a number of useful items in those languages but are consoled by the fact that not much appears to have been written in them. (The one probable exception is Russian. In that particular case we have had to confine our coverage to materials appearing in English within Soviet publications or in English-language digests of the Soviet press.) In addition, the reader should note that we have excluded a variety of periodical articles dealing with Japanese education and the Japanese economy for reasons of space, that materials concerned exclusively with the Ryukyu Islands have intentionally been omitted, and that with a single exception, all master's theses on the occupation have been left out. Readers having a special interest in these subjects should consult the bibliographies described in the first section of our work—in particular, those under entry numbers 1, 2, 8, 15, 22, and 30.

At the outset we also planned to supplement the bibliographical portion of the book with a rather extensive list of individuals who had held high office in the occupation. The hope was that this might provide a useful source of scholarly interviews in the case of those who were still living. A somewhat truncated version of such a list now appears in both classified and alphabetical form as an appendix of this book. It has not been possible, however, to provide current addresses for the names appearing on the list.

Despite these and other shortcomings, it is hoped that our bibliography will prove useful to scholars of all nations and that it will serve to stimulate further academic and public interest in one of the more remarkable historical episodes of our time. We especially hope that it will help our Japanese colleagues acquire a clear and balanced understanding of this segment of their own national history.

In concluding, we wish to acknowledge with deep gratitude the assistance of the following graduate students at the University of Michigan in identifying and annotating entries for this volume: Myrna Ann Adkins, G. A. Benadom, Robert

Introduction

Borgen, John Bowden, Linda Schmitt Gallini, Anthony S. Graefe, P. Hooper Gramlich, Gary Hansjergen, Robert Leutner, Alan Moriyama, Donald R. Neiswender, Koene Rasanen, Elizabeth Sato, Marvin Suomi, Harry R. Wilkinson, and Samuel H. Yamashita. We also are extremely grateful for the invaluable work undertaken by Masashi Nishihara and Mary Tobin Espey, especially during the early stages of this bibliographical project, and have appropriately recognized their contributions on the title page.

ROBERT E. WARD
FRANK JOSEPH SHULMAN

Ann Arbor, Michigan
August 1973

Abbreviations

AFPAC	Air Force Pacific Air Command
ACJ	Allied Council for Japan
AMG	Allied Military Government
ATIS	Allied Translator and Interpreter Section
BCOF	British Commonwealth Occupation Force
CIE	Civil Information and Education (Section)
DRF	Division of Research for the Far East
ECAFE	Economic Commission for Asia and the Far East
EROA	Economic Rehabilitation of Occupied Areas
FEAC	Far Eastern Advisory Commission
FEC	Far Eastern Commission
FTC	Fair Trade Commission
GARIOA	Government and Relief in Occupied Areas
GHQ	General Headquarters
IMTFE	International Military Tribunal for the Far East
IPR	Institute of Pacific Relations
IPS	International Prosecution Section
JCP	Japan Communist Party
LARA	Licensed Agency for Relief of Asia
LDP	Liberal–Democratic Party
NHK	Nihon Hōsō Kyōkai (Japan Broadcasting Corp.)
OIC	Officer in Charge
OIR	Office of Intelligence Research
PIO	Public Information Office
ROK	Republic of Korea
SCAP	Supreme Commander for the Allied Powers
SCAPIN	SCAP administrative directive
SWNCC	State–War–Navy Coordinating Committee

Abbreviations

The names of individual Japanese, Chinese, and Koreans throughout the bibliography are given in Oriental order, that is, one's family name always precedes his personal name (e.g., Tōjō Hideki). To conform with standard Western practice, however, a comma is used to divide a family name from a personal name whenever an Oriental name appears as an author entry within a bibliographical statement (e.g., Tōjō, Hideki). Diacritical marks are included for both personal and place names whenever known except in the case of such conventional anglicized names as Tokyo and Hokkaido.

Bibliographies

Bibliographies devoted specifically or in major part to the Allied occupation of Japan are few in number and limited in scope. The normal sources of bibliographical information such as the *Public Affairs Information Service* and the *Reader's Guide* do, of course, concern themselves with both the period and the subject matter and list many of the relevant materials. Since such items have been examined and, where appropriate, their contents noted in the course of compiling the present bibliography, it has not been thought necessary to list such general and well-known titles here. The list that follows, therefore, is restricted to more specialized and obscure bibliographies. These bibliographies are particularly recommended to the reader since in some cases they have either not been available to us for examination or they include substantial numbers of items that for reasons of space or relative importance it has not been possible to include here.

Ackerman, Edward A. *Japan's Natural Resources and Their Relation to Japan's Economic Future.* 1953. See no. 1818.

1   Akademiia nauk SSSR. Institut narodov Azii. *Bibliografia Iaponii: Literatura Izdannaia v Sovetskom Soiuze na Russkom Iazyke s 1917 po 1958 g*, comp. by V. A. Vlasov, et al. and ed. by M. I. Luk'ianova, et al. Moscow: Izdatel'stvo Vostochnoi Literatury, 1960. 328p.

Compiled by members of the Institute for the Study of the Peoples of Asia of the USSR Academy of Sciences, this publication is the standard bibliography of Russian-language publications on Japan for the period 1917–58. 6249 entries for books, journal articles, and newspaper articles are arranged under 18 major subject categories and are further subdivided by author, then by date. Both the humanities and the social sciences are extensively covered, and under 2 sections in particular—History (see especially p.125–29) and Foreign Affairs (see especially p.221–23)—the interested reader will find citations for works on the Allied occupation. Of particular note are the publications by the Soviet Japanologists Khaim T. Eidus and Leonid N. Kutakov. (Kutakov's subsequently published study *Istoriia sovetsko-iaponskikh diplomaticheskikh otnoshenii* [A History of Soviet–Japanese Diplomatic Relations; Moscow: 1962, 560p.] also should be noted.) None of the entries is annotated, but the entire listing is complemented by an author index. A supplementary volume covering Russian-language publications on Japan written since 1958 and including materials on the occupation is expected to appear in print during the mid-1970s.

Akademiia nauk SSSR. Institut narodov Azii. *See also* no.30.

2 Association for Asian Studies. *Cumulative Bibliography of Asian Studies, 1941–1965: Author Bibliography.* Boston: G. K. Hall, 1969. 4v.

———. *Cumulative Bibliography of Asian Studies, 1941–1965: Subject Bibliography.* Boston: G. K. Hall, 1970. 4v.

The most comprehensive listing available of significant Western-language books and articles on East, Southeast, and South Asia published between 1941 and 1965, these 2 complementary and cumulative sets of the *Bibliography of Asian Studies* for the years 1941–65 are essential bibliographical reference tools. Each set contains approximately 100,000 entries. Pages 274–655 in volume 3 of the subject bibliography list titles dealing with Japan, but while the entries are classified by broad disciplinary subject, there are inconsistencies within the classification scheme and care must be taken to check related subjects in one's search for materials. The *Bibliography of Asian Studies* is published annually, and the issues that have appeared for the years 1966–71 contain 12,000–15,000 entries apiece. Japan is accorded a separate section in each of these volumes, and the yearly listings are indexed by author.

3 Borton, Hugh, et al. *A Selected List of Books and Articles on Japan in English, French, and German.* rev. and enl. ed. Cambridge, Mass.: Harvard Univ. Pr., published for the Harvard-Yenching Institute, 1954. xiv, 272p.

Compiled by Hugh Borton, Serge Elisséeff, William W. Lockwood, and John C. Pelzel, this publication is a useful, general, annotated bibliography classified by subject of works on all aspects of Japanese history, society, and civilization.

4 Brown, Delmer Myers. "Recent Japanese Political and Historical Materials." *American Political Science Review* 43, no.5:1010–17 (Oct. 1949)

A valuable survey of the nature and scope of the documents assembled for use by the International Military Tribunal for the Far East. Beginning with a brief history of the trial of 28 high-ranking Japanese, the author describes the major tribunal documents collected by the University of California at Berkeley. He treats the *Proceedings* (no.1019), exhibits introduced as evidence by the prosecution and the defense, the documents collected by the International Prosecution Section (IPS) of SCAP, several indexes of those documents prepared by the IPS, and the summaries of tribunal proceedings and documents. The author also comments on exhibits of particular interest and value to historians and political scientists. Brown's article, originally a paper read at the first annual meeting of the Far Eastern Association in 1949, provides a useful guide to these important documents.

5 Burton, Peter, and Paul Langer. "Materials for the Study of Contemporary Japan: Japanese Press Clipping Files and Reduced Size Newspaper Reprints." *Far Eastern Quarterly* 14:251–54 (Feb. 1955)

Two excellent press clipping files containing a wealth of material on various aspects of modern Japan are briefly described by the authors. They are the clipping file of Kobe University's Economics and Business Administration Research Institute (Keizai Keiei Kenkyūjo) consisting of over 2,500 bound volumes, and the clipping file of the National Diet Library housed in its Miyakezaka Branch and covering the period since 1947.

Burton and Langer also note the usefulness of the reduced-size reprints (*shukusatsu-ban*) of the major metropolitan newspapers whose value is enhanced by appended detailed chronologies and indexes.

6   Cho, Sung-Yoon. "The Tokyo War Crimes Trial." *Quarterly Journal of the Library of Congress* 24, no.4:309–18, (Oct. 1967)

This exceedingly valuable report provides a survey of the official records of the International Military Tribunal for the Far East (IMTFE) that are available at the Far Eastern Law Division of the Library of Congress. It also evaluates secondary materials in English and Japanese. Since the Far Eastern Law Division has a complete set of the official proceedings, judgment, and opinions and a partial set of exhibits, the comprehensive analysis of this collection is of great benefit to the scholar of the IMTFE. The introductory section is devoted to a historical outline of the proceedings and a description of the basic policy of the 11 prosecuting nations. The author carefully distinguishes at the outset between the Tokyo trials he is examining and those of 5,416 minor Japanese officials (class B and C war criminals) held by the military commissions of 7 Allied nations. His description is confined to the former. The account of the proceedings includes a general breakdown of their contents into 15 parts and the author briefly describes the valuable index to these materials that has been compiled by Paul S. Dull and Michael M. Umemura, entitled *The Tokyo Trials: A Functional Index to the Proceedings of the International Military Tribunal for the Far East* (1957) (no.7). Subsequently, there are a description of that section of the proceedings known as the majority judgment with an outline of its basic arrangement (3 general parts which are subdivided into 10 chapters), a consideration of the Japanese translation of the judgment, entitled *Tōkyō saiban hanketsu* (published in 1949 by the Mainichi Shimbunsha), and a brief discussion of the principles of international law which were raised by the judgment. The author cites significant works that have been written concerning the last-mentioned issue. In addition, he discusses the dissenting opinions of several justices and notes subsequent studies of their positions. The exhibits submitted to the tribunal as listed in its index—"treaties, Imperial rescripts, Imperial ordinances, Foreign Office documents, Home Office analyses, military reports, personnel records of the accused, statistical data, depositions and maps"—are to be found in the National Archives collection, and this report emphasizes the fact that few studies of them have been undertaken as of the time of writing. There is a helpful outline of the tribunal's 2-volume index that should assist the scholar or researcher in locating information relevant to his work. The final section of the report describes important secondary materials concerning the Tokyo trials. The author judges Delmer Brown's article in the *American Political Science Review,* entitled "Recent Japanese Political and Historical Materials," (1949) (no.4) as meriting special attention. He directs the researcher to other important accounts such as Joseph B. Keenan and Brendan F. Brown's *Crimes Against International Law* (1950) (no. 1072), an article by Solis Horwitz in the November 1950 issue of *International Conciliation* (no.1065), John A. Appleman's *Military Tribunals and International Crimes* (1954) (no.1047), and the *Preliminary Inventory of the Textual Records of the International Military Tribunal for the Far East* (no.1020a) compiled by Charles V. Kirchman and Garry D. Ryan of the National Archives in 1965. Several Japanese books on various aspects of this vast subject are briefly described. His report, the author believes, "indicates the scope of the problems yet to be solved and analyzed by more systematic and adequate research of jurists and students of international law and other related fields." The article provides a valuable guide which charts the broad scope of the IMTFE documents and cites important research that has been undertaken to date.

7 Bibliographies

7 Dull, Paul, and Michael Takaaki Umemura. *The Tokyo Trials: A Functional Index to the Proceedings of the International Military Tribunal for the Far East.* Ann Arbor: Univ. of Michigan Pr., 1957. vi, 94p. (Univ. of Michigan, Center for Japanese Studies, occasional papers, no.6)

The first effort to provide a subject index to the 50,000 page-long *Proceedings of the International Military Tribunal for the Far East* (no.1019). While generally following the pattern of the *Subject Index to the Nuremburg Military Tribunal*, this functional index expands the number of subjects and subdivides them in greater detail. However, names of counsel and witnesses other than defendants are not included, nor are rejected documents, the texts of the judgments, the *Proceedings in Chamber,* and documents that were not read into the record. Since pages 41,916 to 42,110 of the *Proceedings* were missing, the authors were unable to include these pages in their index.

8 Eells, Walter Crosby, comp. *The Literature of Japanese Education, 1945–1954.* Hamden, Conn.: Shoe String, 1955. viii, 210p.

An adviser on higher education in the Civil Information and Education Section of SCAP, Eells has compiled an annotated bibliography of 1,428 items of literature on Japanese education that appeared in English from 1945 through 1954. It includes documents, conference reports, books, magazine articles, monographs, and signed book reviews. Some 60 percent of the entries are periodical articles, most of which appeared in the United States or Japan, with some being published in Europe or other Asian countries. More than 200 periodicals of scholarly and general interest were consulted. Approximately one-fifth of the authors are Japanese. Each entry is provided with 3 to 10 lines of annotation. Among the topics treated are SCAP's educational reforms, their effects on the democratization of Japan, the teachers' new role in Japan, Christian educators' contributions to Japanese democracy, various educational missions to Japan and their impressions, and new educational techniques such as audiovisual education.

9 Fishel, Wesley R. "Japan under MacArthur: Retrospect and Prospect." *Western Political Quarterly* 4:210–25 (June 1951)

After commenting on the efforts of both MacArthur and his "tight clique of idolators" to provide the world with a "snow-white view of the Occupation," Fishel notes that until recently there were hardly any critical studies available of postwar Japan or of the occupation itself. For the most part, interested Westerners had to rely on superficial, journalistic accounts published by casual observers or on reports prepared by various sections of SCAP. Civilian and military authorities in Washington and Tokyo failed to inform the public of some of the difficulties inherent in administering a military occupation or to provide any honest appraisals. As a consequence, the general public had an inaccurate and unhealthy view of the activities and accomplishments of the Allied forces in Japan.

The publication of several private studies in 1948 and 1949 appeared at first to provide a welcome supplement to the existing literature. These reports included T. A. Bisson's *Prospects for Democracy in Japan* (no.581), Jerome B. Cohen's *Japan's Economy in War and Reconstruction* (no.1524), Robert K. Hall's *Education for a New Japan* (no. 2054), Edwin Martin's *The Allied Occupation of Japan* (no.561), Helen Mears' *Mirror for Americans: Japan* (no.562), and Harold Wakefield's *New Paths for Japan* (no.576). While informative, however, these works were inadequate because none provided a thoroughly satisfying or complete analysis of the occupation.

Most recently, 4 new books have appeared: W. Macmahon Ball's *Japan: Enemy or Ally?* (no.535); Miriam S. Farley's *Aspects of Japan's Labor Problems* (no.1750); Robert A. Fearey's *The Occupation of Japan, Second Phase: 1948–1950* (no.621); and the 1950 edition of Edwin O. Reischauer's *The United States and Japan* (no.743). All of these, Fishel states, are serious contributions to the study of the occupation. Accordingly, he critically reviews them for the reader, providing an extensive analysis of Ball's work in particular. He then concludes the article with a series of questions about Japan's prospects.

10   Higashiuchi, Yoshio. *Literature on Contemporary Japan*. Tokyo: Tokyo Office of the Hoover Institute and Library, 1951. xiv, 138p.

Based on an examination of the materials which the Tokyo office of the Hoover Institute collected between 1946 and 1951, this publication is an unannotated bibliography of many important studies dealing with the origin, conduct, and aftermath of World War II and with political trends and movements in postwar Japan. Most of the titles cited are of prewar and postwar Japanese-language works. A discussion of SCAP publications, however, also is included, and some of the Japanese-language works deal directly with the Allied occupation of Japan.

11   Ike, Nobutaka. *The Hoover Institution Collection on Japan*. Palo Alto, Calif.: The Institute, 1958. 63p. (Stanford Univ., Hoover Institution on War, Revolution, and Peace, collection survey, 3)

A descriptive survey of the collection on Japan at the Hoover Institution on War, Revolution, and Peace at Stanford University. One short section (p.52–53) notes some of the library's holdings for the occupation period.

12   Institute of Pacific Relations. International Secretariat. *IPR Publications on the Pacific, 1925–1952*. New York: The Institute, 1953. xii, 117p.

All publications of the Institute of Pacific Relations' (IPR) National Councils and the International Secretariat pertaining to the Far East, the Pacific, and South and Southeast Asia are cataloged here. The institute, an unofficial organization, was formed in 1925 "to facilitate the scientific study of the peoples of the Pacific area," and existed till 1958. During these years it conducted an extensive program of research on the political, economic, and social problems of the Asian and Pacific areas, and organized 12 major international conferences in different parts of the world. It also published the proceedings of these conferences and a quarterly journal, *Pacific Affairs,* as well as numerous scholarly books. National councils were established in Australia, China, England, France, India, Japan, the Netherlands, New Zealand, the Philippines, Pakistan, the Soviet Union, and the United States. The catalog includes their publications, a number of which relate to the Allied occupation of Japan. Titles are arranged by area. The bibliography also contains a list of more ephemeral publications by the IPR, its periodicals, Inquiry series, proceedings of IPR international conferences, American IPR studies of the Pacific, and the American IPR pamphlet series. An index of authors is appended.

13   Japan. Diet. Library. *List of Japanese Government Publications in European Languages, 1945–1955*. Tokyo: 1956. viii, 53, 7p.

A list of SCAP publications (1946–52) together with some additional items owned by the American embassy library and by the National Diet Library.

14   ———. Ministry of Agriculture and Forestry. Economic Research Div. *List of Papers and Materials upon Agricultural Economy, January 1938–December 1948*. Tokyo: 1949. 72p.

15   King, Norman D. *Ryukyu Islands: A Bibliography*. Washington, D.C.: Government Printing Office, 1967. iii, 105p. (Dept. of the Army pamphlet 550-4)

King, a former member of the Civil Administration of the Ryukyu Islands and of the Civil Affairs Directorate of the Deputy Chief of Staff for Military Operations, has compiled an extremely comprehensive though unannotated bibliography of nearly 2,100 English-language publications dealing with the Ryukyus. Materials covering the 1945–52 period are found particularly on pages 38–40 ("Military Government 1945–1950," and "Civil Administration 1950–1952"). This pamphlet is an essential reference source that contains considerable information of value to the reader interested in a part of the Japanese islands not really dealt with in this bibliography on the occupation.

Kirchman, Charles V., and Garry D. Ryan. *Preliminary Inventory of the Textual Records of the International Military Tribunal for the Far East.* 1965. See no. 1020a.

Kuroda, Andrew Y. "Periodicals in Occupied Japan." 1949. See no. 2146.

16 Langer, Paul Fritz, and Arthur Rodger Swearingen. *Japanese Communism: An Annotated Bibliography of Works in the Japanese Language, with a Chronology, 1921–1952.* New York: Institute of Public Relations, International Secretariat, 1953. xii, 95p.

This bibliography contains 242 critical entries on Japanese works in American libraries that "deal specifically with the Japanese Communist movement at home and abroad, from its origins ... up to 1951." Communist periodicals are not included except for 200 articles from the journal *Zen-ei* (Vanguard). Entries are listed alphabetically under a variety of topical headings and there are indexes by author and subject. Material on the Communist movement under the occupation is included.

17 Lequiller, Jean. *Bibliographie des ouvrages de sciences humaines consacrés au Japon et publiés entre 1945 et 1948 en français, anglais, et allemand.* Tokyo: 1958. 81p. (Bulletin de la Maison Franco-Japonaise, n.s., t.5, no.1)

A bibliography of publications devoted to Japan published between 1945 and 1958 in French, English, and German.

17a ———, and Pierre Fistie. "Le Japon depuis 1945: état des travaux." *Revue française de science politique* 7, no.4: 890–912 (Oct./Dec. 1957)

This bibliographic essay covers the 134 English- and French-language publications which the authors regard as the most important postwar studies on Japan. The listings are subdivided into history, the American occupation, economic development, economic and social organization, politics and government, and sociological studies. The section on the occupation itself is limited to 17 titles —all of them in English.

18 Liu, James T. C. "The Tokyo Trials: Source Materials." *Far Eastern Survey* 17:168–70 (28 July 1948)

This article considers the identity and contents of materials gathered in connection with the Tokyo trials of war criminals conducted by the International Military Tribunal for the Far East. Documents cited provide insights into the secret policies of the Japanese government before and during World War II. They include records kept by the Ministry of the Imperial Household, and such valuable private documents as the diary of Marquis Kido and the Saionji-Harada memoirs, which provided a detailed narrative of many political crises in presurrender Japan. Also cited as important are a large number of affidavits by Japanese witnesses. Since the trial lawyers chose to use only selected parts of these materials, the author believes these documents are historical materials which warrant further study by scholars.

19 Maki, John McGilvrey. "The Documents of Japan's Commission on the Constitution." *Journal of Asian Studies* 24, no.3:475–89 (May 1965)

The author believes the voluminous documentation produced by the Japanese government's Commission on the Constitution to be indispensable to the scholar concerned with almost any aspect of postwar Japanese politics. His notes on the material to be found in the various parts of the commission's proceedings and reports together with his description of their intricate organization and interrelationships are invaluable to scholars desirous of using the Japanese originals. Maki also comments in detail on the politics surrounding the commission, its functioning, and findings.

20   May, Ernest Richard, and James C. Thomson, Jr., eds. *American–East Asian Relations: A Survey.* Cambridge: Harvard Univ. Pr., 1972. xv, 425p. (Harvard Studies in American–East Asian Relations, 1)

This collection of essays by 18 prominent scholars presents an historiographical survey of American writings on American–East Asian relations from the 1780s to the 1960s. In chapter 15 ("The Truman Era") Robert Dallek of the University of California points out that the American occupation of Japan represents the least studied aspect of our postwar relations with the Far East. "The story of how the most powerful East Asian nation was transformed from a totalitarian enemy into a generally democratic friend," he writes, "goes all but untold." Dallek then notes some of the major questions concerning the subject which have yet to be adequately explored and concludes that until the United States government—the State Department and leading officials in particular—release their papers to researchers, the prospects for the serious study of American–East Asian relations during the Truman era will remain dim.

21   Morley, James William. "Check List of Seized Japanese Records in the National Archives." *Far Eastern Quarterly* 9:306–33 (May 1950)

A preliminary checklist of most of the "over 30,000 volumes of official records which had been seized in Japan by the United States government" and were accessioned from the Foreign Documents Branch of the Central Intelligence Agency on 18 May 1948 by the archivist of the United States. Morley begins by commenting briefly on the general nature of the collection which is located in the War Records Division of the National Archives, and he notes that the collection does not represent all of the records of the Japanese War Ministry and the Navy Ministry and their predecessors. "The records and publications are listed in this check list by their Japanese titles followed by the characters and suggested English translations, with brief descriptive notes attached. They have been grouped under general heads for convenience."

22   Passin, Herbert. *Japanese Education: A Bibliography of Materials in the English Language.* New York: Teachers College Pr., 1970. xi, 135p. (Publications of the Center for Education in Industrial Nations, Columbia Univ.)

A classified but unannotated bibliography listing 1,524 books, articles, and dissertations selected by Passin of Columbia University for inclusion on the basis of their quality and value to the student. Of particular interest is section 3, entitled "The American Occupation," but other sections (e.g., those on students and on teachers) also should be consulted in view of the fact that they contain relevant entries that are not cross-referred from section 3. Since the section on the American occupation lists sources relating to Japanese education during the occupation period that for reasons of space are not included in the present bibliography, interested readers are strongly advised to consult it.

23   ———. "Japanese Education: Guide to a Bibliography in the English Language." *Comparative Education Review* 9:81–101 (Feb. 1965)

This 466 entry bibliography is topically divided into general, historical, the American occupation, moral education, students, teachers, women, and specialized education headings. Brief introductory remarks for each heading point out the most useful and up-to-date works. Listings of unpublished materials are also given. This bibliography has largely been superseded by the author's *Japanese Education: A Bibliography of Materials in the English Language* (no.22).

24   Rabinowitz, Richard William. "Materials on Japanese Law in Western Languages." *American Journal of Comparative Law* 4:97–104 (Winter 1955)

This bibliographic survey of the major fields of law as embodied in the principal codes covers the most important literature under the following headings: Pre-modern Period (i.e., before the Meiji Restoration), General Literature on the Modern Period, Constitutional and Administrative Law, Civil Code, Civil Procedure, Commercial Code, Criminal Law, Code of Criminal Procedure, [and] Private International Law. Rabinowitz points out the usefulness of articles by Blakemore (no.1268) and Oppler (no.1290) and the English-language translation of the *Official Gazette* for the study of legal developments in general during the occupation. Articles by Steiner (no.1292a), Meyers (no. 1287a), and Appleton (no.1267), furthermore, are important for the information they provide about major postwar changes respectively in the Civil Code, the Criminal Code, and the Code of Criminal Procedure. Rabinowitz concludes that the appearance of codes and their relatively frequent revision have provided a major stimulus to writing in Western languages on Japanese law and that we possess as a result adequate translations and commentaries on the major codes of Japan. There is still need, however, for studies that analyze various elements of Japanese law in depth.

Sakamoto, Kusuhito. "Marxian Studies of Agricultural Problems of Post-war Japan." 1955. *See* no.1730a.

25 Shulman, Frank Joseph. *Japan and Korea: An Annotated Bibliography of Doctoral Dissertations in Western Languages, 1877–1969*. Chicago: American Library Assn., 1970. xix, 340p.

A comprehensive, interdisciplinary guide to all Western-language dissertations dealing in whole or in part with Japan and with Korea and submitted to higher-degree granting institutions in 25 countries, among them Japan and the USSR. There are 2,586 titles listed, and for each entry the compiler has provided not only the Ph.D. recipient's name, the thesis title, the name of the institution and the year in which the dissertation was submitted, but also information regarding the location of a published abstract and the best means for obtaining a photographic reproduction of the dissertation typescript, a descriptive annotation, and a listing of related books and articles by the dissertation author. Pages 210–14 identify 37 theses focusing on the occupation, and numerous cross-references lead to closely related entries classified elsewhere within the publication.

26 Silberman, Bernard Samuel. *Japan and Korea: A Critical Bibliography*. Tucson: Univ. of Arizona Pr., 1962. xiv, 120p.

This selected, annotated, and graded guide to the most authoritative and available books and periodical articles on Japan and on Korea contains a number of entries relating to the occupation. Of particular value are the sections entitled "History: The Occupation—1945–1952" listing 31 publications (p.28–29), "Political Patterns: Occupation Period—1945–1952" listing 24 titles (p.70–71), and "Education: Post-war Education" (p.84), and the entire section devoted to works on the Japanese economy (p.84–92).

Supreme Commander for the Allied Powers. Civil Information and Education Section. *A History of Teachers' Unions in Japan*. 1948. *See* no.1785.

27 ———. ———. *Catalogue of Published Documents, December 1945 to 30 April 1947*. Tokyo: 1947. iii, 70p.

This catalog lists 299 unclassified documents published by the Analysis and Research Division of the Civil Information and Education Section from December 1945 through April 1947. The only Civil Information and Education Section unclassified publications that are not included are the daily analyses of the Tokyo press and the analyses of the prefectural press. Under broad topics such as cultural resources research, education research, and information media research are further subdivisions such as aquariums, architecture, and archives, and under these are listed the relevant publications. A majority of the entries are briefly annotated.

Available at the Library of Congress, Washington, D.C. and the Records Center of the National Archives, Suitland, Maryland.

————. Economic and Scientific Section. *Science and Technology in Japan: Reports.* 1947–50. See no.2273.

————. Natural Resources Section. *Japanese Natural Resources: A Comprehensive Survey.* 1949. See no.1822.

Takeshita, K. Lillian. "Recent Works on the New Japanese Constitution." 1953. See no.1217.

28 Taylor, Philip H., and Ralph J. D. Braibanti. *Administration of Occupied Areas: A Study Guide.* Syracuse, N.Y.: Syracuse Univ. Pr., 1948. iv, 111p.

Two political scientists who participated in the occupation of Japan have prepared a useful annotated bibliography on military government with special reference to Germany, Japan, Korea, the Pacific area, and Austria—all countries in which the United States administered military governments in postwar years. There are bibliographical entries on the general subject of military government as related to internal law, personnel training, and America's pre-1945 experience. The section on Japan is a compilation of all published materials, official and nonofficial, available as of mid-1948. These materials are categorized under the following topics: basic documents; organization and structure; general occupation policy; Japanese politics and administration; economics, commerce, industry, finance; education; the constitution; religion and status of the emperor; problems in sociology and social psychology; and critical analysis of the occupation. This section contains approximately 170 entries, mostly articles selected from a wide range of periodicals such as *Far Eastern Survey, Pacific Affairs, Military Review,* the *Nation, Soviet Press Translations,* and *Foreign Affairs.* There is also a section entitled "Guide to Background Materials in Japanese Civilization" which comprises some 40 entries.

29 U.S. Strategic Bombing Survey. *Index to Records to United States Strategic Bombing Survey.* Washington, D.C.: Government Printing Office, 1947.

The U.S. Strategic Bombing Survey was organized by the secretary of war on 3 November 1944 to study the effects of American aerial attacks on Germany and Japan during World War II. Chaired by Franklin D'Olier, the survey was staffed by some 300 civilians, 350 officers, and 500 enlisted men. Between September and December 1945, its survey teams interviewed surviving political, military, and industrial leaders in the 2 countries, inspected bombed industrial areas and cities, and gathered documentary data. The complete files are deposited in the National Archives. This *Index to Records* classifies all of the formal published reports and unpublished documentary data supporting them. It contains 208 reports on the European theater and 108 on the Pacific. They vary in length from 20 to 260 pages; most of the longer ones refer to wartime military operations. The Pacific War reports cover such topics as Japanese morale during wartime, effectiveness of the civilian defense system against air raids, the results of the atomic bombings of Nagasaki and Hiroshima, changes in and corresponding effects on the quantities of available military supplies, the production level of Japanese heavy and light industries caused by bombardment impact of air attacks on transportation, state of the urban economy, the effects of bombardment by naval vessels, interrogations of Japanese officials, and an evaluation of American photographic intelligence of various sites in Japan.

Available at the Library of Congress, Washington, D.C.

30 USSR. Academy of Sciences. Institute of the Peoples of Asia. *Fifty Years of Soviet Historiography of Japan (1917–1966).* Moscow: "Nauka" Publishing

House, Central Dept. of Oriental Literature, 1967. 49p. (Fifty Years of Soviet Oriental Studies, brief reviews)

A particularly useful bibliographical essay on Soviet writings on Japanese history, with considerable focus on twentieth century Japan. A number of the cited works by such authors as I. A. Latyshev (specialist on the 1947 Constitution) and V. A. Popov (specialist on postwar land reforms and peasant movements) deal with the occupation. A selected listing of 106 titles in Russian is appended to the essay.

USSR Academy of Sciences. Institute of the Peoples of Asia. *See also* no.1.

31 Uyehara, Cecil H. *Leftwing Social Movements in Japan: An Annotated Bibliography*. Tokyo: Tuttle, published for the Fletcher School of Law and Diplomacy, Tufts Univ., 1959. 444p.

Part of the studies on Japan's social democratic parties prepared by Allen B. Cole, George O. Totten, and the author, this publication is an extensively annotated bibliographical guide to approximately 1,800 Japanese-language publications on left-wing social movements since World War I. Much of the material deals with the Communist party, but various sections of the work cover such non-Communist groups as the Social Democratic party, the Cooperative Movement, and the Agrarian Movement. Titles related to the occupation are found throughout the volume.

32 Ward, Robert Edward, and Watanabe Hajime. *Japanese Political Science: A Guide to Japanese Reference and Research Materials*. rev. ed. Ann Arbor: Univ. of Michigan Pr., 1961. xi, 210p. (Univ. of Michigan, Center for Japanese Studies, Bibliographic series no.1, rev. ed.)

A largely annotated bibliography of 1,759 Japanese-language publications (primarily books) in the field of political science. Most of the works were published after 1945, and nearly two-thirds of them were not incorporated in the first edition of this bibliography compiled by Ward in 1950. Of particular note to the reader are section 8 dealing with the 1947 Constitution and the amendment controversies and section 27 treating the Allied occupation. Other sections, among them section 18 focusing on the socioeconomic structure and sociopolitical groups and movements and section 24 examining local government and politics, also will be of value.

Major Newspaper and Periodical Sources

The occupation was a subject of close and fairly sustained interest to a small number of newspapers and periodicals. Prominent among the former were such major newspapers of record as the *New York Times* (no.37), the *Christian Science Monitor* (no.33), the *Times* (London) (no.41), and the *Manchester Guardian* (no.36). In addition to carrying the usual wire service reports on developments in Japan, all of these maintained special correspondents on the scene and published with fair although varying frequency special reports and analytic and interpretive commentaries on the news. In so doing these papers also adopted particular editorial stances and viewpoints with respect to the occupation that supplement their reporting and provide a more critical insight into the merits and shortcomings of the policies involved. Such newspapers thus constitute an unusually rich, detailed, and continuous source of information that deserves special mention.

English-language newspapers published in Japan during the occupation period such as the *Nippon Times* (no.38) or the *Pacific Stars and Stripes* (no.40) fall in a somewhat different category, but they, too, supply a great deal of useful information about contemporary developments that is of interest to the scholar.

On a somewhat more restricted and selective basis the same is true of a few periodicals that for a variety of reasons chose to pay an unusual amount of attention to the occupation. Examples would be the *Department of State Bulletin* (no.35a), the *Nation,* or the *New Republic* in this country; *Contemporary Japan* (no.34) or the *Oriental Economist* (no.39) in Tokyo; the *New Times* or *Soviet Press Translations* for the USSR; or *Current Notes on International Affairs* (no.35) for Australia. These journals were certainly not the only ones carrying valuable and fairly numerous articles on the occupation but, over the 6 years and 8 months for which it lasted, their coverage tended to be more continuous and extensive. In many cases they also represent national or other points of view that are of interest to scholars. They have, therefore, been singled out for special mention.

33 Newspapers and Periodicals

33 *Christian Science Monitor*. Boston. daily except Sunday.

The *Christian Science Monitor*'s coverage of the occupation of Japan, while not as extensive as that of the *New York Times* (no.37), is characterized by a very high quality of reporting. In the early months of the occupation, reports on SCAP operations and the Japanese situation appear almost daily. By early 1946, however, the coverage is less complete and has moved off the front page except for major events. The *Monitor*'s correspondents in Japan, Gordon Walker and John Beaufort, take an independent view of the occupation seeking out the news themselves rather than relying on SCAP press releases. In some instances, their independence suggests an overreaction to SCAP policies and views, but the coverage is generally fair and provides an excellent balance for the pro-SCAP views of the *New York Times*. The *Monitor* uses Associated Press and Reuters news releases to cover SCAP policy pronouncements and routine news stories. The *Monitor*'s own correspondents devoted most of their time to in-depth reporting and lead articles that attempt to analyze Japanese opinions of the reform programs and American policies. Many articles focus on the shortcomings of SCAP reforms and the attempts by some Japanese groups to hold on to political and economic power behind the facade of democratization. In a number of his reports during the first year of the occupation, Gordon Walker points out that many of the so-called liberal leaders approved by SCAP were in fact members of the Old Guard that ruled Japan before the war. In his comments on the composition of the Diet after the first election (10 Apr. 1946), he questions whether prewar conservative politicians, such as Yoshida, are capable of passing judgment on a democratic constitution. Walker also criticizes SCAP's activities and the U.S. policy of anticommunism they reflect, for sacrificing progress toward real democracy in Japan to a cold war policy that envisages Japan as a bulwark of democracy in Asia. He believes that this policy allows the conservatives to exploit American fears of communism and causes a polarization of Japanese political forces. On the other hand, he feels that the Communists in Japan are equally harmful, especially in their excessive demands made through the labor unions.

In addition to reports from its Tokyo correspondents, the *Monitor* also carries reports from its Washington writer, Neal Stanford, who covered the proceedings of the Far Eastern Commission and U.S. government news concerning the occupation. Roscoe Drummond in Washington also occasionally devoted his column, "State of the Nation," to the occupation. The *Monitor*'s staff correspondent in Sydney, A. E. Norman, reports on Australian views of the occupation as well as those of other Commonwealth nations. Japan and the occupation are also featured in several series, such as Donovan Richardson's "Leaves from the Editor's Notebook" in February 1947 and the *Monitor*'s editor, Edwin D. Canham's reports on his U.S. Army-sponsored trip to the Far East in February-March 1947.

The *Monitor* devoted a relatively large amount of editorial space to issues pertaining to the occupation from 1945 to early 1948. In the first months of the occupation, the editorials are critical of the Japanese leaders for refusing to admit publicly that they had been defeated. At the same time, editorials find fault with the American policy of an indirect occupation. They state that it is foolish to keep prewar officials in control of Japan (6 Sept. 1945). A later editorial (21 Sept.) notes that "everything that has happened so far has tended to crystallize and bulwark against change . . . in the present economic and social system of Japan which makes a will to war." By the end of 1945, however, the editors take a less critical view of the occupation and find many of its initial steps toward reform praiseworthy. The announcement and publication of the new Japanese constitution brought forth a cry of editorial wrath. In an editorial (8 Mar. 1946) entitled "Japanese Boobytrap" the "gorgeous new Constitution" is denounced as "utterly worthless." The editor states that it is an "American constitution for Japan drawn up in English by men dependent on the pleasure of General MacArthur." He claims that it is presented to the American people as evidence of Japanese reform and democratization and lulls them into a false sense of security. He believes that the only way to radical reform is not through a "streamlined" constitution but through a long occupation. Criticism of the constitution is continued in subsequent editorials (e.g., 12 Oct. 1946).

The *Monitor* is equally skeptical of SCAP's roseate reports of "democratization" as reflected in election results. The editors point out that SCAP has purge powers over all the candidates and characterizes the newly elected Diet as "the MacArthur shogunate." On the other hand, the editors note that there were some positive results from the election, particularly the high voter turnout and participation by women. While the editors are often critical of SCAP policy, they favor some of General MacArthur's actions. An editorial (8 Apr. 1946) praised his speech asking UN members to renounce war. The *Monitor* also supported MacArthur's action in stopping the general strike (1 Feb. 1947). But, they note, that while it was fair and necessary in this one instance, his order applied to only one strike. Therefore, neither government nor union leaders should try to put the order to their own use.

The war crimes trials are given a symbolic and moral interpretation by the editors. They see all nations who have waged war as being on trial in Tokyo. The editors feel that the Allies have right on their side but must be certain that their motives are pure and that there is no hatred, revenge, or narrow nationalism.

On the whole, the *Monitor* looks at the occupation through the eyes of its correspondents and editors and not through SCAP's. It is often critical of what it sees but presents a fairly balanced picture showing positive as well as negative aspects of the occupation.

34 *Contemporary Japan.* Tokyo. quarterly.

Each issue of the periodical *Contemporary Japan* contains a section entitled "Documentary Material" which includes a number of useful documents on the occupation of Japan. The series includes international communiqués by the Allied powers, addresses by officials of SCAP and the Japanese government as well as the U.S. and other Allied governments, and letters by various individuals associated with numerous aspects of the occupation. MacArthur's New Year's messages to the Japanese people as well as addresses commemorating various accomplishments of the occupation may be found in this series. Other materials of note are addresses of various members of the Allied Council for Japan, reports or synopses of reports of the various U.S. advisory missions to Japan in economics, education, labor, civil rights, etc., and such significant documents as the text of the peace treaty with Japan. It should also be noted that the very useful SCAP reports on the first two years of occupation may be found in this series (v.16, July–Sept. 1947, p.402–33 and Oct.–Dec. 1947, p.512–25). The reports were originally published by SCAP under the title *Two Years of Occupation* (nos. 263 and 281).

34a *Current Digest of the Soviet Press* (CDSP). Ann Arbor, Mich. weekly. 1 Feb. 1949—

Published by the ACLS-SSRC Joint Committee on Slavic Studies (and subsequently by the American Association for the Advancement of Slavic Studies), this weekly digest of selected Soviet newspaper and journal articles in translation provides important coverage of domestic developments, documents, indications of official attitudes and policies on both local and foreign affairs, and public declarations of the USSR. The complete texts of major items from *Pravda* and *Izvestia*—the Soviet Union's 2 leading daily newspapers—and the abridged texts or summaries of many other articles in those 2 publications regularly are presented. The digest also selects material from many other Soviet newspapers and a wide variety of journals, focusing on special items or on items of lasting interest to Western readers. In this manner, the CDSP provides a broad picture of the news which has been presented to the Soviet public. Translations, it should be noted, are presented as documentary materials, without any editorial elaboration or comment. Each item, moreover, carries a reference to the Soviet publication in which it appeared, the date, and the page, as well as an indication of the number of words in the Russian-language original and whether the translation is complete or condensed.

In addition to being a reliable and useful source of information on the Soviet Union and on Soviet views and attitudes in general, the CDSP is the major English-language periodical for Soviet articles written between 1949 and 1952 on the Allied occupation of Japan. Considerable attention is paid to Japanese trade union activity, the Japan Communist Party, American plans affecting the Japanese economy, the trial of war criminals at Khabarovsk in December 1949, the American release of prominent war criminals in 1950, the revival of militarism in Japan and American efforts to rearm the country, and the conclusion of a separate peace treaty in September 1951. While most relevant items are signed articles by newspaper correspondents and Soviet specialists on Japan, there also are a number of items which essentially reproduce the text of statements about Japan made by Soviet government officials. All articles are classified, and the specialist on the occupation will therefore find most relevant material under the heading "Foreign Affairs: The Far East" in each weekly issue. There also is a classified quarterly index listing all of the articles within the digest as well as Soviet periodical literature published in such English-language journals as the *USSR Information Bulletin, New Times, Soviet Literature,* and *Soviet Woman*.

Our bibliography on the Allied occupation contains a selection of the most important items which appeared in the CDSP between 1 February 1949 and 13 September 1952. (*See* the Periodical Index for a complete listing of entries.) This represents only a small percentage of the articles, however, which appeared in the Soviet press at that time and which may be found in this authoritative digest.

35 *Current Notes on International Affairs*. Canberra. monthly.

An official monthly record of Australia's diplomatic activities and international developments of significance. It contains a daily chronicle of international events, statements by the Australian minister for external affairs, agreements that Australia has reached with other nations, descriptions of international conferences, unsigned articles, and Australian diplomatic and consular lists. Occasional numbers include texts of communiqués, agreements, resolutions of a binational or multinational character, and a bibliography of contemporary English-language sources on international affairs. The country's involvements in the Pacific War and the subsequent occupation of Japan are frequently reflected in the coverage of such matters as the terms for Japanese surrender, postwar political reforms in Japan, the role of the Far Eastern Commission, and the peace settlement with Japan. In the following sections of this bibliography annotations are provided only for items in the categories of "articles" and "statements" which would be difficult to obtain elsewhere. The texts of treaties and agreements are not noted.

35a *Department of State Bulletin*. weekly.

The *Department of State Bulletin* is a weekly publication that provides both the general public and interested U.S. government agencies with information on pertinent developments in the field of foreign relations and on work carried out by the Department of State and the Foreign Service. It includes press releases on foreign policy issued by the White House and the State Department, and reproduces statements and addresses made by the president, the secretary of state, and other department officials. In addition, the publication contains special articles on various aspects of international affairs, the texts of treaties and agreements to which the United States is or may become a party, and a calendar of diplomatic events and actions.

During the 7 years of the occupation, the *Department of State Bulletin* frequently carried materials directly related to American objectives and SCAP activities in Japan as well as to the peace treaty negotiations with that country. Items of interest to readers of the present bibliography have been incorporated as individual entries and appear throughout the book. For a listing of all such articles, please consult the periodical index.

35b *Far Eastern Economic Review*. Hong Kong. weekly. 16 Oct. 1946– .

The issues of this publication dating from the occupation period were unavailable for consultation at the time this annotation was prepared. From an examination of issues published in 1952 and of various bibliographical sources and published abstracts of specific articles, however, it appears that the journal extensively covered economic developments in Japan during the occupation years. Later issues include considerable commentary on economic news from Japan, occasional surveys of selected aspects of the economy, statistical summaries of many kinds, and reports on specific Japanese industries. As a leading English-language journal on the postwar Asian economy, therefore, it should be regarded as an important secondary source of information despite the relative brevity of its articles.

35c *Journal of Finance and Commerce*. Tokyo. monthly. 15 Aug. 1948–

Published by the *Nippon Times*, this journal provides detailed coverage of the Japanese economy and includes regular statistical summaries, a survey of events affecting the economy in general, and a monthly news commentary. Special articles on particular aspects of the economy and specific industries are common. Detailed summaries and critical analyses of SCAP measures affecting the economy appear fairly regularly, with special attention being paid to such events as the announcement of the Dodge Plan. Lengthy and articulate editorials appear monthly, and not infrequently they deal with occupation policies. The magazine generally seems to maintain its editorial independence: It neither accepts SCAP policies uncritically nor consistently supports the interests of any identifiable sector of the Japanese economy. The publication is a good source both for information on SCAP-related economic developments and for Japanese opinions on SCAP policy.

36 *Manchester Guardian.* daily.

The *Manchester Guardian* reports the occupation of Japan as headline news only through early October 1945. By November 1945, the occupation is relegated to occasional back-page news and is rare and scanty until a final burst of commentary on the peace treaty in August and September 1951. Editorial comment follows this same pattern. The *Guardian*'s initial postwar attitude is that it is preferable to entrust the maintenance of world peace and order to an international coalition of great powers than to hope for eventual Japanese democratization. While faith in General MacArthur's leadership is explicit, and despite occasional editorial wondering at Allied leniency to a former enemy, the paper maintained its skepticism with respect to the ability of SCAP to remold Japanese society according to democratic models. Through 1951 the demise of traditional patterns in Japanese business and politics is disbelieved. However, animosity is not prevalent and Japan is seen in conventional balance-of-power terms as a potential friend and ally. The *Guardian* consistently accepts a commonality of British and American interests in Japan and the Far East and consequently supports without rancor American command in Japan as control by a "like-minded country." Beginning in late 1946, the paper advocates total economic revitalization for Japan and views British concerns about textile competition as petty, self-serving, and inimical to world order. The American and British governmental views on a peace treaty are contrasted and such special areas of interest as the participation of China, the commitment to reparations, and the status of Japanese foreign assets and liabilities are discussed. The *Guardian* is favorable to the Dulles treaty and desires a totally nonpunitive treaty. Almost all editorials, news items, and commentary on the occupation are unsigned. One major exception is an extended article appearing in August and September 1951, by Robert Guillain, entitled "Japan after MacArthur." This analysis expands an earlier concern of the *Guardian* about the motives behind American policy in Japan, and SCAP's tendency to do and undo, to create and then abrogate, certain economic and political reforms. Guillain asserts that American policy is based on securing short-range cold war goals—temporary tactical gains against Russia—rather than long-range goals of stability and improvement for domestic Japan. The *Manchester Guardian* takes a pragmatic, unidealistic approach to the occupation, discounting American protestations of dynamic social evolution but accepting Japan as the best friend the West can hope for in Asia.

37 *New York Times.* daily. (Indexed in the *New York Times Index*, published monthly with annual cumulations from 1945 to 1947, semimonthly with annual cumulations from 1948 to 1952.)

Of all newspapers surveyed, the *New York Times* has the most extensive and comprehensive coverage of the occupation of Japan. Beginning in August 1945, the *Times* carried daily front-page stories about Japan and the occupation. Lead articles and background reports about specific aspects of the occupation, Allied policy, or Japanese attitudes supplement the news coverage. The *Times* prints SCAP's major policy statements as they were made public as well as statements by Japanese leaders. Daily coverage following SCAP operations step-by-step continued through November 1945. Thereafter coverage dropped off rapidly, with only major events, such as the promulgation of the new constitution, making front-page news. From January 1946 news about Japan and American activities there appears on pages 3 or 4. News items focus on the announcement of SCAP reforms, the naming of war criminals and the war crimes trials, and major Japanese political events such as cabinet shifts and elections. In 1947, coverage turns to the problems of Japan's economic recovery, reflecting a change in occupation emphasis. This trend continues into 1948 and 1949 with numerous comments on the problems occasioned by Communist domination of the labor unions. With the outbreak of the Korean conflict in 1950, news about Japan becomes scarce and remains so until the end of the occupation except for a brief period in September 1951 at the time of the San Francisco Peace Conference. In addition to the regular daily coverage of the occupation, the summaries which appear in the "News of the Week in Review" each Sunday provide a concise record of major occurrences during the preceding week. This section also contains lead articles by the *Times*' Tokyo correspondents George E. Jones, Frank Kluckhorn, Lindesay Parrott, and Burton Crane. They present analyses of the outcome of Japanese elections, the content of the new constitution, Japan's lack of strong national leaders, and other timely topics. In general, these articles are more critical of occupation policies and present more of the writer's opinion than do articles by the same correspondents in the *New York Times Magazine*. The "News of the Week in Review" also carries commentary by Washington-based correspondents such as Hanson W. Baldwin as well as political cartoons about Japan from other U.S. newspapers. The editorial viewpoint of the *New York Times* gives unqualified support to practically all SCAP policies and praises General MacArthur's implementation of the policies. Only during the first month of the occupation does the *Times* question MacArthur's wisdom and then only to ask if the reforms are being carried out quickly enough and if there is a master plan for the occupation to guide the reforms. Once the initial postsurrender policy document was made public (26 Oct. 1945), the *Times* gave its full support. For example, the editors of the *Times* favored the retention of the emperor, praised the new constitution comparing its importance to that of the Magna Carta (although later, the editors refer to it as "American-inspired"), and proclaim after each election that democracy has taken root in Japan. This favorable editorial viewpoint toward the occupation carried over to the tone of the news coverage. SCAP reforms were announced in laudatory terms, but there is not much follow-up on their success or failure.

37a *Newsweek.* New York. weekly.

Newsweek's coverage of the occupation reaches its peak of intensity immediately after the surrender, when Japan and the occupation were cover stories for several weeks in a row. Major articles continue to appear until the end of 1945, but coverage is increasingly confined to relatively brief weekly notices of newsworthy SCAP activities, which usually are in the magazine's "Foreign Affairs" section. From early 1946 through mid-1950, few articles of significance appear, except for occasional major stories on such topics as the war crimes trials, disagreements among the Allies over occupation policies, and the new constitution. "Weighing the Year of Atonement," in the 12 August 1946 issue (vol. 28, p.42–44), is one of a small number of articles that attempts to provide a broad review of the occupation. The outbreak of hostilities in Korea and the consequent involvement of Japan as a staging area and as a major source of material for the war effort produces another spate of major articles. Coverage soon thins out, however, until the peace treaty negotiations and the signing of the treaty again attract attention.

Generally speaking, aside from scattered major stories, *Newsweek*'s articles on the occupation tend to be brief, limited in their scope, and written in a popular journalistic style. The magazine's editorial stance seems for the most part to reflect the prevailing SCAP interpretation and assessment of events in Japan at any given time, although the style in which articles were written often results in a somewhat cynical tone. Volumes 26 (July–Dec. 1945) through 39 (Jan.–June 1952) of *Newsweek* cover the occupation period and are fully indexed in the relevant volumes of *The Reader's Guide to Periodical Literature*. A selected number of relevant articles from the journal, it should be noted, are included within the present bibliography in order that they may be brought directly to the user's attention.

38 *Nippon Times* (since 1956 *Japan Times*). Tokyo. daily.

All editorial and news items in the *Nippon Times* are unsigned. News commentary and analysis are common on the editorial page, contributed by a wide range of authors none of whom wrote regularly or extensively during the years of the occupation. However, the attitude of the *Nippon Times* towards the occupation can be divided into 3 periods which correspond to the terms of 3 men who were responsible for the paper. When the *Times* resumed publication in postwar Japan on 1 October 1945, the publisher and printer was a wartime holdover, Kawamura Shōichi. For the first 2 weeks the *Times* advocated a wide variety of social, economic, and political changes under a new cabinet. Criticism of the government is constant but restrained. Although there is regular editorial support for freedom, individual rights, and civil liberties, the paper has a decided traditionalist bent and barely conceals its dislike for SCAP edicts and directives. From 13 October, when Wakamatsu Jintarō took over as publisher and printer, the paper supports without restraint all reforms advocated by SCAP. SCAP directives are published *in toto* every Monday and their contents applauded. There is constant publication of press releases and decisions by all SCAP sections. Commentary on domestic matters is extensive but balanced. The lack of Japanese government initiative in reform is regularly deplored but such aspects as Japan's historical familiarity with democracy, the propriety of older liberals leading Japan in transition, and the need for a blend of the modern and traditional in business and education are stressed. Labor strikes and women's liberation are advocated, as is the need for an efficient police. Reparations are accepted, the united front supported, and the constitution accepted as a Japanese-derived document. From mid-May 1946, there are extensive news and commentary about the war crimes trials. The purges are supported and the allies judged to be "eminently reasonable and just" (14 Dec. 1946). From 13 May 1947, when Togasaki Kiyoshi became president of the paper, there is a drastic change in the content and tenor of the news coverage. There is a gradual tapering off of publications of directives and releases by SCAP and most policies and actions are described as independent actions by the Japanese government. In mid-1947 there are minor criticisms of the extension of the purges and the abolition of the Home Ministry. Direct references to the occupation are rare, but by late 1948 editorial conservatism and anticommunism are pronounced and again in line with the now-changed SCAP desires. Pro-Americanism is again pronounced and all of SCAP's economic policies and recommendations are supported. By early 1950 cold war rhetoric is obvious and an issue-by-issue revision of earlier editorial policy is almost complete—for instance, the dissolution of Zenrōren (National Labor Union Liaison Council) is supported as an attack on labor radicalism and the need for Japanese self-defense actions is noted—and an American-Japanese alliance is advocated from the start of the Korean War. An editorial of 2 September 1950 stated: "The opportunity has come on this fifth anniversary of Japan's formal surrender and immediate rebirth to demonstrate the Japanese people's conviction of their acceptance of democracy by making it unequivocably clear that they want to align themselves with the free nations against the Communist menace which is displaying its ambitions of world domination." Economically, in line with the Dodge proposals, the *Times* advocated "capital accumulation," efficiency, and "rationalization of equipment." Beginning in early 1951 there is unequivocal support for American peace treaty proposals, even those providing for separate treaties and territorial restrictions. The *Times* supports General Ridgway's relaxation of direct control and establishment of committees to review earlier SCAP directives. However, strong assertions of Japanese nationalism and independence are notably absent. Trade with mainland China is renounced as unnecessary. The security treaty is totally supported, and the stationing of American troops in Japan after the peace treaty advocated. In early 1952 the management of the occupation is characterized as "magnanimous and understanding."

39   *Oriental Economist*. Tokyo. weekly.

A weekly Japanese publication concerning business, finance, and governmental activities in all phases of economic endeavor. Regular commentary on and explanation of SCAP economic directives are provided. Statistical information and interpretive economic analysis covering both domestic business and international trade are offered. The *Oriental Economist* was published throughout the occupation and in many respects is the SCAP-sanctioned voice of the Japanese business community. In the controversy about economic revival, the magazine advocated rapid, unlimited production expansion under the most efficient managerial units, thus disregarding considerations of inflation and the "democratization of business."

40   *Pacific Stars and Stripes*. Tokyo. daily. 4 Oct. 1945–

This 4-page daily newspaper was published by the Information and Education Department, Headquarters, Armed Forces in the Pacific at Tokyo. It was intended primarily for American troops stationed in Japan and Korea. It gives regular attention to political events in the United States, Japan, and Europe as well as sports in the United States and feature articles. Among the more notable items covered are the International Military Tribunal for the Far East, the Allied Council for Japan, Japanese government activities, conflicts between the United States and the Soviet Union, independence movements in Southeast Asia, and the growth of Communist power in mainland China. There is also considerable coverage of Japan's war plans prior to 1945. News sources include the Associated Press, United Press, and International News Service as well as its own staff writers. There is little reporting on Korea. There are neither analytical nor critical comments on the occupation.

41 *Times* (London). daily except Sunday. (Indexed in *The Official Index to the Times of London*, published quarterly.)

In comparison with American newspapers, the *London Times* news coverage of the occupation is minimal. After a brief flurry of reporting at the time of the Japanese surrender, the next major events covered are the announcement of the new constitution and the first postwar election in March and April of 1946. The *Times* notes that the new constitution borrowed its theories of government, from the United States, Britain, and France but it gives most attention to the implications of the "no war" clause (Article 9). In an editorial (10 Apr.) discussing the first postwar election the *Times* takes a skeptical stance. It feels that the election turnout may have little to do with democratic ideals and may only be a measure of response to the authority of the emperor voiced in Prime Minister Shidehara's radio broadcast emphasizing the emperor's wish that all people vote. The *Times* stresses that democracy does not come into being overnight but must have time to mature and put down roots. It warns that observers should not be deceived by outward appearances for many prewar attitudes persist. This theme is reiterated the following year in a story on the effects of the new constitution. The article concludes that democracy has only touched the surface of Japanese life and doubts whether the constitution could withstand a serious challenge from either right or left. From 1948 on, attention shifts to economic issues and the peace settlement. The news coverage reflects British concern over Japanese markets, recognizing nevertheless the importance of foreign trade for Japan's economic and political stability. The *Times* also follows rather closely the development of the labor movement in Japan and its close association with left-wing politics. While news coverage is limited, a series of lead articles by the *Times* correspondent in Tokyo, Frank Hawley, examines the labor movement, the activities of the Japan Communist party, and educational reform including a harsh criticism of the Eells plan for university reform.

In November 1948, the *Times* focuses its coverage on the outcome of the Tokyo war crimes trials, giving attention to the dissenting opinion of the Indian representative Pal and to the opinion of Sir William Webb, an Australian judge and president of the tribunal. By mid-1949, when the lines of the cold war had been drawn, the *Times*' editors advocate a longer occupation of Japan to safeguard against extremists of either the right or left. In 1950 the editors begin considering various possibilities for a peace settlement with Japan giving a review of the Commonwealth nations' concerns about an independent Japan. However, the *Times* is also sympathetic to the Japanese position and the problems it faces in regaining sovereignty.

On the whole, the viewpoint of the *Times* differs considerably from that found in American newspapers. There is more concern for the economic aspects of Japan's postwar recovery and the effects of Japan's reentry into world trade. Also there is less enthusiasm for the durable effectiveness of immediate and sweeping reforms. Not being so closely involved in the making and implementation of occupation policies, the British view is more detached and less optimistic than the American, but in an editorial on the occasion of the end of the occupation, the *Times* editors do concede that the American "attempt to graft on democratic institutions has not entirely failed."

Archival Materials

A very high proportion of the written records basic to almost any serious historical or social scientific study of the Allied occupation of Japan is held in governmental collections or archives. The largest and most directly relevant portion was generated by the defense establishment, most notably by the General Headquarters of SCAP, the Joint Chiefs of Staff, the Offices of the Secretaries of War and of the Navy, the Army's Civil Affairs Division, the Navy's Occupied Areas Section, and the Sixth and Eighth Armies. The presidential files and papers are also of great interest. Another very important section of the records originates with the Department of State, its political advisers attached to SCAP's staff, or with numerous agencies within the department concerned with developments in and policies toward occupied areas. The Treasury, the Foreign Economic Administration, and the Office of Strategic Services also contributed less extensive but relevant materials to the total mass of documentation. Some interdepartmental committees, especially the State-War-Navy Coordinating Committee, were of outstanding importance. There is also an international dimension to this literature. The Far Eastern Commission, the Allied Council for Japan, the Combined Chiefs of Staff, and the Pacific War Council all produced records of interest in this connection, as did a succession of high-level international conferences ranging from Casablanca through Potsdam.

The bulk, but not all, of these records is now physically housed in the Washington, D.C. area. Some of the military records have been dispersed to regional depositories in Kansas City and St. Louis, while the Roosevelt papers are at Hyde Park and the Truman papers at Independence, Missouri. General MacArthur's personal and office files are now in part located at the MacArthur Memorial's Bureau of Archives in Norfolk, Virginia (no.46), while another part remains with his family. By far the largest part of the relevant records, however, has been deposited with the National Archives and Records Service (no.48) and falls under the jurisdiction of its Modern Military Records Division. This division is housed in the Archives' new depository at Suitland, Maryland, a suburb of Washington, D.C. A second major collection is to be found in the Department of State's central files, while smaller but important collections are in the possession of the Office of the Chief of Military History (no.49), the Army Library in the Pentagon (no.42), the Historical Office of the Department of State, and the Library of Congress. The McKeldin Library of the University of Maryland at College Park (no.47), also a suburb of the capital, has a unique collection of Japanese-language materials published during the occupation.

Unfortunately, the great bulk of the official documentation relating to the occupation generated by agencies of the U.S. government is not readily available for scholarly use. Much of it is still classified. As a consequence, some form of security clearance is necessary if the scholar is to have meaningful access to the official records. The procedures involved in obtaining this clearance and the feasibility of doing so vary significantly with the department that happens to control access to the particular records sought. The problem is further complicated by the related facts that many of the major collections contain large proportions of action or information copies of documents originating outside of their own department or agency and that the authority to clear such materials for scholarly use legally resides with the issuing agency rather than the agency that happens to have current custody of them. Finally, successful access to various classified materials may oblige the researcher to submit either or both his notes and his final manuscript to official clearance procedures.

The problems involved in alleviating this situation are serious and complex. They range from an insufficiency of funds to bureaucratic indifference or hostility. The sheer bulk of the records involved is truly formidable—about 9,000 linear feet of files, for example, in the main SCAP collection alone. The archival and historical branches of the government do not generally command a high budgetary priority and are starved for both personnel and operating funds. It is partly for these reasons that the so-called automatic downgrading of security classification by steps over a set period of years leading in theory to eventual declassification does not in practice work very effectively. There simply are too many classified documents too interfiled with unclassified materials and too few qualified personnel to take care of the situation.

There are nevertheless a few bright spots with respect to official material relating to the occupation. As of this writing, the Department of State's Historical Office has finally issued the relevant volumes of *Foreign Relations of the United States* for 1947 (no.203b)—twenty-five years after the events described rather than the twenty years they claim to favor or the twenty-two years they normally cite as the interval between the events and the publication of this official record. They have, however, done substantially better with most of the major conference volumes containing the papers relating to such high-level meetings as those at Casablanca, Cairo, Yalta, and Potsdam, and deserve credit for this. Another bright spot is the extent, efficiency, and friendliness of the assistance that scholars working in many of the collections may look forward to receiving from their staffs.

42   Archival Materials

It is also important to note that in addition to the above-mentioned depositories of largely official records, there is a growing number of notable but much smaller collections of materials linked with individual participants in the occupation and with prominent U.S. government statesmen of the period. The Oral History Research Office at Columbia University (no.44), for example, has conducted systematic interviews with at least seventeen former members of SCAP's staff and, under varying conditions, will make the records of most of these interviews available for use by properly qualified scholars. The University of Michigan's Asia Library possesses the papers of the late Commander Alfred Rodman Hussey (no.43), a prominent member of the staff of SCAP's Government Section, while the Hoover Institution on War, Revolution and Peace at Stanford University has a similar but smaller collection of papers given it by Commander Hussey's colleague, Lieutenant Colonel Milo Rowell. The papers of William C. Dixon (a member of the 1946 Mission on Japanese Combines) in the Harry S. Truman Library at Independence, Missouri, Robert L. Eichelberger at Duke University Library (Durham, North Carolina), James V. Forrestal at Princeton University Library, General Walter Krueger in the U.S. Military Academy Library at West Point, General Frank R. McCoy in the Manuscript Division of the Library of Congress, Thomas Vernor Smith (a member of the U.S. Education Mission to Japan) at the University of Chicago Library, Henry L. Stimson at Yale University Library, and Robert E. Wood (chairman of the Board of Directors of Sears Roebuck and Co. and General MacArthur's closest political confidant) in the collection of the Herbert Hoover Library at West Branch, Iowa are but a few additional examples of archival materials which scholars certainly should not overlook even though we have been unable to provide specific entries for them within this bibliography. For further information on the nature and availability of materials of this type, the interested reader should consult the following guides in particular: (1) the annual volumes of *The National Union Catalog of Manuscript Collections* compiled by the Library of Congress, which provides brief descriptions (the size, scope, contents and location of a collection, restrictions on access to its holdings, etc.) of nearly 30,000 manuscript collections housed permanently in over 800 repositories that are regularly open to scholars, and (2) the "news notes" section of the quarterly issues of the journal *American Archivist*, which contains valuable information on recent accessions of manuscript material by various libraries—some of which do *not* list any of their accessions in *The National Union Catalog*.

A series of brief descriptions of particular archival collections which it has been possible for us to examine is provided within this section.

42   Army Library. Pentagon. Washington, D.C.

In addition to the SCAP documents and reports that are widely available in most major libraries, the Army Library in the Pentagon contains a number of further reports issued by the Natural Resources Section, the Economic and Scientific Section, and the Civil Information and Education Section of SCAP. Materials available include studies of the Japanese tax structure, the agricultural programs initiated under the occupation, the 1950 population census of Japan, and a study of the postwar religious situation in Japan. One important series to be found in the Army Library is a collection of bulletins concerning the regulations for the trial of war criminals.

43 Ann Arbor. Univ. of Michigan. Asia Library. Alfred Rodman Hussey, papers.

Hussey was associated with SCAP's Government Section from October 1945, first as a member of the Planning Unit, and then successively as chief, Internal Affairs Unit; chief, Governmental Powers Branch of the Governmental Powers Division; special assistant to the chief, Government Section; and throughout the period, a member of the Planning Group. He left SCAP to return to the United States in July 1948.

Hussey's papers constitute one of the most important collections of materials relating to the activities of the Government Section. Although in some respects fragmentary, the papers shed much light on the internal workings of the section. Several different kinds of material are contained in the Hussey files: copies of formal policy statements and less formal memorandums circulated within the section and between the section and other organs of the occupation; Hussey's own notes and draft proposals on various topics; working drafts of SCAP-initiated legislation; copies of official publications of the occupation and of press releases explaining SCAP policies and innovations; some biographical information on section personnel; and miscellaneous material collected by Hussey in English and Japanese relating to conditions in Japan and the Japanese reaction to occupation activities.

The most important topic covered in the Hussey files is the 1947 constitution. Hussey was a principal author of the so-called MacArthur draft of the constitution and he organized and sometimes annotated the memorandums and drafts among his constitutional materials. These materials include many notes and reports on internal debates on proposed constitutional innovations, on the Konoe-Atcheson talks of October 1945, discussions with the Far Eastern Advisory Commission in January 1946, and on strategies for popularizing and ensuring Japanese acceptance of the new draft constitution. There are also drafts of the constitution at various stages of development. Hussey played a significant role in the establishment of the new Labor Ministry and his files contain extensive materials on this topic. In general, the Hussey papers include letters, memorandums, orders, reports, and official and unofficial policy papers and draft legislation on the following topics:

1. Organization of the occupation, with special reference to the structure, duties, procedures, and personnel of the Government Section
2. Demobilization, war crimes investigations and prosecutions, restitution, and reparations
3. Diet and local election results and campaign practices during the occupation period
4. Diet activities and reorganization
5. The constitution
6. The Imperial Household, its prerogatives, property, membership, and place in the postwar scheme
7. Problems of judicial and police organization and policy, with special attention to civil rights issues
8. Labor unrest, the creation and structure of the Labor Ministry, and attendant legislation
9. Policies and legislation on public welfare and health, relief measures, and education
10. Economic problems, including control of the economy, finance, inflation, commodity allocation, public works, the economic purge, and *zaibatsu* deconcentration
11. Local autonomy and government, the operational role of SCAP in relation to Japanese governmental reorganization, and problems of military government on all levels
12. The political purge and questions of exemptions, amnesty, and noncompliance
13. Venereal disease control (antiprostitution legislation)
14. Civil liberties

44 Archival Materials

15. Press conferences, miscellaneous press translations, and analyses
16. Hussey's drafts of policy statements and memorandums on occupation policies
17. Outlines and materials relating to a projected (but unwritten) book on the occupation—manuscripts, correspondence, and autobiographical information
18. Correspondence, mostly postoccupation
19. Materials relating to Hussey's activities after the occupation

The Hussey papers have been organized by John Bowden of the University of Michigan, and his unpublished M.A. thesis, "The SCAP Files of Commander Alfred R. Hussey" (1968; 114p.), describes and annotates the collection in greater detail. Copies of the dissertation on microfilm and in xerox form are available through the university's Asia Library.

44 Columbia Univ. Oral History Research Office. Oral History Project. New York, N.Y.

The *Oral History Project* at Columbia University includes significant materials relating to the occupation of Japan. Mrs. Beate Gordon, formerly of the Government Section of SCAP, has conducted interviews with participants in the occupation who served with various sections of SCAP and the Far East Command. In the course of these interviews she briefly questions interviewees on their general backgrounds and then concentrates on their experiences in occupied Japan and their impressions of various aspects of the occupation. The taped interviews have then been transcribed and the resulting typescripts average approximately 60 pages apiece. There are 14 completed interviews that relate exclusively to the occupation. Two more interviews (with Eugene Dooman and Charles Kades) were in process. The project also has interviews with Roger Baldwin, Joseph Ballantine, and Sir George Sansom which include considerable material relating to the occupation of Japan. The available interviews are as follows:

44a "Japan, 1947." *The Reminiscences of Roger Nash Baldwin.* Typescript. Oral History Research Office. Columbia Univ. 1954. v.1, pt.3. p.432–503, app.

A considerable portion of Baldwin's reminiscences is devoted to a narrative account of his experiences in Japan during the occupation. This supplements another oral history project interview (1961) (no.44b) that was devoted exclusively to the occupation. Baldwin was a consultant or observer in all of the other ongoing American occupations and thus his analysis of the Japanese situation has a somewhat unusual perspective. The interviews for this extensive report were conducted by Harlan B. Phillips and the account differs from the occupation project interview in that it is not in question and answer form but is an uninterrupted narrative. Consequently this version appears more informal and less restrained.

Baldwin describes the circumstances leading up to his 3-month trip to Japan in a private capacity rather than as a representative of the American Civil Liberties Union and provides a comprehensive account of his experiences during his stay. In addition to his account of specific duties and activities, he provides descriptions of the personalities and attitudes of numerous important SCAP and Japanese officials associated with the occupation, as well as some incisive comments on the nature and operation of the occupation machinery and the general climate of Japan in 1947. There is a particularly thorough study of General MacArthur's personality and role in the occupation, which is extremely complimentary yet also objective. Although critical of many of the general's later actions, Baldwin had great admiration for him in 1947 and attributes the remarkable success of the occupation of Japan as due in greatest part to his leadership. Also included in these reminiscences are notes which he took following several important sessions with General MacArthur regarding censorship, Japan's international relations, the purge, the provost courts, prison cases, public meetings, etc.

Appendix A, entitled "Documents on Japan," may be found in vol.1, part 4 (p.666–726). It covers a variety of materials including some of Baldwin's letters describing assets and liabilities of the occupation, a report to the American Civil Liberties Union on civil liberties in the occupation, and various memorandums and notes to and from SCAP and Japanese officials regarding the author's findings and recommendations.

44b *The Japanese Reminiscences of Roger Baldwin.* Typescript. Oral History Research Office. Columbia Univ. 1961. 118p.

Roger Baldwin's 3-month trip to Japan in 1947 as a private citizen examining civil liberties in occupied Japan is described in this report. As director of the American Civil Liberties Union he had special interest in this area. There is a general discussion of the entire SCAP program, but emphasis is given to those aspects more directly related to civil liberties such as censorship, the maintenance of public order, the judicial system, the administration of the laws, the operations of the G–2 (Military Intelligence) Section of SCAP, and methods of enforcing the provisions of the new constitution. Other topics discussed include the drafting of the constitution, popular reaction to the constitution, the political purges, and reforms in the police and educational systems. The author was primarily concerned with 3 groups during his stay in Japan—occupation officials, Japanese government officials, and citizens' organizations. He provides useful portraits of General MacArthur, Emperor Hirohito, and various occupation officials. In the latter part of the interview, he presents his analysis of the important policy changes which took place midway through the occupation and describes what he conceives to be the achievements and limitations of the occupation, particularly in the field of civil liberties.

44c *The Reminiscences of Ai Kume.* Typescript. Oral History Research Office. Columbia Univ. 1962. 59p.

The first woman lawyer admitted to the bar in Japan here comments on the impact of the occupation on Japanese life. Although not a member of the SCAP staff, she discusses the feelings of the Japanese during the war and their general reaction to the occupying troops after surrender. She is generally favorable to the occupation's programs, particularly the new constitution, the emancipation of women, the numerous legal reforms, and the land reform program. She is somewhat critical, however, of SCAP's educational reforms and also protests against the war crimes trials. The interview provides useful insights into the reactions of an articulate and intelligent Japanese citizen toward the innovations of the occupation.

44d *The Reminiscences of Alvin Graves.* Typescript. Oral History Research Office. Columbia Univ. 1961. 141p.

Alvin Graves held 2 successive positions in occupied Japan—first as a public relations officer for the U.S. Eighth Army in Yokohama and later, in 1946, as deputy head of the Visitor's Bureau, a part of the General Headquarters of SCAP. The author presents an informal narrative account of his impressions. This account evokes the atmosphere of postwar Japan and the aura surrounding MacArthur's office and presents colorful accounts of the personalities and activities of SCAP officials, other foreigners in Japan, and the Japanese people themselves.

44e *The Reminiscences of Burton Crane.* Typescript. Oral History Research Office. Columbia Univ. 1961. 75p.

A *New York Times* correspondent in Japan from the beginning of the occupation records his impressions of the period. Crane emphasizes the economic aspects of the occupation but considers other topics such as the new constitution, education, land reform, and social and political innovations. The main portion of the interview consists of comments on the style of the occupation, the structure and operations of SCAP, the quality of occupation personnel, and the nature of section reports. There are some vivid descriptions of General MacArthur and evaluations of such figures as Generals Marquat, Whitney, and Willoughby, Colonel Kades, and a number of minor officials. Since the author himself covered the meetings of the Allied Council, his account of the activities of the council is authoritative and perceptive. Crane's main criticisms of the occupation concern SCAP's inadequate economic policies and personnel and the manner in which the purges were carried out.

44f *The Reminiscences of Cyrus H. Peake.* Typescript. Oral History Research Office. Columbia Univ. 1961. 56p.

SCAP personnel concerned with constitutional reform and behind-the-scenes events leading up to the adoption of the new constitution are described in detail in this interview. The author, a member of SCAP's Government Section from January 1946 to June 1947, was chairman of the section's committee on the cabinet and he describes the work of this group as well as that of other constitutional drafting committees. Later he was responsible for reviewing legislation under the new constitution while his work in the Government Powers Section involved him with the executive branch of the Japanese government and its committees. Peake also comments briefly on such issues as the political purge, the dissolution of the *zaibatsu*, and the land reform program. The final section presents a general summation of his attitudes toward the accomplishments and failures of the occupation and his estimate of the extent to which the broad goals were attained.

44g *The Reminiscences of Dr. Lauren V. Ackerman.* Typescript. Oral History Research Office. Columbia Univ. 1961. 29p.

Ackerman, who was a member of a 12-man medical mission sent to Japan in 1951 under the auspices of the Unitarian Service Committee, presents an absorbing account of the status of medicine, particularly medical education, in occupied Japan. He describes the activities of the mission's members during their 6-week stay in Japan, emphasizing their relationships with Japanese and with SCAP officials, and presents a résumé of their recommendations for the improvement of medical education in Japan. The interview also includes Ackerman's comments on the effectiveness of the SCAP Public Health and Welfare Section and, in particular, the work of General Sams, the head of this section at the time the mission was in Japan.

44h *The Reminiscences of Douglas W. Overton.* Typescript. Oral History Research Office. Columbia Univ. 1960. 53p.

Overton held 3 occupation-related positions: (1) as first vice consul in the Yokohama Branch of the Office of the U.S. Political Adviser to SCAP from December 1945 to 1949; (2) as a member of the Diplomatic Section of SCAP and its consulate in Tokyo from 1949 to June 1950; and (3) as deputy officer in charge of Japanese political affairs in the State Department in Washington from July 1950 to August 1952. The greatest part of the account concerns his own work—first in Yokohama processing passport applications for Japanese–Americans who had spent the war in Japan, then in Tokyo corresponding with various Allied missions in Japan, later setting up the *zaigai jimusho*, the overseas agencies of the Japanese government similar to consulates, and finally in Washington, working with the still-present Japanese prisoner of war problem and the Okinawan situation. Considerable attention is paid to the relationship between the Diplomatic Section and other SCAP sections and there is also knowledgeable discussion of a variety of topics including Dulles' approach to the treaty question, Japanese reactions to the occupation, the effectiveness of the Far Eastern Commission, MacArthur's dismissal as the supreme commander, and the problem of GI babies born during the occupation.

44i *The Reminiscences of Esther Crane.* Typescript. Oral History Research Office. Columbia Univ. 1961. 59p.

An army civilian employee in Japan during the occupation, Mrs. Crane, the wife of the journalist Burton Crane, was employed initially in the Department of Media Analysis in the Civil Information and Education Section analyzing Japanese newspaper comments on the occupation. Later she worked for the army newspaper *Pacific Stars and Stripes* (no. 40). She comments on a wide variety of topics, notably the structure and operations of the Civil Information and Education Section of SCAP, the new status of women, the peace movement in Japan, and the emperor system.

44j *The Reminiscences of Faubion Bowers.* Typescript. Oral History Research Office. Columbia Univ. 1960. 58p.

One of General MacArthur's military secretaries and a member of the first contingent of Allied troops to land in Japan describes conditions immediately after surrender and his own responsibilities as MacArthur's secretary, which primarily involved making appointments for the general. The account provides an interesting portrait of the supreme commander and his methods of directing the occupation. Included are descriptions of what Bowers perceives to be MacArthur's attitudes toward high-ranking SCAP officials, the emperor, Prime Minister Yoshida, and his analysis of the overall effects of the occupation upon the Japanese people.

44k *The Reminiscences of Harlan Youel.* Typescript. Oral History Research Office. Columbia Univ. 1961. 54p.

Since the speaker spent 1949 in Okinawa and 1950 in Japan, a good part of his reminiscences involve his Okinawan experience. The latter half of the work, however, contains descriptions of his work in Tokyo with the Price Division of the Economic and Scientific Section, the office that was responsible for price controls. After a description of current economic problems such as the food shortage and black marketeering, Youel elaborates upon particular reforms undertaken by the Economic and Scientific Section, especially the dissolution of the *zaibatsu*, the economic purge, land reform, and the Dodge currency reform. Such general topics as the emperor system, the new constitution, the emancipation of Japanese women, and Japanese views on Okinawa are also treated briefly. The author's estimate of the success of the occupation and Japanese attitudes toward occupation reforms are also treated.

44l *The Reminiscences of Harold C. Henderson.* Typescript. Oral History Research Office. Columbia Univ. 1962. 62p.

Henderson was in charge of the Education, Religions, and Arts and Monuments Division of the Civil Information and Education Section at the outset of the occupation. Although he served with SCAP for less than a year, the author was engaged in several important programs, in particular, educational reforms which involved textbook revision and the encouragement of language reform and religious reforms which involved the abolition of state Shinto and the inauguration of various new policies and programs. He also comments briefly on the Civil Information and Education Section's work with regard to the national treasures of Japan. One of the most interesting sections of the interview is a discussion of the initial quality of occupation personnel in all sections and the reasons for later changes in that quality. The material also provides insight into the Civil Information and Education Section's contacts with such Japanese organizations as the Ministry of Education and the Imperial Household.

44m *The Reminiscences of Jake R. Harold.* Typescript. Oral History Research Office. Columbia Univ. 1962. 55p.

A lawyer who was employed in the Labor Division of SCAP's Economic and Scientific Section from 1946 through 1948 presents a well-organized account of labor reforms during the occupation. At first an assistant, Harold later became chief of the Labor Relations Branch of the Labor Division. In the interview he discusses his own role in creating labor relations boards in Japan, in helping to draft important legislation such as the

Trade Union Law and the Labor Relations Adjustment Law, and in developing machinery for conciliation, mediation, and arbitration. Many aspects of the labor reform program are discussed, but those receiving special attention include the development of the Teacher's Union, Communist activity in the labor union movement, and production control. A large portion of the interview is devoted to a description of the educational program of the Labor Division with considerable attention paid to the role of the army in implementing Labor Division programs. Of interest also are comments on relations among various sections of SCAP. The concluding pages present a useful summation of the aims and activities of the Labor Division.

44n *The Reminiscences of Joseph Ballantine.* Typescript. Oral History Research Office. Columbia Univ. 1961. 262p.

The memoirs of this career foreign service officer offer valuable information on a complex and often overlooked aspect of the occupation, namely, presurrender planning for the treatment of a defeated Japan. As acting chairman of the State Department's Post-war Programs Committee, Ballantine is well qualified to describe the programs and policies drawn up beginning in 1943. He outlines the nature and scope of the guidance papers for use by the army and navy and discusses the organization and operations of the State–War–Navy Coordinating Committee. There is considerable emphasis on the different and sometimes conflicting attitudes of individuals within the State Department such as Joseph Grew, Cordell Hull, James Byrnes, and Eugene Dooman. The author attempts to relate these differences to the actual operations of the occupation. After his resignation from the State Department, Ballantine served in the occupation for 3 months in 1946 with the International Military Tribunal for the Far East. He comments on the policies and programs of various sections of SCAP as well as the performance of various officials associated with them. A considerable portion of the report concerns his view of what he considers to be the 2 biggest mistakes of the occupation, i.e., the purge and the economic deconcentration policy, but there is also a consideration of the new constitution and other reform programs.

44o *The Reminiscences of Joseph Gordon.* Typescript. Oral History Research Office. Columbia Univ. 1961. 32p.

The new constitution of Japan is the primary topic of this interview. Initially Gordon was assigned to newspaper translation at the Allied Translator and Interpreter Section of SCAP but later, in 1946, he was transferred and became head of the Interpreters and Translators' Pool of the Government Section of SCAP. His account includes a discussion of his preparatory training in language at the Army Intensive Japanese Language Schools at the University of Michigan and Fort Snelling, an outline of the nature of his responsibilities in SCAP, and a summation of the developments that took place just prior to the adoption of the new constitution. With regard to the constitution, he discusses the background of the document, the controversy surrounding it, and the language difficulties associated with its formulation.

44p *The Reminiscences of Josephine Colletti McKean.* Typescript. Oral History Research Office. Columbia Univ. 1962. 80p.

The author was an education officer with the occupation from 1948 to 1950. In this interview she focuses on her own work in the educational reform program in which she associated primarily with Japanese teachers, principals, superintendents, and representatives of the Ministry of Education. She discusses the effect of particular educational reforms such as in-service teacher training programs and the revision of textbooks and curricula, and gives an overall account of the structure and operations of the new educational system with her own estimates of its favorable and unfavorable aspects.

44q *The Reminiscences of Sir George Sansom.* Typescript. Oral History Research Office, Columbia Univ. 1957. 98p.

A very brief portion of Sir George Sansom's memoirs (p.74–79) concerns his view of the occupation. Although he has many reservations about particular aspects of the occupation, in his general analysis Sansom describes it as a great success. Following this brief summation are candid and colorful remarks on several SCAP officials, notably Generals Willoughby and McCoy, and brief comments on the operations of the Far Eastern Commission.

45 Detroit, Mich. Detroit Public Library. Joseph M. Dodge papers.

The Dodge papers represent one of the most valuable archival sources available for insight into American economic policy toward Japan between 1949 and 1952. In December 1948 President Truman assigned Dodge, who was at that time president of the Detroit Bank and a key adviser on U.S. policy toward occupied Germany, the task of controlling inflation and creating fiscal solvency in Japan. The resultant "Dodge Line" of economic stabilization was one of the most pivotal and controversial aspects of the final occupation years.

Materials in the Detroit collection pertaining to Dodge's activities in Japan are voluminous. They include 9 boxes of documents for 1949; 10 boxes for 1950; 7 boxes for 1951; and 2 boxes for 1952. Another box contains correspondence pertaining to Japan from 1955 to 1961. "Printed material and press notices" for Japan may be found in 9 additional boxes. In all cases, the documents within the various boxes remain in the topical folders in which Dodge himself placed them.

In addition to the information they contain on U.S. economic planning for Japan, the Dodge papers provide insight into such related matters as the Japanese response to the Dodge Line; disagreements within the SCAP bureaucracy over economic and noneconomic policies; and American thinking, especially within the Department of the Army, concerning China and Southeast Asia insofar as these areas were seen as being of importance to Japan. Despite their great bulk and value, however, it is clear that the papers now in the Detroit Library do not represent the complete record of Dodge's activities in Japan. Documents relating to certain sensitive areas with which Dodge was concerned—e.g., Japanese rearmament and postoccupation U.S. aid to Japan—have been removed.

Arrangements to use the Dodge papers should be made through the chief of the Burton Historical Collection, Detroit Public Library, 5201 Woodward Avenue, Detroit, Michigan 48202. Prior permission to examine the papers must be obtained from Dodge's son, whose address is: Joseph J. Dodge, Director, Cummer Gallery of Art, 829 Riverside Avenue, Jacksonville, Florida 32204.

45a Holmes, Lulu H. *Higher Education for Women in Japan, 1946–1948.* Berkeley: Regional Oral History Office, Bancroft Library, Univ. of California, 1968. ix, 54p, 25p.

In an interview conducted by Helene M. Brewer, Lulu Holmes, a SCAP adviser on higher education for women in Japan, presents her recollections of developments with respect to educational conditions for women in Japan during the years 1946–48. She briefly discusses the organizational pattern of SCAP with particular emphasis on the Civil Information and Education Section for which she worked. In addition she describes the goals of the section and the methods adopted to achieve these goals. A general account of the Civil Information and Education Section's reorganization of the Japanese school system is followed by a consideration of reforms that were undertaken in the specific area of higher education for women and the reaction of the Japanese to such reforms. There is also a description of the reorganization and development of several leading women's colleges in Japan by way of concrete illustration. Unlike many of the occupation oral history reports, there is little discussion of personalities and interrelationships within SCAP and more emphasis on the actual implementation of educational reform programs. The final section of the work consists of the text of a report prepared by Holmes in 1966 which summarizes changes in higher education for women in Japan since 1946-48. The report may also be obtained at the Oral History Research Office, Columbia University, New York, NY.

46 MacArthur Memorial. Bureau of Archives. Norfolk, Va.

Numerous materials relating to the occupation may be found in the Bureau of Archives of the MacArthur Memorial. The collection is composed of 18 Record Groups, 4 of which are of particular relevance to the Allied occupation of Japan. Record Group 5 comprises some 40 running feet of documentation and is entitled "Records of General Headquarters, SCAP." This group contains official reports on all SCAP sections as well as on developments in numerous branches of the Japanese government. It also includes documents and reports issued by various independent missions such as the U.S. Personnel Advisory Mission to Japan, and messages and official correspondence of General MacArthur. Record Group 6 (45 ft.), entitled "Records of General Headquarters, Far East Command," relates to military aspects of the occupation between 1947 and 1951. The collection includes general and special orders, interoffice memorandums, and messages sent and received by the Far East Command. Record Group 9 (55 ft.) is entitled "Collection of Messages" and consists of radiograms and cables to and from numerous sections within General Headquarters, SCAP. Record Group 10 (95 ft.) contains some of General Douglas MacArthur's private correspondence from 1932 to 1964. Many of the letters relate directly to his position as the supreme commander for the Allied powers and provide valuable insights into his attitudes toward various aspects of the occupation. There is also a group termed the Blue Binder series which contains collections of messages from various missions, boards, and commissions concerned with occupation matters.

47 McKeldin Library. Univ. of Maryland. College Park, Md.

The University of Maryland's collection of materials relating to the occupation includes a number of special reports issued by the Civil Information and Education Section, the Economic and Scientific Section, and the Natural Resources Section as well as some issues of the *Weekly Bulletin* (no.2186) published by the Public Health and Welfare Section. Materials produced by the Allied Translator and Interpreter Section (ATIS) are particularly numerous. In addition to the various series of *Press Translations and Summaries* (nos.350–51) and *Early Morning Reports,* the McKeldin Library possesses a 2-volume index to ATIS publications as of December 1946 and a number of the ATIS *Monthly Reports* (no.922). The University of Maryland collection also includes a large number of materials relating to military aspects of the occupation, for example, military intelligence reports prepared during the final stages of the war and the early part of the occupation as well as activities reports charting the organization and functions of the U.S. Armed Forces in the Pacific. There are also texts of press releases from General Headquarters, Far East Command from June through September 1948, and various maps of Japan prepared by General Headquarters, U.S. Army Forces, Pacific, from September 1944 through April 1946. There is a particularly good set of SCAP informational materials on Japan and the Japanese government which includes such documents and reports as: *The Cabinet of Japanese Government,* n.d., 31p.; *The Japanese Government Organization Report on 1 September 1946,* 35p.; *Handbook and Laws for the Japanese Diet Elections April 1947,* 97p.; *Local Elections in Japan (1947) Annex 1,* 33p.; *Report on Changes in the Organization of the Japanese Government,* November 1945; and *Japanese Proposed Conversion Plan for Former Army Arsenals into Peace-time Industries,* n.d. The library also possesses an incomplete collection of the corrected verbatim minutes of meetings of the Allied Council for Japan as well as the *Civil Affairs Handbooks* (no. 235) prepared by the army in August 1945 and the War Department *Pamphlets* prepared in September 1945.

The McKeldin Library has what is reputed to be the only extant collection of Japanese galley proofs for materials that were censored by SCAP in the early years of the occupation, as well as English translations of the censored sections and SCAP documents explaining what portions were censored and why. The censored materials include books, magazines, newspapers, letters, and movie scripts. The reasons for censorship were predominantly political and range from the expression of militarist, ultranationalist or rightist views to the advocacy of radical communism. Criticisms of SCAP's social or economic reform programs were also censored. Other censored materials involve criticisms of General MacArthur and of various policies or programs of the occupation or the United States. The materials involved indicate the range of SCAP's control of publication in occupied Japan. The censorship process involved deletion, suppression, or disapproval. The materials are not yet systematically organized.

48   National Archives and Records Service. Modern Military Records Div. Suitland, Md.

The bulk of the official records of the occupation that are apt to be of prime scholarly interest have been deposited in the new archives building at Suitland, Maryland, a suburb of Washington, D.C. They are very extensive, occupying some 4,500 file drawers or 9,000 linear feet of file space. There are also an additional 4 linear feet of comprehensive inventories and packing lists that provide a rough guide to the contents of the collection.

Since these records are the operating files of the General Headquarters of SCAP, they are classified primarily along organizational lines with major holdings for each of the special sections into which General MacArthur's—and, later, General Ridgway's—headquarters was divided, e.g., Government Section, Economic and Scientific Section, Civil Information and Education Section, etc. Within each of these sections the relevant files may be broken down by organizational subdivisions, by chronological order, by subject matter, or by some combination thereof. Actual practice varies widely. There are no records for the supreme commander's own office and those for his chief of staff's office are quite scant as are those for the offices of the assistant chiefs of staff.

The degree of bibliographic control over the contents of this vast collection, and consequently the problems of scholars endeavoring to make use of it, varies widely from section to section. The size and complexity of the collection are such that it has never been financially possible to place the collection under that degree of bibliographic control that the National Archives and Records Service would obviously prefer. As a consequence, it is still extremely difficult to work with some portions of the records, e.g., the files relating to developments at the level of regional or prefectural civil affairs teams. Individual members of the National Archives staff are, however, both very knowledgeable about the contents of the collection and extremely helpful to visiting scholars. Regretably, however, only quite limited sections of the collection are readily available to qualified scholars. Much of the material is still classified and, since classified and nonclassified items are extensively interfiled in the same drawers and folders, the task of segregating the former or of arranging for their declassification has so far greatly exceeded the available resources of money, time, or personnel.

Not all of the SCAP records are kept in the archives at Suitland. Some have been sent to depositories at Kansas City and St. Louis. There exists a *Preliminary Inventory of the Records of General Headquarters, Supreme Commander for the Allied Powers* compiled in 1962 by Helene Bowen (Record Group 331, NM–11, 38p.), a member of the staff of the National Archives and Records Serv-

48a   Archival Materials

ice, that is helpful in understanding the general organization and extent of this record group.

48a   Princeton, N.J. Princeton University Library. John Foster Dulles papers.

The Dulles papers provide a valuable source for the study of the Japanese peace treaty that ended the American occupation in 1952. Dulles was appointed in April 1950 by President Harry S. Truman as Special Adviser to the Department of State and later as personal representative of the president on the Japanese peace treaty with the rank of ambassador. He was given a free hand to negotiate with the Japanese government, as well as with the British, Australian, Philippine and other governments on such vital issues as the continuation of occupation reforms, postoccupation security, reparations, and Japanese recognition of Nationalist China. During his nearly 2 years of effort, Ambassador Dulles regularly consulted with the Senate Foreign Relations Committee and key congressmen on the development of the treaty.

The Correspondence files for the years 1950–52, 1 box on the Japanese peace treaty, and notebooks of press releases and speeches regarding the Far East comprise the bulk of the material available on the termination of the occupation. In addition, portions of numerous interviews available in the Dulles Oral History Project deal with Dulles' role in the Japanese Peace Treaty. The interviews with William J. Sebald, C. Stanton Babcock, George F. Kennan, Allen Dulles, and W. Walton Butterworth are especially noteworthy on Japanese questions.

Permission to use materials in the Dulles papers is required from the Dulles Committee, through Princeton University Library.

49   U.S. Dept. of the Army. Office of the Chief of Military History. Washington, D.C.

The Office of the Chief of Military History contains many of the most widely available SCAP materials such as the historical manuscript series entitled *History of the Non-Military Activities of the Occupation of Japan* (nos.283–337). In addition, there are numerous manuscripts dealing with the activities and experiences of the army ground forces, the army field forces and the field armies during and after World War II. Materials relating to the Sixth and Eighth Armies during and after World War II may also be found in this collection, but many of the most significant documents such as the monograph series of the Historical Section of the Eighth Army Headquarters remain classified and may be used only by persons with security clearance.

Presurrender Planning Before 2 September 1945

The degree of planning for postwar Japan was most unusual. In the United States, for example, systematic planning for the postdefeat treatment of Japan began in the Department of State as early as April 1942. Speculations and recommendations came from private organizations and individuals shortly after this time. Both official and unofficial policy planning for postwar Japan increased in scale and intensity as the war progressed toward an end. Although hostilities ceased with the acceptance by the Japanese government of the terms of surrender set forth in the Potsdam Declaration on 14 August 1945, the formal surrender ceremony did not take place until 2 September 1945. It is this latter date that has been selected as marking the end of the presurrender period and the beginning of the occupation proper.

In this section we have attempted to assemble a reasonably definitive and annotated list of the significant literature relating to the presurrender planning for the postwar treatment of Japan. In our estimation this section constitutes an essential foundation for understanding the nature of subsequent developments during the occupation period proper. The relevant literature is expansive and sometimes difficult to categorize with precision. The simplest arrangement would perhaps have been to classify all materials as either official or unofficial in terms of their authorship. However, a more complicated—but, we hope, also more useful—approach has been adopted. A system of 9 major categories, defined largely but not entirely by subject, has been devised. They are:

1. Planning in the United States
    a. In Official Quarters
    b. In Private Quarters
2. Planning in Japan
3. Planning Elsewhere
4. Major International Conferences and High-level Diplomacy

5. Biographical Literature
6. Materials Associated with SCAP Headquarters
7. Training Arrangements in the United States for the Military Government of Japan
8. The Decision to Use Atomic Weapons
9. General Collections of Official Documents, Speeches, etc.

These categories are not, of course, mutually exclusive. They do permit the arrangement of particular items according to their most outstanding characteristics but, inevitably, there is overlap. Where overlap is substantial, cross-references have been employed, but the reader should be aware that in some cases it has not been readily possible to indicate that relatively minor portions of a work in one category also relate to another category. Therefore, this section should be used as a unit.

It should also be noted that planning for the occupation was a continuous activity. It did not cease with the actual beginning of the occupation on 2 September 1945. In fact, since the end of the war in the Pacific came considerably sooner than was expected at the time, many of the most important plans for the occupation were either devised or put into final form only well after the occupation had formally begun. Consequently, items relating to planning will also be found in later sections.

Planning in the United States

Since the United States bore the major responsibility for the conduct of the war in the Pacific, it is not surprising that she was also involved in wartime planning. Americans attempted to foresee the particular circumstances of Japan and the general circumstances apt to prevail in the international community at the time of Japan's defeat, to determine the nature of the United States' national interests and goals with respect to a defeated Japan, to outline with as much precision and detail as possible the policies best suited to the accomplishment of these goals, and to devise machinery for the implementation of such policies. Postwar planning became an important and relatively popular activity both within the government and in some private quarters.

In the two subsections that follow, an attempt has been made to distinguish between the official U.S. planning process and its results on the one hand, and its private analogues on the other. In fact, while the two processes are organizationally distinguishable, there was some degree of interaction. The governmental planners were usually aware of major viewpoints and writings in the private sector, while the latter watched closely and speculated freely about planning developments within the government and what they portended for the postwar treatment of Japan.

IN OFFICIAL QUARTERS

There have been as yet very few systematic studies of the presurrender planning for the occupation of Japan carried out within governmental circles in the

United States. Of those that are available four volumes of the Foreign Relations of the United States series (v.5 of 1944, v.6 of 1945, v.8 of 1946, and v.6 of 1947—nos.201, 202, 203a, and 203b) plus four monographs (nos.50, 53, 59, and 61) listed below are of outstanding authority and value.

Blakeslee, George H. "Negotiating to Establish the Far Eastern Commission, 1945." 1951. *See* no.853.

Borton, Hugh. "American Occupation Policies in Japan." 1947. *See* no.481.

50 ———. *American Presurrender Planning for Postwar Japan.* New York: Columbia Univ., East Asian Institute, 1967. 37p. (Occasional Papers of the East Asian Institute, Columbia Univ.)

A brief but authoritative report of presurrender planning for American postwar policies for Japan and the Allied occupation of Japan that was originally prepared for a conference on military occupations and political change. There is a chronological account of the planning for the main policies, and the author skillfully analyzes "how the policies were formed first in the Department of State, their development in conjunction with the War and Navy Departments, and finally their acceptance with minor changes by the Allies." The author, a State Department official during this period, presents a careful analysis of the development and implementation of the planning programs involved. An appendix provides a useful outline of the initial postwar objectives of the United States in Japan.

———. "Occupation Policies in Japan and Korea." 1948. *See* no.539.

51 ———. "Preparation for the Occupation of Japan." *Journal of Asian Studies* 25:203–12 (Feb. 1966)

The author who worked with various U.S. presurrender planning agencies gives an account of the establishment and methods of these agencies. Specifically, he writes of the State-War-Navy Coordinating Committee. Borton discusses some of the problems this group faced and the way in which they came up against the problem of the imperial institution. He concludes with a discussion of the way in which General MacArthur and SCAP drafted the new Japanese Constitution.

52 ———. "United States Occupation Policies in Japan since Surrender." *Political Science Quarterly* 62:250–57 (June 1947)

The formulation of U.S. policy in occupied Japan is the topic of this report, and the author analyzes the basic questions confronting the U.S. authorities concerning the military occupation of a former enemy country. He cites the terms of the Potsdam Declaration as one of the more important documents setting guidelines for future policy and also alludes to various documents prepared by the State-War-Navy Coordinating Committee. The article also includes a discussion of the establishment of the Far Eastern Advisory Commission and the Far Eastern Commission which succeeded it.

Brown, Allan R. *The Figurehead Role of the Japanese Emperor: Perception and Reality.* 1971. *See* no.1231b.

Cassidy, Velma H. "American Policy in Occupied Areas." 1946. *See* no.421.

53 Cline, Ray Steiner. *Washington Command Post: The Operations Division.* Washington, D.C.: Dept. of the Army, Office of the Chief of Military History, 1951. xvi, 413p. (U.S. Army in World War II, v.4, pt.2)

A detailed and systematic documentary analysis of that section of the U.S. Army's High Command during World War II called the Operations Division (OPD) of the War Department General

Staff. The author, a Junior Fellow at Harvard University who served in the Office of Strategic Services, presented the original version of this report to Harvard in 1949 as a doctoral dissertation in history entitled "United States Army in World War II; High Command: The Operations Division of the War Department General Staff." The present work covers the origins, development, responsibilities, and characteristics of the OPD from its establishment in March 1942 through its reorganization in 1946. Its predecessor agency, the War Plans Division, is also discussed briefly at the outset. Chapter 16, "Military Planning and Foreign Affairs," discusses the functions of the State-War-Navy Coordinating Committee and presents evaluations of the international conferences of 1944 and 1945. Chapter 17, "Case History: Planning the End of the War against Japan," gives an account of the military strategy to bring about Japan's surrender. This chapter analyzes such topics as initial American strategy, planning for a "prolonged" Pacific War, evaluation of the surrender formula, the use of atomic bombs, the surrender documents, and plans for the occupation.

54 "Concerning Policy toward Japan." *Department of State Bulletin* 13:479–80 (30 Sept. 1945)

A presurrender exchange of letters between Senator Kenneth Wherry and Acting Secretary of State Dean Acheson relating to Wherry's queries concerning Acheson's views on the nature of the impending occupation and the responsibilities of General MacArthur as supreme commander for the Allied powers.

Dunn, Fredrick S. *Peace-Making and the Settlement with Japan.* 1963. See no.2464.

54a Galloway, George Barnes. *Postwar Planning in the United States: An Organizational Directory.* New York: Twentieth Century Fund, 1942. xi, 158p.

In this directory, Galloway provides a nearly complete listing of American agencies engaged in planning for postwar reconstruction as of March 1942. The work of 102 government and private agencies, industrial and financial organizations, trade associations, and transportation agencies is described. In each case, Galloway provides a summary of the organization's activities, its address, the names of its principal personnel, and information on the publications it has produced or is expected to bring out. The directory understandably focuses on postwar planning for the United States and for Europe, but on occasion it refers specifically to planning for Japan as in the case of a Council on Foreign Affairs project chaired by George Blakeslee. Furthermore, it includes information for a number of the agencies which subsequently were to undertake projects on East Asia. For these reasons, this volume is a convenient handbook for those interested in American planning for the postwar reconstruction of Japan.

Ginsburgh, Robert N. *Between War and Peace: An Administrative and Organizational Analysis of Selected Military Government Experiences of the United States Army during the Transition Phase.* 1948. See no.902.

55 Kreps, Leslie Roy. *The Image of Japan in the Speaking of United States Congressmen, 1941–1953.* Ph.D. dissertation, Northwestern Univ., 1957. 370p. (Abstracted in *Dissertation Abstracts* 18: 696 [1958]; University Microfilms order no.24,908)

In this dissertation, Kreps attempts to show that a correlation existed between the accuracy of the image of the Japanese presented in speeches by U.S. congressmen between 1941 and 1953 and the nature of the policies they were advocating. As one example he notes that during World War II, those congressmen who favored relocation of Japanese-Americans invariably used racial stereotypes which depicted the Japanese as treacherous, dishonest, atheistic, and uncivilized. Those congressmen who defended the Japanese-Americans presented a more accurate image. During World War II, the fact that psychological warfare broadcasts presented an accurate image of the Japanese was primarily the result of efforts by Senator Elbert D. Thomas, who had been a missionary in Japan. According to Kreps, in the early 1950's, most congressmen regarded Japan as an ally and expected the Japanese to rearm, despite Japanese reluctance to do so.

Martin, Edwin M. *The Allied Occupation of Japan.* 1948. See no.561.

56 Morgan, Henry G. *Planning the Defeat of Japan: A Study of Total War Strategy.* Washington, D.C.: Dept. of the Army, Office of the Chief of Military History, 1961. x, 197p.

The development of overall Allied strategy against Japan before and during World War II is the primary focus of this work. The author traces the changes in both the strategy and the planning process itself that came about in response to military and political developments before and after Pearl Harbor, and he concludes with an assessment of the strengths and weaknesses of prewar and wartime strategic planning. Chapter 5, "The Last Two Years of War: Reaching the Final Decisions," discusses in some detail the formulation of plans for the projected invasion of Japan, with special attention being given to "Olympic"—the code name for the Sixth Army's planned invasion of Kyushu. Only limited attention is given to postsurrender planning.

57 Morton, Lewis. "Soviet Intervention in the War with Japan." *Foreign Affairs* 40:653–62 (July 1962)

Morton, formerly deputy chief historian of the U.S. Army, describes the military factors that governed American relations with the Soviet Union during the war. He notes that the U.S. decision to seek Soviet participation provides one of the clearest examples in recent history of the subordination of the political to the military considerations of policy.

58 Moseley, Harold W., Charles W. McCarthy, and Alvin F. Richardson. "The State-War-Navy Coordinating Committee." *Department of State Bulletin* 13: 745–47 (11 Nov. 1945)

All 3 writers were at one time staff members of the committee they describe in this article—Moseley from the State Department, McCarthy representing the War Department, and Richardson the Navy Department. Although there is little direct reference to the State-War-Navy Coordinating Committee's (SWNCC) formulation and implementation of policy in occupied Japan, nevertheless students of the occupation will find valuable the discussion of the pre- and postsurrender purposes and authority of SWNCC, its composition, subjects considered by the committee, and the future of the organization. The authors believe that SWNCC will not necessarily be terminated with the advent of peace, but rather will evolve into an agency with the responsibility of a postwar security organization.

59 Svensson, Eric H. F. *The Military Occupation of Japan: The First Years of Planning, Policy Formulation, and Reforms.* Washington, D.C.: 1966. 347p.

This study is concerned primarily with the development of planning and policy formation for the occupation, the entrance of the military forces into Japan, and the execution of some of the significant reform programs that were initiated early in the occupation. The first chapter on early planning for the occupation has been deleted from the volume for security reasons. The portions of the work devoted to presurrender policy formulation thus begin with the establishment of the State-War-Navy Coordinating Committee in December 1944 and the planning that was undertaken at Headquarters, Southwest Pacific Area. They provide useful insights into early planning activities. In his consideration of the occupation proper, the author confines himself to the development of its organizational structure and the initiation of early directives and programs regarding such issues as constitutional reform and reform of the economic and agricultural systems in Japan. In discussing these programs, he describes both their historical backgrounds and the situation as it existed in the immediate postwar period. He then treats problems associated with the inauguration or implementation of the specific reform programs. It is the author's contention that planning and policy formulation were initially hampered by a lack of definition of missions and responsibilities—a deficiency exemplified in the bitter conflict within the U.S. government as to whether the occupation of a defeated nation was properly a function of the military at all, or whether it should be undertaken by civilian agencies. However, he maintains that, even judging from the accomplishments of the early years, the occupation was successful in achieving its primary goals.

The draft manuscript is available at the Office of the Chief of Military History, Washington, D.C.

This report in revised and expanded form was subsequently accepted as a doctoral dissertation (no.60) at the University of Denver in 1966.

60 ———. *The Military Occupation of Japan: The First Years. Planning, Policy Formation, and Reforms.* Ph.D. dissertation, Univ. of Denver, 1966. 427p. (Abstracted in *Dissertation Abstracts* 27: 4205A–6A [1967]; University Microfilms order no.67–4793)

Basing his research on War Department and SCAP records, Svensson examines the political and military circumstances surrounding the formation of policy for the occupation of Japan and the execution of some of the initial, important reforms. He reviews factors that hampered planning for the occupation and describes the plans and materials that were produced in Washington prior to the Japanese surrender by the Civil Affairs Division and the State-War-Navy Coordinating Committee (SWNCC). It is pointed out that SWNCC's failure to complete plans for the occupation before the end of the war enabled SCAP to assume a greater initiative in policy formulation. According to Svensson, MacArthur's headquarters prepared an adequate plan for the initial entry into Japan and smoothly executed it despite the lack of a formal occupation plan.

An earlier version of this study was done in the form of a research paper for the Office of the Chief of Military History (no.59).

U.S. Dept. of Defense. *The Entry of the Soviet Union into the War against Japan: Military Plans, 1941–1945.* 1955. See no.179.

———. Dept. of State. *Occupation of Japan: Policy and Progress.* 1946. See no.468.

61 ———. ———. Office of Public Affairs. *Postwar Foreign Policy Preparation 1939–1945.* Washington, D.C.: Government Printing Office, 1950. ix, 726p. (Dept. of State publication 3580; General Foreign Policy series 15)

This volume records wartime and prewar preparations in the Department of State for the formulation of postwar American foreign policy. Though only secondarily concerned with the development of America's postwar policies for Japan, it is of outstanding importance to students of the occupation. It covers the period from the outbreak of World War II in 1939 through the UN Conference on International Organization convened at San Francisco in June 1945. It begins with a description of initial efforts to seek sound bases for future U.S. foreign policy and goes on to structures, methods, and working relationships that underlay the development of the major U.S. policies for dealing with postwar problems. The roles played by the Advisory Committee on Problems of Foreign Relations within the Department of State (from Sept. 1939 to late 1941) and subsequently by the Advisory Committee on Post-war Foreign Policy (from 1942 to the summer of 1943) are described in parts 1 and 2. Further preparations from the summer of 1943 through the autumn of 1944 are described in part 3, while the last months of the war are treated in part 4. The last third of the volume contains 64 documents relating to postwar planning: memorandums, letters, committee reports, proposals, policy statements, etc. A number of them concern Japan. The volume was prepared by Harley A. Notter, adviser to the assistant secretary for United Nations affairs, Department of State.

62 "U.S. Initial Post-Surrender Policy for Japan." *Department of State Bulletin* 13:423–27 (23 Sept. 1945); also in John M. Maki. *Conflict and Tension in the Far East: Key Documents, 1894–1960.* Seattle: Univ. of Washington Pr., 1961. p.124–32.

The text of the presurrender document which officially set forth U.S. policy for a defeated Japan is divided into 4 major sections. The first section outlines the ultimate objectives of SCAP. The second section specifies the structure and authority of SCAP and its relation to the Japanese government. The third section covers the political goals of the occupation and treats such topics as disarmament and demilitarization, treatment of war criminals, and the encouragement of democratic reforms. The concluding section is devoted to economic policy and covers the economic effects of demilitarization, the possibility of resumption of normal economic activity, reparations payments, and the treatment of Imperial Household property.

62a Vincent, John Carter. "The Post-war Period in the Far East." *Department of State Bulletin* 13:644–48 (21 Oct. 1945)

This article reprints the text of an address delivered at the Foreign Policy Association's forum "Between War and Peace" held in New York on 20 October 1945. Vincent was then director of the State Department's Office of Far Eastern Affairs. The American objective in the Far East, he states, is security; international cooperation is not a goal in itself but a policy in support of that objective. During the course of his remarks on Japan, Vincent also describes and explains the initial postsurrender policy of the American government towards Japan (he had served as chairman of the State-War-Navy Coordinating Committee's Subcommittee for the Far East and had thus been involved in the drafting of the policy [no.62]) and advises "patient but keen attention" to the progress of the occupation itself.

In Private Quarters

The following items relate to the sorts of planning, speculation, and recommendations for the postwar treatment of Japan that were going on in the private sector in the United States before 2 September 1945. Although they represent a broad spectrum of views and policies, they do indicate a good deal of agreement between the private sector and the governmental planners on the identity of the critical issues involved.

63 Aiso, John F. "Japan's Military System Must Be Crushed: Domestic and Economic Reforms Necessary." *Vital Speeches* 10:136–38 (15 Dec. 1943)

The author of a speech delivered at the *New York Herald Tribune* Forum on 17 November 1943 looks forward to the reconstruction of Japan after the war. He discusses several important domestic reforms in the fields of government and education which should receive priority after Japan has been demilitarized. Rather than eliminating the emperor system entirely, he advocates that the Allies dethrone the present emperor, Hirohito, and set up the crown prince as emperor with a liberal regent such as Prince Chichibu. Following his discussion of domestic reform, the author considers the changes that will have to be made in Japan's relations with her immediate neighbors and the other world powers, insisting that Japan must have access to raw materials and free markets in order to survive, yet also advising that the nation be educated so as to cooperate with these nations for their mutual well-being.

64 "Are the Japanese Stalling?" *New Republic* 113:235 (27 Aug. 1945)

Certain delays in the actual surrender of the Japanese are briefly discussed in this editorial. According to the author, sources in Manila claim that the Japanese have been hesitant, not because they intend to renew the war but rather because their defeat utterly stunned them and made them incapable of decisive action for a time.

64a Ballou, Robert Oleson. *Shinto: The Unconquered Enemy*. New York: Viking Pr., 1945. xi, 239p.

Ballou's purpose was to help his readers understand Shinto and the manner in which it has contributed to Japanese militarism. Much of his volume, therefore, consists of a study of Shinto beliefs and institutions—particularly the state-sponsored variety. In chapter 10, however, Ballou recommends what might be done with Shinto after the war. His chief suggestion is that a committee of Western, Chinese, and Japanese scholars be formed to search the Shinto canon for authority to support such concepts as the equality of man, peace, and international cooperation. The emperor may be retained, he feels, if the concept of responsibility originally included in the Chinese concept of the emperor as the Son of Heaven is reemphasized. Ballou presents all of these recommendations because he believes that it would be "folly to discredit the gods of a people whose cooperation is sought." His book includes a large number of translations of Shinto-related materials ranging from the *Kojiki* to wartime propaganda.

65 Bisson, Thomas Arthur. "Making Japan over." *New Republic* 112:744–47 (28 May 1945)

Asserting that the *zaibatsu* and the landlords are "the true essence of modern Japan" around which are grouped all of the other elements of Japan's ruling class (the bureaucracy, the emperor, and the military) and that *zaibatsu* domination of the country has condemned the masses to a life of chronic poverty, Bisson argues that an adequate postwar policy for Japan will require measures that destroy her existing authoritarian system. The colonies of Manchuria, Korea and Formosa in which Japan has tremendous economic interests must be taken away from her, the stranglehold of the *zaibatsu* and of the landlords must be broken through programs of agrarian reform and nationalization as well as through the removal of restrictions on labor organizations, and Japanese businessmen must be prevented from rebuilding the country's arms industry. Such extensive economic reforms cannot be expected of a government staffed by representatives of the *zaibatsu*, the imperial court, and the old bureaucracy; they should be undertaken instead by a government elected by the will of the people and buttressed by a new and democratic constitution. Finally, Bisson indicates that American economic assistance and the removal of all unnecessary barriers to Japanese foreign trade will be important if Japan is to be rebuilt at all after the war.

65a ———. "The Price of Peace for Japan." *Pacific Affairs* 17:5–25 (Mar. 1944); reprinted under the title "The Treatment of a Defeated Nation." In *The Postwar World*, by Hastings Eells, et al. New York: Abingdon-Cokesbury. 1945. p.61–86.

The author, a research staff member of the Institute of Pacific Relations, believes that Japan's defeat is certain and contends that thereafter the United Nations should assume direct responsibility for the type of political and social structure to be established in Japan and should plan to aid the Japanese people in finding new and responsible leadership. He emphasizes the necessity to break what he terms the cycle of Japan's aggression. He suggests that the reformation of Japan—which is required in political, economic, and social fields—

should include the purge of militarists, disarmament, constitutional revision, change in the status of the emperor, and means for Japan's economic self-support.

66 ———. "What Program for Japan?" *Nation* 161:28–29 (14 July 1945)

Looking forward to the imminent end of the Pacific War, the author sharply criticizes what he conceives to be the State Department policy toward a defeated Japan which will oppose only the "militarists" and ignore the guilt of the emperor, the professional bureaucracy, the *zaibatsu* leaders, and the landlords. Supporting his assertion by quotes from important State Department officers, the author indicates their intention to utilize many of these institutions in the postwar government of Japan. In contrast to this "soft" peace, he proposes a 5-point policy toward the conquered nation: (1) that the emperor system be eliminated; (2) that the present constitution be abolished; (3) that a new constitution be drafted by elected representatives of the Japanese people; (4) that the *zaibatsu* armament factories be destroyed and all large industrial factories be nationalized; and (5) that drastic agrarian reforms be undertaken.

Brewer, F. M. "Emperor of Japan." 1945. *See* no.1231a.

66a Byas, Hugh. *Government by Assassination*. New York: Knopf, 1942. ix, 369p.

Byas, a *New York Times* correspondent in Japan before Pearl Harbor, explains Japan's drift towards war during the 1930s through a study of those militarists and nationalists who by assassination or by threat of assassination virtually exercised veto power over the civilian Japanese government. In the course of his presentation, he points out that the emperor was merely a figurehead who reigned but did not rule, and he also argues that Japan should be soundly defeated in order that the Japanese can be taught the penalty of making war. In his conclusions, furthermore, Byas makes certain concrete suggestions for dealing with Japan after the Allied victory. They include the following proposals: (1) Japan should be offered lenient peace terms lest she be encouraged to take revenge upon the West after recovering from her defeat; (2) Japan should be completely disarmed; (3) Japan should be deprived of those colonial possessions which she has used as instruments of war (e.g. the mandated Pacific islands) but should be permitted to retain some sort of control over those which she has gained by peace or in which she has a major economic stake; (4) the emperor should be retained, for he might be the best man to govern the country; and (5) the United States should generally avoid meddling in Japan's internal affairs.

66b "Candidates for Post-war Leadership in Japan: Ozaki and Okano." *Amerasia* 8:227–36 (Aug. 1944)

If a peaceful and democratic Japan is to be built after the war, it is important that there be a genuinely antimilitarist leadership within the country capable of enlisting strong popular support and dealing with the Allies. Attention, therefore, should be paid to those forces within and outside Japan which have consistently maintained an antifascist and an antimilitarist position. There are 2 men who symbolize these potential democratic forces and who can play important roles in Japan's postwar politics provided that they are given the opportunity to present their views to the Japanese people. One is Okano Susumu, a Japanese Communist leader who heads the Japanese People's Liberation Alliance formed in Yenan in February 1944; the other is Ozaki Yukio, a well-known liberal statesman and journalist. These 2 men and the forces they represent constitute a potential alternative to the so-called "Moderates" within Japan's present ruling oligarchy for the leadership of postwar Japan. Since the "Moderates" never opposed the basic aim of Japanese militarism—Japanese domination of East Asia—they may well rule out fundamental economic and social reforms and thereby maintain unchanged the internal conditions which led Japan to war should they be in a position of political power after the Allied victory. For a truly democratic government responsive to the popular will, therefore, the Allies should rely on men such as Okano and Ozaki and give them as much support as possible.

67 Churchill, Arthur C. "Cooperatives in Japan." *Far Eastern Survey* 14:204–7 (1 Aug. 1945)

This article examines the agricultural and industrial organizations in Japan. It considers the historical background of cooperatives, their legal basis in the Cooperative Law of 1900, and changes in their structure and function to meet new demands over the years. The author seeks to explore possibilities for the beneficial use of cooperatives in the forthcoming occupation efforts to develop the Japanese economy along more democratic lines.

68 Colegrove, Kenneth W. "What Shall We Do with the Japanese Emperor?" *Amerasia* 6:376–81 (25 Oct. 1942)

Colegrove, author of several studies on Japanese political structures, details the arguments of the school of opinion that holds that the emperor should be treated as part of the war machine. He contrasts this with the school that believes the emperor should be made to serve as the symbol of national unity for peace in the new world order.

69 Conant, James B. "The Effective Disarmament of Germany and Japan." *Vital Speeches* 11:75–78 (15 Nov. 1944)

In a speech delivered at a meeting of the Foreign Policy Association on 7 October 1944, Conant addresses himself to a consideration of "the premises from which the discussion of the disarmament of Germany and Japan proceeds" rather than providing a detailed blueprint for disarmament itself. Affirming that modern methods of warfare have compelled us to rethink the problems involved in maintaining world peace, he conceives of the problem as twofold: "first the elimination of the most obvious danger to world peace—the renewal of the war by our present enemies; second, the construction of an international organization with power to handle the unpredictable threats to peace which are certain to arise in the not too distant future." The speaker insists that successful disarmament will require a drastic alteration in the industrial potentialities of both countries and maintains that a consideration of economic repercussions must remain secondary to the task of effective disarmament. In looking forward to the postwar period he suggests that military occupation of both countries will undoubtedly be necessary and further recommends that an international armament commission be established to make certain that there will not be a resurgence of the militarists in either nation.

70 Council on Foreign Relations. *Problems of the Peace Settlement with Japan.* New York: The Council, July 1944. 29p.

Six memorandums are presented which deal with various aspects of the problem of a peace settlement with Japan. In "Problems of Japanese Disarmament," Major George F. Eliot concludes that after initial dismantling and destruction of war materiel, policing to ensure against Japanese rearmament would be relatively simple and would not require permanent maintenance of United Nations land forces on the home territory of Japan. The memorandum by Hanson W. Baldwin, entitled "A Security Policy toward Japan," makes recommendations for short- and long-term policy. Military occupation, the author holds, should be brief and accomplish 2 goals: to emphasize their defeat to the Japanese people and to insure full demilitarization. Long-range policies should aim toward continuous demilitarization and gradual readmittance of Japan to the community of nations. Julius W. Pratt's article, "The Future Status of the Japanese Emperor," briefly summarizes various positions advocated in the United States and elsewhere, then argues that harsh treatment of the emperor would not contribute to reforms in Japanese thought or institutions. In his memorandum on "The

Future of the Japanese Mandated Islands" Grayson Kirk summarizes and evaluates several possible dispositions of these territories, all designed to prevent future use of these islands for aggressive military purposes. Another memorandum by the same author, "The Future of the Bonin and Ryukyu Islands," notes the strategic significance of certain major islands in these groups as advance air bases. In the concluding article, "The Future of the Kurile Islands," Julius Pratt recommends that Russia and Japan retain possession of those islands to which their historical and sentimental claims are strongest. According to Pratt, this solution would give Japan possession of all islands south of Shimushiru. No bibliographies are given but several of the memorandums are footnoted.

Eichelberger, Robert L. *Our Jungle Road to Tokyo.* 1950. See no.549.

71   Embree, John Fee. "Democracy in Postwar Japan." *American Journal of Sociology* 50:205–7 (Nov. 1944)
This piece, written in anticipation of an Allied occupation, is a review of the historical development of "limited democracy" in Japan which discusses the symbolic nature of the imperial person, the power of a collective executive, and the special traditional prerogatives of the Departments of the Army and the Navy. While defining the national bureaucratic organization in terms of extraordinary centralization, Embree also stresses the democratic nature of local councils and leadership appointments as well as the existence of a "popularly elected lawmaking body" as part of the central government. The author suggests that the Japanese democratic tradition is deep and strong and is most likely to develop as a result of internally inspired change rather than as a result of military occupation by a foreign power. He anticipates both a Japanese reaction against democracy as an incident of resistance to a prolonged American occupation and an eventual American suppression of the democratic left which will be viewed as revolutionary and subversive.

71a   ———. *The Japanese Nation: A Social Survey.* New York: Farrar & Rinehart, 1945. xi, 308p.
Embree, an anthropologist and one of America's leading academic specialists on Japan during the 1940s, presents a semipopular treatment of Japanese social organization and related economic and governmental factors in order to provide his readers with a basis for interpreting Japanese behavior and for understanding future developments in Japan. In successive chapters—a series of brief essays designed to be introductory rather than exhaustive in nature—he examines Japan's historical background, her modern economic base, the structure of government, the social class system, education, mass communications, the Japanese family and household, religion in Japan, cultural patterns, and national attitudes. Throughout the book Embree seeks to correct prevailing mistaken interpretations of Japanese history, institutions, and character. In his treatment of Japan's governmental structure, for example, he disagrees with those who maintain that the *zaibatsu* have been the predominant influence in Japanese politics, pointing out that the military have probably been the foremost influential group since the 1930s. At the same time, the author notes that the old nobility, the major capitalists, and Japan's military leaders must all be considered when assessing the government's actions and that "even in wartime it is false simplicity to consider the military as being solely responsible for national policy." When discussing the controversial question of Emperor Hirohito's political role, Embree contends that "the existence or nonexistence of an Emperor in Japan has little to do with the basic cause of Japanese foreign policy" and that while the emperor has become the symbol of a new nationalism and accordingly has been a convenient rallying point for Japan's nationalists and militarists, "these military could scarcely have gained the backing they did if internal economic developments and international rivalries and pressures had not played into their hands." Embree limits the number of

specific recommendations he makes for the postwar treatment of Japan. Nonetheless, it is clear that his book was consciously written with those Americans in mind who were then engaged in planning a variety of changes and reforms for occupied Japan—often on the basis of incorrect information and mistaken impressions of the factors that were basic to the Japanese decision to go to war.

72 ———. "Military Occupation of Japan." *Far Eastern Survey* 13:173–76 (20 Sept. 1944)

The author speculates about the forthcoming occupation, discussing possible duration and administration, and particularly emphasizing the importance of well-trained civil affairs administrators, familiar with Japanese language, culture, and history, free from race and class prejudice, and familiar with methods of arbitration. He suggests that there be frequent and direct contact between the civil affairs officers and the Japanese people in order to allay Japanese fears and promote cooperation between the United States and Japan.

73 "Emperor, Zaibatsu, Militarists." *New Republic* 113:255 (27 Aug. 1945); reply by Isidore Epstein entitled "Hirohito and Japanese Anti-Fascists." *New Republic* 113:351–52 (17 Sept. 1945)

The question of who are "war criminals," that is, who possessed real political power in wartime Japan, is briefly considered in this editorial. The author bases his remarks on an article of Mori Ken, a member of the Communist-led Japanese People's Emancipation League, who urges that the Allies not demand the unconditional and immediate overthrow of the emperor or the *zaibatsu* because their guilt is not of the same dimensions as that of the militarists. The author suggests that the Allies heed such sensible advice from Japanese democrats who understand the situation better than foreign observers.

In a strongly worded reply, Isidore Epstein calls the conclusions drawn in the 27 August editorial unfounded and seriously misleading. Quoting a speech entitled "Building a Democratic Japan" which another member of the Japanese People's Emancipation League delivered earlier this year in Yenan, Epstein points out that Japanese democrats are advocating the nationalization of various *zaibatsu* and the abolition of the emperor's prerogatives in addition to the liquidation of the militarists and the reestablishment of a democratic system in Japan.

74 "The Emperor's Authority." *New Republic* 113:235 (27 Aug. 1945)

This brief editorial makes reference to the fact that at the outset of the occupation the Allied powers still have not conclusively understood the power or authority of the emperor in conducting the war or in bringing it to an end.

Feis, Herbert. *The Atomic Bomb and the End of World War II*. 1966. See no.243.

———. *Contest over Japan*. 1967. See no.789.

———. *Japan Subdued: The Atomic Bomb and the End of the War in the Pacific*. 1961. See no.244.

75 Fisher, Galen M. "Japanese Relationships after the War." *Proceedings of the Institute of World Affairs* 20:48–55 (1943)

Six conditions regarding the treatment of a defeated Japan are formulated and discussed in a comprehensive report written midway in the war. Those conditions are: the decisive defeat of the military and the return of conquered territories, the establishment of a civilian regime, the reinforcement of the authority of the Imperial House, full compliance with the conditions of the Atlantic Charter, the promotion of fundamental economic changes within the country, and ultimately the admission of Japan into whatever international agencies may be evolved to keep peace in the future. Such conditions are based on the author's belief that there will be competent and dependable Japanese leaders who will emerge to create a new government and that the "mind set" of a whole people may be changed in a few years by dedicated and diligent occupation authorities.

76 Fleisher, Wilfrid. *What to Do with Japan.* Garden City, N.Y.: Doubleday, Doran, 1945. 178p.

This book provides a thoughtful discussion of how the Allied powers should treat Japan. As a correspondent of the *New York Herald Tribune,* the author lived in Japan for about a decade during the 1930s. Like his earlier book, *Volcanic Isle* (London: Jonathan Cape, 1942. 256p.), which describes his observations of the explosive Japan of the 1930s, this work shows the author's understanding of the Japanese character as well as social and political currents in Japan. It was written after the German defeat and before the Soviet Union's entry into the Pacific War. Suggesting that the emperor be retained to avoid military and political chaos in a defeated Japan and that the Meiji Constitution and undemocratic political institutions be replaced, the author also discusses what the Allied nations should expect of Japan at the time of her surrender, what an Allied military government should try to accomplish in Japan, and at what stage it should consider its task completed and withdraw. He also analyzes what should be done with Southeast and East Asian territories that were formerly conquered by Japan and evaluates the Dumbarton Oaks machinery as an international peace organization. Appendixes include documents and statements concerning the establishment of a postwar international security organization such as the Atlantic Charter of 1941, the Roosevelt plan for world security of 1944, and the Dumbarton Oaks proposals in 1944.

76a ———. "What to Do with Japan." *Life* 18, no.10:88–94, 97 (16 Apr. 1945)

This article consists of excerpts from Fleisher's book *What to Do with Japan* (no.76). The author states that the proper approach to a defeated Japan will be to occupy, disarm, punish, and remodel the country into a peaceful state whose economy is based on agriculture and light industry. The disposal of the rest of the empire, however, will likely become a major source of contention among the Allies. American policy in this respect, Fleisher reports, has still not been determined.

76b "Former Missionaries Declare Politics of Revenge Will Fail in Dealing with Japan." *Christian Century* 62:56 (10 Jan. 1945)

This article summarizes a statement entitled "World Settlement in Japan" issued by 21 former missionaries to East Asia. They denounce plans for the vengeful and punitive treatment of postwar Japan; instead, they argue, there should be a vigorous effort to create "a world community of spirit and interest." Japan need not be reduced to the status of a third-rate agricultural power; a sound defeat and international supervision will be adequate safeguards against the resurgence of militarism. Japan once played a worthy role in the modernization of East Asia, and given the proper encouragement, she may do so again.

76c "The Future of Japan: An American View; A Canadian View." *Pacific Affairs* 17:190–203 (June 1944)

This article presents the reactions of American and Canadian experts on Japan to 2 articles which appeared in the March 1944 issue of *Pacific Affairs*: T. A. Bisson's "The Price of Peace for Japan" (no.65a) and C. N. Spinks' "Indoctrination and Re-education of Japan's Youth" (no.122a). The statement of the American point of view was authored by M. Searle Bates of the International Missionary Council and Kenneth Scott Latourette of Yale University; the Canadian experts preferred to remain anonymous. The Americans were in fundamental disagreement with Bisson only over his recommendation that the imperial institution be abolished. They argue that abolition will only further longterm resentment and animosity, and that a reorientation of Japanese thinking about the emperor and Shinto is both possible and sufficient. They would also recommend that the United Nations not take quite as active a role as Bisson suggests in reshaping the Japanese political and social structure. They find Spinks' article factually sound and easy to agree with. The Canadians generally agree only with Bisson's and Spinks' most drastic recommendations and find conciliatory policies both unwise and improper. Strong Allied control will be necessary for a long time, since the Japanese will emerge from the war intellectually immature and politically bewildered. Not only must the imperial institution be abolished, they argue, but the emperor himself must be held accountable for the deeds and policies carried out during his reign.

Galloway, George B. *Postwar Planning in the United States: An Organizational Directory*. 1942. See no.54a.

Gilchrist, Huntington. "The Japanese Islands: Annexation or Trusteeship?" 1944. *See* no.988a.

77 Godshall, Wilson Leon. "How to Deal with Japan." *Social Science* 18, no.3:120–24 (July 1943)

The author's contention is that "only by the removal of the causes of war in the Far East can an equitable and lasting peace be obtained." First he recommends that Japan be kept from dominating China and the world. Then he advocates the elimination of rivalry over China among the Powers and the application of the Atlantic Charter's principles to the Far East. Finally, with regard to American postsurrender policy toward Japan, Godshall proposes (1) the "complete evacuation of the mainland of Asia" and other areas by Japanese forces; (2) the complete disarmament and demobilization of Japanese military units; (3) the reconstruction of the Japanese economy, with Japanese industry being "channeled into replacement and reconstruction projects for the Far East;" (4) the replacement of the Shinto-militarist system of political values with one upon which a peaceful civilian government can be built; and (5) the retention of the emperor as a stabilizing institution.

78 Gorer, Geoffrey. "The Special Case of Japan." *Public Opinion Quarterly* 7, no.4:567–82 (Winter 1943)

This study, made during World War II, is interesting in terms of presurrender American planning. Gorer points to the need to recognize elements in Japanese culture and society which can be used in rebuilding Japan and at the same time destroy those tendencies which encouraged aggression and militant nationalism. Stripped of its empire, Japan will be difficult to administer, he predicts. Although specific proposals are avoided, many of the problems which the occupation would later face are discussed in rather general terms.

79 Grajdanzev, Andrew J. *Japan's Postwar Agriculture*. New York: Institute of Pacific Relations, International Secretariat, 1945. 27p. (Institute of Pacific Relations, 10th conference, Secretariat paper no.1, 1945)

A research associate of the Institute of Pacific Relations attempts to forecast the postwar conditions of Japanese agriculture. After noting that agriculturally Japan was practically self-sufficient in the 1930s, he considers for the future possible production levels for rice, wheat, barley, beans, corn, sweet potatoes, and Irish potatoes, the possibility of an increase in the cultivated area and in foreign trade, and the possibility of birth control. He suggests that one way to avert the possibility of repeated Japanese aggression is for the United States and Canada to integrate the Japanese economy with their own, thus enabling them to transfer their agricultural surplus to Japan and eliminating the need for Japan to develop markets in Asia by force.

80 Grattan, C. Hartley. "Those Japanese Mandates." *Harper's Magazine* 188:145–53 (Jan. 1944)

The author in an attempt to answer the question of the future of the Japanese mandated islands traces the history of the diplomatic negotiations surrounding those islands since 1898. He is answering arguments by critics like Walter Lippmann who felt that because President Wilson lacked a "positive foreign policy" the islands were given to Japan. In terms of the future the author feels that the United States should either take control of these islands or let a friendly power do so rather than giving them up to some international authority.

81 Haring, Douglas Gilbert, ed. *Japan's Prospect.* Cambridge, Mass.: Harvard Univ. Pr., 1946. xiv, 474p.

This collection of 12 essays was written by 9 professors associated with Harvard University's School for Overseas Administration. The materials contained in the collection were used by the school to train U.S. Army and Navy officers for the duties of military government in a defeated Japan. The scholars concerned concurred in a belief that extensive democratic reform would be required in postwar Japan. Each essay provides historical background and outlines particular aspects of reform considered necessary. Among subjects covered are: Japan's historical tradition, by G. Nye Steiger; population and social structure, by Talcott Parsons; the Japanese farm-tenancy system, by Wakukawa Seiyei; the industrial and commercial complex, by Edward A. Ackerman; the challenge of Japanese ideology and religion, by Douglas G. Haring; military government for Japan in the forthcoming occupation, by Merle Fainsod; prospects for a constitutional democracy, by Frederick M. Watkins; Russian policies in the Far East, by William H. Chamberlin; and international problems, by Carl J. Friedrich. Appendixes include the full text of the Meiji Constitution; an article entitled "Military Government for Japan" by Carl J. Friedrich and Douglas G. Haring, which is a reprint from *Far Eastern Survey* (14 Feb. 1945) (no.231); and a substantial bibliographical list on Japan. The collection is useful to the scholar interested in presurrender planning aspects of the occupation.

81a Heinrichs, Waldo H., Jr. *American Ambassador: Joseph C. Grew and the Development of the United States Diplomatic Tradition.* Boston: Little, Brown, 1966. xiii, 460p.

Chapter 20 of this narrative history of Grew's career focuses on the activities of this former ambassador to Japan during the course of World War II. Heinrichs notes Grew's speechmaking and discusses the opinions concerning the postwar treatment of Japan which Grew advocated in public as well as in private. He points out, for example, that Grew frequently pleaded for tolerance and statesmanship in dealing with a defeated Japan, disagreed with those radical reformers who sought the abolition of the emperor and State Shinto, and argued that the emperor represented an authority which could be used by the United Nations after the war in order to conduct an efficient occupation of Japan, to implement various reforms, and to inaugurate a new order of international cooperation. Heinrichs then discusses Grew's work in 1944 and 1945, first as director of the Office of Far Eastern Affairs, then as American undersecretary of state. He explains how Grew was in a position to oversee the work of the Inter-Divisional Area Committee on the Far East and discusses the role he played in bringing about Japan's surrender. In a concluding paragraph, he also notes that Grew turned down a government suggestion that he return to Japan in September 1945 as MacArthur's political adviser.

82 Holtom, Daniel Clarence. "Shinto in the Postwar World." *Far Eastern Survey* 14:29–33 (14 Feb. 1945)

A general discussion of the role Shinto should play in postwar Japan. Holtom, a leading Western authority on Shinto, favors retaining the emperor in the postwar period, and believes that the Japanese people should be allowed to renovate the religion themselves once the most "dangerous tenets" of Shinto are removed.

82a ———. "The Japanese Mind." *New Republic* 112:742–44 (28 May 1945)

Asserting that the Japanese people

have been subjected to decades of miseducation, Holtom argues that the matter of reeducation deserves high priority if postwar Japan is to be transformed into a peaceful, democratic country. He identifies the most important features of the Japanese "national mind" (in which reeducation must occur) as follows: (1) the Japanese claims to racial uniqueness and superiority which have resulted in intense loyalty to the emperor and the fatherland; (2) the "almost morbid education for death—wherein Buddhist pessimism accentuated primitive impersonality—rather than training in intelligent living for the community;" (3) the long accumulation of bitterness and fear directed toward the white man; (4) the glorification of war and espousal of *Bushidō*, the code of the warrior; (5) the glorification of the emperor; and (6) the subordination of the individual to the state. He concludes that it would be preferable to let Japanese liberals undertake the "redirection and the reconditioning of the 'Japanese mind'" rather than to impose upon the people a reeducation program drawn up by the victorious allies.

83   Howard, Harry Paxton. "Our Allies in Japan." *Commonweal* 36:582–85 (9 Oct. 1942)

This article focuses on the rise of Japanese militarism and its triumph over early forms of Japanese democracy. Drawing on this background, the author calls for an occupation that builds on the foundation of the earlier Japanese democratic experience. He proposes strict limitations on the military and on armaments but counsels that Japan's trade not be restricted and that she be given a secure place in the world community under a new league of nations.

84   Institute of Pacific Relations. (9th conference. Hot Springs, Va. 1945) *Security in the Pacific*. New York: The Institute, International Secretariat, 1945. xiii, 169p.

The report of the ninth conference of the Institute of Pacific Relations, held at Hot Springs, Virginia from 6 to 17 January 1945, and attended by representatives from Australia, Canada, China, France, India, Korea, the Netherlands and the Netherlands Indies, New Zealand, the Philippines, Thailand, the United Kingdom, and the United States. There were approximately 60 papers presented before the conference. Major topics discussed include significant developments in 1944, the future of Japan, economic problems in the Pacific region, the impact of the war upon cultural and race relations, the future of dependent areas, and collective security. Chapter 2, "The Future of Japan," summarizes opinions expressed at conference round table discussions regarding the general principles which should be adopted in developing policy toward Japan and ways in which these principles could be applied. Conference participants speculated on the possible Japanese reaction to total defeat, the impact which defeat could have on different groups in Japan such as the militarists and liberal and radical groups, the prospects of implementing democratic concepts, the immediate post-surrender measures which should be taken, and the measures which should be adopted to deal with repatriation, disarmament, the emperor, and reparations. Disagreement was expressed over the question of whether Japan would ever become "non-aggressive." However, there was consensus regarding the desirability of an active role for the United Nations in dealing with Japan as well as the desirability of encouraging democratic forces, developing economic recovery measures, and building a trustworthy international security system. Lists of participating members and of the papers presented are appended.

85   Jaffe, Philip J. *New Frontiers in Asia: A Challenge to the West*. New York: Knopf, 1945. vi, 375p.

The author, an editor of *Amerasia*, develops the argument that India, China, and Japan constitute "new economic frontiers" in Asia. He maintains that Anglo-American cooperation in extending assistance for the development of India and China and the establishment of a peaceful and trustworthy Japan would serve to benefit not only those countries but also industrialized nations such as America, Great Britain, and the Soviet Union. He then discusses the task confronting the Allied powers, that is, to "establish the kind of worldwide political and economic framework within which a democratic Japan can function." Reviewing the roots of Japanese aggression, Jaffe refers to the oligarchical control of the country by the militarists, bureaucrats, imperial nobles, and industrialists, who, he believes, jointly tried to solve the country's economic problems by external expansion. He then examines "democratic forces" in Japan and discusses Ozaki Yukio's liberal political activity, Okano Susumu's (Nosaka Sanzō) campaign in China through his Japanese People's Emancipation League, and the activities of Japanese trade and peasant unions. The author suggests that it will be necessary to reform the status of the emperor, revise the constitution, purge militarist leaders, release political prisoners, undertake agrarian reforms, and ensure democratic control of the national economy. However, he stresses that effective and lasting reforms must be carried out by the Japanese themselves.

86 "Japan: An Opportunity for Statesmanship." *Life* 19:22–23 (16 July 1945)

The concept of an extensive postwar occupation of Japan is rejected in this editorial and the classic pattern of disarmament, territorial restrictions, punishment of war criminals, and reparations is advocated. Rapid recognition of a sovereign Japanese government which could design policies for reconstruction with aid from nongovernmental sources is suggested. Fundamental to these proposals is the idea that the consequences of defeat will produce substantial societal change, regardless of American intervention.

87 "The Japanese: Their God-Emperor Medievalism Must Be Destroyed." *Fortune* 25:53–57, 162–69 (Feb. 1942)

Using Japanese history as a basis for a discussion of why "Japan must be crushed," this article pictures the Japanese as "immersed in a national cult of violence," having learned little from their contacts with and imitation of the West other than to become aware of their weakness. A series of pictures displays the author's image of the Japanese as a people whose "minds are full of Ghosts." In addition to defeating Japan militarily, the article discusses the importance of destroying the "cult of the God Emperor" and replacing it with a new leadership which is guaranteed a fair deal in world markets.

88 "Japan's Choice." *Nation* 161:103–4 (4 Aug. 1945)

The Potsdam ultimatum offering Japan a choice of unconditional surrender or "prompt and utter destruction" is considered in this brief editorial. The author believes that the ultimatum was inadequate because of its failure "to drive a sharp wedge between the Japanese people and their rulers." According to the author, such a wedge might have been driven by a clearcut statement from the Allies to the Japanese people indicating Allied repudiation of the emperor and the industrialists as well as the militarists.

89 "Japan's Peace Strategy: The Suzuki Cabinet." *Amerasia* 9:163–73 (1 June 1945)

In appraising the significance of the Suzuki government, the author explains that, unlike Nazi Germany, no worldwide sentiment has developed in favor of destroying the political and industrial roots of Japanese aggression along with Japan's military establishment. He notes that the Suzuki cabinet cannot lead Japan along the road to democracy for 2 reasons. First, they are strongly opposed to democratic processes of government and have always used every available means to suppress popular movements. Second, they would unquestionably be powerful opponents of the measures of social and economic reform required to raise the living standards of the Japanese people and give Japan a stable and expanding economy.

90 Johnstone, William Crane. *The Future of Japan.* London: Oxford Univ. Pr., 1945. viii, 162p.

The author, associated with the Institute of Pacific Relations, evaluates various proposals for dealing with postsurrender Japan and offers some proposals of his own. Beginning with the spectrum of Japan's possible reactions to defeat, his discussion covers such matters as the coming occupation, disarmament, reparations, economic controls, the imperial position, and issues relating to the social, political, and economic reconstruction of the nation. The author's proposals reflect an astute perception of the Japanese mind and of political currents in Japan. He appears particularly concerned about a possible revival of Japanese aggression against the United States and strongly recommends that all autocratic leaders such as militarists, *zaibatsu* leaders, and imperial court officials be replaced. Many of his proposals turned out to be similar to those actually adopted during the postwar Allied occupation. An exception to this was the author's overestimation of the role of the United Nations in handling postwar Japan and his suggestion that it oversee the military control of the country.

91 ———. "The Hot Springs Conference." *Far Eastern Survey* 14:16–22 (31 Jan. 1945)

An unofficial private conference of representatives of the Allied nations (excluding the USSR) held in Hot Springs, Virginia, from 6 through 17 January 1945 is described in this account. Although the agenda concerned various crucial problems of the war in the Pacific relating to numerous Asian nations and to the eventual peace settlements, a considerable portion of the article deals with Japan, particularly the future of a defeated Japan. While not specifically identifying speakers by their country, the author nevertheless presents their various and sometimes conflicting suggestions offered at round table discussions concerning the armistice terms, the occupation of Japan by the Allies, reparations payments, and the military disarmament of the nation. There was also discussion of the most suitable manner in which to encourage democratic groups in Japan and to change the direction of the Japanese economy. Although no definitive program of action was announced, the meetings appear to have been highly useful and to have resulted in various constructive proposals regarding the treatment of a defeated Japan.

Jones, Francis C., Hugh Borton, and B. R. Pearn. *The Far East 1942–1946.* 1955. *See* no.505.

92 Katayama, Koshi. "Is a Democratic Revolution Possible in Japan." *Free World* 2:128–31 (Mar. 1942)

A description of what the author considers to be the "long history of the democratic struggle of the Japanese people." Events in modern Japanese history such as the peasant revolts during the Tokugawa period and in the first 10 years of the Meiji Restoration, the Russo-Japanese War, the rice riots in 1918, and the Manchurian Incident of 1931 are viewed as part of the Japanese people's struggle for liberty and democracy. The period from 1931 to the time the article was written is seen as the most difficult time for democratic forces in Japan. The author declares that World War II is a war between fascism and democracy and if the Japanese militarists are defeated the democratic forces will revolt against the "military despots" and succeed in founding a democratic Japan.

93 Kerr, George H. "Sovereignty of the Liuchiu Islands." *Far Eastern Survey* 14:96–100 (25 Apr. 1945)

A general history of the Ryukyu (Liuchiu) Islands and U.S. involvement there. Particular emphasis is placed on Perry's negotiations to open ports in the 1850s, and Grant's arbitration of the Sino–Japanese dispute over their control in the 1870s. Postwar possibilities for control of the Ryukyus are briefly discussed.

94 Kirchwey, Freda. "The Emperor's Rescript." *Nation* 161:170 (25 Aug. 1945)

A brief criticism of the emperor's rescript announcing the surrender of Japan in "one of the trickiest bits of imaginative writing that ever came out of Tokyo." The author urges that one of General MacArthur's priorities should be the exposure of the deception prompted by this statement and the reaffirmation of the fact that Japan has been totally defeated and driven to unconditional surrender.

95   Lamott, Willis Church. *Nippon: The Crime and Punishment of Japan.* New York: Day, 1944. 258p.

Lamott, a missionary teacher in Japan during the 1920s and 1930s, provides a detailed analysis of the Japanese national character and psychology in order to set forth both the causes for Japan's aggression and the principles which should be followed in dealing with her after the war. He describes the country's educational system as one "of transmission, mental regimentation and the importation of officially selected and officially approved ideas," and accordingly recommends that it be thoroughly overhauled. Likewise, after describing the nature of emperor worship and the related mythology, he argues that the emperor must be stripped of his aura of divinity if Japan is to be reconstructed along democratic lines. Lamott warns against the dangers of "political scene-shifting" by present leaders in Tokyo and advocates a number of changes in the Meiji Constitution and Japanese political practice designed to break the hold of the militarists on the administration and make the government more responsive to popular will. Finally, the author proposes the abandonment of old-fashioned imperialism, the creation of a global plan for collective security, and the establishment of a regional organization for Asia in order to insure permanent peace in the Pacific.

95a   ———. "What *Not* to Do with Japan." *Harper's Magazine* 190:585–91 (June 1945); abridged and published under the same title in *Reader's Digest* 47:23–26 (Aug. 1945)

Lamott anticipates a military invasion of Japan and contemplates American policy towards that country after her defeat. He feels that a policy of minimal restructuring of education and the imperial institution will be followed by a hands-off policy during which the Japanese would regain sovereignty and undertake their own reconstruction.

95b   ———. "What of Postwar Japan?" *Asia* 42:573–75 (Oct. 1942)

Lamott cautions his audience against assuming that the defeat of the Japanese militarists will necessarily discredit them. After all, he writes, the military is "the constant, not the variable, in Japanese life." The future of the imperial institution, in turn, remains unclear, but it is certainly central to any change occurring within Japan. Revolution will follow the defeat, Lamott continues, but it will lean towards communism instead of being democratic or liberal in nature.

96   Lattimore, Owen. "The Sacred Cow of Japan." *Atlantic Monthly* 175:45–51 (Jan. 1945)

Lattimore, who was an Asian affairs specialist for the U.S. government during World War II, complains about the West's general ignorance of Japan. Along with comments on events leading up to the war, he suggests that Japan's basically fascist society and emperor system must be drastically reformed after the war to bring out the democratic potential in the Japanese people. This article is a chapter from Lattimore's book *Solution in Asia* (1945) (no.97).

97   ———. *Solution in Asia.* Boston: Little, Brown, 1945. 214p.

This book elaborates upon ideas developed from lectures which the author presented in the spring of 1944. A student of Asia, the author was a State Department official in Japan at the time this book was published. Prior to that he worked as an editor of the journal *Pacific Affairs*. Concentrating on Japan and China, he analyzes the recent histories of these countries, the history of Western involvement in Asia, and the events which led up to World War II. He finds that "military aggression was the only possible outcome of Japan's social system, and it will be renewed unless the Japanese are allowed to change the system." The thrust of the book is critical and prescriptive. The author advocates several policies which he believes the Allies should pursue once victory in Asia is achieved. Chief among them are an international security force to keep Japan under observation; industrial disarmament but not deindustrialization, which would cause the starvation of millions; and internment of the emperor and his heirs under supervision of a United Nations commission. The author sees the emperor as the fount of militarist power, and he fears that, if we were to make use of him to implement occupation policy, after our withdrawal the power to manipulate him would not pass to the representative of a democratic government but would revert to the militarists.

An integrated Asian policy rather than compartmentalized policies toward China, Russia, Japan, and colonial countries is urged. The author stresses the need for coordination of U.S. policies toward Asia with other countries' policies, especially those of Britain and the Soviet Union through the United Nations and through multinational consultations. In his view, Asia will become a testing ground for determining the degree to which the capitalist and collectivist worlds can cooperate. Failure in Asia, he affirms, would doom hope for a cooperative world order.

Martin, Edwin M. *The Results of the Allied Occupation of Japan: An Interim Report.* 1947. *See* no.512.

98 "The Meaning of Victory." *Life* 19: 34 (27 Aug. 1945)

The terms of the Japanese surrender are examined in terms of their avoidance of limitations on the imperial system. The necessity of convincing the Japanese to separate church and state and to sanctify the individual rather than the group is stressed.

99 Mears, Helen. "The Japanese Emperor." *Yale Review* 33:238-57 (Winter 1944)

In suggesting that the emperor be retained, Helen Mears points out that if the Japanese people acquiesce in the smashing of their military machine under the emperor's leadership, that move will be not only what the United Nations wants but also a highly important first step in freeing the Japanese system without challenging the fundamental loyalties and customs upon which national discipline and unity have depended.

100 ———. "The Japanese Riddle." *Atlantic Monthly* 172:100-104 (Sept. 1943)

An attempt to understand the Japanese national character based on an extended visit to prewar Japan. The author observes that the Japanese solve unpleasantness and problems of human relations by pretending that they do not exist and by denying individual emotions and ideas. The Japanese also are trained to accept poverty. These qualities seem to make for good soldiers but can backfire under duress when the Japanese are apt to be unadaptable and emotionally unstable.

101 Moulton, Harold Glenn, and Louis Marlio. *The Control of Germany and Japan.* Washington, D.C.: Brookings Institution, 1944. xi, 116p.

This carefully organized analysis considers the use of various types of economic controls against Germany and Japan to prevent their rearming after an Allied victory has been achieved. Part 1 discusses the German case. Part 2, dealing with Japan, first analyzes the economic position of that country in 1930 and concludes that up to that time Japan's colonies had been an economic burden. After 1930, when Japan undertook a concentrated program for the development of war power, figures indicate that her strength as a war power rested upon the industries and natural resources of the colonies and annexed areas, especially Manchuria and Korea. The authors discuss the proposed reduction of Japan to preimperial status and conclude that Japan could not be a strong military power without colonial or foreign supplies. Japan's future, they hold, will depend chiefly upon the development of primary industries in Japan proper and the expansion of foreign trade. In part 3 economic control measures are assessed as having limited value as they cannot be enforced unless backed by adequate military power. Some such measures, however, are considered as useful supplements to a system of military controls. Various types of military controls are discussed and alternative U.S. defense policies are analyzed. Participation in cooperative programs for controlling Germany and Japan and for developing a collective security system is advocated in the interest of cost and efficiency. The authors, both economists, were on the staff of the Brookings Institution when this book was written. Moulton had previously published several economic studies for that institution, including analyses of the economic positions of Germany and Japan. Marlio, a French economist, engineer, and industrialist had extensive experience in both government and industry. He came to the United States during World War II and joined the Brookings staff in 1941. Except for the last chapter dealing with American policy, which was written by Moulton, this study is a collaborative effort.

102 "A New Far Eastern Policy? Japan versus China." *Amerasia* 8, no.12:179–89 (9 June 1944)

In view of the possibility that a politically reliable Japan—purged of her militarists—may remain the dominant nation in Asia after the war, the authors of this article focus their attention on the appointment of Joseph C. Grew, former ambassador to Japan, to the position of director of the U.S. State Department's Office of Far Eastern Affairs. They note that Grew replaces the strongly pro-Chinese director Stanley Hornbeck, and that this appointment may be indicative of the government's rejection of the popularly accepted belief that China automatically will emerge at the end of the war as the leading power in East Asia. Grew's background and his views of postwar Japan and of the emperor are discussed, and *Amerasia* offers a number of recommendations regarding the composition of the postwar Japanese government, American policy toward the emperor, and American participation in the development of a democratic Japan.

103 "The New Japanese Line." *Nation* 161:195–96 (1 Sept. 1945)

The writer briefly discusses the attitudes of the defeated Japanese just prior to the beginning of the occupation. He notes the attitude of resignation encouraged by the newspapers and the early attempts to establish democratic political parties but cautions against interpreting these changes as anything more than surface compliance with the wishes of the Allies. He also warns the Allies not to be taken in by Japanese efforts to create dissension among them, for example, by Japan's request that SCAP permit its forces in Manchuria to retain their arms in order to protect the local population against the Soviet army.

104 "A New State Department Approach to the Japanese Emperor." *Amerasia* 8:75–76 (3 March 1944)

A presurrender discussion of an alleged change in the State Department's policy toward Japan—particularly toward treatment of the emperor in a defeated Japan. The author views the new policy as a more flexible one based on 2 premises: (1) the belief that the Japanese people themselves must decide on the emperor, once the militarists have been eliminated, and (2) the view that the emperor should not be attacked in America since he may be helpful after the surrender. However, the writer considers State Department policy to be incomplete insofar as it is more concerned with the military defeat of Japan than with its development in the postwar period.

105 "Occupying Japan." *Nation* 161:168–69 (25 Aug. 1945)

In looking forward to the imminent

occupation of Japan, the author of this editorial believes that the problems and responsibilities of such an occupation will be far greater in Japan than is the case in Germany due to the fact that the Japanese did not suffer the overwhelming military defeat the Germans did. In considering the occupation program itself, he strongly advocates that General MacArthur utilize the expertise of such men as Herbert Norman of the Department of External Affairs of Canada or Laurence Salisbury of the Institute of Pacific Relations rather than rely on Undersecretary Joseph Grew or his associate, Eugene Dooman. Throughout the editorial he emphasizes the fact that the United States must not let the fear of social change intimidate it into making concessions to "big business leaders, landlords, and princes" whose power should be eliminated.

106 "The Offensive against Japan: Japan's Political Strategy." *Amerasia* 7:379–81 (Nov. 1943)

The author points out that while Japan has gone on the defensive militarily, she is still very much on the offensive politically and is skillfully exploiting the relatively weak position of the United Nations in the colonial world. He notes that thus far we have done little to counteract this political offensive with a positive program of our own.

107 Olds, C. Burnell. "Potentialities of Japanese Liberalism." *Foreign Affairs* 22:433–43 (Apr. 1944)

A review of Japanese history for the purpose of showing that the Japanese have always been under the power of a small but powerful military caste, that since the Restoration a strong progressive element has attempted to curb military dictatorship in the interests of popular government, and that the democratic impulse is still alive and following defeat could reassert itself. Essential conditions for the establishment of a new order in Japan are outlined.

108 Pacificus, *pseud.* "Dangerous Experts." *Nation* 160:128–29 (3 Feb. 1945)

An editorial highly critical of 2 foreign service officers—one, an American, Eugene Dooman, in charge of State Department relations with the army and navy civil affairs sections, and the other, an Englishman, Sir Paul Butler, adviser to the Foreign Office on Far Eastern matters. The author is apprehensive about their possible influence in formulating plans for the future occupation of Japan. He characterizes both men as conservatives who would retain the present ruling groups with the exception only of the militarists, and he warns that such a policy could lead to civil war or further international conflict.

108a ———. "How to Deal with Japan." *Nation* 159:436–37 (14 Oct. 1944)

The anonymous author of this article reports on some of the U.S. State Department's proposals and indicates that various government officials have as their ultimate objective the creation of a liberal, peaceful and responsible Japan. He points out, however, that there has been very little recognition of the fact that Japanese militarism is rooted in Japan's inability to resolve her economic problems peacefully and that the country's leading economic interests have been exploiting both the peasants and the workers. Furthermore, he asserts, Japan will eventually be dominated by the *zaibatsu* if the State Department carries out all of its policies without any restraint. Accordingly, the author is pleased to note President Roosevelt's decision to shift some of the responsibility for postwar economic planning from the State Department to the Liberated Areas Section of the Office of Far Eastern Affairs FEA)—an office which has been ordered to plan for a thoroughgoing renovation of the Japanese economy. However, Eugene Dooman, a State Department official, is opposed to the policy of transforming Japan into an agricultural country incapable of waging modern warfare (as advocated by Stanley Hornbeck) and may seek to influence FEA's policies accordingly.

109 Peffer, Nathaniel. *Basis for Peace in*

the Far East. New York: Harper, 1942. 277p.

Published in cooperation with the International Secretariat of the Institute of Pacific Relations, Peffer's study seeks to ask and answer 2 important questions: Why the United States is fighting in the Pacific, and how an enduring peace can eventually be insured. The author, an academic specialist in international relations, first traces in detail the steps which culminated in the outbreak of war, then discusses the principles he recommends for a peace settlement. Peffer believes that Japan must be taught that war does not pay. Accordingly, he advocates that her cities be devastated by air bombardments and that her industrial complex be completely destroyed. He also suggests that she be deprived of all territorial possessions, that the remnants of her navy be sunk, and that her entire merchant marine be turned over to the Chinese. Then, if the Japanese abandon their militarist ambitions and demonstrate their intention of becoming "a member of good society," an effort should be made to help Japan meet her legitimate economic needs and to prosper in non-aggressive ways by providing her with loans and technical advice and by assuring her free and equal access to markets and raw materials throughout Asia. Since his study covers the entire Far East, Peffer also makes a number of interesting recommendations regarding the future of China and of Southeast Asia.

109a ———. "The Japanese Hope: A Liberal Core." *New York Times Magazine* p.6, 23 (2 Sept. 1945)

The author, a professor of international relations at Columbia University, says that the basic questions facing the Allies are: what kind of peace do we want with Japan? and how shall we insure future peace? Essentially, these questions mean what groups do we want to be dominant in postwar Japan? He views the emperor's role as determined by the men around him. Under the occupation he foresees a temptation to fall back on those men who have run Japan before for the sake of order and smoothness of operation. To fall back on these men, he warns, poses a great danger because the old top-level bureaucrats are closely allied with the military and *zaibatsu* and were a part of the oligarchy which led Japan to war. The occupation must turn instead to the liberals who are to be found in the middle levels of the civil bureaucracy. By using these men, the author claims, the occupation can nurture embryonic liberalism in Japan and bring about a great change in the national spirit. This change will make possible a complete social reconstruction and remove Japan forever from the medieval spirit of its past.

109b ———. "Occupy Japan?" *Harper's Magazine* 188:385–90 (Apr. 1944)

According to Peffer, the idea of occupying Japan after the war "is fantastic and had better be dropped." He feels that the utter devastation Japan is likely to suffer in the process of being defeated will suffice to accomplish the Allies' aim: to prevent Japan from rearming and from again becoming a menace to world peace. Peffer assumes that an armed invasion will be necessary to defeat Japan; to plan beyond that bloody task and to seek the introduction of a long-term occupation is folly. Furthermore, the American position in Japan would be like that of the Japanese in China, but worse, "for the Chinese are not a warlike people and the Japanese are." Peffer envisions even greater difficulties with the government and administration of an occupation than with invasion and pacification. The practical problems alone are insurmountable. The aftereffects could be worse: democracy would be associated with humiliation, and militarism would be associated with a "golden age" to be restored as soon as possible. Peffer recommends in conclusion that the Allies "defeat Japan, defeat it thoroughly, make it acknowledge defeat in surrender, and then let well enough alone."

110 "Postwar Treatment of Japan." *International Conciliation* no.410:231–43 (Apr. 1945)

An article originally printed in January 1944 which summarizes the contents of reports by 53 groups of university students concerning the postwar treatment of a defeated Japan. Specific topics for consideration include the treatment of Japanese leadership, territorial settlements, reparations payments, the punishment of war criminals, and the prevention of further military aggression. The article also discusses the groups' recommendations for steps that should be taken to establish a democratic and peace-loving Japan through programs for relief and rehabilitation, the establishment of equal trade rights, the abolition of discrimination against racial groups in the United States, and the encouragement of Japan's participation in international organizations.

110a Price, Willard. *Japan and the Son of Heaven.* New York: Duell, Sloan, and Pearce, 1945. viii, 231p.

Price considers the future of the emperor to be the single most important problem of the Pacific peace. His book describes the emperor both as an individual and as an institution in an effort to clarify the factors which must be taken into account when determining the fate of the imperial dynasty. While Hirohito is portrayed sympathetically, the imperial institution is seen as being central to most of what is wrong with the Japanese political institution. State Shinto and the present concept of imperial divinity are both comparatively recent phenomena, Price points out. They were conscious creations designed solely to legitimize despotism. Only by abolishing the imperial system altogether, therefore, can a resurgence of aggressive Japanese nationalism be prevented.

The Reminiscences of Joseph Ballantine. 1961. See no.44n.

111 Rosinger, Lawrence K. "Breaking Up the Japanese Empire." *Foreign Policy Reports* 20:62–71 (1 June 1944)

The article attempts to analyze "the nature of Japan's colonial rule in Formosa, Manchuria, Korea, and the Pacific islands, the resulting reactions of the conquered peoples, and the contributions of the colonies to Tokyo's power of aggression." After looking at each of the 4 areas in this fashion, the author considers unsettled questions related to the empire, examining future possibilities and the role of the Big Four.

112 ———. "People—Not Emperor—Hold Key to Peaceful Japan." *Foreign Policy Bulletin* 23, no.12:2–3 (7 Jan. 1944)

The comments of former ambassador to Japan, Joseph Grew, concerning treatment of a defeated Japan are briefly considered in this article. The author agrees with Grew's general position that the United States should offer the Japanese people hope for the future rather than simply punish them for the war. However, he questions the former ambassador's assertion that "Japanese emperor worship may be a force for keeping the peace if the emperor is 'a peace-seeking ruler not controlled by the military'," and advocates that the United States not take any stand on the emperor's future at this stage of events, but determine her attitude toward specific Japanese political institutions when the nation has been conquered.

113 ———. "Public Discussion Needed to Clarify Policy on Japan." *Foreign Policy Bulletin* 24, no.39:1–2 (13 July 1945)

In an article written toward the close of the war, the author insists that the United States clarify its policy toward a defeated Japan. He advocates that punishment be meted out to all those responsible including the imperial court and industrial circles, and he states that in the formulation of this aspect of policy "perhaps the most important principle to recognize is that Japanese aggression has been supported by virtually the entire nation—not simply a small militaristic clique." He also urges that the United States continue to insist upon an unconditional surrender, for to settle for any-

114 ———. "Roosevelt Defines U.S. Security Needs in the Pacific." *Foreign Policy Bulletin* 23:1–2 (18 Aug. 1944)

President Roosevelt's remarks concerning U.S. policy toward a defeated Japan and their variance with the tone of some of the State Department releases are briefly discussed. The author alludes to the fact that the president seems to recognize that "it is up to the Japanese nation to prove to us it can be trusted" rather than emphasizing his trust in the moderate civilian elements or a peace-seeking emperor with whom the United States can cooperate.

115 ———. "Victory over Japan Ushers in Acute Period in Far East." *Foreign Policy Bulletin* 24:1–3 (17 Aug. 1945)

A brief discussion of the Japanese surrender and its impact on the Japanese people as well as Allied governments. The author describes the Allied position regarding the status of the emperor as it was elaborated in Secretary of State Byrnes' note of 11 August issued on behalf of the Big Four. The author maintains that the note shows that the Big Four intend to use the emperor to implement their policies but will not make any long-term pledges regarding his status.

116 ———. "What Future for Japan." *Foreign Policy Reports* 19:141–54 (1 Sept. 1943)

Rosinger considers numerous problems which would have to be faced once Japan was defeated in World War II. He notes the importance of Asia's modernization and of the necessity of making the peace with Japan a "joint peace of the United Nations" with "common understanding of what is meant by Japan's 'unconditional surrender'." The following questions are examined in this article: Should Japan be disarmed? Should Japan's industry be destroyed? Should the United Nations control Japan's foreign trade? Should Japan lose its empire? Should Japan pay reparations? Should there be a military occupation of Japan? With whom should we conclude peace? Are the Japanese people responsible for the war? What path for a new Japan? Will Japan have a revolution? What can we do for Japan?

117 Roth, Andrew. *Dilemma in Japan.* Boston: Little, Brown, 1945. 302p.

This book analyzes political and social developments in Japan during the 1930s and suggests policies that should be adopted toward a defeated Japan. Apparently it was written in July 1945 and published in September of that year. Although not considering the Potsdam Declaration of 26 July 1945, the author, a Japanese specialist associated with the Institute of Pacific Relations, correctly estimates how such a declaration could conceivably set the stage for a "conditional unconditional surrender" whereby a defeated Japan could retain the emperor system. To insure a peaceful Japan, he suggests full disarmament, supervision of industries, punishment of war criminals, and military occupation of the country. However, as a key to lasting peace, he strongly urges that the entire Japanese political and economic system be drastically reoriented. In this respect he is critical of Undersecretary of State Joseph C. Grew and his "Japan crowd" in the department for their associations with the "old gang" of conservative and *zaibatsu*-connected leaders in Japan, to which association he attributes their interest in establishing political stability in postwar Japan at the expense of political reform. Roth's praise of Communist party members as hopeful prodemocratic and anti-militaristic leaders is said to have induced some SCAP personnel to help such persons as Okano Susumu (Nosaka Sanzō, subsequently chairman of the Japan Communist party) return to Japan from China soon after the war. The book reportedly was widely read by SCAP officials during the initial phase of the occupation and was reviewed favorably in the 24 November 1945 issue of the *Asahi Shimbun*. Later, however, the author was prevented by SCAP from re-entering Japan and the Japanese version of his book was banned from sale by SCAP order.

118 Rowe, David Nelson. *Collective Security in the Pacific.* New York: Institute of Pacific Relations, American Council, 1945. 14p. (Institute of Pacific Relations, 9th conference, U.S. paper no.10, 1945); reprinted under the title "Collective Security in the Pacific: An American View." *Pacific Affairs* 18:5–21 (Mar. 1945)

Rowe, concerned with guaranteeing postwar security in the Pacific, calls for the establishment of a Pacific regional organization that would function in conjunction with the international structure outlined in the Dumbarton Oaks draft. He indicates the probability that Japan would be downgraded to a fifth-rank power after her defeat and that peace in the postwar period would be secured only by arrangements agreed upon by the United States, the Soviet Union, and Great Britain. He urges the adoption of a cautious approach regarding Japan's future and warns that Japanese rearmament can be prevented only by strict prohibitions. The maintenance of American bases in the western Pacific and the establishment of mobile amphibious power for American forces is regarded as necessary to insure postwar control of Japan.

119 ———. "Ultimatum for Japan." *Far Eastern Survey* 14:217–19 (15 Aug. 1945)

A lucid description of the contents and possible effects of the Berlin Proclamation issued under the authority of the United States, the Chinese Republic, and Great Britain concerning the terms under which Japan has now been given an opportunity to end the war. After a discussion of other efforts to convince the Japanese to surrender, particularly the informal broadcasts of Captain E. M. Zacharias of the U.S. Navy, the author analyzes the text of the proclamation itself. He criticizes the vagueness of such terms as "advisors of the Emperor" which he conceives of as absolving the emperor from guilt, yet at the same time he points to the constructive elements of the proclamation. There is a discussion of what the document implies regarding the future occupation of Japan, with particular emphasis on the economic effects of determining Japan's boundaries so as to include only the 4 main islands.

120 Salisbury, Laurence E. "The Zaibatsu as War-Makers." *Nation* 161:30–32 (14 July 1945)

The big industrialists and financiers of the *zaibatsu* organizations are characterized as one of Japan's ruling coalition of 4 groups, the other 3 being the military, the bureaucrats, and the politicians. The author argues against what he terms a common notion in Washington that distinguishes the militaristic *zaibatsu* groups from the moderate, antimilitarist *zaibatsu* groups that do not warrant punishment. He maintains that all of the *zaibatsu* not only failed to oppose military aggression after 1931 but also directed that aggression to enhance their own power and profits. In conclusion, he warns that if their activities are not properly regulated by SCAP during the occupation, the *zaibatsu* will once again resume inordinate power in Japan and prepare for the next war.

120a Sands, William Franklin. "Japan's Future." *Commonweal* 42:264–66 (29 June 1945)

Sands begins by praising William C. Johnstone's book *The Future of Japan* (no.90) for correctly emphasizing the central problem of postwar Japan: the future of the imperial institution. Johnstone argues that the total abolition of the institution is essential, and he thus disagrees with the position taken by Owen Lattimore in his work entitled *Solution in Asia* (no.97). Sands considers the latter book as the more intelligent and expert of the two. Nevertheless, he asserts, Westerners are abysmally ignorant of Japan and of the Japanese, and important decisions about the country's future must be made with great care.

120b Smith, Kingsbury. "Our Government's Plan for a Defeated Japan." *American Mercury* 58:29–35 (Jan. 1944)

Smith asserts that the American government is anxious that Japan *not* surrender until after she has been thoroughly defeated, for many American officials are convinced that lasting peace cannot be secured until the Japanese militarists are not only discredited in the eyes of the Japanese people but also are completely destroyed and rendered incapable of reviving aggression in the future. He predicts that a stern peace marked by territorial dismemberment, complete disarmament, and heavy reparations will be imposed. The Japanese people, however, will not be treated cruelly, and the suggestion in some quarters that China be permitted to absorb Japan has been rejected. Smith also indicates that the United States is prepared to let the Japanese people determine the future of their emperor and choose their own form of government (providing that it is non-militaristic and non-fascist in nature) but that American planners envisage the creation of an Allied Pacific Control Council to control Japan for an indefinite period of time.

121 "Soft Peace for Japan?" *Nation* 160:683–84 (23 June 1945)

The advocates of a "soft" peace who would bar an unconditional surrender and strive to save Japanese "face" are criticized in this editorial. The author suggests that the recent arrest of 6 leading critics of the State Department who had protested against such a compromise might indicate the ascendancy of what he terms reactionary and pacifist groups who favor accommodation with the enemy. He contends that a "peace that maintained Japan's semifeudal social system would inevitably breed another war" and urges that stern measures be taken to insure a lasting peace.

122 Spinks, Charles Nelson. "The Liberal Myth in Japan." *Pacific Affairs* 15:450–56 (Dec. 1942)

Spinks, a navy officer, states, in regard to postwar planning, "We must recognize that we have no really liberal allies within the fabric of Japanese life ... with whom we can work later for the establishment of a democratic liberal Japan." Supposed liberals from the time of Fukuzawa and Ōkuma on have always supported foreign expansion because of the Japanese provincial ignorance of colonial realities and samurai militaristic tradition.

122a ———. "Indoctrination and Re-education of Japan's Youth." *Pacific Affairs* 3:56–70 (Mar. 1944)

Spinks describes the development of the Japanese educational system and the increasing role of nationalistic and militaristic indoctrination within it. He points out that an abrupt and wholesale enforcement of "democratic" education will simply not be enough to undo years of damage. Despite the great likelihood that defeat will discredit the old ideology in the minds of most Japanese, the author continues, the people will be intellectually immature and in need of firm guidance. The introduction of democratic principles and modern Western ideas should be gradual, and the pace of any contemplated reforms should be dictated by the ability of the Japanese to understand and assimilate them.

123 Steiner, Jesse Frederick. "Japanese Attitudes and Problems of Peace." *American Sociological Review* 10:288–94 (Apr. 1945)

This article presents an analysis of the rationale behind Japanese attitudes toward the divinity of the emperor, democratic forms of government, military aggression, and the military code of death. In the light of his explanation of these issues, the author discusses the ramifications of 2 possible courses of action open to the Allies regarding the surrender of Japan. The first of these is to insist upon an unconditional surrender and the second is to settle for some kind of negotiated peace. The author discusses the implications of both alternatives, suggesting that a policy be carefully drawn up well before the surrender itself and that it be a policy which will insure lasting peace in the Pacific.

Taylor, Philip H. "The Administration of Occupied Japan." 1950. See no. 927.

124 "Terms for Japan." *New Republic* 113:119–20 (30 July 1945)

Written immediately prior to the surrender of Japan, this editorial focuses on several important aspects of the peace terms for Japan and the eventual occupation. After emphasizing the necessity for a concentrated effort on the part of the Allies, the author briefly discusses some options that are open with regard to the terms of peace. He suggests that a temporary Allied military government be established which would encourage latent democratic elements in Japan. Moreover, he emphasizes the importance of destroying the power of the financial and industrial barons as well as that of the military.

Timperley, Harold J. "Peace Aims in the Pacific." 1942. See no.178b.

125 "A Trustworthy Japan: Prospects and Prerequisites." *Amerasia* 8:339–48 (1 Dec. 1944)

This article is a presurrender discussion of some important aspects of the occupation of Japan. Juxtaposed with a consideration of the prewar power of the *zaibatsu* and the militarists, the author discusses the presence of liberal elements and democratic forces within Japanese society in the early nineteenth century in such areas as education, labor, and politics. The latter half of the article is devoted to an explicit discussion of the forthcoming occupation itself and the author suggests the necessity of reform in the spheres of politics, education, industry, and agriculture, and the creation of healthy social, economic, and political structures in Japan. He emphasizes throughout, however, that Allied occupation authorities should not enforce such reforms upon the country but rather should allow and encourage such reforms to be carried out by the Japanese people themselves in order to effect lasting change. He also stresses the importance of establishing a wider framework of economic and political stability throughout Asia within which a democratic Japan might function successfully.

126 Van Patten, Louise M. "Japan: An American Problem." *Far Eastern Survey* 14:114–17 (9 May 1945)

The results of a number of public opinion surveys in the United States are examined to determine attitudes of Americans towards Japan, the Japanese people, and Americans of Japanese descent before, during, and at the end of World War II. The author contrasts American attitudes towards Japanese and Germans and discusses various attitudes in this country towards the future treatment of a defeated Japanese nation.

127 Ward, Robert Edward. "The Potential for Democratization in Prewar Japan." In *Public Policy* 17:105–43 (1968)

A study linked to the occupation in the sense that it attempts to investigate the preexisting potential for democratization that existed in Japan before 1945 and thus served as a foundation for the varieties of democratic reforms attempted by the occupation authorities.

———. "Reflections on the Allied Occupation and Planned Political Change in Japan." 1968. See no.759.

128 Ward, Robert Spencer. "Can Japan Win by Losing?" *Asia and the Americas* 45:234–38 (May 1945)

The author argues that even more necessary than the impending military defeat of Japan will be the need for the Allies to effect a total defeat of the political objectives of the Japanese empire. He elaborates these objectives through a detailed discussion of the aims and activities of the Greater East Asia Co-Prosperity Sphere and the nature of the Japanese expansion into Southeast Asia. He recommends that economic and political reforms be inaugurated as soon as possible in Japan and in the other nations of the Far East through the establishment of aid programs and the setting up of a formal United Nations Organization.

129 "What to Do with Japan." *Fortune* 29:181–84, 289 (Apr. 1944)

The author suggests some considerations the United States might bear in mind with respect to the treatment of a defeated Japan. After insisting upon the necessity of an unconditional surrender by Japan, he proceeds to discuss postsurrender problems and insists that "success will depend not only on how wisely we act in Japan but also on how positively we participate in Asia," particularly in China. Moreover, he advises that the Allied powers take as little direct action as possible in reshaping the nation during the occupation and insists that the Japanese themselves deal with the problems of rebuilding their nation. Warning that too great an involvement on the part of the occupying authorities with specific reform programs might antagonize the people and foster noncooperation, civil disobedience, and assassination, he suggests that we make our ideas widely known and leave it to the Japanese to implement them. The only exception to this policy, he concludes, should be an Allied program for the permanent demilitarization of Japan.

130 Widgery, Alban G. "Influences for Peaceful Organization in Postwar Japan." *South Atlantic Quarterly* 42, no.4:338–46 (Oct. 1943)

Widgery tries to analyze the ideological influences which might be encouraged after the war to create a peaceful Japan. He sees Shinto as the main influence in Japan. Though it was long ago taken over by military leaders, Shinto in its purest form is simply an attitude of sincerity and purity of intention, an ideal which could well be adapted to peaceful ends. Buddhism, Confucianism, and Christianity are not seen as important. The author also feels that loyalty to the emperor is deeply rooted in Japanese life. Though the emperor himself has been controlled by militarists, he ought to be retained as monarch of a demilitarized state. Finally, the militarist-capitalist alliance is criticized for virtually enslaving the Japanese masses.

131 Wildes, Harry Emerson. "The Japanese Press." *Free World* 10:56–60 (Aug. 1945)

The quality of Japanese newspapers is analyzed from the standpoint of their value as a resource in the occupation effort to promulgate an understanding of democracy in Japan. Although Japan had not yet surrendered at the time, the author is confident surrender would occur imminently and suggests that Americans must consider methods and means of operation in the defeated country. After briefly outlining how Japanese newspapers can be utilized to reeducate the Japanese citizenry, the author discusses the quality of various newspapers as well as the strict censorship imposed upon them in the prewar and wartime periods. There is a valuable summation of the general policies of significant Japanese newspapers and the author expresses his confidence that the continuance of 2 of these papers, under strict American supervision, can serve the occupation well.

132 ———. "Who Signs the Treaty?" *Asia and the Americas* 45:421–24 (Sept. 1945)

Speculating as to which Japanese will sign the peace treaty with the United Nations, the author concludes that it will be the emperor's brother, Prince Chichibu, and presents a brief sketch of the prince's personality and political views before and during the war. He also discusses the personalities and attitudes of other possible delegates, i.e., Shidehara Kijūrō, Ozaki Yukio, Prince Tokugawa Iyemasu, Prince Saionji Hachirō, and Sawada Setsuzō. The author predicts that this group will appear at the conferences "ostensibly liberal, vociferously apologetic for the errors of the militarists, and profuse in promises that Japan will mend its ways."

132a Wolfe, Henry Cutler. "Suzuki-san, Our Major Problem in Japan: On the Common Man Depends the Success of

Our Occupation." *New York Times Magazine* p.5–7, 29+ (26 Aug. 1945)

Wolfe describes the Japanese social system as being shaped like a pyramid: beneath a small ruling elite are the impoverished masses. The average Japanese is kept in serfdom by a combination of religious mysticism, force, and thought control. Despite the harshness of his everyday existence, the common man does not readily complain; he is diligent, cheerful, and clean. He is dangerous not because he is inherently bad but because his masters have made him so. The occupation cannot count on the small number of more enlightened people in Japan for support, Wolfe predicts, for there will be attempts to destroy any one who cooperates with the occupation. The common man, therefore, must first be shown that his overlords have lost the war, and then he must be won over to the Allied side by improvements in his standard of living.

Planning in Japan

Making the final decision to surrender was as difficult and potentially fatal a problem as has faced any modern Japanese government. It involved the fate of the empire, the future of the dynasty, the lives and fortunes of many members of the ruling elite groups, and the well-being and indeed the survival of millions of Japanese subjects. Individual, highly placed Japanese had been persuaded from early in the war that the nation's future depended upon the government's willingness and ability to negotiate a peace settlement with the Allies on as favorable terms as possible before the final invasion of the home islands was launched. The struggle to bring about such a negotiated settlement and the nature of its terms gradually came to be the focal point of domestic Japanese politics. When one refers to "presurrender planning in Japan," therefore, the question of how and on what terms to end the war is the principal and overwhelming issue involved. Beyond making plans for ending the war, the Japanese had a few postwar planning activities of a more specific and long-term sort, but little has been written about them so far.

Among the items that follow, Butow's study (no.136) is still by far the best and most impressive account of Japan's presurrender circumstances and plans. The books by Kase (no.143) and by the Pacific War Research Society (no.148) complement the Butow study nicely. The autobiographical accounts by two of Japan's wartime ministers of foreign affairs, Shigemitsu and Tōgō (nos.149 and 150), provide inside stories of great interest and value. Mention should also be made of the series of reports by the U.S. Strategic Bombing Survey (nos. 152–60). These reports provide unique insights into the physical, economic, and psychological circumstances of Japan in the closing months of the war.

133 Bisson, Thomas Arthur. "Japan's Strategy of Revival." *New Republic* 113: 242–44 (27 Aug. 1945)

In the period immediately following the surrender of Japan, the author outlines what he considers to be the strategy adopted by Japan's rulers to insure their survival in the postwar period. According to him, there are 3 aspects of this plan which have been implemented already: "first, preservation of the inviolability of the Emperor; second, maintenance of the

Imperial throne; third, interposition of the Imperial government between the Supreme Allied Commander and the Japanese people for the effectuation of all measures, military and political, decreed by the victorious powers." He warns the United Nations of the great danger of treating the emperor as a puppet, particularly for the purpose of effecting political reform, and suggests that instead the Allies make use of a broad, popular movement to establish a genuinely democratic governmental structure. Finally, there is a discussion of the terms of the Potsdam Declaration. It is criticized for its failure to make clear the guilt of the imperial clique and the *zaibatsu* along with its condemnation of the militarists.

134 Brooks, Lester. *Behind Japan's Surrender*. New York: McGraw-Hill, 1968. xviii, 425p.

This account of events in Japan preceding surrender to the Allies gives special attention to the obstacles to surrender raised by terrorism, assassinations, and an attempt at an armed coup d'état. The author participated in the early years of the occupation of Japan as editor of an army magazine. He has returned to Japan several times since and conducted research for this book there in 1965. The narrative proceeds from the assumption that Japan's rebellious military leaders and their followers were behaving understandably, given their refusal to allow even the possibility of defeat. In a description of events leading to Japan's capitulation, the author includes characterizations of some of the men who played important roles in the final days of imperial Japan, including those who planned and led the unsuccessful coup d'état.

The scholarly value of the book is diminished by the lack of footnotes but a description of major references is given on a chapter by chapter basis at the end of the book. The author has relied chiefly upon some 40 interviews conducted in 1965, official documents, Japanese and English newspapers, and secondary sources written primarily in English. An extensive bibliography and an index are provided. The book has been translated into Japanese under the title *Shūsen hiwa* (Tokyo: Jiji Tsūshinsha, 1968. 552p.).

135 Burks, Ardath Walter. "Survey of Japan's Defeat." *Far Eastern Survey* 15: 248–50 (14 Aug. 1946)

In this article a former member of the U.S. Strategic Bombing Survey discusses the results of SCAP's research concerning the events which brought about Japan's defeat. This evidence shows that: (1) Japan was not fully mobilized economically at the time of Pearl Harbor; (2) the balance of naval air power was won at Midway; and (3) the role of the atomic bomb was "useful but not essential."

136 Butow, Robert Joseph Charles. *Japan's Decision to Surrender*. Stanford, Calif.: Stanford Univ. Pr., 1954. xi, 259p. (Hoover Library on War, Revolution, and Peace, publication no.24)

In careful and scholarly detail the author has pieced together a record of the events and personalities behind Japan's decision to surrender. The book is based on Butow's doctoral dissertation by the same title, submitted to Stanford University in 1953. The narrative briefly notes the early successful months of Japan's military ventures, describes the crises which grew out of mounting defeats, and then discusses in detail the efforts of a few key men toward ending the war and the obstacles which they encountered. The author records the steps by which a small faction within the Japanese ruling elite committed the Japanese government to salvaging the nation through negotiation. He describes the launching of peace feelers in Sweden and Switzerland, the quest for Soviet aid and later for Soviet mediation, and the final reliance upon the influence of the emperor and the throne to overrule the militarists and accept the terms of the Potsdam Declaration. The author concludes that the emperor was able to play a decisive role in this particular episode because of the confluence of several factors: the prestige of the throne; the dangerous and complex national situation which precluded the resignation of the cabinet; and the unanimous decision of the ministers, who were irreconcilably divided among themselves, to accept the emperor's unofficial and extralegal pronouncements.

The author has made extensive use of documents and records both in English and Japanese, especially interrogations and statements of individuals involved personally in the events recorded here. He also interviewed 22 such persons in 1951 and 1952. Sources are carefully footnoted throughout the book. The value of the book is further enhanced by 11 appended documents, including the Cairo Declaration, the Potsdam Declaration, Japan's first surrender offer and the U.S. reply, President Truman's statement announcing Japan's acceptance of the Potsdam accord, notification to the Japanese government, Japan's final note, the Imperial Rescripts of 14 August and 2 September 1945, and the Instrument of Surrender. Scholars will find much that is of interest and value in this perceptive and detailed account. This book has been translated into Japanese under the title of *Shūsen gaishi, mujōken kōfuku made no keii* (Tokyo: Jiji Tsūshinsha, 1958. 342p.).

———. *Tojo and the Coming of the War.* 1961. See no.1053.

137 Craig, William. *The Fall of Japan.* New York: Dial, 1967. xiv, 368p.

This first book by a young historian describes in journalistic and somewhat sensational style the desperate situation of Japan during the last years of the Pacific War. Events treated include a brief history of the kamikaze units, the dropping of the atomic bombs on Hiroshima and Nagasaki, the emperor's decision to surrender, reaction to this decision in the United States and Japan, and incidents relating to the surrender of troops and freeing of prisoners in Japan and throughout Asia. Although the product of some research, this narrative is essentially a popular account. Little analysis is provided and the narrative is replete with brutally detailed descriptions of kamikaze raids, atomic bomb victims, assassinations, suicides, etc. The author has provided extensive notes on his source materials which include personal interviews as well as documents and secondary sources in both English and Japanese. A selected bibliography is appended.

138. ———. "The Fall of Japan." *Saturday Evening Post* 240:36–56 (26 Aug. 1967)

In this excerpt from his book, *The Fall of Japan* (no.137), published in 1967, Craig details the Japanese response to the ultimatum presented them by the Potsdam Conference and their subsequent reactions to the occupation forces.

Feis, Herbert. *The Atomic Bomb and the End of World War II.* 1966. See no.243.

———. *Japan Subdued: The Atomic Bomb and the End of the War in the Pacific.* 1961. See no.244.

139 Fishel, Wesley R. "A Japanese Peace Maneuver in 1944." *Far Eastern Quarterly* 8:387–97 (Aug. 1949)

The first Japanese attempt to surrender which came to a climax in October 1944 is briefly described in this article. The author outlines the background of the Japanese officials involved and events leading up to the efforts of the Japanese to enter into negotiations with the Chinese at their Chungking headquarters, which they hoped would eventually lead to an end of the war. Fishel reproduces the text of a peace missive signed by Miyagawa Tadamaro on 14 October 1944 requesting that the Chinese make preparations for official peace negotiations. The author offers suggestions as to why the Japanese peacemakers attempted to negotiate with the Allied government via the Chinese and also discusses reasons why these efforts were doomed to failure.

140 Fromm, Joseph. "Sabotage of Recovery within Japan." *World Report* 4, no. 1:10–11 (6 Jan. 1948)

Joseph Fromm describes the release of Japanese government wartime stockpiles to major industrial firms that took place from 14 August to 28 August 1945. The *zaibatsu* were allowed to take over the scarce commodities involved at no cost or at very low cost, it is claimed. Huge profits at government and, ultimately, public expense resulted.

141 Gustafson, Philip H. "What if We Had Invaded Japan?" *Saturday Evening Post* 218:18–19, 33–34 (5 Jan. 1946)

Philip Gustafson, a naval officer assigned to the SCAP staff, describes the sophisticated defense network awaiting the proposed Allied amphibious invasion of Japan. From interviews with Japanese officers as well as data collected by the staff of SCAP, he explains why General MacArthur's intelligence officers estimated Allied casualties would have been more than one million.

142 James, David H. *The Rise and Fall of the Japanese Empire*. London: Allen & Unwin, 1951. 409p.

In this general history of Japan emphasis is placed on the Shōwa era (1926–) and on Japanese aggression prior to World War II. Chapters 21 and 22 deal with the surrender of Japan in August 1945. James notes the negotiations of Japanese government officials concerned with the acceptance of "unconditional surrender" and the preservation of the imperial institution. The public reactions to surrender and to the imperial broadcast of 14 August are discussed. The author recalls the days prior to the arrival of American occupation forces and his experience as a prisoner at Ōmori prison camp. Details of troop landings and of the release and care of prisoners of war are presented.

143 Kase, Toshikazu. *Journey to the Missouri*, ed. by David N. Rowe. New Haven, Conn.: Yale Univ. Pr., 1950. xiv, 282p.

Intended primarily for the American public, this revealing account deals with the causes of Japan's entry into war and her defeat and with the efforts of responsible Japanese to bring the war to an end through a negotiated surrender. The author is an American-educated former diplomat who served in the Japanese Foreign Office for some 20 years. He knew many of the personalities involved in this account and participated personally in many of the events described. Following his recollections of the surrender ceremony aboard the U.S.S. *Missouri*, Kase describes the outbreak of hostilities in Manchuria and the subsequent rise of the military to a position of political dominance within Japan. Important events in Japanese politics and diplomacy from the 1930s through the Pacific War are described and related to world events. The efforts of Foreign Office diplomats to attain peace are described in some detail, along with a description of the important role of the Lord Privy Seal in this endeavor. The author's attitude throughout is strongly pro-American, pro-British, and anti-Russian. He blames the Japanese militarists for starting the war and for delaying surrender. He also stresses the emperor's lack of responsibility for the decision to go to war while attributing power and influence to the throne in the decision to surrender.

The book was published in England under the title *Eclipse of the Rising Sun* (London: Jonathan Cape, 1951. vi, 282p.). The English edition does not carry the editor's foreword by David N. Rowe, which appears in the American edition. A Japanese edition of the book is entitled *Mizurī-gō e no dōtei* (Tokyo: Bungei Shunjū Shinsha, 1951. 338p.).

144 Katō, Masuo. *The Lost War: A Japanese Reporter's Inside Story*. New York: Knopf, 1946. 264p.

A well-informed account of the rise and fall of Japan's militaristic regime in the 1930s and 1940s. The author was a leading journalist of Dōmei News Service. Particularly relevant to the study of the occupation are his reports in the last 2 chapters wherein he describes the circumstances of Japan's decision to surrender and captures vividly the atmosphere in Japan in the closing days of the war from 15 August through Japan's formal surrender on 2 September 1945. Katō relates the unfavorable rumors about Allied troops coming to Japan, the apprehensions of women and even government officials about the Allied troops' behavior, the persistently defiant conduct of unhappy young Japanese soldiers against the government's cease-fire orders, the impressive efficiency with which the American occupation forces began to work in Japan, and the actual good behavior of the troops subsequent to their landing. The author was one of 10 Japanese journalists who were allowed to cover the Allied landings at Atsugi on 28 and 30 August and to report the surrender ceremony on the *Missouri* on 2 September 1945. His observations of some of the major events such as the Potsdam Declaration, the Japanese government's response to it, the Manila Surrender Mission, and his knowledge of the extent to which such events were reported to the Japanese public are particularly interesting.

145 Kawai, Kazuo. "Militarist Activity between Japan's Two Surrender Decisions." *Pacific Historical Review* 22:383–89 (Nov. 1953)

The editor of a Japanese English-language newspaper during the war describes the conflict between civilian leaders who were resigned to Japan's surrender and military leaders who wanted to continue fighting. After the midnight session of the Imperial Council on 9–10 August, some military leaders issued statements implying that Japan planned to remain in the war even though a decision to surrender had been made. Because of the resulting confusion, the emperor made his famous radio statement on 15 August announcing the Japanese surrender.

146 ———. "*Mokusatsu:* Japan's Response to the Potsdam Declaration." *Pacific Historical Review.* 19:409–14 (Nov. 1950)

This article argues that Japan never rejected the Potsdam Declaration but rather took an attitude of *mokusatsu* or withholding comment. Some Japanese leaders had already begun moving towards surrender as early as the spring of 1944 and the Japanese Foreign Office and other civilians wanted to begin discussions with the Allies on the basis of the Potsdam Declaration, but the military objected and the result was *mokusatsu*. Both the Japanese military and the Allied leaders took this silence for outright rejection, and the war accordingly was continued.

147 Maki, John McGilvrey. *Japanese Militarism: Its Cause and Cure.* New York: Knopf, 1945. 258p.

Written prior to the end of the war, this book attempts to spell out the elements of Japanese society and ideology which would have to be altered by an occupation force in order to ensure peace once military victory over Japan is achieved. The elements discussed are major currents in Japanese history in which the author perceives antidemocratic, militaristic tendencies. These elements are the political and economic oligarchy, political control by a military class, emperor worship, and foreign influences coupled with antiforeignism. In the author's view, military defeat will create a foundation for an attack on these elements of Japanese society by seriously undermining the position of Japanese militarists for the first time in that country's history. The principal problem confronting a genuine democratic revolution in Japan is described as that of new leadership. The author notes that prewar "liberals" did not form a cohesive group and few, except for Communists and Socialists, strongly held their political philosophy. Academics who were driven underground during the war might, according to this author, emerge as leaders of a group opposing the militarists. He argues that regardless of which group holds political power, the basis of government must be widened through institutional change and political education if the oligarchical pattern is to be broken. Since it is foreseen that the Allies will not allow Japan to rebuild her heavy industry to the point where it might again be of use to the military, a cloudy economic future for Japan is forecast. Abolishing or greatly modifying the emperor's position is mandatory in the author's view, but he stresses that it is best accomplished by the Japanese themselves. Other alternatives he sees as temporary or potentially dangerous.

The author is a scholar of Japanese politics who was a student at the University of Washington when he undertook the research upon which the book is based. The approach is largely historical, and no footnotes or bibliography are included. It may best be described as an informed opinion on the major problems which an occupation force in Japan would face, combined with a recommended course of action.

148 Pacific War Research Society, comp. *Japan's Longest Day*. Tokyo: Kodansha International, 1968. 339p.

The 24 hours during which Japan finally decided upon surrender to the Allies (noon of 14 Aug. to noon of 15 Aug. 1945) are reconstructed in a dramatic, detailed, hour-by-hour account. Fourteen Japanese scholars who compose the Pacific War Research Society of the Bungei Shunjū Publishing Company (Bungei Shunjū Senshi Kenkyūkai) drew upon 79 personal interviews with participants and witnesses to piece together this history. The results of their joint effort comprise one of the most complete accounts of this subject available. The first section describes key events leading up to the decision to surrender that transpired prior to 14 August 1945. The bulk of the book is devoted to an account of events on 14–15 August culminating in the broadcast of the imperial rescript announcing surrender to the Japanese people. Each hour between noon, 14 August and noon, 15 August is treated in a separate chapter. Conversations between key participants and accounts of their personal reflections are reconstructed. The narrative fully conveys the tension and conflict of the period. The attempted coup by military elements trying to prevent surrender is described in detail, as are the official meetings and proceedings which led to the final surrender decision. This publication is a careful and accurate translation of the original Japanese volume, *Nihon no ichiban nagai hi* (Tokyo: Bungei Shunjū Shinsha, 1965. 228p.).

Rosinger, Lawrence K. "Occupation Paves Way for Stern Political Moves in Japan." 1945. *See* no.404.

Schoenberger, Walter S. *Decision of Destiny*. 1969. *See* no.246b.

149 Shigemitsu, Mamoru. *Japan and Her Destiny: My Struggle for Peace*. Ed. by F. S. G. Piggott, tr. by Oswald White. London: Hutchinson, 1958. 392p.

A translation of the author's *Shōwa no dōran* (The Disturbed Years of the Shōwa Era) (Tokyo: Chūō Kōronsha, 1952. 2v.). Shigemitsu was a Japanese diplomat who served as ambassador to China, the Soviet Union, and Great Britain in 1932–41 and, finally, as foreign minister from 20 April 1943 to 7 April 1945, from 17 August to 17 September 1945, and from 10 December 1953 to 23 December 1956. He presents his version of Japanese political history from the Manchurian Incident of 1931 to his resignation from the Higashikuni cabinet on 17 September 1945. His memoirs are written on the basis of personal experience, memory, and official notes made at the International Military Tribunal for the Far East. Shigemitsu was convicted and sentenced as a war criminal at this trial and was not released until November 1950. The author describes how Japan developed its expansionist policy, the effects of the domestic political situation on Japan's foreign policy, the Tokyo–Berlin–Rome axis, the formation of Tōjō's war cabinet, and the deterioration of the "war of Greater East Asia" from Japan's point of view. He also discusses his role in various political events during these turbulent years. Of particular interest to students of the occupation of Japan is the last chapter, which describes how the Suzuki cabinet attempted to terminate the war, the abortive coup d'état attempted by extremists in the army and navy on the night of 14 August, and

150 Tōgō, Shigenori. *The Cause of Japan.* Tr. and ed. by Tōgō Fumihiko and Ben Bruce Blakeney. New York: Simon & Schuster, 1956. v, 372p.

This translation of *Jidai no ichimen* (Tokyo: Kaizōsha, 1952. 360p.) reproduces the second and third parts of the book's Japanese edition. Part 1 in the English version covers events leading to the outbreak of the Pacific War, beginning with Tōgō's appointment to the post of foreign minister. Part 2 deals with events leading to the end of the war. A career diplomat, Tōgō served as foreign minister first at the time of Pearl Harbor and then at the end of the Pacific War. He played a major role in bringing about Japan's decision to surrender. No record of events during the occupation or of his trial by the war crimes tribunal is included. An extensive translator's introduction describes the circumstances under which the book was written, gives some biographical background about the author, and summarizes the history of events which set the scene for the beginning of the author's chronicle. Tōgō died before polishing his manuscript; nevertheless, the account is carefully written and very readable. Helpful explanatory notes are scattered throughout the text and several useful documents are appended, including a list of chief figures of the Japanese government and High Command, July 1940 to August 1945; the Japanese–American draft understanding (9 Apr. 1941); and the decisions of the imperial conferences of 2 July and 6 September 1941. The 2 who translated and edited the volume were well qualified for the task. Tōgō Fumihiko, son-in-law and adopted son of Tōgō Shigenori, is a career diplomat and member of the Japanese Permanent Delegation at Geneva. Ben Bruce Blakeney served as defense council for Tōgō Shigenori and others in the Tokyo war crimes trials. He became a lecturer in American law at Tokyo University in 1949 and has also been engaged in the general practice of law in Tokyo.

151 U.S. Army Air Force. *Mission Accomplished.* Washington, D.C.: Government Printing Office, 1946. vi, 110p.

One of the first attempts made by the United States to determine the factors which led Japan to a war with the United States and to probe the attitudes which prevailed among the Japanese about their prospects as the war progressed. The report does not specifically focus on the occupation, but it does describe in useful fashion the state of Japanese society and morale during the war and at the beginning of the occupation. One hundred sixty-two high-ranking civil, military, and industrial leaders of Japan during World War II were interrogated for this study, along with 3 European missionaries working in Japan. In part 1, 51 individuals provided intelligence on the reaction of Japanese leadership to several phases of the war. Members of Japan's highest political echelons such as Marquis Kido, Prince Konoe, Admiral Toyoda, and Fleet Admiral Nagano discussed internal dissent regarding the decision to go to war. Military commanders discussed the difficulties that Japan faced as the American campaign progressed from a "defensive phase" to a "holding phase" and then to an "offensive phase." The Japanese recounted the fear of American air raids which they had entertained as early as October 1943. They regarded the fall of Saipan as the turning point of the war and analyzed the effects of American air supremacy on Japanese ability to continue the war both in terms of war production and morale. Finally, they described the imperial conferences leading to acceptance of the Potsdam terms. In part 2, 107 less important Japanese were asked some 13 questions such as "What were the main factors in the defeat of Japan?"; "When did the Japanese definitely decide that further resistance was futile?"; "Did you ever believe that the defeat of Japan was inevitable?"; etc. Answers reveal that the majority of those interrogated had not expected a Japanese victory. Part 2 is followed by statements by 4 Japanese Christian leaders and 3 European missionaries commenting on the effect of the Allied air attacks on the religious life of the people.

———. Strategic Bombing Survey. *Index to Records to United States Strategic Bombing Survey.* 1947. See no.29.

152 ———. ———. *Japan's Struggle to End the War.* Washington, D.C.: Government Printing Office, 1946. v, 36p. (Pacific War Report no.3)

The first third of this brochure outlines the Japanese political scene in the last year of the war and the principal efforts to stop the war. The belief on the part of a number of highly placed Japanese in the futility of continued resistance was attributed by the authors to the effects of U.S. air power in: (1) blockading the home islands; (2) undercutting hard-core militarists through American victories in the Pacific; and (3) demoralizing the population. The first appendix contains Japanese estimates of U.S. and Japanese military strength and national resources at the outbreak and conclusion of the war, and a memorandum of conversations in February 1945 between 24 of the leading Japanese military-political figures.

153 ———. ———. Chairman's Office. *The Effects of Atomic Bombs on Hiroshima and Nagasaki.* Washington, D.C.: Government Printing Office, 1946. v, 46p. (Pacific War report no.13)

This report describes in detail U.S. bombing raids against Japan, their physical effects, their effects on Japanese morale, and the role they played in Japan's decision to surrender. There is a section comparing the atomic bomb to other weapons. The final chapter is an examination and evaluation of various defense measures against atomic explosion, including shelters, decentralization, civilian defense, and active defense. The conclusion of the study states that, as defensive weapons, atomic bombs are useful primarily as deterrents to potential aggression. It is also asserted that as the developer and exploiter of atomic weapons, the United States must take the lead in establishing and implementing international guarantees to prevent their future use.

154 ———. ———. ———. *Summary Report (Pacific War).* Washington, D.C.: Government Printing Office, 1946. iii, 32p. (Pacific War report no.1)

This summary report of the Pacific War provides a description of the strategic plans of Japan and the United States, the way in which the United States gradually achieved air superiority over increased territory which finally included the Japanese home islands, and the way in which that air superiority was exploited. The results of air attacks, including the effects of the atomic bombings, are briefly reported. There is also an assessment of the degree to which the Pacific study modifies the conclusions and recommendations of the earlier European study.

155 ———. ———. Civilian Defense Div. *Summary Report Concerning Air-Raid Protection and Allied Subjects in Japan.* Washington. D.C.: Government Printing Office, 1946. 19p. (Pacific War report no.10)

The lack of a unified command system for civilian defense activities is regarded in this report as the cause of poor air-raid protection in Japan. The confused status of civilian defense, particularly at the top level, the decentralization of authority, and usurpation of functions are noted. A summary of civil defense activities undertaken before, during, and after American air raids is also included. Among these activities are evacuation from urban areas, air-raid warnings, shelters, fire fighting, medical services, and repair. Some measures taken by the Japanese government to protect factories and utilities are described. In conclusion, it is stated that in many Japanese cities, people panicked and failed to obey instructions during severe air raids. This conduct is contrasted to that of the Germans.

156 ———. ———. Manpower, Food, and Civilian Supplies Div. *The Japanese Wartime Standard of Living and Utilization of Manpower.* Washington, D.C.: Government Printing Office. 1947, xi, 146p. (Pacific War report no.42)

The decline in the Japanese standard of living in terms of food, civilian supplies, and the wartime utilization of manpower are described and analyzed as factors in Japan's decision to surrender. A wealth of statistical information supplements the text of the study. Nearly 200 tables and figures are included throughout the text and in appendixes.

157 ———. ———. Morale Div. *The Effects of Strategic Bombing on Japanese Morale.* Washington, D.C.: Government Printing Office, 1947. vi, 262p. (Pacific War report no.14)

A history of Japanese morale during the Pacific War is constructed from a cross-sectional survey of Japanese civilians, special interrogations, and a variety of Japanese documents. After a summary of conclusions and a discussion of the purposes and methods of the survey, various findings are analyzed in detail. Subjects dealt with include the morale of the nation as a whole, the direct effects of bombing, relationships between bombing experiences and morale, the morale of the labor force, problems of evacuation, the effects of the atomic bombs on morale, the apparatus of morale control, the role of propaganda, and the role of morale in Japan's surrender. Attitudes toward the future, the emperor, and occupation forces in the postsurrender period are also explored. The air attacks against Japan's 66 largest cities are credited as the most important factor which caused doubt among the Japanese people concerning their eventual military victory and made them willing to terminate the war. In 20 appendixes the methods and materials used in this study are described in detail. Two notes appended to the study are taken from a diary by Itō Toyojiro and provide examples of "subversive letters."

158 ———. ———. Naval Analysis Div. *Interrogations of Japanese Officials.* Washington, D.C.: Government Printing Office, 1946. 2v. (Pacific War report no.72)

These interrogations of 118 Japanese naval officers were conducted in Tokyo during October, November, and December 1945 by officers of the Naval Analysis Division. Lists of interrogations are provided, arranged by subject matter. Indexes of major battles and operations and of Japanese officials are also included in the first volume. Interrogations 1 through 70 appear in volume 1; nos.71 through 118 are in volume 2. The format is consistent throughout: the name and rank of the person being questioned are given, followed by the identity of the interrogator and the names of any other Allied officers present. A summary of the statement precedes the transcript of questions and answers, all in English. Short biographical sketches of the Japanese officers, stressing their military careers during the Pacific War, are provided at the end of the second volume.

159 ———. ———. Over-All Economic Effects Div. *The Effects of Strategic Bombing on Japan's Economy.* Washington, D.C.: Government Printing Office, 1946. ix, 244p. (Pacific War report no.53)

This account is both a description of the damages inflicted on the Japanese economy by U.S. military operations and an assessment of the role which such economic destruction played in the final outcome of the Pacific War. Japan's economic position in 1941, the economy under the stress of war, the course of air attacks against the Japanese economy, and the record of damages are all examined. The final chapter is a review of the considerations which were fundamental in the selection of bombing targets during the war. Three appendixes containing approximately 250 tables supplement the text. Included in the appendixes are an analysis of Allied economic intelligence concerning Japan, an appraisal of Japan's gross national product and its components from 1940 to 1945, and a note on statistical sources. The bulk of the appended tables provide statistics on various aspects of Japanese economic development for the decade preceding 1945.

160 ———. ———. Physical Damage Div. *A Report on Physical Damage in Japan.* Washington, D.C.: Government Printing Office, 1947. v, 225p. (Pacific War report no.96)

161 Zacharias, Ellis M. "Nippon's Five Secret Peace Bids." *United Nations World* 3:25–29 (Aug. 1949)

Zacharias, deputy director of the Office of Naval Intelligence, describes secret diplomatic negotiations which clearly indicated Japan's intention to surrender months before the atomic bomb was dropped. Unfortunately, a promised continuation was not published and the article is incomplete. These diplomatic maneuverings involved a diverse cast, including the pope, the archbishop of Tokyo, the emperor of Japan and his "brilliant mother," Stalin, Douglas Fairbanks, Jr., and others. Some of their roles are not at all clear. As early as December 1944, American intelligence learned that moderate Japanese leaders planned to form a cabinet replacing the ardent militarists. Fairbanks advocated sending a secret mission to negotiate with his friend, the peace-loving mother of Emperor Hirohito. President Roosevelt is said to have been guilty of ignoring these diplomatic paths to peace.

161a ———. "Eighteen Words That Bagged Japan." *Saturday Evening Post* 218:17, 117–20 (17 Nov. 1945); abridged and published under the same title in *Reader's Digest* 47:93–98 (Dec. 1945)

Zacharias relates the story of his 21 July 1945 radio broadcast over the Pacific transmitter of the Office of War Information in which he said (in Japanese), "As you know, the Atlantic Charter and the Cairo Declaration are the sources of American policy." He asserts that this broadcast may have played the decisive role in ending World War II, for the message indicated to the Japanese government that the United States knew of Japan's desire to end the war as well as of Japan's need for clarification of the term "unconditional surrender" and for information on the Allied postsurrender plans. Furthermore, the Japanese wanted assurances that the emperor could remain on the throne. Zacharias then discusses the events that led up to this particular broadcast and some of the developments which followed it.

Planning Elsewhere

The United States was not alone in its concern about the postwar treatment of Japan. Its major allies were also very much interested and had plans and policies that differed from those of the United States in varying degrees. The extent to which they would be able to implement these plans became a serious source of dissension among the so-called United Nations.

A number of the principal sources relating to such Allied plans and policies have been assembled below. Related materials for later periods will be found in the section on international aspects (p.260).

162 Australia. Dept. of External Affairs. "Japanese Surrender: Statement by the Prime Minister (The Rt. Hon. J. B. Chifley) in the House of Representatives on 29th August, 1945." *Current Notes on International Affairs* 16:169–74 (Aug./Sept. 1945)

Prime Minister Chifley addressed the lower house of the U.S. Congress on 29 August 1945 on diplomatic events that led to the Japanese surrender and the Australian response thereto. He also explained the Australian position on the postwar control of Japan. The address stresses the Australian government's views on the emperor's war guilt and its desire to be represented at the surrender ceremonies in Japan and Singapore and to participate in the military control of Japan.

163 ———. ———. "Some Views on the Post-war Treatment of Japan." *Current Notes on International Affairs* 16:6–17 (Jan. 1945)

This article summarizes a variety of official and unofficial views on the post-surrender treatment of Japan. The official views are those of President Roosevelt; Generalissimo Chiang Kai-shek; Joseph Grew; Vere Redman, director of the Far Eastern Division of the British Ministry of Information; and Sir George Sansom. The unofficial views are those of prominent specialists such as Nathaniel Peffer, Thomas A. Bisson, Charles Nelson Spinks, and Professor S. R. Chow. Chinese newspapers and miscellaneous articles are also examined in this connection. Subjects discussed include the disposal of Japanese territories, disarmament, control arrangements, reparations, the political structure of postwar Japan, Japan's economic future, and its future relations with international organizations. Many of the views examined were expressed between 1942 and 1944 in publications such as *Foreign Affairs, International Affairs,* and *Pacific Affairs,* and as papers presented at Institute of Pacific Relations' conferences.

164 Australian Institute of International Affairs. *Australia and the Pacific.* Princeton, N.J.: Princeton Univ. Pr., 1944. x, 203p.

Ten papers, which were prepared by members of the Australian Institute of International Affairs and presented to the eighth conference of the Institute of Pacific Relations held in Quebec in December 1942, are reprinted here in modified form. All assume an eventual Allied victory over Japan and exemplify Australian views of their country's position in the Pacific in the postwar period. Although no specific Australian role is indicated or advocated for the postwar period, closer relations between Australia and the United States and an expanded role for Australia are called for and the view is expressed that Japan should be stripped of all her conquered territories. K. H. Bailey, W. D. Forsyth, P. D. Phillips, Julius Stone, and W. G. K. Duncan are the contributors of the first 5 papers concerning the political context, while G. L. Wood, S. M. Wadham with K. H. Northcote, Roland Mountain, and Walter Hill present economic papers. The last paper was jointly authored by members of the institute.

———. A Study Group. *Australia's Interests and Policies in Regard to Problems of Economic and Social Reconstruction in the Pacific.* 1947. See no.772.

Beloff, Max. *Soviet Far Eastern Policy since Yalta.* 1950. See no.775.

———. *Soviet Policy in the Far East, 1944–1951.* 1953. See no.776.

164a "Chinese Views on Japan's Post-war Government." *Amerasia* 8:22–24 (21 Jan. 1944)

In his most recent New Year's message to the Chinese army and the people of China, Chiang Kai-shek expressed his belief that the Japanese militarists must be liquidated, that Japan's postwar political system must be purged of all aggressive elements, and that the Japanese people should be allowed to decide on the form of their future government. In turn, Sun Fo, the president of the legislative Yuan of the Chinese government, recently wrote an article in which he called for a end to the military clique, the emperor, and the cult of emperor worship and for the establishment of a democratic-republican Japan. In this fashion prominent Chinese spokesmen have publicly declared themselves in favor of a democratic Japan and have stated that they regard the imperial institution as a dangerous and integral part of aggressive Japanese militarism. By way of contrast, certain American and British circles continue to place all of the blame for the war on the militarists and are anxious to preserve the imperial institution.

165 Chou, Keng-sheng. *Winning the Peace in the Pacific: A Chinese View of Far Eastern Postwar Plans and Requirements for a Stable Security System in the Pacific Area.* New York: Macmillan, 1944. xi, 98p.

A professor of international law and international relations discusses the problems of postwar planning in the Pacific from a Chinese point of view. Chou was educated in Japan, England, and France and was a resident of the United States at the time this book was written. He outlines 4 essential requirements for permanent order in the Pacific: complete disarmament of Japan after her defeat; readjustment of the relationship of China to other world powers, including abolition of the unequal treaties and of inequitable treatment of Chinese abroad; solution of the racial and national problems of the region exacerbated by colonialism; and establishment of a regional organization to ensure security and maintain peace. Among his recommendations for the postwar treatment of Japan are limiting Japanese territory to the boundaries established before 1894, investigation of the actual role of the emperor in the conduct of the war before deciding on the fate of the imperial institution, and reparations in the form of industrial materials and machines to aid China in her postwar economic recovery. An admirer of democratic institutions, the author envisions postwar China as a leading example of constitutional democracy in Asia and thus as a stabilizing factor in a new world order. This booklet is an expanded version of the author's paper, "A Permanent Order for the Pacific," submitted to the eighth conference of the Institute of Pacific Relations in 1942.

166 Chow, S. R. "The Future of Japan: What Happens When Defeat Is Accomplished?" *Contemporary China* 4 (30 Apr. 1945); also in *Asiatic Review* n.s. 41:284–89 (July 1945)

An article by a professor of international law discusses the treatment of Japan after surrender. He advocates the return of all Japanese territory acquired after 1879 and wholesale repatriation of Japanese living in these areas, total and immediate disarmament, and prolonged military control of approximately 20 years duration (although not necessarily prolonged occupation of the Japanese homeland). He also considers the necessity of establishing some economic controls in order to prevent a resurgent Japan. Finally, there is a discussion of the role of the emperor, and the author cites various opinions from several Chinese and American journals and newspapers as to how he should be treated at the termination of the war.

166a ———. "The Pacific after the War." *Foreign Affairs* 21, no.4:71–86 (Oct. 1942)

Without achieving a permanent order in the Pacific, Chow argues, a lasting peace will be impossible. For such a permanent order, the following 4 essential requirements must be met: (1) Japan must be defeated and completely disarmed; (2) a fundamental adjustment must be made in China's relationship with the foreign powers; (3) there must be an equitable solution of the region's racial and national problems; and (4) a regional organization must be formed to establish security and peace. With regard to Japan, the author rejects the contention of those who advocate a policy of moderation and generosity towards Japan and who are reluctant to assign an international force to police the country after she has been disarmed. He also asserts that Japan must be required to relinquish all territories that she has acquired since 1894 and perhaps the Ryukyu Islands as well. Chow's article presents an important Chinese viewpoint on the postwar settlement. In a revised and enlarged form, it was subsequently presented as a data paper at the December 1942 Institute of Pacific Relations conference.

167 Craigie, Sir Robert Leslie. *Behind the Japanese Mask.* London: Hutchinson, 1945. 172, 2p.

The British ambassador to Japan from 1937 to 1942 recounts the sequence of political events in Japan that led to the Pacific War and describes Anglo–Japanese relations during that time. He also follows through his personal experiences the intricacies of the struggle in Japan between proponents and opponents of the war. He gives a keen profile of the leading figures in the 1930s and early 1940s. The book was written before Japan's surrender, although the end of the war was in sight. In the final chapter, which is of interest to students of the occupation, the English diplomat suggests the nature of a postwar occupation for Japan. He maintains that the Allied objectives should be to create conditions in which the Japanese would find ways to govern themselves by democratic methods. He suggests that priority be given to economic recovery, that constitutional and legislative reforms be deferred, and that the imperial rule be preserved with the possible abdication of Emperor Hirohito and succession by the crown prince with Prince Chichibu as regent. He advocates the elimination of political corruption, a cabinet responsible to Parliament, civilian control over the military, the elimination of ultranationalistic textbooks, and reeducation of the Japanese people. "Behind the mask of inscrutability," the author views, there are good qualities of the Japanese people such as kindliness, courage, and loyalty that should serve as the basis on which to build a new nation.

Dallin, David J. *Soviet Russia and the Far East.* 1948. See no.780.

168 Ehrman, John. *Grand Strategy.* London: HMSO, 1956. xvi, 422p. (History of the Second World War, United Kingdom Military series, v.6)

The last volume of the official British history of World War II. The first 4 chapters deal with Britain's part in the Allied victory in the European theater, and the remaining 6 with the Allied victory in the war against Japan. These last chapters begin with a description of the Allied reconquest of central Burma from October 1944 to May 1945. They then consider the development of the American strategy with Russian and British participation in the Pacific War from October 1944 to June 1945 and the Allied plan to recapture Singapore and invade Japan from June to August of 1945. The British part in the initial decision to use atomic bombs is reviewed, referring in particular to the Potsdam Conference, Japanese peace feelers, and the Japanese response to the Potsdam Declaration.

Evatt, Herbert V. *Australia in World Affairs.* 1946. See no.786.

169 "Factors in the Settlement with Japan." *Pacific Affairs* 18:40–54 (Mar. 1945)

An article which summarizes the conclusions reached by a Chatham House study group that met in London early in 1944 to discuss the problems that might be involved in the treatment of a defeated Japan. It suggests alternatives which Japan might adopt in the political sphere, such as the adoption of a democratic or Communist system of government. The report considers the pros and cons of an Allied promotion of Japan's economic revival, as well as the matter of the disposal of the armed forces, constitutional reform, and the promotion of a social revolution involving the emancipation of women, and reform of the educational and religious systems. It sees a cure for Japanese ills in a reeducation and liberation of thought by the Allies.

169a "Far Eastern Melting Pot." *Economist* 149, no.5322:250–52 (25 Aug. 1945)

In the first half of this article dealing with the impact of the Japanese surrender in Japan and in China respectively, the author strongly criticizes the manner in which the Japanese have sought to save face when surrendering but praises the Allies for their decision to retain the emperor. Only the emperor could have persuaded the country's military commanders to lay down their arms, and without his imperial rescript, the Japanese armies stationed in China, Malaya and Indonesia might have continued the war. The emperor's authority also will be essential to the smooth establishment of the occupation forces and of Allied controls in Japan. The article questions the ability of the Japanese national structure to survive the impact of this unprecedented defeat and notes that economic and political developments in East Asia during the coming months may well be crucial in this regard. Finally, there is an indication that the Soviet Union will have a strong, if indirect, influence on Japanese politics in the immediate future.

Feis, Herbert. *The Atomic Bomb and the End of World War II*. 1966. See no.243.

———. *Contest over Japan*. 1967. See no.789.

———. *Japan Subdued: The Atomic Bomb and the End of the War in the Pacific*. 1961. See no.244.

"The Future of Japan: An American View; A Canadian View." See no.76c.

Greenwood, Gordon, ed. *Australian Policies toward Asia*. 1954. See no.793.

169b Keeton, George W. "What Can We Do with Japan?" *Contemporary Review* 144:21–25 (July 1943)

Keeton offers suggestions for presurrender planning and discusses problems which will require detailed consideration. With regard to Japan's postwar political structure, he points to 3 alternative possibilities: (1) a United Nations decision to maintain a modification of the existing regime; (2) the possibility of Japan's going communist; and (3) a United Nations effort to encourage the liberal, Western forces in Japan to take control and at the same time to arrange for a Pacific security pact similar to the Atlantic Charter. In the area of economic problems, Keeton notes that a primary motive for Japan's expansionism was the vulnerability of her supplies of raw materials and food. The postwar settlement, therefore, should pay some attention to these needs. The postwar educational system in turn should be geared to educating the Japanese to standards of behavior generally accepted by the United Nations. Keeton feels that foreign teachers might be useful in promoting this particular goal, as might be increased efforts to Christianize the country. Finally, Keeton expresses his concern over the matter of emigration. Since most countries will not welcome a massive inflow of Japanese nationals, a specific solution for that problem is very difficult. At the very least, however, the problem should be considered in conjunction with any UN efforts to combat overpopulation as a whole in Asia.

169c Knight, F. J. "Japan's Post-war Leader?" *World Review* (London) 2:27–29 (Nov. 1944)

Knight speculates that Prince Konoe Fumimaro will be called upon to assume a role of leadership in Japan's postwar government. He is characterized as being "clever, sophisticated and of distinguished aristocratic family" and as having "dabbled" with liberalism during his youth. Other biographical information also is provided.

170 Mateveev, Illarion. "The Kurile Islands." *Far Eastern Survey* 13:227–28 (29 Nov. 1944)

An account of the Kuriles in light of the possibility of their postwar restoration to the Soviet Union. The article focuses on their basic geographical features and their cultural history.

170a Phillips, Philip David. "The Pacific through Australian Eyes." *Austral–Asiatic Bulletin* 6, no.2:14–21 (Mar. 1945)

This review of certain contemporary Asian developments includes a 1 page section on Japan. Phillips writes that the discussion of Japan within the Australian press and by the Australian public has been "meagre, indeed, almost non-existent" where matters involving the post-

171 **Presurrender Planning**

war treatment of the Japanese militarists, government, and people are concerned. He attributes this situation to Australia's traditional dependence upon imperial authority and to the preoccupation of most Australians with domestic concerns.

171 Redman, H. Vere. "The Problem of Japan." *International Affairs* 20:19–31 (Jan. 1944)

The text of an address given by the author at Chatham House in September 1943. The writer predicts some probable aspects of the situation in a defeated Japan considering the psychological state of the people and the dislocation and economic deterioration that will occur. Without committing himself to either position, he discusses the pros and cons of the destruction of the imperial myth and of the position of the emperor. He also speculates about what will be done with the military leaders and what means will be taken to break the political power of the gendarmerie and the police. Finally, in the crucial sphere of education, he suggests that the Allies seek not to revolutionize the Japanese educational system but only to rid it of its nationalistic bias and to allow the changing social and political climate to effect deeper changes.

172 Reed, John Jay. *American Diplomatic Relations with Australia during the Second World War*. Ph.D. dissertation, Univ. of Southern California, 1969. 360p. (Abstracted in *Dissertation Abstracts International* 30:4923–A [1970]; University Microfilms order no.70–8540)

Examining the alliance between the United States and Australia that developed as a consequence of the outbreak of World War II in the Pacific, this study includes some information of the postwar plans regarding Japan of the 2 countries.

173 Royal Institute of International Affairs. *Japan in Defeat: A Report by a Chatham House Study Group*. London: Humphrey Milford, published for Oxford Univ. Pr., 1945. xiii, 132, 2p.

A report of a study of Japanese affairs conducted by a group of 10 specialists headed by Sir Paul Butler, who was adviser on Far Eastern affairs to the British Foreign Office in 1944. It was done in association with the inquiry initiated by the Institute of Pacific Relations regarding the future of Japan and was submitted to the institute's ninth international conference in January 1945. Undertaken when Japan's defeat was approaching, the report is intended to forecast the reactions of the Japanese people to defeat and to suggest what seemed likely to occur in Japan after the war. From this perspective, the report covers various aspects of Japanese society such as the throne, the military, nationalist societies, the administration, liberals, Japan's attitude toward foreign powers, religion, education, women, the economic outlook, finance, population problems, and the social position of the peasant. For each subject, there is a thoughtful discussion of probable postsurrender conditions. The study carefully avoids advocating specific policies that should be adopted by the Allied governments toward the control of Japan, but, nevertheless, suggests several alternatives. For instance, there is cautioning against premature tampering with institutions such as the throne, the army, big business families, and the educational system, and the suggestion that these institutions might function as stabilizing elements during an immediate postwar period of political and social chaos. While it does not completely negate the possibility of a direct Allied military occupation, the report implicitly recommends that the Allied control be indirect in the light of the inherent complexities caused by difficulties of language and the Japanese psychology. Although perhaps too pessimistic, this general estimate of postwar conditions reflects deep insight into Japanese affairs. In 1948 the major portion of the report was incorporated in revised form into Harold Wakefield's *New Paths for Japan* (1948) (no.576).

174 Sansom, Sir George B. *Postwar Relations with Japan*. London: Royal Institute of International Affairs, 1947. 18p. (Institute of Pacific Relations, 10th conference, supplementary paper, 1947)

A reproduction of a paper of the same title submitted to the eighth conference of the Institute of Pacific Relations held at Mont Tremblant, Quebec, Canada in December 1942. The author predicts the defeat of Japan, outlines measures to apply to postwar Japan, and discusses relations between Japan and the rest of Asia and between the Allies and Japan. He suggests that Japan be disarmed and expresses the opinion that a defeated and disarmed Japan will not represent a serious menace to the peace of the Far East. He urges the United Nations to take measures in the postwar period to enlist Japanese cooperation for insuring security and welfare in the Pacific area. In order to persuade the Japanese that cooperation with the West is beneficial to Japan, he argues that there must be free channels of communication between the West and the Japanese people. He states that the denial of free expression, which, to him, was the most reactionary feature of Japanese domestic policy, has been the greatest obstacle to positive change, and that the "remarkable incapacity" of the Japanese to understand the essentials of cultures other than their own must be remedied before Japan can make a useful contribution to postwar reconstruction and reform. While admitting that harsh peace terms and a military occupation would be necessary, Sansom does not believe that punitive measures alone would provide the means of reforming Japanese political thinking; rather, a "nice mixture of persuasion and coercion" is necessary to show the Japanese what to put in the place of the "distasteful features" of their system.

174a ———. "Japan in the Postwar World." U.S. Office of Education *Bulletin* 7:9–16 (1945)

Sansom argues that Japan's loss of her empire will be the most important consequence of her surrender inasmuch as it will mean the loss of her major source of food and raw materials for some time. While the Japanese will naturally recognize the need for a change in their leadership, the Allies will have to encourage them if the resulting changes are to be more than superficial in nature. The major tasks of the United Nations will be to set a good example of international behavior and to undo the indoctrination of the Japanese people. Although Japanese thinking is still largely feudalistic, there are liberals who may be encouraged to take an initiative, and the fact that Shinto was largely an artificial, official creation will make it relatively easy to disestablish. None of these reforms, however, will be accepted by the Japanese if they feel that they will compromise their country's strength too drastically.

175 Scott, J. W. Robertson. "Japan's Future and Our Own." *Hibbert Journal* 43: 204–11 (Apr. 1945)

The author, then editor of the *Countryman*, examines the future of Japanese-American relations after the war and the role of Japan in Asia. He traces briefly Japan's history before the war emphasizing the rise of militarism and violence in domestic politics. Scott feels that the British and Americans in order to insure democracy in Japan must convince the Japanese "that our way of life is not only superior but has been the source of our success against them."

176 Shearer, J. O., and F. L. W. Wood. *Collective Security in the Pacific*. Wellington: New Zealand Institute of International Affairs, 1945. 12p. (Institute of Pacific Relations, 9th conference, New Zealand paper no.2, pt.1, 1945)

Two New Zealanders express their point of view regarding the adoption of measures to promote security in the Pacific after the war. Observing that regional security can be maintained only within the framework of world security arrangements, the authors support the Moscow Declaration of 30 October 1943, which favors the establishment of a world peace organization. They also uphold the spirit of the Canberra Pact which appeals for the equality of nations, thus rejecting the concept of Big Power guardianship. They suggest that security in the Pacific be preserved both by establishing defense zones, one for the South and

Southwest Pacific covering New Zealand and Australia, and another for Southeast Asia and Indonesia, and by effective control of Japan. Before a peace settlement with Japan is signed, they urge that Japan's military power be reduced to a minimum. They believe, however, that Japan's future form of government should be determined by the Japanese themselves.

177 Somerville, John C. "Post-war Japan." *National Review* (London) 125: 65–70 (July 1945)

This essay, written prior to the termination of the war, discusses some aspects of the Allied treatment of a defeated Japan. The author recommends that the entire army, navy, and air force be completely disbanded, along with the Diet and the House of Peers. He strongly advises that the emperor be retained since his removal might plunge his people into chaos, and suggests that an oligarchy which would consist of Japanese with international experience be set up to rule the country until democracy takes a firm hold. The article also includes a brief discussion of the treatment of the former Japanese territories of Manchuria, Formosa, and Korea (Chōsen).

178 Sun, Fo. "The Mikado Must Go." *Foreign Affairs* 23:17–25 (Oct. 1944)

In anticipation of an American defeat of Japan, the author marshals the reasons why he is strongly in favor of the disenthronement of the Japanese emperor. According to him, "the imperial idea is the essence of Japanese aggression" and must be totally destroyed in order to destroy the aggressive, warmongering elements at the heart of the present Japanese nation. He briefly describes the arguments of such men as Joseph Grew who favor the retention and "use" of the emperor and points out what he conceives to be their fatal flaws, that the emperor would be used not only by the liberals but also by the reactionary ultranationalist groups. In looking forward to other postsurrender measures to be taken, he urges firm Allied control of Japan's heavy and chemical industries.

178a Timperley, Harold John. *Japan: A World Problem.* New York: Day, 1942. ix, 150p.

Timperley, an Australian journalist residing in the United States, asserts that the Japanese are obsessed with the idea of world domination because they have a deep-rooted feeling of racial superiority and a long-held dream of empire. He notes, moreover, that there can never be a durable peace in East Asia, and hence in the entire world, until the power of the Japanese military oligarchy is broken. In his concluding chapter, therefore, Timperley presents a number of recommendations for the postwar treatment of Japan. First, he states, the Japanese should be encouraged to initiate constitutional reforms which would eliminate the hold that the military has had over the country's civilian government. Next, some form of international peace-keeping arrangement backed by overwhelming force must be provided to guarantee Japan's security against foreign aggression. Finally, in addition to introducing measures that would readjust her "distorted and ill-balanced economic system," Japan must be allowed to share in the advantages offered by the Atlantic Charter—"access, on equal terms, to the trade and to the raw materials of the world" —in order that the Japanese may exploit appropriate economic opportunities.

178b ———. "Peace Aims in the Pacific." *Asia* 42:398–99 (July 1942)

Timperley presents a consensus of public opinion about the postwar settlement for Asia and in the course of his discussion indicates that any proposals involving Japan must provide for her legitimate political, economic and security needs. He makes a number of specific recommendations as well, and they include the following: (1) a complete Japanese withdrawal from China, Manchuria, Formosa, Korea, and the mandated islands; (2) a Chinese declaration of her moral and legal rights to compensation for damages incurred as a consequence of Japanese aggression, followed by a waiving of all claims for reparations in recognition of Japan's inability to make substantial payments; (3) constitutional changes which would deprive the military oligarchy from maintaining control of the Japanese government; (4) the extension of loans and trading opportunities to Japan; and (5) legislative action by various Western governments which would result in a liberalization of their present immigration policies. The editors of *Asia* invited readers of the journal to express their reactions to Timperley's views as well as to statements in a companion piece by Taraknath Das entitled "Asia Wants Freedom Now." Several pertinent replies including letters from Tyler Dennett, Quincy Wright, George H. Blakeslee, and H. D. Fong, therefore, appear in the August (p.464–65, 495) and September (p.545–46) issues of the journal.

178c Tsang, Chih. "Reparations for China." *Asia and the Americas* 44:306–7 (July 1944)

In an extract from his forthcoming book *China's Postwar Markets* (New York: International Secretariat, Institute of Pacific Relations, distributed by Macmillan, 1945; xi, 239p.), Tsang explains that China's postwar industrialization and rehabilitation will necessitate the import of large volumes of capital and consumer goods and that reparations would serve as a good means for offsetting the expected trade imbalance. While confiscated Japanese investments in Manchuria, Formosa, and China proper could be considered as reparations items, they can be used only for the further development of the regions in which they are found and cannot be used immediately as a means of paying for China's postwar purchases. Reparations in kind or in cash from Japan, therefore, would be very useful. Their amount, however, should be commensurate with Japan's productive capacity, they should consist primarily of industrial plants and equipment or of cash receipts from the export of Japanese goods to the United States and Great Britain, and they should be limited in duration to a maximum of 10 years. At the time he wrote this article, Tsang was serving as the general secretary of the Universal Trading Corporation—the official purchasing agency of the Chinese government.

179 U.S. Dept. of Defense. *The Entry of the Soviet Union into the War against Japan: Military Plans, 1941–1945.* Washington, D.C.: Government Printing Office, 1955. v, 107p.

This well-documented report reconstructs the major official military advice given on the question of Soviet entry into the war against Japan. The documents are mainly concerned with high-level military activities centered in Washington, although the views and recommendations of the Pacific theater commanders are also included. The survey reveals that America became interested in the possibility of Russian participation in the Pacific War immediately after the Pearl Harbor attack but that the Soviet Union remained reluctant to consider or discuss joining the Allied forces in the Pacific through 1942. The report indicates, however, that by the end of 1943 Anglo-American military planners had reason to believe that the Soviet Union would participate in the Pacific War after the defeat of Germany. There were active diplomatic maneuvers in Washington, London, and Moscow during 1944 to encourage Russian participation in the Pacific War and to obtain Russia's agreement to the American use of air bases in Siberia. On the other hand, the report also notes the presence of a paper submitted to the Joint Chiefs of Staff (JCS 1176) arguing that Russian participation, though desirable, would not be essential. The report then examines the decisions reached at the Yalta and Potsdam Conferences of 1945 regarding joint U.S.-Soviet military effort in the Pacific and studies Pacific strategy including that for the invasion of the Japanese islands. The work was translated into Japanese in a special supplement of *Sekai shūhō*, a weekly magazine, of 11 November 1955.

———. Dept. of State. *Foreign Relations of the United States, Diplomatic Papers, 1944.* v.5, *The Near East, South*

Asia, Africa, The Far East. 1965. See no.201.

179a "Victory in the East." *Economist* 149, no.5321:217–18 (18 Aug. 1945)

Now that Japan has announced her surrender, the Allies must work out appropriate arrangements for laying the foundations of peace in East Asia. The militarists must be eliminated, and a final decision ought to be made about the future role of the emperor. While it will be necessary to control the industrial enterprises which enabled Japan to go to war, the Allies should not forget that industry will be vital for a peaceful economy as well. The major difficulties in arriving at an amicable peace settlement will center around territorial issues in view of the existence of 2 rival and competing centers of power (Communist and Nationalist) in China.

Walter, Austin F. *Australia's Relations with the United States: 1941–1949.* 1954. See no.841.

179b "What Can Be Done with a Defeated Japan?" *Dublin Review* 215:21–26 (July 1944)

According to this report of "a correspondent from Japan," the first task of the United Nations is to discredit the Japanese militarists by inflicting complete defeat on Japan. Secondly, efforts must be made to see that the Japanese people place their faith in elements within Japan sympathetic to Anglo–American ideals, and an attempt accordingly must be made to build up such elements in the public esteem. The appeal of the Soviet Union (at this time still a nonbelligerent in Asia) should not be underestimated. The writer concludes that the Japanese should be reminded of the fact that their arts and literature have done more to spread the glory of the emperor around the world than their military efforts. They should therefore cultivate the arts of peace and not of war.

180 "What Government in Japan?" *New Statesman and Nation* n.s.30:139–40 (1 Sept. 1945)

The author surveys political developments since the Restoration and the possibility of establishing democracy in postwar Japan. An examination of the roles of the Imperial Household Ministry, the army, the cabinet, the bureaucracy, and big business in government reveals that the democratic tradition in Japan before the occupation was weak and superficial. However, according to the author, "the occupying armies will have, from the outset, to rely on the use of [existing] Japanese officials and institutions." This viewpoint indicates a difficult and unprofitable job ahead for the Allies. It is predicted that China will play the dominant postwar role in Japan.

181 Whyte, Sir Frederick. *The Rise and Fall of Japan.* London: Royal Institute of International Affairs, 1945. 59p.

A brief and balanced picture of the road that Japan followed from the Meiji Restoration through her defeat in World War II. It was completed a few weeks after Japan's surrender. Having described Japan's national interests in Asia and her foreign policy from 1868 through 1941, the author discusses both .the domestic and the international factors that led Japan to "overreach herself." The third and last chapter examines the course Japan might follow in the future and the responsibility of the United Nations toward Japan. The author warns that the United Nations should not make the same mistakes in Japan as the Allied powers did in Germany after World War I by attempting to compel drastic change in the political system of a defeated nation. He points out that the United Nations' real "predicament" is the problem of finding the right political group with which to work toward the building of a new Japan. Although he suggests that the United Nations might undertake reforms in Japan in such areas as disarmament, the purge of militarist leaders, and a change in the status of the emperor, he stresses that the Japanese themselves will have to create a new political system that is suitable for them.

Major International Conferences and High-Level Diplomacy

Some of the principal decisions affecting Allied policies toward postwar Japan were taken at or in connection with a series of summit and other high-level conferences held during the war. The doctrine of unconditional surrender emerged, for example, from the Casablanca Conference in January 1943; Japan's postwar territorial boundaries were fixed at the Cairo, Yalta, and Berlin Conferences; while the terms of surrender were set forth in the Potsdam (or Berlin) Proclamation.

There follows a list of primary and secondary sources relating specifically to these conferences and their results. Perhaps most notable among them are the several volumes of conference papers in the Foreign Relations of the United States series. At this writing such volumes have been issued for the Washington (1941–42) and Casablanca (1943) (no.197), Cairo and Teheran (1943) (no.198), Malta and Yalta (1945) (no.199), and Berlin (1945) (no.200) Conferences.

182 Armstrong, Anne. *Unconditional Surrender: The Impact of the Casablanca Policy upon World War II.* New Brunswick, N.J.: Rutgers Univ. Pr., 1961. xiv, 304p.

A balanced and scholarly reappraisal of the effect of the Allied demand for the unconditional surrender of Germany and Japan, a formula which developed at the Casablanca Conference of January 1943. The author inquires into the conditions under which the United States adopted this policy, the aims and motives of the United States, the nature of the American policy-makers' thinking about European history, and how the formula of unconditional surrender was developed through successive Allied conferences such as Yalta and Potsdam. There is little reference to the Japanese case; the author examines primarily the effects of the Casablanca policy upon Germany. However, the study of the origins, meaning, and results of the policy as well as the analysis of the reactions of Churchill, Stalin, Roosevelt, and the German generals offer fresh insights that are relevant to the study of the Japanese surrender.

183 Beitzell, Robert Egner. *Major Strategic Conferences of the Allies, 1941–1942: Quadrant, Moscow, Sextant, and Eureka.* Ph.D. dissertation, Univ. of North Carolina at Chapel Hill, 1967. 518p. (Abstracted in *Dissertation Abstracts* 28:3594A–95A [1968]; University Microfilms order no.68–2153)

Diplomatic relations among the United States, Great Britain, and the Soviet Union from Pearl Harbor through the Teheran Conference in December 1943 are reviewed here. The intricate bargaining during the strategic conferences centering about Stalin's territorial claims to Eastern Europe, the Anglo-American agreement to assault first Germany by striking at North Africa in 1942 and then Japan, the subsequent agreement to replace this plan with the plan to conduct a cross-channel operation in 1943, and the decision to postpone this operation until 1944 are depicted. It is emphasized that the Teheran meeting was more important than the Yalta or Potsdam Conferences in determining the postwar condition of Europe. Beitzell shows that during this conference Roosevelt became convinced that Soviet-American cooperation had been achieved; he accepted Stalin's territorial demands and decided to isolate Churchill and invade France. The mixed Anglo-American reaction to Stalin's August 1943 proposal for a foreign ministers conference and a Big

Three meeting is described. One of the most significant events of the Moscow Foreign Ministers Conference was the Russian pledge to declare war on Japan after Germany's surrender.

184 Burns, James MacGregor. *Roosevelt: The Soldier of Freedom 1940–1945.* New York: Harcourt, Brace, Jovanovich, 1970. xiv, 722p.

Concluding the first complete biographical account of President Franklin D. Roosevelt (v.1, *Roosevelt: The Lion and the Fox*, 1956), this carefully researched and well-written book focuses on Roosevelt's war leadership, his visions and strategy, and the dualism between ideals and *realpolitik* that beset him during the days of World War II. The author, a professor of government at Williams College, studies Roosevelt's activities in relation to the domestic scene as well as to the international developments of the period and provides insights into the origin of the cold war, the transformation of the American presidency, and the significant changes that occurred in American society. Information on the fighting with Japan, the president's policies vis-à-vis Tokyo, and such conferences as Casablanca and Teheran is included, but the main emphasis of the book lies elsewhere.

Byrnes, James F. *All in One Lifetime.* 1958. See no.206.

———. *Speaking Frankly.* 1947. See no.207.

Churchill, Winston L. S. *The Second World War.* 1948–53. See no.208.

185 Feis, Herbert. *Churchill, Roosevelt, Stalin: The War They Waged and the Peace They Sought.* Princeton, N.J.: Princeton Univ. Pr., 1957. xi, 692p; 2d ed. 1967. xi, 702p.

The author carefully traces the development of relations among Great Britain, the United States, and the Soviet Union from January 1942 to May 1945, i.e., from the start of the wartime coalition through the surrender of Germany. He examines the difficult beginnings of cooperation among the Allies, how accord developed through various international conferences, and how it waned later in the war. Students of the Pacific War can observe how the Allies made decisions with respect to the eastern front, e.g., the formulation of strategic plans to speed the surrender of Japan, Soviet participation in the war, the use of atomic bombs against Japan, conditions for the surrender of Japan, territorial settlements after Japan's surrender, etc. Much of the author's information is derived from official and private collections of papers and correspondence, e.g., those of the State Department, Averell Harriman, and President Truman.

186 Hoska, Lukas Ernest, Jr. *Summit Diplomacy during World War II: The Conferences at Tehran, Yalta, and Potsdam.* Ph.D. dissertation, Univ. of Maryland, 1966. 281p. (Abstracted in *Dissertation Abstracts* 27:3100A [1967]; University Microfilms order no.67–2334)

The extent to which strategy was developed and basic international agreements were achieved at Teheran, Yalta, and Potsdam is examined here. Hoska reviews the methods of negotiation, both formal and informal, used by each of the participants as well as their respective roles, missions, and objectives. In his discussion of each conference, he considers the question of bases and military strongholds in Japan, the disposition of Japanese territory in China and Korea, and Soviet aims in the Far East and notes actions and events which affected the policies of each of the Allies.

186a Inahara, Katsuji. "Their Crimea Conference." *Contemporary Japan* 14:1–15 (Jan./Mar. 1945)

Within this article the editor of *Contemporary Japan* (who is also the author of several works on international problems) speculates on the probable content of the discussions at Yalta. It is clear to him that the purpose of the United Nations is not only to "break the backs" of both Germany and Japan but also to keep them in "backless" positions in the future. Nations that are taking an equivocal stand on such a policy are being pressured to align themselves with the Allies by declaring war or else they will be excluded from UN membership. The fact that the Chungking government has been invited to the San Francisco conference proves that Japan was under discussion at Yalta, although both Churchill and Roosevelt have denied that fact. Inahara assumes that the "secret understanding" alluded to by Roosevelt in his report to Congress refers to some sort of agreement between Roosevelt and Stalin regarding the future of Japan. Inahara concludes that "the Crimea decision on the organization of a United Nations' world security organ amounts to an attempt to deny Japan and Germany their rightful privileges to prosper in their spheres of the globe."

187 Keck, Daniel Newton. *Designs for the Postwar World: Anglo-American Diplomacy, 1941–1945*. Ph.D. dissertation, Univ. of Connecticut, 1967. 291p. (Abstracted in *Dissertation Abstracts* 28: 3746A–47A [1968]; University Microfilms order no.68–1363)

Keck reviews diplomatic relations between Great Britain and the United States from the Atlantic Conference in August 1941 to July 1945, just before the Potsdam Conference. Noting that wartime diplomacy was strongly characterized by personal elements, he evaluates the personal relationship between Churchill and Roosevelt, their relations with Stalin, and their diplomatic roles. Aspects of consensus and conflict among these wartime leaders regarding the type of postwar world they envisaged are depicted. Three issues are chosen for study: the nature of postwar Europe with respect to the future of Germany, France, and Poland, and of national spheres of influence; relationships between the Western allies and the Soviet Union; and concepts of a world security organization.

188 Kecskemeti, Paul. *Strategic Surrender: The Politics of Victory and Defeat*. Stanford, Calif.: Stanford Univ. Pr., 1958. ix, 287p.

A staff member of the RAND Corp. presents a theoretical analysis of strategic surrender. He treats surrender as a strategic problem for the losing side in a military situation where the winning side is completely victorious, and he attempts to theorize about general conditions that determine whether or not the cessation of hostilities will involve surrender. He believes that such general conditions include "strategic constraints" and the political objectives and attitudes of the belligerents. In theorizing about these conditions, Kecskemeti pays heed to 4 historical cases of surrender during World War II, namely, the French, Italian, German, and Japanese surrenders. The Japanese surrender is treated in chapter 6 (pages 155–214) where the author discusses the United States' surrender policy toward Japan, Japan's peace policies as seen in the dispatch of "peace feelers" to Moscow, and the Japanese reaction to the atomic bombs. The author provides a good evaluation of the American surrender policy. He also reappraises the significance of the rule of unconditional surrender in World War II and its role in prolonging the war, pointing out the fallacies of the formula.

189 McNeill, William H. *Survey of International Affairs 1939–1946: America, Britain, and Russia, Their Cooperation and Conflict, 1941–1946*. London: Oxford Univ. Pr., 1953. xviii, 819p.

The third of an 11-part wartime survey sponsored by the Royal Institute of International Affairs and edited by Arnold Toynbee. The author, an American professor, has reconstructed international events from December 1941 through December 1946, with special emphasis upon agreement and discord among the United States, Great Britain, and the Soviet Union. The volume consists of 4 parts: part 1, "Cooperation to Fight the War, December 1941–December 1943"; part 2, "Cooperation as Peace Loomed, December 1943–February 1945"; part 3, "Breakdown of Allied Cooperation, February 1945–December 1946"; and part 4, "Reflections and General Observations." The first part treats the political obstacles to Allied cooperation in the war against Japan and the Cairo and Teheran Conferences of 1943; the discussion in the second part concerns Allied cooperation in the military campaign against Japan and the Yalta Conference in 1945; the third part analyzes the Potsdam Conference in 1945, the surrender of Japan, Allied difficulties in the Far East, and the beginning of the cold war from early 1946.

190 May, Ernest Richard. "The United States, the Soviet Union, and the Far Eastern War, 1941–1945." *Pacific Historical Review* 24:153–74 (May 1955)

This study of American efforts to draw the Soviet Union into the war against Japan lends support to the theory that it was military expediency rather than President Roosevelt's concern for amicable Soviet–American relations that determined much of American wartime policy vis-à-vis Soviet activities in East Asia. The Yalta agreement over the disposition of Japan's territorial possessions is cited as one example of the Allied willingness to meet most Soviet demands in order to secure Soviet collaboration in the final battle for Japan. At the same time, however, May openly wonders why Stalin's demands were "astonishingly mild" when he appeared to be in an exceptional bargaining position in early 1945. May explains that Stalin may have feared a Japanese decision to ask the United States and Great Britain for peace terms which would leave Japan in a strong position on the Russian frontiers. For this reason, May continues, it may be presumed that Stalin cautiously asked only for the restoration of rights and territories once held by the Tsars rather than for a guaranteed share in the occupation of Japan or for a division of postwar Japan into occupied zones.

191 Millot, Bernard. *La guerre du Pacifique*. Paris: Robert Laffont, 1968. 2v.

Millot, a cartographer at the National Geographic Institute in Paris, records the events of the Pacific War, beginning with the attack on Pearl Harbor and continuing through the beginning of the American occupation of Japan. His first volume, subtitled "Le déferlement japonais," covers the period from December 1941 through September 1943; the second, subtitled "Le raz de marée américain," deals with the period from October 1943 to September 1945. The volumes are primarily an examination of the progress of military campaigns and developments in the battles of the Pacific War. However, chapter 12 in the second volume contains a brief discussion of the Yalta Conference of February 1945 and the Soviet decision to enter the Pacific War. The last chapter, chapter 14, is a review of the Potsdam ultimatum and Japan's capitulation, the favorable attitude of the Japanese toward General MacArthur at the outset of the occupation, and the causes of Japan's defeat.

192 Neumann, William L. *After Victory: Churchill, Roosevelt, Stalin, and the Making of the Peace*. New York: Harper and Row, 1967. xii, 212p.

In this book, William Neumann, a specialist in diplomatic history at Goucher College, deals with the history of peacemaking efforts by the leaders of the United States, Britain, and the Soviet Union during World War II. The first 7 chapters are concerned primarily with events in Europe while the final 3 are of relevance to students of Japan. Chapter 8 deals with the Yalta Conference and describes the events leading to the adoption of a secret agreement providing for the entry of the Soviet Union into the war against Japan. A copy of the agreement is included, along with other related protocols. Chapter 9 gives a short account of the Potsdam Conference. In chapter 10 the circumstances in which the peace treaty with Japan was concluded are discussed briefly. Although it does not focus directly on the occupation of Japan, the book provides a clear view of the international milieu at the end of the war. The text is not footnoted but a useful bibliographic essay and detailed index are provided.

193 ———. *Making the Peace 1941–1945: The Diplomacy of the Wartime*

Conferences. Washington, D.C.: Foundation for Foreign Affairs, 1950. 101p.

The author attempts to reconstruct what really went on among Allied participants in the wartime conferences. He does so by critically reviewing memoirs written by the participants. The conferences studied are the Atlantic Conference in August 1941, the Moscow Conference in September 1941, the Washington Conference of December 1941 to January 1942, the Hopkins mission, the Casablanca Conference of January 1943, the Eden mission to Washington in March 1943, the Quebec Conference in August 1943, the Moscow Conference in 1943, the Cairo Conference in 1943 and the Crimean Conference of February 1945. Most of the subjects treated pertain to European questions and postwar international organization. However, there are several portions treating Allied strategies against Japan. Throughout the work the author tries to reveal points of disagreement among the Big Three which were not officially acknowledged. He concludes that Western diplomacy with the Russians during the war failed to achieve a lasting peace.

194 Smith, Daniel M., ed. *Major Problems in American Diplomatic History: Documents and Readings.* Boston: Heath, 1965. x, 677p., maps.

A professor of American diplomatic history, the editor selects 21 critical events that affected the international relations of the United States from 1776 through 1963. He provides basic documents related to those events as well as various evaluations of them. The eighteenth event is the Yalta Conference of 4–11 February 1945. Included are extracts from the Agreement Regarding Entry of the Soviet Union into the War against Japan and extracts from 2 essays, one by Chester Wilmot in *The Struggle for Europe* (New York: Harper, 1952), pages 639–58, and the other by Forrest C. Pogue, "Yalta in Retrospect," in *The Meaning of Yalta* (1956) (no.195), pages 188–208. Wilmot, an English writer close to British officials during the war, holds that the Yalta Conference was Stalin's greatest victory. He criticizes Roosevelt for failing to develop closer Anglo-American diplomatic collaboration and for the "naive" belief that Stalin's friendship could be won through concessions. Pogue maintains that Yalta was a defensible attempt to secure Russian cooperation and to set limits on Soviet expansion through minimal concessions to their terms.

195 Snell, John L., ed. *The Meaning of Yalta: Big Three Diplomacy and the New Balance of Power.* Baton Rouge: Louisiana State Univ. Pr., 1956. xiii, 239p.

A reappraisal of the Yalta Conference of February 1945. Four scholars prepared 6 chapters covering different aspects of the subject. Chapter 4, entitled "Yalta and the Far East," is by George A. Lensen. He first reviews the historical development of Far Eastern tensions and then discusses the increasing American interest in Russian participation in the war against Japan, an interest which, he believes, commenced as early as 8 December 1941, one day after the Japanese attack on Pearl Harbor. Lensen then defines the national interests of each of the Allied powers in the Far East and discusses military matters considered at the conference as well as political commitments undertaken by the Allied governments. Finally, he evaluates the aftermath of the Yalta Agreement. The author concludes that postwar conflict was engendered not by the Yalta Agreement itself but by the Allied failure to live up to that agreement and by the "imperfect" elements of the agreement that reflect "man's inability to gaze into the future" of relationships among the Allied nations. This chapter, together with chapter 2—"What to Do with Germany?" by John L. Snell—and chapter 3—"Russian Power in Central-Eastern Europe," by Charles F. Delzell—were originally presented before the 1955 convention of the Southern Historical Association held in Memphis, Tennessee.

U.S. Dept. of Defense. *The Entry of the Soviet Union into the War against*

Japan: Military Plans, 1941–1945. 1955. See no.179.

196 ———. Dept. of State. *Agreement Regarding Japan between the Leaders of the Three Great Powers: The United States of America, the Union of Soviet Socialist Republics, and the United Kingdom of Great Britain and Northern Ireland.* Washington, D.C.: Government Printing Office, 1946. 4p. (Dept. of State publication 2505; Executive Agreement series 498)

This publication reprints the full texts in English and Russian of the Yalta Agreement of 11 February 1945 specifying the conditions on which the Soviet Union agreed to enter the war against Japan on the side of the Allies.

———. ———. *Occupation of Japan: Policy and Progress.* 1946. See no. 468.

197 ———. ———. Bureau of Public Affairs. Historical Office. *The Conferences at Washington, 1941–1942, and Casablanca, 1943.* Washington, D.C.: Government Printing Office, 1968. lxx, 895p. (Foreign Relations of the United States: Diplomatic Papers; Dept. of State publication 8414)

Official American records of the first 3 conferences in which President Roosevelt and Prime Minister Churchill participated after the United States joined the war: the first Washington Conference, 22 December 1941–14 January 1942; the second Washington Conference, 19–25 June 1942; and the Casablanca Conference, 14–24 January 1943. The introduction discusses sources consulted in compiling this record. The volume is divided into 3 sections, one for each conference. Each section contains editorial footnotes and preconference papers, proceedings of the conference, and relevant conference documents and supplementary papers. The supplementary papers include not only official agreements that were then made public but also numerous items of confidential correspondence, telegrams, reports, and talks. The preconference papers for the first Washington Conference reveal that the Soviet Union contemplated acting against Japan as early as 6 January 1942. These conferences concerned a number of strategic problems as well as political issues. Of particular importance for students of the occupation of Japan is the Casablanca Conference which resulted in the adoption of an unconditional surrender policy for both Germany and Japan. Statements and press communiqués on this subject are included.

198 ———. ———. ———. ———. *The Conferences at Cairo and Teheran, 1943.* Washington, D.C.: Government Printing Office, 1961. lxxviii, 932p. (Foreign Relations of the United States: Diplomatic Papers; Dept. of State publication 7187)

The official American record of the Cairo and Teheran Conferences held in 1943 describes those meetings in detail. The Cairo Conference was held in 2 sessions from 22 to 26 November and from 2 to 7 December 1943 before and after the Teheran Conference of 27 November–1 December. All of the meetings were attended by President Roosevelt, Prime Minister Churchill, and their top advisers including the Anglo-American Combined Chiefs of Staff. The documents compiled in this volume are based largely on American sources, published and unpublished, but some derive from other Allied sources including published Russian materials. Preconference papers, background documents, and conference proceedings have been carefully collected so as to reconstruct an accurate picture of the conference. A useful introduction explains the nature of the sources consulted. The first Cairo Conference is particularly relevant to the study of the occupation of Japan, as it involved Generalissimo Chiang Kai-shek and discussed problems of the war against Japan. It includes discussions on plans for the occupation of Japan, the postwar status of the emperor, and plans for Russian participation in the war against Japan. There is also a section on postconference papers consisting of memorandums and telegrams issued after the second Cairo Conference.

199 ———. ———. Historical Div. *The Conferences at Malta and Yalta, 1945.* Washington, D.C.: Government Printing Office, 1955. lxxviii, 1,032p. (Foreign Relations of the United States: Diplomatic Papers; Dept. of State publication 6199)

Two summit conferences of the Allied powers in early 1945 are documented in great detail: the Malta Conference held from 30 January to 2 February in which Roosevelt conferred with Churchill on the wars against Germany and Japan; and the Yalta Conference, which took place on 4–11 February bringing together Roosevelt, Churchill, and Stalin. The records are divided into 3 major parts: preconference documents, the Malta Conference, and the Yalta Conference. Within each group are collected documents, correspondence, messages, agreements among the countries concerned or within the delegations of the respective countries, including "top secret" communications and conference minutes. Among the sources of the materials are the State Department files, the Bohlen collection, the Hiss collection, the Matthews files, Moscow embassy files, FEC (Far Eastern Commission) files, White House files, Joint Chiefs of Staff files, and the Hopkins files. The development of the Yalta Agreement with respect to Russian entry into the war against Japan is treated at length.

200 ———. ———. ———. *The Conference of Berlin (The Potsdam Conference), 1945.* Washington, D.C.: Government Printing Office, 1960. 2v. (Foreign Relations of the United States: Diplomatic Papers; Dept. of State publications 7015 and 7163)

The official U.S. government records of the Conference of Berlin, better known as the Potsdam Conference, are presented here. The Berlin Conference, held from 16 July to 2 August 1945, was a complicated series of bilateral, tripartite, and quadripartite meetings, participated in by officials of the United States, Britain, the Soviet Union, and Poland. This 2-volume compilation of records concerns both preconference and conference diplomacy, seen primarily from the American standpoint. There is a comparison of the notes taken by different participants in the conference and examination of a wide range of published and unpublished materials. The introduction discusses the nature of the sources consulted, indicating that most of the documents were originally of a confidential nature. The preconference papers comprising volume 1 include correspondence among the leaders, memorandums, and cables exchanged among American leaders as well as among the Allied leaders, recommendations submitted to President Truman by his advisers and the secretary of state, general background reports presented to the president on international developments that led to the conference, preparation of the agenda for the conference, appointment of delegations, and final physical arrangements. Volume 2 contains records of negotiations during the conference, including the presidential log, minutes and other records of conference proceedings, conference documents, and supplementary papers. Of particular interest for students of the Pacific theater of World War II are preconference recommendations and reports on the war against Japan in section 4 of volume 1 and conference documents in section 7 of volume 2. Discussed therein are Japanese peace feelers via the Soviet Union toward the end of the war, the origins and development of the Potsdam Declaration calling for Japan's unconditional surrender, Allied policies and strategies in the war against Japan, the use of atomic weapons, and the release of tankers from Europe to the Pacific. Both volumes were summarized in Japanese in the magazine *Sekai Shūhō* in 1961.

201 ———. ———. ———. *Foreign Relations of the United States, Diplomatic Papers, 1944.* v.5, *The Near East, South Asia, Africa, the Far East.* Washington, D.C.: Government Printing Office, 1965. viii, 1,345p. (Dept. of State publication 7859)

This volume is concerned with United States' relations with countries of the

Near East, South Asia, Africa, and the Far East including Japan. Most of the sections on Japan refer to the wartime treatment of each other's nationals, prisoners of war, protests of the bombing of allegedly nonmilitary objectives, and military conduct of a similar kind. However, the last 2 sections (p.1183–289) concern the background of the occupation. The first (p.1183–86) treats the American and British governments' decision not to reply to Japanese peace feelers received through Sweden. It sets forth an exchange of messages between the American and British governments from 26 September to 10 October 1944. The second (p.1186–289) treats in detail presurrender policy planning in regard to the postwar treatment of Japan and areas under Japanese control. It includes correspondence and negotiations among various offices of the State, War, and Navy Departments and telegrams and agreements between Allied governments dating from 10 December 1943 through 10 December 1944. Of particular significance is a series of position papers by the Inter-Divisional Area Committee on the Far East and the Postwar Programs Committee setting forth drafts of departmental policies on such matters as the extent and nature of the impending occupation of Japan, composition of forces, the extent of freedom of worship to be permitted in Japan, the status of the emperor, reparations, disarmament, war criminals, and the mandated islands. There are also memorandums on the scope and responsibilities of a civil affairs administration and recommendations by the Committee on Post-War Programs regarding surrender terms, the nature of a Japanese Instrument of Surrender, what Japanese authority should sign the instrument and who should receive it, and what nations should control and decide policy toward a defeated Japan.

202 ———. ———. ———. *Foreign Relations of the United States, Diplomatic Papers, 1945.* v.6, *The British Commonwealth, the Far East.* Washington, D.C.: Government Printing Office, 1969. vii, 1,436p. (Dept. of State publication 8451)

A most important document for the study of the occupation. It treats United States' diplomatic relations during the year 1945 with the British Commonwealth and the Far East. The section on Japan (p.316–1016) sets forth in its first quarter diplomatic communications between Japan and the United States relating to treatment of prisoners of war, attacks on hospital ships and other nonmilitary objectives, and the Japanese government's protest over the atomic bombing of Hiroshima. The remaining three-quarters of this section (p.475–1016) are devoted to questions of terminating the war and planning for the occupation of Japan. Particular groups of documents are concerned with: (1) reports (originating on 30 Jan. 1945) of unofficial overtures from Japanese sources to the U.S. Office of Strategic Services in Switzerland indicating a Japanese interest in making peace; (2) postwar policy planning with respect to Japan (continued from *Foreign Relations . . . 1944.* v.5. [no. 201]) p.1186–289; (3) the surrender of Japan; and (4) relinquishment by the Swiss government of representation of American interests in Japan and Japanese occupied territory. The second and third categories are of particular relevance to the study of occupied Japan and contain all available official information, including telephone and memorandums of oral conversations, from the State, War, and Navy Departments, the president, and the British, Russian, Swiss, Swedish, Chinese, Japanese, and other governments with which Washington was in contact with respect to the termination of hostilities. The records indicate something of the intricate process through which the United States developed and executed its postsurrender policies toward Japan in the fields of political and economic reform, disarmament, reparations, war criminals, etc., and the developments that led to friction among the Allies in respect to the establishment of the Far Eastern Commission and the Allied Council for Japan.

203 ———. ———. ———. *Foreign Relations of the United States, Diplomatic Papers, 1945.* v.7, *The Far East, China.* Washington, D.C.: Government Printing Office, 1969. vi, 1506p. (Dept. of State publication 8442)

This volume is entirely devoted to American policy planning and decisions with respect to China in 1945. The documents refer to political, military, and economic conditions in China both prior and subsequent to the Japanese surrender. Of particular relevance to occupied Japan is the fourth section, entitled "Questions Involving Japanese Surrender Arrangements" (p.492–526). This section concerns disputes among the Chinese, British, and French over their participation in the acceptance of the Japanese surrender. It includes a number of telegrams exchanged among Secretary of State Byrnes, U.S. Ambassador in France Caffrey, President Truman, Prime Minister Attlee, President of the Chinese Executive Yuan Soong, and President Chiang Kai-shek from 9 August through 6 September 1945. There is also an exchange of telegrams concerning a proposed joint statement with reference to the surrender of Japanese troops to Chiang Kai-shek.

203a ———. ———. ———. *Foreign Relations of the United States, 1946.* v.8, *The Far East.* Washington, D.C.: Government Printing Office, 1971. viii, 1137p. (Dept. of State publication 8554)

Fully one-half of this volume on American relations with various countries in East and Southeast Asia deals specifically with occupied Japan. Pages 85–382 cover the occupation and control of Japan as a whole during 1946 and include such important documents as (1) the report on the proposed reform of the Japanese governmental system prepared by the State-War-Navy Coordinating Subcommittee for the Far East (SWNCC 228); (2) the Draft Treaty on the Disarmament and Demilitarization of Japan drawn up by the U.S. government early in 1946; (3) a report by Dr. George H. Blakeslee on the Far Eastern Commission's trip to Japan, 26 December 1945–13 February 1946; (4) SWNCC's recommendations for the treatment of the imperial institutions; (5) numerous memorandums and statements on the draft constitution and its submission to the Japanese Diet; (6) the texts of statements by various foreign governments—especially those of Great Britain, the USSR, and China—on American policy in Japan; and (7) a considerable number of telegrams and memorandums exchanged by the secretary of state and members of the Office of Political Adviser in Japan. Part 2 (p.382–471) concentrates on the apprehension and punishment of Japanese war criminals. This section contains a significant number of statements and memorandums pertaining to foreign views of Japanese war criminals and the participation of the representatives of the USSR, Great Britain, India and other nations on the War Crimes Tribunal. The summary of testimony presented from 19 to 25 November 1946 before the Tribunal by Mr. Joseph W. Ballantine, Special Assistant to the Secretary of State, also is featured. The third and final section (p.471–604) considers the matter of war claims and reparations and is a continuation of p.989–1016 in volume 6 of *Foreign Relations . . . 1945* (no.202). Of particular interest is SWNCC report 236/10 entitled "Interim Reparations Removal Program for Japan," SWNCC report 227/13 entitled "Final Policy Concerning Restitution of Looted Property from Japan," and the texts of several memorandums and notes regarding the legal status of Japanese property seized by the Russians in Manchuria and the postwar reparations claims of the Soviet government.

203b ———. ———. ———. *Foreign Relations of the United States, 1947.* v.6, *The Far East.* Washington, D.C.: Government Printing Office, 1972. ix, 1,159p. (Dept. of State publication 8606)

This volume is the latest one on Asia in the Foreign Relations series to appear in print before the present bibliography went to press. Like the preceding ones, it is an invaluable documentary source for understanding the occupation of Japan. Pages 156–345 deal with the occupation and control of the country as a whole and contain numerous exchanges between occupation personnel in Tokyo and government officials in Washington on the one hand, and between various foreign governments and American authorities on the other hand. Among the subjects of particular concern are: (1) the disposition of property belonging to the imperial household and to convicted war criminals; (2) Japanese fishing and whaling operations—especially the proposed Japanese whaling expedition to the Antarctic; (3) the role of the Far Eastern Commission in the occupation; (4) relations between SCAP and the Allied Council for Japan; (5) the restoration of private trade between Japanese and foreign businessmen and the establishment of an export-import revolving fund; (6) the question of the Japanese working of phosphate deposits on Angaur Island; (7) the increasingly hostile attitude of the Soviet Union towards United States policy in Japan; and (8) the question of Japan's postwar economic recovery. Pages 345–446 comprise a second section of the volume and examine Allied war claims, Japanese reparations and restitution, and the desired levels of industry and of production within Japan. The third and final section of the documentation (pages 446–595) covers the efforts of the United States in behalf of an early peace treaty with Japan. The materials include (1) General MacArthur's memorandums of 21 March and 1 September on the drafts of the proposed treaty; (2) memorandums and statements issued by the various Allies (particularly Australia, China, Great Britain, and the USSR) that are essential for understanding their positions; (4) lengthy memorandums on the manner of preparing the treaty and on the legal situation resulting from a peace settlement in which certain Allies refuse to participate; (5) the results of a planning staff study of questions involved in the Japanese peace settlement that advises against an early termination of Allied control over Japan; and (6) a 29 October memorandum on the treaty by Robert A. Fearey of the Division of Northeast Asian Affairs.

Wilkinson, Harry R. *The Soviet Union and the Allied Occupation of Japan: Prelude.* 1971. See no.888a.

203c Winnacker, Rudolph A. "Yalta: Another Munich?" *Virginia Quarterly Review* 24, no.4: 521–37 (Autumn 1948)

In order to provide a better understanding of American policy at Yalta, Winnacker discusses and analyzes the procedures employed in reaching decisions there as well as the decisions themselves. While most of his discussion focuses on Eastern Europe, he does refer to Japan and to the concessions made to the Soviet Union in the Far East. In this regard, he explains that in February 1945, American leaders were extremely anxious to secure Soviet help in the final military push against Japan and were hesitant about committing American troops to fight the Japanese on the mainland. He points out, moreover, that the Russians were capable of implementing unilaterally nearly all of the demands which the United States acknowledged at Yalta and that without some agreement full Communist control in Manchuria and northern China was to be expected and the Kuomintang would not have had any opportunity even to reattempt the reintegration of those areas into China proper. Of all the Far Eastern territory yielded at Yalta, only the Kurile Islands might have been occupied ahead of the Soviets. Some agreement with the Russians, therefore, was better than nothing at all.

204 Woodward, Sir Llwellyn. *British Foreign Policy in the Second World War.* London: HMSO, 1962. iv, 592p. (History of the Second World War)

Written primarily on the basis of materials contained in the British archives, this publication is an offical British record of World War II in the series *History of the Second World War.* There is frequent overlap with Sir Winston Churchill's 6-volume *The Second World War* (1948–54) (no.208). In 31 chapters, the volume narrates the events which took place mainly in Europe from September 1939 to the Potsdam Conference of July–August 1945. Students of the Pacific War will find chapters 8 and 31 relevant. Chapter 8 discusses the Far Eastern situation that led to Japan's Pearl Harbor attack in 1941, and chapter 31 notes briefly in 4 pages the relevance of the Cairo and Potsdam Declarations to the Allied war against Japan.

Woodward's publication represents an abridgment of a larger work written between 1942 and 1950 for official use. The more complete version began to appear under the same title in 1970 (London: HMSO), and three of its volumes have been published to date. The Far Eastern situation prior to the outbreak of World War II is treated in chapters 22–24 (in vol.2), but a fourth volume that would presumably cover the Yalta and Potsdam conferences in detail was unavailable for examination when the present bibliography went to press.

Biographical Literature

The wartime period is rich in biographical literature produced by a wide variety of participants. It is probably no exaggeration to estimate, however, that upwards of eighty percent of these materials refer to the European and Atlantic theaters of combat. The Pacific theater was a distinctly secondary area of operations and importance for all but those immediately involved. It is a particularly interesting comment on the degree of Eurocentrism afflicting the U.S. government to see how relatively little attention was paid the war against Japan at the highest levels in Washington and how late in the war such a shift of focus took place.

Among the items that follow, the memoirs by Grew, Hull, Leahy, Stimson, and Truman (nos.211–13, and 216–17) are particularly relevant to the subject of presurrender planning. Most of these volumes also contain sections relating to one or more of the major international conferences treated in the preceding section.

205 Arnold, Henry Harley. *Global Mission*. New York: Harper, 1949. xii, 626p.

The autobiography of a well-known general of the air force and member of the Joint Chiefs of Staff. The last 2 chapters refer to the Potsdam Conference, which he attended, and to the air raids against Japan and the atomic bombing. There are some interesting, if casual, observations about Russian operations and his views on Japan's approaching surrender are useful.

206 Byrnes, James Francis. *All in One Lifetime*. New York: Harper, 1958. x, 432p.

The secretary of state who served from July 1945 to January 1947 recounts his 50 years' experience in public office. Starting his appointment as court stenographer in 1900, he describes his election to the House of Representatives in 1910, election to the Senate in 1931, appointment as an associate justice of the Supreme Court in 1941, director of Economic Stabilization in 1942, director of War Mobilization in 1943, secretary of state in 1945, and finally election as governor of South Carolina in 1950. Byrnes writes of some of the characteristics of different public offices and of the virtues and weaknesses of those in public office with whom he became associated. Part 5, which treats his years as secretary of state, records his participation in the decision on the use of atomic bombs in Japan, the Potsdam Conference, the Japanese surrender, foreign ministers' conferences in London, Moscow, and Paris, the United Nations, etc. While not dealing directly with the occupation, this account is useful in discerning what efforts the United States made to negotiate with Russia in the interest of international security. This part understandably overlaps with Byrnes' earlier memoirs, *Speaking Frankly* (1947) (no. 207). The book contains a detailed index.

207 ———. *Speaking Frankly*. New York: Harper, 1947. xii, 324p.

The secretary of state from July 1945 to January 1947 here sets forth an intimate and candid account of American diplomacy from the beginning of 1945 through June 1947. It is essentially a record of his efforts to meet the Russian challenge in settling World War II and establishing a postwar peace. The description of his participation in the Yalta Conference, the Potsdam Conference, foreign ministers' conferences in London, Moscow, and Paris in 1945–46, and the UN General Assembly in London in 1946 aids the reader a great deal in grasping the atmosphere of each conference. He contends that the sense of unity prevailing among the Allied powers at Yalta did not prevail through subsequent conferences and that the Russians were "after everything they could gain" from the power vacuum in central Europe. Byrnes urges a greater role by the United Nations to counter this Russian advance.

Chapter 11, "Toward Peace in Asia," is particularly useful for students of the Allied occupation of Japan. There are informative references to the circumstances of Byrnes' reply to the Japanese note of 10 August 1945, the subsequent Soviet–American struggle over the control mechanisms for the occupation of Japan, the disposition of the Japanese mandated islands, and how the author feels a peace treaty with Japan should be concluded. This book has been translated into Japanese under the title of *Sotchoku ni kataru* (Nagoya: Chūbu Nihon Shimbunsha, 1947).

208 Churchill, Winston L. S. *The Second World War*. Boston: Houghton Mifflin, 1948–53. 6v.

In these memoirs of World War II, Churchill records his observations from 1919 through 1945, considering the Second World War as a continuation of the First. Each volume has a subtitle: volume 1, "The Gathering Storm"; volume 2, "Their Finest Hour"; volume 3, "The Grand Alliance"; volume 4, "The Hinge of Fate"; volume 5, "Closing the Ring"; and volume 6, "Triumph and Tragedy." Most of the text pertains to political and military developments on the European and Atlantic fronts but several chapters relate to the war against Japan. Japanese military preparations in 1941 and the Pearl Harbor attack are described in volume 3; while the Japanese invasions of Malaya, Singapore, Burma, and the Netherlands East Indies, as well as the consequent Australian anxieties, are treated in volume 4. The Cairo and Teheran Conferences in late 1943 are discussed in detail in volume 5, including differences between Churchill and the Chiefs of Staff on strategy against Japan. Recorded also are differences between Churchill and Roosevelt on the conduct of the war against Japan in March 1944. Particularly relevant are chapters 18 and 19 in volume 6, which deal with the Allied plans for the attack on Japan in 1945 and the discussions at Potsdam with respect to the prospects for a speedy termination of the war without Russian assistance and the decision to use the atomic bomb against Japan. There is an index. Scattered throughout the volumes are a considerable number of Churchill's directives, telegrams, notes, and other correspondence. The whole series has been translated into Japanese under the title of *Dainiji Taisen kaikoroku* (Tokyo: Mainichi Shimbunsha, 1950–56. 6v.).

209 Deane, John Russell. *The Strange Alliance: The Story of Our Efforts at Wartime Cooperation with Russia*. New York: Viking, 1947. viii, 344p.

The commanding officer of the U.S. Military Mission in the Soviet Union during World War II vividly recounts his experiences in Moscow working with Russian military personnel. His task was to facilitate Soviet–American collaboration in war efforts. The work consists of 4 parts. Part 1 describes his job from his arrival in Moscow in October 1943 and particularly his work on the lend-lease program for the Soviet Union. Part 2 relates the collaboration between the 2 countries in the European theater. Part 3, which is most relevant for students of the occupation of Japan, treats Soviet–American cooperation in the Pacific War. In this part he notes that, although Stalin mentioned as far back as August 1942 Russia's intention to participate eventually in the war against Japan, the USSR delayed doing so until the summer of 1945. In addition he elaborates upon his contention that Soviet–American planning for combined operations in the Pacific was impossible due to each nation's differing concepts of joint operations. He includes observations on the Yalta and Potsdam Conferences and his own participation in them. Also interesting are his descriptions of communications on 10–11 August 1945 among Averell Harriman, George Kennan, and top Russian leaders on the treatment of the Japanese offer to surrender.

Eichelberger, Robert L. *Our Jungle Road to Tokyo*. 1950. See no.549.

210 Forrestal, James. *The Forrestal Diaries*, ed. by Walter Millis with the collaboration of E. S. Duffield. New York: Viking, 1951. xxiv, 581p.

A collection of diaries that James Forrestal kept from July 1944 through January 1949 while he was secretary of the navy (May 1944–July 1947) and secretary of defense (Sept. 1947–Mar. 1949). Entries were not written daily, but the continuity of the account is maintained by the editor, Walter Millis, who lucidly describes political developments, both domestic and foreign. The diaries contain summaries of major decisions made at various meetings Forrestal attended such as cabinet and State–War–Navy Coordinating Committee meetings, discussions with Presidents Roosevelt and Truman, remarks by himself and a number of leaders he encountered, and impressions and ideas he himself had entertained. With the assistance of the book's excellent index, students of the occupation of Japan may benefit from accounts of activities preceding actual American decisions. Under the entry of "Japan" in the index, for example, there are references to the atomic bombings, the invasion of Japan, Japan's surrender, the control system for Japan, disarmament, reparations, etc. Forrestal's diaries also reveal American concern with the status of the emperor and Russian objectives in the Far East. There is also a reference to American interception of Japanese official coded messages in 1945 and its contribution to successful Allied strategy for bringing about Japan's surrender.

211 Grew, Joseph Clark. *Turbulent Era: A Diplomatic Record of Forty Years, 1904–1945*. Ed. by Walter Johnson. Boston: Houghton Mifflin, 1952. 2v.

This 2-volume memoir by a former prominent American diplomat stands as one of the most significant records of American diplomatic activity during the first half of this century. The author began his diplomatic career in 1904 as a clerk to the consulate-general in Cairo and subsequently served in Mexico City, St. Petersburg, Berlin, Vienna, Paris, Copenhagen, and Berne, before he was appointed ambassador to Turkey in 1927 and ambassador to Japan in 1932. His assignment in Tokyo was abruptly terminated in December 1941 when the Pacific War broke out. His mission in Japan up to 1942 is described in his *Ten Years in Japan* (New York: Simon & Schuster, 1944. xii, 554p.). During the war he served as director of the Office of Far Eastern Affairs in the Department of State from 1 May through 20 December 1944, at which time he was appointed undersecretary of state, serving in this capacity until 15 August 1945. He was regarded as head of the "Japan crowd" in the State Department. These 2 volumes of memoirs are based on his diary, letters, copies of his dispatches to Washington, and memory. They are particularly important for students of the occupation. Set forth in chapters 35 and 36 of the second volume are addresses, reports, and letters which Grew wrote from 1942 to 1945 regarding Japan's military strength, the character of Japanese leadership, the lack of congruity between Japanese militarists and the people, the importance of regarding the emperor as an asset rather than a liability in terminating the war and steering Japan into peaceful and constructive channels, postsurrender reforms that Japan should undertake, and the origins of the Potsdam Declaration. Chapter 37 presents his own memorandums, and memorandums received from other departments from April to June 1945. These contain interesting information relating to the Yalta Agreement and Soviet policy in the Far East in postwar years. Editorial notations have been added by the author and his editorial assistant, Walter Johnson.

212 Hull, Cordell. *The Memoirs of Cordell Hull*. New York: Macmillan, 1948. 2v.

These voluminous memoirs (123 chaps. in 1,804p.) by the secretary of state who served from March 1933 through November 1944, represent an excellent record of American diplomatic history during the 1930s and 1940s. Chapter 113, "Unconditional Surrender," and chapter 114, "Toward Victory in the Orient," should draw the attention of students of the occupation. These chapters describe the diplomatic history of the principle of unconditional surrender as applied to the Axis powers after being originally formulated at the Casablanca Conference in January 1943. He discloses the positions on terms for ending the war against the Axis taken by Churchill and Stalin as well as by the president and other prominent American leaders. He also discusses the State Department's original formula for an armed occupation of Japan in the postwar period, which recommended no partitioning of Japan, retention of the imperial system, and control of the Japanese government by Allied civil affairs officers with policy matters referred to the State Department. Hull's personal contribution to the Potsdam Declaration consisted of sending a cable on 16 July 1945 to Secretary of State Byrnes in Potsdam urging that for tactical reasons the Potsdam Declaration not include any Allied commitment with regard to the status of the emperor in a conquered Japan. A Japanese translation appeared under the title of *Kaisōroku* (Tokyo: Asahi Shimbunsha, 1949).

Krueger, Walter. *From Down Under to Nippon: The Story of the Sixth Army in World War II*. 1953. See no.906.

213 Leahy, William D. *I Was There: The Personal Story of the Chief of Staff to Presidents Roosevelt and Truman, Based on His Notes and Diaries Made at the Time*. New York: McGraw-Hill, 1950. xi, 527p.

The chief of staff to Presidents Roosevelt and Truman from 1942 to March 1949 recounts on the basis of notes and diaries his public service from January 1941, when he was assigned to be ambassador to the Vichy regime in France, through the victory over Japan in August 1945. The author attended most of the Allied summit conferences held during the war. Of particular interest to those studying the occupation of Japan are the last 6 chapters, 18 to 23, where Leahy records his observations of the Yalta Conference, atomic bombs, and the Japanese surrender. Throughout these chapters the admiral asserts his long-held conviction that Japan could have been defeated without Russian participation or without the invasion of the home islands of Japan. Official communications with Presidents Roosevelt and Truman and the French Admiral Darlan in 1940–49 are appended, plus lists of principal personalities who attended the top Allied conferences in 1943–45.

Murphy, Robert D. *Diplomat among Warriors*. 1964. See no.733.

214 Sherwood, Robert E. *Roosevelt and Hopkins: An Intimate History.* New York: Harper, 1948. xii, 979p.; rev.ed. 1950. xix, 1,002p.

Harry L. Hopkins, President Franklin D. Roosevelt's aide and closest personal adviser, died in 1945 before writing his memoirs. This biography, carefully researched and written by Robert Sherwood at the request of Hopkins' widow, is based on Hopkins' voluminous papers and on numerous interviews conducted by Sherwood with Hopkins' friends and acquaintances. The author himself was a personal friend of Hopkins. Although the book is largely tangential to the subject of the Allied occupation of Japan, this record of an important presidential intimate provides a wealth of background material concerning the international milieu during and immediately after World War II. Of especial note for occupation scholars may be the account of events surrounding the Yalta Conference and Russian–U.S. relations. The volume is divided into 5 parts. The first deals with Hopkins' life before 1941. Part 2 deals with events in 1941 including the Atlantic Conference and the outbreak of the Pacific War. Part 3 recounts important events of 1942. The Casablanca, Cairo, and Teheran Conferences are described in Part 4 along with other events of 1943. Part 5, covering 1944 and 1945, includes a description of the Yalta and San Francisco Conferences. A mission by Hopkins to Moscow in May and June 1945 was credited with saving the San Francisco Conference. The account throughout is filled with the texts of valuable statements, documents, and informal communications between Hopkins and various notables. The author's attitude toward Hopkins and President Roosevelt is friendly, but the text never degenerates into indiscriminate praise. Explicit chapter headings, extensive footnotes gathered at the back of the volume, and an index enhance the usefulness of the book for research purposes. It has been translated into Japanese under the title of *Rūzuberuto to Hopukinzu* (Tokyo: Misuzu Shobō, 1957), and was awarded a 1949 Pulitzer Prize for biography.

215 Stettinius, Edward R., Jr. *Roosevelt and the Russians: The Yalta Conference.* Garden City, N.Y.: Doubleday, 1949. xvi, 367p.

The American secretary of state from November 1944 to April 1945 describes the Yalta Conference (4–11 Feb. 1945) in which he participated. Stettinius describes conference developments on a day-to-day basis and frequently discusses the personalities of the leaders as well as the general atmosphere pervading the gatherings. The author believes that the Allied conference was the most important held during the war years and that a number of important solutions were reached. He is also convinced that the conference will become "'a symbol' of a wise and courageous attempt" by Roosevelt and Churchill "to set the world on the road to lasting peace." There is an analysis of the breakdown of Allied unity soon after the conference, and the Russian entry into the Pacific War is discussed in chapters 4 and 14. The text of an "Agreement on Terms for Entry of the Soviet Union into the War against Japan" signed on 11 February 1945 is appended. A Japanese version of the work is entitled *Yaruta kaidan no himitsu* (Tokyo: Rokkō Shuppansha, 1953. 250p.).

216 Stimson, Henry Lewis, and McGeorge Bundy. *On Active Service in Peace and War.* New York: Harper, 1947. xxii, 698p.

A biography of Stimson, secretary of war from January 1940 through September 1945, which Stimson wrote in collaboration with McGeorge Bundy, then a Harvard University professor. The book begins with Stimson's appointment in 1905 as U.S. attorney for the southern district of New York under President Theodore Roosevelt and covers the following 40 years which Stimson spent largely in public life. Chapter 23, "The Atomic Bomb and the Surrender of Japan," makes extensive reference to Stimson's article (no.247) in the February 1947 issue of *Harper's Magazine.* It concerns Stimson's role in the American decision to use the atomic bomb in order to effect a prompt Japanese surrender; his 2 July 1945 memorandum for the president proposing a strategy to lead Japan to unconditional surrender without invading her home islands, i.e., the Potsdam Declaration; his participation in the Potsdam Conference; and his defense of the use of atomic bombs against Japan.

217 Truman, Harry S. *Memoirs.* Garden City, N.Y.: Doubleday, 1955. 2v.

President Truman recounts in his 2-volume memoirs the trying years in the White House from 12 April 1945, when he took the oath of office, through 20 January 1953, when he was succeeded by General Eisenhower. The first volume is subtitled "Year of Decisions" and covers Truman's presidential experiences in 1945. The second volume, subtitled "Years of Trial and Hope," records the remaining years of his presidency. The memoirs are detailed and include quotations from official documents and his personal letters. Students of the occupation will find this work helpful in describing the president's views, motives, and alternatives with respect to Japan. He discusses Allied policy to end the war, the Potsdam Declaration, atomic bombings, Soviet attempts to share control of Japan, Japan's Manila Mission, the surrender ceremony on the *Missouri*, MacArthur's record in Japan, the MacArthur–Harriman discussions on the Far Eastern situation in 1950, the peace treaty with Japan, etc. The account is particularly helpful in understanding relations between Washington and SCAP in Tokyo.

218 USSR. Ministry of Foreign Affairs. Commission for the Publication of Diplomatic Documents. *Stalin's Correspondence with Churchill, Attlee, Roosevelt, and Truman, 1941–45.* New York: Dutton, 1958. 2v.; reprinted in New York: Putnam, Capricorn Books, 1965. 2v.

A collection of 900 items of correspondence exchanged between Joseph Stalin and the heads of the American and British governments between July 1941 and December 1945. It was originally compiled in Russian by the Ministry of Foreign Affairs of the Soviet Union and published by the State Political Books Publishing House, Moscow in 1957. In the same year it was reproduced in English in 2 volumes by the Foreign Languages Publishing House in Moscow under the title *Correspondence between the Chairman of the Council of Ministers of the USSR and the Presidents of the USA and the Prime Ministers of Great Britain during the Great Patriotic War of 1941–45.* Volume 1 of the American edition (virtually identical with the Soviet edition) collects 516 items of Stalin's correspondence with Winston Churchill and Clement R. Attlee from July 1941 through November 1945, while volume 2 presents 384 messages between Stalin and Franklin D. Roosevelt and Harry S. Truman from August 1941 to December 1945. A wide variety of subjects are covered, ranging from condolences on the death of prominent officials to discussion of policies, proposals for draft communiqués, and arrangements for coordinated military operations. Each message is numbered in chronological order. Most of them are classified "personal and secret." There are some editorial footnotes. A serious drawback is the absence of an index which makes it difficult to locate subjects. Particular note should be taken of the correspondence between Truman and Stalin after 12 August 1945. This correspondence discusses preparations for the acceptance of the forthcoming Japanese surrender and the draft text of General Orders no.1 to be issued by SCAP to the Japanese government upon its formal surrender. Stalin's confidential message to Truman of 16 August 1945 reveals the Russian desire to occupy all the Kurile Islands and the northern half of Hokkaido. The request was rejected by Truman on 18 August. Subsequent correspondence refers to procedural difficulties encountered at the Council of Foreign Ministers in London and Truman's attempt to persuade Stalin to accept the establishment of the Allied Council for Japan and the Far Eastern Commission.

219 Wilhelm, Maria. *The Man Who Watched the Rising Sun: The Story of Admiral Ellis M. Zacharias*. London: Watts, 1967. 238p.

This popular biography largely parallels and abridges Zacharias' own account of his career in naval intelligence as described in *Secret Missions* (1967) (no.220). Included is the story of his entrance into the navy, his assignment to Japan as a language officer, his prediction of the attack on Pearl Harbor, his wartime service at sea and as an intelligence officer, and his broadcasts to Japan attempting to induce a surrender during the weeks prior to 14 August 1945. The last chapter contains an account of Zacharias' activities after his retirement in 1946 until his death in June 1961. His lectures and written works continually stressed his firm conviction that a competent intelligence service could be the most effective deterrent to war. A short list of suggested readings and an index are provided.

220 Zacharias, Ellis M. *Secret Missions: The Story of an Intelligence Officer*. New York: Putnam, 1946. viii, 433p.

This autobiographical account of a naval intelligence officer recounts his career from his assignment to Japan as a language officer in 1920 through the end of World War II. As deputy director of naval intelligence, Zacharias broadcast several appeals to the Japanese in the last months of the Pacific War to explain Allied surrender terms and to conduct a psychological campaign against the Japanese High Command. His account provides interesting glimpses into intelligence operations and their relationship to other military and diplomatic operations. Of relevance to students of the surrender and occupation of Japan is the last section of the book dealing with events presaging the end of the war, such as Zacharias' radio broadcasts and the Potsdam Declaration. Texts of the author's 14 broadcasts to Japan are appended. It is translated into Japanese under the title of *Nihon to no himitsusen* (Tokyo: Nikkan Rōdō Tsūshinsha, 1958. 324p.).

Materials Associated with SCAP Headquarters

Before the entry of American troops into Japan and the formal surrender ceremony on 2 September 1945, a number of arrangements had to be made between General MacArthur's headquarters and the Japanese government. These arrangements involved the provision of information as to the strengths and dispositions of Japan's armed forces, the location of mine fields off the Japanese coast, the condition and capacities of Japanese airfields and harbor facilities, the dates and places of entry of American troops into Japan, the care and release of Allied prisoners of war, the disarmament of Japanese forces, and arrangements relating to the formal surrender ceremony, the composition of the Japanese delegation, the role of the emperor, instructions to the Japanese populace, etc.

Some of these arrangements were made by radio. A number were made, however, through face-to-face conversations between a Japanese presurrender mission and American representatives at Manila on 19–20 August 1945. The following items relate to communications of this sort.

221 Supreme Commander for the Allied Powers. *Documents Presented at Manila, Philippine Islands, 19 and 20 August 1945 to Japanese Representatives for Arrangement of the Surrender of the Japanese Armed Forces to the Supreme*

Commander for the Allied Powers. 1945. Record Group 5, Box 1. MacArthur Memorial, Bureau of Archives, Norfolk, Va. 1 folder.

This folder contains drafts of important documents related to the surrender of Japan. Materials include the text of the Proclamation by the Emperor of Japan, the Instrument of Surrender, and General Orders no.1, Military and Naval issued by the Imperial General Headquarters ordering the cessation of hostilities. The collection also includes the texts of SCAP directive nos.1 and 2 and Annex B to directive no.2 concerning the prompt and orderly establishment of the occupation forces in Japan.

222 ———. *Incoming Messages.* Aug.–Sept. 1945. Record Group 9. MacArthur Memorial, Bureau of Archives, Norfolk, Va. 1 folder.

These unclassified radiograms, arranged in chronological order, emanate from the emperor, the Japanese cabinet, and Imperial General Headquarters during the period just prior to and immediately after Japan's capitulation. Certain ones are addressed to the Japanese people and were intercepted by the U.S. Army Signal Corps shortly before surrender, but the majority are addressed to SCAP and concern the Potsdam Declaration, the cessation of hostilities, the terms of surrender, troop demobilization, arrangements for the Japanese emissaries to Manila, preparations for the forthcoming occupation, and the locations of prisoners of war and civilian internee camps in Japan, Korea, and Taiwan. Some concern illegal acts committed by U.S. soldiers in Japan and requests for the exemption of certain buildings and areas in Japan from requisition by SCAP authorities.

223 ———. *Japanese Surrender File: Correspondence.* Aug.–Sept. 1945. Record Group 5, Box 1. MacArthur Memorial, Bureau of Archives, Norfolk, Va. 1 folder.

Messages and documents relating to military and diplomatic aspects of the cessation of hostilities, the surrender of Japan, and the surrender ceremony itself are collected in this folder. Materials include the text of the Potsdam surrender ultimatum to the imperial Japanese government and numerous messages exchanged among various SCAP personnel as well as messages from SCAP to the Japanese government and to other Allied governments regarding the terms of surrender, troop conduct, and the instructions issued to SCAP's advance party. Also included are details of the surrender ceremony and lists of the Japanese surrender delegation and Allied personnel to be present at the ceremony.

224 ———. *Outgoing Messages.* 15 Aug.–9 Oct. 1945. Record Group 9. MacArthur Memorial, Bureau of Archives, Norfolk, Va. 1 folder.

Unclassified messages from SCAP to the Japanese government and to the emperor. They are arranged in chronological order and provide an indication of Allied actions and policies in the closing stages of the war and the beginning of the occupation. They relate to such issues as the surrender, cessation of hostilities, the Manila Mission, communication procedures between SCAP and the government of Japan, evacuation of prisoners of war and civilian internees, surrender ceremony preparations, the Allied landing in Japan, procurement of supplies, repatriation, and the control of civil disorder in Japan and other areas of East Asia.

225 ———. *Requirements of the Supreme Commander for the Allied Powers Presented to the Japanese Representatives at Manila, Philippine Islands, 20 August 1945.* Aug. 1945. Record Group 5, Box 1. MacArthur Memorial, Bureau of Archives, Norfolk, Va. 5, 3, 5, 5p.

This set of 4 documents issued by SCAP to the Japanese government's representatives at Manila immediately prior to the occupation outlines the initial arrangements for the establishment of the occupation and the expected role of the Japanese government. Document 1, entitled "Orientation, Agenda, and Requirements (Revised)," outlined the methods and places of arrival of U.S. military forces in Japan and demands information from the Japanese government pertaining to air fields, naval bases, harbor facilities, troop barracks, officers' quarters, etc. Document 2, entitled "Requirements for Entry and Operations of an Advance Party Representing the Supreme Commander for the Allied Powers within the Tokyo Bay Area," considers necessary provisions for SCAP's advance party in Tokyo. Document 3, "Requirements for Entry of the Supreme Commander for the Allied Powers and His Accompanying Forces," deals with the arrival of the main occupying forces and the duties of the Japanese government at this time. Document 4, "Requirements for Entry and Operations of Initial Occupation Forces in the Kanoya Area of Southern Kyushu," outlines measures of security and assistance to be taken by the Japanese for the advance party then contemplated for this particular area in southern Kyushu, i.e., police escort, free communications facilities, removal of all mines, provision of adequate accommodations, billets and camp area facilities, and the provision of local guides. There is a Japanese translation of these requirements and appended are maps of the Tokyo Bay area and a document providing specific information concerning logistic requirements for the occupation.

226 ———. *Reports of General MacArthur.* Washington, D.C.: Dept. of the Army, 1966. 5v. in 4.

An official record of the military operations that General Douglas MacArthur conducted in the southwest and western Pacific in 1941–45 and a Japanese account of the corresponding period. Originally put together in galley proof as *The Campaigns of MacArthur in the Pacific* (no.227) by General MacArthur's headquarters in Tokyo in 1950 and withheld from circulation, the report is published here exactly as in the earlier version except for an added foreword and indexes. The work was compiled first by MacArthur's Southwest Pacific Area G–3 Section and later by his G–2 (Intelligence) Section, headed by Major General Charles A. Willoughby who acted as chief editor. Volume 1 records the operations of forces under MacArthur's command from the Japanese attack on Luzon in 1941 through their victory in 1945, while the supplement to volume 1 describes such military aspects of the occupation of Japan as the advance planning in Manila, the landing in Japan, command structure, the release of prisoners of war, the demobilization of Japan's armed forces and their repatriation, the military government system, and occupation security and intelligence measures. It covers the period through December 1948. Volume 2, part 1 describes Japanese operations in the southwest Pacific from 1941 through September 1944 as reconstructed by Japanese officers' notes, statements, diaries, etc., as well as by Japanese governmental and military documents. Volume 2, part 2 describes Japanese operations from October 1944 through August 1945.

All 4 books are documented, using both English and Japanese sources, and are well illustrated. Particularly interesting from the standpoint of the Allied occupation of Japan are chapters 13 and 14 of volume 1, which concern Allied plans for the invasion of Japan and events leading to Japan's surrender; the supplement to volume 1; and chapters 20 and 21 in volume 2, part 2 which treat developments in Japan leading to the surrender. They cover such topics as the Potsdam Conference, Japanese imperial conferences, the palace guard rebellion, and the Japanese surrender mission to Manila. The last volume contains an article by Matsudaira Yasumasa, former minister of the Imperial Household, on the emperor's role during the Pacific War. It should be noted that while these volumes are ostensibly official publications, the Department of the Army specifically disclaims any responsibility for their accuracy.

227 U.S. Army. Southwest Pacific Area. G–2 Section. *The Campaigns of MacArthur in the Pacific.* Tokyo: 1950. 2v. in 6.

The galley proof of a history of the

Pacific War temporarily withheld from publication. This draft version, called "Semi-final-Mock-up," may be found in the Bureau of Archives, MacArthur Memorial, Norfolk, Virginia. The work was later published in 1966 by the Department of the Army under the title *Reports of General MacArthur* (no.226), the only changes being in title, an additional foreword, indexes, and a reorganization of the volumes. The published collection consists of four books in 2 volumes, volume 1 and volume 1 supplement, and volume 2, parts 1 and 2. It includes a treatment of the Japanese Presurrender Mission to Manila in August 1945, the Blacklist Plan for the military phases of the occupation of Japan, and some discussion of the initial stages of the occupation proper.

228 ———. ———. ———. *Historical Record Index Cards*. July 1941–Nov. 1945. Record Group 3. MacArthur Memorial, Bureau of Archives, Norfolk, Va. 12 ft. (approx.)

This collection provides the actual texts of radiograms, Public Relations Office broadcast messages and releases, reports, and State-War-Navy Coordinating Committee directives and memorandums. Records are filed chronologically and the vast majority refer to campaigns in the Pacific theatre. The final 18 record cards, dating from 15 August 1945 to 4 November 1945, concern presurrender policies for the occupation of Japan, negotiations with the Japanese government for the cessation of hostilities, SCAP liaison with other foreign nations during the occupation, plans for troop landings in Japan, suggested candidates for the position of political adviser to SCAP, and reports on negotiations for the establishment of the Far Eastern Advisory Commission.

Training Arrangements in the United States for the Military Government of Japan

The United States began to train officers for service with military government units in postwar Japan as early as May 1942. Ultimately as many as 2,500 officers received such training at the School of Military Government at Charlottesville, Virginia, the civil affairs training schools (CATS) at six major universities, and the Civil Affairs Holding and Staging Area (CASA) at Monterey, California. Such activities also constituted one aspect of the presurrender planning for the occupation of Japan.

In any event a good deal of this elaborate training proved to be irrelevant. Most of it was based on the assumption of an actual invasion of Japan and was intended to equip the students to administer conquered areas immediately in the rear of the combat lines, a situation that never materialized. Many of the students never got to Japan, and those who did were incorporated into General Headquarters, SCAP or the Sixth and Eighth Armies under circumstances notably different from those anticipated at the schools. The most important consideration, though, was the fact that a system of military government was never established in Japan. The Japanese government remained in existence after the surrender and functioned continuously and effectively. As a consequence the role of Americans was confined to the setting of general policies and the supervision of their execution by the Japanese. The situation was thus fundamentally different from that in Germany.

229 "AMG Plans for Japan." *Nation* 160: 667 (16 June 1945)

A letter to the editor from a young officer in training for service with the future military government of a defeated Japan criticizes that training program for being "too shortsighted, too exclusively interested in military expediency and... extremely one-sided about political matters." The writer claims that those in charge of training are strongly conservative and he is particularly critical of their suggestion that as military governors the officers should make an accommodation with the *zaibatsu* combines and control the economy through them.

229a Bloch, Henry Simon, and Bert F. Hoselitz. *The Economics of Military Occupation: Selected Problems.* rev. ed. Chicago: Univ. of Chicago Pr., 1944. xii, 157p.

While this scholarly study does not make specific recommendations for economic policies in occupied Japan, it describes and analyzes certain economic problems common to all military occupations. The authors base their discussion on data derived from historical sources, from the recent experiences of the Allies in areas wrested from Axis control, and from partial revelations of German, Italian, and Japanese practices in their respective areas of military control. Topics covered include military currency, exchange rates, banking, taxation, production control, and price control and rationing. Chapter 8, "Economic Problems and Policies in the Pacific," includes a more detailed treatment of Japan's economy and economic policies in occupied areas and of the use of military currency in areas occupied to date by American forces. As a concise statement of the theoretical and practical types of information available to economic planners towards the end of World War II, the entire volume is valuable for those interested in American presurrender planning for Japan.

Braibanti, Ralph J. D. *The Occupation of Japan: A Study in Organization and Administration.* 1949. *See* no.895.

230 Friedrich, Carl Joachim. "Military Government as a Step toward Self-Rule." *Public Opinion Quarterly* 7:527–41 (Winter 1943)

The role of military government in a defeated nation is discussed in this article by the director of the School for Overseas Administration at Harvard University. Friedrich treats various interpretations of the nature and objectives of military government and describes problems which arise in connection with restoring law and order and encouraging self-rule in an occupied country. He concludes that the military government of occupied countries will be an extremely delicate task and can have only a limited though vital role in the development of self-government in the occupied lands.

231 ———, and Douglas G. Haring. "Military Government for Japan." *Far Eastern Survey* 14:37–40 (14 Feb. 1945)

In an article written prior to the occupation, the authors discuss the training of future civil affairs officers for Japan, outlining their administrative responsibilities and describing their training in the 3 categories of area studies, language, and military government. The description is based on the program at Harvard University which was similar to those conducted at Yale, the University of Michigan, the University of Chicago, Northwestern, and Stanford Universities.

———, et al. *American Experiences in Military Government in World War II.* 1948. *See* no.900.

232 Holborn, Hajo. *American Military Government: Its Organization and Policies.* Washington, D.C.: Infantry Journal Pr., 1947. vii, 243p.

The author, who worked in the Office of Strategic Services and had close contact with American military government operations during World War II, critically examines the policies and practices of American military governments in Europe and Asia. The first 3 chapters are an evaluation of American military government planning after December 1941, when the secretary of war approved plans to train officers for civil affairs and liaison. These chapters also provide a description of the functions of the Combined Civil Affairs Committee, which was a joint Anglo-American endeavor to conduct civil affairs operations. Chapters 4 through 9 are an examination of the Allied military governments in Germany, Austria, and Italy. Chapter 10 deals with the American experience in the Far East. In this chapter, reference is made to the civil affairs training schools of the army and navy, the Civil Affairs Holding and Staging Area and its functions, the decisions by the Joint Chiefs of Staff to create a Joint Civil Affairs Committee on 1 May 1945, the implications of the Potsdam Declaration for the status of the emperor, and the Far Eastern Commission. Noting that the occupation of Japan is, in general, satisfactory, Holborn states that a much less satisfactory situation exists in divided Korea.

233 Mason, John Brown. "Lessons of Wartime Military Government Training." *Annals of the American Academy of Political and Social Science* 267:183–92 (Jan. 1950)

In an article devoted to a description of wartime programs for the training of military government or civil affairs officers for future work in various occupied territories, a section is devoted to those concerned with Japan. Following a useful description of the civil affair training programs in various American universities, there is a brief consideration of the Japanese program. The author, however, believes it is impossible to evaluate the effectiveness of the officers' instructions in Japanese civil affairs since the program for Japan "was planned for action in a gradual invasion accompanied by prolonged fighting" and "the training had little relation to the actual task awaiting the officers, with the exception of language study." Moreover, he asserts, many officers trained for Japan qualified for early demobilization in Europe and never saw Japan, while others were not needed because early surrender necessitated a much smaller number of U.S. officers than was originally estimated.

234 "Military Occupation and Government of Enemy Territory." In U.S. War Dept. *Basic Field Manual.* v.7, Military Law. pt.2, Rules of Land Warfare. 2 Jan. 1934. p.69–81.

A prewar statement of army policy for the occupation of a defeated nation. The scope and legitimate activities of an occupation are delineated. Separate sections deal with the administration of occupied territory, the effects of occupation on the population, the extent to which indigenous officials should be allowed to continue exercising their duties, and the treatment of enemy property. The document was prepared while General Douglas MacArthur was chief of staff.

Montgomery, John D. "Administration of Occupied Japan: First Year." 1949. *See* no.908.

The Reminiscences of Joseph Gordon. 1961. *See* no.44o.

235 U.S. Army. Service Forces. *Civil Affairs Handbooks, Japan.* Washington, D.C.: Army Service Forces Hdqters., July 1944–Mar. 1945. (Army Service Forces Manual M 354–1A to 354–18C)

This group of handbooks on Japanese civil affairs constitutes a series in the U.S. Army Service Forces manuals that were prepared for the Military Government Division, Office of the Provost Marshall General. The purpose of the handbooks was to facilitate American military commanders in conducting military government operations with maximum effectiveness and a minimum of human misery and material damage. Treated as restricted materials at the time of their publication, the handbooks were not intended as policy statements but rather as reference books containing basic factual information that might be needed for planning and policy-making in the occupied area in question. Most of the volumes were prepared by the Research and Analysis Branch of the Office of Strategic Services. Japanese civil affairs are covered under 18 rubrics. They are: (1) geographical and social background, (2) government and administration, (3) legal affairs, (4) government finance, (5) money and banking, (6) natural resources, (7) agriculture, (8) industry and commerce, (9) labor, (10) public works and utilities, (11) transportation systems, (12) communications, (13) public health and sanitation, (14) public safety, (15) education, (16) public welfare, (17) cultural institutions, and (18) Japanese administration of occupied areas. Within each section there are often subsections. For example, in section 2 one finds (2a) government and administration, and (2b) local government. The length varies from 58 to 350 pages. Each handbook attempts to describe features of Japanese society, with special reference to the operations of the Japanese government and the roles and responsibilities of different organs of that government. The series provides factual and statistical information on Japan in the early 1940s based primarily on Japanese sources, public and private, such as the 1940 census reports, *Teikoku tōkei nenkan* (Statistical Yearbook of Imperial Japan), and Japanese books and newspapers. The territory covered includes Manchuria, Korea, Taiwan, and the Southeast Asian region—all of which were then under Japanese control. Most of the handbooks print photos of major establishments and sometimes essential equipment and machines being used in Japan. Some of the handbooks carry in an appendix some basic Japanese words and expressions that may be of use for American civilian officers working in Japanese territories.

236 ———. Civil Affairs Training School. Univ. of Michigan. *Final Report of the Civil Affairs Training School, Far Eastern Program (Japan), University of Michigan, Submitted 15 October 1945.* Ann Arbor: 15 Oct. 1945. v, 97p.

This final report on the training program which prepared civil affairs officers for military government duties in occupied Japan includes a history of the program and facts concerning its establishment and administrative operation. The Universities of Michigan, Chicago, Northwestern, Stanford, Yale, and Harvard administered programs dealing with Japan; only at Michigan and Chicago, however, were personnel trained as civil censorship officers to supervise the censorship of postal and cable communications in Japan. The content of the curriculum, which dealt with Japanese language instruction, area studies, military government, and civil censorship, is examined. The relations of the Michigan program to the Office of the Provost Marshall General, the School of Military Government in Charlottesville, Virginia, and to the Judge Advocate General's School in Ann Arbor are explained. Various appendixes, giving lists of textual materials available for use by the school, of lecture topics, of enrolled officers, and of teaching personnel, are included.

237 ———. War Dept. *United States Army and Navy Manual of Military Government and Civil Affairs, 22 December 1943.* Washington, D.C.: Government Printing Office, 1943. ix, 86p. (War Dept. Field Manual 27–5 and Navy Dept. OpNav 50E–3)

This manual is a revised prescription of guiding principles and policies which should be utilized in areas occupied by U.S. forces for the planning and implementation of military government and the control of civil affairs. It is designed for use by the War and Navy Departments, theater commanders and their subordinates. The manual consists of 7 chapters: (1) general; (2) civil affairs responsibility; (3) organization of military government; (4) personnel; (5) planning; (6) proclamations, orders, ordinances, and instructions; and (7) military commissions, provost courts, and claims. Definitions of military government, occupied territory, and civil affairs are given in the first chapter. In the second chapter 24 specific areas over which civil affairs officers should exercise responsibility are listed. These include political order, supervision of military and civil courts, civilian supply, public health, communications, public finance, agriculture, labor, education, and records. Other subjects mentioned in the manual deal with the qualifications of civil affairs officers, sources of information for planning, and the form and content of civil affairs orders.

The Decision to Use Atomic Weapons

From the American standpoint the making of the decision to drop atomic bombs on Hiroshima and Nagasaki was closely interwoven with and related to the origins and timing of the Potsdam Proclamation. The latter cannot be fully understood without reference to the former. It is for this reason that a brief section on the literature of "the atomic decision" is included at this point, despite the fact that, strictly speaking, it relates more to the conduct of the war than to the topic of presurrender planning. In this connection special mention should be made of the two versions of the Feis book (nos.243 and 244) and the reader's attention should also be called to the publications of the U.S. Strategic Bombing Survey (nos.152–60).

238 Alperovitz, Gar. *Atomic Diplomacy: Hiroshima and Potsdam; The Use of the Atomic Bomb and the American Confrontation with Soviet Power*. New York: Simon & Schuster, 1965. 317p.

Alperovitz, a Fellow of King's College at Cambridge University, analyzes American policy toward the Soviet Union after April 1945, when, he believes, President Truman began to change President Roosevelt's policy of "cooperation" with the Russians and assume a tougher stance. The author feels that the prospect of possessing the atomic bomb, rather than the death of Roosevelt, was a factor which significantly influenced Truman's decision to adopt a strong policy aimed at forcing Soviet acquiescence to American plans for eastern and central Europe. In this regard, he disagrees with the conclusion of Herbert Feis, a leading specialist on this period, who wrote *Churchill, Roosevelt, Stalin* (1957) (no.185) and *Between War and Peace: The Potsdam Conference* (Princeton, N.J.: Princeton Univ. Pr., 1960. viii, 367p.). In his examination of developments at the Potsdam Conference, Alperovitz notes the extent to which Truman alternately adhered to the subtle policy of opposition to the Russians suggested by Secretary of War Stimson and to the advice of Secretary of State Byrnes who urged strong opposition. Truman's postponement of the Potsdam Conference until July is regarded as a tactic to delay a showdown with Stalin with the hope that the successful testing of the atomic bomb would strengthen the United States' bargaining power vis-à-vis the Soviet Union. The author is critical of the American decision to use the atomic bomb against Japan, asserting that Truman and his senior advisers knew that Japan would probably surrender without recourse to this measure.

239 Baldwin, Hanson Weightman. *Great Mistakes of the War*. New York: Harper, 1949. 114p.

The author, who served as military and naval correspondent for the *New York Times* from 1937 to 1942 and thereafter as military affairs editor, critically reviews a number of key wartime decisions of the U.S. government. He argues that, being idealists rather than realists, the Americans were lacking in an overall long-range strategy for the war in both Europe and the Pacific. What he calls America's "political mistakes" during the war include insistence on unconditional surrender for Germany, the loss of eastern and central Europe by failing to invade the Balkans, the failure to develop a politically viable China policy, an unreasonable defense of the Philippines, appeasement of Russia at the Yalta Conference so that it would enter the Pacific War, and, finally, the use of atomic bombs against Japan. Regarding the atomic bombing as "the penalty of expediency," he contends that the atomic bomb was used without fair and proper warning to the Japanese and that Japan would have surrendered even if the bomb had not been dropped. He is also critical that America first demanded unconditional surrender and then later made it conditional by agreeing to the retention of the imperial system.

239a Batchelder, Robert C. *The Irreversible Decision, 1939–1950*. Boston: Houghton-Mifflin, 1962. 306p.

This book, based on the dissertation the author prepared for a Ph.D. in social ethics at Yale University, examines the historical events and moral principles involved in the decision to use the atomic bomb against Japan. Part 2, "The Decision to Drop the Atomic Bomb, 1945," is a straightforward narration of the series of meetings, decisions and developments in the war which resulted in the bombing. Part 3, "Dropping the Atomic Bomb: Right or Wrong?", examines among other things the ethical considerations underlying the motives for using the bomb, and attempts to determine the role of the bombing in Japan's decision to surrender. The author considers in his concluding chapters the effect of the development and use of atomic weaponry on postwar society and international politics.

240 Bresler, Robert Joel. *American Policy toward International Control of Atomic Energy 1945–1946*. Ph.D. dissertation, Princeton Univ., 1964. 178p. (Abstracted in *Dissertation Abstracts* 26: 1750–51 [1965]; University Microfilms order no.65-2115)

The evolution of American policy regarding international control of atomic energy in 1945–46 is examined here. Discussed are the decision to use the atomic bomb against Japan, the decision not to exchange scientific information with the Soviet Union, and the failure of the Acheson-Lilienthal-Baruch proposals to specify when the United States would relinquish its atomic deterrent. Bresler indicates in this discussion his belief that Secretary of State Byrnes regarded the atomic bomb as a political weapon and therefore considered it unwise for the United States to commit itself to a policy of international control of atomic energy. Chapter 2 is a review of the decision to use the atomic bomb against Japan and the role of the Potsdam Conference in this regard.

241 Compton, Arthur Holly. *Atomic Quest: A Personal Narrative*. New York: Oxford Univ. Pr., 1956. xix, 370p.

One of the civilian scientists who helped develop atomic energy during World War II, the author gives a personal narrative of how it was done and the moral struggle he and his colleagues experienced in developing a weapon of "wholly unprecedented destructive power." The fourth chapter describes the "heart-searching decision" made by top American leaders concerning the use of the atomic bomb against Japan. Compton defends the American use of the atomic bomb to terminate the war. He presents the top military strategists' concern to win the war with the least amount of destruction and the fewest number of American casualties. He relates the discussions held by members of the Interim Committee (composed of Henry L. Stimson, George L. Harrison, James F. Byrnes, Ralph A. Bard, William L. Clayton, Vannevar Bush, Karl T. Compton, James B. Conant, and the author) from May to August 1945 as to the wisdom of using the atomic bomb. He also describes the report of the Scientific Panel which was opposed to the use of the bomb. He reconstructs developments at the Potsdam Conference in connection with the arrival of news of the first successful atomic test and the development of a new strategy to bring about Japan's surrender. The author visited Japan in 1954 and reaffirms his conviction regarding the wisdom of the atomic bombing through his exchange of views with Japanese reporters and others.

242 Compton, Karl T. "If the Atomic Bomb Had Not Been Used." *Infantry Journal* 60:16–17 (Feb. 1947); reprinted from *Atlantic Monthly* 178, no.6:54–56 (Dec. 1946)

Compton, president of Massachusetts Institute of Technology, adviser to the War Department on the atomic bomb, and observer on General MacArthur's staff, defends the atomic bombing of Japan. He argues that it was no worse than the bombing of Tokyo; that it brought an end to the war; and that otherwise the Japanese would have continued fighting to the last man.

243 Feis, Herbert. *The Atomic Bomb and the End of World War II.* rev. ed. Princeton, N.J.: Princeton Univ. Pr., 1966. vi, 213p.

A revised edition of a book originally published in 1961 under the title of *Japan Subdued* (no.244). Most of the original material is retained, but Feis has extensively rewritten chapter 4, which presents the background of the decision to drop the atomic bomb, and chapter 17, which contains his conclusions concerning the use of the atomic bomb against Japan. However, most of the points made in the previous edition remain unaltered.

244 ———. *Japan Subdued: The Atomic Bomb and the End of the War in the Pacific.* Princeton, N.J.: Princeton Univ. Pr., 1961. 199p.

This scholarly narrative describes the plans and acts of the Allied and Japanese governments in 1945 leading to an end of the war in the Pacific. The book is divided into 4 parts. Part 1 discusses 3 alternatives available to the Allies for ending the war—combined assault, inducement, or shock, i.e., the atomic bomb. Part 2 relates the diplomatic maneuverings behind the policy decisions made at Potsdam, and part 3 gives an account of the days between the decision to drop the bomb and Japan's formal surrender. Part 4 consists of reflections on the use of the atomic bomb against Japan. The author notes the extensive presurrender planning by the Allies, particularly the United States. He summarizes and analyzes the initial occupation policies set forth by the U.S. Initial Post-Surrender Policy for Japan and comments, sometimes critically, on their long-range effects. The author concludes that the Japanese government would not have surrendered before July 1945 either unconditionally or with specific guarantees for continuation of the imperial dynasty. He concurs with the conclusion of the U.S. Strategic Bombing Survey that Japan would have surrendered by November or December 1945 without use of the atomic bomb, even if Russia had not entered the war. Finally, he agrees that to end the war victoriously as soon as possible was justification for dropping the bomb, but he holds that the Japanese should have been forewarned of its nature and destructive power.

Official documents, diplomatic records, and memoirs provide much of the material upon which this informative and balanced account is based. The author also draws upon personal experience and expertise. A modern historian associated with the Institute of Advanced Studies at Princeton when this book was written, he had previously worked as an adviser on economic affairs for the State Department from 1931 to 1944 and had served as special consultant to the secretary of war from 1944 through 1947.

245 Fogelman, Edwin, ed. *Hiroshima: The Decision to Use the A-Bomb.* New York: Scribner, 1964. ix, 116, ix p. (Scribner Research Anthologies)

A collection of 19 essays and letters related to the subject of the atomic bombing of Hiroshima. They are grouped in 4 different categories: American decision-making on the Hiroshima bombing, the American scientists involved in developing atomic bombs, the Japanese reaction, and various observations concerning the social and moral implications of atomic bombing. The selection of material is balanced. All materials are excerpted. The sources on which this anthology is based include: Harry S. Truman's *Memoirs* (1955) (no.217), Henry L. Stimson's and McGeorge Bundy's *On Active Service in Peace and War* (1947) (no.216), James F. Byrnes' *Speaking Frankly* (1947) (no.207), J. Robert Oppenheimer's letter to the Atomic Energy Commission, Arthur H. Compton's *Atomic Quest* (1956) (no.241), Tōgō Shigenori's *The Cause of Japan* (1956) (no.150), Kase Toshikazu's *Journey to the Missouri* (1950) (no.143), Hanson W. Baldwin's *Great Mistakes of the War* (1949) (no.239), and Patrick M. S. Blackett's *Fear, War, and the Bomb* (New York: Whittlesey, 1949. 244p.).

246 Knebel, Fletcher, and Charles Waldo Bailey (II). *No High Ground*. New York: Harper and Row, 1960. ix, 272p.

An account of how the decision was made to drop atomic bombs on Hiroshima and Nagasaki. The authors describe the Japanese overtures for surrender which Allen Dulles, the European director of the Office of Strategic Services, received in July 1945 during the Potsdam Conference. They further discuss the progress of the Manhattan project, the people who planned the first atom bomb, and disagreements among Truman's top aides as to the wisdom of dropping the bombs and the steps to be followed if and when they were dropped. The views of political and military leaders such as Henry Stimson, Cordell Hull, James Byrnes, William Leahy, and Leslie Groves as well as those of scientists such as Arthur Compton and J. Robert Oppenheimer are studied closely. The book was translated into Japanese and published under the title of *Mohaya kōchi nashi* (Tokyo: Kōbunsha, 1960. 279p.).

246a Kolko, Gabriel. *The Politics of War: The World and United States Foreign Policy, 1943–1945*. New York: Random, 1968. x, 685p.

A study of American wartime policy which describes the actual condition of the world in 1943, 1944, and 1945 as much as it does the way in which the United States at that time "defined and quite as often misconceived the course of global realities." Chapter 21 (p.522–48), entitled "The Far East after Yalta: The Dilemma of China and the Future of Japan," includes 1 section dealing with both the role of the atomic bomb in America's Far Eastern policy and American planning for postwar Japan. Chapter 22 (p.549–67)—"July 1945: The War with Japan and the Potsdam Conference"—focuses on Japan's unsuccessful attempt to negotiate a peace prior to the destruction of Hiroshima and Nagasaki. Throughout this chapter, Kolko is critical of the American failure to realize how desperately serious the Japanese were about surrendering. He concludes, moreover, that the United States could have won the war in the Pacific without Russian intervention and without the use of the atomic bomb had the Americans been willing to explore significant alternatives open to them during that summer.

246b Schoenberger, Walter Smith. *Decision of Destiny*. Athens: Ohio Univ. Pr., 1969. viii, 330p.

This study analyzes the domestic and international forces which led President Truman to authorize the use of the atomic bomb against Japan. It finds that a major factor in Truman's decision was the longstanding Allied commitment to demanding an unconditional surrender of Japan combined with a general agreement among the decision makers that Japan would fight to the last. In tracing the progress of the secret Manhattan atomic bomb project during the war in both its scientific and political dimensions, Schoenberger demonstrates that the program developed an internal momentum of its own which became an additional factor in Truman's decision. The author also analyzes in some detail the Allied debates over war policy and the growth of a peace faction within the Japanese government in order to clarify the factors which must be considered in coming to any conclusions about the moral justifications for using the bomb against Japan. Schoenberger's book concludes with an extensive listing of pub-

247   Stimson, Henry Lewis. "The Decision to Use the Atomic Bomb." *Harper's Magazine* 194:97–107 (Feb. 1947)

The events leading up to the American bombing of Hiroshima and Nagasaki in August 1945 are described by the man who was secretary of war at that time. He describes plans and preparations in the development of the bomb, emphasizing the roles of the Scientific Panel and the Interim Committee which advised the president concerning progress in developing the bomb and its possible effects. The central portion of the report discusses United States policy toward Japan in July 1945 and the reasons why it was deemed necessary to use the bomb to effect the surrender of Japan. Relevant memorandums from the author to the president are presented and the report concludes with a personal statement wherein the author states that in his estimation the reasons for the use of the bomb "have always seemed compelling and clear . . . in order to end the war in the shortest possible time and to avoid the enormous losses of human life which otherwise confronted us."

248   Strauss, Lewis L. "A Thousand Years of Regret." In his *Men and Decisions.* Garden City, N.Y.: Doubleday, 1962. p.163–200.

A personal secretary to President Hoover, special assistant to Secretary of the Navy James Forrestal during World War II, and later chairman of the Atomic Energy Commission, the author has written some 19 essays citing examples from his own career that illuminate the process whereby men reach important decisions. He also considers the consequences of these decisions. In this essay, which constitutes chapter 9 of the volume, Strauss argues that the United States decided to drop the atomic bombs on Japan in August 1945 in spite of convincing military and political reports that Japan would surrender without such bombing. He also notes that the Russians knew from May 1945 on that the Japanese were desperate in their efforts to end the war but that Stalin merely hinted at this to his Allies, even at the Potsdam Conference. These desperate efforts by the Japanese were also monitored by American cryptographers and made known to Secretary of the Navy Forrestal in July 1945. However, Forrestal was reluctant to appear at the Potsdam Conference without invitation. Thus he deliberately delayed his arrival at Potsdam until some 48 hours after the conference issued a declaration demanding the unconditional surrender of Japan's armed forces, thus depriving the conference of a chance to take alternative policies into consideration.

General Collections of Official Documents, Speeches, etc.

For those interested in the official texts of major documents, speeches, and communiqués involved in the postwar planning process or in facsimile versions of the actual surrender documents signed aboard the U.S.S. *Missouri*, the following entries should prove helpful. Numerous documents relating to this subject also will be found in items listed in the section containing general collections of official documents (p.148).

249   Ausubel, Nathan, ed. *Voices of History, 1945–1946: Speeches and Papers of Roosevelt, Truman, Churchill, Attlee, Stalin, De Gaulle, Chiang, and Other*

Leaders Delivered during 1945. New York: Gramercey, 1946. xix, 810p. (Voices of History)

The last of a 5-part series entitled Voices of History. As the subtitle suggests, the full or partial texts of addresses, declarations, joint communiqués, directives, or messages by a selection of chiefs of state during 1945 are compiled here. Arranged in chronological order, almost all of the documents are quoted from official sources. Entries under August and September are particularly relevant to Japan. Among them are the Soviet Union's declaration of war on Japan (8 Aug.), the Japanese surrender offer (10 Aug.), Emperor Hirohito's broadcast on the surrender (14 Aug.), MacArthur's directions to Japan for a Manila meeting (15–18 Aug.), Prince Higashikuni's speeches to the Japanese people and troops (17 Aug.), the emperor's and prince's addresses to the Diet (4 and 5 Sept. respectively), and the United States' and MacArthur's statements on the occupation of Japan (6 and 9 Sept. respectively). All are published without specific comment, but general comments are given on monthly developments for each of the 12 months.

Foreign Affairs Assn. of Japan, ed. *The Japan Year Book 1946–1948.* 1949. See no.550.

250 *International Declarations* No. 1– (Sept. 1945–)

This publication succeeds *Peace Aims Documents* published by the National Peace Council during World War II. In this first issue are 6 documents pertaining to the defeat of the Axis: the Atlantic Charter of 14 August 1941; the Declaration of Philadelphia adopted by the conference of the International Labor Organization on 10 May 1944; the Crimea Declaration of 11 February 1945; the Act of Chapultepec adopted by the Inter-American Conference on War and Peace on 3 March 1945; the Potsdam Conference declarations issued on 2 Aug 1945; and, finally, the Potsdam Proclamation to Japan issued on 26 July 1945.

250a "Japan Officially Surrenders." *Current History* 9, no.50:338–42 (Oct. 1945)

Provided among the documentary material within this issue of *Current History* are the complete text of the surrender agreement signed aboard the U.S.S. *Missouri* on 2 September and the text of the Japanese general order no.1 detailing the surrender procedure of Japan's military forces and acknowledging the subordination of the Japanese government's authority to that of the supreme commander for the Allied powers.

"Japan seit seiner Kapitulation." 1947. See no.504a.

250b "Japan Surrenders." *Current History* 9, no.49:184–92 (Sept. 1945)

Provided within this collection of documentary materials are the texts (with brief explanatory introductions) of (1) the Potsdam declaration of 26 July calling upon Japan to surrender; (2) President Truman's statement of 6 August informing the American people of the explosion of an atomic bomb over Hiroshima and calling the great potentialities of this bomb to their attention; (3) the Soviet declaration of war on Japan, dated 8 August 1945; (4) the Japanese surrender offer of 10 August broadcast by Japan's Dōmei news agency to the United States, Great Britain, the USSR, and China; (5) the 11 August reply of the Allies to Japan through U.S. Secretary of State James F. Byrnes; (6) Japan's surrender message of 14 August; (7) President Truman's proclamation on 14 August of Japan's official surrender; (8) Secretary of State Byrnes' 14 August instructions to the Japanese; and (9) Emperor Hirohito's radio broadcast of 14 August in which he announced the surrender to the Japanese people.

251 Maki, John McGilvrey. *Conflict and Tension in the Far East: Key Documents, 1894–1960.* Seattle: Univ. of Washington Pr., 1961. ix, 245p.

A collection of treaties, agreements, and official policy statements concerned with international relations in East Asia and accompanied by brief introductory notes. Chapter 5, entitled "Japan's Wartime Diplomacy: 1941–45," includes the Soviet denunciation of the Neutrality Pact with Japan, 6 April 1945, and the Soviet Declaration of War against Japan, 8 August 1945. Chapter 6—"Japan: The Lost War and the Peace"—contains: (1) the Cairo Conference declaration of 1 December 1943, (2) President Truman's statement of 8 May 1945 on the meaning of unconditional surrender for Japan, (3) the Yalta Agreement, (4) the Potsdam Declaration, (5) the Imperial Rescript on the End of the War, 14 August 1945, (6) the U.S. Initial Post-Surrender Policy for Japan, (7) the Treaty of Peace with Japan (San Francisco, 1951), (8) the Treaty of Peace between the Republic of China and Japan (Taipei, 1952), (9) the Joint Declaration between the USSR and Japan (Moscow, 1956), and (10) the Reparations Agreement between the Philippines and Japan (Manila, 1956). Maki, compiler of these documents, is professor of Japanese government and politics at the University of Washington.

252 National Archives, ed. *The End of the War in the Pacific: Surrender Documents in Facsimile.* Washington, D.C.: Government Printing Office, 1945. 24p. (National Archives publication no.46–6)

This pamphlet contains a brief description of the termination of hostilities at the end of the Pacific War, a radio script of the ceremonies that opened an exhibit of Japanese surrender documents, and facsimiles of the surrender documents themselves. Documents include the credentials of the Japanese signatories of the Instrument of Surrender, the Instrument of Surrender itself, Emperor Hirohito's rescript announcing the surrender as well as an English translation thereof, and the instruments of surrender for Japanese forces in the Philippines, South Korea, and Southeast Asia.

Available at the Reference Branch, Office of the Chief of Military History, Washington, D.C.

253 New Zealand. Dept. of External Affairs. *Select Documents on International Affairs, 1945.* Wellington: Government Printer, 1945. 67p. (Dept. of External Affairs publication 13)

This publication contains the texts of 7 international documents of major importance published in 1945. Included are the Three-Power Proclamation to Japan issued at Potsdam on 26 July 1945, the Soviet-Chinese treaty of 14 August 1945, and the United States Initial Post-Surrender Policy for Japan of 22 September 1945. No commentary is provided.

254 United Nations. *Instrument of Surrender.* Washington, D.C.: Government Printing Office, 1945. 8p.

Facsimile copies of the official documents pertaining to the Japanese surrender are collected here. They are: (1) the Instrument of Surrender signed 2 September 1945; (2) Emperor Hirohito's proclamation of surrender; and, (3) the emperor's letter of credentials which authorized Shigemitsu Mamoru, foreign minister, and General Umezu Yoshitarō, chief of the General Staff of the Imperial Japanese Army, to represent the Japanese government and the Japanese army, respectively, and sign the Instrument of Surrender. Both the English and Japanese texts of the emperor's proclamation and the letter of credentials are included.

255 U.S. Congress. Senate. *Surrender of Italy, Germany, and Japan: World War II.* Washington, D.C.: Government Printing Office, 1946. iv, 111p. (79th Cong., 1st sess., 1946. Senate document no.93)

On 4 October 1945 Senator Barkley presented before the Senate this set of documents relating to the defeat of the Axis powers. It comprises the Instruments of Surrender, armistice terms, surrender instructions, and statements by Allied leaders. The section on Japan (pt. 3) contains 16 documents, including the Potsdam Declaration, General MacArthur's statement on the Japanese Surrender Mission to Manila, his and Admiral Nimitz's addresses at the surrender ceremony on 2 September 1945, the Japanese imperial rescript on surrender, and President Truman's address on surrender.

256 ——. Dept. of State. *The Axis in Defeat: A Collection of Documents on American Policy toward Germany and Japan.* Washington, D.C.: Government Printing Office, 1945. v, 118p. (Dept. of State publication 2423)

All major documents relating to American policy toward Germany and Japan that were issued from 1941 through 1945 are collected here. The work consists of 3 parts: "General Policy," "Surrender," and "Occupation." The first part comprises communiqués and declarations issued after conferences of the major powers occurring between 1941 and 1945, such as the Atlantic Charter of 14 August 1941 and the declarations following the Moscow, Cairo, Teheran, Crimea, and Yalta Conferences. The portion of the second part that concerns the Japanese surrender includes the texts of the Potsdam Declaration, the Japanese offer of surrender (10 Aug. 1945), Japanese acceptance of the Potsdam Declaration (14 Aug. 1945), Japanese surrender documents (1–2 Sept. 1945), and President Truman's radio address (1 Sept. 1945). Finally, the third part contains 4 relevant documents. They are: the American proposal for a Far Eastern Advisory Commission (21 Aug. 1945) released 10 October 1945, the United States Initial Post-Surrender Policy for Japan (29 Aug. 1945), the authority of General MacArthur as supreme commander for the Allied powers (6 Sept. 1945), and the SCAP "Bill of Rights" directive to the Japanese government (4 Oct. 1945).

——. ——. *Occupation of Japan: Policy and Progress.* 1946. See no.468.

257 ——. ——. *Surrender by Japan: Terms between the United States of America and the Other Allied Powers, September 2, 1945.* Washington, D.C.: Government Printing Office, 1946. 7p. (Dept. of State publication 2504; Executive Agreement series 493)

This publication presents a photostatic copy of the Instrument of Surrender signed by 4 Allied powers and Japan at the surrender ceremony held aboard the U.S.S. *Missouri* on 2 September 1945. Thereby Japan proclaimed its unconditional surrender to the Allied powers and pledged to "carry out the provisions of the Potsdam Declaration in good faith," and accepted the subjugation of the authority of the emperor and the Japanese government to SCAP. There are also photostatic copies of the Japanese and English texts of a proclamation made by the emperor on the same day accepting the terms of surrender and all provisions of the Instrument of Surrender.

258 ——. ——. Office of Public Affairs. Div. of Publications. *In Quest of Peace and Security: Selected Documents on American Foreign Policy, 1941–1951.* Washington, D.C.: Government Printing Office, 1951. vi, 120p. (Dept. of State publication 4245; General Foreign Policy series 153)

This publication collects full texts or excerpts from 34 documents central to American foreign policy from 1941 through 1951. It consists of 3 parts: part 1 presents wartime documents including the communiqués of the Casablanca, Moscow, Cairo, Teheran, Yalta, and Berlin (Potsdam) Conferences as well as President Roosevelt's speech on "The Four Freedoms" and the text of the Atlantic Charter, both from 1941. Part 2 relates to defeated and occupied areas; it contains the texts of the Japanese Instrument of Surrender of 2 September 1945, the Principles for a Japanese Peace Treaty, and a U.S. memorandum of 24 November 1950 to governments represented on the Far Eastern Commission. Part 3 sets forth documents regarding "security against aggression" such as aid policies, the Point Four Program of 1949, peace resolutions adopted by the United Nations General Assembly in 1949 and 1950, disarmament speeches, and American cultural exchange programs. Little commentary is added.

The Occupation Period,
2 September 1945–28 April 1952

For present purposes the occupation may be said to have begun formally on 2 September 1945 with the completion of the ceremony of surrender aboard the U.S.S. *Missouri*. It lasted for 6 years and 8 months, terminating on 28 April 1952 when the Treaty of San Francisco (signed on 8 Sept. 1951) took legal effect, thus ending the war and restoring Japan to sovereign status in the eyes of all but the few belligerent powers that failed either to sign or to ratify the peace treaty.

Most of the literature in Western languages about the Allied occupation both dates from and relates to this period of slightly less than 7 years. There is, of course, overlap at both ends. Some accounts written during the occupation treat presurrender planning and other relevant events that took place before 2 September 1945. Similarly, there are an appreciable number of retrospective studies written after 1952 that cover the occupation proper and sometimes its antecedents as well—although these are not nearly so numerous as the historical and social scientific importance of the developments concerned would lead one to expect. In the entries that follow an effort has been made to identify such overlapping items through cross-referencing.

The principal problem for the bibliographer of the occupation, however, is less one of periodization than of categorization. It flows from the astonishing scale and complexity of the activities undertaken by the headquarters of SCAP. The 2 major initial goals of the occupation are frequently summarized in overly simple terms as the demilitarization and democratization of Japan. At a later date these goals underwent important changes: some measure of remilitarization was substituted for demilitarization, and economic rehabilitation was added as a third goal. The pursuit of these aims involved the occupation authorities in positive interventions in almost every significant area of political, economic, and social organization and action in Japan. This occupation was unique in the scope and penetration of both its ambitions and its actual undertakings. As a consequence it is no simple matter to categorize the literature that seeks to describe and analyze such sweeping endeavors. So much of it reflects the complexity of its subject matter and defies simple categorization.

In the sections that follow every effort has been made to classify items primarily under subject heads describing their principal content or emphasis and to compensate for minor additional emphases by cross-references. There still remains a very sizeable category that can only be denominated as "general" in coverage. The items therein have been grouped together and, wherever possible, subclassified into groups that seemed to offer the maximal possible research utility for average scholarly purposes.

General Materials

This category has been somewhat arbitrarily defined as consisting of items that devote substantial attention to three or more different aspects of the Allied occupation of Japan. Since so many of the items concerned take the form of reports or serials intended to summarize complex processes of events over set periods of time or of newspaper or periodical commentaries written to keep readers abreast of a cluster of recent and rapidly changing activities, the coverage is frequently very broad. In an attempt to bring as much order and precision as possible into this unwieldy class of materials, the following system of 8 subcategories of classification has been devised:

1. SCAP: Situation and Progress Reports
2. SCAP: Official History of the Occupation
3. SCAP: Reports by Subordinate Headquarters
4. SCAP: Press Releases and Conferences
5. SCAP: Analyses and Translations of the Japanese Press
6. SCAP: Administrative Directives to the Japanese Government
7. General Collections of Official Documents
8. Calendar of General Commentaries 1945–72

It will be noted that, with the exception of the last, all of these subcategories are substantive in nature. In the case of the last category, a chronological arrangement seemed to offer the greatest potential advantage from the standpoint of most students of the occupation period.

SUPREME COMMANDER FOR THE ALLIED POWERS (SCAP) SITUATION AND PROGRESS REPORTS

The occupation produced a considerable number of general situation and progress reports, some serial in nature. These reports were more frequent in the earlier and more critical years than toward the end of the occupation when both political power and initiative had begun to return to the Japanese government. In fact their relative paucity after 1948 is a serious hindrance for students of the occupation. It is only partially compensated by the existence of the enormous *History of the Non-Military Activities of the Occupation of Japan* (1952) (nos.

283–337) that will be described in the following section. Many entries in the section dealing with SCAP's organization, staff, and functions (p.296) are closely related to those in this section and should be consulted.

Perhaps most notable and generally useful among such progress reports are the *Summation of Non-Military Activities in Japan and Korea* (no.262) and the *Political Reorientation of Japan* (no.279). Both of these, unfortunately, cover only the period up to September 1948.

259 Supreme Commander for the Allied Powers. *Japanese File: Correspondence, 1945–1947*. Record Group 5, Box 1. MacArthur Memorial, Bureau of Archives, Norfolk, Va. 1 folder.

Letters and reports are chronologically arranged here and deal mainly with important Japanese individuals or groups. The contents include brief intelligence reports on totalitarian elements in the prewar Japanese army and on the careers of several prominent Japanese religious and political leaders, lists of important persons in the Japanese government in 1945 and 1946, a roster of the House of Representatives in 1947 that indicates members' previous business and political experiences, and SCAP memorandums describing the Nippon Kyōdōtō (Cooperative party of Japan) and the Shin Nippontō (New Japanese political party). A large part of the materials concerns American and Japanese positions on the issue of war criminals and there is a copy of the SCAP press release of 18 January 1946, citing names, ranks, and current addresses of 110 additional war criminal suspects. The file also includes the texts of SCAP directives nos.2 and 3 to the Japanese government, and a report submitted to the supreme commander by a former Tokyo Imperial University professor on the subject of reform of the Japanese family system.

260 ———. *Occupation Reports: Japan and Ryukyuan*. 1947. Record Group 5, Box 76. MacArthur Memorial, Bureau of Archives, Norfolk, Va. 1 folder (23, 17, 93p., app.)

A report presented by SCAP to Kenneth C. Royall, secretary of the army. It is divided into 3 main sections. According to a letter of 11 October 1947 from General MacArthur which is also included in the file: "Section 1 indicates the progress made during the Occupation to achieve the political and economic objectives of the United States. Section 2 outlines the present situation and more prominent immediate problems, and Section 3 deals with future plans including requirements, industrial levels, financial aspects and potential contributions to the economic recovery of the Far East." Section 1 covers a wide range of subjects including presurrender conditions, the new constitution, the courts of law, local government and the neighborhood associations, the political purge, the economic deconcentration program, agricultural production and food problems, forestry, industry, reparations, mineral resources, civil transportation and communications, public finance, labor, foreign trade, and social aspects of the occupation.

———. *Reports of General MacArthur*. 1966. See no.226.

261 ———. *Summary of Data on Problems of Major Interest, Supreme Commander for the Allied Powers/Far East Command, for Members of the Armed Forces Committee, House of Representatives, Congress of the United States*. Tokyo: Sept. 1947. Record Group 5, Box 76. MacArthur Memorial, Bureau of Archives, Norfolk, Va. 35p.

This booklet prepared by SCAP's General Headquarters provides a comprehensive outline of the organizational structure and operation of the occupation to date. Information is carefully organized under a variety of headings.

Introductory charts in section 1 present the organizational structure of the General Headquarters, Far East Command, and the General Headquarters of SCAP whereas 2 maps indicate the deployment of forces throughout the Far East Command and the deployment of occupation forces in Japan and Korea. They are followed by accounts of personnel data for military and civilian SCAP personnel as well as other special groups in Japan, a description of the bases of the Far East Command, and problems associated with training as well as various other matters concerned with the military theater in the Far East. Section 2 concentrates on key problems confronting the occupation authorities in the areas of economic deconcentration and recovery, food production, natural resources, reconstruction problems, public health and welfare, and social conditions. Section 3, entitled "The Possibility of a Balanced Japanese Economy," discusses the nature of Japan's prewar and postwar economy, defines what SCAP believes are the requirements for a balanced Japanese economy, forecasts Japan's foreign trade from 1948 to 1953, and discusses Japan's balance of payments, problems in establishing foreign exchange rates, production levels, and levels of consumption. Engineering matters relevant to the occupation are discussed prior to a consideration of the Far East air and naval forces. The fourth and final section of the report concerns non-military aspects of the occupation, including descriptions and diagrams relating to the new political life of Japan, the structure of the Japanese government, the responsibilities of the Diplomatic Section of SCAP, and information relating to reforms in education, religion, media, labor, natural resources, public health, and welfare. It also discusses the progress of the repatriation program and procedures of demobilization. Formerly restricted, this report provides a valuable, if brief, summation of occupation activities. There is an indication in the introduction that the report included appendixes to sections 1 and 3 but these are missing from the document at Norfolk.

262 ———. *Summation of Non-Military Activities in Japan and Korea.* Mimeographed. Tokyo: SCAP, Sept./Oct. 1945–Aug. 1948. nos. 1–35. monthly.

SCAP's comprehensive monthly report on nonmilitary activities in postwar Japan and Korea. Although Japan is covered from September 1945 to August 1948, Korea is omitted from the series after March 1946, the words "and Korea" being deleted from the original title. The reports describe the existing situation in Japan rather than explain SCAP directives to the Japanese government. Individual numbers vary in length from 200 to 340 pages, and cover 4 general categories of information. The first category, entitled "General," presents a concise summary of the entire issue and discusses SCAP organization and operations. The other categories, political, economic, and social, give more detailed information on particular topics. The political section discusses developments with respect to national and local government, political parties, the Diet, the purge, the police, prisons, accidents, legal affairs, war criminals, etc. The economic section also covers a wide range of topics such as agrarian reform, production and distribution by industrial sectors, export-import ratios, etc. The last category, social, treats public health, public welfare, education, religion, public libraries, and communications media, etc. Each August issue (no.11, Aug. 1946; no.23, Aug. 1947; and no.35, Aug. 1948) contains an appended review of the previous occupation year. Each issue also contains approximately 100 charts, graphs, and maps relevant to the material discussed.

263 ———. *Two Years of Occupation.* Tokyo: SCAP, Aug. 1947. 3v.

A brief self-appraisal by SCAP of its activities and reform programs during the first 2 years of the occupation. It comprises 3 slender volumes, covering economic, political, and social aspects respectively. Volume 1 reviews the activities of the Civil Communications, Civil Property Custodian, Civil Transportation, Economic and Scientific,

Natural Resources, and Reparations sections. The work of the General Procurement Agent is also treated in this volume. Volume 2 discusses SCAP reform programs undertaken by the Government Section, covering constitutional reform and other legal and judicial reforms, the purge, the elections of 1946 and 1947, the creation of a Labor Ministry and the promotion of local autonomy. The nature of the new constitution and the general framework of the purge program are discussed in appendixes. A description of Government Section activities is followed by an evaluaton of the work carried out by the International Prosecution Section and the Legal Section. Volume 3 presents a report by the Civil Information and Education Section covering religion, education, public opinion, and media analysis. It also deals with the Public Health and Welfare Section. All reports are too brief to be of academic value but are useful for general information.

———. Allied Translator and Interpreter Section. *Monthly Report.* 1945–46. See no.922.

264 ———. Civil Affairs Div. *Monthly Activities Report.* Tokyo: SCAP, 1946–51. monthly.

Each regional and district civil affairs team submitted a monthly report in mimeographed form to General Headquarters, SCAP, which provides a useful outline of the activities of regional occupation forces and offers a summary of regional and district trends. The report also notes local noncompliance with SCAP directives. The civil affairs regions were Chūgoku, Hokkaido, Kanto, Kinki, Kyushu, Shikoku, Tōhoku, and Tōkai-Hokuriku. Reports consist of a general résumé of the months' operations followed by a series of titled annexes. Annex A, "Legal and Governmental Activities," concerns Japanese government administration, activities of local government groups, political parties, and other such matters. Annex B1, "Public Health Activities," concerns local endeavors in implementing public health programs and related reforms; Annex B2, "Public Welfare Activities," relates to the work of welfare agencies in the area. Annex D is an economic summary which includes a summation of progress in agriculture, fisheries, forestry, mining and geology, price and distribution, industry, customs, and labor. Annex E1 contains pertinent information on civil education activities —both scholastic and social—and Annex E2 relates to civil information activities. Annex F contains a summation of the civil affairs teams' surveillance of Japanese tax administration.

Available at the Washington National Records Center, Suitland, Maryland.

265 ———. Civil Information and Education Section. *Activities Report.* Tokyo: SCAP; Nov. 1945–Dec. 1946, Jan. 1949, May 1951. weekly.

A weekly report prepared by the Civil Information and Education Section's Press and Publication Branch, this series discusses work completed and work still in progress with respect to Japanese publications, translating selected materials, publishing materials for the use of SCAP agencies as well as American and Japanese official and nonofficial groups, and setting up programs and conferences. There is also a description of current administrative or organizational problems and a report of the current responsibilities of the branch's personnel. Any press releases that were made during the previous week are noted and the reports also provide lists of books and other publications that received clearance from SCAP. Later editions of the series are entitled *Weekly Report* (no.272) but the format is similar to earlier issues.

Available at the Washington National Records Center, Suitland, Maryland.

266 ———. ———. *C I and E Bulletin.* Tokyo: SCAP, 2 June 1947–21 Dec. 1949. 3v. bimonthly.

A bimonthly mimeographed bulletin published by the Civil Information and Education Section and designed to provide information for the military government teams (MG teams) of the Eighth Army. The bulletin was intended to "report succinctly the essential detail of developments of interest to MG Teams; provide interpretative background; afford a medium for interchange of news and ideas; and from time to time offer information as to availability of reference materials on related subjects" (v.1, no.1, p.1). Japanese education and plans for its reform are the primary topic of this bulletin; coeducation, the PTA, teacher evaluation, textbook rewriting, Boy Scouts and Girl Scouts, and library facilities are some of the other topics covered. Also included are such matters as the rural land reform program, the agricultural co-op program, public health service, revision of the civil code, and constitutional revision. The bulletin contains additional items, one being "MG Reports" which describe military government teams' activities in the various prefectures, such as the planning of children's art exhibits. Another item is the "Bulletin Supplement," appending Civil Information and Education Section reports, educational documents, and speeches by prominent American visitors or SCAP officials. Still another item is the Civil Information and Education Section's radio program texts. Sketchy as each report is, it is useful for understanding the objectives and activities of the Civil Information and Education Section at local levels. The bulletin grew in size as the occupation progressed, beginning with some 10 pages but later nearly doubling its length, and adding much material to its supplementary sections. For a partial listing of the articles appearing in the different issues, see Walter Crosby Eells, *The Literature of Japanese Education, 1945–1954* (no.8), p.138–42.

Available on microfilm from the National Archives, Washington, D.C.

267 ———. ———. *Mission and Accomplishments of the Occupation in the Civil Information and Education Fields*. Tokyo: SCAP, 1 Oct. 1949. 25p.

A brief account of the functions and responsibilities of the Civil Information and Education Section of SCAP and its achievements from 1945 to 1949. It is arranged by the section's individual divisions, i.e., Information Division, Education Division, Religions and Cultural Resources Division, and Public Opinion and Sociological Research Division.

268 ———. ———. *Mission and Accomplishments of the Occupation in the Civil Information and Education Fields*. Tokyo: SCAP, 1 Jan. 1950. 28p.

A later edition of a slightly shorter report (no.267) published on 1 October 1949. It summarizes the Civil Information and Education Section's activities from the start of the occupation through 1949. Following a discussion of the establishment and organizational structure of the section, the report considers the responsibilities of its 4 divisions: Information, Education, Religions and Cultural Resources, and Public Opinion and Sociological Research. Under the Information Division are data on information programs; SCAP's regulation of newspapers, magazines, books and radio broadcasting; and the information centers established throughout Japan. The Education Division's restructuring of school administration, reordering of school finances, and reorganization of the educational system are described as are the Religions and Cultural Resources Division's activities in establishing religious freedom, separating church and state, eliminating militarism and ultranationalism, and assisting Christian missions in Japan. The final section briefly describes the Public Opinion and Sociological Research Division's role in conducting attitude surveys of the Japanese people. Twelve charts provide information on such topics as the location of the Civil Information and Education information centers, the nature of the Civil Information and Education Section exhibits, the structure of the new Ministry of Education, and production of textbooks.

Available at the Library of Congress, Washington, D.C.

269 ———. ———. *Monthly Summary*. Mimeographed. Tokyo: SCAP, Sept. 1945–May 1951. monthly.

Monthly summaries of the activities of the Civil Information and Education Section of SCAP have been collected in these mimeographed volumes. Accounts vary from 8 to 20 pages in length and provide detailed descriptions of past problems, current developments, and future activities of the section proposed during the previous month. The reports are divided according to topics which represent the Civil Information and Education Section's most important responsibilities, i.e., information, education, and religions, and within each of these general categories there are described the activities of the information centers, the content of newspaper and magazine releases, the progress of educational and cultural programs, and developments in Japanese religions as well as Christian religions in Japan. Other related topics include youth activities, educational exchange programs, United Nations Economic, Scientific, and Cultural Organization affairs, the dissemination of religious materials, and library affairs. The monthly series provides excellent statistical information on these topics and an account of progress made. Issues often include supplements which present the texts of important letters, speeches, or newspaper articles during the month, relevant statistical information, and special reports undertaken by various divisions within the section.

This series is available at the Washington National Records Center, Suitland, Maryland. The Library of Congress, Washington, D.C. possesses a less complete collection.

270 ———. ———. *Special Reports.* July 1946–50.

Various research units of the Civil Information and Education Section collected information and prepared studies that were eventually issued by the section's Analysis and Research Division as special reports. Most of these provide some background information, a description of the immediate postwar situation, and of later developments under the occupation on a vast variety of topics. Reports available at the Washington National Records Center in Suitland, Maryland include studies of teacher indoctrination (Mar. 1946), women's legal status in Japan (Mar. 1946), Japanese cultural organizations (Apr. 1946), fine arts magazines (July 1946), the reeducation of Japanese servicemen (July 1946), public opinion agencies in Japan (Aug. 1946), women's sections of the 5 major political parties (Nov. 1946), surveys of opinions and attitudes expressed in letters by Japanese to occupation authorities (8 reports) (1946), libraries in Japan (Mar. 1947), neighborhood associations (Jan. 1948), a history of teachers' unions in Japan (Mar. 1948), religions in Japan (Mar. 1948), economic aid to students in Japan (May 1948), education in the new Japan (v.1 and 2, May 1948) (no.2124), a survey of certain publications with wide labor readership (July 1948), the report of the educational exchange survey (Sept. 1949), Japan: some psychological perspectives (Oct. 1949), the development and present status of *romaji* in Japan (Dec. 1950), and plans for fiscal year 1952 (Apr. 1951). Reports on various organizations are also included—i.e., the Harmonization Society (Kyōchō Kai) (Apr. 1946), the Jōmō newspaper (Apr. 1946), the Japan Public Opinion Research Institute (Nippon Yoron Kenkyūsho) (Apr. 1946), other public opinion agencies (Mar. 1946), and the newspaper collection of Tokyo Imperial University (Apr. 1946). There is also a catalog of research materials prepared in March 1946 which cites statistics and reports that were produced by the Civil Information and Education Section's Research and Information Division since its inception.

A number of these special reports may also be found at the McKeldin Library of the University of Maryland, College Park, Maryland. Maryland's collection consists of the following:

Survey of Opinions and Attitudes Expressed in Letters by Japanese to Occupation Authorities: no.4 (25 Mar. 1946) 39p.

Survey of Opinions and Attitudes Expressed in Letters by Japanese to Occupation Authorities: no.5 (30 Apr. 1946) 74p.

Preliminary Survey of Japanese Advertising (3 July 1946) 14p.

Public Opinion Agencies in Japan (19 Aug. 1946) 47p.

Summarized History of the Ministry of Education (19 Aug. 1946) 80p.

Survey of Opinions and Attitudes Expressed in Letters by Japanese to Occupation Authorities: no.7 (31 Aug. 1946).

Jiji News Agency Public Report on "Trends of Democratization in the First Year of the Occupation" (1 Oct. 1946) 89p.

Public Opinion Organizations of All Types in Japan (31 Oct. 1946) 11p.

Women's Sections of the Five Major Political Parties: Liberal Party, Communist Party, Social Democratic Party, Cooperative Democratic Party, and Progressive Party (Nov. 1946) 20p.

Zoos, Aquariums, and Botanical Gardens in the Kyoto-Nara-Osaka Area (21 Nov. 1946) 15p.

Shakai Undō Tsūshin (Social Movement News) (10 Dec. 1946) 10p.

The Jiji Shimpo Publishing Company (12 Dec. 1946) 15p.

Women's Organizations in Tokyo (Jan. 1947) 36p.

Kaigai Shuppanbutsu Yunyū Kyōkai (The Foreign Publications Importers Assn.) (14 Jan. 1947) 4p.

Kodansha Magazines: no.1 (14 Jan. 1947) 6p.

Hokkaido Magazines (31 Jan. 1947) 15p.

Libraries in Japan (containing 3,000 volumes or over) rev. (28 Feb. 1947) 95p.

Organization, Membership, and Activities of Women in Major Labor Federations (30 July 1947) 17p.

Survey of Opinions and Attitudes Expressed in Letters by Japanese to Occupation Authorities: no.16 (14 Nov. 1947) 3p.

Japanese Educational Institutions under the Jurisdiction of Ministries Other Than the Ministry of Education (30 Apr. 1948) 78p.

Rural-Urban Circulation of Principal Dailies in Japan (5 May 1948) 28p.

Economic Aid to Students in Japan (10 May 1948) 95p.

271 ———. ———. *Weekly Summary.* Mimeographed. Tokyo: SCAP, Oct. 1945–Jan. 1946. weekly.

This mimeographed series presents a brief report of the significant activities of all divisions of the Civil Information and Education Section of SCAP for the preceding week. Early reports are a few pages in length but later issues range from 30 to 40 pages. Methods of organization and reporting vary considerably. In general, rather than discussing the Civil Information and Education Section's activities according to particular divisions, the report arranges the vast array of material according to the nature of the reform program or subject under consideration, for example, suppression of militarism and ultranationalism, dissemination of democratic ideals, information programs, press and publications, motion pictures, important religious, political, social, or cultural organizations, etc. Many accounts indicate programs that are completed and those still in progress. There are also editorials on the latest developments in politics, journalism, and education, and résumés of important conferences that have taken place during the week.

Available at the Washington National Records Center, Suitland, Maryland.

272 ———. ———. Education Div. *Weekly Report.* Tokyo: SCAP, 1945–51. weekly.

Progress in the SCAP program to reform the Japanese educational system is noted in this series of detailed weekly reports submitted by the Education Division to the chief of the Civil Information and Education Section. Reports note work in progress, completed programs, and the future programs planned on the local as well as national levels. The great range of topics includes primary and secondary education and higher education, vocational education, adult education, textbook revision, media education, health and physical education, youth organizations and student activities, scientific education, libraries, and teacher training.

Available at the Washington National Records Center, Suitland, Maryland.

273 ———. Economic and Scientific Section. *Mission and Accomplishments of the Occupation in the Economic and Scientific Fields.* Tokyo: 26 Sept. 1949. 30p.

274 ———. ———. *Mission and Accomplishments of the Supreme Commander for the Allied Powers in the Economic and Scientific Fields.* Tokyo: SCAP, 1950. 47p.

This report is divided into 2 main sections—the first providing 16 charts and graphs indicating Japan's economic situation and the second offering a narrative account of economic reform measures undertaken by SCAP. The charts and graphs cover a wide range of subjects, including population statistics, industrial production figures, consumer price indexes, and import-export data. Most of the graphs cover the period from the beginning of the occupation through 1949. The second part of the report provides a brief description of the economic situation at the close of the war. It describes problems confronting occupation authorities and discusses ways in which SCAP authorities attempted to solve these problems in order to enable Japan to achieve a self-supporting economy. Topics emphasized include finance, taxation, industry and utilities, shipping, tourist and trade services, foreign trade and commerce, foreign exchange funds, labor, and scientific and technical activities.

Available at the Washington National Records Section, Suitland, Maryland.

275 ———. ———. *Mission and Accomplishments of the Supreme Commander for the Allied Powers in the Economic,* *Scientific, and Natural Resources Fields.* Tokyo: SCAP, 1952. ii, 79p.

This report is in two parts. The first half concerns economic and scientific matters and the second, natural resources. The report presents the reforms SCAP has attempted in these fields and estimates the degree to which they have succeeded. The first part covers such subjects as finance, taxation, price and distribution, industry and utilities, foreign trade and commerce, shipping, tourism, foreign exchange, democratization of business organizations, the labor force, labor conditions, and scientific and technical activities. The second part is presented under 4 headings: agriculture, fisheries, forestry, and mining and geology. Thirty-eight useful charts are provided.

276 ———. ———. *Progress Report.* Mimeographed. Tokyo: SCAP, 20 June 1946. 22p.

The functions of the Research and Statistics Division in collecting and interpreting economic statistics on all phases of the Japanese economy are outlined in this brief mimeographed report. There is a critical examination of existing Japanese statistical reports and procedures concerning such topics as industry, population, labor, prices, distribution, foreign trade, and financial statistics. There are also an evaluation of the accuracy of these reports and procedures and recommendations of new reporting procedures deemed necessary by the division. The broad topic of industry is broken down into specific industrial sectors such as textiles, electrical equipment, copper, and iron and steel. There is also an outline of studies of Japanese businesses in connection with the deconcentration program.

Available at the Washington National Records Center, Suitland, Maryland.

277 ———. Government Section. *A Brief Progress Report on the Political Reorientation of Japan.* Tokyo: SCAP, 10 Oct. 1949. 60p.

A summary statement of what SCAP felt it had accomplished in its attempts to reform the Japanese government. After critically outlining the structure of prewar government in Japan, it describes how the legal bases of government have changed under the occupation forces' directorship. The report refers not only to the scope of the legislative, executive, and juridical responsibilities of the national government but also to the principles underlying local government and the civil service. It then discusses the rise of new political leadership as a result of the purge of militarists and ultranationalists and the introduction of popular elections, as well as the development of new political movements and increased public political consciousness. The final 2 chapters are devoted to a discussion of General MacArthur's attitude toward Japan's political reorientation and a description of the *modus operandi* between the SCAP authorities and Japanese government officials.

278 ———. ———. *A Brief Progress Report on the Political Reorientation of Japan.* rev. ed. 31 Dec. 1949. Record Group 5, Box 93. MacArthur Memorial, Bureau of Archives, Norfolk, Va. 76p.

A revised version of an earlier report issued on 10 October 1949 under the same title (no.277). It follows the text of the earlier report almost exactly, but there are minor additions and the subheadings of chapters are arranged in a somewhat different fashion.

279 ———. ———. *Political Reorientation of Japan, September 1945 to September 1948: Report.* Washington, D.C.: Government Printing Office, 1949. 2v. Reprint eds.: (1) St. Clair Shores, Mich.: Scholarly Pr., 1968; (2) Westport, Conn.: Greenwood, 1970.

The report prepared by SCAP's Government Section on its activities during the first 3 years of the occupation. It is one of the most comprehensive and useful reports published by SCAP and is indispensable for understanding the reasoning behind the occupation's policies and the Japanese response to those policies. The first volume, consisting of 12 chapters, deals descriptively with various phases of Japan's political development such as diplomatic relations, the purge, the new constitution, the national executive, the Diet, the judicial and legal systems, the civil service, local government, law enforcement, elections, political parties, and political education. Treatment of each subject is preceded by a brief historical description of presurrender conditions. The general tone of the report is one of satisfaction with Japan's political progress and hopefulness for the country's future. The second volume consists of appendixes that include the texts of the basic diplomatic documents that led to Japan's surrender, and of documents relating to the elimination of the old order, the new constitution, governmental reorganization, and political policy. The latter volume also contains the texts of some 50 statements by General MacArthur, documents revealing the history, administrative structure, and personnel of the Government Section of SCAP, and the English language texts of 45 laws implementing the new constitution.

For a description and brief review of this 2-volume publication, see Sir George B. Sansom's article in the September 1951 issue of *Pacific Affairs* entitled "The Political Orientation of Japan" (no.662).

280 ———. ———. *Review of Government and Politics in Japan.* Tokyo: SCAP, Nov. 1948–Feb. 1951. monthly.

Comprehensive monthly reports prepared by the Government Section to summarize political developments within the Japanese government and to outline the activities of political parties during the preceding month. Reports range from 75 to 150 pages in length and provide a detailed narrative account of major developments in the Japanese political sphere for this period. Along with accounts of current cabinet activities, biographical sketches of cabinet members, and an outline of general policy, considerable attention is devoted to financial and economic problems with which the government must deal, the police system, activities of major political parties and any changes in their composition, the current situation in the Diet, and brief reports on such issues as repatriation, the purge, or illegal transactions. During periods before or after national and local elections, there is considerable coverage of their preparation and results. Later reports (from May 1949) also present the texts of important SCAP and U.S. government statements on the political situation in Japan as well as press comments on these. Included are reports entitled *United States' Views on Japan's Resumption of International Responsibilities* (May 1949) and *Discussions of Peace Issues* (Feb. 1950). Throughout the series are tables which are helpful in charting the results of local elections.

This series is available at the Washington National Records Center, Suitland, Maryland. The reports for September 1948, February 1949, and April 1949–April 1950 may be found at the Bureau of Archives, MacArthur Memorial, Norfolk, Virginia (Record Group 5, Boxes 95–98, 15 binders).

———. Natural Resources Section. *Mission and Accomplishments of the Occupation in the Natural Resources Field.* 1949. See no.1824.

———. ———. *Mission and Accomplishments of the Occupation in the Natural Resources Field.* 1950. See no.1825.

———. ———. *Mission and Organization of the Natural Resources Section.* 1947. See no.1826.

———. Public Health and Welfare Section. *Bulletin.* See no.2186.

———. ———. *Mission and Accomplishments of the Occupation in the Public Health and Welfare Fields.* 1949. See no.2187.

———. ———. *Mission and Accomplishments of the Occupation in the Public Health and Welfare Fields.* 1949. See no.2188.

281 ———. Public Information Office. *Two Years of Occupation.* Mimeographed. Aug. 1947. Record Group 5, Box 105. MacArthur Memorial, Bureau of Archives, Norfolk, Va. 1 binder; also in *Contemporary Japan* pt. 1, 16:402–33 (July/Sept. 1947); pt. 2, 16:512–25 (Oct./Dec. 1947)

The complete text of a mimeographed report prepared by the Public Information Office, the last 3 sections of which were later published independently under the title *Two Years of Occupation* (Aug. 1947) (no.263). Composed of 6 major sections and prefaced by a general introduction, the report provides a brief but comprehensive outline of the structure and operations of the occupation program through August 1947. The first section, entitled "Major Commands (with Tokyo Headquarters)," describes the structure and operations of the Far East Air Forces and the Naval Forces Far East, and includes a description of the training of forces, the quality of personnel, special services program to date and an estimate of future work. The third major section, entitled "Far East Command: Special Staff Sections," describes the accomplishments and future tasks of such specialized Far East Command sections as the Central Purchasing Office, the Chaplain Section, the Chemical Section, the Civilian Personnel Section, the Engineering Section, the Medical Section, the Ordnance Office, the Provost Marshall Section, the Quartermaster Section, the Office of the Signal Officer, the Special Services Section, the Transportation Section, and the Troop Information and Education Section. In general it treats activities in the first and second years of the occupation. The final 3 sections, later published, concern economic, political, and social aspects respectively. Section 4 (v.1 of the published work) reviews the activities of the Civil Communications, Civil Property Custodian, Civil Transportation, Economic and Scientific, Natural Resources, and Reparations Sections. The work of the General Procurement Agent is also treated in this section. Section 5 (v.2 of the published work) discusses SCAP reform programs undertaken by the Government Section, covering constitutional reform and other legal and judicial reforms, the purge, the elections of

1946 and 1947, the creation of a Labor Ministry, and the promotion of local autonomy. The nature of the new constitution and the general framework of the purge program are discussed in appendixes. A description of Government Section activities is followed by an evaluation of the work carried out by the International Prosecution Section and the Legal Section. Section 6 (v.3 of the published work) presents a report by the Civil Information and Education Section covering religion, education, public opinion, and media analysis. It also deals with the Public Health and Welfare Section. All reports are quite brief.

282 ———, and Far East Command. *Selected Data on the Occupation of Japan*. Tokyo: SCAP, 1950. v, 214p.

A report on the achievements and activities of the Allied occupation of Japan to mid-1950. The report, prepared jointly by SCAP and the Far East Command, consists of 2 parts. The first section, which takes up the greater part of the report, covers SCAP activities, giving a succinct account of overall policies and programs. Topics are arranged in 17 sections which include constitutional revision, legal and administrative reform, educational innovations, religious freedom, public health improvements, natural resources, economic democratization, fair trade, industrial relations, communications, custody of civil property, war crimes trials, demobilization of the Japanese military organization, civilian censorship, repatriation, and SCAP personnel matters. The second part briefly delineates the activities of the U.S. Far East Command. Its structure and personnel are discussed along with the operation of its military intelligence service and problems of the logistical support of the occupation. There are 38 useful charts on selected aspects of the occupation, to which is added an 85-page discussion of the changes in the organizational structure of SCAP and the Far East Command between 1946 and 1950.

U.S. Dept. of State. *Occupation of Japan: Policy and Progress*. 1946. See no.468.

———. Army. Southwest Pacific Area. *The Campaigns of MacArthur in the Pacific*. 1950. See no.227.

SCAP OFFICIAL HISTORY OF THE OCCUPATION

There exists in typescript, and now on microfilm, an official *History of the Non-Military Activities of the Occupation of Japan*. It consists of fifty-five monographs on as many aspects of the occupation's organization and activities. The monographs are of widely differing quality and scholarly utility. In the section that follows, there is one general entry describing the series as a whole, its organization, and availability. It is followed by separate, short-title entries for each of the fifty-five monographs that comprise the series. It should be understood that a full citation of any monograph would include the series title and author as well as the title of the particular monograph concerned.

Supreme Commander for the Allied Powers. General Headquarters. Statistics and Reports Section. *History of the Non-Military Activities of the Occupation of Japan*. Tokyo: SCAP, 1952.

This work consists of fifty-five monographs which were prepared by the Statistics and Reports Section (later called the Civil Historical Section) of SCAP and edited by William E. Hutchinson. The collection is an official record of SCAP's activities in Japan, and it describes the rationale behind many of the most significant occupation policies and reform programs. Data for these monographs were originally collected by SCAP's special staff sections and cover the nonmilitary activities of the occupation of Japan from 1945 through July 1951.

The monographs generally begin with a description of the historical background of the subject to be treated, then explain the occupation's objectives and comment upon the effects of occupation policies and the Japanese reaction to them. The monographs present a comprehensive description of the occupation's programs rather than a critical analysis of its policies. Each report contains extremely useful appendixes that set forth statistical data, charts, legal documents, reports, speeches, SCAP directives, etc., relevant to the subject of the monograph. Those SCAP staff members who took part in the compilation of the work are acknowledged at the beginning of the first monograph, which is an introduction to the series.

Of the fifty-five monographs, the complete texts of eleven are still under security classification, and one of the monographs (monograph 42) (no.324) is partially classified. A twelve-page section, entitled "Title of Monograph," at the beginning of the whole series was consulted for annotations for these twelve monographs; it provides a brief summary of the contents of each monograph.

Since its originally planned system for volumes and parts within volumes did not materialize, SCAP then arbitrarily assigned numbers 1 through 55 to those entries as an alternative. Consequently, many monographs indicate a volume and part, but many others do not. When used, volume numbers are often confused and inconsistent, thus making it extremely difficult to comprehend the internal ordering of subseries. Helpful for clarification are the call numbers that were given to most of these monographs for its historical manuscript file by the Office of the Chief of Military History in Washington, D.C. According to this call number system, the fifty-five monographs seem to range between 8-5/AA1/v1/c1/3462 (monograph 1) and 8-5/AA16/v4/c1/3566 (monograph 55), although this is not verifiable due to the inclusion of classified monographs in the series. When ordered according to the last four-digit number, and volume and part numbers, if available, this historical monograph series seems to be arranged according to a subject index. Generally speaking, volumes are grouped under several subject headings, although there are inconsistencies.

In the following arrangement, roman numerals in parentheses after the monograph numbers refer to volume, and arabic numerals or alphabetical letters refer to parts within the volumes. Where volume or part indications are not provided, a blank space has been left. The series is ordered as follows: Political—monographs 6(III,1) and 12(V,3); Political and Legal—monographs 7(III,A), 8(III,B), 9(III,C), 10(III,E), 11(III,F), and 13(V,6); Civil Liberties—monographs 14(V,1), 15(V,4), and 55(V,2); Social—monographs 16(XI,), 31(XI,A), 32(XI,D), and 33(XI,G); Public Health and Welfare—monographs 18(,), 19(VIII,); Reform of Business Enterprise—monographs 24(X,A), 25(X,C), and 26(X,D); Labor and Agrarian Reforms—monographs 27(,), 28(XI,A), 29(XI,B), and 30(XI,D); Finance—monographs 37(XIII,A), 38 XIII,B), 39(XIII,C), and 40(XIII,D); Natural Resources—monographs 36(,), 42(XIV,B), and 43(XIV,C); Fuel and Power—monographs 41(,),

General Materials 287

44(,), 45(,), and 46(XV,B); Industry—monographs 47(XVI,A), 48(XVI,B), and 49(XVI,C); Commerce—monographs 50(,), 51(,), and 53(XVII,D). Unclassified monographs—monographs 1, 2, 3, 4, 5, 17, 21, 22, 23, 34, 35, and 54.

The original manuscript of this series is kept at the World War II Record Division, National Archives, Washington, D.C. Declassified monographs are available on microfilm for public purchase through the Washington National Records Center.

283 Monograph 1. *Introduction, 1945–1951.* 1952. 58p.

The first monograph describes in a general way the condition of the Japanese nation and people from 1945 until 1950. It provides an outline of the basic legal and organizational structure through which SCAP implemented its policies of demilitarization and democratizaton. Democratization programs are discussed under 5 subheadings: (1) removal of obstacles, (2) the constitution, (3) local autonomy, (4) education, and (5) economic reform.

284 Monograph 2. *Administration of the Occupation, 1945–July 1951.* 1952. 179, 43p.

Following a description of the origins of occupation authority, this monograph presents a detailed but succinct discussion of the development of SCAP's overall structure. Its methods of operation are also described and particular attention is given to the control of Japan's foreign relations during the occupation. The appendixes include charts of the organizational structure of SCAP, detailed organization charts of the special staff sections, and brief and incomplete lists of staff personnel in major positions at various times during the occupation.

285 Monograph 3. *Logistic Support, 1945–1951.* 1952. 146, 82p.

This monograph deals with problems related to the maintenance and support of SCAP administration and operations, discussing such questions as real estate, labor, transportation, communications, utilities, and other general supply systems. The text and appendixes include some 20 statistical tables related to the procurement of supplies for the occupation program, Japan's termination of war expenses, and information on occupation employees.

286 Monograph 4. *Population.* 1952. 139p., app.

This monograph is classified, but, according to SCAP's notation, it is composed of 2 parts. Part 1 concerns presurrender statistics of the Japanese population and provides information on prewar and wartime trends in population and the factors affecting such trends. Part 2 discusses population at the outset of the occupation, occupation policies regarding population censuses, social and economic statistics, repatriation, mortality decline, and urban and rural population trends.

287 Monograph 5. *Trials of Class "B" and "C" War Criminals.* 1952. 4, 243p.

This monograph concerns trials of class "B" and class "C" Japanese war criminals—those who committed atrocities or inhuman acts against particular races or groups, civilian populations, or prisoners of war. The report consists of 2 parts. Part 1 discusses Japan's violation of the laws of war during World War II, Allied protests against Japanese offenses, the reasons why the Allies felt the war crimes trials necessary, and the legal framework within which the trials were conducted. Part 2 considers representative cases such as command responsibility trials, POW (prisoner of war) camp trials, trials for ceremonial murders, trials for medical experiments on war prisoners, etc. The final 2 short chapters are concerned with statistics of trials, sentences, and procedures of review, clemency, and parole. Documents con-

288 Monograph 6. *Local Government Reform, 1945–December 1950.* v.3, pt.1. 1952. 48, 132p.

This monograph consists of 2 parts. The first treats the presurrender status of Japanese local government. It discusses the historic origins of local government, the Taika Reforms, the governmental system under the shogunate, the prefectural, city, town, and village assemblies, and the role of the chief executives at each level, and, finally, considers the tendency toward greater centralization during World War II. It also gives a useful account of the historical development of neighborhood associations and their operations. The second section, dealing with postwar local government, analyzes the process and effects of the purge program, and describes the new local government system under the Local Autonomy Law of 1947. In addition, it considers such matters as the new financial burdens of supporting police and educational systems and the problem of administrative inefficiency caused partly by the inappropriately large number of local governments for a country of Japan's small size. The appendix includes a bibliography of some 40 Japanese and English publications on local government that were issued between 1888 and 1948, the texts of Ministry of Home Affairs instructions, SCAP directives on local government, and the full text of the Local Autonomy Law of 1947.

289 Monograph 7. *The Purge, 1945–December 1951.* v.3, pt. A. 1952. 144, 129p.

This report first discusses legal precedents for the purge, followed by a comprehensive coverage of the political and economic aspects of the purge program itself and a description of the Appeals Board system and the depurge program. The monograph also deals with the elimination of "undesirable" organizations such as Dai Nippon Butokukai, terroristic groups, and some labor organizations. Nine tables in the text and one table in the appendixes give a useful summation of the purge and depurge programs; the appendixes also include major SCAP directives and imperial ordinances related to the purge, as well as the text of a questionnaire for purge eligibility, and lists of purged offices, groups, and organizations.

290 Monograph 8. *Constitutional Revision, 1945–December 1951.* v.3, pt.B. 1952. 88, 72p.

The monograph first treats constitutional developments in the pre-1945 period, then basic U.S. policy for constitutional revision and the Japanese government's reaction to it. After tracing the origins of the constitution, it comments on such provisions as the status of the emperor, rights and duties of the people, and local self-government. It concludes with a discussion of some of the questionable aspects of the constitution that are still debated, including the cabinet's power to dissolve the lower house of the Diet without a preceding Diet vote of nonconfidence, the constitutionality of rearmament, and the treatment of the Communist party.

291 Monograph 9. *National Administrative Reorganization, 1945–1949.* v.3, pt.C. 1952. 92, 148p.

A comprehensive analysis of the transformation of the executive branch of the national government as defined in the Meiji and the postwar constitutions. It considers both the presurrender status and postsurrender status of the emperor, the privy council, the *jūshin* (senior statesmen), the cabinet, and the ministries. It also gives detailed descriptions of the scope of power of the postwar ministries, thus indicating the increased authority of the postwar prime minister and the cabinet, and the proportionally reduced power of the emperor. The appendixes include a bibliography of both English and Japanese materials on this topic which appeared prior to 1945, as well as complete lists of prime ministers, privy council presidents and cabinet ministers, laws and imperial ordinances that established the prewar and postwar executive organs, a chronology of the order in which the new ministries were created, and a list of the relevant major SCAP directives.

292 Monograph 10. *Election Reform 1945–November 1951.* v.3, pt.E, 1952. 91, 71p.

Analyzes the occupation reforms of the electoral system, and the effects of these reforms upon the elections that took place in Japan between 1945 and 1951. Specific electoral studies include the national elections of 1946, 1947, 1949, and 1950, and the local elections of 1947 and 1951. The report covers a wide range of issues such as election legislation, election violations, election expenses and party finances, composition of the Diet, election administration, election districts, local referenda, etc. It contains some 30 useful tables on various aspects of electoral results, plus relevant legislation (including the Election Law of 1925), cabinet ordinances, and SCAP directives related to the subject.

293 Monograph 11. *Development of Political Parties, 1947–November 1951.* v.3, pt.F. 1952. 200, 103p.

This report considers the development of political parties during the occupation period from various angles. The monograph presents a general survey of major and minor political parties and analyzes the effects of the purge upon party development. It also compares various features of several parties: their organizational structure, local branches, the role of women in the party, etc. Excellent genealogical charts of political party development from 1880 to 1950 are found in the appendixes, together with charts showing the organization of the major postwar parties, their party constitutions, and legal documents regarding the purge.

294 Monograph 12. *Development of Legislative Responsibilities, 1945–October 1950.* v.5, pt.3. 1952. 77, 80p.

This monograph deals with the 2 national legislatures: the imperial Diet which lasted until 1947 and the national Diet which replaced it in 1947. It explains why the imperial Diet had no power to terminate the war, how the purge severely affected the membership of the imperial Diet, and the manner in which legislative innovations including constitutional revision were enacted by the imperial Diet. It also discusses SCAP innovations in the national Diet system, in such areas as the relations between the two houses, the Diet's relations with the cabinet, committee systems, and the establishment of the new Diet powers of judicial investigation and filibustering. Appended are useful tables on party strength in both of the houses in the first 8 national Diets, the text of the Diet Law of 1947, and the rules of the 2 houses as of 1947.

295 Monograph 13. *Reorganization of Civil Service, 1945–1951.* v.5, pt.6. 1952. 92, 115p.

A useful account of the occupation reform of the Japanese civil service. It analyzes the role of Japan's new constitution in the reorganization process, the role of the U.S. Personnel Advisory Mission, and the functions of the newly created National Personnel Authority. In addition, it discusses recruitment, compensation systems, and position classification. The monograph is supplemented by statistical data on civil service personnel from 1932 to 1952, and by relevant documents, legal and otherwise, from both SCAP and Japanese sources.

296 Monograph 14. *Legal and Judicial Reform, 1945–December 1950.* v.5, pt.1. 1952. 117, 115p.

Gives an overall picture of the legal and judicial reforms that were undertaken during the occupation rule. Topics treated include SCAP's initial action for the removal of restraints on civil liberties, civil and criminal code revisions, and the legal protection of such liberties of the individual as petition, habeas corpus, and criminal indemnity. The monograph discusses the new judicial organization and new criteria for court officials, as well as the reforms related to public procurators and lawyers. It concludes with illustrations of court procedures. Appended are major SCAP directives concerned, letters exchanged between the Japanese prime minister and the supreme commander on this topic, and major laws dealing with civil and criminal procedures, court organization, and lawyers.

297 Monograph 15. *Freedom of the Press, 1945–January 1951.* v.5, pt.4. 1952. 194, 34p.

After briefly touching upon the effects of the war on newspaper and other publication industries, the monograph lays out the SCAP blueprint for freedom of the press and discusses the problems of the postwar publication industries. It considers both the problems of management, which was affected by radical reorganization and shortages of printing materials, and the problems of labor, which articulated its interests through new union organizations. Aspects also treated are the replacement of the Dōmei News Service by new agencies, relations between the national press and smaller local presses, publishers' efforts to improve the quality of their publications, the purge of important personnel, the removal of Communist employees, foreign publications authorized by SCAP for circulation in Japan, and the copyright law. The appendix includes SCAP directives, the Publishers' Code, the Canons of Journalism, and excellent tables on average newspaper circulation, newsprint allocation for newspapers, magazines and books, circulation of daily papers, circulation of the Big Three papers by prefectures, and foreign books authorized for publication in Japan.

298 Monograph 16. *Theatre and Motion Pictures, 1945–December 1951.* 1952. 64, 32p.

This report describes occupation reform programs in the theatrical and movie media. It discusses SCAP's purge of "authoritarian" elements of content, personnel, and legislation related to movies and the theater, as well as its efforts to encourage the production of new kinds of programs in such areas as documentaries, newsreels, and foreign films. It considers such management problems as shortages of material, financial difficulties, and labor-management relations. There are interesting tables on Japanese movie production from 1945 to 1950 and export figures for 1941 and the years from 1947 to 1950. In addition, it includes the Motion Picture Code of Ethics of 1949 and SCAP directives, one of which provides a list of some 240 films banned in 1945 as undemocratic.

299 Monograph 17. *Treatment of Foreign Nationals.* 1952. 165p., app.

A classified monograph which covers the following subjects: (1) the problems confronting SCAP with respect to foreign nationals and solutions devised to meet those problems; (2) SCAP responsibility for the repatriation of all imprisoned and interned citizens of Allied powers and the nationals of friendly powers; (3) SCAP responsibility for repatriating enemy nationals; (4) SCAP procedures for determining the citizenship of foreign nationals residing in Japan; (5) the establishment of occupation courts to provide for criminal and civil jurisdiction over members of the occupation forces and the placement of all other foreign nationals under the legal jurisdiction of the Japanese courts; (6) the preservation of law and order among foreign nationals by the Japanese government with the aid of SCAP; (7) the activities of SCAP in controlling all foreign nationals and foreign shipments entering or leaving Japan; and (8) the responsibility of SCAP for the welfare of foreign nationals electing not to be repatriated.

300 Monograph 18. *Public Welfare, 1945–December 1949.* 1952. 114, 131p.

This monograph discusses the efforts that the occupation authorities made to improve public welfare conditions in post-surrender years. The study reveals SCAP's activities in this field, which range from concern for repatriates, foreign nationals, disabled veterans and homeless children to providing emergency relief and housing, and organizing fund-raising campaigns for welfare purposes. Also covered are welfare-related legislative measures such as the Daily Life Security Law (1946), the Law for the Welfare of Disabled Persons (1949), the Child Welfare Law (1947), and the Disaster Relief Law (1947). Other concerns of SCAP were the development of adequate facilities for the training of social workers, and the encouragement of public and private relief agencies such as the Red Cross, CARE, LARA (Licensed Agency for Relief of Asia), and UNICEF. The monograph includes 11 tables in the text and 12 tables in the appendixes on the welfare issues mentioned above. Related SCAP directives and the texts of welfare laws are appended.

301 Monograph 19. *Public Health, September 1945–December 1950.* 1952. v.8. 233p., app.

This monograph gives a comprehensive picture of public health conditions in Japan in 1945 and occupation efforts to improve them. Among the topics covered are public health administration under the Ministry of Welfare, health centers, specialized disease control programs for smallpox, venereal disease, and tuberculosis, etc., sanitation and port quarantine services, hospital and clinic administration, dental services, pharmaceutical affairs, nursing and midwifery, veterinary services, laboratory services, nutrition surveys, public health education, and narcotics control regulations. Twenty-eight tables in the text and 16 tables in the appendixes provide statistical data on the subjects mentioned above, and related SCAP directives and Japanese laws are appended.

302 Monograph 20. *Social Security, 1945–March 1950.* v.8, pt.C. 1952. 106, 38p.

The establishment of an extensive social security system in postwar Japan was another of SCAP's reform programs. This monograph treats such subjects as the improvement of the medical insurance program and the provision of social insurance for public and private employees and the self-employed. Under these general headings are included such items as unemployment insurance, workmen's compensation, health insurance, seamen's insurance, the government pension system, government mutual aid associations, and the national health insurance system. The monograph also discusses the discontinuation of military pensions and the compensation of undemobilized personnel. Additional analyses of the subject matter are provided by 33 tables and the appended digests of insurance benefits.

303 Monograph 21. *Foreign Property Administration.* 1952. 199p., app.

A classified monograph. SCAP's notation indicates that the report covers both the presurrender and postsurrender conditions of foreign property in Japan, United Nations property, Axis property, and other foreign property confiscated or damaged during the war. The monograph also discusses SCAP's policies on the administration of such foreign properties in Japan.

304 Monograph 22. *Reparations.* 1952. 102p., app.

A classified document which treats occupation policies concerning Japan's payment of reparations and the removal of reparations in kind from specific industries.

305 Monograph 23. *Japanese Property Administration.* 1952. 83p., app.

A classified monograph which deals with SCAP activities in the administration of Japanese property with a view to liquidating property that belonged to ultranationalistic, terroristic, and secret, patriotic organizations. It also considers occupation efforts to establish control over the importation and exportation of goods, the regulation of foreign exchange and financial transactions, and the protection of Japanese-owned patents, trademarks, and copyrights.

306 Monograph 24. *Elimination of Zaibatsu Control, 1945–June 1950.* v.10, pt.A. 1952. 188, 223p.

This monograph describes SCAP programs for eliminating *zaibatsu* control and decentralizing economic power. It discusses the recommendations of the Edwards Mission and the evaluation of these recommendations by SCAP authorities. SCAP policies of economic democratization are then discussed through a consideration of the liquidation of holding companies, the surveillance of restricted concerns, the surveillance of *zaibatsu* entrepreneurs, the termination of family control, and the prohibition of the use of *zaibatsu* names and trademarks. Also referred to are the disposition of securities, and the dissolution of the East Asia Shipping Co. and of the Mitsui and Mitsubishi trading companies. Thirty tables, statistical and otherwise, are incorporated in the text and the appendixes. The appendixes also include the text of the Edwards Mission report (1946), the Yasuda plan for dissolution (1945), some 25 legal documents of SCAP and the Japanese government regarding the eradication of *zaibatsu* power, and a list of name changes by major *zaibatsu* concerns in 1945–50.

307 Monograph 25. *Deconcentration of Economic Power, 1945–December 1950*. v.10, pt.C. 1952. 89, 116p.

This monograph treats the occupation's attempt to eliminate operating holding companies, as distinct from the *zaibatsu*, which are pure holding companies. It gives an elaborate and useful account of how the Deconcentration Law of 1947 came to be enacted, how the deconcentration program had to be modified in 1948 when its shortcomings became manifest, how the Deconcentration Review Board was set up, and finally how the program was completed on the basis of the review board's recommendations. It gives detailed information on those companies such as the Japan Steel Co., whose designations for dissolution were cancelled. The appendixes contain detailed tables on the final reorganization of 13 operating holding companies, as well as the text of the Deconcentration Law, the public notices of the Holding Company Liquidation Public Commission, and the commission's fact-finding report on 11 companies.

308 Monograph 26. *Promotion of Fair Trade Practices, 1945–October 1951*. v.10, pt.D. 1952. 118, 135p.

This monograph describes another economic reform program of the occupation which attempted to foster new democratic institutions and practices to take the place of former monopolistic ones. The Anti-Monopoly Law of 1947 and the establishment of a Fair Trade Commission (FTC) are discussed, and an explanation is given of how the occupation tried through legislation to ensure fair trade practices, both domestic and international. The monograph gives an extensive account of the FTC's procedures, its supervision of patents and trademarks, and its power to enforce its decisions. It presents a generally favorable evaluation of the effect of the fair trade program upon Japan's economic recovery. The full texts of the Anti-Monopoly Law of 1947 and 8 other related laws are appended.

309 Monograph 27. *The Rural Land Reform, 1945–June 1951*. 1952. 128, 147p.

This monograph is concerned with one of the 2 basic agrarian reform plans that SCAP implemented. Defining SCAP's primary objectives with respect to rural land reform in the light of its perception of prewar land tenure problems, the paper evaluates the first and second land reform programs. The latter half is devoted to an analysis of administrative and procedural problems encountered by the second reform program, such as land commission elections, corrective and supplementary legislation for the functioning of land commissions, acquisition and transfer of land, tenant-landlord relationships, and adjustment to long-range requirements. The socioeconomic effects of the reform are also discussed. In the text and the appendixes are 22 tables and 2 charts which provide a general picture of the prereform tenure conditions and the changes effected by the SCAP program. The monograph also includes relevant SCAP directives, the Owner-Farmer Establishment Special Measures Law of 1946, and the Agricultural Land Adjustment Law of 1938 with postwar legislative amendments.

310 Monograph 28. *Development of the Trade Union Movement, 1945–June 1951.* v.11, pt.A. 1952. 119, 71p.

This report gives an overall picture of the occupation's labor program and the development of the Japanese labor movement. It explains that SCAP first acted to abolish proscriptive labor legislation, the patriotic labor organizations, and the labor-boss system, and then attempted to establish a new labor law and a Labor Ministry. The monograph describes the characteristics of the new unions and the subsequent development of national labor federations, and discusses the persistent reaction against Communist influence in the labor movement, the question of participation in international labor organizations, labor disputes, their effects on production, and the formation of employers' associations. The appendixes contain useful labor statistics from 1945 to 1951, the texts of the Labor Union Law and related documents, SCAP directives, and a selection of SCAP's letters on labor problems to the Japanese prime minister in 1948.

311 Monograph 29. *Working Conditions, 1945–September 1950.* v.11, pt.B. 1952. 132, 78p.

The improvement of labor conditions was another program of change undertaken by SCAP. This monograph provides a concise description of the immediate postwar manpower conditions, such as surplus labor, labor drift to rural areas, and low labor productivity. It discusses SCAP's efforts to eliminate undemocratic labor practices, encourage protective legislation, and recruit manpower into new industries. The Labor Standards Law, the Accident Compensation System, the Unemployment Insurance System, SCAP reforms in the wage structure, and the functions of the Ministry of Labor are comprehensively treated. The appendixes include 10 statistical tables on labor and industry mainly for the years 1945 through 1950, SCAP directives, the Labor Standards Law, and the Employment Security Law of 1947. Source materials consulted are cited at the outset of the report.

312 Monograph 30. *Agricultural Cooperatives, 1945–December 1950.* v.11, pt.D. 1952. 65, 56p.

The agricultural cooperative program, which was the second of SCAP's 2 basic agrarian reforms, is comprehensively treated in this monograph. It considers the Agricultural Cooperative Association Law which eliminated the prewar "authoritarian" agricultural associations; it further discusses problems of implementation involved in the cooperative movement, such as the establishment of a federation of cooperative associations, the management of its finances, and the regulation of its activities. Although viewing the last as one of the most formidable problems, nevertheless the monograph regards the overall operation of the program as successful, and concludes that the program has contributed to the democratic development of the rural community. The appendixes include 8 statistical tables on the cooperative program, and the texts of the Agriculture Cooperative Association Law, the Agriculture Organization Liquidation Law of 1947, and the Cabinet Order for Establishing the Standards for Financial Activities of Agricultural Cooperative Associations and Federations Thereof, which was enacted in 1950.

313 Monograph 31. *Education, 1945–September 1949.* v.11, pt.A. 1952. 320, 332p.

The first half of this monograph summarizes the history of the Japanese educational system prior to 1945, beginning with the establishment of the first school for Buddhist priests in the seventh century by Prince Shōtoku. The second half is devoted to educational developments from 1937 to 1949. After showing how the rise of the militarists and ultranationalists led to the breakdown of education, it presents a comprehensive coverage of the occupation's efforts to reform the educational system through elimination of ultranationalistic and Shinto elements, the purge, the creation of a teacher's union, the dispatch of the U.S. Education Mission to Japan, administrative decentralization, basic legislative reform, modification of textbooks, language reform, etc. Appended are 24 useful tables and charts on various aspects of Japanese education such as the school systems of 1937 and 1945, school conditions, student conditions, school curriculums, school finances, educational background of teachers, etc. Included also are the texts of SCAP directives and Japanese legal documents relevant to education.

314 Monograph 32. *Religion.* v.11, pt.D. 1952. 56, 81p.

This monograph presents the occupation objectives regarding religious affairs, the most significant of which were the establishment of religious freedom, the separation of church and state, and the creation of equality among religions. It discusses the effects of occupation policies upon Japanese society, namely, the return of state-owned land to the religious groups which had previously owned them, the change in the relationship between Shinto and the state, the administration of cemeteries, and the settlement of financial problems. The role of religion in education, social services, youth activities, new religions, and relations among the various religious sects are considered, as well as the postwar status of Buddhism, Christianity, and Shinto. The appendixes include the texts of the Religious Organizations Law of 1939, the Religious Corporations Ordinance of 1945, the Imperial Rescript of 1 January 1946, the Religious Juridical Persons Law of 1951, and relevant SCAP directives.

315 Monograph 33. *Radio Broadcasting, 1945–1951.* v.11, pt.G. 1952. 54, 106p.

The monograph deals with the occupation authorities' attempt to democratize Japanese society by means of reforming the Japan Broadcasting Corp. (NHK). A brief account of the changes that occurred in radio programs during the preoccupation days after Japan's surrender is followed by a description of the occupation's efforts to popularize programs concerning public affairs, to present SCAP information, and to introduce new radio programs. Other aspects covered are the enactment of radio and broadcasting legislation, the establishment of a Radio Regulatory Commission, and the reorganization of the Japan Broadcasting Corp. The appendixes include a table on NHK's record of earnings from 1935 to 1950, the NHK charter, SCAP directives related to this subject, and the full texts of the Radio Law, the Radio Broadcast Law, and the Radio Regulatory Commission Establishment Law, all promulgated in 1950.

316 Monograph 34. *Price and Distribution Stabilization: Non-Food Program.* 1952. 199p., app.

This classified monograph reflects SCAP attempts to implement programs facilitating Japan's economic restoration. Programs discussed pertain to price, subsidies, distribution, allocation, rationing, and incentive goods. Programs for the recovery and distribution of surplus war goods are also covered.

317 Monograph 35. *Price and Distribution Stabilization: Food Program.* 1952. 204p., app.

This classified monograph deals with food programs of the occupation and discusses the immediate postsurrender situation in Japan and SCAP policies with regard to food prices, subsidies, distribution of food, the allocation of various incentive goods, and rationing. The recovery and distribution of surplus war goods also are examined.

318 Monograph 36. *Agriculture, September 1945–December 1950.* 1952. 300, 108p.

This monograph is concerned with SCAP's program to increase agricultural productivity. It covers legislative and administrative aspects of land development and reclamation, protective measures against natural disasters, and improvements in the utilization of agricultural resources. It also discusses agricultural research on soils, fertilizers, seeds, insects, and diseases. Two other reform programs discussed are the insurance program for crops and livestock and the food collection program. Crop production statistics for 1946–49 are presented in the concluding chapter, and these statistics are discussed in terms of their impact upon the population. Twenty-eight tables and 19 figures in the text provide statistical information on Japan's agricultural production, and these tables are supplemented by 58 tables in the appendixes. The appendixes also contain the texts of the Agricultural Improvement Bureau Law and the Agricultural Improvement Promotion Law of 1948.

319 Monograph 37. *National Government Finance, 1945–March 1951.* v.3, pt.A. 1952. 175, 90p.

A monograph that "traces the major fiscal policies and programs of the Japanese Government as they affected budgetary relationships and the national economy" for the period from 1945 to 1951. Following an aggregate analysis of yearly budgets, the monograph discusses the reform of the budgetary system, whereby major expenditures were allocated for stabilization subsidies, public works, support of the occupation forces, reconversion finance, and national support of local government activities. In addition, considerable attention is paid to the reforms of the national tax structure and administration, as well as to national debt policies including the Dodge Plan. The text presents 14 charts and graphs on government expenditures for 1945–50, tax conditions, tax organizations, and the national debt, while the appendixes provide 18 statistical tables on various aspects of Japan's financial situation, relevant SCAP directives, the Finance Law of 1947, and the Ministry of Finance Establishment Law of 1947. Source materials are cited in the introductory section of the report.

320 Monograph 38. *Local Government Finance, 1945–March 1951.* v.13, pt.B. 1952. 70, 114p.

The reform of local government finance is treated under 3 categories: the reform of the local fiscal system, the budgetary reform of local governments, and the reform of local taxation. The first category concerns the reallocation of fiscal functions and the enactment of measures to strengthen the local revenue systems, while the second deals with major expenditures and revenue items. The last category is concerned with legal measures such as the Emergency Local Tax Law of 1946, the Local Tax Laws of 1947, 1948, and 1950, as well as the Shoup Mission's recommendations. Hokkaido, Tokyo, and Osaka are treated as prefectures, and all cities, towns, and villages as municipalities. Included in the text are charts and graphs on local government expenditures, revenues, the sources of taxes collected in 1945, and the distribution of tax revenues. Eleven useful statistical tables are appended, together with tax legislation, a relevant SCAP directive, and the text of the 1950 Civil Information and Education Section press conference on the Shoup Mission recommendations.

321 Monograph 39. *Money and Banking, 1945–June 1951.* v.13, pt.C. 1952. 71, 22p.

The banking system reform is the main subject of this monograph, which includes the establishment of the reconversion finance bank, the formation of the 3 principles of economic stabilization of 1948, the 9-point stabilization program of the same year, and the reform of the securities market. It deals with the problem of monetary inflation, the impact of the Korean War upon Japan's economy, and the results of the 1951 SCAP–Far Eastern Commission mission to Washington to promote Japanese-American economic cooperation. The monograph provides 3 charts concerning commercial imports and exports, bank loans, and the national money supply, as well as 15 tables that indicate the various types of banks, the relationship between the *zai-*

322 *batsu* and the banks, and money rates. SCAP directives related to these subjects are also appended.

322 Monograph 40. *Financial Reorganization of Corporate Enterprises.* vol.13, pt.D. 1952. 99, 57p.

This monograph concerns SCAP's efforts at the financial reorganization of corporate enterprises, in order to save these enterprises from bankruptcy and to recast their capital structures in financially sound terms. It discusses the Enterprise Reconstruction and Reorganization Law and the Special Composition Law of 1946, as well as SCAP standards for the complex reorganization of corporate enterprise. The report covers such topics as SCAP revisions in the accounting systems of the various enterprises, the formation of second companies from a parent company, and the revaluation of a company's fixed assets. Despite the many difficulties encountered in the financial reorganization program, the SCAP reforms are viewed as successful. Fifteen tables are included, covering the progress of the reorganization of special accounting companies, special losses, changes in capital structures, the creation of second companies, and the financial conditions of 650 corporations. The appendixes also present 2 tables on special losses, related legislation, and the imperial ordinances of 1946 concerned with the finances of corporate enterprises.

323 Monograph 41. *The Petroleum Industry, 1945–June 1951.* 1952. 100, 4p.

The monograph discusses how the petroleum industry was rebuilt and developed under the direction of SCAP in postsurrender years. The revival and renovation of domestic industry is given considerable space in this monograph, which covers the exploration for new reserves, advances in techniques of drilling and production, and improved management of the domestic petroleum industry. Other subjects covered are the limitations of the synthetic liquid fuel industry, the transportation and storage of crude oil, the development of the petroleum refining industry, and the importation of petroleum. Charts and graphs are inserted which give the location of petroleum reserves and refineries, and the organization of petroleum industries, while 12 tables provide statistical figures on postsurrender conditions of the Japanese petroleum industry. The appendixes include tables on petroleum sources for Japan proper between 1931 and 1950, as well as statistics on petroleum deliveries by the U.S. government to Japan.

324 Monograph 42. *Fisheries, 1945–1950.* v.14, pt.B. 1952. 204, 58p.

This monograph concerns SCAP's policy on Japanese fisheries. This policy was intended to maximize the production level while at the same time maintaining maximum conservation of fishing resources. After discussing changes in the authorized fishing areas in the postwar period and petroleum shortages at that time, the monograph treats production problems such as the allocation of petroleum and cordage, the building of vessels, and black market control of fisheries. Attention is also given to the whaling industry and the development of marine resources. In the last chapter, the monograph considers the democratization of the fishery rights system by the replacement of the former fisheries associations with fisheries cooperatives. Twenty-two charts and graphs and 10 tables provide graphical and statistical information on fishing areas, fisheries and whaling production, the allocation of petroleum, abaca, cotton, etc., and the organization of the Fisheries Agency. Appended are 19 tables of SCAP directives and the text of the Fisheries Cooperative Association Law. A few portions of the monograph are considered classified and omitted from the reprinting. Those portions are pages 24, 119–27, 137–39, and 156.

325 Monograph 43. *Forestry, September 1945–January 1951.* v.14, pt.C. 1952. 134, 128p.

The monograph explains SCAP efforts to improve the quality of forestry in Japan. It consists of 2 parts: Part 1 discusses the presurrender status of Japanese forestry with respect to prewar production and consumption patterns, wartime government control, conservation methods, types of ownership, and prewar administration of forest land. Part 2 covers postwar aspects of forestry, including occupation policies toward timber production and the utilization of resources, reorganization of distribution channels, the dissolution of the timber control companies, reforestation programs, forest insurance, and the Forest Industries Association Law. Included also are the reform of the Bureau of Forestry, and SCAP efforts to provide flood control through forest extension programs. Twelve charts and graphs are included. The appendixes comprise 23 tables, the texts of SCAP recommendations on forest tax reform and improved forest planting, and Japanese legislation on forestry.

326 Monograph 44. *Rehabilitation of the Non-Fuel Mining Industries.* 1952. 104p., app.

This monograph is classified. It pertains to postwar conditions in nonfuel mining industries, considering SCAP policy and programs and analyzing the variety of occupations, methods of production, governmental activity in mining, labor conditions in the mines, dissolution of mining monopolies, and the financial problems of mining.

327 Monograph 45. *Coal.* 1952. 72p., app.

This monograph is classified. SCAP notes, however, indicate it covers policies toward the rehabilitation of coal production, the procurement of critical supplies, and the reorganization of the coal mining industry. It also discusses the reduction in financial support by the Japanese government during the occupation period.

328 Monograph 46. *Expansion and Reorganization of the Electric Power and Gas Industries, 1945–March 1950.* v.15, pt.B. 1952. 86, 27p.

This monograph concerns SCAP policies regarding the development of the electric power and gas industries in post-war years. It discusses the rehabilitation of these industries, patterns of production and consumption, as well as methods of rationing, reorganization, and financial assistance. The discussion is supplemented by 12 charts and graphs and 5 tables in the text, and by 14 tables in the appendixes. Some statistical figures cover the period prior to 1945 but most involve the years after 1945.

329 Monograph 47. *The Heavy Industries, 1945–1950.* v.16, pt.A. 1952. 163, 47p.

SCAP policies and problems concerned with the postwar development of Japanese heavy industries are related in this monograph. Heavy industries covered are iron and steel, nonferrous metals, industrial machinery, shipbuilding, transportation machinery, chemicals, rubber, and cement. For each industry, the monograph analyzes such aspects as the production conditions of the immediate postwar period, rehabilitation difficulties, industrial involvement with reparations programs, and export trading conditions. There are some 45 useful charts, graphs, and tables in the text and the appendixes. The production figures include the period from 1930 to 1950.

330 Monograph 48. *Textile Industries, September 1945–December 1950.* v.16, pt.B. 1952. 146, 57p.

The rebuilding of the textile industries in Japan is the subject of this monograph and numerous aspects are discussed. Among them are SCAP's policy for reconversion to peacetime production; the effects of the reparations programs on the textile industry, anti-*zaibatsu*, and economic deconcentration programs of SCAP; price controls within the textile industries; and changes in textile labor conditions. The monograph discusses particular kinds of textile industries—silk, cotton, rayon, wool, and hard and bast fiber, as well as the processes of dyeing and finishing fabrics. It also analyzes the export figures on various textiles. Quarterly production of different textile products for 1946–50 is given in charts, while 32 tables refer to yearly production and import and export statistics for the period 1946–50. The appendixes provide an additional 27 statistical tables on working conditions and living accommodations provided by particular kinds of textile industries, as well as major textile production figures for 1930–50 and relevant SCAP directives.

331 Monograph 49. *The Light Industries, 1945–March 1951*. v.16, pt. C. 1952. 159, 17p.

The monograph discusses the rehabilitation of light industries in postwar Japan. Particular kinds of light industries are considered separately: synthetic dyestuffs, inedible fats and oils, industrial explosives, pottery, porcelain, sheet glass, refractories, processed foods, pulp, paper, bicycles, sewing machines, agricultural implements, watches, clocks, light electrical equipment, and optical instruments. The discussion of respective industries generally covers their situations at the beginning of the occupation and the effects of the reparations and deconcentration programs upon their output. The report also covers SCAP's elimination of the private control associations, production, exports, and imports. Statistics for the period 1945–50 are provided in the text, whereas similar data for 1930–50 are appended in 17 statistical tables.

332 Monograph 50. *Foreign Trade*. 1952. 265p., app.

This classified monograph discusses presurrender conditions of foreign trade in Japan, covering developments in foreign trade, commercial organizations, and the government controls of such organizations, the government's tariff policy and customs service, and the status of foreign trade at the end of the war. In addition, it discusses postsurrender trade conditions and describes SCAP measures enacted to solve problems connected with Japan's foreign trade. These measures include the promotion of private trade, the transfer of trade from government channels to private channels, the participation of foreign firms in trade activities, the reform of foreign trade enterprise, and the regulation of shipping and customs.

333 Monograph 51. *Land and Air Transportation*. 1952. 133p., app.

This monograph is also classified. SCAP notes indicate that the following topics are discussed: the abolition and subsequent reestablishment of civil aviation, the reorganization of the Ministry of Transportation, the improvement of state and private railways, labor conditions within the transportation industry, the implementation of programs for the rehabilitation of the prewar transportation plan, and the financial reform of land transportation.

334 Monograph 52. *Water Transportation, 1945–1951*. v.17, pt.C. 1952. 118, 25p.

The monograph reflects SCAP concern over water transportation in postwar years. It discusses the administration and operation of the merchant fleet and port facilities, SCAP regulation of domestic cargo bookings, and the entry and exit of foreign vessels. Other subjects treated are reform of water transportation enterprises, including the dissolution of the East Asiatic Steamship Co., the reorganization of harbor transportation companies, and the rehabilitation of the merchant marine and harbors, as well as transportation for repatriates and the utilization by SCAP of water transportation facilities. Charts and graphs provide statistics on ships sailing under SCAP-authorized flags, ships of the merchant fleet that were 100 gross tons or over, the number of Japanese merchant and exnaval ships used for the return of repatriates, and cargo carried in coastal trade. Twenty-nine tables are added in the text and the appendixes to substantiate the main report.

335 Monograph 53. *Communications, 1945–December 1950*. v.17, pt.D. 1952. 226, 40p.

Occupation policy with regard to the telecommunications system is discussed in this monograph. Among the topics covered are the rehabilitation of plants for the manufacture of communications equipment, the improvement of public telecommunications service, and the reinforcement of specialized telecommunications services such as radio systems for the police, the coastguard, fishermen, and those people concerned with railroads, air navigation, and meteorological work. SCAP's concern for the improvement of international communications and the international postal service is also discussed here. Thirty relevant figures and tables are provided, and related SCAP directives are appended.

336 Monograph 54. *Reorganization of Science and Technology in Japan, 1945–September 1950.* 1952. 112, 56p.

This report focuses on SCAP reforms of Japanese science and technology in the light of the U.S. demilitarization policy. It describes the U.S. occupation of laboratories of military significance such as those concerned with atomic energy, aviation, cyclotrons, or electronics, and also discusses the American investigation of wartime progress made by Japanese scientists. The monograph explains why the occupation authorities found it necessary to reorganize the administrative system of Japanese research organizations and discusses the formation of the Japan Association for Science Liaison, the Scientific and Technical Policy Comrades' Association, the Renewal Committee for Science Organization, and the Japan Science Council. It also indicates that aid in this endeavor was provided by the U.S. National Academy of Science. With SCAP's encouragement, technological reorganization was undertaken by the Japanese Ministry of Commerce and Industry. Set forth in the appendixes are SCAP directives, related laws, and the names of members of various Japanese committees and of members of the U.S. Scientific Mission to Japan.

337 Monograph 55. *Police and Public Safety, 1945–October 1951.* v.5, no.2. 1952. 160, 241p.

This monograph treats SCAP reforms of police administration. After introducing basic SCAP policies toward police reform such as the reorientation of police service and a SCAP directive on respect for the civil liberties of citizens, the monograph discusses special study commissions whose purpose was to plan for the decentralization of police administration. It also considers the significant features of the new Police Law of 1947 and related legislation, the effects of the new decentralized police service system, and subsequent tendencies away from decentralization. Other subjects covered are the training of policemen, the introduction of policewomen, police equipment, legal measures to prevent increased incidents of crime, the prevention of juvenile delinquency and civil disorder, the *oyabun-kobun* (patron-protégé) system, and law enforcement to improve traffic safety. The monograph also concerns maritime safety and fire prevention, discussing both legislative reinforcement and the improvement of training and equipment. The text and the appendixes together contain 17 tables, while the appendixes also present related SCAP directives, the texts of 23 laws relevant to police and public safety services, and the rules and regulations of the National Public Safety Commission.

SCAP REPORTS BY SUBORDINATE HEADQUARTERS

At the outset the principal commands serving under General MacArthur in the occupation of Japan were the Sixth and Eighth Armies. The former was deactivated in Japan at the end of 1945, leaving only the Eighth Army plus the supreme commander's headquarters in Tokyo to man the occupation. Both armies had extensive responsibilities for the inauguration and conduct of local military government activities within the boundaries of their commands. These responsibilities involved the establishment of military government (later civil affairs) teams throughout the country and the local supervision of and reporting on the imple-

338 The Occupation

mentation of SCAP policies at the prefectural, city, town, and village levels. The supreme commander's headquarters itself, which set overall policy for the occupation, did almost nothing directly with respect to the control or surveillance of the local consequences of national reform programs. Accordingly, the reports of these subordinate headquarters do something to fill the gap between high-level planning in Tokyo and grass roots implementation in the prefectures. In general, however, this aspect of the occupation is very poorly documented. The interested reader will find related materials in the sections on local government and administration (p.441) and on organization, staff, and functions (p.296).

338 Frank, Benis M., and Henry I. Shaw, Jr. *Victory and Occupation.* Washington, D.C.: Historical Branch, G-3 Div., Hdqters., U.S. Marine Corps, 1968. 945p. (History of U.S. Marine Corps. Operations in World War II, v.5)

The final work in a 5-volume history of Marine Corps operations during World War II, this volume covers the activities of the corps in the Okinawan invasion and the occupations of Japan and north China as well as the corps' postwar demobilization and reorganization programs. Part 4, entitled "Occupation of Japan," details the initial planning and operations of the corps in Japan, its deployment in Kyushu through December 1945, and its last months in Japan. The authors describe the landing of troops at Yokosuka (Tokyo Bay) on 30-31 August 1945 for the purpose of taking control of the important Japanese naval base there and their subsequent landings at Sasebo and Nagasaki in late September. The activities of the marines in disposing of all war materiel found within various military installations on Kyushu, in ensuring full Japanese compliance with the surrender terms, and in such varied activities as the apprehension of war criminals and the repatriation of Koreans and Chinese living in Japan are depicted. As the occupation wore on, the need for large numbers of combat troops steadily lessened and by early 1946 most of the marines stationed on Kyushu were withdrawn from Japan. Much of the authors' account is drawn from Shaw's earlier work, *The United States Marines in the Occupation of Japan* (1962) (no.338b).

Krueger, Walter. *From Down under to Nippon: The Story of the Sixth Army in World War II.* 1953. See no.906.

338a Rogers, Charles A. *Occupation Diary, First Cavalry Division.* Pomona, Calif.: First Cavalry Div. Assn., 1950. 58p.

338b Shaw, Henry I., Jr. *The United States Marines in the Occupation of Japan.* rev. ed. Washington, D.C.: Historical Branch, G-3 Div., Hdqters., U.S. Marine Corps, 1962. 29p. (Marine Corps Historical Reference pamphlet)

One in a series of regimental histories of the U.S. Marine Corps during World War II, this is a concise narrative of the major events which took place when Marine air and ground units were deployed to the main islands of Japan shortly after that country's surrender. The text is based on official records, interviews with participants in the operations described, and reliable secondary sources. Shaw describes in detail the landing of the marines at Yokosuka to seize the vital naval base there and at Sasebo and Nagasaki a few weeks later. He explains that the seizure of ports of entry in the Tokyo Bay area was regarded as a matter of top priority in view of the military's belief that the chances for a successful and bloodless occupation of Japan and the peaceful surrender of outlying garrisons would be greatly improved if Tokyo were occupied without incident. Furthermore, he points out that the marines involved in the Kyushu operation during the fall of 1945 supervised the execution of SCAP directives to the Japanese government instead of institinstituting direct military rule there. This action was in accordance with MacArthur's policy of using, but not supporting, that government. Throughout this study, Shaw refers to the various activities undertaken by the Marines in disposing vast stockpiles of military material, in reestablishing the Japanese civilian economy, and in supervising the repatriation of foreign civilians and prisoners of war as well as in handling the large numbers of Japanese who returned from overseas. For the most part, however, the author's focus is on the deployment of the Marines and not on their interaction with the Japanese. For a related study which is based in part on the present work, see Benis M. Frank and Henry I. Shaw's *Victory and Occupation* (1968) (no.338).

339 U.S. Army. Eighth Army. *Collection of Messages*. Jan. 1947–Apr. 1951. Record Group 9. MacArthur Memorial, Bureau of Archives, Norfolk, Va. 15 folders.

The majority of these unclassified radiograms were sent from the Eighth Army to MacArthur as commander in chief of the Allied forces in the Pacific and some few to him as supreme commander for the Allied powers. There are also some cables from the Far East Command to the Eighth Army. Messages are filed chronologically and are generally of 2 types. The first, occurring largely in 1947 and early 1948, concern army personnel matters—transfers, arrivals, departures, court martial cases, etc. The second, far more numerous, concern Eighth Army activities in occupied Japan. They include brief reports on Japanese war criminals, repatriation activities, election irregularities noted in 1947, the reception and control of commercial entrants to Japan, Japanese–Korean antagonism, and the activities of Koreans in Japan. The subjects which receive the most attention are reports regarding strikes by Japanese workers, labor union demonstrations and elections, and reports on Communist activities in the labor unions. The final messages relate more to the worsening Korean situation than to the occupation of Japan.

———. ———. ———. Hdqters. *Eighth Army Military Government Organization and Activities*. 1947. See no. 928.

———. ———. ———. ———. *Operational Directives*. 1945–49. See no. 929.

340 ———. ———. ———. ———. Military Government Section. *Military Government Bulletin*. Mimeographed. Tokyo: June 1948–June 1949. irregular.

This mimeographed serial was issued sporadically depending upon material available and need for an issue at a particular time. Usually issues appear monthly and range from 40 to 60 pages each. The series was nondirective in nature and was created "as a means for providing an informal source of information and exchange of ideas of interest to military government personnel." Nevertheless, it presents considerable information about the structure and operations of the military government teams in Japan. Information is arranged under several major categories. Under civil education, various programs such as in-service teacher training and the Japanese Girl Scout program are considered, while under civil information are included the activities and programs of the Civil Information and Education Regional Information Centers. The category of economics includes discussion of recent developments in agriculture, food distribution, mining, forestry and petroleum, whereas the last 4 general units—finance and civil property, legal and government, public health, and public welfare—pertain to the activities of local military government teams in these areas. The bulletin provides an overall picture of military government team activity on the prefectural and local level, with specific activities of particular teams frequently cited by way of illustration.

This serial is available at the Washington National Records Center, Suitland, Maryland.

341 ———. ———. ———. Historical Section. *The Amphibious Eighth*. Tokyo: 1947? 127p.

An illustrated record of the U.S. Eighth Army. The book begins with 7 September 1944 when the Eighth Army, which had been activated on 10 June 1944 at Memphis, Tennessee, came to Hollandia, New Guinea under the command of Lieutenant General Robert L. Eichelberger. It covers the fighting against the Japanese in the Philippines and ends in late 1947, the end of the second year of their occupation of Japan. It presents short biographies and pictures of all leading officers including generals, their commanders, chiefs of staff, and wartime and peacetime section chiefs. It also describes the army's operations in New Guinea and the Philippines, its composition, its responsibilities in occupied Japan, and the distribution of responsibilities among the Eighth Army, "I" Corps, IX Corps, and the British Commonwealth Occupation Force.

342 ———. ———. ———. "I" Corps. *Military Government in "I" Corps: Honshu and Kyushu, Japan.* n.p.: The Corps, 21 July 1948. 40p.

The U.S. Army's "I" Corps, which was under the Eighth Army, was in charge of 3 regional military government teams. These 3 regional teams coordinated 12 prefectural military government teams in central Honshu and all 7 of the prefectural teams in Kyushu. This short publication was designed primarily for the orientation of visitors and newly assigned personnel, and presents a summary of the accomplishments of "I" Corps in various aspects of its work. These accomplishments include economic and political reforms, land reform, public health and welfare improvements, and civil education. The report describes the nature of the problems involved and the progress made by SCAP between August 1945 and April 1948. Accounts are often given with breakdowns according to prefecture.

———. ———. Far East Command. *Japan: Friend and Ally.* 1952. *See* no. 2497.

343 ———. ———. Far East Command. Military History Officer. *The Far East Command, 1 January 1947–30 June 1957.* 30 June 1957. Record Group 6, Box 9. MacArthur Memorial, Bureau of Archives, Norfolk, Va. 75p.

This overall summary of the aims, activities, and accomplishments of the Far East Command from its inception to January 1947 to its discontinuation 10 years later provides an outline of the occupation of Japan and places U.S. policy in Japan in the larger context of overall Far Eastern policy. There is general discussion of conditions in Japan and Korea at the conclusion of the war followed by an account of the establishment of the Far East Command and a description of its work in civil affairs and military government in occupied Japan, Korea, and the Ryukyus. The bulk of the report deals with the Korean conflict, but these sections also contain information on the situation in Japan and a description of the effects of the Korean War on that country. The concluding sections discuss the issue of the Far East Command's security as well as changes in its command and organization and offer a résumé of its accomplishments. There is also a description of successive commanders in chief, headquarters, and major commands within the Far East Command plus a chronology of important events.

344 ———. ———. 93d Military Government Co. *Quarterly Digest of 93d Military Government Co. Activities, Kyushu, Japan, Jan.–Mar. 1946.* Kumamoto, Japan: 1946. iii, 400, 14p.

The 93d Military Government Company was attached to the U.S. Army's "I" Corps on 31 December 1945, and, effective 20 January 1946, was assigned to Kumamoto and Oita prefectures to assist the occupation programs. On 2 March 1946, the company's assigned control areas were changed to Kumamoto and Kagoshima prefectures. This report is a weekly summary of the company's activities in the first 3 months of 1946 in these prefectures. It is helpful in understanding what went on at prefectural levels during the occupation period. The report gives a fairly detailed account of the company's administrative and organizational structure and changes therein. It provides a list of personnel involved, as well as weekly prefectural progress reports in the areas of public health, education, natural resources, repatriation, labor, housing, prices, and industries. Statistical information is given in connection with various surveys such as local elections, civilian communicable disease, relief supply recipients, educational institutions, fishing boats in operation and the amounts of fish caught, and labor conditions. The report is supplemented with 14 pages of illustrations showing scenic views of Kyushu as well as military government officers at work. While the data are useful, the editing is poor.

345 ———. ———. Sixth Army. *Report of the Occupation of Japan: Sixth U.S. Army, 2 September 1945–30 November 1945.* Yokohama? Bunjudō 8th U.S. Army Printing Plant, n.d. 99p.

346 ———. ———. ———. Hdqters. Sixth Information and Historical Service. *Sixth Army Occupation of Japan.* Typescript. 1946. 102p., maps, illus.

The role of the Sixth Army in the concluding months of the war and the first crucial months of the occupation of Japan is recounted in this report, prepared by Commanding General Walter Krueger. The account of the final months of fighting provides interesting insight into the nature and extent of the preparation to invade Japan but the major portion concerns Sixth Army activities in Kyushu after the commencement of the occupation. Following a description of the forces of the Sixth Army assigned to the occupation (the "I" Corps, "X" Corps, and the Fifth Marine Amphibious Corps) the author discusses the responsibilities of these occupying troops in the 4-fold job of (1) maintaining law and order, (2) destroying enemy equipment, (3) demobilizing the enemy's armed forces, and (4) establishing a peaceful and workable economy for the Japanese people. There are accounts of the attitudes of the Japanese civilian population toward the occupying forces, as well as a discussion of initial difficulties to be overcome with respect to demobilization, disarmament, and repatriation. The educational and recreational facilities provided for the troops are also briefly described. The report concludes with the transfer of the Sixth Army command on 31 December 1945 and its inactivation in Japan. Maps and illustrations provide information on the planned assault on Japan, strategic moves of armed forces in the Pacific area, current progress of the demobilization effort, etc.

Available at the Reference Branch, Office of the Chief of Military History, Washington, D.C.

SCAP PRESS RELEASES AND CONFERENCES

General MacArthur and his staff were very much interested in their public relations. Although General MacArthur himself held but a single press conference during his sixty-seven months in Tokyo, he and his staff were keenly concerned about the extent and quality of their press coverage. In pursuance of this interest the supreme commander himself made frequent statements for publication while highly placed members of his staff often held press conferences. The resulting output of official viewpoints was very sizeable and covered an enormous variety of topics. The following entries may be supplemented by reference to the "Documentary Materials" section of the journal *Contemporary Japan* (no.34) which throughout the occupation routinely carried a number of the more important press releases of this sort.

347 Supreme Commander for the Allied Powers. Civil Information and Education Section. *Press Conferences.* Tokyo: SCAP, Dec. 1945–Mar. 1947. 4 folders.

This collection includes typewritten copies and mimeographed versions of press releases and press conferences held by various officials associated with SCAP, particularly the Civil Information and Education Section, the Economic and Scientific Section, the Public Health and Welfare Section, and the International Military Tribunal for the Far East. While some entries provide the entire text of the conference or statement, the majority are Civil Information and Education Section summaries. Topics cover the spectrum of SCAP activities in Japan and include the labor situation, educational reform, measures of public safety, price control and rationing, elections, current political developments, land reform, and the deconcentration program. There are also a few entries which concern press conferences held by foreign officials in Japan, e.g., the commander-in-chief of the British Pacific fleet.

Available at the Washington National Records Center, Suitland, Maryland.

348 ———. Public Information Office. *Press Releases.* 1945–49. Record Group 5, Box 105. MacArthur Memorial, Bureau of Archives, Norfolk, Va. 1 folder.

Miscellaneous press releases from SCAP headquarters and from the Army News Service in Washington are chronologically arranged in this folder along with several news releases by the Okayama daily English news service. The collection includes a very small percentage of SCAP press statements, but topics treated relate to MacArthur's statements regarding the progress of the occupation, the eventual reduction of its size, New Year's and surrender anniversary messages, the nature of the draft constitution of Japan, the restoration of trade between Japan and foreign countries to private hands, political decisions of the Far Eastern Commission, and future military commitments of the United States to Japan.

SCAP ANALYSES AND TRANSLATIONS OF THE JAPANESE PRESS

The most detailed and continuous—although not necessarily the best informed—commentary on the occupation appeared, of course, in the Japanese press. For some years the plans, pronouncements, and activities of the occupation and its leaders made front-page news throughout the country. The occupationaires, being extremely interested in the nature of Japanese reactions to their initiatives and programs, found the Japanese daily and periodical press one of their most convenient means of assessing such responses. Since very few of them could read Japanese, they speedily arranged for the regular translation into English of major sections of the vernacular press as well as for informed commentaries on and analyses of its significance. These translations were assembled in summarized abstracts and widely distributed in SCAP offices. These files today constitute a major source of detailed information in English about the programs, personalities, and plans of the occupation and about Japanese reactions thereto. The reader is also referred to the section on mass media and censorship (p.678).

349 Supreme Commander for the Allied Powers. Allied Translator and Interpreter Section. *Press Analysis.* Tokyo: SCAP, Oct. 1945–Oct. 1948. nos.1–915.

The Media Analysis Division of the Allied Translator and Interpreter Section issued this report starting early in the occupation. It provides the section's analysis of important editorials and news articles appearing in Japanese and English-language newspapers published in Tokyo on such issues as revision of the constitution, reform of education, dissolution of the *zaibatsu*, progress of the occupation, and developments in political parties. Each issue begins with a summation of current trends in Tokyo's leading newspapers, i.e., their political and social positions, their economic stance, and their degree of dependence or independence and particular newspapers' positions are discussed and sometimes quoted. Although the *Press Analysis* is similar in many ways to the Allied Translator and Interpreter Section's *Press Translations and Summaries* (no.351) and the *Early Morning Report,* it differs insofar as it generally notes and analyzes only dominant notes in Tokyo's daily press, whereas the others are intended to provide a synopsis of all significant news—not only in Tokyo, but in Japan as a whole. The Library of Congress collection is not complete but is missing numbers 61, 364–435, 486–516, 659–90, and 815–20.

350 ———. ———. *Press Translations.* Tokyo: SCAP, 5 Nov. 1945–22 Apr. 1946.

For a description of this series, see SCAP's *Press Translations and Summaries: Japan* (no.351).

351 ———. ———. *Press Translations and Summaries: Japan.* Tokyo: SCAP, 5 Nov. 1945–22 Aug. 1949.

This series consists primarily of full translations or summaries of articles in the Japanese-language daily press and other periodicals, both national and provincial. Approximately 1,500 publications were scanned each month "for material of possible interest to the Occupation." The periodicals surveyed included the major Tokyo dailies, such as *Asahi Shimbun, Mainichi Shimbun, Yomiuri Hōchi, Jiji Shimpo,* and *Tōkyō Shimbun,* the leftist dailies *Mimpō* and *Akahata,* other major-city dailies, a host of prefectural papers, and a broad range of journals, reviews, and popular magazines such as *Keizai, Chūō Kōron, Genron, Chijo, Seinen Bunka, Sobieto Bunka, Minshu Hyōron, Sekai Hyōron, Hataraku Fujin, Asahi Hyōron,* and many others. Throughout the series, each translation or summary of an article or editorial includes the source, author, and date of original publication in Japanese. The format changes considerably during the years of publication, but the main body of translated material is consistently subdivided into 4 rough topical categories, with items classified under the following headings:

1. *Economic.* This category includes news items and articles dealing with economic matters, broadly defined. A good deal of statistical material is presented in full, including government budget figures, data on land ownership and reform programs, war costs and reparations, banking and finance, and the general state of the postwar economy, as well as more specific information on the condition and recovery of various industries. Items on the implementation of SCAP economic directives and the Japanese reaction to them are translated or summarized, as are items on wage and salary levels, employment rates, consumer prices and the black market, local government spending, etc. For a short time (5 Nov.–22 Nov. 1945) there was a separate finance series, but this was merged with the economic series.

2. *Political.* This section provides ample coverage of the passage of the Shōwa Constitution, with full translations of early drafts and revisions, as well as the full texts, draft and final, of selected pieces of important legislation. Government and party reorganization, SCAP purges, local and national elections (often including biographical material on candidates), the growing influence of labor and leftist parties, the political effects of SCAP innovations and reforms, and public opinion surveys are among other areas treated.

3. *Social.* This tends to be a catchall category, but includes interesting information on living standards, labor movements, housing problems, changing social patterns, the "family sys-

tem," and, of course, the social effects of SCAP-initiated reforms.

4. *Editorial*. This final section includes summaries and full translations of editorial comment on all areas of Japanese society and occupation policy, taken from newspapers and journals across the political spectrum.

The format of the *Press Translations* series changes enough so that it may be slightly confusing. Through 5 April 1946, under the overall title *Press Translations*, the contents are arranged in separate series under the subtitles, economic, political, social, and editorial series. Reports consisting of up to 6 or 7 "items" (usually unrelated) are numbered consecutively in each separate topical series, and each report is also given a number in an overall Press Translations series. The items themselves range in length from a few lines to several pages.

From 5 April to 22 April 1946 (roll 11 of the microfilm edition), still under the title *Press Translations*, there was published daily (except Sunday) a single folder bringing together the day's translations and summaries, arranged and numbered according to their respective series. In addition, there is a title page listing significant items among those translated, and a 1- or 2-page ATIS daily commentary summarizing and commenting on significant developments reported in the translations. The items included in each daily folder may be dated from a day to a week or more earlier than the folder itself.

After 22 April 1946, the series as a whole is titled *Press Translations and Summaries: Japan*. The daily folders are henceforth numbered in their own series, but the contents of each folder is the same as before. For a time a monthly summary of significant developments was published toward the end of each month but this was soon dropped. Beginning with no.104 (4 Sept. 1946) there was included an early morning edition (title varies), which consisted of items of immediate interest from the day's Tokyo newspapers. A weekend edition, published on Monday, was added as well giving items from Sunday's and Monday's Tokyo papers. A press analysis was incorporated in the daily folders after no. 759 (1 Nov. 1948), apparently, like the morning edition, originally published in a separate, numbered series (no.349), and now merged with this publication. Hereafter there also was published every Tuesday, beginning 2 Nov. 1948 (no. 760), an expanded 3-part analysis consisting of the usual daily press analysis, a prefectural press analysis, and a publications analysis. The last two were taken over from two Civil Information and Education series of the same name (nos. 352 and 353), and focus on 1 or 2 major topics or problems treated in a number of Japanese publications in the preceding months.

This series is available on 75 rolls of microfilm from the National Archives. Less complete runs are available at the McKeldin Library of the University of Maryland (no.1 of 23 Apr. 1946 through no.683 of 4 Aug. 1948 with some 60 numbers missing) and the Library of Congress (no.1 through no.1009 of 9 Aug. 1949, but with a large number of missing issues).

352 ———. ———. *Prefectural Press Analysis*. Tokyo: SCAP, 20 Feb. 1946– Nov. 1948. nos.1–283. irregular.

Irregularly issued every 3 or 4 days by the Analysis and Research Division of the Civil Information and Education Section, this publication is generally 3 or 4 pages in length and performs the same task at the prefectural level that the *Press Analysis* (no.349) performs for the Tokyo area. The contents of the news articles and editorials appearing in local papers throughout Japan are described and analyzed and often there is an attempt to relate this information to larger occupation activities and objectives. Subjects for attention reflect the wide scope of SCAP's interests and concern many aspects of Japan's political, social, and economic life that received significant attention in the press. Frequently, the reports provide English translations from the local press but the bulk of the material relates more to SCAP's attitude toward the news than to the editorials or articles themselves.

Available from the Army Library, the Pentagon, Washington, D.C.

353 ———. ———. *Publications Analysis.* Tokyo: SCAP, 26 Dec. 1945–29 Oct. 1948. nos. 1–218. irregular.

Concentrating on the contents of magazine articles appearing in Japan, this series of Civil Information and Education Section reports was issued irregularly—sometimes daily and sometimes once every 4 to 6 days. Early issues concentrate on special reports on particularly important magazines or those with a large circulation, describing the nature of the journal and the positions of its editors on various topics. Later, with the rapid increase in the number of publications, the format of the report changed. One or more topics were emphasized in each issue and the positions of several important periodicals on the topic were noted. Topics analyzed run the gamut of SCAP concerns including current politics, the agricultural reform program, domestic industries, the current fiscal situation, labor unions, postwar social and legal problems, and Japanese reaction to the occupation. Magazines analyzed initially are generally women's or family magazines but in later years a change may be noted, with an increase in the number of business and economic periodicals as well as political and social journals. The writers strive to outline as objectively as possible the ideas and attitudes of Japanese writers and publishers covered.

Available at the Library of Congress, Washington, D.C.

———. Civil Information and Education Section. Public Opinion and Sociological Research Div. *Current Japanese Public Opinion Surveys.* 1948–49. See no. 2303.

SCAP ADMINISTRATIVE DIRECTIVES TO THE JAPANESE GOVERNMENT

The basic mission of the supreme commander and his headquarters was to make or perfect plans for the achievement of the principal goals of the occupation and to supervise the execution of these plans by the Japanese government. In a formal sense such plans were transmitted to the Japanese government in the shape of administrative directives called SCAPINs. A separate category of such directives applying to housekeeping arrangements within SCAP or to directives supplementary to a basic SCAPIN were known as SCAPIN-As. With the passage of time this formal and relatively public mode of communicating with the Japanese government was superseded by more cloistered devices such as private meetings and even telephone conversations.

354 Supreme Commander for the Allied Powers. *Catalog of Administrative Directives (SCAPIN-A's) to the Japanese Government.* Tokyo: SCAP, 1947–51. 4v.

A collection which summarizes the texts of SCAP's Administrative directives nos. 1 (3 Sept. 1945) through 7480 (26 Nov. 1951). Volume 1 includes SCAPIN-A's nos. 1 (3 Sept. 1945) through 2000 (15 Aug. 1946); volume 2, SCAPIN-A's nos. 2001 (15 Aug. 1946) through 4000 (23 June 1947); volume 3, SCAPIN-A's nos. 4001 (23 June 1947) through 6000 (11 Sept. 1948); and volume 4, SCAPIN-A's nos. 6001 (11 Sept. 1948) through 7480 (26 Nov. 1951).

355 ———. *Catalog of Directives to the Japanese Government.* Tokyo: SCAP, 1952. 2v.

A collection which lists all of the SCAP directives (SCAPINs) to the Japanese government issued during the occupation period, and provides a brief description of their contents. Volume 1 covers SCAPINs nos.1 (2 Sept. 1945) through 2159 (21 June 1951), and volume 2 covers SCAPINs nos.2160 (6 June 1951) through 2204 (26 April 1952). SCAPINs are arranged in numerical order, and directives for revision and rescission of SCAPINs are inserted immediately after the original SCAPIN number, thus making such changes of status easier to follow. Each directive is shown with its official title, date of issuance, and the particular section of SCAP involved. The list contains cross-references to related SCAPINs, SCAPIN-As, and SCAPINs that rescind the original directive.

356 ———. *Directives of the Supreme Commander for the Allied Powers, 1945–1947*. Tokyo: Nippon Times, n.d.

A collection of directives issued to the Japanese government by SCAP up to the end of 1947. It is classified in some 32 general categories such as political, economic, press and information, and welfare. The collection is poorly edited. Directives are arranged unsystematically and many pages are missing. In the edition covering 1945 the directives are prefaced by the texts of major documents such as the Cairo Declaration, the Potsdam Declaration, the Instrument of Surrender, and the U.S. Initial Post-Surrender Policy for Japan. No SCAPIN numbers are given but only AG (Adjutant General's Section) numbers are provided. In addition to the collection of directives issued in 1945 the series includes the following SCAP publications published in Tokyo by the Nippon Times: *Directives of the Supreme Commander for the Allied Powers, January–June 1946* 280p., *Directives of the Supreme Commander for the Allied Powers, July–December 1946* 168p., *Directives of the Supreme Commander for the Allied Powers, January–June 1947* 79p., and *Directives of the Supreme Commander for the Allied Powers, July–December 1947* 96p.

357 ———. *Index of Directives to the Japanese Government*. Tokyo: SCAP, 1950. ii, 51p.

An index of SCAPINs nos.1 (2 Sept. 1945) through 2133 (15 Dec. 1950) plus some 390 directives for rescissions of earlier directives. The index is arranged by subject, and subjects are itemized in considerable detail. Agriculture, for example, is classified into census, finance, production implements, land, organizations, production, products, subsidies, taxation, and use of air fields. Within such classifications each heading is further subdivided; for instance, under land, there are subheadings on ownership, reform, and tenancy.

Available on microfilm from the National Archives, Washington, D.C.

358 ———. *SCAP Directives to the Imperial Japanese Government*. Tokyo: SCAP, n.d. 7v.

A collection of SCAPIN texts extending only from SCAPIN no.1 (2 Sept. 1945) to SCAPIN no.666 (28 Jan. 1946). Directives are listed consecutively and each volume contains 100 SCAPINs, with the exception of the final volume which contains SCAPINs nos.601 to 666.

359 ———. *SCAP Directives to the Imperial Japanese Government*. Tokyo: SCAP, 1945–52.

A collection of the texts of the entire set of SCAPINs, nos.1 (2 Sept. 1945) to 2204 (26 Apr. 1952), including attached documents. From SCAPIN no. 1693/1 (29 May 1947) on, the directives were addressed to "the Japanese Government" rather than to "the Imperial Japanese Government," and the title was correspondingly changed. This carefully compiled collection is the most authoritative publication of SCAPIN texts. SCAPINs, or SCAP instructions, are those directives issued in written form during the occupation period to implement SCAP policies. They were issued in most cases in the name of the adjutant general or assistant adjutant general, on behalf of the supreme commander, and they originated in different SCAP offices such as the Government Section or the Economic and Scientific Section. Some of the SCAPINs are general in scope, but the majority deal with very specific aspects of the occupation policy, discussing procedures and time limits for particular projects. They also include supporting documents such as reports and memorandums. Subject matter includes the surrender and disarmament of the Japanese armed forces (SCAPIN no.1), the purge (SCAPINs nos.93, 115, 548, etc.), the dissolution of the *zaibatsu* (SCAPINs nos.162, 244, 1363, etc.), rural land reform (SCAPINs nos.411, 1855), educational reforms (SCAPIN no.178), and the separation of state and religion (SCAPIN no.448). Some directives instruct the Japanese government to provide SCAP with information on certain subjects, while others revise or rescind earlier directives.

SCAPINs are to be distinguished from SCAPIN-As, or administrative directives of SCAP, which were issued primarily for SCAP to meet the technical needs of its administration. Besides the procurement of space and facilities for SCAP use, SCAPIN-As were also issued to supplement SCAPINs, to clarify ambiguous aspects of SCAPINs, and to deal with questions and requests of the Japanese government. The first date of issue of both SCAPINs and SCAPIN-As was 2 September 1945, whereas the last SCAPIN, no.2204, was issued on 26 April 1952, and the last SCAPIN-A, no. 7480-A, appeared on 26 November 1951. Numerous SCAPINs and SCAPIN-As were issued in the early years of the occupation, from 1945 through 1947, and the numbers greatly decreased from 1948 through 1952.

Available on 6 rolls of microfilm from the National Archives, Washington, D.C.

360 ———. *SCAPINs*. Tokyo: SCAP, 1952. xi, 528p.

A collection of the texts of 900 SCAPINs relating to the Economic and Scientific Section of SCAP. A very useful work which covers almost the entire period of the occupation, from 4 September 1945 to 8 March 1952. The table of contents arranges SCAPINs in numerical order, inserts directives for rescissions immediately after the original numbers, and also indicates the subject matter of each instruction and its date of issuance.

361 ———. *Supplement to Index of Directives to the Japanese Government*. Tokyo: SCAP, 31 May 1948. Record Group 5, Box 69. MacArthur Memorial, Bureau of Archives, Norfolk, Va. 23p.

This index of SCAPINs nos.1550–1901 inclusive supplements the *Index of Supreme Commander to the Allied Powers Directives to the Japanese Government* (not included in this bibliography) for SCAPINs nos.1 through 1549 of 28 February 1947. Pages 1 through 20 of the supplement contain the actual index and the final 3 pages correlate SCAPIN numbers with adjutant general's file numbers. SCAPINs rescinding earlier numbers are included although not indicated in the index as rescissions. The index is arranged alphabetically according to the subject of the directive.

362 ———. *Supplement to Index of Directives to the Japanese Government*. Mimeographed. Tokyo: SCAP, 30 Sept. 1949. Record Group 5, Box 69. MacArthur Memorial, Bureau of Archives, Norfolk, Va. 10p.

SCAPINs nos.1954–2048 inclusive are indexed in this mimeographed booklet which supplements the *Index of Supreme Commander for the Allied Powers Directives to the Japanese Government* (not included in this bibliography) for SCAPINs nos.1 through 1953 of 31 December 1948. Topics are arranged in alphabetical order and SCAPINs rescinding earlier numbers are included in the listing.

363 ———. *Supplement to Index of Directives to the Japanese Government*. Tokyo: SCAP, 13 July 1950. Record Group 5, Box 69. MacArthur Memorial, Bureau of Archives, Norfolk, Va. 4p.

364 The Occupation

This index supplements the *Index of the Supreme Commander for the Allied Powers Directives to the Japanese Government* (not included in this bibliography) for SCAPINs nos.1 (2 Sept. 1945) through 2069 (31 Dec. 1949) and covers SCAPINs nos.2070 (1 Jan. 1950) through 2111 (30 June 1950) inclusive. Some of the SCAPINs concerned rescind earlier ones. Topics are arranged in alphabetical order according to subject.

364 ———. *Supplement to Index of Directives to the Japanese Government.* Tokyo: SCAP, 1951. 3p.

An index of SCAPINs nos.2134 (4 Jan. 1951) through 2159 (21 June 1951), plus 19 directives for rescissions, which constitutes a supplement to SCAP's earlier publication, *Index of Directives to the Japanese Government* (no.357), published in December 1950. Not included are SCAPINs nos.2160 (6 June 1951) through 2204 (26 Apr. 1952) for which reference should be made to SCAP, *Catalog of Directives to the Japanese Government*, volume 2 (no.355). The index is arranged by subject.

This index is available on microfilm from the National Archives, Washington, D.C.

GENERAL COLLECTIONS OF OFFICIAL DOCUMENTS

An official operation of the scale and importance of the Allied occupation of Japan is inevitably the product of a great many prior governmental decisions, both domestic and international in nature. It also generates many more such decisions in the course of its activities, including its termination. All such decisions are embodied in documents of greater or lesser degrees of formality and public status. We are fortunate where the occupation of Japan is concerned in having a number of excellent collections of the relevant documentation.

In addition to the items noted below, the interested reader is referred to the section including a general collection of official documents, speeches, etc., on p.108, to the excellent selection of such documents in the second volume of the *Political Reorientation of Japan* (1949) (no.279), and to the "Documentary Materials" section of the journal *Contemporary Japan* (no.34). The fifty-five monographs comprising the *History of Non-Military Activities of the Occupation of Japan* (1952) (nos.283–337) also frequently have very useful documentary appendixes. Needless to say, all relevant volumes of the Foreign Relations of the United States series (nos.197–203b) are similarly useful.

365 Dutt, Vidya Prakash, ed. *East Asia: China, Korea, Japan, 1947–50.* Bombay: Oxford Univ. Pr., 1958. vii, 747p. (Indian Council of World Affairs, Delhi. Select Documents on Asian Affairs)

The second volume in a series of Select Documents on Asian Affairs prepared by the Indian Council of World Affairs. It contains political, economic, and diplomatic documents of major significance for the 3 East Asian countries which appeared largely between 1947 and 1950. The section on Japan, pages 455 to 728, has 38 documents grouped in 6 categories: (1) constitutional developments; (2) political "democratization"; (3) economic "democratization"; (4) political developments; (5) economic stabilization; and (6) selected speeches and messages of General MacArthur. Included are the full texts of the Constitution of Japan, the Diet Law, the Police Law, the Labor Standard Law, MacArthur's letter dated 24 July 1948 to Prime

Minister Ashida concerning revision of the National Public Service Law, the Soviet statement on Japanese industry issued 23 September 1948, several policy statements by Prime Ministers Katayama and Yoshida, SCAP programs and policies on Japanese economic stabilization, and the Shoup Tax Mission report on taxation reforms. This volume is a useful collection of documents regarding the Allied occupation of Japan.

366 Japan. Ministry of Foreign Affairs. Special Records Div. *Documents Concerning the Allied Occupation and Control of Japan.* Tokyo: Tōyō Keizai Shimpōsha, 1949–51. 6v.

A collection of important Allied and Japanese documents pertaining to the Allied occupation and control of Japan. The first of the 6 volumes gives both English and Japanese texts while the remaining ones have no corresponding Japanese texts but contain introductory comments for the Japanese reader. The volumes are classified by subject: (1) basic documents; (2) political, military, and cultural; (3) financial, economic, and reparations; (4) commercial and industrial; (5) civil property; and (6) aliens. Included are SCAP directives (SCAPINs), memorandums issued by SCAP sections to ministries of the Japanese government (section memos), memorandums from the Commander Naval Forces, Far East, from the Eighth Army, and from the military government, as well as Japanese laws, regulations, and other materials. Volume 1 also contains the Cairo and Potsdam Declarations, the Yalta Agreement, communications exchanged between the Allies and Japan regarding the latter's surrender, the Instrument of Surrender, Terms of Reference for the Far Eastern Commission and the Allied Council for Japan, and the U.S. Initial Post-Surrender Policy for Japan.

367 ———. Prime Minister's Office. Bureau of Statistics. *Japan Statistical Yearbook* (*Nihon tōkei nenkan*). Tokyo: Nihon Tōkei Kyōkai, 1950– . No.1, 1949– . Annual.

The most comprehensive official compilation of basic Japanese statistics and a continuation of *Nihon Teikoku tōkei nenkan* (Statistical Yearbook of the Japanese Empire), which was published between 1882 and 1940. Figures within the statistical tables are given for the title year as well as for the decade preceding the title year. These tables cover a wide range of subjects from agriculture, manufacturing, and trade, to labor, wages, and prices. Headings and subheadings are in both English and Japanese. War-damage statistics, it should be noted, are included in no.1 (1949), and beginning with no.2 (1950) basic international statistics are appended.

368 McNelly, Theodore Hart, ed. *Sources in Modern East Asian History and Politics.* New York: Appleton-Century-Crofts, 1967. xviii, 422p.

A collection of primary sources accompanied by brief editorial notes that is designed to provide supplementary reading for courses in the history, politics, and ideologies of modern East Asia. Several of its documents and statements deal with the defeat and occupation of Japan as well as with the democratization of the country. They are: (1) the Konoe Memorial (14 Feb. 1945); (2) the Potsdam Proclamation; (3) the imperial rescript at the end of the war (14 Aug. 1945); (4) "On Being a Good Loser," by Yoshida Shigeru (from his *The Yoshida Memoirs: The Story of Japan in Crisis* [1962] [no.769]); (5) Diet Resolution Rescinding the Imperial Rescript on Education (19 June 1948); (6) Senate Journal Resolution 94 (Senator Richard Russell's proposed congressional resolution of Sept. 1945 calling for the trial of Emperor Hirohito as a war criminal); (7) Rescript on the Construction of a New Japan (the Imperial New Year's Day Rescript of 1946 in which the emperor renounced his divinity); (8) Reform of the Japanese Governmental System (SWNCC–228); (9) the Treaty of Peace with Japan; and (10) the Japan Supreme Court decision in the Sunakawa case, 16 December 1959. The text of the postwar constitution of Japan is also included in this collection as Appendix A of the volume.

369 New Zealand. Dept. of External Affairs. *Select Documents on the Surrender and Control of Japan.* Wellington: Government Printer, 1947. 63p. (Dept. of External Affairs publication 29)

Beginning with the Potsdam Declaration of 26 July 1945, the documents selected include the Japanese acceptance of the Potsdam Declaration, the Instrument of Surrender, the U.S. Initial Post-Surrender Policy for Japan, the scope of authority of General MacArthur as supreme commander of the Allied powers, the terms of reference of the Far Eastern Advisory Commission, the Far Eastern Commission, and the Allied Council for Japan, selected SCAP directives to the Japanese government, and a joint statement on the British Commonwealth Occupation Force in Japan issued by the United Kingdom, Australia, India, and New Zealand on 31 January 1946. Little commentary is provided.

370 U.S. Congress. Senate. Committee on Foreign Relations. *A Decade of American Foreign Policy: Basic Documents, 1941–49.* Washington, D.C.: Government Printing Office, 1950. xiv, 1,381p. (81st Cong., 1st sess., 1950. Senate document no.123)

Prepared at the request of the Senate Committee on Foreign Relations by the staff of the committee and the Department of State, this voluminous collection of documents treats both American and international materials. Included are presidential addresses, congressional resolutions, communiqués and declarations issued by international conferences, treaties, agreements, proposals, letters, white papers, etc. Documents were selected in terms of their usefulness to the Congress in its deliberations on foreign policy. The collection contains a total of 313 documents which are grouped under 8 major categories: (1) wartime documents looking toward peace; (2) conferences on the peace settlement; (3) the United Nations, basic organization; (4) United Nations, specialized agencies; (5) the inter-American system; (6) defeated and occupied areas; (7) other areas of special interest to the United States; and (8) current international issues. Documents related to Japan are found in parts 1, 6, and 8. These include decisions of the Cairo, Teheran, Potsdam, and Yalta Conferences, the text of the Japanese Instrument of Surrender, major decisions on the occupation of Japan by the American government and the Far Eastern Commission in 1945–47, the charter of the International Military Tribunal for the Far East, decisions and policies on Japanese reparations by the American government and the Far Eastern Commission in 1946–49, and the trusteeship agreement for the former Japanese mandated islands. There is a summary index but no editorial notes are provided. The collection was later reproduced in slightly modified form and reduced size under the title of *Recent American Foreign Policy: Basic Documents 1941–1951* (no. 373).

371 ———. Dept. of State. *American Foreign Policy 1950–1955: Basic Documents.* Washington, D.C.: Government Printing Office, 1957. 2v. (Dept. of State publication 6446; General Foreign Policy series 117)

This 2-volume collection of 20 parts is the successor to an earlier publication of the same nature prepared by the Senate Committee on Foreign Relations, *A Decade of American Foreign Policy: Basic Documents, 1941–49* (1950) (no. 370). It includes major documents from American, foreign, and international sources that have significant bearing upon the formulation and development of American foreign policy. The volumes contain some pre-1950 and post-1955 documents as well. They cover a wide range of subjects such as objectives of American foreign policy, the United Nations, postwar settlements, basic security treaties of the United States, developments in almost all nations of the world and these nations' relations with the United States, disarmament, control of atomic energy, foreign aid, trade policies, organization of the Department of State, etc. Sections relevant to the occupation of Japan may be found in part 3 (p.425–83), which concerned the peace settlement with Japan, and in part 14 (p.2405–48), which presents documents concerning American foreign policy toward Japan. There are no editorial notes but there is a useful summary index at the end of the second volume.

―――. ―――. *Occupation of Japan: Policy and Progress.* 1946. See no. 468.

―――. ―――. Bureau of Public Affairs. *Foreign Relations of the United States, Diplomatic Papers, 1945.* v.6, *The British Commonwealth, the Far East.* 1969. See no.202.

―――. ―――. ―――. *Foreign Relations of the United States, Diplomatic Papers, 1945.* v.7, *The Far East, China.* 1969. See no.203.

―――. ―――. ―――. *Foreign relations of the United States, 1946.* v.8, *The Far East.* 1971. See no.203a.

―――. ―――. ―――. *Foreign relations of the United States, 1947.* v.6, *The Far East.* 1972. See no.203b.

372 ―――. ―――. Office of Public Affairs. *Documents and State Papers.* Washington, D.C.: Government Printing Office, Apr. 1948–June 1949. 896p. 15 nos. (Dept. of State publications 3109, 3114, 3142, 3171, 3236, 3284, 3301, 3363, 3438, 3440, 3484, 3500, and 3525)

Prepared and edited by the Department of State, this monthly periodical was to "provide, as a complement to the *Department of State Bulletin* (no.35a), long-range information in the field of international relations, the Department of State, and the Foreign Service." After its fifteenth issue (June 1949), the publication was combined with the *Department of State Bulletin* beginning with the issue of 3 July 1949. Each issue of *Documents and State Papers,* approximately 50 pages long, contains 3 to 6 items. They include documentary reports, policy papers, texts of treaties and international agreements, basic background studies, and a record of participation in UN activities. There is also a brief annotated calendar of international meetings. In the 15 issues are 7 items related to Japanese affairs: (1) "Program for Reeducation in Japan: A Survey of Policy," no.1, April 1948, pages 3–31; (2) the text of the "Basic Initial Post-Surrender Directive to Supreme Commander for the Allied Powers for the Occupation and Control of Japan" (a directive from the State, War, and Navy Departments approved on 1 Nov. 1945 and dispatched on 8 Nov. 1945 by the Joint Chiefs of Staff), no.1, April 1948, pages 32–45; (3) the text of "Prohibition of Military Activity in Japan and Disposition of the Japanese Military Equipment" (a policy decision adopted by the Far Eastern Commission (FEC), 12 Feb. 1948), no.2, May 1948, pages 99–101; (4) the text of "Restitution of Looted Property" (an FEC decision of 29 July 1948), no.6, September 1948, pages 424–26; (5) the text of "Activities of the Far Eastern Commission, Second Report by the Secretary General" (a report published together with appended documents under the same title, as Department of State publication 3420, Far Eastern series 29 (no.859), no.10, January 1949, pages 615–22; (6) the text of "Private Commercial Entrants to Japan" (SCAP circular no.1, 14 Jan. 1949), no.11, February 1949, pages 666–72; and (7) the text of "Policy towards Patents, Utility Models, and Designs in Japan" (a policy decision approved by the Far Eastern Commission 17 Mar. 1949), no.14, May 1949, pages 795–97. All items but the first are directives and were reprinted from the documents indicated.

373 Wilcox, Francis O., and Thorsten V. Kalijarvi. *Recent American Foreign Policy: Basic Documents 1941–1951.* New York: Appleton–Century–Crofts, 1952. xviii, 927p.

Essentially a condensed version of *A Decade of American Foreign Policy: Basic Documents, 1941–49* (1950) (no. 370) prepared by the U.S. Congress, Senate Committee on Foreign Relations.

Wilcox, chief of staff of the committee, and his staff associate, Kalijarvi, reduced the volume in size in order that it might be published for wider circulation. The general format and the 8 major categories of the original work are retained but extensive editing and excerpting have eliminated material that was judged to be less important. The book also adds some 60 documents for 1950 and early 1951, producing a total of 245 documents. Editorial notes are provided for each document to explain its historical significance and provide background knowledge.

CALENDAR OF GENERAL COMMENTARIES, 1945–72

This category is a residual one representing the balance of the general literature on the occupation after subtracting the items classified in the immediately preceding sections. A great deal of the entries represent what was then contemporary reporting on the current scene in Japan. It is, of course, particularly true of materials written during the occupation period proper, although one does encounter some more systematic and scholarly accounts as well. These latter tend quite naturally to cluster, however, in the postoccupation period.

Perhaps the most noteworthy aspect of the literature represented in this section is the paucity of scholarly studies of a nature and scale that transcend the format of articles or isolated chapters. The exceptions are few, the most outstanding being the contributions of Professors Kawai (no.714) and Reischauer (nos.741–43). Former Prime Minister Yoshida's memoirs, although greatly abridged in this English-language version, are also of value as a uniquely informed account from a Japanese viewpoint (no.769). The entries in the section on the international aspects (p.260) and the section on political parties and elections (p.452) are in many cases closely related to those in this section and should also be consulted. The same is true of the entries in the section providing a calendar of general commentaries on the economy, 1946–72 (p.481). It parallels the present section on the economic side and should be used in conjunction with this section.

Where an entry covers developments over a span of several years, it has been classified under the year of publication or, when possible, under the last of the years actually treated.

1945

374 "The Army Way." *Nation* 161:677 (22 Dec. 1945)

Occupation policy is categorized on 3 different levels in this editorial. The first level is that aspect of American policy which is determined to thwart Soviet Communist aspirations in Japan. The second, according to the author, "has the surprisingly fresh flavor of enlightened democratic thinking" and is responsible for many social and political reform programs. The third level of policy is the implementation of these enlightened programs and the author here takes the position that the army is not a suitable instrument for such a complex task of social engineering. Nevertheless, he concludes that the overall impact of the occupation upon Japan has been beneficial.

374a Bogdanov, Nikolai. "In Vanquished Japan." *USSR Information Bulletin* pt.1 "A Country after War" 5, no.113:6–7

(27 Oct. 1945); pt.2 "Failure of the Kamikaze" 5, no.114:6–7 (30 Oct. 1945); pt.3 "The People and the Rulers" 5, no.115:6–7 (1 Nov. 1945)

Bogdanov, a member of the first Soviet delegation to arrive in Japan after the war, describes war-ravaged Tokyo in this 3-part series of articles that originally appeared in the Russian-language newspaper *Krasnaya Zvezda*. He writes in particular about his impressions of the impoverished and suffering Japanese—a people whom he depicts as one "turned primitive"—and speculates on the lack of concern by Japanese officials for the plight of their people.

375 Bolles, Blair. "Will State Department Changes Stiffen Policy on Japan?" *Foreign Policy Bulletin* 24:4 (14 Sept. 1945)

The author suggests that the State Department policy toward a defeated Japan will take a sterner direction due to the recent resignation of 2 influential State Department officers, Joseph C. Grew, former Undersecretary of State, and Eugene Dooman, adviser on Japanese affairs. According to the author, their departure from office "gives new authority to a group of men in the Department who have less faith in our recent enemy," namely Dean Acheson, the new undersecretary, and John Carter Vincent, chief of the Division of Chinese Affairs. The article concludes with brief speculations as to the kind of military occupation that will be necessary for Japan.

Butow, Robert J. C. *Tojo and the Coming of the War*. 1961. See no.1053.

375a "Can Democracy Be Imposed by a Victor's Decree?" *Christian Century* 62: 1228 (7 Nov. 1945)

This editorial praises MacArthur's initial reform efforts, including the enfranchisement of women, the encouragement of labor activity, and the enactment of guarantees for the freedom of thought and of the press. While it is probably impossible to "order" democracy, the editors concede, these steps should be hailed as the first clear indication of the direction in which American policy in Japan is heading.

376 Chamberlin, William Henry. "The Occupation of Japan." *Common Sense* 14, no.11:10–13 (Dec. 1945)

Chamberlin was a correspondent for the *Christian Science Monitor* in Tokyo from 1934 until 1939. He claims that the occupation of Japan is progressing more successfully than that of Germany. He cites 2 reasons: a single central control and the method of maintaining the Japanese administration. He criticizes those who attack the course plotted for the occupation. On one side, he denounces those who want "an eye for an eye and a tooth for a tooth." On the other, he belittles the left and their "vaguely defined social revolution." He also cautions critics by saying that Japan cannot become a duplicate of the United States. He advises that Japan be allowed to rebuild her foreign trade and shipping and that the future of the *zaibatsu* be left to the Japanese Parliament.

377 "Civil versus Military Control." *Forum* 104:262–67 (Nov. 1945)

An interesting juxtaposition of editorial statements of several leading American newspapers regarding the controversy between General MacArthur and Acting Secretary of State Dean Acheson over American policies in occupied Japan. The immediate issues are an announcement of MacArthur's indicating that American forces would be drastically reduced within 6 months' time and the consternation this statement caused in the State Department. However, the article also considers such related aspects as the nature of a military occupation, the relationship between military and diplomatic phases of an occupation, and the effects such a dispute has on internal congressional affairs. Some of the newspapers whose editorials are included are the *Washington Post*, the *Philadelphia Inquirer*, and the *San Francisco Chronicle*.

378 "The Control of Japan: 1. Political and Constitutional Reform." *Contemporary China* 5 (29 Oct. 1945)

The first and only part of what was originally intended to be a 3-part discussion of basic control policies of the Allies for Japan viewed from the standpoint of the Chinese. Under the topic of political and constitutional reform, the anonymous author discusses the Meiji Constitution, the institution of the emperor, the Diet, the cabinet, the Privy Council, political parties, war criminals, and ultra-nationalistic and militaristic organizations. He gives a brief history of each and offers suggestions for their reform or elimination.

379 Corey, Herbert. "Japan and the End of the World." *Free World* 10:34–36 (Sept. 1945)

Immediately after the surrender, the author discusses the pressing problem of "what to do with Japan." He deals with such social issues as the treatment of the emperor and the punishment of the warlords, suggesting that the former be retained but the latter severely punished. He concludes with a brief discussion of the implications of the atom bomb not only for the Japanese cities concerned but also for the entire world in future times.

380 "Cross-Currents in Japan." *Nation* 161:244–45 (15 Sept. 1945)

The author of this brief editorial criticizes General MacArthur's leniency toward former militaristic groups. He illustrates this by citing SCAP's use of several thousand members of the Kempeitai or gendarmerie which the author characterizes as the Japanese counterpart of the Gestapo. Moreover, he attempts to predict possible changes in occupation policy resulting from the resignation of Eugene Dooman as chairman of the State-War-Navy Coordinating Committee and his replacement by the China specialist, John Carter Vincent.

381 Embree, John Fee. "How to Treat the Japanese: A Complex Issue." *New York Times Magazine* p.5, 51 (9 Sept. 1945)

In this article the author considers what attitudes should shape American policy toward Japan. An anthropologist specializing in Japanese studies, he takes an optimistic view of Japanese cooperation with the occupation. Citing the example of the defeated followers of Saigō Takamori after the Satsuma Rebellion in 1877, he states that the Japanese will be docile and law abiding after the defeat. He believes that the victors should not be vengeful but should treat the citizens as patriotic individuals who supported their government. A fairly small occupation force should be sufficient and he believes that establishment of a truly democratic government will be impossible as long as occupying forces remain in Japan. While he holds that Japanese political institutions are the most responsive to public pressure of any in Asia, he points out that whatever political system evolves in Japan will reflect traditional values and will probably utilize a revolving leadership. He concludes that there is every reason to be optimistic about the development of democracy in Japan because there already exists a trend away from authoritarianism and feudalism and toward a representative form of government.

381a "Fate of Japan." *Canadian Forum* 25:152 (Oct. 1945)

Even though they recognize the fact that Canada has little voice if any in determining occupation policy, the editors of *Canadian Forum* still are alarmed at the tendencies which are becoming evident in MacArthur's policies. It appears that Japan's social and economic patterns will be left essentially unchanged, and MacArthur is showing favor toward antidemocratic elements as well. "After all," the editors conclude, "what else could be expected from the hero of the Republican party?"

382 "Getting Tough with Japan." *New Republic* 113:363–64 (24 Sept. 1945)

This brief editorial outlines the difficult nature of the Allied situation in Japan just after the surrender—a situation which warranted extreme caution on the part of General MacArthur. However, the author insists that now the supreme commander must act decisively to encourage democratic forces and to mete out punishment to the Japanese industrialists as well as the militarists. If not, he suggests that the general be replaced or supplemented by a capable civil administrator.

383 "Good Faith with Japan." *Christian Century* 62:1119–20 (3 Oct. 1945)

The uproar created by MacArthur's statement that no more than 200,000 American occupation troops would be needed in Japan in 6 months' time is the focal point of this article. Causes of this uproar include the dismay of the professional military at the thought that a vast standing army would not be needed, the feeling that MacArthur's statement was an expression of personal political aspiration, and the desire of certain Americans to seek revenge and a vengeful peace with Japan.

384 "How We Fumble in Japan." *New Republic* 113:733–34 (3 Dec. 1945)

The author of this editorial is extremely critical of the American occupation 3 months after its beginning. After outlining the immediate problems to be met by the Allies in effecting the transition from war to peace, the author criticizes the lack of real political, social, and economic reforms to date, the unwillingness of the Americans to allow the Far Eastern Commission any measure of authority, SCAP's decision to use the existing Japanese government, and the lack of communications even between American officials in Washington and Tokyo. He suggests that commissions of experts from the United States and other Allied powers be called in to analyze the situation and make recommendations for its improvement.

384a Janeway, Eliot. "America's Moral Crisis." *Asia and the Americas* 45:466–69 (Oct. 1945)

In the course of discussing some of the problems created by the war, Janeway, a well known writer on economic and political matters, talks about American policies for occupied Japan. He asserts that the Japanese decision to surrender caught the United States unprepared and that as a result we are allowing the Japanese to set the pattern for the postwar years. American leaders are "more interested in what the Japanese are thinking than in how Japan is to function" and are anxious for the Japanese to take the initiative and relieve them of unwelcome responsibilities. If the United States bases its policies upon its shortsighted interpretation of Japanese opinion and Japanese purposes, Janeway continues, we are bound to restore to Japan the implements of power. Accordingly, it is important that American officials disregard Japanese opinion and, furthermore, allow Japan to experience a period of intellectual disorder and political disunity. Only in this fashion will she be able to change her ways and abandon militarism.

384b "Japan's Revolution Goes Forward." *Christian Century* 62:1435 (26 Dec. 1945)

This editorial contrasts the occupation policies of retribution and suppression carried out in Germany with those followed in Japan. Allied policies in Japan, the editors point out, are directed towards liberating the masses and raising their standard of living.

384c "Japanese Reconversion." *Fortune* 32:224 (Nov. 1945)

This brief article notes that the devastation which Japan suffered greatly exceeds the predictions made by outsiders. With characteristic industry, however, the Japanese are using their gold reserves and a small inflow of dollars to balance their international accounts.

385 Jones, George E. "Suzuki-san Learns the Meaning of Defeat." *New York Times Magazine* p.9, 41 (4 Nov. 1945)

As the winter of 1945 approaches, the writer finds that life is grim for the Japanese common man. Food and shelter are scarce. High prices on the black market force people to sell art goods and silks for chocolate and cigarettes. The author observes that most Americans

386 Kaplan, Benz. "Tojo Doesn't Live Here Anymore." *Free World* 10:32–36 (Dec. 1945)

One of the vanguard of 200,000 American troops to land in Japan here presents his impressions of the newly defeated nation in diary form. In an informal account, he describes his own landing, that of General MacArthur, first encounters with Japanese, the ruins of Tokyo, Yokohama, and Kawasaki, and the living conditions of the first occupation forces.

387 Kluckhorn, Frank L. "Fear Dominates Japan Today." *New York Times Magazine* p.6–7, 50 (30 Sept. 1945)

The author, one of the *Times*' correspondents in Tokyo, believes that the occupation must not only cope with the material problems of Japan but also must institute educational and psychological reforms. He sees the dominant emotion in Japan as fear of an unknown future. This uncertainty is compounded by severe shortages of food and housing. The occupation faces the problem of remaking a people's way of life and thought. Kluckhorn believes that SCAP officials will find this task difficult because of the vastly different cultural background of the Japanese. The people have been taught blind obedience for centuries so there is no nucleus from which to create a democratic movement.

388 ——. "First Impressions of Conquered Japan." *New York Times Magazine* p.8, 49 (9 Sept. 1945)

The author was one of the first 2 Americans to enter Tokyo after the surrender. He records his nervousness under the hostile stares of Japanese civilians and soldiers but even amid the great destruction in Tokyo he finds evidence of the energy and industry of the Japanese people. Most of the rubble has been cleared away and makeshift dwellings erected. Of special interest is his translation of an editorial from the *Hōchi Shimbun* which describes for its Japanese readers the attitudes necessary for democracy. The author sees Japan's most immediate problems as being hunger and overpopulation. He takes an optimistic attitude toward the success of the occupation, citing General MacArthur's greatest ability as "being able to get along with people he wants to get along with."

389 ——. "The Menacing Shadow: Japan's Old Order." *New York Times Magazine* p.5, 42 (16 Sept. 1945)

Writing in the early weeks of the occupation, the author raises the question of whether a liberal order can ever be instituted in Japan. He points out many elements of the old order, such as the Black Dragon Society, the coalition of militarists and bureaucrats, and the *tonarigumi* ("neighborhood associations") system which still remain in Japan. He expresses the fear that these elements will outlast the occupation and regain control of the Japanese people using the centuries-old device of thought-control. In order to avoid this, the author believes that the occupation must work to reeducate the Japanese people, making them aware of the evils of militarism and of the atrocities committed by the militarists. Reeducation could be carried out through the mass media as well as by using the authority of the emperor to institute changes in attitude through the *tonarigumi* system.

Kodama, Yoshio. *I Was Defeated.* 1959. See no.1073.

389a Kornhauser, Arthur William. "Can Japanese Militarism Be Uprooted? Poll of Experts." *American Magazine* 140: 40–41, 112–14 (Oct. 1945)

Kornhauser presents the results of a poll of experts on Japan who addressed themselves to questions dealing with various aspects of the occupation. A large majority of these individuals favor a liberal policy aimed at rehabilitating Japan; most likewise feel there is at least a fair chance of Japan's becoming a trustworthy member of the international community within 10 to 15 years. The experts are divided on other questions relating to such topics as the future of democracy in Japan, the reforms which should be pursued, and the position of the emperor. All generally agree that the nature of Japanese society and Japan's international behavior will be determined by the fate of peace elsewhere in the world. The experts polled are listed at the conclusion of the article, although none are cited by name in the text itself.

Krueger, Walter. *From Down under to Nippon: The Story of the Sixth Army in World War II*. 1953. See no.906.

390 Li-em, Channing. "Re-education of Japan." *Forum* 104:193–97 (Nov. 1945)

The first section of this article is devoted to an analysis of what the author believes to be the Japanese characteristics responsible for their prewar and wartime behavior. He characterizes the Japanese as sadistic and believes that, in general, they fear and worship power. The second section discusses what should be the Allied attitudes toward a defeated Japan and the author strongly recommends that we keep Japan completely disarmed and weak, that we anticipate a lengthy period of military occupation to insure that reforms are implemented, and that we reeducate the Japanese so that Japan may eventually become a responsible and democratic nation.

391 "Life in Tokyo." *Life* 19:105–13 (3 Dec. 1945)

The everyday life style of the Japanese in their devastated homeland is reviewed here. The status of the emperor, reform of the police, the extent of starvation and lack of housing, fraternization of occupation troops with Japanese women, and the revival of the Communist party are mentioned.

392 Lyell, Thomas Reginald Guise. "Japan: A Problem in Reconstruction." *Asiatic Review* n.s. 41:375–78 (Oct. 1945)

An essay written at the outset of the occupation discussing the Allied reconstruction of Japan and emphasizing the necessity for a thorough understanding of the Japanese character by the occupation authorities in order to bring about permanent and meaningful change. The author presents a skeleton outline of Japanese cultural and political history, then advocates various reforms in the educational and religious spheres as well as the mass media that might be effected to help change the former group mentality to a spirit of healthy individualism. He sees this change as a crucial consideration in the success of the occupation.

393 Matsumoto, Tsuyoshi. "No Surrender at All." *Nation* 161:311–12 (29 Sept. 1945)

The author suggests that Japan has not surrendered to the Allies in spirit but has only laid down its obsolete weapons of war "having been forced by the atom bomb to accept the 'changed situation'." He draws parallels between Japan's present course of action and its behavior at other times in its history, notably with the advent of Admiral Perry in 1853, when the rulers outwardly adapted the country to Western demands for an expedient length of time. Finally, he expresses his concern that occupation authorities have continued to use the same ruler, the same political machinery, and the same system of government to effect drastic social and political changes in the Japanese nation.

394 Morley, James William. "The First Seven Weeks." *Japan Interpreter* 6, no. 2:151–64 (Summer 1970)

A brief but insightful investigation of a much-neglected problem by an outstanding student of Japanese politics and political history. The 7 weeks involved are the first 7 weeks of the Allied occupation of Japan and the problem is the identification of the attitudes, motives, and plans with respect to the occupation of the men who led the Japanese government at that time. Morley emphasizes such matters as Prince Konoe's fear of a left-wing revolution, the general and basic concern with the need to preserve the imperial system, and the attempts made by both political and business leaders to influence the course of SCAP policy.

395 Morris, Frank D. "Seventy Million Problem Children." *Collier's* 116:22–23, 53–54 (1 Dec. 1945)

Morris comments on the enigmatic qualities of the Japanese people and their intellectual and spiritual understanding of democracy. Political and educational reform and the emancipation of women are discussed in this context.

395a Morris, John. "Some Thoughts on the Japanese Problem." *United Empire* 36: 226–28 (Nov. 1945)

In this luncheon address delivered on 17 October 1945, Morris offers his opinion on a variety of issues facing the occupation. He generally favors the view that the emperor was little more than a tool of the militarists, but feels that the Japanese concept of the emperor should be changed. The Japanese army has been demobilized, but since it was not defeated in battle, he warns, it is still potentially dangerous. He shares the American hope that Japan can be democratized, but doubts whether the Japanese truly understand what democracy is. In any case, he concludes, the final result of the democratization program will undoubtedly differ from American expectations.

Mosley, Leonard O. *Hirohito, Emperor of Japan.* 1966. See no.1243.

396 Mydans, Shelley. "The Japanese Mind in Defeat." *Life* 19:26 (3 Sept. 1945)

The author discusses the Japanese proclivity for hysteria and obsession in times of extreme emotional stress. She anticipates a long period of tension and hate toward America which can be mitigated only by spontaneous goodwill and honest dealings with the Japanese people. Mydans notes the history of an emperor without secular power and concludes that the American supreme commander could gain legitimacy by maintaining the emperor as a spiritual institution.

Oda, James S. "Hirohito's Possible Successor." 1945. See no.1244.

397 "Our Occupation Policy for Japan." *Department of State Bulletin* 13:538–45 (7 Oct. 1945)

An NBC interview with John C. Vincent, director of Far Eastern Affairs in the State Department, Major General John H. Hilldring, director of Civil Affairs in the War Department, and Captain R. L. Dennison, navy representative on the Far Eastern Subcommittee of the State-War-Navy Coordinating Committee, regarding American objectives and activities in postwar Japan. The 3 men comment on such topics as General MacArthur's relationship with the State Department, the possible length of the occupation, and SCAP's attitude toward the emperor, the *zaibatsu* combines, and those Japanese imprisoned by the militarist governments of Japan during the 1930s. There is a brief comparison of the German and Japanese occupations, as well as a discussion of possible reforms in the landholding and educational systems of Japan.

398 Parrott, Lindesay. "We Bring a Revolution to the Japanese." *New York Times Magazine* p.9, 51–52 (14 Oct. 1945)

The author, a *New York Times* correspondent, characterizes the occupation as a "quiet revolution" which is altering the whole structure of Japanese society. While on the surface, life goes on as usual with the Japanese people trying to eke out an existence, there are far-reaching psychological changes taking place. The occupation reforms are aimed at destroying Japan's war potential and creating the groundwork for a democratic structure. Thus far, he believes, the reforms have been aimed at guaranteeing civil liberties and revising the educational system. Meanwhile, the new Japanese leaders are waiting and watching to see the extent of the occupation reforms.

399 Petrov, D. "Eliminating Sects of Aggression or Preserving Them?" *New Times* no.9(19):28–30 (1 Oct. 1945)

In a review of *The Control of Germany and Japan*, by Harold G. Moulton and Louis Marlio (1944) (no.101), the reviewer concentrates chiefly on one central idea, i.e., the authors' "anxiety to prevent any change in the economic system of Germany and Japan." He maintains that such a policy has support in some American circles which would use Japan as a buffer state to control Soviet activities in the Far East. Contrary to such a policy, the author insists that militarists, ultranationalists, and *zaibatsu* leaders must be eliminated entirely in order to rebuild a democratic Japan.

400 "Policy for Japan." *New Republic* 113:419 (1 Oct. 1945)

The author of this brief editorial finds reassurance in the policy declaration of the American government regarding the postwar treatment of Japan. He commends the Americans for welcoming the participation of the other Allied powers, for their decision "to use the existing form of government in Japan, not to support it," and for their program to dissolve the *zaibatsu* banking and industrial combines.

401 Redman, H. Vere. "Japan's Surrender: What Next?" *Asiatic Review* n.s. 41:407–9 (Oct. 1945)

An article written immediately after the surrender and focused on what the author considers Japan's lack of a feeling of guilt for the war. In order to insure the future good behavior of the Japanese, he believes the occupation authorities should attempt to create such a sense of guilt in the Japanese people, and he advocates vigorous and immediate prosecution of war criminals as one effective means of doing this. War criminals are categorized into 2 types: (1) those who directly perpetrated atrocities on their own responsibility, and (2) those holding supreme responsibility for the outbreak of the war.

402 Reynolds, Thomas F. "Our Japanese Policy." *New Republic* 113:307–9 (10 Sept. 1945)

The author of this article analyzes U.S. policy in Japan as one aimed to promote social evolution as opposed to economic revolution. He defends on pragmatic grounds the use of Emperor Hirohito to end the war and views this as part of a larger program to achieve stability so that whatever liberal forces may have been latent in Japan can begin functioning. According to the author "until the amorphous mass of Japanese citizens can be indoctrinated with the concept of individual rights in a slow-moving social evolution, Japan will remain dangerous soil, capable of again becoming a menace to world peace." He views the existing Higashikuni cabinet as a short-term expedient with few long-range political connotations.

403 Rosinger, Lawrence K. "Long Range Plans on Japan Needed to Assist MacArthur." *Foreign Policy Bulletin* 24:1–2 (21 Sept. 1945)

The article mentions several steps already taken by SCAP in controlling and redirecting the Japanese information media and speculates on what the author terms the long-range character of American policy, i.e., "whether the United States will be satisfied simply to disarm Japan technically or will seek far-reaching alterations in Japanese society." The author believes that the length of the occupation will be a key factor in determining U.S. policy and advocates a sufficiently long period of military occupation in order to make reform permanently effective.

404 ———. "Occupation Paves Way for Stern Political Moves in Japan." *Foreign Policy Bulletin* 24:1–2 (7 Sept. 1945)

The causes of Japan's military surrender are briefly discussed before the author considers the general aims of the occupation as determined from state-

405 Roth, Andrew. "The Prisoners We Forgot." *Nation* 161:305–6 (29 Sept. 1945)

The author strongly urges that SCAP attend to the important business of freeing Japanese political prisoners—those "thousands of Japanese democrats, liberals, and leftists who had dared to fight the ruling clique and its ruthless police." He categorizes these arrests in 4 great waves—one in the late twenties, one in the early thirties, one in 1937–38, and a large raid on Pearl Harbor Day, and briefly notes the kinds of citizens imprisoned at these times. Since no specific action has yet been taken by SCAP in spite of President Truman's assurance that they would be freed, the author strongly urges the occupation authorities to free and then make use of these "champions of democracy" to create a new Japan rather than rely on the "fawning opportunists that come crawling to the American authorities" now that the Americans are in power.

406 Salisbury, Laurence E. "Regeneration of Japan." *Far Eastern Survey* 14:249–51 (12 Sept. 1945)

This article, written immediately after the surrender of Japan, discusses the occupation that will soon commence. The author describes the 2 general alternatives open to MacArthur: retention of the former regime after elimination of the obviously war guilty or the inauguration of sweeping changes in government personnel "so as to permit the emergence of domestic groups which could initiate a domestic program designed to eliminate the economic basis for aggression." He then discusses the unrealistic attitudes toward Japan's defeat evidenced by various important Japanese officials and dignitaries and advocates that these individuals immediately be eliminated from government in the forthcoming occupation. In conclusion, he advocates that SCAP give support to those liberals who actually represent the popular movements that must have arisen against the oligarchy and totalitarianism of the prewar and wartime periods.

406a Shalett, Sidney M. "The Occupation of Japan." *Forum* 104:162–64 (Oct. 1945)

Shalett offers his observations on the beginning of the occupation. His topics include MacArthur's qualifications, the size of the occupation forces, the need to impress upon Japan the reality of her defeat, the physical condition of the country after prolonged bombing, and the future of the Emperor. Japan will never become an American-style democracy, the author concedes, but at least her "trouble-making proclivities" may be curbed.

407 "Showdown in Japan." *Nation* 161:215–16 (8 Sept. 1945)

This editorial considers the initial directions of the occupation as determined by the Allied decision to work through the emperor and the existing governmental structure. The author urges that the supreme commander turn his attention to the task of demilitarizing and democratizing Japanese industry as one of his most important priorities. He also suggests that SCAP discover whatever democratic groups remain in the country and utilize them in implementing Allied programs of reform.

407a Smith, Roy, and Arthur Kruse. "Debate Japan Occupation." *City Club Bulletin* n.s. 12:59–60 (29 Oct. 1945)

A debate presented before the City Club of Chicago on 15 October 1945.

408 Stone, Isidor F. "Behind the MacArthur Row." *Nation* 161:297–99 (29 Sept. 1945)

The author evidences skepticism concerning a White House statement outlining the nature of occupation policy in Japan, chiefly because of his belief that the kinds of changes that must be effected in Japanese society necessitate a total military government. He protests against the decision to retain the machinery of the Japanese government and expresses strong reservations about the Allies being able to break the power of the aristocrats, the bureaucrats, and the industrialists "if we confine ourselves to operating through a government which remains their instrument." In the author's opinion, the reason for abandoning the original plan for a military government is connected with United States–Soviet relations, which he views as crucial in determining Japan's future. In conclusion, he warns against the reactionary elements in the State and War Departments in Washington who are attempting to equate advocacy of a "hard" peace with communism and who wish to maintain the status quo by settling for a "soft" peace and "bringing the boys back home."

Supreme Commander for the Allied Powers. *Incoming Messages.* 1945. See no.222.

Supreme Commander for the Allied Powers. *Outgoing Messages.* 1945. See no.224.

Svensson, Eric H. F. *The Military Occupation of Japan: The First Years of Planning, Policy Formulation, and Reforms.* 1966. See no.59.

———. *The Military Occupation of Japan: The First Years. Planning, Policy Formation, and Reforms.* 1966. See no. 60.

409 "The Task of the Occupation Forces." *Amerasia* 9:247–51 (Sept. 1945)

This article discusses 2 related aspects of occupation policy. The first is SCAP's decision to use the emperor as what the author defines as the chief instrument of Allied control and to leave the whole sociopolitical structure of Japan intact. Although conceding that this may have been justified in the immediate postwar period, he warns against prolonging such a policy which will only strengthen the imperial institution and the ruling oligarchy—both of which were partially responsible for Japan's former militarism. The second aspect of the occupation discussed is the degree of control exercised by Allied governments over the supreme allied commander and his staff. The author suggests that this is minimal and also criticizes the fact that "the American people are being kept in ignorance of the means being taken to implement a foreign policy that is of vital concern to their own future security." The article advocates that an Allied policy be formulated which would give every opportunity to latent democratic forces within Japanese society to make themselves felt as a viable political force and to participate actively in the future administration of Japan.

410 Tench, C. T. "Advance Party: Mission Surrender." *Infantry Journal* 59: 30–36 (Aug. 1946)

This account of the 48 hours of activity of the advance party of SCAP, headed by the author and sent to check on Japanese arrangements and facilities for the mass airborne landings that initiated the occupation of Japan and the arrival of General MacArthur, is written in a very informal style. It describes the apprehensions of the colonel and outlines preparations undertaken after his arrival. Several near-incidents and how they were averted are also depicted.

Tregaskis, Richard. "Road to Tokyo." 1945. See no.927a.

411 "Unregenerate Japan." *Nation* 161: 273–74 (22 Sept. 1945)

An editorial protesting current Japanese propaganda that is issued to American newspapers in the form of declarations of innocence on the part of Japanese statesmen and industrialists. The author believes these misleading statements confuse the American public and lead them to support current SCAP policy which is tending to absolve the *zaibatsu* leaders, court figures, and political leaders from war guilt.

411a "U.S. Occupies Japan." *Life* 19:29–41 (10 Sept. 1945)

This photoessay documents the arrival of the American occupation forces

412 Van Der Water, Margorie. "Psychology in Japan." *Science News Letter* 48: 234–36, 238 (Oct. 1945)

Written soon after the inauguration of the Allied occupation, this article examines the general psychological outlook of the former enemy. The first half of the report discusses presurrender efforts headed by U.S. Navy Captain Ellis Zacharias to wage a psychological campaign that would induce the enemy to surrender. The latter half discusses what the author conceives to be the real attitude behind the surface friendliness of the now defeated Japanese and methods which might be adopted by occupation personnel to ascertain true Japanese attitudes. She insists that there should be freedom of the press and academic freedom in the new democratic Japan.

413 Whyte, Sir Frederick. "The Prospect in the Far East." *Contemporary Review* 168:193–97 (Oct. 1945)

The author lays the blame for Japan's wartime activities on the quality and characters of her leaders—"reckless and headstrong men who knew little of the world outside Japan and less of true statecraft." He advocates an occupation which will be neither so short as to be merely a brief embarrassment nor so long that domestic problems become distorted by the alibi of foreign control. The author calls for Allied unity in a program of political and social reeducation that will be initiated and maintained by the Allies but carried out by the Japanese. The article closes with a plea for the need to put aside petty national economic biases and work to integrate Japan into a healthy worldwide industrial trade system.

Wildes, Harry E. "Who Signs the Treaty?" 1945. See no.132.

414 "Winning the Peace in Japan." *Amerasia* 9:243–47 (Sept. 1945)

In detailing Japan's peace treaty as well as the complex task of the occupation forces, the author notes that it is essential that we do not allow ourselves to be maneuvered into the position of supporting the old ruling oligarchy as the sole source of power and authority in Japan.

1946

415 "America's Eastern Empire." *Labour Research* 35, no.11:166–67 (Nov. 1946)

This article briefly reviews recent developments in occupied Japan with specific reference to agrarian reform, the elections, the labor movement, various labor strikes, and action vis-à-vis the emperor and the *zaibatsu*. The author is critical of SCAP, asserting that "General MacArthur's conception of 'democracy' is strictly an American one, and [that] little effort has been made from above to strike at the real roots of Japanese Fascism and aggression."

415a Angus, H. F. *Japan: Our Problem.* Toronto: Canadian Institute of International Affairs, 1946. 16p. (Behind the Headlines, 6, no.3)

Pointing out that Canada, "as a Pacific country, has vital interests at stake in the [coming] peace settlement of the United Nations with Japan," Angus asserts that the prospects of peace in the Pacific depend largely on the occupation's success in resolving the basic problems that caused Japan to go to war. He first reviews the major highlights of modern Japanese history, focusing on the international economic situation of the 1920s and 1930s which caused Japan's aggressive overseas expansion. Then, under the heading "The Problem of Peace," he touches upon the position of the emperor, democracy in Japan, the importance of disarming Japan, the necessity for Japan to revive her foreign trade, reparations and war crimes, and peace aims. The coming few months, Angus concludes, will be crucial for the future of both Japan and her neighbors.

415b "Are We Winning the Peace in Japan? An Appraisal of American Occupation Policy." *Amerasia* 10:43–71 (Feb. 1946)

The entire February issue of this periodical is devoted to an attempt to describe the "actual situation" in Japan after 5 months of American occupation. The author first discusses the continued prominence of such former elements and institutions as the imperial system, the *zaibatsu*, the landed interests, and the court circle. He speaks of the reemergence of ultranationalist parties and groups, all of which, in his opinion, serve to keep the former governmental power structure in being. The actual situation in Japan is then compared with SCAP's announced aims for reform and the author criticizes the disparity between the two. To support his argument, he analyzes in detail 3 major aims of the occupation: dissolution of the *zaibatsu*, the land reform program, and the purge of militarist and ultranationalist elements. There is also a brief discussion of SCAP programs concerning the armed forces, the secret police, the educational system, and Shinto, as well as an analysis of the current Japanese political scene. This analysis includes an examination of the composition and programs of what are termed the 4 major political groups in Japan— the Progressive party (*Shimpotō*), the Liberal party (*Jiyūtō*), the Social Democratic party (*Shakaitō*) and the Communist party (*Kyōsantō*). There is also a discussion of the Communist party's attempts to form a People's Front coalition. The article concludes with a discussion of United States versus Allied direction of the occupation, criticizing U.S. efforts to prevent Soviet and British participation and urging that the United States encourage such participation in the future.

416 Ashmead, John. "The Japs Look at the Yanks." *Atlantic Monthly* 177:86–91 (Apr. 1946)

An account of a navy interpreter's rambles through postwar Japan, which narrates how he discovers the wonders of Japanese art and plumbing and how he makes friends by distributing chocolate bars. Ashmead concludes that "the women are much easier to talk to on political subjects."

417 Baba, Tsunego. "Mr. Baba on Politics." Tr. by S. Fujii. *Free World* 11:28–31 (Feb. 1946)

This article was translated from the Japanese by Fujii Shuji after appearing in Japan in the first issue of *Shinsei* (The new life) in November 1945. Baba discusses the "state of confusion" in Japan after the war, maintaining that Japanese bureaucrats always "attempt to please their superior" instead of remembering their duty to the people. He also gives examples to demonstrate the idea in Japan "which makes much out of Government but nothing of the people." After pointing out the problems, Baba notes what must be done before the "true Japan" can emerge.

418 Bickerton, Max. "Japan under Control." *New Statesman and Nation* pt. 1, 32:222 (28 Sept. 1946); pt. 2, 32:242 (5 Oct. 1946)

The author emphasizes the rapid changes since the end of the war, particularly the union movement and the political and economic emancipation of women. In part 1 there is a cursory examination of political activities, particularly the 10 April 1946 election, which stresses the view that the purges and the election of the Yoshida cabinet are indicative of a gradual, but not substantial, swing away from traditional patterns. Part 2 discusses the humanization of the emperor, Japanese reaction to that phenomenon, American maneuvers to force acceptance of SCAP's own constitutional draft, and criticisms of the failure to effectuate any basic reforms of the *zaibatsu* or the agrarian system. The author believes that "the original genuine upsurge of popular democratic enthusiasm has been largely aborted" and that there is an ever-present danger of an accommodation between SCAP and reactionary Japanese elements.

419   Busch, Noel Fairchild. "A Report on Japan." *Life* 21:104–10, 112+ (2 Dec. 1946)

Busch attributes the success of the occupation to the cooperation of the Japanese and the effective leadership of General MacArthur. The organization and functioning of the Allied Council is discussed, particularly the activities of the Soviet delegation. The importance of creating a permanently demilitarized society is stressed. The author reviews the relationship between SCAP and the Far Eastern Commission, noting MacArthur's effective independence. The work of SCAP's Civil Information and Education Section in educational reform and of the Economic and Scientific Section in *zaibatsu* liquidation and union reorganization is highlighted. The need for General MacArthur to balance the autocracy of military government with a gradual relinquishment of direct control of Japanese society is examined.

420   Caiger, George. "Democracy and the Japanese." *Austral–Asiatic Bulletin* 6:17–23 (Apr. 1946)

The substance of an address delivered before the New South Wales branch of the Australian Institute of International Affairs, this is an intelligent, well-written paper aimed at providing some understanding of Japan's cultural differences in the face of current Allied policy for that country. Caiger sums up his views by stating, "I received the impression that the idealism of the Americans, their fascination for a 'project', rather ran away with them, and that they were largely ignorant of the basic Japanese outlook, failing to appreciate the tremendous problems involved. It is becoming more obvious that whatever form of democracy Japan achieves, it will not closely resemble any existing form, and the less it does the more likely it is to be successful."

421   Cassidy, Velma Hastings. "American Policy in Occupied Areas." *Department of State Bulletin* 15:291–96 (18 Aug. 1946)

Cassidy, a research associate in the Foreign Policy Studies branch of the State Department's Office of Public Affairs, outlines the basic objectives of American policy in Germany, Austria, Japan, and Korea. She broadly defines these objectives as: "to create conditions under which political and economic democracy can flourish and to prepare for the eventual peaceful cooperation of these countries in international affairs." The bulk of the report is an explication of specific policies in the different occupied nations. There is a discussion of the establishment of the State–War–Navy Coordinating Committee and the nature and function of this organization in policy formulation. In considering the occupation of Japan, the author treats the Allied Council for Japan and the Far Eastern Commission and, finally, discusses the coordination and execution of the State Department's political, economic, and cultural policies in Japan and Korea.

422   Clifton, Allan Stephen. *Time of Fallen Blossoms*. London: Cassell, 1950. xiv, 204p.

Clifton, one of the few Australians to participate in the postwar occupation of Japan, recounts his personal experiences as an interpreter for SCAP during the first year of the occupation. His narrative is a simple commentary concerning the people, the events, and the conditions which he encountered among the Japanese, as the conquered nation struggled to accept its defeat and create some semblance of normality in the lives of those who had survived the holocaust. His description of SCAP reforms and policies provides a strong but definitely secondary theme throughout his narration; his primary concern is to describe the people with whom he came in contact and his sympathetic, slightly romantic reaction to them.

423   Dempsey, David. "Occupation Policy: Germany and Japan." *Antioch Review* 6:143–54 (Spring 1946)

The occupations of Germany and Japan are considered separately in this report and discussion of the Japanese experience focuses around corrective measures initiated by SCAP against the basic political and economic evils of Japan. The author cites recommendations of various authorities and juxtaposes the actual steps already taken by SCAP with regard to such topics as Japan's former colonial possessions, state Shinto, the imperial system, educational and agrarian reforms, and the *zaibatsu* organizations. The author points out that U.S. policy is still in the phase of removing the onerous prewar and wartime controls and recommends a program of positive assistance as well.

423a Dorget, Guy. "Notes sur la politique américaine au Japon." *Politique étrangère* 11, no.3:292–304 (July 1946)

Dorget discerns in American policy towards Japan 2 tendencies: the idealist-democratic (supported by American public opinion) and the realistic-conservative (supported by the financial, industrial, and governmental oligarchy). With this dichotomy in mind, he proceeds to discuss various aspects of occupation policy. Such problems as the future of the imperial institution, the treatment of war criminals, press freedom, and educational reform attract much of his attention. Dorget also discusses agrarian reform, trust-busting, and monetary reforms. With the convening of the Far Eastern Commission, Japan is becoming the object of competition among the Allies, but in Dorget's view MacArthur's power will remain supreme. The article concludes with a generally positive appraisal of the work of the occupation to date.

424 England, H. G. "The Punishment of Germany and Japan." *Hibbert Journal* 44:146–51 (Jan. 1946)

The author outlines the principles by which he feels policies toward a defeated Germany and Japan should be carried out. He bases them on the following: (1) abasement of pride, (2) forgiveness and love of enemies, (3) mutual dependence and need for cooperation, and (4) just reward of labor. Discussing the use of nuclear bombs against Japan, he feels there was justification for their use and that those innocent people who suffered will "receive their comfort and ample compensation in paradise."

425 "Ersatz Democracy for Japan." *Amerasia* 10:111–24 (Oct. 1946)

An article that is highly critical of the occupation with respect to the formulation and implementation of its policy. The author believes that "United States policy shifts from passive tolerance to active support of the old guard," and cites May 1946 as the decisive point of change. He discusses the results of the May elections, and the "*zaibatsu* cabinets" under Shidehara and Yoshida, as well as SCAP's activities in the drafting and adoption of the new constitution and its programs concerning the dissolution of the *zaibatsu*, land reform, and the promotion of the labor union movement. The author is also critical of SCAP for what he terms its disregard of the recommendations of the Far Eastern Commission. By way of a solution, he advocates the nationalization of basic industry and finance, real support of the labor union movement, and a really thorough political purge, as well as greater U.S. cooperation with the member nations of the Far Eastern Commission.

425a "First Year of Allied Occupation of Japan: Report of the Supreme Commander for the Allied Powers." *Department of State Bulletin* 15:460–61 (8 Sept. 1946)

This statement by a spokesman for SCAP was released on 29 August 1946 and summarizes in positive and very general terms SCAP's demobilization, disarmament, and reform activities.

426 Gayn, Mark J. "Japan: Bastion for World War III?" *Forum* 106:329–30 (Oct. 1946)

Reprinted from the author's column in the *Chicago Sun*, this article contrasts the initial mood of the occupation with the present one a year after Japan's surrender. The former mood is described as one of hope in effecting drastic political, social, and economic reforms, whereas the latter is characterized by a preoccupation with fortifying the country as a bastion against Soviet incursions. The author views this change in priorities as detrimental to the implementation of some of the more important reforms—particularly in the encouragement of the labor union movement.

427 ———. *Japan Diary*. New York: Sloane, 1948. x, 517p.

An eyewitness report in diary form by a *Chicago Sun* correspondent on events in Japan from December 1945 to October 1946 and in Korea from October to December 1946. Over two-thirds of the book concerns Japan. The author's style is lively and he views the occupation with some degree of cynicism and disillusion. His frequent trips to various local areas in Japan enabled him to present a valuable account of rural events and conditions at the time. His meetings with members of the occupation staff and various Japanese leaders also added a useful dimension to an understanding of what occurred in the SCAP High Command and in top Japanese government circles. Gayn maintains that the occupation's democratization program was a failure because it delegated authority to old style, antidemocratic leaders, who "sabotaged" all effective reform programs. Another reason for the failure, he suggests, is that "reformers" in General Headquarters were forced out as the military staff became predominant over the civilian staff. The book was translated into Japanese under the title *Nippon nikki* (Tokyo: Chikuma Shobō, 1952. 2v.).

428 ———. "Japanese Journey." *Forum* 105:638–39 (Mar. 1946)

This article, reprinted from a feature story in the *Chicago Sun*, describes the author's recent journey through the villages of rural Japan. He concludes from his experiences that the accomplishments of the occupation are more evident on paper than in actuality and attributes this failure to 2 factors: SCAP blunders and the tremendous vitality of traditional Japanese forces. The author is especially critical of SCAP's failure to effectively destroy the *zaibatsu* combines and advocates that punishment be meted out to those involved with any part of the prewar and wartime governing apparatus. He particularly recommends that officials on local levels be carefully and continually scrutinized by SCAP authorities.

429 ———. "Our Balance Sheet in Japan." *Collier's* 117:12–13, 81–82 (23 Mar. 1946)

An evaluation of the occupation after its first 6 months of operation is presented here, with emphasis placed on the attempt to encourage individual self-expression and the development of indigenous leadership. Gayn suggests that the American method of operating through existing Japanese leadership structures has permitted active subversion of the spirit of most democratic reforms. The alleged failure of educational reforms, land reform, and *zaibatsu* liquidation is noted as is the revival of nationalist organizations.

429a "General MacArthur's Emancipation of Japan: An Address by Dr. Arnold D. A. de Kat Angelino, Famed Netherlands Far Eastern Expert." *Knickerbocker Weekly* 6, no.6:10–11 (1 Apr. 1946)

This article reviews the highlights of a Dutch scholar's address at a Foreign Policy Association discussion meeting in New York on 16 March 1946. He is reported to have paid high tribute to MacArthur for the success of the occupation to date in such areas as demilitarization, the dissolution of ultranationalistic societies, and the enfranchising of Japanese women. He is also said to feel that the Japanese are sincere in their cooperation with SCAP because defeat has smashed their self-confidence and they now realize that they are dependent on foreign goodwill for almost everything.

429b Gorbatov, Boris. "Japan Today." *USSR Information Bulletin* 6, no.40: 339–41 (23 Apr. 1946)

Gorbatov, a correspondent for *Pravda*, attacks the continued existence of "Tennoism" and conservatism in early postwar Japan. He first provides a sarcastic report of the emperor's initial visit among the people to inspect war ruins, then reports on the unpopular and undemocratic nature of the Shidehara government. He also describes the displeasure of an unnamed Japanese cabinet official with Japan's new constitution which he regarded as a "document of bloody revolution," but Gorbatov notes that Japanese reactionaries should be pleased with the document as it retains the monarchy and the peerage.

430 Green, Owen Mortimer. "Japan in Defeat." *Fortnightly* 166, no.955:7–13 (July 1946)

A brief review of Japan's first year under the Allied occupation. Green notes that the destruction of Japan's military machine has proven easier than had been expected; lauds such reforms as the political purges, the decrease in censorship, and the abolition of Shinto as the state religion; and comments on the efforts to break up the *zaibatsu* and to carry out a comprehensive land reform. Part of the article discusses the new constitution—"the climax of General MacArthur's work"—which Green regards as being insufficiently Japanese in spirit. Finally, the author describes some of the economic and psychological readjustment which Japan is undergoing and concludes that it would be wise for the Allied powers to deal charitably with her when the terms of a peace treaty eventually are drafted.

431 Halliwell, Martin. "Japan, 1946." *Spectator* 176, no.6152:527–28 (24 May 1946)

The author of this article feared that the occupation was proceeding much too smoothly. Japanese reactionaries were acting obsequiously to encourage the rapid termination of the occupation and Japan's return to its former ways. Halliwell recommends, therefore, that the Allies remain in Japan for at least 25 years. Since Japanese industry was virtually destroyed during the war, he suggests that reparations take the form of coal, timber, medical supplies, and the labor of unrepatriated Japanese. He is worried that Asian nations, not appreciating Western good intentions, still respect Japan. Finally, he applauds MacArthur's brilliance and courage as head of SCAP.

432 Hart, Richard Harry. *Eclipse of the Rising Sun*. New York: Foreign Policy Assn., 1946. 96p. (Headline series, no. 56)

This brief overview of the first year of the Allied occupation is no.56 in the Headline series published by the Foreign Policy Association "to enable readers to reach intelligent and independent conclusions on the important international problems of the day." This volume should not be confused with another book by the same name, which is the British edition of Kase Toshikazu's book, *Journey to the Missouri* (1950) (no.143), published in London by Jonathan Cape. Richard Hart has been connected with public libraries since 1929, specializing in informal educational work with adults. During and immediately following World War II he was engaged in a project of writing and research about Japan for the War Department, and he also lectured and broadcast about American–Japanese relations. Basically favorable toward the occupation and its reform programs, the account first summarizes Japan's surrender and initial occupation tasks such as troop surrender and repatriation, war crimes trials, and disposition of the Japanese empire. Following a brief outline of occupation organization, the author describes various reforms implemented and planned in government and politics, in the economy, and in education and religion. The text is supplemented by a statement by Owen Lattimore on Japan's future, the preamble of the proposed Japanese constitution, summaries of principal sections of the new constitution and Bill of Rights, and a short annotated list of suggested readings.

432a "Has Democracy Taken Root in Japan?" *Christian Century* 63:1027 (28 Aug. 1946)

While democratic institutions still have little more than a foothold in Japan, Japan's great strides toward recovery contrast vividly with the chaos and disintegration evident in Germany. Japan nonetheless still faces grave economic problems, and the food shortage remains particularly acute. Meanwhile, the emperor's renunciation of his divinity has opened the way for Christianity. American Protestantism, however, has so far made little effort to exploit this opportunity in order to make its contribution to the spiritual foundations of democracy in Japan.

433 Horner, Francis J. "Japan Today." *Asiatic Review* 42:277–81 (July 1946)

In his account of occupied Japan, Horner details the many problems General MacArthur and his staff must confront. The greatest of them, he states, is understanding the Japanese psychology.

434 Horton, Douglas. "The Emperor and Democracy in Japan." *Congregational Quarterly* 24:134–38 (Apr. 1946)

Horton briefly discusses the emperor and the traditional Japanese concept of deities, then indicates his belief that the abolition of the imperial institution would considerably retard the democratization of a defeated Japan. He also speaks of a positive need for Christianity within the country and criticizes all of the reforms carried out in accordance with SCAP directives.

434a "Japan under Control." *Economist* 151:202–3 (10 Aug. 1946)

Since the April 1946 general election, support for the Yoshida government has weakened. If a new election were held at present, the Social Democrats would score heavy gains because they have been appealing to many groups suffering from economic problems which the conservative parties have not dealt with. The Social Democrats, however, have yet to find a way to appeal strongly to the workers. Despite such political tensions, Japan still is in a better overall state than Germany, since the country is united under one political authority, will soon have a new constitution, and is not embroiled in any significant territorial disputes. Furthermore, the Japanese are far more fortunate in some respects than the Germans, for "they have one master and they know who he is."

435 Johnson, U. Alexis. "Seventeen Days in Japan." *American Foreign Service Journal* 23:7–10, 57–64 (July 1946)

Johnson, American consul at Yokohama, gives an impressionistic account of his first postwar trip to Japan. He reports on the devastated condition of the major cities and discusses the immediate Allied concern for the release of all prisoners of war held in Japan. The author takes pains to stress the cooperation of Japanese officials and private citizens with the initial skeleton force of occupation personnel.

436 Johnstone, Anne, and William Crane Johnstone. *What Are We Doing with Japan?* New York: Institute of Pacific Relations, American Council, 1946. 64p. (Institute of Pacific Relations pamphlet no.19)

Reforms undertaken during the first year of the Allied occupation of Japan are recounted here. Topics treated include a brief history of presurrender maneuvers by both the Allies and Japan, the nature of indirect Allied rule over Japan, the basic directives of the opposition, and social, political, and economic reforms. The extent of constitutional revision, agrarian reform, the dissolution of *zaibatsu*, reparations, and the political ferment of early 1946 are examined in detail. Allied indifference to political developments in Japan is termed "fatal" for the next generation, for this indifference could permit a resurgence of the quiescent but by no means extinct Old Guard at the expense of the weak and inexperienced democratic elements.

437 La Cerda, John. *The Conqueror Comes to Tea: Japan under MacArthur.* New Brunswick, N.J.: Rutgers Univ. Pr., 1946. 224p.

This collection of loosely organized anecdotes and observations conveys some of the flavor of early occupation days in Japan but contains little of scholarly interest. A broad range of topics is haphazardly touched upon, including the Japanese personality, prostitution, the imperial family, government and politics in Japan, MacArthur and the press, labor unions, the war crimes trials, and Christian missionaries. General MacArthur's opening address to the Allied Council for Japan is appended.

438 Lamott, Willis Church. "Japan Follows a Pattern." *Virginia Quarterly Review* 22:370-82 (Summer 1946)

This article attempts to penetrate behind the surface reasons for the rapid conversion of Japan to a democratic state. The author believes this conversion to be due to the government leaders' self-interest as well as strong pressure from SCAP. He discusses and compares the changes that were undertaken by the Meiji Restoration of 1868 and the revolutionary changes wrought by the occupation authorities. There is a consideration of the continued dominance of the conservative Old Guard in government and industry with the suggestion that Japan may be adapting itself "to the dominant political philosophy of the world until a position is attained from which power can be exerted and advantage gained." He believes that the U.S. occupation authorities must put forth a prolonged effort to gradually educate the people in true democratic ways of thought and action to insure a real and lasting democratic reconstruction of the country.

439 Lin, Hu. "How to Deal with Japan." *Foreign Affairs* 24:253-61 (Jan. 1946)

In a discussion of Allied treatment of a defeated Japan the Chinese author of this report begins by stating that the Chinese "now wish to destroy only Japan's aggressive ambitions, not to annihilate the Japanese as a nation or as a people." He recommends a humane occupation which would eradicate militarism and change the Japanese pattern of thinking. There is a review of the background of what he deems necessary reform, i.e., that the emperor system be unconditionally abolished, that land reform be effected, that the economic system be completely revised, eliminating the *zaibatsu* and destroying all heavy industry, and that widespread educational reform be effected. His final remarks concern the authority directing the occupation. The author strongly recommends that broad occupation policies be formulated jointly by the principal members of the United Nations sitting in Tokyo, not Washington, and that they should delegate responsibilities to General MacArthur as supreme commander.

440 Lipp, Frederick J. "Yuhoko and the State: Current Reactionary Trends in Japan." *Free World* 12:23-26 (Dec. 1946)

Slightly more than a year after the beginning of the occupation the author, a former U.S. Navy correspondent in Tokyo, discusses the political reforms enacted by SCAP and the current political stance of the Japanese government. He characterizes MacArthur's political reforms as "a remarkable piece of political engineering" on paper and devotes the rest of his report to a study of why so many reforms have proved ineffective. He cites the political immaturity of the people and the continued use of former government bureaucrats as compelling reasons, and he discusses the unfortunate implications of the change in U.S. policy toward conservatism as a result of growing Soviet–American conflict. He voices alarm at the continuous increase of power by the ultraconservatives and support of that power by the conservative government presently in office.

441 Matsumoto, Toru, and Marion Olive Lerrigo. *A Brother Is a Stranger.* New York: Day, 1946. xiii, 318p.

Matsumoto, a Japanese Christian who was in the United States at the outbreak of the Pacific war and was interned for the next three and a half years, devotes most of this memoir to a description of his childhood in Japan. The closing chapters (p.272–318), however, describe his reactions to the Japanese surrender and reproduce a series of conversations with American friends and acquaintances about the future prospects of Japan as seen by a Westernized Japanese. The topics discussed include the imperial system and Japanese attitudes toward it, likely obstacles to the democratization of Japan, the Japanese social system, and the Japanese tendency toward fatalism.

442 Matsumoto, Tsuyoshi. "A Plan for Japan." *Asia and the Americas* 46:170–72 (Apr. 1946)

In detailing his 10-point plan for a new Japan, Matsumoto states that the foundation for a strong Japan still exists but what it needs is a new purpose, a new way of utilizing its dynamic power, and a new leadership. During the war, Matsumoto Tsuyoshi taught Japanese to U.S. Army personnel.

443 May, Henry F., Jr. "MacArthur Era, Year One." *Harper's Magazine* 192:226–73 (Mar. 1946); abridged and published under the same title in *Reader's Digest* 48:55–58 (June 1946)

This account of the early mood of the occupation is based on the author's experiences during a recent visit to Japan. The bulk of the article centers on the friendliness and cooperation that the Japanese have shown to their conquerors. The author attempts to analyze this phenomenon. He provides several explanations. Some Japanese are acting in compliance with official policy, out of commercial motive, or merely in awe of American military power, and their attitudes are merely superficial. Others, however, have a genuine liking and admiration for the Americans due to the good conduct of American troops in Japan and to the existence of liberal and pro-Western sentiment carried over from the 1930s. The author recommends that the occupation authorities attempt to work through the latter group of Japanese if they are to create a truly democratic society within the country.

444 Mears, Helen. "Our Far-Flung Correspondent: Tokyo Revisited." *New Yorker* 22:100–109 (19 Oct. 1946)

In the first of 2 brief reports from Tokyo, the author comments on the overwhelming presence of Americans in Tokyo, on various housing, food, and clothing problems that the Japanese are continuing to face, and on the general behavior of American GIs in Japan.

445 ———. "Our Far-Flung Correspondent: You in Tokyo." *New Yorker* 22:84–93 (23 Nov. 1946)

Titled after a pamphlet given by SCAP's Office of Civilian Personnel to Americans upon their arrival in Tokyo, this second of 2 brief reports from Tokyo focuses on the adjustment of American civilians to life in postwar Japan. The author depicts a very comfortable style of living for SCAP personnel and points out, among other things, how involved Americans have become in black-market speculation.

Montgomery, John D. "Administration of Occupied Japan: First Year." 1949. *See* no.908.

446 Morris, John. "Japan under the Occupation." *Fortnightly* 166:301–8 (Nov. 1946)

An analysis of the general conduct of the occupation written from a British viewpoint. The author defines and discusses the tasks of the occupation as being 2-fold—the first, the immediate military problem of destroying Japan's actual capacity to again menace the peace, and the second, the long-term educational objective of destroying Japan's will to disturb the peace of the world. Although he generally considers the first year of the occupation to be a success, nevertheless, he suggests that it might be improved if SCAP were to allow a greater degree of participation by the other Allied powers. He forecasts some form of occupation for 15 or 20 years in order to insure a reeducation of the Japanese in the democratic way of life.

447 ——. *The Phoenix Cup: Some Notes on Japan in 1946.* London: Cresset, 1947. x, 224p.

An informal report of the author's experiences during a 6-month stay in occupied Japan as a special correspondent for the News Division of the British Broadcasting Corporation. In an objective and absorbing account, he presents a portrait that is focused upon the Japanese people and their reactions to defeat in the immediate aftermath of the war. As a British citizen, his evaluation of the American occupation troops and the impact of their presence in Japan is notably objective. Although such economic and political matters as food shortages and political elections are considered, they are usually discussed in relation to particular persons or events in the author's experience. The book is successful in evoking the general atmosphere of Japan in 1946.

448 Nehmer, Stanley. "Japan under MacArthur." *Current History* 11:118–27 (Aug. 1946)

This article presents a brief description of what the author, a State Department official, considers the 10 major steps taken by SCAP in the first 8 months of the occupation for the purpose of restructuring Japanese life. The 10 major areas of SCAP activity are summarized as: the establishment of civil liberties, the purge of war criminals, the weakening of Shinto, the promulgation of a new constitution, the holding of national elections, the dissolution of the *zaibatsu*, the encouragement of agrarian reform, the establishment of inflation controls, the creation of a program to alleviate the problem of food shortages, and the encouragement of an eventual trade revival. For each of these topics, the author discusses the relevant SCAP directives and the effects of the new reforms upon Japanese society.

449 Noble, Harold J. *What It Takes to Rule Japan.* New York: U.S. Camera, 1946. 96p.

A U.S. Marine Corps major, the author gives his observations on the Pacific War and postsurrender Japan. He regards the Japanese as a formidable enemy. He analyzes the merits and demerits of Japanese military operations in the first half of the book, and in the second half he discusses the problems of ruling a defeated Japan. Such problems as the language barrier, a lack of experience of military rule on the part of the Americans, and the lack of Japanese leadership for progressive reform are cited. The author also holds that there should be a single command system under General MacArthur to rule Japan, that Emperor Hirohito should retain the throne, and that democracy cannot be imposed upon the Japanese. He suggests that the occupation be conducted with cold logic and avoidance of emotional fervor. There are approximately 30 pages of pictures illustrating the bitterness of battles in the Pacific islands, prewar Japanese daily life, the devastation of Tokyo and Hiroshima caused by American bombings, the Japanese surrender, and the beginning of the occupation. The text of this publication, it should be noted, first appeared in the 29 September 1945 issue of the *Saturday Evening Post*.

449a "Non-military Activities in Japan and Korea." *Department of State Bulletin* pt.1 "Political Activities in Japan" 14: 749–51 (5 May 1946); pt.2 "Economic Activities in Japan" 14:804–6 (12 May 1946); pt.3 "Social Activities in Japan" 14:807–8 (12 May 1946); pt.4 "Legal and War Crimes" 14:808–12 (12 May 1946)

This article consists of excerpts from issue no.5 of SCAP's *Summation of Non-Military Activities in Japan and Korea* (no.262) covering developments in a wide range of areas during the month of February 1946. A map of SCAP admin-

449b "Occupation Policy in Japan." *Economist* 150:82–84 (19 Jan. 1946)

MacArthur's purge directive of 4 January 1946 is said to highlight a basic contradiction in American policy. In order to carry through the reforms needed to pacify and democratize Japan, MacArthur must rely on old-style Japanese bureaucrats and politicians. Otherwise, chaos might result which would damage MacArthur's reputation at a time when he is being considered at home as a potential presidential candidate. Generally speaking, however, SCAP personnel are dedicated reformers of New Deal type. This accounts for the occupation's policy of branding the capitalists, the landowners and the military as "enemies of the people." Nevertheless, SCAP is criticized daily in the American press for allowing old Japanese political and business leaders to continue in positions of influence. The unavoidable contradictions in Allied policy, then, are such that the best course is to withdraw from Japan as soon as possible in order to allow the Japanese to work out their own solutions.

450 "The Outlook in Japan." *World Today* 2:512–23 (Nov. 1946)

A discussion of social and political developments in the occupation program 1 year after Japan's surrender. The article considers the problems of reeducating the Japanese under 2 aspects. The first concerns straightforward political decisions such as the demobilization of the armed forces, the apprehension of war criminals, and the enactment of a new constitution. The second relates to the more complex matter of adjusting traditional Japanese culture to a political and social revolution. The author particularly emphasizes the controversy over romanizing the Japanese script, altering the position of the emperor, and conducting war crimes trials. He concludes that in the first year of the occupation the worst social and political abuses have been abolished and the worst men eliminated from public life.

451 Parrott, Lindesay. "Can We Prevent a Japanese Hitler?" *New York Times Magazine* p.12, 46–47 (10 Mar. 1946)

The author reports that after 6 months, the American occupation of Japan has made some progress, but the contrast between the wealthy black market profiteers and the impoverished former soldiers reveals that many problems are yet to be solved. The author investigates what the common man believes about democracy and its chances for survival in Japan. He sees the greatest danger in the Japanese tendency to equate democracy with disrespect for the law. He stresses the need for more well-informed American military government personnel who can interpret democracy to the people. He concludes that regardless of the negative or positive aspects of the occupation, it will take at least a generation to see if democracy has taken root in Japan.

452 ———. "Japan a Year after: Still a 'Gamble'." *New York Times Magazine* p. 18, 45 (25 Aug. 1946)

Reviewing the first year of the occupation, the author states that the demilitarization of Japan has been accomplished. He believes that with the introduction of the "American-inspired" constitution, the second goal of preparing the ground for a new regime is well on its way to completion. It is also confirmed by the success of the first postwar election. In the author's opinion the third goal of creating a new democratic system still has not been reached. The basic problem is how to achieve the economic stability necessary for a sound political system.

453 Penrose, William O. "Japanese Reeducation: The Imperial Carp vs. Civil Rights." *Harvard Educational Review* 16:160–66 (Summer 1946)

Identifying the imperial carp as the symbol for emperor worship and the traditional Japanese national polity, the author illustrates the conflict of this symbol with another symbol—the American flag, which represents the democratic form of government. In an informal narrative description of the life of an ordinary Japanese citizen, the author tries to convey the effects of the occupation reforms upon his life. Such reforms concern the lifting of restrictions on political, civil, and religious liberties and the abolition of the thought police. The 10 April elections are viewed as Japan's first step toward responsible popular government. The latter part of the article discusses educational reforms and while the author concludes that changes have been of a negative character thus far (i.e., rooting out nationalistic and militaristic influences) he believes that positive changes are imminent. The article includes a summary of the major recommendations for Japanese education as presented by Kermit Eby, a member of the U.S. Education Mission to Japan.

454 Pevsner, J. "Japan after Capitulation." *Soviet Press Translations* 1:12–25 (30 Nov. 1946)

In an article published by *Pravda* in March 1946, there is an analysis of the actions that have been taken by the Allies in order to break the power of the "reactionary cliques, responsible for the war in the Far East." The report is highly critical not of SCAP but rather of the present Japanese government under Shidehara. The author characterizes this government as preoccupied with preserving untouched the administrative machinery of the old system. Moreover, he provides prewar and present production figures issued by the Japanese press and discusses the methods currently being used to convert the economy to a peacetime basis. There is coverage of General MacArthur's attempts to dissolve the *zaibatsu* combines, the initial SCAP efforts at land reform, and recent developments in the leading political parties. In the opinion of the author, the Shidehara government has been unable to cope with the political and economic problems facing Japan. The final section of the report describes the postwar activities of the Japan Communist party in its efforts to overcome the ultraconservative groups still in power in Japan. The author concludes by affirming his faith that the alliance of the 4 great Allied powers will ultimately succeed in the democratization of Japan.

455 "Policies and Principles." *Time* 47: 25–26 (14 Jan. 1946)

Time reviews the first report issued by General MacArthur on the progress of the occupation. The existence of a gap between SCAP directives and their implementation is noted. The position of the Allied Council and the Far Eastern Commission as policy-making bodies with power to oversee SCAP activity is discussed.

455a "Premier Shigheru Yoshida's Broadcast Address on the Eve of the First Anniversary of Japan's Unconditional Surrender, August 14, 1946." *Contemporary Japan* 15:393–94 (Sept./Dec. 1946)

Great changes, according to Prime Minister Yoshida Shigeru, have occurred in Japan during the course of 1 year. Demilitarization, sweeping changes in the structure and leadership of government, the dissolution of the *zaibatsu*, the land reform, the purges, and the apprehension of suspected war criminals are among the major developments. Japan's reconstruction as "a new nation of culture and a new democratic state," however, is still far from complete. The rehabilitation of the economy is only beginning, and there is need to approve the new constitution, which promises a great future for Japan. Yoshida also comments on Japan's postwar international position. She is now cut off and quarantined from the rest of the world, he points out, and only by faithfully carrying out the terms of the Potsdam Declaration will Japan be able to bring this unfortunate situation to an end.

455b Price, Willard. *Key to Japan*. New York: Day, 1946. viii, 309p.

While much of this book may be characterized as travelogue or popular history, Price uses his description of people, places, and events as a vehicle for communicating his views on the Japanese national character and on what the occupation should try to achieve in Japan. As in many of his other works, he sharply criticizes SCAP's decision to permit the continued existence of the imperial institution, which he feels will remain a potential rallying point for Japanese militarism and authoritarianism. He also consistently portrays the Japanese as a formidable people in both war and peace.

456 Profumo, J. D. "Japan under MacArthur." *Journal of the Royal Central Asian Society* 34:175–85 (Apr. 1947)

This article is a lecture given by Profumo before the Royal Central Asian Society in December of 1946. Profumo had been the prime minister's representative to SCAP during the first phase of the occupation. In his talk Profumo reviews the political, economic, and social situation in Japan. He discusses the occupation itself and the goals of demilitarization and democratization.

456a Redman, H. Vere. "Japan and the Japanese." *Journal of the Royal United Service Institution* 91:112–19 (Feb. 1946)

This article, the text of a lecture which the author delivered on 14 November 1945, covers a variety of topics dealing with Japanese society. The cramped living conditions of the Japanese, Redman states, are conducive to a "highly developed social sense," but at the same time they severely restrict the freedom of the individual. The Japanese family system is very representative of social customs, and the low position of women and a strong sense of fixed social order are noteworthy elements of family life. Law in Japan is seen as a protection for the vast body of customary procedure and as a servant of an omnipotent state. The author's talk concludes with a discussion of religion in Japan centering upon state Shinto.

The Reminiscences of Alvin Graves. 1961. *See* no.44d.

The Reminiscences of Joseph Ballantine. 1961. *See* no.44n.

"Reports from a Neglected Area." 1946. *See* no.972a.

457 Rosinger, Lawrence K. "Can U.S. Do More to Back Democratic Elements in Japan?" *Foreign Policy Bulletin* 26: 2–3 (1 Nov. 1946)

The author criticizes SCAP's exaggeration of democratic developments in Japan and its enthusiastic support of the Yoshida government. He believes that it is contrary to previous policy statements wherein the United States pledged itself "to use the existing form of government in Japan, not to support it." He cites instances where the United States has supported a strong Japanese right wing out of fear of a very weak left wing and warns that such a policy will serve to destroy the moderate progressive elements in the Japanese society. Finally he advocates that the United States move toward a greater measure of civilian control of the occupation, giving the State Department the predominant role in the formulation of policy and relegating the army to action as a police force.

458 ———. "Will U.S. Occupation Bring Fundamental Changes to Japan?" *Foreign Policy Bulletin* 26, no.1:1–2 (18 Oct. 1946)

In an attempt to shatter American complacency regarding the success of the occupation that has been fostered by overly simplistic statements from SCAP headquarters, the author urges that one look at 2 distinct spheres of the occupation: "the sphere of paper directives and laws and the sphere of reality." Sometimes, he believes, the 2 overlap and impressive results are achieved, but often, particularly with respect to social reforms, the 2 spheres are widely divergent. He illustrates his point by citing rural attitudes toward some of the democratic reforms initiated, and he urges renewed energy in the business of effectively implementing reform programs in Japan.

459 Roth, Andrew. "Japan Unchanged." *New Statesman and Nation* 31:240–41 (6 Apr. 1946)

The author takes a pessimistic view of the occupation to date, suggesting that there exists a cabal of prewar Japanese leaders which has successfully avoided the Allied purge and has worked to sabotage democratization, while retaining the substance of power in their own hands. To support this position, he cites as evidence SCAP's failure to change the system of land tenure and the retention of wartime police personnel in security and liaison capacities. He predicts that increased tension between the Union of Soviet Socialist Republics and the United States will encourage occupation authorities to water down planned democratization programs and to accept continued reactionary rule in Japan.

460 Sano, Manabu. "Democratic Revolution in the Making." *Contemporary Japan* 15:175–88 (May/Aug. 1946)

A Japanese Socialist presents his interpretation of the changes wrought in the postwar political and social structure of Japan. He views postwar Japan as in the throes of a fourth revolution in its history, which he categorizes as a democratic revolution in contrast to its 3 predecessors. He predicts drastic changes in the constitution and the role of the emperor, and looks forward to an economic democracy for both urban and rural sectors of Japanese society.

461 Schwartz, Doris. "Letters from an Army Nurse in Japan." *New York Times Magazine* p.21, 57 (14 Apr. 1946)

In excerpts from her letters, Schwartz records her impressions of life in the Japanese countryside. The comments reveal the occupation personnel's initial apprehensiveness of the Japanese people and an American tendency to be patronizing once they got acquainted.

462 Snow, Edgar. "Is Japan Drifting toward Socialism?" *Saturday Evening Post* 218:20, 129–30 (22 June 1946)

In a critical look at the reforms of SCAP, Snow, a world correspondent for the *Post*, attempts to forecast what is likely to develop when the occupation ends. He notes that many reforms remain only on paper because of indifference and deliberate sabotage by the Japanese bureaucracy and because of a lack of thoroughness in punitive measures by the Allies. Fundamental policies such as land reform, disposition of government property, and the rights of organized labor versus capital present growing dilemmas which can hardly be solved within the limits of accepted American economic practice alone.

463 ———. "What the Jap Is Thinking Now." *Saturday Evening Post* 218:9–11, 36+ (11 May 1946)

Snow, a *Post* correspondent, describes the impact of the war on a rural Japanese village and its reaction to various directives from SCAP. From his conversations with different groups within the community, he relates their opinions about their government, the emperor, and the occupation.

464 Spencer, Joseph E. "Japan and the Peace." *Proceedings of the Institute of World Affairs* 21:167–70 (1946)

A round table discussion on Japan headed by D. C. Holtom is briefly summarized in this article. Topics considered in the discussion include the economic situation of Japan, its population problems, and certain Japanese social, religious, and educational factors that must be understood by the architects of the occupation before they can effect any lasting change in the country.

465 Strauss, Harold. "Right Face in Japan." *Nation* 163:606–9 (30 Nov. 1946)

The author attempts to describe and analyze the reasons behind what he characterizes as a drastic change in the complexion of occupation policy after 20 May 1946 which affected not only SCAP policies concerning Japan but also U.S. relations with the other Allied powers, particularly the Soviet Union. He characterizes this change as one from toleration of moderate socialist objectives to one of opposition to them and discusses

SCAP's labor and price control policies as well as its stand during the recent elections as illustrative of its growing conservatism. The author concludes that the real test of SCAP intentions will come in 1947 when growing Socialist strength may cause a new election. SCAP's reaction to this situation, he affirms, will indicate its true character.

465a "Summary of Non-Military Activities in Japan for May 1946." *Department of State Bulletin* 15:127–30, 132 (21 July 1946)

This article is based on issue no.8 of SCAP's *Summation of Non-Military Activities in Japan and Korea* (no.262) covering significant developments during May 1946. Among the subjects covered are the formation of the Yoshida cabinet, labor demonstrations, the apprehension of war criminals, problems of food shortages, industrial production, finance, and the reparations question.

466 Supreme Commander for the Allied Powers. *Two Memoranda of General C. Whitney to MacArthur about Interviews with Japan's Prime Minister Shidehara, January 25, 28, 1946.* Record Group 5, Box 80. MacArthur Memorial, Bureau of Archives, Norfolk, Va. 1 folder.

The file contains a biographical report on members of the Shidehara cabinet compiled by the Office of the Chief of Counterintelligence of General Headquarters on 23 October 1945. The report is intended to indicate the previous experience and political outlook as well as the present positions of Shidehara and the various ministers in his cabinet. Sources of biographical information are cited and generally are drawn from Japanese periodicals and the *Who's Who in Japan*. Also included are 2 memorandums to SCAP from General Courtney Whitney, chief of the Government Section, regarding talks with Prime Minister Shidehara which took place in January 1946, concerning the provisions of the SCAP directive relating to the purge of political figures in the Japanese government.

467 Tiltman, Hessell. "Letter from Tokyo —Learning Democracy." *New Republic* 115:229–30 (26 Aug. 1946)

In a letter written from Tokyo the author presents a few firsthand observations of the occupation. Although acknowledging the fact that SCAP has effected a number of important changes, nevertheless he warns against thinking that Japanese society can be transformed in a few months or even years. The latter part of the letter relates to Japanese attitudes regarding their present situation as affected by Soviet-American tensions. The author describes the fear many Japanese have of aligning themselves with either power. Finally, he suggests that to really effect lasting democratic reform Japan must vastly raise the quality of its legislators.

468 U.S. Dept. of State. *Occupation of Japan: Policy and Progress.* Washington, D.C.: Government Printing Office, 1946. iv, 173p. (Dept. of State publication 2671; Far Eastern series 17)

A general outline of Allied policy toward the occupation of Japan is presented along with a report of progress up to the middle of 1946. The document begins with a presentation of major official policies and decisions that led to the establishment of the Allied occupation, such as the Cairo and Yalta Conferences and the Potsdam Declaration, the Far Eastern Advisory Commission, the Far Eastern Commission, and the U.S. Initial Post-Surrender Policy. This section on policy development is followed by a description of SCAP's structure and SCAP's directives with respect to various aspects of Japanese society. They include demilitarization, constitutional reform, the growth of party government, electoral practice, war criminals, reparations, education, economics, the *zaibatsu*, labor, and international trade. The report concludes with President Truman's Army Day speech on 6 April 1946 relating to the American role in the Far East in the attainment of a lasting peace. The appendixes comprise the texts of 39 major documents prepared by the Allied nations, the United States, or Japan, in

1943–46. Beginning with the Cairo Declaration of 1943, the documents range from the text of the first Japanese offer of surrender made to the United States through the Swiss government on 10 Aug. 1945, to a summary of the U.S. Education Mission to Japan's report in April 1946. Other important documents are SCAP directives on the purge, the Japanese draft constitution as submitted to SCAP on 22 April 1946, the imperial rescript of 1 January 1946, the charter of the International Military Tribunal for the Far East as amended on 26 April 1946, the initial reparations policy formulated by the Far Eastern Commission on 13 May 1946, and so forth. A very useful publication.

469 ———. ———. "Occupation: Why? What? Where?" *Foreign Affairs Outlines: Building the Peace* no.10:1–4 (Autumn 1946) (Dept. of State publication 2627)

American participation in the Allied occupation of "defeated countries," namely, Germany and Japan, and of "liberated countries," namely, Austria and Korea, is briefly outlined. The article describes the basic principles of U.S. foreign policy as well as various army and navy programs begun in 1942 for training occupation personnel. There is also a consideration of methods of occupation, the role of SCAP in Japan, problems of occupation, demilitarization and democratization, and length of occupation.

470 ———. ———. "What We Are Doing in Japan—and Why." *Foreign Affairs Outlines: Building the Peace* no.12:1–4 (Autumn 1946) (Dept. of State publication 2633; Far Eastern series 15)

The work of 160,000 Americans in uniform and 2,000 American civilians in the occupation and control of Japan is briefly discussed. Items include the objectives, the estimated length and machinery of the occupation, the origin and development of the Allied policy of occupation (viewing the Cairo Conference of 1943 as the starting point of policy formulation), and areas of SCAP concern related to the reform of Japanese society. In connection with the last item, reference is made to disarmament, dissolution of economic combines, reparations, agrarian reforms, SCAP's "bill of rights" directive, the abolition of state Shinto, the purge, the elimination of the secret police, the establishment of democratic electoral systems, prosecution of war criminals, and educational reform. The occupation is viewed as "a long and difficult job" lying ahead.

471 "U.S. in Japan." *Life* 20:32 (18 Feb. 1946)

This editorial commends the leadership of General MacArthur. It suggests the need for a long-term plan for Japan's future which would allow the development of light industry while shifting heavy industry to other Asian nations. The creation of the Far Eastern Commission is discussed and the hope expressed that this body will create substantive Allied policy rather than bicker about reparations distribution.

472 Van Kirk, Walter W. "Winning the Peace in Japan." *Christian Century* 63: 106–8 (23 Jan. 1946)

Van Kirk analyzes occupation policies, praising MacArthur's leadership and the creation of a new constitution. The banning of fascist organizations, the purging of certain individuals, the liquidation of *zaibatsu* control in the economy, and the creation of a free and democratic press are examined. Allied directives on education are seen as the key to the creation of an intellectually free society.

473 Walser, T. D. "Revenge or Peace in Japan." *Christian Century* 63, no.40: 1178–79 (2 Oct. 1946)

This article, an attack on occupation policies, levels 3 major criticisms against Allied activities in Japan. They concern forced Americanization, the war crimes trials, and the economic policies of Ambassador E. W. Pauley. The author sees MacArthur's democratization policy as American style democracy or nothing at all. In his view Japan was partially forced to war by the threat of economic strangulation, and thus the war crimes trials were too harsh. Finally, he questions the economic policies of Pauley as leading to the economic enslavement of the country. Walser was a Presbyterian minister in Tokyo prior to World War II and at this writing served as secretary of the Fellowship of Reconciliation in New York City.

474 Westerfield, Hargis. "Failures in GI Orientation: The Japanese Story." *Free World* 11:62–63 (Apr. 1946)

An American soldier tells of the undesirable behavior of GIs in Japan after World War II. He attributes part of the reason for the soldiers' conduct to weak American army orientation programs including lack of language training. He points out attitudes which could be formed by the Japanese in response to their contact with these Americans.

475 Wheeler, Post. *Dragon in the Dust.* Hollywood, Calif.: Marcell Rodd, 1946. 253p.

In the preface of his book, Wheeler, a member of the diplomatic corps who served in the American embassy in Tokyo intermittently after 1906, addresses himself to the question of the nature of Allied policy for the defeated nation, and he urges the adoption of harsh measures against a people whom he characterizes as untrustworthy and devious. Specifically, he recommends the abolition of the imperial institution, unremitting scrutiny and control of the Japanese people, and abolition of every vestige of Shintoism. To provide support for his argument that strong measures should be employed by the occupation against the Japanese, Wheeler describes events and emotions that transpired during his various sojourns in Japan and attempts to demonstrate that these experiences were components of a broad trend of deception, militarism, and arrogance that led the nation into war. On the basis of his description, it appears that Wheeler hoped to influence the fundamental character of the Allied occupation rather than provide any detailed commentary concerning the specifics of occupation policy.

476 Wincelberg, Simon. "Visiting Professor." *American Mercury* 75:50–56 (July 1952)

The author, a free lance writer, presents an informal account of his experiences as a language teacher in Japan during the initial months of the occupation. Although officially a part of the Public Relations Section of SCAP's Division Headquarters in Niigata, he taught English conversation to the city's most prominent individuals. The account is anecdotal and does convey in a humorous manner something of the atmosphere of the early occupation in the outlying areas.

1947

477 Allen, Lafe Franklin. "Democracy in Japan." *Commonweal* 46:542–46 (19 Sept. 1947)

The author, a former military officer in Japan, is optimistic about the prospects for a democratic Japan as long as the occupation is not ended "before our reforms have had time to jell." After a discussion of the techniques of repression employed by the prewar and wartime Japanese governments, Allen turns to SCAP's efforts to redirect the Japanese toward democracy. He then offers examples of the results of these efforts: the high (72.1%) turnout of voters in the April 1946 elections, the enthusiasm with which workers have greeted unionization, the vigorous press criticism of the government, and the fact that Japan elected its first Socialist premier in May 1947. After making a plea that Japan be allowed "an honest chance to regain her footing economically," Allen closes with several further paragraphs of glowing praise for the Japanese people's intelligence and willingness to learn.

477a Arnold, David. "What Is MacArthur up to?" *Soviet Russia Today* 16:10–11, 30 (Dec. 1947)

A strongly critical analysis of the conduct of the occupation. The author believes that all of the occupation policies have been shaped toward building Japan into an anti-Soviet base. He condemns MacArthur's "one-man rule" in Japan and discusses Soviet claims to a greater voice in the occupation. He further criticizes what he terms MacArthur's preservation of the foundations of the old order, his ineffectual purge of the militarists, the incomplete program for *zaibatsu* dissolution, and the inadequate reparations program. Finally, the article considers what the author sees as the flagrant injustices of the proposed arrangements for a peace conference.

478 Baldwin, Roger Nash. "New Liberties in Old Japan." *Survey Graphic* 36: 421–25 (Aug. 1947)

The president of the American Civil Liberties Union gives his impressions of reform in occupied Japan. He begins with a glowing account of the popularity of MacArthur, the friendliness of occupation troops, the civil liberties guaranteed in the new constitution and the new status of the emperor. "These amazing accomplishments... are due both to directives conceived in the best American tradition and to the inherent desires of long suppressed popular forces in Japan itself." Still, the author finds that all is not perfect. He criticizes occupation censorship, the trial of Japanese before American provost courts, limits on the civil liberties of occupation personnel, and various Japanese problems not related to the occupation such as police abuses and discrimination against minority groups in Japan.

479 Behrstock, Arthur. "Japan Goes American." *American Magazine* 143:14–18 (May 1947)

480 Beuschlein, Alice. "United States Policy and Japan." *Proceedings of the Institute of World Affairs* 23:89–92 (1947)

Professor Delmer Brown was the chairman of this panel discussion concerning how and to what extent Allied policy is being implemented in Japan. Topics which are briefly considered include measures enacted to promote economic stability, the educational reforms, and the changing role of Shinto in Japanese religious life.

481 Borton, Hugh. "American Occupation Policies in Japan." *Department of State Bulletin* 17:1001–5 (23 Nov. 1947); also in *Proceedings of the Academy of Political Science* 22:397–405 (Jan. 1948)

This report, prepared by the special assistant to the director of the Office of Far Eastern Affairs, is an excellent overall summation of the occupation. The author concisely discusses the concepts upon which occupation policy was based, the development of the hierarchy of authority among the Allied powers, and the establishment of such advisory bodies as the Far Eastern Advisory Commission and the Far Eastern Commission. After a consideration of the activities and recommendations of these bodies as well as their limitations, there is a detailed presentation of SCAP activity in the political and economic spheres with particular reference to the provisions of the new constitution and the establishment and operations of the Inter-Allied Trade Board for Japan. The concluding section of the report outlines the difficulties associated with the negotiation of a peace treaty with Japan.

482 Brumbaugh, Thoburn T. "Perilous Opportunity in Japan." *Christian Century* 64:172–73 (5 Feb. 1947)

Concern over the unsettled economic situation in Japan is expressed by Brumbaugh. He examines occupation directives which seek both to liberalize and free Japanese society and to suppress radicalism in business, politics, and social relations. He emphasizes the spiritual reconstitution of Japan and notes MacArthur's active participation in promoting Christianity and in calling for missionaries.

Busch, Noel F. "Occupation of Japan." 1947. *See* no.2284.

483 Buss, Claude A. "The Problems of the United States in the Pacific." *Proceedings of the Institute of World Affairs* 23:121–37 (1946)

A large portion of this article on U.S. policy in the Far East is devoted to the occupation of Japan. It outlines the structure and responsibilities of the various organizations involved—SCAP, the Allied Council, and the Far Eastern Commission—and discusses their achievements in the economic and political spheres. In addition, the author mentions the criticisms directed at the occupation and discusses the bitter disagreements in the Allied Council between the United States and the USSR regarding Allied policy and its implementation.

484 Canham, Erwin D. "Can This Be Japan?" *Christian Science Monitor* magazine section 39, no.128:2–3 (26 Apr. 1947)

The editor of the *Christian Science Monitor*, at the conclusion of a tour of the Far East, gives his glowing report on U.S.–Japanese amicability during the occupation. The plush life-style of the higher occupation officers is mentioned along with the "charm" of traditional Japan. The degree to which Japan would adapt to democracy is seen as crucial for the world's future.

485 Chaze, Elliott. *The Stainless Steel Kimono.* New York: Simon & Schuster, 1947. x, 207p.

This fast-moving, hilarious account about American paratroopers on duty in northern Japan is by a former reporter for the Associated Press who arrived in Japan a few months after the occupation had begun. While commenting on the obedience, patience and passive resistance of the Japanese whom he met, he makes no attempt to present the reader with more than a superficial understanding of Japan or of the Japanese as a conquered people. Most of his narrative is concerned with the way in which he and his buddies lived in Japan until their transfer back to the States. Chaze's book, therefore, is useful for understanding the lives and attitudes of many young Americans who participated in this particular army of occupation.

486 Close, Upton. "Japan Remade—and China: The One Laurel on Our Crown." *Vital Speeches* 14:41–44 (1 Nov. 1947)

An author and lecturer, Close delivered this speech to the Executives' Club of Chicago on 3 October 1947. He attempts to prove his contention that "Japan is the only place in the world where our going to war has in any way helped democracy or civilization." After categorizing the Japanese as a "feminine-minded people given to extremes of fury and docility," he attributes the success of the occupation to the leadership of General MacArthur, who refused to tolerate the "crowd of radicals" from the State Department, the New Deal bureaucrats, and the civilians who were attempting to bring chaos into Japan just as they did in Germany. It is the author's opinion that Japan is only one of the modern nations suffering from a lack of moral authority and he advocates the establishment of a new moral force in Japan in the form of Christianity.

487 Cochrane, Robert B. "MacArthur Era: Year Two." *Harper's Magazine* 195:277–84 (Sept. 1947)

The second year of the occupation is seen as one of crisis by the author, a former war correspondent and also former head of the Tokyo bureau of the *Sun* papers of Baltimore. The author attributes this crisis to General MacArthur's determination to maintain his free hand in the occupation at all costs. He discusses the most significant reforms ordered by MacArthur at the outset of the occupation and is highly critical of MacArthur's insistence that the emperor be freed of war guilt and retained in power. Moreover, he compares the aims of SCAP directives with the actual accomplishments to date, particularly criticizing the economic reforms. He believes that such specialized areas are outside the competence of the military. In conclusion, he recommends 4 steps that SCAP should take to meet the impending crisis: (1) the reduction of occupation troops, (2) the substitution of a civilian administration for the present military one, (3) the formulation of an immediate decision regarding reparations payments, and (4) transference of the Far Eastern Commission from Washington to Tokyo.

488   Cole, Taylor, and John H. Hallowell, eds. *Post-war Governments of the Far East*. Gainesville: Journal of Politics, Univ. of Florida, 1947. 271p.; reprinted from *Journal of Politics* 9, no.4:1–271 (Nov. 1947)

A reprint of the *Journal of Politics* 9, no.4 (Nov. 1947) which consists of an introduction and articles on the postwar governments of various East Asian countries. The chapter "Post-war Government and Politics of Japan" (p.565–87) is by John W. Masland, a political scientist who served in the Government Section of SCAP. (For a full annotation of the chapter, see entry no.513 within this bibliography.) The introduction to the book by Paul Clyde discusses Japan briefly (p.485–90) and Japan is mentioned in passing in a few of the other chapters, notably those on the USSR and Korea.

489   Colton, Kenneth E. "The Sun Rises for Japan." *Annals of Iowa* 39, no.2: 138–44 (Oct. 1947)

The article, consisting primarily of a very informal letter originally not intended for publication, presents Colton's personal impressions of the ceremonies held in Tokyo on 3 May 1947 to mark Japan's adoption of a constitution and her formal transformation from an empire into a republic. Noting the unenthusiastic reception accorded by most Japanese as well as the dismal weather that particular day, Colton's account tended to take a dim view of the entire proceedings.

490   Costello, William. "Report from Tokyo." *New Republic* 116:7 (10 Feb. 1947)

General MacArthur's prevention of the threatened general strike and its effects upon the current political and economic situation in Japan are the basic topics of this brief report. The author is extremely critical of the Yoshida cabinet's inability to prevent political and economic chaos and he discusses recent events which indicate increased popular dissatisfaction with the government in power. He interprets MacArthur's recent action as a resumption of responsibilities which Yoshida is incapable of handling.

491   Council on Foreign Relations. "American Responsibilities in the Far East: 1. The Occupation of Japan." In *The United States in World Affairs 1945–1947*. New York: Harper, published for the Council, 1947. p.254–73.

The development of Allied policy concerning Japan in the immediate postwar period is reviewed here, and 3 general policy areas are examined, including organizational and intellectual demilitarization, social and political democratization, and peacetime economic reorganization. Allied criticisms of American command are examined and the creation of the Far Eastern Commission and the Allied Council is noted. The authors discuss the difference between long-range economic and political reform and temporary institutional tinkering. The new constitution and the elections of 1946 and 1947 are analyzed. In conclusion, MacArthur's opinion that the occupation should be phased out in late 1947 is noted.

492   Crofts, Alfred. "Can Japan Come Back?" *China Monthly* 8:81–83, 100–102 (Mar. 1947)

The author addresses himself to Japan's condition a year and a half after defeat and to her prospects for the future. He offers numerous examples of the extent of devastation brought by total defeat to all aspects of Japanese national life, but balances them with further examples and analyses suggesting that Japan is nevertheless capable of accomplishing a full recovery in short order. He cites as positive factors the people's acceptance of defeat and their "earnest personal feelings [which] work against any future military establishment," occupation reforms and technical assistance, the prosperity of Japan's farmers and fishermen, and the fact that inflation has virtually wiped out Japan's burden of war debt. He concludes that "Japan is at full nadir—lower she cannot go; the only course is upward."

493 "Democracy in Japan." *Economist* 153:668–69 (25 Oct. 1947)

In what he terms a "tentative and provisional estimate of the stability of the new regime," the author examines the government of occupied Japan as contrasted with that of the war years. He discusses SCAP's demilitarization and democratization programs as well as the social changes that have been ordered by SCAP directives, particularly agrarian reform, the dissolution of the *zaibatsu* combines, and other economic reform programs. The author concludes that "it is on the success of its social policy rather than on its purely political constitutional innovations that the viability of the American-sponsored new order in Japan depends."

493a Duboscq, André. *Les japonais*. Paris: Société d'Editions Françaises et Internationales, 1947. 203p. (Problèmes internationaux)

This survey history of Japanese civilization by a veteran French specialist in Asian affairs includes material on the beginnings of the Allied occupation. Duboscq praises SCAP's early accomplishments in such areas as the demilitarization of the country and the introduction of various reforms. Duboscq also believes that the Japanese people are sincerely anxious to make those reforms work, but at the same time, he warns of the danger of an excessively rapid and therefore superficial democratization of the Japanese government and of Japanese society.

494 Dupays, Paul. *MacArthur assagit le Japon; chronique historique. Parfait accord du Mikado avec le régime démocratique, fin 1945–1946–1947*. n.p.: Éditions de la Critique; dépositaire Hachette, Londres, 1952. 113p.

495 Fertig, Norman. "Japan in Defeat." *Proceedings of the Institute of World Affairs* 22:46–48 (1947)

This round table discussion headed by Arthur G. Coons, formerly of the Reparations Commission, is focused upon Japan's problems as a defeated land. The panel members briefly discuss the current economic situation, possible effects of atomic radiation on soil fertility, and the political and social significance of the new constitution.

496 "For and against MacArthur." *Economist* 153:721–22 (1 Nov. 1947)

In a thoughtful appraisal of the effects of the occupation thus far, the author, formerly a correspondent in Japan, discusses the political and economic difficulties which Japan must yet face. Although commending General MacArthur as having done a remarkably good job, nevertheless, the author points out that in many areas, particularly the crucial economic and political arenas, reforms which have taken place on paper have not actually been effected. He concludes with the wish that the supreme commander "were not so addicted to wishful thinking and were not so surrounded by men who encourage him in this vice."

497 Frederick, James O. "Japan Finds a Level." *Commonweal* 47:112–15 (14 Nov. 1947)

In a brief analysis of the effects of the occupation, the author claims that the Allied powers have brought about a reversal in Japanese social, political, and economic spheres—removing power and prestige from the militarists and *zaibatsu* leaders and allocating benefits to the laborers and farmers. Believing that "the impact of the occupation was even greater than that of the war," he discusses the results of particular SCAP reforms, particularly the land reform program, as well as various political and fiscal reforms.

498 Galbraith, T. D. "Impressions of Japan To-day." *United Empire* 38:9–14

(Jan./Feb. 1947); abridged version published under the title "Conflicting Ideas on Japan" in *Great Britain and the East* (Far East Issue) 63:52F–F53 (Jan. 1947)

In September 1946 Galbraith visited Japan as a member of the Parliamentary delegation specifically invited by SCAP to spend several days within the country. In an address which he subsequently delivered before the Royal Empire Society, he commented on the quality of MacArthur's leadership, Japanese living conditions, various changes in women's status and the introduction of universal suffrage, and such problems as the fuel and transportation shortages which hampered efforts to promote economic recovery. Galbraith was generally complimentary of SCAP's work, but from the text of his lecture and from the published remarks of Society members in the ensuing discussion, it is clear that at that time there already were certain differences of opinion in England over the way in which the occupation should be run.

499 Green, Owen Mortimer. "Japan Resurgent." *Eastern World* 1:7 (May 1947)

While Japan's postwar recovery has been extraordinary, her recent achievements are still small when compared with those of her past. The Japanese response to MacArthur's reforms has been remarkably positive; the political world may still be highly unstable, but the Japanese—especially the peasants—are not inclined towards communism. A peace treaty must come soon, however, for it is certain that no one will benefit any longer from Japan's continued isolation from the outside world.

499a ———. "Peace Prospects for Japan." *Eastern World* 1:10–12 (Sept. 1947)

Green notes that the Allies are displeased with the United States for her acting as if she alone were responsible for the victory over Japan. America dominates the occupation, and trade with Japan in turn is being dominated by the dollar. Green tends to doubt that there has yet been the sort of revolution in Japan which MacArthur claims to have occurred. Furthermore, while Japanese industry obviously has recovered to some extent from the war, a truly balanced rehabilitation of the country's economy will depend on an early peace.

Gulick, Addison. "The Problem of Right and Wrong in Japan and Some of Its Political Consequences." 1947. *See* no.1929.

500 Horner, Francis J. "Japan Today." *Asiatic Review* 43:75–77 (Jan. 1947)

Some 15 months after the start of the occupation, Horner observes that the Japanese are beginning once again to take up the affairs of life with initiative and purpose. He credits much of the success to General MacArthur but points out that credit must also be given to Japanese adaptability, industry, and especially to the realistic outlook of their leaders.

501 ———. "Japan's Difficult Democracy." *Asiatic Review* 43:173–75 (Apr. 1947)

Horner examines the difficulties the Japanese face in realizing a true democracy as people with so long a tradition, so utterly different a mentality, and a past so opposite to that of the United States.

502 Hutchinson, Paul. "Is MacArthur Attempting the Impossible?" *Christian Century* 64:72–73 (15 Jan. 1947)

The effects of the occupation are questioned in this article, and the author cautions against premature congratulations and points out both economic privations and the constraints on democracy imposed by SCAP. He considers Japanese enthusiasm for democracy to be superficial and sloganistic. Occupation methods are praised for creating conditions whereby indigenous democratic forces can develop and grow. Hutchinson questions whether the most undemocratic of means—a military occupation and dictatorship—can accomplish democratic aims.

503 James, Weldon. "Democracy: So Sorry." *Collier's* 119:21–23, 63–65 (25 Jan. 1947)

James comments on the results of extensive interviews in Minakami, a rural Japanese community. These interviews indicate that occupation policy is not understood and that the lives of most people remain unaffected by the American-sponsored reforms.

504 ———. "MacArthur's Democracy." *Collier's* 119:24–25, 65–69 (28 June 1947)

James undertakes a review of occupation reforms, stressing that an adequate understanding of democracy has not yet been inculcated into the Japanese people. General MacArthur's continuous competition with the Soviets for the loyalty of the public is discussed. A variety of changes ranging from the liberation of political prisoners to the emancipation of women is examined.

"Japan, 1947." *The Reminiscences of Roger Nash Baldwin*. 1954. See no.44a.

504a "Japan seit seiner Kapitulation." *Europa-Archiv* 1, no.8/9:397–403 (Feb./Mar. 1947)

A chronological table of modern Japanese history (with emphasis on developments during World War II) is followed by a discussion of the postwar occupation, focusing on the participation of the Allies in the occupation machinery, the demilitarization of Japan, the problem of reparations, the liquidation of the *zaibatsu*, developments in the domestic political arena, and various reforms including the introduction of a new constitution. An appendix of documents (p.404–11) provides in German translation several important texts relating to postwar Japan. They include (1) the provisions of the Yalta agreement in regard to Japan, (2) the text of the Instrument of Surrender, (3) extracts from the communiqué of the Moscow Conference of Foreign Ministers, dated 28 December 1945, (4) the Allied ultimatum to Japan of 26 July 1945, better known as the Potsdam Declaration, (5) the White House declaration of occupation policy in Japan, dated 6 September 1945, and (6) the text of the new constitution.

The Japanese Reminiscences of Roger Baldwin. 1961. See no.44b.

505 Jones, Francis Clifford, Hugh Borton, and Bertie Reginald Pearn. *The Far East 1942–1946*. London: Oxford Univ. Pr., 1955. xiv, 589p. (Survey of International Affairs 1939–1946, v.7)

The seventh of an 11-volume series, entitled Survey of International Affairs 1939–1946, edited by Arnold Toynbee and sponsored by the Royal Institute of International Affairs. The series deals with World War II. However, the title of this particular volume is somewhat misleading. The work covers domestic and international developments in East and Southeast Asian countries, 2 of which are studied through 1947 rather than 1946 (Japan and Korea). Approximately half of the volume is devoted to a discussion of developments during and after the Pacific War. In part 1, "The Far East during the War," F. C. Jones analyzes Japan's conquest of Southeast Asia and discusses Japanese diplomacy from 1942 to 1945. In part 2, "The Far East after the War," Hugh Borton writes on "Japan under the Allied Occupation, 1945–47." The subjects discussed include conditions in Japan at the time of surrender, occupation policies, SCAP organization, SCAP's steps toward democratization, Allied participation in policy formulation, political reforms, the brief ascendancy of the Social Democrats following the April 1947 general elections, economic and trade conditions in 1945–47, economic reforms, and some social developments such as religious freedom.

505a Kagawa, Toyohiko. "We Have Abandoned War in Japan." *Christian Century* 64:1483 (3 Dec. 1947). Reply by Kikuchi Akira: *Christian Century* 64:1617 (31 Dec. 1947)

In this brief article Kagawa, a Japanese Christian leader, asserts among other things that "by the abandonment of war, we in Japan have emerged from the era of barbarism. Thus we have been accorded a chance to make ourselves the most progressive and civilized of all the nations. . . . The ideal we pursue is that of making Japan a state with which God can be pleased." Kikuchi replies to Kagawa by arguing that "Japan is a sort of huge concentration camp. If the controlling power feels that a militarized Japan is essential . . . we shall again see the resurgence of militarism in Japan." He feels that the true role of Christianity within the country is not that of making pledges of peace but rather one of preparing for the coming conflict with the rising tide of communism in Asia.

505b Keeton, George W. "Japan since the Surrender." *Great Britain and the East* (Far East Issue) 63:42F–F43 (June 1947)

Keeton first notes that the Japanese have obtained an incorrect impression of the "true situation" because SCAP has controlled policy towards Japan since her surrender and has not permitted Great Britain and the Commonwealth countries to participate within the occupation in anything other than a purely subordinate capacity. He then discusses the alternatives for the Allies with regard to the form of government that postwar Japan would have and points out that the decision was made to establish a "liberal" regime within the framework of a constitutional monarchy in the hope that such a regime would cooperate peacefully with the United States. Because "liberal" institutions have "no roots in popular goodwill," however, they will probably fail in the long run. Keeton refers in passing to a variety of occupation reforms and indicates that the restoration of Japan's industrial and commercial structure is necessary for the country's peaceful evolution. He concludes on a pessimistic note, predicting that once the occupation forces withdraw, the extreme left and the extreme right within Japan will engage in a struggle for political power that may climax in the outbreak of another war in East Asia.

506 Kelley, Frank Raymond, and Cornelius Ryan. *Star Spangled Mikado.* New York: McBride, 1947. 282p.

Two newspaper correspondents, one representing the *New York Herald Tribune* (Kelley) and the other an Irish journalist, present an informal portrait of some of the leading personalities—both American and Japanese—of the occupation. General MacArthur himself receives the most coverage, but there are also chapters devoted to General Tōjō, Prince Konoe, the emperor, Kumazawa (a pretender to the throne), and some of the leading officials in the SCAP headquarters in Tokyo. In the concluding portion of the book the authors consider more specifically political issues, i.e., the character of the postwar parties, the operations of the Diet, the provisions of the new constitution, and a future peace treaty with Japan. Appendixes include the text of the Potsdam Declaration, a partial text of the Moscow Conference communiqué, the U.S. Initial Post-Surrender Policy for Japan, and the Constitution of Japan.

507 Kern, Harry F. "Trouble in Japan: How the Struggle to Win the Peace Now Threatens the Success of the American Occupation." *Newsweek* 29:36–43 (23 June 1947)

In this 3-part article, the foreign editor of *Newsweek* expresses skepticism concerning the quality of occupation policies and advocates both an early peace treaty and a prolonged American presence in Japan. Part 1 of the article is a scathing analysis alleging both a lack of Japanese philosophical conversion and failure on the part of the occupation to counteract the tendency of the people to act according to traditional patterns rather than as individuals. Part 2, devoted to Japanese economic problems, discusses inflation, the lack of substantial American credit, and the weak economic leadership of SCAP. Part 3 is critical of the occupation purges, claiming that these weakened the leadership potential and created a group of shadow leaders, who were increasingly unfriendly toward the United States. In 2 addenda to the article Kern also criticizes the secrecy of SCAP leadership and the isolated position of General MacArthur which prevents him, in Kern's opinion, from receiving comprehensive information and competent advice.

508 Kudryavtsev, V. "The Governmental Crisis in Japan." *Soviet Press Translations* 2:104–6 (15 Sept. 1947)

The author presents his interpretation of the events which led up to the resignation of the Yoshida government and its replacement by the coalition headed by the Socialist Katayama. In an article published in the 3 June 1947 issue of *Izvestia*, he describes the growing inadequacy of the "reactionary" Yoshida government to cope with the pressing political and economic problems of the nation. According to the author, since the Americans can no longer use the Liberal party for their political purposes, they are resorting to a maneuver to force the new leadership "to adopt a policy resembling the policy of the Liberal Party." There is considerable attention paid to the development of the 4-party coalition and speculation as to its political future. The author is hopeful that the coalition will have some measure of success in quelling the forces of reaction in Japan.

509 Lauterbach, Richard Edward. *Danger from the East*. New York: Harper, 1947. xi, 430p.

The author, a Luce publications correspondent, presents a highly readable, informative account of postwar Japan. Korea and China are also discussed but approximately one-half of the book is devoted to occupied Japan. Its value is enhanced by the many documents appended, including the Cairo Conference communiqué, the Yalta Agreement, the Potsdam Proclamation, the Imperial Rescript Announcing Surrender to the Japanese People, the Instrument of Surrender, the U.S. Initial Postsurrender Policy for Japan, and the Japanese draft constitution. The "danger" referred to in the title relates to the danger for all nations which fail to recognize that Asia is in revolution. It refers also to the danger of those who would despair of winning our ideological battle with the Soviet Union in Asia, resorting instead to the atomic warfare for which we are better prepared. Descriptive accounts of the emperor and MacArthur as personalities and as grand figures in Japanese life and politics are followed by chapters dealing in some detail with the new constitution, educational reform, political reforms, the land reform program, and the labor movement. The Allied Council is also discussed as a testing ground of American–Soviet cooperation.

The author is openly skeptical of the progress claimed by SCAP in its reform programs. Although he admits that it has done a good job compared to other occupations, he observes a wide gap between theory and practice, policy and administration. He partially attributes this gap to the insufficient number of trained personnel who might effectively implement policy.

Basically critical of U.S. unilateral control of the occupation, the author states, "We have treated Japan as a colony and we have accepted Japan's problems as our own, forgetting that the whole world must be considered in any settlement of the Japanese problem." He advocates preparing Japan for world citizenship by transferring control from the U.S. military to a UN commission. In remarks addressed to the Tokyo Press Club in March 1947, MacArthur himself favored Allied troop withdrawal and UN administration as soon as a peace treaty was signed.

509a Lee, Clark Gould. *One Last Look Around*. New York: Duell, Sloan & Pearce, 1947. xiii, 295p.

Approximately half of this book deals with early postwar Japan. Lee begins with accounts of Japan's surrender and the arrival of the first American occupation troops. Succeeding chapters include discussions of the emperor (who the author feels must be held accountable for the war), the devastated condition of Japanese industry, Tokyo Rose, the arrest of Tōjō, and rumors about atrocities committed by American troops in Japan. Perhaps the most interesting chapter of all recounts Lee's interview with Tōjō at his home the day before the latter's arrest and suicide attempt.

510 Liu, James T. C. "Japan's Political and Economic Struggle." *China Monthly* 8:160–61, 171–72 (May 1947)

Japanese politics in 1946, according to this article, were characterized by stability and a good working relationship between the government and occupation authorities. By the spring of 1947, however, economic problems had brought about a situation of near-crisis in the political sphere. Liu describes the increasing militancy of labor groups, which led in turn to a strengthening of the Socialist and Communist politicians' resolve to gain control of the government, and the resulting disputes and negotiations on the question of coalition government.

511 Maki, John McGilvrey. "Japan: Political Reconstruction." *Far Eastern Survey* 16:73–77 (9 Apr. 1947)

The contradiction between democratic reform and reactionary counterreform in Japan is explained in terms of 3 sources of conflict: (1) the domestic struggle between those in power and their opponents; (2) the dilemma in SCAP created by a strategic commitment to revolutionary change in Japanese politics and a tactical unwillingness to support such change; and (3) the contacts between occupation and Japanese political forces. Maki believes that the occupation's retention of prewar governmental and bureaucratic structures will produce mutual interests between the government and SCAP and reduce SCAP's ability to work with progressive Japanese forces. He criticizes as unnecessary actions such as the banning of demonstrations on 20 May 1946 and the ardent berating of communism by George Atcheson before the Allied Council, stating that these actions undermine belief in the American protestations of democratic intent. He calls for a program beyond mere anticommunism and pro-Americanism to inspire confidence among the Japanese and to encourage their renunciation of traditional patterns of behavior.

———. *Japanese Nationalism in Transition.* 1947. See no.1949.

512 Martin, Edwin M. *The Results of the Allied Occupation of Japan: An Interim Report.* Mimeographed. New York: American Institute of Pacific Relations, 1947. 69p. (Institute of Pacific Relations, 10th conference, U.S. paper no.4, 1947)

The chief of the Division of Japanese and Korean Economic Affairs, Department of State, examines various SCAP policies. Subjects covered include SCAP's work in the areas of demobilization, repatriation, the trial of war criminals, reparations, Japan's territorial changes due to defeat, demilitarization, and democratization. At the outset Martin describes the origins of American policy toward defeated Japan, tracing policy preparations back to 1942. However, he deals primarily with Japan's democratization, discussing the political and military purges, educational reform, reorganization of the political structure and process, the deconcentration of financial combines, development of organized labor, and agrarian reform. There is also a consideration of the difficulties involved in achieving economic recovery, including the prohibition of foreign trade, coal shortages, labor unrest, financial problems, inadequate transportation, and the poor distribution system.

513 Masland, John Wesley, Jr. "Post-war Government and Politics of Japan." *Journal of Politics* 9:565–87 (Nov. 1947); reprinted in Taylor Cole and John H. Hallowell, eds. *Post-war Governments of the Far East.* Gainesville, Fla.: Journal of Politics, Univ. of Florida, 1947. p.565–87.

The occupation reform of the Japanese political structure is carefully and comprehensively analyzed in this report. The author divides Japan's political development into 2 categories for consideration—the first relating to changes in the structure of government and the second to the emergence and development of political parties and new political leaders. The constitution of 1946 is the chief topic in the first category and the author describes in detail its provisions on the emperor, the Diet, the cabinet, the judiciary, the Bill of Rights, and the process of amendment. Within the second category, there is a discussion of the imperative need for new political leadership, particularly in the light of the purges of former leaders. After a detailed discussion of the number and nature of the most significant of the postwar political parties, the author concludes by describing postwar trends in the cabinet and reaffirms the necessity for the emergence of responsible Japanese leadership if the occupation reforms are to succeed.

514 Maurer, Herrymon. "The U.S. Does a Job." *Fortune* 35:134–43, 179–89 (Mar. 1947).

Viewing the occupation of Japan as essentially a missionary enterprise, the author maintains that SCAP "is often dynamic, not infrequently paternal, and almost always evangelical." He has a totally positive view of the occupation, believing that the various reforms effected in postwar Japan (including even the drafting of the constitution) may be attributed mainly to the Japanese government's acting on mere suggestions from SCAP authorities. Included in the report are brief summaries of political and social innovations, SCAP's position vis-à-vis the Communist party, the *zaibatsu* combines, and Shinto, and a discussion of the various individual SCAP sections and their responsibilities. Finally the author discusses the difficulties of a meaningful and permanent democratization of the Japanese state that will endure beyond the conclusion of the occupation.

515 Mydans, Shelley. "Conquerors: In Japan They Wrestle with Domestic Problems." *Life* 22:19–20, 22 (5 May 1947).

This article by the wife of the head of *Life*'s Tokyo bureau describes the problems encountered by American civilians living in Japan under the occupation. The author's day-to-day domestic routine was an endless round of encounters with Japanese servants and repairmen who were not only caught up in the bewildering upheavals of postsurrender Japan but also found themselves having to deal with foreigners making incomprehensible demands. Mydans' descriptions of her problems in adjusting to the role of "conqueror" and of her dealings with the SCAP bureaucracy are both instructive and entertaining.

Nehmer, Stanley. "The Occupation of Japan: The Third Phase." 1947. See no. 1476.

Parrott, Lindesay. "Japan Still Worships at Shinto Shrines." 1947. See no. 2324.

516 ———. "The Old Is on Trial, the New Is Being Tried." *New York Times Magazine* p.12–13, 46 (5 Jan. 1947).

In a review of the events of the first 16 months of the occupation, the author sketches vignettes of the types of changes that have occurred: the formation of labor unions, new schools, and the breaking up of the *zaibatsu*. He finds that the apathy caused by years of wartime hardship is disappearing and reforms are taking hold rapidly. Nevertheless, he notes that much remains to be done. Some of the old bureaucracy remains, land reform is yet to be carried out, and Shinto is still a powerful force. Most of the problems are economic, and their solution poses difficulties for the stability of the government. In summary, he characterizes Japan as "a land in which medievalism is challenged by the impact of Western ideas."

517 "Progress of Occupation in Japan." *Armed Forces Talk* no.198:1–11 (1947).

Distributed by the Army Department to various field commanders for the purpose of keeping American military personnel informed of developments in Japan, this publication seeks to answer in general terms such questions as what progress has been made in demilitarizing, democratizing, and rehabilitating postwar Japan.

518 Quigley, Harold S. "Democracy Occupies Japan." *Virginia Quarterly Review* 23:521–31 (Autumn 1947)

In the author's analysis of the occupation of Japan, he defines the endeavor as "an attempt of Occidental cultures to set the direction of an older Oriental culture by fiat and friendly council." In addition to discussing negative measures such as the disarmament and demobilization programs, the dissolution of the *zaibatsu* and the secret police, and the purge, he also considers such positive aspects as the encouragement of labor unions and political parties, the enfranchisement of women, and the formulation of a new constitution. He emphasizes throughout the article the underlying dilemma inherent in a situation whereby SCAP, which advocates a relatively socialistic legislative program, is at the same time highly antagonistic to Socialists and protective toward the conservative bureaucracy. As Quigley interprets the situation, "the revolutionists in SCAP are drafting the new laws, but the conservatives are supervising their execution." He concludes by indicating that it is still too early to appraise the results and that the test of the occupation's success will come after, not during, its duration.

519 Ray, Donald P. "Our Progress in Japan." *World Affairs* 110:109–13 (Summer 1947)

A brief discussion of the important political and social changes that have revolutionized Japanese society. It includes recommendations for the promotion of greater economic stability. The author urges that SCAP authorities begin thinking of postoccupation Japan and make every effort to educate the Japanese people in the spirit of democracy so that occupation innovations will be retained after the normal occupation is over.

The Reminiscences of Cyrus H. Peake. 1961. *See* no.44f.

520 Rosinger, Lawrence K. "The Occupation of Japan." *Foreign Policy Reports* 23:50–59 (15 May 1947); extracted and published under the title "Post-war Politics in Japan." *Great Britain and the East* (Far East Issue) 63:F39–40F (Aug. 1947)

The author begins his report by discussing the preplanning stages and organizational framework of the occupation as well as its principal programs and their implementation. The political and economc spheres receive particular emphasis. The author considers the operations of the Japanese government, the development and character of political parties, the new role of the emperor, and the reforms initiated by the SCAP-inspired constitution. Following his discussion of contemporary politics is an analysis of the economic situation, discussing Japan's relative economic status vis-à-vis other Asian nations, the purges of the *zaibatsu* leaders, SCAP's land reform program, the reparations issue, and the present inflation and food shortage. Rosinger believes that American policy toward Japan has been and will become increasingly influenced by the trend of U.S.–Soviet relations. He warns that "if the U.S. were to become permanently committed to Japanese right wing elements because of fear of the Japanese Left and Russia, the use of constructive liberal forces would be frustrated." In concluding, he affirms that the occupation will succeed only if SCAP vigorously pushes the reforms it has initiated on paper and encourages the rise of new Japanese leaders to carry them out.

521 Sibiryakov, A. "The Situation in Japan." *Soviet Press Translations* 2:8–10 (15 Apr. 1947)

This article describing important domestic political events in Japan appeared in the 13 February 1947 issue of *Trud*. In an indictment of the Yoshida cabinet, the author cites various unsuccessful efforts of the leftist organizations and political party factions to overthrow the "reactionary" government. There is considerable attention to what he considers the betrayal of the right-wing Socialists who agreed to participate in a coalition government headed by Yoshida. The article concludes with a brief description of MacArthur's directive to forbid the general strike by government workers, which the author fears will encourage the forces of feudal reaction in Japan.

522 Smith, Thomas Vernor. "Consent and Coercion in Governing." *Pacific Spectator* 1:315–25 (Summer 1947)

This article is a consideration of some of the paradoxical elements of the term "military government." The author, who was familiar with both European and Japanese occupation endeavors, discusses the theoretical implications of the term "military," which suggests control by coercion, and the term "government," which for the American people implies control through the consent of the people. He then discusses some concrete examples of military government, illustrating the defects in the occupation of Germany, where Allied rule is based more on coercion than on consent, and pointing up the successes in the occupation of Japan, where the American conception of military government is based on consent.

523 Steele, Archibald T. *Present-Day Japan*. Mimeographed. New York: American Institute of Pacific Relations, 1947. 21p. (Institute of Pacific Relations, 10th conference, U.S. supplementary paper, 1947)

Six articles written by Steele which first appeared in the *New York Herald Tribune* are reproduced here. They are: (1) "Japan—Two Years after the War"; (2) "The U.S. Military Government Teams and Their Influence on the Japanese"; (3) "Thinking and the Re-Education of Japan"; (4) "Inflation and American Responsibility for Japan's Economic Recovery"; (5) "Japan's Overpopulation Problem"; and (6) "The 'MacArthur Era' and the Future of Japan." Each article provides some insight into different aspects of the problems which confronted defeated Japan. Steele, generally in favor of the way the American-dominated occupation was being conducted, notes the absence of open opposition among the Japanese and states: "The amazing compliance of the Japanese people is as frightening as it is impressive." While appreciative of the need for military government teams to prod local government officials to execute SCAP directives, he believes there is gradual progress being made toward democratization. He is critical of the inadequate "channels" of communication linking lower-ranking SCAP officials, military government workers, and the Japanese to MacArthur. He also criticizes the occupation personnel and conflicting viewpoints in General Headquarters. Convinced that it will take 20 to 25 years to reform Japanese society, he suggests that the country's new educational system be continued for some time under American or UN supervision, that the Japanese be encouraged to travel and study in the West, that they be encouraged to develop healthy political and economic leadership, and, finally, that U.S. personnel remain in Japan to check internal disorder or the rise of militarism.

524 Stewart, Maxwell S. "Our Record in Japan." *Nation* 165:95–98 (26 July 1947)

The paradoxical elements of the occupation resulting from SCAP's interest in promoting democratic reforms and at the same time in combating the Communist threat are discussed in this report. The author considers the implementation of the demilitarization and education programs, the formulation of the new constitution, and the development of a strong labor union movement. He then illustrates what he considers to be the chief defects in the administrative structure and general operations of SCAP by describing its economic policy which has failed to set up an effective control system for the *zaibatsu* or to reduce the inflationary spiral. According to the author, these goals should be priorities of SCAP in order to insure political and social reforms, but he concedes that the general goals of the occupation have been kept in sight thus far. Finally, he advocates that the responsibility of the occupation be transferred to the United Nations before the American impact becomes too pronounced in the country.

Supreme Commander for the Allied Powers. *Two Years of Occupation.* 1947. See no.263.

———. *Two Years of Occupation.* 1947. See no.281.

———. Diplomatic Section. *Atcheson Correspondence.* 1945–47. See no. 926.

525 Taylor, Philip H. "Policy Snags in Japan: Efficiency of Administration and Controls Put under Spotlight." *Christian Science Monitor* magazine section 39, no.51:3, 14 (25 Jan. 1947)

Philip H. Taylor, associate professor of international relations at Syracuse University, is highly critical of SCAP for various weaknesses in its administrative organization. He is particularly disturbed by the continuing interference of the military general staff in nonmilitary activities and distinctly civil affairs, and he feels that appropriate administrative reforms could eliminate the constant confusion, unnecessary duplication of effort, and unlimited friction that are seriously delaying or entirely preventing the satisfactory fulfillment of the occupation mission.

526 Tiltman, Hessell. "Letter of the Week: Tokyo Breakdown." *New Republic* 116:3, 46 (10 Feb. 1947)

In a letter discussing the current scene in Tokyo, the author charges that many of the successes of the occupation have occurred only on paper. In order for the occupation to succeed, certain fundamental conditions which have not yet been realized must first be achieved. In addition to carrying out an effective purge, Tiltman writes, MacArthur all along should have been taking steps to build and strengthen democratic forces. Instead, according to the author, SCAP, "by attempting the first operation while shying . . . from the second, is creating a vacuum." Eventually, he predicts, the ultraconservatives will again hold the reigns of power in Japan.

527 U.S. Dept. of State. Div. of Research for Far East. *Situation Report—Japan: Comments on Current Intelligence.* 11 Oct. 1946–14 Mar. 1947. nos.3479.16–3479.25. unpublished.

Political developments in Japan reported in these issues include such subjects as: "The Role of the Bureaucracy in the Yoshida Cabinet," "The House of Councillors Law," "The Peace Settlements in Japanese Politics," "The Threatened February 1 Government Workers Strike in Japan," "Japanese Expenditure for Allied Occupation," and "Problems of Recovery in the Japanese Coal Industry." Each issue varies in length from 5 to 32 pages and treats 1 to 3 subjects. With the 28 February 1947 issue, the title changed to *Situation Report—Japan.*

Available at the National Archives.

528 Van Benschoten, Arnold. "Success of a Mission." *United States Naval Institute Proceedings* 73:529–37 (May 1947)

The author draws upon his experience of 10 months in military government work in Hyōgo prefecture to sketch a picture of the outlying areas in occupied Japan. He focuses upon Hyōgo which he deems a representative cross section of Japan, describing the duties of the military government teams in assisting tactical forces in SCAP's demilitarization program and the numerous mutual misunderstandings between Japanese and Americans before a gradual lessening of mistrust occurred. He concludes that the occupation of Japan has been much more successful than that of Germany. The account is informal and contains a number of personal anecdotes about occupied Japan.

529 Vining, Elizabeth Gray. "One World in Tokyo." *Woman's Home Companion* 74:30, 127–30 (May 1947)

The tutor to the crown prince of Japan narrates some of her experiences during the first few months of her stay in Tokyo. She describes the way Japan looked upon her arrival, some of the

530 Wang, Yun-sheng. "Japan's Dangerous Road." *China Magazine* 17:10–15 (Sept. 1947)

The editor in chief of the Shanghai *Ta Kung Pao* is skeptical regarding the permanence of democratic change in occupied Japan without a more thorough elimination of the feudal foundations of Japanese society. He maintains that the Japanese people are easily misled by force characteristics of the Japanese imperial family, and her desire to communicate the meaning of democracy to those whom she met.

and that prewar forces are still in positions of power.

531 Woollacott, Derrick. "The Japanese Peasant: A Recruit for Democracy?" *Geographical Magazine* 20:246–51 (Oct. 1947)

This photo-essay consists of photographs of Japanese farm life accompanied by a brief text emphasizing the importance of the peasant to Japan's postwar recovery and the question of whether the conservative peasantry can become a positive force for the further democratization of the country.

1948

532 Baker, Frayne. "Occupation of Japan." *Army Information Digest* 3:2–7 (Jan. 1948)

This optimistic account by General MacArthur's public information officer describes the accomplishments of the occupation. The author views the occupation not only as a military mission but also as an experiment to change a formerly semifeudal society into a modern democratic state in a short period of time. It is his opinion that "the undertaking has assumed more of the character of the liberation of an oppressed people than the occupation of a conquered foe" and he briefly lists the most important innovations made by the Allies in the political, social, and economic spheres toward such a liberation. In concluding the article, he warns the Japanese to guard against totalitarian forces from the political right or left.

533 Baldwin, Roger Nash. "Japan's American Revolution." *Current History* 14:100–102 (Feb. 1948); abridged and published under the same title in *Reader's Digest* 52:75–79 (Mar. 1948).

In a brief, informal account of the social and political changes wrought by the occupation, Baldwin focuses on the personality of General Douglas MacArthur and lauds his leadership in bringing about Japan's postwar transformation. Baldwin also notes the lack of Communist success in Japan, the transformation of Emperor Hirohito into a national democratic symbol, and the role played by Lieutenant General Robert Eichelberger, commander of the Eighth Army.

534 ———. "The Nisei in Japan." *Common Ground* 8:24–29 (Summer 1948)

Most of the article deals with the problems of nisei who were caught in Japan during the war and who lost their American citizenship by being naturalized without their knowledge or by working in certain wartime jobs. It touches also on the problems of the occupation nisei (those Japanese–Americans employed by SCAP as interpreters, translators, and censors) and "returned students" (Japanese who had studied abroad) and comments on the perplexities of those American soldiers and occupation nisei who sought to marry Japanese civilians. Baldwin, who regarded the nisei as occasionally overzealous ambassadors of democracy, served as director of the American Civil Liberties Union and visited Japan in order to help nisei who were stranded there.

535 Ball, William Macmahon. *Japan: Enemy or Ally?* New York: Day, 1949. xii, 244p.

The author, an Australian diplomat, represented the British Commonwealth on the Allied Council for Japan from July 1946 through August 1947. In this work, he presents his analysis of the structure and operation of the Allied occupation from its inception through 1948. In discussing the manner in which the Allied policies of demilitarization and democratization were implemented, the author tends to be critical of the shifting positions of the American-dominated SCAP organization. Moreover, he is doubtful about the success of the democratization program. Subjects are treated primarily in terms of the interests of the Allied Council for Japan (ACJ), and there is considerable emphasis on formal decisions of SCAP, the Japanese government, the Far Eastern Commission (FEC), and the ACJ, with little attention to the reaction of the Japanese people to the occupation programs of change. The author proposes that an Allied control body be established in Tokyo to replace the ineffective ACJ and FEC. He also warns against helping Japanese reactionaries and *zaibatsu* groups to revive and reestablish industrial and economic supremacy in East Asia, as they might again be used for aggressive Japanese expansion. The appendixes include the full texts of the Constitution of Japan promulgated on 3 November 1946, the report of the Johnston Committee (an advisory group sent to Japan by the Department of the Army to study measures for Japan's economic recovery) dated 19 May 1948, and the U.S. Statement on Japanese Industrial Reconstruction, issued at the FEC meeting of 9 December 1948. The book was first published in Australia in 1948, and the chapter regarding "Major Developments in 1948" as well as the last 2 appendixes were added to the American edition that appeared later in the same year. It was also translated into Japanese under the title, *Nihon, teki ka mikata ka* (Tokyo: Chikuma Shobō, 1953. 266p.).

536 ———. "Reflections on Japan." *Pacific Affairs* 21:3–19 (Mar. 1948)

This article presents the personal and unofficial views of the occupation held by the former representative for the United Kingdom, Australia, New Zealand, and India on the Allied Council for Japan. Ball served in that capacity from March 1946 to September 1947. The author gives his interpretation of the overall progress of the occupation, the durability of its social, political, and economic reforms, and the effectiveness of the purge program. Finally he looks ahead to speculate about Allied postpeace treaty control of Japan. The author's observations about the occupation are tempered by his belief that Japanese patriotism is still a powerful force, that the society is still saturated with a militarist and expansionist spirit, and that, since SCAP elected to work through the Japanese government rather than supplant it, it was compelled to identify more and more with conservative Japanese even when it would have preferred to enforce more liberal measures.

537 Ballantine, Joseph W. "The New Japan: An American View." *Far Eastern Survey* 17:286–88 (22 Dec. 1948)

A brief article attempting to explain the factors underlying the U.S. efforts to rehabilitate Japan and to relate this policy to general American policy in the Far East. Addressing himself to the arguments of those Asians who had misgivings about occupation reforms and were apprehensive about a resurgent Japan, the author, a former Foreign Service officer, attempts to refute their objections. Topics discussed are SCAP's control of Japan's war-making potential, the country's economy, and its political and social institutions. Special emphasis is given to SCAP policies of educational reform as indicative of the underlying spirit of the occupation reform.

538 Bisson, Thomas Arthur. *Is Democracy Winning Japan?* New York: Institute of Pacific Relations, 1948. 48p.

539 Borton, Hugh. "Occupation Policies in Japan and Korea." *Annals of the American Academy of Political and Social Science* 255:146–55 (Jan. 1948)

This report is an overall analysis of the occupation program. It includes a discussion of the 4 most important documents which formulated basic occupation policies, namely, the Potsdam Declaration, the Instrument of Surrender, the U.S. Initial Post-Surrender Policy for Japan, and the Moscow Declaration of Foreign Ministers. It provides a description of Japanese attitudes toward the occupation authorities, and a discussion of democratic developments in the social and political institutions of Japan as seen through such topics as the general elections, the reemergence of political parties, and educational reforms. Problematic aspects still confronting the occupation such as the continued influence and power of the bureaucracy and the unhealthy economic situation are also treated. Finally, there is a discussion of the steps that have been initiated and the problems still to be overcome in connection with the signing of a peace treaty.

540 Briggs, Everett F. *New Dawn in Japan*. New York: Longmans, 1948. 249p.

541 Brines, Russell. *MacArthur's Japan*. New York: Lippincott, 1948. 315p.

A journalistic and balanced, though somewhat superficial, account of the occupation forces and conditions in Japan from 1945 through the middle of 1948 by the chief of the Associated Press, Tokyo bureau. The author was an AP correspondent in Tokyo from 1939 to 1941 and was among the first foreign journalists to reenter Japan after the war. He remained in Tokyo through 1951. The book characterizes a defeated Japan as: "the setting sun," MacArthur as: "the first American Emperor," and the emperor as: "the puzzled Mikado," etc. The author treats a variety of topics including the background and personality of MacArthur, conditions in Japan immediately subsequent to surrender, the dissolution of the *zaibatsu*, Japan's economic dilemma, the labor movement, the Diet, the bureaucracy, elections, land reform, education reform, and the Communist threat. In his discussion, the author provides some historical background for the various subjects he covers, particularly comparing present conditions to conditions in the late 1930s. Also interesting is his discussion of the change in the personalities of Americans who came to Japan from 1945 to 1948 and of the Japanese reactions to them.

542 Brumbaugh, Thoburn T. "Behind America's Shield of Steel." *Christian Century* 65:651–53 (30 June 1948)

The author discusses the creation of an American military shield in East Asia to protect against "ideological and military aggression and bulwark, if necessary, our own aggressive purposes." Japan is considered to be a strong part of this shield and her receptivity to Christian democracy is discussed in terms of the success of land reform and the creation of dignity for the common man. American social and economic responsibilities in Japan are seen as requiring a strong commitment for a decade or more.

543 Busch, Noel Fairchild. *Fallen Sun: A Report on Japan*. New York: Appleton–Century, 1948. 258p.

This collection of informal journalistic accounts appeared in *Life* and *Horizon* in 1946 and 1947. It relates to the occupation, the Japanese people, and the future of Japan. Generally favorable toward occupation policies, the report is more descriptive than interpretive and is somewhat superficial. The author covers such topics as the atmosphere in occupied Tokyo, the war-torn landscape, SCAP operations and personalities, the Allied Council for Japan and the Far Eastern Commission, the cooperative attitude of the Japanese toward efforts being made by various sections of SCAP in reforming Japan, Japanese behavior patterns, and ways of living.

544 Clark, Blake. "Yokosuka: Pilot Plant of Democracy." *Forum* 110:34–37 (July 1948); abridged and published under the title "Adored by Each Citizen of Yokosuka." *Reader's Digest* 53:51–54 (Sept. 1948)

The rehabilitation of the former Japanese naval base of Yokosuka is briefly described as an example of the beneficial aspects of the occupation. The author notes the social and economic demoralization of this important city in the immediate postwar period and contrasts it with the changes effected under SCAP officer Captain Benton Decker. He describes American efforts to improve sanitary conditions, to rebuild hospitals, to develop new industries as a substitute for the former armament industries, to encourage the formation of women's clubs for civic work, and to improve the educational system. The author maintains that by positively helping to rebuild Japan, such constructive programs will ultimately reduce the cost of the occupation for the United States.

545 Clune, Frank. *Ashes of Hiroshima: A Post-war Trip to Japan and China.* Sydney: Angus & Robertson, 1950. xviii, 301p.

The author is an Australian journalist who travelled to Japan and China as a war correspondent from 14 September to 1 November 1948. The account is useful in understanding Australian views regarding postwar Japanese conditions, the role of the British Commonwealth Occupation Force (BCOF), and SCAP's policy of occupation. Clune records his impressions and observations in considerable detail. In Japan, he visited Iwakuni Air Base, Kure, Hiroshima City, and Tokyo in that order. He describes interviews with General MacArthur, BCOF leaders, members of the Australian Mission in Tokyo, the mayor of Hiroshima City, and a Jesuit priest in Hiroshima. He regards SCAP as "the kindest conqueror the world has ever known," describes with somewhat patriotic touches the Australian presence in Japan, and optimistically anticipates that Japan will be Australia's ally in the future.

546 Costello, William. *Democracy vs. Feudalism in Post-war Japan.* Tokyo: Itagaki Shoten, 1948. 237p.

The author was a CBS correspondent in occupied Japan. He presents an informal journalistic account of the first 3 years of social turbulence under the occupation. Rather than describing and analyzing specific occupation reforms, he concentrates on treating the social climate of the country in an attempt to delineate what he conceives to be the differences between an operative democracy and "Japan's unique form of 20th century feudalism." Alleging that among many Japanese there is lip service paid to democracy in public and determination to forestall its every form in private, the author insists that the democratization of Japan will be accomplished only when the attitudes of the Japanese people are changed. In a conversational account interspersed with various episodes and anecdotes based on his experiences, the author discusses the operations of the present government, the new public personality of the emperor, some changes brought about by the new constitution, recent activities of revived reactionary forces, and SCAP efforts to eliminate such feudal remnants as the *oyabun-kobun* system. The book has been translated into Japanese under the title of *Shisō no nairan: sengo Nihon ni okeru minshushugi to hōkenshugi* (Tokyo: 1949).

547 ———. "Japanese 'Plunderbund'." *New Republic* 118:15–16 (5 Jan. 1948)

The recent disclosure of a scandal regarding Japanese military supplies is seen as a refutation of the popular notion that the occupation has been "an unadulterated success." After describing the illicit operations whereby the *zaibatsu* appropriated vast quantities of looted goods after the war, the author discusses recent efforts on the part of the judicial branch of the Japanese government to investigate the scandal and urges SCAP to render as much assistance as possible to apprehend those guilty. If not, he warns that there will be a resurgence of Japan's war mongers and cartelists.

548 Council on Foreign Relations. "America's Record in Japan and Korea." In *The United States in World Affairs 1947–1948.* New York: Harper, published for the Council, 1948. p.137–67.

This 4-part article provides an examination of the results of the first year and a half of the occupation. In the first section, the political reforms initiated by SCAP are delineated; the purge, the renunciation of imperial divinity, the postwar party alignment, and the results of the general elections in 1946 and 1947 are examined. The instability of democratic government is exemplified by means of an examination of the Katayama cabinet. Economic reform is discussed in the second part, with emphasis on the elimination of the landlord-tenant land tenure system and on the liquidation of *zaibatsu* control provided for in directive FEC–230 (Anti-Monopoly Act and the Economic Decentralization Act). Progress towards a reparations settlement is also noted. A brief general survey of postwar Japanese economic output is undertaken in the third section, with emphasis on reforms promoting self-sufficiency and the elimination of American subsidies. Finally, the difficulties involved in concluding a peace treaty are analyzed. Soviet, American, and Chinese proposals concerning the method of negotiating the treaty and its substance are presented.

548a Crofts, Verna I. "Japan as I Saw It." *Chicago Schools Journal* 30:57–60 (Oct. 1948)

Crofts describes the Japanese people and their attitudes towards the occupation during the year (1946/47) she worked as a teacher in the U.S. Army's education program at Kobe. She first notes the reverence with which the Japanese treat MacArthur, then describes the good relationships that have developed between American GI's and the Japanese civilian population. She also briefly comments upon some of the changes in the Japanese schools and points out how energetically American military government teams have been seeking to introduce principles of education and sanitation throughout the countryside. Crofts concludes by calling the "ubiquitous young G.I." America's most successful "good-will ambassadors" in Japan, for on account of their generous and kind-hearted nature, they have convinced the Japanese that the Americans are not cruel or evil people.

549 Eichelberger, Robert L. *Our Jungle Road to Tokyo*. Written in collaboration with Milton Mackaye. New York: Viking, 1950. xxvi, 306p.

Eichelberger recounts in readable style his experiences during the Pacific War and the occupation of Japan. He was commanding general of the U.S. Armed Forces in Australia from 1942 to 1944 and then commanding general of the Eighth Army from 1944 to 1948. There is more reminiscence than critical analysis in this account of his observations and experiences. The Eighth Army, established on 9 September 1944, played a major role in the Philippines campaign. After the Japanese surrender it became responsible for maintaining the security of Japan and for ensuring the Japanese government's compliance with the orders of the occupation forces. This responsibility was shared by the Sixth Army until it was deactivated in January 1946. The last 3 chapters are of special interest to students of the occupation. The general describes the Eighth Army's duties in Japan as planned prior to the Japanese surrender and its revised assignment as a peaceful occupant after the surrender, MacArthur's landing at Atsugi, the surrender ceremony on the *Missouri*, the release of Allied prisoners, his conversation with former Prime Minister Tōjō, the Tokyo war trials, and the achievements of military government teams. The general evaluates the occupation highly and regards Japanese cooperation with occupation policies favorably. Writing before the outbreak of the Korean War, he warns against an early peace treaty with Japan due to the "shaky" situation in the Far East.

549a Fellers, Bonner Frank. "Our New Friends, the Japanese." *Nation's Business* 36, no.2:41–43, 68+ (Feb. 1948)

Fellers predicts that "the new Japan, provided we don't blunder, will eventually emerge as a Christian democracy, and a staunch friend of the United States." The militarists have been discredited, he says, and the "inbred" cruelty of the Japanese has been undermined by occupation reforms. Despite the persistence of "religious patriotism," the Japanese will naturally swing toward Western ideology as a final step in the borrowing process they began in the 1870s. They will reject Communist ideology because of a deep-seated distrust of Russia.

550 Foreign Affairs Assn. of Japan, ed. *The Japan Year Book 1946–1948*. Tokyo: The Association, 1949. xv, 614, 350p.

A compendium of useful factual information on a wide range of topics concerning Japan. Topics treated include politics, society, economics, geography, history, culture, agriculture, education, and religion, as well as useful information for the tourist. A comprehensive introductory explanation is provided for each subject providing statistical information from as far back as 1935. Most useful are the voluminous appendixes which include the texts, full or partial, of major directives of SCAP, the new Japanese constitution and the Meiji Constitution, as well as major laws and ordinances. Other documentary materials include the texts of the Cairo and Potsdam Declarations, the Instrument of Surrender, the U.S. Initial Post-Surrender Policy for Japan, the imperial announcement renouncing the emperor's divinity, and the indictments submitted to the International Military Tribunal for the Far East. For developments from 1949 to 1952, see *The Japan Year Book, 1949–52* (1952) (no.674).

551 Gilbert, Scott. "Four Tales of Japan." *United Nations World* 2:36–39 (Apr. 1948)

Subtitled "It took Captain Brown a Long Time to Learn That Democracy Cannot Be Imposed on a People Unprepared for It," this story by a former U.S. Marine captain consists of 4 vignettes describing an American occupation officer's attempts to relate to the Japanese. The first part concerns his requisitioning some heating equipment from a Japanese city council. The second describes the poverty and hopelessness of a bombed out family in Nagasaki. The third is the officer's attempt to encourage independent thought in his interpreter. Finally, the petty crimes of Japanese individuals against their own people are described.

552 Gilmore, Robert John, and Denis Ashton Warner, eds. *Near North: Australia and a Thousand Million Neighbors*. Sydney: Angus & Robertson, 1948. xvi, 368p.

Two Australian journalists edited this collection of 18 articles written by 13 men (including themselves) with journalistic experience in the Asian and Pacific theaters during World War II. The articles are designed to provide a political and social picture of the Near North, a term generally used by Australians for East, South, and Southeast Asia. The countries and areas covered are Malaya, Hong Kong, Burma, India, Indochina, China, the Philippines, Timor, New Guinea, and Japan. The last 3 articles pertain to postwar Japan. Denis Warner, then chief of the Reuters-Australian Associated Press Bureau in Tokyo, writes on political, historical, and social conditions in postwar Japan. He describes the operation of MacArthur's headquarters, discusses the question of why MacArthur retained the emperor, and supports the view that Japan is "America's latest colony." A second article is contributed by Jack Percival, a British correspondent, who focuses on political aspects of postwar Japan. Subjects dealt with include the triple turnover of prime ministers in the first year after the surrender, MacArthur's policy of democratization, the separation of Shinto from the state, immature political parties, the American brand of democracy being implanted in Japan, and the ineffectual Allied Council for Japan. A third article by Robert Gilmore relates briefly the role and function of the British Commonwealth Occupation Forces (BCOF) in Japan. He reports that the landing at Kure near Hiroshima of the Australian advance party of BCOF on 13 February 1946 was an historic event for Australia but was also "tragically Australian" in its utter lack of any sense of mission. Gilmore also writes that BCOF is being run on a tight budget alongside the rich Americans.

552a Green, Leslie C. "Law and Administration in Present-day Japan." In *Current Legal Problems 1948*, ed. by George W. Keeton and G. Schwarzenberger on behalf of the Faculty of Law, University College, London. London: Stevens, 1948. p.188–205.

Green, an assistant lecturer at University College in London, critically surveys the manner in which the occupation authorities have set about their task. He first focuses on the nature of the Meiji constitution and explains how the manner of its application had made it necessary for SCAP to supplant it. He then discusses the initial postsurrender policy for Japan, the new constitution, and some of SCAP's activities—in particular those centering around demilitarization, the purging of suspected militarists, and the prosecution of war criminals. Green criticizes the United States for deliberately minimizing the role which the other Allied powers could play within the occupation, writing that one is left with the impression that "by and large the law of the United States is the law of Japan." In concluding he states, "The lasting character of the changes brought about in Japanese law cannot yet be judged. We must wait until after the occupation forces and the American authorities have departed. In the meantime let us remember that one swallow does not make a summer, and a mass of democratic laws and pious aspirations does not make a democracy."

553 Green, Owen Mortimer. "Reconstruction in Japan." *Fortnightly* 163:385–90 (June 1948)

This article attempts to describe the factors contributing to political and social unrest in Japan during the occupation. It discusses problems of industrial production and population growth as well as the difficulties SCAP encountered in implementing its programs of *zaibatsu* dissolution and land reform. The author expresses the misgivings of the British concerning an alleged American intent to build up Japan as the workshop of the Far East since this might provide unwelcome competition to manufacturers in the Commonwealth countries. He also recommends that SCAP free Japanese trade and advocates an early signing of a peace treaty so that Japan might begin to handle her own affairs. He concludes by questioning General MacArthur's belief that the occupation has wrought a "spiritual revolution" in the Japanese and suggests that traditional values are still prevalent among the people.

554 Gresham, Alan. "Impressions of Japan." *Contemporary Review* 174:204–8 (Oct. 1948)

An impressionistic account of occupied Japan which emphasizes the instability and chaos of the society. The author describes the increasing Westernization of Japanese life and concludes that a Japanese version of a modern democratic society is emerging.

555 Grilli, Marcel. "A Summary of Achievement: The First Anniversary of the Japanese Constitution." *Military Government Journal* 1:16–17, 26 (June 1948)

Written after the first anniversary of the promulgation of Japan's constitution, this article attempts to enumerate the various beneficial changes that have been effected by means of that document as well as other occupation reforms. Discussing only the content of the various new laws and organizations but not their implementation, the author considers such political reforms as the change in imperial status, the restructuring of the Diet, the reorganization of the judicial branch of government, the establishment of a new criminal code and public service laws, the decentralization and reform of education, the land reform program, and the laws passed for the dissolution of the *zaibatsu*. According to the author's somewhat optimistic description, all of these reforms have been successful in creating a new social, political, and economic order for Japan.

555a Guillain, Robert. "La reprise japonaise." *Politique étrangère* 13, no.1:49–64 (Feb. 1948)

Guillain views with skepticism the prospects for a genuine democratization of Japan since the Japanese "resist by not resisting" and the Americans involved in the reform effort are too few in number to be truly successful. The prospects for economic recovery, on the other hand, are generally good. The "substantial" progress to date has rested on the industrious nature of the Japanese peasantry and the rapidity with which reconstruction was undertaken in all areas of the Japanese economy. This progress, however, is being threatened at present by the cost of the occupation itself, which must be borne by the Japanese government, and by inflation. In any case, Guillain concludes, the most crucial determining factor in Japan's future and that of the occupation will be Soviet–American rivalry and tensions.

556 "Interview with the First Japanese Editor to Visit U.S. since 1941." *United States News* 25:38–41 (17 Sept. 1948)

Suzuki Bunshirō, editor of the *Asahi*, traveled to the United States in 1948 as correspondent for 7 Japanese newspapers. The interview covers 8 areas: the lack of animosity on the part of the Japanese towards the occupation, the reaction of the Japanese public to wartime bombing and to the prosecution of the war, the reasons for the rise of militarism and nationalism in prewar Japan, the influence of communism in postwar Japan, the continuing spread of Russian influence in Asia, the problem of inflation in Japan and the need for U.S. capital, the present position of the emperor, and the Japanese attitude toward the *zaibatsu*. The interview closes with expressions of thanks to the United States and encourages continued American influence in Japan.

557 "Japan: One or Many?" *Time* 51:25–26 (31 May 1948)

This article discusses General MacArthur's role as a guide to occupation reforms. The restoration of civil rights is examined, as is the attempt to maintain moderates in positions of power. The activity of the Deconcentration Review Board in the area of *zaibatsu* liquidation is mentioned. *Time* considers trade revival to be the key to general economic revival.

557a *The Japan Who's Who and Business Directory, 1948.* Tokyo: Tokyo News Service, 1948. ii, 352, 199p.

The first who's who and business directory in English to appear in postwar Japan, this reference work is a valuable publication for the student of the occupation period. Part 1 consists of a listing of approximately 2000 businessmen, politicians, high government officials (both national and local), men of letters and arts, scientists, educators, prominent religious and social leaders, and journalists. For each individual, it provides his present position, his place and date of birth, the college from which he graduated, his present address, and the important events that have marked his life as well as the major positions that he has held to date. Part 2—the business directory—includes such materials as (1) a listing of the chambers of commerce and industry in Japan, and of Japanese trade and economic bodies; (2) lists of firms requiring deconcentration; (3) a classified and detailed list of Japanese industrial companies and business firms with their addresses, a statement of their activities, their capital as well as their assets and liabilities, and the names of their major executives; and (4) lists of the mayors of leading cities and of the governors of prefectures. An index of companies facilitates the use of this directory.

558 "Japanese Cabinets since the Surrender." *Current Notes on International Affairs* 19:187–90 (Apr. 1948)

This article reviews briefly the successive postwar cabinets of Prince Higashikuni, Shidehara, Yoshida, Katayama, and Ashida. It regards the Higashikuni cabinet as having performed a useful role in the early stages of the occupation by bringing about a smooth transition. SCAP's purge directive of 4 January 1946, it states, caused drastic reorganization of Japanese political parties, contributing indirectly to the growth of liberal elements in the April 1946 election. It also refers to SCAP's intervention in a general strike planned for February 1947 and to the ineffective coalition represented by the Katayama cabinet.

559 Ladejinsky, Wolf Isaac. "Trial Balance in Japan." *Foreign Affairs* 27:104–16 (Oct. 1948)

Three years after the start of the occupation, the author, a former agricultural consultant on SCAP's staff, presents a thoughtful analysis of its accomplishments. A description of the latitude of General MacArthur's authority is followed by a brief analysis of the new constitution and a discussion of the basic objectives of the occupation and their implementation. Those areas emphasized are: the elimination of the *zaibatsu*, the reconstruction of the labor movement, the inauguration of the land reform program, and the reform of education. The author believes that there is no reason why the military occupation cannot be terminated shortly, although he maintains that a generation must pass "before we can know how deeply its spirit has been accepted and how lasting its effects will be on Japan."

Latourette, Kenneth S. "Peace with Japan." 1948. *See* no.2334.

560 McEvoy, Dennis. "Let's Get out of Japan." *Forum* 110:148–50 (Sept. 1948); abridged in *Reader's Digest* 53:49–51 (Oct. 1948)

Although acknowledging the importance of Japan's remaining anti-communist, the author argues against the conclusion that a continued American presence will insure such an anti-communist stance. Believing that Americans are now endangering the fruits of the occupation and retarding Japan's economic recovery by a prolonged and expensive occupation, he advocates that the United States "follow the recommendations of General MacArthur and send home the army of American civil servants and troops," thereby allowing the Japanese to run their own affairs. In conclusion, he proposes that a small Allied supervisory commission remain to see that the occupation reforms are not jeopardized.

561 Martin, Edwin M. *The Allied Occupation of Japan*. New York: American Institute of Pacific Relations, 1948. xiv, 155p.

The first in an Institute of Pacific Relations series of studies on occupation reforms, this is a "concise review of the aims, methods, and accomplishments of the military occupation of Japan" as of 1948. The author, a State Department official during this period, is concerned more with describing the actual operating conditions of the occupation and the goals it intended to achieve than with evaluating its results. The book considers presurrender planning activities and the formulation of Allied policy as well as issues concerning demobilization, the war crimes trials, reparations, and territorial changes. Matters relating to the democratization of the country are given greatest emphasis and there is particularly good coverage of economic matters—i.e., the reorganization of economic institutions, the development of labor organizations, and agrarian reform. Appended are the texts of the Basic Post-Surrender Policy for Japan, 26 June 1947; the Agreement of the Foreign Ministers at Moscow on Establishing the Far Eastern Commission and the Allied Council for Japan, 27 December 1945; and the Basic Initial Post-Surrender Directive to SCAP for the Occupation and Control of Japan, 8 November 1945.

562 Mears, Helen. *Mirror for Americans: Japan*. Boston: Houghton Mifflin, 1948. xiv, 329p.

This critical appraisal of the occupation and U.S. policy toward Asia by a correspondent for the *Saturday Evening Post* examines and compares U.S. and Japanese points of view on American policies toward Asia and concludes that "the first step for 'educators' is to discover how well their practice squares with their principles from the point of view of those they seek to educate." Drawing examples from nearly every facet of American policy toward Asia, Helen Mears illustrates a wide gap between official preachments and practice. It is her conviction that Americans made their own wartime propaganda the accepted interpretation of Japanese actions and motives. They then structured a corrective and punitive occupation based on this erroneous interpretation and on an overly idealized view of the American system. This account seems aimed primarily at exploding myths, exposing half-truths and lies, and reappraising American activities from an Asian viewpoint. Topics covered include the mandated islands of the Pacific, Japan's annexation of Korea vis-à-vis Western colonialism in Asia, the role of trade in the international relations of Japan and the United States, and Western versus Japanese interests in China. The broad coverage and loose organization of the book, combined with its ambiguous chapter headings, sparseness of credited sources, and lack of an index handicap the reader and lessen the usefulness of the book for research purposes. Appendixes include the Atlantic Charter and several excerpts from U.S. government documents on Pearl Harbor. SCAP reportedly forbade the translation of this book into Japanese. After the occupation ended, however, a translation did appear under the title of *Amerika no hansei: Amerikajin no kagami to shite no Nihon* (Tokyo: Bungei Shunjū Shinsha, 1953. 415p.).

563 Menken, Jules. "The Problem of Japan." *National Review* (London) 130: 461–67 (June 1948)

The author briefly discusses problems related to SCAP's decision to retain the emperor and to dissolve Japan's *zaibatsu* combines, and he describes what he considers 2 fatal errors in Allied attitudes toward Japan. The first is the American desire to fortify Japan as a bastion against Soviet communism and the second is the Australian fear and hatred of Japan and the resultant desire to keep her perpetually weak. He suggests that the Allied powers should have a regard for Japan's historical role in the Far East and formulate a measured and moderate Allied policy which would have lasting effects upon the country's political and social development.

564 Mignone, Frederick. "The Parallel Problems of Italy and Japan." *South Atlantic Quarterly* 47:298–313 (July 1948)

The postwar conditions of Japan and Italy are compared in an article which focuses on the economic dilemmas in both countries, the unstable political control maintained by their governments, and the efforts of the Communists to overthrow the parties in power. The author discusses the common problems they share such as drastic food shortages, physical destruction as a result of the war, and mounting inflation. A brief discussion of the proliferation of new political parties and organizations in both countries is discussed, with special attention paid to the activities of the Communist party. There is also consideration of the marked growth of labor unions in Italy and Japan and the Communist influence in such organizations. The author suggests somewhat similar solutions to the economic problems of these countries, namely that the United States work with other democratic nations to promote economic stability through the development of a healthy export-import trade relationship and the provision of large amounts of aid to bolster their national economies.

565 "On International Themes." *Soviet Press Translations* 3:367–68 (15 June 1948)

Translated from a story in *Izvestia* on 22 April 1948, this article presents a brief analysis of the Ashida government. According to the author, the programs sponsored by this government are utterly contrary to the Allied policies of demilitarization and democratization as set forth in the Potsdam Declaration. Moreover, the American authorities are accused of trying to set the Japanese people against the USSR and to convert Japan into a bastion against communism.

565a "Remaking Japan." *Statist* 148:614–15 (18 Dec. 1948)

Japan's captors have avoided the twin mistakes made in postwar Germany, Austria, and Korea: the establishment of occupation zones and the dismantling of industrial facilities. Japan's reconstruction, however, has been uncomfortably slow on account of the loss of her prewar markets, the negative effects of SCAP's antitrust measures, unsettled conditions in Asia, and increased competition from other countries in such areas as fishing and the production of textiles and other inexpensive consumer goods. The article concludes with a prediction that occupation controls will rapidly be loosened during the coming months.

566 Sano, Manabu. "The Evolution of the Democratic Revolution." *New Leader* 31, no.15:8–9 (10 Apr. 1948)

The organizer of the postwar Farmer-Labor Vanguard party comments favorably on the dissolution of the *zaibatsu*, SCAP's land reform program, the growth of the labor unions, and other features of democratization, but he feels that many of these developments have not gone far enough. "Many intellectually honest Japanese," he writes, "are beginning to feel a sense of uneasiness [and] are asking whether the revolution has not failed to fit some of the realities of a Japan whose level of social life is dropping readily." Concerned about problems of domestic unemployment and curtailed economic production, Sano calls for increased economic activity. He also urges that the civil service system be reorganized, notes that it will still be some time before a political party truly representative of the Japanese people emerges, and asserts that more must be done to enable those Japanese who are interested in American culture to secure publications and appropriate informational materials from abroad.

567 Sansom, Sir George B. "Conflicting Purposes in Japan." *Foreign Affairs* 26:302–11 (Jan. 1948)

Some important aims of the occupation as well as the peace treaty that will be drawn up and the various economic and strategic problems that arise in connection with these aims are the focus of this article. The author is specifically concerned with the 2-fold Allied intent: (1) to make the Japanese people unwilling to go to war again, and (2) to make them unable to go to war. With regard to the first aim he cautions against the belief that democracy has taken deep and lasting root in Japan after a few short years of foreign control. Concerning the second aim which involves controlling the industrial activity of Japan, he points out the contradictory situation facing the United States. On the one hand "only foreign aid can make possible a dangerous revival of expansionist policies in Japan," yet, on the other hand, a certain amount of foreign aid will be necessary in order to rebuild the economy to a level at which Japan will be self-supporting and no longer a financial drain on the United States. Such a dilemma, he suggests, will have to be approached at the peace conference and solved in such a way that the Allies, particularly the Asian Allies, will be satisfied and the economy of Japan will be safeguarded.

568 Schwartz, Charles. "Japan's Chance for Freedom." *Military Government Journal* 1, no.10:9–10 (Aug. 1948)

Schwartz points out that if the Japanese are provided with enough to eat, an honest government, and some basis for expecting a brighter future, democracy may work in Japan.

568a "La situation au Japon." *Chronique de politique étrangère* 1, no.5:86–96 (Sept. 1948)

This article is one of several chapters on the problems of the postwar world which appeared in this publication of the Institute for International Relations in Bruxelles, Belgium. It first briefly discusses the terms of the Japanese surrender, then summarizes and comments upon various aspects of the occupation including (1) the relationship of SCAP to the

Allied Council for Japan and the FEC, and (2) the new constitution, several extracts from which are provided in French translation. A brief discussion of the possible terms of a Japanese peace settlement concludes the article.

569 Sneider, Richard L. "Japan: An Experiment in the Development of a Democratic Society." *Columbia Journal of International Affairs* 2:21–36 (Winter 1948)

A detailed discussion of several important facets of the occupation program which relate to Allied efforts to establish a democratic and peaceful government in Japan. The author considers the dual roles and responsibilities of SCAP and the Japanese government in the program, changes in SCAP's procedures of policy making and operations over the course of time, the quality of SCAP personnel, and the hierarchy of responsibility within its organizational structure. There follows an appraisal of SCAP's performance in effecting legislative changes and insuring the proper administration of those new measures. The author distinguishes between the political elements of the democratization program, which involve free elections, a democratic constitution, and civil rights; and the economic elements, which involve reform of industry and agriculture. He devotes considerable attention to the implications of these reforms and the opposition to them by powerful antidemocratic forces within the Japanese government.

Supreme Commander for the Allied Powers. Government Section. *Political Reorientation of Japan, September 1945 to September 1948.* 1949. See no.279.

570 Takagi, Yasaka. "Defeat and Democracy in Japan." *Foreign Affairs* 26:645–52 (July 1948)

Four major reforms which the occupation has effected in Japan are discussed in this article. They are: (1) the establishment of democratic instruments of government; (2) the advancement of labor unions; (3) the land reform program; and (4) the field of education. The latter part of the article is devoted to what the author defines as "the awakening of the concept of individual personality" which he believes is different from traditional Japanese behavior yet essential for the true democratization of Japan. In his concluding remarks, the author states his belief that "Japan needs Protestant Christianity" in order for her people to grasp the real meaning of democracy.

571 Thomas, Elbert D. "Leadership in Asia under a New Japan." *Annals of the American Academy of Political and Social Science* 255:156–65 (Jan. 1948)

A loosely structured article discussing Japan's past, its present period of occupation, and its future as an important Asian power. With respect to Japan's past history, the author considers the country's prewar pattern of militaristic action as having been carried out partially in imitation of Western military examples. Regarding the present period, he categorizes the occupation objectives as falling into 3 broad areas—demilitarization, political and social reorientation, and economic reconstruction. The author warns that although economic conditions in Japan must be attended to, they should not be given total priority over political and social reforms. In the concluding section he describes why, in his opinion, the United States must consider Japanese development as our responsibility and stresses the need for increasing cooperation and friendship between the 2 countries for their mutual advantage.

572 "Three Years after the Rout of Japanese Imperialism." *New Times* no.37:1–2 (8 Sept. 1948)

The American occupation of Japan is viewed as an attempt to turn the country into a colony of American monopolies and a strategic base for American expansion in the East. In order to accomplish such an aim, the writer believes, Americans have been forced to rely more and more upon the reactionary Japanese forces of imperialism and militarism and to subvert the growth of the national liberation movement in Asia.

"Trends in United States Policy towards Japan." 1948. See no.1516.

573 U.S. Dept. of the Army. Civil Affairs Div. *Occupied Japan: A Summary.* Washington, D.C.: 1948. 11p.

574 Vandenbosch, Amry. "The Flaming East." *Annals of the American Academy of Political and Social Science* 257:23–36 (May 1948)

Vandenbosch discusses postwar Allied policy in Asia and reviews the basic wartime policy statements issued at Cairo, Yalta, and Potsdam as well as the surrender terms for Japan. The responsibility for the functioning of occupation policies shared among SCAP, the Allied Council, and the Far Eastern Commission is explained, and selected democratic reforms are analyzed. The author explains the limitations of a military occupation and the obstacles to a rapid conclusion of a peace treaty with Japan.

575 Varshavsky, A. "In Tokyo." *New Times* no.37:19–23 (8 Sept. 1948)

A correspondent in Tokyo describes his view of the situation in that city 3 years after the termination of the war. He discusses housing conditions, educational facilities, city transportation, and police activity in Japan's capital city. He considers the Americans to be shockingly lax in rebuilding the city except for those parts which they themselves intend to utilize. He also accuses occupation officials of turning popular suffering to their private profit and living a life of luxury while the masses starve.

576 Wakefield, Harold. *New Paths for Japan.* London: Royal Institute of International Affairs, 1948. viii, 223p.

The first part of the book is a reprint in revised form of the major portion of an earlier publication by the Royal Institute of International Affairs, entitled *Japan in Defeat: A Report by a Chatham House Study Group* (1945) (no.173). While the first part deals with the sociopolitical and cultural conditions of Japan at the end of the war, the second part describes postwar developments up to the summer of 1947. The author, an Englishman, evaluates Allied occupation policies on such issues as the war crimes trials, constitutional revision, political and economic readjustment, and national reeducation. While generally supporting the occupation program, the author further suggests that Japan be given an incentive to pursue constructive national goals. One such incentive would be its admission into the United Nations so as to encourage positive participation in the international community. The work is based on such sources of information as the *New York Times*, the *Christian Science Monitor*, the *Nippon Times*, and news releases of the Dōmei News Service, plus a few government documents.

577 Warner, Dave. "A Long Look: Japan and Korea." *Military Government Journal* 1, no.7:14 (May 1948)

Warner writes of the considerable appeal that American popular culture has for both the Japanese and the Koreans, as well as of the need for qualified people seriously interested in working for the various subdivisions of SCAP's Civil Information and Education Section.

578 "Washington Now Plans to Lighten the Japanese Occupation Load." *Newsweek* 32:52 (25 Oct. 1948)

This review of possible future shifts in American occupation policy in Japan emphasizes 6 points: (1) the abandonment of the idea of rapidly adopting a peace treaty; (2) the reduction of American military responsibility for economic rehabilitation; (3) the establishment of a permanent national police force of 150,000 men; (4) encouragement to Japanese officials to operate more independently of occupation supervision; (5) the discontinuation and reversal of the purges; and (6) attempts by the United States to insure the cooperation of other allies in occupation decisions.

578a Woddis, Jack, and Neil Stewart. "Wall Street over the Far East." *Labour Monthly* 30:344–47 (Nov. 1948)

It is increasingly clear, the authors argue, that the role envisaged by the

United States for Japan is that of "the military, political, and economic fulcrum" of U.S. Far Eastern policy. Japan is evidently to be rearmed for the purpose of crushing colonial liberation movements, and will be the base for an attack on the Soviet Union. As the future "industrial workshop of the Far East," Japan is already becoming an extension of the American economy.

Yanaga, Chitoshi. "Japan: Tradition and Democracy." 1948. *See* no.1987.

1949

579 "Allied Policy in Japan: Theory and Practice." *World Today* 5:190–201 (May 1949)

The author first describes Allied objectives and the policies adopted to attain those objectives and later considers the implementation of those policies and their present and future effects upon Japanese society. Particularly emphasized are the changes in the emperor's role, political developments as a result of a new American-sponsored political system, the reparations issue, land reform, and educational programs. The occupation is divided into 3 phases: (1) the demilitarization program, (2) the democratization program, and (3) changes in occupation aims. In this third phase, according to the author, "the emphasis has been less on making Japan democratic than on making her economically self-supporting." This aim has often been termed a reversal in SCAP policy, particularly economic policy. In the final section, he considers to what extent the Americans have succeeded in democratizing Japan, pointing out the many and serious problems associated with such an undertaking. However, he is cautiously optimistic about the chances of some democratic reforms lasting after the American withdrawal.

580 Ballantine, Joseph W. "Report on Japan." *American Foreign Service Journal* 26:9–11, 38+ (Oct. 1949)

Ballantine discusses the possibilities of implementing democratic reforms aimed at the individual in Japan. He notes the need for cultivation of a public consciousness among the Japanese and the reforms in education made with this need in mind. The necessity for continual American encouragement of liberal elements among the people and for a continuous supply of Western intellectual and scientific materials is explained. The author analyzes the ambivalence of the American goal regarding Japanese economic revitalization vis-à-vis the extensive tariff protection of U.S. markets.

581 Bisson, Thomas Arthur. *Prospects for Democracy in Japan.* New York: Macmillan, 1949. viii, 143p.

A concise critical analysis of occupation policies and achievements in Japan during the first 2 and a half years since surrender is attempted here by a former official of the Government Section of SCAP. Once a research associate of the Institute of Pacific Relations and a member of the U.S. Strategic Bombing Survey group that visited Japan in 1945, the author describes the kind of Japanese leadership that the occupation forces faced at the time of their arrival and the basic objectives pursued by the occupation. Bisson maintains that SCAP was led by the ease and speed with which the military surrender finally took place to underestimate the determination and skill with which the Japanese ruling oligarchy intended to fight for the preservation of its control over political and economic institutions. He points out that the Old Guard managed to maintain its dominance through the 1946 and 1947 general elections. Bisson is critical of the ineffectiveness of the purge, the inadequacy of *zaibatsu* dissolution, and the failure to destroy fully authoritarian agencies such as neighborhood associations, labor bosses, and the Agricultural Association. Bisson is also critical of the Katayama cabinet for not executing reform measures effectively and for not adequately meeting pressing economic problems. He also notes that the postwar rulers of Japan succeeded in watering down SCAP's major directives and in obstructing the emergence of a democratically-controlled economy. Finally, he deplores a shift in occupation policy emphases after 1948 which encouraged the continued dominance of conservative leaders and delayed the achievement of original SCAP aims.

582 Bolles, Blair. "U.S. Reshapes Policy in Asia." *Foreign Policy Bulletin* 28:1–2 (3 June 1949)

A section of this report is devoted to the effects of the American anti-Communist policy in Japan in terms of United States' relations with other Allied powers and Far Eastern nations. The author contends that such recent American decisions as the ban on strikes by government employees and the curtailment of the reparations program have disturbed many of these nations. Finally, he implies that there is a possibility that in the next 6 months the military occupation will end and General MacArthur will be replaced by a civilian commissioner.

Buck, Pearl. "The Good People of Japan." 1949. *See* no.2283.

582a Chenery, William Ludlow. "Red Shadow over the Pacific." *Collier's* 120: 26, 41+ (13 Sept. 1947)

Chenery finds the Japanese still appreciative of the occupation for the protection it guarantees them against possible Soviet aggression. In any case, Allied control of the country must be continued since Japan will have to grapple with tremendous food shortages for some time to come. Chenery then describes at some length various American efforts to combat these shortages and to rebuild Japan's productive capacity. He concludes that while SCAP is making progress on many fronts, "the cloud of Russian intentions and ambitions" overshadows everything and necessarily delays the day when Japan will regain complete independence.

583 Council on Foreign Relations. "American Policies in the Far East (II): Changes in Occupied Japan." In *The United States in World Affairs 1948–1949*. New York: Harper, published for the Council, 1949. p.288–306.

The delay in concluding a peace treaty with Japan which resulted from disagreement among the major powers concerning procedures is examined here, as are the changes in SCAP policy following the acceptance of a prolonged occupation. The completion of demilitarization and of legislated democratic reform and the shift among occupation personnel to a concern with economic recovery is analyzed. The reports of the Draper and Johnston Missions are examined, and specific economic reforms which had been undertaken, including tax reform, the reconstitution of international trade, and the completion of *zaibatsu* decentralization in accordance with directive FEC–230 are noted. The reasons for which the comprehensive reparations program was abandoned and the resultant antagonism expressed by other Asian nations are noted. Comments are offered concerning the continued instability and polarization of the political scene in Japan with reference to the elections of January 1949.

584 ———. "Search for a Far Eastern Policy: 3. Problems of Japan and Korea." In *The United States in World Affairs 1949*. New York: Harper, published for the Council, 1950. p.448–60.

A comparison of techniques used during the occupations of Germany and Japan is followed by a cursory discussion of the inculcation of conservative democracy in Japan. The unsatisfactory rate of economic recovery and price stabilization is noted. The increasingly important role of Japan in Asian cold war politics is emphasized, and the possibility of concluding a peace treaty without Soviet participation is examined. The permanent success of occupation reforms is seen to depend on the incorporation of Japan into a Pacific collective security network.

585 Crockett, Lucy Herndon. *Popcorn on the Ginza: An Informal Portrait of Postwar Japan.* New York: Sloane, 1949. xi, 286p.

The author, an American Red Cross worker in Japan, records her impressions of the early years of the Allied occupation. In anecdotal fashion, she places emphasis on the everyday encounters of occupation personnel and their families with Japan and the Japanese. Her observations are generally entertaining but superficial. Concrete improvements introduced by the occupation forces in such fields as health and agriculture are seen as taking hold, but her conclusions about the possibility of democracy in Japan are largely negative. She claims that feudalistic mentality and customs still maintain their hold on the Japanese people.

586 "Democratic Traditions in Japan." *External Affairs* 1:12–13 (Nov. 1949)

This brief article consists of 2 letters concerning a "festival for democracy" sponsored by the civil affairs team in Shizuoka prefecture. It is an interesting comment on Allied judgments of the success of the democratization of Japan. The first letter from E. H. Norman, head of the Canadian Liaison Mission to Japan, is a congratulatory one in which he emphasizes the democratic aspects of Japan's own history; the second, and more interesting, is a reply from Moses Burg, chief of the Civil Information Section of the civil affairs team in Shizuoka, indicating that the festival was a success in that "for once, the Japanese were able to think and speak of democracy with a feeling of pride, self-respect, and intimacy" rather than inferiority and unfamiliarity.

586a Deverall, Richard L. G. "Storm Signals over Japan." *America* 80:622–24 (12 Mar. 1949)

The author writes of Soviet attempts to make capital out of Japan's difficulties and American economic mistakes in the occupation.

586b "Dilemma in Japan." *Economist* 156:357–58 (26 Feb. 1949)

This article denounces the remarks of the United States secretary of the army who is alleged to have stated that Japan might be viewed as "expendable" in the event of war with the Soviet Union. It is dangerous to talk about such things, the article maintains, at a time when Japan is still completely dependent on the United States for her defense. The great majority of the Japanese people accept the current *status quo*, but should American defense guarantees begin to look unreliable, the number of those who look to the Communist powers of Asia for support will increase. If America finds it impossible to pledge protection to Japan, the article concludes, it must be prepared to create a Japanese defense force in spite of objections at home and especially in Australia.

587 Dozier, Edwin Burk. *Japan's New Day.* Nashville: Broadman, 1949. 154p.

588 Eidus, Khaim. "General MacArthur's Campaign against the Japanese Working Class." *Soviet Press Translations* 5:74–76 (1 Feb. 1950)

Eidus examines alleged American–Japanese repressive policies against the exercise of certain democratic rights by the working class in an article that was originally published in the 12 November 1949 issue of *Trud*. The suppression of the Communist party by police terrorism and arrest is strongly emphasized. The layoff of 1,500,000 workers, undertaken as a measure to promote economic stabilization, is regarded as an attempt to weaken the labor movement, as is a ban against striking and collective bargaining by 2,500,000 state employees. Vehement criticism of right-wing Socialists for their attempts to gain control of labor organizations is recorded. Also mentioned is a government crackdown on intellectuals and the dismissal of many left-wing personnel from the educational system. In conclusion, the author lists organizations and groups that continue to fight against American reactionary activity.

Fairbank, John K., et al. *Next Step in Asia.* 1949. See no.788.

589 Green, Owen Mortimer. "De-mok-ra-sie." *Nineteenth Century and After* 145: 133–37 (Mar. 1949)

The Far Eastern correspondent for the *Observer* begins by discussing the general elections that were held in late January 1949. He notes that they followed the expected course, with the Democratic Liberals being returned in large numbers and with Prime Minister Yoshida gaining solid support within the Diet. At the same time, however, the Communists have increased their membership in parliament from 4 to 35 and have doubled their vote within Japan. Their gains within the cities are indicative of the widespread economic distress that continues to confront many urban wage-earners. The cities remain largely in ruins, and exports are not too encouraging. Green then turns his attention to the British government's failure to play an active and independent role in the occupation. It has only tagged along behind the United States and, as a consequence, has succeeded in irritating British Far Eastern circles and especially Australia. Finally, the author comments on some of the efforts to terminate the occupation. "Beneath all other symptoms of unrest in Japan," he asserts, "the deepest, most universally felt is the chafing against the Allied occupation. In this there is no difference between Communists and others." Russia's insistence that the peace treaty terms be fixed by the Council of Ministers in which she could use her veto, rather than by a majority of the Far Eastern Allied Committee in Washington, has caused the delay in the formal conclusion of peace. SCAP's increasingly liberal measures, however, are evidence of the present Allied policy to work towards the day when Japan will be independent and sovereign once again.

590 ———. "Japan, 1945–9." *Contemporary Review* 176:138–42 (Sept. 1949)

Green calls for the return of Japan to the circle of "independent friendly nations." While acknowledging the efficacy of the occupation-inspired freedoms and Japan's substantial economic recovery, he doubts MacArthur's claim of a spiritual conversion of the Japanese people and indicates that enough punishment has been exacted. The author emphasizes his conviction that Japan will make more progress, both politically and economically, along lines approved by the United States if the occupation were soon ended. Finally, he cites the activity of the Communists in taking advantage of legitimate public resentment toward the United States as another impelling reason to end the occupation.

591 Hamilton, Mary Glenn B. "Military Government in Japan." *Military Government Journal* 2:1–2 (Jan./Feb. 1949)

A brief analysis of reforms enacted by the Eighth Army Military Government Section, which for 3 years was under the leadership of Brigadier General Rex W. Beasley. Considering only the more successful achievements of the army, the author discusses the economic reforms affecting such industries as electrical power production and coal mining, changes in the Japanese labor system, agricultural reform, improvement of the public health system, innovations in Japanese fishing and forestry, and SCAP encouragement of local participation in educational and political decision-making.

592 Kagawa, Toyohiko. "Japan's Postwar Balance Sheet." *Christian Century* 66:110–11 (26 Jan. 1949)

Kagawa reviews the bloodless democratic revolution led by General MacArthur and lists a wide variety of completed reforms. He comments that a spiritual revolution has not followed and the result is the initiation of a process of self-destruction in Japan. He discusses rising crime rates, moral deterioration, and the popularity of materialism throughout society. The author places the blame for these problems on the refusal of conservatives and capitalists to accept the changes in Japan which have moved farmers, workers, and cooperative institutions to the fore.

593 Kantor, Ken. "Uncle Come-come." *New York Times Magazine* p.78–79 (25 Sept. 1949)

This article concerns a Japanese teacher of English conversation who regularly appears on national radio. The author feels that this popular program is influential in spreading democratic ideas in Japan. He sees the teacher, Joe Hirakawa, as a model for the new Japanese, a mixture of East and West.

594 Kerr, William Campbell. *Japan Begins Again*. New York: Friendship Pr., 1949. 180p. Japanese translation under the title *Nihon no sai shuppatsu* (Tokyo: Shinkyō Shuppansha, 1951. 241p.)

This general work on modern Japan contains 3 chapters of interest to the student of the Allied occupation. Chapter 1 (p.1–14) is entitled "The Empire Is No More" and discusses the immediate postwar economic, political, psychological and religious picture. Chapter 7 (p.93–118) focuses more specifically on postwar reconstruction with reference to farming, public welfare, prison reform, the new constitution, and noteworthy educational and religious developments. Finally, chapter 8 (p.119–46)—"All Japan for Christ"—discusses the reorganization of Christian missionary activities in Japan and the work of the missionaries in serving Japanese youth, the Korean and Okinawan communities within Japan, and others in need of their help.

595 Ketzel, Clifford. "The Occupation of Japan." *Proceedings of the Institute of World Affairs* 25:38–41 (1949)

A round table discussion headed by James T. Watkins concerning the occupation's objectives and their implementation is briefly summarized. The greatest divergence of opinions occurred with respect to the question of what Japan's economic position in the postwar world should be. Also considered were questions concerning reparations payments and Japan's political stance in the face of the intensifying cold war and the gradual disintegration of Nationalist China.

596 Krylov, V. "The Struggle Continues." *New Times* no.23:22–25 (1 June 1949)

A letter from a Tokyo correspondent presents a leftist analysis of the contemporary scene there. Concentrating on political and economic developments, the author discusses the activities of the newly formed Yoshida cabinet and its current efforts to thwart the development of the Communist party. However, the author maintains that such efforts are ineffective and the Communists are daily growing stronger. He discusses the marked increase of labor disturbances and the dire economic situation in the country and cites the recent May Day demonstrations as evidence of the vigor and the size of what he terms Japan's genuine democratic forces.

597 Kudryavtsev, V. "Campaign against the Democratic Rights of the Japanese People." *Soviet Press Translations* 4: 462–65 (1 Sept. 1949); abridged version published under the same title in *Current Digest of the Soviet Press* 1, no.26:27–28 (26 July 1949)

Police efforts to control demonstrating workers in a series of clashes in Tokyo and Kobe are the focal point of this article that was originally published in the 23 June 1949 issue of *Izvestia*. The author accuses SCAP and the reactionary Japanese government of attempting to rebuild the Japanese military in total disregard of the provisions of the Potsdam Declaration in order to reimpose complete repression upon the country.

598 ———. "The Fourth Anniversary of the Defeat of Militarist Japan." *Soviet Press Translations* 5:5–7 (1 Jan. 1950)

Kudryavtsev emphasizes the decisive contribution made by Soviet forces in Manchuria which aided in the defeat of Japan in 1945. His conclusion notes both the Soviet attempts to call a meeting of the Council of Foreign Ministers in order to draw up plans for a peace treaty and the American unwillingness to negotiate except within the context of the Far Eastern Commission. The American decision to prolong the occupation is regarded as a conscious aspect of the U.S. imperialist policy in Asia. The occupation authorities and the Yoshida government are represented as reactionary and oppressive vis-à-vis the desires of the

Japanese people for independence, democracy, and peace.

This article was originally published in the 3 September 1949 issue of *Izvestia*.

599 ———. "Japan in the Plans of American Imperialism." *Soviet Press Translations* 5:233–35 (15 Apr. 1950); abridged version published under the title "Japan in American Imperialist Plans" in *Current Digest of the Soviet Press* 1, no. 51:26 (17 Jan. 1950)

Kudryavtsev deals with American attempts to create an alliance with Japan to provide "cannon fodder" for her imperialist aims in Asia in an article originally published in the 17 December 1949 issue of *Izvestia*. Cited as examples of this policy are the establishment of a heavily armed national police force and attempts to destroy the Japanese democratic movement. In regard to the second category, the author discusses suppression of the Korean minority and police terrorism directed against the Communist party. He also considers American attempts to create postwar Japanese trade patterns which would exclude traditional Chinese markets and create competition with the British in Southeast Asia.

600 "Long Road to Recovery." *Newsweek* 34:28–31 (12 Sept. 1949)

Skepticism of MacArthur's confidence in the Japanese ability to recover is expressed here. The continued presence of over 5,500 administrative personnel from the SCAP bureaucracy is noted as one justification for this skepticism. The authors emphasize the continued Communist threat and discuss the reorganization of a large, well-armed national police force. Improvement in industrial production is noted, but the weakness of the export trade sector is regarded as highly significant.

601 Ludmer, Henry. "Japan as Seen by a Foreigner." *Ohio Journal of Science* 49:209–20 (Nov. 1949)

Ludmer categorizes the major problems confronting the occupation authorities in Japan as follows: (1) the geographical problem of how to make use of Japan's strategic location without increasing her military potential; (2) the political problem of how to stop Communism without encouraging the growth of authoritarianism in any form; (3) the economic problem of how to attain economic and financial stability in the long run; (4) the social problem of taking care of the annual population increases without accompanying increases in land and capital resources and without causing social unrest; and (5) the military problem of how to provide Japan with appropriate means for self-defense without encouraging the revival of Japanese militarism and without endangering neighboring Asian countries. Ludmer served in the Pacific Military Intelligence Research Section of the United States Army in 1945 and is the author of publications dealing with Japanese taxation.

602 Martin, Charles. "The Rebirth of a Nation." *Proceedings of the Institute of World Affairs* 26:51–65 (1950)

This article provides a comprehensive outline of the organizational structure of the occupation, its objectives, its operations, and the effects it has produced on Japanese society. The author treats the occupation's organization in 4 major parts: SCAP, General Headquarters, the Eighth Army, and the military government teams. Of particular interest is a detailed description of the various sections of General Headquarters and their areas of responsibility. The author then discusses what he terms the evidences of Japan's rebirth as demonstrated by the creation of a peaceful and nonaggressive Japan, the establishment of a democratic nation through drastic change in government, the encouragement of an economically viable Japan, and the formation of a redirected religious outlook.

603 Matsuoka, Yōko. *Daughter of the Pacific*. New York: Harper, 1952. 245p.

The autobiography of a Japanese woman educated in prewar America. Pages 195–245 cover the period from Japan's surrender to 1949, when the author revisited the United States. She witnessed some of the important events of the occupation and provides a somewhat superficial but interesting Japanese view of them.

603a Mears, Helen. "We're Giving Japan Democracy, but She Can't Earn Her Living." *Saturday Evening Post* 221:12 (18 June 1949); Reply of Douglas MacArthur with Editorial Comment: *Saturday Evening Post* 222:4 (30 July 1949)

Mears argues in this editorial that while the occupation has provided the Japanese with a vast array of new freedoms and democratic principles, it has failed to give them even a prewar standard of living. Inflation nullifies labor's gains; government spending is astronomical (and supported by the American taxpayers) largely because of the high cost of the occupation's reforms; and Japan has no national income to speak of. MacArthur's policies were to promote "the well-being and happiness of the individual," but according to Mears, "up to now our policies have . . . conspicuously failed to do so."

In his reply to her criticisms, MacArthur first of all notes that Mears has not been in Japan since July 1946—and not "recently," as the *Post*'s editors state. He disputes her implication that the costs of maintaining the occupation and financing its various reforms are keeping the Japanese standard of living low. In any case, freedom and democracy are not commodities whose worth may be measured on the basis of cost. MacArthur also disputes Mears' contention that the Communists the "laughing their heads off" at the problems plaguing the occupation; it is more likely, indeed, that they take comfort in articles such as those by Mears.

604 Nehmer, Stanley. "Japan under Occupation." *Current History* 17:273–76 (Nov. 1949)

In line with SCAP's optimistic analysis of the results of the Allied occupation to date, the writer lists all of the accomplishments that have been effected in the social and political realms, particularly concentrating upon the effects of the new constitution. There follows a description of the less satisfactory economic situation and a discussion of the steps taken by the U.S. government for the rehabilitation of the dangerously tottering economy. This section is best documented, providing sound statistics and clear descriptions of U.S. appropriations and the accomplishments of the Dodge and Shoup Missions. In the final section of the article, the author defines the nation's most important problem as "her fast-growing population and her crucial dependence upon foreign trade for food and raw materials," but he is optimistic concerning Japan's chances for achieving a successful and self-sustaining democracy.

605 "New Door to Asia." *Time* 52:32–36 (9 May 1949)

The importance of Japan as the last bastion against communism in East Asia is stressed. The idea of a "bloodless revolution," which is inculcating democracy in Japan, is examined as is the need to change the Japanese from believers in conformity to practitioners of individualism. Economic reform is mentioned in terms of current unemployment and hunger problems, and the Dodge Mission is explained. The article notes domestic Communist activity, MacArthur's reaction to it, and his promises for true freedom in Japan.

606 Park, Richard. "Transition in Japan." *Far Eastern Survey* 18:225–26 (21 Sept. 1949)

The occupation's transitional phase in which "controls and supervision, held by the Supreme Commander for the Allied Powers, are being returned gradually to the Japanese Government for autonomous operation" is succinctly and accurately described. As a former military government officer in Japan, the author is well qualified to comment upon resulting revisions of the administrative organization of the occupation. He describes the changes that will result in the abolition of the 45 prefectural civil affairs teams as of 30 November 1949 and the elimination of the Eighth Army's

Civil Affairs Section as of 31 December 1949. Noting that most qualified senior civil affairs officers judge such a transition well timed or even long overdue, the author regards 1950 as a year of crisis in Japan's political and economic life which will offer Japan an opportunity to confirm or destroy Allied confidence in the nation.

"A Peace Treaty for Japan." 1949. *See* no.2343.

607 *Political Handbook of Japan. 1949.* Tokyo: Tokyo News Service, 1949.

This book contains many useful data on both the political scene and the press in Japan as of 1949. Included are a detailed description of the election of 1947 and the major political parties, some information on the small parties, and material on the occupation's political reforms. Data on the press include descriptions of major newspapers, a list of magazines according to their subject, and information on circulation and popularity of various publications. The book concludes with a section entitled "Who's Who of Leaders in Politics and Press of Japan."

607a "Prime Minister Shigeru Yoshida's Administrative Policy Speech Delivered at the Opening of the Sixth National Diet, November 8, 1949." *Contemporary Japan* 18:567–72 (Oct./Dec. 1949)

Yoshida opens his address with both a wish that the peace treaty be concluded at the earliest possible date and a statement of his pride in Japan's unarmed status. Economic planning, he then says, is being undertaken in accordance with Dodge Plan recommendations and those of the Shoup Mission regarding tax reforms. Government expenses are being cut back; controls on certain commodities are being adjusted or eliminated; and every effort is being made to promote foreign trade. Land reform is proceeding apace. Yoshida finds the new labor movement "wholesome and constructive" as well. Admittedly, industrial rationalization is promoting unemployment, but the government is countering it with public works and relief programs, for otherwise social unrest would lead to the infiltration of radical foreign ideologies. A terroristic, destructive minority is attempting to cause trouble, Yoshida warns, but he is confident that most Japanese people will ignore the "malcontents" and devote themselves to national recovery.

607b Rowe, David Nelson. "Where Can We Stand in Asia?" *Virginia Quarterly Review* 25, no.4:526–43 (Autumn 1949)

The Communist surge to victory in China has forced the United States to decide whether it would be best to withdraw entirely from Asia at this point or to commit American resources to holding the small and weak rim countries of Asia against Communism. This dilemma can most easily be seen in the case of Japan, where recent discussions have centered on the desirability of defending Japan in the event of war. Rowe strongly advocates that Japan not be allowed to fall into Communist hands by default, but he points out that the necessity of defending Japan will require an extension of the occupation period and may alienate some of the Japanese who are growing weary of the occupation. Rowe then seeks to explain how the United States has gotten into its present dilemma. He notes that Japan must be defended by others against external aggression because the Allies have reduced the country to a state of complete military impotence. Furthermore, Japan's economic problems must be resolved if the political and social reforms undertaken by SCAP are to succeed. For this to occur, however, it will be necessary either for the United States to open its markets to Japanese cotton textiles and cheap manufactured goods or for Japan to expand its trade with the Communist states of Asia—a step which would provide them with the material required for consolidating their power. Since the United States cannot permit the latter, it is apparent that continued Communist victories on the mainland will prevent "any reasonably satisfactory solution of the Japanese problem." Rowe concludes the article by noting how America's willingness to let the Russians take over Manchuria in accordance with the Yalta Agreements and the subsequent U.S. decision to withdraw American Marines from north China have contributed to the present disaster, and he urges that the United States do its best to defend Japan, Formosa, and other parts of Asia against the further spread of Communism.

608 Sansom, Sir George B. "Can Japan Be Reformed?" *Far Eastern Survey* 18: 258–59 (2 Nov. 1949)

George B. Sansom, eminent author and historian, reviews W. Macmahon Ball's book, *Japan: Enemy or Ally?* (1949) (no.535) in an attempt to find some explanation of the facts Ball puts forth about the occupation. He states that the occupation has failed only when it has undertaken aims impossible of realization, taking no account of normal human behavior, of predictable economic pressures, and of plain strategic compulsions.

608a "SCAP's Progress." *New Statesman and Nation* 38:604–5 (26 Nov. 1949)

After summarizing the activities of the occupation to date and the shifts in SCAP policy, this article analyzes the current situation in Japan. Most of the occupation's reforms are said to have failed or to have been consciously dropped, and the Yoshida government is alleged to be extremely reactionary. Should the issue of a separate peace with China and the Soviet Union escalate into a violent open debate within Japan, it could bring about the collapse of that government and a negation of much of what SCAP has worked for.

609 Sheean, Vincent. "MacArthur in Tokyo." *Holiday* 6:99–113 (Dec. 1949)

After giving a brief picture of the physical aspects of Tokyo, Sheean comments on the new freedoms available to the Japanese under the occupation—freedom to speak frankly and to partake of their love of pleasure without fear, in addition to others. In spite of economic hardships, he views the Japanese as being in high spirits. The author believes the development and use of Shinto, which he outlines, by those in power were primarily responsible for the psychological attitude which made possible Japan's war against the United States. He sees Shinto as MacArthur's chief problem in Japan, and feels that the central concern should be to completely eradicate it. MacArthur's efforts toward setting up democracy, such as his encouragement of labor unions and free speech, are examined. Finally, a picture of MacArthur himself is drawn, emphasizing his role in the war, his changing public image, his intelligence, and his "unwavering patriotism."

610 Slocum, Winthrop. "The Naval Technical Mission to Japan." *United States Naval Institute Proceedings* 75, no.1:1–11 (Jan. 1949); abstracted in *Journal of the Royal United Service Institution* 94:231–36 (May 1949)

Early in the fall of 1945, the members of the U.S. Naval Technical Mission to Japan ("Nav Tech Jap") were sent to East Asia to gather intelligence on wartime Japanese work in the field of naval technology. For this purpose they surveyed all of the Japanese scientific and technological developments that were of interest to the U.S. Navy and Marine Corps, interrogated numerous Japanese naval and civilian personnel, and sought to appraise the technological status of both the Japanese navy and industry. This article provides an interesting and informative review of the mission's activities and illustrates SCAP's interest not only in demilitarizing Japan but also in gathering as much information as possible about that country's military developments for possible future use by the U.S. Armed Forces. The author first served as liaison officer to G-2, SCAP, and subsequently as deputy chief, then as chief, of the entire mission.

611 "Statement Issued by U.S. Under-Secretary of the Army Tracy Voorhees at the Press Conference Held in Tokyo, September 10, 1949." *Contemporary Japan* 18:404–12 (July/Sept. 1949)

During a brief stay in occupied Japan, the undersecretary of the army called a press conference and outlined his attitudes and those of leading officials of the Department of the Army on the occupation. Voorhees answers questions concerning the possible duration of GARIOA (Government and Relief in Occupied Areas) and EROA (Economic Rehabilitation of Occupied Areas) appropriations to Japan, the possibility of U.S. aid to Japan after the signing of a peace treaty, the Army Department's plans for reduction of its personnel on the occupation staff, the transferral of the occupation civil affairs administration to civilian control, the state of Japan's economic recovery, etc. Throughout the conference, Voorhees expresses his admiration for General MacArthur's leadership and his estimation of the occupation as a resounding success.

Supreme Commander for the Allied Powers. Civil Information and Education Section. *C I and E Bulletin.* 1947–49. See no.266.

———. Commander in Chief. Aide-de-Camp. *Master Files.* 1945–49. See no. 925.

———. Government Section. *A Brief Progress Report on the Political Reorientation of Japan.* 1949. See no.277.

———. ———. *A Brief Progress Report on the Political Reorientation of Japan.* rev. ed. 1949. See no.278.

612 "Time to Leave Japan." *New Republic* 120:5–6 (30 May 1949)

Arguing that there is no longer any clear justification for the occupation since the Japanese now live in a demilitarized state under a democratic constitution, the author of this editorial nevertheless does not believe that the democratization of Japan has been accomplished. Recently, he believes, in response to a wave of reaction in the United States against the liberalism of MacArthur's programs, there has been a swing to the right in Japan. The author is apprehensive regarding the election of Yoshida who espouses reactionary programs and concludes that "continued reform is the one chance for democracy in Japan and a precondition of peace."

613 U.S. Dept. of State. *Messages.* 2 July 1946–30 Dec. 1949. Record Group 9. MacArthur Memorial, Bureau of Archives, Norfolk, Va. 26 folders.

The majority of these unclassified radio messages are from the State Department to SCAP and the Far Eastern Commission. A few are from the supreme commander to the State Department or from the Economic Control Administration to the State Department. The State Department messages are generally excerpts from or summaries of articles that appeared in U.S., Soviet, English, or Chinese newspapers and periodicals on U.S. occupation policy and internal developments in Japan. Other information includes excerpts from the Allied Council for Japan minutes, information on personnel of the International Military Tribunal for the Far East, reparations requests from various Allies, and information on State Department personnel in Japan. Messages from SCAP to the State Department include a statement of MacArthur's views on the draft constitution (26 July 1946), and one on the reestablishment of trade procedures between Japan and other nations. Messages are filed chronologically.

613a U.S. Naval Technical Mission to Japan. *History of Mission: November, 1946.* n.p.: The Mission, 1946. 47p.

614 Vaughn, Miles W. "American Policy and Future Security of Japan." *Contemporary Japan* 18:155–73 (Apr./June 1949)

In a general résumé of the occupation, the author briefly discusses the new status of the emperor, the reparations program, Japan's economic and political liberation, the new labor laws, and some important provisions of the postwar constitution—emphasizing how all of these have been inaugurated for the unselfish goal of rebuilding a healthy and peaceful Japan. By analogy he likens American policy in Japan to American policy all over the world and portrays the Soviet Union as an international troublemaker intent upon world conquest. The author concludes with a consideration of America's role in a postoccupation Japan. In view of Japan's own lack of defense and with no indication that it will be permitted to rearm in the foreseeable future, he envisages "some sort of agreement under which the U.S. will guarantee Japan's territorial integrity" and allows that there may be permanent bases there.

615 Walliser, Blair A. "Sunset in the East." *National Geographic Magazine* 89:797–812 (June 1946).

The author stresses the sincerity of Japanese efforts to cooperate with occupation officials and SCAP directives. He attempts to capture the mood of uncertainty that underlies all Japanese efforts to adhere to the spirit of the imposed reforms—for instance the inability of most Japanese to pay more than lip service to democracy because of a fundamental lack of understanding of the theory and institutions of American democracy. The author sees a need to mix Western and traditional Japanese elements in every aspect of the reform program in order to create stable and lasting changes.

616 Waln, Nora. "The Grass Roots Revolution in Japan." *Atlantic Monthly* 184: 56–60 (Dec. 1949)

An informal and impressionistic account of life in a Japanese village during the occupation. While mainly describing traditional Japanese rituals such as the bath or family laws, the author does comment briefly upon the effects of the SCAP-sponsored land reform program.

617 Yanaga, Chitoshi. *Japan since Perry*. New York: McGraw-Hill, 1949. x, 723p.

In his final chapter, Yanaga deals with the occupation and reconstruction of Japan. In describing occupational objectives and directives, he discusses government and politics in Japan, the new constitution, and educational reforms.

1950

Ball, William M. *Notes on Nationalism and Communism in the Far East*. 1950. *See* no.773.

618 Bisson, Thomas Arthur. "Asia in Change." *Pacific Spectator* 4:68–80 (Winter 1950)

Pages 75 through 77 of this general essay on East Asia concern Japan. Three books are used as a focal point for the discussion—Russell Brines' *MacArthur's Japan* (1948) (no.541), Mark Gayn's *Japan Diary* (1948) (no.427), and W. Macmahon Ball's *Japan, Enemy or Ally?* (1949) (no.535). The author considers the occupation of Japan and discusses the different outlooks and conclusions of the 3 writers with respect to such issues as the rooting out of former militarists from the government, the land reform program, and the SCAP program for economic recovery.

618a Blunden, Edmund. "A Lecturer in Japan." *United Empire* 41:296–99 (Sept./Oct. 1950)

Blunden, a British cultural attaché in Tokyo from 1948 to 1950, delivered this luncheon address before the Royal Empire Society on 22 June 1950. He begins with a discussion of the history of British teaching in Japan and current American education reform programs. He then relates his experiences in giving public lectures in English literature in Tokyo: the Japanese reaction was highly favorable, and sometimes as many as 2,000 people attended. Communism, he judges, is not the threat in Japan that many make it out to be, for it is little more than non-destructive play-acting. The most important thing for the occupation and for foreigners in general to realize is that the Japanese are an intelligent, capable, and disciplined people.

619 Borton, Hugh, ed. *Japan*. Ithaca, N.Y.: Cornell Univ. Pr., 1951. viii, 320p.

Twenty scholars of Japan contributed the 23 chapters in this introductory survey of Japan from the earliest periods through the middle of 1950. Subjects discussed range from Japanese topography to architecture and from financial development to scientific research in Japan. The last chapter, 23 (p.298-311), written by Jane M. Alden, focuses upon Japan's experience with the Allied occupation and includes brief descriptions of the machinery for the formulation of Allied policy, objectives of the occupation, the organization of SCAP headquarters, SCAP's relations with the Japanese government, and the accomplishments of the occupation. Alden evaluates the occupation favorably, stating that by 1950 its mission was completed and that its termination was delayed only as a result of the inability of the Allied powers to agree upon a peace treaty for Japan.

This collection of articles first appeared in the 1951 edition of the *Encyclopedia Americana*.

619a Buck, Philip Wallenstein, and John Wesley Masland, Jr. *The Governments of Foreign Powers*. rev. ed. New York: Holt, 1950. xi, 948p.

Chapters 26-29 (p.591-620) of this textbook deal with Japan. The first 2 chapters summarize the development of the Japanese government from the Meiji Restoration through the end of World War II. Chapter 28, in turn, provides a detailed, comprehensive, and well-organized account of the American administration of Japan. This particular chapter concludes with 2 observations: (1) that there was a shift in occupation policy from an emphasis on democratization to efforts that would promote economic recovery, and (2) that it should be kept in mind that the occupation's reforms were alien-authored measures derived from alien notions of man's relationships to the state. Chapter 29 attempts to assess the results of SCAP's reforms and speculates on their chances for survival once the occupation ends. The results so far have been uneven, the authors conclude. Japan's future will depend on how quickly her economic recovery proceeds and how well the people understand their responsibilities and their rights in a democratic society.

619b "Can We Keep Japan's Friendship?" *Christian Century* 67:692 (7 June 1950)

This editorial calls for a revision of the optimistic judgments normally heard about the success of the occupation in the light of a growing awareness that not everything is going well. In particular the magazine calls attention to the strong opposition in Japan to the continued maintenance of American bases there after the peace treaty is signed.

620 "Declaration of the Soviet Representative in the Allied Council for Japan." *Soviet Press Translations* 6:45-48 (1 Feb. 1951)

This statement by the Soviet member of the Allied Council for Japan, A. Kislenko, made in regular session, 20 December 1950, concerns the repressive measures taken by American occupation authorities and the Japanese government against trade unions, the Communist party, and other democratic organizations. Kislenko makes 5 protests and cites Far Eastern Commission resolutions (usually the Basic Post-Surrender Policy for Japan) which have been violated. His protests are against: (1) the forcible disbanding of the Zenrōren trade union council; (2) the banning of 1,200 progressive publications, including the Communist party newspaper *Akahata*; (3) the dismissal of workers and employees, teachers, and students for their political views; (4) police terrorism and coercion (the author lists 6 specific examples); and (5) the restoration of political rights to 10,000 wartime fascist leaders.

This article originally appeared in the 21 December 1950 issue of *Pravda*.

621 Fearey, Robert T. *The Occupation of Japan, Second Phase: 1948-1950*. New York: Macmillan, 1950. xii, 239p.

This study of the Allied occupation covers the period up to mid-1950 before the outbreak of the Korean War and supplements another earlier work sponsored by the Institute of Pacific Relations, Edwin M. Martin's *The Allied Occupation of Japan* (1948) (no.561), which deals with the period up to the end of 1947. While Martin's work emphasizes a description of the occupation's aims, Fearey devotes a large proportion of this volume to an analysis of occupation programs in terms of their impact on the Japanese people and to an appraisal of their accomplishments, weaknesses, and prospects. He had been private secretary to Ambassador Joseph C. Grew in Tokyo and had subsequently worked in the Office of Northeast Asian Affairs of the Department of State. In October 1945 he was transferred from Washington to the staff of George Atcheson, Jr., State Department representative in SCAP. The author was also a member of the Dulles peace mission to Japan. Fearey begins with changes in the mechanisms for the formulation and execution of Allied occupation policy and then discusses SCAP activities in the areas of demobilization, the Tokyo trials, reparations, and democratization programs such as educational reform, governmental reorganization, labor reform, and agrarian reform. There follow assessments of the political and economic scenes and of Japanese economic prospects. While noting that progress has been slow, the author is hopeful of a definite improvement in the future. There is a chapter on a peace treaty with Japan, with the central problem foreseen by the author as Japan's security. Finally, he observes developments in Japan in the first half of 1950 and reports the growth of "a discernible restiveness which accentuated the urgency of a peace settlement at the earliest practicable time." The book has been translated into Japanese under the title of *Nihon senryō: sono seika to tenbō* (Tokyo: Kōbundō, 1952. 238p.).

622 "Five Years after the Surrender of Imperialist Japan." *New Times* no.35: 1–2 (30 Aug. 1950)

SCAP is accused of "disrupting the democratization of Japan . . . patronizing war criminals and suppressing the rights of the people" 5 years after the beginning of the occupation of Japan. American refusal to work with the Allied Council for Japan and the Far Eastern Commission is considered only one manifestation of SCAP's dictatorial manner. The final paragraphs discuss what the author terms American intervention in Korea, which he views as another imperialist effort to subjugate Asia.

622a Gaddis, John Wilson. *Public Information in Japan under American Occupation: A Study of Democratization Efforts through Agencies of Public Expression.* Genève: Impr. Populaire, 1950. vi, 199p.

First submitted as a doctoral dissertation to the Institut Universitaire des Hautes Etudes de l'Université de Genève, this study is concerned with the philosophy, methods, and international implications of the American effort to purge the Japanese of their autocratic ideology and to indoctrinate them in peace and democracy.

623 Green, Owen Mortimer. "Japan and Korea." *Fortnightly* 174:84–89 (Aug. 1950)

The beginning of hostilities in Korea is considered in the light of its effect upon the signing of an Allied peace treaty with Japan. The author discusses the historical relationships between Japan and Korea as well as the Japanese reaction to a possible large scale war in Korea and presents reasons why he believes the hostilities may serve to postpone a peace treaty with Japan. He then gives a general summation of the occupation, dividing it into 3 significant periods for consideration. The first period extends to 1946, at which time the stunning psychological impact of defeat had generally worn off. The second period lasts from 1946 to 1948 when reparations were stopped, production began to rise, and recovery seemed possible. The third period, beginning in 1949, has been marked by a substantial reform of the tax structure and a curbing of Japan's inflationary spiral. Finally, as an illustration of the success of the occupation, the author points to the poor showing of the Communists in the recent Upper House elections.

624 Greene, Marc T. "Japan Today and Tomorrow." *Eastern World* 4:19–20 (July 1950)

A correspondent's admiring account of the extraordinary progress of Japan after 5 years of the "MacArthur Policy." It is based on an interview with the supreme commander as well as on personal observations. Stress is laid on MacArthur's hopes for land reform, education reform, and the role of a free press. The writer expresses his fear that the growing prosperity may be blighted by population pressure and Communist influence.

625 Guillain, Robert. "Japanese Uncertainties." *International Affairs* 26:329–38 (July 1950)

The author, a Frenchman who was detained in Japan throughout the war, presents an analysis of that country after subsequent visits during the Allied occupation. There is an objective and intelligent discussion of the aims of the occupation, as well as a consideration of its actual accomplishments and the reasons for important changes in SCAP policy. The author maintains that the imposition of order upon postwar Japanese society was as important an Allied contribution to Japan as was the reintroduction of democratic principles. Although hopeful about the success of democracy in the country, he nevertheless identifies 3 chief evils that are vitiating the progress of Japanese democracy: (1) corruption in the government, (2) the persistence of old Japanese political ways, and (3) the return of the Old Guard bureaucrats and *zaibatsu* leaders. In accord with his belief that "the future of Japanese democracy will largely depend on economic recovery," the author outlines in detail some of the problems of the Japanese economy and some possible solutions to those problems. Lastly, he discusses Japan's future role in international politics, suggesting that the majority of Japanese favor a policy of neutrality—remaining aloof from any political alliances with the Big Powers. In the author's opinion "an independent Japan, belonging neither to the 'Western' nor the 'Eastern' camp, might set a very important precedent in Asia."

626 Holland, Charles D. "Japan's Rising Millions Spell Danger." *Great Britain and the East* 66:37 (Apr. 1950)

Although Japan has made considerable economic progress under the occupation, the steady increase of her population poses a major problem for the country and "export or perish" may well become her postwar motto. Holland then turns to a discussion of the political situation and concludes that the occupation has not yet made much headway in democratizing Japan. There is considerable anxiety over what will happen after the occupation ends in particular because of the growing strength of the Japan Communist Party, and the conclusion of a peace treaty together with the withdrawal of American military forces will inevitably be followed by a struggle between those on the right and the left ends of the political spectrum.

627 "Japan: One Step Forward, Two Steps Backward?" *Eastern World* 4, no. 12:6–8 (Dec. 1950)

The occupation can take pride in the land reform and an impressive array of liberal legislation and newly-guaranteed civil rights. The current political atmosphere, however, gives cause for considerable pessimism. The emperor is still held in awe, and the industrialists and bureaucrats remain very powerful. The Korean War has led both to rearmament and a "Red scare." It is clear, furthermore, that Japan is to become an American satellite. Military necessity, the article concludes, has undone most of the reforms; it is unfortunate that the other Allies have been unwilling or unable to resist this tendency.

628 *The Japan Who's Who.* 1950–51 ed. Tokyo: Tokyo News Service, 1950. iv, 576p.

This revised edition of a 1948 publication (see no.557a) provides an alphabetical listing of approximately 3200 well-known Japanese who were active towards the end of the occupation period. Standard biographical information is given for each individual. While members of the Allied occupation forces are excluded from the volume, a number of important Western businessmen and journalists working in Japan do appear within it.

"Japan's Christian University." 1950. See no.2070.

629 Kagawa, Toyohiko. "The Social and Economic Outlook in Japan Today." *Journal of the Royal Central Asian Society* 37, pt.2:124–31 (Apr. 1950)

The text of a talk given by Kagawa at the 1 March 1950 meeting of the Royal Central Asian Society, this is a brief discussion of important developments during the occupation period with some focus on the economic situation, the effect of the new constitution on Japanese life, the state of Christianity in Japan, and the nature of Communist influence within the country. Kagawa also includes comments on his own involvement in the campaigns to increase the number of adherents to Christianity and in the organization of consumers' cooperative associations.

Kawai, Kazuo. "Japan: A Focal Point in the Cold War." 1950. See no. 798.

630 King, John K. "Japan: Occupation and Problems of Peace." *Proceedings of the Institute of World Affairs* 26:43–47 (1950)

A brief summation of a round table discussion on postwar Japan headed by John M. Maki. The discussion was intended not to anticipate answers but rather to isolate and view problems associated with the occupation of the country. It sets forth the comments of the various members of the group concerning such issues as Japan's future role in the Far East, its procurement of raw materials necessary for economic survival, the effectiveness of the political and social reforms of the occupation, future U.S.–Japanese relations, and the possibility of the eventual admission of Japan into the United Nations.

630a Maack, Dorothy Howerton. "American Family Life in Japan." *Journal of Home Economics* 42:792–93 (Dec. 1950)

This article describes the special problems of those Americans who lived in Japan not as occupation personnel but rather as "commercial entrants." Such families often found themselves in ambiguous situations: for instance, they were under the jurisdiction of both Japanese and SCAP military law. The high cost of living, the difficulties of adapting Japanese housing to American needs, problems with Japanese servants, shopping for food, and recreational activities are other topics briefly discussed by the author.

631 Mears, Helen. "The Russians Are Making the Most of Our 'Imperialist Rule' in Japan." *Saturday Evening Post* 222, no.44:12 (29 Apr. 1950)

Mears contends within this editorial that the occupation has thus far advanced Soviet interests more than American ones. Despite occupation reform efforts, "the Japanese are worse off than in a period of prewar depression" and Japanese poverty contrasts sharply with the affluent lifestyle of Americans living in Japan. Accordingly, there are many occasions for the Communists to charge that the Americans are imperialists. It is for this reason, Mears concludes, that U.S.–Soviet relations in Japan have been generally peaceful except in regard to their differences over Emperor Hirohito.

631a "Occupation." *Commonweal* 52:260 (23 June 1950)

This editorial attributes the continuation of the occupation to the cold war and feels that the prolonged and increasingly abrasive presence of American troops has undermined the logic and philosophy of the occupation itself.

The Occupation

Osborne, John. "'My Dear General'." 1950. *See* no.970.

631b "Peace Festival Proscribed." *Christian Century* 67:988 (23 Aug. 1950). Reply by Robert H. Grant: *Christian Century* 67:1172 (4 Oct. 1950)

The editors of *Christian Century* question the wisdom of the decision—presumably SCAP's—to cancel the annual 6 August peace festival in Hiroshima. SCAP feared "that Communists and North Koreans resident in Japan might take the opportunity to carry out undesirable activity," but the editors maintain that to proscribe a peace festival, especially in Hiroshima, is to suggest to the Japanese that SCAP's desire for Japan's becoming a nation of peace-lovers is less ardent than it might otherwise seem.

In his reply, Grant, an American missionary residing in Kyoto, attributes the cancellation of the Hiroshima peace festival to Japanese police officials rather than to SCAP. He feels in any case that the Japanese are not yet fully capable of counteracting or seeing through Communist propaganda in an atmosphere of skepticism where "because no one knows what to believe, no one believes anything."

632 "Planning a Japan without MacArthur," *U.S. News and World Report* 28:22–23 (16 June 1950)

In anticipation of the retirement of General MacArthur from the Japanese scene, this article speculates on the probable consequences for future occupation policy. A separate peace treaty between the United States and Japan is thought to be the most probable outcome, although the turning over of power to the Japanese government without a treaty and with American troops remaining in Japan is also considered possible. Future Japanese–American friendship is deemed so important as to require that Japanese interests be given considerable attention.

633 Pratt, Julius William. "The Government of Japan." In *Foreign Governments and Their Backgrounds*, by John Clarke Adams, et al. New York: Harper, 1950. p.771–867.

Pratt reviews in detail the democratic reconstruction of occupied Japan as well as the postwar political parties. He notes that although there have been many hopeful developments, Japan's theoretically democratic government still functions under a dictatorship as absolute as that of any shogun.

634 Quigley, Harold S. "American Policy and Japanese Politics." *Political Quarterly* 21, no.1:29–39 (Jan./Mar. 1950)

Quigley felt, in 1950, that "the occupation's basic objective—the advancement of democratic ideals and institutions—is not being realized." MacArthur's rule is viewed as not unlike the feudal shogunate in its military and undemocratic nature. Also, the reformist goals of the occupation are virtually a utopian dream. Finally, the occupation has been caught between its radical legislative program and the conservative Japanese administration it works through.

The Reminiscences of Esther Crane. 1961. *See* no.44i.

634a Sayre, John Nevin. "Miracle of Reconciliation." *Reconciliation* 27, no.1:741–43, 755 (Jan. 1950)

The author undertook a 5-week long visit to Japan during which he had the opportunity to talk with the emperor and empress, Prime Minister Yoshida, General MacArthur, various Buddhist and Christian leaders, a number of students, and other people in all walks of life. His conversations, Sayre writes, have convinced him that the Japanese are very much in favor of peace and support the renunciation of war clause in the postwar constitution.

634b Sheerin, John B. "Dulles on Japan." *Catholic World* 171:324–25 (Aug. 1950)

This piece is a subsection of a longer editorial entitled "Truman Saves Korea" (p.321–25). Sheerin notes that the target of the Communist thrust in Korea is Japan. The question now is where Japan will stand if she is forced to choose between Russian communism and American democracy. Sheerin is worried, for Japan is not only extremely poor and faced with continuing food shortages, but also is ruled at present by a group of extremely conservative Japanese politicians. The common people are beset with "a great moral perplexity" and are unhappy about the present status of the emperor, who (in the author's opinion) should "be granted some degree of authority" since he is evidently sincere and loyal to MacArthur.

635 Sissons, David C. S. "SCAP's Statements on the Occupation of Japan." *Australian Outlook* 4:29–40 (Mar. 1950)

Sissons challenges MacArthur's published statements to the effect that the Japanese have had a change of heart and that democracy and pacification have taken root in Japan under SCAP's guidance. He adduces as evidence the reluctance of the government to part with the Meiji Constitution, various administrative efforts to undermine occupation reforms, and indications that the court system strays from Anglo–American ideals of jurisprudence. The basic soundness of democracy itself, MacArthur says, guarantees its durability. Sissons, however, argues that adequate living standards and economic stability are prerequisites for democracy's survival and that it is not yet clear that the occupation has succeeded in guaranteeing either.

636 Supreme Commander for the Allied Powers. Government Section. *Proceedings of the Diet and Related Matters.* 1948–50. Record Group 5, Box 79. MacArthur Memorial, Bureau of Archives, Norfolk, Va. 1 folder.

This miscellaneous collection of mimeographed reports and correspondence charts some of the activities of the Diet in the later years of the occupation. Arranged in no discernible order, materials include drafts of Prime Minister Yoshida's addresses to the Diet and radio addresses, letters from Yoshida to General MacArthur, and Diet communications with particular divisions of SCAP.

A large portion of the materials in the collection are reprints of Diet proceedings and summaries of legislation. There is also a special report on the emperor's tour of Kyushu in May and June 1949. Topics covered run the gamut of occupation activities, but those receiving special emphasis include provisions of the National Public Service Law, the 9-point stabilization program, the issue of Diet dissolutions, labor-related activities and legislation, fiscal measures, programs of taxation, the peace treaty, the future national security of Japan, and Japanese participation in international conferences. The entire collection may also be found at the Records Center of the National Archives in Suitland, Maryland.

——, and Far East Command. *Selected Data on the Occupation of Japan.* 1950. See no.282.

Taylor, Philip H. "The Administration of Occupied Japan." 1950. See no.927.

637 Tormey, Gertrude. "Nine Days in Japan in April 1950." *Education* 71:38–44 (Sept. 1950)

In this exerpt from the diary of an American teacher in Japan, an impressionistic mosaic of Japanese life in the latter days of the occupation is presented. Experiences such as a trip to Hiroshima, meetings with Japanese school officials and students, visits in Japanese homes, and participation in holiday activities are related. The excerpt gives an indication of the dimensions of the responsibilities of a teacher serving with the occupation and provides some estimate of the probability of occupation social reforms successfully taking root.

638 Tracy, Honor Lilbush Wingfield. *Kakemono: A Sketch Book of Post-war Japan.* New York: Coward–McCann, 1950. vii, 205p.

A well-known British author who visited various parts of Japan during the Occupation—including Tokyo, Kyoto, Kure, Hiroshima, and Yokohama—describes her travels in a humorous vein.

She sees both favorable and unfavorable dimensions of occupied Japan, not only in culture and customs but also in the Japanese style of politics and the occupation's reforms. Her accounts are candid on-the-spot reports, and she comments, for example, on SCAP's struggle to cope with graft and black marketing among Japanese leaders, relations between MPs and GIs, Japanese attitudes toward "de-mok-ra-shi" (democracy as pronounced by the Japanese), the atmosphere in the press club, and visits to military government team headquarters. The book has been translated into Japanese under the title of *Kakemono: senryō Nihon no omote ura* (Tokyo: Bungei Shunjū Shinsha, 1952. 292p.).

639 U.S. Dept. of the Army. Civil Affairs Div. *Weekly Report on Japan to the Far Eastern Commission.* Washington? 1948–50. nos.107–263. weekly.

640 Vosburgh, Frederick G. "Japan Tries Freedom's Road." *National Geographic Magazine* 97:593–632 (May 1950)

The author attempts a survey of 4 years of the occupation noting changes and emphasizing the benevolence of MacArthur's rule. Some of the examples cited are the humanizing of the emperor, the land reform program, and SCAP's distribution of food and medical treatment. He discusses the Communist threat to Japan and pays attention to the difficulties in repatriating prisoners from Soviet-controlled parts of Asia.

641 Wheeler, Romney. "We Are Kidding Ourselves in Japan." *American Mercury* 71:712–19 (Dec. 1950)

A newspaperman who served for a year and a half on MacArthur's civilian staff presents a pessimistic appraisal of the effects of the occupation. Although conceding that the democratization effort has been "vigorous and well meaning enough," the author charges that many reforms have been ineffective and that one of the distinguishing features of the occupation program "has been a really magnificent ability to work at cross purposes." He includes numerous examples of such confusion, drawn largely from SCAP reforms in labor, education, and public health, as well as the creation of the new American-made constitution. He concludes that we have managed to create a maximum of confusion in Japan with a minimum of good and suggests that our well-meaning efforts will not have been entirely in vain if we place more responsibility in Japanese hands and if "we will now think more in terms of what Japan *needs* and less in terms of what we *want*."

1951

642 Allison, John M. "The Next Phase in Japan." *Far Eastern Survey* 20:199 (7 Nov. 1951)

In an address to the Far East–America Council of Commerce and Industry, 19 October 1951, Allison, deputy to John Foster Dulles, details the factors responsible for proposed revisions of certain occupation measures.

643 Brown, Margery Finn. *Over a Bamboo Fence: An American Looks at Japan.* New York: Morrow, 1951. 239p.

The purpose of this army wife's narrative is to provide an account of her personal experiences in a country whose history and customs were unknown to her at the time of her arrival in the autumn of 1946. Her descriptions reveal that prior to her departure from Japan in May 1948, Mrs. Brown had encountered and had sought to comprehend many of the concepts and orientations inherent in Japanese life and tradition, including the concepts of *on*, *giri*, and *shibui*. Her emphasis throughout is on the experiences and emotions of individual Japanese who struggled to resurrect their lives in accord with and occasionally despite SCAP directives. This book was translated into Japanese under the title *Kakinegoshi* (Tokyo: Nihon Shuppan Kyōdō Kabushiki Kaisha, 1952. 229p.).

644 Cohen, Jerome Bernard. "Lessons in Guidance." *Saturday Review of Literature* 34:48, 55–56 (14 Aug. 1951)

Ostensibly a review of Robert Textor's book, *Failure in Japan* (1951) (no.670), this brief article provides a thoughtful analysis of that work and in addition presents some of the reviewer's own perceptions of the occupation. Characterizing Textor's analysis as "one-sided and severe" as contrasted with the "very laudatory self-evaluations of high Occupation officials," Cohen suggests that a few years' distance will provide a better perspective and that the credits will probably outweigh the debits. Although conceding some of Textor's arguments against the limitation of freedom and the curtailment of labor union activity, he points to the numerous social, economic, and political benefits that have been conferred on Japan during the occupation. Finally, Cohen argues against Textor's desire to civilianize and prolong the occupation and believes that the time has come to leave the governing of Japan to the Japanese.

645 Cousins, Norman. "A Tough One for History." *Saturday Review of Literature* 34:22–23 (3 Mar. 1951)

In an editorial describing his recent visit to Japan, the author expresses amazement at the speed and extent of Japan's economic recovery which he believes took place largely during the previous year. In an informal account he describes his general impressions of the people, the streets of Tokyo, the atmosphere of Hiroshima, all of which he believes reflect a spirit of "recovery and well-being." He comments that he has observed little or no interest in the Korean War among the Japanese populace but rather a determination to remain aloof from that crisis.

646 Eichler, David K. "The Future of the New Japan." *Yale Review* 41:161–80 (Winter 1952)

Eichler describes the geographical, sociological, and economic difficulties Japan must face now that the occupation is ending. In noting the legal and political reasons for American insistence on a peace treaty, he examines General MacArthur's view that the Japanese have undergone a political and spiritual reformation. The author served with the Far Eastern Commission for 4 years.

Eidus, Kh. "The American Policy for a Militarized Fascist Japan." 1951. *See* no.2471c.

Fishel, Wesley R. "Japan under MacArthur: Retrospect and Prospect." 1951. *See* no.9.

647 Gibney, Frank. "The Birth of a New Japan." *Life* 31:134–53 (10 Sept. 1951)

The author reviews the postwar progress of Japan, praising the pragmatism and adaptability of the Japanese. The retention of traditional patterns of personal obligation is noted, and the extent of economic and social changes since the Meiji Restoration explained. Gibney discusses the rapidity with which the institutions of democracy were adopted and the tendency of SCAP to reform by edict. The disparity between legal and spiritual acceptance of democracy is stressed and examples of disorders caused by sudden freedom are given. Gibney also analyzes the change in American policy from advocacy of permanent disarmament and neutrality in 1945 to advocacy of rearmament in 1950. Japan's future role is seen as democracy's answer to Asian communism.

648 Hsu, Immanuel C. Y. "Japan: A Progress Report." *Current History* 21:137–42 (Sept. 1951)

In a thoughtful article, a former member of the Far Eastern Commission considers the occupation of Japan, concentrating upon the hierarchy of responsibility and actual use of power therein. He then discusses the international position of Japan during the past 6 years and its future position in view of the forthcoming peace treaty. In considering the first topic, the author states that "the work of General MacArthur, as the military occupant, has been unique in that it deviates drastically from the established rules of international law on military occupation." Although not denying the benefits the supreme commander has brought to Japan, nevertheless, the author declares that he has completely reversed the line of authority which should run down "from the Allied Powers to the Far Eastern Commission, through the U.S. Government to the Supreme Commander." In considering the second topic, there is a discussion of the diplomatic and political background of the treaty negotiations with particular emphasis upon the problem of Japan's future security and the contradiction inherent in the constitutional renunciation of war and the maintenance of a self-defense force. The author concludes that "in the interest of power politics and in the name of humanitarian magnanimity, the West is reviving Japan, much to the fear and suspicion of other Asian nations."

649 Hudson, Geoffrey. "Japan and Asia." *Twentieth Century* 150:127–33 (Aug. 1951)

The first part of this article attempts to explain the changes which took place in the American attitude toward Japan during the course of the occupation, a change resulting chiefly from the Communist takeover in China and increased Soviet strength in the Far East. In the latter part of his report, the author points not only to recent occupation reforms but also to various elements in Japan's past history which in his opinion qualify the nation for its present lead over all other Asian nations in both industry and government organization. In predicting the country's future, he suggests that there will be a swing to the right in the sphere of internal politics but believes that the country will remain firmly in the democratic tradition barring an acute economic or political crisis.

649a "Japan under Ridgway." *Economist* 160:1218–19 (26 May 1951)

The adoption of a new constitution, the implementation of a widespread land reform, and the passage of legislation enabling industrial workers to organize trade unions were the three most important measures undertaken by the occupation in order to promote democracy in Japan. The survival of democracy will depend most upon the lasting impact of the second and third of these changes, but in themselves they do not insure democracy's continued success. A serious decline in the Japanese economy could greatly offset their effect, and as Japan is the key to eastern and southern Asia in the struggle against Communism, it is important that Japan be able to increase its trade with other countries in order to maintain and develop a healthy economy.

650 "Japan without MacArthur." *U.S. News and World Report* 30:23 (20 Apr. 1951)

Half of this brief article is a summary of the results of the occupation thus far in such areas as land reform, a revived economy, government under a democratic constitution, and friendly Japanese–American relations. The second half is a comparison of the governing styles of General MacArthur and his successor, General Ridgway. The author predicts that the military occupation is coming to a close and a peace treaty is about to be negotiated.

651 "Japan's Uncertain Future." *U.S. News and World Report* 31:15–19 (7 Sept. 1951)

An interview with Joseph Fromm, regional editor of *U.S. News and World Report*, concerning his impressions of the results of the occupation. His major contentions are: that the United States will keep up to 4 divisions of troops in Japan after the peace treaty; that the Japanese plan to resume trade with China in iron ore and soybeans; that there is bound to be some political instability and Japanization of occupation reforms after the treaty is signed; that the imperial institution will be retained as a symbol of stability; that a revival of militarism based on the national police force is possible; that the *zaibatsu* system will continue to be strengthened; that the current living standards and economic output of Japan are rapidly improving and are no longer problem areas; that the Communist party has lost strength in Japan and is of little immediate threat; and finally, that the liberation of women is a significant reform and of a permanent nature.

652 Jones, E. Stanley. "Report from Japan." *Christian Century* 68:710-11 (13 June 1951)

A comment is offered here on the trenmendous progress of the Japanese since the war. The desire in Japan to have security and protection without rearmament, preferably under UN tutelage, is also noted. Jones considers moral and spiritual regeneration to be the primary need of the Japanese people and mentions his own experiences converting many to Christianity.

653 Kawai, Kazuo. "American Influence on Japanese Thinking." *Annals of the American Academy of Political and Social Science* 278:23-31 (Nov. 1951)

The permanent influence of American democratic ideals on Japanese society is analyzed in the context of the cold war battle for the loyalty of Asia. Aspects favorable to the acceptance of American influence are cited: the ability of the occupation to win the trust and confidence of the Japanese—a factor which has accentuated indigenous democratic tendencies, and has created new vested interest groups; the success of economic rehabilitation; the traditional fear of Russia; and the desire for world respect, which will promote the permanence of American influence. The author also examines tendencies which will oppose this influence: democratic reform is stifled by the emphasis on economic revival; strong conservative resistance to communism leads to an opposite reaction; fear for national security leads to the popularity of neutrality; traditions of close contact with China and of totalitarianism are still strong; and continued economic, social, and intellectual problems could lead either to a resurgence of nationalism or to the adoption of Communist ideology.

Latourette, Kenneth S. *The American Record in the Far East, 1945–1951.* 1952. *See* no.804.

654 Lukyanov, M. "Japan: The Revived Hotbed of Aggression in the Far East." *Soviet Press Translations* 6:507-20 (1 Oct. 1951)

This article on the American–Japanese alliance analyzes in depth the results of occupation policy. Agrarian reforms are regarded as antidemocratic for they allegedly result in the replacement of landlords by the bourgeois-kulak element which is detrimental to the peasants. The strengthening of the *zaibatsu* is examined with emphasis on the failure of *zaibatsu* liquidation and of industrial decentralization and on the pervasiveness of the financial and market control exerted by American monopolies. Lukyanov presents data to support his contentions that Japanese industry has surpassed prewar levels of production of military supplies and that Japan serves as an arsenal for the United States. He also presents evidence of buildups in army and navy units by the Japanese and of their close cooperation with American air force contingents. The final section of the article is devoted to the existence of "democratic" forces in Japan. Topics such as wage rates, discrimination against women, the suppression of the Japan Communist party, current levels of strikes and protests, and activities in regard to the peace movement are noted. In conclusion, the friendship and goodwill of the Soviet Union are emphasized as are repeated Soviet efforts to bring about a general peace treaty.

This article appeared originally in *Voprosy Ekonomiki*, no.7, 1951.

MacArthur, Douglas. *Official Correspondence of General MacArthur. 1945–51. See* no.945.

655 "MacArthur's Legacy in Japan." *New Statesman and Nation* 41:439-40 (21 Apr. 1951)

This review of the occupation at the time of MacArthur's removal criticizes MacArthur and Dulles for purposefully preserving Japan's war potential as an American asset. The existence of a 75,000-man National Police Reserve under recently depurged leadership, the

Morris, J. Malcolm. *The Wise Bamboo.* 1953. See no.909.

656 Mukai, Hiroo. "Letter from Tokyo." *Pacific Spectator* 5, no.4:420–25 (Autumn 1951)

A letter surveying the literary scene in modern Japan, primarily before World War II. There are a few comments about postwar Japanese literature, however, including the mention of some writers currently popular (e.g., Dan Kazuo and Koyama Itoko) and praise for a tendency to lessen the distinction between "pure" and "popular" literature.

656a Nagato, Masaji. "Democratic Progress Reviewed." *Contemporary Japan* 20: 444–51 (Oct./Dec. 1951)

Nagato, the recently depurged former editor-in-chief of the *Mainichi Shimbun*, presents his assessment of the progress of democratization in Japan. By now, he writes, unregenerate militarists comprise only about 1 percent of the entire population, and the new Japanese democracy is more revolutionary than that of almost any other country. To prove this assertion, he offers a number of examples of sweeping reforms in the areas of labor, education, and the family system, and draws attention to the abolition of the aristocracy and the "humanizing" of the imperial family. Much more needs to be done, Nagato concedes, but overly critical foreigners should take into account Japan's sincerity and diligence and not forget that democracy took a long time to develop in the West.

657 Ozaki, Yukio. "Reminiscenses." *Contemporary Japan* 20:156–68 (Apr./June 1951)

The first section of this piece is entitled "On Rearmament" and discusses the author's views of the United Nations and his feeling that "Japanese rearmament must be organized in such a fashion as to enable the country to contribute to world peace and coordinate with the United Nations." The next section is called "On Peace and Religion." Here the writer identifies himself as a pacifist with no religion and maintains that "the mightiest enemy of world peace is no other than narrow-minded patriotism." The third section, "On Japanese Language," suggests that "one of the major causes for defeat could be discovered in the defective nature of [the] language." It studies the defects of the Japanese language in historical perspective and shows the discrepancy between ideology and organic function upon which the Japanese are attempting to run democracy. "Guided by their self-centered conception, the Japanese are apt to disregard the basic principles of democracy." The author discusses problems resulting because a new system was brought to Japan before ideological changes were made, and he calls for basic improvement of the language as a first step toward reorientation.

658 Parrott, Lindesay. "Japan at Her New Time of Decision." *New York Times Magazine* p.9, 56–57 (15 Apr. 1951)

Although Japan has made notable strides toward democracy, it still faces a number of problems after the peace treaty. The author notes that democracy is not homegrown, but imposed on Japan. Reports of its successful adoption are somewhat exaggerated by occupation spokesmen. The author finds the basic sentiment of the Japanese people to be "Japanism" or patriotism. He concludes that perhaps Japan's greatest problem is the weakness of her leadership: there are no outstanding figures comparable to those who led the Meiji Restoration.

659 ———. "Problems and Prospects of the New Japan." *New York Times Magazine* p.14–15, 61 (25 Nov. 1951)

In this article the author presents a concise factual summary of the most important aspects of modern Japan: the land, the people, the political system, and the economy. In his conclusion, he states that Japan's future depends on the improvement of the economic situation. Japan must trade to be strong and her success at trading depends on the willingness of Western nations to trade.

Princeton, N.J. Princeton University Library. John Foster Dulles papers. *See* no.48a.

660 Quigley, Harold S. "Evaluating the Japanese Occupation." *Far Eastern Survey* 20:176–78 (10 Oct. 1951)

Quigley reviews 2 studies on the occupation, *The Occupation of Japan*, by Robert A. Fearey (1950) (no.621) and *Failure in Japan*, by Robert B. Textor published in 1951 (no.670). In disagreement with the point of view running through both books, he points out that neither we nor other peoples may elect to impose ourselves as mentors upon the highly cultured Oriental peoples; only as invited advisers, freely sought and sincerely wanted, can we function effectively.

661 Rudnev, A. "Occupied Japan." *New Times* no.29:23–26 (18 July 1951)

In a letter from Tokyo the author contrasts the appalling poverty of Japanese citizens with the affluence of their American conquerors. He claims that government spending is aimed not at alleviating the dire circumstances of the people but at rebuilding the Japanese army. All spheres of culture and education are being Americanized. The writer describes the efforts of SCAP and the Japanese government to quell Communist publications and demonstrations and discusses the manner in which cheap American books and movies are being forced upon an unwilling Japanese people.

662 Sansom, Sir George B. "The Political Orientation of Japan." *Pacific Affairs* 24:306–12 (Sept. 1951)

A distinguished Asian specialist describes and comments upon the 2-volume publication of SCAP's Government Section, entitled the *Political Reorientation of Japan* (1949) (no.279). Although judging the body of the work to be straightforward, he notes that "the prefatory sections at moments strike a note of complacency." There follows a brief review of the work's 12 sections, noting the contents and style of each. Sansom concludes with an observation that the occupation was on the whole benevolent and effective but that at times "idealism seems to have outrun practical wisdom."

663 ———. "Recent Impressions." *Contemporary Japan* 20:1–4 (Jan./Mar. 1951)

These impressions were written following a December–January visit by George Sansom to Japan after an absence from that country of 5 years. He was favorably impressed by the signs of improvement in material conditions in Japan but noticed that a "strange confusion prevails in the world of thought." He discusses possible causes for this situation, considering what effects might be attributed to the Allied occupation, but concluding that the trouble is largely economic. He does not see the occupation policy of democratization as having produced firm and widespread political convictions among the Japanese.

664 ———. "A Recent Visit to Japan." *Journal of the Royal Central Asian Society* 38:267–76 (Oct. 1951)

In a meeting before the Royal Asian Society on 3 May 1951, George Sansom talks about a recent trip to Japan. He discusses the political situation and new political problems which are emerging, the influence of the occupation, the economic situation, and the threat of communism to Japan.

664a Scalapino, Robert Anthony. "Democracy in Asia: Past and Future." *Far Eastern Survey* 20:53–57 (21 Mar. 1951)

After discussing the general prospects for democracy in Asia, Scalapino turns his attention to Japan, which he sees as an ideal laboratory for "isolating and exposing the real sources of the democratic problem in Asia." He first briefly outlines the history and traditions of

Japanese government and politics, then proceeds to a discussion of the democratizing efforts of the occupation. "Postwar Japan," Scalapino argues, "is a proving ground for implanting democracy by direct occupation." There are, however, some basic problems to be overcome. Chief among these is the contradiction between the necessarily authoritarian nature of the occupation and the democracy it is trying to encourage. In addition, the uniqueness of American political and economic forms makes their transplantation difficult. Nevertheless, the experience and insight gained during the occupation of Japan can be put to good use in other, less developed, Asian countries.

665 Schmid, Peter. *Japan heute: Nippon lächelt wieder*. Stuttgart: Deutsche Verlags-Anstalt, 1951. 186p.

666 Smythe, Hugh H. "How Democratic Is Japan?" *Nation* 173:168–70 (1 Sept. 1951)

Smythe questions the effectiveness of a wide range of SCAP-initiated democratic reforms including those dealing with rearmament, restrictions on labor union activity, and recentralization of education. He discusses patterns of nationalist and material motivation, deplores the lack of powerful Japanese progressive sentiment, and anticipates a revival of totalitarian regimentation.

667 "Some Aspects of the Occupation of Japan." *External Affairs* 3:305–8 (Sept. 1951)

A review of legal and operational aspects of the occupation beginning with the Cairo, Yalta, and Potsdam agreements and relating to the goals of demilitarization and democratization. A discussion of the powers exercised by SCAP is followed by an explanation of the structure and functions of the Far Eastern Commission and the Allied Council for Japan. The author notes the ineffectiveness of these organizations in the face of American opposition. Finally, the structure of SCAP is examined and a brief review of its policies is presented.

667a Sprout, Harold, and Margaret Sprout, comps. & eds. *Foundations of National Power: Readings on World Politics and American Security*. 2d ed. New York: Van Nostrand, 1951. xxiv, 810p. (Van Nostrand Political Science series)

This collection of selected readings covering all parts of the world contains excerpts from several books and articles on the geography, resources, and people of Japan; Japanese institutions, ways, and traditions; and Japan's adjustment to defeat as well as developments during the occupation period. Included are readings taken from (1) chapter 1 of D. G. Haring's *Japan's Prospects* (no.81); (2) chapter 1 of Thomas A. Bisson's *Prospects for Democracy in Japan* (no.581); (3) Harold H. Fisher's "Soviet Policies in Asia" (*Annals of the American Academy of Political and Social Science* no. 263: 188–201 [May 1949]); and (4) chapter 8—"The Future of Japan"—of W. Macmahon Ball's *Japan: Enemy or Ally?* (no.535).

668 Steiner, Jesse Frederick. "Impression of Post-war Japan." *Contemporary Japan* 20:145–55 (Apr./June 1951)

Steiner begins by contrasting facets of the old Japan and new Japan existing today, noting the unequal progress in the rural and urban areas. The bulk of the article then concentrates on the changing attitudes of the Japanese during the postwar years. He notes an appreciation of the freedom to voice political opinions, but shows the difference in attitude between the younger and older generations. He discusses instances where aspects of the new democratic government have been disappointing, pointing to a feeling that many features of the Japanese government must be changed when a peace treaty is ratified. The interrelation of governmental structure and the new democracy to the economic situation is described, along with the strains caused by the slow progress toward economic recovery. In addition to the threat to democracy resulting from the economic plight of a large part of the better educated classes in Japan, the author discusses dangers from both the left and right. He demonstrates how Communist philosophy appeals to some traditional Japanese ways of thinking noting that the "red menace to free government" might become stronger if economic conditions deteriorate. The real threat, however, he sees on the right. The article, nevertheless, ends on a positive note.

669 Supreme Commander for the Allied Powers. Diplomatic Section. *Correspondence of Political Adviser to SCAP.* 1947–51. Record Group 5, Box 100. MacArthur Memorial, Bureau of Archives, Norfolk, Va. 1 binder.

A collection of letters, telegrams, memorandums, reports, and speeches associated with SCAP's political adviser, William J. Sebald. Spanning the period from October 1947 to March 1951 and chronologically ordered, the documents relate to a variety of topics which concerned Sebald. They include the text of Sebald's New Year's message of December 1947, speeches delivered by him to the Allied Council for Japan on the activities of the council and its perception of the Japanese labor movement, correspondence with various foreign missions in Japan and with UN Secretary General, Trygve Lie, regarding appeals for contributions for its emergency relief program as well as memorandums concerning the treatment of German assets in Japan, and the establishment of the Fukuoka Division of the Diplomatic Section of General Headquarters. Later memorandums and correspondence concern proposals for Japanese membership in such organizations as the United Nations Educational, Scientific, and Cultural Organization, the World Health Organization, the World Meteorological Organization, the International Film Festival, its participation in the twelfth International Penal and Penitentiary Congress, and meetings of the International Penal and Penitentiary Commission, as well as the International Convention for the Regulation of Whaling. There are also SCAP memorandums discussing the establishment of Japanese overseas agencies in the United States and other nations.

———. Government Section. *Review of Government and Politics in Japan.* 1948–51. See no.280.

670 Textor, Robert B. *Failure in Japan: With Keystones for a Positive Policy.* New York: Day, 1951. xxiv, 262p.

A civilian employee with the Civil Information and Education Section of SCAP for more than 2 years presents a critical analysis of the Allied occupation of Japan. Following an introduction by Owen Lattimore which compares and contrasts the economic and political situations in wartime and postwar Japan and Germany, there is a general description of American aspirations and intentions in Asia, particularly in Japan, and an outline of what the author conceives to be the vital changes that must be made in Japan's present power structure. Convinced that the occupation started successfully but has deteriorated seriously in later years, the author devotes the greatest part of the book to a presentation of 6 keystones which he believes would constitute sound bases for a positive Japan policy. The first of these concerns the Japanese economy which the author insists must be rid of excessive concentrations of economic power and freed from domination by American business. The second keystone relates to political and personal freedoms and the author criticizes restrictive SCAP policies on civil liberties and urges that the rights of free expression and peaceable assembly be encouraged. Labor is the third area considered, and in this chapter the author protests the occupation's drastic curtailment of what he considers to be numerous legitimate activities of organized labor and urges SCAP to encourage political responsibility and participation by organized labor. In the fourth area, termed the availability of information, there is an appeal for an expanded and enriched information program making materials on democratic thought available to the Japanese public. The author also argues for the development of cultural exchange and research programs between Japan and the United States. Under a fifth rubric termed "civilianization," the author maintains that civilian supremacy in the occupation must be established by replacing military personnel with qualified civilians where any civil function is concerned. The final category—increasing internationalization—points up the need for encouraging the participation of other Allied nations in the formulation of occupation policy and for increasing Japan's internal autonomy where possible before the final peace settlement with Japan is reached. The author believes that General MacArthur's departure from Japan in 1951 may clear the way for a more effective occupation policy. A first appendix provides information on the specific organization and operation of the occupation in Tokyo and Washington, and a second furnishes a list of Japanese companies undergoing deconcentration. This work was translated into Japanese under the title of *Nihon ni okeru shippai* (Tokyo: Bungei Shunjū Shinsha, 1952. 364p.).

670a Tiltman, Hessell. "Japan: The Strictly Democratic 'Banzai'." *Reporter* 4, no. 6:17–21 (20 Mar. 1951)

Tiltman finds that the occupation's efforts to democratize Japan have met with only qualified success. Its technical, medical, and public health programs have been enthusiastically welcomed by the Japanese. Likewise, the land reform has already benefitted the peasantry. Political democracy, however, has made little headway, for political power still centers on the big industrialists and bureaucrats, the constitution is rarely read and little understood, and popular loyalty to the emperor remains unshaken despite his "humanization." Tribute must be paid, Tiltman states, to the "high Christian and moral concepts" that have guided MacArthur and to the devoted and sincere efforts of countless Americans in the occupation, but the results so far have been uneven.

671 U.S. Dept. of State. *In-Messages.* Jan. 1950–Apr. 1951. Record Group 9. MacArthur Memorial, Bureau of Archives, Norfolk, Va. 10 folders.

These unclassified, chronologically ordered radio messages are from the State Department to SCAP. Many of the later messages concern the worsening Korean situation, but earlier ones contain press reports on occupation programs and related issues such as the rearmament of Japan, the texts of presidential statements on U.S. foreign policy, the White House announcement of the 14 October 1950 conference between President Truman and General MacArthur, trade agreements between Japan and other nations, and the establishment of new diplomatic missions in Japan.

672 ———. ———. *Out Messages.* Jan. 1950–Apr. 1951. Record Group 9. MacArthur Memorial, Bureau of Archives, Norfolk, Va. 5 folders.

These folders are chronologically arranged and consist of radiograms from the Diplomatic Section of SCAP to the State Department on a variety of topics related primarily to Japan and peripherally to the Korean conflict. The most numerous messages contain SCAP summaries of Japanese press releases regarding political, social, and economic reform programs of the occupation and recent changes in those programs as well as coverage of national and international events, the reaction of the Japanese to the outbreak of hostilities in Korea, and the question of the rearmament of Japan. Soviet reaction and press comments on various occupation activities are also noted. Other messages are reports by SCAP on such issues as activities in the Diet, changes in the cabinet, developments in various political parties, changes in the national budget, press conferences of various Japanese political and business officials, activities of the Japan Communist party, proceedings of the Allied Council for Japan, the status of various trade and diplomatic missions in Japan, relations between Japan and Korea, interest among some Japanese in reestablishing trade relations with the People's Republic of China, the outlawing of the Japan Communist party, and recent developments on the peace treaty issue.

Yoshida, Shigeru. "Japan and the Crisis in Asia." 1951. *See* no.2442.

1952

673 Dewey, Thomas Edmund. *Journey to the Far Pacific.* Garden City, N.Y.: Doubleday, 1952. 335p.

While Dewey's Far Eastern tour took him to Korea, Okinawa, Taiwan, the Philippines, and Southeast Asia as well as to Japan, this record of his travels includes a substantial section on the latter. In addition to making general observations on conditions in Japan and the activities of the occupation, he discusses in some detail the land reform, which he calls "the brightest spot in the whole picture" since it deprived the communists of their best chance to make headway in Japan. His tour of the country, during which he made a point to visit rural areas as well as major cities, included interviews with various Diet members, Prime Minister Yoshida, and the emperor. Dewey left Japan feeling optimistic about the country's future. Nevertheless, he did see "small but ugly clouds" on the Japanese horizon, and he expressed concern in particular about strong communist influence among Japanese teachers.

673a Dilley, Opal Lawrence. *After Many Long Years.* New York: Pageant, 1952. 119p.

An almost blindly favorable account of the Allied occupation is presented by the wife of a SCAP employee. The author's subjects include the SCAP machinery, educational reforms, food supplies, public health improvements, guarantees of freedom of the press and free expression, democratic elections, economic reconstruction, and constitutional reform. Data based on statistical information are often provided. However, the author's style is stilted and she tends to present a grossly simplistic picture of the occupation program, referring to the occupation forces, for example, as "disciples of mercy and apostles of peace." Her approach is based on the belief that after many years as a backward and helpless state, Japan is finally being saved morally and spiritually by the forces of the Allied powers.

674 Foreign Affairs Assn. of Japan, ed. *The Japan Year Book, 1949–52.* Tokyo: The Association, 1952. xvii, 778, 555p.

Material covered in this yearbook is similar to that in the 1946–48 edition (no.550). However, a special chapter, entitled "Allied Occupation and Control of Japan" (chap.4, p.233–58), provides a summary of the aims of the occupation, SCAP structure, SCAP reforms ranging from constitutional revision to public welfare improvements, SCAP measures on commercial entrants, judicial practices, tourism, etc. President Truman's address at the San Francisco Peace Conference is also reprinted. Appendixes include SCAP letters and memorandums issued from 1948 to 1951, laws and ordinances enacted from 1948 to 1952, and "documentary materials." Included among these are Joseph Dodge's statement on the Japanese budgetary reform, the Far East Command headquarters' report on Japanese prisoners of war, the prime minister's speeches before Diet sessions, the address by Yoshida Shigeru, the chief Japanese delegate at the San Francisco Peace Conference, the text of the Peace Treaty with Japan, and the text of the United States–Japan Security Treaty and the Administrative Agreement.

675 Itō, Nobutaka (Nobufumi). *New Japan: Six Years of Democratization.* Tokyo: Japan Peace Study Group, 1952. 243p.

The democratic institutions and legal framework constructed during the Allied occupation of Japan are summarized in this book. Topics are arranged under the 3 general headings of political, economic, and social democratization. Following a brief descriptive account of Japan's surrender and the occupation period, the author discusses such issues as the new constitution, local self-government, agrarian reform, economic deconcentration, the new commercial code, labor legislation, the new civil and criminal laws, and the new education system. Some descriptive and explanatory background is given in each case, but little critical discussion is offered. As the author himself says, "This book contains . . . only the facts, leaving the final judgment to the readers." His own impression is that development of a democratic spirit among the Japanese will take a long time but that the democratic framework set up could lead to true democracy in Japan if the international environment is encouraging.

676 "Japan under the Occupation." *Current Notes on International Affairs* 23: 531–54 (Oct. 1952)

Political developments in Japan during the Allied occupation are reviewed here. The Allied machinery for the occupation of Japan is described with references to the Potsdam Declaration, the Far Eastern Commission, the Allied Council for Japan, and SCAP and its special staff sections and military government teams. This description is followed by a general account of occupation reforms such as demilitarization, democratization, constitutional revision, the new status of the emperor, the purge, war criminals, and educational reforms. The article also discusses the development of Japanese party politics under SCAP control.

677 John, Arthur. "Japan: The Imposed Reformation." *Australian Quarterly* 24: 22–30 (Mar. 1952)

This article speculates on the possible fate of occupation reforms after the signing of the peace treaty. The reforms are seen as an amazingly well-received attempt to impose American values on the Japanese, but some changes will probably be made (e.g., improving the status of the emperor and revising Article 9 of the constitution), some reforms never took hold (e.g., dissolution of the *zaibatsu*), and others will prove too expensive (e.g., expanded education). The author concludes that the reforms will last only if world conditions remain reasonably peaceful and prosperous.

678 Langer, Paul Fritz. "The Japanese Political Scene." *Journal of International Affairs* 6:163–72 (Spring 1952)

Writing in 1952, Langer analyzes the Japanese political scene since the conclusion of World War II. Most of his article deals with the major political parties and the Yoshida cabinet. Langer predicts the continued success of the conservatives either by coalition or by the formation of a new conservative party. He concludes that "democracy may face a difficult time in Japan."

679 Martin, Howard H. "Blueprint for the New Japan." *Education* 72:394–404 (Feb. 1952)

An extensive and detailed review of the occupation is presented here. Martin begins with an historical presentation stressing the development of commerce and industry since the Meiji Restoration, the acquisition of the Japanese empire, and Japan's conduct in World War II. He then discusses the signing of the peace treaty in relation to concurrent security negotiations throughout the Pacific area. Various policies of the occupation are examined in terms of their effect on Japan, including: (1) territorial redistribution and its effect on population and resource availability; (2) agricultural self-sufficiency involving production increases and trade patterns; (3) reform of the land tenure system based on a tenant-landlord relationship; (4) the possible use of Hokkaido as a place for domestic migration and industrial development; (5) Japanese emigration patterns to the United States, Asia, and Latin America; (6) the importance of past and future American financial assistance; (7) the development of new patterns of raw material and power fuel acquisition; (8) the revival of manufacturing in all areas except armaments; and (9) the revival of Japan as a significant participant in world trade. Martin concludes that a determination to rehabilitate the national economy in order to restore a high standard of living and the desire for achievement of a high and honorable status among nations are dominant forces in postwar Japan.

680 Parrott, Lindesay. "Japan's Mood as a New Chapter Opens." *New York Times Magazine* p.7, 53 (27 Apr. 1952)

The author, who has been the *Times*' correspondent in Tokyo since September 1945, looks back over the years of the occupation and concludes that it has had little impact on the Japanese people. He views the occupation not as a basic restructuring of Japanese society but as giving different aspects of it a chance to grow. Japan still faces the age-old problems of too many people and too few resources. The author asserts that in light of its history, Japan will respond to these problems with increasing isolationism and by becoming a selfish ally of the West. Moreover, he warns that Japan may revert to her former use of business combines and other such prewar practices after the United States' trade subsidies stop. However, he believes that in spite of the above tendencies, the fact of Japan's defeat and the threat of communism in Asia may change Japan's outlook and cause it to become a bulwark of democracy in the Far East. This apparent change in the Japanese national character is due to their ability to adapt foreign things to their own use.

681 Price, Willard. "Cruising Japan's Inland Sea." *National Geographic Magazine* 104, no.5:619–50 (Nov. 1953)

Towards the end of the occupation period, Price and his wife spent 6 weeks sailing on a private boat from Osaka to Shimonoseki. This article is a popularized account of that voyage. Much of what they have to say deals with the various scienic places that they visited and with the reception accorded them by Japanese communities along the route. The account, however, also does contain some information on the state of Japan's postwar recovery after several years of SCAP reforms and Japanese efforts to rebuild their country.

682 ———. *Journey by Junk: Japan after MacArthur*. New York: Day, 1953. 317p.

A trip by small boat through the Inland Sea provides the backdrop for this informal account of Japan near the end of the Allied occupation. The author is a free-lance writer and photographer on an assignment for the *National Geographic Magazine*. His anecdotal travelogue is punctuated with impressionistic accounts of the status of Japanese women, deconcentration of the *zaibatsu*, birth control, and the land reform program.

In the final chapters of the book the author voices concern over what he perceives as the growing influence of communism and a resurgence of Japanese militarism and emperor worship. He sees the latter as indirectly encouraged by the occupation policy of respect toward the emperor. The revival of militarism he sees as being encouraged by the occupation. He points to Article 5 in the peace treaty which expresses Japan's right to self-defense, to the return of purged nationalists and militarists to citizenship and participation in government, to the newly formed National Police Reserve, which at the time of writing was being equipped with arms and munitions from the United States, and to the rebuilding of Japan's munitions industry, which was beginning to supply armaments for the UN forces in Korea. According to his calculations, in the early 1950s Japan was spending 200 billion yen annually for defense, one-fourth of the national budget. The lowering of Japanese living standards which he predicts as a result of rearmament will, in his view, lead to further unrest and ultimately to policies of expansion and aggression.

Beyond discouraging Japan's rearmament, he advocates such measures as emigration and birth control. These measures, he argues, would decrease population pressure, another force which he sees as driving the nation to expansionism.

682a "Re-examination of Post-war Legislations." *Contemporary Japan* 21, no. 10/12:631–40 (1952)

This article is an English-language summary of the conclusions of a roundtable discussion among a group of Tokyo University law professors that was directed at assessing the legislation sponsored by the occupation. The transcript of the discussion itself appeared in the February 1952 issue of *Juristo* and covered the following topics: (1) the new constitution; (2) local autonomy; (3) the reform of the police system; (4) the revision of the code of criminal procedure; (5) postwar labor laws; (6) the reorganization of the educational system; and (7) postwar amendments to the civil code. The participants agree on the general conclusion that since the postwar legislation is mostly modeled after American laws and therefore lacks an adequate foundation in the Japanese tradition, many of the new laws are difficult to apply in practice. Accordingly, before condemning them, it is necessary to try modifying them in order that they may be more applicable to the realities of postwar Japan. Changes in their original objectives, however, are considered unacceptable since the consensus of the group is that the majority of the new laws are just and based on noble ideals.

683 Shiba, Kimpei. *I Cover Japan*. Tokyo: Tokyo News Service, 1952. v, 268p.

The managing editor of the *Nippon Times* writes casually and humorously about activities in occupied Japan "primarily for entertainment with persons who know little about us in mind." He treats the popularity of the American brand of democracy in postwar years, public baths, traditional human relationships as observed in *Kabuki* and the occupation's reactions to them, *harakiri*, geisha society, the prime minister's job, police operations, woodblock prints, Japanese battleships sunk in the Pacific War, etc.

684 Smythe, Hugh H. "Successor to the Samurai." *United Nations World* 6:15–18 (June 1952)

Smythe attempts a critical review of the effects of occupational reforms, concentrating on the activities and political style of Prime Minister Yoshida Shigeru. Following a short biographical sketch, he asserts that Yoshida is a direct successor to the Japanese tradition of authoritarian leadership. His actions concerning the abrogation or modification of occupation reform legislation are treated at length, particularly vis-à-vis such matters as the introduction of the special law dealing with public disorder, the call for restoration of Kigensetsu (Empire Day—the annual celebration of Emperor Jimmu's accession to the throne), the recentralization of public education, and government encouragement of *zaibatsu* control in economic affairs. The author contends that the Japanese people as a whole know nothing of democracy and have no strongly articulated opinions that must be considered by the government. He concludes that Yoshida is not suppressing any substantial popular desires by undertaking modification of occupation reforms.

684a ———. "Japan: Point of No Return?" *New Republic* 126:13–14 (28 Jan. 1952)

Smythe, a teacher of social sciences at Yamaguchi National University, criticizes the undemocratic character of recent legislative recommendations made by the Japanese government. Among the items he cites are the elimination of the Women's and Minors' Bureau and the Public Utilities Commission, the reduction of the compulsory school period, restrictions on freedom of the press and freedom of assembly, centralization of the police force, and the encouragement of cartels.

684b Stahmer, Hans Georg. *Japans Niederlage—Asiens Sieg: Aufstieg eines grösseren Ostasien*. Bielefeld: Deutscher Heimat-Verlag, 1952. 318p.

Stahmer, the German ambassador to Japan from December 1942 until the end of the war, recounts the history of Japan from the months immediately preceding Pearl Harbor through the early 1950s. Chapter 4—entitled "Japan's Ascent from the Abyss"—discusses the major developments in Japan under the occupation, particularly the democratization program, the war crimes trial, the country's economic recovery, and the San Francisco Peace Treaty.

685 Tokumaro, N. "New Occupation of Japan." *New Times* no.24:22–23 (11 June 1952)

In an attack on the American conduct

of the occupation, the author repeats accusations that SCAP officials are living comfortably among the poverty of the Japanese, that American occupation personnel are undisciplined and extremely unpopular, that the so-called peace treaty is in reality a ruse to keep Japan subjugated to the American yoke, and that occupation officials are giving every encouragement to the reactionaries, militarists, industrialists, and imperialists who are still largely unpunished for their part in the war.

686 Vinacke, Harold M. *The United States and the Far East, 1945–1951.* Stanford, Calif.: Stanford Univ. Pr., 1952. vi, 144p.

Vinacke originally presented this publication as a data paper for the eleventh international conference of the Institute of Pacific Relations in October 1950. It was later revised to include events until the summer of 1951. The occupation is surveyed in the chapter, "Postwar Policy toward Japan," pages 67–81. Presurrender goals, early demilitarization and reform programs, and finally the policy of economic recovery are described, shifts in policy being seen as largely the result of American relations with Communist powers. Japan is mentioned briefly in other chapters and the last chapter has a section entitled "Steps toward a Treaty with Japan" (pages 129–33) which describes mainly the military problems involved.

Vining, Elizabeth G. *Windows for the Crown Prince.* 1952. See no.1264.

687 Willoughby, Charles A. "Tribute to Japan." *Reader's Digest* 60:55–59 (Feb. 1952)

Willoughby writes a testimonial to the goodwill and cooperative spirit of the Japanese which greatly facilitated implementation of occupation reforms. He speaks of the failure of the Communist attempt to use former prisoners of war from Siberia to gain support throughout Japan. The Japanese provision of bases for American men and supplies during the Korean War is praised. Willoughby also notes the extent to which the occupation employed existing leadership to reestablish an ordered society. In conclusion, he comments on 2 goals which he feels should be encouraged during future American–Japanese cooperation in East Asia, namely: (1) Japan must be made militarily secure—specific mention is made of developing a 250,000-man army; and (2) Japan must expand, economically and geographically. Willoughby hints that Japan, as a vital American ally, should be allowed to regain a geographical and economic position in East Asia comparable to her position in the prewar era.

1953–72

688 Amravati, Mallappa. *Relations between Japan and the United States since 1945 with Special Reference to the Peace Treaty and the Security Pact.* Ph.D. dissertation, New Delhi, Indian School of International Studies, 1969. iv, 391p.

In this doctoral thesis the period of the Allied occupation is represented as a time during which the ruling conservative leadership in Japan attempted to survive by consciously subverting the occupation reforms. The author claims that the same group strove to exploit the cold war in order to regain great power status for Japan. These efforts successfully culminated in the conclusion of the peace treaty with the Western bloc and in the military alliance with the United States. The thesis treats a wide range of subjects including Japanese reaction to the surrender, differences among the Allied powers as to the Allied occupation machinery, SCAP reforms, Japanese response to the reforms, the shift in American policy toward Japan after 1947, differences within the American government and among the Allies regarding the Japanese peace settlement, an evaluation of the San Francisco Peace Conference, and Japanese views on the peace treaty and the security pact with the United States.

688a *Asahi Shimbun*. Staff. *The Pacific Rivals: A Japanese View of Japanese–American Relations*. Tr. by Peter Grilli and Murakami Yoshio. New York: Weatherhill/Asahi, 1972. xvi, 431p.

This book is a translation of *Nippon to Amerika* (Tokyo: Asahi Shimbunsha, 1971), which itself consisted of a series of articles appearing in the *Asahi Shimbun* between January and July 1971. The articles cover a broad range of topics more or less centering on the general theme of Japanese–American relations. Part 3, "The Occupation and Its Legacy" (p.109–209), contains 32 brief articles dealing with every major aspect of occupation policy. An introductory article characterizes the occupation as "a further extension of the U.S. policy—the same as that which led to the Pacific War—to dismantle the Japanese government and military machine." The attitudes of the occupation, it continues, were derived from "the missionary zeal and pioneer vigor that had developed from the American experience." The articles which follow consist of interviews with Japanese officials and intellectuals, anecdotes chosen to dramatize the content of occupation reforms and the Japanese reactions to them, material drawn from publications of the occupation period, and sometime vigorously opinionated editorial commentary. Generally speaking, the occupation's social and political reforms are viewed favorably, and the "reverse course" that began even before 1952 to lessen their impact is deplored. American conceptions of the world political situation and of Japan's international role, however, are criticized.

689 Bakke, Edward Wight. *Revolutionary Democracy: Challenge and Testing in Japan*. Hamden, Conn.: Archon Books, 1968. x, 343p.

The author asserts that the reforms instituted by the occupation constituted a revolution on a scale far beyond the Japanese powers of assimilation. Comparing Western historical development with Japanese conceptions of individualism, rule of law, foundations of government, etc., he identifies and traces in their varying strengths indigenous traditions and traits predisposing for or against the abruptly introduced changes. Although he notes the shock effect of the radical reforms, he contends that in the long run their acceptance depends on the degree to which they can be and are integrated with the continuing experience-produced values and practices all Japanese know and understand.

690 Ball, William Macmahon. "Today's Japan: A Return to the Past." *Nation* 178:253–56 (27 Mar. 1954)

A contributing editor of the *Nation* and the former representative of the British Commonwealth in the Allied Control Commission in Japan writes of his impressions of Japan following his first visit to that country in six years. He notes the vast material improvements that have occurred, but feels that the Japanese are more anxious, restless, and unhappy than they had been in 1947 because they are again responsible for making their own decisions. "This inner conflict," he points out, "is most evident in the worried search for a foreign policy." There is considerable concern about where their alliance with the West against the Communist world will lead them. Ball then comments on what he sees as signs of the government's efforts to eliminate some of the occupation's reforms. Past leaders are again in key positions, and the government is seeking to impose new restrictions on the political activities of school teachers and to reestablish a single, centralized control of the police. In addition, scandals are rocking both government and business circles. These are having a definite negative impact on public opinion, producing "a revulsion against the whole idea of parliamentary government and a yearning for the strong, honest patriot who will send corrupt politicians packing."

691 Beardsley, Richard King, John Whitney Hall, and Robert Edward Ward. *Village Japan*. Chicago: Univ. of Chicago Pr., 1959. xx, 498p.

This study of a social microcosm,

the village of Niiike, a small rice-growing community in Okayama prefecture, is based primarily on interviews, questionnaires, and firsthand observation by the authors—professors of anthropology, history, and political science at the University of Michigan—and by others, using the field station established in Okayama as a base from April 1950 to July 1954 and revisited up to 1957. It portrays all aspects of activity, organization, and the way of life in a rice-growing village. Although no large or important group of occupation forces were in Okayama, the impact of the Allied occupation on village life in Japan is treated in some detail. Included are the effects of the occupation on local office holders, on inheritance laws, on political participation, and on education. The Local Autonomy Law and land reform are both studied from the standpoint of their effect on rural villages. Villagers' attitudes toward occupation reforms such as attempts to reform the legal system are also noted.

692 Beasley, William Gerald. *The Modern History of Japan*. New York: Praeger, 1963. xi, 352p. (The Praeger Asia–Africa series)

Beasley, noting the postwar period to be the continuation of the story of Japan's attempts to come to terms with the modern world, discusses demilitarization, political and constitutional reform, the judiciary, and the reform of labor laws, land tenure, and education under the occupation. Beasley is professor of Far Eastern history at the School of Oriental and African Studies, University of London.

693 Bennett, John W., and Ishino Iwao. "Futomi: A Case Study of the Socioeconomic Adjustments of a Marginal Community in Japan." *Rural Sociology* 20:41–50 (Mar. 1955)

The authors, conducting a research program to assess the effects of the land reform program, report on how a rural Japanese community confronted the economic hardships of the immediate postwar years and on its responses to the various reforms of the occupation. They note, for example, that while the economic situation was insecure and the cause of genuine needs, the prevailing values kept individuals and families from accepting public support.

694 Blanchod, Frédéric Georges. *Vagabondage au Japon*. Lausanne: Marguerat, 1953. 225p.

695 Borton, Hugh. *Japan's Modern Century: From Perry to 1970*. 2d ed. New York: Ronald, 1970. x, 610p.

In examining Japan's reorientation under the occupation, Borton, director of the East Asian Institute, Columbia University, notes that the docile submission of the military and civilian populace was due to several factors: first, the Japanese were accustomed to obeying their superiors; second, the physical and psychological state of shock of most of the people; and third, the personality, attitude, and reputation of General MacArthur.

696 ———. "Past Limitations and the Future of Democracy in Japan." *Political Science Quarterly* 70, no.3:410–20 (Sept. 1955)

The author argues that even prewar party cabinets were basically controlled by Japan's oligarchs and that SCAP therefore had to create a democratic government largely from scratch with a new constitution, labor unions, reformed education, etc. These reforms, however, were weak because they were forced on Japan by a military occupation and because the men who control the Japanese government are more important than the formal political structure. Since postwar government has been controlled by conservatives, certain reforms (e.g., educational) have been undone while others (e.g., labor unions, land reform, women's rights) seem to have taken hold. The author concludes that Japan "may settle down to a moderate form of democracy well to the right of center."

697 Bowers, Faubion. "Twenty-five Years Ago: How Japan Won the War." *New*

York Times Magazine p.5–7, 35–44 (30 Aug. 1970)

An impressionistic, critical, and opinionated version of the occupation by a man who served as an interpreter and aide for General MacArthur in its early days. Bowers deplores the arrogance of the American undertakings in Japan and the alleged ignorance and offensiveness of many of the high officials involved. He concludes with respect to the occupation that "America attempted the impossible . . . but Japan nevertheless accomplished a miracle of its own."

698 Bronfenbrenner, Martin. *Prospects of Japanese Democracy.* Toronto: Canadian Institute of International Affairs, 1955. 16p. (Behind the Headlines, 15, no.3)

Bronfenbrenner, a University of Wisconsin faculty member at the time he prepared this pamphlet, presents an overview of postwar Japan's political structure and economic situation, and assesses the prospects for Western-style democracy within the country. His discussion touches upon the party system, the constitution, Japan's economic problems, the weakness of democratic tradition, extremism in politics, and the position of Japan in the cold war. Reference frequently is made to the impact of various occupation policies upon the country, with Bronfenbrenner noting, on the one hand, the relative success of reform programs in counteracting landlord influence and, on the other, the problems that have arisen out of the occupation's efforts to encourage Japanese trade unionism. Bronfenbrenner is critical of the failure of the Americans to practice what they preached as may be seen, for example, in SCAP's refusal to allow the Japanese Diet to consider any measure not approved in advance by the occupation authorities or to amend any occupation-approved measure without occupation approval of the amendment. He argues that practices such as these, together with petty offenses by occupation personnel and American objections to Japanese trade with Communist countries, have led to "an understandable revulsion against everything American, democracy included." Nonetheless, the author is optimistic about the prospects of Japanese democracy provided that existing occupation-influenced democratic institutions "can maintain their present foothold and survive their present 'time of troubles'."

698a ———. "Balm for the Visiting Economist." *Journal of Political Economy* 71: 293–97 (June 1963)

Bronfenbrenner offers "ten commandments" to be followed by economists advising foreign governments, especially those of underdeveloped countries, and illustrates the consequences of failing to heed them with examples drawn from the occupation period in Japan. The failure to understand both Japanese banking and record-keeping practices and Japanese attitudes toward competition undermined SCAP antitrust and monetary reform efforts. The condescending attitude of SCAP personnel towards their Japanese counterparts resulted in an early loss of sympathy among Japanese intellectuals; and this in turn led to planning and legislation which was badly or incompletely thought out as well as to a legacy of anti-Americanism within Japanese intellectual circles. Furthermore, the failure to make proposals intelligible to their intended audiences led to their rejection. As an example Bronfenbrenner points to the value-added tax controversy of 1950–52. In addition, suspected or actual influence-peddling and other self-serving activities of various members of SCAP's industrial division aroused Japanese mistrust and hostility. SCAP's educational reforms foundered because of a too-close adherence to American models. Finally, Bronfenbrenner points to the lavish housing which SCAP provided its dependents as an instance of the kind of conspicuous consumption visiting advisers should avoid.

699 Burks, Ardath Walter. *The Government of Japan.* 2d ed. New York: Crowell, 1964. xvi, 283p. (Crowell Comparative Government series)

This monograph describes the government of Japan, with emphasis on the period of readjustment since the conclusion of the treaty of peace. Some information is included on the occupation, but it is scattered throughout the text.

700 Cameron, Meribeth E., Thomas H. D. Mahoney, and George E. McReynolds. *China, Japan, and the Powers: A History of the Modern Far East.* 2d ed. New York: Ronald, 1960. xiii, 714p.

A history of Western relations with East Asia in which one chapter—chapter 31, "Japan since Pearl Harbor"—is devoted to a review of the Japanese surrender, the major features of occupation policy and reforms, and Japan's postwar economic and political recovery.

701 Chatterjee, B. R. *Changes in Power Politics in the Far East: Japan, 1944–1954.* Meerut City, India: Jai Prakash Nath, 1955. 46p.

702 Chéroy, Jacques, *pseud.* "Les Américains au Japon." *Revue du Paris* 61:105–21 (Jan. 1954)

This review of the American occupation of Japan seeks to assess some of the results of American efforts to reform and transform the country. Most of the author's attention focuses on the major political and economic changes of the period.

702a ———. *Où va le Japon?* Paris: Hachette, 1954. 384p.

This straightforward account and analysis of recent Japanese history includes a detailed study of the occupation presented in part 3, entitled "L'ère MacArthur" (p.161–315). Chéroy first reviews major developments before 1948, with particular focus on the new constitution, labor and land reforms, and the guarantee of individual freedoms. The United States is considered to have acted with good intentions, but the reintroduction of democracy meant little to most Japanese as long as economic conditions within the country remained bad. Chéroy then examines some of the major changes in American policy after 1948, when SCAP began emphasizing economic growth and accorded those measures designed to implement Japan's economic recovery higher priority than the various freedoms previously accorded labor unions and other groups. The impact of the Korean War also is considered, for the war demonstrated to the United States the need for military bases in Japan and a longterm defense alliance with that country. Finally, the author discusses the treaty of peace that was concluded at San Francisco and explains why some Japanese were unhappy with its provisions. Throughout his account, Chéroy comments on the nature of the Allied occupation. He points to many significant accomplishments and notes how unusual it was for the people of a defeated nation to extend as much cooperation to the victors as the Japanese did. Nevertheless, he continues, there were many weaknesses in America's policies. SCAP failed to realize that not everything which was good for the United States was appropriate for Japan and, as a result, naively exported American ideas and ways and sought to graft them onto Japanese institutions. Furthermore, the Americans may be criticized for having failed to emphasize economic recovery earlier than they actually did and for not reconciling their economic policies with aspects of their program for the democratization of Japanese life and society.

703 Clyde, Paul Hibbert. *The Far East: A History of the Impact of the West on Eastern Asia.* 3d ed. Englewood Cliffs, N.J.: Prentice-Hall, 1958. xxviii, 836p.

A historical account of Japan and of China in which one chapter (chap. 36) is devoted to a summary account of the major features of the occupation including changes in the political and social structures, land reform, *zaibatsu* dissolution, and postwar economic recovery.

704 Cole, Allan Burnett. *Japanese Society and Politics: The Impact of Social Stratification and Mobility on Politics.* Boston: Graduate School of Boston Univ., 1956. 158p. (Boston Univ. Studies in Political Science, 1)

Cole begins this work by introducing approaches to the study of Japanese sociopolitical behavior noting the severe institutional changes occasioned by the occupation, the "reverse course" in Japan, and the relevance of the Japanese experience for other societies in the process of modernization. He continues by outlining briefly the theories and definitions of such terms as "strata" and "classes" as used in the study. The period since 1945 is described as one of the 2 periods of extensive vertical mobility in Japan. The American occupation of Japan is used as a way of explaining the significance of Japanese social stratification and mobility for politics, noting that occupation policies affected almost every facet of Japanese life. Cole maintains that there was a "calculated intention to strengthen those classes or strata which, it was hoped, would be the most likely exponents of more democratic politics." The effect which the postwar democratization program had on the position and downward mobility of the imperial and titled nobility is discussed along with the fact that democratization has not strengthened significantly the middle stratum of the middle class. Postwar changes in the Japanese bureaucracy resulting from democratization are examined as are changes in the military and police. The deconcentration, purge, and reconcentration of the *zaibatsu* and the ensuing sociopolitical effects are discussed. The growth of the labor movement as one of the 3 greatest sociopolitical changes in postwar Japan is studied. The author also examines the social and political effects of the land reform program.

705 Colton, Kenneth E., Hattie Kawahara Colton, and George O. Totten, eds. "Japan since Recovery of Independence." *Annals of the American Academy of Political and Social Science* 308:1–175 (Nov. 1956)

This issue of the *Annals* concentrates on the social and institutional changes in Japan since the official termination of the Allied occupation in 1952. The various articles were written by 9 Japanese, 8 Americans, and 1 American-trained British scholar. Most contributors include a discussion of occupation reforms and policy changes as a basis for studying the current trends. Throughout the issue the reader will note both the stability of Japanese political, economic, and social institutions in the midst of military defeat, foreign occupation, and reassertion of independence and the continuing debate on whether a "revision" of occupation reforms is called for. "Transition seems to be characteristic not only of political development but of the economy, education, the family, and the full gamut of Japanese life." The major areas examined in the article are: constitutional and governmental developments, domestic politics, economic problems and developments, social and educational developments, and foreign relations.

706 Dangerfield, Royden. *The New Japan*. New York: Foreign Policy Assn., 1953. 62p. (Headline series, no.102)

Dangerfield presents a brief study of modern Japanese history, concentrating on the effects of the occupation on Japanese economic and political development. The establishment of SCAP is explained and its policies concerning demilitarization, the promulgation of a new constitution, and selected social changes are noted. A variety of long-range problems which the occupation attempted to alleviate, including population and food shortages, the continued low level industrial production, trade imbalances, raw material shortages, and future defense and internal security considerations are examined. The United States–Japan Security Treaty and Japanese relations with other Asian countries are explained.

707 Dening, Sir Esler. *Japan*. London: Ernest Benn, 1960. 263p. (Nations of the Modern World)

Sir Esler Dening, former British ambassador to Japan and chief political adviser to the supreme allied commander in Southeast Asia, presents an introductory survey of Japan. Part 1 is a brief survey of Japanese history. The next 3 sections provide discussions of a variety of subjects dealing with postwar Japan, including economic conditions, the arts, education, foreign relations, and Japan's international position. Chapters 6 to 9 focus on postwar domestic political changes. The machinery for the Allied occupation of Japan and Great Britain's part in the control of Japan, the process of establishing the Constitution of Japan, new constitutional provisions for the imperial family and the status of the emperor, the abolition of the peerage, and the operations of party government are briefly examined.

707a Dower, John. "Occupied Japan and the American Lake, 1945–1950." In *America's Asia: Dissenting Essays on Asian–American Relations*, ed. by Edward Friedman and Mark Selden. New York: Pantheon, 1971. p.146–206.

Dower's study is essentially a critique of many commonly held interpretations of American policy vis-à-vis occupied Japan. In order to eliminate the possibility of any Japanese aggression in the future, Dower argues, the United States initially carried out an extensive program designed to demilitarize and democratize the country. Within a short time, however, as the cold war intensified, American strategy changed and the need for an economically strong buffer state to Communist expansion in Asia became a primary concern of American policy-makers. Dower's article itself centers around 5 themes. In his first section, entitled "Control of Japan," the author discusses the Soviet–American confrontation over the problem of Allied participation in the occupation and points out how the United States denied her allies any meaningful role. Part 2, "The American Lake," shows how America's unilateral control over Japan was part of a vaster pattern of expanding American power in which the United States assumed virtual control over the Pacific Ocean north of the equator. Part 3, "The Workshop in the Lake," focuses on the reverse course in occupation policy that involved a shift away from reform and towards economic rehabilitation and development. Involving such matters as the abandonment of the *zaibatsu* dissolution program and the imposition of curbs on labor union activity, this shift constituted a unilateral revision of some of the basic premises of the occupation. The final 2 sections, "The Occupation in World Opinion" and "The Other Side of the Lake," survey the reaction of various countries to American occupation policies (particularly after 1947) and suggest a link between Japan's postwar revival and the outbreak of the Korean War.

707b ———. "The Superdomino in Postwar Asia: Japan in and out of the Pentagon Papers." In *The Senator Gravel Edition: The Pentagon Papers*, ed. by Noam Chomsky and Howard Zinn. Boston: Beacon, 1972. v.5, p.101–42.

In his introduction, Dower writes that the study of postwar Japan is virtually inseparable from an examination of U.S.–Japanese relations and that the publication of the Pentagon Papers, together with certain other materials which have recently become available, now makes it possible to structure the general course of Japan's postwar development in a more meaningful way. In each of the 6 sections of his article, Dower draws upon the Pentagon Papers to document the view that American policy-makers had of Japan as the superdomino in Asia, to relate this view to the American creation around 1949 of a United States–Japan–Southeast Asia nexus "aimed at the creation of a capitalist bloc in Asia and an economic and military noose around China," to show how the United States has influenced domestic developments in postwar Japan even after the termination of the occupation, to point out certain important features in the U.S.–Japan military relationship, to explain American attitudes toward such matters as the potential of the Japanese masses for revolutionary action, and to examine Japan's emergence as a "superpower" during the late 1960s. Section 3 of Dower's article focuses on the occupation period itself. Within it he ascribes the "reverse course" in Allied occupation

The Occupation

policy to "U.S. support for the emergence of a dependable, capitalist ruling class in Japan" composed essentially of members of big business, the bureaucracy, and the conservative party. While only a few of the Pentagon Papers deal at any length with occupied Japan, those that he cites document this aspect of U.S. policy by indicating (among other things) how much the United States wanted Japan to produce goods and services important to the United States and the economic stability of the non-Communist part of Asia and how anxious American policy makers were that Japan develop an effective military force as well as the capacity for producing low-cost, military material.

Edwards, Marie A. *Political Activities of Japanese Postwar Labor Unions*. 1956. See no.1749.

708 Eskelund, Karl. *The Emperor's New Clothes*. London: Burke, 1955. 192p.

708a Eunson, Roby. *100 Years: The Amazing Development of Japan since 1860*. Tokyo: Kodansha International, 1965. 192p.

This centennial pictorial history of Japan chronologically records the most significant developments between the mid-1860s and the early 1960s. Chapter 9, entitled "The Occupation," provides a 4 page introductory summary of the period together with 27 photographs including ones relating to the war crimes trial, the land reform, the elections, the labor movement, the food crisis, and the activities of American troops in Japan.

Gibney, Frank. *Five Gentlemen of Japan: The Portrait of a Nation's Character*. 1953. See no.1928.

708b Gibson, James B. "The Occupation of Japan: Ten Years Later." *World Affairs* 118:109–11 (Winter 1955)

The author, who was at one time attached to the Liaison and Investigation Office of SCAP's Civil Information and Education Section, assesses the impact of the occupation on Japanese life and the permanence of such SCAP measures as reforms in health, welfare and education, the extensive purges, and the enactment of a new constitution. He finds that the occupation's overall impact has been tremendous, but that it is extremely difficult to determine conclusively how well the Allied goals have been served. Some of the changes envisioned by SCAP exist only on paper, and others have consistently been underfunded. Nonetheless, while it might appear to the casual observer that the reforms of the occupation are being systematically reversed one by one, in reality the majority of them are not.

709 Goodman, Grant Kohn, comp. *The American Occupation of Japan: A Retrospective View*. Lawrence: Univ. of Kansas, Center for East Asian Studies, 1968. viii, 41p. (International Studies, East Asian series, research publication no.2)

This small book is a compilation of papers and commentaries which were presented as a panel at the 1968 meeting of the Association for Asian Studies. Following an introduction by the compiler, 3 papers and 2 commentaries are given. All are by respected scholars of Japan, several of whom participated in the Allied occupation. The papers presented are: "The American Occupation of Japan: Political Retrospect," by Robert E. Ward (no.760); "The American Occupation of Japan: Economic Retrospect," by Martin Bronfenbrenner (no. 1635a); and "The American Occupation of Japan: Social Retrospect," by Edward Norbeck (no.734a). Brief commentaries are offered by John M. Maki and Harry Emerson Wildes. The papers, all brief but insightful, analyze different reform programs and possible explanatory factors behind their relative success or failure. Several of the panel members stress the degree to which the occupation was a mutual undertaking by Americans and Japanese.

710 Hall, John Whitney. *Japan: From Prehistory to Modern Times*. New York:

Delacorte Pr., 1970. xiv, 397p. (Delacorte World History, 20)

A brief treatment of the occupation focusing on the reforms enacted by the Allies and the factors behind Japan's postwar recovery concludes this historical narrative of Japan by Hall, Griswold Professor of History at Yale University. This book was originally published in Germany under the title *Das japanische Kaiserreich* (Frankfort: Fischer Bücherei, 1968. 380p.).

711 ———, and Richard King Beardsley, eds. *Twelve Doors to Japan*. With chapters by Joseph K. Yamagiwa and B. James George, Jr. New York: McGraw-Hill, 1965. xxi, 649p.

This introduction into the various aspects of Japanese culture notes the effects of the occupation on the following facets of Japanese society: geography, cultural anthropology, history, language, literature, visual arts and culture, religion and philosophy, education, politics, law, and economic development. The authors are all distinguished scholars in their respective fields.

711a Iino, David N. "Freedom and Authority in the Realization of Values." In *Freedom and Authority in Our Time: Twelfth Symposium of the Conference on Science, Philosophy and Religion*, ed. by Lyman Bryson, et al. New York: Conference on Science, Philosophy and Religion in Their Relation to the Democratic Way of Life, 1953. p.717-32.

Iino, a lecturer at the International Christian University in Tokyo, concludes a generally theoretical article with a 10 page treatment of freedom in Japan. The occupation has brought to Japan an array of freedoms hitherto unknown, particularly in the social and intellectual spheres, but it remains to be seen whether the Japanese people have the requisite self-discipline and moral will to avail themselves of these freedoms properly and in the pursuit of positive ideals. Christianity, Iino feels, is ideally suited to fill the gaps in Japanese ethical thought.

712 Ike, Nobutaka. *Japanese Politics: An Introductory Survey*. New York: Knopf, 1957. xiv, 300, ix p.

Ike analyzes the way in which power is exercised in Japan in terms of the historical, social, ideological, and institutional setting and the dominant political forces—business, labor, and agriculture. In noting significant differences between the prewar and the postwar political situations, he points out that the postwar freedom of political expression has done much to relieve tensions, and the emergence of the Socialist party provides those who find the traditional order to their disliking with a vehicle for registering political protest.

713 Jasay, A. E. de. "Reform and Recovery in Japan." *Australian Quarterly* 25: 61-68 (Dec. 1953)

This article argues that the democratic reform and the economic recovery of Japan are mutually exclusive. The occupation reforms, Jasay believes, destroyed the Japanese economy by being anti-big business (e.g., the purge of *zaibatsu* executives, the holding company liquidation measures, etc.) and by interfering with foreign trade. The occupation's shift in emphasis to economic recovery came too late, and the author therefore concludes that "probably nothing short of the spectacular can break Japan's vicious circle of undercapitalization, overpopulation, and political catastrophe."

714 Kawai, Kazuo. *Japan's American Interlude*. Chicago: Univ. of Chicago Pr., 1960. vii, 257p.

The impact of the occupation upon Japanese society and Japanese reactions to the American influence of the occupation period are the primary subjects of this penetrating study. Born in Japan but educated in America, the author was a professor of history and political science from 1932 to 1941 before serving as editor in chief of the *Nippon Times* from 1946 to 1949. Drawing from this rich background, he provides a balanced and scholarly analysis of the situation. Among the subjects covered are: the Japanese people's surprisingly subservient attitude toward the occupation forces, the character of the occupation administration headed by General MacArthur, factors that contributed to a smoother democratization process than was initially expected, political implications of constitutional revision, the new image of the emperor, and the purposes and actual consequences of various reforms—political, economic, agrarian, educational, and so forth. While generally supporting the occupation's programs of change, the author draws attention to factors that do not necessarily promise the eventual success of democracy in Japan. Particularly stimulating are his discussion of the impact of the democratization process on social change and his interpretation of the historical reaction by the Japanese to social progress since the Meiji period. Excellent bibliographical notes are added.

715 Keene, Donald Lawrence. "Literary and Intellectual Currents in Postwar Japan and Their International Implications." In *Japan between East and West*, by Hugh Borton, et al. New York: Harper, published for the Council of Foreign Relations, 1957. p.153–98.

Focusing on modern Japanese writers and critics, Keene's article presents a study of some of the literary and intellectual currents in postwar Japan. It begins with a discussion of popular reading habits and the manner in which writers make their living. It then groups the important contemporary authors and characterizes their writings, tastes, and attitudes. This in turn is followed by an examination of postwar Japanese criticism and the relationship between literature and politics. While Keene does not make any specific reference to the occupation, the article does provide the reader with a means for understanding literary trends during that particular period.

716 Kennedy, Malcolm D. *A History of Japan*. London: Weidenfeld & Nicolson, 1963. 365p.

In his year by year account of Japan under foreign occupation, Kennedy examines the policies and reforms of SCAP and the Japanese reaction to them. Malcolm Kennedy is the author of numerous studies on Japan.

716a Kolko, Joyce, and Gabriel Kolko. *The Limits of Power: The World and United States Foreign Policy, 1945–1954*. New York: Harper and Row, 1972. 820p.

This study of the global context of postwar U.S. foreign policy presents a history of the crucial decade of 1945–54, when most of America's basic problems—and failures—emerged. While coverage for this period is worldwide, the authors' focus is upon developments in Europe and East Asia respectively. Two chapters in all deal exclusively with Japan. Chapter 11 (p.300–25), entitled "The Dilemma of Japan," covers the first 2 years of the occupation and considers American wartime planning for postwar Japan, the Allies and the occupation, the occupation government, SCAP's relations with the Allied Council, the dilemmas of reform and reconstruction, labor conditions, occupation reforms, and the limits and context of the reforms. Chapter 19 (p.510–33)—"The Restoration of Japan"—in turn examines the 1947–51 period and covers the American response to Japan's economic crisis, Japan's economic recovery, the workers' response to developments affecting their lives, the Dodge Plan, the role of the left in a reconstructed Japan, and the peace treaty. Throughout their book, Joyce and Gabriel Kolko seek to pinpoint the goals that motivated the conduct of American policy, and in the case of Japan, they conclude that the United States succeeded in achieving most of its objectives by 1952 in large measure because no other country was powerful enough to prevent it. When the occupation ended, "politically the conservative ruling class was firmly entrenched in power and the working class, for the first time, was effectively subjugated. And, above all, the Japanese economy had been reintegrated into the American economic orbit."

Kreps, Leslie R. *The Image of Japan in the Speaking of United States Congressmen, 1941–1953.* 1957. See no.55.

717 Kublin, Hyman, ed. *Japan, Selected Readings.* Boston: Houghton Mifflin, 1968. 244p.

A selection of readings covering all of Japanese history, edited and annotated by Kublin and intended primarily for secondary school students. Section 5, "The Making of a New Japan," covers the occupation with a general introduction (pages 179–81) and the following selections: "Long Live Peace" (pages 185–87), an essay by a 15-year old schoolboy from rural Japan; "Rights and Duties" (pages 188–91), excerpts from the new constitution; "His Imperial Japanese Majesty" (pages 192–96), taken from an article by A. M. Rosenthal in the *New York Times Magazine*, 19 May 1963; "The Old and the New" (pages 197–204), from David Plath's book, *The After Hours: Modern Japan and the Search for Enjoyment* (Berkeley: Univ. of California Pr., 1964. 221p.); "The Ever-expanding Market" (pages 205–8), from *Japan: Growing Market for U.S. Exports* (Washington, D.C.: United States–Japan Trade Council, 1966); "The College of One's Choice" (pages 208–12), from Victor Kobayashi's article in *Educational Forum*, volume 28; and "Which Way for Japan" (pages 213–16), from Yoshida Shigeru's book, *The Yoshida Memoirs* (1962) (no.769).

718 Kuwabara, Takeo. "Tradition versus Modernization in Postwar Japan." *Diogenes* (Montreal) no.40:129–47 (Winter 1962)

At the beginning of this article, Kuwabara, a vice-president of the Science Council of Japan, points out that such occupation changes as the establishment of the new constitution, the acceleration of the labor movement, and the punishment of militarist leaders have had a positive impact on Japan, but he reminds the reader that not all of the changes were fully acceptable to the Japanese. Kuwabara then discusses attitude changes among the Japanese following the end of the occupation and comments on these throughout the remainder of the piece, referring in particular to the conflict between tradition and modernization that has become a significant factor in postwar Japanese culture and thought.

719 Langdon, Frank. *Politics in Japan.* Boston: Little, Brown, 1967. xiii, 290p. (Little, Brown series in Comparative Politics)

A detailed structural-functional analysis of postwar Japanese politics with particular emphasis on the behavioral aspects of the Japanese and on their political structures. Information about the occupation may be found in chapter 2, "Origins of the Political System," and in other portions of the book. The occupation as a subject in its own right, however, is not studied in particular detail.

720 Langer, Paul Fritz. *Japan, Yesterday and Today.* New York: Holt, Rinehart and Winston, 1966. iii, 250p. (Contemporary Civilizations series)

Langer's account presents a general introduction to the land, life, people, history, and modern institutions of Japan. Considerable information on the occupation and its effects may be found particularly in the chapter on political institutions, where SCAP, various political reforms and the constitution are discussed, and in the chapter on Japan's economic institutions, which contains a section on the Japanese economy under the occupation with particular focus on the land reform, labor policy, and the deconcentration of the *zaibatsu*.

721 Latourette, Kenneth Scott. *The History of Japan.* rev. ed. New York: Macmillan, 1957. 299p.

A revised edition of Latourette's historical account that was first published in 1918 under the title *The Development of Japan*. The final chapter describes some of the characteristics and developments of the American occupation.

722 Lens, Sidney. "What Happened to the MacArthur Revolution?" *Progressive* p.12–14 (Dec. 1953)

Lens discusses the changes in American occupation policies that have occurred since 1948, pointing out that the initial objective of organizing the labor unions and clipping the wings of both the militarists and the *zaibatsu* was abandoned 3 years after the surrender of Japan. He claims that these changes have halted the process of democratization within the country and that the United States is "back in the old groove again, upholding the status-quo and supporting reaction and militarism."

722a Lequiller, Jean. *Le Japon.* Paris: Editions Sirey, 1966. ix, 621p. (L'histoire du XXe siècle)

Written by a former director of the Institut Franco–Japonais in Tokyo, this work presents a detailed account of modern Japanese history through the early 1960s. Two chapters within it focus specifically on the occupation period. Chapter 23—"Le shogun MacArthur et ses réformes"—deals with the Japanese acceptance of their defeat, SCAP, the demobilization and political reforms, the economic chaos of the immediate postwar years and American assistance, the trade unions, agrarian reform, the liquidation of the *zaibatsu*, education, and the new position of the emperor. Chapter 24 in turn examines the year 1948 as a turning point, the subsequent reconstruction of the economy, MacArthur's control of the extreme left, the Korean War, and Japanese rearmament and the peace treaty. Lequiller's account is generally straightforward and factual, but on p.490–93 he does express his personal views of the America occupation as he seeks to sum up its impact and consequences. Among his major points are the following: (1) Many of the reforms undertaken during the first few years of the occupation were hastily conceived and implemented. Nonetheless, one must remember that at that time, many Americans were predicting that the occupation would be quite short and, accordingly, felt the need to move swiftly. (2) SCAP paradoxically sought to impose a liberal regime on the Japanese by authoritarian means. Since there were few Japanese liberals who could draft and carry out a series of drastic reforms, the Americans had to substitute themselves for the Japanese and through their efforts seek to create the necessary conditions for the birth of a liberal and democratic Japan. (3) While MacArthur explicitly sought to create a "spiritual revolution" in Japan through the destruction of the old system of values and the introduction of American ideas, SCAP in reality failed to furnish an appropriate substitute. Such Western concepts as democracy, justice, and social progress were terms bandied about by many Japanese but truly understood and assimilated by only a few among them. (4) Despite the weaknesses of SCAP's organization and the fact that many of the reforms were drawn up or imposed much too quickly, the reforms generally have been far more effective and lasting than most critics predicted. They tended to meet actual needs and accordingly have been accepted (but sometimes modified) by the majority of the Japanese people.

723 Lewe van Aduard, Evert Joost. *Japan, From Surrender to Peace.* The Hague: Martinus Nijhoff, 1953. xv, 351p.

This factual and concise account of the occupation is presented by a Dutch diplomat stationed in Tokyo from 1949 to 1952 as deputy chief of the Netherlands Mission in Japan. He offers conventional but comprehensive coverage of the occupation programs of reform in 1945–47. The latter half of the volume is devoted to diplomatic negotiations after 1948 among the Allied powers and between the Allies and Japan that ultimately led to the conclusion of the peace treaty in 1952. There is a perceptive account of the relationship between domestic happenings in Japan and international maneuverings during 1948, particularly the taut Russo–American relations, as well as a clear description of initial Japanese reluctance toward the American-sponsored idea of a "separate peace," the role of the Dulles mission, and the reaction of the Allied nations to the peace proposal. In his final chapter, the author offers a long and rather trite discussion concerning the "hopeful but uncertain" future of Japan.

724 Linebarger, Paul Myron Anthony, Djang Chu, and Ardath Walter Burks. *Far Eastern Government and Politics*. 2d ed. Princeton, N.J.: Van Nostrand, 1956. 643p. (Van Nostrand Political Science series)

Designed as a textbook on East Asian politics, this volume treats the politics and governments of China and Japan in 2 separate sections, but the authors acknowledge joint effort and responsibility for the entire book.

In the section dealing with Japan several chapters are devoted to a discussion of the cultural background and history of Japanese politics from early times to the modern period and World War II. The last 3 chapters deal with the occupation government and politics and their impact on postoccupation Japan. The authors believe that such time perspective is invaluable for understanding continuities and change in Japanese politics. The continuity of Japanese government under the occupation and the dominant position of the United States are stressed as points of departure for the discussion of the occupation of Japan as contrasted with the occupation of Germany. The organization and operation of SCAP are discussed, as are the makeup and roles of the Far Eastern Commission and the Allied Council for Japan. The purges and constitutional reform are described and analyzed as the first stages of Allied occupation policy, followed by an account of continuities and changes in the postwar institutions of the emperor, the Diet and cabinet, the civil service and local government, political parties, and the economic system as it relates to the political system. The last chapter deals with developments in postoccupation Japan. A moderate reversal of occupation policy is seen in trends toward constitutional revision and rearmament. The last pages of the book touch upon a variety of topics, giving summary descriptions and making appraisals and predictions. Some of the topics included are public administration, the functioning of the Diet, the conservative party coalition, the left- and right-wings of the political spectrum and their prospects, the recentralization of local government, the role of the press, and rural traditionalism. The authors conclude that the occupation probably accomplished much less change than its defenders claim but much more than its detractors and most Japanese realize. The value of the presentation is considerably enhanced by several useful organizational charts, extensive footnotes, and a variety of appended documents. Among the appendixes are the Imperial Rescript Announcing Surrender to the Japanese People, major points incorporated in the government section of the new constitution, the constitution of Japan, a list of Japanese premiers from 1885 to 1953, and the party composition of the Diet from 1947 to 1953. The comparative approach which is utilized throughout the book also lends a valuable perspective to the events and institutions analyzed. The scholar of Japan as well as the general reader should find this account useful and informative. The authors may be forgiven for a few mistaken prognostications, such as their view that, by mid-1956, constitutional revision was a "sure thing."

725 McNelly, Theodore Hart. *Contemporary Government of Japan*. Boston: Houghton Mifflin, 1963. xi, 228p.

An introduction to the institutions of Japanese government as they function today in their historical and social setting. Chapter 2—"The American Occupation and the New Constitution" (based in part on the author's article, "The Japanese Constitution: Child of the Cold War" [1959] [no.1194])—and chapter 3—"The Throne and Popular Sovereignty"—provide a useful survey of the impact of the occupation upon Japanese political institutions and of the creation and nature of the postwar constitution. Information on other areas of occupation reforms, e.g., police, education, and local government, may be found elsewhere within the text.

726 Maki, John McGilvrey. "Democracy in Japan, 1945–1955." *United Asia* 7: 298–302 (Dec. 1955)

The author traces the growth of democracy in Japan from 1945 to 1955. He looks at this phenomenon in terms of the right-wing and left-wing extremism Japan has experienced. He also studies the influence of the Allied occupation upon democracy in Japan. He feels what people see as antidemocratic developments in Japan such as the Defense Agency Law and the Police Law are in fact signs of democratic stability in Japan. The fact that these measures were legally established seems to Maki to be evidence that the democratic process works in Japan. Maki sees Japan as an experiment in democracy in which concepts of democracy were transplanted to a society which had previously little tradition of democratic thought.

727 ———. *Government and Politics in Japan: The Road to Democracy.* New York: Praeger, 1962. xi, 275p.

John Maki, professor of Japanese government and politics at the University of Washington, has written a study of the origins, character, and operation of democracy in Japan. The early chapters of this book focus on the occupation period: chapter 2 examines the complex interplay between the Allied authorities and the Japanese government and people in the democratic revolution; chapter 3 studies the response of the Japanese to the occupation and attempts to explain the country's readiness for change immediately after the war; and chapter 4 discusses the origins of the 1947 constitution and the principles governing its operation. Succeeding chapters, on the structure of the government, new patterns of Japanese society, and political parties and elections, also incorporate some information related to developments in Japan between 1945 and 1952.

728 Martin, Kingsley. "Japan's Destiny." *New Statesman and Nation* 50:351–52 (24 Sept. 1955)

This article considers the rapid and continuing recovery of Japan in the context of a cold war where both East and West are "willing to pay heavily to win to their side the support of a highly disciplined, industrious and potentially decisive ex-enemy." The author believes Japan's destiny lies in combination with other countries of Asia, not as a junior partner of the United States. He ends on the note that "Japan today awaits its new Shogun." The author believes in the capacity of Japanese democrats to achieve fundamental national change, but only if they are given time and spared the reemergence of a powerful army. He fears that the United States is subverting both conditions by pressing Japan to become a powerful military ally.

729 Mendel, Douglas Heusted. "Revisionist Opinion in Post-treaty Japan." *American Political Science Review* 48:766–74 (Sept. 1954)

Mendel analyzes some results of a 2-pronged voter and leadership survey of posttreaty Japanese political opinion made by the author between the fall of 1952 and the late summer of 1953. He notes that revisionism is not an ephemeral posttreaty phenomenon but a complex, deeply rooted amalgam of Japanese nationalism and justified criticism of occupation excesses.

730 Miller, Perry. "Teacher in Japan." *Atlantic Monthly* 192:63–65 (Aug. 1953)

Miller, a professor of American literature, conducted seminars at the Universities of Tokyo and Hiroshima where he found the students honest, friendly, and anxious to learn about American—not just European—culture. But he also observed some skepticism. The Japanese with their like of abstract "isms" found the twists in occupation policy confusing. They also asked whether America had renounced war, monopolies, religion in public schools, etc.

Mishima, Sumie Seo. *The Broader Way: A Woman's Life in the New Japan*. 1953. See no.2260.

731 Morris, Ivan Ira. "L'évolution politique du Japon d'après-guerre." *Politique étrangère* 21:323–40 (May/June 1956)

In this article Morris describes the occupation, the political scene of the mid-1950s, and the status of the left- and right-wings in Japanese politics. The occupation is seen as divided into an early reformist stage which worked for democratization, decentralization, and demilitarization and a subsequent conservative stage concerned with economic revival and anticommunism. In describing political developments after 1951, Morris is generally critical of the conservative trend in Japan, pointing out that communism is not much of a threat because of the weakness of the Japan Communist party.

732 Mukherjee, Asoke Kumas. *The Japanese Political System*. Calcutta: World Press Private, 1966. 165p.

In this institutional analysis of the Japanese political system, Mukherjee notes the impact of occupation policy on the postwar development of this system. Chapters 4–8 deal primarily with SCAP activities: chapter 4 is a review of occupation objectives, policy, and administraton; chapters 5–8 are concerned with the development of the new constitution, the bargaining involved in its creation, and the political results of its promulgation. Basic principles of popular sovereignty, the renunciation of war, the guarantee of civilian rule, judicial independence, and autonomous local government are discussed. One chapter is devoted to the enumeration and explanation of the civil rights and duties of citizens under the new constitution.

733 Murphy, Robert Daniel. *Diplomat among Warriors*. Garden City, N.Y.: Doubleday, 1964. x, 470p.

A combination of an autobiography and observations on foreign affairs in which the author participated. Murphy, a career diplomat, began his career in 1917, served in Europe during and after World War I, and acted as President Roosevelt's personal representative in French Africa during World War II, participating in the Potsdam Conference in 1945. His considerable experience in working with and among military men lay behind his assignment in 1952 as the first postoccupation American ambassador to Japan. It was expected that this experience would be useful in working out details of the administrative arrangements for the United States–Japan Security Treaty. Later he also became a negotiator in the Korean armistice agreement and assistant secretary of state for UN affairs. Murphy records his professional experiences and memoirs in 29 chapters. His observations on the Potsdam Conference (chap. 20) and his ambassadorial assignment in Tokyo (chap. 24) are particularly relevant to the study of the occupation of Japan. In the former chapter Murphy describes the conference, including the report received by the Americans regarding the success of the atomic test in New Mexico, while in the latter chapter he gives his impressions of the results of MacArthur's occupation reforms, referring to freedom of expression, the new status of the emperor, the origins of Article 9 of the Japanese constitution, Russian efforts to assist Communist infiltration in Japan, Yoshida's political techniques, etc. A Japanese translation appeared under the title of *Gunjin no naka no gaikōkan* (Tokyo: Kajima Kenkyūjo Shuppankai, 1964. 590p.).

733a Mydans, Carl. *More than Meets the Eye*. New York: Harper, 1959. 310p.

Mydans, a photographer for *Life* magazine, devotes several chapters of this book to an account of his experiences in Japan during the early years of the occupation. He arrived there even before MacArthur and describes in some detail the conditions he found in Tokyo and the reactions of the Japanese to their first contacts with Americans. An interview with ex-Prime Minister Suzuki Kantarō is one of the more interesting episodes that Mydans relates. His descriptions of domestic life in Tokyo after the arrival of his wife and of their travels around Japan provide insights as well into conditions during the immediate postwar period and into the attitudes of the Japanese towards their conquerors.

734 Nish, Ian Hill. *A Short History of Japan.* New York: Praeger, 1968. 238p. (Praeger Short Histories)

This historical survey by an English specialist on modern Japan includes 1 chapter devoted to the occupation. Entitled " 'Enduring the Unendurable,' 1945–54" chapter 12 (p.192–206) discusses SCAP's major reforms and subsequent efforts to rebuild the country's economy, the drafting of the Japanese peace treaty, and the "reverse course" carried out by the Japanese government after 1951 when it reversed some of the policies of the occupation period and withdrew some of its more radical reforms.

734a Norbeck, Edward. "The American Occupation of Japan: Social Retrospect." In *The American Occupation of Japan: A Retrospective View*, comp. by Grant K. Goodman. Lawrence: Univ. of Kansas, Center for East Asian Studies, 1968. p.27–33.

Norbeck's survey concludes that the important social reforms undertaken by the occupation were largely a success. The intent of SCAP's directives in the field of education (e.g., the prohibition of the teaching of morality) has been carried out in spite of their controversial nature; such actions as the provision of a constitutional guarantee of religious freedom, the end of national support of Shrine Shinto, and the associated prohibition of emperor worship have been retained; the legal validity of the land reform's provisions has been upheld by the Japanese Supreme Court; and post-occupation efforts among certain groups to revise those features of the Civil Code which extended increased individual freedom to Japanese citizens (e.g., the abolition of primogeniture and the extension of equal legal rights to women) have failed. These various reforms, Norbeck argues, were successful largely because the major social reforms were congruent with essentially unplanned trends of change in Japan and because many of the attitudes and values held by Americans and Japanese in the late 1940s were essentially compatible in nature.

735 Ohe, Seizō. "Socio-Political Experiment in Postwar Japan." *Ethics* 66, no.4: 250–61 (July 1956)

Ōe Seizō of Nihon University analyzes the essential features of Japan's postwar sociopolitical transformation and seeks to derive from it some perspectives for Japan's future development. He begins with a brief historical review in which he characterizes Japanese history before 1868 as a history of cultural development basically following the same line as that of Europe, and Japanese history after 1868 as a "process of Westernization still suffering from an inner spiritual antinomy." He then asserts that the revision of the fundamental idea of the Japanese state as evidenced by changes in the emperor's status, reforms in the traditional family system, and the abolition of Shinto as the state religion was the central feature of the occupation period. These changes, he observes, were "nothing but the final liquidation of what had been left unliquidated by the Meiji Restoration." Finally, Ōe discusses the spiritual situation of present-day Japanese youth and some of the ways in which Japanese society may develop in the future.

735a Ostwald, Paul. *Japans Weg von Genf nach San Francisco.* Stuttgart: W. Kohlhammer Verlag, 1955. 122p.

Ostwald studies the political causes and political outcome of Japan's involvement in World War II from the time of the Manchurian incident through the conclusion of peace in 1951. Chapter 4 (p.92–112) focuses on the postwar period and summarizes relevant developments under 3 headings: (1) The Unconditional Surrender; (2) The New Constitution; and (3) Peace at San Francisco.

736 Overton, Douglas W. "The Political Structure of Japan: Democratic or Paternalistic." *Proceedings of the Academy of Political Science* 26:89–96 (Jan. 1955)

In answering the question as to whether Japan is currently a democratic country the author considers 2 significant elements—the effects of the constitution of 1947 and the vestiges of paternalism which remain in Japan. He briefly highlights some of the more significant provisions of the constitution and views that document as "a most advanced charter for democratic procedures." On the other hand, he discusses certain obstacles to democracy in paternalism and traditional Japanese dependence upon groups and also cites Japan's military security problems as hindering democratic tendencies. He ends with the conclusion that "self-interest, rather than any idealistic attachment to theories will be the principal bulwark of democracy in Japan."

737 Passin, Herbert. *The Legacy of the Occupation: Japan*. New York: Columbia Univ., East Asian Institute, 1968. 45p.

This perceptive evaluation of the occupation and its reforms is a slightly revised version of a paper prepared for the Conference on Military Occupations and Political Change, 20–23 April 1967, sponsored by the Committee on Comparative Politics of the Social Science Research Council. The author, a professor of sociology at Columbia University, discusses the strategy and assumptions underlying the occupation and evaluates the effects of the occupation in relation to the effects of such phenomena as deferred change, the release of latent forces, culture contact, and changes that had nothing to do with the occupation. He examines and evaluates major occupation reforms as experiments in guided social change. Among the reforms discussed are constitutional change, the land reform program, changes in the civil code affecting family structure and the status of women, and economic reforms. In this brief but insightful analysis the author raises several important questions to be addressed by scholars of the occupation in the process of evaluating the assumptions, objectives, and results of occupation programs.

Pfaff, William. "The Third Revolution." 1953. *See* no.2530.

738 "Post-war Democratization in Japan." *International Social Science Journal* 13, no.1:7–91 (1961)

A collection of short articles on various occupation "democratization" projects that appeared as part 1 in this issue of the *International Social Science Journal*. Each article is by a well-known Japanese scholar who describes 1 area of reform and the extent to which it had taken hold by the late 1950s. The articles, which are individually listed and annotated within this bibliography (note the cross-reference numbers), are as follows: "The Constitution" (p.7–20), by Takayanagi Kenzō (no.1216); "Law" (p.21–34), by Kawashima Takeyoshi (no.1286); "Economics" (p.35–43), by Tsuru Shigeto (no.1668); "Japanese Education" (p.44–56), by Makino Tatsumi (no.2087); "Family Life" (p.57–64), by Tanimo Setsu (no.1982); "Rural Society" (p.65–77), by Fukutake Tadashi (no.1926); and "Development of Democratic Consciousness among the Japanese People" (p.78–91), by Takahashi Akira (no.1980).

739 Quigley, Harold S., and John E. Turner. *The New Japan: Government and Politics*. Minneapolis: Univ. of Minnesota Pr., 1956. viii, 456p.

This comprehensive and balanced account is devoted in large part to a description and analysis of occupation reforms affecting the political and governmental system in postwar Japan. The authors were at the time professors of political science at the University of Minnesota. Quigley also served as a research consultant to SCAP in 1946 and 1947. Following several introductory chapters which describe prewar and wartime government in Japan, the bulk of the book is devoted to a discussion of occupation policies and administration and their effects, both short- and long-term. Dealt with in some detail are the purges, the new constitution, civil rights legislation, the emperor, the cabinet, the national bureaucracy, the Diet, elections, major political parties, the courts, and local government. At least one chapter is devoted to each of these topics; the new constitution is dealt with in 4 of the 23 chapters. Much of the presentation involves description of new legal and political institutions, supplemented with narrative accounts of their establishment. Japanese government and politics are viewed as passing out of a feudal-militarist pattern and into a new era. The authors make no predictions about the stability of the new Japan fashioned by the Allied occupation, but they are confident that a real transition from the old pattern is taking place. Their major reservations about the occupation revolve around the attempt to foster democracy by military control. The authors conclude that the traditional Japanese attitude of subservience to government authority which contributed to the smoothness of the occupation has yet to be replaced with the spirit of free inquiry and criticism necessary for democratic government.

740 Quo, Fang-quei. *Japanese Liberalism: A Case Study in the Transplantation of Political Theory*. Ph.D. dissertation, Univ. of Southern Illinois, 1964. 207p. (Abstracted in *Dissertation Abstracts* 25: 5366 [1965]; University Microfilms order no.65–1334)

In an attempt to derive a theory for the transplantation of alien political ideas into a society with a different cultural and historical background, Quo examines the transformation of liberalism in Japan and offers an explanation for the repeated failure of this concept to become integrated into prewar Japanese society. In chapter 6, entitled "Mass Liberalism," the successful adoption of liberalism in the aftermath of World War II is attributed to the "artificial revolution" initiated by the occupation authorities. The author concludes that the difficulty of transplanting alien political ideas into a society with different traditions can be reduced to the problem of devising appropriate and successful political techniques.

741 Reischauer, Edwin Oldfather. *Japan: Past and Present*. 2d ed. rev. New York: Knopf, 1954. xi, 292, xi p.

In his chapter on the occupation, Reischauer describes the successes and failures of the occupation forces during this period of rapid change and evolution in Japanese society. He notes that the unexpected accomplishments of the occupation were due to the pressures of war and defeat, the reforms of the occupation authorities, and the active cooperation of the Japanese people.

742 ———. *Japan: The Story of a Nation*. New York: Knopf, 1970. xi, 345p.

Basically Reischauer's earlier work, *Japan: Past and Present* (1954) (no. 741), revised to such an extent that the title too has been changed. A nontechnical survey of all of Japanese history, the book has 2 chapters dealing largely with the occupation, "Occupation" (p. 218–41) and "Recovery" (p.242–84). The first of these chapters is an account of occupation policy from a generally American point of view, dividing the occupation into the usual 3 stages of demilitarization, reform, and recovery, and describing the various American-led programs at each stage. The second chapter begins by stating, "The Americans do deserve credit for formulating and guiding the democratic reforms of the occupation period, but the Japanese deserve most of the credit for their success." This chapter describes how the Japanese, working under the American occupation, rebuilt Japan, and includes an analysis of the economic strengths underlying apparent destitution, social and intellectual breaks with tradition, and the internal revival of prewar democratic politics. It is an excellent introductory survey of the occupation period sympathetic to both the American and Japanese points of view.

743 ———. *The United States and Japan*. 3d ed. Cambridge, Mass.: Harvard Univ. Pr., 1965. xxv, 396p. (The American Foreign Policy Library)

In his introduction Edwin O. Reischauer states, "This volume centers upon the most crucial phase of Japanese–American relations, that is our occupation of Japan 1945 to 1952." In this third revised edition, some sections are carried over from earlier editions published in 1950 and 1957 respectively. Chapters 1 and 2 and parts 2 and 3 deal with prewar Japan and derive from the 1949 edition. Materials added in the 1956 edition—chapters 3, 10, 11, and 12—describe the American occupation of Japan and its immediate effects. Part 5, "The Postwar Japanese," was newly written for this edition. Reischauer describes the objectives, effects, and significance of the occupation within a changing international context. He summarizes the extent of the wartime damage inflicted upon Japan, the qualities of the Japanese which aided their recovery, the impact of General MacArthur's role in the occupation, and some of the problems which impaired the effectiveness of the occupation. In chapter 11, entitled "Retribution and Reform," occupation programs such as the dismantling of the Japanese empire, demilitarization, the war crimes tribunals, the purges, reparations, constitutional and other legal and political reforms, educational reforms, social and economic reforms, and the land reform program are described and evaluated. Reischauer regards occupation policy as a success in restoring a balance between democratic and authoritarian forces. He is optimistic about a Japanese future in peaceful alignment with the free world and the United States.

The book is not footnoted, but an index and an annotated list of suggested reading are included. Among the documents appended are the Potsdam Proclamation, the U.S. Initial Post-Surrender Policy for Japan, the postwar Constitution of Japan, the Treaty of Peace with Japan, and the Treaty of Mutual Cooperation and Security between the United States of America and Japan (1960).

Richie, Donald. *This Scorching Earth.* 1956. *See* no.913.

744 Robinson, Laura. "A Visit to Occupied Japan." *Georgia Review* 7:180–87 (Summer 1953)

This chatty travelogue offers a montage of images of Japan in 1951 (or early 1952) accompanied by short discourses on Japanese culture and history. The author concludes that "it is hard to see what will happen after the Occupation ceases," and that the Japanese "will play a game of watchful waiting to see how successfully democratic principles and international cooperation work in the rest of the world."

745 Rōyama, Masamichi. "Prospects of Constitutional Democracy in Japan." *Japan Quarterly* 1:1–7 (Oct./Dec. 1954)

The author describes the growing debate over constitutional revision in Japan inspired by conservative opposition to occupation reforms on the grounds that they constitute "excessive democratization." He concludes that the prospects for democracy in Japan depend both on a careful balancing of capitalist economic and political interests with those of the working classes and on the question of the role in East-West relations which Japan will play in a world "charged by the advent of Communism in Asia."

746 Scalapino, Robert Anthony. "The United States and Japan." In *The United States and the Far East,* ed. by Willard L. Thorp. 2d ed. Englewood Cliffs, N.J.: Prentice-Hall, 1962. p.11–73.

In this essay on American–Japanese relations between the mid-1850s and the early 1960s, Scalapino devotes considerable attention to the occupation, focusing on initial occupation policy, the treatment of war criminals, the emperor, the democratization program, political reform, economic and social change, occupation policy revision after 1946, reparations and trade, and the San Francisco treaty.

747 Scarangello, Anthony. *A Fulbright Teacher in Japan.* Tokyo: Hokuseido Pr., 1957. iv, 148p.

Essentially the personal observations of an American residing in Tokyo during the late 1940s and early 1950s, this publication is a narrative account that contains information on some of the occupation reforms and related activities. The author devotes 4 out of 11 chapters to a description of the behavior of the American GIs, which he regards as generally commendable, the educational reforms, the democratization of the imperial system and Japanese reactions to the new status of the emperor, and the reconstruction of Hiroshima and Nagasaki. The occupation is viewed as an overall success, and the lack of hostility on the part of the Japanese towards the Americans frequently is noted.

Schwantes, Robert S. *Japanese and Americans: A Century of Cultural Relations.* 1955. See no.832.

748   Sebald, William J., and Russell Brines. *With MacArthur in Japan: A Personal History of the Occupation.* New York: Norton, 1965. 318p.

This book provides a personal record of the occupation operations as observed by a top-ranking American diplomat. Sebald worked in the Office of the Political Adviser to SCAP from January 1946 to September 1947, and as chief of the Diplomatic Section of SCAP and chairman of the Allied Council for Japan from September 1947 to April 1952. In organizing background material for the book, he was assisted by Brines, an AP correspondent who resided in Japan from 1939 to 1941 and again from 1945 to 1951. The work provides interesting information concerning the diplomatic maneuverings that went on among the Allied nations as well as the communications among officials in Washington, the Japanese government, and SCAP. Sebald begins his study with an account of Japan in the prewar period from 1925 to 1939 when he was intermittently in Kobe as a naval language officer and a practicing attorney. He subsequently contrasts the Japan of that time with occupied Japan and relates some of his own experiences as "an Occupation diplomat" working with General MacArthur and George Atcheson, Jr., communicating with the State Department, negotiating with the Japanese government, quarreling with the Russian representative on the Allied Council for Japan, and indirectly assisting in the preparation for the war crimes trials. His account also covers his role in the Korean War, the San Francisco peace treaty, the United States–Japan Administrative Agreement of 1952, and his views on the dismissal of MacArthur and the appointment of Ridgway as his successor. For Brines' own record of the occupation of Japan, see his *MacArthur's Japan* (1948) (no.541). The present work has been translated into Japanese under the title of *Nihon gaikō no kaisō* (Tokyo: Asahi Shimbunsha, 1966. 270p.).

749   Sheldon, Walter J. *The Honorable Conquerors: The Occupation of Japan 1945–1952.* New York: Macmillan, 1965. xvi, 336p.

A popular account of the Allied occupation of Japan. The author, a SCAP official and resident in Japan for some 10 years, regards the occupation as uniquely successful yet notes the incomplete meeting of Japanese and American minds in the postwar period. He attempts to "recapture the sights, sounds, smells and atmosphere of those days" by describing several significant events as they appeared to Japanese and Americans in various social positions. Topics referred to are the emperor's decision to surrender on the night of 14 August 1945 and his public announcement on the following day, the surrender ceremony on the *Missouri,* the "MacArthurian style" of work, the Japanese government's *modus operandi,* the Tokyo war trials, the purge, the activities of labor unions, *zaibatsu* dissolution and other forms of economic deconcentration, the Korean War, democratization, the San Francisco peace treaty, and the American influence on Japanese life. Personalities in SCAP and the Japanese government are described.

749a   Sissons, David C. S. "Japan 1945–1962." *British Survey* no.157:1–20 (Apr. 1962)

The occupation's activities may be broken down into the 2 broad categories of demilitarization and democratization,

Sissons writes. The demilitarization program included at first strict measures against economic institutions believed to have been partly responsible for the triumph of militarism. These measures, however, were largely abandoned by 1947 since the extent of Japan's economic weakness had become evident by that time and the cold war had begun to dictate a policy of rapid economic rehabilitation. In the political sphere, liberal democratizing policies were followed for much of the occupation period. Sissons notes, nevertheless, that a "reverse course" was already evident by the end of the occupation. The gradual dismantling or adaptation of SCAP-ordered institutions and programs to Japanese ways after 1952 is Sissons' major topic in the concluding portions of this article.

Soukup, James R. *Labor and Politics in Postwar Japan: A Study of the Political Attitudes and Activities of Selected Labor Organizations*. 1957. See no.1779.

750 Storry, Richard. *A History of Modern Japan*. Harmondsworth, Middlesex: Penguin, 1960. 287p. (Pelican book, A475)

In his review of occupation policies and the Japanese reaction to them, Storry describes the stages through which the Japanese passed in their reaction to SCAP as apprehension, admiration, disappointment, and boredom. Richard Storry is a Fellow of St. Anthony's College, Oxford.

751 Strauss, Harold. "Editor in Japan." *Atlantic Monthly* 192:59–62 (Aug. 1953)

The author, an editor for the Knopf publishing company, visited Japan in the autumn of 1952 and interviewed a number of leading novelists: Oka Shōhei, Ishikawa Tatsuzō, Kawabata Yasunari, and Osaragi Jirō. He comments on the aesthetics and economics of postwar Japanese writers, some of whom seem very Westernized and others very traditional.

752 Sullivan, Sister Maria Regina, S.J. *United States–Japanese Relations and Public Opinion, 1945–1955*. Ph.D. dissertation, St. John's Univ., 1959. vi, 241p.

This dissertation covers the following subjects: (1) Japan during World War II; (2) fundamental principles of the occupation; (3) demilitarization and democratization; (4) the period of Japan's recovery and her stabilization; and (5) Japan viewed as a possible bastion of the Western world in the Far East.

753 Terasaki, Gwen. *Bridge to the Sun*. Chapel Hill: Univ. of North Carolina Pr., 1957. 260p.

The personal experiences of the American wife of Terasaki Hidenari between 1930 and 1950 are related in this informal narrative. Terasaki was a member of the Japanese diplomatic corps who served as liaison officer between the emperor and SCAP until his death in 1950. Much of the book is devoted to an account of this couple's life during his diplomatic assignments in the United States, China, and Japan. They were in Japan continually from 1942, and their wartime experiences occupy a large portion of the book. During the latter part of the war the Terasakis left Tokyo and lost contact with their friends and associates. They returned to the capital after Japan's surrender, and soon after Terasaki became liaison officer between the emperor and SCAP. He apparently did not discuss his work with his wife, for few observations about it are offered in this account. Several notables such as Shigemitsu Mamoru and Admiral Nomura are referred to in some anecdotes. However, the book is essentially a personal, informal narrative concerning the experiences and impressions of the author herself and it contains little that is of scholarly interest.

754 Tiedemann, Arthur Everett. *Modern Japan: A Brief History*. Princeton, N.J.: Van Nostrand, 1955. 192p. (An Anvil original, 9)

Part 1, chapter 4 of this brief account of Japanese history since the mid-1800s reviews the structure of the occupation, some of the economic and political reforms, initial and subsequent American policy towards Japan, and the San Francisco peace treaty. Part 2, a collection of selected readings, includes the texts of the 1947 constitution, the Treaty of Peace, and the Security Treaty between the United States and Japan (1951), and a translation of poems composed by Emperor Hirohito between 1946 and 1955 which were studied by many Japanese for clues to his views on current affairs.

Truman, Harry S. *Memoirs.* 1955. See no.217.

755 Tsuji, Kiyoaki. "Postwar Political Trends in Japan." *United Asia* 8:221–25 (Sept. 1956)

Writing in 1956 the author, a professor at Tokyo University, traces the 10 years of Japanese politics since the end of World War II. He is concerned about the "retrogression of democratic trends in Japanese politics" and tries to trace how the original occupation goals of democratization and demilitarization have changed. Specifically, he contrasts the policies and goals of the Yoshida cabinet and the Hatoyama cabinet. He concludes that both external and internal factors have caused Japanese democracy to undergo modifications. He fears what he terms the "reactionary tendency of Japanese domestic policies."

756 Tsuru, Shigeto. "A New Japan? Political, Economic, and Social Aspects of Postwar Japan." *Atlantic Monthly* 195: 103–7 (Jan. 1955)

Tsuru, a leading Japanese economist, praises the occupation for concentrating on the fundamental reform of Japanese society and notes that, while Japan had recovered economically by 1953, he is not sanguine about the future. Many reforms have been swept away because they were not executed on Japanese initiative, and the economic recovery— itself largely a result of the Korean War —may not prove permanent.

757 Vinacke, Harold M. *Far Eastern Politics in the Postwar Period.* New York: Appleton–Century–Crofts, 1956. xiii, 497p.

A narrative rather than analytical study focusing on political developments in various East and Southeast Asian countries after World War II. Chapter 15 —"Japan: Through Occupation to Independence"—discusses the meaning of "unconditional surrender" for Japan, the initial Allied postsurrender policy for that country, international aspects of the occupation, the demilitarization and democratization of Japan, the 1947 constitution and the Japanese renunciation of war, and selected economic reforms. Chapter 16, entitled "Post-Treaty Japan," also focuses to a considerable extent on the occupation, studying among other things the consequences of the failure to conclude an early peace, the emphasis on economic recovery after 1947, internal Japanese politics during the late 1940s, and the negotiation of the peace treaty.

758 Ward, Robert Edward. "The Legacy of the Occupation." In *The United States and Japan*, ed. by Herbert Passin. Englewood Cliffs, N.J.: Prentice-Hall, 1966. p.29–56.

A professor at the University of Michigan discusses the impact of the American-dominated occupation of Japan from 1945 to 1952 upon present relationships between the United States and Japan. He treats the goals and nature of the occupation, its shifting policies, and the implications of the San Francisco peace settlement, before analyzing the "continuing consequences of defeat and Occupation." Along with these subjects such matters as the psychological impact of Japan's defeat, Japanese pacifism, and the consequences of democratization are also discussed. In the author's view, the most important legacy of the occupation lies in the establishment of broad congruities between the national interests of the 2 nations. He expresses optimism about the future of Japanese–American relations despite the presence of neutralist tendencies in Japan. This article and 5 others in the book were originally prepared for the twenty-eighth national meeting of the American Assembly of Columbia University held in 1965. The entire book has been translated into Japanese under the title of *Nihon to Amerika* (Tokyo: Nan'undō, 1967. 288p.).

———. "The Potential for Democratization in Prewar Japan." 1968. *See* no.127.

759 ———. "Reflections on the Allied Occupation and Planned Political Change in Japan." In *Political Development in Modern Japan*, ed. by Robert E. Ward. Princeton, N.J.: Princeton Univ. Pr., 1968. p.477–535.

A retrospective analysis of the Allied occupation of Japan viewed as a massive experiment in planned political change. The author seeks to describe the presurrender plans of the United States for the postsurrender treatment of Japan, compare them with actual changes in the system over the intervening years, determine the strategies by which such changes were induced, and investigate the extent to which they were attributable to exogenous factors such as the presence and activities of the occupation rather than more long-term endogenous factors. He concludes that the occupation was a necessary condition and catalyst for these changes but not in itself a sufficient cause.

760 ———. "The American Occupation of Japan: Political Retrospect." In *The American Occupation of Japan: A Retrospective View*, comp. by Grant K. Goodman. Lawrence: Univ. of Kansas, Center for East Asian Studies, 1968. p.1–9.

Characterizing the occupation as "a remarkably successful experiment in directed or planned political change," Ward points to the longlasting and pervasive impact of the Allied political reforms. The doctrine of popular sovereignty has been solidly established in Japanese public law and judicial practice, Japan now has a responsible form of government and its citizens are constitutionally guaranteed a variety of civil and political rights, a competitive party system exists, there has been an appreciable degree of decentralization of political, administrative and fiscal authority, public opinion has become a powerful factor in political life, and innovations in such areas as education, the status of women, and rural life have significantly strengthened the existing democratic political system. Despite certain shortcomings, Ward continues, Japan's postwar political performance must be considered impressive. The essential political structure established as part of the occupation's program to democratize the country remains intact, recent Japanese efforts to revise the political structure have been more notable for their moderation than for any attempt to revert to prewar institutions and practices, and the postwar democratic system of government represents a distinct break with Japan's prewar authoritarian past. The success of the occupation's political reforms, however, should not be attributed exclusively to SCAP's presence and influence. Such domestic factors as the existence of a prewar liberal element in Japan's political tradition and the familiarity of the Japanese with modern political institutions provided the occupation with a basis on which to build a democratic society. In short, then, the occupation served as an essential catalyst and successful form-giver but it definitely was not a *deus ex machina*.

761 ———, ed. *Five Studies in Japanese Politics*. Ann Arbor: Univ. of Michigan Pr., 1957. 121p. (Univ. of Michigan, Center for Japanese Studies, occasional papers, no.7)

Three of the studies in this volume are oriented toward politics in Japan and 2 toward legal problems. Paul S. Dull's article (no.1320) is based on his experiences as a research associate at the Center for Japanese Studies field station in Okayama City, Japan, and examines the local political "boss" in Japanese politics by means of a case study. Alfred B. Clubok's paper (no.1355) derives from library research and provides insights into the geographical and demographic patterning of "conservative" political strength in Japan as manifested in 5 general elections of members of the House of Representatives from 1947 to 1955. William C. Amidon's piece (no.

986a), entitled "The Issue of Sakhalin in Russo–Japanese Relations," explores the political history and contemporary economic and political significance of the island. Sugai Shūichi of Kyoto University's Law School (no.1348) writes of the Japanese police system in an effort to "assess the innovations introduced by the Occupation into the Japanese police system and to examine their effect." His study examines the extent to which the "reverse course" movement has affected the reforms initiated by the occupation and is "presented as an indication of the fate of the whole Occupation system." The bibliographical essay by Dan F. Henderson is entitled "Japanese Legal History of the Tokugawa Period: Scholars and Sources."

762 ———, ed. *Political Development in Modern Japan*. Princeton, N.J.: Princeton Univ. Pr., 1968. 637p. (Studies in the Modernization of Japan, 4)

In this analysis of the principal agencies for political development in modern Japan, articles by Henderson and Ward are noteworthy. Henderson deals with law and political modernization in Japan and Ward (no.759) treats the problem of the amenability of the developmental process to external control and manipulation. He provides a case study of the Allied occupation viewed as an experiment in planned political change.

763 ———, and Dankwart A. Rustow, eds. *Political Modernization in Japan and Turkey*. Princeton, N.J.: Princeton Univ. Pr., 1964. viii, 502p. (Studies in Political Development, 3)

This comparison of political modernization in Japan and Turkey examines in a series of papers by noted specialists the environmental and foreign factors that stimulated political, social, and cultural changes of a modernizing sort, investigates the relationship between economic and political aspects of modernization, and puts forth general conclusions about the process of political modernization in the 2 countries.

764 Watanabe, Masaharu, and Hugh H. Smythe. "After the Japanese Occupation." *Current History* 24:32–38 (Jan. 1953)

Written nearly a year after the conclusion of the occupation, this article by 2 professors of social science at Yamaguchi National University attempts to describe the reforms made by the occupation forces and to evaluate their effect on Japanese society after the termination of the occupation. They are particularly concerned with the land reform program, the *zaibatsu* deconcentration program, the position of the emperor, and the curtailment of the militarists and the bureaucrats. The authors are pessimistic regarding the efficacy of land reform and they maintain that the *zaibatsu* have survived despite the Law for the Elimination of Excessive Holdings. They judge that the policy regarding the emperor has succeeded thus far, but the elimination of the military has only partially succeeded. In conclusion, they believe Japan is heading for a difficult and dangerous future unless corrective measures are taken.

765 Wildes, Harry Emerson. *Typhoon in Tokyo: The Occupation and Its Aftermath*. New York: Macmillan, 1954. v, 356p.

The author was a regional specialist on Japan in the Office of War Information during World War II and served in the Government Section of SCAP during the occupation. Largely on the basis of personal research and extensive travelling and interviewing in Japan, Wildes, the author of *Social Currents in Japan* (Chicago: Univ. of Chicago, 1927. ix, 375p.) offers a critical analysis of the organization and operations of the SCAP administration; he also comments adversely upon the effects of occupation policy in Japan. He presents profiles of prominent SCAP officials and leaders of Japanese political and business circles and discusses the relations between SCAP and Japanese leaders. While consideration is given to the purge, the new role of a humanized emperor, the puppet Diet, and modes of operation within SCAP and Japanese governmental offices, greater attention is paid to a description of actual conditions in the country such as persistent political strife, official malfeasance, unsuccessful local autonomy, undemocratic police, the growing underground empire of criminals, low judicial dignity, insufficient concern for public health, undemocratic consequences of land reform, and what the author considers to be a shift in SCAP policy which was first favorable to left-wing social forces, especially the Communists, and later critical or antagonistic toward them. He praises Generals Ridgway and Clark who, unlike MacArthur, went out of the capital city to observe social realities in the country itself. He claims that contrary to MacArthur's assertions, a revolution has not been accomplished in Japan. Rather, the author views it as a rennaisance of the old order. He gives credit for the successes of the occupation to devoted and understanding "middle-brass Occupationnaires" and to an amazingly cooperative Japanese populace. This book was translated into Japanese under the title of *Tōkyō sempū* (Tokyo: Jiji Tsūshinsha, 1954. 318p.).

766 ———. "War for the Mind of Japan." *Annals of the American Academy of Political and Social Science* 294:1–7 (July 1954)

The former chief of SCAP's Political and Social Affairs Division, Civil Historical Section, discusses the struggle between democracy and communism for the control of postwar Japan. Wildes criticizes the occupation authorities for the inadequacy of their efforts at understanding Japanese ethics, needs, and modes of thought and at bringing democracy to the country, as well as for their failure to combat Soviet propaganda alleging that the United States was converting Japan into a colony and turning the islands into a military base. At the same time, however, he also notes serious Soviet blunders and inconsistencies and the ineptness of Japan's Communist leadership, which spoiled their effectiveness as propagandists. Wildes concludes with a plea for new and concerted action against communism, and he proposes various courses of action that must be undertaken if the United States is to win the war for the mind of Japan.

767 Yanaga, Chitoshi. *Japanese People and Politics.* New York: Wiley, 1956. viii, 408p.

In this book Yanaga of Yale University surveys modern Japanese political behavior. He argues that the basic character of Japanese society and institutions could hardly have been altered so radically by the occupation's efforts as to produce overnight a democratic system of government. Thus, the occupation's reform programs are placed within the larger perspective of Japanese political traditions. Though there are no chapters specifically on the occupation, there are frequent references to this period throughout the publication. The first 4 chapters attempt to analyze the nature of Japanese society and are followed by chapters on the constitution, the emperor, the Diet, political parties, the bureaucracy, the economy, law, and foreign relations.

768 Yoshida, Shigeru. *Japan's Decisive Century, 1867–1967.* New York: Praeger, 1967. v, 110p.

A personal account of major events and themes in modern Japanese history with considerable emphasis on postwar developments. Yoshida Shigeru, prime minister of Japan during much of the occupation era, includes a lengthy discussion of many of the economic and political problems that confronted a defeated Japan and some of the reforms that were undertaken by the Allied powers. He also appraises occupation policy, terming it an overall success, and notes how invaluable American aid was for Japan's recovery. Other accounts of the occupation are much more detailed than Yoshida's narrative, but his is extremely useful for anyone interested in understanding the views that influential Japanese leaders of the period had of MacArthur, the Allies, and the occupation reforms.

This book is a revised version of an article entitled "Japan's Decisive Century" which Yoshida originally wrote for and published in the 1967 volume of the *Britannica Book of the Year* (Chicago: William Benton, 1967), p.17–48.

769 ———. *The Yoshida Memoirs: The Story of Japan in Crisis*. Tr. by Yoshida Kenichi. Boston: Houghton Mifflin, 1962. vii, 305p. German-language translation by Kurt Reis published under the title *Japan im Wiederaufsteig: Die Yoshida-Memoiren*. Düsseldorf: E. Diederiches, 1963. 283p.

The career diplomat who came to lead Japan first as foreign minister and later as prime minister during most of the turbulent postwar occupation period describes his diplomatic and political experiences and political developments in Japan from the 1930s to the mid-1950s. The work is invaluable for understanding a Japanese evaluation of the occupation and postwar Japanese developments. Beginning with his personal account of the growth of Japanese expansionist policies in the 1930s, Yoshida describes his role as ambassador to Great Britain from 1936 to 1939 and his acquaintance with such prominent persons as Prince Konoe, General Anami, and Ambassadors Sir Robert Craigie and Joseph Grew. He goes on to depict the beginnings of the occupation and to record his impressions of General MacArthur and his aides. He reviews his own contacts and negotiations with SCAP and comments on the occupation reform programs with particular reference to constitutional revision, the purge, educational reform, police reform, the self-defense forces, and agricultural and labor reforms. There is a critical discussion of SCAP's policy on the *zaibatsu* and labor and left-wing groups which he regards as having culminated in the rapid growth of Communist forces. However, the author stresses his respect for MacArthur. He considers the occupation as having been successful because occupation aims were identical to those of the Japanese government.

The former prime minister also gives his views on food shortage problems, the peace treaty negotiations, Japan's territorial problems, and the postoccupation Security Treaty between Japan and the United States and the concurrent Administrative Agreement. He comments on the San Francisco peace treaty and describes his visits to major Western capitals in 1954. In a postscript he analyzes the occupation in relation to Japan's political turmoil in 1960. It is a much condensed and substantially edited translation of the author's original 4-volume *Kaisō jūnen* (Reminiscences of Ten Years) (Tokyo: Shinchōsha, 1957–58).

International Aspects

Although primarily an American operation in terms of both its planning and execution, the occupation of Japan also had international aspects of major importance. They may be viewed either externally from the standpoint of the occupation as an aspect of U.S. or other overall national foreign policies or internally in terms of the extent and form of non-American participation in the planning and administration of the occupation. In the two following subsections we intend to treat the literature relating to both of these categories.

Foreign Policies of the United States and Other Nations

From both the official and unofficial American standpoints there was at the outset a notable tendency to regard the occupation of Japan in relatively isolated and self-contained terms. It was seen not so much as an element in U.S. global or regional foreign policy or strategy but as a remote and somewhat exotic exercise in the demilitarization and subsequent democratization of a recent and still potentially dangerous enemy state. This view was, of course, an artifact of our persistent Eurocentrism. Our eyes then, as usual, were focused on western and central Europe and particularly on Russian activities in those areas. It was only with the advent of the cold war and its gradual expansion to Pacific Asia that the government of the United States began seriously to examine the strategic realities of the situation in the western Pacific and, against this background, to reassess the potential roles that Japan could play. The eventual result was, of course, a reversal of the national attitudes and policy toward Japan. Given the importance of the episode, the surprising thing is the paucity of the relevant literature.

One has the impression that the other major powers—less engrossed than was the United States in the particularities of the occupation—were much more apt to view the situation and role of postwar Japan in the larger rather than the narrower context. The literature reflects this view.

Although this external view of Japan's potentially larger role in the international relations of eastern Asia was constantly present in some quarters at least, the issues and viewpoints tended to be more salient at some times than at others. They were especially so at the beginning and end of the occupation period and in 1948 when the United States' policies were undergoing a decisive shift from looking upon Japan as a defeated and still possibly dangerous enemy to viewing the country as a potential ally. Readers interested in this subject are referred, therefore, to the section on planning elsewhere (p.71), to the entire category providing a calendar of general commentaries, 1945–72 (p.152), and, in particular, to items listed for the years 1945, 1948, 1951, and 1952, and to the section on the economy 1948 (p.490). Items set forth in the sections on the termination of the occupation (p.727) and on the security treaty and Japanese rearmament are also relevant in many instances. Many of the articles in the following section, on international participation (p.281), relate to the subject matter of this section as well.

770 Ashida, Hitoshi. "Japan: Communists' Temptation." *Contemporary Japan* 20:15–24 (Jan./Mar. 1951)

In this article a member of the House of Representatives in Japan and a former premier discusses the Communists' threat to Japan, outlining his views on the proportions of and reasons for this threat and suggesting necessary steps to effectively deal with it. He studies America's policy of "a balance of power" and maintains that the Communists' activity in Korea is a first step toward driving the United States out of Japan and the western Pacific. The author also examines the importance of Japan's geographic position in terms of the struggle between America and the Communist powers. Ashida views a country with no self-defense as an irresistible temptation for an invader and states that even though Japan at present has no choice but to depend on the occupation forces, "even powerful America will not be able to devote sufficient attention to the defence of Japan, should a third World War break out." The problem, then, he maintains, is whether the Japanese constitution permits self-defense. He points out why he feels Article 9 of the constitution does not mean abandonment of the right of self-defense. He concludes his examination of the self-defense problem by asserting that the key to this problem is men rather than arms, money, or constitutional right.

770a Atcheson, George, Jr. "American Attitudes on Allied Occupation of Japan." *Department of State Bulletin* 16: 596–98 (30 Mar. 1947)

This article contains the substance of remarks which the U.S. representative to the Allied Council for Japan made at the council's regular meeting on 19 March 1947. During a recent trip to the United States, Atcheson found that many high officials and ordinary citizens expressed considerable interest in the occupation in spite of the fact that there was less press coverage of developments in Japan than he would have preferred. The American people, he states, are not vengeful; they are impressed by the cooperative spirit of the Japanese, sympathetic to Japan's current problems, and pleased with her progress towards democracy.

771 "Australia Watches Japan." *New Statesman and Nation* 36:518–19 (11 Dec. 1948)

The correspondent reports that the Australian government is dissatisfied with American occupation policies, which are perceived as favoring a rapid reconstitution of Japanese political and economic potential as an anti-Russian measure. He indicates that in Australia, fear of Japan outweighs fear of Russia.

772 Australian Institute of International Affairs. A Study Group. *Australia's Interests and Policies in Regard to Problems of Economic and Social Reconstruction in the Pacific*. Mimeographed. Sydney: The Institute, 1947. 62p. (Institute of Pacific Relations, 10th conference, Australian paper no.2, 1947)

The areas of Japan, China, Southeast Asia, and Papua and New Guinea are examined in their relation to Australian policy in the 4 chapters of this paper. The first chapter, entitled "Australian Policy towards Japan," contributed by N. D. Harper, is a discussion of Australia's prewar, wartime, and postwar policies toward Japan. Harper observed that, although Australian interests in the prewar Far East—primarily in economics and security—were substantial and were usually promoted by trade with Japan, her security interests were threatened by Japan's emergence as a Pacific power. He contends that Australia's postwar policy toward Japan was strongly influenced by memories of Japanese aggression in the southwest Pacific and by changes in the Australian outlook on world affairs. This postwar policy toward Japan favors the "total elimination" of Japanese militarism. Although Harper calls for the revival of a stable Japanese economy as a contributing factor to a political power balance in the Pacific, he supports the Australian government in its disagreement with SCAP regarding policies that favor granting permission to Japan to resume external trade and the withdrawal of American troops from Japan in the near future.

Ball, William Macmahon. *Japan, Enemy or Ally?* 1949. See no.535.

773 ———. *Notes on Nationalism and Communism in the Far East*. New York: Institute of Pacific Relations, International Secretariat, 1950. 41p. (Institute of Pacific Relations, 11th conference, secretariat paper no.7, 1950)

A professor of political science at Melbourne University and former British Commonwealth representative on the Allied Council for Japan discusses the political situation in the postwar Far East, with special emphasis on Japan, China, Malaya, and Indonesia. After noting that the East Asian scene after World War II represents a complex mingling of 3 social forces, namely, anticolonialism, the struggle against poverty, and anti-Western influence, Ball describes economic conditions, the origins of social revolutionary activities in Asia before Communist inroads, and prospects for Asian unity. In reference to Japan, he states that although the Japanese have been politically and socially reformed and reoriented under the Allied occupation, it is difficult to tell whether changed Japanese political behavior is "a discreet and tactical submission to the exigencies of the Occupation" or a sincere response to new national circumstances. He contends that if China is ruled by the Communists, it will exert a strong influence on political movements in Japan.

774 Ballantine, Joseph W. "The Far East." In *A Foreign Policy for the United States*, ed. by Quincy Wright. Chicago: Univ. of Chicago Pr., 1947. p.129–38. Together with "Discussion of the Far East." p.139–61.

Ballantine's paper presents the objectives of American foreign policy in Asia now that the United States has come to bear "a major responsibility for establishing and maintaining peace, order, and stability in the Pacific area." In the course of his presentation, Ballantine briefly describes in generally favorable terms the goals and activities of the occupation and notes that the Japanese have shown a remarkable willingness to cooperate with SCAP in making "a good start . . . toward the achievement of American political and military objectives." At the same time, however, he warns that without "wise and sympathetic guidance," the Japanese may revert to their old ways or convert to communism.

Japan was the major topic of the discussion that followed Ballantine's talk. The discussants included several university professors and other students of Asian and international affairs as well as the author himself. A broad range of topics was covered including the length of the occupation, the quality of the Japanese political leadership, difficulties facing SCAP's democratization program, and the need for rehabilitating the Japanese economy.

775 Beloff, Max. *Soviet Far Eastern Policy since Yalta*. New York: Institute of Pacific Relations, International Secretariat, 1950. 34p. (Institute of Pacific Relations, 11th Conference, secretariat paper no.2, 1950)

Beloff surveys the development of Soviet foreign policy toward the Far East from early 1945 through June 1950. He examines the background of the Yalta Agreement of 11 February 1945 and the Soviet efforts in August 1945 to participate equally in the occupation of Japan. The tensions which developed from 1948 to 1950 between Moscow and the Japan Communist party, between Moscow and Washington over Allied policy toward Japan, and between SCAP and the Japanese Communists are described. Beloff notes that after the war the Soviets quickly abandoned their wartime policy of cooperation with the United States and adopted the concept of "two battling worlds." Russian moves in Korea, events in Manchuria, the Communist success in mainland China, the Soviet–Chinese agreements of 1950, and the Soviet position in Southeast Asia are discussed, as are Russian disputes with the West over European problems and the relation of these disputes to Russian actions in the Far East.

776 ———. *Soviet Policy in the Far East, 1944–1951*. London: Oxford Univ. Pr., 1953. viii, 278p.

A balanced appraisal of Soviet policy in East and Southeast Asia from the Yalta Conference in February 1945, when Russia agreed to enter the war against Japan, to the San Francisco Peace Conference in September 1951. Warning that Soviet policies cannot be understood simply by knowledge of the ideological position that Moscow professes, the author examines the development of Soviet policy toward China, Japan, and Korea by inquiring into domestic conditions in Asia as well as into Russian relations with various Western governments. The chapter on Soviet policy toward Southeast Asia is written by Joseph Frankel. In chapter 6, which deals with Soviet policy toward Japan, the author covers such subjects as the Soviet move to denounce the Russo–Japanese neutrality pact, the attitudes of the Russian participants at the Potsdam Conference toward atomic bombs, Russian reactions to Japan's move to end the war, the Soviet opposition to the Far Eastern Advisory Commission, its views and actions in the Far Eastern Commission and the Allied Council for Japan, the Soviet criticism of SCAP reform programs, and Russian connections with the Japan Communist party. There is a good discussion of Moscow's attitudes and actions on the question of a peace treaty with Japan. The author believes that the Soviet Union

777 The Occupation

lacked a firm policy toward occupied Japan and a peace treaty with Japan. The book has been translated into Japanese under the title *Sovieto no Ajia seisaku* (Tokyo: Nihon Gaisei Gakkai, 1957. 454p.).

Butler, Sir Paul. "Satellite Japan." 1947. See no.1464a.

Byrnes, James F. *All in One Lifetime.* 1958. See no.206.

———. *Speaking Frankly.* 1947. See no.207.

777 Cheng, Peter Ping-chii. *A Study of John Foster Dulles' Diplomatic Strategy in the Far East.* Ph.D. dissertation, Univ. of Southern Illinois, 1964. 674p. (Abstracted in *Dissertation Abstracts* 25:6043 [1965]; University Microfilms order no. 65–1320)

John Foster Dulles' general principles, policies in the Far East, and strategy in 4 major Far Eastern crises—Korea, Quemoy, Japan, and Indochina—are examined here, as are opinions expressed among his critics and supporters from 1950 to 1959. According to Cheng, Dulles' major contributions to American Far Eastern policy include support for the extension of the policy of military containment to the Far East and his commitment to peaceful means of uniting divided nations in the Far East.

Clune, Frank. *Ashes of Hiroshima: A Post-war Trip to Japan and China.* 1950. See no.545.

778 "Consolation Prize in Japan?" *Economist* 157:439–40 (27 Aug. 1949)

The occupation of Japan is discussed in relation to the drastically changing international situation, particularly in China. This change in the international sphere is viewed as responsible for the basic change in Allied policy in occupied Japan. The American troops are viewed not only as policing the Japanese but also protecting them from outside invasion. The author questions the willingness of the Japanese to ally themselves with the Americans but concludes that, in the eyes of the Japanese, American power is nearly undefeatable. This notion plus the strong indigenous anti-Communist feeling in Japan makes it reasonable to assume that a future military alliance would have real support in Japan and that the Japanese "may be counted as willing supporters of policies designed to preserve their country from Communist conquest."

779 Council on Foreign Relations. "The World at the Crossroads: 3. East Asia on the Eve." In *The United States in World Affairs 1950.* New York: Harper, published for the Council, 1951. p.174–89.

In this discussion concerning the success with which communism was spreading in East Asia, Japan is cited as a strongpoint in the United States' defense system. Attempts by the Soviets and by Japanese Communists to hinder the implementation of occupation policies are noted. The possibility of concluding a peace treaty without participation by the Soviet Union and Mainland China is considered, as is the possibility of Japanese rearmament.

780 Dallin, David J. *Soviet Russia and the Far East.* New Haven, Conn.: Yale Univ. Pr., 1948. ix, 398p.

A general introductory survey of the Soviet Union's policies toward the Far East and its relations with China, Korea, and Outer Mongolia. The period covered is from the 1930s, when Russia attempted to appease a militant Japan, through early 1948. The author presents a picture of Soviet efforts to extend the Russian sphere of influence southward. The Yalta and Potsdam Conferences and subsequent Russian participation in the war against Japan are described in chapter 11 while Soviet policies toward postwar Japan are treated in chapter 14. A Japanese translation has appeared under the title of *Soren to Kyokutō* (Tokyo: Hōsei Daigaku Shuppankyoku, 1950. 2v.).

781 Daoust, George Arlington, Jr. *The Role of Air Power in U.S. Foreign Policy in the Far East, 1945–1958.* Ph.D. dissertation, Georgetown Univ., 1967. 235p. (Abstracted in *Dissertation Abstracts* 28:

3243A–44A [1968]; University Microfilms order no.68–1901)

The extent to which postwar American foreign policy-makers place reliance on the use of air and sea power and on the atomic bomb as means of controlling the vast expanses of ocean in the Far East is examined here. Daoust discusses the policy of massive retaliation enunciated in 1954 and concludes that when air power does not fulfill its role as a deterrent, the commitment of ground forces is the only viable alternative to massive retaliation. He bases his conclusion on observations made during the 3 postwar crises in the Far East—Korea (1950–53), Indochina (1954), and Taiwan (1958).

782 Deverall, Richard L. G. *Red Star over Japan*. Calcutta: 1952. 352p.

Deverall, onetime chief of Labor Education on General MacArthur's staff, presents a documented, geopolitical analysis of the position and role of the Soviet Union in Asia during the late 1940s and early 1950s. The primary purpose of the book is to provide an examination of the activities of Communist elements in Japan and in the USSR. Deverall regards postwar Soviet activity in Asia as a major threat to Western security, emphasizes the penetration of Communist forces into Japan, and warns of the dangers of Japan becoming a Soviet satellite.

783 Dooman, Eugene H. "A Letter to My Japanese Friends." *Contemporary Japan* 19:1–18 (Jan./Mar. 1950)

Dooman, who was an adviser on Far Eastern affairs at the Potsdam Conference in 1945, states that "the supreme interest of the United States in Japan is the common security." He comments on the feasibility of occupation efforts to create a democracy in Japan and notes reasons why Americans have difficulty understanding Japanese patterns of behavior. Dooman sees much the Japanese should cherish in their history and culture, even though they are remorseful about the war. The importance of political parties as a means toward political stability is discussed. After outlining American policy in the Far East, the author discusses its implications for Japan, particularly in terms of Soviet expansionism. The need for restoration of a viable Japanese economy and the value of encouraging Japan's trade with democratic countries are studied. The general tone of the article seems optimistic regarding what can be accomplished under the occupation and chances for Japan to create a "stabilizing power in East Asia."

784 Dulles, John Foster. "Japan and the Philippines." *Far Eastern Survey* 20:115 (13 June 1951)

This article contains excerpts from remarks by Ambassador John Foster Dulles before the Philippine Institute of Pacific Relations, Manila, 12 February 1951 and briefly explains the American view on reparations and the security question of the islands off the Asiatic mainland.

785 Dutt, Vidya Prakash. *India's Foreign Policy with Special Reference to Asia and the Pacific*. Mimeographed. New Delhi: Indian Council of World Affairs, 1950. 45p. (Institute of Pacific Relations, 11th conference, Indian paper no.2, 1950)

India's desire for peace and nonalignment is explained here as the author reviews the international situation in Asia. Topics examined include the impact of Sino–American tensions, the rise of Asian nationalism and anticolonialism, the need for economic reconstruction, overseas Indians, and recognition of Communist China. With reference to Japan, Dutt stresses the Indian government's support for "a speedy peace treaty which would allow her economic rehabilitation, political self-determination, and evacuation of occupation forces."

786 Evatt, Herbert Vere. *Australia in World Affairs*. Sidney: Angus & Robertson, 1946. xi, 213p.

A collection of 20 speeches, statements, radio addresses, and articles dating from early 1945 to mid-1946 made or written by Evatt, the Australian foreign minister. The collection conveys the

Australian political outlook, particularly relating to the issue of security in the Pacific. Of special interest are the author's statements on Japanese war criminals, Australian–American cooperation for peace and security in the Pacific, and his article entitled "Has the Menace of Japan been Removed?" The last is a reprint from the *New York Times Magazine* of 3 February 1946 (no.787).

787 ———. "Japan Is Still a Menace." *New York Times Magazine* p.10, 46 (3 Feb. 1946)

Evatt, writing as foreign minister of Australia, wants more power for the Far Eastern Commission. He believes that all nations who helped in Japan's defeat should have a voice in policy-making. He advocates a hard-line policy against Japan, going beyond complete demilitarization to the dismantling of all industries with possible military potential. He warns that the Japanese have not admitted defeat and fears they are still expansionists who are waiting for a chance to trick the West again.

788 Fairbank, John King, et al. *Next Step in Asia.* Cambridge, Mass.: Harvard Univ. Pr., 1949. v, 90p.

A collection of papers by 4 authorities on Asia developed from a symposium presented at the 1949 Harvard Summer School Conference on American Policy in the Far East and subsequently published in cooperation with the International Secretariat of the Institute of Pacific Affairs. The papers are: (1) "Communism in China and the New American Approach in Asia," by John K. Fairbank (Harvard Univ.); (2) "Problems of Economic Development in the Far East," by Harlan Cleveland (Economic Cooperation Administration); (3) "Japan and Korea as American Policy Problems," by Edwin O. Reischauer (Harvard Univ.); and (4) "The Asiatic Context of Our Far Eastern Economic Policy," by William L. Holland (Institute of Pacific Relations). All address themselves to the need of creating a new, integrated American foreign policy towards postwar Asia.

Reischauer's article is the only one among the 4 to focus on the occupation of Japan. In it he compares the U.S. occupation of Japan with that of South Korea, praising American planning and personnel in the former and attacking it in the latter. The American effort to democratize and transform Japan, he asserts, has gotten off to a good start. He is critical, however, of the American effort to proceed unilaterally, pointing out the risk involved in making the reform a vital test of American postwar foreign policy and of democracy. Reischauer also discusses the major reasons for the American success and the Japanese willingness to cooperate, and he concludes with an account of the reforms that have been undertaken and of the problems that must still be resolved.

789 Feis, Herbert. *Contest over Japan.* New York: Norton, 1967. 187p.

The occupation is viewed in this book as a contest between the United States and the USSR over Allied policy in Japan. A brief outline of U.S. relations with both Japan and the Soviet Union prior to the occupation is followed by a useful description and summation of relevant official texts such as the Cairo Declaration, the Yalta Agreement, and the Potsdam Declaration as well as various other diplomatic documents. Also included as appendixes are copies of the aforementioned documents and others, notably the demobilization directive, the U.S. Initial Post-Surrender Policy for Japan, and the Moscow Agreement.

The author, a modern historian who was a member of the Institute of Advanced Studies at Princeton from 1950 to 1963, drew on his own personal experience to write this account. After serving as an adviser in economic affairs for the State Department from 1931 to 1944, he worked as a special consultant to the secretary of war from 1944 to 1947. In narrative form he presents a description of the abortive London Conference in which the divergence between U.S. and Soviet government policies became manifest. The greater part of the book is then devoted to a description of diplomatic maneuverings after that time, particularly those associated with the Moscow negotiations. A summary account of the provisions agreed upon by the Moscow Conference is followed by a discussion of initial reactions in the United States, USSR, and Great Britain. The final chapter describes and assesses the operation in Japan of the Allied Council and the Far Eastern Commission. The author concludes that the council did nothing to produce cooperation or understanding between the United States and Russia, nor did it immunize Japan from the impact of the cold war. Both the council and the commission are seen as arenas where U.S. and Russian interests continually clashed, and the declining roles of these organizations in the face of the cold war are noted. An account of the San Francisco Peace Conference appears at the end of the book, followed by the conclusion that developments in U.S. and Russian relations with Japan since that time have validated American avowals that its policies were directed toward the emergence of a democratized, peaceful, and independent Japan.

790 Feraru, Arthur N. "Public Opinion Polls on Japan." *Far Eastern Survey* 19:101–3 (17 May 1950)

Detailing the results of public opinion polls on Japan, Feraru, a graduate student of international relations, points out that the majority of Americans approved of the handling of the Japanese occupation, stressing particularly the excellent leadership of General MacArthur.

791 "Foreign Minister's Statement on Japan." *China Magazine* 18:58–60 (July 1948)

In this short statement by the Nationalist Chinese minister of foreign affairs, Wang Shih-chieh, on 5 June 1948 the Chinese endorsement of the Potsdam Proclamation of 26 July 1945 concerning the state of the postwar Japanese economy and reparations is reaffirmed and the countenancing of any Japanese rearmament disavowed.

791a "The 'Fortune' Survey." *Fortune* 32: 303, 305–6+ (Dec. 1945)

This public opinion survey of American views by Elmo Roper includes a number of items concerning Japan in a series of questions on topics related to the war, the occupations of Japan and Germany, and future prospects for peace.

792 Gardner, D. H. *Canadian Interests and Policies in the Far East Since World War II*. Mimeographed. Toronto: Canadian Institute of International Affairs, 1950. 15p. (Institute of Pacific Relations, 11th conference, Canadian paper no.1, 1950)

Canadian policies toward the Far East are examined here in national interest terms. The author believes that Canada's foreign policy has been basically determined by her unique relationships with the United States, Great Britain, and the Commonwealth. However, Gardner stresses Canada's concern with Pacific security, citing her participation in the Far Eastern Commission, the Tokyo trial, and the dispatch of a Canadian reparations mission to Japan. The Canadian position is described as favorable to the development of a viable Japanese economy enabling Japan to become a trading partner, the transfer of islands formerly under Japanese mandate to United States' trusteeship, and the rapid conclusion of a peace treaty with Japan with or without the participation of Mainland China and the Soviet Union.

792a Gibson, Tony. "Chinese Students and America's Japan." *Eastern World* 2, no. 8/9:17–18 (Aug./Sept. 1948)

Gibson's topic is the evidently widespread opposition of Chinese students to the occupation's treatment of Japan. A group at St. John's University in Shanghai, for instance, asserts that the real goal of the United States in rebuilding Japan is to seize Far Eastern markets and military bases, and that the American-sponsored renewal of Japanese militarism will lead once again to war with China. Gibson finds that such sentiments are not confined to Shanghai, but have resulted in large student demonstrations and strikes elsewhere in China. These demonstrations, he observes, bode ill for the future of U.S.–China relations.

793 Greenwood, Gordon, ed. *Australian Policies toward Asia: Australian Papers, Institute of Pacific Relations Conference, 1954.* Melbourne: Australian Institute of International Affairs, 1954. 1v.

Seven Australian papers presented to the twelfth conference of the Institute of Pacific Relations at Kyoto in 1954. Two have particular relevance to the study of the occupation of Japan: "Australia and U.S. Pacific Policy, 1951–4," by N. D. Harper, a senior lecturer in history at the University of Melbourne, and "Australia's Relations with Japan since 1945," by W. Macmahon Ball and H. A. Wolfsohn, both political scientists at the University of Melbourne. Ball represented the British Commonwealth on the Allied Council for Japan in Tokyo. Discussing historical changes in the Australian assessment of the broad strategic picture in the Pacific, Harper reviews relations between Australia and the United States since 1942, when the former appealed for assistance in the wake of Japan's southward expansion. He notes that the first major Australian conflict with American Pacific policy arose over the postwar position of Japan and the terms of the Japanese peace treaty. The previous agreement between the 2 countries on occupation policy which culminated in the Far Eastern Commission's Basic Post-Surrender Policy for Japan of 19 June 1947 broke down as the United States made a reassessment of Far Eastern tensions and began to make Japan "the workshop of East Asia" against Communist threats. There is also a discussion of Australian concern over MacArthur's "unlimited" control over SCAP policies. The ANZUS (Australia, New Zealand, United States mutual security) pact is regarded as a *quid pro quo* for Australian acceptance of the peace treaty, which seemed to Australians "astoundingly lenient."

Ball and Wolfsohn in their paper review Australian relations with Japan in 3 periods: 1945–47, 1947–50, and 1951 and after. They describe the efforts of the Australian government in 1945–47 to become independent of British policy and to claim to be "a party principal" in decisions about postwar Japan and to press for Japanese reparations. They characterize Australia's attitude toward Japan in 1947–50 as one of "anxious and subdued compliance with American policy" due to rising Communist threats. The peace treaty debates, maintain the authors, represent the dilemma facing Australian policy as a result of Australia's opposition to Japan's rearmament on the one hand and its appreciation of the necessity for Japan's rearmament on the other. They hold that throughout the postwar period Australian policy toward Japan has been shaped mainly by fear of the revival of Japanese militarism.

794 Harper, Norman Delholm. "Australian Policy towards Japan." *Australian Outlook* 1, no.4:14–24 (Dec. 1947)

The postwar balance of military and economic power in the Pacific was modified by (1) the decline of British and Dutch influence, (2) the emergence of Russian influence, and (3) Chinese instability. The author feels that Australian security can be best insured by working through the British Commonwealth and encouraging a prosperous, peaceful Japan. It is feared that militarism may reappear in Japan as a result of American efforts to use Japan as a bulwark against communism. However, revival of Japanese trade and industry (at least light industry) is encouraged because a prosperous Japan will be more stable and a good trading partner for Australia.

Holman, D. S. "Japan's Position in the Economy of the Far East." 1947. See no.1127.

Hunt, Frazier. *The Untold Story of Douglas MacArthur.* 1954. See no.957.

795 "Japan: Costly Base for U.S." *U.S. News and World Report* 28:26–27 (17 Feb. 1950)

This brief report notes a change in American attitudes toward Japan with respect to the resumption of Japan–Mainland China trade. There is some indication that the Chinese market will be replaced by permanently increased U.S.–Japan trade. The article also discusses reports of an alleged U.S. attempt to secure permanent air bases at Itazuke, Yokota, and Misawa, a naval base at Yokosuka, and headquarters for 75,000 troops at Yokohama. These attempts are said to be part of an American plan to maintain Japan as its outer defense line in case of a Soviet attack. The reactions of Japanese to these reports are also presented.

796 "Japan Could Arm Millions, but Is Her Price Too High?" *U.S. News and World Report* 29:22 (15 Dec. 1950)

This report discusses reasons for the American interest in rearming a sizable Japanese army for the support of the UN operations in Korea. The author states that Japan has the potential to supply and train 200,000 troops and that the old army command could be rapidly reactivated. Two problems associated with such a policy, however, are that the raw materials to sustain a remilitarized Japanese economy are not readily available and that the constitution and adverse public opinion might make such an action impossible.

797 " 'Japanese Comeback'." *Economist* 157:595–96 (17 Sept. 1949)

After defining current American policy in Japan as "the restoration of Japan to the status of a friendly nation and the utmost expansion of Japanese industry and trade," the author of this article outlines the objections of the nations of the Far Eastern Commission to this policy. He summarizes the positions of the Philippines and Australia and the more complex one of Great Britain, wherein the economic and political reactions are at odds with one another. In order to allay any mistrust of a revived and independent Japan he suggests that an American and Commonwealth base be maintained in Japan after the termination of the occupation.

798 Kawai, Kazuo. "Japan: A Focal Point in the Cold War." *World Affairs Interpreter* 21:246–64 (Oct. 1950)

The author analyzes the occupation goal of making Japan a bulwark against communism. Although the health of the Japanese people is better and new construction is progressing rapidly, the economy is still sick, and the Communist party—though weakened—remains a threat. He foresees the possibility of many people jumping the gap from fascism to communism in a search for a panacea. Though Secretary of State Acheson promised the military protection of Asia, he sees this as ineffective in forestalling the advance of communism and predicts the imminent demise of Formosa.

799 Keeton, George W. "Peace-Making with Japan." *World Affairs* (London) 2:337–43 (Oct. 1948)

Focusing his attention on Sino–Japanese relations, the author—principal of the London Institute of World Affairs—speculates how a reconstructed Japan could be a threat to China. He compares Japan with postwar Germany and also touches upon the differences among the United States, the members of the British empire, and the Soviet Union over Allied occupation policies and the lack of a formal peace treaty with Japan.

800 Kennan, George Frost. *Memoirs, 1925–1950.* Boston: Little, Brown, 1967. 583p.

A record by a distinguished American diplomat of his own diplomatic career from 1925 to 1950. Largely based on his diaries, telegraphic dispatches, reports, and position papers, Kennan, an expert on Russian affairs, recounts his diplomatic experiences in major capitals of the world including Moscow, Prague, Berlin, Lisbon, Tokyo, and Washington. His thoughts on America's world policy are particularly enlightening. In chapter 16, entitled "Japan and MacArthur," the former ambassador to Moscow discusses American interests in postwar Europe and Asia and compares the American occupations of Germany and Japan. He refers in the latter case to conflicts among the State and War Departments and SCAP and reveals how, as chief of the State Department's Policy Planning Staff, he helped to bring about an important shift in American occupation policy toward Japan in late 1948 and 1949, i.e., from favoring a disarmed and neutral Japan to espousing an armed and pro-American Japan. He himself regards this achievement as "after the Marshall Plan, the most significant constructive contribution I was ever able to make in government." He describes his delicate mission to Japan in February 1948, when he met MacArthur and succeeded in reconciling the views of SCAP and the State Department regarding the timing of a peace treaty for Japan and the substance of such a treaty.

801 Krane, Jay B. "Polls, Press and Occupation Policy." *Columbia Journal of International Affairs* 2:71–75 (Winter 1948)

A brief examination of American attitudes toward the occupations in both Germany and Japan. The author considers 2 media of public opinion—polls and newspapers—and discusses popular attitudes as depicted by the results of Gallup and Fortune polls from 1945 through 1947 and by the amount of space devoted to Japan and Germany as shown in the Twohey weekly surveys of American newspaper editorial columns and front pages. He concludes that both types of surveys demonstrate a clear pattern of popular uncritical acceptance of occupation policies in Germany and, even more so, in Japan.

Kudryavtsev, V. "The Japanese Problem in Sino–American Relations." 1947. See no.1475.

802 Kurata, Seiji. "Die sowjetische Politik gegenüber Japan 1945–1954." *Osteuropa* 5, no.5:345–51 (Oct. 1955)

A study of postwar Soviet policy towards Japan. It includes a discussion of official views on the Allied occupation (including its actual organization and American programs for democratization, economic reform, and demilitarization), on the conclusion of a peace treaty with Japan, and on the nature of Soviet–Japanese relations following the occupation period.

803 Langer, Paul Fritz. "The Soviet Union and Japan." *Journal of International Affairs* 8, no.1:21–31 (1954)

Langer writes about the importance of Japan in the cold war maneuvering between the Soviet Union and the United States. He reviews the disagreements between both powers over the workings of the occupation and the way both powers have attempted to influence the Japanese political scene. He also analyzes the importance of Japan for both the United States and the Soviet Union.

804 Latourette, Kenneth Scott. *The American Record in the Far East, 1945–1951.* New York: Macmillan, 1952. vi, 208p.

In this account of America's postwar Asian policy written on behalf of the American Institute of Pacific Relations, Latourette, professor of history at Yale University, discusses both the major principles by which the United States governed its policies in East, South, and Southeast Asia during the immediate postwar period and their application in the various parts of Asia. Chapter 9 (p.139–70), entitled "The Record in Japan," presents a general summary of the motivations underlying American policy in Japan, the problems faced in rebuilding that country, and the accomplishments of the occupation authorities in a wide range of activities.

805 Lattimore, Owen. "Japan Is Nobody's Ally." *Atlantic Monthly* 183:54–58 (Apr. 1949)

Drawn from the author's book, *The Situation in Asia* (1949) (no.806), this article is divided into 4 sections and examines American policy in Japan. Lattimore believes that this policy "is based on the assumption that as Japan goes, so can Asia be made to go." In section 1 he maintains that there is a dangerous fallacy in the American assumption that Japan can be made the workshop of Asia and a bulwark against Russia. In the analysis of the occupation in section 2, there is a distinction drawn between the initial period when some democratic reforms were initiated and the latter period which reflected the preoccupations of the Eightieth Congress and catered to American business. The 2 final sections are concerned with our future policy in Japan, and the author warns that "a Japan made strong enough by American subsidy to hold an economic ascendancy over the rest of Asia, and strong enough to be an American ally against Russia if it wants to be, is automatically a Japan strong enough to doublecross America and make its own deals both with Russia and with the rest of Asia." He insists that Americans should not make Japan "or any other single country" the primary instrument of American policy nor can the United States singlehandedly make Japan the workshop of Asia.

806 ———. *The Situation in Asia.* Boston: Little, Brown, 1949. 244p.

Following a review of the recent history of Asia, the postwar situation is analyzed as a product of 2 forces—nationalism and revolution. The effects of these forces on Russia, Japan, and China are described and related to prescriptions for American policy in Asia. The author, a geographer and historian, served as editor of *Pacific Affairs* from 1934 to 1941 and lectured at Johns Hopkins University from 1938 to 1963. He was deputy director of Pacific Operations for the Office of War Information from 1942 to 1944 and served as a member of the reparations mission to Japan in 1945 and 1946.

Japan is dealt with directly only in chapter 6, "Japan Is Nobody's Ally" (no. 805). The author assumes that Japan will follow Asia, not vice versa, and he doubts that Japan can be made into a politically reliable bulwark against Russia. He criticizes the U.S. goal of making Japan a strong ally and prescribes policies which would allow Japan more independence in its foreign affairs. He does not address himself specifically to occupation policies and programs but advocates an internationally accepted peace treaty and quick end to the occupation, closure of U.S. bases in Japan and Korea, and adjustment of American relations with Russia and independent "third countries."

This book was translated into Japanese under the title *Ajia no jōsei* (Tokyo: Nihon Hyōronsha, 1950. 271p.).

807 Leathem, Samuel. *New Zealand's Interests and Policies in the Far East.* Wellington: New Zealand Institute of International Affairs, 1950. 24p. (Institute of Pacific Relations, 11th conference, New Zealand paper no.1, 1950)

New Zealand's policies toward countries in East and Southeast Asia from 1945 to 1950 and her responses to significant events in these regions are described here. After briefly reviewing general political developments in Asia during the postwar period, Leathem, a research secretary of the New Zealand Institute of International Affairs, explains some of the reasoning behind the Pacific Pact proposed by Foreign Minister F. W. Doidges of New Zealand. It was supported by Parliament but denounced by some extraparliamentary groups including the Communist party. The paper emphasizes New Zealand's fear of a resurgence of Japanese military power. Both New Zealand and Australia demand the inclusion of effective security provisions in any peace treaty with Japan. Both are also concerned over MacArthur's tendency to side with the more conservative political groups in Japan.

808 Lee, Jin Won. "Brief Survey of Korean–Japanese Relations (Postwar Period)." *Koreana Quarterly* 1, no.1:64–85 (1959)

A member of St. Anthony's College at Oxford University, England, Lee provides a picture of the postwar Japanese attitude toward Korea through a survey of the conditions of the Korean minority in postwar Japan, the problem of the "peace line" between Japan and Korea, and the question of property claims and rights involving both the Japanese and Korean governments.

809 Leng, Shao-chuan. *Japan and Communist China*. Kyoto: Doshisha Univ. Pr., 1958. ii, ii, ii, 166p.

810 Levi, Werner. *Australia's Outlook on Asia*. East Lansing: Michigan State Univ. Pr., 1958. v, 246p.

In this work a political scientist traces postwar changes in Australian attitudes and policies toward the countries of East, South, and Southeast Asia. His study is analytical rather than descriptive, examining the psychological background of Australians in their reactions to Asian affairs. Australian concern with stability and security in the western Pacific is given special attention. Of interest to the study of occupied Japan is chapter 10, entitled "Japan, Friend or Foe?" in which Levi succinctly reviews Australian–Japanese relationships from 1945 through 1957. He indicates that Australia became critical of Great Britain in 1945 for not arranging for Australia to play an appropriate role in the control of Japan. As a result, Great Britain had Australia represent the British Commonwealth on the Allied Council for Japan. The author also notes differences which arose between Australia and the United States even before Japan's surrender on the formula for the control of postwar Japan. Involved were Australia's demand for the dethronement and trial of the emperor, the abolition of the *zaibatsu*, and a radical democratization of the social structure. After Japan's surrender Australia was also opposed to the Council of Foreign Ministers' handling of Japanese problems and to the Big Power veto in the Far Eastern Commission and the Allied Council for Japan. Levi also notes the growing dissatisfaction by Australians with occupation decisions made "high-handedly" by the United States and willingly followed by the Japanese government. Japanese whaling expeditions to the Antarctic and the disposal of Japanese territories are cited as examples. The diplomacy among the Allies, particularly Australia and the United States, with respect to the conclusion of a peace treaty with Japan is also discussed.

Lin, Hu. "How to Deal with Japan." 1946. See no.439.

811 Lippmann, Walter. *Commentaries on American Far Eastern Policy*. Mimeographed. New York: American Institute of Pacific Relations, 1950. 65p. (Institute of Pacific Relations, 11th conference, U.S. paper no.3, 1950)

Thirty-two articles which first appeared in Lippmann's newspaper column, "Today and Tomorrow," in the *New York Herald Tribune* are compiled here. These articles, which appeared between 6 September 1949 and 10 August 1950, are discussions of American diplomacy in Asia, relations with Russia, and security in the Pacific. Approximately half are concerned with the Korean War. There are 4 selections concerning American relations with Japan: "The Japanese Conundrum" (23 May 1950); "The American Commitment in Japan" (12 June 1950); "After Japan What Then?" (13 June 1950); and "Korea and Japan" (27 June 1950). The major theme of all 4 is a contention that the Russian possession of the atomic bomb and the power of the Communists in China have shaken the balance of power in East Asia, causing disagreements within the American government regarding the timing of a peace treaty with Japan, and have necessitated a revision in American thinking concerning the withdrawal of American military forces from Japan following the conclusion of a peace treaty. Lippmann notes that the Korean incident strongly argues against the complete and permanent disarmament of Japan.

812 Liu, James T. C. "Resurgent Japan: A Chinese View." *Far Eastern Survey* 17:269–71 (8 Dec. 1948)

An article discussing the occupation reforms from the Chinese point of view and expressing a growing dissatisfaction in China that the author claims is paralleled in Australia, the Philippines, and India. He cites specific political, economic, and military aspects of the occupation which dismay the Chinese, including the preservation of the emperor system as a rallying point of the *zaibatsu*, the catering to landlord and bureaucratic interests, the revival of a large Japanese police force supplied with American surplus arms, and the revival of the Japanese steel and chemical industries. He suggests that the United States may secure Japanese friendship at the price of alienating China.

813 McClurkin, Robert J. G. "Relations between Japan and the United States." *Annals of the American Academy of Political and Social Science* 294:14–22 (July 1954)

While not focusing on the occupation period, the author—acting director of the Office of Northeast Asian Affairs of the U.S. State Department—constantly refers to the occupation throughout this article. He notes that relations between the 2 countries now rest upon (1) a set of psychological and emotional ties resulting from hundreds of thousands of individual contacts between Americans and Japanese during the occupation; (2) their common national interests (among them a common recognition of the danger of international communism); and (3) their economic links with each other. He also comments briefly on existing treaties and agreements between Japan and the United States that incorporate many of the understandings which are essential to the continuation of amicable relations between the two.

814 McDonald, William J. "Some Legal Aspects of Recent United States–Japanese Relations." *Politeia* 4, no.2/3:180–88 (1952)

The author argues on philosophical and religious grounds for a moralistic approach to the problems of state. He uses the recent relations between Japan and the United States as an example of "the perennial necessity, especially in times of emergency and crisis, of some kind of return to natural law concepts."

815 Morley, James William. *Soviet and Communist Chinese Policies toward Japan, 1950–1957: a Comparison.* New York: Institute of Pacific Relations, International Secretariat, 1958. 46p. (Institute of Pacific Relations, 13th conference, secretariat paper no.3, 1958)

Morley of the East Asian Institute, Columbia University, notes that from 1950 until the summer of 1954, the Russians and the Communist Chinese developed and maintained a strikingly common front in their policies toward Japan. This unanimity extended to their propaganda attacks on the conservative leadership of Japan and on American activities there, as well as their attempts to win friends among the Japanese people.

Murphy, Robert D. *Diplomat among Warriors.* 1964. *See* no.733.

816 Natarajan, L. *From Hiroshima to Bandung: A Survey of American Policies in Asia.* New Delhi: People's Publishing House, 1955. 175p.

The Indian author analyzes American policies in Asia from the time of the Japanese surrender through the Asian–African Conference in Bandung, Indonesia in 1955. Critical of American efforts to establish military predominance in Asia, he holds that India and China have the historic task of forging an alliance for peace in Asia by persuading the United States to withdraw its military forces and bases from Okinawa, Formosa, Korea, and Japan. In chapter 3, "Atomic Diplomacy," the author claims that as the Allied Council for Japan was shown to be ineffective, American occupation policy moved further away from its professed aims of democratization and demilitarization. The suppression of mass demonstrations by American troops, press censorship, depressed economic conditions, and the construction of strong military bases by American occupation forces draw strong criticism. The author bases his comments on American correspondents' reports in such leading newspapers as the *New York Times*, *New York Herald Tribune*, and the *Christian Science Monitor*. A Japanese version of this work has been published as *Hiroshima kara Bandon e* (Tokyo: Iwanami Shoten, 1956. 246p.).

817 New Zealand. Institute of International Affairs. *New Zealand and the Pacific*. Mimeographed. Auckland: The Institute, 1947. 45p. (Institute of Pacific Relations, 10th conference, New Zealand paper no.1, 1947)

This paper consists of 3 monographs: "New Zealand and Security in the Pacific," by Willis Airey; "Trusteeship and New Zealand's Pacific Dependencies," by Ernest Beaglehole; and "New Zealand's Economic Interest in the Far Eastern Settlements," by C. G. F. Similin. Only Airey includes some discussion regarding the future of Japan. He reviews New Zealand's relations with Great Britain and her prewar support of the League of Nations. It is his contention that the future of Japan is crucially linked to the future security of all nations in the Pacific and that New Zealand must have some voice in the formation of Allied policy toward Japan to guarantee her future national security. He points out that some groups in New Zealand fear that a predominant American influence in Japan may help permit the survival of reactionary Japanese elements and that these groups have suggested the negotiation of a peace treaty as soon as possible and the transfer of control of the occupation to the United Nations.

818 Noble, Harold J. "Russians Are Very Busy in Japan." *Saturday Evening Post* 219:14–15, 115–20 (23 Nov. 1946)

Noble, a *Post* correspondent, describes the strategic interest of the Russians in Japan and their links with the emerging Japan Communist party. Their program has 4 integral parts. First, they strive for every possible weakening of Japanese economic capacity. Second, they try to obstruct the American occupation program and to undermine American prestige. Third, they do all they can to develop the Japan Communist party as an agitating agency. Fourth, they engage in espionage activities to learn all they can of the American forces. He states that if we deny the Japanese a role in world trade, we will foster unemployment, hunger, and a dangerous mixture of nationalism and communism.

819 Olver, A. S. B. *Outline of British Policy in East and Southeast Asia, 1945–May 1950*. London: Royal Institute of International Affairs, 1950. 83p. (Institute of Pacific Relations, 11th conference, United Kingdom paper no.1, 1950)

A research secretary of the Royal Institute of International Affairs describes British policy toward Asia. In chapter 2, which deals with British interests in Japan, Olver notes that Britain's primary postwar interest in Japan, other than a general desire to see the country democratized and disarmed, revolves around economic concerns. He states that, although the United Kingdom has little effective control of the occupation of Japan, it supports most of the policies and actions of SCAP. Reference is made to the conflict in Britain between the desire of the government to allow Japan's revived economy to aid in the reconstruction of Southeast Asia and the fear among British textile industries that unfair Japanese competitive techniques will be employed in this region. Britain's opposition to any restrictions on Japan's external trade and merchant shipping is also discussed.

820 Onoe, Masao. "Postwar Relations between Japan and the Soviet Union." *Review* (Tokyo) no.4:17–39 (May 1965)

In reviewing the political aspects of postwar Russo–Japanese relations, Onoe of Kobe University examines the territorial issues, the problems of Japan's national security, and the Soviet intention to neutralize Japan. He discusses the Soviet refusal to sign the San Francisco peace treaty and its subsequent effect on ties between the 2 countries.

821 "Our Ex-enemy." *China Magazine* 17:1–4 (Sept. 1947)

This expression of Nationalist Chinese sentiment against a rejuvenated Japan, while reflecting a highly bipolarized view of the world, calls for the formulation of American policies for Japan on the basis of historical rather than immediate strategic considerations. It rejects the American notion of building a strong Japan to counter an increasingly belligerent USSR.

822 "Peace and Protection for Ex-enemy." *Newsweek* 35:23–27 (20 Feb. 1950)

Newsweek reports on the changes in occupation policy resulting from a re-evaluation of American foreign policy goals in Asia which were expanded to include the prevention of the spread of communism, the use of nationalism to counter communism, and an attempt to alienate Communist China from Russia. In this context plans for rapid settlement of a peace treaty are noted as is the possibility of a separate bilateral treaty allowing the permanent installation of American military bases in Japan. Importance is attached to the creation of a strong, centralized police force to control internal Communist activity.

"Plans for a Stronger Japan." 1948. See no.1509.

823 "Protest of Representatives of Chinese Public Opinion against American Policies in Japan." *Soviet Press Translations* 3: 419–20 (15 July 1948)

An article which appeared in *Pravda* on 12 July 1948 and which summarizes a statement made by 282 Chinese professors, economists, newspaper editors, and others that was published in the Shanghai newspaper, *Ta Kung Pao*, on 11 June 1948. It is strongly critical of what the authors term American aid and encouragement in the rearmament of Japan. They cite various steps that have been taken such as the reinforcement of Japan's great naval bases at Yokosuka and Sasebo, the procurement of minelayers and submarines, and the retention of much presurrender military equipment. In the Russian article the Chinese writers are said to believe that the American development of renewed Japanese war potential is in preparation for a future U.S.–Japanese military alliance. In addition, mention is made of the persecution that Chinese residents in Japan are being subjected to without SCAP objection. Finally, the authors urge vigorous resistance to the revival of a militarist Japan.

Reischauer, Edwin O., et al. *Japan and America Today*. 1953. See no.2532.

824 Reitzel, William, Morton A. Kaplan, and Constance G. Coblenz. *United States Foreign Policy 1945–1955*. Washington, D.C.: Brookings Institution, 1956. 535p.

Postwar American foreign policy goals and decisions are examined here vis-à-vis the developing cold-war environment and the American desire to achieve worldwide containment of communism. Chapter 9 is a discussion of the organization and policies of the occupation and the changes made in these policies to meet basic security needs in East Asia. The occupation is characterized as an American venture in which authority is both concentrated and isolated. Leadership purges and *zaibatsu* liquidation are noted. The emphasis in 1948 on economic reorganization and revitalization is discussed in light of the financial burden imposed on the United States by the occupation. Soviet reluctance to participate in treaty negotiations after 1947 is explained, and the American desire to build a strong and friendly Japan is linked to the development of the threat of Soviet communism throughout the world.

825 "The Report Delivered by Ambassador George Atcheson, Jr., Chairman of the Allied Council for Japan at the Council Session, March 19, 1947." *Contemporary Japan* 16:110–13 (Jan./Mar. 1947); also in *Department of State Bulletin* 16: 596–98 (Mar. 1947)

At the suggestion of the supreme commander, Atcheson outlines to the Allied Council his observations during a recent visit to the United States as to the "general attitudes and opinions of American governmental officials and the American people in regard to the Allied Occupation of Japan." He describes the American government and its people as wholeheartedly in support of the occupation of Japan; even in discussing the recent threatened strike of government workers, the ambassador remarks that "opinion was unanimous in supporting General MacArthur's intervention and stoppage of the strike."

826 Romulo, Carlos P. "Our Fight against

Japan Has Just Begun." *New York Times Magazine* p.8, 46 (21 Oct. 1945)

Romulo, resident high commissioner of the Philippine Islands, believes that the Japanese will always remain a threat in the Pacific. He views their current meekness and politeness as a mask to fool the Allies. Behind this mask, he maintains, they are still spiritually arrogant and militaristic. Because the author believes that Westerners can never learn to deal adequately with the Japanese mind, he suggests that the Chinese be put in charge of the reeducation of the Japanese and take a leading part in the occupation.

827 Rosecrance, Richard Newton. *Australian Diplomacy and Japan, 1945–1951.* Parkville: Melbourne Univ. Pr., 1962. xv, 288p.

A stimulating study of Australian policy toward Japan in the postsurrender period. The author, a political scientist, presents carefully documented facts and balanced interpretations to describe postwar developments in Australia's efforts to ensure her security in the western Pacific in cooperation with the United States. The author claims that Australia's policy toward Japan underwent a drastic change in the 6 years after the war— from "a cathartic and enduring occupation of Japan" with total reformation of the nation to "a short, beneficent occupation" with the dilution of major economic and military reforms and the recreation of a Japanese war potential. There is a penetrating analysis of the Australian government's stands on various related issues based on the records of the Far Eastern Commission and the Allied Council for Japan. The author also analyzes the emergence of the ANZUS (Australia, New Zealand, United States mutual security) treaty in relation to a peace treaty with Japan and Australia's historical interest in a Pacific security pact. Australian national interests are well explained and Australian–American diplomatic maneuverings are closely examined. However, the author relies heavily on Australian and American sources of information and little on Japanese sources. This tends to simplify his presentations regarding developments within Japan and to overemphasize the effects of American–Australian relations on the San Francisco Peace Conference in September 1951. A useful bibliography is added, and the full text of the peace treaty with Japan is appended.

828 ———. *Australian Foreign Policy and the Problem of Japan: 1945–1951.* Ph.D. dissertation, Harvard Univ., 1957. ix, 429p.

This dissertation has been published under the title of *Australian Diplomacy in Japan, 1945–1951* (no.827).

829 Ryan, R. S. "Some Thoughts on Japan." *Australian Outlook* 3, no.1:62–69 (Mar. 1949)

The author criticizes the popular Australian desire to keep Japan down as both impossible and undesirable because Australia needs prosperity and stability in the western Pacific which in turn requires a prosperous and stable Japan. Japan is seen as basically primitive and feudal, overpopulated, poor in both natural and capital resources, but strong in its labor force. Because of SCAP demilitarization and democratization policies, the author is basically optimistic that Japan will not follow the example of post-World War I Germany, but still recommends that occupation or at least supervision of Japan should last 15 or 20 years.

830 Number not used.

831 Scheuer, Stewart. "Japan: The United States Redeemed." *Columbia Journal of International Affairs* 5, no.1:53–64 (Winter 1951)

This article by a graduate student who served in the occupation contrasts America's prewar and postwar Far Eastern policy as it related to Japan. China is seen as the crucial area of conflict of Japanese–American interests. The 1930s are termed the "climax of unreality in U.S. Far Eastern policy," whereas Japan's actions are seen as realistic in view of the economic pressures upon her. The occupation is viewed as an effort to urge the worldwide community to accord to Japan precisely the concessions for which she went to war.

832 Schwantes, Robert Sidney. *Japanese and Americans: A Century of Cultural Relations*. New York: Harper, published for the Council on Foreign Relations, 1955. x, 380p.

Published for the Council on Foreign Relations, this book is a fascinating survey of the cultural relations between Japan and the United States from Perry's arrival in Japan to the mid-1950s. The occupation is but part of the picture. Certain sections discuss it in some detail, for example, "Revolution by Directive: Occupation Reforms" (p.104–16) and "New Education for Japan?" (p.121–28). More frequently, though, it is mentioned only in passing where the author describes such matters as teacher exchange, student exchange, movies, music, and missionaries.

833 Scott, John Richard. *The Effect of the Cold War upon the Occupation of Japan*. Ph.D. dissertation, Univ. of Illinois, 1952. 368p. (Abstracted in *Dissertation Abstracts* 12:750 [1952]; University Microfilms order no.4012)

The effects of great power politics upon the occupation of Japan from the Japanese surrender to the San Francisco Peace Conference in 1951 are the subject of this thesis. Following an analysis of the relationships among the Big Powers prior to the Japanese surrender, topics such as the initial conflict among the Allies over the control of the occupation, the roles of the Allied Council for Japan and the Far Eastern Commission, and the criticism of America's unilateral approach to the occupation are examined. Scott notes that SCAP shifted its emphasis from reform to economic recovery as the cold war developed, and that cold war considerations were reflected in the negotiations concerning the restoration of Japan's sovereignty. He evaluates the San Francisco conference as primarily a product of the power struggle between the East and West camps.

834 Stuart, J. Leighton. "Campaign by Chinese Students against American Policy in Japan." *Department of State Bulletin* 18:813–14 (20 June 1948)

In an address to the Chinese people, the American ambassador to China defends American policy in occupied Japan. He deplores the agitation of Chinese student groups and claims this agitation "is seriously damaging the traditional cordiality between the United States and China." In the remaining sections of the article the ambassador argues against the Chinese charge that the Americans are fostering the restoration of Japanese militarism and economic imperialism and insists that Japanese economic recovery must be encouraged in order to avoid unrest and chaos throughout the country.

835 Tompkins, Pauline. *American–Russian Relations in the Far East*. New York: Macmillan, 1949. xiv, 426p.

The history of American–Russian rivalry and cooperation in East Asia is traced from the beginning of the nineteenth century. In chapter 14 their relations during World War II and immediately thereafter are discussed and their positions toward Japan noted. The abortive Far Eastern Advisory Commission and subsequent Far Eastern Commission and Allied Council, the American control of occupation policy, and the resultant Allied dissatisfaction are examined. The American decision to regard Japan as a potential ally is explained and is related to 4 other considerations: (1) increasing Soviet–American antagonism; (2) General MacArthur's paternalistic leadership and reliance on domestic conservatives; (3) the abandonment of reparations and the commitment to extensive reindustrialization; and (4) the postponement of a peace conference. The author notes the possibilities for a reemergence of nationalism and militarism.

836 Ulyanov, A. "The Second Anniversary of the Victory over Japan." *Soviet*

Press Translations 2, no.20:254–58 (1 Dec. 1947)

Essentially a statement of the thesis that Russian intervention in the Pacific War was the factor primarily responsible for the Allied victory over Japan. This was published originally in the 3 September 1947 issue of *Trud*.

U.S. Dept. of State. Bureau of Public Affairs. Historical Office. *Foreign Relations of the United States. Diplomatic Papers, 1945*. 1967. See no.887.

837 ———. ———. Office of Northeast Asian Affairs. *United States Relations with Japan, 1945–1952*. New York: American Institute of Pacific Relations, 1953. 59p.

Intended for the Conference on Japanese–American Relations, held in Honolulu, January 1953, this publication is one of the background papers. The conference was jointly sponsored by the Japan Institute of Pacific Relations and the Institute of Pacific Relations of Hawaii. Rather than discussing problems of the period from 1945 to 1952, the paper describes U.S. intentions as of late 1952 toward various problems in Japan which relate to American interests. While the report discusses economic and cultural matters as well, the greatest emphasis is placed on political aspects of U.S.–Japanese relations. America's general objectives toward Japan are described as helping to build a Japan which is independent, economically viable, democratic, and a trusted member of the society of nations. The paper discusses such subjects as the Japanese peace treaty, the Security Treaty between the United States and Japan, the Administrative Agreement, Japan's application for membership in the United Nations, territorial problems, high seas fisheries in the north Pacific Ocean, and the civil air transport agreement between the 2 countries.

838 "Unizonia in Japan." *Economist* 154: 746–47 (8 May 1948)

After discussing the reasons why American control of occupied Japan developed as a unilateral operation, the author analyzes the present implications of such a position, i.e., as a means of excluding the increasingly menacing Russians from influence in Japan. The author complains, however, that such a policy also excludes the British, Australians, and Chinese from their rightful place in the endeavor. The latter half of the report concerns the future peace treaty and it is noted that U.S.–Soviet positions are not in accord on the matter. The author anticipates a bitter struggle on this issue and cannot predict the outcome. In discussing Japan's economic rehabilitation and future the author suggests that the United States, Britain, Australia, and other interested nations consider the nation's particular problems within the framework of an extended Marshall Plan for world trade recovery.

Vaughn, Miles W. "American Policy and Future Security of Japan." 1949. See no.614.

839 Vinacke, Harold M. *The United States and the Far East*. Mimeographed. New York: American Institute of Pacific Relations, 1950. 53p. (Institute of Pacific Relations, 11th conference, U.S. paper no.1, 1950)

A professor of political science at the University of Cincinnati examines the way in which American policy toward Asia developed after 1945. In his comparison of American policies toward Europe and Asia, Vinacke contends that American objectives in Europe were designed to contain Soviet expansionism and to build barriers to the spread of Soviet rule by promoting economic rehabilitation in western Europe, whereas in Asia the United States developed a separate policy for each of the Asian countries and failed to coordinate these policies. The discussion of American policy toward China, Korea, Japan, and Southeast Asian countries is based on this contention. Vinacke observes that the outbreak of the Korean War brought about a change in American policy from "country" policies to an overall policy toward Asia, based on the desire to contain Soviet and Chinese Communist expansion. In this context he analyzes the shifts in emphasis in American policy for Japan, first in 1947–48 when the emphasis on political reforms was supplemented by emphasis on economic rehabilitation, and again in 1950 when an emphasis on the military rearmament of Japan became manifest. He notes that MacArthur held the opinion through 1949 that an early peace treaty with Japan and subsequent withdrawal of American military forces would be beneficial to both countries.

840 ———. *The United States and the Far East, 1945–1951.* Stanford, Calif.: Stanford Univ. Pr., 1952. vi, 144p.

Reviewing American foreign policy toward Asia since the end of World War II, the author, a political scientist, examines how American policy has been conducted with respect to Southeast Asia, China, Korea, and Japan and argues that our policy toward China has been a failure and that there should be an overall coordinated Far Eastern policy to "contain" communism. The fifth chapter pertaining to American policy toward Japan examines the Potsdam Declaration of 1945 and the relationship among SCAP, the 4-power Allied Council for Japan in Tokyo, and the 11-nation Far Eastern Commission in Washington. This chapter also describes SCAP-sponsored reform programs, the changed American policy on Japan's disarmament, military arrangements for Japan's peace and security, etc. The work was originally prepared as a data paper for the eleventh international conference of the Institute of Pacific Relations held in India in 1950.

841 Walter, Austin Frederic. *Australia's Relations with the United States: 1941–1949.* Ph.D. dissertation, Univ. of Michigan, 1954. 411p. (Abstracted in *Dissertation Abstracts* 14:1247 [1954]; University Microfilms order no.8432)

Walter examines the important military, political, and economic relations that developed between Australia and the United States from 1941 to 1949. He evaluates these relations in terms of the concept of small power–big power relationships and notes their respective economic philosophies and programs. Chapters 3 through 6 provide a discussion of the Australian and American positions regarding the status of Pacific island bases and territories formerly occupied by Japan, the machinery and policies devised for the Allied occupation of Japan, and the nature of the peace settlement with Japan.

842 Wang, Yun-sheng. "Japan: Storm Center of Asia." *Pacific Affairs* 21:195–99 (June 1948)

A letter to the editor of *Pacific Affairs* by the editor in chief of the Shanghai *Ta Kung Pao*, expressing his hearty agreement with W. M. Ball's article of March 1948 (no.536) which speaks of the "ominous reappearance of the Rising Sun." Wang strongly criticizes the United States for promoting the recovery of Japan by every means in her power and warns that a resurgent Japan will arouse the animosity of all Asian peoples.

843 ———. "Japanese Thought: 1947." *China Magazine* 17, no.10:27–31 (Oct. 1947)

Wang, editor in chief of the Shanghai *Ta Kung Pao*, visited Japan for 2 weeks in 1947 at the invitation of General MacArthur. In this article he first presents a Japanese view of the occupation, then analyzes General MacArthur's own motives and presents the Chinese reaction to the occupation, emphasizing the problems that may arise if Japan is allowed to rebuild. The article concludes with a discussion of the question, Restoration for What?

———. "Japan's Dangerous Road." 1947. See no.530.

843a Welles, Sumner. *Where Are We Heading?* New York: Harper, 1946. 397p.

This important analysis of American foreign policy and international diplomatic trends by a former U.S. undersecretary of state is sharply critical of America's vacillating foreign policy. In chapter 6, "The Nationalist Surge in Asia," he describes and comments on the immediate postwar scene in the Philippines, China, Korea, Japan, India and Indonesia. With respect to Japan, he first reviews the early stages of MacArthur's administration and asserts that it has been highly efficient in a military sense on account of its successful implementation of a number of major political and economic reforms. The nature of the policy underlying the occupation, however, comes in for attack. "The basic error in our approach to the ultimate solution of the Japanese problem," Welles writes, "seems to me to lie in the assumption . . . that Japan can be prevented from again becoming a menace . . . through the enforcement of an occupation policy which is limited largely to strategic and security considerations and to the more superficial aspects of political reform." If Japan is to be transformed and democratized, attention must be paid to the needs of the Japanese people particularly in the areas of health, social welfare, education, economic security, and individual freedoms. Accordingly, Welles recommends that the Economic and Social Council of the United Nations be asked to survey the present and future needs of the Japanese people as a whole and urges that the occupying forces implement whatever policy decisions the UN makes.

844 Wheeler, Romney. "Stalin's Target for Tomorrow." *Harper's Magazine* 202: 28 33 (Jan. 1951); abridged and published under the same title in *Reader's Digest* 58:65–68 (Mar. 1951)

The writer, formerly attached to MacArthur's civilian staff in Tokyo, believes that the possibility of a Communist conquest of Japan is a real and present danger. He cites 1950 as the year in which communism made its most rapid advance in Japan—when criticism of Japan's government was replaced by criticism of the Allied occupation. Pointing to the increasing population problem and the related problem of unemployment, the author demonstrates how such conditions can foster communism. He discusses recent Communist activity among farmers and laborers before presenting a summation of SCAP's record throughout the occupation. Although acknowledging the importance of the political, social, and economic reforms enacted thus far, the author insists that to avoid a Communist takeover in Japan, practical steps should be initiated immediately to control the expanding population and to encourage the Japanese people to develop their own version of democracy rather than to adhere strictly to the American version.

845 Yarovoi, V. "England and Post-war Japan." *Soviet Press Translations* 2:1–4 (15 Mar. 1947)

This article, translated from the 18 January 1947 issue of *Izvestia*, attempts to analyze Great Britain's foreign relations with the United States, particularly in the Far East. The author points out that although Britain recognizes the leading role of the United States in the Far East and also agrees with American policy in eliminating the most obvious Japanese reactionaries from power, nevertheless, there are many areas of importance where British and American interests are not in accord with one another. He cites the most significant areas of difference as the revival of Japanese imperialism and Japanese foreign trade, the establishment of a maximum level of Japanese industrial production, the problem of reparations, and the issue of economic disarmament. The article concludes with a general summation of the policy of both countries on these vital issues.

846 Zhukov, E. "Manoeuvers of the Japanese Reactionaries." *New Times* no.12 (22):3–6 (15 Nov. 1945)

Exclusive control of the occupation by a single Allied power, the United States, is sharply criticized in this article.

The author insists that such an arrangement ignores the substantial contribution of the USSR to the war effort. Moreover, he claims, such single-handed supervision "cannot ensure that radical reconstruction of Japan which is demanded by the interests of all the United Nations." He cites the continued presence of former militarists, the gendarmerie, and the *zaibatsu* leaders on the Japanese scene as evidence that the American occupying authorities cannot or will not eliminate such reactionary forces on their own accord.

INTERNATIONAL PARTICIPATION

While the occupation of Japan was essentially an American operation, there was also a measure of Allied participation. The fact that this was not more extensive and influential was a persistent cause of dissension between the United States on the one hand and its erstwhile Allies on the other.

In an institutional sense formal provision was made for Allied participation in the determination of policies for the occupation by the establishment of three international agencies with carefully restricted authority: the Far Eastern Advisory Commission or FEAC (established on 30 Oct. 1945 and superseded by the Far Eastern Commission), the Far Eastern Commission or FEC (26 Feb. 1946–28 Apr. 1952), and the Allied Council for Japan or ACJ (5 Apr. 1946–28 Apr. 1952). At a lower level invitations were also extended to the major Allied powers to provide troops to participate in the actual occupation under the overall command of General MacArthur. Only the British accepted this invitation and they provided from February 1946 a force of about 36,000 men at peak strength, composed primarily of Australian troops with the addition of Indian forces at a later date. These men were known as the British Commonwealth Occupation Force or BCOF. They had a separate zone of occupation and garrison but no military government duties or responsibilities therein.

The items that follow relate primarily to the FEC and ACJ and secondarily to the FEAC and the BCOF. In some cases they also provide insights into the larger role of Japan in the overall foreign policies of the states involved. In this sense they interrelate with the items in the preceding section. Since both the FEC and ACJ were concerned with the policies of the occupation in general, discussions in both of these bodies ranged broadly over many aspects of SCAP activities. Entries in this section, therefore, often supplement those in the preceding calendar of general commentaries (p.152).

One other aspect of the occupation that was notably international in character was, of course, the Tokyo war crimes trials. They are treated separately in a section devoted to the war crimes trials (p.340). Similarly, there is also a separate section devoted to the peace treaty (p.728), another aspect of the occupation involving extensive international interests and participation.

847 "Allied Control Council for Japan." *International Organization* 1:169 (Feb. 1947)

The structure and operations of the Allied Control Council are briefly outlined in this report and the author describes the council's role as an advisory and consultative body. The relationship between General MacArthur and the council is also briefly and impartially discussed.

848 "Allied Council for Japan." *Current Notes on International Affairs* 21:441–54 (July 1950)

The work of the Allied Council for Japan from 1946 through May 1950 is reviewed. The article states that the council's contribution to occupation policy for Japan has been "largely a negative one," particularly since the relations between the United States and the Soviet Union have greatly deteriorated. It reports that the council had only 4 items on the agenda in 1948 and discussed only 2 subjects in 1949. All council members who represented the United States, the Soviet Union, China, and the British Commonwealth from 1946 to 1950 are listed. Major subjects taken up by the council are briefly described including the purge, radio broadcasting, public health, land reform, resumption of private trade, police reform, and repatriates detained in Soviet-controlled territory.

849 "Allied Council for Japan." *International Organization* 1:547–48 (Sept. 1947)

The discussions of the council during May of 1947 concerning Japanese wage-price policy are briefly considered and some attention is given to the criticism of SCAP policy by the Soviet member, Lieutenant General Derevyanko. Other areas of Soviet–American contention are also mentioned.

850 "Allied Council for Japan." *International Organization* 2:151–52 (Feb. 1948)

The most notable activities of the Allied Council during the latter part of 1947 are briefly discussed. The author notes the resignation of W. Macmahon Ball as the British Commonwealth representative, the appointment of William J. Sebald as chairman of the council, the disagreement between the American and Soviet members concerning the repatriation of Japanese war prisoners still held in Russian-controlled areas, and the criticism of SCAP editorial policy by several of the members of the council.

851 "America's Empire." *New Statesman and Nation* 32:371–72 (23 Nov. 1946)

Such recent developments as the conclusion of a new treaty with China and the efforts made to secure control over the former Japanese mandate in the Pacific are indicative of an imperialistic American expansion in Asia of unequalled size and rapidity. Indeed, the control of Japan is now virtually the exclusive prerogative of General MacArthur, who regards the actions of the Allied Council as both a nuisance and an unnecessary interference with his routine of administration, and the Japanese are being thoroughly indoctrinated in the American way of life. The occupation may theoretically be one calling for active Allied participation. In reality, however, every precaution is being taken against the infiltration of British and Soviet ideas, and the British troops stationed in Japan are not being permitted to take part in the military government or reorganization of the country.

Ball, William M. *Japan, Enemy or Ally?* 1949. See no.535.

851a Bell, A. T. J. "Royal Engineers in the British Commonwealth Occupation Force." *Royal Engineers Journal* 65, no. 1:1–14 (1951)

Studies the activities of those members of the British Army's Corps of Royal Engineers who were in Japan between the middle of 1947 and early 1949.

852 Blakeslee, George Hubbard. *The Far Eastern Commission, A Study in International Cooperation: 1945 to 1952.* Washington, D.C.: Government Printing Office, 1953. v, 240p. (Dept. of State publication 5138; Far Eastern series 60)

The author was a member of the U.S. delegation to the Far Eastern Commission (FEC). As political adviser to the FEC chairman, he also served as the U.S. member of the FEC's Steering Committee for the whole period of its existence. He presents an informative account of the historical background of the FEC, its development, the subjects dealt with, decisions reached, and an overall summation of the commission's limitations and achievements. Although emphasis is placed on the relation of the U.S. government to the FEC and the report tends to give a favorable picture of the Western nations' roles as opposed to the Soviet role, the account of the commission's decision-making process reveals interesting interrelationships among the members and between the FEC and SCAP. Views of member nations are also indicated by citing the minutes of the meetings. Among major issues discussed are constitutional reform, demilitarization, Japan's external contacts, Japanese fishing and whaling on the high seas, reparations, food problems, and labor policy. The author also gives an overall evaluation of the record of the FEC.

853 ———. "Negotiating to Establish the Far Eastern Commission, 1945." In *Negotiating with the Russians*, ed. by Raymond Dennett and Joseph E. Johnson. Boston: World Peace Foundation, 1951. p.119–37; also published under the title, "The Establishment of the Far Eastern Commission." *International Organization* 5:499–514 (Aug. 1951)

The author is one of 10 contributors to a book that focuses on U.S.–Russian relations between 1943 and 1947 with regard to various topics such as military assistance in 1943–45, the Nuremberg trial agreements, atomic energy, and cultural exchange. As a former professor of international relations, an officer in the Department of State, and political adviser to the chairman of the Far Eastern Commission (FEC), Blakeslee describes the negotiations that took place among the 4 powers (the United States, the Soviet Union, Great Britain, and China) and particularly between the United States and the Soviet Union regarding Allied policy for the occupation of Japan. He outlines diplomatic developments beginning with 21 August 1945, when the United States proposed its draft terms of reference for the establishment of a Far Eastern Advisory Commission, and ending with 26 December of that year, when the Moscow meeting of foreign ministers adopted the terms of reference of the Far Eastern Commission and of the Allied Council for Japan (ACJ). He also reveals the concessions that were made by all parties involved concerning, for example, the structure, responsibilities, and location of the FEC and the ACJ, as well as the relationship between the FEC, the ACJ, and SCAP. The article is more descriptive than analytical or evaluative, presenting a quite impartial picture of the negotiations. The author, however, does not document his citations.

Borton, Hugh. "American Occupation Policies in Japan." 1947. *See* no.481.

———. "United States Occupation Policies in Japan since Surrender." 1947. *See* no.52.

854 "The British Commonwealth Occupation Force for Japan." *Current Notes on International Affairs* 17:27–28 (Jan. 1946)

The composition, responsibilities and chain of command of the British Commonwealth Occupation Force are briefly described. Its relationships to the Joint Chiefs of Staff in Australia, SCAP, and the U.S. Occupation Forces in Japan are also clarified.

854a "British Commonwealth Occupation Force in Japan: Summary of Agreement between U.S. and Australia." *Department of State Bulletin* 14:220–22 (10 Feb. 1946)

This press release dated 31 January 1946 contains the following 3 items: (1) a summary of the agreement by which the United States government accepted the participation of a British Commonwealth force in the occupation and in which the responsibilities of that occupation army are detailed; (2) a statement by MacArthur welcoming Commonwealth participation; and (3) a note to the effect that while both China and the Soviet Union have been invited to participate, China has indicated its present inability to send troops and the USSR has failed to accept the invitation.

Buss, Claude A. "The Problems of the United States in the Pacific." 1947. See no.483.

Byrnes, James Francis. *All in One Lifetime*. 1958. See no.206.

855 ———. *Moscow Meeting of Foreign Ministers, December 16–26, 1945*. Washington, D.C.: Government Printing Office, 1946. 18p. (Dept. of State publication 2448; Conference series 79)

Secretary of State James Byrnes attended the second meeting of the Council of Foreign Ministers held in Moscow in December 1945. This publication is the radio report which he gave to the nation on 30 December 1945 upon his return from Moscow. Byrnes reports that the meeting brought about a better understanding among the United States, the Soviet Union, and Great Britain. He explains the agreement reached with the concurrence of China regarding the authority and composition of a Far Eastern Commission and an Allied Council for Japan and the relationship between these 2 organizations and General MacArthur as supreme commander for the Allied powers. The text of their agreement, entitled Soviet–Anglo–American Communiqué, signed on 27 December 1945, is appended.

———. *Speaking Frankly*. 1947. See no.207.

855a "Canada and the Far Eastern Commission." *External Affairs* 1, no.B:3–7 (Dec. 1948)

After summarizing the terms of Japan's surrender as laid down by the Potsdam Declaration, the author reviews the purpose of the Far Eastern Commission, its establishment, Canadian participation in it, and some of the commission's activities in the field of economic reform. He points out that the FEC has approved various policy decisions of considerable importance to Canada on the matter of Japanese disarmament, and concludes that Canada's participation in the FEC will remain the principal means by which she can express her views on Japan until the convening of a full-fledged peace conference.

855b Capper, D. P. "Japan in Transit." *National Review* (London) 132:425–31 (Apr. 1949)

Capper comments very favorably on the progress of postwar reconstruction in Japan but at the same time expresses resentment of the manner in which the Americans dominated the occupation. Outside of the Tokyo–Yokohama area and the zone occupied by the British Commonwealth Occupation Force, "British uniforms were as rare as Japanese generals in Piccadilly" Square. Capper also describes the American requisitioning of housing and grounds in the Yokohama area and refers to "the self-consciously Olympian figure of General MacArthur."

Clune, Frank. *Ashes of Hiroshima: A Post-war Trip to Japan and China*. 1950. See no.545.

856 "Communiqué on the Moscow Conference of Three Foreign Ministers Released by SCAP Headquarters, December 30, 1945." *Contemporary Japan* 15:146–51 (Jan./Apr. 1946)

Issued just after the meeting in Moscow of the foreign ministers of the USSR, the United Kingdom, and the United States from 16 through 26 December 1945, this report summarizes the agreements reached on a number of important topics. Following a brief discussion of the preparation of peace treaties with Italy, Rumania, Bulgaria, Hungary, and Finland, the communiqué describes the establishment of the Far Eastern Commission to replace the Far Eastern Advisory Commission. The structure and functions as well as the location of this new organization are briefly discussed and the report also describes the establishment of the Allied Council for Japan. The concluding passages of the document briefly touch upon the situation in Korea and China.

856a Dai, Poeliu. "The Far Eastern Commission and Its Recent Developments." *American Journal of International Law* 42, no.1:148–55 (Jan. 1948)

In this brief résumé of FEC activities, the technical counselor to the Chinese Commission on the Treaty of Peace with Japan first reviews the establishment of the Far Eastern Commission, its functions, its voting procedure, the committees which the FEC has organized, and their activities. He points out that the formulation of the "Basic Post-Surrender Policy for Japan," approved by the FEC on 19 June 1947, was the most significant policy decision that the Commission had reached to date, and he discusses this policy at some length. Dai also refers to the Commission's concern with the timing of the first postwar general elections, the constitution, the questions of reparations and of looted property, the problem of determining Japan's peaceful needs, and the problem of defining Japan's appropriate industrial level. The FEC, Dai concludes, represents "a compromise and a careful balance between two divergent views—the one tending to ascribe to the controlling authorities the role of absolute and unhampered leadership for the sake of deficient action while the other favoring a greater degree of joint cooperation among the principal Allies who have contributed their due shares to the defeat of the enemy."

"Declaration of the Soviet Representative in the Allied Council for Japan." 1951. See no.620.

"Exercise of Criminal and Civil Jurisdiction over Nationals of Members of the United Nations: Far Eastern Commission Policy Decision." 1950. See no. 1298a.

856b "Far Eastern Advisory Commission: Terms of Reference." *Department of State Bulletin* 13:561, 580 (14 Oct. 1945)

Transmitted by the United States government on 21 August 1945 to the governments of China, the United Kingdom and the USSR and released to the press on 10 October, this document provides for the establishment of the Far Eastern Advisory Commission and indicates its functions, composition, location, organization, and the procedure for its termination.

857 Far Eastern Commission. *Activities of the Far Eastern Commission: Report by the Secretary General, February 26, 1946–July 10, 1947*. Washington, D.C.: Government Printing Office, 1947. viii, 109p. (Dept. of State publication 2888; Far Eastern series 24)

This report by Secretary-General Nelson T. Johnson of the Far Eastern Commission is intended to acquaint the general public with the importance of the commission in formulating Allied policies for the control of Japan. The first 32 pages provide a summary of the history and organizational structure of the FEC and describe its accomplishments from its inception on 26 February 1946 to 10 July 1947. These accomplishments relate to the commission's Basic Post-Surrender Policy for Japan, Japanese constitutional revision including the review policy decision, reparations policies, economic reconstruction policies, democratization policies with particular reference to labor unions and the educational system, policy on war criminals, policy for the treatment of non-Japanese nationals in Japan, and, finally, policy on Japan's disarmament. The remaining two-thirds of the report is an appendix of 45 items, 41 of which are the texts of the FEC's formal policy decisions. Other items include the terms of reference of the FEC of 27 December 1945, a full list of all FEC personnel from the organization's beginning, FEC consultations on 20 March 1946 regarding the date of the twenty-second general election, and SCAP's reply to it (29 Mar. 1946). The report provides useful material for the student of the occupation.

———. "Basic Post-Surrender Policy for Japan." 1947. See no.899.

858 ———. *Far Eastern Commission Minutes and Minutes of the Various Committees.* Washington, D.C.: The Commission, 1946–52.

A basic and valuable collection of the proceedings of the Far Eastern Commission and of its several committees. The difficulties of obtaining permission to declassify them under the regulations of 13 different nations, however, have prevented their being made available for scholarly use. Complete sets exist in the Department of State's central files and in the National Archives.

859 ———. *The Far Eastern Commission: Second Report by the Secretary General, July 10, 1947–December 23, 1948.* Washington, D.C.: Government Printing Office, 1949. viii, 65p. (Dept. of State publication 3420; Far Eastern series 29)

This report follows a first report submitted in July 1947, *Activities of the Far Eastern Commission: Report by the Secretary General, February 26, 1946–July 10, 1947* (no.857). The second report covers FEC activities for the period indicated in the title. The first 15 pages are devoted to a description of the 13 policy decisions which the FEC made during this year and a half. They are concerned with Japan's disarmament, the reduction of her industrial war potential, principles of Japanese farmers' organizations, policies for Japan's trade, food supply for Japan, etc. Appendixes, which constitute the remaining two-thirds of the report, present these 13 decisions plus the text of the Potsdam Declaration, the terms of reference for the FEC, the organization of the FEC, a complete list of FEC personnel since its foundation in February 1946, and, finally, activities of the Inter-Allied Trade Board of Japan.

860 ———. *The Far Eastern Commission: Third Report by the Secretary General, December 24, 1948–June 30, 1950.* Washington, D.C.: Government Printing Office, 1950. viii, 48p. (Dept. of State publication 3945; Far Eastern series 35); summarized and published under the title "Third Report on the Activities of Far Eastern Commission: December 24, 1948–June 30, 1950." *Department of State Bulletin* 23:288–93 (21 Aug. 1950)

The third public report by the secretary-general of the Far Eastern Commission covering its activities for the period mentioned in the title. During this period the FEC membership increased from 11 to 13 nations, the Republic of Burma and the former Dominion of Pakistan being admitted on 17 November 1949. The Soviet Union boycotted meetings after 19 January 1950, when the commission voted down the Soviet demand to expel the Republic of China from the FEC. Nine policy decisions of the FEC were formulated during this period. The report describes them and appends the verbatim texts of each. These decisions pertain to Japanese war criminals, agrarian reform, patents, trademarks, restitution of looted property, and access to Japanese technological information. In addition to the texts of policy decisions mentioned above, the appendixes present basic documents that led to the formation of the FEC and a list of all the FEC personnel from the organization's beginning in 1946.

———. "Reduction of Japanese Industrial War Potential." 1947. *See* no.1002.

861 "Far Eastern Commission." *Current Notes on International Affairs* 21:265–75 (Apr. 1950)

Major policy decisions by the Far Eastern Commission up to March 1950 are reviewed. These decisions pertain to basic occupation policy for Japan, disarmament, reparations, democratization, review of the Japanese Constitution, and the resumption of Japan's participation in international meetings. The article views the work of FEC as a considerable achievement in the light of the vetoes granted the 4 major powers. A total of 63 policy decisions adopted by the FEC from its establishment in February 1946 through March 1949 are listed in an appendix to this issue on pages 305–7.

862 "The Far Eastern Commission." *International Organization* 1:176–78 (Feb. 1947)

Details concerning the establishment of the Far Eastern Commission are followed by a description of its various functions in this brief outline. The author also cites some of the more important policy directives issued by that organization concerning food supplies, the interim reparations program, extraordinary tax laws, the handling of aliens in Japan, and the basic principles of a new constitution.

863 "Far Eastern Commission." *International Organization* 1:376–77 (June 1947)

Some significant activities of the Far Eastern Commission during 1946 and 1947 are considered in this report. It provides a description of topics considered by the commission such as the trade union movement, atomic energy research, restitution of property, and revision of the educational system. There is also an account of the FEC's policy decision which established the Inter-Allied Trade Board for Japan on 10 October 1946 in order to provide consultation among the Allies regarding the disposition of exports available from Japan and the provision of imports required for Japan.

864 "Far Eastern Commission." *International Organization* 1:552–54 (Sept. 1947)

This brief article summarizes the report by the secretary-general of the United Nations on the activities of the Far Eastern Commission, 26 February 1946–10 July 1947, which was released on 17 July 1947. The article mentions 8 categories of FEC activity determined by the secretary-general and also cites the specific accomplishments of the organization that are considered in the UN report.

865 "Far Eastern Commission." *International Organization* 2:156–57 (Feb. 1948)

A brief account of policy decisions taken by the Far Eastern Commission concerning interim export-import policies for Japan, the reduction of Japanese industrial war potential, and the supply of food available for the civilian population of Japan during the latter half of 1947.

866 "Far Eastern Commission." *International Organization* 2:394–96 (June 1948)

The major policy decisions of the commission from January through April of 1948 are discussed in this brief report. Topics considered include the programs to prohibit future Japanese military activity and to dispose of military equipment, a plan for the restitution of looted property, and U.S. proposals to bring about the revival of the Japanese economy. The activities of the Inter-Allied Trade Board for Japan concerned with the reopening of the country to private trade are also noted.

867 "Far Eastern Commission." *International Organization* 3:180–82 (Feb. 1949)

This brief report summarizes 13 policy decisions that were adopted by the Far Eastern Commission from 10 July 1947 to 23 December 1948, dividing them into 3 categories relating to the 3 goals of disarmament, democratization, and the establishment of a self-sustaining economy for Japan. The report also briefly touches upon U.S.–USSR disagreement over a Soviet proposal regarding the restoration and development of Japanese industry and the reasons why the United States recently withdrew its support of directive FEC–230, which demanded the dissolution of some *zaibatsu* combines. Finally, there is mention of the activities of the Inter-Allied Trade Board for Japan during this same period.

868 "Far Eastern Commission." *International Organization* 3:380–81 (May 1949)

This account of the activities of the Far Eastern Commission from December 1948 through March 1949 includes discussion of American–Soviet disagreements within the commission between Ambassador Panyushkin of the USSR and Major General McCoy of the United States. The most hectic dispute concerned the establishment of an effective

9-point economic stabilization program proposed by the Americans on 10 December 1948. There is also mention of the FEC's decision of 16 March 1949 to eliminate paragraph 1a regarding the trials of Japanese war criminals. This decision affected those involved in the "planning, preparation, initiation or waging of a war of aggression or a war in violation of international treaties, agreements and assurances, or participation in a common plan of conspiracy for the accomplishment of any of the foregoing."

869 "Far Eastern Commission." *International Organization* 3:564–66 (Aug. 1949)

The most significant activities of the Far Eastern Commission from March 1949 through May of that year are briefly noted. Matters discussed are the FEC's endorsement of General MacArthur's land reform program, the announcement of the end of reparations withdrawals from Japan, and the U.S. recommendation of 6 May to the FEC suggesting that Japan be permitted to attend international meetings and conventions to which it was invited, subject to SCAP supervision.

870 "The Far Eastern Commission and the Allied Council for Japan." *Current Notes on International Affairs* 17:19–26 (Jan. 1946)

This short article describes the formation of the Far Eastern Advisory Commission on 29 October 1945 and the terms of reference for the subsequent Far Eastern Commission and Allied Council for Japan. It also treats Australia's participation in these international bodies as well as its policies on the control of postwar Japan. The article stresses the role played by the minister for external affairs, Evatt, in defining occupation policy during October and November of 1945. Parliamentary opinion in Britain is quoted as to the "particular interest" of Australia and New Zealand in the peace terms to be imposed on Japan. After noting Evatt's general progress report of 28 November the article summarizes Australian proposals on Allied occupation policy for Japan issued on 29 November and discusses Australian objections to the veto power given the 4 major powers on the Far Eastern Commission. The full text of the communiqué of the Moscow Conference of 28 December 1945 is appended to this issue on pages 37–40.

871 "The Far Eastern Commission and the Allied Council for Japan." *Current Notes on International Affairs* 17:595–609 (Oct. 1946)

The activities of the Far Eastern Commission (FEC) and the Allied Council for Japan (ACJ) are reviewed with Australian evaluations and comments. The article emphasizes the importance of the commission, describes Australia's role in the formulation of basic policy for Japan through the FEC, and discusses the FEC's policy discussions regarding Japan's new constitution, an Inter-Allied Trade Board for Japan, and reparations. A similar report is given on the ACJ with particular reference to proposals by the Commonwealth representative, W. Macmahon Ball, with respect to land reform. The article opposes the veto accorded the 4 major powers and the limitations on Australian participation. Appended are the full text of the new Japanese constitution, proposed terms of reference for an Inter-Allied Trade Board for Japan, the texts of the notes exchanged in August 1945 between the Japanese government and the Allied powers regarding the former's acceptance of the Potsdam Declaration, and the text of the Instrument of Surrender of 2 September 1945.

871a "Far Eastern Commission: Summary Report on Trip to Japan." *Department of State Bulletin* 14:370–74 (10 Mar. 1946)

This paper on the FEC's tour of Japan in January 1946 consists of 2 parts. The first is an itinerary indicating where the commission went and with whom it conferred. The second is a selection of communications including: (1) general exchanges between the commission and General MacArthur, among them a document entitled "Long-Term Agenda for the Commission FEAC–10/2," dated 9 November 1945; (2) exchanges between the commission and its Washington office regarding Soviet participation on the commission; (3) an exchange between the commission and General MacArthur regarding Allied participation in SCAP; and (4) an exchange between the commission and MacArthur regarding Axis nationals in Japan.

871b "Far Eastern Rivalries." *Economist* 149, no.5333:667–68 (10 Nov. 1945)

During the 3 months since Japan's surrender, the "political pattern of the Far East has been settling more and more into one of separate spheres of influence." Japanese military forces have formally surrendered to the Allied authorities designated in the Instrument of Surrender which General MacArthur drew up, and those same authorities have assumed direct responsibility for policy within their respective areas. As a result, while the Russians have taken over certain parts of the prewar Japanese empire, the Americans have been left with absolute control over Japan itself. Dissatisfied with this arrangement, the Soviet Union has come to insist that all of the Allies be permitted to share in making policy for the future of Japan. In this regard, they are actively supported by the British Commonwealth—in particular by the Australians, who are very resentful of the exclusion of their troops from the occupation and of the absence of any direct Australian representative from the circle of MacArthur's political advisers. The United States has come under considerable pressure from her allies, and an Allied commission for Japan is now to be set up.

871c "Four-power Farce in Japan." *Economist* 158:323–24 (11 Feb. 1950)

The Allied Council for Japan has been reduced to impotence. Its proceedings have become a series of farcical 30-second assemblies and generally constitute a propaganda platform for both the United States and the Soviet Union. Most of the blame for this development is attributable to MacArthur, who has resented the Council's existence and has limited its role to that of an advisory agency. The Council's only accomplishment as a result has been its admirable recommendations for land reform laws tabled by W. Macmahon Ball and substantially accepted by MacArthur despite Japanese efforts to sabotage them.

Frederick, James O. "Payment from Japan." 1948. *See* no.1125.

Green, Owen M. "De-mok-ra-sie." 1949. *See* no.589.

872 Hsu, Immanuel C. Y. "The Allied Council for Japan." *Far Eastern Quarterly* 10:173–78 (Feb. 1951)

The author of this article was a member of the Chinese Mission in occupied Japan and worked with the Chinese delegation to the Allied Council for Japan for over 2 years. He presents an objective and useful analysis of the Allied Council. Following a description of the establishment of the Allied Council for Japan, the author discusses the nature of the council's meetings and the increasing friction that developed between the members culminating in the Soviet Union's boycott of the meetings in December 1949. The author judges the Allied Council for Japan to have been "outstandingly ineffective" and attributes this to the power politics of the nations sitting on it, i.e., the United States, the Soviet Union, the British Commonwealth, and China. In conclusion he views the Council as "a mirror reflecting the political realities of East–West conflicts."

873 Johnson, Nelson Trusler. "The Far Eastern Commission." *American Foreign Service Journal* 24:11–12, 50–51 (Dec. 1947)

The activities of the Far Eastern Commission (FEC) concerning the Japanese fulfillment of surrender terms are presented as is a review of SCAP directives since February 1946. Johnson discusses the organization and operation of the FEC and comments on specific decisions concerning the promulgation of a new constitution, educational reform, and economic rehabilitation.

874   Levi, Werner. "International Control of Japan." *Far Eastern Survey* 15:299–302 (25 Sept. 1946)

This brief article concerns the 2 official groups which represented international involvement in the occupation—the Far Eastern Commission and the Allied Council in Tokyo. The author discusses the circumstances of their formation and describes the organizational structure and powers of these bodies, emphasizing how, in practice, they were essentially consultative and advisory bodies which did not impinge upon SCAP's authority in any serious way. He contrasts these 2 bodies with their postwar Eastern European counterparts and views these councils as manifestations of the careful balance of national interest among the Big Powers.

874a   "Liaison with the Supreme Commander for the Allied Powers." *Department of State Bulletin* 15:164–65 (28 July 1946)

This policy statement, approved by the Far Eastern Commission on 18 July 1946, makes arrangements for liaison between the FEC and SCAP. These arrangements include provisions for the regular exchange of information between the 2 organizations, for the appointment of Allied personnel to the SCAP staff, and for *ad hoc* consultation between members of SCAP and the FEC.

875   MacArthur, Douglas. "Statement by General MacArthur." *Department of State Bulletin* 17:221–22 (3 Aug. 1947)

This statement of the supreme commander of the Allied powers, made on 12 July 1947, comments on a policy decision to be adopted by the Far Eastern Commission concerning the postsurrender treatment of Japan. MacArthur praises the document as "one of the great state papers of modern history," illustrating the fact that the great nations of the world are able to work together on vital international issues. Furthermore, he praises the balance of the commission's recommendation—neither insisting on harsh and unjust treatment of the former enemy nor allowing the preservation of former institutions and leadership responsible for the war. Asserting that the disarmament and demilitarization programs have already been implemented, MacArthur urges revived dedication to the other phases of the occupation program.

875a   "MacArthur's Incubus." *Plain Talk* p.17–20 (Nov. 1949)

The Far Eastern Commission, according to this article, has been the greatest impediment to MacArthur's policies in Japan. After briefly discussing the origins and history of the FEC, the article attempts to show how it has been prevented from taking any constructive action on problems brought before it by one Soviet veto after another. This difficulty has arisen from the fact that at the time the FEC was organized, no one foresaw the change in Soviet attitudes which would lead to serious conflicts in policy over the occupation of Japan.

875b   McCoy, Frank R. "Clarification of Press Policy Relating to FEC Decisions." *Department of State Bulletin* 19:806 (26 Dec. 1948)

McCoy issued this statement on 10 December 1948 in response to a Soviet press release that dealt, contrary to FEC rules, with a policy proposal which had not been approved by the commission. The proposal in question, made by the Soviet representative, had provided (1) that no limitations be placed on the development of peaceful Japanese industry, and (2) that a longterm control system be established to inhibit the revival of war industries in Japan. McCoy wished to make clear in his statement the objections of the Far Eastern Commission to the provisions. The first one is meaningless, for no limits had ever been considered: the second one falls outside the jurisdiction of the FEC, since it applies to the posttreaty period.

876   "Occupation of Japan." *New Statesman and Nation* 32:301–2 (26 Oct. 1946)

This letter from a British officer is bitterly critical of the pervasiveness of American control of the occupation. The author feels that the total lack of influence by the British will serve only to bring ridicule on Great Britain which will in turn prove prejudicial to future economic and political dealings between the 2 countries.

876a Piggott, F. J. C. "Occupying Japan." *Army Quarterly* 54:109–17 (Apr. 1947)

This intelligently written account describes several aspects of the occupation of Japan as seen by a divisional staff officer between February and December 1946. Divided into 8 short sections, the article focuses in particular on the composition of the British Commonwealth Occupation Force (BCOF), BCOF's contact with the United States army, activities in Tokyo, such problems as those raised by the existence of a large number of Koreans and Formosans in Japan, Japanese reactions to the occupying forces, and the British position on the accomplishments of the occupation to date.

"Policy Statements by Far Eastern Commission on Japanese Constitution." 1947. *See* no.1201.

876b "Procedural Organization of Allied Council for Japan: Remarks by American Representative and Chairman of the Council." *Department of State Bulletin* 15:382–84 (25 Aug. 1946)

This article consists of remarks made by George Atcheson, Jr., at a special meeting of the Allied Council for Japan on 13 August 1946. Atcheson devotes most of his talk to justifying the predominant role of the United States in the occupation, but reminds council members that MacArthur welcomes advice and counsel from all sources, particularly the council and the FEC.

The Reminiscences of Burton Crane. 1961. *See* no.44e.

The Reminiscences of Douglas W. Overton. 1960. *See* no.44h.

The Reminiscences of Sir George Sansom. 1957. *See* no.44q.

877 "Review of the Organization and Accomplishments of the British Commonwealth Occupation Force." *Current Notes on International Affairs* 19:516–19 (Aug. 1948)

A statement by Australian Defense Minister J. J. Dedman on 15 July 1948, regarding the functions of the British Commonwealth Occupation Force operating in Japan since early 1946. It reports that the BCOF is a valuable experiment for future regional defense and that Australian forces constituted the major component of BCOF with 37,000 men at its peak in late 1946. This number was greatly reduced in 1947.

878 Rosinger, Lawrence K. "United States Accepts Allied Control of Japan." *Foreign Policy Bulletin* 25:2–3 (4 Jan. 1946)

This brief report discusses the implications of the Moscow Agreement under whose terms control of the occupation is to become more diversified through the establishment of the Far Eastern Commission and the Allied Council for Japan. The author sees the agreement as a compromise between the original American view relegating all other nations to an advisory capacity and the other Allied nations' interest in asserting greater control themselves. He briefly mentions MacArthur's objections to the new arrangements but stresses the general's willingness to try to make them work, concluding with the observation that the new arrangement must be put into effect with the highest amount of tact and goodwill on the part of all nations involved to insure international cooperation.

879 ———. "U.S. Defense of Japanese Regime Disturbs Allies." *Foreign Policy Bulletin* 26:2–3 (25 Oct. 1946)

A remark of U.S. Ambassador George Atcheson, Jr., to the Allied Council to the effect that "Japanese aims have become virtually identical with Allied aims" serves as the convenient starting point of a discussion of the operation of the

Allied Council 5 months after its establishment. The author believes that the statement has come to reflect the general position of the United States in the council which regards "criticism or questioning of the Japanese authorities as a reflection on the United States." He believes that this position has led to considerable frustration, not only on the part of the Soviet representative to the council, General Derevyanko, but also of the British Commonwealth representative, W. Macmahon Ball, and the Chinese member, General Chu Shih-ming. The article concludes with a brief consideration of the U.S. defense of the present Yoshida government, warning that, if criticism of the Japanese government is to be taken as criticism of the United States, then "the meetings of the Council can be nothing more than forums at which the Soviet, American and other representatives will match wits and display increasing anger."

880 ———. "U.S. Proposes Allied Advisory Council on Japan." *Foreign Policy Bulletin* 25:1–2 (19 Oct. 1945)

The 9 October proposal of Secretary of State Byrnes to establish a Far Eastern Advisory Commission is succinctly but thoroughly treated. The article discusses the experience and qualifications of Major General Frank Ross McCoy, who will be the American member of the Washington-based commission, and the main features of the proposed commission—its limitations as well as its powers. The author then discusses the reactions of the other Allied nations to the U.S. proposal—particularly that of Great Britain, which has shown interest in creating a control body rather than an advisory one. Finally, in the face of the monumental tasks of the occupation, the author advocates increased international cooperation and the use of administrative and technical personnel from other Allied countries—particularly China, Britain, and the Soviet Union, which would make the occupation a truly cooperative effort and increase its efficiency as well.

881 Singh, Rajendra. *Post-war Occupation Forces: Japan and South-east Asia.* New Delhi: Combined Inter-Services Historical Section, India and Pakistan, 1958. xxxiv, 317p. (Official History of the Indian Armed Forces in the Second World War, 1939–45. Campaigns in the Eastern Theatre)

A useful, official record of the activities of the British Commonwealth forces in postwar Japan and Southeast Asia. The volume, prepared as part of the official history of the Indian armed forces in World War II, describes the responsibility of the Indian forces in the military administration of territories occupied by the Allied powers in Japan and Southeast Asia from February 1946 through August 1947, when India became independent. It consists of 2 parts. The first records the activities of all contingents of the British Commonwealth Occupation Force (BCOF) under MacArthur, as supreme commander for the Allied powers. Bisheshwar Prasad, the general editor of the official history, presents introductory notes on the nature of the Allied occupation of Japan, basic objectives of the occupation, and SCAP machinery. He reports on the negotiations between Washington and SCAP on the one hand, and between Washington and Canberra on the other, regarding the participation of the British Commonwealth forces in the occupation of Japan—negotiations which culminated in the MacArthur–Northcott Agreement of 30 January 1946. The book also treats the roles of the Allied governments or their liaison missions in Tokyo, the British Commonwealth occupation policy, the supreme control of BCOF by the intergovernmental Joint Chiefs of Staff set up in Australia and its organization, the breakdown of BCOF by military components and nationality, dependent families, welfare of the troops, postal and financial arrangements made for the troops, how Indian units were formed to serve in Japan, and the nature of their work in Shikoku and southern Honshu such as disposal of Japanese war equipment, supervision of repatriated Japanese soldiers, control of black market activities, and control of Japanese general elections. The second part of the work concerns the participation of Indian units in the control of Southeast Asia under the command of Lord Mountbatten. There are detailed accounts of the recovery of Allied prisoners of war, the restoration of order in French Indochina, Thailand, and the Netherlands East Indies, and of the repatriation of Japanese prisoners of war.

881a ———. "British Commonwealth Occupation Force in Japan." *Journal of the United Service Institution of India* 79: 155–62 (July 1949)

881b ———. "JCOSA: An Experiment in Joint Control." *Journal of the United States Service Institution of India* 81: 154–56 (July/Oct. 1951)

On the organization of the Joint Chiefs of Staff Australia on behalf of Great Britain, Australia, New Zealand, and India for the purpose of participating in the Japanese occupation after the war and on the reasons for its failure.

"Some Aspects of the Occupation of Japan." 1951. *See* no.667.

882 Stratton, Samuel S. "The Far Eastern Commission." *Far Eastern Survey* 17: 190–93 (25 Aug. 1948)

In this article the deputy secretary-general of the Far Eastern Commission discusses the accomplishments of that body, considering the policy decisions handed down by the FEC in the 3 broad areas of disarmament, democratization, and economic recovery. The article discusses the FEC's role in the formulation of a new constitution and an interim reparations program, and in taking the first steps toward the resumption of Japanese foreign trade. The author treats such unresolved issues as the formulation of a final reparations program and notes the diminishing effectiveness of the commission in the second and third years of the occupation of Japan. The prevailing tone of the article is one of confidence regarding the effectiveness of the FEC as "one of the few remaining indications of the thesis that successful postwar settlements must be built upon the unity of the great powers."

882a ———. "The Far Eastern Commission." *International Organization* 2:1–18 (Feb. 1948)

The deputy secretary-general of the Far Eastern Commission presents an overall review of the accomplishments of the FEC to date within this particular article. He begins by describing the background of the commission's creation and how the interests of the United States as the chief contributor to victory against Japan and as the principal occupying power were safeguarded under the new arrangements. He then discusses many of the FEC's activities, focusing in particular upon the new constitution and various economic matters brought before the commission. He points out that all 44 FEC policies to date have been passed without a dissenting vote and that in general the approved policies have followed fairly close along the lines of either original U.S. policies set up before the FEC was organized or else U.S. proposals subsequently submitted to the FEC for consideration. In most cases, furthermore, FEC deliberations have been friendly and constructive—in part because of the closed-door nature of the meetings at which they were held. Stratton concludes by speculating on the commission's future and states that "the fact that the Commission *has* worked suggests that, given the same approach, patience and determination, it will be possible for these same Allies to write a peace treaty with Japan that will safeguard the vital interests of all of them, including the United States, and thus lay the basis for lasting peace in the Pacific."

883 Supreme Commander for the Allied Powers. *Far Eastern Commission Messages*. 1945–50. Blue Binder series. MacArthur Memorial, Bureau of Archives, Norfolk, Va. 7 folders.

Unclassified communications between the Joint Chiefs of Staff in Washington and the commander in chief of Allied forces in the Pacific and SCAP dealing with the establishment and activities of the Far Eastern Commission (FEC). The messages, filed chronologically, report the communiqué of the Moscow Conference which established the FEC, information on Washington's liaison arrangements with the FEC, and FEC policies on such matters as Japan's new constitution, establishment of the Inter-Allied Trade Board for Japan, treatment of aliens in Japan, and a postsurrender policy for Japan. One message, dated 10 December 1948, contains the text of a State Department explanation of the U.S. withdrawal from the FEC's agenda of FEC directive 230, the basic policy statement on deconcentration.

―――. Monograph 2. *Administration of the Occupation, 1945–July 1951.* 1952. See no.284.

884 ―――. Allied Council for Japan. *Verbatim Minutes of the First Meeting* through *Verbatim Minutes of the One Hundred and Sixty-fourth Meeting.* Tokyo: Allied Council for Japan, Office of the Secretariat, 1946–52.

A complete collection of the verbatim minutes of all 164 meetings that the Allied Council for Japan held in Tokyo between 5 April 1946 and 23 April 1952. As an advisory body to SCAP, the council discussed a wide range of subjects. The minutes present a vivid picture of the interaction of the member nations—the United States, the British Commonwealth, China, and the Soviet Union—and their reactions to current social and political conditions in Japan. Subjects covered include the effectiveness of the purge program, Allied food policy for Japan, rural land reform, the resumption of relations between Japanese labor organizations and their foreign counterparts, measures for the prevention of diseases in Japan, the process of liquidation of *zaibatsu* concerns, and exports and imports.

By and large, the first 47 meetings of the council (up to Nov. 1947) consisted of lengthy and substantive discussions, generally lasting for a full 2 hours, often more, and the minutes of these meetings average 40 pages in length. After November 1947, however, the council frequently had no business on its agenda and, if it met at all, the members engaged in propagandistic debates. SCAP acted through the United States representative who was concurrently chairman of the Allied Council. SCAP and the Soviet Union dominated the agenda throughout the entire period, and the minutes reveal the growing Soviet antagonism towards SCAP policies. The minutes further show that the Soviet member boycotted the council from the 102d meeting (21 Dec. 1949) through the 131st meeting (17 Jan. 1951) during which time the United States had placed on the agenda the item, Concerning Treatment of Convicted Japanese Prisoners of War in Soviet Russia. After each meeting's minutes are appended summaries of the council's various recommendations to SCAP, SCAP reports to the council, and SCAP's letters to the Japanese government and other governments.

Available on microfilm from the National Archives, Washington, D.C.

―――. Civil Information and Education Section. *Memos and Correspondence with Various Missions in Japan.* 1948–51. See no.2159.

―――. Diplomatic Section. *Correspondence of Political Adviser to SCAP.* 1947–51. See no.669.

885 ―――. ―――. *Correspondence with SCAP Missions.* 1945–51. Record Group 5, Boxes 101–5. MacArthur Memorial, Bureau of Archives, Norfolk, Va. 29 folders.

These folders contain collections of correspondence between the Diplomatic Section of SCAP and the various foreign missions in Japan. Materials are arranged chronologically and the series covers communications with the Australian Mission from 1946 to 1951, the Belgian Mission from 1947 to 1951, the Brazilian Mission from 1949 to 1951, the British Mission from 1945 to 1951, the Canadian Mission from 1945 to 1951, the Chinese Mission from 1945 to 1951, and the Danish Mission from 1948 to 1951. Correspondence generally relates to the establishment of new missions in Japan, the appointment of the heads of missions, changes in important personnel, requests made to the supreme commander by the missions for various kinds of information, and requests for clearance of their nationals for entry into Japan and Japanese citizens for entry into their respective countries.

"The Task of the Occupation Forces." 1945. See no.409.

886 Tiltman, Hessell. "Letter from Tokyo: What Is the Council?" *New Republic* 115:414–15 (30 Sept. 1946)

The activity of the Allied Council for Japan is the focal point of this letter. The writer suggests that the council has minimal power and is often little more than a stage for bitter American–Soviet wrangling. The letter also describes the writer's observations with respect to the plans of the big industrialists of Japan to regain power in the postwar period. According to him, such industrialists are confident that they will be aided by their American counterparts in this endeavor. The last portion contains a brief description of Nosaka Sanzō, Japanese Communist leader in the Diet, outlining his plans for future political action.

887 U.S. Dept. of State. Bureau of Public Affairs. Historical Office. *Foreign Relations of the United States, Diplomatic Papers, 1945.* v.2, *General: Political and Economic Matters.* Washington, D.C.: Government Printing Office, 1967. vi, 1577p. (Dept. of State publication 8314)

Of particular interest among these U.S. government papers is the documentation on American participation in 2 foreign ministers' meetings: the first session of the Council of Foreign Ministers held in London, 11 September–2 October 1945 (p.99–560), and the Moscow Conference of Foreign Ministers held 16–26 December 1945 (p.560–826). Both meetings were largely devoted to the settlement of European problems but were also concerned with problems of Allied policy toward Japan. A detailed index at the end of the volume is helpful in locating subjects regarding the control of Japan as well as Allied reactions to the proposals involved. Included are discussions of the control machinery for Japan and the establishment of the Far Eastern Commission and the Allied Council for Japan.

887a Walsh, J. M. "British Participation in the Occupation of Japan." *Army Quarterly* 57:72–81 (Oct. 1948)

After discussing the terms for the occupation of Japan, Walsh focuses on the participation of the British Commonwealth Occupation Force within it and on arrangements among the member units of the BCOF. He points out that Australian influence has been predominant within the BCOF from the outset and views their participation in the occupation as a unique unifying experience for the various Commonwealth countries. Walsh's account is accompanied by a foldout sketch-map depicting Shikoku and southern Honshu, the areas where the BCOF was stationed.

888 Wells, Roger H. "Interim Government and Occupation Regimes." *Annals of the American Academy of Political and Social Science* 257:66–69 (May 1948)

Part of a more inclusive article discussing Allied control commissions in conquered enemy states through the winter of 1947. It points up differences between the occupations of Japan and the European countries and, in addition, discusses the formation and operational procedures of the Far Eastern Advisory Commission, its successor the Far Eastern Commission, and the Allied Council for Japan. The author has some criticisms of the Far Eastern Commission but in general believes it to be an effective and useful body. He concludes that the Allied Council for Japan was "used as a forum for airing American–Soviet differences and for Soviet charges that the United States military government was supporting reaction in Japan." The final section of the report on Japan considers various criticisms of the American role in the Far Eastern Commission and the Allied Council for Japan and briefly discusses some of the less desirable aspects of the occupation such as the resurgence of the old bureaucracy or the worsening economic situation.

888a Wilkinson, Harry Richard. *The Soviet Union and the Allied Occupation of Japan: Prelude.* M.A. thesis, Univ. of Michigan, Center for Japanese Studies, 1971. v, 160p.

Relying heavily on Russian scholarship and strongly reflecting the Soviet point of view, Wilkinson's thesis traces and analyzes Soviet behavior towards the defeat and occupation of Japan from the time of the Yalta Conference in February 1945 through the Moscow Conference of the Council of Foreign Ministers in December 1945. It also includes a pre-Yalta historical perspective on Soviet–Japanese relations. The author contends that the Soviet entry into the war against Japan was militarily significant and consistent with agreements negotiated between the USSR and the Western Allies. Furthermore, he argues that the virtual exclusion of the Soviet Union from planning for the treatment of postwar Japan, while a logical reaction to Soviet behavior in Eastern Europe and Germany, was a contributing factor in the rapid, postwar deterioration of U.S.–Soviet relations. There are 3 appendixes to this work which contain short translations by the dissertation author of relevant Soviet studies. They are: (1) Sergei B. Sosinskii. "The Far Eastern Agreement." In his *Aktsiia "Argonavt."* Moscow: Izdatel'stvo Mezhdunarodnye Otnosheniia, 1970. p.69–89; (2) Khaim T. Eidus. "Introduction." In his *S.S.S.R. i IAponiia: Vneshnepoliticheskie Otnosheniia posle Vtoroi Mirovoi Voiny.* Moscow: Izdatel'stvo "Nauka," 1964. p.3–10; and Khaim T. Eidus. "Policy of the USSR." In *ibid.* p.11–19.

Available at the Asia Library, Univ. of Michigan, Ann Arbor, Michigan. The author's prior permission is required for borrowing it on interlibrary loan.

Organization, Staff, Functions

The structure of the occupation was national in scale and complex in form. It ranged from the supreme commander for the Allied powers and his General Headquarters in Tokyo—both commonly, if confusingly, referred to by the acronym SCAP—through the separate headquarters of the Eighth (and, briefly, the Sixth) Army to the regional and prefectural military government or civil affairs teams scattered throughout the forty-six prefectures of postwar Japan. The administrative staff attached to SCAP in Tokyo by 1949 numbered about 5,500, while the strength of the occupation's armed forces proper ranged from perhaps 500,000 down to about 150,000 depending on the period concerned. The mission and functions of this enormous apparatus were set forth in general terms in a presidential order of 6 September 1945 known as U.S. Initial Post-Surrender Policy for Japan and spelled out in considerably more detail in a Joint Chiefs of Staff order (1380/15) of 3 November 1945 entitled Basic Initial Post-Surrender Directive to Supreme Commander for the Allied Powers for the Occupation and Control of Japan (the texts of both may be found in Supreme Commander for the Allied Powers, Government Section, *Political Reorientation of Japan,* v.2, p.423–26, 429–39; no.279). The presidential order was later paraphrased and formally adopted as the Basic Post-Surrender Policy for Japan by the Far Eastern Commission on 19 June 1947 (*See* no.899).

The following section sets forth the literature dealing with these matters of organization, staff, and functions. It includes serials and files of administrative nature circulated internally within SCAP and its subordinate sections and headquarters. Related materials may be found in the section on SCAP's situation and progress reports (p.113), SCAP—official history of the occupation (p.123), and reports by subordinate headquarters (p.137). Also included is a selection of materials on the lives and attitudes of American military personnel in Japan.

889 "Army Acts to Improve Conduct in Japan." *Christian Century* 63:956 (7 Aug. 1946)

This editorial praises the successful efforts of the United States Army to lower the rate of venereal infection among American military personnel in Japan. The magazine takes note, however, of rumors that Japanese women have been discovered sharing quarters in post barracks with servicemen, and it calls upon the Army to tighten its discipline in this regard.

890 Bennett, John W. "Community Research in the Japan Occupation." *Clearinghouse Bulletin of Research in Human Organization* 1, no.3:1–5 (Winter 1951)

The author, who served as chief of the Public Opinion and Sociological Research Division of SCAP's Civil Information and Education Section between 1949 and 1951, discusses the aims, methods, and results of the division's research. Projects mentioned are case studies of village fishing rights, the effect of land reform on rural communities, and the interrelation of 4 neighboring forestry-agriculture villages. Stress is placed on the indispensability of the division's Japanese staff, due to the linguistic weakness of the American researchers and the breadth of the assigned projects. The basic social problems are seen as being rooted in an excessive population existing in a marginal economy.

891 ———. *Social and Attitudinal Research in Japan: The Work of SCAP's Public Opinion and Sociological Research (PO and SR) Division*. Columbus, Ohio: Ohio State Univ., Dept. of Sociology, Feb. 1952. 13p. (Ohio State Univ. Research Foundation project 483, report no.1; Office of Naval Research project NR 176–110, interim technical report no.1). Reprinted under the same title in *Journal of East Asiatic Studies* (Manila) 2, no.1:21–33 (Oct. 1952)

This report evaluates the activities of SCAP's Civil Information and Education Section in the area of research on Japanese social relations. After describing the development of survey research from a public opinion and sociological research unit within the Analysis and Research Division of the Civil Information and Education Section in early 1946 to full division status in October 1948, the report describes the functions of the division and its studies of Japanese attitudes toward prostitution, overpopulation, the social position of women, the *zaibatsu*, and international problems. Some of the research projects conducted by the division in cooperation with other SCAP sections are also treated. They include: *The Japanese Village in Transition*, by Arthur F. Raper, Tamie Tsuchiyama, Herbert Passin, and David L. Sills (1950) (no.1729b), *Some Aspects of the Fishery Right System in Selected Japanese Fishing Communities* (1948) (no.1860), *A Preliminary Study of the Neighborhood Associations of Japan* (1948) (no.1330), and *The Japanese Labor Boss System: A Description and a Preliminary Sociological Analysis* (1952) (no.1754b). In conclusion, the report notes the nature of contemporary research by Western scholars on Japanese society and the significance of this division and its work in this respect. It also comments on the findings and research methodologies involved.

Bennett, John W., and Ishino Iwao. *Paternalism in the Japanese Economy: Anthropological Studies of Oyabun–Kobun Patterns.* 1963. See no.1912.

892 Berrigan, Darrell. "Japan's Occupation Babies." *Saturday Evening Post* 220:24–25, 117–18 (19 June 1948)

Berrigan's subject is the children fathered by American troops in Japan. According to military law, he notes, soldiers have no obligation beyond a moral one to support these children, and most do not. The article consists primarily of a series of anecdotal examples of the difficulties faced by the children and their mothers, especially in those cases where the fathers were black. Neither the Japanese nor the American government is doing much to ease their plight, and private agencies cannot meet the need.

893 Braibanti, Ralph J. D. "Administration of Military Government in Japan at the Prefectural Level." *American Political Science Review* 43:250–75 (Apr. 1949)

This study of the administration of military government at the local (prefectural) level provides valuable information on an often overlooked aspect of the occupation. Divided into 7 sections, it provides a comprehensive picture of the structure and operations of the lowest level of SCAP's administrative structure. Part 1 briefly discusses the relevance of operations at this level to the final success of the occupation, and part 2 describes the initial structure of prefectural government units and the major changes which took place on 1 July 1946. Part 3 examines the chain of authority within the 5 layers of administration of the occupation (i.e., the descending hierarchy from SCAP in Tokyo to the Eighth Army, corps headquarters, regional headquarters, and the prefectural team). The author describes it as revealing "a standard Army pattern of line command which is characterized by vertical organization wherein all policy emanates from the highest authority." Parts 4 and 5 examine the limited range of administrative action which the prefectural team has at its disposal. The author defines and describes it under 4 headings: (1) surveillance, (2) reporting of noncompliant behavior, (3) the rendering of informal nonmandatory advice and assistance to Japanese prefectural governments, and (4) limited responsibility in the conduct of judicial proceedings for the trial of offenses committed by Japanese nationals. The final section discusses relations between military government officials at the local level and Japan's postwar political parties.

894 ———. "Occupation Controls in Japan." *Far Eastern Survey* 17:215–19 (22 Sept. 1948)

An examination of SCAP's administrative structure which defines 4 procedural mechanisms by which SCAP operates, the first being an injunction or prohibition; the second, mandatory directives of a positive nature; the third, judicial procedures; and the fourth, consultative or advisory assistance. The article emphasizes the inadequate communications between SCAP in Tokyo and the 46 prefectural field offices of SCAP. The author believes it will delay the Japanese government's early assumption of full governing responsibility.

895 ———. *The Occupation of Japan: A Study in Organization and Administration.* Ph.D. dissertation, Syracuse Univ., 1949. xxii, 970p.

Braibanti discusses the organizational and administrative aspects of occupation operations in Japan. He begins with an account of the training of military government personnel; the work of top-level policy formulating organizations such as the State-War-Navy Coordinating Committee, the Far Eastern Commission, and the Allied Council for Japan; and problems related to the effective implementation of military government. He then discusses the conflict between the nature of military government and its administration of civil affairs, problems of procedural controls over the Japanese government, problems of coordination among different levels of military government, the role of the Eighth Army, and the role of the Counterintelligence Corps. He also examines Japanese attitudes toward military government, military government operations at the prefectural level, and relations among the different branches of the occupation forces.

896 ———. "The Role of Administration in the Occupation of Japan." *Annals of the American Academy of Political and Social Science* 267:154–63 (Jan. 1950)

After identifying 3 major areas of crucial importance in the Allied occupation of Japan—(1) the formulation and development of an occupation policy, (2) the calculation of the effect of this policy on the government and people of Japan, and (3) the construction of an administration which serves as a link between the first and second problems—the author focuses on the last of these 3 aspects. He discusses the administration of the occupation under 5 general topics. The first and perhaps most significant of these topics is a definition and explanation of a set of criteria for effective occupation administration under which are included the necessity to preserve the self-respect of the vanquished people, the maximum use of noncoercive techniques, the establishment of a positive relationship between the governmental institutions and the cultural milieu of the country, and the use of democratic techniques in governing. The second general topic is concerned with an explanation of the "paradox of democratization by force," whereas the third briefly discusses the structure of the occupation as a supervisory rather than operational endeavor. The fourth topic relates to such techniques of control as the SCAP directive, the formal advisory commissions, and other informal contacts between SCAP and the Japanese government, and the last general topic discusses the problems encountered in trying to maintain consistency among the various levels of administration. The author was himself a military government officer in Japan for a year and a half.

Bronfenbrenner, Martin. "The American Occupation of Japan: Economic Retrospect." 1968. *See* no.1635a.

Chaze, Elliott. *The Stainless Steel Kimono*. 1947. *See* no.485.

897 Crawford, Robert H. "Why Occupations Decline." *Military Government Journal* 2:3–4 (Fall 1949)

This article represents one of the few critical analyses of the Allied occupation to be found in a periodical which usually presents very optimistic accounts of SCAP's successes. The author, who served with SCAP from 1946 to 1948, discusses what he considers to be the defects impeding the accomplishment of military government aims in Japan—"first, our unwillingness to recognize unhappy situations when we see them and second, the danger of concluding that once an order has been made, there can be no change." Moreover, he concludes, among SCAP personnel there is not an adequate supply of trained supervisory personnel to accomplish the necessary reforms. Speaking from personal experience and citing incidents of administrative inefficiency and incompetence, the author suggests that one solution to the problem would be "the elimination of the 'life work' ideal for civilians in an Occupation" and the replacement of permanent employees by qualified civilian specialists who would serve for a limited period of time.

Crofts, Verna I. "Japan as I Saw It." 1948. *See* no.548a.

898 Falk, Ray. "Teaching 'Demokratzi' to the Japanese." *New York Times Magazine* p.12–13, 54–56 (12 June 1949)

The author, a free-lance correspondent, bases this report on his observations of the military government team in Ibaraki prefecture. He believes that it is the local military government teams which have the most impact on the daily lives of the Japanese. He outlines the organization and training of the team and sketches a typical day of the commander. In addition he describes the basic duties of each of the specialized officers. While he observes that most of the local teams are effective in introducing reforms, he finds the Japanese eager to carry out surface change but stubborn at the core. He is critical of some military government commanders who try to be empire builders and of the time-consuming official reports required by military government headquarters and by SCAP.

899 Far Eastern Commission. "Basic Post-Surrender Policy for Japan." *Department of State Bulletin* 17:216–21 (3 Aug. 1947); reprinted under the title "Decision of the Far Eastern Commission Concerning Basic Post-war Policy in Japan, June 19, 1947" in *International Organization* 2:207–13 (Feb. 1948), and under the title "Basic Occupation Policy for Japan" in *Current Notes on International Affairs* 18:420–25 (June/July 1947)

The text of a Far Eastern Commission (FEC) document which was adopted on 19 June 1947, and which outlines the commission's general policies relating to postwar Japan. It consists of a preamble offering a general introduction and 4 main sections. Section 1 discusses the general objectives of the FEC and the means whereby they shall be achieved. Section 2 considers the establishment of the Allied command and the formulation of a military occupation under the supreme commander. Section 3 summarizes the political changes that shall be effected and part 4 elaborates the commission's economic policy including such matters as reparations payments and restitution of stolen property. This FEC document is substantially identical with the earlier U.S. Initial Post-Surrender Policy for Japan of 29 August 1945 (no.62).

900 Friedrich, Carl J., et al. *American Experiences in Military Government in World War II*. New York: Holt, 1948. xii, 436p. (American Government in Action series)

American policy regarding military governments and the institution of this form of government in Europe and the Pacific during the months from the early summer of 1943 until the summer of 1946 are examined by those who actually participated in their establishment. The volume consists of 4 parts. Part 1 is a treatment of general problems of military government such as American goals, the place of the concept of democratization in American foreign policy and military government, the relationship between political intelligence and military government, and the military occupation policies of the Axis powers. Parts 2 and 3 are descriptive accounts and evaluations of experiences in Italy, France, Austria, and Germany. Part 4 portrays the American military governments in Guam, Japan, and Korea. The section on Japan in chapter 15 (p.318–54) was written by Arthur D. Bouterse (chief, Public Welfare Subsection, SCAP), Philip H. Taylor (chief, Southeast Asia Section, Far East Branch, G–2, War Dept.), and Arthur A. Maass (military government post liaison officer for Kanagawa prefecture). These 3 men describe in considerable detail the history of the evolution of military government for Japan. Topics covered include the sources from which the personnel for military government in Japan were recruited, the confusion created by the early Japanese surrender, the Military Government Section of the U.S. Army Forces in the Pacific, which functioned from 5 August to 4 October 1945, and its replacement by SCAP's special staff sections, the origins of SCAP directives, the special staff sections of SCAP and their relations with the general staff, and relations between SCAP and the Japanese government and between SCAP and the military government teams. The problems faced by SCAP, including the need for the replacement of the "tactical" form of military government organization utilized in Japan by a "territorial" form of organization better suited to settled areas like Japan, are critically examined. There is also a discussion of the conflict between law and order policies and democratization policies and of SCAP's initial lack of concern regarding public utilities and the food situation.

901 "General of the Army Douglas MacArthur's Announcement on 'Pro-Fraternization' Regulation, September 23, 1949." *Contemporary Japan* 18:437–39 (July/Sept. 1949)

This announcement outlines the changes in SCAP's fraternization regulations. There is a 7–point explication of the relaxation of restrictions for occupation personnel allowing them permission to use Japanese hotels, inns, and theaters not specifically posted off limits, to compete with or against Japanese in sports, and, "when authorized by local commanders," to invite Japanese to organized social activities. Following the 7 points are 3 points relaxing restrictions for non-occupation personnel authorized by SCAP to be in Japan. In the final paragraphs of this pronouncement, MacArthur discusses SCAP's recent steps "to return to the Japanese Government those functions and responsibilities which it demonstrates capacity to handle."

902 Ginsburgh, Robert Neville. *Between War and Peace: An Administrative and Organizational Analysis of Selected Military Government Experiences of the United States Army during the Transition Phase*. Ph.D. dissertation, Harvard Univ., 1948. 507p.

Chapter 6 of this dissertation, which is an administrative study of the Japanese occupation, was written in May 1947 but is followed by a postscript describing occupation activities until the summer of 1948. Ginsburgh analyzes the evolution of American and Allied occupation planning, the organization and functioning of American agencies concerned with the occupation, and the relation of these agencies with international supervisory bodies. He concludes that occupation planning was adequate, given the suddenness of the Japanese capitulation, but he criticizes the long and complex chains of command through which policies were executed and altered and the lack of firm guidance and up-to-date intelligence available to local military government teams.

Available at the Harvard University Archives, Widener Library, Cambridge, Massachusetts.

902a Grauer, Alvin. *So I Went to Japan: The Delights, Despairs, and Minor Perils Experienced by Allied Personnel Stationed in Post-war Japan*. Tokyo: Nippon Times, 1947. 66p.

This general introduction to Japan and Japanese life immediately after the war is a whimsical account divided into 3 major chapters: the occupation, Japanese life, and Japanese customs. The sections dealing with the occupation itself average only 2 pages in length and have the following titles: "Morning, Quonset Area"; "Is This Trip Necessary?"; "The Marines Have Landed"; "Hiroshima, City of Horror"; "Nara, Dearly Beloved"; "When Budda [sic] Smiles"; "Fuji—Jewel of Japan"; "Back from Hakone"; "We Visit"; and "Step Right up and Call Me Taro-san".

902b Gray, Gordon. "Military Government: East and West." *Military Government Journal* 1:8–12 (Jan. 1948)

The assistant secretary of the army reviews some of the functions and activities of the U.S. Office of Military Government. While his focus is on Europe, he does provide some information with regard to Japan, writing that "One is struck immediately by the similarity of the Military Government problem" in both Germany and Japan, and that the continuing shortage of food represents the major headache in both countries for the occupation authorities.

902c Hallett, Robert M. "GI's Buy up Japan: Barter for Souvenirs Goes on Apace." *Christian Science Monitor* magazine section p.5 (15 June 1946)

Hallett finds that American soldiers are busily purchasing souvenirs of all kinds from hard-pressed Japanese throughout the country. Most of the sales are made after lengthy bargaining sessions in sign language that become major social occasions punctuated by laughter and good-natured arguments. Hallett believes that the friendly relationships thus established helped, especially in the early days of the occupation, to calm the fears people had of the Americans as a consequence of wartime Japanese propaganda.

903 Hilldring, John H. "American Policy in Occupied Areas." *Department of State Bulletin* 15:47–48 (14 July 1946)

The assistant secretary of state and chairman of the State-War-Navy Coordinating Committee (SWNCC) succinctly outlines the planning and implementation of American policy in all occupied areas including Germany, Austria, Japan, Korea, and the Venezia Giulia of Italy. He emphasizes the State Department's role in the development and promulgation of that policy and outlines the organizational structure and responsibilities of the newly created Office of the Assistant Secretary of State for Occupied Areas, which was created to coordinate all of the department's activities concerned with occupations. He briefly discusses the State Department's efforts to coordinate the activities of the U.S. government and the Far Eastern Commission but concentrates on the structure and operations of SWNCC. In his description of that organization, he affirms that it provides a much needed working link between the armed services and those responsible for foreign policy but insists that "since 70–85 percent of the Occupation problems presented to the State, War, and Navy Departments are political, the Department of State should occupy the position of leadership."

904 Hille, Henry L., Jr. "Eighth Army's Role in the Military Government of Japan." *Military Review* 27:9–18 (Feb. 1948)

After briefly describing and analyzing the formal mission and history of the Eighth Army's activities in Japan, the author, a lieutenant colonel in its Corps of Engineers, describes the organization of the Army's military government activities. He includes a map showing the location of military government teams as reorganized on 1 January 1947 and a chart entitled "Command Channels for Military Government Teams" as of the same date. He also discusses the problems faced by the occupation in the areas of economics, public health and welfare, information and education, repatriation, administration, and procurement. Hille concludes that the mission of military government demands that "a positive, constructive role" be played by military government units in the field. Upon their success or failure in carrying out this role will depend the outcome of the units' various efforts to teach the Japanese people "democracy as we understand it."

Holborn, Hajo. *American Military Government: Its Organization and Policies*. 1947. See no.232.

905 James, Weldon. "Main Street Moves to Japan." *Collier's* 119:16–17, 102–5 (14 June 1947)

The author discusses the standard of living of occupation personnel in Japan. He indicates that most officials take advantage of the occupation to live in a way that would be beyond their resources in the United States. Examples of graft and immoral behavior are given.

Kelley, Frank R., and Cornelius Ryan. *Star Spangled Mikado*. 1947. See no.506.

906 Krueger, Walter. *From Down under to Nippon: The Story of the Sixth Army in World War II*. Washington, D.C.: Combat Forces Pr., 1953. xv, 393p.

The U.S. Sixth Army's 3 years in the Pacific War are recorded here by its commanding general from activation on 25 January 1943 through deactivation on 31 December 1945 at Kyoto. This careful and detailed account, based on official reports and the author's recollections, describes the bitter fighting and trying experiences which his army endured. He also recounts the brilliant strategies planned by General MacArthur. Approximately the last tenth of the book is devoted to the Sixth Army's duties in Japan. It describes the Sixth Army's part in the projected Olympic and Coronet operations to assault the Japanese islands and in the Blacklist Plan for the occupation of Japan. It then describes the cancellation of these operations because of Japan's surrender and the Sixth Army preparations for landing in Japan and stationing the Marine Amphibious Corps, "I" Corps, and "X" Corps in western Japan. The author also refers briefly to the duties of the Sixth Army in cooperation with the Counterintelligence Corps to check the extent to which the Japanese government complied with SCAP instructions to demobilize Japanese armed forces, to hand over materiel, to convert industries for peaceful purposes, to repatriate Orientals and Europeans, and to sponsor lectures on democracy for the Japanese. Appended are a list of officers transferred to the headquarters of the Sixth Army, lists of major units of the Third and Sixth Armies, and a list of Sixth Army casualties.

MacArthur, Douglas. "Statement by General MacArthur." 1947. See no.875.

907 Maki, John McGilvrey. "United States Initial Postsurrender Policy for Japan." In *Essays on Modern Politics and History Written in Honor of Harold M. Vinacke*, ed. by Kim Han-Kyo. Athens: Ohio Univ. Pr., 1969. p.30–56.

A historical and analytical account of the drafting and significance of this basic U.S. policy statement which provided the fundamental guidance for the conduct of the Allied occupation of Japan. Maki considers it to be one of the outstanding documents of American diplomatic history.

Martin, Charles. "The Rebirth of a Nation." 1950. See no.602.

908 Montgomery, John Dickey. "Administration of Occupied Japan: First Year." *Human Organization* 8:4–16 (Summer 1949)

Montgomery, who was with the Seventy-sixth Military Government Company at the Civil Affairs Staging Area, Presidio of Monterey, California and who went to Japan as an administrative officer and labor economist, provides an informative look at the problems and processes involved in setting up and carrying out the administration of occupied Japan. He sees the American military government as an active agent in far-reaching culture changes both planned and unplanned, the latter including unpredicted consequences of the planned program. The assumptions concerning Japanese culture on which planning was based and fundamental aspects of this culture are examined. Problems of the preoperational phase of the occupation, particularly concerning the military government officers rushed to the Civil Affairs Staging Area, are discussed. The organization and administration of the military government are outlined and organizational deficiencies noted. Problems with communication and policy uncertainty at the local levels are among the difficulties discussed. Two case studies are included to demonstrate the gap between policy formation and policy implementation. The disunity occasioned by the impact of "civilian" politics upon the "military" is considered. The author calls for further study of the planned and unplanned effects which the introduction of foreign institutions will have on the Japanese culture.

909 Morris, J. Malcolm. *The Wise Bamboo*. Philadelphia: Lippincott, 1953. 253p.

The author was manager of the Imperial Hotel in Tokyo from 1945 to 1951, first as a soldier, then as a civilian. He describes the problems he faced in dealing with occupation VIPs, Russians, female visitors, judges of the International Military Tribunal, etc.

Moseley, Harold W., Charles W. McCarthy, and Alvin F. Richardson. "The State-War-Navy Coordinating Committee." 1945. See no.58.

910 "Occupation of Japan." *New Statesman and Nation* 32:170 (7 Sept. 1946)

A letter from a British Commonwealth Occupation Force officer criticizes directives pertaining to the conduct of occupation personnel. He maintains that Allied personnel in their dealings with Japanese are required to steer a middle course between authoritarian and militaristic policies on the one hand and benevolent, educational, "cultural penetration" on the other. The author feels that the result of this mixed policy will be to minimize the long-range constructive effects of the occupation and that a valuable opportunity is being lost to practice a more effective brand of "cultural penetration."

911 "Occupation Official Says the Plushy Life Is All that Holds Most Americans in Japan." *U.S. News and World Report* 27, no.9:38 (26 Aug. 1949)

An unnamed occupation official is reported to have remarked that "the only reason a lot of us don't quit and go home is that it's so plushy out here." The article maintains that Americans in fact have little left to do now that the initial years of the occupation are over.

912 Parrott, Lindesay. "GI's Are Great Guys: Yanks Make a Hit with the Kids of Japan." *New York Times Magazine* p.29 (17 Mar. 1946)

Six months after the Japanese surrender, the occupation "is busily replaying the pleasant age-old comedy of the soldier and the kid." The American GI has impressed the Japanese with his generosity and good manners; whatever the outcome of the occupation, therefore, the soldiers and Japanese children will retain pleasant memories of one another.

The Reminiscences of Alvin Graves. 1961. See no.44d.

The Reminiscences of Burton Crane. 1961. See no.44e.

The Reminiscences of Douglas W. Overton. 1960. See no.44h.

The Reminiscences of Esther Crane. 1961. See no.44i.

The Reminiscences of Faubion Bowers. 1960. See no.44j.

913 Richie, Donald. *This Scorching Earth.* Rutland, Vt.: Tuttle, 1956. 317p.

This historical novel by Donald Richie, a feature writer for the *Pacific Stars and Stripes* in 1946–49 and a film critic, takes the occupation of Japan as its subject. Focusing on the office of a so-called Special Services Section in the headquarters of SCAP in Tokyo and an American military base in Yokohama, the author describes the relationships among middle-ranking officers and people around them, their social life, and their attitudes toward Japanese culture and society. The novel is somewhat satirical. It features a major from Texas who preaches democracy and practices black marketing, a colonel who is relieved of his post for being too American, a secretary who enjoys her popularity among military men, and a Japanese woman who feels caught between an American soldier she loves and a Japanese university student she is supposed to marry.

Sebald, William J., and Russell Brines. *With MacArthur in Japan: A Personal History of the Occupation.* 1965. See no.748.

914 Shepard, Whitfield P. "Japan Takes a Step." *Military Government Journal* 2:8 (Winter 1949)

A brief discussion of the abolition of the civil affairs teams in each of Japan's 46 prefectures and the transference of their authority to 8 regional civil affairs teams to be comprised mainly of civilians. According to the author, who is chief of the Civil Affairs Section of the Eighth Army, this transition, effective 1 January 1950, marks the end of the Eighth Army's involvement with civil affairs. Such a change, he believes, will be beneficial insofar as it will allow the Japanese to begin to regain their independence and initiative in such matters.

Singh, Rajendra. *Post-war Occupation Forces: Japan and South-east Asia.* 1958. See no.881.

Smith, Thomas V. "Consent and Coercion in Governing." 1947. *See* no.522.

914a ———. "Government of Conquered and Dependent Areas." In *Civil-Military Relationships in American Life*, ed. by Jerome Gregory Kerwin. Chicago: Univ. of Chicago Pr., 1948. p.91–115.

Smith's article originally was one of several lectures delivered at the University of Chicago that dealt with the problem of how to avoid militarism and to continue the fundamental American tradition of civilian control of government policy while maintaining a huge postwar military establishment with its pervasive influence in government, science, education and industry. Smith focuses on the role which Americans have played in governing Germany, Italy, and Japan, and he considers in particular the educational and religious policies of the military government authorities in each of these areas. He concludes that military government was conducted with reasonable conformity to various American constitutional principles including the separation of powers and the separation of church and state, and is generally impressed with the manner in which the occupation of Japan has been carried out to date.

915 "Soft Life for Occupation Workers." *U.S News and World Report* 26:26–27 (4 Mar. 1949)

Claiming that the standard of living is much higher for American occupation forces in both Germany and Japan than for those with comparable jobs in the United States, the author asserts that the administrative capacities of occupation forces have suffered as a consequence. He suggests that occupation personnel are coming to be viewed as conquerors who have a vested interest in maintaining their jobs and inflated standards of living.

915a "Some of Our Soldiers." *Commonweal* 44:349 (26 July 1946)

When American soldiers in Japan are reported to be "raping, thieving, and bullying," this editorial observes, the official response is that only a small minority do so. Similar reports about Russian soldiers in other places, however, are treated as typical of Russian behavior in general. The editors are bemused by this double standard and at the same time wonder if the U.S. Army is incapable of disciplining its own troops.

916 Supreme Commander for the Allied Powers. *Circulars*. 8 Apr. 1946–23 Dec. 1947. Record Group 5, Box 76. MacArthur Memorial, Bureau of Archives, Norfolk, Va. 2 folders.

These circulars, like the SCAP *Memos* (no.919), were published sporadically. Circulars are generally brief, ranging from 2 to 5 pages apiece. Subjects covered include regulations on working hours of civilian personnel; entry and exit of individuals, aircraft, and surface vessels into, from, and over Japan; foreign quarantine regulations for Japan; international air traffic regulations in Japan; regulations for the importation of noncommercial media and materials, mass communication, and regulations for the sale in Japan of translations, reproduction and performance rights to foreign copyrighted material; conduct of international trade by private commercial representatives; the establishment of a Japanese Export-Import Revolving Fund; and matters regarding air traffic in Japan. There is also a diagram of the hierarchy of responsibility within the Tokyo General Headquarters of SCAP.

917 ———. *General Orders*. 2 Oct. 1945–6 Apr. 1951. Record Group 5, Box 76. MacArthur Memorial, Bureau of Archives, Norfolk, Va. 1 folder.

These orders, issued by command of the supreme commander, are arranged in chronological order and relate directly to the activities of the various divisions of SCAP. Initial orders concern the official establishment of various sections of SCAP such as the General Headquarters, Economic and Scientific Section, the Civil Information and Education Section, the Natural Resources Section, the Government Section, and the Legal Section (all issued 2 Oct. 1945). The collection also treats the establishment of such special staff sections as the Office of Civilian Personnel (14 Nov. 1945) and the official charter of the International Military Tribunal for the Far East (19 Jan. 1946). There are also orders announcing the appointment of various staff members. Later orders concern such matters as the discontinuance of the secretariat of the International Military Tribunal for the Far East (12 Feb. 1949) and the General Accounting Section (13 May 1949) as well as the discontinuation of the Statistics and Reports Section and its replacement by the Civil Historical Section (16 Jan. 1950). Amendments and recissions of earlier orders are also included.

918 ———. *Index of Joint Chiefs of Staff Directives to Supreme Commander for the Allied Powers.* Mimeographed. 31 Dec. 1948. 42p. Record Group 5, Box 69. MacArthur Memorial, Bureau of Archives, Norfolk, Va.

This mimeographed booklet supersedes a previous index dated 1 June 1948 and provides a comprehensive index of all directives to SCAP issued by the Joint Chiefs of Staff. Subjects are arranged in alphabetical order and general topics are broken down into subdivisions, e.g., under labor there are subdivisions for conditions, control, law, and organizations. References indicate the directive number as well as the serial number, section number, and paragraph where a particular topic may be found.

919 ———. *Memos.* 8 Oct. 1945–7 Nov. 1946. Record Group 5, Box 76. MacArthur Memorial, Bureau of Archives, Norfolk, Va. 1 folder.

This file contains miscellaneous SCAP memorandums filed in chronological order. It covers a variety of topics principally indicating the locations of various foreign liaison offices and the Japanese foreign office, announcements of new liaison officers, and the reorganization of foreign governments' representation in Japan. Memorandums directly related to SCAP staff sections contain instructions on topics ranging from vaccination requirements to procedures of communication with the press and offices of the Japanese government.

———. Monograph 1. *Introduction, 1945–1951.* 1952. See no.283.

———. Monograph 2. *Administration of the Occupation, 1945–July 1951.* 1952. See no.284.

———. Monograph 3. *Logistic Support, 1945–1951.* 1952. See no.285.

920 ———. *Staff Memos.* Mimeographed. 10 July 1945–15 Mar. 1951. Record Group 5, Boxes 75–76. MacArthur Memorial, Bureau of Archives, Norfolk, Va. 5 folders.

The materials in this mimeographed collection are chronologically ordered and were issued sporadically—sometimes as often as 5 times a month and sometimes only once a month—depending on circumstances. Memorandums vary in length but are generally from 2 to 5 pages long. They may be divided into 2 general categories: (1) those outlining programs and responsibilities to be undertaken by various agencies of the occupation, and (2) those concerning the structure and operations of the SCAP organization itself. The earliest memorandums regarding occupation programs provide a systematic outline of activities on demilitarization and democratization and indicate the particular section of SCAP responsible for such activities, i.e., Legal Section, Government Section, Cultural and Educational Section, or the Engineering and Scientific Section. Topics cover a wide range of issues including the political purge, repatriation, preparation for the war crimes trials, the deconcentration of the *zaibatsu*, the control of civilian communications, the inauguration of civilian supply and relief programs, and the initiation of various economic, financial, and political reforms. Later memorandums are more specifically concerned with detailed accounts of a particular aspect of a program. The memorandums also contain periodic lists of the names of the top secret control officers appointed for each staff section.

The second category of memorandums concerns the nature and function of the entire SCAP operation in Japan. They outline particular aspects of staff responsibilities as well as proper procedures to take in various circumstances and discuss programs for management improvement. They cover a variety of topics including the administration of discipline, private residence policies, legal assistance for SCAP personnel, a list of legal holidays, official relations and contacts with foreign missions, payment of officers, officer promotions, reserve duty, travel regulations within Japan and, internationally, procedures for sending communications and supply policies. The memorandums also provide information on matters concerning SCAP policy for nonoccupation personnel and for exchange clearance for nonoccupation personnel wishing to enter or leave Japan. Revisions of earlier staff memorandums are noted in the series.

921 ———. *Tokyo and Vicinity Telephone Directory.* Tokyo: SCAP, 1945–52. irregular.

During the occupation period SCAP issued telephone directories at frequent intervals as its organizational structure and personnel changed. Approximately 30 such directories were issued and some 19 of them may be found within the National Archives, Library of Congress, and the Army Library. The titles vary. The most common are: *Tokyo and Vicinity Telephone Directory; Tokyo, GHQ, Telephone Directory;* and *Greater Tokyo Area Occupation Forces, GHQ.* Each directory gives classified and alphabetic lists of telephone numbers for all sections of SCAP headquarters and the Far East Command headquarters as well as for the Allied Council for Japan. They run from the office of the commander in chief down to the heads of branches and give the names and assignments of ranking personnel in each office.

922 ———. Allied Translator and Interpreter Section. *Monthly Report.* Tokyo: SCAP, Oct. 1945–Nov. 1946. monthly.

This brief, monthly report outlines the structure and operations of the section, noting personnel changes that have taken place in previous weeks and discussing the activities of each of the various divisions, i.e., those responsible for translation as well as the production, information, and forward units.

Available at the McKeldin Library, University of Maryland, College Park, Maryland.

923 ———. Civil Affairs Div. *Comparative Data: Japan and Germany, Estimates of Appropriate Funding.* n.d. Record Group 5, Box 106. MacArthur Memorial, Bureau of Archives, Norfolk, Va. 1 chart.

A chart providing comparative data on U.S. funding in occupied Japan and Germany. Covering the fiscal years 1948, 1949, and 1950, it cites the Government and Relief in Occupied Areas funds spent for each of those years as well as funds from the Economic Cooperation Administration for both Japan and Germany. In addition, the chart provides data on population estimates, per capita expenditures, and arable land for both countries for the same time period.

———. Civil Information and Education Section. *Activities Reports.* Nov. 1945–Dec. 1946, Jan. 1949, May 1951. See no.265.

924 ———. ———. *Information Programs.* Mimeographed. Tokyo: SCAP, Nov. 1948. 158p.

This mimeographed pamphlet issued by the Information Division of the section contains descriptions of all but one of the Civil Information and Education Section's national information programs in operation in 1948. A brief introductory note explains the nature and significance of the programs which supplement SCAP activities in the political, social, and economic fields. Programs are arranged under general topics which include agricultural cooperatives, general price stabilization, public health, safety and welfare, reconstruction and housing, and women's affairs. Each program is described individually; there is a brief background account, an outline of the division's general and specific objectives in inaugurating the program, the main themes of the program, the group to whom it is intended to appeal, the media involved in the program's propagation, and a description of progress already made and goals still to be achieved.

Available at the Washington National Records Center, Suitland, Maryland.

925 ———. Commander in Chief. Aide-de-Camp. *Master Files.* Nov. 1945–Mar. 1949. Record Group 5, Box 1. MacArthur Memorial, Bureau of Archives, Norfolk, Va. 3 folders.

Three folders, arranged chronologically, contain a variety of materials relating to the work of Colonel Herbert B. Wheeler, the aide-de-camp in the Office of the Commander in Chief, General Headquarters, SCAP. The first file covers the period from late 1945 through 1946 and includes various orders for the purchase of occupation supplies; some random statistics on food deficits in vital urban areas; a partial English translation of a Japanese book on the career of General MacArthur by Yamazaki Kazuyoshi which was examined and censored by SCAP; partial lists of the general and special staff section officers for General Headquarters, Allied Forces in the Pacific; directories of Japanese personnel in the Central Liaison Office in Tokyo; and lists of military and civilian personnel from the Netherlands, France, China, the United Kingdom, and the Soviet Union. There is also some interesting correspondence between SCAP and 4 members of the defense counsel staff concerning their resignation from the International Military Tribunal for the Far East in May of 1946. The second file, covering 1947, consists of a number of miscellaneous documents on assorted topics, some of them relating to Korea rather than Japan. The greater part of the materials in this folder consist of reports and correspondence from the Civil Information and Education Section to the commander in chief's office on such topics as the American publishers' press conference with Japanese newspapers, the language reform situation, and the quality of articles on the occupation appearing in United States' newspapers and magazines. There are also included documents and letters concerning Japanese newspapers and SCAP attitudes toward them. There is a Civil Information and Education Section report to General Headquarters on the scope of the expert consultants program, with particular emphasis on the forthcoming education mission and a list of possible American members for that mission. Other topics covered in the second file are land reform, the establishment of military occupation provost courts, and the propagation of Christianity in Japan. Rosters from the Public Information Office which indicate the location of all foreign correspondents for the months October through December of 1947 may also be found in the file. In contrast to the first 2 files, the third file dealing with 1948 contains only a few charts and diagrams concerning current and proposed public works budgets for education as compared with construction costs, changes in salaries and the cost of living. There is also a brief report by the Natural Resources Section on the results of the second Japanese Antarctic whaling expedition and several miscellaneous papers.

926 ———. Diplomatic Section. *Atcheson Correspondence.* 1945–47. Record Group 5, Box 100. MacArthur Memorial, Bureau of the Archives, Norfolk, Va. 1 binder.

Memorandums, letters, and reports written and received by George Atcheson and correspondence related to him are collected in this binder and chronologically arranged. They cover the period from September 1945 through October 1947. Most of the materials relate to his responsibilities as State Department political adviser to SCAP and chairman of the Allied Council for Japan. They concern arrangements for a 4-man deputation of American Christian leaders to confer with their Japanese counterparts, current Japanese attitudes on the imperial institution, details of the projected peace treaty with Japan, an interim reparations directive, control and ownership of radio broadcasting in Japan, Joseph Keenan's difficulties as the chief of counsel for the International Military Tribunal for the Far East, and broad policy changes by SCAP in the course of the occupation.

———. Economic and Scientific Section. *Labor Division Manual*. 1949. See no.1787.

927 Taylor, Philip H. "The Administration of Occupied Japan." *Annals of the American Academy of Political and Social Science* 267:140-53 (Jan. 1950)

A critical account of the administration of the Allied occupation by an author with considerable experience in SCAP—first as editor in chief of SCAP's monthly *Summation* (no.262) for Japan from 1945 to 1946 and then as chief of the Operations Department, School for Government of Occupied Areas. The author stresses several factors that are of prime importance in determining the direction of the occupation, particularly the preeminent position of General MacArthur and the collapse of the Allies' wartime cooperation. He then discusses in detail the initial organization and early policy documents preparing for the occupation as well as the establishment of the Far Eastern Commission and SCAP. He briefly outlines the responsibilities of members of these organizations. There is a clear summation of the successes and failures of the occupation to date, discussed under 3 broad policy objectives: demilitarization, democratization, and the establishment of a self-sustaining economy. The last portion of the article is devoted to an explanation of the causes behind the change in policy that occurred in 1948-49 and a description of some important results of that change. In the concluding section the author speculates about the future of American policy toward Japan and suggests that the United States does not have the exclusive right to make policy decisions for Japan. He maintains that such a course of action will not be beneficial to Japan, to the United States, or to the other Asian nations who have a vital interest in the future of their former enemy.

927a Tregaskis, Richard. "Road to Tokyo." *Saturday Evening Post* pt.1, 218:20, 121-22 (29 Sept. 1945); pt.2, 218:20, 105-6 (6 Oct. 1945); pt.3, 218:20, 106-7 (13 Oct. 1945); pt.4, 218:18, 111-14 (20 Oct. 1945); pt.5, 218:20, 114-16 (27 Oct. 1945)

This series of articles chronicles Tregaskis' observations as a reporter assigned to MacArthur's headquarters in Manila and subsequently in Tokyo during the weeks immediately before and after the surrender. The first 2 articles, datelined Manila, describe the frantic confusion of the headquarters immediately after the Japanese surrender—an event which came much earlier than expected. The military government section was initially understaffed; soon, however, it was overwhelmed by a sudden increase in manpower and many last minute changes in plans. Tregaskis then notes a trend toward the "mollification" of American policy. The primary example he cites is the decision that was made to govern Japan indirectly. The next 2 articles are datelined Yokohama. They recount Tregaskis' arrival in Japan with the first groups of military government officers and describe the activities of the occupation in its early days. The last article in the series deals largely with the disappointment and annoyance of the military government officers at the decision to rule through the existing Japanese government. Their resentment, Tregaskis indicates, was due not only to a feeling that their training and preparation was going to waste but also to a fear that SCAP was "giving Japan back to the Japanese."

928 U.S. Army. Eighth Army. Headquarters. *Eighth Army Military Government Organization and Activities*. Tokyo: SCAP, Sept. 1947. 28p., charts.

This brief pamphlet describes the nature and function of military government in occupied Japan. There is a brief discussion of the hierarchy of responsibilities within the military government echelons extending from the commanding general of the Eighth Army down to the prefectural teams. The bulk of the pamphlet is devoted to a summary of military government activities in its principal areas of interest, i.e., economics, public health, repatriation, civil information and education, public welfare, and legal and government matters. Two charts provide a diagram of the organizational structure of Eighth Army Headquarters and a map indicates the location of military government teams as of 1 July 1947.

Available at the Washington National Records Center, Suitland, Maryland.

929 ———. ———. ———. ———. *Operational Directives.* Tokyo: SCAP, 1945–49. irregular.

Issued on an irregular basis these directives were sent from the Eighth Army Headquarters to all military government teams and regions in Japan. Included in the collection are operational directives, amendments to, and recisions of earlier directives sent from the office of the commanding general to members of the Eighth Army in Japan. Directives are generally limited to a few pages and serve to explain the army's role in implementing a particular aspect of the occupation—whether it be in accord with a SCAP directive or a Japanese government program. Directives in this limited collection concern the inventory and transfer of looted property, food distribution, repatriation, building policies of the Japanese government, national elections, agricultural reform, control of population movements, transportation control, restaurant control, etc.

Available at the Washington National Records Center, Suitland, Maryland.

930 ———. ———. Far East Command. Military Intelligence Section. Historical Section. *Summary of Activities, G–2 Historical Section, February 16–March 16, 1947.* Mar. 1947. Record Group 6, Box 4. MacArthur Memorial, Bureau of Archives, Norfolk, Va. 24p.

A brief outline of the G-2 Historical Section's activities during the preceding month, divided into 4 main parts. Part 1 provides a roster of personnel and an organizational chart. Part 2 describes the projects with which the section was occupied during the period concerned including intelligence reports, the surveillance of the official historical records of the Japanese government, and assignments from the War Department. Part 3 discusses the progress made on each of these projects, and part 4 describes recent acquisitions of the section's library in Tokyo. Three appendixes provide SCAP directives concerning official Japanese war records and other official documents, miscellaneous sources of information, and further information on War Department assignments.

931 ———. ———. Pacific Air Command. *General Information for Dependents of Military Personnel Planning to Come to Japan.* Tokyo: 1946? 17p.

Wells, Roger H. "Interim Government and Occupation Regimes." 1948. See no.888.

Wildes, Harry E. *Typhoon in Tokyo: The Occupation and Its Aftermath.* 1954. See no.765.

931a Worden, William L. "G.I. Is Civilizing the Jap." *Saturday Evening Post* 218: 18–19, 103–4 (15 Dec. 1945)

Worden finds that the living example of the American soldier is proving to be an effective force for democratization. The Japanese are waiting to be told what to think, but their "slippery countrymen" in both the press and the government are evading their responsibilities. The press is confused by its new freedom and contributes nothing but anti-American half-truths and innuendo, while being unable or reluctant to make constructive contributions that would discredit the old and build up the new. The behavior of the GIs, therefore, remains the only good source of information about the meaning and practice of democracy.

Yoshida, Shigeru. *The Yoshida Memoirs: The Story of Japan in Crisis.* 1962. See no.769.

The Supreme Commander for the Allied Powers

Only two men held the post of supreme commander for the Allied powers: General Douglas MacArthur for the first sixty-seven months of the occupation and General Matthew B. Ridgway for the last thirteen. Since after June 1950 the Korean War had forcibly diverted much of the supreme commander's attention away from a prime focus on Japan and since the occupation was at that time in its terminal stages and marked by an increasing reversion of both initiative and power to Japanese rather than American hands, General Ridgway had relatively little to do with any of the major innovations or programs associated with the occupation. His mission was rather to conduct the Korean War and to preside over Japan's transition from occupation to independence and to a new role as an American ally. As a consequence his imprint on the occupation and the literature connected therewith was light.

General MacArthur, on the other hand, practically personified the American occupation of Japan. The literature reflects this point. Few have found it possible to discuss the period seriously without devoting substantial attention to his role as supreme commander. As a consequence, most general and many specialized accounts contain sections devoted to MacArthur. The interested reader is advised at minimum, therefore, to consult also the appropriate sections under "General Materials" (p.113) as well as no.46 (p.30). This last entry describes the notable collection of MacArthuriana assembled at the MacArthur Memorial in Norfolk, Virginia.

The following items have been classified under 3 headings: (1) Douglas MacArthur, primary materials; (2) Douglas MacArthur, secondary materials; and (3) Matthew B. Ridgway.

DOUGLAS MACARTHUR

Primary Materials

This section consists of speeches and writings by General MacArthur and files of his personal correspondence, appointment books, etc. A good deal of the material is located at the MacArthur Memorial in Norfolk, Virginia. His speeches have been arranged chronologically rather than alphabetically. The reader's attention is also called to the collection of statements by General MacArthur published as Appendix F (p.736–89) of volume 2 of *Political Reorientation of Japan, September 1945 to September 1948: Report* (1949) (no.279).

MacArthur, Douglas. "The Surrender of Right to Make War." 1946. *See* no. 1005.

932 "General Douglas MacArthur's Message on the First Surrender Anniversary, September 2, 1946." *Contemporary Japan* 15:394–96 (Sept./Dec. 1946)

Commemorating the first anniversary of the signing of the surrender terms on the battleship *Missouri*, the supreme commander discusses the implementation of the philosophical principles which were outlined at Potsdam and reaffirmed on the *Missouri*. He maintains that the impact of these new principles can be visualized only if one understands the Japanese philosophy as it evolved since feudal times, and he briefly describes this previous philosophical position as militaristic and ultranationalist. He views the revolution of the spirit of the Japanese people brought about through the occupation as "an unparalleled conclusion in the social history of the world" and urges the Allied powers to persevere in their monumental task of guiding the Japanese people to reshape their lives and institutions to conform to the ideals of a democratic society.

933 "General of the Army Douglas MacArthur's New Year's Message to the Japanese People, January 1, 1947." *Contemporary Japan* 16:101-2 (Jan./Mar. 1947)

MacArthur uses the occasion of the New Year's celebration to look back upon the spirit of reform of the previous year and to look forward to future developments. He speaks of the complexities of reform, of the "crosscurrents of decision and indecision, of progress and retrogression" which have marked the postwar period yet is optimistic regarding the overall success of the great reforms "designed to uplift the dignity and wellbeing of the individual and to establish a free society."

934 "General of the Army Douglas MacArthur's Message to the U.S. Congress in Compliance with the Request of the War Department (Released to the Press, February 20, 1947)." *Contemporary Japan* 16:106-10 (Jan./Mar. 1947)

After briefly outlining the general philosophy of the Allied occupation of Japan and discussing some of the pressing political and economic problems to be solved by the SCAP organization, MacArthur emphasizes to the Congress the fact that food and other emergency relief supplies will continue to be needed in Japan and that these will have to be provided through appropriations from the United States. He views such aid as our national responsibility and is confident that the United States will live up to such responsibilities.

934a "General of the Army Douglas MacArthur's Statement anent the House of Representatives Election of April 25th, April 27, 1947." *Contemporary Japan* 16:226 (Apr./June 1947)

MacArthur characterizes the election as the last preparatory step before the adoption of the new constitution. The constitution itself, he notes, is among the most liberal and progressive charters in the world and "reflects one of the great spiritual reformations of mankind." The basic issue in the election, according to MacArthur, was a choice between political philosophies. The totalitarian extreme right had already been discredited, but the Japanese people firmly and decisively rejected as well the extreme left Communist philosophy and chose instead a moderate course that insures the preservation of freedom and the enhancement of individual dignity.

MacArthur, Douglas. "Statement by General MacArthur." 1947. *See* no.875.

935 "General of the Army Douglas MacArthur's New Year's Message to the Japanese People, January 1, 1948." *Contemporary Japan* 17:97-98 (Jan./Mar. 1948)

MacArthur's understanding of the aims and accomplishments of the occupation is summarized in this brief message to the Japanese people. He classifies the major reforms in 3 general categories —economic, political, and social—briefly relating the progress that has been initiated by the Allied powers and assuring the Japanese that they themselves must take the responsibility to safeguard these reforms.

936 "General of the Army Douglas MacArthur's Message to the Japanese People Issued on the Occasion of the First Anniversary of the New Constitution, May 2, 1948." *Contemporary Japan* 17:208-11 (Apr./June 1948)

The main portion of MacArthur's address to the Japanese people consists of a discussion of the nature of the democracy which the Allied powers are attempting to establish in Japan and a review of the progress that has been made by the Japanese people during the past year. He concentrates particularly upon economic reforms that have been initiated and especially commends the Japanese people for their growing consciousness of public responsibility which will help to prevent a resurgence of totalitarian forces in the future.

"General Douglas MacArthur's Review of the War Crimes Sentences Issued on November 24, 1948." 1948. *See* no. 1014.

937 "New Year's Message Issued by General Douglas MacArthur, Supreme Commander for the Allied Powers on January 1, 1949." *Contemporary Japan* 18:126–28 (Jan./Mar. 1949)

Like previous New Year's messages, this address by MacArthur to the Japanese people concentrates on the progress of the preceding year and looks forward to the ensuing year. MacArthur believes that since political reform has largely been completed, the emphasis has shifted from political to economic reconstruction and that such reconstruction will present a difficult challenge to the Japanese people. At the conclusion of his address, he restores to the Japanese people "the unrestricted use and display of your national flag within your country's territorial limits."

938 "General MacArthur's Message to the People of Japan Issued on the Constitution Day, May 3, 1949." *Contemporary Japan* 18:274–75 (Apr./June 1949)

Marking the second anniversary of the birth of a new Japan, the supreme commander lauds the Japanese people for their unceasing efforts to effect political stability and social progress in their nation. He states that Allied forces still occupy Japan not due to any fault of the Japanese but rather "to events and circumstances elsewhere beyond your capacity to influence or control." He characterizes the occupation as having changed over the years "from the stern rigidity of a military operation to the friendly guidance of a protective force."

939 "General of the Army Douglas MacArthur's Statement Issued on the Fourth Anniversary of Japan's Surrender, September 2, 1949." *Contemporary Japan* 18:398–404 (July/Sept. 1949); reprinted under the title of "MacArthur's Four Years in Japan." *U.S. News and World Report* 27, no.11:61–63 (9 Sept. 1949)

As is usual with such commemorative addresses to the Japanese people, MacArthur presents an overall summation of the progress of the Allied occupation in achieving its goals in the political, social, and economic spheres. In this address, the economic realm is emphasized and the recent problems and solutions to those problems are discussed. The author makes particular reference to the increase of the Japanese population and discusses the issue of the eventual revival of Japan's foreign trade. After condemning Communist efforts to thwart occupation objectives, he praises the American people for a great and noble effort and the Japanese people for "having faithfully fulfilled their surrender commitments and earned the freedom and dignity and opportunity which alone can come with the restoration of a formal peace."

940 "General MacArthur's New Year's Message to the Japanese People, January 1, 1950." *Contemporary Japan* 19:136–39 (Jan./Mar. 1950)

As is customary in such addresses, the supreme commander attempts to sum up all significant accomplishments in occupied Japan to date. He emphasizes the fact that the previous year has witnessed progressive and far-reaching relaxation of occupation controls and expresses his pleasure that the Japanese economy is approaching a condition where "the stability of the price structure derives from the equilibrium of normal economic forces rather than from artificial devices." He suggests that the coming year will present 2 difficult problems which concern "the global ideological struggle" and the "international procedural conflict delaying call of a Japanese peace conference."

941 "General MacArthur's Statement on the Third Anniversary of Japan's New

Constitution, May 3, 1950." *Contemporary Japan* 19:302–4 (Apr./June 1950); reprinted under the title "Illegalize the Japanese Communist Party: The Pawn of an Alien Power." *Vital Speeches* 16: 458–60 (15 May 1950)

After some cursory remarks concerning the nature and effective operation of Japan's constitution, MacArthur discusses the activities of the Communist party in occupied Japan. The general is vehement in his disapproval of Communist goals and methods in Japan but expresses his confidence in the Japanese people's ability to withstand such a menace.

942 "General Douglas MacArthur's New Year's Message to the People of Japan, January 1, 1951." *Contemporary Japan* 20:120–21 (Jan./Mar. 1951)

In what was to be his final New Year's message to the Japanese people, MacArthur praises Japan's continued progress toward its ultimate goal of national stability and particularly emphasizes Japan's economic recovery. The final section of the brief address concerns Japan's renunciation of war as an instrument of national policy. Although MacArthur conceives this concept to be "one of the highest, if not the highest ideal the modern world has ever known," nevertheless he allows that if threatened by the forces of international lawlessness, "it will become your duty within the principles of the United Nations in concert with others who cherish freedom to mount force to repel force."

942a MacArthur, Douglas. "The Battle to Save the Republic: Drift toward Totalitarian Rule." *Vital Speeches* 17, no.23: 713–16 (15 Sept. 1951)

In an address delivered in Cleveland on 6 September 1951, MacArthur lashes out at the failure of American political and military leaders to seize the opportunity after World War II to "consolidate the victory into a truly enduring peace." Communism has made rapid gains as a result, and the United Nations is inherently weak. Japan's postwar recovery, however, is a bright spot in this otherwise bleak picture. Fortunately Japan was spared the dreadful consequences of a Soviet military occupation. Under United States guidance, she has erected free institutions similar to American ones, has cooperated in the enactment of many important reforms, and has accepted many of the Christian virtues embodied in the American character. MacArthur also praises the new defense relationship between Japan and the United States.

943 MacArthur, Douglas. *General Douglas MacArthur's Private Correspondence.* 1932–64. Record Group 10. MacArthur Memorial, Bureau of Archives, Norfolk, Va. 96 boxes. 95 ft.

This voluminous collection of MacArthur's private correspondence is filed chronologically and includes materials received by the general as well as written by him. The greater portion of the collection consists of letters and cables sent to MacArthur from family friends, armed service associates, congressmen, government officials, international leaders, university professors, businessmen, journalists, churchmen, and well-wishers. Most of the letters are written in a congratulatory tone to commend MacArthur on the success of the occupation, his birthday, or his election to honorary societies, to confer honorary degrees upon him, or to request his presence at a ceremony or event. Later letters frequently comment on the possibility of MacArthur as a presidential candidate. There are many brief remarks regarding particular aspects of the occupation which the writer praises, e.g., enfranchisement of women, the improvement of education, the initiation of a democratic voting system, etc., but there is little critical analysis or exploration of significant aspects of the occupation either in letters written to MacArthur or in his terse replies, which most often simply acknowledge his gratitude at expressions of confidence and encouragement.

944 ———. "General MacArthur Replies." *Fortune* 39:74–75, 188+ (June 1949)

In reply to a previous and critical

economic report on SCAP in the April 1949 issue of *Fortune* (no.1560), the supreme commander outlines his view of the current economic situation. He absolves SCAP from direct responsibility for Japan's economic affairs until 1949 and insists that U.S. policy intended that whatever recovery was possible would have to be based on indigenous Japanese resources. There is a brief description of Japan's dire economic situation at the termination of the war and of SCAP's economic policy from 1945 through December 1948. MacArthur then discusses the implications of the U.S. Interim Economic Stabilization Directive which made the rehabilitation of the Japanese economy an explicit occupation objective. In the final section of his report, MacArthur answers 8 criticisms that were made in the earlier article concerning rampant inflation, industrial stagnation, taxation, overdependence on the United States, increasing costs of the occupation, and a lethargic and inefficient bureaucracy. His views on such issues as employment, *zaibatsu* war guilt, and corruption in Japanese politics may also be found. The supreme commander concludes by expressing his belief that Japan's economic problems are formidable and his confidence that SCAP and Japanese officials will continue to make great and rapid progress in solving them. This article is excerpted in Japanese in the August 1949 issue of *Chūō Kōron*.

945 ———. *Official Correspondence of General MacArthur.* 1945–51. Record Group 5, Box 1. MacArthur Memorial, Bureau of Archives, Norfolk, Va. 1 folder.

A small segment of MacArthur's correspondence during the occupation years, consisting mainly of letters but with a few telegrams and cables as well. Most are letters received by MacArthur but a few letters from him are included. The file is arranged chronologically and the range of topics and individuals included is vast. Many letters from important U.S. and international figures thank the general for his hospitality during their stay in Japan and commend him for the success of the occupation. Letters of particular interest include correspondence from Emperor Hirohito; the adjutant general's report of the visit of the Far Eastern Advisory Commission to Japan; Joseph B. Keenan's comments on the new constitution; an interview with Madame Chiang Kai-shek; Prime Minister Yoshida's New Year's greetings to MacArthur in December 1945 enclosing a copy of a Japanese translation of the soon-to-be-released Imperial Rescript of January 1, 1946; correspondence from General Eisenhower and former President Herbert Hoover; a letter from Roy S. Campbell, chairman of the Deconcentration Review Board, on the mission's work; a memorandum from Claude Buss of the Civil Information and Education Section, General Headquarters, Supreme Commander for the Allied Powers; correspondence concerning a Japanese peace conference proposal from Wang Shih-chieh of the Chinese Mission in Japan; a memorandum from R. J. Wysor, project manager for Overseas Consultants, Inc. concerning reparations; correspondence with a U.S. Congressman concerning immigration laws between the United States and Japan; a letter from William Greene, president of the American Federation of Labor; a letter from Ambassador Edwin Pauley, U.S. reparations representative, on his views on the philosophy of reparations; and one from President Manuel Roxas of the Philippines discussing rehabilitation and reconstruction in the Philippines. There is also correspondence from Carlos P. Romulo, Philippines delegate to the United Nations and the Far Eastern Commission discussing the Far Eastern Commission and its interest in the formulation of a new constitution for Japan. While most letters are of a commendatory nature, there are 2 letters of complaint from the British member of the International Military Tribunal for the Far East concerning the accommodation of British personnel in Tokyo. Other notable correspondence is from various army and navy officials, Secretary of War Kenneth C. Royall, Madame Chiang Kai-shek, George Atcheson of the State Department, British

Prime Minister Clement Attlee, and various ambassadors from Europe, Asia, and Australia. Several of MacArthur's Christmas and New Year's messages and surrender anniversary messages to the members of the Far East Command and the Japanese people may also be found. Some of MacArthur's more important letters are addressed to Prime Minister Yoshida advising a general election in the near future (1947), and to President Harry Truman discussing the progress of the occupation.

946 ———. *Duty, Honor, Country: A Pictorial Autobiography.* New York: McGraw-Hill, 1965. 218p.

A pictorial biography compiled by *Time,* Inc. Pictures are well selected and are captioned with appropriate excerpts from MacArthur's *Reminiscences* (1964) (no.947). The book is divided into 5 parts and the fourth part, 20 pages long, covers the general's years in occupied Japan. The brevity of this part attests to the striking infrequency of his public appearances during his years as supreme commander for the Allied powers. Pictures show him attending the surrender ceremony on the *Missouri,* speaking to the Allied Council for Japan in Tokyo, and meeting with American dignitaries such as Generals Eisenhower and Marshall, W. Averell Harriman, Herbert Hoover, and John Foster Dulles.

947 ———. *Reminiscences.* New York: McGraw-Hill, 1964. viii, 438p.

MacArthur narrates his own career from 1880 through 1964, desiring "to leave it as a heritage to my wife and son." The book is neither a comprehensive balanced record of his career nor a critical or profound self-analysis. It is, as the title suggests, a recollection of major events in which he was involved. There are numerous quotations, often long, from speeches, reports, statements, letters, and other documents, written by both Americans and non-Americans, that praise his own personal qualities, actions, and achievements. The book understandably tends to provide a very favorable picture of the general and his career.

It consists of 10 chapters, the seventh of which relates to the occupation of Japan. This chapter refers to the Manila Mission, the surrender ceremony on the *Missouri,* meeting with the emperor, the emperor's New Year's message in 1946, constitutional revision, the Tokyo war crimes trials, educational reforms, economic democratization, new social status for women, his disagreements with other Allies (particularly the Russians) over occupation policies, his relations with Washington, etc. There are extensive citations from Major General Courtney Whitney's *MacArthur: His Rendezvous with History* (1956) (no.981), Kase Toshikazu's *Journey to the Missouri* (1950) (no.143), messages from President Truman, letters from Prime Ministers Yoshida Shigeru and Suzuki Kantarō, and Karl T. Compton, president of the Massachusetts Institute of Technology, statements of Field Marshall Viscount Alanbrooke, and several of MacArthur's own statements on the Tokyo trials, the constitution, etc. A Japanese version has been published under the title of *Makkāsā kaisōki* (Tokyo: Asahi Shimbunsha, 1964. 2v.), and approximately one third of it appeared in *Asahi Shimbun* as a 169-part series from 6 January to 23 June 1964.

MacArthur Memorial. Bureau of Archives. Norfolk, Va. *See* no.46.

Mears, Helen. "We're Giving Japan Democracy, but She Can't Earn Her Living." [With reply of Douglas MacArthur.] 1949. *See* no.603a.

948 Supreme Commander for the Allied Powers. *General MacArthur's Guest Book.* Nov. 1944–Apr. 1951. Record Group 5, Box 111. MacArthur Memorial, Bureau of Archives, Norfolk, Va. 1v.

General MacArthur's guest book offers significant though partial insights into the visitors he saw during the years of the occupation. Although it begins with November 1944 in the Philippines, the vast majority of entries occur from September 1945 to April 1951. Entries generally include the signature, date, and address of the visitor and often his official title. The overwhelming majority of names entered in the book are non-Japanese, although the names of major and minor Japanese officials and members of the Diet may be found. Although the emperor's signature is not entered in the volume, Crown Prince Akihito's may be found. Among the many visitors are high ranking officers in the U.S. Armed Services, ambassadors and members of foreign missions in Japan, United Nations' delegates, numerous international news correspondents, business leaders, religious leaders, congressmen, members of special missions to Japan, and American university presidents and professors. There may also be found several entertainers and sports figures who visited occupied Japan.

949 ———. Commander in Chief. *Extra Copies of Letters and Personal Messages.* June–Sept. 1949. Record Group 5, Box 2. MacArthur Memorial, Bureau of Archives, Norfolk, Va. 1 folder.

Copies of letters written, with one exception, by General MacArthur between 16 June 1948 and 3 September 1949 to 4 individuals—Stephen Early, the undersecretary of the Department of National Defense; Tracy Voorhees, assistant secretary of the army; Dean Acheson, secretary of state, and George Kennan, director of the Political Planning Staff of the Department of State. The exception is a reply to MacArthur's letter by Early. They present statements of MacArthur's understanding of the character and philosophy of the occupation of Japan as contrasted with that of Germany. Opposing what he defines as a misunderstanding of the Japanese situation in some quarters of the State Department that would favor a change in the structure of the occupation to render it more like the German occupation, MacArthur summarizes his position by affirming that "to speak of civilianizing the Occupation is to speak in riddles" since in many respects the occupation has been a civilian operation from its inception.

950 ———. Military Section. *Daily Appointments.* May 1945–Apr. 1951. Record Group 5, Boxes 2–3. MacArthur Memorial, Bureau of Archives, Norfolk, Va. 10 folders.

Records indicating General MacArthur's daily appointment schedule are filed chonologically in these folders. Each day's appointments are recorded separately with the date and time of the appointment but there is rarely indication of the purpose of the visit. With the exception of such Japanese dignitaries as the emperor, Prime Minister Shidehara, Princes Konoe and Higashikuni, and Prime Minister Yoshida, there are relatively few appointments with Japanese officials. The majority of the supreme commander's visitors over the course of the occupation appear to have been SCAP personnel and high ranking American military officers such as Generals Willoughby, Stilwell, and Wedemeyer as well as important foreign dignitaries such as President Osmeña, Syngman Rhee, General Derevyanko, and W. Macmahon Ball. In addition various governmental figures, State Department officials as well as congressmen, and heads of numerous special missions (e.g., Pauley, Strike, Ladejinsky, and Buss) frequently saw MacArthur. There are also notations of several interviews with correspondents from the major American newspapers and wire services as well as those of various other countries and considerable time was spent by the general with missionary groups.

———. Public Information Office. *Press Releases.* 1945–49. See no.348.

951 Whan, Vorin E., Jr., ed. *A Soldier Speaks: Public Papers and Speeches of General of the Army Douglas MacArthur.* New York: Praeger, 1965. xxix, 367p.

A collection of General MacArthur's representative public speeches and reports arranged in chronological order. It was prepared as a study of MacArthur's career for cadets of the U.S. Military Academy at West Point. Some 70 statements trace the development of his thoughts and views. The period 1908 to 1964 is divided into 9 parts. The fifth pertains to his years as supreme commander for the Allied powers and comprises 15 speeches that he made between 1945 and 1950. These include his statement upon the completion of Japanese demobilization (16 Oct. 1945), his decision authorizing the death sentence for General Homma (21 Mar. 1946), his opening speech delivered at the Allied Council for Japan (5 Apr. 1946), his speech at the Philippines' independence ceremony in Manila (4 July 1946), his statement on the first anniversary of Japan's surrender (2 Sept. 1946), his statement on the postsurrender policy for Japan adopted by the Far Eastern Commission (3 July 1947), and his message to the Japanese people on the third anniversary of the Japanese Constitution (3 May 1950). For each statement the editor has added a short descriptive note providing background information.

Secondary Materials

This section assembles the literature about General MacArthur that focuses specifically on his personality, career, and role in the occupation. Most of the accounts are polemic in nature—either strongly for or against MacArthur. Few people were neutral on this score. There are a number of biographies but, until very recently, none that might be described as scholarly or approaching the definitive in character. James' study (no.958) has gone far toward filling this gap, but, unfortunately, at this writing only the first volume has been published and it stops with 1941. The accounts by Generals Whitney and Willoughby (nos.981 and 983) are also notable because of their authors' long and intimate associations with General MacArthur.

952 "Authority of General MacArthur as Supreme Commander of the Allied Powers." *Department of State Bulletin* 13: 480 (30 Sept. 1945)

Prepared jointly by the State, War, and Navy Departments, this is the text of a message transmitted to General MacArthur on 6 September 1945 through the Joint Chiefs of Staff. It clarifies the nature of his authority and stipulates that (1) the authority of the emperor and of the Japanese government is subordinate to that of the supreme commander of the Allied powers, (2) the control of Japan should be exercised through the Japanese government to the extent that such an arrangement produces satisfactory results, and (3) the statement of Allied intentions regarding Japan contained in the Potsdam Declaration are to be carried out.

Baldwin, Roger N. "Japan's American Revolution." 1948. *See* no.533.

952a Bezrodnov, I. "Under General MacArthur's Rule." *New Times* no.50:18–21 (10 Dec. 1947)

General MacArthur is accused of performing the roles of Japanese emperor, government, and constitution singlehanded, of actively encouraging the *zaibatsu* magnates while attempting to subvert the labor union movement, and of ignoring the lawful interests of the laboring peasant. He is depicted as encouraging Japanese reaction and thwarting true democratic reform programs.

Bolles, Blair. "U.S. Reshapes Policy in Asia." 1949. *See* no.582.

Bowers, Faubion. "Twenty-five Years Ago: How Japan Won the War." 1970. *See* no.697.

953 Caulfield, Genevieve. "MacArthur, Father and Leader of Postwar Japan." *Catholic World* 173:246–51 (July 1951)

Caulfield stresses the importance of MacArthur's leadership to the eventual success of occupation policies. MacArthur's lack of sentimentality and his basic sense of justice are praised; his dismissal as Supreme Commander for the Allied Powers is regarded as a powerful psychological blow to the Japanese trust in American intentions.

"Concerning Policy toward Japan." 1945. *See* no.54.

Costello, William. "Report from Tokyo." 1947. *See* no.2314a.

954 Creel, George. "General MacArthur." *Collier's* 121:18–19, 56–62 (15 May 1948)

Creel discusses General MacArthur's role in developing a democratic Japan and preventing Communist success. The purge of Japanese wartime leadership and the granting of civil liberties to the rest of the Japanese public are explained. A variety of press criticisms of General MacArthur is answered with emphasis on the devotion of the supreme commander for the Allied powers to the tenets of democracy and capitalism.

955 Dyer, Armel. *The Oratory of Douglas MacArthur.* Ph.D. dissertation, Univ. of Oregon, 1968. 342p. (Abstracted in *Dissertation Abstracts* 29:986A [1968]; University Microfilms order no.68–11,950)

General MacArthur's public speeches are analyzed in terms of Aristotelian and Ciceronian concepts of rhetoric. Following a discussion of the special requirements and characteristics of speechmaking in the military, Dyer examines General MacArthur's oratory in terms of the Aristotelian concepts of "speaker-audiences-speeches" and speech "occasions." He also analyzes his speeches according to the Ciceronian divisions of *invento* (content), *dispositio* (arrangement), *elocutio* (style), *memoria* (preparation), and *pronuntiatio* (delivery). His findings indicate that the general employed all 3 forms of Aristotelian proof: *logos* (logical), *pathos* (emotional), and *ethos* (ethical), and that the greatest strength of MacArthur's speeches stemmed from his use of ethical proofs. According to Dyer, most of these speeches were well organized and purposeful and often had a conclusion with high emotional appeal. He concludes that MacArthur's style was more Rhodian than Attic, that he observed the principles of composition, that he often used parallelism and repetition, and that his "complete grasp of ideas, resulting in his projection of carefully structured, logically related units" was the most important factor in his superior delivery. The use of "polysyllabic and unusual words" and the combination of abstract ideas and stylistic devices are referred to as "MacArthurisms."

Greene, Marc T. "Japan Today and Tomorrow." 1950. *See* no.624.

955a Gribachev, P. "MacArthur, 'Paleface Mikado'." *Current Digest of the Soviet Press* 2, no.27:3–4 (19 Aug. 1950)

This condensation of an article appearing in the 12 July issue of *Literaturnaya gazeta* characterizes MacArthur as an egotist, coward, and maniac patron of Japan's reactionary elements. He seldom comes into contact with the people, "surpassing in this the 'divine' Emperor of Japan himself," and like the recent militarists he "dreams of absorbing the whole of Asia." MacArthur also is accused of turning Japan into a military and economic outpost of the United States.

956 Gunther, John. *The Riddle of MacArthur: Japan, Korea, and the Far East.* New York: Harper, 1951. xiv, 240p.

This concise account by an acute American journalist represents a favorable but balanced analysis of General MacArthur, his personal qualities, and his SCAP operations. Although reference is made to the Korean and Formosan situations, emphasis is placed upon occupied Japan and American policy in Asia. Sent on an Asian tour by *Look* magazine in 1950, the author found the MacArthur story to be one of the worst-reported stories in history. He therefore sets forth a detailed description of the character, work pattern, and legends of this "Caesar of the Pacific," frequently contrasting him with Franklin D. Roosevelt. There are also discussions of MacArthur's relations with the press and a profile of his SCAP section chiefs. Reflecting the timing of his visit to the Far East during the Korean War, Gunther evaluates the record of the occupation in terms of its durability in the struggle between American democratic ideals and the "rapacious" growth of Communist ideology. As Gunther sees it, the major problem confronting MacArthur is how to restore Japanese sovereignty while preserving the disarmament provision of the Japanese Constitution, protecting her security, and keeping her as America's ally against the Soviet Union. The author's observations of the atmosphere in Tokyo, the emperor, the imperial family, and Japanese leaders, especially Yoshida Shigeru, are interesting. The book has been translated into Japanese under the title of *Makkāsā no nazo* (Tokyo: Jiji Tsūshinsha, 1951. 368p.).

957 Hunt, Frazier. *The Untold Story of Douglas MacArthur.* New York: Devin-Adair, 1954. 533p.

This detailed but somewhat tedious biography of General MacArthur covers his life from his birth in 1880 through 1954. The book consists of 4 parts, only the last of which concerns students of the occupation. In it the author deals with the Allied powers' efforts from the beginning of 1945 to win the Pacific War, MacArthur's plans to invade Japan in late 1945, the surrender ceremony on the *Missouri*, MacArthur's maneuverings to save Japan from communism, the outbreak of the Korean War, MacArthur's dismissal as the supreme commander in the Far East, and his speeches and political activities in the United States. There is little reference to occupation programs for the political, social, and economic reorientation of Japan. The basic theme pertains to how MacArthur successfully fended off Russian moves to limit American influence in the Far East and how Washington reacted to his activities and pronouncements. Inaccurate and undocumented statements are unfortunately frequent.

958 James, D. Clayton. *The Years of MacArthur: v.1: 1880–1941.* Boston: Houghton Mifflin, 1970. xx, 740p.

A carefully researched and dispassionate evaluation of the man who was to head the postwar occupation of Japan, this book is the first of a 2-volume definitive biography of General Douglas MacArthur written by an associate professor of history at Mississippi State University. Volume 1 takes the reader only as far as the attack on Pearl Harbor. It is important, nevertheless, for understanding the occupation because of the light that it sheds on MacArthur's character and quality of leadership and the information that it provides on his family background, his days at West Point, his years in the Philippines and his attachment to the islands, and his tenure as chief of staff under Presidents Hoover and Roosevelt. The reader will also find MacArthur's prewar views of Japan to be of considerable interest. The author indicates how aware MacArthur was of the growing Japanese threat to American interests, how he supported Stimson in the latter's efforts to persuade President Hoover to impose economic sanctions on Japan at the time of the Manchurian crisis, and how he worked to strengthen Philippine defenses against Japan prior to the outbreak of the war.

959 "Japan Asks: After MacArthur, What?" *Business Week* p.153–54 (21 Apr. 1951)

The impact and implications of the removal of General MacArthur as supreme commander for the allied powers are the focal point of this brief article. Mention is made of the Japanese fear that his removal signals a change in American policy toward communism in Asia. However, it is pointed out that the peace treaty will be negotiated on schedule and the American commitment to protect Japan will remain firm. It is likely that MacArthur's replacement, General Ridgway, will be primarily concerned with the Korean War and that Japan will be allowed more political independence prior to the signing of the peace treaty.

"Japan, 1947." *The Reminiscences of Roger Nash Baldwin*. 1954. See no.44a.

"Japan: One or Many?" 1948. See no.557.

"Japan without MacArthur." 1951. See no.650.

The Japanese Reminiscences of Roger Baldwin. 1961. See no.44b.

959a "Jeeps, MP's and Japanese Cops Make a Daily Parade of MacArthur Trip to Work." *United States News* 24:68 (19 Mar. 1948)

This brief article describes MacArthur's aloof working style and the pomp and deference which surround his movements in the streets of Tokyo.

960 Kelley, Frank Raymond, and Cornelius Ryan. *MacArthur: Man of Action*. Garden City, N.Y.: Doubleday, 1951. 191p.

The 2 correspondents who wrote *Star-Spangled Mikado* (no.506) in 1947 present another account of the same subject, General MacArthur, this time giving a biographical sketch of his professional career as a man of courage. The authors begin their narrative with a description of MacArthur's childhood and proceed through his romances, his career in World War I, his West Point days, his years as chief of staff, his military experiences in the Philippines and the Pacific War, and his achievements as chief of the Allied occupation. In 3 chapters treating his years in the occupation, the authors picture the general's masterly performance in organizing occupation operations, meeting with the emperor, carrying out various programs of reform, understanding the oriental mind, and rebutting Russian needling in the Allied Council for Japan. Anecdotes and episodes about MacArthur are inserted throughout the text. The general's remarks made in 1935 on the art of war, his commentary on Genghis Khan in 1935, and his speech on the *Missouri* on 2 September 1945 are appended.

———, and ———. *Star Spangled Mikado*. 1947. See no.506.

961 Kenney, George Churchill. *The MacArthur I Know*. New York: Duell, Sloan and Pearce, 1951. 264p.

The air commander who helped to turn the tide of General MacArthur's Pacific War operations in July 1942 gives a popular and personal account of MacArthur. His admiration for the general began with his first impressions and related to MacArthur's brilliant military accomplishments, his leadership qualities, and his oratory. Accounts of MacArthur's performance in the surrender ceremony on the *Missouri*, the Korean War, etc., are included. Only 1 chapter out of 13 is devoted to the occupation period. Outlined therein are the achievements of MacArthur's administration of occupied Japan such as the liberation of Allied prisoners, the purge of Japanese war leaders, the release of Japanese political prisoners, the dissolution of the "thought control police," the destruction of *zaibatsu* industries, land reform, the abolishment of Shinto as the state religion, educational reform, universal suffrage, and the war crimes trials. The author stresses that the occupation was successful due to MacArthur's understanding of how to deal with Asians. The discussion tends to be superficial and laudatory.

962 Kudryavtsev, V. "Revelations by General MacArthur." *Soviet Press Translations* 4:264–66 (1 May 1949); abridged version published under the same title in *Current Digest of the Soviet Press* 1, no.10:33 (5 Apr. 1949)

The author of this article, which originally appeared in *Izvestia* on 9 March, presents his version of an interview which General MacArthur had with Ward Price, Tokyo correspondent of the English newspaper, the *Daily Mail*. The author claims that General MacArthur, unaware that his remarks would be published, indicated the true nature of American intentions in Japan—that is, "not the democratization and demilitarization of Japan, but its conversion into a military springboard for the United States in the Far East." In the author's opinion, this interview only corroborates what the Soviets have known for a long time.

963 Lauterbach, Richard Edward. "Letters to MacArthur: Japs Ask Him Favors and Tell Their Troubles." *Life* 20:4, 7 (14 Jan. 1946)

This brief report discusses the nature of the personal letters—both in English and in Japanese—sent to MacArthur during the first few months of the occupation. Many of them express their approval of the occupation and the war crimes trials; others complain of such matters as food rationing and the bureaucracy and request MacArthur's assistance in efforts to obtain various favors from SCAP authorities.

964 Lee, Clark Gould. "Some Plain Talk about MacArthur." *Cosmopolitan* 120: 28, 82, 84 (Apr. 1946)

Correspondent Clark Lee discusses 10 widely repeated stories and rumors about General MacArthur. He notes that the tales have gained widespread, if not unanimous, acceptance among navy men in the Pacific and have been extensively retold in the United States.

965 ———, and Richard Henschel. *Douglas MacArthur*. New York: Holt, 1952. x, 370p.

This biography of General MacArthur was prepared by 2 correspondents. Clark Lee provides a descriptive profile and Richard Henschel a pictorial sketch. Lee worked for the Associated Press and later for the International News Service in occupied Japan. He devotes only 1 chapter out of 19 to MacArthur's role in Japan. There he presents an informative description of high-ranking personalities on MacArthur's staff such as Generals Charles Willoughby, Courtney Whitney, Richard Sutherland, Edmond Almond, and Walton Walker. Lee claims that press censorship often took place in Japan without MacArthur's knowledge. There is no substantial discussion of the occupation's reform programs.

966 "MacArthur: Fact and Legend." *United States News* 24:13–14 (16 Apr. 1948)

An appraisal of MacArthur's work in Japan, undertaken when he was being suggested as a possible candidate for president in 1948. It discusses his alleged method of operating in secret and through a limited number of loyal subordinates. Also considered are the present effectiveness of major reforms such as the promulgation of a new constitution, SCAP's land reform program, the breakup of the *zaibatsu*, and trade union formation. The article concludes that while MacArthur has succeeded in destroying the old mode of Japanese traditionalism, he has not yet shaped a new society.

966a "MacArthur Points the Way." *Christian Century* 62:1056–57 (19 Sept. 1945)

MacArthur's speech to the Japanese on the occasion of Japan's formal surrender was "a conjunction of far-seeing statesmanship, sound Christian philosophy, moving eloquence and practical handling of an intricate concrete situation." MacArthur has already begun the reeducation of the Japanese people with his quiet entry into Tokyo and his personal calm and dignity.

966b "MacArthur Upholds Disarmament and Right of Self-Defense." *Christian Century* 67:68 (18 Jan. 1950)

The editors of *Christian Century* wonder about the Japanese reaction to MacArthur's New Year's message (no. 940). The general devoted most of his message to a tribute to Japan's recovery and democratization. He closed it, however, with statements that on the one hand praised the Japanese for adopting the anti-war clause of the new constitution and on the other affirmed that the clause should not be taken to deny "the inalienable right of self-defense against unprovoked attack." The editors warn that MacArthur may be undermining the very provisions of the Japanese constitution which his message professed to praise.

967 McEvoy, J. P. "General MacArthur Reports on Japan." *Reader's Digest* 56: 9–14 (May 1950)

In this interview with General MacArthur, emphasis is placed on the general's opinions concerning the future of Japanese society and the permanence of occupation reforms. The occupation's attempt to create ties between all segments of the population and the new constitution is stressed as is the new order of society. The probability of a dominating role for the Communist party is evaluated within the context of the stabilizing party system. MacArthur emphasizes the necessity of Japanese neutrality and the need for continued disarmament as a practical means of maintaining peace in Asia and as a stimulus for world peace.

967a Naoi, Takeo. "Japan: 'Orphan in the Pacific'." *New Leader* 34, no.19:16–17 (7 May 1951)

The 11 April dismissal of MacArthur as supreme commander of the Allied powers came as a stunning shock to all of Japan. Every segment of the population expressed grief at MacArthur's departure and gratitude for the work he had done. While not an object of affection in part because he was so aloof, Naoi points out, MacArthur was a symbol of stability in Asia, protecting Japan against the Communist threat, and his departure has left many Japanese uneasy and apprehensive about the future.

968 Okazaki, Katsuo. "The Late General MacArthur and Japan." *Contemporary Japan* 28, no.1:1–9 (Sept. 1964)

Okazaki Katsuo, former ambassador to the United Nations, describes the deep respect the Japanese people hold for General MacArthur and the vital decisions MacArthur made in the interest of Japan.

969 Osborne, John. "MacArthur and Asia." *Life* 29:126–41 (25 Sept. 1950)

The magic of General MacArthur's leadership and his opinions concerning strategy against communism in Asia are discussed. Osborne emphasizes the relationship of MacArthur to his Tokyo staff and the respect he has earned at all levels of Japanese society.

970 ———. " 'My Dear General'." *Life* 29:127–39 (27 Nov. 1950)

Osborne utilizes a sampling of letters between General MacArthur and Prime Ministers Yoshida, Ashida, and Katayama to indicate the locus of power in occupied Japan and to illuminate the extent of SCAP-Japanese cooperation. The author comments on the circumstances behind each exchange of letters which cover the period from 27 December 1946 through 12 October 1950. The letters deal with such matters as the exact applicability of the penal and criminal code to the imperial family, the strengthening of local government, the purging of prominent political figures such as Hatoyama Ichirō and Matsumoto Jiichirō, and the creation of a police system balanced between local and national control.

971 Pearl, Jack. *General Douglas MacArthur*. Derby, Conn.: Monarch, 1961. 144p.

A former managing editor of *Saga* and *Climax* magazines, Pearl has written a popular biography of General MacArthur. The story begins with the general's West Point days and describes his brilliant military career in Europe during World War I, in the Pacific during World War II, and in the Korean War. MacArthur's strategies in the battles of the Philippines and Korea are particularly glorified. Only 5 pages (p.109–13) are devoted to MacArthur's task as supreme commander for the Allied powers. In these pages, the author praises MacArthur's brave entry into postsurrender Japan on 30 August 1945, and his efficient transformation of Japan from a feudal to a democratic society, briefly citing his occupation reforms. There are many exaggerated and inaccurate statements.

972 Pratt, John M., ed. *Revitalizing a Nation*. Chicago: Heritage Foundation, 1952. 120p.

A collection of portions of speeches, policy statements, and remarks made by General Douglas MacArthur on public occasions plus informal letters. The book consists of 2 parts, with the first part being a collection of remarks and the second being a pictorial collection highlighting scenes of MacArthur's life. The editor groups different paragraphs of MacArthur's public pronouncements under several topics and captions them. His purpose is to use MacArthur's "teachings" as sources of moral and spiritual strength for American readers. The utterances selected here refer to a variety of topics which include among others the evil nature of war, the virtues of human freedom, the evil of communism, American ideals, patriotism, the Korean War, defense of Asian and Pacific nations, denouncement of governmental rule by propaganda, aid to Europe, and taxes. The second chapter, 11 pages long, focuses on MacArthur's favorable evaluation of Japan as a spiritually reborn nation. No sources are cited for the quotations included.

The Reminiscences of Alvin Graves. 1961. See no.44d.

The Reminiscences of Faubion Bowers. 1960. See no.44j.

The Reminiscences of Sir George Sansom. 1957. See no.44q.

972a "Reports from a Neglected Area." *Commonweal* 45:219–20 (13 Dec. 1946)

Reporting on the progress of the occupation, this editorial notes that MacArthur has been able to build on certain initial advantages. First, as various commentators have pointed out, the Japanese blame their wartime leadership rather than the Americans for the destruction of their cities and for their present plight; furthermore, they seem to be very enthusiastic about MacArthur himself and the United States in general. Second, speaking in practical terms, MacArthur has been able to "run the whole show." Nevertheless, the editors ask whether a military occupation can succeed in imposing democracy, whether an unarmed Japan can survive in close proximity to the U.S.S.R., and whether the economy can be rebuilt in order to guarantee Japanese survival without a reappearance of the kinds of conflicts Japan faced before the war.

Ridgway, Matthew Bunker. *The Korean War*. 1967. See no.984.

973 Robb, Stephen. *Fifty Years of Farewell: Douglas MacArthur's Commemorative and Deliberative Speaking*. Ph.D. dissertation, Indiana Univ., 1967. 284p. (Abstracted in *Dissertation Abstracts* 28: 3812A [1968]; University Microfilms order no.68–2348)

Robb analyzes the rhetoric of General MacArthur's commemorative speeches as well as that of his deliberative speeches, and maintains that the deliberative addresses made after his recall as supreme commander in April 1951 really served to stifle debate, for MacArthur with his regal temperament, authoritarian propensities, and "romantic self-image," refused in effect to debate with opponents. He claims that the ideas expressed in these speeches are evidence that General MacArthur's 14-year "self-imposed exile in the Far East" had removed him intellectually from his audiences. A pervasive similarity in the general's commemorative addresses is also noted, and as an example, the resemblance between the "Duty, Honor, Country" speech delivered at West Point in 1962 and the 1935 "Farewell to the Rainbow" speech is outlined. Robb concludes that these speeches are "curiosities which offer insight into the mind of General MacArthur who frequently applied nineteenth-century prose to twentieth-century problems."

974 Rovere, Richard H., and Arthur M. Schlesinger, Jr. *The General and the President and the Future of American Foreign Policy*. New York: Farrar,

Straus and Young, 1951. vii, 336p.; *The MacArthur Controversy and American Foreign Policy.* rev. ed. New York: Farrar, Straus and Giroux, 1965. xv, 366p.

A staff member of the *New Yorker* and an associate professor of history at Harvard University describe the background and nature of the controversy between General Douglas MacArthur and President Harry Truman that led to MacArthur's dismissal as supreme commander for the Allied powers in Japan as well as supreme commander of UN forces in Korea and commander in chief of U.S. forces in the Far East. The authors include an analytical and highly critical biographical sketch of MacArthur as a military statesman and administrator, and they also discuss his character and some of his basic attitudes in witty but scarcely objective terms. MacArthur's role in the occupation of Japan, however, is not examined in any detail.

975 ———, and ———. "The Story of Douglas MacArthur." *Harper's Magazine* 203:21–35 (July 1951)

In an article apparently initiated after MacArthur's dismissal as supreme commander for the Allied powers, the authors present a comprehensive picture of MacArthur's personality and lifework. After a discussion of his family background and early career, there is an account of his involvement in the occupation. Characterizing his position in Japan as America's first proconsulship, the authors nevertheless favorably view his leadership and believe his redistribution of land holdings to have been his most enduring reform. They claim that it was during the occupation that MacArthur's devoted political following became a cult which surrounded the general in protective adoration and refused to brook any criticism of the occupation. The latter part of the article concerns the Korean War.

976 Ryan, Cornelius. "MacArthur: Man of Controversy." *American Mercury* 71: 425–35 (Oct. 1950)

This portrait of General MacArthur includes his early career and wartime experiences as well as his position as the supreme commander in occupied Japan, and it provides some fresh insights into the personality of this controversial figure. Ryan, the coauthor of a book, *MacArthur: Man of Action* (1951) (no.960), strives to be impartial in his description of the general—presenting the criticisms of his detractors as well as the adulation of his supporters. With regard to MacArthur's conduct of the occupation, the author briefly outlines the criticism of those who believe he is being too egotistical and dictatorial and contrasts this with the widespread approval of MacArthur evidenced by the Japanese people themselves.

977 Scalapino, Robert Anthony. "What Trends Will Emerge in Post–MacArthur Japan?" *Foreign Policy Bulletin* 30:2–3 (18 May 1951)

In the aftermath of General MacArthur's dismissal by President Truman, the author analyzes the attitudes of the Japanese toward this complex and controversial figure. He believes that MacArthur still has strong support among most Japanese due to 3 important factors which he characterizes as "symbolism, power, and personality." Nevertheless, he maintains that the general is not without his critics in the country—among the Social Democrats, the Communists, most labor unions, "and many other movements which might be considered to the left of center." He alleges that Japanese of higher education or sophistication also have their reservations. He concludes that the varying Japanese opinions will undoubtedly be subject to changes depending on the nature of future domestic and foreign developments.

Sissons, David C. S. "SCAP's Statements on the Occupation of Japan." 1950. *See* no.635.

977a Sommers, Martin. "Reconversion of Douglas MacArthur." *Saturday Evening Post* 218:12–13, 41+ (25 May 1946)

Much of this article recounts an interview that Sommers had with MacArthur in Tokyo. The general, he finds, is impatient with the "kick-em-in-the-face boys," who demand a punitive occupation and peace settlement. The Japanese admire winners and are already on our side, for they recognize that they were betrayed by their military. In response to criticism of SCAP's decision to retain the imperial institution, MacArthur argues that the emperor has never been much more than a powerless figurehead and is now a valuable stabilizing symbol. If the occupation lasts longer than 5 years, MacArthur continues, it will lose its effectiveness and will engender resentment among the Japanese. Sommers also points out that MacArthur is immensely proud of the anti-war Japanese constitution and concludes that MacArthur, once a "relentless warrior," now sees his role as that of leading the world toward the renunciation of war.

977b Splane, Russell. "Our Far-flung Correspondents: SPUSA." *New Yorker* 24, no.9: 90, 92 (10 Apr. 1948)

In this report dated 20 March 1948, Splane describes the reactions of both Americans and Japanese in Tokyo to MacArthur's 9 March announcement that he would be willing to run for the presidency if nominated. The Japanese press treated the announcement as a major news event, Splane notes, giving it more attention than the announcement of the new Ashida cabinet, which was made on the same day. Japanese editorial writers generally greeted the announcement with a mixture of approval and regret, pleased on the one hand with the possibility of an American president familiar with Japan but disturbed on the other at the potential departure of MacArthur as supreme commander of the Allied powers. Splane also notes that some Japanese were already beginning to refer to MacArthur by the initials SPUSA, or "Supreme President, U.S.A."

Stoddard, George D. "MacArthur and the U.S. Education Mission to Japan." 1946. *See* no.2114.

Truman, Harry S. *Memoirs*. 1955. *See* no.217.

Vining, Elizabeth G. *Quiet Pilgrimage*. 1970. *See* no.1264a.

978 Weldon, James. "General's General: Douglas MacArthur." In *Men Who Make Your World*, by Overseas Press Club of America. New York: Dutton, 1949. p.51–67.

The associate editor of the *Louisville Courier-Journal* sketches and evaluates the career of Douglas MacArthur. More than half of the article is devoted to a description of MacArthur's life prior to and his appointment as supreme commander for the Allied powers in August 1945. MacArthur's impressive record at West Point, his familiarity with Asian culture, his courage, moralistic thinking, and other "god-like" attributes are discussed. The second part, treating his occupation years, views him as soldier turned statesman. While favorably evaluating the occupation reforms in general, the author is critical of MacArthur for the "most glaring defect" of his performance in Japan, namely, a failure to appreciate the role of the free reporter in a democratic society. He describes MacArthur's skill in giving the impression to visitors in Tokyo that the occupation was a perfect operation with which no one could find fault.

979 "What Keeps General MacArthur in Japan." *U.S. News and World Report* 26:20–21 (17 June 1949)

The following reasons are presented as an explanation of why General MacArthur chooses to remain in Japan: his position as supreme commander allows him a proper stage upon which to pursue a life of mystery, drama, and personal power; he has a strong sense of duty and considers himself the symbol of U.S. activity in Japan so that his return home would seem an abandonment of Japan by the United States; and, finally, he has taken it upon himself to guide occupation policy directly and therefore is not anxious to leave before that policy is totally implemented.

980 Whitney, Courtney. *MacArthur Advancing Freedom's Frontiers.* n.d. Record Group 5, Box 100. MacArthur Memorial, Bureau of Archives, Norfolk, Va. 97p.

A typewritten account of General MacArthur's role in directing the occupation of Japan, apparently done after the end of the occupation by a close associate and great admirer of the general. Beginning with a description of MacArthur's entry into Japan, the work discusses the initial establishment of the occupation, MacArthur's style of leadership and the nature of his direction of the occupation, the development of the occupation's goals and programs in the early years, and significant changes adopted in the face of developing cold war tensions. The writer provides numerous anecdotes drawn from his close relationship with MacArthur in the capacity of chief of the Government Section during the occupation. The final chapter, entitled "His Finest Hour," describes the dismissal of MacArthur by President Truman on 11 April 1951, an action which Whitney views as "shameful treatment."

981 ———. *MacArthur: His Rendezvous with History.* New York: Knopf, 1956. xi, 547, xiii p.

This statement of unqualified admiration for General MacArthur is eloquently written by a person regarded as MacArthur's closest confidant in the General Headquarters administration. Whitney, who organized guerrilla warfare against the Japanese in the Philippines under MacArthur's direction during the Pacific War, served as chief of the Government Section of SCAP from December 1945 through April 1951. Although not documented, the book provides a highly informed and intimate account of MacArthur's thoughts, remarks, and behavior, including his sense of history. The author covers the period from 27 July 1941, when MacArthur was called to active service to head the American and Philippine forces in the Far East, through December 1954. The work is divided into 4 parts: World War II, Japan, Korea, and America. The part on Japan describes the surrender ceremony on the *Missouri*, MacArthur's style of work and life in Tokyo, his principles for the reform of Japan, the reform programs undertaken, meetings with Japanese leaders, the controversy over constitutional revision, SCAP's conflict with Communist groups including the Russian delegate to the Allied Council for Japan, and MacArthur's diplomacy with Moscow and London as well as with Washington. With respect to each topic the author succinctly records the achievements of MacArthur and the motives lying behind his actions. Based largely on the author's personal files, it is an authoritative if uncritical biographical account of the general. The section on Japan has been translated into Japanese under the title of *Nihon ni okeru Makkāsā* (Tokyo: Mainichi Shimbunsha, 1957. 198p.).

982 ———. "MacArthur: The Man." *Reader's Digest* 68:121–26 (Feb. 1956)

Whitney, who joined MacArthur's staff early in World War II and stayed with him through the occupation, gives personal glimpses of the general from his arrival in Japan until his removal as supreme commander. This article consists of excerpts from the author's book-length study *MacArthur: His Rendezvous with History* (no.981).

"Why General MacArthur Wishes to End Military Rule in Japan." 1947. See no.2331b.

983 Willoughby, Charles A., and John Chamberlain. *MacArthur, 1941–1951.* New York: McGraw-Hill, 1954. xiii, 441p. British edition published under the title *MacArthur: 1941–1951; Victory in the Pacific* (London: Heinemann, 1956. xiii, 441p.)

A well-documented but subjective account of General MacArthur's actions and achievements covering the period from 1941 through his dismissal as supreme commander for the Allied powers in April 1951. During this decade Willoughby served in the G–2 (Intelligence) Section of MacArthur's headquarters and was assistant chief of staff, G-2, until 1951. A member of the original "Bataan gang," he analyzes and explicates the planning and execution of MacArthur's campaigns from Bataan to the Korean War with frequent references to G-2 intelligence reports. Throughout the chapters devoted to MacArthur's strategic maneuvers in the Western Pacific and in Korea, the author expresses unbounded admiration for his chief's professional skill. Chapters 12 to 14 cover SCAP operations in Japan. The first refers to the planned Olympic and Coronet operations, Japan's surrender, the Japanese surrender mission to Manila, and the ceremony on the battleship *Missouri*. Chapter 13 describes how MacArthur and his headquarters staff fought to preserve Japan's security by driving out "Communist suspects" within SCAP, pursuing the Sorge spy case, confronting the Russian delegate at the Allied Council for Japan about the treatment of Japanese detainees in Siberia, and closely watching the movements of Japanese Communists. The last of these chapters —on the Allied occupation—discusses SCAP's efforts at political reform such as the purge, constitutional revision, greater local autonomy, and greater power for the Diet. Although his frequent reference to intelligence reports assists the reader in understanding the factors which entered into SCAP's decisions and policies, the 3 chapters on Japan fail to demonstrate as deep an understanding of this subject as do the chapters dealing with military strategy. A Japanese translation of selected sections of this work appears under the title of *Makkāsā senki* (Tokyo: Jiji Tsūshinsha, 1956. 3v.).

983a "You Can't Please Back-seat Drivers.' *Saturday Evening Post* 218:132 (27 Oct. 1945)

This editorial approves of the competent job MacArthur is doing in Japan and disapproves of the unpleasant attacks often heard accusing him of treating the Japanese too lightly. MacArthur is following his orders as supreme commander for the Allied powers to the letter, the magazine asserts; his mission is clear—to demilitarize and democratize the Japanese—and he is fulfilling it well. The motives of his critics vary, but the editors sense a strong leftist flavor in their anti-MacArthur campaign.

MATTHEW B. RIDGWAY

Apart from reporting in the daily news columns very little has been written with specific reference to General Ridgway's role as supreme commander for the Allied powers. The principal exceptions appear to be his own two books listed below.

"Japan without MacArthur." 1951. See no.650.

Ridgway, Matthew Bunker. "Korea and Japan: Military Operations, Armistice Negotiations, Relations with People." 1952. See no.2533.

984 ———. *The Korean War: How We Met the Challenge. How All-out Asian War Was Averted. Why MacArthur Was Dismissed. Why Today's War Objectives Must Be Limited.* Garden City, N.Y.: Doubleday, 1967. 291p.

Matthew B. Ridgway presents a study of the Korean War which focuses on the American response to the outbreak of hostilities in Korea, the manner by which an all-out Asian war was averted, General MacArthur's dismissal from his command in 1951, and the implications of the war for subsequent American military and policy objectives. His account of MacArthur's controversial role as the supreme commander of UN forces in Korea is both critical and illuminating, and Ridgway frequently elucidates such important aspects of MacArthur's character as his need for adulation, his faith in his own infallible judgment, and his tendency to isolate himself from others.

985 ———. *Soldier: The Memoirs of Matthew B. Ridgway as Told to Harold H. Martin.* New York: Harper, 1956. ix, 371p.

Ridgway recollects his military career in the European and Pacific theaters during World War II. He succeeded General Douglas MacArthur on 12 April 1951 as supreme commander for the Allied powers and served in that capacity until Japan was restored its independence in April 1952. During this time he concurrently commanded the Eighth Army and was the commander in chief of the UN Command in Korea. His observations of this period are set forth in chapter 27, where he refers to his work with John F. Dulles and Yoshida Shigeru on treaty arrangements for Japan and also to his meeting with the emperor. Appendixes include the full text of Ridgway's address made before a joint session of Congress on 22 May 1952, where he reported on Japanese–American relations as well as the Korean situation.

985a "Statement Issued by the Supreme Commander for the Allied Powers Matthew B. Ridgway Concerning the Ratification of the Japanese Peace Treaty, April 27, 1952." *Contemporary Japan* 21, no.1/3:158–59 (1952)

This statement announces the effective date and time (28 April 1952, 10:30 P.M. Tokyo time) of the peace treaty and hence of the termination of the occupation. At that time American forces in Japan will assume the status accorded them by the new security treaty. Ridgway calls this an "historic moment" and offers the opinion that the objectives for which MacArthur and his assistants labored "will have been in large measure attained," thanks to the cooperation and loyalty of the Japanese government and public-spirited Japanese citizens. He hopes that the American troops remaining in Japan can be withdrawn shortly, for their presence will continue to present problems and will be a magnet for attacks by Communists and "other subversive groups."

Punitive and Precautionary Aspects

Although constructive and reconciliatory in ultimate intent, the occupation of Japan also had a number of punitive aspects. They were particularly salient during the first two years when the United States viewed Japan primarily as a recently defeated and potentially still dangerous enemy. More than punishment was involved in such measures, however. They were also intended to guard against a future revival of military strength and aggressive disposition or capacity in Japan. In this sense they had precautionary as well as retributive characteristics. The principal measures involved were the territorial dismemberment of the Japanese empire, the demilitarization program, the war crimes trials, the purge, reparations payments, and the repatriation program. Separate sections are devoted to the literature on each of these subjects. It should be pointed out that many of the entries in the section containing general materials (p.113) also devote substantial attention to one or more of these subjects.

Territorial Dismemberment of the Japanese Empire

The basic decisions with respect to the dissolution of the Japanese empire were taken prior to the end of the war, particularly at the Cairo, Yalta, and Potsdam

(Berlin) Conferences. As a result of these agreements Japan, upon surrender, immediately lost control of Taiwan, the Pescadores, Korea, the puppet state of Manchukuo, and all of her rights and interests elsewhere in China and eastern Asia. In addition to these losses, certain domestic Japanese territories were also taken by the victorious powers. The USSR, acting on the basis of the Yalta Agreement, took possession of southern Sakhalin, the Kuriles, Habomai, and Shikotan. The United States occupied the prefecture of Okinawa, Amami Oshima, Marcus Island, the Bonins and Volcanos, and the former Japanese mandated islands in the western Pacific. These dispositions prevailed without serious challenge throughout the occupation. The only territorial issues that aroused sustained interest and attention during this period concerned the former mandated islands which Japan held in trust from the League of Nations and Soviet control over the so-called Northern Territories. The basic issue in the first case was whether they should be retained outright by the United States or, alternatively, be administered as a strategic trusteeship under the United Nations. The available literature from the occupation period concentrates on these two questions.

Some of the entries in the sections on presurrender planning (p.34, 71, 81, and 91) also provide background information on this subject. The general territorial issue emerges again in wider context in connection with the section on the peace treaty (*see* p.728) which, among other things, had the function of formalizing the new titles to former Japanese territories.

986 "Agreement at Yalta on the Kuriles and Sakhalin." *Department of State Bulletin* 14:189–90 (10 Feb. 1946)

This article summarizes Secretary of State Byrnes' news conference of 29 January 1946 at which he stated that the Yalta Agreement specifies the return of Southern Sakhalin, the Kuriles, and other northern islands to the Soviet Union. In Byrnes' opinion, this agreement will have to be formalized by treaty, despite the fact that the territories are theoretically being returned to their rightful owner. He notes as well that the Yalta Agreement provided for Soviet entry into the war with Japan. The text of the agreement may be found in *Department of State Bulletin* 14:282 (24 Feb. 1946).

986a Amidon, William C. "The Issue of Sakhalin in Russo–Japanese Relations." In *Five Studies in Japanese Politics*, ed. by Robert Edward Ward. Ann Arbor: Univ. of Michigan Pr., 1957. p.60–99. (Univ. of Michigan, Center for Japanese Studies, occasional papers, no.7)

The first part of this article presents the historical development of Sakhalin as an issue in Russo–Japanese relations, beginning in the seventeenth century, and includes discussion of the agreements made at Yalta in 1945 and negotiations undertaken since that time. The second part is an evaluation of the strategic and economic importance of Sakhalin.

987 Austin, Warren. "Submission of U.S. Draft Trusteeship Agreement for Japanese Mandated Islands." *Department of State Bulletin* 16:416–23 (9 Mar. 1947)

This statement by the U.S. representative to the United Nations was made before the Security Council on 26 February 1947. The draft trusteeship agreement relates only to the former Japanese mandated islands received from the League of Nations, i.e., the Marshalls, the Marianas, and the Carolines. The statement presents the reasons why the United States believes it should have control of the islands and outlines a proposed program of supervision and administration. Following the general statement are comments on the draft agreement explaining in more detail the particular provisions of the 16 articles.

Ballantine, Joseph W. "The Future of the Ryukyus." 1953. *See* no.2510.

987a Berrigan, Darrell. "Russia Builds a Base in Japan." *Saturday Evening Post* 220:28–29, 155–57 (8 Nov. 1947)

On the basis of interviews with Japanese repatriates and escapees, Berrigan reports that the Soviet Union is making rapid progress in building up her military installations on her newly-acquired islands north of Hokkaido. The most serious problems created by Soviet acquisition of the northern territories, aside from the military threat and the maltreatment of the Japanese remaining there, is the economic impact on northern Hokkaido. The loss of extensive fishing grounds and the influx of a large refugee population have resulted in high unemployment and serious food shortages in the villages and towns along the northern coast. Berrigan also notes that many citizens groups have been formed in the area to agitate for the islands' return to Japanese jurisdiction.

Council on Foreign Relations. *Problems of the Peace Settlement with Japan.* 1944. *See* no.70.

988 Fifield, Russell Hunt. "The Coming Settlement with Japan." *Contemporary Review* 177:144–49 (Mar. 1950)

Fifield, reviewing the territorial disposition of the former Japanese empire, discloses how historical precedent, strategic interest, economic necessity, and common ancestry were involved to justify the disposition of the various areas. The importance of strategic considerations is particularly evidenced in the probability that only the island areas returned to Japan will be demilitarized.

Garbuny, Siegfried. "Japan: Regeneration." 1946. *See* no.1453.

988a Gilchrist, Huntington. "The Japanese Islands: Annexation or Trusteeship?" *Foreign Affairs* 22:635–42 (July 1944)

This article is devoted for the most part to recounting the prewar history of the Japanese mandated islands as background for a brief discussion of the islands' postwar fate. Gilchrist notes 3 possible alternatives: (1) outright annexation by the United States, (2) direct international control and administration, and (3) a modification of the old mandate system. He chooses the third as the most practical and as being of greatest advantage to the United States.

989 Japan. Ministry of Foreign Affairs. Public Information Bureau. *The Northern Islands: Background of Territorial Problems in the Japanese–Soviet Negotiations.* Tokyo: Bunshodo, 1955. 28p.

989a Johnstone, William Crane. "Future of the Japanese Mandated Islands." *Foreign Policy Reports* 21:190–207 (15 Sept. 1945)

Johnstone first presents a brief history of the Japanese mandated islands, including a summary of the conditions under which they were entrusted to Japan and the violations which she was charged with committing after her withdrawal from the League of Nations in 1933. The remainder of the article is devoted to summarizing and analyzing a report of the Subcommittee on Pacific Bases of the House Committee on Naval Affairs, "considered by many a tentative blueprint for United States security in the Pacific." The report recommends that the United States retain "at least dominating control" over the islands within the rules laid down by the United Nations, and it discusses at length both the legal problems involved in transferring the mandate to the United States and the future strategic value of the islands.

Kajima, Morinosuke. *Modern Japan's Foreign Policy.* 1969. *See* no.1070.

990 Keesing, Felix M. "The Former Japanese Mandated Islands." *Far Eastern Survey* 14:269–71 (26 Sept. 1945)

Written by an anthropology professor at Stanford, this article is a brief survey of the Marshalls, the Carolines, the Marianas, and the Palau Islands from a geographical viewpoint. Keesing proposes that these islands be divided into separate civilian and military zones during the postwar period.

990a Langen, Benita. *Die Gebietsverluste Japans nach dem Zweiten Weltkrieg: Eine völkerrechtliche Studie.* Berlin: Duncker und Humblot, 1971. 241p. (Schriften zum Völkerrecht, 19)

Originally presented as a doctoral dissertation to the faculty of law and political science at the University of Bonn, this work is a detailed and at times technical study of Japan's loss of her overseas empire from a legal point of view. Chapter 1 surveys developments during the occupation period and indicates what was accomplished at the San Francisco Peace Treaty Conference. Chapter 2 examines Chinese and Soviet claims respectively to Taiwan and to Southern Sakhalin and the Kurile Islands, the steps that led to their annexation, and Japanese renunciation of these territories. Chapter 3, in turn, focuses on the question of Japanese sovereignty over Korea and the reestablishment of an independent Korean regime. Finally, chapter 4 studies the transfer of the mandated islands to the United States and the American administration of the Ryukyu and Bonin Islands.

991 Lattimore, Eleanor. "Pacific Ocean or American Lake?" *Far Eastern Survey* 14:313-16 (7 Nov. 1945)

An article which speculates about U.S. treatment of territory that was formerly a part of the Japanese empire, warning against an occupation policy of "expansion and aggrandizement" that would be the result of sole U.S. control over this territory. The author suggests that an international trusteeship system be established as soon as possible to govern the various islands formerly under Japanese control, and briefly discusses the various kinds of trustee arrangements that might be established.

Mateveev, Illarion. "The Kurile Islands." See no.170.

Nomura, Kichisaburō. "A Peace Treaty and Japan's Security." 1950. See no.2350.

992 Ōhira, Zengo. "The Territorial Problems of the Peace Treaty with Japan." *Far Eastern Economic Review* 25:17-20, 26 (3 July 1958)

A professor of international law at Hitotsubashi Academy, Tokyo, Japan discusses his views of the main characteristics of the peace treaty with Japan and of the territorial clauses of that treaty. He calls the peace treaty a "dictated peace." The 4 territorial problems of the peace treaty which he examines involve Korea, Formosa, Sakhalin and the Kurile Islands, and Okinawa and Ogasawara.

992a "The Pacific Islands in the Peace: An Australian View." *Round Table* 36, no.141:35-39 (Dec. 1945)

This study of the future of various Pacific islands includes a brief discussion concerning the mandated Marianas, Marshalls, and Carolines. The United States claim to these islands is accepted as natural on account of their strategic importance. American fortification of some of these islands, however, would be inconsistent with the terms of administration if the United States were to receive them as a mandate. Controlling them as a trusteeship would resolve this particular problem.

992b Robbins, Robert R. "United States Trusteeship for the Territory of the Pacific Islands." *Department of State Bulletin* 16:783-90 (4 May 1947)

Robbins traces the steps leading to the UN approval on 2 April 1947 of the trusteeship agreement for the former Japanese mandated islands. His discussion begins with a description of the islands and a summary of their history to date. The remainder of the article is devoted to a detailed study of the changes that the agreement underwent during the course of its movement through the

United Nations decision-making process. Generous quotations from relevant debates as well as from the text and proposed amendments are provided.

993 Roucek, Joseph S. "Some Geographic Factors in the Strategy of the Kuriles." *Journal of Geography* 51:297–301 (Oct. 1952)

This article describes the importance of the Kurile Islands for Japan, the USSR, and the United States. Roucek writes of the historical background of the Kuriles and the reasons why both Japan and the USSR claim these islands. He also discusses the political and strategic factors which make these islands important in the maneuvering of the cold war.

993a Stephan, John Jason. *Sakhalin: A History*. Oxford: Clarendon Press, 1971. xiv, 240p.

Chapter 8 (p.142–66) of this study, the first comprehensive history of Sakhalin ever to be published, describes in detail the blitzkrieg invasion and occupation of the southern half of the island by Soviet military forces in August 1945. Military government was established on August 27th, all radios, arms and automobiles were immediately confiscated, and publication of the local newspaper *Karafuto Nichinichi Shimbun* was suspended. Shortly thereafter, initial efforts were made with the help of former Japanese officials as well as Japanese businessmen and technical experts to resurrect the area's civil administration and to reconstruct its economy along communist lines. In February 1947 this part of the island was administratively absorbed into the Union of Soviet Socialist Republics. While a number of the former Japanese bureaucrats, community leaders and business managers as well as many of the disarmed soldiers were sent to labor camps in Siberia, from which many never returned, the vast majority of the civiliaan population remained on the island and continued their normal pursuits until their repatriation in the late 1940s.

993b Sugiyama, Shigeo. "Diplomatic Relations between Japan and the Soviet Union with Particular Emphasis on Territorial Questions." In *Japan in World Politics*, ed. by Young C. Kim. Washington, D.C.: Institute for Asian Studies, 1972. p.21–39.

Sugiyama of Hosei University first summarizes and analyzes the origins of the dispute between Japan and the USSR over the status of the Kurile Islands and Southern Sakhalin. He concludes that the Instrument of Surrender signed on 2 September 1945, the peace treaty itself, and the earlier Allied agreements at Cairo, Yalta and Potsdam all failed to provide for the formal transfer to the Soviet Union of sovereignty over those areas. Sugiyama next examines the treatment of the territorial question in the Soviet–Japanese Joint Declaration of 19 October 1956 and the negotiations leading up to it. In his opinion, the declaration clearly left the question of sovereignty over the disputed areas unresolved and, in fact, tacitly acknowledged the justice of some of the Japanese claims. The author concludes with a detailed refutation of the legal arguments used by the Soviet Union to support its current refusal to reopen debate on the territorial issue, and he briefly summarizes the positions of the Japanese political parties on this particular question.

994 Sutton, Joseph Lee. "Territorial Claims of Russia and Japan in the Kurile Islands." In University of Michigan, Center for Japanese Studies. *Occasional Papers*, v.1. Ann Arbor: Univ. of Michigan Pr., 1951. p.35–61.

This article presents the history of Russian activities involving the Kurile Islands, beginning with the early Russian explorations of the area, and the historical background for the territorial claims of both Russia and Japan in these islands. The role of the Kuriles during World War II and their occupation by the Russians are discussed. The questions concerning disposition of the islands after the war and their place in the Yalta Agreement are also examined. The author comments on the strategic value of the Kuriles to Russia, Japan, and the United States and concludes the article with a section on the future of the Kuriles, noting that they "have not passed permanently from the international scene."

994a Tabata, Shigejirō. "Re-examination of Japan's Territorial Problems." *Contemporary Japan* 23, no.7/9:569–72 (1955)

This article by a professor of law at Kyoto University was translated from the May 1955 issue of *Chūō Kōron*. Tabata finds it ironic that those who are now demanding the return of Southern Sakhalin and the Kuriles are the same people who strongly supported the 1952 peace treaty in which Japan renounced her claims to those islands. In any case, now is not the proper time to press for reversion inasmuch as the Soviet Union would fear the use of the territories as U.S. bases. The article also includes a detailed analysis of the treaties and agreements which relate to the legal status of the disputed islands.

995 Takano, Yūichi. "The Territorial Problems between Japan and the Soviet Union." *Japanese Annual of International Law* 3:52–64 (1959)

This discussion focuses on the 1956 Russo–Japanese Joint Declaration signed with a view to restoring diplomatic relations between the two countries, on Russo–Japanese negotiations over the legal status and territorial future of southern Sakhalin and the Kurile Islands (including Habomai and Shikotan), on the failure of the San Francisco Peace Treaty to stipulate the countries in whose favor Japan renounced title to her overseas territories, and on various interpretations of the peace treaty's territorial clause. Several short appendixes—including the letters exchanged between Matsumoto Shunichi and Andrei Gromyko in September 1956, and articles drawn from various treaties dealing specifically with Sakhalin and the Kuriles—supplement this essay by Professor Takano, a specialist in international law at Tokyo University.

995a Tamura, Kōsaku. "Origins of the Northern Territorial Issue and Its Legal Status." *Japan Annual of International Affairs* no.2:73–96 (1962)

Tamura attempts to determine the legal status of Southern Sakhalin, the Kurile Islands, and certain islands off the coast of Hokkaido which are still under Soviet control. On the basis of a detailed analysis of Allied agreements concluded during the war, the provisions of the San Francisco Peace Treaty, and earlier treaties and agreements between Japan and Russia, he concludes that the Soviet Union has no clear legal claim to any of the disputed territories, least of all those adjacent to Hokkaido. He also asserts that the Soviet government is demonstrating both expansionist tendencies and irresponsibility in continuing its refusal even to negotiate with Japan on the territorial issue.

995b "Trusteeship Agreement for the Former Japanese Mandated Islands Approved at the 124th Meeting of the Security Council." *Department of State Bulletin* 16:791–92, 794 (4 May 1947); also in *International Organization* 2:410–14 (June 1948)

The complete text of the agreement designating the United States as the administering authority over the Pacific Islands formerly held by Japan under a mandate from the League of Nations.

Ulanovsky, Yu. B. "Territorial Issues in the Japanese Peace Settlement." 1952. *See* no.2457.

996 United Nations. Security Council. "Discussion of the Draft Trusteeship Agreement for the Former Japanese Mandated Islands." *United Nations Security Council Official Records* (Second Year, nos.20, 23, 25, 26, 30, and 31) (26 Feb.–2 Apr. 1947). Also published in a French-language edition.

The draft trusteeship agreement for the former Japanese mandated islands, submitted by the United States to the 113th meeting of the Security Council held on 26 February 1947, was debated in 5 subsequent meetings and, after some revision, was adopted unanimously. The 5 meetings in question were the 116th, 118th, 119th, 123rd, and 124th, held on 7, 12, 17, 25 March and 2 April 1947, respectively. The *Official Records* give a complete record of Security Council debate on this subject. Representatives of Australia, Belgium, Brazil, China, Columbia, France, Poland, the USSR, Syria, the United Kingdom, and the United States took part. The agreement designated the United States to administer the former Japanese mandated islands in the Pacific under United Nations trusteeship and became effective on 18 July 1947.

997 U.S. Dept. of State. *Draft Trusteeship Agreement for the Japanese Mandated Islands.* Washington, D.C.: Government Printing Office, 1947. 20p. (Dept. of State publication 2784; Far Eastern series 20); also in *Department of State Bulletin* 15:889–91 (17 Nov. 1946), and in *International Organization* 2:410–14 (June 1948)

The UN decision to grant the United States trusteeship over the former Japanese mandated islands is recorded here. The publication includes the full text of the draft trusteeship agreement with article-by-article commentaries submitted to the United Nations Security Council by the United States representative on 26 February 1947. The text of President Truman's statement made on 6 November 1946 concerning a draft trusteeship agreement and the statement made by the U.S. representative on the Security Council on 17 February 1947 are also included.

998 ———. ———. Bureau of Public Affairs. Historical Office. *Foreign Relations of the United States, Diplomatic Papers, 1945.* v.1., *General: The United Nations.* Washington, D.C.: Government Printing Office, 1946. lviii, 1611p. (Dept. of State publication 8294)

This volume includes for the most part official documents concerning the United Nations Organization and the role of the United States in creating it. It has a section, however, on the disposal of the former Japanese mandated islands in the Pacific of interest to students of the occupation.

998a Uyehara, Shigeru. "The Peace Conference and the Residents of Southern Kurile." *Democratic Japan* (Tokyo) no. 1:9–10 (Jan. 1950)

Uyehara indicates that a movement among the former residents of "Southern Kurile" (i.e., the islands of Etorofu, Kunashiri, Shikotan, and Habomai, which were seized by the Soviet army in August 1945) for the return of the islands to Japan has recently grown in strength and intensity. He briefly discusses the historical, botanical, and topographical features of those 4 islands which prove that they are a part of Hokkaido and not of the Kurile Islands referred to in the Yalta Agreement. Since the Cairo Agreement only specified that those territories acquired by Japan through invasion or the use of force would be returned to their rightful owners, Uyehara concludes, "it is believed [that] the problem of the return of Southern Kurile will automatically clarify itself" during the coming peace treaty negotiations.

THE DEMILITARIZATION PROGRAM

Initially the primary mission of the occupation was to demilitarize Japan to a point where it could never again constitute a threat to the maintenance of peace in the western Pacific area. The program involved at the outset the disarmament and demobilization of Japan's armed forces and a massive destruction of arms and facilities for their manufacture. At a later stage Article 9 of the new constitution added to this a formal and permanent renunciation of the use of force or the threat of force as an instrument of national policy and a commitment never again to maintain an army, navy, or air force—at least for other than defensive purposes. The relevant literature is set forth below.

The Occupation

In the later years of the occupation and partially as a result of shifts in American policy toward Japan, a controversy over rearmament arose in Japan and elsewhere. This controversy is treated separately in the section on the Security Treaty, the Administrative Agreement, and Japanese rearmament (p.781). A number of entries in the section containing general materials (p.113) are also relevant.

"Abolish the Yasukuni Shrine." 1945. See no.2198.

999 Acheson, Dean Gooderham. "Japanese Vessels Available for Delivery to U.S., U.K., U.S.S.R., and China." *Department of State Bulletin* 16:717–18 (20 Apr. 1947)

This statement by the U.S. acting secretary of state was released to the press on 11 April and declared that SCAP was now preparing to turn over to the Allied governments 140 surface vessels which had previously been exempted from the directive to destroy all combatant vessels of the Japanese fleet.

Conant, James B. "The Effective Disarmament of Germany and Japan." 1944. See no.69.

"Constitution Proposed for Japan Bans War." 1946. See no.1172a.

Council on Foreign Relations. *Problems of the Peace Settlement with Japan*. 1944. See no.70.

999a "Curb on War Potential of Japan Urged by Ambassador Panyushkin." *USSR Information Bulletin* 8, no.19: 591, 618 (6 Oct. 1948)

Alexander Panyushkin, the Soviet representative to the Far Eastern Commission, presents his government's view on the development of postwar Japanese industry. He argues that there should not be any specified level for "peaceful" industry nor any restrictions on Japanese exports. The Soviet Union, however, is anxious for a complete prohibition on the production of war material and does seek an FEC "control" measure whereby Japanese compliance could be assured.

999b Dionisopoulos, P. Allan. "The No-War Clause in the Japanese Constitution." *Indiana Law Journal* 31:437–54 (Summer 1956)

The author begins by examining the events leading to the inclusion of Article 9 in the Japanese postwar constitution and the principle of self-defense existing in international law. Questions raised before Prime Minister Yoshida about the problem of "self-defense" are discussed as are the contradictions involved in this war-renouncing clause. The second section of the article outlines the gradual process of rebuilding Japan's military force. The roles played by Japan's various political parties in this regard are noted. The effect on this buildup of the Mutual Security Act enacted by the U.S. Congress in 1953 is studied, and Prime Minister Yoshida's developing policies are discussed. The transition by 1 July 1954 from complete demilitarization and demobilization to the existence of a 3-pronged self-defense force is demonstrated. Part 3 questions the wisdom of U.S. activities concerning this no-war clause but justifies them in terms of the definite goals of the United States at the end of World War II and the fact that "hindsight has the advantage over foresight."

999c "Draft Treaty on the Disarmament and Demilitarization of Japan." *Department of State Bulletin* 14:1113–14 (30 June 1946)

This item reprints the text of a U.S. draft treaty circulated to the governments of China, the Soviet Union, and the United Kingdom, and released to the press on 21 June 1946. The treaty deals with such matters as the disarming and demobilization of Japanese military and paramilitary forces, the dismantling of war industries, and a quadripartite inspection system to be set up at the conclusion of the occupation period.

1000 Engineers Joint Council. National Engineers Committee. *Report on the Industrial Disarmament of Japan, Submitted to the Secretaries of State, War, and Navy.* New York: The Committee, 1946? 37p., tables, app.

A 6-man committee under the chairmanship of Carlton S. Proctor submitted this report to the secretaries of state, war, and navy. The purpose of the committee's study was "to prescribe a plan for the control of the Japanese nation which will eliminate its threat or challenge to world peace for generations to come." The report specifically deals with controls for industrial war potential. Three factors essential for such production, i.e., raw materials, processing equipment, and energy are studied in relation to Japan's 4 most important industries —(1) mineral and metal industries, (2) heavy chemical industries, (3) fuel industry, and (4) electrical power industry. The study is supplemented by general recommendations regarding the construction industry, scientific research, and nuclear energy. The concluding section of the report summarizes the findings and recommendations of the committee and 5 appendixes present statistical data on Japan's mineral and metal industries, chemical and fuel supplies, and the power industry.

Available at the Reference Branch, Office of the Chief of Military History, Washington, D.C.

1001 Far Eastern Commission. "Prohibition of Military Activity in Japan and Disposition of the Japanese Military Equipment." *Documents and State Papers* 1, no.2:99–101 (May 1948); also in *Current Notes on International Affairs* 19:203–5 (Apr. 1948)

The text of the policy decision approved by the Far Eastern Commission on 12 February 1948, released to the press on 23 March 1948, and subsequently published by the Office of Public Affairs of the U.S. State Department in this documentary series appears here. The FEC decision prohibits the reestablishment of such organizations as the War and Navy Ministries, the Japanese Imperial High Command, and the Supreme Military Council, and it forbids the resumption of military training by the civilian population. Furthermore, all military equipment seized from the Japanese armed forces was ordered either destroyed or confiscated for use by the occupation forces.

1002 ———. "Reduction of Japanese Industrial War Potential." *Department of State Bulletin* 17:513–16 (14 Sept. 1947)

This 12-point program was approved by the Far Eastern Commission on 14 August 1947 and contains a detailed description of the commission's recommendations for the reduction of Japanese industrial war potential. The report distinguishes between primary and secondary war facilities and provides explicit directions for their disposition. It also discusses the disposal of war-supporting industries and the handling of property of nationals who are members of the United Nations, and outlines a general reparations policy. There is also a detailed section concerning future restrictions on Japanese industrial capacity to prevent a resurgence of militarism.

1003 Fukase, Tadakazu. "Théorie et réalités de la formule constitutionnelle japonaise de renonciation à la guerre." *Revue du droit public et de la science politique en France et à l'étrangère* 79:1109–59 (Nov./Dec. 1963)

The first part of this study seeks in part to determine from a theoretical point of view the historical origins of the renunciation of war as found in Article 9 of the Japanese constitution. Fukase, a member of the Law Faculty at Hokkaido University, traces this concept back to the French Revolution, when it was first incorporated in the French constitution of 1791, and points out that the constitutions of Brazil (1891), Spain (1931), Thailand (1932), and the Philippines (1935) all contained similar clauses. In part 2 Fukase analyses the political realities of a country's renunciation of war and discusses, among other things, the apparent contradiction in the establishment of a 250,000-man defense force, the Japanese government's reinterpretation of Article 9, Japan's progressive rearmament, various juridical issues involving Article 9, and public opinion in Japan towards the retention or elimination of this article from the postwar constitution.

Garbuny, Siegfried. "Japan: Regeneration." 1946. *See* no.1453.

1004 Kluckhorn, Frank L. "The Japanese Menace: The Militarists." *New York Times Magazine* p.7, 36 (2 Sept. 1945)

Controlling the Japanese military establishment is the major problem facing the Americans, reports the author, one of the *Times'* correspondents in Japan during the early months of the occupation. The military is upheld by state Shinto and the samurai tradition. The author believes that the emperor was kept a virtual prisoner by the militarists, who are characterized as being tricky, persistent, and narrow in outlook. They believe that Japan is destined to rule the world. Since domination by the military has long formed the basis of Japanese life, the author warns that it will be extremely difficult to restructure Japanese social organization. Nevertheless, he reports that some experts say it will be possible to keep Japan weak by regulating and restricting the inflow of raw materials. Another hopeful force is the disillusionment of the Japanese people with the military due to defeat in the war. The best course, the author concludes, is for the Allied occupation to apply stern measures to break up the military establishment.

Krainov, Pavel. "Peace Is Sole Objective in Policy of USSR in the Far East." 1948. *See* no.2333a.

1005 MacArthur, Douglas. "The Surrender of Right to Make War." *Vital Speeches* 12:389–91 (15 Apr. 1946)

In a speech delivered before the Allied Council for Japan on 4 April 1946, the supreme commander for the Allied powers briefly discusses the role and responsibilities of the council as an advisory and consultative body. He then gives a concise summation of the goals of the occupation—those concerning disarmament and demobilization which have been largely accomplished as well as the ongoing programs associated with the democratization of the Japanese nation. Following a discussion of "sharp and ill-conceived criticism of the Occupation policies" he returns to the question of Japan's political reform and emphasizes the importance of the new constitution that will be submitted to the next national Diet. The concluding sections of MacArthur's talk deal specifically with the provision renouncing war, and he commends this proposal to the thoughtful consideration of all of the peoples of the world, suggesting that the United Nations Organization will succeed only if it accomplishes for all nations what Japan has accomplished in its new constitution —the renunciation of war as a sovereign right.

1006 McNelly, Theodore Hart. "American Influence and Japan's No-War Constitution." *Political Science Quarterly* 67: 589–98 (Dec. 1952)

In view of increasing international tensions, the author affirms at the outset that "the conviction is growing among the Western powers that for self-defense in the present world situation, Japan must have an effective army and navy." However, he asserts, a principal hindrance to rearmament is the Japanese constitution itself which renounces war and the maintenance of armed forces. The bulk of this article is a thorough account of the history of the adoption of this controversial portion of the constitution and the various stages whereby the SCAP-originated document became the postwar constitution of Japan.

1007 ———. "The Renunciation of War in the Japanese Constitution." *Political Science Quarterly* 77, no.2:350–78 (Sept. 1962)

A detailed and documented article concerning the origins and subsequent controversy surrounding Article 9, the peace chapter, of Japan's postwar constitution. Washington intended to demilitarize Japan but not permanently disarm her. The idea appears to have been suggested first by Prime Minister Shidehara to General MacArthur, who directed that a clause renouncing war be included in the constitution. This decision has since been regretted by many Japanese and Americans. Legal problems regarding Japan's self-defense force and the stationing of American troops in Japan also are described.

1008 Nishijima, Yoshiji. "The Peace Constitution Controversy." *Japan Quarterly* 10:18–27 (Jan./Mar. 1963); reprinted in Betty B. Burch and Allan B. Cole, eds. *Asian Political Systems: Readings on China, Japan, India, Pakistan.* Princeton, N.J.: Van Nostrand, 1968. p.141–50.

Nishijima finds that Article 9, the antiwar clause, has become the primary focus of debate in the continuing controversy over revision of the postwar constitution. Those who favor revising Article 9 generally argue that the realities of the postwar world demand that the constitution be altered to account for Japan's defense needs. Those opposed contend that the conflict between Japanese rearmament and Article 9 should be resolved rather by disarming Japan and adopting a strictly neutralist position in world affairs. A small but influential third group asserts that Article 9 is merely the statement of an ideal and may reasonably be retained even if Japan's defenses are expanded. Nishijima provides in outline form a useful summary of the current points being made by the pro- and antirevision forces, and summarizes the opinions most frequently heard on the question in the public hearings held by the Constitution Research Council in 1958–61.

Ozaki, Yukio. "Reminiscences." 1951. *See* no.657.

1008a Panyushkin, Alexander S. "The Position of the Soviet Delegation in the Far Eastern Commission." *USSR Information Bulletin* 8, no.4:115–16 (28 Feb. 1948)

In this statement of 19 February 1948 to the Far Eastern Commission, Ambassador Panyushkin clarifies the Soviet position on the prohibition of military activity in Japan, the disposition of Japanese military equipment, and the procedure to be followed in the admission of Pakistan to membership in the commission. Panyushkin's statement was issued to counter "incorrect" reports which had previously appeared in the American press.

"Protest of Representatives of Chinese Public Opinion against American Policies in Japan." 1948. *See* no.823.

1009 Sissons, David C. S. "The Pacifist Clause of the Japanese Constitution: Legal and Political Problems of Rearmament." *International Affairs* 37, no.1: 45–59 (Jan. 1961)

Focusing on the origins and subsequent controversy surrounding the issue of Japan's renunciation of war, David Sissons studies and traces the progressive reinterpretation of Article 9 of the constitution by successive Japanese governments and the Supreme Court between 1946 and 1960. The author first discusses how the concept of a constitutional prohibition of war originated, the reactions of the Japanese cabinet to MacArthur's draft of the "Pacifist Clause," and Prime Minister Ashida's addition of important qualifying phrases to the clause prior to the constitution's passage through the Diet. He then examines Prime Minister Yoshida's view that the renunciation of war did not mean the abandonment of Japan's right of self-defense and the interpretations of this view by ensuing cabinets. Finally, Sissons notes some of the cases brought before the Supreme Court that have been connected with Article 9—among them Suzuki Mosaburō's suit of 1952 and the Sunakawa Trespass case—and shows how court actions have supported the government's contention regarding the constitutionality of its self-defense measures.

Slocum, Winthrop. "The Naval Technical Mission to Japan." 1949. *See* no. 610.

1009a Stead, Ronald Maillard. "Top Secret out." *Christian Science Monitor* magazine section p.3 (27 Sept. 1947)

The naval base at Kure, Stead writes, used to be a top secret area. Now, however, this former center of Japan's naval greatness has become "a scrap iron merchants' El Dorado" as the remnants of Japan's fleet are cut apart for scrap under SCAP direction. Stead feels that it would be educational for Japanese from all over the country to visit Kure and observe the systematic destruction of what was left of Japan's vaunted naval power.

1010 Supreme Commander for the Allied Powers. Military Intelligence Section. *Final Report: Progress of Demobilization of the Japanese Armed Forces*. Tokyo: 31 Dec. 1946. 96p., charts, maps.

This comprehensive final report records the demobilization of the Japanese armed forces from the initiation of the program to its completion. Material is divided into 5 general sections. Section 1 describes the demobilization machinery and discusses relevant SCAP directives, the establishment of the Demobilization Board, and the responsibilities of SCAP personnel involved as well as those of the personnel of the Local Assistance Bureau of the Japanese Home Ministry. Section 2 records the progress of the program and the various related activities undertaken throughout Japan, while section 3 discusses demobilization from overseas areas. Sections 4 and 5 discuss procedures of demobilization for the air force and navy. Various charts and maps provide data on trends of demobilization, military personnel demobilized, and geographic areas involved.

Available at the Reference Branch, Office of the Chief of Military History, Washington, D.C.

1010a "USSR Invites FEC to Discuss Proposal on Japan." *USSR Information Bulletin* 8, no.22:701, 716 (17 Nov. 1948)

Alexander Panyushkin, the Soviet representative to the Far Eastern Commission, clarifies his country's definition of the war industries which are to be prohibited in the redevelopment of the Japanese economy. Specifically, these industries are the "primary war facilities" and the "secondary war facilities" that are defined in the 18 August 1947 decision of the FEC entitled "Reproduction of Japanese Industrial War Potential."

1010b Walker, Gordon W. "Exit Jap Fleet." *Christian Science Monitor* magazine section p.4 (5 Apr. 1947)

While the Allies had initially believed that the Japanese fleet was completely destroyed during the course of the war, a small number of serviceable ships and ships under construction in fact remained at the Kure naval shipyards on the day Japan surrendered. Now, however, even these remnants of the imperial fleet, which became Allied property in accordance with the surrender terms, are being reduced to scrap. Walker reports that the scrapping operation is scheduled to be completed by the fall of 1948, but Japan's naval war potential will essentially be eliminated by June 1947.

THE WAR CRIMES TRIALS

Numerous trials of alleged war criminals were conducted by the victorious Allied powers following the surrender of Japan. By far the most conspicuous of these trials was the marathon trial held in Tokyo by the International Military Tribunal for the Far East (Tokyo war crimes trial) from February 1946 to November 1948. This trial was the Far Eastern equivalent of the Nuremberg trials and involved twenty-eight of Japan's most eminent prewar and wartime leaders. In addition to it there were hundreds of other trials of less well-known defendants conducted by the Eighth Army at Yokohama and by other commands elsewhere in eastern and southeastern Asia.

In the sections that follow the literature on such trials has been divided into a first category composed solely of the official documentation relating to the trials of the twenty-eight alleged major offenders in Tokyo and the comparable trial of General Yamashita in Manila, and a second category assembling a variety of unofficial commentaries upon all of the war crimes trials.

Official Documentation

The International Military Tribunal for the Far East (IMTFE), established on 19 January 1946 by special proclamation of General Douglas MacArthur, was set up in accordance with the provisions of the Potsdam Declaration and the Japanese Instrument of Surrender signed on 2 September 1945. The tribunal, better known as the Tokyo war crimes trial, provided the machinery through which the trial of twenty-eight Japanese wartime leaders accused of war crimes by eleven Allied nations was conducted. The charter of the International Military Tribunal for the Far East was defined in General MacArthur's proclamation and stipulated the initial terms of reference for the tribunal. These terms were revised on 26 April 1946 (General Orders no.20, GHQ, SCAP). Eleven judges, one from each of the eleven nations represented on the tribunal, were appointed by the supreme commander on 15 February 1946 (General Orders no.7, GHQ, SCAP). On 29 April 1946 an indictment was filed by the International Prosecution Section of SCAP. Like the panel of judges, the prosecution was composed of eleven members representing eleven Allied nations. Its chief of counsel was an American, Joseph B. Keenan. According to the indictment, fifty-five criminal acts had been committed by the defendants between 1 January 1928 and 2 September 1945.

The court was officially opened on 3 May 1946. The indictment was read on 3 and 4 May and the accused pleaded innocent. The prosecution presented its case from 4 May 1946 through 24 January 1947, and the defense its case from 27 January 1947 through 9 January 1948. Between 12 January and 10 February 1948 evidence was presented in rebuttal and reply, and from 11 February to 16 April 1948 summations and arguments were offered by both sides. On 4 November 1948 Sir William F. Webb, the Australian president of the tribunal, read the judgment of the majority of the eleven judges. The Indian member of the court, Justice R. M. Pal, filed a lengthy dissenting opinion. The French and Dutch judges presented dissenting opinions on parts of the majority judgment. The Philippine justice submitted a separate concurring opinion. The president of the court also filed a separate statement. On 12 November 1948 the tribunal was officially closed. The sentences pronounced by the tribunal and ordered by SCAP were carried out on 23 December 1948.

The prosecution and defense staffs gathered and presented many documents: 4,336 exhibits were admitted as evidence; 419 witnesses testified in court; and 779 witnesses gave evidence in depositions and affidavits. The transcript of the Proceedings (no.1019) alone fills 48,412 mimeographed pages in 113 volumes.

In addition to the IMTFE proceedings in Tokyo, the United States also conducted a major war crimes trial in Manila against General Yamashita Tomoyuki, wartime commander of Japanese forces in the Philippines and Malaya.

1011 "Answer to Soviet Protest on MacArthur Clemency Circular." *Department of State Bulletin* 23:60–61 (10 July 1950)

Two notes are presented here: one from the Soviet government dated 11 May 1950, protesting MacArthur's circular no.5, "Clemency for War Criminals," of 7 March 1950, and the second a U.S. response dated 6 June. The Soviets contend that SCAP jurisdiction over the sentencing of criminals tried by the International Military Tribunal of the Far East is strictly limited to action before approval of sentence is given by the charter of that tribunal and by a 3 April 1946 decision of the Far Eastern Commission. Because MacArthur approved the sentence of all 16 criminals, the Soviets claim he acted illegally when he released them. The American response states that SCAP has the right to reduce or alter, except to increase in severity, any sentence of war criminals, at any time, under the charter of the International Military Tribunal. American officials contend that the sentences have not been altered; rather, parole has been granted to the 16 criminals, allowing them to serve the remainder of their sentences outside prison under periodic supervision. They are subject to reincarceration if parole is violated.

1011a "Apprehension, Trial, and Punishment of War Criminals in the Far East." *Department of State Bulletin* 16:804–6 (4 May 1947)

This 12 December 1946 policy decision of the FEC defines and categorizes various war crimes and delegates to SCAP the task of organizing a military tribunal and establishing procedural rules. Provisions also are included which establish appropriate procedures for dealing with war crimes and criminals outside of SCAP's own jurisdiction. The Far Eastern Commission urges that all investigations be initiated without delay.

1012 Australia. Dept. of External Affairs. "War Crimes." *Current Notes on International Affairs* 16:217–20 (Oct./Nov. 1945)

Terms of reference for the trial of Axis war criminals are presented here. Included are: the Moscow Declaration of October 1943; actions being taken by the United Nations War Crimes Commission; a report of a conference of national war crimes officers held in London, 31 May 1945; an agreement on the prosecution and punishment of major war criminals signed by Great Britain, France, the United States, and the Soviet Union on 8 August 1945; the activities of the Australian War Crimes Commission established in September 1945; its *Report on Japanese Atrocities* (also called the Webb Report); and, finally, the establishment of Australian military tribunals to try Japanese war criminals apprehended by the Australian military forces.

1013 Bernard, Henri. *Memorandum, Dissenting Judgment.* Tokyo: International Military Tribunal for the Far East, 1948. 23p.

The dissenting opinion filed by French Justice Bernard from the majority judgment includes substantial criticism of both the judicial procedures adopted by the tribunal and the sentences which were imposed. Justice Bernard maintains that the defendants were not given adequate opportunity at the preliminary examination to obtain and organize evidence for their defense and that the decision by the prosecution not to prosecute the emperor was unfair to the accused. He also denounces the way in which the judgment was prepared and adopted, asserting that dissenting opinions were ignored by the majority of the judges and that personnel in organizations outside the tribunal provided support for the majority opinion. The Japanese text of his opinion is printed in Asahi Shimbun Hōtei Kishadan, *Tōkyō Saiban* (Tokyo: Tōkyō Saiban Kankōkai, 1962. v.3, p.195–214).

Brown, Delmer M. "Recent Japanese Political and Historical Materials." 1949. See no.4.

Cho, Sung-Yoon. "The Tokyo War Crimes Trial." 1967. See no.6.

Dull, Paul, and Michael Takaaki Umemura. *The Tokyo Trials: A Functional Index to the Proceedings of the International Military Tribunal for the Far East.* 1957. See no.7.

1014 "General Douglas MacArthur's Review of the War Crimes Sentences Issued on November 24, 1948." *Contemporary Japan* 17:433–34 (July/Dec. 1948)

MacArthur's official statement in connection with his responsibility to review the sentences passed on the Japanese war criminal defendants by the International Military Tribunal for the Far East discusses the unique nature of the proceedings and the extraordinary difficulties which arise in trying men for a nation's conduct. In commenting on the trials, however, he affirms that "I can find nothing of technical commission or omission in the incidents of the trial itself of sufficient importance to warrant my intervention in the judgments which have been tendered."

1015 "General Tomoyuki Yamashita *vs.* Lieutenant General Wilhelm D. Styer." *United States Supreme Court Records.* Lawyers' ed. 327:499–545 (Oct. 1945 term)

The text of the case of General Yamashita argued and decided in the Supreme Court of the United States in February 1946.

1016 International Military Tribunal for the Far East. *Judgment of the International Military Tribunal for the Far East.* Tokyo: The Tribunal, 12 Nov. 1948. 1,218, 130p.

The 10 chapters of the majority judgment of the tribunal, read from 4 November through 12 November 1948, are printed here. The judgment begins with a description of the establishment, jurisdiction, and proceedings of the tribunal. It provides background information concerning the tribunal's understanding of its task. The authors of the judgment assert that while Japan agreed to become a member of "civilized communities" by joining the League of Nations and ratifying international laws concerning the conduct of war, it systematically violated these laws after 1930. Aggressive Japanese conduct directed against China, the Soviet Union, and areas in the Pacific is discussed. Tribunal findings and verdicts are listed. Major documents related to the tribunal, including the text of the Potsdam Declaration, the Instrument of Surrender, and the charter of the tribunal, are appended. No index is provided. The judgment was originally read into the *Proceedings* (1946–48) (no.1019) on pages 48, 415–49, 858, and was later published by various institutions including the U.S. War Department (1948, 7v.). A Japanese version appears in *Tōkyō Saiban hanketsu* (Tokyo: Mainichi Shimbunsha, 1949. 320p.).

1017 ———. *Tokyo War Crimes Trials, Documents, Exhibits for the Defense.* (Defense document nos.1–3,088) Tokyo: The Tribunal, 27 Jan. 1947–10 Feb. 1948. 23v.

The defense documents compiled here were presented in court between 27 January 1947 and 10 February 1948 and are arranged according to their defense document numbers, not their exhibit numbers. It should be noted that not all of the documents collected here were accepted as court exhibits; the first one accepted was registered as exhibit no. 2283. The documents include affidavits, the sworn depositions of the defendants, diaries, memoirs, excerpts of past remarks, political and military records, telegrams, treaties, reports, etc. Original materials written in Japanese were translated into English by the Defense Language Branch. The defense exhibits that were actually read in the tribunal sessions are covered in the *Proceedings* (1946–48) (no.1019) on pages 17, 264–38, 931. A total of 1,411 defense exhibits are indexed in *Tokyo War Crimes Trials, Documents, Exhibits for the Defense: Index 1947–48)* (no.1033).

1018 ———. *Tokyo War Crimes Trials, Documents, Exhibits for the Prosecution.* (Exhibit nos.1–2,282) Tokyo: The Tribunal, 4 May 1946–24 Jan. 1947. 22v.

The prosecution, working in conjunction with the International Prosecution Section of SCAP, prepared over 12,000 documents to support its case. Of these 2,282 were presented before the court and accepted as exhibits for the prosecution during the period 4 May 1946 to 24 January 1947. All of these 2,282 prosecution exhibits are included here, and are arranged by exhibit number. Records of decisions of Allied conferences, imperial ordinances, memorandums exchanged among Japanese high ranking officials, minutes of government meetings such as the cabinet and Privy Council, diaries, memoirs, books, affidavits, and depositions are among the items included. The documents vary in length from one to several hundred pages. The exhibits that were actually read in court are cited in the *Proceedings* (1946–48) (no.1019) on pages 105–16, 259; for a list of exhibits, see *Tokyo War Crimes Trials, Documents, Exhibits for the Prosecution, Index* (1946–47) (no.1032).

1019 ———. *Tokyo War Crimes Trials, Proceedings.* (818 sessions) Tokyo: The Tribunal, 3 May 1946–16 Apr. 1948. 113v. Available on microfilm (36 reels) from the Photoduplication Service, Dept. C–2, Library of Congress, Washington, D.C. 20540.

The official record of the tribunal covering 818 sessions in 417 days from 3 May 1946 when the indictment was read until 16 April 1948 when the summations for the prosecution and the defense were completed is presented in these volumes. This record does not include the proceedings of the last 7 sessions conducted in November 1948 when the judgment was read. Verbatim minutes were typed, mimeographed, numbered consecutively, and issued by session. The volumes contain a variety of material, including a copy of the indictment, a discussion of the legal basis of the tribunal's jurisdiction, debates on legal technicalities, testimony of witnesses, a record of exhibits presented, arguments concerning the introduction, identification, and acceptance of evidence, and the summations by both sides. Evidence presented relates to Japanese attitudes toward war; military and economic aggression in China and other parts of Asia; atrocities; Japan's relations with countries such as Germany, Italy, France, the British Commonwealth, the United States, the Soviet Union, the Netherlands, Portugal, and Thailand; the Japanese constitution; government structure; imperial ordinances; the political role of the military; the scope of cabinet responsibility; and the relationship of the defendants to these matters. An official Japanese translation of the proceedings was issued in 1948 under the English title *Japanese Record of Proceedings of the International Military Tribunal for the Far East.* This translation was reprinted in 1968 under the title *Kyokutō Kokusai Gunji Saiban Sokkiroku* (Tokyo: Yūshōdō Shoten. 10v.).

1020 Jaranilla, Delfin. *Separate Opinion Concurring, the Majority Judgment.* Tokyo: International Military Tribunal for the Far East, 1948. 35p.

This concurring opinion by the Philippine justice on the tribunal is a defense of its legality. Justice Jaranilla is particularly critical of the argument presented by the Indian Justice R. M. Pal which stated that the tribunal had exceeded its jurisdiction. However, Jaranilla disagrees with one conclusion reached by a majority of the judges, namely, that conspiracy constitutes a crime only when it is committed against peace; he contends that crimes of conspiracy are committed through acts of general military aggression as well as through acts directed against peace. On the basis of this contention, he maintains that the sentences imposed on the defendants were too generous and therefore inappropriate. A Japanese version of this opinion appears in Asahi Shimbun Hōtei Kishidan, *Tōkyō Saiban* (Tokyo: Tōkyō Saiban Kankōkai, 1962. v.3, p.176–92).

1020a Kirchman, Charles V., and Garry D. Ryan. *Preliminary Inventory of the Textual Records of the International Military Tribunal for the Far East.* Record Group 238. General Services Administration, National Archives and Record Service, NM 62 (1965). 5p.

A listing of all of the International Military Tribunal for the Far East documents found in the holdings of the National Archives at Suitland, Md.

Liu, James T. C. "The Tokyo Trials: Source Materials." 1948. *See* no.18.

New Zealand. Dept. of External Affairs. *Annual Report of the Department of External Affairs, 1 April 1948 to 31 March 1949.* 1949. *See* no.2342.

1021 Pal, Radhabinod B. *Dissenting Opinion of Judgement and Decision of the International Military Tribunal for the Far East in the Case of the United States of America, the Republic of China, et al. against Araki Sadao, Dohihara Kenji, et al.* Tokyo: International Military Tribunal for the Far East, 1948. 12v.

The Indian member of the tribunal wrote a lengthy dissenting opinion from the judgment. In his 12-volume work, Pal questions the fundamental *raison d'être* for a tribunal conducted only by victorious powers and asserts that the jurisdiction of the tribunal does not cover wars waged by Japan prior to 1941, that the charter of the tribunal does not adequately define war crimes, and that the tribunal can try the accused only on charges of "war crimes in stricto sensu," such as mistreatment of prisoners of war and civilians, not on charges of crimes which endangered peace and promoted aggression. He explains at length that according to international law and precedent, wars waged by states are not illegal. This explanation contradicts the fundamental argument of the prosecution, and on the basis of this explanation, Pal advocates that all the accused be acquitted. He strongly condemns President Truman for his decision to use the atomic bomb against Japan, comparing this action to Hitler's policy of genocide. The opinion consists of 7 parts: (1) preliminary legal problems; (2) the definition of wars of aggression; (3) regulations concerning evidence and procedure; (4) overall conspiracy; (5) the scope of International Military Tribunal for the Far East jurisdiction; (6) war crimes in a strict sense; and (7) recommendations. Pal declares that the prosecution failed to produce convincing evidence that a conspiracy existed among the Japanese, the Germans, and the Italians to achieve world domination. As a result of the controversial nature of this opinion, it is said that it was barred from publication for some time. In 1950, however, public awareness was stimulated when Pal's opinion was upheld by a distinguished British political leader, Lord Hankey, in his book, *Politics, Trials, and Errors* (Oxford: Pen-in-Hand, 1950. xiv, 150p., and Chicago: Regnery, 1950. xiv, 150p.). The full text of the original report, *The International Military Tribunal for the Far East: Dissentient Judgment* (Calcutta: Sanyal, 1953. xvii, 701, 23p.) was reprinted in India in 1953. Pal's statement became known to the Japanese public when it was translated in its entirety into Japanese under the title of *Nihon muzairon* (Japan Not Guilty) (Tokyo: Nihon Shobō, 1952. 626p.). Additional and more accurate versions appeared in Asahi Shimbun Hōtei Kishadan, *Tōkyō Saiban* (Tokyo: Tōkyō Saiban Kankōkai, 1962. v.3, p.345–935), and in Tōkyō Saiban Kenkyūkai, *Kyōdō Kenkyū Pāru Hanketsusho* (A Joint Study of Pal's Judgment) (Tokyo: Tokyo Saiban Kankōkai, 1966. p.147–737).

1022 Röling, Bernard V. A. *Opinion of Mr. Justice Roling, Member for the Netherlands.* Tokyo: International Military Tribunal for the Far East, 12 Nov. 1948. 249p.

In his presentation, Bernard V. A. Röling takes issue with the judgment adopted by a majority of the tribunal members. He contends that the jurisdiction of the tribunal was restricted to the Pacific War, a war fought between Japan and those nations that signed the Instrument of Surrender, and argues that judgment concerning other wars fought in the Far East was beyond the jurisdiction of the tribunal. He also challenges the concepts of "crimes against peace" and "responsibility for war," maintaining that it is impossible to define these concepts. A substantial portion of his report is devoted to observations concerning the facts presented at the tribunal and to his disagreement with specific verdicts. He asserts that Oka, Satō, and Shimada should have been sentenced to death, while Hata, Hirota, Kido, Shigemitsu, and Tōgō should have been acquitted. A detailed justification of his assertions is included. A Japanese version of his statement appears in Asahi Shimbun Hōtei Kishadan, *Tōkyō Saiban* (Tokyo: Tōkyō Saiban Kankōkai, 1962. v.3, p.215–344).

1023 Supreme Commander for the Allied Powers. *International Military Tribunal for the Far East, Established at Tokyo January 19, 1946*. Washington, D.C.: Government Printing Office, 1947. 16p. (Dept. of State publication 2765; Treaties and Other International Acts series 1589)

Contains the official texts of 3 documents relating to the International Military Tribunal for the Far East. They are: a special proclamation to establish the tribunal, issued by General MacArthur on 19 January 1946; the charter of the tribunal, issued as SCAP General Orders no.1 (19 Jan. 1946); and the amended charter of the tribunal, issued as General Orders no.20 (26 Apr. 1946).

———. *Japanese File: Correspondence, 1945–1947.* See no.259.

———. Monograph 5. *Trials of Class "B" and "C" War Criminals.* 1952. See no.287.

1024 ———. Government Section. *The Case of General Yamashita: A Memorandum.* Tokyo: SCAP, 1950. 82, 4p.

Brigadier General Courtney Whitney, who was chief of SCAP's Government Section, prepared this memorandum (22 Nov. 1949) for SCAP in order to defend the legality of the trial and conviction of General Yamashita Tomoyuki, which was conducted by an American military commission at Manila in 1945. The memorandum was intended primarily to rebuff arguments against the validity of such a trial advanced by Captain Adolf F. Reel, one of the 5 members of defense counsel for the general. These arguments by Reel were expounded in his controversial book, *The Case of General Yamashita* (no. 1089), which was published in 1949. In view of the wide publicity given Reel's book and SCAP's concern over the apparent continued suspicion among the Japanese people concerning the fairness of the trial, General Whitney advances counterarguments on the basis of the official record of the trial, the past history of military tribunals, and the 1929 international agreements on the conduct of war. His discussion is followed by 3 appendixes setting forth the opinions of the U.S. Supreme Court justices on an appeal made by General Yamashita's defense to bring the case before a civilian court, the report of the United Nations War Crimes Commission on the Yamashita case, and a summary of the trial record prepared by the Pacific Office of the Theater Judge Advocate of the U.S. Army Forces. Finally, General Whitney reproduces a statement issued by Major George F. Guy, another member of defense counsel, on 7 November 1945. This statement appeared in the *Nippon Times* on the same date and is a justification of the trial of General Yamashita.

1025 ———. International Prosecution Section. *Analyses of Documentary Evidence.* Tokyo: International Military Tribunal for the Far East, 1947. 27v. (IPS document no.0012)

Basic descriptive information concerning the documents numbered from 1 to 4,100 which were prepared by the

International Prosecution Section is given here. Each description gives the title of the document concerned and describes its nature. The author(s), date, and location of the original document are also given.

1026 ——. ——. *Chronological Summary*. Tokyo: International Military Tribunal for the Far East, 1947. (IPS document no.0001)

Oral and documentary evidence presented by the prosecution up to 10 December 1946 are summarized here in chronological order starting with the Tanaka cabinet of 1928 and ending with the Suzuki cabinet of 1945. References to relevant exhibits or pages in the *Proceedings* (1946-48) (no.1019) are included.

1027 ——. ——. *Decision of Imperial Conferences, Cabinet Meetings, and Other Conferences and Meetings Which Appear in the Prosecution's Evidence*. Tokyo: International Military Tribunal for the Far East, June 1947. 283p. (IPS document no.0004)

The arguments conducted and the decisions agreed upon at various imperial conferences and at meetings of such high-level government bodies as the Privy Council, the cabinet, and the Supreme War Council are recorded here. In each of the 14 chapters, material pertaining to the sessions of a particular government body is presented. It is organized in chronological order and is limited to testimony and documents submitted by the prosecution. Exhibit numbers and page references to the *Proceedings* (1946-48) (no.1019) are also given.

1028 ——. ——. *General Index of the Record of the Defense Case*. Tokyo: International Military Tribunal for the Far East, 10 Oct. 1947. 152p. (IPS document no.0008)

The defense case was divided into 6 "phases": (1) general problems; (2) Manchuria and Manchukuo; (3) China; (4) the Union of Soviet Socialist Republics; (5) the Pacific War, and, (6) individual defenses. Statements and testimony relating to the first 4 of these phases and to the Tripartite Pact subdivision of the Pacific War phase are indexed here. This material was read before the tribunal by several defense counsels between 24 February and 19 June 1947, and is cited in the *Proceedings* (1946-48) (no.1019) on pages 17,004-24,758. In the index, statements and testimony are divided according to a detailed list of topics and by the names of witnesses. Cross-references to pages in the *Proceedings* are given.

1029 ——. ——. *General Index of the Record of the Prosecution's Case*. Tokyo: International Military Tribunal for the Far East, 30 June 1947. 101p. (IPS document no.0005)

The record of the prosecution's case reported in pages 1 to 16,997 of the *Proceedings* (1946-48) (no.1019) and presented from 3 May 1946 through 31 January 1947 is indexed here. The treatment is divided by the 14 phases of the case, and includes entries for many related names, places, and institutions with references to pertinent pages in the *Proceedings*.

1030 ——. ——. *Narrative Summary of the Record*. Tokyo: International Military Tribunal for the Far East, 1947. 6,000p.

This digest of the *Proceedings* (1946-48) (no.1019) was prepared by the International Prosecution Section to assist both prosecution and defense attorneys in preparing their summations. The pages in the *Proceedings* and the numbers of the court exhibits which provided the basis of this digest are indicated. The compilation of this summary was discontinued with page 37,167 of the *Proceedings* and does not cover that section of the defense case covered in pages 37,168 to 38,947.

1031 ——. ——. *Tokyo War Crimes Trials, Addendum to Revised Index of Documents by Defendants*. Tokyo: International Military Tribunal for the Far East, 23 May 1947. 7p.

1032 The Occupation

A sequel to the *Revised Index of Documents by Defendants* (1947) (no. 1039) of 14 April 1947.

1032 ———. ———. *Tokyo War Crimes Trials, Documents, Exhibits for the Prosecution: Index.* Tokyo: International Military Tribunal for the Far East, 4 May 1946–24 Jan. 1947. 322p.

A total of 2,282 prosecution exhibits accepted by the tribunal from 4 May 1946 when the prosecution opened its case through 24 January 1947 when the prosecution rested are indexed here. These exhibits are described in the *Proceedings* (1946–48) (no.1019) on pages 105–16,259. This index is simply a listing of exhibits according to exhibit numbers assigned by the tribunal, and it provides information concerning the numbers originally given by the prosecution to each document and the pages in the *Proceedings* where each document is cited "for identication" and/or "in evidence." No dates are given.

1033 ———. ———. *Tokyo War Crimes Trials, Documents, Exhibits for the Defense: Index.* (Exhibit nos.2,283–3,915) Tokyo: International Military Tribunal for the Far East, 26 Feb. 1947–16 Apr. 1948. 270p.

This index of exhibits includes a listing of 1,411 defense exhibits and 222 prosecution exhibits, which were accepted as evidence by the tribunal from 26 February 1947 through 10 February 1948. They are arranged according to the order in which they were accepted. In addition to exhibit numbers, the index includes the title of the document, the original number the document was given by either the prosecution or defense, and the pages of the *Proceedings* (1946–48) (no.1019) at which it is cited as evidence or for purposes of identification.

1034 ———. ———. *Tokyo War Crimes Trials, Index of Documents Not Specifically Linked to One or More of the Defendants.* Tokyo: International Military Tribunal for the Far East, 26 May 1947. 17p.

This working list of prosecution documents is grouped according to 8 topics. It was "prepared for the purpose of re-evaluation of files material only" and is not as complete as *Index to Documents (by Phase and Subject)* (no.1036). The 8 topics are: (1) the Japanese constitution, governmental and army organization, collections of official announcements, Foreign Ministry business reports, post-surrender activities, etc.; (2) propaganda, censorship, matters of internal politics, ultranationalist societies; (3) China; (4) collaboration with Germany and Italy; (5) France, Thailand, Netherlands, Portugal; (6) the Soviet Union; (7) preparations for war and aggression against the United States and Great Britain; and (8) class "B" and "C" offenses. Documents grouped under these topics are divided into 2 categories, one for those documents introduced before the court as evidence and one for those documents which were not. Those introduced as evidence were given exhibit numbers. This index does not include: (1) any documents which appeared in *Revised Index of Documents by Defendants* (1947) (no.1039); (2) German documents (document nos.4,000 to 4,100); (3) documents numbered between 4,100 and 11,900 which were assigned to attorneys; (4) some 100 documents numbered between 1 and 4,000 which were of no value as evidence or for reexamination.

1035 ———. ———. *Tokyo War Crimes Trials, Index of Witnesses.* Tokyo: International Military Tribunal for the Far East, 1948. 34, 117p.

The names of witnesses who testified for the prosecution or defense from 17 June 1946 through 10 February 1948 are indexed in this document. Prosecution witnesses who testified between 17 June 1946 and 30 January 1948 are included in one section, and defense witnesses who testified from 28 February 1947 through 10 February 1948 are in another. In each section witnesses are listed in alphabetical order, together with the name of the person who directed the testimony, the names of those who cross-examined the witness, and the page(s) in the *Proceedings* (1946–48) (no.1019) where the testimony is recorded.

1036 ———. ———. *Tokyo War Crimes Trials, Index to Documents (by Phase and Subject).* Tokyo: International Military Tribunal for the Far East, 20 Mar. 1947. 20p.

Prosecution documents numbered from 1 to 2,969 and 4,000 to 4,095 are indexed here under 13 main headings with detailed subheadings. They pertain to all phases of the prosecution's case. The main headings are: (1) the Japanese constitution and the functions of offices held by defendants; (2) Manchurian military aggression, 1931–45; (3) all-China military aggression, 1941–45; (4) economic aggression in China, 1932–45; (5) narcotics in China and elsewhere, 1932–45; (6) preparations for war; (7) preparing Japanese opinion for war; (8) relations with Germany, Italy, France, and Thailand; (9) relations with the Soviet Union; (10) relations with the United States and British Commonwealth; (11) relations with the Netherlands and Portugal; (12) class "B" offenses; and (13) class "C" offenses, 1931–45.

1037 ———. ———. *Tokyo War Crimes Trials, Japanese Cabinet Officials, 1927–1945.* Tokyo: International Military Tribunal for the Far East, n.d. 4p.

The names of members of the 17 cabinets formed between 20 April 1927 when the Tanaka cabinet was established and 16 August 1945 when the Suzuki cabinet resigned are listed together with their ministerial positions. The chart also includes the names of the occupants of the 11 top military positions in Japan during the administration of these cabinets and of the Higashikuni cabinet (17 Aug. to 5 Oct. 1945). The military positions identified are: army chief of staff, army vice-chief of staff, army vice-minister, chief of Military Affairs Bureau, chief of staff Kwantung Army, commander in chief Kwantung Army, inspector general of Military Education, navy chief of staff, navy vice-chief of staff, navy vice-minister, and chief of Naval Affairs (*Gummu*) Bureau.

1038 ———. ———. *Tokyo War Crimes Trials, Numerical List of IPS Documents Introduced as Court Exhibits.* Tokyo: International Military Tribunal for the Far East, 9 Dec. 1947. 32p.

Intended primarily as a cross-reference to the 2-volume *Index of Exhibits* (nos.1032 and 1033), this list contains all the International Prosecution Section documents placed in evidence by the prosecution up to the end of November 1947. The documents are arranged by document number, with exhibit numbers listed if applicable. Exhibits for identification only are noted with an asterisk. The last prosecution document given is no.8,279, which is exhibit no.1,901. The last exhibit recorded is no.2,112, i.e., document no.8,260.

1039 ———. ———. *Tokyo War Crimes Trials, Revised Index of Documents by Defendants.* Tokyo: International Military Tribunal for the Far East, 14 Apr. 1947. 46p.

This index represents a revision of the *Index to Documents (by Defendants)* issued on March 15, 1947 and includes a listing of the numbers of all documents prepared for the defense of each of the 28 accused. The documents are classified according to defendants and are grouped according to those introduced as evidence and those which were not. Defense documents are arranged by defense document numbers and, for those introduced as evidence, by exhibit numbers as well. The system thus clarifies the relationship between defense document numbers and exhibit numbers, and also indicates whether a given document was used in the defense of more than one defendant. Documents for identification only are marked with an asterisk.

1039a Takayanagi, Kenzō. *The Tokio Trials and International Law: Answer to the Prosecution's Arguments on International Law Delivered at the International Military Tribunal for the Far East* on 3 and 4 March 1948. Tokyo: Yuhikaku, 1948. iv, 111, 137p. In English and Japanese.

This book consists of 2 lengthy addresses which Takayanagi, Japan's leading specialist in Anglo–American law, made before the Tokyo tribunal during the winter of 1948. Takayanagi delivered his remarks in English (slightly polished Japanese translations accompany the texts of those particular speeches within this volume), and he argued against Chief of Counsel Joseph B. Keenan's assertion that the conspiracy committed by the defendants (as charged in count no.1) was known to and well recognized by most civilized nations. Takayanagi stated that the doctrine of criminal conspiracy was a "peculiar product of English legal history" and that it was a dangerous doctrine. His reasoning eventually won the support of 2 of the tribunal's justices—Pal of India and Webb of Australia—but Keenan was able to persuade the majority of judges that there was indeed such a crime in international law.

1040 Tōjō, Hideki. *Affidavit of Hideki Tojo, Individual Defense.* Tokyo: International Military Tribunal for the Far East, 19 Dec. 1947. 246p. (Defense document no.3,000)

This affidavit of former Prime Minister Tōjō Hideki, prepared with the aid of his defense counsels, Kiyose Ichirō and George F. Blewett, is a review of various topics including Tōjō's personal history, his military policies, disposal of prisoners of war, the motives behind the formulation of the Greater East Asia policy, and the circumstances surrounding the imperial conference, of 5 November and 1 December 1941 which preceded the attack on Pearl Harbor.

1040a "Trial of Far Eastern Criminals." *Department of State Bulletin* 14:846–48, 853 (19 May 1946)

This article consists of 2 items relating to the war crimes trials: (1) "The Indictment—Statement by Joseph B. Keenan, Chief of Counsel for the Prosecution," which details and explains the charges according to the Charter of the International Military Tribunal for the Far East; and (2) a document summarizing the indictment and listing the defendants and their former positions.

1040b "Trial of Far Eastern War Criminals." *Department of State Bulletin* 14: 361–64 (10 Mar. 1946)

This item contains the texts of 2 documents: (1) General MacArthur's proclamation of the establishment of the International Military Tribunal for the Far East, and (2) the Charter of the tribunal declaring the constitution of the tribunal, its jurisdiction, provisions for a fair trial, the powers of the tribunal, the conduct of the trial, and the judgment and subsequent sentencing of all those who are found guilty.

1041 U.S. Army Forces in the Pacific. *Regulations Governing the Trial of War Criminals.* Mimeographed. n.p.: 1945. 1v.

A collection of mimeographed bulletins regarding regulations for the trial of those apprehended as war criminals in the Pacific and in the China theaters. Documents date from 24 September 1945 to 27 December 1946 and are issued either by General Headquarters, U.S. Army Forces, Pacific or later by General Headquarters, SCAP. Each bulletin sets forth official policies concerning various aspects of war crimes trials such as the establishment of military commissions, their jurisdiction over persons and territory, membership of the commission, prosecutors, powers and procedures of commissions, the conduct of trials, rights of the accused, submission of evidence, judgment, and sentences. One bulletin lists minor revisions or additions to earlier orders.

Available at the Army Library, the Pentagon, Washington, D.C.

1042 ———. Dept. of State. *Trial of Japanese War Criminals: Documents.* Washington, D.C.: Government Printing Office, 1946. iv, 104p. (Dept. of State publication 2613; Far Eastern series 12)

A collection of 3 major documents relating to the International Military Tribunal for the Far East. A list of 11 judges representing the Allied nations is followed by the full text of the "Opening Statement of the Prosecution," by Joseph B. Keenan, chief of counsel of the prosecution. Some of the important topics which this statement deals with include the general organization of the prosecution documents prepared; the basis of the 3 groups of crimes according to which charges were made (i.e., group 1, crimes against peace; group 2, murder; and group 3, conventional war crimes and crimes against humanity); the total 55 counts of the indictment; and appendixes of additional documents used to support charges. The second document presents the full text of the charter of the International Military Tribunal for the Far East as amended on 26 April 1946 (SCAP General Orders no.20). The third document is the full text of the tribunal's indictment no.1, which is comprised of the total 55 counts of the indictment along with the names of war criminals tried. The subsequent 5 appendixes are: Appendix A, summarizing particulars supporting several counts of the indictment; Appendix B, listing articles of treaties violated by Japan; Appendix C, listing official assurances violated by Japan; Appendix D, listing official assurances violated by Japan and incorporated in group 3; and Appendix E, outlining the statement of individual responsibility for crimes set out in the indictment. This last appended document lists the 28 accused and describes the positions they held between 1928 and 1945 which led to their indictment.

———. ———. Historical Div. *Foreign Relations of the United States, 1946.* v.8, *The Far East.* 1971. See no.203a.

1043 ———. Supreme Court. "Judicial Decisions *in re* Yamashita [and] *in re* Homma." *American Journal of International Law* 40, no.2:432–82 (Apr. 1946)

A collection of the official judicial decisions and the dissenting opinions regarding the Yamashita and Homma cases.

1044 Webb, Sir William F. *Webb's Judgment.* Tokyo: International Military Tribunal for the Far East, 1948. 658p.

A separate statement filed by the Australian justice and president of the tribunal stresses that the tribunal is a military court of the Allied powers and that the charter of the tribunal constitutes a part of international law. Webb also remarks that, although the emperor should not have been prosecuted, "justice requires me to take into consideration the Emperor's immunity when determining the punishment of the accused found guilty." He states he did not agree with the sentences imposed by the majority judgment and suggests that life imprisonment may be a more effective "deterrent" to crimes against humanity than capital punishment. He also gives a detailed account of his reasoning with respect to the verdicts for each of the 25 defendants. The initial portion of his judgment dealing with general matters has been translated into Japanese in Asahi Shimbun Hōtei Kishadan, *Tōkyō Saiban* (Tokyo: Tōkyō Saiban Kankōkai, 1962. v.3, p.164–75).

Unofficial Commentaries

The bulk of the entries that follow relate to the proceedings of the International Military Tribunal for the Far East in Tokyo. A few treat the trial of General Yamashita Tomoyuki in Manila and the trial in Khabarovsk (USSR) of former army officers accused of engaging in bacteriological warfare. An even smaller number focuses on the trials of less important offenders grouped as class "B" and "C" war criminals.

1045 "Advocate of Plague." *Current Digest of the Soviet Press* 2, no.9:28–29 (15 Apr. 1950).

The American prosecutor Joseph B. Keenan, who "has been distinguished for his weakness toward eminent war criminals" ever since the opening of the Tokyo war crimes trial, is accused of seeking to defend Emperor Hirohito from just prosecution for his wartime activities. Keenan rejected reports on Japanese bacteriological warfare which the Soviet government presented during the Tokyo trial, and he now is refusing to accept the "irrefutable proof established by the Khabarovsk trial of the establishment of the criminal Japanese bacteriological detachment No.731 which was formed on direct instructions of the Emperor Hirohito." The article accordingly asserts that Keenan is biased against the Soviet Union and accuses the Americans of defending the emperor and other war criminals in order that they may be used for "new, barbarous aggression." This article first appeared in the 23 February issue of *Izvestia* and has been translated here in full.

1045a Allen, Lafe Franklin. "Japan's Militarists Face the Music." *American Foreign Service Journal* 24:14–17, 41–44 (Aug. 1947).

Allen describes the proceedings of the International Tribunal for the Far East and the American determination to allow both prosecution and defense full opportunity to express opinions. The role of chief prosecutor, held by Joseph B. Keenan, is highlighted and the prosecution arguments are outlined. Defense preparation and legal tactics used to challenge the punishment of the Japanese for breach of existing international law are discussed. Allen regards Japanese press coverage of the trials as an inducement for domestic democratic reform.

1046 ———. "Judgment Day in Tokyo." *Military Government Journal* 2:7–8, 12 (Fall 1949).

The proceedings of the International Military Tribunal for the Far East are briefly summarized in this article. The author gives a general summation of the sentences passed upon the Japanese defendants and a brief and rather biased description of the attitudes of such important persons as General Tōjō and Marquis Kido during the trial. While critical of the fact that Emperor Hirohito and members of the *zaibatsu* were not put on trial at the same time, the author nevertheless views the trials as generally fair proceedings which, he hopes, will "convince the Japanese people beyond a shadow of a doubt that international lawlessness does not pay."

1047 Appleman, John A. *Military Tribunals and International Crimes.* Indianapolis: Bobbs-Merrill, 1954. xv, 421p.

In chapter 22, on the International Military Tribunal for the Far East, the author examines the court's composition and its rules of procedure. He sharply criticizes the attitude and rulings of the court's president, particularly his disregard for the rights of the defense counsel. After discussing the majority and the dissenting judgments of the tribunal, the author concludes that the legal concept of aggressive war as a criminal action has been enhanced as a consequence of the proceedings.

"Are We Converting Japan into an Allied Colony?" 1946. See no.1297.

1048 Berezhkov, V. "The Tokyo Trial." *New Times* no.5:6–9 (28 Jan. 1948).

The author complains about the 2-year duration of the Tokyo trials of major Japanese war criminals, the domination of the trials by MacArthur and his appointees, and the dishonest whitewashing tactics of the American defense lawyers and their Japanese colleagues. The concluding paragraphs discuss American collusion with *zaibatsu* bosses and militarist leaders and this unholy alliance is viewed as the reason why such groups have not been brought to trial in Tokyo.

1048a Bergamini, David. *Japan's Imperial Conspiracy.* New York: Morrow, 1971. xxxviii, 1239p.

Bergamini challenges the validity of the commonly held view that Japan's aggressive military activities from the 1930s on were in effect beyond Emperor Hirohito's control and were only reluctantly approved by him. From the evidence, Bergamini believes, it is clear that Hirohito could easily have been convicted by the International Military Tribunal for the Far East for actively participating in and perhaps even leading a long-term conspiracy in support of aggressive Japanese expansionism. The emperor escaped trial, nevertheless, for 2 reasons. First, the Allies decided that his presence on the throne was needed to legitimize occupation control and to preserve domestic order. Second, a concerted effort was made by people close to Hirohito in the court and the imperial household to disguise and deny the emperor's complicity in the planning and execution of the war. Bergamini marshalls some evidence in support of his thesis, but willingly admits that certain crucial arguments have necessarily had to be based either on educated guesswork or on interviews with people wishing to remain anonymous. The author's journalistic style and his handling of evidence somewhat diminish the soundness of the book as a scholarly source, but Bergamini demonstrates at the very least a need for increased academic attention to the role of the imperial court in presurrender Japanese politics.

The introduction to *Japan's Imperial Conspiracy* is by Sir William Flood Webb, the Australian member and presiding judge of the Tokyo war crimes trial. In it Webb briefly explains the legal background of the trial and expresses his opinions on the legal implications of the decision not to prosecute the emperor. Webb finds much to recommend in Bergamini's book and praises him for rejecting both the wartime image of the Japanese as "cold and calculating schemers" and the "postwar apology for the Japanese as fanatic emotional blunderers."

1049 Blakeney, Ben Bruce. "International Military Tribunal." *American Bar Association Journal* 32:475–77, 523 (Aug. 1946)

The arguments to dismiss charges on the basis of lack of jurisdiction by the defense counsel for General Umezu made before the International Military Tribunal for the Far East on behalf of all defendants represented by American counsel are presented here. Blakeney attempted to base his motion on the fact that war has never been considered a crime but rather a legitimate national policy based on force. He maintains that war is an act of nations rather than individuals and that individuals cannot be held responsible. The idea that killing in war is not murder and the concept that wartime offenses must be punished by a military commission designated and appointed by the victorious belligerent are discussed. The author utilizes American and international legal covenants in his argument, and deplores the tendency of the prosecution to create *ex post facto* law in these trials.

1050 Blewett, George F. "Victor's Injustice: The Tokyo War Crimes Trial." *American Perspective* 4:282–92 (Summer 1950)

Blewett, defense attorney for Tōjō in the Tokyo war crimes trial, notes that the trial can only be a source of disquiet and uneasiness. He points out that not only were basic departures from long-accepted Western legal traditions tolerated, but a patently double standard was also applied to the leaders of the victorious and defeated nations.

1051 "Bring the War Criminals to Justice." *New Times* no.6:3–5 (8 Feb. 1950)

Accusing the wartime Japanese of formulating hideous plans for the conduct of biological warfare, this editorial insists that those war criminals responsible, including Emperor Hirohito, be tried for their offense. It is stated that such a procedure has the full approval of the Far Eastern Commission and is blocked only by the United States.

1052 Browne, Courtney. *Tojo: The Last Banzai*. New York: Holt, Rinehart and Winston, 1967. viii, 260p.

This popular biographical account of the career of Tōjō Hideki deals with the occupation period only in the last section of the book and then only with respect to Tōjō's imprisonment and trial by the war crimes tribunal. The author, an English journalist, relied in large part on source materials written in English, but he also interviewed Mrs. Katsuko Tōjō. The account is generally sympathetic. Tōjō is pictured as an honorable human being with a warrior's code of ethics and mode of thinking, caught up in events over which he had limited control. Much of his testimony, it is noted, was devoted to exonerating the emperor and assuming full responsibility for Japan's decision to go to war. The author himself makes no explicit judgment as to the utility or legality of the war crimes tribunal, but he notes that Tōjō's testimony and lack of remorse seem to have freed the Japanese people from any feeling of war guilt at the same time that they restored Tōjō's own reputation as an honest man and a soldier.

1053 Butow, Robert Joseph Charles. *Tojo and the Coming of the War*. Princeton, N.J.: Princeton Univ. Pr., 1961. 584p.

The author, a professor of history at the University of Washington, presents in this book a thoroughly researched, carefully documented account of Tōjō Hideki's career and the role of the military in Japanese affairs of state in the modern century. The interrelationship of man and events stressed in this book makes it as much a historical analysis as a biographical account. Although only the last 3 chapters out of 16 deal directly with the occupation period and specifically with the war crimes tribunal, much of the data utilized throughout the book to describe and analyze prior events are taken from war crimes trial and occupation documents and records. Much confusion and many misconceptions on the parts of both Japanese and Americans are brought to light by this account of the war and its aftermath. It would seem that a comparison of Japanese and English transcripts of the tribunal proceedings documents frequent breakdowns in communication and further misunderstandings. Also, the author's close calculation of the timing of sequences of events frequently reveals plausible explanations for events previously disputed or misinterpreted. It would appear, for example, that the delivery of Japan's final note to the U.S. secretary of state 1 hour after the attack on Pearl Harbor was the result of sheer mishandling by the Japanese embassy in Washington, not a calculated act of duplicity.

Tōjō's personal aims in testifying before the war crimes tribunal are described as exonerating the emperor, blaming the war on the Western powers, and rehabilitating his own reputation before being hanged. He is revealed here as a reflector, not a creator, of national thought, far from the Hitler–Mussolini pattern. In the author's words: "It was not his to command or dictate. He was one among many and not even first among equals. He was a militarist—misguided, naive, and narrow in outlook; he regarded war as a legitimate instrument of national policy; he apparently believed what he had told the court." This statement is as close as the author comes to disagreeing explicitly with the tribunal's judgment of Tōjō as a war criminal, although the evidence presented here would not tend to support the court's judgment.

The book has much information and insight to offer the scholar of the Allied occupation. The author takes special care to evaluate all available interpretations and evidence before drawing and documenting his own conclusions. The bibliography and footnotes provide an extensive record of relevant documents and secondary source materials in both English and Japanese. He has also interviewed 56 persons and corresponded with 66 persons, both American and Japanese, who have personal knowledge of the events analyzed.

1054 Chiang, Wen-hsien. *Dohihara Kenji and the Japanese Expansion into China, 1931–1936*. Ph.D. dissertation, Univ. of Pennsylvania, 1969. 336p. (Abstracted in *Dissertation Abstracts International* 30: 2591A–92A [Dec. 1969]; University Microfilms order no.69–21,334)

The role of General Do(h)ihara Kenji as chief of the Kwantung Army's Mukden Special Service Organ in 1931–36 is studied in this thesis. Examining 4 events of the period—the Nakamura incident, the Mukden incident, the abduction of Henry P'u-yi, and the North China autonomy scheme—the author finds that the International Military Tribunal for the Far East correctly judged Doihara guilty of conspiracy against China but maintains that the tribunal failed to see the motives behind Doihara's role, thus going too far in sentencing him to death. It is argued that Doihara was not as guilty in the Nakamura incident and the North China autonomy scheme as the tribunal judged. Chinese, Japanese, and English materials are used in the study.

1055 Comyns-Carr, A. S. "The Judgment of the International Military Tribunal for the Far East." *Transactions of the Grotius Society* 34:141–51 (1948)

This article by a British participant in the International Military Tribunal for the Far East is in 2 parts. The first compares legal aspects of the Tokyo and Nuremberg tribunals, and the second recounts and comments on information unearthed in the course of the Tokyo trials on events leading up to the Pacific War.

1056 ———. "The Tokyo War Crimes Trial." *Far Eastern Survey* 18:109–14 (18 May 1949)

A thoughtful, well-written account of the International Military Tribunal for the Far East, presented by a member of the British prosecution staff during the Tokyo trials. At the outset the author declares his intention "to draw attention to certain points without expressing an opinion on them." There is a valuable comparison of the Tokyo trials with those at Nuremberg, Germany, wherein he points out similarities and differences between the two regarding such matters as indictment and procedure. Following this comparison, the author discusses various pleas of the 25 defendants, the tribunal's decision regarding responsibility for prisoner of war treatment, and the question of the emperor's responsibility for the war. The final section of this useful report discusses the historical evidence amassed from various important documents used during the trials regarding events which took place in Japan of the 30s, the army's path to power, Japan's role in the Axis, and the internal political situation in Japan immediately prior to Pearl Harbor. According to the author's general description of the trials, "by trial and error a system was gradually worked out which aimed at incorporating from the methods of all the nations assembled those best suited to the purpose in hand."

1057 "A 'Dead Man' Speaks." *Life* 24: 87–91 (26 Jan. 1948)

This article criticizes the personnel of the International Military Tribunal for the Far East for allegedly abandoning the cause of promoting democracy among the Japanese people in favor of personal feuding, noting the animosity existing between U.S. prosecutor, Joseph Keenan, and tribunal president, Sir William Webb. The testimony of Tōjō Hideki is presented to substantiate *Life*'s claim that the trials are producing public nostalgia for Japan's past greatness.

1058 Dickinson, George. "Japanese War Trials." *Australian Quarterly* 24:69–75 (June 1952)

The author, an Australian army lawyer who helped defend accused Japanese war criminals, criticizes the Australian war crimes court for modifying rules of evidence so that both unfair and irrelevant evidence was introduced even though many of the suspects tried were merely "the pawns in a war game." He also condemns the Australian press for its exaggerated reporting and concludes that war crimes courts ought to be conducted by neutrals.

Evatt, Herbert V. *Australia in World Affairs.* 1946. See no.786.

"Far Eastern Commission." 1949. See no.868.

1059 Feldhaus, J. Gordon. "The Trial of Yamashita." *Current Legal Thought* 13: 251–62 (Aug. 1947)

This report by a member of the defense counsel for General Yamashita was abstracted from the *South Dakota Bar Journal* of October 1946. The author presents a brief biography of the defendant, particularly stressing his responsibilities and activities during the war. He later describes the charges made against Yamashita as well as the proceedings of the trial which condemned him to death. The author then elaborates upon his contention that Yamashita had been deprived of a fair trial and mentions 5 grounds upon which the defense counsel attempted to appeal the decision.

1059a Fuqua, Ellis E. "Judicial Review of War Crime Trials." *Journal of Criminal Law and Criminology* 37:58–64 (May 1946). Also published in *Illinois Law Review* 40:546–53 (Mar./Apr. 1946)

Using the trial of General Yamashita Tomoyuki as a case in point, Fuqua opens by stating that the methods adopted by the United States and the other Allies for prosecuting war criminals represent "one of the most critical developments in the aftermath" of World War II particularly insofar as international military justice is concerned. He briefly reviews the events preceding Yamashita's trial, then focuses his attention on the decision of the United States Supreme Court to deny his petition for a writ of habeas corpus as well as to hold that the military commission sentencing him was lawfully created to try him and that the trial procedure itself was proper and valid. Critical of the absence of legal provisions for the judicial review of the trial of an enemy combatant by a duly authorized military commission with appropriate jurisdiction, the author argues that this is contrary to traditional American concepts of a fair trial and suggests that changes are in order.

1060 Golunsky, S. "The Trial of the Japanese War Criminals." *New Times* no.18: 6–10 (1 May 1947)

After a brief discussion of the organization and conduct of the Tokyo trials, the author concentrates upon the Japanese war criminals and the prewar and wartime events that have been discussed during the trials. He divides the 28 major war criminals into 5 groups and describes them as: (1) leading Japanese statesmen, (2) Japanese army and navy leaders, (3) Japanese diplomats, (4) economic officials, and (5) ideologists of Japanese imperialism and aggression. The remaining portion of the article analyzes information concerning Japanese prewar and wartime activities that has been revealed by the defendants.

1061 Hanayama, Shinshō. *The Way of Deliverance: Three Years with the Condemned Japanese War Criminals*. Tr. by Suzuki Hideo, Noda Eiichi, and James K. Sasaki. Tr. rev. by Harrison Collins. New York: Scribner, 1950. xv, 297p.

A Buddhist theologian and Tokyo University professor of literature recounts his experiences as prison chaplain for a group of accused Japanese war criminals beginning with his assignment to Sugamo Prison in February 1946 and ending with the execution of 7 A-class criminals on 23 December 1948. The account, largely based on the author's diary, makes little reference to the proceedings of the International Military Tribunal for the Far East held from 3 May 1946 to 12 November 1948. It is devoted primarily to a description of the author's contacts with 34 men who were executed, namely, 27 younger prisoners who were sentenced by the American military courts to death and executed between May 1946 and November 1948 and 7 A-class war criminals judged guilty by the International Military Tribunal. The author also records remarks and poems left by these prisoners and stresses how many of them came to accept the Buddhist faith. It is translated from an original Japanese work, entitled *Heiwa no hakken* (The discovery of peace) (Tokyo: Asahi Shimbunsha, 1949. 319p.).

1062 Hankey, M. *Politics: Trials and Errors*. Chicago: Regnery, 1950. xiv, 150p.

While the author's general criticism of

the Nuremberg and Tokyo trials focuses on the partiality of the justice given, his specific complaint in the case of Shigemitsu relates to the paucity of the evidence against him. A strong case for his innocence is presented. Without the dedicated work of American defence lawyers, the trial would have been only an exercise in vengeance. This book has been translated into Japanese as *Sensō saiban no sakugo* (Tokyo: Jiji Tsushinsha, 1952. 256p.).

1063 "Have We Lost the Peace?" *Christian Century* 66:838–39 (13 July 1949)

The occasion for this editorial is a decision by the United States Supreme Court that convicted war criminals have the right to appeal their convictions through the federal court system. The decision came 6 months after 7 convicted Japanese were hanged following a denial on technical grounds of their right to appeal to the Supreme Court. The magazine sees this latest decision, which amounts to a reversal of the earlier fatal ruling, as further evidence of a growing fear among the victorious powers of World War II that "morally" they have "lost the peace." The cause of this fear is a realization that the means by which victory was achieved and the ends to which victory has been put are perhaps of dubious morality.

1064 Heller, Maxine Jacobson. *The Treatment of Defeated War Leaders*. Ph.D. dissertation, Columbia Univ., 1965. 500p. (Abstracted in *Dissertation Abstracts* 26: 4786 [1966]; University Microfilms order no.65-13,954)

This study deals with the treatment of leaders of defeated nations after the Napoleonic Wars and World Wars I and II. It includes a discussion of the debates among the Allied powers concerning the possibility of a war crimes trial in Tokyo and the fate of the Japanese emperor. After outlining the way in which Napoleon, the Kaiser, and Nazi and Japanese war leaders were treated, Heller concludes that in each case the victors sought to remove leaders who could conceivably precipitate further conflict and often punished them in one way or another. They would then seek to justify this action to the people of the country involved, and attempt to prove the merit of their cause through documentation of the defeated leaders' alleged war crimes.

1064a Hessel, Eugene A. "Let the Judges Do the Hanging!" *Christian Century* 66: 984–86 (24 Aug. 1949)

Hessel's subject is the war crimes trials being conducted in Manila. He first enumerates a series of "characteristics of these trials which make it difficult to arrive at justice," including the time that has elapsed since the alleged crimes were committed, the vindictive nature of the prosecution, and the problems of pinpointing responsibility. He then provides a defense of one of the accused, Ichinose Haruo, and a critique of the prosecution's tactics and unwillingness to consider what Hessel regards as the overwhelming testimony to Ichinose's innocence and true Christian character.

"Hirohito: Criminal or Puppet?" 1950. *See* no.1235.

1064b Hogan, Willard N. "War Criminals." *South Atlantic Quarterly* 45, no. 4:415–24 (Oct. 1946)

In his defense of the war crimes trials, Hogan focuses on the question whether the various trials in Europe and the Far East are "a proper and wise use of the judicial process." After an extended discussion of the charges and legal principles involved, he argues that it is important to make the trials a matter of record and to give the accused the opportunity to offer any defense which they may have. He recognizes that there are objections to the fact that the Allies are applying their own standards of justice and that the tribunals are composed solely of members of the victor nations, but contends that the Axis nations might have done the same had they won the war. Finally, he points out that there are only 3 alternatives available—(1) letting the Nazi and Japanese leaders go free, (2) executing them without appropriate trials, and (3) proceeding with formal indictments and open trials—and that the war crimes trials are "soundly conceived in relation to the choices that are available."

1065 Horwitz, Solis. "The Tokyo Trial." *International Conciliation* no.465:473–584 (Nov. 1950)

The entire issue of this journal presents an invaluable analysis of the IMTFE in Tokyo. The complex and controversial subject is discussed under 5 categories: (1) the origin and authority of the trial, (2) the charter of the tribunal and the trial machinery, (3) the defendants and the indictment, (4) the trial itself, and (5) judgment and sentences. The author, a member of the prosecution staff throughout the trial, considers the activities of the Far Eastern Commission which led to their policy decision on the "Apprehension, Trial, and Punishment of War Criminals in the Far East" and the special SCAP proclamation establishing the International Military Tribunal for the Far East. Following it are the provisions of the charter and amendments suggested by the Allied delegations, a discussion of the selection of the defendants, and a description of the offices they held in prewar and wartime Japan. The author briefly describes the tribunal's attitudes toward the emperor and the industrialists in terms of their war guilt. The bulk of the report is devoted to the proceedings of the trial itself and the judgment and sentences passed. In describing the proceedings, the author first sets forth the facts (organized into 14 phases) which the prosecution attempted to establish. Following it is the case for the defense which was organized into 7 parts, as well as evidence used in rebuttal, evidence in mitigation, and final arguments. Concluding this section is a brief discussion of the difficulties of the trial that resulted from the necessity to use both Japanese and English and from the fact that, aside from the Nuremberg trials, there were no legal precedents upon which the tribunal could rely. The second major topic, that of the judgment and sentences, is considered under 3 broad categories: (1) rulings on questions of law, (2) findings on issues of fact, and (3) verdicts and sentences. There is consideration of the dissenting as well as concurring opinions of the 11 members of the tribunal with regard to the various rulings and verdicts. Whereas the account of the trials is matter-of-fact and the tone as dispassionate as possible, in his brief concluding remarks the author presents his own attitudes towards the Tokyo trial, affirming its relevance and discussing its significant contributions to world peace and security. Appended are 3 useful sections: Appendix A discussing the location and availability of the historical materials involved; Appendix B providing a brief discussion of the prewar and wartime positions of each of the defendants; and Appendix C indicating on a chart the final charges and sentences of each of the defendants.

1065a "Ill-Starred Defenders of War Criminals." *Current Digest of the Soviet Press* 2, no.11:22–23 (29 Apr. 1950)

Supporters of peace and democracy throughout the world have warmly welcomed the Soviet note of 1 February 1950 to the governments of the United States, Great Britain, and the People's Republic of China proposing the formation of an international military court for the trial of a group of Japanese war criminals headed by Emperor Hirohito. The American ruling circles, however, have refused to cooperate. Nonetheless, the article continues, Hirohito cannot be "held aloof" from responsibility for wartime Japanese activities in the area of bacteriological warfare, for his sanction was required for any declaration of war or the commencement of military operations. For this reason, "however the Japanese militarists and their American patrons may excel in their defense of the criminals against mankind, they cannot escape the irrefutable facts expounded in the Soviet government's note." This article originally appeared in the 10 March issue of *Izvestia* and is an abridged translation of the Russian text.

1065b "Indictment in the Case of Former Servicemen in the Japanese Army . . . Charged with Preparing and Using Bacteriological Weapons. . . ." *Current Digest of the Soviet Press* 1, no.52:35–43 (24 Jan. 1950)

The complete text of a story which appeared in the 24 and 25 December 1949 issues of *Pravda* and *Izvestia*, this article presents the indictment against several Japanese who stood trial in Khabarovsk at that time. These men were accused of planning to employ weapons of bacteriological warfare on a wide scale in wars of aggression against the Soviet Union and other countries. The article discusses in considerable detail (1) the organization of special formations for preparing and waging bacteriological warfare, (2) Japanese criminal experiments on live human beings, (3) the Japanese use of bacteriological warfare against China, (4) increased Japanese preparation for bacteriological warfare against the Soviet Union, and (5) the responsibilities of each of the men on trial.

1065c "International Hangings." *Commonweal* 49:165 (26 Nov. 1948)

This editorial raises questions about the justice of the death sentences handed down at the Tokyo and Nuremberg war crimes trials. It finds in them "a smell of self-righteous pride, a perfume rarely absent in circles of liberal world reform."

1066 "The International Military Tribunal for the Far East." *Current Notes on International Affairs* 19:231–41 (May 1948)

The character and the work of the International Military Tribunal for the Far East are reported here. It covers the period from 19 January 1946, when General MacArthur issued an order establishing the tribunal, through 16 April 1948, when the prosecution and defense rested to await the verdict which was delivered in November. After a brief description of the charter of the tribunal and the composition of the court, the nature of the indictment against 28 political and military leaders of prewar Japan is described with added biographical information regarding the 25 who were actually tried. The prosecution and defense phases of the trial are summarized.

1067 "International Military Tribunal for the Far East." *International Organization* 1:176 (Feb. 1947)

A summation of the nature and scope of the Tokyo war crimes trials, including such particulars as the provisions for the selection of members of the tribunal, the kinds of war criminals tried, and a list of the defendants and the prosecuting nations.

1068 "International Military Tribunal for the Far East." *International Organization* 3:184–86 (Feb. 1949)

The specifics of the November 1948 final verdict against 28 Japanese war criminals are discussed in this report. The article enumerates the Japanese defendants, the charges against them, and the sentences they received. There is also brief mention of the law on which the judgment of the tribunal was based and the reasons why 2 of the 11 members of the International Military Tribunal entered minority judgments exonerating the defendants in question.

1068a Ireland, Gordon. "Uncommon Law in Martial Tokyo." *Year Book of World Affairs* 4:50–104 (1950)

By applying "correct" legal principles to the facts and events of the Tokyo war crimes trial, the author, a visiting professor of law at the Catholic University of America, shows that "the International Military Tribunal could not apply international law and did not apply common law." Ireland first presents a critical description and analysis of the trial under several successive headings: creation of the tribunal, the charter of the tribunal, the trial, the judgment, separate opinions, the sentences, courtroom proceedings, defense counsel, attacks on jurisdiction, [and] appeal to United States supreme court. He then points out that all of the convictions depended on the questionable premise that aggressive war was illegal by international law. Finally he lists 10 serious violations of common law which occurred during the Tokyo trial. They included (1) the change of judges during the course of the trial, (2) the absence of participating judges from some of the court sessions, (3) the failure of two of the judges—the French and Soviet members—to understand English, one of the official languages, in which motions and arguments were made by the counsel, as well as the inability of most if not all of the judges to comprehend Japanese, the other official language, (4) the decision to conduct the trial while various defendants were absent on account of illness, (5) the prosecution's use of statements made by the defendants, who had not been warned that their testimony could be used against them, for the purpose of incriminating these same defendants, (6) the court's admission of both hearsay evidence and improperly authenticated documentation, and (7) the admission of evidence by affidavit—an act which denied the defendants the opportunity to be confronted with the witnesses against them and to cross-examine these same witnesses. Ireland concludes that the judgment of the International Military Tribunal for the Far East was not an example of international law but rather "a round-about subterfuge by which victorious nations through legal forms avenged themselves on enemy leaders who committed the real crime of being beaten."

1068b "Jap War Criminals Await Trial." *Life* 19:29–33 (12 Nov. 1945)

This photoessay consists of a brief introductory article and a series of photographs taken at the prison camp for alleged war criminals on Ōmori Island. Among the individuals pictured are former prime ministers Tōjō Hideki and Suzuki Kantarō, Kishi Nobusuke (minister of commerce at the time of Pearl Harbor and a future prime minister of Japan), several other members of the Pearl Harbor cabinet, and a number of lower-ranking men.

1069 "Joseph Keenan Meets the Press." *American Mercury* 70:456–60 (April 1950)

This reprint of a "Meet the Press" interview with Joseph Keenan, chief prosecutor in the trials of Japanese war criminals, includes the following opinions expressed by Keenan: Emperor Hirohito should not have been tried as a war criminal because he sincerely desired peace; there is no evidence that the Japanese used bacteriological warfare in World War II; the war crimes trials were justified because they were murder trials, not punishment of a defeated nation; and General MacArthur has done an excellent job as occupation commander and is irreplaceable.

1069a "Justice Demands International Trial of Japanese War Criminals." *USSR Information Bulletin* 10, no.4:112–13 (24 Feb. 1950)

This *Pravda* editorial of 4 February 1950 demands that high Japanese officials engaged in plans through August 1945 to conduct bacteriological warfare against China and the Soviet Union be brought to trial before an international tribunal. The remaining "criminals" in addition to the 12 convicted recently at Khabarovsk are Emperor Hirohito and Generals Ishii, Kitano, Wakamatsu and Kasahara.

1070 Kajima, Morinosuke. *Modern Japan's Foreign Policy*. Rutland, Vt.: Tuttle, 1969. 327p.

A prominent Japanese politician and businessman as well as chairman of the Liberal Democratic party's Foreign Relations Research Committee, Kajima Morinosuke is the author and compiler of a collection of essays which he has written over a 15-year period dealing with Japan's contemporary foreign policy and its future trends. Chapter 5, entitled "The Need to Reexamine 'Tokyo Trial'" (written in February 1959), argues for a review of the verdicts and minority opinions of the Tokyo war crimes trial and attacks the verdicts which held Japan to be solely responsible for the Pacific War. Chapter 11, "Russo–Japanese Relations," contains a brief section on the Soviet refusal to sign the San Francisco Peace Treaty and to relinquish control over certain islands north of Hokkaido. None of the remaining essays, however, deals in any important respect with issues closely related to the occupation period.

1071 Katona, Paul. "Japanese War Crime Trials." *Free World* 12:37–40 (Nov. 1946)

A lawyer and journalist presents "the basis and background of the trials which, with Nuremberg, create a new concept of war and of personal responsibility for war." Following a historical description of the development of the concept of war crimes trials beginning after World War I, Katona concentrates on the trial of General Yamashita Tomoyuki which occurred before the Tokyo and Nuremberg trials and was thus the first major war crime trial of World War II. He outlines the proceedings of the trial and concludes that Yamashita was not proven guilty of the charges against him but was convicted for other reasons. There is also a brief description of the conduct of the Tokyo war crimes trials. The author outlines some of the legal problems they created, i.e., the problem of *ex post facto* law, principles of jurisdiction, and the question of whether an individual acting in his capacity as an official of the state may be held individually and criminally responsible for acts committed in this capacity.

1072 Keenan, Joseph Berry, and Brendan Francis Brown. *Crimes against International Law*. Washington, D.C.: Public Affairs Pr., 1950. x, 226p.

Assessing the value of the Tokyo war crimes trial in retrospect, the authors justify the work undertaken by the court. Keenan was chief of counsel for the United States and for the Prosecution Section of the Military Tribunal while Brown was his juridical consultant. The work, based on Keenan's statements at the trial and Brown's memorandums, reiterates in effect the position taken by the United States, rejecting the doctrine against *ex post facto* law. It evaluates highly the prosecution's job, but is critical of the defense for its efforts to acquit the accused by "interposing a fundamentally false theory of law which vitiates the criminality of the alleged offense for the reason that the society in question had no protesting criminal law." The authors discuss the historical significance of the trial, the linkage of the Potsdam Declaration to the charter of the tribunal, the source of General MacArthur's authority over the tribunal, the basis of the charter for the tribunal, the history of the concepts of wars of aggression, crimes of conspiracy, and crimes against humanity, and the principle of superior orders as contrasted to individual responsibility. Appended are the texts of Brown's testimony before the Subcommittee on Genocide of the Senate Foreign Relations Committee on 25 January 1950, the statement on the source and scope of General MacArthur's authority, and the rules of proceedings for the International Military Tribunal for the Far East.

1073 Kodama, Yoshio. *I Was Defeated*. Tokyo: 1959. xiii, 228p. Translation and publication arranged by Fukuda Taro.

An autobiography translated from the original Japanese work, *Ware yaburetari* (Tokyo: Kyōyūsha & Tōkyō Shuppansha, 1949. 303p.). The memoir was written while Kodama was detained in Sugamo Prison outside Tokyo from late 1945 until late 1948 as a class "A" war crimes suspect by the International Military Tribunal for the Far East. Kodama was a prominent rightist leader who advocated the establishment of "Imperial politics." During the 1930s and the first half of the 1940s, he had a variety of military assignments in China and India and served the government in an advisory capacity. The autobiography reveals his version of the history of nationalism and militarism during this period as well as his reactions to significant events during the war years. It also gives his observations on political developments in the postsurrender period. Kodama disapproves of Japan's conduct of the war, blaming the bureaucrats, militarists, and imperial court officials for their poorly coordinated military operations, lack of devotion to the war, and, above all, for embarking on an unreasonable military adventure without sufficient material support. In the fourth and last part of the book he describes events that took place immediately after the Japanese surrender, referring, for instance, to his ill-fated attempt to save a score of young rebellious soldiers who committed suicide at Atagoyama Hill outside Tokyo. He also describes his role as a counselor to Prime Minister Prince Higashikuni including his successful attempt to have the prince and MacArthur meet in Yokohama without public knowledge. He writes that he was impressed with the disciplined entry of American soldiers into Japan after the war. However, he says that he became restless with the occupation authorities' "softness" on communism, contending that, due to a lack of real knowledge of Japan and the Japanese, Americans were making in Japan the same kind of mistakes that the Japanese had made in China. Prince Higashikuni is regarded as being the first Japanese prime minister who served the genuine interests of the people. The publication of the Japanese version of this book was banned by SCAP until 1949.

1074 ———. *Sugamo Diary*. Tokyo: 1960. xv, 275p. Translation and publication arranged by Fukuda Taro.

An English version of the author's *Shibafu wa fumaretemo* (Tokyo: Shinyūkan Shimbunsha, 1956. 250p.), a diary he kept from 25 January 1946 to 24 December 1948, while he was interned in Sugamo Prison as a class "A" war crimes suspect by the International Military Tribunal for the Far East. His diary reveals a grim but fascinating picture of life in the prison—the behavior of other war crimes suspects, their reactions to the tribunal, attitudes toward the American military police officers working in the prison, their self-criticisms, etc. There are also humorous touches. The diary shows Kodama as a man of composure and courage at a time when he was facing possible execution. He was released on 24 December 1948 and is presently a prominent leader in the rightist movement. Another manuscript he wrote while imprisoned in Sugamo was published in English under the title *I Was Defeated* (1959) (no.1073).

1075 Kudryavtsev, V. "The Verdict against Japanese Militarism." *Soviet Press Translations* 4:70–71 (1 Feb. 1949)

In an article originally appearing in the 3 December 1948 issue of *Trud*, the author comments upon the Tokyo trials of war criminals concluded in November of that year. He outlines the verdicts meted out to the 25 leading war criminals, viewing these verdicts as "a triumph for the advocates of peace and security." Nevertheless, the author is extremely critical of the forces of reaction in Japan and their "overseas patrons" who refuse to punish the war criminals still at large and are intent upon thwarting the efforts of the Soviets to demilitarize and democratize Japan.

1076 Kuhn, Arthur H. "International Law and National Legislation in the Trial of War Criminals: The Yamashita Case." *American Journal of International Law* 44:559–62 (July 1950)

Kuhn discusses the legality from the standpoint of international law of the trial of General Yamashita for permitting civilian massacres while commanding general in the Philippines.

1077 Liu, James T. C. "The Tokyo Trial." *China Monthly* 8:242–47 (July 1947)

Liu focuses on the preliminary defense presentation at the war crimes trial. He first discusses the controversy stirred by a sensationalistic account of the defense's opening arguments that was published in the U.S. Army newspaper *Stars and Stripes* on the day before the arguments began. He then devotes the remainder of the article to summarizing and commenting upon the defense presentation itself, focusing on the statements made by Kiyose Ichirō, Takayanagi Kenzō, and the American lawyers for the defense. Liu is highly critical of the Japanese statements, which both challenged the legality of the proceedings and argued that alleged Japanese aggression were acts of self-defense.

1078 ———. "The Tokyo Trial: Second Look." *China Monthly* 8:279–80 (Aug. 1947)

In this article, Liu sympathizes with the indifference felt by most Americans and Japanese toward the war crimes trials, whose length and complexity have made the proceedings both boring and incomprehensible to the general public. He argues, however, that the trials are immensely important in that they will help to establish definitions of the concepts of aggression and international morality. Furthermore, they will produce an otherwise unobtainable mountain of useful and interesting data which future historians can use for detailed accounts of the war and of Japanese and Chinese history.

1079 "Major Japanese War Criminals: International Tribunal's Findings." *Current Notes on International Affairs* 20:330–45 (Mar. 1949)

Covered in this article are the findings of the International Military Tribunal for the Far East on the several counts of the indictment, the verdicts, and the sentences for each of 25 major war criminals. Included also are the separate opinion of the president of the tribunal and the dissenting opinions of the Indian, French, and Dutch judges. The article also notes such developments as the appeal of the verdicts to the U.S. Supreme Court. The full text of the indictments submitted to the tribunal is appended.

1080 Markov, M. "The Approaching Trial of Major Japanese War Criminals." *New Times* no.8:7–10 (15 Apr. 1946); reprinted in *USSR Information Bulletin* 6, no.46:403–5 (18 May 1946)

Arguing for a just and speedy punishment of Japan's war criminals, the author discusses the approaching war crimes trials. He considers the numerous individuals who are to be tried but criticizes the American occupation authorities for retaining the emperor as titular head of Japan, thus making his trial as no.1 war criminal impossible. The author further discusses other prominent officials who ought to be tried but remain free. There is criticism regarding the manner in which the trials will be conducted, but the author maintains that "the Tokyo trial of the war criminals is destined to play an important role in strengthening the position of the progressive forces."

1081 ———. "Falsification of History at the Tokyo Trial." *New Times* no.17:7–11 (21 Apr. 1948)

Analyzing the accuracy of reports about the prewar and wartime activities of Japan and Germany that have been revealed in the Tokyo trials, the author vehemently contests the American claim that the aggressive actions of Germany and Japan were not closely and deliberately coordinated. He attempts to prove that there was extensive and intimate cooperation between the 2 Axis powers throughout the war. In his concluding remarks the author relates the above information to his contention that Japan rendered Germany very substantial military assistance and made extensive preparations for an attack on the Soviet Union.

1081a ———. "Mamoru Shigemitsu and His Patrons." *Current Digest of the Soviet Press* 3, no.24:11–12 (28 July 1951)

According to this 2700-word article which appeared in the 7 June issue of *Literaturnaya gazeta*, MacArthur freed the former Japanese foreign minister on 21 November 1950—well before the expiration of his sentence as a war criminal—because the U.S. State Department could not get along without his services. Indeed, the United States has long sought to assist Shigemitsu and intervened on his behalf during the Tokyo war crimes trial. Markov then reviews Shigemitsu's role during the prewar and wartime eras and comments critically as well on SCAP's general program for depurging many Japanese militarists, on the U.S. draft of a peace treaty, and on American plans for reviving Japanese militarism. He concludes by advising his readers that "the war criminal Mamoru Shigemitsu, walking about free, is a sinister symbol of Wall Street's policy in Japan. Let the patrons of the war criminals remember that the people have warned them of the heavy responsibility they have taken upon themselves in releasing the enemies of mankind and entering into a criminal alliance with them."

1081b *Materials on the Trial of Former Servicemen of the Japanese Army Charged with Manufacturing and Employing Bacteriological Weapons.* Moscow: Foreign Languages Publishing House, 1950. 535p.

This volume provides considerable documentation on the trial of Japanese militarists charged with planning and waging biological warfare during World War II. Held in Khabarovsk on 25–30 December 1949, the trial proceedings showed how Japanese units in Manchuria began preparations for germ warfare as early as 1931 and how they subjected crops, cattle, Chinese and Soviet citizens, and American prisoners of war on various occasions to germs producing plague, anthrax, typhoid, and cholera. The proceedings furthermore indicate that relevant documents about these activities were given to Joseph B. Keenan, the chief American prosecutor at the Tokyo war crimes trial, but that the documents were not submitted to the tribunal and that the United States accordingly has kept Emperor Hirohito and General Ishii Shirō (the person who authorized and directed bacteriological warfare against China) from receiving just punishment.

1081c Mayevsky, V. "Monstrous Crimes Committed by Japanese Barbarians." *USSR Information Bulletin* 10, no.3:93 (10 Feb. 1950)

The trial and conviction in Khabarovsk of former Japanese army officers for allegedly planning for and engaging in bacteriological warfare against the Soviet Union is recounted in this article. Mayevsky refers specifically to the bacteriological experiments and operations of detachments 731 and 100 of the Kwantung Army in Manchuria.

1082 Minear, Richard Hoffman. *Victor's Justice: The Tokyo War Crimes Trial.* Princeton, N.J.: Princeton Univ. Pr., 1971. xv, 229p.

Richard Minear, a member of the History Dept. at the Univ. of Massachusetts and the author of *Japanese Tradition and Western Law* (Cambridge, Mass.: Harvard Univ. Pr., 1970. xi, 244p.), presents a polemical account of the background, proceedings, and judgment of the Tokyo trial from its charter and simultaneous Nuremberg "precedent" to its present-day effects. He examines the trial from the viewpoints of history, international law, and the legal process in general, and he discusses the motives of the trial's proponents, the trial's prejudged course (its choice of judges, procedures, decisions, and omissions), General MacArthur's review of the verdict, and the criticisms of the 3 dissenting judges. Finally, he points out the dangers that were and continue to be inherent in such an international, political trial.

1082a "Note of Soviet Government to U.S. Government." *Current Digest of the Soviet Press* 2, no.20:33 (1 July 1950)

This note of 11 May, reproduced here in full from the 13 May issues of *Pravda* and *Izvestia*, strongly criticizes the SCAP circular of 7 March 1950, stating that all war criminals then serving sentences in Japan could be released before the expiration of their sentence. Such a decision, the Soviet government asserts, constitutes a gross violation of international law since it changes or completely annuls the verdict of the International Military Tribunal for the Far East and contradicts as well the Far Eastern Commission's resolution entitled "On the Arrest, Trial, and Punishment of War Criminals in the Far East." MacArthur has exceeded his authority, and the United States government therefore is urged to take immediate steps to declare the circular null and void.

1082b "Note of the Soviet Government to the Government of USA." *USSR Information Bulletin* 11, no.5:153 (8 Mar. 1951)

This note of 12 February 1951 protests the decision by SCAP to release Shigemitsu Mamoru from prison prior to the completion of his original sentence. According to the Soviet government, the Far Eastern Commission made no provision for the preterm release of convicted Japanese war criminals.

1083 "Observations on the Trial of War Criminals in Japan." *External Affairs* 1: 12–23 (Feb. 1949)

The first section of this discussion of the work of the International Military Tribunal for the Far East presents a comprehensive, chronological history of the establishment, operations, judgment, and sentencing of prisoners by that body. Individuals involved in both prosecution and defense are listed and the rationale for the existence and operation of such a body is given. The second section is a presentation of selected documentary material used as evidence in the trials. The author attempts to assess the historical value of such materials which include firsthand interviews with wartime leaders, previously secret government documents, the Saionji-Harada memoirs, and the diary of Marquis Kido. Brief mention is made of the trials of individuals charged with atrocities. In addition, 2 pages of personal information about each of the 28 Japanese leaders tried for major war crimes are presented. The article makes no judgment regarding the effect of the trial on Japanese public opinion or political education but merely indicates that it was reported and commented on at length in the Japanese press.

1084 Piggott, Francis Stewart Gilderoy. *Broken Thread: An Autobiography.* Aldershot, England: Gale & Polden, 1950. xix, 424p.

This autobiography of a former British military attaché in Tokyo touches only tangentially upon the occupation period. The major portion of the book is a personal account of Piggott's life and career, beginning in 1887 with a 3-year childhood visit to Japan. His father, a barrister, served during this period as an adviser to Itō Hirobumi during the drafting of the Japanese Constitution of 1889. Piggott served officially in Japan from 1904 to 1906 as a language officer. His career after 1906 took him back and forth between Japan and England. Piggott left Japan for the last time in 1939, and his account of events thereafter deals primarily with his activities in England. The final chapter, an epilogue, summarizes briefly the history of Anglo–Japanese relations from 1868 to 1950. He comments upon the Tokyo war trials and notes that he wrote affidavits on behalf of several Japanese defendants. A copy of his affidavit on behalf of General Homma Masaharu is appended, along with relevant correspondence. Also appended is Lord Hankey's affidavit on behalf of Shigemitsu Mamoru.

1085 Potter, John Deane. *The Life and Death of a Japanese General.* New York: New American Library, 1962. 191p. (Signet book. P2226); also published under the title *A Soldier Must Hang: The Biography of an Oriental General.* London: F. Muller, 1963. xiii, 210p.

On Yamashita Tomoyuki.

Price, Willard, and John Goette. "How Long Hirohito?" 1945. *See* no. 1251.

1085a Quentin-Baxter, R. Q. "The Task of the International Military Tribunal at Tokyo." *New Zealand Law Journal* 25: 133–38 (7 June 1949)

For the crime of preparing and launching an aggressive war, the author asserts, the tribunals could validly punish the leaders of Japan, Germany, and other nations which had solemnly renounced the recourse to war as an act of national policy by subscribing to the Pact of Paris. He also states that the Nuremberg and Tokyo trials have established the principle that punishment may be dealt out not only to subordinates who violate the laws of war but also to those senior officials who bore the chief responsibility for all the evils which war entails. At the same time, however, the legal proceedings must be manifestly just if the principles asserted are to have value or significance. Quentin-Baxter then reviews the historical background to World War II which the Tokyo tribunal had to examine and notes that the tribunal found Japan's activities during the 1920s and 1930s to be part of a single scheme for aggression, concluded that the central scheme of aggression was conceived and promoted by a group within the Japanese army and its naval and civilian supporters, and discovered that the Japanese armed forces had systematically violated the laws and customs of war in every country where they were present. Finally the author assesses the general value of the Tokyo trial and notes that the proceedings could be used to reeducate the Japanese people.

1086 Raginsky, M. "Monstrous Atrocities of the Japanese Imperialists." *New Times* no.2:3–7 (8 Jan. 1950)

In an examination of "conclusive and incontrovertible evidence" gathered at the International Military Tribunal, this article accuses the Japanese of intending to use bacteriological weapons against their enemies during the war. The author describes specific details of such a plan revealed in the preliminary investigation and testimony given by former generals Yamada, Kajitsuka, Takahashi, and Kawashima. He asserts that it was the Soviet intervention in Manchuria which prevented such plans from being realized but warns that the real initiators of bacteriological warfare are currently being protected by General MacArthur.

1087 ———, and S. Rozenblit. "What People Expected of the International Military Tribunal in Tokyo." *Soviet Press Translations* 3:421–25 (15 July 1948)

In an article appearing in *Pravda* on 2 June 1948, just prior to the conclusion of the Tokyo trials, the authors argue that, contrary to what the Americans allege, Japan was in fact an aggressor against the Soviet Union in spite of the so-called neutrality pact. Therefore, they reason, the Soviet peoples have a right to expect stern punishment for the chief Japanese war criminals. They urge the 11–nation international war tribunal to condemn severely Japanese aggression and avenge all who have suffered from it.

1088 Rama Rao, T. S. "The Dissenting Judgment of Mr. Justice Pal at the Tokyo Trial." *Indian Year Book of International Affairs* 2:277–91 (1953)

Justice Pal offered the only dissenting judgment at the International Military Tribunal for the Far East in Tokyo, and that judgment, which expresses a different view of facts and law from those of the majority of the Tokyo tribunal and the Nuremberg tribunal, is examined here. The author discusses Pal's views on the questions of whether the International Military Tribunal established under the charter promulgated by SCAP can go beyond existing rules of international law and define new crimes and whether these new laws can be used retrospectively to punish prisoners. The dissenting justice answered both of these questions in the negative. In addition to examining the legislative power of victor nations, the concept of crimes against peace as set up by the Pact of Paris in 1928 and the question of the legality under international law of holding individuals responsible for acts of a state are considered. The author outlines Justice Pal's view of the facts leading to Japan's part in World War II and maintains that Pal does not advocate a static view of international law but shows how changes can be made. The article concludes with the observation that, under the current decisions of the military tribunals, "the only crime evolved in the international sphere is the crime of losing a war."

1089 Reel, Adolf Frank. *The Case of General Yamashita*. Chicago: Univ. of Chicago Pr., 1949. vi, 324p.

The author gives a critical analysis of the trial of General Yamashita Tomoyuki, wartime commander of Japanese forces in Malaya and the Philippines. The trial was conducted by an American military commission in Manila in 1945 and General Yamashita was sentenced to death and executed. The author, a lawyer who had been a U.S. Army captain during the Pacific War, served as one of the 5 members of defense counsel for the general. The report is a very readable narrative, but it is also intended to be a serious critique of the nature of such a trial, whereby a military court tries a foreign soldier after the cessation of hostilities. On the basis of his frequent and close contact with the general, the author presents a favorable picture of his character. Moreover, the author relates how his own efforts in 1946 to have the case transferred from the military court to the U.S. Supreme Court were frustrated. More legalistic arguments for such a transferral are not included in the narrative but are appended. The book later became so controversial that SCAP felt impelled to prepare a memorandum to correct the "gross misrepresentations" of Reel's account of the Yamashita trial. SCAP presents its views in a publication of the Government Section entitled, *The Case of General Yamashita: A Memorandum* (no.1024) published in 1950. Reel's book was translated into Japanese under the title of *Yamashita saiban* (Tokyo: Nihon Kyōbunsha, 1952. 2v.). The book was barred from publication during the occupation years.

1090 ———. "Even His Enemy." *Ohio Bar Association Report* 19:163–75 (3 June 1946)

One of General Yamashita's defense lawyers discusses his trial and conviction as a war criminal in this report. After a brief description of the Japanese general's wartime career, the author discusses the reasons of the defense for appealing the case to the U.S. Supreme Court and the unsuccessful outcome of that appeal. He also presents at length the dissenting opinions of 2 justices of the Supreme Court. He is extremely critical of the type of trial to which Yamashita was subjected and believes the general was condemned to death without regard for due process of law. In concluding, he suggests that the case against another Japanese general, Homma, while stronger than that against Yamashita, was apparently conducted in the same unfair fashion as Yamashita's.

The Reminiscences of Joseph Ballantine. 1961. See no.44n.

1090a "Remember?" *New Republic* 115: 895 (30 Dec. 1946)

This brief editorial on the trial of ex-Premier Tōjō and 15 other suspected war criminals indicates that the Japanese people are continuing to crowd the spectators' gallery (primarily in order to sit and study the war criminals themselves) even though the press is becoming apathetic about the proceedings. While the trials are supplying a complete and objective account of Japanese wartime aggression, the editorial continues, SCAP is encouraging the Japanese to regard the 1931–1945 period as a "recent unpleasantness" which would best be forgotten as soon as possible.

1091 Riley, Walter Lee. *The International Military Tribunal for the Far East and the Law of the Tribunal as Revealed by the Judgment and the Concurring and Dissenting Opinions.* Ph.D. dissertation, Univ. of Washington, 1957. 218p. (Abstracted in *Dissertation Abstracts* 18: 1481 [1958]; University Microfilms order no.58–1092)

Riley evaluates the Tokyo war crimes trial as one of the most momentous developments in the history of international law, basing his judgment on the decision of the tribunal to declare aggressive war a crime under international law and to charge those who initiate war with individual responsibility. He maintains that there was no legal precedent for this decision, and that when the tribunal said "according to law" it meant "according to the law laid down in the Charter of the International Military Tribunal for the Far East." He suggests that if the accused in the Tokyo trial had been tried and sentenced by any procedure under joint or several military jurisdictions there would have been no juridical protest. Although he would not disagree with the sentences imposed on the accused, he questions the wisdom of interpreting these sentences as derivatives of international law.

1091a Röling, Bernard V. A. "The Tokyo Trial in Retrospect." In *Buddhism and Culture: Dedicated to Dr. Daisetz Teitaro Suzuki in Commemoration of His Ninetieth Birthday*, ed. by Yamaguchi Susumu. Kyoto: Nakano Press, 1960. p.247-66.

The author, who served as the representative for the Netherlands on the International Military Tribunal for the Far East, reviews the principal weaknesses of the Tokyo trial (most notably, the absence of representatives for the neutral countries on the bench) and points to the unprecedented character of both the Nuremberg and Tokyo tribunals. He nonetheless feels that the motivation for the establishment of the tribunals was valid and justifies their existence.

1092 Russell, Edward Frederick Langley. *The Knights of Bushido: The Shocking History of Japanese War Atrocities*. New York: Dutton, 1958. xiv, 335p.

The author records the history of atrocities committed by Japanese soldiers against Asians and members of the Allied forces during the Pacific War. The book begins with an account of the Japanese soldiers' savage conduct in China in the 1930s and then refers to their treatment of prisoners of war and civilian populations in Asia in the 1940s. Major events covered are the Thai-Burmese railroad construction, the murder of American airmen in Burma and French Indochina, the massacre or cruel treatment of Allied prisoners of war in the Philippines and the western Pacific islands, the "death marches" in the Philippines, war crimes on the high seas, cannibalism, vivisection, and mutilation. The last chapter briefly describes the events that led to the formation of the International Military Tribunal for the Far East and lists the sentences given to the 28 Japanese leaders tried by the tribunal. It also provides valuable information on the military courts established by the British, the Americans, and the Australians in Singapore and Manila. Various legal arguments are appended. The author claims that his descriptions are primarily based on evidence and documents provided at various war crimes trials and on affidavits and statements made by witnesses of such crimes. However, perhaps due to the narrative nature of his account, the sources are not cited for all of the incidents discussed. The general tone of the work is somewhat emotional. It constitutes a companion to the author's earlier book, *The Scourge of the Swastika* (New York: Philosophical Library, 1954. 259p.), which pertains to the history of Nazi war crimes.

1092a Schroeder, Paul W. *The Axis Alliance and Japanese-American Relations, 1941*. Ithaca: Cornell Univ. Pr., published for the American Historical Assn., 1958. ix, 246p.

Most of this study deals with the reasons for Japan's entry into the Axis Alliance, the American reaction to that event, and the manner in which the alliance actually functioned during World War II. In an epilogue (p.217-29), however, Schroeder discusses the Tokyo war crimes trials with particular reference to the interpretation placed on the Tripartite Pact by both the prosecution and the tribunal. His primary disagreement is with the tribunal's treatment of the alliance as a criminal compact made between aggressor nations primarily for the furtherance of their illegal aggressive purposes. Japan's reasons for entering into the alliance were far too ambiguous to characterize them so simply, he argues. Furthermore, the tribunal's contention that Japan actively cooperated with Germany and Italy is contradicted by Japan's repeated refusals to attack the USSR in accordance with German pleas. Schroeder concludes that scholarly attention to the trials is long overdue since they have important implications for international law and provide new insights into the history of the period as a whole.

1092b "Sentence Japanese War Criminals." *Christian Century* 65:1262 (24 Nov. 1948)

This editorial welcomes the convictions handed down by the International

War Crimes Tribunal in Tokyo as "another precedent for holding accountable the men who are responsible for starting wars," but the decision to exempt the emperor from the trials is held to have weakened the concept of personal accountability for war guilt. The magazine reminds its readers that "the moral law, on which all justice is based, makes no exceptions."

1093 Sleeman, Colin, ed. *Trial of Gozawa Sadaichi and Nine Others.* London: William Hodge, 1948. lxxii, 245p. (War Crimes Trials series, v.3)

The trial of Gozawa Sadaichi, commanding officer of a wartime internment camp, and of several of his subordinates was the first war crimes trial to be held in the Far East. At their trial before a British court in Singapore on 21 January–4 February 1946, these men were accused of starving, overworking, and generally maltreating the hundreds of prisoners (largely Indian troops) who were interned on one of the Palau Islands between June 1943 and September 1945. The trial resulted in the death by hanging of one of the defendants—Nakamura Kaniyuki (the first Japanese war criminal to be sentenced to death)—and in sentences of imprisonment for most of the others. The present volume provides the complete text of the trial's proceedings as well as a lengthy introduction discussing both the Japanese wartime mentality and the historical background of the case at hand.

1093a ——, and S. C. Silkin, eds. *Trial of Sumida Haruzo and Twenty Others (The "Double Tenth" Trial).* London: William Hodge, 1951. xxxii, 324p. (War Crimes Trials series, v.8)

This trial derives its name from the date 10 October 1943 (the anniversary of the establishment of the Republic of China), when the kempeitai in Singapore staged a massive search of the Changi Internment Camp housing over 3000 European civilians. The Japanese security police, and in particular its chief, Sumida Haruzō, had long suspected the camp-mates of engaging in an anti-Japanese conspiracy. They therefore took advantage of an act of sabotage involving six Japanese oil tankers anchored in Singapore harbor to arrest certain camp members and to extract confessions of illegal activities from most of them. Fifteen people in all died during the course of the extended investigation. The postwar trial held at the Supreme Court Building of Singapore in March and April 1946 charged several members of the kempeitai with arresting, ill treating, and torturing 57 civilian prisoners. The trial was conducted in accordance with the normal procedure in military courts for the trial of minor war criminals. Eight men in the end were sentenced to death and six others to varying terms of imprisonment. The present volume contains an introductory essay and the full text of the proceedings. Sleeman and Silkin, the editors, served respectively as prosecutor and as member of the military court at the trial itself.

1093b Solow, Herbert. "A Rather Startling Result." *Fortune* 39, no.4:158–66 (Apr. 1949)

This critical account of the Tokyo and Nuremberg war crimes trials asserts that the net result of these 2 tribunals has been "a loss for U.S. politics in the Orient and for world order." Solow argues that the Tokyo trial hurt the United States politically by making Tōjō an anti-democratic martyr, by failing to provide the Japanese with truly democratic political education, and by making the United States appear more vengeful when SCAP confirmed the death sentences for a number of the defendants while the Russians cleverly opposed capital punishment. Solow is also critical of the trial on juridical grounds. Several of the judges, he points out, had openly expressed their belief that Japan was guilty of war prior to their appointment to the tribunal, while some of the judges —including the presiding officer—failed to attend the tribunal's hearings for weeks on end. The defense was subjected to various discriminatory rules of procedure, moreover, and the court admitted as evidence unsworn and unidentified prosecution documents. As a result, the conviction of wartime Foreign Minister Shigemitsu in particular may well have been invalid. Furthermore, the tribunal itself was biased in its composition on account that it excluded judges representing the nation whose nationals were being tried as well as those of neutral countries. "Based solely on power," Solow concludes, "these were victors' political tribunals, capable of giving the vanquished anything from mercy to vengeance, but inevitably something that few can regard as legal justice."

1093c "Soviet Government's Note to U.S. Government." *Current Digest of the Soviet Press* 2, no.35:20 (14 Oct. 1950)

First published in the 28 August issue of *Pravda*, this is the text of an official note dated 25 August in which the Soviet government again criticizes the SCAP circular permitting Japanese war criminals to be released before the expiration of their sentences. It reiterates the Soviet view that MacArthur has exceeded his powers and has violated the charter of the International Military Tribunal for the Far East, rejects the American view that premature release is not an alteration of one's sentence, and asserts that the U.S. government's reference to the fact that the practice of the early release of prisoners exists in many countries is irrelevant in this particular case.

1094 Spurlock, Paul E. "The Yokohama War Crimes Trials: The Truth about a Misunderstood Subject." *American Bar Association Journal* 36:387–89, 436–37 (May 1950)

Spurlock, former reviewer of the records and sentences of the Yokohama trials for the American Eighth Army, describes the process of punishing lesser Japanese war criminals. He reviews the work of the War Crimes Branch for the Pacific Theater through December 1945 and the subsequent creation of the Eighth Army Military Commission for the conduct of trials, and the Legal Section of SCAP for the investigation and prosecution of war criminals. Prosecution and defense procedures are examined and points such as the right of the prosecution to draw inferences from a defendant's refusal to testify and to introduce affidavits as evidence, as well as the protection against retrial if found innocent are noted. The trial method is explained and both the efforts of defense counsel and the process of reviewing every case, which frequently resulted in a reduction of sentence, are stressed.

1095 Sutton, David Nelson. "The Trial of Tojo: The Most Important Trial in All History?" *American Bar Association Journal* 36:93–96, 160–65 (Feb. 1950)

The legal basis of the International Military Tribunal for the Far East and its composition and functioning are examined. The 28 defendants are identified and the reasons for their selection as defendants presented. Sutton discusses the extraordinary difficulties involved in preparing and conducting the trial. Contradictions between Anglo–American and Japanese legal procedures, the dearth of court officials familiar with Japanese customs and society, the scarcity of available documentation, and the necessity of examining testimony covering the 17-year period from 1928 to 1945 are noted. The author explains why the basic charge of "conspiracy to wage wars of aggression and the waging of wars of aggression" was proven to the satisfaction of the court. In this explanation he reviews the history of Japanese aggression from 1928 through the attack on Pearl Harbor. Sutton contends that the evidence of wartime atrocities is overwhelming and thus justifies the harshness of the sentences. He presents 3 findings by the tribunal which he feels will be important to international law in the future: (1) the charter authorizing the International Military Tribunal was based on existing international law; (2) aggressive war is an international crime; and (3) claims of national self-defense must be adjudicated before an impartial tribunal and must demonstrate the good faith of the defendant.

1096 Sveshnikov, I. "Japan's Undeclared Wars on the Soviet Union." *New Times* no.46:15–20 (10 Nov. 1948)

At the close of the International Military Tribunal for the Far East the author asserts that the trial proved beyond any possibility of doubt that the Japanese committed acts of aggression against the Soviet Union and the Mongolian People's Republic. Most of the article consists of a detailed account of these acts of aggression which the author claims were revealed at the Tokyo trials. He asserts that those who would disagree with his conclusions are "friends and defenders of the Japanese major war criminals" who are deliberately falsifying the facts of history and misrepresenting actual events.

1097 Tallow, Adamin A. *Command Responsibility: Its Legal Aspect*. Manila: published by the author, 1965. xxxii, 472p.

A doctoral dissertation submitted to the University of Santo Tomas in the Philippines in 1958, this work presents a detailed study of the principle of command responsibility in connection with war crimes, in particular, the responsibility that a military officer assumes for maintaining strict discipline among his subordinates. The author, a veteran of World War II, first examines various definitions of command responsibility, individual soldiers' responsibilities, war criminals, "acts of state," international law, and "unconditional surrender." He then inquires as to the laws under which the United States may proceed against war criminals, the nature of war crimes and war criminals, what courts have jurisdiction over war criminals, and whether chiefs of state are liable. The book also discusses various opinions, policies, and decisions concerning command responsibility as applied by the war crimes tribunals at Nuremberg, Tokyo, and Manila. Included are the opinion of Justice Pal, the Indian member of the International Military Tribunal for the Far East, regarding Tōjō and "acts of state" (chap. 10); the dissenting opinions of Justices Murphy and Rutledge, in the case of the USA vs. Yamashita Tomoyuki; the concluding arguments by the defense and prosecution in the case of Yamashita (chap. 18); and the judgment of the Tokyo trial (chap. 16).

1098 Trainin, A. "From Nuremberg to Tokyo." *New Times* no.12:11–14 (17 Mar. 1948)

Expressing the sentiments similar to those in an earlier article in the same periodical by V. Berezhkov (1948) (no. 1048), this article attempts to compare the Nuremberg and Tokyo trials. Although British and American lawyers defended fascist imperialists and industrialists in both trials, the author feels that the Tokyo trials are worse because "the structure and proceedings of the Tokyo Tribunal . . . are marked by tendencies which have very little in common with the principles of international justice established by Nuremberg." He cites unwelcome changes in the appointment of judges and changes in procedure and concludes that the trials can be defined as a "judicial tragedy."

1098a "Trial of Former Japanese Soldiers Charged with Preparing and Using Bacteriological Weapons." *Current Digest of the Soviet Press* 2, no.1:21–27 (18 Feb. 1950)

This series of articles provides detailed summaries of the trial in Khabarovsk of several Japanese servicemen accused of preparing to undertake bacteriological warfare against the Soviet Union. Included are the cross-examinations of the defendants, a speech delivered by the state prosecutor L. N. Smirnov, and the conclusion of the trial at which the defendants made their last speeches. There is no commentary or analysis of the proceedings. These articles appeared in full in the 26–31 December 1949 issues of *Pravda* and *Izvestia*.

1099 "Trial of Japanese War Criminals." *Department of State Bulletin* 20:569–71 (1 May 1949)

This article reprints FEC press releases of 1 April and 16 March 1949 summarizing recommendations of the Far Eastern Commission to member governments in regard to the termination of war crimes proceedings. The primary decision thus announced is that no further trials of "Class A" war criminals are to be initiated. The 16 March press release in turn summarizes the results of the proceedings already completed against this same class of Japanese criminals.

1099a "Trial of the Japanese Agents." *USSR Information Bulletin* 6, no.60:23 (11 Sept. 1946)

A Moscow correspondent describes the trial and conviction of 8 "White Guard" Russians who had served in the Japanese intelligence service. These men were convicted by the Military Collegium of the Supreme Court of the USSR on charges of espionage and sabotage, primarily in Manchuria. Sentences of the defendants ranged from death for 6 of them to terms of 20 and 15 years at hard labor respectively for the other two.

1099b Tsai, Paul Chung-tseng. *Judicial Administration of the Laws of War: Procedures in War Crimes Trials.* LL.D. thesis, Yale Univ., 1957. 789p.

This comprehensive analysis of war crimes trials procedures concludes with a formulation of standards for such trials. Information on the proceedings of the International Military Tribunal for the Far East may be found throughout the dissertation.

1100 "Two Japanese War Criminals." *New Republic* 114:269 (25 Feb. 1946)

An editorial comment on the procedures of the military tribunal established to try 2 major Japanese war criminals. Although acknowledging the reprehensibility of the 2 Japanese—Generals Yamashita and Homma—nevertheless, the writer points out the fact that there were 2 dissenting opinions in the U.S. Supreme Court's ruling in response to the generals' appeal. Both dissenting judges indicated that the procedures of the military tribunal were sloppy and even in violation of basic Anglo-Saxon principles of law insofar as the Japanese were given no time to formulate their defense, hearsay evidence was introduced, and cross-examination was extremely limited.

"USSR Motives on Trying Emperor of Japan Questioned." 1950. *See* no.1263.

1101 Vasilyev, A. N. "The Tokyo Trial of the Chief Japanese War Criminals." *Soviet Press Translations* 3:195–202 (1 Apr. 1948)

An article in 2 parts which appeared first in *Pravda* on 19 and 20 February 1948. It reports the speech of Vasilyev, who was the chief prosecutor for the Soviet Union at the Tokyo war crimes trials. The Soviet prosecutor analyzes the evidence of Japanese aggression against his country from the turn of the century up to the end of the war. Numerous border skirmishes and naval encounters between Japan and the USSR in the Far East are cited as examples of Japanese aggression. The author insists that Japan be chastized and that severe punishment be meted out to the chief Japanese war criminals. Those who he believes have been most responsible for aggression against the USSR are former Prime Minister Tōjō, former Chief of the General Staff Umezu, and former ministers and ambassadors Araki, Itagaki, Hiranuma, Minami, Shigemitsu, Hirota, Ōshima, Hashimoto and Tōgō.

1101a ———. "The Atrocities of the Aggressors Have Been Exposed!" *Soviet Press Translations* 5:411–13 (1 July 1950); abridged version published under the title "Misdeeds of Aggressors Have Been Exposed" in *Current Digest of the Soviet Press* 2, no.19:35 (24 June 1950)

The published proceedings of the Khabarovsk trial (no.1081b) show that Japan planned bacteriological warfare not only against the Soviet Union but also against the United States, Great Britain, and other nations. The trial disclosed as well the criminal role of Emperor Hirohito and of the Japanese Generals Ishii, Kitano, Wakamatsu, and Kasahara, who were the inspirers and organizers of the use of bacteriological weapons. These men should be brought to trial before a special international military court, as the Soviet government proposed in its 1 February 1950 note to various foreign governments, but the ruling circles of both the United States and Great Britain are refusing to cooperate. Indeed, Vasilyev concludes, the U.S. is presently utilizing the services of Japanese and German bacteriologists in order to prepare for bacteriological warfare itself. This article originally appeared in the 10 May issue of *Pravda*.

1101b ———. "On Rapid Trial and Punishment of War Criminals: On the Results of the Tokio Trials." *Current Digest of the Soviet Press* 1, no.25:11–15 (19 July 1949)

Vasilyev's article is a condensed translation of an analysis of the Tokyo war crimes trial which first appeared in the March 1949 issue of *Sovetskoye gosudarstvo i pravo*. The author focuses his attention on the defense's delaying tactics and on the weaknesses of the Anglo-American court procedure which resulted in the trial's lasting a full 2 and a half years. He criticizes, for example, the procedure of reading entire documents in court, the complicated and lengthy procedures in examining the various witnesses, and the Tribunal's unwillingness to limit the defense in any way. Nevertheless, Vasilyev concludes, the trial did make a major contribution to world peace, for it condemned Japanese aggression as well as those responsible for it and acknowledged the fact that Japan was guilty of aggression against the Soviet Union in addition to several other countries.

1102 "The Verdict Pronounced by the International Military Tribunal for the Far East on the Twenty-five Japanese War Crimes Suspects, November 12, 1948." *Contemporary Japan* 17:416–32 (July/Dec. 1948)

This material is excerpted from the much lengthier official verdicts pronounced by the International Military Tribunal for the Far East. The document briefly summarizes the wartime careers of the major war criminals, and indicates the charges against them and the sentences they finally received. Japanese so considered are: Araki Sadao, Doihara Kenji, Hashimoto Kingorō, Hata Toshiroku, Hiranuma Kiichirō, Hirota Kōki, Hoshino Naoki, Itagaki Seishirō, Kido Kōichi, Kimura Heitarō, Kaya Okinori, Koiso Kuniaki, Minami Jirō, Matsui Iwane, Muto Akira, Oka Takazumi, Sato Kenryo, Shigemitsu Mamoru, Shimada Shigetarō, Shiratori Toshio, Suzuki Teiichi, Tōgō Shigenori, Tōjō Hideki, Umezu Yoshijirō, and Ōshima Hiroshi.

1103 Wadsworth, Lawrence W., Jr. *A Short History of the Tokyo War Crimes Trials with Special Reference to Some Aspects of Procedures*. Ph.D. dissertation, American Univ., 1955. 238p.

This treatment of the International Military Tribunal for the Far East contains chapters on (1) the origins of the Tokyo trials, (2) the establishment of the tribunal as well as its powers and functions, (3) the indictment, (4) the cases for the prosecution and for the defense, (5) the court procedure and actual conduct of the trials, and (6) the judgments and sentences.

1104 Walkinshaw, Robert B. "The Nuremberg and Tokyo Trials: Another Step toward International Justice." *American Bar Association Journal* 35:299–302, 362–63 (Apr. 1949)

The author analyzes the place of the Nuremberg and Tokyo trials in the evolution of international criminal law. The position of the London Agreement of 8 August 1945 as the legal basis for the establishment of the International Military Tribunal for the Far East is clarified, as is the format of approval granted by the Japanese government for the establishment of this tribunal. The method by which membership on the tribunal was decided is discussed and the manner of indictment delineated. The author stresses the differences in spirit and function between the trials in Tokyo and those in Nuremberg. The Tokyo trial is criticized on a procedural basis but is regarded as the preferable method of punishing wartime leaders. The difficulties created by testimony delivered in the Japanese language and those stemming from the search for witnesses to testify regarding events in China are mentioned. Walkinshaw asserts that a common body of international law is developing which is directed against the waging of aggressive war, and he discusses the possibilities of future international sanctions against aggression.

THE PURGE

Entries in this section relate to SCAP's purge program that eventually dissolved numerous organizations and removed or excluded upward of 200,000 individuals from public office or from certain private managerial positions. The basic attempt was to facilitate the emergence of new and more democratic leadership elements. The program operated at both the national and local levels.

Entries in the section providing a calendar of general commentaries (p.152) and the section on political parties and elections (p.452) also frequently treat this program.

Andō, Nisuke. *Surrender, Occupation, and Private Property in International Law: An Evaluation of Some United States Practices during the Occupation of Surrendered Japan.* 1971. See no.2236.

1105 Baerwald, Hans Herman. *The Purge of Japanese Leaders under the Occupation.* Berkeley: Univ. of California Pr., 1959. 111p. (Univ. of California Publication in Political Science, 8)

A study of the purge program by an individual who worked in the Statistics and Review Branch of the Government Section of SCAP. The author describes the emergence of the purge program, the criteria for purging, problems of administration, limitations of the purge, and its impact. Emphasis is placed on evaluating the effectiveness of the purge. Among the topics treated are the status of the emperor; individual responsibility for wartime conduct; the Hatoyama case; enlargement of the scope of the purge to include local government officials, economic leaders, and mass media personnel; the functions of screening committees and appeals boards; supervision of purgees' activities; the backgrounds of the total of 210,288 purgees; and material relating to their subsequent activities. The concluding chapter discusses the process of depurging and domestic and international factors that undermined the success of the purge program. Baerwald's book is a revision of the doctoral dissertation he submitted under the same title to the University of California at Berkeley in 1956 (202p.).

1106 "Behind the Japanese Purge: American Military Rivalries." *Newsweek* 29:40 (27 Jan. 1947); reply with rejoinder 29:44 (10 Feb. 1947)

Internal SCAP rivalries and the economic significance of the 4 January and 21 November 1946 and the 4 January 1947 purge ordinances are the focal points of this article. The claim is made that 30,000 businessmen are to be purged and that 250,000 will be prevented from assuming high economic positions. It is contended that the extent of this purge is the result of the close relationship between General Whitney, chief of the Government Section, and General MacArthur and that such purges are not in America's best interest for they will result in economic disorganization and will create advantages for left-wing groups in Japan.

In a reply published 2 weeks later, MacArthur briefly explains his purge directives, justifying them as a purge of the active exponents of militarism and aggression from the postwar Japanese economy. He also indicates personal surprise in learning that his action was interpreted as antagonistic to the American capitalist ideal, for he believes that the purge will not hinder the development of a peaceful industrial economy in Japan. A rejoinder, which appears together with MacArthur's reply, reaffirms the author's contention that the purge is working to the detriment of American interests. It also cites such new developments as the power and initiative shown by extreme leftists in a threatened general strike as well as the general support that the leftists are now receiving in the Soviet press.

1107 Bisson, Thomas Arthur. "The Economic Purge in Japan." *Far Eastern Quarterly* 12:279–99 (May 1953)

This article examines one of the main methods used by the occupation to accomplish the dissolution of the *zaibatsu*, namely, the purging of "old-line combine men" from positions of major business responsibility in order to encourage the emergence of new business leaders. The author considers specifically the 2 lines of attack developed by the occupation to deal with this problem: the major purge directive known as SCAPIN no. 550 and the *Zaibatsu* Appointees Law, a Diet enactment. In examining SCAPIN no.550, he outlines how the purge was carried out, which leaders were purged, and what was meant by "public office." In the conclusion various aspects of the economic purge operation are evaluated and the underlying weaknesses noted.

1108 "The Japanese 'Purge'." *Current Notes on International Affairs* 19:335–38 (June 1948)

This short article explains the reasons for the purge of Japanese leaders and gives a summary description of the 198,022 individuals purged under SCAP's directive of 4 January 1946 (SCAPIN no.550). It holds that, while the purge may have decreased the efficiency of government and industry by removing skilled and competent men, it was a necessary preliminary step to the reform and democratization of Japan and "to an infusion of new blood."

Kern, Harry F. "Trouble in Japan: How the Struggle to Win the Peace Now Threatens the Success of the American Occupation." 1947. *See* no.507.

1109 Kinoshita, Hanji. *Purge Policy and After*. Tokyo: Nihon Taiheiyō Mondai Chōsakai, 1954. 40p. (Japan papers, 9)

A preparatory paper for the twelfth conference of the Institute of Pacific Relations held in Kyoto in 1954.

1110 Montgomery, John Dickey. *Forced to Be Free: The Artificial Revolution in Germany and Japan*. Chicago: Univ. of Chicago Pr., 1957. 209p.

The author's extensive research on the Allied occupation programs in Germany and Japan has been combined in a book that provides considerable insight into both programs. It concentrates on one important aspect of both military occupations—the elimination and replacement of former leaders. According to the author, the thesis of his report is "that the Allied program for the occupation of Germany and Japan after World War II constituted the first halting effort to induce 'artificial revolution' on behalf of democracy; that this effort was only partially successful, and that these experiences, whether successes or failures, may have both immediate and long range implications for the conduct of America's present foreign policy." He attempts to analyze the nature of the 2 artificial revolutions which he believes came to be limited, with few exceptions, to the "negative devices of denazification and its Japanese equivalent, the political purge." Consequently, his study is primarily a detailed and penetrating interpretation and comparison of the Allied attempts to destroy in Germany and Japan the totalitarian leadership and replace it with a responsible democratic leadership. In the author's opinion, these attempts were only partially successful for 3 main reasons: (1) the elite groups were not adequately

1111 ———. *The Purge in Occupied Japan: A Study in the Use of Civilian Agencies under Military Government.* Chevy Chase, Md.: Johns Hopkins Univ. Operations Research Office, 1954. xviii, 381p. (Johns Hopkins Univ. Operations Research Office. Technical memorandum ORO-T-48 [FEC])

A detailed study of the Allied occupation's purge program carried out in postwar Japan. It represents a meticulous investigation of the subject and offers a balanced evaluation of the purge policy. It treats such subjects as the objectives of the purge policy, the way in which the policy was conducted, the political effects of the purge, public reactions, effects of the economic purge, local effects of the purge, and recommendations for future purge policy. The research was conducted in Japan during 1952. Political and economic analyses as well as public opinion surveys were carried out together with the collection and examination of SCAP and Japanese government records. Montgomery often compares the purge programs as applied in Japan and Germany. While favoring swift, decisive, and categorical purges through civilian governmental instrumentalities as in Japan, the author is critical of the limited removals at the local level and opposes giving important policy-making positions to protegés and relatives of purgees. He recommends that, when an occupation lasts for a long time, a systematic program of depurging be undertaken to avoid setting purgees apart as objects of special public sympathy when the occupation is terminated. There are some 80 excellent tables on various aspects of the subject as well as appended documents relating to SCAP directives, Japanese government orders, political purgees and their subsequent electoral records, individuals purged, reactions to the purge, public opinion analyses, and postpurge activities of purgees. For a more explicit comparative study of the Allied purges in Germany and Japan, see his *Forced to Be Free* (no.1110) published in 1957.

1111a Obama, Toshie. "A Warning to Financial Leaders." *Contemporary Japan* 19:571–73 (Oct./Dec. 1950)

Obama, an adviser to the *Nippon Sangyō Keizai Shimbun* who had recently been granted amnesty from the purge, devotes most of his comments to what he sees as the detrimental impact of the purge upon financial circles. The removal of the top leadership has left only mediocre and inexperienced people in charge. The purgees who have been reinstated have so far tended to be large shareholders, useful for their stimulation of capital accumulation but not necessarily in other ways. The best financial experts were associated with the great *zaibatsu* financial bodies or with quasi-governmental organizations now defunct, and consequently they have no positions to return to at all. The purge, moreover, is contributing to a delay in financial reorganization that could turn Japan's present economic weakness into a chronic malady. This article originally appeared (in Japanese) in the December 1950 issue of *Kaizō*.

"Occupation Policy in Japan." 1946. See no.449b.

1111b "The Political Purge Demanded in the Two Directives to the Shidehara Government." *Nation* 162:57 (19 Jan. 1946)

This brief editorial explains that recent purge directives have greatly enhanced the prospects of the liberal progressive forces in the coming elections because the purge has made all active exponents of militarism, fascism and aggressive nationalism ineligible for public office. If the Socialists and Communists can successfully gain electoral support in the countryside, the next Diet will be dominated by a leftist government.

1112 "Purging the Japanese Fascists." *New Republic* 114:37–38 (14 Jan. 1946)

A brief editorial expressing approval of MacArthur's insistence that the Japanese government be purged of all Fascists, particularly military men and former members of secret societies. According to the author, such proposals indicate that there are some new policymakers in the State Department and that MacArthur is receiving and following their good advice.

1113 Quigley, Harold S. "The Great Purge in Japan." *Pacific Affairs* 20:299–308 (Sept. 1947)

An analysis of the occupation's purge operation, providing a detailed description of SCAPIN no.550, entitled "Removal and Exclusion of Undesirable Personnel from Public Office," and discussing its implementation. The purge is divided into 2 phases—the first phase beginning with SCAPIN no.550 on 4 January 1946 and the second beginning on 4 January 1947, when the issuance of 4 imperial ordinances and a supplementary cabinet ordinance greatly increased the scope of the purge. There is some discussion of the procedures of the local screening committees and of the Central Committee in Tokyo. The article provides statistics on the number of persons screened—both those passed and those barred—for ministries and other government organizations. There is also a brief discussion of reactions to the purge programs observed in the editorials of such leading Japanese newspapers as the *Asahi Shimbun*, the *Tōkyō Shimbun*, the *Mainichi Shimbun*, *Akahata*, and the *Minami Nippon Shimbun*.

The Reminiscences of Joseph Ballantine. 1961. See no.44n.

1114 Supreme Commander for the Allied Powers. *Miscellaneous Papers and Documents.* Tokyo? 1945–48. 2 reels.

This microfilmed collection of mimeographed monographs and documents relates to SCAP's program to purge Japanese political leaders. It consists of 2 reels. The first contains primarily materials that SCAP obtained or prepared in 1945–48, apparently for its own use, in order to carry out the purge. Most of this material provides biographical data on ultranationalist leaders. Some of the selections are monographs, while others are translations from Japanese and German data. Many of them are still in draft form with handwritten corrections added on the manuscripts. Included on this reel are: (1) Marius B. Jansen's monograph, *The Japanese and Sun Yat-sen* (Cambridge, Mass.: Harvard Univ. Pr., 1954. ix, 274p.), which investigates the relations between Sun Yat-sen and the Japanese in bringing about the Chinese Revolution of 1911; (2) an anonymous monograph, *History of the Purge*, which describes the history of the Dai Nippon Butokukai (Great Japan Military Virtue Association) from its emergence in the early twentieth century to its dissolution upon SCAP orders; (3) extracts from General Karl Haushofer's *Dai Nihon* (Berlin: E. S. Mittler und Sohn, 1913. xvii, 377p.), analyzing the Japanese government of the pre–1945 period and illustrating how Japan's political ideology, leadership, and national interests in Asia and the Pacific were in conflict with those of the United States; (4) a list of 44 Japanese "secret" societies, which strangely includes such major political parties as the Minseitō and the Seiyūkai; and (5) biographical notes on additional ultranationalist personalities and societies, translated from Yoshihisa Kuzuu's *Tōa senkaku shishi kiden* (Biographies of Early Patriots in East Asia) (Tokyo: Kokuryūkai Shuppanbu, 1935–38. 3v.) and collected from foreign sources such as George T. Ladd's *In Korea with Marquis Ito* (New York: Scribner, 1908. x, 477p.), Benoît Favre's *Les sociétés secrètes en Chine* (Paris: G. P. Maisonneuve, 1933. vii, 222p.), and the *Newspaper Digest*. This collection, although far from systematic, is useful in understanding how SCAP collected information before taking action on prospective purgees.

The second reel is a collection of some 40 items composed not only of official documents of SCAP and the Japanese government concerning the purge program but also of draft documents, memorandums which circulated within SCAP and within the Japanese government, memorandums between SCAP and the Japanese government, and assorted newspaper articles. This collection, far more systematic than the first one, includes: (1) extracts of "U.S. Post-Defeat Policy Relating to Japan" (SWNCC 150/4A, 12 Oct. 1945), and of "Basic Directive for Post-Surrender Military Government in Japan Proper" (JCS 1380/15, 3 Nov. 1945); (2) SCAP directives on the purge issued in 1946; (3) a SCAP press release of 4 January 1946 on "SCAP's Issuance of Order on the Dissolution of Japanese Organizations;" (4) the draft paper, "Dissolution of Ultranationalistic Societies," which was to become part 5 of the official history of SCAP's Government Section published in July 1949; (5) imperial ordinances, laws, and cabinet orders; (6) Ministry for Home Affairs notifications, Prime Minister's Office notifications, Attorney General's Office notifications, and a list of 161 organizations dissolved by 17 different orders issued between February 1946 and August 1948; (7) memorandums from the Attorney General's Office of the Japanese Government to SCAP's Government Section in 1948; (8) memorandums from Hans H. Baerwald, Statistics and Review Branch of the Government Section, to the Public Administration Division of the same section; (9) a memorandum from the Home Affairs Ministry to prefectural governors in 1946; (10) a memorandum from the Attorney General's Office to the prefectural governors in 1946; and finally (11) articles by Tanaka Sōgorō and Kashikawa Gorō that appeared in the *Nippon Times* on 16 and 17 April 1948 respectively.

————. Monograph 6. *Local Government Reform, 1945–December 1950.* 1952. See no.288.

————. Monograph 7. *The Purge, 1945–December 1951.* 1952. See no.289.

————. Monograph 12. *Development of Legislative Responsibilities, 1945–October 1950.* 1952. See no.294.

————. Monograph 23. *Japanese Property Administration.* 1952. See no. 305.

————. *Two Memoranda of General C. Whitney to MacArthur about Interviews with Japan's Prime Minister Shidehara.* 1946. See no.466.

1115 ————. Government Section. *Materials on the Depurge.* Tokyo: SCAP, July 1951–Oct. 1951. 1 folder.

This chronologically arranged collection has no official title. It includes letters, memorandums, and other miscellaneous papers relating to correspondence between the Government Section of SCAP and the Liaison Bureau of the Japanese Ministry of Foreign Affairs in 1951. All materials concern the depurging of various Japanese officials—former army and navy officers, former police personnel, former officials of secret military and ultranationalistic societies, governors of Japanese occupied territories, etc. The collection contains lists of the categories and numbers of purgees as well as of the names of a number of former officials who were purged.

Available at the Washington National Record Center, Suitland, Maryland.

1115a "Trouble Coming in Japan." *Christian Century* 64:133 (29 Jan. 1947)

This editorial acknowledges the fact that the occupation of Japan has been "brilliant" in comparison with that of Germany. Nevertheless, it criticizes the recent SCAP decree banning from future participation in public life all individuals having the slightest connection with the presurrender government. Only men lacking experience and appropriate knowledge will be eligible for high office in government and business, the editors warn, and "a creeping and cumulative paralysis" will be the result.

Reparations Payments

The initial intention of the United States and its Allies was to exact very substantial payments of reparations in kind from the defeated Japanese government as well as to confiscate practically all of Japan's overseas assets. This policy is embodied in the first of a series of official reports on the feasibility and scale of such a program known as the Pauley report. In the course of 1947 and 1948 this policy was progressively modified, although interim reparations deliveries continued to be made. These changes resulted in part from the recommendations of two further official reparations surveys—by the Strike (or Overseas Consultants) Mission and the Johnston Committee. Reparations deliveries and the entire associated program were ended in the spring of 1949 as a result of unilateral action by the U.S. government. Many entries in the section providing general commentaries on the economy (p.481) are closely related to the subject of reparations.

Acheson, Dean G. "Japanese Vessels Available for Delivery to U.S., U.K., U.S.S.R., and China." 1947. See no.999.

1116 "Agreement for Reparations and Economic Cooperation between Japan and the Union of Burma, Signed at Rangoon, November 5, 1954." *Contemporary Japan* 23, no.4/6:427–29 (1955)

The text of the agreement designed to implement the provisions of Article 5, paragraph 1(a) of the peace treaty calling upon Japan to provide Burma with appropriate reparations payments.

1116a Ajia Kyōkai. "Japan's War Reparations—Achievements and Problems." *Asian Affairs* 4:99–111 (Mar. 1960)

After describing the provisions that have been made for Japan to pay reparations to Burma, Indonesia, the Philippines, and Vietnam, the authors provide a detailed review of the methods and schedules involved in reparations payments. They note that the renewal and promotion of Japanese trade with Southeast Asia is a positive consequence of the reparations program, but that there are major problems involved in determining what kinds of goods and services should be supplied under the reparations agreements.

1117 "Announcement of the U.S. Government, Issued through the State Department by Major General Frank McCoy, U.S. Representative on the FEC Concerning the Japanese Reparations, May 13, 1949." *Contemporary Japan* 18:277–82 (Apr./June 1949); also published under the title "Japanese Reparations and Level of Industry" in *Department of State Bulletin* 20:667–70 (22 May 1949) and under the title "United States Note on Japanese Reparations" in *Current History* 17:39–42 (July 1949)

In a brief but concise summation of United States' policy regarding reparations at meetings of the Far Eastern Commission, the author attempts to illustrate why the United States has come to some new conclusions regarding this matter. He then outlines these new conclusions: (1) the Japanese economy shows little prospect of being balanced in the near future and thus will require all resources at its disposal; (2) the burden of removing further reparations could seriously jeopardize the economic objectives of the occupation; (3) there is little prospect of Far Eastern Commission agreement on a reparations schedule; and (4) Japan has already paid substantial reparations through the expropriation of its former overseas assets. Finally, McCoy announces that the United States "has no intention of taking further unilateral action under its interim directive powers to make possible additional reparations removals from Japan," that is, that it will cease the removal of industrial plants for reparations.

1118 Bennett, Martin Toscan. "Japanese Reparations: Fact or Fantasy?" *Pacific Affairs* 21:185–94 (June 1948)

The author of this article believes that the reparations policy toward Japan should revert to the basic philosophy underlying the Pauley report and warns against the continued presence of incentives for aggression in Japan. He considers one such incentive to be the fact that Japan is still stronger than her Asian neighbors and recommends that the United States direct Japanese reparations in such a manner as to supply industrial facilities to the areas against which Japan committed the most violent aggression. The article contains a detailed analysis of the provisions of the Overseas Consultants, Inc. report of 26 February 1948 as well as a discussion of the Pauley Mission, the backgrounds of its members and the report it issued, and of the Strike group which visited Japan in 1947 and became known as the Special Committee on Japanese Reparations.

1119 ———. "Postwar Treatment of Japan." *Annals of the American Academy of Political and Social Science* 246:117–24 (July 1946)

This report presents personal observations of the Japanese reparations program by an adviser on industrial matters to Ambassador Pauley of the U.S. Reparations Mission. The author was a first-hand observer of the course of military and industrial disarmament. In his report he provides a summary of prewar and wartime economic conditions in Japan, emphasizing the way in which the rest of Asia became increasingly dependent on Japan during this period. According to the author, one of the important tasks of the reparations program is to reverse this trend of dependence and "encourage the other Asian nations to develop the economic potential inherent in their physical and human resources." The article discusses the specifics of physical disarmament of Japanese industry and also briefly considers various proposals for the decentralization of ownership control by the *zaibatsu*. The author strongly urges a reparations program that is in line with the terms of the Cairo and Potsdam Declarations.

1120 Bisson, Thomas Arthur. "Reparations and Reform in Japan." *Far Eastern Survey* 16:241–47 (17 Dec. 1947)

A former special adviser in the Government Section of SCAP argues for the elimination of Japanese reparations. His argument is based on economic recovery criteria and he reviews the economic "debacle" of postwar Japan through the summer of 1947. Bisson blames the slow pace of recovery on inadequate SCAP supervision and deliberate Japanese sabotage and bungling done to ensure a lenient peace settlement. The Strike report of September 1947 and the earlier downward revision of the Pauley reparations levels by the Far Eastern Commission are noted. An extensive program of American loans and credits is advocated to facilitate recovery. Bisson believes that the future of Pacific security depends on this recovery but questions the ability of the domestic leadership which has worked to "sabotage recovery to get a soft peace" to provide democratic leadership in the future.

1121 Brenn, Bruce M. "United States Reparations Policy toward Japan, September 1945 to May 1949." In *Studies in Japanese History and Politics*, ed. by Richard K. Beardsley. Ann Arbor: Univ. of Michigan Pr., 1967. p.71–113. (Univ. of Michigan, Center for Japanese Studies, occasional papers, no.10)

Tracing the various changes in American reparations policy during the period covered, the author stresses that early recommendations for the transfer of excess industrial facilities to other Asian nations were based on inaccurate estimates of what surplus equipment and machinery Japan might have and of the capability of Japan's underdeveloped neighbors to utilize them. The realization that heavy reparations demands upon the Japanese would necessitate considerably greater American economic assistance to Japan was the key factor in bringing about the changes that occurred in U.S. policy.

Council on Foreign Relations. "American Policies in the Far East (II): Changes in Occupied Japan." 1949. *See* no.583.

1122 Eichler, David K. "Negotiating the Japanese Reparations Settlement." *Military Government Journal* 1:2–6 (Sept./Oct. 1948)

Just reparations for Japan's wartime enemies, industrial disarmament of Japan, and the creation of a healthy economy in Japan are the 3 topics of this report. The author, deputy secretary-general of the Far Eastern Commission, discusses the role of the FEC in determining the extent and destination of Japanese reparations payments. There is a chronological account of the various U.S. economic missions sent to Japan (the Pauley Mission, the Strike Mission, and the Johnston Committee) as well as a summation of their recommendations. In addition to providing some insight into the difficulties of determining how much should be exacted from Japan in reparations, the author also examines the problems associated with negotiating reparations shares —for example, the allocation of fair portions to those countries which formerly suffered from Japan. In a very objective analysis, he discusses the merits and drawbacks of the various conflicting reports and advocates that unflagging efforts be made to "reconcile the divergencies of viewpoint and judgment which they represent into a national economic policy for Japan." The article includes a useful chart citing the specific figures recommended by the various groups for reparations removals in Japan's 5 key industries, i.e., (1) iron and steel, (2) light metals, (3) metal-working machinery, (4) shipbuilding, and (5) chemicals.

1123 Falco, Tom. "Can Japan Pay Her War Bill? Big Business Surveys Japanese Reparations." *Military Government Journal* 1:3–4 (July 1948)

The complex and controversial issue of reparations payments is clearly outlined in this brief article. The author discusses the most important programs put forth: the State–War–Navy Coordinating Committee's (SWNCC) policy document 236/43 and the proposals of the Overseas Consultants, Inc., and the Johnston Committee. He then compares and contrasts their significant similarities and differences. There are statistics elaborating in detail the stern SWNCC proposals as well as the more lenient ones submitted by the Overseas Consultants and Johnston groups. Finally, some attention is given to what the author considers to be the main reasons behind the recent changes in attitude: the belief that Japan will be able to stand on its own without massive American assistance only through a revival of its economy and the conviction that a strong Japan will be a bulwark against Soviet Communist incursions in East Asia.

Far Eastern Commission. "Reduction of Japanese Industrial War Potential." 1947. *See* no.1002.

1124 ———. "Restitution of Looted Property." *Documents and State Papers* 1, no.6:424–26 (Sept. 1948)

The text of a policy decision regarding the restitution of Allied industrial and transportation machinery, cultural objects, and other property seized by the Japanese. The decision was approved by the Far Eastern Commission on 29 July 1948, was released to the press on 9 August 1948, and subsequently was published in this series by the Office of Public Affairs of the U.S. State Department.

1125 Frederick, James O. "Payment from Japan." *Commonweal* 47:534–36 (12 Mar. 1948)

Disagreement among the representatives of the Far Eastern Commission regarding reparations from Japan is considered in this brief but informative article. The author discusses the historical background of the reparations issue and then outlines the findings of the Pauley Mission and the various positions of the member nations of the Far Eastern Commission, particularly the Soviet Union. He briefly relates Soviet claims and American objections to those claims and concludes by discussing the detrimental effect which the continued threat of reparations has had upon the Japanese economy.

1126 Gayn, Mark J. "Japan: Full Speed Astern." *New Republic* 119:13–16 (9 Aug. 1948)

The author discusses 2 major areas that have been affected by the reversal of SCAP's 3-year old policy for Japan—reparations and the decentralization of the *zaibatsu* combines. Regarding the reparations issue, there is a detailed description of the original Pauley program as well as the Strike report which succeeded it. The author then describes the measures that initially were taken to dissolve the *zaibatsu* as elaborated in the directive FEC-230 and the later reversal of this plan as a result of the Draper Mission. In the author's opinion "the new policy takes the accent off reform and puts it on reconstruction" and he warns against the dangers of the resurgent Japan that this will insure.

Hall, Peirson M. "The Japanese Zaibatsu." 1946. *See* no.1801.

1127 Holman, D. S. "Japan's Position in the Economy of the Far East." *Pacific Affairs* 20:371–80 (Dec. 1947)

An examination of U.S. policy in the shaping of Japan's postwar economy and its effect on U.S. relations with China and Korea. The article discusses the reparations programs, particularly emphasizing the Pauley plan, and considers their political as well as economic consequences. Included is a useful summary of Japan's economic situation during 1947, along with a discussion of possibilities for its future economic development. The author argues that the contribution Japan could make towards the economic recovery of the Far East through revival of her industries would be much greater than that achieved through reparations. He urges building up Japan as an area of relative political and economic stability in the Far East to offset growing chaos on the Asian continent.

1127a Inaba, Shūzō. "Reparations and Japan's Economy." *Contemporary Japan* 21, no.1/3:108–13 (1952)

This article by the director of the Association for the Study of the National Economy originally appeared in Japanese in the May 1952 issue of *Sekai*. According to Inaba, the history of German reparations after World War I demonstrates that reparations are impossible unless the defeated country is economically solvent, and that reparations demands may lead to reactionary feelings if they are too vindictive. Although the harsh reparations program originally planned for Japan has been considerably softened, he notes, the peace treaty specifies that Japan is still committed to fulfilling her reparations obligations, however difficult that may be. Japan owes a moral obligation and must "pay her way out," but the existing claims are beyond her present means. The South Asian countries are mistaken if they believe that Japan's high rate of growth and her high living standards mean that she can easily pay up. Inaba concludes that the only way out for Japan is to show her sincerity and good faith and to present a true picture of her difficulties to the various creditor nations.

1127b "Interim Principles for Restitution of Identifiable Property Confiscated in Japan from Allied Nationals." *Department of State Bulletin* 16:708–9 (20 Apr. 1947)

This FEC policy decision of 6 March 1947 deals with property belonging to Allied nationals which was located in Japan at the outbreak of hostilities and was subsequently seized or confiscated by the Japanese government. The decision establishes procedures for the identification and return of such property.

1128 Itagaki, Yoichi. "Reparations and Southeast Asia." *Japan Quarterly* 6:410–19 (Oct./Dec. 1959)

The author, a leading authority in Japan on the economy of Southeast Asia, analyzes Japan's policies toward various Southeast Asian countries in terms of her reparations payments after the war. The author first analyzes the amount and terms of the reparations which were paid to Burma, the Philippines, Indonesia, and Vietnam. An analysis of Japanese economic cooperation in these countries follows. Itagaki concludes with general statements both on the question of reparations and upon Japan's new role in Southeast Asia.

1129 Japan. Ministry of Foreign Affairs. *Japanese Reparations.* Tokyo: The Ministry, 1950. 89p.

1129a "Japan Drafts Property Compensation Law." *Department of State Bulletin* 25:429–32 (10 Sept. 1951)

The draft text of the proposed Allied Powers Property Compensation Law is reproduced within this issue of the *Bulletin*. Its provisions include a statement of the principles of compensation, the means for determining the scope of damage and the location of damaged Allied property of all kinds, the calculation of the amount of damages in each particular case, and the procedures for making claims and paying compensation.

1130 *Japan's International Economic Position.* Mimeographed. New York: Institute of Pacific Relations. International Secretariat, 1947. 9p. (Institute of Pacific Relations, 10th conference, supplementary paper, 1947)

Written by a non-American economist, this paper questions the wisdom of Edwin Pauley's recommendations to the president concerning Japanese reparations and suggests alternative measures. Pauley proposed the reduction of Japan's heavy industry to a minimum and urged that capital equipment from the iron and steel, electric power, chemical, and machine tools industries be taken from Japan and used to promote industrialization in China, Korea, and the Philippines. The anonymous author expresses doubts concerning these proposals, questioning whether this capital equipment can be transplanted and used effectively by the Asian countries claiming reparations. He argues that the kinds of equipment needed in these nations can only be removed from Japan at the risk of impeding Japan's economic recovery. He suggests that reparations be limited to the materials that Japan would have to discard under the disarmament program and that the objectives of reparations, one of which is to speed the economic recovery of the Far East, would be better served by industrial revival in Japan rather than by industrial transplants to other Asian nations.

1130a "Japanese Blueprint: Overseas Consultants, Inc. Will Determine How Much Industrial Capacity Japan Can Afford for Reparations." *Business Week* p.88 (9 Aug. 1947)

This article briefly reports on the visit of a 30-man team of American industrial executives and engineers known as "Overseas Consultants, Inc." Their mission is to conduct an industrial survey of Japan in order to determine how much the country can afford to part with by way of reparations while still retaining the capacity for becoming self-supporting. The survey, the article concludes, will become the basis of the American position in the upcoming reparations discussions held by the Far Eastern Commission.

1130b "Japanese Reparations Goods." *Department of State Bulletin* 16:433–34 (9 Mar. 1947)

The text of the policy decision approved by the Far Eastern Commission on 13 February 1947, this document provides instructions regarding the dismantling, packing, and shipping of reparations goods to various foreign countries.

1130c McCoy, Frank R. "Transfer of Japanese Industrial Facilities to Devastated Countries." *Department of State Bulletin* 16:674–75 (13 Apr. 1947)

In this statement of 3 April 1947 to the members of the Far Eastern Commission, McCoy announces the American government's decision to issue an interim directive to SCAP authorizing that Japanese industrial facilities be made immediately available to advance reparations transfers to China, the Philippines, the Netherlands (for use in the Indies), and Great Britain (for use in Burma, Malaya, and its colonial possessions in the Far East). These 4 states, McCoy declares, are in urgent need of the equipment for the purpose of economic rehabilitation. A further delay in their transfer until the commission reaches an agreement as to the assignment of reparations shares to various countries would merely result in the deterioration of assets usable for relief purposes.

1131 Markov, M. "Reparations from Japan." *New Times* no.37:8–11 (10 Sept. 1947)

The author favors the exacting of reparations from Japan and strongly disapproves of American attempts to cancel such payments. He charges that the United States is neglecting the victims of Japanese aggression in order to accommodate the Japanese industrialists, their true allies. He outlines the recommendations of the Pauley Mission and claims the Japanese government put forth an even bolder proposal to retain Japanese industrial equipment—both proposals receiving American sympathy. The author condemns America for taking unilateral action in the matter and claims that it is yet further evidence of that nation's interest in the economic domination of a conquered country.

1132 Mears, Helen. "Footnote on Reparations and Reform in Japan." *Far Eastern Survey* 17:108–10 (5 May 1948)

A member of SCAP's Labor Advisory Committee writes to refute an earlier article by Thomas A. Bisson (no.1120) appearing in the December 1947 issue of the same periodical. Bisson's article viewed the then-current economic crisis in Japan as due to a deliberate sabotage plot by the Japanese in order to gain an easy reparations program and a soft peace. In a balanced report of the conditions of the Japanese economy since the war, the author critically examines SCAP economic policy, concentrating on the Pauley report as an economic program whose enactment would have seriously jeopardized Japan's peacetime economy, and on the later Strike report, which argued for changes in the Pauley proposals, a halt to the reparations program, and active SCAP support of industrial revival. The author warns against a prolonged occupation of Japan that might well result in "a continued lowering of the people's standard of living and the reemergence of Japan as a pawn in Far Eastern power politics."

1133 Miyata, Kiyozo. "Reparations and Japan's Economy." *Asian Affairs* 1, no.3:233–45 (Sept. 1956)

A professor of economics at Kobe University examines the effect that the payment of reparations will have on Japan by describing the uniqueness of the Japanese reparations program, the underdeveloped nature of the countries of Southeast Asia which are recipients of Japanese funds, the content of the reparations, and the impact of the program upon Japanese firms, Japan's industrial structure, and the national economy.

Ōhira, Zengo. "Settlement of the U.S.A.'s Postwar Assistance to Japan." 1962. *See* no.1654a.

1134 Ohkita, Saburō. "Japan Views Her Reparations." *Contemporary Japan* 16:11–26 (Jan./Mar. 1947)

A systematic analysis of the effects of the reparations program on Japanese industry. The author discusses the recommendations of the Pauley Commission and the interim reparations program of the Far Eastern Commission, and then describes their consequences on particular industries such as the army and navy arsenals, light metal plants, the machine tool industry, sulphuric acid plants, shipbuilding, the ball-bearing industry, iron and steel, power generating plants, civilian munitions plants, and the synthetic rubber and petroleum industries. The article provides statistics of production limitations under the interim reparations program, and compares them to prewar levels.

1135 Overseas Consultants, Inc. "Japan's War Reparations: A Survey of the Japanese Industrial Potential." *Military Government Journal* 1, no.7:11–13 (May 1948)

This study describes the objectives of the survey conducted by the Overseas Consultants, Inc. and some of the group's recommendations. Two charts showing Japanese industries, their capacity, and their value accompany the article.

1136 ———. *Report on Industrial Reparations Survey of Japan to the United States of America.* New York: Overseas Consultants, Inc., Feb. 1948. 224p., 46 exhibits.

This report of the Overseas Consultants, Inc. charts the findings and recommendations of the group's 5-month study in Japan of Japanese industrial plant and potential. The group was headed by Clifford S. Strike and other members were drawn from such organizations as Standard Research Consultants, the American Appraisal Co., F. H. McGraw and Co., and Stone and Webster Engineering Co.

The study is divided into 3 main sections. Section A designates those plants and facilities which the mission believes should be retained in Japan and those which should be made available for reparations, a task which involved a study of all facilities in such industries along with estimates of their capacities and values. Section B offers an estimate as to productive facilities which should be retained in Japan in order to permit the country to achieve a self-supporting economy. Section C contains exhibits which provide statistical data on the quality, quantity, and productive capacity of various Japanese industries.

In marked contrast to the Pauley Mission's recommendations made in 1946, the Overseas Consultants' report concludes that a strong industrial Japan would be less dangerous to the peace and prosperity of the Far East than a continuance of the present state of instability and economic maladjustment. The members of the Overseas Consultants, Inc. thus address themselves to the enormously difficult problem of restoring the economy of Japan to a self-supporting basis and "recommend against the removal of productive facilities (except primary war facilities) which can be effectively used in Japan."

Available at the Washington National Records Center, Suitland, Maryland.

1137 Ozawa, Takeo. "Japanese Foreign Debts and Reparations Problems." *Asian Affairs* 1:274–89 (Sept. 1956)

Ozawa, the General Affairs Counselor in the Foreign Ministry's Asian Affairs Bureau, divides Japan's foreign debts into 2 categories: those which were caused directly or indirectly by the war, and those that were incurred before the war (e.g., foreign currency bonds). In itemizing the debts in the first of these 2 categories, he notes that they include (1) reparations payments to various Southeast Asian nations, (2) the return and compensation for the Allied nations' assets in Japan, (3) relief to maltreated Allied prisoners of war, (4) compensation for the damages done to persons and properties during the war, and (5) payment for aid received from the United States and Great Britain during the occupation period (e.g., GARIOA funds and the goods released after the war by the British Commonwealth Occupation Force). After discussing each of these items at some length, he points out various problems which Japan is facing in settling all of its foreign debts.

1138 Pauley, Edwin W. *Report on Japanese Assets in Manchuria to the President of the United States, July 1946.* Washington, D.C.: Government Printing Office, 1946. xi, 255p., app.

From May to July 1946, the U.S. Reparations Mission, headed by Ambassador Edwin W. Pauley, conducted an extensive survey of Japanese assets in Manchuria subject to Japanese reparations. The mission was organized on 30 April 1946, and visited Tokyo, South Korea, and major Manchurian industrial and mining cities including Mukden, Fushun, Kiaoyang, Changchun, and Kirin. It had 35 members, including well-known American engineers specializing in various fields of industry. Their report notes that the situation in Manchuria was far from promising due to the fighting between the Chinese Communists and Nationalists and the removal by the Russians of indispensable industrial equipment. The necessity for the immediate transfer from Japan of power equipment for coal-mining industries, which are vital to the restoration of Manchuria's industrial complex, is stressed. The rehabilitation of power installations in Manchuria is urged. In the 18 chapters of the report, detailed accounts are given of conditions in areas such as electric power, coal, steel, railways, cement, food, textiles, pulp, and radios. Fourteen documents regarding plant inspection, Japanese investments in Manchuria, and other pertinent data are appended.

1139 ———. *Report on Japanese Reparations to the President of the United States, November 1945 to April 1, 1946.* Washington, D.C.: Government Printing Office, 1948. ix, 52, 200p. (approx.) (Dept. of State publication 3174; Far Eastern series 25)

The 15-member U.S. Reparations Mission to Japan, organized in November 1945 and headed by Ambassador Pauley, filed its recommendations on an American policy regarding reparations from Japan on 1 April 1946. The report contains a 52-page statement entitled "Comprehensive Program," which summarizes the mission's findings and recommendations. It concerns a considerable range of reparations problems: disposition of industries, Japan's foreign trade, merchant shipping, finance, and mineral resources. The statement expresses a conviction that the war only damaged the direct war economy, that Japan still retains great productive potential, that a surplus is available for reparations, and that Japan's reparations to neighboring Asian countries would contribute to political stability in East Asia. This general summary is followed by 52 reference materials, which include the mission's interim report of 18 December 1945, the text of the U.S. preliminary statement on American reparations policy for Japan, the interim program presented to the Far Eastern Commission on 12 January 1946, and more detailed statements on recommended policies for specific items such as iron, textiles, fisheries, the pulp industry, forest products, war-connected plants, exports and imports, foreign assets, the *zaibatsu*, patents and trademarks, petroleum, coal, and copper.

1140 Petrie, W. F. "Reparations since the Surrender: Changes in the Attitude towards Japanese." *Australian Outlook* 4, no.1:51–61 (Mar. 1950)

This article presents an Australian view of the problem of collecting reparations from Japan. Early postwar planning called for the payment of reparations to poorer Asian countries so as to create an economic balance in the Far East. In 1947, however, American policy changed to opposing reparations and encouraging reconstruction of Japanese industry. This change in policy was in part to help contain communism and in part because the Japanese made their country seem poorer than it really was. As a result the interests of less developed Asian countries were ignored and the author feels that in the future Australia may be threatened by reborn Japanese economic and military might.

1140a "Recommendations by Ambassador Pauley on Japanese Reparations." *Department of State Bulletin* 15:957–59 (24 Nov. 1946)

This article is a summary description of the report (no.1139) submitted on 17 November 1946 by Edwin W. Pauley and his colleagues dealing with the subject of postwar Japanese reparations.

1141 Reday, Joseph Z. "Reparations from Japan." *Far Eastern Survey* 18:145–51 (29 June 1949)

Discussing the question of reparations from Japan, Reday notes that it constitutes probably the biggest gap between American and Allied thinking on Japan. A possible line of action, he suggests, is that of reparations from current Japanese industrial output. Joseph Reday was formerly chief of the SCAP division that handled reparations affairs in Tokyo.

1141a "Release of Earmarked Gold in Japan." *Department of State Bulletin* 21: 637–38 (24 Oct. 1949)

This article consists of 3 items: (1) a directive dated 3 October 1949 ordering SCAP to release to France and Thailand gold which had been earmarked for them by the Japanese government before the end of World War II; (2) a statement by Frank R. McCoy at a FEC meeting on 15 September announcing the intention of the United States government to issue the above directive; and (3) a detailed list of the quantities of gold involved, and when and why they were earmarked for transfer.

1141b "Reparations Agreement between Japan and the Republic of Indonesia, Signed at Djakarta, January 20, 1958." *Contemporary Japan* 25, no.2:306–8 (Apr. 1958)

The text, without additional commentary, of the 11 articles implementing Article 4, paragraph 1(a) of the treaty of peace between Japan and Indonesia providing for Japanese reparations payments over a number of years.

1141c "Reparations Agreement between Japan and the Republic of the Philippines Signed at Manila, May 9, 1956." *Contemporary Japan* 24, no.4/6:362–69 (1956); also in John M. Maki. *Conflict and Tension in the Far East: Key Documents, 1894–1960.* Seattle: Univ. of Washington Pr., 1961. p.150–55.

The text of the agreement containing 14 articles together with an annex, both of which stipulate the provisions for Japanese payments to the Philippines for losses incurred by the latter during the course of World War II. There is no accompanying commentary.

1142 "Reparations from Japan." *Economist* 149, no.5336:779–80 (1 Dec. 1945)

Appearing at the time that Edwin Pauley was conducting a preliminary survey of Japan's capability to afford reparations, this article suggests that there may be major limitations on the amount she ultimately will pay. The author first points out that the Japanese have already been deprived of valuable assets through the loss of their empire and that this should be fully taken into account when reaching any settlement. As the major claimant, moreover, China was indicating that she not only wished to receive large quantities of equipment for her own development programs but also was anxious to deindustrialize Japan and thereby reduce the power of her major Asian competitor. By implication, this course of action was one which some of the Allies would be likely to reject. Finally, the United States as the nation principally responsible for Japan was showing signs of increasing concern about Japan's future. The Americans not only wanted to modernize and democratize the country, but they were also loath to have reparations claims strip her of most of her capital equipment or reduce her to destitution for an indefinite period of time if such action were to mean that a decent minimum standard of living could not be maintained without considerable American relief aid.

1142a "Reparations from Japan." *Economist* 161, no. 5643:903–4 (20 Oct. 1951)

After reviewing Japan's postwar economic progress and noting that the Japanese will shortly begin a new drive to expand their foreign trade, the article explains the fears that many in England have of renewed Japanese competition. The Lancashire textile industrialists in particular are concerned, and there is growing alarm that Japan will be able to secure control of various overseas markets as a consequence of the reparations agreements she is to conclude with certain Asian countries.

1142b "Report of Edwin W. Pauley on Industrial Conditions in Manchuria." *Department of State Bulletin* 15:1154–55 (22 Dec. 1946)

This article, a digest of Pauley's report on Manchurian industry (no.1138), describes the extensive damage suffered by industrial installations in Manchuria during the period of Soviet occupation and sharply criticizes those responsible for the pillage and destruction that occurred. Statistical summaries are provided where appropriate.

1142c "The Report Prepared by the Johnston Committee and Submitted to United States Secretary of the Army Kenneth Royall (Released to the Press), May 19 1948: The Text of the 'Summary of the Report'." *Contemporary Japan* 17:211–14 (Apr./June 1948)

In a useful summation of the report of the Johnston Committee, this document touches upon the major observations and recommendations of the committee—particularly with regard to Japan's current and future economic situation, and the issue of reparations. The report urges that the United States now assist in the recovery of Japan and settle the issue of reparations by retaining any plants which are needed in bringing about the recovery of Japan. The final sections of this summarized report concern the committee's findings in Korea and include some comparisons with the Japanese situation.

1143 "Restitution of Looted Property." *Department of State Bulletin* 15:163–64 (28 July 1946)

According to this policy statement approved by the Far Eastern Commission on 18 July 1946, steps should be taken immediately to restore to their rightful owners property held by the Japanese which can be identified as having been obtained by fraud or duress from Allied nationals. The kinds of property to be returned include industrial and transportation machinery and equipment; gold and other precious metals, gems, foreign securities or currency, and other foreign exchange assets; cultural objects; and agricultural products and industrial raw materials. The statement also outlines procedures for filing claims and for the delivery of looted property.

1143a "Restitution of Looted Property." *Department of State Bulletin* 21:790 (21 Nov. 1949)

This article describes FEC decisions, released to the press on 25 October 1949, modifying earlier decisions regarding the distribution of funds received from the liquidation of property looted by the Japanese but unidentified as to proper owner. The funds were originally to have been distributed by 1 October 1949 among the countries looted by Japan during the war and in proportion to the recognized national reparations shares of those countries. The new decisions change the deadline to 1 April 1950 and allow the countries involved to work out among themselves a schedule of shares in the absence of a formal decision on reparations shares by the FEC.

1143b "Restitution of Looted Property in Japan: A United States Directive." *Department of State Bulletin* 18:482–83 (11 Apr. 1948)

This U.S. interim directive, dispatched by the Joint Chiefs of Staff to SCAP on 17 March 1948, provides an addendum to former directives dealing with the recovery of goods taken by the Japanese from the overseas territories which they occupied. Procedures for the return of property and the destruction of unclaimed property are briefly outlined.

1143c "Restoration and Protection of Allied-Owned Trade-marks in Japan." *Department of State Bulletin* 21:308–9 (29 Aug. 1949)

On 28 July 1949, the Far Eastern Commission approved a policy decision regarding Allied-owned trademarks. This article consists of the text of that decision and a digest and analysis of it. The decision provides that trademark rights lost during the war be restored to their Allied owners and that measures be taken to insure against Japanese piracy of Allied trademark rights and against the mismarking of goods.

1144 "Reversal on Japan." *Economist* 154: 670–71 (24 Apr. 1948)

The recommendations of the Overseas Consultants, Inc. and the subsequent Hoffman group on the issue of Japanese reparations are briefly discussed. The rationale behind America's abandonment of her previous stern reparations policy is explained and the new, more lenient approach is contrasted with an earlier approach advocated by the Draper Mission. The author acknowledges that many Asian allies of the United States will find its new policy distasteful but asserts that fear of Russia is greater than fear of disturbing these small nations.

1145 "A Review of the Japanese Reparations Problem." *China Economist* 1:338–42 (21 June 1948)

This article summarizes a report by Professor Wu To which first appeared in the 5 June 1948 issue of *Hsin Lu Weekly*, a publication of the Social and Economic Research Institute of Peiping. Wu strongly criticizes SCAP for its delays in distributing reparations materials and payments, evidently because of its decision to promote the rehabilitation of the Japanese economy. Detailed analysis of the reports submitted by the Pauley and Draper Missions is included as evidence to support these criticisms. The article then presents a summary of Wu's recommendations calling for (1) immediate decisions on the specific materials to be included in reparations transfers and on the allotment of shares among the Allied powers, and (2) the inclusion of bullion and finished products in reparations transfers, in addition to industrial equipment. Finally Wu argues that the economic rehabilitation of Japan and the reparations question should be treated as separate and distinct issues, and that once China receives her share of reparations, adequate measures must be taken to insure their advantageous use.

1145a "The Selection of Plants for Reparations Removals, Destruction, or Retention in Japan." *Department of State Bulletin* 16:1201 (22 June 1947)

The text of a policy decision approved by the Far Eastern Commission on 22 May 1947 detailing how SCAP should determine what is to be done with Japanese plants, machinery, equipment, and other industrial facilities.

1146 "Should We Strip Japan of Tools?" *Christian Century* 63:1492 (11 Dec. 1946)

Edwin W. Pauley's proposal to strip Japan of her war potential, the editors contend, will deprive her of her peace potential as well. "Doubling unemployment by taking reparations on this scale will make Japan a festering Asiatic slum," they warn, and the damage to the economy caused by such punitive measures will nullify American gains to date.

1147 Snow, Edgar. "Hon. Spoils Rot in Japan." *Saturday Evening Post* 218:22–23, 141–42 (15 June 1946)

Edgar Snow, a world correspondent for the *Post*, notes that the Japanese have still not been presented with a reparations bill 9 months after the start of the occupation because the Allies can't agree on how to divide the spoils. The Japanese government, he explains, will continue to procrastinate and sabotage proposed reforms until they are told the full extent of the reparations program, and the longer the final decision is delayed, the more rapidly the spoils deteriorate. In examining the final American recommendations for reparations, he indicates their effects on both Japanese and Allied interests.

1148 Strike, Clifford S. "Revenge is Expensive." *American Magazine* 144:50–51, 82–84 (Sept. 1947)

Strike argues that the United States should stand firm against the demands of her allies that Japan be stripped of her remaining industrial resources as part of the reparations program. It was a mistake to give the Soviet Union free rein in Germany to loot and demolish German plants and machinery, and this mistake should not be repeated in the case of Japan. Soviet claims to a share of confiscated Japanese industrial materials are particularly weakened in Strike's opinion by the wholesale looting and confiscation carried out by Soviet military forces in Manchuria. He believes that the United States should oppose the demands of other members of the Far Eastern Commission even if a separate peace treaty is the result, for a self-sustaining Japanese economy is a prerequisite for any permanent change in Japanese ideology.

Supreme Commander for the Allied Powers. Monograph 21. *Foreign Property Administration*. 1952. See no.303.

———. Monograph 22. *Reparations*. 1952. See no.304.

1149 ———. *Reparations Messages*. 1946–49. Blue Binder series. MacArthur Memorial, Bureau of Archives, Norfolk, Va. 2 folders.

Several unclassified messages from SCAP to the War Department and from the department to SCAP concerning the issue of reparations. The SCAP messages summarize the recommendations of Ambassador E. W. Pauley while the Army radiograms outline the report on Japanese reparations by Overseas Consultants, Inc. and a State Department position paper read to the Far Eastern Commission by General McCoy.

1150 ———. *Vested Assets in Japan: Final Report of Trusteeship.* n.p.: 1952. 1v.

SCAP's liquidation policy for German assets in Japan is exhaustively treated in this report which consists of 11 major sections. A description of general Allied policies in this matter is followed by a description of controlled property; policies related to patents, trademarks and copyrights; the property of individuals; government owned and controlled property; claims; accounting methods; and eventual distribution of the proceeds. The final section presents the "Report of Audit" prepared by the Office of the Comptroller at the Far East Command headquarters.

Available at the Library of Congress, Washington, D.C.

Tsang, Chih. "Reparations for China." 1944. See no.178c.

U.S. Dept. of State. Historical Div. *Foreign Relations of the United States, 1946.* v.8, *The Far East.* 1971. See no. 203a.

1151 "U.S. Repudiates Philippine and Chinese Complaint on Japanese Reparation Removals." *Department of State Bulletin* 20:831–33 (26 June 1949)

A detailed repudiation of Philippine and Chinese claims for continued Japanese reparations is presented here. State Department officials delineate American policy concerning the abandonment of reparations. The policy is based on recognition of the vital need for a balanced Japanese economic revival and on the lessening of American willingness to continue extensive financial support. The Philippine and Chinese criticisms of 19 and 26 May 1949 are refuted as follows: (1) the Potsdam Declaration provided first for economic recovery and then for reparations; (2) the elimination of reparations after 4 years is not an abrogation of Far Eastern Commission directives; (3) economic recovery is not based on remilitarization; (4) Japan's recovery is in the best interests of all Asian nations; and (5) the United States is not rejecting Philippine rehabilitation.

1152 Vaughn, Miles W. "The Report of the 'Johnston Committee'." *Contemporary Japan* 17:119–23 (Apr./June 1948)

None of the actual recommendations of the Johnston Committee is considered in this report. Rather, the author briefly discusses the program "as part of a world program on the part of the United States to further world peace and prosperity," whereby the United States will fill the role of a "friendly banker and economic counsellor" for all Asian nations.

1153 "The War Reparations Situation." *Oriental Economist* 27:181–84 (Apr. 1959)

In detailing Japan's reparations agreements with Burma, the Philippines, and Indonesia, the author discusses the amounts paid to date, the effect of reparations on normal trade, and the manner for procuring reparations items.

1153a Yamamoto, Noboru. "Reparation and Economic Cooperation: Influence of Japan's Reparations on the Economic Development of Southeast Asia." *Asian Affairs* 1, no.3:246–59 (Sept. 1956)

Professor Yamamoto of Keio University focuses his attention on the role that reparations have played in promoting economic cooperation between Japan and the nations of Southeast Asia. He first points out the significant difference between the reparations burden levied on Germany following the First World War and the reparations demanded from Japan after World War II, noting that in the latter case they do not exceed the limit which would injure Japan's economic viability and that they have taken the form primarily of payments in kind and in services rather than in cash. Furthermore, they have "evolved from the hitherto nature of a penalty to a new pattern which includes the proposition of giving economic aid." Yamamoto then outlines the reparations agreements which have been concluded with Burma and the Philippines and considers the economic effects of these reparations on the recipient countries. He concludes that reparations have enabled the states of Southeast Asia to obtain vitally needed materials, techniques and capital for economic development, and that these reparations can contribute to long-term economic stability and to a sense of cooperation and solidarity between the Japanese and Southeast Asian peoples.

Yanaga, Chitoshi. *Big Business in Japanese Politics*. 1968. See no.1815a.

THE REPATRIATION PROGRAM

The repatriation program that permanently returned to their homeland about six million Japanese, both military and civilian, from stations and residences scattered throughout eastern and southeastern Asia and the western Pacific was in part punitive and precautionary in intent. Repatriation was in this sense compulsory, even for Japanese civilians long resident overseas who lost practically all of their assets and belongings as a consequence. The program may also in some way be regarded as a humanitarian endeavor. Strangely enough, it is this aspect that acquired the greatest and most durable salience after the war and is reflected in most of the following entries. The particular point at issue was the continued attempt by SCAP and the Japanese government to induce the USSR to return to Japan several hundred thousand prisoners taken during or immediately after its brief war with Japan. These efforts continued into the early 1950s.

1154 "Allied Council for Japan." *International Organization* 4:339 (May 1950)

This brief notice records the fact that at a meeting of the Allied Council for Japan on 1 March 1950, the British Commonwealth representative urged SCAP to take action on Japanese charges that war prisoners in the Soviet Union had been denied repatriation unless they agreed to join the Japanese communist party upon their return. The United States representative agreed to suggest to the Japanese government that an investigation be undertaken, and the government did so on the following day.

1154a "Australian Journal Exposes American-Provoked 'Question of Repatriation of Japanese from USSR'." *Current Digest of the Soviet Press* 2, no.7:16–17 (1 Apr. 1950)

Originally appearing in the 5 February issues of *Pravda* and *Izvestia*, this article presents the findings of the monthly journal *Australian Democrat* (Melbourne) in regard to the controversy over the repatriation of Japanese prisoners of war. Anti-Soviet American and Japanese officials in Tokyo are alleged to be conducting a carefully worked out campaign to create anxiety and concern among the Japanese people, and they are preparing lists of unrepatriated prisoners of war which contain the names of people known to be dead. "It is being said loudly in journalistic circles in Tokyo," the article concludes, "that the whole question of repatriation from Siberia is being used by the Americans as a maneuver to eliminate the influence on the Japanese people of the repatriates who have returned to their homeland healthy and happy."

1154b Blakemore, Thomas L., Jr. "Recovery of Japanese Nationality as Cause for Expatriation in American Law." *American Journal of International Law* 43: 441–59 (July 1949)

Blakemore discusses the problem involving the nationality status of several thousand nisei who discovered after World War II that certain actions taken by them or by others on their behalf during the course of the war either had seriously clouded their claims to American citizenship or had resulted in an apparently irrevocable expatriation. The problem, as the author explains, was that "of the effect on American nationality of the reacquisition of Japanese nationality obtained through a process known to Japanese law as 'recovery'." In this article, Blakemore describes the Japanese legal institution of "recovering one's nationality" (*kaifuku*) and its relationship to other phases of Japanese nationality law. He then considers the application of "recoveries" of those articles of law and of Section 5 of the American Nationality Acts of 1907 and 1940 which deal with expatriation. Finally, he examines certain troublesome categories of ostensible "recoveries" as well as "recoveries" obtained during minority, and explores various possibilities for challenging the apparent loss of American nationality which has resulted.

1154c Carey, Jane Perry Clark. "Displaced Populations in Japan at the End of the War." *Department of State Bulletin* 13: 530–37 (7 Oct. 1945)

An adviser on displaced populations in the Department of State, Carey presents a thorough report on the historical background and current situation of various groups of displaced persons in Japan. She begins by describing the situation for the largest group of foreigners displaced in Japan, the Koreans, then discusses the Chinese, Australians, various Europeans, and the Americans. Although the report concentrates mainly on the fate of these foreigners during the war years, it provides some useful information on the displacement of the indigenous population during that period and indicates the vast scope of SCAP's future task of repatriation.

1155 Deverall, Richard L. G. *Japan's Soviet Held Prisoners of War*. Bombay: National Information and Publications, 1951. 33p.

1155a ———. *Stalin's Prize: Japanese Prisoners-of-War*. Baltimore: Uptown Pr., 1951. 22p.

1155b Gane, William Joseph. *Foreign Affairs of South Korea, August, 1945, to August, 1950*. Ph.D. dissertation, Northwestern Univ., 1951. 444p. (Abstracted in Northwestern Univ. *Summaries of Doctoral Dissertations* 19:352–57 [1951])

This study of the activities of the foreign office of the United States Army Military Government in Korea and of UN efforts to secure unity and independence for all of Korea pays considerable attention to 2 subjects of interest to the student of the occupation of Japan: (1) the repatriation program for Japanese civilian residents and military personnel that was managed by the U.S. Army Military Government, and (2) the supervision of relations between South Korea and Japan by SCAP, which tended to view Korean–Japanese problems primarily from the standpoint of Japanese needs. Gane notes that SCAP's financial and export control policy which affected Koreans returning from Japan may have promoted Japan's postwar economic recovery but inhibited postwar reconstruction in South Korea.

1156 I., V. "MacArthur's Parrots." *New Times* no.18:26–27 (1 May 1950)

This editorial deals with "slanderous lies concerning the repatriation of Japanese war prisoners from the Soviet Union." Insisting that repatriation of Japanese prisoners of war has been completed, the author presents several quotations from the Soviet newspaper affirming this and accuses the Americans and their Japanese "parrots" of malicious fabrication.

1157 Ishida, Gladys. *The Japanese American Renunciants of Okayama Prefecture: Their Accommodation and Assimilation to Japanese Culture*. Ph.D. dissertation, Univ. of Michigan, 1956. 339p. (Abstracted in *Dissertation Abstracts* 17: 1406–7 [1957]; University Microfilms order no.21,138)

The behavior of the Japanese–Americans who renounced their American citizenship and returned to Okayama prefecture during the war is described in this study. Ishida briefly reviews the history of these Japanese in America, discussing the circumstances surrounding their emigration, the nature of their communities in the United States, their wartime relocation, etc. She then describes significant differences in behavior and adjustment exhibited by *kibei* (Japanese–Americans reared or educated in Japan) and *nisei* (second-generation Japanese–Americans) in Okayama, and concludes that the behavior of the *kibei* indicates a harmonious integration of 2 cultures, while that of the *nisei* does not. Her study is based on interviews with some 27 renunciants and their parents.

1158 Japan. Ministry of Foreign Affairs. Public Information Div. *Announcement of Japanese Foreign Ministry and Letters of Foreign Minister to President of United Nations General Assembly on Repatriation Problem*. Tokyo: The Ministry, The Division, 1951. 32, 20p.

1158a "Japanese Come Home from Lost Empire." *Life* 20:17–23 (11 Feb. 1946)

This article consists mostly of photographs taken by Alfred Eisenstadt at the Hario repatriation camp in Kyushu. At that time the camp was handling 9,000 repatriates a day.

Mitchell, Richard H. *The Korean Minority in Japan*. 1967. See no.2261.

1159 Noble, Harold J. "Japs Hate Their Heroes." *Saturday Evening Post* 219:18–19, 143–44 (12 Oct. 1949)

Noble, a correspondent in Tokyo, describes the problems facing returning Japanese soldiers. He notes that while their return is one of the most impressive accounts of the mass movements of people over the seas, it only serves to increase unemployment and food difficulties. The civilian populace treat the former soldiers with contempt. Many who had lauded their heroes to fantastic heights now hate them for the hardships which the nation has suffered.

1160 Norbeck, Edward. "Edokko: A Narrative of Japanese Prisoners-of-War in Russia." *Rice University Studies* 57, no.1:19–67 (Winter 1971)

Based upon information gathered by Norbeck in Tokyo in 1959, this publication is a description of the main events in the wartime and postwar experiences of one group of Japanese soldiers who were sent as prisoners of war from Manchuria to Siberia in the autumn of 1945. The thoughts, social relations, and behavior of these men are recounted, and the type of life that they experienced as laborers and the type of indoctrination that some among them underwent in one camp is vividly described. The narrative concludes with the repatriation of Makoto, Norbeck's principal informant, who initially received a cold reception from his family and friends in Tokyo on account of their fear that he, like many others returning from the Soviet Union, had become a Communist during his stay in Siberia.

The Reminiscences of Douglas W. Overton. 1960. See no.44h.

1161 "Report Compiled on the Japanese Prisoners of War in USSR by General Headquarters, Far East Command, Military Intelligence Section, General Staff, SCAP, Made Public on February 1, 1950." *Contemporary Japan* 19:140–49 (Jan./Mar. 1950)

This report, made public at a meeting of the Allied Council for the Far East, discusses the past experiences and present situation of approximately 700,000 Japanese civilian and military personnel who were interned by the USSR after the war. Statistics were compiled from various Japanese government bureaus such as the Japanese Demobilization Bureau and were checked through a nationwide survey of the families of the missing persons, as well as interrogations of the thousands of Japanese who were eventually repatriated. The bulk of the report relates accounts of conditions in the prisoner of war camps and condemns the USSR for using the Japanese prisoners to increase Soviet production.

1162 "Request to USSR for Information on Japanese Prisoners of War." *Department of State Bulletin* 20:635–36 (15 May 1949)

This letter of 25 April 1949 from William J. Sebald, chief of the Diplomatic Section of SCAP, to Lieutenant General K. N. Derevyanko, Soviet member of the Allied Council for Japan, requests the Soviet government to provide complete information on the names and conditions of all Japanese prisoners of war held in Soviet-controlled territories in accordance with the Allied Council discussions of 29 October 1947.

1162a Sebald, William Joseph. "Information Requested on Japanese Held in Soviet Territory." *Department of State Bulletin* 23:256–57 (14 Aug. 1950)

In this statement made before the Allied Council for Japan on 2 August 1950, the American representative attacks the USSR's refusal to answer the assertions of the United States government that there are large numbers of Japanese war prisoners still awaiting repatriation from Siberia. The United States has made repeated requests for information about these prisoners, Sebald points out, but the Soviet authorities have remained silent. The text of an American note of 9 June reminding the Soviet Union of its failure to answer previous queries follows Sebald's remarks.

1162b ———. "Soviet Union Still Refuses to Cooperate in Repatriation of Japanese." *Department of State Bulletin* 22: 24–28 (2 Jan. 1950)

This article reprints a statement made by Sebald, United States member on and chairman of the Allied Council for Japan, at a meeting of the Council on 4 December 1949. The statement strongly denounces the Soviet Union for its delays in repatriating Japanese military and civilian personnel in Soviet-held areas and for refusing to issue detailed rosters of prisoners and fatalities. Sebald also describes and criticizes the Soviet treatment of prisoners as reported by returnees and accuses the Soviet authorities of indoctrinating prisoners before their release.

1163 "Statement by William J. Sebald, Deputy for SCAP, Chairman and Member for the United States at the Allied Council for Japan at the 113th Meeting of the Council on May 10, 1950." *Contemporary Japan* 19:305–14 (Apr./June 1950)

Sebald's remarks concentrate upon the issue of repatriation, alleging that several thousand Japanese prisoners of war are alive and are still being held by the Soviet authorities. He sharply criticizes the USSR for allowing such a situation to continue and claims such behavior is in violation of the Geneva Convention for the protection of victims of war. Following Sebald's statement to the council are his letters to the Soviet member of the Allied Council for Japan, Lieutenant General Derevyanko, on this same matter and the text of a resolution passed by the Japanese Diet "for the acceleration of repatriation of unrepatriated Japanese and investigation into their actual situations through the United Nations."

Stephan, John J. *Sakhalin: A History*. 1971. See no.993a.

Supreme Commander for the Allied Powers. Monograph 17. *Treatment of Foreign Nationals*. 1952. See no.299.

1163a Tanaka, Kōichi. "Prisoners of War in Soviet Russia." *Democratic Japan* (Tokyo) no.10:11–12 (Jan./Feb. 1951)

Tanaka strongly attacks the continuing refusal of the Soviet Union to allow a United Nations inspection team to investigate charges that over 300,000 Japanese war prisoners remain in Soviet hands.

1164 "USSR Fails to Account for Prisoners of War." *Department of State Bulletin* 23:430–36 (11 Sept. 1950)

Included here are the texts of notes addressed to United Nations Secretary-General Trygve Lie by the United Nations representatives of Australia, New Zealand, and the United States. The notes call for placing the "Failure of the Union of Soviet Socialist Republics to Repatriate or Otherwise Account for Prisoners of War Detained in Soviet Territory" on the provisional agenda of the fifth session of the General Assembly. Attached are the texts of 10 documents relating to the repatriation of both German and Japanese prisoners of war. Among these are the agreement between the Soviet Union and SCAP of 19 December 1946; Tass News Service announcements concerning prisoners of war dated 22 April and 9 June 1950; a resolution adopted by the Japanese Diet on 2 May 1950; and an exchange of notes between the United States and the Soviet Union in June and July 1950.

1165 "USSR Urged to Supply Information on Detention and Repatriation of Japanese." *Department of State Bulletin* 22: 102–3 (16 Jan. 1950)

In this note from the State Department to the Soviet Embassy in Washington, a request is made for information on the identification and well-being of Japanese prisoners of war. The discrepancy between the Japanese claim of 472,000 prisoners under Soviet detention and the Russian acknowledgment of 95,000 prisoners is noted.

1165a Viktorov, Ya. "Sebald's Deliberate Lies." *Soviet Press Translations* 5:523–26 (1 Oct. 1950); abridged version published under the same title in *Current Digest of the Soviet Press* 2, no.34:29–30 (7 Oct. 1950)

On 2 August 1950, William J. Sebald, the United States representative to the Allied Council for Japan, stated that there still were 370,000 Japanese prisoners of war in the Soviet Union (no. 1162a). In reacting to this assertion, Viktorov accuses Sebald of deliberately lying and states that Sebald personally knows that the repatriation of Japanese nationals has been completed. SCAP's figures, as Viktorov demonstrates, have been fabricated, and the United States simply wishes "to distract the attention of the Japanese people from the infamous deeds being done by the American occupational authorities in Japan and from the crude and reactionary policy of the U.S.A., aimed at the political and economic enslavement of the Japanese people." Indeed, Viktorov concludes, the United States has decided to raise the question of Japanese nationals in Siberia at the same time that it is failing to explain the fate of 500,000 Japanese who allegedly died in Southeast Asia. Viktorov's article first appeared in the 25 August issue of *Pravda*.

1165b "Voices of Repatriates from the U.S.S.R.: A Symposium." *Contemporary Japan* 22, no. 7/9:539–43 (1953).

This item consists of 3 reports by Japanese repatriates from the Soviet Union excerpted from a larger collection of such reports appearing in the January 1954 issue of *Chūō Kōron*. The 3 repatriates, who returned to Japan in December 1953, are a former journalist from Southern Sakhalin, an army private captured in Manchuria, and a woman who was teaching in Dairen during the summer of 1945. Their reports describe conditions in the prisons and labor camps as well as Soviet efforts at indoctrination (or the absence thereof). All of the individuals emphasize the lack of racial prejudice among their captors.

Wagner, Edward W. *The Korean Minority in Japan, 1904–1950.* 1951. See no.2277a.

1166 Waln, Nora. "Japanese Prisoners Home from Russia." *Atlantic Monthly* 184:28–30 (Nov. 1949).

A touchingly human though not very analytical description of Japanese repatriates from Russia to occupied Japan. Most of them tell how helpful the Americans are, but a few seem sympathetic to communism.

1167 Warner, W. F. "Repatriate Organizations in Japan." *Pacific Affairs* 22:272–76 (Sept. 1949).

Following a summation of SCAP's repatriation of more than 5 and one-half million Japanese to their homeland, the author discusses the social rehabilitation of these individuals. He maintains that the greatest aids in such an endeavor are the cohesive force of the Japanese family and the repatriate organizations "designed to unite individuals with similar backgrounds and ideas" and ranging from local groups to national associations. He focuses on these organizations, categorizing them in 3 main groups: those organized for a specific purpose, those emphasizing the members' occupation, and those instituted on a geographical basis, and defines their aims as social, political, or economic. In concluding, the author notes that the Japanese government and civilian agencies have accomplished much in rehabilitating repatriates —but not enough. He also criticizes SCAP for barring all former military leaders from public office since, in doing so, it has removed much of Japan's best potential leadership.

Political, Legal, and Administrative Aspects

If at the outset the primary goal of the occupation had been the effective demilitarization of Japan, it was—in a mechanical sense at least—speedily achieved. A second goal, that of democratization, then came to absorb more and more of the attention of SCAP. It was not isolated from the earlier emphasis on demilitarization. It was widely assumed among the American planners of the occupation that a democratic government was less apt to display aggressive tendencies than an authoritarian one. A shared system of governmental and social organization also seemed to offer a more promising foundation for future American–Japanese relations than did the continuance of prewar political institutions in Japan. These views were quite apparent in both the official and private plans for the postwar treatment of Japan developed in the United States before the end of the war (*see* the sections on presurrender planning [p.34, 81, 91, 100, and 108]).

Against this background it is hardly surprising that SCAP very early in the occupation made it clear to the Japanese government that it expected far-reaching changes in the Japanese political system and that they should be uniformly democratic in tendency. SCAP not only demanded such changes but for the first few years of the occupation took strong and positive initiatives to make certain that the types and scale of the political changes undertaken accorded with American notions of what was appropriate. Such pressures gradually abated in the course of 1947 and most of the major political reforms were accomplished—at least in an institutional sense—by the end of that year. Thereafter, the primary emphasis shifted to the economic sphere.

The literature relating to the occupation's endeavors to effectuate changes in the political, legal, and administrative spheres is collected below. Many of the entries in the section providing general materials (p.113) and the section on the supreme commander (p.311) also relate to this subject.

Constitutional Change

The most fundamental political and legal change required of the Japanese government by SCAP was the total revision of the Meiji Constitution of 1889–90. A so-called model of the sort of democratic constitution desired was written by the Government Section of SCAP and transmitted to the Japanese government under circumstances involving an appreciable amount of suasion. This document with very few changes was subsequently adopted by the Japanese government as its own initial draft of a revised constitution and submitted to the national Diet for approval. Following lengthy consideration and debate and some amendment by this body, it was adopted as the new constitution of Japan on 3 November 1946 and took effect the following 3 May. Thereafter, in part because of the circumstances attending its drafting and adoption, the new constitution became a subject of considerable political controversy within Japan, especially after 1952. This controversy culminated in the appointment of a cabinet commission—the Commission on the Constitution or *Kempō Chōsakai*—in 1957 to reexamine the constitution and its origins and the eventual submission of an enormous final report by this body in 1964. The new constitution has not yet, however, been amended in any respect.

The following entries represent the literature on both the origins of Japan's new postwar constitution and the subsequent history of the ensuing constitutional controversy. Many of the general works on the occupation (p.113) devote substantial attention to these matters, as do those in the other subsections of the present section.

Ashizu, Yoshihiko. "The Shinto Directive and the Constitution: From the Standpoint of a Shintoist." 1960. See no.2198a.

Bisson, Thomas A. "Making Japan over." 1945. See no.65.

Blakemore, Thomas L. "Post-war Developments in Japanese Law." 1947. See no.1268.

1168 Brown, Richard Gerard. *Ministerial Responsibility in Japan.* Ph.D. dissertation, Northwestern Univ., 1952. 503p. (Abstracted in Northwestern Univ. *Summaries of Doctoral Dissertations* 19:347–51 [1951])

In his examination of the status of ministerial responsibility in Japan after September 1945, the author refers to Japanese history, philosophical concepts, culture, and most importantly, to political developments during the occupation period. His conclusions are as follows: (1) the establishment of parliamentary government is a fundamental principle of the new Japanese constitution; (2) ministerial responsibility to the Diet is collective rather than individual; (3) cabinet ministers are individually responsible to the prime minister who in turn is responsible to the Diet; (4) the opposition parties in the Diet are ineffective; (5) the new constitution has impaired the *Tennō* system, which was an element of strength in the Meiji Constitution; (6) parliamentary government in Japan could be enhanced through development of an effective opposition in the Diet; (7) tradition is a potent force in Japanese parliamentary government; and (8) parliamentary government under the new constitution could be enhanced through a moderate strengthening of the *Tennō* system. In his study, Brown utilized a wide range of official and unofficial American, Australian, British, French, and Japanese documents as well as his experiences as a parliamentary liaison officer with the Government Section of SCAP.

1169 Cho, Sung-Yoon. "Constitutional Revision in Japan." *Quarterly Journal of the Library of Congress* 23:332–36 (Oct. 1966)

This study is limited to a brief discussion of the reasons for establishing the Commission on the Constitution and to a summary of the debate on the subjects of the emperor system and Article 9 of the constitution. Cho is a legal specialist in the Far Eastern Law Division of the U.S. Library of Congress.

1170 Colton, Hattie Kawahara. "The National Diet after Independence." *Annals of the American Academy of Political and Social Science* 308:18–27 (Nov. 1956).

This article describes the nature of the Japanese national Diet after the end of World War II, examines the activities of the Diet since independence, discusses proposals for changes in the system, and notes some of the major problems facing this branch of government. The issues, problems, and interparty and intraparty struggles of the fifteenth, sixteenth, nineteenth, twenty-second, and twenty-fourth Diet sessions are studied. Proposed constitutional changes resulting from the fact that "no post-occupation government has found it easy to steer a legislative program through the Diet" are discussed along with proposals for changes in the House of Councillors' electoral system. Specific problems examined by the author are problems of the standing committee system, procedures relating to bills of individual Diet members, and the problem of keeping order during Diet sessions.

1171 ———. "The Working of the Japanese Diet." *Pacific Affairs* 28, no.4:363–72 (Dec. 1955)

A detailed description of the operation of Japan's Parliament, particularly after the peace treaty. The roles of the speaker, various committees, party discipline, personal cliques, opposition parties, bureaucrats, and physical violence are all described. The author concludes that power is weighted in favor of the executive and the Diet has been lacking in responsible criticism and debate but that these problems are common to most Western democracies.

Colton, Kenneth E. "The Sun Rises for Japan." 1947. See no.489.

1172 *The Constitution of Japan, Effective May 3, 1947*. Washington, D.C.: Government Printing Office, 1947. iv, 13p. (Dept. of State publication 2836; Far Eastern series 22) Also published in *International Affairs* 17:649–58 (Oct. 1946) and, together with the brief imperial rescript causing the constitution to be promulgated, in *Contemporary Japan* 15:396–407 (Sept./Dec. 1946)

The English-language version of Japan's new constitution, promulgated on 3 November 1946 and effective as of 3 May 1947, appears in these publications. The constitution consists of a preamble and 103 articles brought together under 11 chapters. They concern the emperor (chap. 1), Japan's renunciation of war (chap. 2), the rights and duties of the people (chap. 3), the Diet (chap. 4), the cabinet (chap. 5), the judiciary (chap. 6), finance (chap. 7), local self-government (chap. 8), the amendment process (chap. 9), the supreme law (chap. 10), and supplementary provisions (chap. 11). A number of other works cited within this bibliography—e.g., Hugh Borton's *Japan's Modern Century* (no.695), John Maki's *Government and Politics in Japan: The Road to Democracy* (no. 727), and Yanaga Chitoshi's *Japanese People and Politics* (no. 767)—also contain the text of the postwar constitution.

1172a "Constitution Proposed for Japan Bans War." *Christian Century* 63:356 (20 Mar. 1946)

This editorial praises the draft constitution as a model for other countries. Its similarities to American and European documents are described and commented on; but in its clause renouncing war, the magazine feels, the draft surpasses all of its counterparts.

1173 Cornwall, Peter George. "Japanese Political Reaction to Constitutional Revision 1945–46." In *Studies in Japanese History and Politics*, ed. by Richard K. Beardsley. Ann Arbor: Univ. of Michigan Pr., 1967. p.39-70. (Univ. of Michigan, Center for Japanese Studies, occasional papers, no.10)

The author reviews all published constitutional revisions and contrasts each of them with the official Japanese government draft that was approved by General MacArthur. The drastic difference in style and intent among them is attributed to various SCAP pressures. The progress of the revised constitution through the Privy Council and the Diet under the scrutiny of the Far Eastern Commission as well as SCAP is noted, and the nature of government explanations to legislative questions raised about the constitution is analyzed.

Dionisopoulos, P. Allan. "The No-War Clause in the Japanese Constitution." 1956. *See* no.999b.

1174 ———. "Revisionist Tendencies in Post-Occupation Japan." *Western Political Quarterly* 10:793-801 (Dec. 1957)

The author traces the political trends in terms of possible revision of the 1947 constitution from the end of the occupation through the 1956 elections. He writes briefly of the circumstances surrounding the origins of the constitution and examines the policies toward revision of the Yoshida and Hatoyama cabinets. He concludes that recent political developments indicate 3 things: (1) the House of Councillors will be the scene of political struggles in the future; (2) revision cannot occur at the present time; and (3) Japan is a 2–party system in appearance only.

1175 Far Eastern Commission. "Toward Formulating a New Japanese Constitution: Policy Statements by Far Eastern Commission on Japanese Constitution." *Department of State Bulletin* 16:802-6 (4 May 1947)

The position of the Far Eastern Commission vis-à-vis the MacArthur-sponsored draft of the postwar constitution is outlined in this article. Recommendations concerning the review of the Meiji Constitution and the contents of the new constitution are listed. A section dealing with the apprehension, trial, and punishment of war criminals and a brief section outlining policy regarding the peacetime economic needs of the Japanese people are also included.

1175a Fernbach, Alfred P. "Japanese Government under the 1946 Constitution." In *The Study of Comparative Government: An Appraisal of Contemporary Trends. Essays Written in Honor of Frederic Austin Ogg*, ed. by Jasper Berry Shannon. New York: Appleton-Century-Crofts, 1949. p.87-106.

After briefly reviewing Japan's modern political history and the occupation's goal of eliminating those authoritarian and feudal aspects of Japanese government which had been responsible for her recent military aggression, Fernbach summarizes the circumstances under which the postwar constitution was drafted and presents a detailed analysis of the document's important provisions. He asserts that SCAP's efforts at reshaping the entire governmental framework of Japan was the major positive political achievement of the occupation and that the new constitution represented a complete break with the past. He then summarizes the more important legislative and administrative steps taken between 1946 and 1948 to implement various constitutional changes. A new Imperial House Law and the National Public Service Law, for example, were passed; likewise, there were significant changes in local government and a complete reorganization of the Diet and of major governmental ministries. The author concludes, however, that there still is a need to recast Japanese education and to rehabilitate the country's economy if democratization is to be insured.

Fukase, Tadakazu. "Théorie et réalités de la formule constitutionnelle japonaise de renonciation à la guerre." 1963. *See* no.1003.

1175b Fukui, Haruhiro. "The Liberal-Democratic Party and Constitutional Revision." In *Papers on Modern Japan 1968*, ed. by David C. S. Sissons. Canberra: Dept. of International Relations, Research School of Pacific Studies, Australian National Univ., 1968. p.26–45.

This study examines the issue of constitutional revision and its relationship to the organizational structure of and factional rivalries within the Liberal Democratic Party. Fukui finds that until the outbreak of the Korean War (which prompted SCAP to encourage a limited remilitarization of Japan), the constitution was not the object of much controversy. With the end of the occupation, however, many conservative politicians made the revision of the SCAP-dictated constitution a primary objective. Fukui traces the development of the revision issue in the politicking which resulted in the merger of the Liberal and the Democratic parties in 1955, and he summarizes the activities of the LDP Constituent Committee and the Commission on the Constitution. A table is appended summarizing the findings of a number of public opinion polls taken between 1952 and 1963 on the question of constitutional revision.

―――. *Party in Power: The Japanese Liberal-Democrats and Policy-Making*. 1970. *See* no.1367a.

1176 Grassmuck, George. "Western Influences in Japanese Constitution-making." *India Quarterly* 3:362–81 (Oct./Dec. 1947)

The author first describes briefly the history of constitution-making in Japan prior to World War II. According to the Meiji Constitution the emperor was the supreme sovereign and the power of the people was not specified. After Japan was defeated, the intention of the "conquerors" was to change this concept. The new constitution promulgated in November 1946 is viewed here as a plan of government "adorned by the flowery phrases of law" resulting from the efforts of the occupying forces as well as Japanese governmental leaders. As a conveyor of many of the social and economic reforms desired by SCAP, the constitution is looked at here as an instrument for educating the people of Japan. The position of the emperor, the Bill of Rights and Duties, the Diet, the cabinet, the judiciary, and the concept of federalism as created by the new constitution are examined. The document is criticized as containing occidental solutions for problems in an oriental setting. The significance of Japanese political parties is also noted.

1177 Grover, Verinder. *The Constitution of Japan*. Delhi: Atma Ram, 1964. ii, 184p.

Grover reviews the political history of Japan, emphasizing institutions and constitutionalism and examining in detail the negotiations and framing of the 1947 constitution. Separate chapters on the imperial system, cabinet, Diet, judicial system, and civil rights are included, and the history and postwar functioning of political parties, the electoral system, local government, and a national bureaucracy are discussed.

1178 Henderson, Dan Fenno, ed. *The Constitution of Japan: Its First Twenty Years, 1947–67.* Seattle: Univ. of Washington Pr., 1969. xv, 323p. (Univ. of Washington, School of Law, Asian Law series, no.1)

Eleven Japanese and American scholars of constitutional law and political science here reappraise the 1947 constitution of Japan. Among them are: John M. Maki, Takayanagi Kenzō, Yokota Kisaburō, Satō Isao, Ukai Nobushige, B. J. George, Jr., and the editor. None of them provide an extensive discussion of SCAP's involvement with the drafting of the constitution; rather, their articles reflect their common desire to discern the extent to which the American-directed constitution has become rooted in Japanese soil and to clarify the kinds of problems that have occurred in the process of transition from the Meiji Constitution. The volume consists of 4 parts. Part 1 is a review of the "constitutional style" that has grown out of 20 years of practice of the postwar constitution and an analysis of the developments in constitutional revisionist opinions. Part 2 focuses upon the significance of the expansion of judicial power under the constitution, with a study of judicial review that involved political questions, administrative actions, and treaties. Part 3 is an examination of the relationship between individual liberties and the public welfare. Part 4 is an evaluation of documents published by the Commission on the Constitution from 1957 to 1964. The 11 articles in the first 3 parts were originally presented before the Washington Law Review Symposium sponsored by the Asian Law Program of the School of Law, University of Washington in 1968. They subsequently appeared in the *Washington Law Review* 47, no.5:887–1167 (June 1968). The article in part 4, "The Documents of Japan's Commission on the Constitution," by John M. Maki, is a reprint from the *Journal of Asian Studies* 24:475–89 (1965) (no.19).

1179 Herzog, Peter, S. J. "Political Theories in the Japanese Constitution." *Monumenta Nipponica* 7, no.1/2:1–23 (Jan. 1951)

The postwar constitution, as Herzog points out, was created in order to implement certain of the terms of Japan's surrender and was in conformity with the terms of the Potsdam Declaration. Not only were those who drafted it concerned with providing the country with the blueprint for a new form of government, but they also wished to instill among the Japanese people a new view of political life. The author accordingly notes that the constitution had as its primary objectives the transformation of Japan into a democratic and peace-loving nation, and with this in mind he presents an examination of 4 of the concepts which formed the basis of the new constitution: the idea of a Bill of Rights, parliamentarianism, judicial supremacy, and popular sovereignty.

1180 Hoshii, Iwao. "Japan's Controversial Constitution." *Orient/West* 7, no.5:11–23 (May 1962)

Hoshii Iwao, a former professor at Sophia University and a member of the Research Division of the Fuji Bank at the time this article was written, discusses the issue of constitutional revision—a subject of considerable controversy and debate in Japanese political circles. After presenting a history of the moves to amend the constitution, he reviews the circumstances under which the document was drafted during the occupation period. Considerable attention is paid to Article 9, the so-called war renunciation clause. He also focuses upon the constitutional position of the emperor, the failure of the Diet and of the courts (including the Supreme Court) to play the role constitutionally assigned to them, and the problems that resulted from the constitution's lack of detailed guidelines for the successful implementation of the local autonomy principle. While critical of the constitution for being "little else but a hopeful statement of abstract principles and a soulless inventory of procedural amenities unrelated to the actual political situation of the country," he is particularly angered at the manner in which Japanese politicians and bureaucrats have implemented and interpreted the constitution. Their failure to live up to its principles, he concludes, is responsible for many of its insufficiencies.

1180a Inomata, Kōzō. "In Defence of the Constitution." *Contemporary Japan* 24, no.4/6:200–15 (1956)

This article by a member of the Central Executive Committee of the Social Democratic Party expresses the official opinion of that party on the problem of constitutional revision. The major impetus for the conservatives' efforts to revise the constitution, according to Inomata, is their desire to modify the constitutional prohibition on rearmament (Article 9). The conservatives argue that a new constitution is necessary to "consummate" Japan's independence, but while it is true that Japan is only nominally sovereign, Inomata replies, it is not because of the constitution but rather on account of the current policies of the conservatives. Inomata notes the formation of a "Federation for Defense of the Constitution" by the socialists and the progressives in response to the conservatives' call for revision. The article also discusses in some detail both the circumstances surrounding the adoption of the constitution in 1947 and the major developments in the conservatives' current campaign for revision.

1181 Isozaki, Tatsugorō. "Dissolution of the House of Representatives and Dissolution of Local Self-Government Assembly." *Osaka University Law Review* no. 3:1–14 (1955)

A study of the dissolution of the House of Representatives on the one hand and of prefectural, city, town, and village assemblies on the other. The author, a professor of law at Osaka University, focuses on the regulations concerning the two and through a step-by-step comparison delineates the major differences between them.

1182 Japan. Commission on the Constitution. *Constitution of Japan: The Original Draft Constitution Prepared by SCAP.* Tokyo: Secretariat of the Commission, n.d. 22p.

A reprint of the original and basic draft for a new Japanese constitution written by the Government Section of SCAP between 4 and 10 February 1946. The reprint served as source material for the work of the Commission on the Constitution organized by the Japanese government in 1957. No commentary is provided. The draft contains 92 articles organized into 11 chapters.

1183 ———. ———. *Papers.* Mimeographed. Tokyo: 1961. 1v.

Approximately 100 problems regarding the constitution of Japan are listed and discussed in this collection of 10 papers, each referring to one of the first 10 chapters of the constitution. Points of a controversial nature or points of suggested revision originally raised by experts testifying before the commission or by the commission's own members are here summarized in English by 4 Japanese scholars: Matsumoto Kaoru of Waseda University, Hayakawa Takeo of Kobe University, Tanaka Hideo of Tokyo University, and Hokama Hiroshi of Chuo University. The reasons for suggested revisions are concisely set forth. Among the points recommended for further investigation are whether the emperor's status should be that of Head of State, whether Article 9 renouncing war should be amended, and whether the Diet should be bicameral or unicameral. This document served as the basis for a subsequent questionnaire prepared by the commission in 1962 for the purpose of ascertaining the views of Western scholars on the Japanese constitution.

1184 ———. ———, ed. *Comments and Observations by Foreign Scholars on Problems Concerning the Constitution of*

Japan, 1946. Tokyo: Secretariat of the Commission, 1964. 284p.

In 1962 the Commission on the Constitution solicited comments on the Japanese constitution from 35 Western scholars of constitutional law and political science. Their replies are published in this volume. The commission sent study missions to the United States and Canada in March–May 1962, and to Europe in October–December of the same year. Among those who responded in oral or written form are Gabriel A. Almond, B. James George, Jr., Karl Loewenstein, John M. Maki, James W. Morley, Harold S. Quigley, Robert A. Scalapino, and Robert E. Ward from the United States; Mario Battaglini of Italy; Maurice Duverger of France; O. Hood Philips and Richard Storry of Great Britain; Konrad Hesse, Karl-Heinz Seifert, and Gerhard Mueller of West Germany; and Frank Scott of Canada. They responded primarily to a questionnaire prepared by the commission posing problems raised earlier by Japanese scholars and experts. The text of the questionnaire for the European scholars is appended. The responses are usually given in the authors' native language.

1185 ———. ———, ed. *Comments and Observations by Foreign Scholars on Problems Concerning the Constitution of Japan, 1946 (Supplement).* Tokyo: Secretariat of the Commission, 1964. 7p.

This supplement to the preceding item (no.1184) contains the views of a French scholar, C. Eisenmann, on the Japanese constitution of 1947.

1186 ———. Ministry of Foreign Affairs. Bureau of Public Information and Cultural Affairs, ed. *Japan's Problems.* rev. ed. Tokyo: The Ministry, The Bureau, 1954. 114p.

A revision of a book published in 1953. It comprises 7 articles by prominent Japanese specialists on problems facing Japan. Written for the general foreign reader, they are of an introductory nature. In treating their respective subjects, all articles cover the occupation period to varying extents and some give an appraisal of occupation programs. The more relevant ones are: "Japanese Constitution and Political Parties," by Miyasawa Toshiyoshi; "Democratization of Japanese Administration of Justice," by Tanaka Kōtarō; and "An Appraisal of Educational Reforms in Japan," by Hidaka Daishirō. Miyasawa writes that the Japanese constitution of 1947 was based on the MacArthur draft, and that the Japanese government and political parties could not ignore MacArthur's desire for a constitution that deprived the emperor of political power despite the fact that public opinion favored the emperor's position as set forth by the Meiji Constitution. Tanaka holds that the courts and judges which have been entrusted with increased powers under the new constitution have yet to acquire a social position corresponding to their new responsibilities. Hidaka provides a rather extensive evaluation of SCAP's educational reform programs. He is critical, for instance, of SCAP's decision to recognize the teachers' right to strike, its prohibition of Japanese history courses in primary schools, and the elimination of some science courses from the high school curricula.

The Japanese Reminiscences of Roger Baldwin. 1961. *See* no.44b.

1187 Kaneko, Eiichi. "Japan and the 'Peace' Constitution." *Canadian Forum* 36:200–201 (Dec. 1956)

Recent gains of the opposition parties in the upper house of the Diet are seen as insuring that the "peace clause" will remain in the constitution for at least another 3 years. This clause, though instigated by the occupation, has the overwhelming support of the Japanese people. Changes in the international scene have led to the creation of the self-defense forces. The United States, in league with the leaders of Japanese industry and government, seeks to align Japan with the "free world." Realizing that they have nothing to gain from this alignment, many common people strongly dissent. A case in point is the Sunagawa riots over the expansion of the American-operated Tachikawa air base.

1188 Kasteleiner, Rolf H. *Die staatsrechtliche Entwicklung Japans seit 1945.* Inaugural-Dissertation, Philipps-Universität Marburg/Lahn, 1952. 98p.

Part 1 of the dissertation studies Japan's constitutional development from the end of World War II to May 1947, when the new constitution came into effect, and it includes information on the Allied occupation, the organization of SCAP, military occupation policy, and various events of those two years. Part 2 focuses on the Japanese constitution of 1947 and on its effect upon Japan's constitutional development during the following five years.

Available at Marburg/Lahn, Universitätsbibliothek, no.XVIII B.

1189 Kawai, Kazuo. "Sovereignty and Democracy in the Japanese Constitution." *American Political Science Review* 49: 663–72 (Sept. 1955)

Kawai explains that the present constitution's treatment of the status of the emperor is highly vulnerable on substantive, procedural, and historical grounds. He notes that while the constitution was intended to establish democracy in Japan, it ran counter in almost every way to the means by which the Japanese liberals had been trying to make democracy palatable to their countrymen.

1190 Kinoshita, Hanji. "Constitutional Developments in Post-war Japan." *Indian Year Book of International Affairs* 5: 156–71 (1956)

Pointing to demilitarization and democratization of Japan as the primary objectives of occupation policy, Kinoshita examines the Potsdam Declaration and other documents as reflections of these 2 ultimate goals. He then outlines the fundamental points considered necessary by the Allied powers for the constitution of Japan. A discussion follows of the events leading to the Matsumoto draft, which was found inadequate for democratization by General MacArthur and was replaced by the MacArthur draft, the "most radical of all drafts except that of the Communist Party." Steps taken to push forward the democratization of Japan's political system are enumerated as the political background of the new constitution. Major portions of the new constitution, including the preamble, are quoted and discussed. The author sees the 3 most important subjects and changes in the constitution when compared with the old Meiji Constitution as: (1) the new status and role of the emperor; (2) the renunciation of war; and (3) the respect shown for fundamental human rights. He concludes with a brief look at the late "reverse course" in Japan and its implications.

1191 Kobayashi, Naoki. "The Establishment of the Constitution: An Analysis." *Journal of Social and Political Ideas in Japan* 1, no.2:14–17 (Aug. 1963)

In this article which was translated from the May 1962 issue of *Shisō*, Kobayashi answers critics who charge that the new constitution was "forced" upon the Japanese people. He reviews the political scene in 1945–46 and claims that at that time "there existed no democratic bodies qualified to initiate constitutional reforms." He also feels that the changes brought about under the constitution, particularly that concerning the status of the emperor, reflected the feelings of the majority of the Japanese people.

1192 Kudryavtsev, V. "MacArthur and the Japanese Constitution." *Soviet Press Translations* 4:395–98 (1 July 1949); abridged version published under the same title in *Current Digest of the Soviet Press* 1, no.20:14–15 (14 June 1949)

The constitution of 1947 is the subject of this article originally appearing in *Izvestia* on 13 May 1949. From the fact that MacArthur "in general" said nothing about the constitution in a speech given on the second anniversary of that document, the author concludes that MacArthur is no longer proud of SCAP's role in its adoption and rather is intent on subverting it. He cites various examples of American and reactionary Japanese violation of the constitution—for example, the issuance of an order forbidding collective bargaining and strikes, the disparity still existing between men and women in Japanese business, and the allocation of considerable authority to the Japanese emperor.

MacArthur, Douglas. "The Surrender of Right to Make War." 1946. *See* no. 1005.

McNelly, Theodore Hart. "American Influence and Japan's No-War Constitution." 1952. *See* no.1006.

1193 ———. *Domestic and International Influence on Constitutional Revision in Japan, 1945–1946.* Ph.D. dissertation, Columbia Univ., 1952. 451p. (Abstracted in *Dissertation Abstracts* 12:747–48 [1952]; University Microfilms order no. 4216)

After examining the roles of various groups that participated in constitutional revision in 1945–46, the author concludes that the new constitution of Japan was "almost entirely a MacArthur product." McNelly explores and describes the abortive attempt of Prince Konoe to devise a new constitution, the Shidehara cabinet's proposals for constitutional revision, various proposals made by political parties and private groups, and the secret drafting of a new constitution by the Government Section of SCAP. The author claims that "the new Japanese Constitution owes almost nothing to the effort of the Japanese people or to the Allied Powers."

1194 ———. "The Japanese Constitution: Child of the Cold War." *Political Science Quarterly* 74, no.2:176–95 (June 1959)

A carefully documented history of Japan's constitution from the end of World War II until the late 1950s. The postwar international context—specifically, efforts to keep Soviet hands off Japan—is emphasized along with MacArthur's personal role. Largely ignoring instructions from Washington, MacArthur seems to have forced the new constitution on Japan and viewed it as a victory over possible Russian intrigues. Conservative Japanese efforts first to write a more moderate constitution and, after the occupation, to revise the constitution are also described.

1195 ———. "Political Reform in Japan: SCAP Report." *Far Eastern Survey* 19: 161–64 (13 Sept. 1950)

McNelly describes the role of General MacArthur's headquarters in the drafting of Japan's new constitution as revealed in the 2-volume report, *Political Reorientation of Japan, September 1945 to September 1948: Report* (no.279) prepared by the Government Section of SCAP. Theodore McNelly formerly served with the occupation forces in Japan.

———. "The Renunciation of War in the Japanese Constitution." 1962. *See* no.1007.

Maki, John McGilvrey "The Documents of Japan's Commission on the Constitution." 1965. *See* no.19.

1196 ———. "The Prime Minister's Office and Executive Power in Japan." *Far Eastern Survey* 24:71–75 (May 1955)

Maki evaluates apparent signs that the executive branch of the Japanese government has been moving in the direction of a position of control and domination akin to that of the presurrender period. His examination of the functions and the political influence of this unit sheds light not only on the current role of the Japanese executive but also on the general course of democratic government and political movements in Japan.

1197 Matsumoto, Kaoru. "Question of Constitutional Revision in Japan." *Waseda Political Studies* 5:1–27 (1962)

The 3 main questions which are set forth by the author are the imposed constitution, the renunciation of force, and the role of the emperor. He expresses the opinion that the Japanese people and the Diet in particular were not truly free to amend or reject the constitution as they saw fit. He questions the occupation's shift in policy which allowed for defense forces in response to the Korean incident but in contradiction to the renunciation of arms. Along with the question of the role of the emperor in the Japanese nation, he deals with several other questions such as the judiciary, human rights, and the roles of the cabinet and the prime minister.

1198 Miller, Frank Owen. *Minobe Tatsukichi: Interpreter of Constitutionalism in Japan.* Berkeley: Univ. of California Pr., 1965. xi, 392p. (Publications of the Center for Japanese and Korean Studies)

The author of this study of a prominent constitutional scholar, Professor Minobe Tatsukichi (1873-1948), is concerned primarily with Minobe's organ theory of the state. Miller discusses at length the continental European theories, mostly German, which exerted a formative influence on Minobe, as well as his methodology and general theory of law and the state. In addition, he treats the opposing school of constitutional thought, that of Hozumi and Uesugi, and the conflict between the 2 schools which culminated in the famous Minobe affair of 1935. In the concluding chapter, Miller first relates Minobe's activities in the immediate postwar period up to his death in 1948, and secondly, provides an "assessment" of Minobe's relationship to the issue of constitutional revision in postwar Japan. Miller's book is a revision of the 551 page doctoral dissertation he submitted under the same title to the University of California at Berkeley in 1961.

Monnier, Claude. *Les Américains et Sa Majesté l'Empereur: Étude du conflit culturel d'où naquit la constitution japonaise de 1946.* 1967. See no.1242.

Mukherjee, Asoke K. *The Japanese Political System.* 1966. See no.732.

1199 Nakasone, Yasuhirō. "Reasons for Constitutional Revision." *Contemporary Japan* 24, no.7/9:401-13 (1956)

In detailing the reasons for requiring the revision of the Japanese constitution, Nakasone points out that either democracy or pacificism must, in practice, conform with the prevailing conditions of a particular country. He notes that it may be well to remember that the Allies incorporated in the constitution their covert intention to enervate Japan with the concepts of democracy and pacifism.

1200 "The New Japanese Constitution." *Current History* 10:447-55 (May 1946)

The text of the proposed constitution made public on 6 March 1946 by the Shidehara cabinet for submission at the next session of the Diet. The draft consists of a preamble together with 95 articles organized into 11 chapters. No commentary is provided.

Nishijima, Yoshiji. "The Peace Constitution Controversy." 1963. See no. 1008.

1201 "Policy Statements by Far Eastern Commission on Japanese Constitution." *Department of State Bulletin* 16:802-3 (4 May 1947)

This policy decision outlines the Far Eastern Commission's attitudes toward the draft constitution. The commission requests SCAP to inform the Japanese government that "the Far Eastern Commission must be given an opportunity to pass upon the final draft of the constitution to determine whether it is consistent with the Potsdam Declaration and any other controlling document before it is finally approved by the Diet and becomes legally valid." The statement expresses concern that the Japanese public may have misunderstood SCAP statements and be under the impression that the draft already has the approval of the powers represented on the commission. The latter section of the report outlines what the Far Eastern Commission considers should be basic principles for a new Japanese constitution.

1202 Quigley, Harold S. "How New Is the New Japan?" *Virginia Quarterly Review* 33:17-27 (Winter 1957)

Working from the premise that democracy was not new to Japan with the constitution of 1947, the author, a professor emeritus at the University of Virginia and a former research consultant for the Civil Intelligence Section of SCAP, concludes that revision of the constitution will occur because it is an American document and does not truly express a Japanese interpretation of democracy. Most of the article does not specifically deal with the occupation or its policies.

1203 ———. "Japan's Constitutions: 1890 and 1947." *American Political Science Review* 41:865–74 (Oct. 1947)

A comparative analysis of Japan's 2 constitutions with emphasis on the current constitution. The analysis includes a discussion of the 2 documents, the models upon which they were based, and the attitudes of various segments of the Japanese population toward the new constitution. Special attention is devoted to the changed status of the emperor, the renunciation of war as a means of settling international disputes, civil rights provisions, parliamentary government, the repudiation of the former dualism between civilian and military cabinet members, judicial independence and the right of judicial review, provisions for local self-government, and procedures for amending the constitution.

1204 ———. "Revising the Japanese Constitution." *Foreign Affairs* 38:140–45 (Oct. 1959)

Quigley, a former research consultant to SCAP, examines a report by the Japanese Research Council into the origin, operation, and possible revision of the constitution. The following aspects are reviewed: (1) the attitude toward the emperor system; (2) the proper interpretation of Article 9, the no-war provision; (3) SCAP's intentions in writing a draft constitution; (4) General Whitney's attitude toward cabinet acceptance of the draft; and (5) SCAP's authority to prepare a draft.

1205 Reid, Ralph Waldo Emerson. *Post War Constitutional Reform in Japan, 1945–1947*. Ph.D. dissertation, Harvard Univ., 1949. 861p.

This study consists of an historical treatment of the drafting process of the postwar constitution, an extensive summary and analysis of its contents, comparisons with the Meiji Constitution, and a discussion of potential constitutional, political, and social problems facing Japan. The appendix contains the texts of various documents relevant to the constitutional reform process, from the Potsdam Declaration to postwar legislation.

Available at the Harvard University Archives, Widener Library, Cambridge, Mass.

The Reminiscences of Cyrus H. Peake. 1961. See no.44f.

The Reminiscences of Joseph Gordon. 1961. See no.44o.

1206 Röhl, Wilhelm. *Die japanische Verfassung*. Frankfort: Metzner, 1963. 273p. (Die Staatsverfassungen der Welt, 4)

Intended to provide the German reader with an introduction to the postwar Japanese constitution, the author presents an historical review of the document's origins, discusses the efforts of various political groups to change the constitution, and examines some of its most controversial provisions. The study includes an annotated translation of portions of the constitution as well as a number of useful appendixes (all in German), among them the text of the Potsdam Declaration and various drafts of proposed constitutional revisions.

———. *Fremde Einflüsse in modernen japanischen Recht*. 1959. See no. 1291.

Rosinger, Lawrence K. "Rightist Victory Must Not Act as Break on Japanese Democracy." 1946. See no.1396.

1207 Rowe, David Nelson. "The New Japanese Constitution." *Far Eastern Survey* pt.1, 16:13–17 (29 Jan. 1947); pt.2, 16:30–34 (12 Feb. 1947)

The various ways in which political reforms could be implemented in Japan and the significantly new features of the postwar constitution are discussed in this 2-part article. In part one, the preparation of the postwar constitution is cited as an example of the difficulty involved in developing satisfactory reforms. Clarification of wartime and immediate postwar American thinking concerning the principles to be incorporated into the new constitution is coupled with an examination of the actions of General MacArthur and of SCAP personnel who prepared the constitution and forced Japanese acceptance of it. The dissatisfaction of the Yoshida government with the constitution and its hesitancy to accept the document are regarded as indications of the Japanese failure to have guilty feelings about the war. In part 2, some of the provisions of the postwar constitution are compared and contrasted with those of the Meiji Constitution. These include the ones dealing with: (1) the imperial system; (2) the shift of sovereignty from the emperor to the people; (3) the composition and powers of the Diet; (4) the provisions for a civilian cabinet; (5) the renunciation of war and armed forces; and (6) the strengthening of the autonomy of local governments. Rowe's observations lead him to conclude that the constitution is necessary as a foundation for long-range political reeducation, but he notes that the creation of a new constitution should not be misconstrued as a sign of rapid or permanent change in Japanese attitudes.

Rōyama, Masamichi. "Prospects of Constitutional Democracy in Japan." 1954. *See* no.745.

1208 Satō, Isao. "Future Prospects of Constitutional Revision." *Journal of Social and Political Ideas in Japan* 1, no.2:11–14 (Aug. 1963)

In an article translated from the January 1962 issue of *Sekai*, Satō discusses the question of constitutional revision in Japan. He reviews past periods when constitutional revision was discussed and claims that at no time was the public fully informed about the issues at hand. Hence, he calls for a genuine public discussion on this question perhaps in the form of an election. He also urges the government's Commission on the Constitution to include views of those political parties not represented on that commission.

1209 Satō, Tatsuo. *The Origin and Development of the Draft Constitution of Japan*. Tokyo: Foreign Affairs Assn. of Japan, 1957. 55p. Reprinted from *Contemporary Japan* pt.1, 24, no.4/6:175–99 (1956); pt.2, 24, no.7/9:371–400 (1956)

Satō traces the process by which a constitution was drafted in postwar Japan. He explains the establishment and functioning of the "Matsumoto Committee," which was formed to discuss constitutional revision independent of SCAP control. Two drafts by the committee, based on the principles of imperial sovereignty, increased cabinet power, cabinet responsibility to the Diet, and strengthened civil rights, are discussed; the rejection of these drafts by General MacArthur and the subsequent preparation of a model draft by SCAP are analyzed. The presentation to the Japanese government and the negotiations concerning disputed points which occurred prior to publication of the draft and its submission to the Diet are also discussed. Difficulties involved in translation and pressure by SCAP for Japanese adoption of the draft are noted. The process of deliberation and amendment which occurred in both houses of the Diet is analyzed and questions regarding the locus of sovereignty and the nature of the national polity (*kokutai*) are highlighted. Complete texts of the original MacArthur draft and the final constitution are appended.

1210 Scalapino, Robert Anthony. "The Japanese Diet Today." *Parliamentary Affairs* 5:347–55 (Summer 1952)

After discussing the flaws in the Meiji Constitution which the author considers basically authoritarian, Scalapino describes the changes which the occupation brought to the Japanese Diet. Because they were borrowed to some degree from American institutions, the nature of the Supreme Court, the relation between the upper and lower houses of the

Diet, and the committee system are all unclear. Despite uncertainty about how these problems will be worked out, the author has "cautious hope" for the future of parliamentarianism in Japan.

1211 Shimizu, Nozomu. "Die Entwicklung der japanischen Verfassung seit 1946." *Öffentliche Verwaltung* 11:401–8 (June 1962)

Shimizu begins this article by pointing out that the postwar constitution has been a controversial document even though it has gone unchanged through the first 15 years of its existence. He then focuses his discussion on 3 important topics—(1) the emperor system and popular sovereignty; (2) Article 9 and the question of Japanese rearmament; and (3) the activities of the cabinet's Commission on the Constitution headed by Professor Takayanagi—and describes the issues surrounding each of them. Throughout his presentation, Shimizu provides the reader with the results of polls showing Japanese attitudes on such matters as the best type of defense for Japan, the advisability of rearming, and the role of the emperor. He also makes frequent comparisons between the Meiji and postwar constitutions in order to point out major differences between them.

The author, a faculty member at Waseda University, served as visiting professor at Bonn University at the time he prepared this article for publication.

Sissons, David C. S. "The Pacifist Clause of the Japanese Constitution: Legal and Political Problems of Rearmament." 1961. *See* no.1009.

1212 Sugihara, Yasuo. "The Control of the Constitutionality of Laws under the Constitution of Japan." *Hitotsubashi Journal of Law and Politics* 2:1–13 (Apr. 1963)

Sugihara's study focuses on Article 81 of the postwar constitution, which stipulates that the Supreme Court is the court of last resort with the power to determine the constitutionality of any law, order, regulation, or official act. He discusses the various theoretical and legal questions which have arisen in connection with the interpretation of this constitutional provision including (1) the type of system provided for in Article 81; (2) the organs which are to exercise the power of control over the constitutionality of laws; (3) limits upon the control of the constitutionality of laws; and (4) the effects of a court decision that a particular law is unconstitutional.

Supreme Commander for the Allied Powers. Monograph 8. *Constitutional Revision, 1945–December 1951.* 1952. *See* no.290.

———. Monograph 12. *Development of Legislative Responsibilities, 1945–October 1950.* 1952. *See* no.294.

1213 Tabata, Shinobu. "The Development of the Separation of Powers in Japan." *Doshisha Law Review* international ed. no.3:13–22 (1958)

Tabata Shinobu, professor of constitution and political science at Doshisha University, discusses the introduction of the concept of the separation of powers into Japan during the early Meiji period and, by comparing various aspects of the Meiji and postwar constitutions, shows how this concept has been incorporated into Japanese law. He points out that the new constitution provides the Japanese people as a whole with considerable sovereignty and a wide range of political and other fundamental rights, and he indicates how the Diet has been able to enhance its authority vis-à-vis other governmental bodies during the postwar era.

1214 ———. "Two Treatises on Japanese Constitution: 1. The Japanese Constitution and World Peace. 2. Revision of the Japanese Constitution, Especially of the Peace Clause." *Doshisha Law Review* international ed. no.1:23–30 (1956)

In this 2-part article, Tabata of Doshisha University discusses the significance of Article 9 (the peace clause renouncing war) and criticizes those people who seek to revise the new constitution in order to permit Japanese rearmament.

1215 Tagami, Jōji. "Some Problems on the Constitution of Japan." *Annals of the Hitotsubashi Academy* 1:147–62 (Apr. 1951)

In reviewing the provisions of the old and new constitutions, Tagami points out certain concepts and ordinances in the new constitution that prevent debate or revision.

1216 Takayanagi, Kenzō. "Post-war Democratization in Japan: The Constitution." *International Social Science Journal* 13, no.1:7–20 (1961)

A law professor and chairman of the cabinet's Commission on the Constitution, the author participated in the 1946 Diet deliberations over its ratification. In this article, he discusses some of the major political problems arising under the new constitution. They include the problems of interpreting the Bill of Rights, determining the Head of State, and the role of parliamentarianism in postwar Japan. Takayanagi also examines Article 9, which he considers a "lofty ideal," and confirms Prime Minister Shidehara as the originator of the concept.

1217 Takeshita, K. Lillian. "Recent Works on the New Japanese Constitution." U.S. Library of Congress. *Quarterly Journal of Current Acquisitions* 10:143–46 (May 1953)

The author, who is assigned to the Orientalia Division of the Library of Congress, outlines the more than 50 works received by the Library of Congress which were written by Japanese authors concerning the new constitution. A brief sketch of the constitution is given at the beginning and end of the article.

1218 Ukai, Nobushige. "Constitutional Trends and Developments." *Annals of the American Academy of Political and Social Science* 308:1–9 (Nov. 1956)

Ukai examines the question, What are the real political implications of the revisionist tendencies since independence? In order to answer this question he compares the 1947 Japanese constitution with the constitution of 1889 in terms of 3 principles which differ radically in the 2 documents. They are popular sovereignty, renunciation of war, and fundamental human rights. He then comments on the constitutional revisions which were considered in 1948 and 1949 and discusses the movement to revise the constitution after independence. He outlines the reasons for the desire to revise the constitution stated in the draft proposals of the Constitution Investigation Committee of the Liberal party dated 5 November 1954. In considering the political significance of the postindependence revisionists, the author summarizes their plans under 3 headings: Diet over the people, cabinet over the Diet, and emperor over the cabinet. Ukai presents an evaluation of the proposals for revision and concludes with comments on the future of the constitution.

1219 ———. "The Individual and the Rule of Law under the New Japanese Constitution." *Northwestern University Law Review* 51:733–34 (Jan./Feb. 1957)

After noting that the postwar constitutional reforms were in line with the trends toward greater freedom characteristic of Japan's modern political history, Ukai contrasts the rule of law concept adopted by the new constitution from Anglo–American law with the German *Rechtsstaat* principle espoused during the Meiji period. He concedes that the Meiji Constitution did contain some guarantees of personal rights but states that it tried to restrict those freedoms according to the will of the state. In contrast, the postwar constitution provides firmer as well as more extensive guarantees and provides for the invalidation of legislative and administrative actions which are contrary to various constitutional provisions. A full third of the rights which are specified in the new constitution guarantee the personal liberty of individuals from government excesses—a particularly significant matter in light of the cruel and arbitrary manner in which the prewar government had wielded its power and had encroached upon personal freedom. Furthermore, in view of the fact that the police had commonly used torture in order to obtain confessions, it is noteworthy that the new constitution forbids the infliction of torture by any public officer and provides guarantees against self-incrimination. Japan lacks a liberal tradition which is as strong as that of the United States, however, and it therefore will be important that the Japanese people take appropriate steps to insure that the new constitutional provisions are fully carried out.

1219a Wagatsuma, Sakae. "Guarantee of Fundamental Human Rights under the Japanese Constitution." *Washington Law Review* 26, no.2:145–65 (May 1951)

Wagatsuma, a professor of law at Tokyo University, first describes the Meiji Constitution's provisions for the guarantee of human rights and the major defects in both the machinery of political justice and the police system which frequently enabled the government to infringe upon many of the rights actually enjoyed by Japanese citizens. He then outlines the guarantee of human rights according to chapter 3 of the new constitution and describes in general terms the legislative reforms effected to implement it. While not greatly enlarging the sphere of guaranteed rights, the author states, the postwar constitution guarantees them as "rights which are inviolable even in accordance with law" rather than merely as "rights which cannot be restricted except in accordance with law." Under the Meiji Constitution, he continues, individual rights often were violated primarily because of the poor implementation of existing guarantees. In contrast, the Japanese people are now constitutionally permitted to sue the state for damage suffered through illegal acts of public officials; the Supreme Court has the power to pass upon the constitutionality of all laws and ordinances; the code of criminal procedure has been thoroughly revised in order to improve the existing machinery of criminal justice; and the police system has undergone drastic changes affecting the nature of its activities and its authority. Wagatsuma concludes with a discussion of the Japanese people's rights of subsistence and shows how such postwar legislation as the land reform and directives for the dismemberment of the *zaibatsu* have had a positive impact in this regard.

1220 Ward, J. M. "A New Constitution for Japan." *Australian Outlook* 1:7–16 (Sept. 1947)

This article discusses the origin and content of the new constitution and its degree of acceptance by the Japanese. Ward analyzes in detail the differences between the constitutions of 1889 and 1947. Given the evident lack of enthusiasm for it which he finds among Japanese politicians, he also speculates on the future of the latter once the occupation comes to an end. He concludes that "to regard this constitution of a few months' standing as likely to be confirmed by general satisfaction with its provisions is quite unjustified" and "that no set of institutions can guarantee liberty in a society where the foundations of liberty are weak."

1221 Ward, Robert Edward. "The Commission on the Constitution and Prospects for Constitutional Change in Japan." *Journal of Asian Studies* 24, no.3:401–29 (May 1965)

In this essay on the postwar constitution, Ward discusses the present status of the revisionist movement and some of the changes that have been advocated in order to explain why there is considerable Japanese sentiment for constitutional revision but no accompanying formal government effort to achieve it. He first notes that strong opposition to the new constitution goes back to the early days of the occupation and was found among people in high political circles who in public posed as its official sponsors. He then discusses the steps that led to the establishment in 1956 of the Commission on the Constitution (*Kempō Chōsaki*), the membership of this commission, and some of the significant disagreements and rifts among its members as well as major areas of consensus. Ward also summarizes the recommendations of the revisionists, who comprised the majority of the commission's membership, with respect to such matters as the position of the emperor, the rights and duties of the people, demilitarization, local self-government, and the amendment process. In discussing the nature of the commission's final report (submitted in 1964) and its implications, the author speculates on the report's political consequences and points out the major legal and political problems that confront the proponents of revision. Barring a serious economic depression or a widespread resurgence of nationalism, he concludes, the immediate prospects for constitutional change are very limited.

1222 ———. "The Constitution and Current Japanese Politics." *Far Eastern Survey* 25, no.4:49–58 (Apr. 1956)

This analysis of Japanese political trends during the immediate postoccupation period focuses upon the broad issue of constitutional revision. The author notes the controversy surrounding the constitution since its promulgation and the desire of its critics for changes that would bring it into accord with Japanese political traditions, ideals, or practices. He then analyzes 4 major bases for revision advocated by the conservatives within the country: (1) the alien authorship of the constitution, a fact substantiated by the disclosure and publication in 1954 of the complete and official text of the MacArthur draft, upon which the present constitution is based; (2) the issue of the emperor's proper legal and theoretical role within the state and its variance with present constitutional provisions; (3) the extremely controversial issue of national defense and rearmament and the limitations imposed by Article 9; and (4) the need for an overall revision of Japan's administrative structure, which would increase the cabinet's power and the centralization of authority at the expense of the Diet and local autonomy. In concluding his essay, the author first discusses some of the legislative obstacles that stand in the way of achieving revision and then predicts that the issue of constitutional revision will continue to be prominent in Japanese politics and that its chances appear to be excellent in the long run.

1223 ———. "The Origins of the Present Japanese Constitution." *American Political Science Review* 50:980–1010 (Dec. 1956)

In a comprehensive discussion of the origins of Japan's new constitution, the author divides his material into 5 general sections. The introductory section briefly discusses possible international implications of the fact that the constitution had alien authors—i.e., SCAP staff members. The author also stresses the need for Americans to know the actual facts of the matter in so far as they can be determined. The second section includes a consideration of the terms upon which Japan surrendered to the Allied powers, which determined the subsequent legal rights of the Allies "to control and impose reform" on Japan. There is a description of the initial steps of SCAP and the Japanese government to formulate a new constitution, and the roles of both parties are analyzed until 1 February 1946, when "developments took a new and surprising turn." Section 3 is an attempt to reconstruct events that are extremely difficult to verify and the author emphasizes the fact that conclusions must remain tentative. Nonetheless, there is a careful analysis of changes and developments within the SCAP organization after 1 February 1946, as well as a consideration of SCAP's rivalries with the Far Eastern Commission and other international agencies and a considered estimate of the roles of the Department of State and the interdepartmental agency known as the State–War–Navy Coordinating Committee which had some bearing on the turn of events. Section 4 emphasizes the dominating role of the Government Section of SCAP in preparing the draft constitution, subsequent meetings with Japanese government officials, and the various complex procedures which took place before the constitution was finally adopted. This section contains much detailed information on various versions considered with differences and similarities carefully pointed out. The final section provides a brief summary of the adoption of the new constitution and the author emphasizes the external and internal importance to Japan of the formulation of this constitution. In the final paragraphs he considers what effects the manner in which the constitution was formulated might have on future Japanese political developments and on U.S.-Japanese relations. He concludes that SCAP played far too dominant a role in the formulation of the constitution and that, "In retrospect, one can only wish that the Japanese, with advice and guidance of a more open and far less compulsive sort, had been permitted to work out their own Constitution over a suitable period of time."

1224 Williams, Justin. "The Japanese Diet under the New Constitution." *American Political Science Review* 42:927-39 (Oct. 1948)

This article presents a detailed appraisal of the Diet Law, describing the events preceding its passage by the imperial Diet on 19 March 1947, the reaction on the part of various influential members of the Diet to the bill, and the nature of the Diet Law's provisions. The author considers that there are 41 radically changed provisions of the new law and cites several practices and procedures that were formerly imposed on the Diet which have been omitted from the new law. Examples of such practices include the division of the houses into sections, prorogation of the houses, and restrictions on petitions. Finally, the author considers in detail the numerous new aids, devices, and facilities allowed by the new law, such as the establishment of the franking privilege for members of the Diet, the establishment of standing committees, and beneficial changes in the methods of handling bills. He concludes with a general comparison of the former Law of the Houses and the new Diet Law.

1225 ———. "Making the Japanese Constitution: A Further Look." *American Political Science Review* 59:665-79 (Sept. 1965)

This reexamination of the making of the postwar constitution by a former chief of the Legislative Division of the Government Section, General Headquarters, SCAP challenges the views of several American scholars and the findings of the Japanese Commission on the Constitution. The author criticizes those who believe that MacArthur was instrumental in devising either the substance or the procedure of a radical plan for incorporating Western political philosophy in the revised constitution, that he schemed against the Moscow Agreement's provisions regarding the constitution-making prerogatives of the Far Eastern Commission, that he contravened American policy by preparing a model constitution, and that he imposed an alien form of government upon the Japanese. Williams argues that SWNCC 228, the document on the reform of the Japanese governmental system which MacArthur received from Washington in January 1946, stipulated that Japan was to receive a Western-style constitution. He asserts that MacArthur obeyed both the spirit and the letter of his orders on constitutional change and that the U.S. government was determined to prevent the Far Eastern Commission from obstructing him in his task. Without a model, the author continues, Japan's conservative leaders would have been unable to agree upon the radical changes that were demanded of them. Finally, Williams asserts that the Japanese people freely and openly accepted the draft constitution, which their elected representatives had approved, as a direct consequence of Yoshida's persuasive appeal to public opinion.

1226 Yamada, Y. "The New Japanese Constitution." *International and Comparative Law Quarterly* 4:197-206 (Apr. 1955)

The author, then assistant professor of administrative law at Kobe University, writes about the new Japanese constitution. He first describes the 2 guiding principles of that document—pacificism and democratic government—and the ways in which these ideas are embodied in specific articles. He then touches upon the questions of sovereignty, judicial review, and the separation of powers.

1227 Yokota, Kisaburō. "Sovereignty under the New Constitution." *Contemporary Japan* 16:134–47 (Apr./June 1947)
This article attempts to define the meaning of the concept of sovereignty under the new constitution. Through an analysis of the use of the term in the preamble and Article 1 of the new constitution, the author determines that sovereignty is considered to reside in the people as opposed to the emperor. He analyzes and refutes the position of those conservatives in the government who propose that the concept of sovereignty is solely a Western one not applicable to Japan and insist that the principle of *kokutai* is more relevant.

THE IMPERIAL SYSTEM

One of the most difficult and thorny problems confronting the Allies upon Japan's surrender was the question of what to do about the emperor—first, in a short-term sense, should he be forced to abdicate; tried as Japan's foremost war criminal; or retained in office and exploited as a means of insuring Japan's peaceable compliance with the terms of surrender? and second, in a long-term sense, what, if anything, should be done about the future of the imperial system; should it be discarded or retained; and, if the latter, what status and power should attach to it? A lively controversy developed on these scores both in the United States and elsewhere. It is described in the following literature. The interested reader will find that some of the entries in the sections on presurrender planning (p.34 and 71) relate to this matter, as do others in the section on general materials (p.113), and the section on religion (p.694).

"Advocate of Plague." 1950. *See* no. 1045.

Aiso, John F. "Japan's Military System Must Be Crushed." 1943. *See* no.63.

1228 Allen, Lafe Franklin. "Ex-God of Japan." *Forum* 110:135–38 (Sept. 1948)
The new role of the emperor of Japan in the postwar period is informally discussed, and the author emphasizes its striking contrast to his position in the period before the occupation. There is a brief consideration of particular changes made by the new constitution in the emperor's status and responsibilities. The article concludes with a description of his subjects' various attitudes towards their emperor, ranging from their former reverence to complete repudiation.

1229 Baker, Alonzo Lafayette. *The Influence of the Divine Emperor Doctrine upon Japan.* Ph.D. dissertation, Univ. of Southern California, 1948. 421p. (Abstracted in Univ. of Southern California. *Abstracts of Dissertations . . . 1948.* p.147–50)
The extent to which the doctrine of a divine emperor influenced the course of Japanese history from the Meiji Restoration to the end of World War II is examined, and the functions of the educational system and state Shinto, 2 bulwarks of the imperial institution, are emphasized. Although Baker emphasizes the role of this doctrine in prewar Japan, he also briefly examines efforts by the occupation to weaken its influence and discusses SCAP's orders to disestablish state Shinto, humanize the emperor, reduce Japan's war potential, decentralize *zaibatsu* groups, and democratize the general political structure. He concludes that although the Allied powers have undertaken commendable reform policies and achieved considerable progress in 2 and a half years, the occupation must

continue for several decades "if a resurgent oligarchy is not to assume power again."

1230 Ball, William Macmahon. "Emperor and Government in Japan." *Australian Outlook* 2, no.2:67–77 (June 1948)

A chapter from Ball's book, *Japan: Enemy or Ally?* (1949) (no.535), which supports the decision to retain the emperor despite the risks involved. Hirohito, the author argues, was not a completely helpless pawn before the war and the occupation must purge the imperial system of the militarism and superstition that envelope it. Even a constitutional emperor can be manipulated by "feudal" interests. Finally, Ball suggests that the Diet and cabinet are not very powerful and that the "feudal" bureaucracy must be reformed if Japan is to become truly democratic.

1231 Bayles, William. "Hirohito." *American Mercury* 63:278–85 (Sept. 1946)

This article, based on Bayles' impressions during a tour of Japan as an official observer for the U.S. War Department, discusses the emperor as the keystone of Japan's politico-social structure. Bayles points out that he finds no proof that Hirohito's power is waning, rather he seems to be stronger than ever before.

Bergamini, David. *Japan's Imperial Conspiracy*. 1971. See no.1048a.

Bisson, Thomas A. "Japan's Strategy of Revival." 1945. See no.133.

1231a Brewer, F. M. "Emperor of Japan." *Editorial Research Reports* v.2 1945: 121–38 (14 Aug. 1945)

Divided into 3 sections, this report is a straightforward, factual account designed primarily for journalists who are expected to be writing about the subject. Part 1, entitled "The Allies and the God-Emperor of Japan," discusses the Allied terms of surrender accepted by Japan, conflicts of opinion among Allied statesmen on the treatment of the emperor, and American policy on the emperor between 1941 and 1945. Part 2 describes the place of the emperor in Japanese life, focusing on the mythological basis of the god-emperor tradition, the history of the imperial institution, and emperor worship in twentieth century Japan. Part 3—"The Emperorship and a New Japan"—in turn examines some of the obstacles to democratic tendencies in Japan, methods by which the Japanese people could adopt a new constitution under which the emperor's role would be limited, and the views of such men as Sun Fo, Owen Lattimore and John Maki who have been advocating the abolition of the imperial institution in Japan.

1231b Brown, Allan Robert. *The Figurehead Role of the Japanese Emperor: Perception and Reality*. Ph.D. dissertation, Stanford Univ., 1971. 283p. (Abstracted in *Dissertation Abstracts International* 32:5867A [1972]: University Microfilms order no.72-11,514)

Through a survey of general and scholarly publications, an analysis of relevant documents, and a series of interviews, Brown attempts to determine the nature of the American image of the emperor's role with particular reference to its perception within policy making circles. An effort is then made to trace the evolution of the decision, made during the course of presurrender planning, to retain both the imperial system as an institution and Hirohito as emperor after the war. The nature of the American image is thus examined within the context of an actual policy decision. This role perception is then compared with the reality presented by the record of the emperor's actual participation in the political process that resulted in Japan's decision to go to war. In his conclusions, Brown indicates that the American image of the emperor was not entirely consistent with political reality, for Hirohito's role had been defined by too many people in greatly oversimplified terms and had been too literally limited. The dissertation also suggests that the emperor possessed a greater degree of personal influence than that for which the perception of his "figurehead" role had allowed.

"Chinese Views on Japan's Post-war Government." 1944. See no.164a.

Council on Foreign Relations. *Problems of the Peace Settlement with Japan.* 1944. See no.70.

1232 Craemer, Alice R. "Shall We Retain the Japanese Emperor? Yes!" *Forum* 104:144, 146–50 (Oct. 1945)

After a comprehensive description of the role of the emperor in Japan from the twelfth century until the end of World War II, the author sets forth reasons why, in her opinion, the Allies are justified in retaining the emperor as the titular head of Japan. There is an analysis of the institution itself and contrasted with it, a portrait of the present emperor, Hirohito, and his activities prior to and during the war. Although insisting that the decision regarding the fate of the emperor must ultimately be made by the Japanese people themselves, the author nevertheless suggests that the Allied decision was wise as well as expedient, in so far as the emperor provides the necessary stability and order within Japan at a crucial time in the nation's history.

For an article expressing the opposite viewpoint on this subject, see Mary Katharine Strong's "Shall We Retain the Japanese Emperor? No!" (no.1257) in the same issue of *Forum*.

1233 Crane, Burton. "Educating a Prince." *New York Times Magazine* p.28–30 (1 Dec. 1946)

In this human interest story, one of the *Times'* Tokyo correspondents reports on his visit to the Peers School (Gakushuin) where he observed how Crown Prince Akihito is being educated. He relates several anecdotes which show how well the crown prince is adapting to student life. He sees Akihito as a serious student aware of his future responsibilities.

Embree, John F. *The Japanese Nation: A Social Survey.* 1945. See no.71a.

"Far Eastern Melting Pot." 1945. See no.169a.

"The Future of Japan: An American View; A Canadian View." 1944. See no. 76c.

1234 Griggs, Thurston. "Notes on the Japanese Emperor." *American Perspective* 3:43–49 (Apr. 1949)

In reviewing the emperor concept, Griggs notes that the failure to define Hirohito's responsibility for acts executed in his name during the war obscures his present status and function. He points out that in retaining Hirohito, the Allies have inherited a powerful myth. Whether the myth can be made innocuous and supplanted by better controlled forces remains to be seen.

Heinrichs, Waldo H., Jr. *American Ambassador: Joseph C. Grew and the Development of the United States Diplomatic Tradition.* 1966. See no.81a.

1235 "Hirohito: Criminal or Puppet?" *U.S. News and World Report* 28:20–21 (17 Mar. 1950)

The occasion for this article reviewing SCAP changes in the imperial institution was the Russian demand that Hirohito be tried as a war criminal. The writer asserts that the United States has supported the imperial system in the conviction that it has become impossible again to use the emperor as a rallying point for the revival of a Japanese police state. Moreover, the emperor is viewed as an important symbol of the unity of the Japanese people.

1236 Holtom, Daniel Clarence. "The 'New' Emperor." *Far Eastern Survey* 15:69–71 (13 Mar. 1946)

In an article written prior to the issuance of the new constitution, the author discusses the necessity of drastically restricting the authority of the emperor in order to achieve the occupation's goal of a stable democratic society. He advocates changes in the terminology referring to the emperor, destruction of his powers through thorough revision of the constitution, abolition of the Imperial House Law and the enactment of laws for commoners and the imperial family alike, the drafting of a new law of succession, and the appropriation of former Imperial Household property for public use. The author criticizes the mild changes regarding the emperor's powers that were purported to be effected in the first Japanese drafts of a new constitution and insists that fundamental changes be made.

Horton, Douglas. "The Emperor and Democracy in Japan." 1946. *See* no.434.

"Ill-Starred Defenders of War Criminals." 1950. *See* no.1065a.

1237 Ishida, Takeshi. "Popular Attitudes toward the Japanese Emperor." *Asian Survey* 2:29–39 (Apr. 1962)

In tracing changes in popular attitudes toward the emperor in postwar Japan, Ishida points out that there is a fundamental imbalance between the centralization and stabilization of political power in Japan on the one hand, and the lack of a unifying, broadly accepted value system on the other. The existence of this vacuum in the value system is one of the reasons why the vague and emotional symbolism of the emperor can still find support.

1238 Jones, George E. "Hirohito: The Man and the Emperor." *New York Times Magazine* p.10–11, 54–55 (23 Sept. 1945)

The author as the first American newsman invited to visit the Imperial Palace grounds gives his impressions of the emperor's environment and his role in Japanese life. He sees the emperor as an introvert isolated from the people over whom he holds spiritual authority but who, in his symbolic role, may hold the key to Japan's future and peace in Asia. The author reports that informed Japanese admit that the emperor was misled by the military. He notes that the people regard him as the ruler who brought peace to Japan. The author concludes that the occupation authorities must deal firmly with the emperor but at the same time must work to explain this unique institution to the American people. The occupation's aim must be to humanize the role of the emperor, not to try him as a war criminal.

Kawai, Kazuo. "Sovereignty and Democracy in the Japanese Constitution." 1955. *See* no.1189.

1238a ———. "The Divinity of the Japanese Emperor." *Political Science* (Wellington, N.Z.) 10, no.2:3–14 (Sept. 1958)

Kawai seeks to determine whether the Japanese people on the whole have accepted the new concept of the emperor propagated by the occupation authorities. He first explains that for most Japanese, the "divinity" of the emperor had merely meant that greater sanctity was attached to the emperor's person than to any one else on account of his *ex officio* status as high priest of the nation. Accordingly, the "humanization" of the emperor did not come as a great shock to the Japanese; indeed, most people had always realized that he was a mortal being. Kawai finds, nonetheless, that the emperor's renunciation of his divinity had "some limited degree of usefulness" insofar as it emphasized the human size of his nature and accelerated the development of the rational and progressive aspects of the emperorship. While the older and less educated segments of the population still preserve the traditional attitudes towards the emperor, younger people in general accept the new conceptions, thereby guaranteeing their eventual dominance.

1239 Kobayashi, Shyōzō. "On the Emperor-as-symbol in the Constitution of Japan: Note on Its Difference from the Emperor-as-god and from the Emperor-as-human Being." *Waseda Political Studies* no.6:25–40 (1968)

Concerned with the role of the emperor in Japanese society today, the author examines the concept of the symbolic emperor and the way it differs from the concept of the emperor as held under the Meiji Constitution. Kobayashi tries to distinguish the emperor-as-symbol from the emperor-as-human being. In the course of his article, the author touches on popular opinion of the emperor, the influence of General MacArthur and the occupation, the question of sovereignty, and the role of this "new" emperor in Japanese society.

Lamott, Willis. *Nippon: The Crime and Punishment of Japan*. 1944. *See* no. 95.

1240 Lauterbach, Richard Edward. "Memo to Mrs. Vining." *New Republic* 116, no. 9:12–14 (3 Mar. 1947)
A foreign correspondent writes to the woman who has been sent to Tokyo as a private tutor to Crown Prince Akihito about Akihito's upbringing before the end of World War II and his education during the first year of the occupation.

Materials on the Trial of Former Servicemen of the Japanese Army Charged with Manufacturing and Employing Bacteriological Weapons. 1950. *See* no.1081b.

1241 Matsumoto, Tsuyoshi. "We Fight the Emperor: A Declaration of Independence by One of His Subjects Who Are Revolting against His Name." *Asia and the Americas* 45:417–20 (Sept. 1945)
A Japanese living in the United States and committed to the Allied viewpoint attempts to define his attitude toward the imperial institution and the present emperor of Japan and to suggest the future fate of the emperor. He distinguishes between the present emperor, Hirohito, whom he claims is an innocent man used by the militarists, and the imperial institution which he believes the Allies are fighting to destroy. He suggests that the emperor be given the option "to abdicate and become a common man to be judged strictly on his individual merits and demerits or remain as Emperor of Japan and be taken as fully responsible for Japan's crimes against humanity."

1242 Monnier, Claude. *Les Américains et Sa Majesté l'Empereur: Étude du conflit culturel d'où naquit la constitution japonaise de 1946.* Neuchâtel, Switzerland: Éditions de la Baconnière, 1967. 222p. (Histoire et société d'aujourd'hui)
A useful account by a Swiss scholar of the circumstances underlying the drafting and adoption of the constitution in 1946–47. Although the principal concern is with the position of the emperor, the author also provides a quite extensive description of the total process of constitutional revision including the attitudes and activities of the principal figures involved on both the American and Japanese sides, the Konoe and Matsumoto draft constitutions as well as those prepared by a variety of political parties and other groups, the state of contemporary public opinion, and the actual course of American–Japanese negotiations on this subject from the beginning of the occupation to the publication of the 5 March 1946 draft. An attempt is made to portray the entire process in an appropriate social and cultural context.

1243 Mosley, Leonard Oswald. *Hirohito, Emperor of Japan.* Englewood Cliffs, N.J.: Prentice-Hall, 1966. ix, 371p.
A journalistic and rather superficial biographical account of Emperor Hirohito from his birth in 1901 through January 1946 when he formally denied the divinity of the emperor. In 24 chapters Mosley describes the emperor's boyhood, education, relationship with his parents and brothers, daily activities, reaction to rising militarism in the 1930s, and his political role before, during, and after World War II. Chapters 20 to 24 (p.293–350) are particularly relevant to a study of the occupation of Japan. Chapter 20 describes the moves begun after May 1945 by the emperor, imperial court officials, and some cabinet members to end the war, and their development up to the time of the Potsdam Conference. Chapter 21 discusses the reaction of the emperor and other officials to the Potsdam Declaration of July 26 and the atomic bombing of Hiroshima. There is a description of the emperor's decisive role on 10 August in persuading cabinet members and imperial conference mem-

bers to accept the declaration. Chapter 22 describes the continued irresolution of the Supreme War Council concerning the acceptance of the declaration, the emperor's role in persuading them to accept it, and his subsequent public radio announcement of the surrender on 15 August. Chapter 23 describes the surrender ceremony aboard the U.S.S. *Missouri* on 2 September and MacArthur's treatment of the emperor. A final chapter analyzes the process whereby SCAP fostered the denial of the emperor's divinity. The role of General Courtney Whitney, chief of the Government Section of SCAP, is particularly stressed although it has not yet been determined whether SCAP or the Japanese initiated the emperor's renunciation of divine status. The appendixes give the texts of the Yalta Agreement, the Potsdam Declaration, Japan's first surrender offer, Japan's final note of acceptance of the Potsdam Declaration, and the Imperial Rescript of 15 August 1945.

"A New State Department Approach to the Japanese Emperor." 1944. *See* no. 104.

1243a Noble, Harold J. "Meet Busy Little Hirohito Today." *Saturday Evening Post* 219:18–19, 105 (10 Aug. 1946)

Basing his conclusions on interviews with court officials and relatives of the imperial family, Noble judges the emperor to be a "sad and lonely man." His brief visits among the people since the surrender have humanized and popularized him, but the traditions of the court and of Japanese society have isolated him as well; he had no close friends and little freedom. His situation contrasts strongly with the freedom and activity allowed other members of the royal family. Although a good case can be made for holding the emperor morally and legally responsible for the war, Noble notes, he is needed on the throne to facilitate the occupation's programs. Even if he would like to abdicate, therefore, he is doomed to his solitary existence.

1244 Oda, James S. "Hirohito's Possible Successor." *New Republic* 113:342–43 (17 Sept. 1945)

A brief description of the prewar and wartime activities of Prince Chichibu, the younger brother of the present Emperor Hirohito and a possible successor to Hirohito or regent for the crown prince. According to the author, the prince's detention during the last 2 years was due to his close ties with army extremists. He predicts that as war criminals are brought to trial in the course of the occupation, the prince's "political machinations" will be exposed.

1245 Ōkubo, Genji. *The Problems of the Emperor System in Postwar Japan: Surveyed from an Examination of Arguments on the Subject.* Tokyo: Japan Institute of Pacific Studies, 1948. 87p. (Pacific Studies series)

Ōkubo first surveys recent opinions on the legal responsibility of the emperor for the declaration of war and asserts that Hirohito's voluntary admission of his responsibility for World War II would greatly retard or defeat the "spiritual revolution of militarism." He then compares the attitudes of the different political parties towards the emperor system through an examination of the discussions on the draft constitution held in the Diet in 1946. He concludes with the belief that if the democratization of Japan is steadily pushed forward, the Japanese people will come to realize that sovereignty under the new constitution now rests with them rather than with the emperor as in the past.

1246 Packenham, Compton. "To the Japanese, the Emperor Links the Living with the Dead." *Newsweek* 31:37 (7 June 1948)

Packenham, a Tokyo bureau chief, writes about the retention of traditional ideas vis-à-vis the postwar functions of the imperial institution. The concept of *kami* is explained in terms of its relationship to the emperor and the usefulness of the imperial institution as a means for facilitating the adoption of occupation policy is emphasized. Mention is also made of the distinction between democratizing the person of the emperor and altering his position as head of the national family.

1247 Parrott, Lindesay. "At Long Last Hirohito Begins to Enjoy Life." *New York Times Magazine* p.12–13, 42–44 (12 May 1946)

This article, one of several aimed at explaining the imperial institution and the role of the emperor to the American people, shows how Hirohito has made a conscious effort to become "one of the people." Since disavowing his divinity, he has allowed himself to be photographed on vacation with his family. The author reports that Hirohito makes regular visits throughout Japan as part of the effort to democratize and humanize the role of the emperor.

1248 ———. "Mr. Hirohito Is Still the 'Sun God'." *New York Times Magazine* p.15 (22 May 1949)

Although under the new constitution the emperor's position is completely divorced from politics, the author reports that the Japanese people still regard him as something more than a symbol of national unity. There is, however, political opposition to the emperor's democratization from the extremists on both the left and right who call for his abdication. The author feels that the emperor is of great psychological importance to the Japanese and functions as a symbol, a safety valve, and a force for order.

1249 "The 'Peace-Loving' Emperor of Japan." *Amerasia* 8, no.1:6–8 (7 Jan. 1944)

The author criticizes those who advocate that the emperor be retained in order to serve as a unifying and stabilizing political force in postwar Japan. He points out that they ignore the fact that in modern Japanese history the emperor has always served as the instrument of absolutism and national chauvinism. When Allied propaganda fails to attack the imperial system, it plays directly into the hands of "the fascist leaders of Japan —both military and civilian—who rely on the power of emperor-worship to prevent the growth of a democratic movement in Japan." Accordingly, the author advocates that we stop relying upon the emperor and an autocratic system of government and recommends that we appeal instead to the common people of Japan for the necessary support in rebuilding the country after the war is over.

1250 Price, Willard. "Behind the Mask of Modern Japan." *National Geographic Magazine* 88:513–35 (Nov. 1945)

In an article concerning the imperial institution as a socioreligious phenomenon, the author estimates the institution to be of such pervasiveness and power as to make it the primary and most difficult concern of the occupation. Price relies on personal experiences to relate a series of examples and anecdotes criticizing the inculcation of the emperor myth as an aspect of political socialization through the educational system. The institution of the emperor is considered to have been the vital cog in the presurrender system because it legitimized a privileged position for the military class.

———. *Japan and the Son of Heaven.* 1945. See no.110a.

1251 ———, and John Goette. "How Long Hirohito?" *Free World* 10:40–44 (Sept. 1945)

This article consists of 2 brief reports expressing opposite views on SCAP's decision to retain the emperor of Japan. Price, arguing that the Mikado must go, suggests he should be tried as a war criminal. Alleging that "there is no place for the Emperor above, along with, or below the government of occupation," he insists that after the present emperor is removed, the question of resuming the monarchy should be left to the Japanese people to decide at the termination of the occupation. Goette, defending the Allied wisdom of preserving the imperial institution, cites various historical parallels. As an alternative, he suggests the Allied powers punish the real Japanese war lords through the offices of the emperor rather than holding their own war crimes trials.

1252 Rosinger, Lawrence K. "Hirohito's Denial of Divinity Reveals Ferment in Japan." *Foreign Policy Bulletin* 25:1–2 (11 Jan. 1946)

Two topics are briefly discussed in this article: (1) the significance of the emperor's New Year's message denying his divinity, and (2) the implications of the postponement of the Diet elections. The author cautions against interpreting the emperor's statement as positive proof of a more liberal political orientation. Rather, he views it as a shrewd and far-seeing move to reduce the restlessness of the people and build up popular confidence in his abilities as a national leader. The latter part of the article discusses the reasons why the elections have been postponed–in the author's opinion chiefly "to permit the forward looking elements in Japan to develop more strength" against the entrenched conservative parties. Finally, he cautions against excessive optimism regarding political reforms, pointing to the extremely precarious economic situation.

———. "People—Not Emperor—Hold Key to Peaceful Japan." 1944. *See* no.112.

1253 Samuels, Veronica. "Hiro-Hito, le premier souverain mortel d'une dynastie de dieux." *Historama* no.193:90–97 (Oct. 1967)

Sands, William F. "Japan's Future." 1945. *See* no.120a.

1254 Smythe, Hugh H. "The Japanese Emperor System." *Social Research* 19, no.4: 485–93 (Dec. 1952)

Smythe points to a revival of prewar attitudes towards the emperor. "A new pattern of life was introduced into the country during the six and one-half years of occupation, yet there is still a deep belief in the continued descendence of the Emperor . . . from the ancestral gods." Occupation reforms humanized the emperor, but various incidents mentioned demonstrate a return to emperor worship. This apparent inconsistency is explained in terms of the Japanese "familial state" ideology which taught that the emperor is the hereditary father of an obedient and reverent nation. This view of the nation has deep roots in Japan and cannot be easily changed.

1255 ———, and Watanabe Masaharu. "Japanese Popular Attitudes toward the Emperor." *Pacific Affairs* 26:335–44 (Dec. 1953)

This article argues that occupation efforts to "democratize" the emperor were unsuccessful. Public opinion surveys made between 1945 and 1948 show overwhelming support for the emperor system, as do interviews by Japanese sociologists and popular criticism of students who demonstrated against the emperor in 1951. The authors conclude that "the emperor is being enveloped in an atmosphere reminiscent of the past, and is on the verge of becoming once again a subject whose discussion is taboo."

1256 Soong, Norman. "Will Emperor Hirohito Abdicate?" *China Magazine* 18:42–45 (July 1948)

The author reviews various opinions concerning the abdication of the emperor. He discusses the issue of the emperor's personal and symbolic responsibility for the conduct and loss of the war and affirms that a political and moral clearing of the slate through an abdication will allow greater future freedom of action for the Japanese.

1257 Strong, Mary Katharine. "Shall We Retain the Japanese Emperor? No!" *Forum* 104:145, 150–57 (Oct. 1945)

The Allied decision to retain the emperor—even temporarily—is sharply criticized in this article. Taking the position that the emperor is the symbol of Japanese nationalism, feudalism, and aggression, the author advocates the immediate removal of this most important member of a dangerous social edifice. She emphasizes the fact that he has been and remains "the keystone of the entire Japanese religious, economic, political, and social structure" and believes that SCAP's permissive attitude toward the emperor has increased his power and strengthened his autocracy rather than having a weakening effect in accord with the general intentions of the occupation. Following this article is an English translation of the Imperial Rescript Announcing Japanese Surrender.

For an article expressing the opposite viewpoint on this subject, see Alice R. Craemer's "Shall We Retain the Japanese Emperor? Yes!" (no.1232) in the same issue of *Forum*.

1258 Suda, Ryūsuke. "The Role of the Emperor in Postwar Japan." In *Social and Economic Aspects of Japan: Seijo Gakuen Jubilee Year 1917–1967*, ed. by Uchida Naosaku and Ikeda Kōtarō. Tokyo: Economic Institute of Seijo Univ., 1967. p.221–38.

Suda Ryūsuke, associate professor of constitutional law at Seijo University, presents a brief, legal analysis of the postwar status of the imperial system. He discusses the changes wrought by the new constitution and examines the various constitutional provisions concerned with the emperor, namely (1) his derivation of power from the will of the people; (2) his role as a symbol of the state; (3) succession to the throne; (4) the obligation of the emperor to secure the advice and approval of the cabinet before acting on state matters; (5) the character of the imperial powers; (6) the emperor's right to act freely in private; and (7) democratic control of all imperial property.

Sun, Fo. "The Mikado Must Go." 1944. See no.178.

1259 Takayanagi, Kenzō. "The New Emperor System." *Japan Quarterly* 9:265–74 (July/Sept. 1962)

Formerly chairman of the Commission on the Constitution, Takayanagi writes of the way in which a new role for the emperor was created during the occupation period. He begins by tracing developments at the end of the war concerning the imperial institution. An account is given about the controversy over the retention of the emperor and the role played by General MacArthur and SCAP. Takayanagi ends by discussing the status of the emperor in present day Japan and the controversy over the kind of role he should or should not be playing.

"The Task of the Occupation Forces." 1945. See no.409.

1260 Tibesar, L. H. "Hirohito: Man, Emperor, 'Divinity'." *Review of Politics* 7: 496–504 (Oct. 1945)

Shortly after the cessation of hostilities with Japan the author discusses the personality and spiritual-political role of the emperor of Japan. He expresses the belief that the emperor was used by the ultranationalists and militarists for their own purposes and need not be held responsible for the war. He comments upon the so-called divinity of the emperor, and the fact that it was questioned by most educated Japanese years before his postwar proclamation renouncing divinity. In the concluding section, the author contends that "it was most certainly a very wise decision that prompted the Allied powers to retain the Emperor of Japan," but concludes that the occupation authorities will not be able to establish democracy in Japan until they have established the Christian concepts upon which democracy is based.

1260a Titus, David Anson. "Emperor and Public Consciousness in Postwar Japan." *Japan Interpreter* 6:182–95 (Summer 1970)

Basing his conclusions on a survey of popular attitudes toward the emperor and the imperial institution conducted in 1964, Titus finds that only a small proportion of the Japanese people still retain images of the emperor recognizably similar to those inculcated in the presurrender period. The vast majority of the respondents were aware of his new constitutional position as "symbol of the state," and only a small proportion —mostly people in the higher age brackets—chose to call him a "god manifest." The old attitude of reverence, Titus states, has been replaced either by affection or by indifference. These findings testify to "the extraordinary flexibility of the imperial institution in reshaping its own image to the needs of a 'popular' monarchy in a consumer-oriented, dynamic, 'modern' society." Such flexibility, Titus argues, has been one of the factors that has contributed to the workability of the SCAP-initiated reforms in Japan's political system.

1261 Tolischus, Otto D. "The God-Emperor: Key to a Nation." *New York Times Magazine* p.8, 32–33 (19 Aug. 1945)

This article focuses on the importance of the emperor and of emperor worship as embodied in state Shinto. The author, who was the *Times'* Tokyo correspondent before the war, explains that the emperor is the foundation of an autocratic system which might better be described as a theocracy. He claims that the Japanese spiritual world is totally different from ours; Shinto has no ethics or morality and the Japanese believe themselves to be descended from gods. After describing the beliefs and practices of Shinto, the author concludes that state Shinto or emperor worship will be the greatest block to democracy in Japan. He points out that most of the political power in Japan lies with the emperor's councilors and not with the emperor himself. His advisers use the emperor as a "divine shield" to promote their own policies. The only way to avoid future misuse of the emperor's authority, the author says, is to do away with the emperor. However, if the emperor must stay on the throne, the author suggests 2 other options. First, the Allies must make the emperor responsible for the defeat and convince the Japanese people that he was. Second, the Allies must lay a foundation for a responsible democratic government which transfers ultimate sovereignty to the people.

1261a "Transformation of Hirohito." *Christian Century* 62:1147 (10 Oct. 1945)

The editors of *Christian Century* recognize that Emperor Hirohito's visit to General MacArthur's headquarters was an unprecedented type of action from the standpoint of traditional Japanese etiquette. It is a hopeful first step, therefore, toward casting aside "the medieval mumbo-jumbo that has surrounded the Japanese throne."

1262 Tsuneishi, Warren Michio. *The Japanese Emperor: A Study in Constitutional and Political Change.* Ph.D. dissertation, Yale Univ., 1960. 307p. (Abstracted in *Dissertation Abstracts* 27:1884A [1966]; University Microfilms order no. 66-12,883)

In this examination of the constitutional and political status of the emperor under the Meiji and the postwar constitutions, the author first analyzes the emperor's position with respect to civilian and military elements in the prewar and wartime governments. He then discusses the changes affecting the emperor brought about by SCAP, such as the destruction of the dual power structure of civilian and military elites, the elevation of the cabinet to executive supremacy, the humanization of the emperor, and the establishment of popular rather than monarchical sovereignty. In the final section of the dissertation, the author emphasizes the emperor's loss of legitimacy in the postwar period.

U.S. Dept. of State. *The Conferences at Cairo and Teheran, 1943.* 1961. See no.198.

1263 "USSR Motives on Trying Emperor of Japan Questioned." *Department of State Bulletin* 22:244 (13 Feb. 1950)

State Department officials respond here to the Soviet proposals of 1 February 1950 that the emperor and several former generals be tried by a special military court on charges of crimes against humanity. They state that such a request is in direct contradiction to the Far Eastern Commission decision of 3 April 1946 to exempt the emperor from indictment as a war criminal. The suggestion is made that the Soviet proposals are intended to divert public attention from the failure of the Soviet government to explain the fate of 370,000 still-missing Japanese prisoners of war.

1264 Vining, Elizabeth Gray. *Windows for the Crown Prince*. Philadelphia: Lippincott, 1952. 320p. Abridged version published in the *Reader's Digest* 61:141-68 (Oct. 1952).

Vining provides a detailed account of her personal experiences in Japan from October 1946 to the end of 1950. During this interval she served as tutor to the crown prince and was in constant contact with both Japanese elite and SCAP personnel. Observations concerning individuals within these groups and more general comments and evaluations concerning a variety of SCAP policies provide a conspicuous but secondary component of her reminiscences.

1264a ———. *Quiet Pilgrimage*. Philadelphia: Lippincott, 1970. vi, 410p.

This autobiography deals extensively with the author's experiences in Japan from late 1946 through December 1950 —the years when she was employed by the Japanese government as a tutor to Crown Prince Akihito. In *Windows for the Crown Prince* (no.1264), a book for which she is well known, Mrs. Vining focused her attention on matters concerning the crown prince. By way of contrast, part 3 (p.189-293) of this particular work provides extensive information about her personal life in occupied Japan and her own contacts with a number of important personalities other than the prince. Mrs. Vining begins her account with an explanation of how Emperor Hirohito's request that the Education Mission headed by Dr. George Stoddard seek an American tutor for Prince Akihito eventually led to her going to Japan. She then describes the home in which she lived for four years, her relations with the Imperial Household, her teaching in Koganei (a western suburb of Tokyo) where she taught the prince both in private lessons and together with his classmates at the Gakushuin (Peers' School), her numerous meetings respectively with the emperor and General MacArthur, and her summers at the mountain resort of Karuizawa. Her remarks range from comments on the deprivations that most Japanese had to endure after the war to brief assessments of the occupation itself. The two chapters which she devotes to Emperor Hirohito and General MacArthur and her opinions of these men are particularly noteworthy.

1265 "What Future for Japan?" *New Republic* 113:270-71 (3 Sept. 1945)

The author of this editorial discusses some aspects of the treatment of a defeated Japan, emphasizing the controversy in government circles as to what should be the treatment of the emperor. Acknowledging the fact that the issue is a complex one, the author protests against the efforts of those seeking to whitewash Hirohito and insists that he should "accept his fair share of the responsibility for the war crimes in which he participated."

CHANGES IN THE LEGAL SYSTEM

The enactment of a fundamentally new and democratic constitution required extensive changes in the system of supporting laws and, in particular, the basic revision of the six codes of Japanese law. This revision was a major undertaking that has so far received insufficient scholarly attention abroad. The relevant literature is described below.

1266 Abe, Haruo. "Criminal Justice in Japan: Its Historical Background and Modern Problems." *American Bar Association Journal* 47:555-59 (June 1961)

In his address the Public Prosecutor for the Ministry of Justice outlines the system of criminal justice in Japan, describes its historical development, and discusses some of its present problems. In referring to the occupation, he asserts that SCAP's failure to pay sufficient attention to Japan's cultural and historical background at the time it was undertaking a series of drastic socio-legal reforms led to the enactment of a defective Code of Criminal Procedure. In particular, the present code suffers from a fundamental disharmony between the Continental European and the Anglo–American legal systems, which were abruptly merged upon the recommendation of the foreign legal advisers attached to SCAP's Legal Section. To support his contention, Abe cites a few of the problems with which the Japanese judiciary must presently contend.

1267 Appleton, Richard B. "Reforms in Japanese Criminal Procedure under Allied Occupation." *Washington Law Review* 24, no.4:401–30 (Nov. 1949)

Faced with the need to provide Japan with a modern system of criminal procedure which would clarify the true facts in various criminal cases and would apply as well as execute the laws equitably and speedily, the Diet enacted a new code of criminal procedure in July 1948. In addition, it passed several other laws which accomplished related reforms, among them a new juvenile law, a reformatory law, a Habeas Corpus law, and a law concerning the inquest of prosecution. All of this legislation introduced into Japan important institutions and ideas derived from the Anglo-Saxon tradition. Within the present article, Richard Appleton, an attorney in the Legislation and Justice Division of SCAP's Legal Section, clarifies the nature and objectives of these Allied-instigated reforms and provides a detailed discussion of the provisions in the new code that cover the organization and working of the criminal investigation, the indictment, the trial, and the appeals. This important and authoritative study should be read in conjunction with a succeeding article in the *Washington Law Review*, Howard Meyers' "Revisions of the Criminal Code of Japan during the Occupation" (no.1287a).

1268 Blakemore, Thomas L. "Post-war Developments in Japanese Law." *Wisconsin Law Review* no.4:632–53 (July 1947)

Although this report was written at a time when much of the occupation's legal program was still being planned, it is a careful analysis of the situation to date. The author presents a brief outline of the history of Japanese jurisprudence before World War II and then discusses changes made as a result of the occupation. The provisions of the new constitution are described and compared with those of the Meiji Constitution. Then there is a discussion of public law that covers provisions regulating the legislative, executive, and judicial branches of the national government as well as local government. Some consideration is also given to new attitudes toward government economic control and nationalization of industry. Finally, there is an analysis of changes in private law and civil liberties. In concluding, the author warns that "the basic occupational objective of democratization will be unsecured if SCAP withdraws, leaving merely the machinery for protection of civil liberties without the men who are of a mind to operate it." He suggests that real legal reform will be effected by a reorientation of the present legal profession and the development of new methods of legal education.

1269 ———, and Yazawa Makoto. "Japanese Commercial Code Revisions Concerning Corporations." *American Journal of Comparative Law* 2:12–24 (Winter 1953)

Two of the individuals involved in the occupation reforms discuss the story of the conception, enactment, content, and acceptance of major revisions in the Japanese Commercial Code. At first, they explain, SCAP paid little attention to reforming this area of Japanese law. Only in the course of implementing some advanced antitrust legislation late during the occupation period did the code come under the scrutiny of the Anti-Trust and Cartels Division of SCAP's Economic and Scientific Section. Accordingly, a committee was established in 1949 to work out appropriate revisions, and these were subsequently incorporated in a law passed by the Diet. The authors categorize the reforms into 3 major categories: (1) the rearrangement of corporate powers as between the shareholders meeting, the board of directors, and the corporate auditors; (2) the provision of new methods of attracting and inducing capital investment; and (3) the strengthening of the rights of individual shareholders. After discussing these reforms at length, they note the mixed reaction among Japanese corporations which had to implement them. Blakemore and Yazawa also point out that the draftsmanship as well as the contents of the code revisions suffered because they were prepared by only a small committee which had to work under considerable time constraints and without the benefit of general public discussion. There are clamors for the revision of the new corporation laws, the authors conclude, and some changes are likely to be made now that the occupation is over.

1270 Blakeney, Ben Bruce. "A Sketch of the Development of Japanese Law." *Japan Quarterly* 7:491–505 (Oct./Dec. 1960)

Blakeney, who served as chief defense counsel at the International Military Tribunal for the Far East, analyzes the development of Japanese law since the beginning of Japanese history. While writing about the influence of Chinese law, Blakeney concentrates upon the Japanese "native law" tradition and upon the various influences of Western law. The largest section of the article deals with the 1232–1867 period of "feudal law." He ends his article by discussing some of the newer Western concepts of law which came in after the Meiji Restoration and during the Allied occupation of Japan.

1271 Coleman, Rex. "Japanese Family Law." *Stanford Law Review* 9:132–54 (Dec. 1956)

This article was expressly prepared to help American attorneys familiarize themselves with the status of marriage and divorce under existing Japanese law in order that they could handle domestic law cases involving returning servicemen who had been married or divorced while in Japan. The article is of value as well to specialists working on the occupation in view of its information on SCAP-initiated changes in the Civil Code that affected Japanese family law. Coleman first describes the nature of Japan's postwar legal system, then compares relevant provisions in the prewar and postwar Civil Code under the headings (1) marriage and its formation, (2) annulment, (3) the effect of marriage on matrimonial property, and (4) divorce. He points out how influential Japanese custom and tradition continue to be in the area of marriage and divorce and notes, among other items, various provisions that reflect the idea of female equality which the reformers were seeking to foster. In concluding, Coleman warns the reader to remember "that the changes imposed by the 1948 Code were to a large extent the reforms of American supervisors. Provisions which are not suited to the Japanese social order may well be exchanged for others more akin to the terms of the old Code."

1272 *The Criminal Code of Japan, as Amended in 1947, and the Minor Offenses Law of Japan.* Tr. by Thomas L. Blakemore. Tokyo: Nippon Hyōronsha, 1950. v, 186p. Text in Japanese and English.

Part 1 of this publication contains the text in both English and Japanese of the Criminal Code of Japan (Statute no.45 of 1907), the principle repository of substantive law in the criminal field. The code was amended in 1947 by the deletion of provisions for several crimes, by an increase in certain penalties, and by the elimination of a number of provisions which were regarded as too unfavorable to the criminal. Part 2 provides the text of the Minor Offenses Law (Statute no.39 of 1948). This is a fresh act of legislation which replaced the Police Offenses Ordinance (Ministry of Home Affairs Ordinance no.16 of 1908), whose abolition was necessitated by its incompatibility with the spirit and provisions of the postwar constitution. There are no explanatory comments to accompany either text.

1273 De Becker, E. V. A. *The Patent, Trade Mark, Design, and Utility Model Laws of Japan.* Tokyo: Maruzen, 1949. vii, 256p.

Incorporating the minor legal changes effected during the occupation period, the present volume provides the texts of the patent, trade mark, design, and utility model laws; the law concerning patent attorneys; and the regulations for registration tax and fees. Included as appendixes are (1) The Law for the Prevention of Unfair Competition; (2) The Cabinet order of 12 August 1949 regarding the postwar disposition of industrial property rights owned by Allied nationals; and (3) an outline of probable legislation regarding Allied nationals' trade marks, based on SCAPIN 2042 of 9 September 1949.

1274 ———. "Post-war Trends in Japanese Law." *Transactions of the Asiatic Society of Japan* ser.3, 3:27–45 (Dec. 1954)

This article surveys many of the legal changes resulting from occupation reforms. After briefly stating the occupation's goals, the author reviews the postwar constitution chapter by chapter and describes different categories of ancillary laws.

1275 Fuetō, Toshio. "Japan: Revision of the New Civil Code." *American Journal of Comparative Law* 6:559–65 (Autumn 1957)

Fuetō of Yamaguchi University reports on Japanese reactions to the country's new Civil Code during the immediate postoccupation period. His study focuses on the abolition of the "family system," the legal changes that gave people more freedom in matters of marriage and divorce, and the establishment of the principle of equal succession—the primary objects of popular controversy—and he reports on field observations that he undertook to determine public sentiment towards the new code. The author notes that the greatest divergence in opinion is found between the urban and rural sectors of the population. He concludes that the code will be increasingly accepted as long as the Japanese continue to create an industrialized and urbanized society this is conducive to egalitarian and individualistic principles. Otherwise efforts to amend the revised code and to reintroduce prewar concepts may become successful.

1276 Henderson, Dan Fenno. *Conciliation and Japanese Law: Tokugawa and Modern.* Seattle: Univ. of Washington Pr., published for the Assn. for Asian Studies, 1965. 2v. (Assn. for Asian Studies, monographs and papers, 13)

This study traces the development of conciliation (or mediation) in Japan from its Tokugawa origins to its role in modern social and legal practices. The author, a practicing lawyer and political scientist, focuses on trial practice during the Tokugawa period in volume 1 of his work. Volume 2, in turn, discusses modern Japanese analogies to Tokugawa conciliation, examines statutory conciliation in Japan, and evaluates modern practices of conciliation as they have developed in formal procedural law under the postwar constitution. The second volume also contains an extensive, unannotated bibliography of Japanese- and Western-language sources and writings on modern (1868–1964) Japanese law. The entire publication represents a substantial revision of the author's doctoral dissertation which was submitted in 1955 to the University of California at Berkeley under the title "The Pattern and Persistence of Traditional Procedures in Japanese Law."

1277 Japan. Attorney General's Office. *The Constitution of Japan and Criminal Laws.* Tokyo: Japan Trade Guide Publishing Co., 1951. v, 198p.

In addition to the postwar constitution, this volume contains the texts of several of the criminal laws that either were drafted during the occupation period or that underwent substantial change at that time. These laws are as follows:

(1) The Penal Code (Law no.45 of 1907 with subsequent amendments); (2) The Code of Criminal Procedure (Law no.131 of 1948); (3) The Criminal Indemnity Law (Law no.1 of 1950); (4) The Minor Offenses Law (Law no. 39 of 1948); (5) The Juvenile Law (Law no.168 of 1948); (6) The Reformatory Law (Law no.169 of 1948); (7) The Prison Law (Law no.28 of 1908 with postwar amendments); (8) The Offenders Prevention and Rehabilitation Law (Law no.142 of 1949); (9) Law for the Immediate Aid to Offenders, etc. (Law no.203 of 1950); (10) The Rehabilitation Worker Law (Law no. 204 of 1950); (11) Law for Establishment of [the] Attorney-General's Office (Law no.193 of 17 Dec. 1947); and (12) The Public Procurator's Office Law (Law no.61 of 1947).

1278 ———. ———. *The Constitution, Penal Code, and Essential Laws for the Correction of Offenders in Japan.* Tokyo: Japan Trade Guide Publishing Co., 1950. iv, 85p.

Compiled for the 12th International Penal and Penitentiary Congress (The Hague, 1950), this volume contains the essential laws relating to the correction of offenders that were in force near the end of the occupation period. In addition to the 1947 constitution and the 1907 penal code, it includes the texts of the Prison Law of 1908, the Juvenile Law of 1948, the Reformatory Law of 1948, and the Offenders Prevention and Rehabilitation Law of 1949.

1278a ———. ———. *The Civil Code of Japan.* Tokyo: Attorney General's Office, 1949. 2v. (Codes and Statutes of Japan, nos. 4 & 5)

The text of the prewar Civil Code (Laws no.89 of 1896 and no.9 of 1898) in its amended form as accepted by the occupation authorities is presented here in an English-language translation without any accompanying commentary or annotations. A second edition of the code was brought out by the Attorney General's Office in 1951 and is identical in all respects except for the addition of the following 3 appendixes: (1) Law Concerning the Application of Laws in General (*Hōrei*) (Law no.10 of 1898); (2) The Nationality Law (Law no.147, promulgated on 4 May 1950); and (3) The Old Nationality Law (Law no.66 of 1899).

1278b ———. ———. *The Code of Criminal Procedure (Law no.131, Promulgated on July 10, 1948).* Tokyo: Attorney General's Office, 1948. ii, 125p. (Codes and Statutes of Japan, no.1)

The complete text of the code dealing with such matters as defense by counsel, the nature of acceptable evidence, trials, and the procedure for appeals.

1278c ———. ———. *The Commercial Code of Japan.* Tokyo: Japan Trade Guide Publishing Co., 1951. iv, 200p.

Complete translations of the Commercial Code of Japan, the Law on Bills, and the Law on Checks may be found in the present volume. Book 1 of the code is concerned with general provisions and Book 2 with companies. Both books were extensively amended after World War II and in the present compilation, their translations are based chiefly on those made by the Legislation and Opinion Division of the Attorney-General's Office. Book 3 deals with commercial transactions and Book 4 with maritime commerce. Both of these have undergone scarcely any amendment since 1945, and their present texts are based on the translation prepared by the Codes Translation Committee of the League of Nations Association of Japan. The Law of Bills and the Law on Checks, while independent of the Commercial Code, are incorporated in this compilation because they are important pieces of legislation having hitherto been regarded as substantially part of the Commercial Code. The laws are based respectively on the Convention Providing a Uniform Law on Bills of Exchange and Promissory Notes, 1933, and on the Convention Providing a Uniform Law on Checks, 1933. Indexes facilitate the use of the volume.

1279 ——. ——. Bureau of Civil Affairs. *Nationality Law and Other Regulations Concerned*. Tokyo: The Office, The Bureau, 1951. 28p.

1280 ——. Ministry of Finance. Bureau of Taxation. *Internal Revenue Code of Japan*. Tokyo: The Ministry, The Bureau, 1951. 1262p.

Provides the complete text in English-language translation of the following laws: income tax law, corporation tax law, accessions tax law, net worth tax law, assets revaluation law, travelling tax law, registration tax law, liquor tax law, commodity tax law, sugar excise law, gasoline tax law, playing-set tax law, stamp tax law, bourse tax law, special taxation measures law, national tax collection law, anti national tax evasion law, and the tax agent law. Many of these laws were amended or changed during the occupation period, but there is no indication what these changes were.

1281 —— Ministry of Justice. Immigration Bureau. *Laws and Regulations for Immigration Control in Japan*. Tokyo: The Ministry, The Bureau, 1952. 86p.

The text of the Immigration Control Act as promulgated on 4 October 1951 and amended on 28 April 1952 and 31 July 1952. It covers the entry and exit of aliens, proceedings of deportation, regulations regarding immigration, liabilities of the master of a vessel, and departure and repatriation of Japanese nationals.

——. Ministry of Labor. Liaison Affairs Section. *The Japan Labor Legislations*. 1950. See no.1756.

1282 ——. Prime Minister's Office. Pension Bureau. *The Pension Law*. Tokyo: The Office, The Bureau, 1951. 76p.

The text of the Pension Law (Law no.48 of 14 Apr. 1923) with subsequent amendments drawn up for civil servants of the government.

1283 ——. Supreme Court, comp. *The Code of Civil Procedure*. Tokyo: Supreme Court, 1950. 189p.

Compiled by the Liaison Section in the General Secretariat of the Supreme Court, this volume presents the text of the code without any accompanying commentary. The code was promulgated in 1890 and subsequently was amended on several occasions, among them in 1948 and 1949.

1283a ——. ——. *The Penal Code of Japan (Law no.45 of 1907 as Amended by Law no.77 of 1918, Law no.61 of 1941 and Law no.124 of 1947)*. Tr. by the Attorney General's Office of Japan. Tokyo: Supreme Court, 1950. 30p.

An unannotated translation of the code covering such crimes as arson and fire by negligence, forgery, fraud and blackmail, illegal arrest and confinement, homicide, kidnapping and abduction, perjury, theft and robbery, and the violation of secrecy, as well as crimes relating to civil war, gambling and lotteries, and places of worship and graves.

The Japanese Reminiscences of Roger Baldwin. 1961. See no.44b.

1284 Kanayama, Masanobu. "The Reformation of Japanese Civil Law and Its Spiritual Base." *Doshisha Law Review* international ed. no.1:31–50 (1956)

This article is essentially a critique of postwar reforms in Japanese family law and in the laws of property and succession. The author, Kanayama of Doshisha University, points out that the legal system of each nation is customarily rooted in that country's socioeconomic, cultural, and religious heritage, and he shows how the prewar legal system devised during the late Meiji period satisfactorily met Japanese needs. In contrast, he continues, many of the postwar legal changes that were forced upon the Japanese people have failed to recognize the natural relationship that should exist between law and human life. As a result, considerable confusion has developed and the need for either a reconsideration of the new civil law or a change in the traditional Japanese way of life has become increasingly urgent.

1285 Katō, Masao. "Japanese Farmers' Families and Succession Law: Based on the Survey Made by Japan Association of Private Law." *Doshisha Law Review* international ed. no.1:62–79 (1956)

This article by an assistant professor of civil law at Doshisha University discusses some of the advantages and disadvantages of reforms in inheritance practices among Japanese farmers following the enactment of the new constitution and a new civil law.

1286 Kawashima, Takeyoshi. "Post-war Democratization in Japan: Law." *International Social Science Journal* 13, no.1: 21–34 (1961)

An overview of the democratization of Japanese law during the occupation. Kawashima outlines the changes that have occurred by examining the status of the emperor, the role of the executive branch of government, the administration of justice, and the power of the Diet under both the Meiji and the 1947 constitutions. He also briefly examines the constitutionality of the defense corps and of postwar changes in farm tenancy and in labor relations practices. He concludes with an analysis of problems which have arisen as a result of the new laws and their implications with respect to democracy in Japan.

1287 Maki, John McGilvrey. "Japan's Subversive Activities Prevention Law." *Western Political Quarterly* 6:489–511 (Sept. 1953)

The first major act of the Japanese government after the occupation was this law which allowed it to restrict or even to dissolve certain terrorist organizations. The author points out that at the very beginning of the occupation an end was ordered to all restrictions on political freedoms. The new law of the postoccupation government was appealed on constitutional grounds. This test of the occupation-instituted constitution failed as the reaction to the activities of the Japan Communist party and the Korean incident caused civil liberties to yield to internal security.

1287a Meyers, Howard. "Revisions of the Criminal Code of Japan during the Occupation." *Washington Law Review* 25, no.1:104–34 (Feb. 1950)

The Law for the Partial Amendment of the Criminal Code, promulgated by the Diet on 26 October 1947, represented the most extensive revision of the prewar Criminal Code carried out during the occupation period. In this article, the former chief of the Criminal Affairs Branch, Courts and Law Division, Government Section of SCAP, categorizes and discusses the changes incurred by this important law. He divides them into 2 groups: those amendments which radically diverged from the old code's provisions and accordingly represented substantial changes in Japanese criminal law, and those amendments which were primarily technical in scope and affected the application of the law itself. Under the first category, Meyers discusses 7 major changes. The first of these involved the abolition of the special protection afforded the imperial household by articles 73–76 of the old code—provisions which made it a special crime, for example, to insult members of the imperial family and to trespass on imperial property. The second, a change enacted in accordance with Article 9 of the postwar constitution, deleted all references in the code to the act of damaging or destroying Japan's war potential and limited punishable crimes relating to war primarily to those involving conspiratorial actions that would result in another state's declaring war upon Japan. The deletion of provisions in the old code which made acts against foreign diplomatic representatives a *special* crime and that restricted free speech and expression (articles 105a, b, and c—"Offenses against Peace and Order"—and Chapter 34, "Crimes against Reputation") were the third and fourth major changes respectively. Criminal penalties for adultery also were eliminated. The final 2 major changes which Meyers enumerates involved the special provisions regarding members of a household and the extra-territorial application of Japanese law to aliens. Specifically, Japanese criminal laws henceforth were to be applied more or less equally to all citizens regardless of their family relationship to the injured party or criminal in question, and non-Japanese who carried out criminal acts against Japanese nationals outside of Japan were to be tried only by the courts and under the law of the country where the acts had been committed. The revisions of a technical nature—the second category which Meyers examines—sought in turn to modernize the Criminal Code in order to meet existing needs. Provisions were made for restoring civil rights to criminals, penalties were increased where needed, judges were given greater discretion to suspend execution of sentences, and the concept of double jeopardy was applied more broadly.

1288 *The New Commercial Code of Japan, Amended in 1948.* Tr., ed., and rev. by Fukuda Sumio. Tokyo: Tokyo News Service, 1948. 22, 378, 34, 17p.

Complete translations of the Commercial Code of Japan, the Law on Bills, and the Law on Checks may be found in the present volume. In addition, the publication contains an historical introduction on the drafting and amending of the code, the text of the Law Relating to *Yugen-Kaisha* (Book 4, Part 2 of the code) which is not to be found in the translation of the code published by the Attorney General's Office in 1951 (no.1278c), and two appendixes. The historical introduction is useful for pointing out the significant changes in the rules on companies that occurred during the postwar period with regard to such matters as incorporation and registration, the acquisition of property, public notices, and the reorganization of companies.

Oppler, Alfred C. "Courts and Law in Transition." 1952. *See* no.1309.

1289 ———. "Human Rights among the Japanese." *Military Government Journal* 1, no.7:1–4, 23 (May 1948)

Prepared by the chief of the Courts and Law Division of SCAP's Government Section, this is an informative summary of the major reforms affecting the judiciary and Japanese law as of early 1948. Oppler first reviews the enactment of such legislation as the Court Organization Law, the Judges Impeachment Law, and a law concerning the status of judges and other court officials. He then focuses on the revision of the various codes and the laws connected with the basic revisions. "Whether the new laws will be mere blueprints or will be properly applied and penetrate the life of Japan's society," he concludes, "will depend in the last analysis on the Japanese people themselves."

1290 ———. "The Reform of Japan's Legal and Judicial System under Allied Occupation." *Washington Law Review* 24, no.3:290–324 (Aug. 1949)

This important survey of the major judicial and legal reforms enacted to implement the postwar constitution was prepared by the chief of the Legislation and Justice Division, Legal Section of SCAP. It first notes that the occupation authorities had to take into consideration the 2 factors on which the Japanese legal system was based: the continental European character of many of the laws, and the strength of indigenous customs and traditions. It also points out that the revision of the basic legal codes was carried out largely by regular Diet legislation with SCAP acting merely in an advisory and controlling capacity. The article then briefly examines the provisions and the legislative implementation of the new constitution—the document which laid the legal foundations for subsequent changes in many areas of Japanese life and which necessitated a wide range of administrative and legal reforms. Oppler's main focus within the article, however, quickly turns to the actual reforms carried out between the autumn of 1946 and the summer of 1948. These sought to implement the constitution by freeing the judiciary of executive control and by strengthening its prerogatives, by promoting fundamental human rights, and by protecting the individual from undue governmental interference in his private life. The major reforms are categorized as follows: (1) legislation to insure the independence and high caliber of the judiciary; (2) the clear-cut separation of the public procurators from the courts, to which they had been attached in the past, through the passage of the Public Procurator's Office Law of 1947; (3) the elevation of the legal profession and the effort to free lawyers from the type of government supervision formerly exercised by the Minister of Justice; (4) the revision of Books 4 and 5 of the Civil Code (covering the fields of domestic relations and inheritance)—a revision that replaced the "house" (*ie*) with the modern small family, abolished all restrictions on the legal status of women, and reformed the *koseki* (family registration) system; (5) sweeping reforms of the substantive as well as procedural elements of the criminal law; (6) the passage of a *Habeas Corpus* act in 1948; (7) the revision of the Code of Civil Procedure; and (8) reforms affecting administrative procedures. Oppler concludes his article on an optimistic note as he speculates about the willingness of the Japanese to retain these various reforms long after the occupation itself is over.

Rabinowitz, Richard W. "Materials on Japanese Law in Western Languages." 1955. See no.24.

1291 Röhl, Wilhelm. *Fremde Einflüsse im modernen japanischen Recht*. Frankfort: Metzner, 1959. 72p. (Schriften des Instituts für Asienkunde in Hamburg, 4)

This study of the European and American influences upon Japanese law during the first half of the twentieth century includes considerable information on American efforts to change many Japanese laws during the occupation period in order to eliminate feudalism and to democratize Japan. The discussion covers not only private law, the Civil Code, commercial laws including the anti-monopoly laws, criminal law, and labor legislation, but also the constitution and parliament, the administration of the government, and the police system in Japan.

1291a Salwin, Lester N. "The New Commercial Code of Japan: Symbol of Gradual Progress toward Democratic Goals." *Georgetown Law Journal* 50: 478–512 (Spring 1962)

The chief of the Trade Laws Branch of SCAP and a special assistant for legal affairs to the chief of SCAP's Economic and Scientific Section between 1946 and 1952 presents a very informative account of the revision of Japan's Commercial Code. He begins by discussing the major characteristics of the old code in which the organization and management of companies were regarded primarily as matters of private concern to the promoters and directors of the firms in question. The occupation authorities regarded this and other corporate practices as obstacles to their program for the long-range democratization of the Japanese economy. As a result of action undertaken late during the occupation period, a law for the partial amendment of the code (largely affecting Book 2 of the code) was approved by the Diet on 2 May 1950 and promulgated as Law no.167 of 1950. Salwin summarizes the major revisions, dividing his discussion into 2 categories: under "shareholders' rights" he focuses on (a) shareholders' access to corporate books and records, (b) preemptive rights, (c) capital stock, (d) voting, (e) shareholders' objections to merger, and (f) shareholders' meetings; under "shareholders' remedies," in turn, he refers to (a) standards governing the responsibilities of a company's directors and officers, (b) action for damages, (c) injunctive relief, (d) the removal of directors, (e) court-appointed inspectors, and (f) wrongful or unauthorized corporate acts. He notes, furthermore, that an advisory council subsequently appointed by the Ministry of Justice to review and make recommendations for changes in the code did not advocate any significant amendments except for the section dealing with preemptive rights. The council's position, therefore, may be interpreted as an indication of the lasting quality of the postwar legislative reforms, but Salwin cautions that the permanence of the revised code will depend upon a continuing gradual movement toward democratization of Japanese society in general.

Solomon, Albert H. "Revision of the Japanese Mining Law under the Occupation." 1951. *See* no.1821.

1292 Steiner, Kurt. "The Revision of the Civil Code of Japan: Provisions Affecting the Family." *Far Eastern Quarterly* 9: 169–84 (Feb. 1950)

Following a clear and concise explanation of the history and significance of the family system in Japanese life, the author discusses in some detail the changes of the Civil Code necessitated by the new constitution. He outlines the conservative and liberal attitudes toward revision of the old laws, and he briefly examines the relationship between some provisions of the new constitution and the Civil Code before its revision with regard to such issues as the choice of spouse and the inequality of the sexes with regard to property and inheritance, choice of domicile, and divorce. The author concludes with the observation that "the revision of the civil code marks a step forward not only in the legal but also the political and social development of Japan," but he warns that although the lawmaker's task is completed, the greater one of the educator and the statesman in implementing the law has only begun.

1292a ———. "Postwar Changes in the Japanese Civil Code." *Washington Law Review* 25, no.3:286–312 (Aug. 1950)

Steiner, the author of an article detailing the effect of the revised code upon the Japanese family (no.1292), first briefly discusses the family system and its importance in Japan, the Civil Code before revision, and the constitution and the temporary adjustments in the Civil Code that were pursuant to its enforcement. He then examines in some detail the amendments in Books 4 and 5 of the code which relate to family relationships and which were necessary in order to democratize the legal relations among Japanese family members. Some of these changes dealt with matters of divorce, adoption, succession, the Family Registration Law, and the extent of parental power in general. Steiner suggests that the urban intelligentsia and many members of the middle class and the industrial working class have long felt that the traditional family system was anachronistic. Accordingly, by doing away with all legal sanctions against nonconformity, the revised code will "considerably hasten the adjustment of the [more conservative] farmers and fishermen to the freer urban concept." The code, Steiner concludes, will survive because its reform was in line with tendencies active in Japanese society for some years and because it is enjoying considerable popularity despite objections to it by powerful conservative forces within the country.

Supreme Commander for the Allied Powers. Monograph 14. *Legal and Judicial Reform, 1945–December 1950.* 1952. *See* no.296.

———. Monograph 17. *Treatment of Foreign Nationals.* 1952. *See* no.299.

1293 ———. *Preparatory Material for the Revision of Japanese Civil Law.* Tokyo: SCAP, 1947? 5, 152, 17, 50, 38p.

A microfilmed collection of mimeographed papers relating to the revision of the Japanese Civil Code. It contains 4 categories of material but the collection is unsystematically organized. The first is a 5-page statement, entitled "Revisions of Civil Code," issued jointly by SCAP's Civil Information and Education Section and its Government Section on 1 August 1947. It contains 7 major points which SCAP suggests as possible guidelines for Diet debate and public hearings relating to the revision of the Civil Code on the basis of a brief 10-article Law for the

Temporary Adjustment of the Civil Code which was put into effect on 3 May 1947. The second is an English translation of the bill for the partial amendment of the Civil Code submitted to the Diet in July 1947. The third is a collection of 11 bills relating to the Civil Code. They include an amnesty bill, a Public Procurator's Office bill, a bill for the enforcement of the court organization law, and a bill for the temporary adjustment of the Code of Civil Procedures pursuant to the enforcement of the constitution of Japan. The last category of material is an opinion paper, entitled "Recovery of Japanese Nationality as Cause for Loss of American Nationality," prepared by Thomas L. Blakemore, Foreign Service auxiliary officer, Office of the U.S. Political Adviser, Tokyo, in May 1946. The author discusses the Japanese processes of naturalization and of recovery of nationality and the legal effect of such recovery as well as the manner in which the American nationality acts of 1907 and 1940 have been applied to Japanese–Americans who seek to recover Japanese citizenship.

1294 ———. Government Section. *Subject Index of Laws Enacted by Japanese Diet from the Beginning of Occupation to June 1951.* Mimeographed. Tokyo: SCAP, 1951. 61p.

This mimeographed document provides a useful index to all laws enacted by the Japanese government during the occupation of Japan. There is an introductory index indicating the dates of each Diet session and the number of laws passed during that session. The main body of the work arranges the 1,459 laws passed during this period according to subject. It indicates the law number and cites the edition of the *Official Gazette* in which the text of the law appeared.

Available at the Law Division of the Library of Congress, Washington, D.C.

1294a Takayanagi, Kenzō. "Contact of the Common Law with the Civil Law in Japan." *American Journal of Comparative Law* 4:60–69 (Winter 1955)

In an address delivered at the Opening Session of the Fourth Congress of the International Academy of Comparative Law, the author first describes how the system of Japanese law came to be based during the Meiji era on the continental European tradition of civil law and how there subsequently was an unprecedented inflow of American laws and institutions during the occupation period. He then illustrates how the Japanese are dealing with these imported American institutions, referring in particular to (1) the Supreme Court, (2) rule-making power, (3) contempt of court, (4) *Habeas corpus*, (5) taxpayers' suits, (6) administrative commissions, and (7) administrative law. Takayanagi points out some of the major problems which have arisen from the efforts to graft aspects of Anglo–American law onto the Japanese legal system. He also criticizes the occupation authorities for not carefully determining in advance how the institutions they were introducing would work in Japanese society, and concludes that Japan will remain a country of civil law in part because the occupation was too short to effect any radical reform in the legal education which trains Japanese to work with principles and institutions which are not rooted in the Anglo–American tradition.

1295 Von Mehren, Arthur Taylor, ed. *Law in Japan: The Legal Order in a Changing Society.* Cambridge, Mass.: Harvard Univ. Pr., 1963. xxxviii, 706p.

A product of the Japanese–American Program for Cooperation in Legal Studies, this book represents a major effort to consider law as a part of the social order, rather than as a technical body of rules. There are 17 essays by Japanese legal scholars on various aspects of Japanese law and a summary of the discussion of their papers by a group of 40 Japanese and American scholars. The essays are arranged in 3 groups: the legal system and the law's processes; the individual, the state, and the law; the law and the economy. They range from such problems as the role of law in Japanese society and the law and the family to discussions of Japanese legal education and labor relations.

1296 Wagatsuma, Sakae. "The Japanese Legal System, 1945–1955: Changes in Retrospect." *Monumenta Nipponica* 12, no.1/2:105–19 (Apr./July 1956)

This article is an adapted translation of Wagatsuma's introduction to a series of studies by Japanese scholars reviewing postwar Japanese legislation which appeared in the journal *Juristo* (no.100 [15 Feb. 1956]) under the title "Sengo hōsei no hensen, kaiko to tembō." It focuses on the major changes in the Japanese legal system between 1945 and 1955 and considers the overall character of the legislation enacted during that decade. It also reviews some of the results of changes introduced by SCAP. Wagatsuma concludes that many of the reforms have been of great benefit to the Japanese people but notes that not all of the principles of the postwar constitution could be realized on account of the changing world situation and its adverse impact upon Japan.

1296a ———. "Democratization of the Family Relation in Japan." *Washington Law Review* 25, no.4:405–26 (Nov. 1950)

This study of the revised Civil Code written by a law professor at Tokyo University who served on the subcommittee which drafted the changes supplements Kurt Steiner's article entitled "Postwar Changes in the Japanese Civil Code" (no.1292a). Wagatsuma first focuses his attention upon the public reaction to the amended version. Many people, he points out, approved the revision because they considered it essential to the renovation of the House (*Ie*) system, but others felt that the changes were too drastic while still others criticized the revision as not thoroughgoing insofar as it permitted certain features of the *Ie* system to be retained. Wagatsuma then examines the immediate and potential impact of the code upon Japanese family life. Family life, he explains, is intrinsically influenced by tradition and may at first not be greatly affected by many of the changes. In the long run, however, the impact is bound to be felt in view of the increasing popular dissatisfaction with such traditional restrictions as those which had been imposed on the freedom of marriage and on the rights of the wife in Japanese society. Indeed, the revision of the code was not as revolutionary an action as it might seem, for even before the war serious efforts had been made to amend it in order to bring about greater democratization of Japanese family relations.

———. "The Family System under the New Civil Code." 1947. *See* no. 1984a.

The Judicial System

The new constitution also required far-reaching changes in the Japanese judicial system. The courts became an independent and equal branch of the government, the old separate administrative court was abolished, and a system of judicial review was instituted. Efforts were made also to alter the status and role of lawyers. Finally, the presence of foreign troops manning the occupation raised unprecedented problems of legal jurisdiction over members of these forces and their dependents. The literature on these subjects is not extensive. It is listed below.

1297 "Are We Converting Japan into an Allied Colony?" *Christian Century* 63: 292 (6 Mar. 1946)

This editorial contends that the United States has blundered twice in 1 week with respect to Japan. First, the Americans executed General Yamashita after the Supreme Court refused to review his "highly irregular" trial. Second, General MacArthur decreed an exemption of all United Nations nationals and institutions from Japanese jurisdiction. That decree will stigmatize the present Japanese government for acquiescing in a return of the hated principle of extraterritoriality and will result in Japan's being turned into an Allied colony.

1297a Cho, Sung-Yoon. *Jurisdiction over Foreign Forces in Japan, 1945–1960.* Ph.D. dissertation, Tulane Univ., 1963. 356p. (Abstracted in *Dissertation Abstracts* 24:3404–5 [1964]; University Microfilms order no.64–1804)

This study examines the problems of criminal and civil jurisdiction which resulted from the presence of foreign troops on Japanese soil from 1945 until 1960. Cho focuses on what he believes to be the fundamental aspects of the problem of jurisdiction—namely, the relation of international and municipal law—and discusses Japanese attitudes and actions regarding this problem.

1298 Dionisopoulos, P. Allan. "Judicial Review and Civil Rights in Japan: The First Decade with an Alien Doctrine." *Western Political Quarterly* 13:269–87 (June 1960)

In his analysis the author refers to both the specific articles of the Japanese constitution which defined the Supreme Court as the keeper of the constitution and the cases in which judicial review was used. He views the progress of judicial review as timid, due to the fact that the constitution was conceived in haste which necessitated the use of an Anglo–Saxon model for which the Japanese were not prepared.

1298a "Exercise of Criminal and Civil Jurisdiction over Nationals of Members of the United Nations: Far Eastern Commission Policy Decision." *Department of State Bulletin* 23:664–65 (23 Oct. 1950)

This article reprints a policy decision approved by the FEC on 21 September 1950 and released to the press on 3 October 1950. The decision permits Japanese courts to exercise criminal jurisdiction over all United Nations nationals in Japan except for members of the armed forces, those attached to the occupation forces, those on official business in Japan, and members of the immediate families and dependents of these same groups. The decision also makes specific procedural recommendations to be followed in criminal and civil cases involving UN nationals.

1299 Gokijo, Kakiwa. "The Judicial System of New Japan." *Annals of the American Academy of Political and Social Science* 308:28–39 (Nov. 1956)

The secretary-general of the Supreme Court of Japan begins this article by noting the differences between the prewar and postwar functions, structure, and operations of Japanese courts. He presents in table form the classification of the courts as created by the Court Organization Law which went into effect with the constitution in 1947 and then describes the qualifications, tenure, and duties of judges and other court officials. The jurisdiction of the courts and the various types of court actions are also outlined. Criminal cases and civil cases are studied. The role of family courts, the disposition of juvenile problems, and lay participation in the operations of the judicial system are summarized. In conclusion, the author views the major marked difference between the present and prewar Japanese courts as "the devotion given to protecting fundamental human rights."

1300 Itoh, Hiroshi. *Japanese Supreme Court: Judicial Decision-making Analysis.* Ph.D. dissertation, Univ. of Washington at Seattle, 1968. 256p. (Abstracted in *Dissertation Abstracts* 29:3652A–53A [1969]; University Microfilms order no. 69–7059)

The nature of Japanese judicial decision-making after 1946, when the role of the judiciary was significantly expanded under the new constitution, is examined here. After a review of Japanese literature on this subject, Itoh traces the development of Japanese studies concerning the judicial decision-making process and indicates that past studies have been limited to questions of law and fact in particular cases. In an attempt to show that judicial decision-making requires more than facts and simple questions of law, the author analyzes the diverse factors that are involved in the decision-making process. He examines the consistency and predictability of judicial outcomes on the basis of his assumption that there is a high degree of correlation between judicial value judgments and the voting behavior of judges. Using Guttman's Scalogram analysis he analyzes civil liberties and civil rights cases decided by the Japanese Supreme Court between 1947 and 2 June 1958. To test the popular opinion that there is no bloc of similarly minded justices on the Supreme Court, he applies a modified block analysis technique to the cases decided during this period. The final section is an analysis of judicial behavior on the political-question doctrine within the context of a judicial activism versus judicial restraint dichotomy.

Japan. Ministry of Foreign Affairs. *Japan's Problems*. 1954. See no.1186.

1301 ———. Supreme Court. *The Court Organization Law and Regulation Concerning the Departmental Organization of the General Secretariat of the Supreme Court.* Tokyo: The Court, 1950. 65p.

The organization of the Supreme Court and its inferior courts (high courts, district courts, family courts, and summary courts) as well as the provisions for court officials and judicial apprentices, for the conduct of court business and expenses, and for judicial administration are stipulated in the text of the Court Organization Law (Law no.59 of 1947) presented in this volume. The texts of the Law for the Enforcement of the Court Organization Law (Law no.60 of 1947), and of Supreme Court Regulation no.5 (1 Dec. 1947) concerning the departmental organization of the Court's General Secretariat also are included.

1302 ———. ———. *Japanese Judicial System under the New Constitution.* Tokyo: 1953. 18p.

This summary review of the postwar judicial system focuses on the judicial power of the courts, the system of the courts and their jurisdiction, the judges and other personnel of the courts, and the participation of laymen in judicial proceedings. The authors point out how greatly judicial power has been expanded under the new constitution so that the settlement of all legal disputes and the interpretation and construction of all statutes and ordinances are now referred to the Supreme Court. They also indicate how the status of the Supreme Court judges has been elevated and discuss both the authority and limitations of the Supreme Court and the qualifications of its judges. Page 18 contains a statistical table of the civil and criminal cases handled by all of the courts in Japan between 1948 and 1952.

1303 ———. ———. *Outline of Civil Trial in Japan.* Tokyo: The Court, 1950. 17p.

This pamphlet deals with changes in civil proceedings from prewar to postwar practices. It gives brief sketches of the various types of civil actions, proceedings, appeals, and special actions.

1303a ———. ———. *Rule of Criminal Procedure (Supreme Court Rule no.32, 1948).* Tokyo: Attorney General's Office, 1949. ii, 103p. (Code and Statutes of Japan, no.2)

The text of the rule of criminal procedure containing provisions for such matters as defense and assistance, the detention of the accused, the examination of witnesses, the preservation of evidence, public trials, and appeals.

1304 ———. ———. *The Rule of Criminal Procedure (The Rule for Enforcement of the Rule for Criminal Procedure). The Code of Criminal Procedure (The Law for Enforcement of the Code of Criminal Procedure).* Tokyo: The Court, 1950. x, 491p. In English and Japanese.

Compiled by the Liaison Section of the Supreme Court's General Secretariat, this volume contains not only the Rule of Criminal Procedure (Supreme Court Rule no.32, 1948, with four amendments dating from 1949 and 1950) and the complete text of the Code of Criminal Procedure but also the text of the Law for Enforcement of the Code of Criminal Procedure. The Japanese and English-language texts are placed side by side. There are no accompanying comments or explanations.

1305 ———. ———. Bureau of Criminal Affairs. *Recent Developments in the Field of Criminal Justice in Japan*. Tokyo: The Court, 1950. 52p.

The impact of the 1947 constitution on matters involving criminal justice in postwar Japan is examined here at some length. A comparison is made of the number of courts and judges and of the jurisdiction of the courts in prewar and postwar times; there is a discussion of the Penal Code and the Code of Criminal Procedure; the increase in the number of crimes and hence in the number of criminal cases and the case load of the judges is depicted; and the outstanding features of criminal justice in Japan (e.g., the percentage of those acquitted and of those who file higher appeals) are pointed out. Finally, the authors describe the chief characteristics of the new Code of Criminal Procedure and the impact that the innovations within the code have had. Among the code's postwar features which they point to are (1) the abolition of the preliminary examination system (*yoshin*) and the adoption of the principle of proceedings centering around the public trial in the first instance; (2) the adoption of rigid rules of evidence and the strengthening of the principle of direct examination; (3) introducing the reviewing character of *kōso* appeal (first appeal); (4) the promotion of the principle of equality of both parties to litigation; and (5) the provisions for the guarantee of human rights.

1305a Johnson, Chalmers Ashby. *Conspiracy at Matsukawa*. Berkeley: Univ. of California Pr., 1972. x, 460p. (Publications of the Center for Japanese and Korean Studies)

Johnson uses an exhaustive case study of the investigations and trials growing out of the alleged sabotage of a passenger train at Matsukawa in August 1949 to examine the functioning of the Japanese procuratorial and judicial system. SCAP legal reforms (especially the introduction of the Anglo-American adversary proceedings into Japanese criminal trials) figure prominently in this particular case. As Johnson contends, these reforms were largely responsible both for the protracted nature of the entire case (it remained before the courts until 1970) and for the ultimate exoneration of the alleged conspirators. It was not only the specific content of the changes SCAP made in the Japanese system of criminal justice which created difficulties. The very breadth and comprehensiveness of these changes also complicated the proceedings inasmuch as it took several years for the Japanese judges and procurators involved to become fully versed in all the details of the new system. During the course of his study, Johnson also points out that the gradual accumulation of precedents eventually resulted in a better integration of the SCAP reforms with Japanese legal proceedings. The concluding chapter of his book summarizes the author's evaluation of the impact the reforms had upon the Matsukawa case and generally upon the administration of justice in postwar Japan.

1306 Kakudo, Toyoji. "The Doctrine of Judicial Review in Japan." *Osaka University Law Review* no.2:59–78 (1953)

The author focuses on current Japanese interpretations of Articles 81 and 98 of the new constitution. The former article, he explains, provides the Supreme Court with the "power to determine the constitutionality of any law, order, regulation, or official act." The latter stipulates that no law or government act contrary to the provisions of the constitution, the supreme law of the land, can have legal force or validity. Kakudo notes that there are significantly different interpretations of these articles and classifies the opposing views into 3 categories, pointing out that these differ particularly with regard to the circumstances under which a law can be declared unconstitutional.

1307 Maki, John McGilvrey. *Court and Constitution in Japan: Selected Supreme Court Decisions, 1948–1960.* Seattle: Univ. of Washington Pr., 1964. xlvi, 445p.

The impact of the 1947 constitution on postwar Japanese life is illustrated in this representative collection of 26 constitutional decisions of the Supreme Court of Japan. All of the decisions were published originally in *Saikō Saibansho hanreishū* (Collection of Supreme Court precedents. Compiled under the direction of the Committee on Supreme Court Precedents, v.1– . Tokyo: 1947– .) and deal with such constitutional problems as land reform, censorship, civil rights, new relationships among the branches of government, the relationship between individual freedoms and society, and the nature of the new freedoms guaranteed under the constitution. Several of the cases treated in this compendium had their origins during the occupation period or were directly related to the stationing of American forces in Japan. Among these, perhaps the most relevant ones to the student of the occupation are: case 16, "Just Compensation" in Article 29 and the Land Reform; case 17, The Meaning of "Minimum Standards of Wholesome and Cultured Living" in Article 25 (concerning the violation of the occupation's Staple Food Management Law regulating the purchase and sale of rice and other staple food items); and case 23, The Constitutionality under Article 9 of U.S. Bases in Japan (The Sunakawa Decision). An extensive introduction by Maki discussing the history, philosophy, and nature of the constitution and the Supreme Court also may be found in this volume.

1308 Meyers, Howard. "The Japanese Inquest of Prosecution." *Harvard Law Review* 64:279–86 (Dec. 1950)

The author, formerly chief of the Criminal Affairs Branch of SCAP's Government and Legal Section, writes about the establishment of the inquest of prosecution in Japan. Meyers describes the structure and methods of this system. He feels it was immediately accepted by the Japanese and provided a way in which the Japanese people could question the operations of law enforcement. Meyers also feels that the success of this system indicates that the postwar trend of protecting the rights of the individual still exists.

1309 Oppler, Alfred C. "Japan's Courts and Law in Transition." *Contemporary Japan* 21, no.1/3:19–55 (1952)

The author of this article served as division chief at different times in the Government Section and in the Legal Section, General Headquarters of SCAP, from February 1946 until being appointed legal adviser, G–5, General Headquarters, Far Eastern Commission. Writing at the time of "reorientation, reevaluation, and transition," after the ratification of the peace treaty when controls were relaxed, he considers the legislative reforms resulting from the occupation and the role of Japan's new judiciary. He examines the reform of the basic codes such as civil, criminal, and procedural codes and explains why future improvement is still needed. While briefly treating the background and content of various code reforms, Oppler maintains that "this whole reform work stands or falls with an independent judiciary." In this regard he first examines the nature and scope of judicial independence under the new constitution. In considering the relationship between the judiciary and other branches of the government, he also looks at the matter of selection of judges. He then moves on to the position of the individual judge. In studying the responsibilities of the Supreme Court he covers the power of judicial review and notes the court's emphasis on protecting the constitutional rights of the suspect and accused in a criminal procedure and the individual's right to personal liberty. The magnitude of the problem caused by the great backlog of civil and criminal cases is discussed and factors placing "an ever-increasing burden on the courts and law enforcement agencies" are outlined.

Though the author concludes that no final evaluation of Japan's courts and laws can be given during this period of transition, he declares that the Japanese themselves will freely determine the choices for further improvement.

———. "The Reform of Japan's Legal and Judicial System under Allied Occupation." 1949. See no.1290.

1310 Parker, James Perkins. "The Japanese Supreme Court Mission: Towards a New Legal Order in Japan." *American Bar Association Journal* 36:916–18, 975 (Nov. 1950)

The tour of American judicial institutions made by 6 Japanese judges is reported here and regarded as a harbinger of the maturation of an independent and democratic Japanese judiciary. Parker considers the contradictions between traditional Japanese and American legal codes and procedures, emphasizing the continued slow pace of court action. In addition, he notes the lack of a continuous trial system, of an arraignment and plea system in criminal cases, of provision for punishment of contempt, and the scarcity of men pursuing the legal profession in Japan. The objectives and composition of the mission are analyzed and the participation of its members in seminars, demonstrations, and professional gatherings is mentioned.

1311 Rabinowitz, Richard William. "The Historical Development of the Japanese Bar." *Harvard Law Review* 70:61–81 (Nov. 1956)

In this article Rabinowitz traces the history of the Japanese Bar since the Tokugawa period. He covers the role of the lawyer, the beginning of Japanese law codes, the influence of Western law, and the reforms brought about during the occupation period. He lists factors which he feels retarded the development of the legal profession in Japan. He concludes that there was no occupational monopoly for the lawyers, and that professional organizations were never strong. He also cites the type of higher education available for lawyers.

1312 ———. *The Japanese Lawyer: A Study in the Sociology of the Legal Profession.* Ph.D. dissertation, Harvard Univ., 1956. x, 438p.

Rabinowitz examines the "lawyer role" and the execution of this role in Japan. Although his approach is primarily contemporary, he provides historical materials which illustrate the changes in the role of the lawyer and the nature of the legal system initiated by occupation reforms.

Available at the Harvard University Archives, Widener Library, Cambridge, Massachusetts.

Sugihara, Yasuo. "The Control of the Constitutionality of Laws under the Constitution of Japan." 1963. See no. 1212.

Supreme Commander for the Allied Powers. Monograph 14. *Legal and Judicial Reform, 1945–December 1950.* 1952. See no.296.

1313 Suzuki, Hisakazu. "Judicature of Past Ten Years." *Contemporary Japan* 23, no.10/12:676–85 (1955)

Here the chief of the Information and Liaison Office of the Japanese Ministry of Justice writes first of the disintegrated state of public order following Japan's defeat in 1945 and relates the circumstances involved in the firing of a judge of the Kyoto District Court on orders of the occupation forces. He then discusses the large scale legal reform begun by the occupation in February 1946 and notes the occupation control of public procurators. The effect of the new Code of Criminal Procedure which came into force in 1949 and the workings of the jury system in Japan are studied. The "offensive movement for the revolution by violence of the leftists" in 1952 is noted along with the partial amendment in 1953 of the Code of Criminal Procedure. The last part of the article reviews a serious case which arose in 1954 and caused "reflection upon the nature of the work of criminal investigation and prosecution." The author begins his 10-year survey by showing the bitter reminiscences of the judges but ends with comments on their "satisfaction and delight in the later developments." A page of statistics on law cases and officials concludes the article.

1313a Takayanagi, Kenzō. "The Judiciary under the New Constitution." *Contemporary Japan* 16:235–51 (July/Sept. 1947)

The author, a legal adviser to the Foreign Ministry and a professor at Tokyo University, begins by criticizing the tendency of Japanese legal experts to pay too much attention to abstract, metaphysical questions such as the definition of sovereignty. He himself prefers the analysis and criticism of concrete issues. One such issue is the position of the judiciary under the new constitution, to which the remainder of the article is devoted. In his opinion, the most important aspects of the new judicial system include (1) control and surveillance over both the legislative and executive branches of government; (2) guarantees against encroachment by the executive; (3) rule-making power within the legal process; (4) the power to rule on the constitutionality of legislative and executive measures; (5) Cabinet nomination of Supreme Court judges (a system he feels, however, may lead to political abuse); and (6) fixed retirement ages for judges as well as provision for impeachment and recall.

1314 Tanaka, Kōtarō. "Democracy and Judicial Administration in Japan." *International Commission of Jurists Journal* 2:7–19 (Winter 1959/Summer 1960)

The author, who was at the time chief justice of the Supreme Court of Japan, writes of the changes judicial administration has undergone and the kinds of problems it faces in the future. He discusses the role of an independent judiciary, the problem of the separation of powers, and the role of the courts and judges in Japanese society.

1315 ———. "Democratization of Japanese Administration of Justice." In *Japan's Problems*, ed. by Japan. Ministry of Foreign Affairs. Bureau of Public Information and Cultural Affairs. Tokyo: The Ministry, 1954. p.13–26.

Tanaka Kōtarō, chief justice of the Japanese Supreme Court, describes judicial reform under the new constitution. He notes that while the system has been transformed, its substance is still not entirely free from traditions and old habits. He suggests that the judicial branch take a universal point of view on 2 things: first, be critical from an international standpoint and examine the things actually being done; second, acknowledge a basic rule of justice and freedom for all mankind.

LOCAL GOVERNMENT AND ADMINISTRATION

The occupation authorities initiated a sweeping program of political decentralization in Japan based upon the assumption that democratic institutions and values were most secure if firmly established at the grass roots level of politics. As a consequence serious efforts were made to increase the autonomy of cities, towns, and villages—and, secondarily, of prefectures—at the expense of national authority. The endeavor involved changes of an institutional, legal, political, and fiscal nature. They are described in the following literature. The interested reader is also referred to the section on reports by subordinate headquarters of SCAP (p.137) and to the section on land reform (p.544).

Beardsley, Richard K., John W. Hall, and Robert E. Ward. *Village Japan*. 1959. *See* no.691.

Braibanti, Ralph J. D. "Administration of Military Government in Japan at the Prefectural Level." 1949. *See* no.893.

1316 ———. "Executive Power in Japanese Prefectural Government." *Far Eastern Quarterly* 9:231–44 (May 1950)

In an examination of the scope and nature of prefectural power in Japan, the author describes the political power structure of Japanese prefectures in the pre-surrender period and contrasts this with the occupation period. He contends that the decentralization of the government brought about by the occupation has greatly reshuffled the power of prefectural governors. There is a comprehensive explanation of the particular provisions wrought by the SCAP system including both positive executive powers as well as restraints on that power and means of redress. The concluding paragraphs provide a clear summation of postwar changes in prefectural executive power.

1317 ———. "Neighborhood Associations in Japan and Their Democratic Potentialities." *Far Eastern Quarterly* 7:136–64 (Feb. 1948)

The first half of this comprehensive report is devoted to a definition of the neighborhood association (*tonarigumi*) in Japan and an outline of its historical development. The latter half discusses the effects of surrender upon the associations, early negative occupation policy toward the neighborhood associations, and later experiments with their democratization. The author affirms that whether or not the value of the neighborhood associations is recognized by SCAP authorities, nevertheless, such associations are an important and useful organization in occupied Japan which "will not remain neglected by the Japanese Government when it regains its autonomy." The article is a valuable examination of an important Japanese institution that survived not only the war but also the occupation.

1318 Brett, Cecil Carter. *The Government of Okayama Prefecture: A Case Study of Local Autonomy in Japan*. Ph.D. dissertation, Univ. of Michigan, 1956. 305p. (Abstracted in *Dissertation Abstracts* 17:1371 [1957]; University Microfilms order no.21,152)

Brett examines the government of Okayama prefecture in an attempt to indicate the extent to which occupation reforms promoting local autonomy were successful. He discusses government functions, the executive and legislative branches, formal and extralegal methods by which laws were made, and national-prefectural relations with respect to agriculture, education, and police. His findings indicate that the populace had little effective control over the prefectural administration, that little use was made of initiative or referendum, that the legislative branch was subordinate to the executive, and that the elected prefectural governor served the central government rather than the prefecture. He concludes that the achievement of the occupation reforms of decentralization and democratization fell short of expectations. He also states that hierarchical bureaucratic characteristics and traditional authoritarian habits of thought and behavior were still evident in prefectural government.

1319 ———. "The Japanese Prefectural Legislature." *Parliamentary Affairs* 11:23–38 (Winter 1957/58)

On the basis of research done between 1953 and 1955, the author points out that, while the occupation introduced prefectural legislatures, they are Western in form only but Japanese in content. Contrary to occupation intentions, these legislatures have not developed into powerful bodies because of authoritarian Japanese political traditions. Most of the article is devoted to a detailed account of a typical assembly session, followed by a description of the formal legislative process. The author sees the operation of prefectural legislatures as being largely formalistic and takes this as typically oriental.

Bronfenbrenner, Martin. "The Japanese Value-added Sales Tax." 1950. See no.1677.

Dore, Ronald P. *Land Reform in Japan*. 1959. See no.1703.

1320 Dull, Paul Shirley. "Maeda Shoichi: A Case Study of a Japanese Political Boss." In *Five Studies in Japanese Politics*, ed. by Robert E. Ward. Ann Arbor: Univ. of Michigan Pr., 1957. p.15–20. (Univ. of Michigan, Center for Japanese Studies, occasional papers, no.7)

Based upon research carried out in Okayama prefecture, this chapter is a case study of political bossism during the occupation period. The sources and range of power of one local leader—Maeda Shoichi—are examined, his techniques of control and community position are described, and some of the motives for his activities are assessed. For the student of the occupation, this study is important for understanding the problems encountered by the occupation authorities in their efforts to democratize Japanese local government. The Local Autonomy Law, Dull points out, did indeed increase the power of local legislative bodies at the expense of the central government. Nevertheless, he concludes, studies such as his show that a more democratic use of authority within the villages and *buraku* of Japan did not automatically result.

1321 ———. "The Political Structure of a Japanese Village." *Far Eastern Quarterly* 13:175–90 (Feb. 1954)

The village government of Kamo-son, Tsukubo-gun, Okayama-ken is described in this article in order to show the forms and functions of village administration in Japan as designed by postwar occupation reforms and the actual workings of this political structure. The study is divided into an examination of "the formal administrative structure and the system of political relationships out of which real decisions are made." Officials, village government offices, and a variety of administrative agencies are discussed. Dull maintains, "Despite reforms intended to democratize village government, older methods of reaching decisions and executing policies are still used." He notes the difficulty caused by the existence of an older rural Japan side by side with a new Japan that is becoming increasingly Westernized, industrialized, and urbanized.

1322 ———. "The *Senkyoya* System in Rural Japanese Communities." In Univ. of Michigan, Center for Japanese Studies. *Occasional Papers*, v.4. Ann Arbor: Univ. of Michigan Pr., 1953. p.29–38.

This article is based upon research undertaken while Dull was a research associate at the University of Michigan's Center for Japanese Studies' field station at Okayama. He begins by pointing out problems with the manner in which the political processes in Japan have usually been studied. He then describes the *senkyoya* system in Japan, noting the functions of the *senkyoya* or "those concerned in political (and, specifically, electoral) affairs below the level of officialdom" and outlining the workings of the system. The final section of the piece discusses changes in the *senkyoya* system occasioned by Japan's defeat in World War II and the subsequent occupation such as the succession of younger men to the role of *senkyoya*, the reasons for this shift, and the impact on the system of the enfranchisement of women. He also comments on techniques which have changed as the *senkyoya* system has been modified and on the attempts made by Socialist parties and the Communist party to take advantage of changes.

1323 Hashiguchi, Makoto. "Modernizing Our Local Government." *Contemporary Japan* 15:337–45 (Sept./Dec. 1946)

An analysis of 4 bills concerned with the reform of local government organization: a bill amending the law on the organization of Tokyo metropolis, a bill amending the law on the organization of cities, a bill amending the law on the organization of towns and villages, and a bill amending the law on the organization of urban and rural prefectures. All 4 bills were passed by the Japanese Diet on 20 September 1946 with SCAP approval. The author discusses these bills as they served to extend participation in government by the local populations, as they extended the powers of the deliberative organs of government, as they served to democratize the executive organs of government, and as they promoted better relations between the deliberative and executive organs of the government.

Huberman, Morris A. "Backwoods Japan during American Occupation." 1947. See no.1841.

Isozaki, Tatsugorō. "Dissolution of the House of Representatives and Dissolution of Local Self-Government Assembly." 1955. See no.1181.

1324 Japan. Prime Minister's Office. Secretariat. Local Autonomy Section. *Laws Concerning Local Autonomy.* Tokyo: 1948.

Kluckhorn, Frank L. "The Menacing Shadow: Japan's Old Order." 1945. See no.389.

1325 Masland, John W. "Neighborhood Associations in Japan." *Far Eastern Survey* 15:355–58 (20 Nov. 1946)
A concise report by a member of the SCAP staff on the role of the neighborhood associations (*tonarigumi*) in Japanese society. It includes a description of their history and organizational structure and devotes special attention to their operation during and after the war. The author argues that such associations are characteristic of a totalitarian system of government and contrary to the principles of democratic society, and, as such, should be outlawed by the occupation.

1326 Nishikawa, Kiyoharu. "Local Governments and Their Financial Administration in Post-war Japan." *Public Finance* 18, no.2:110–19 (1963)
Nishikawa of Osaka City University gives a Marxist analysis of how the local autonomy which the occupation had originally encouraged broke down before the centralization of power in the hands of conservative leaders. The article is followed by a French résumé on page 119. The occupation's reforms, the steps taken by the central government to undo these reforms, and the weakness of the opposition are described. The trend toward centralization is regarded as part of a program of "capitalistic 'rationalization'" which serves only the interests of "great enterprises and local bosses."

Raper, Arthur F. "Some Recent Changes in Japanese Village Life." 1951. See no.1964.

1327 Steiner, Kurt. "The Japanese Village and Its Government." *Far Eastern Quarterly* 15:185–99 (Feb. 1956)
Japan is presented here as a predominantly rural society that is becoming more and more urbanized. Steiner very briefly outlines the historical development of the Japanese village and describes the organization and activities of the *buraku*, showing how the traditional Japanese family system has retained much of its vigor within the *buraku*. He comments on various changes made by the occupation, noting the commissions created under it and describing features of the Local Autonomy Law. The lack of distinction "between the village as an autonomous entity and as a national agency" is discussed, and the author explains why "inter-governmental relations still bear a closer resemblance to their prewar counterpart than they do to the plans of the Occupation reformers." The lack of financial independence of the Japanese village is outlined, and the 2 forms of citizen participation in Japanese local government—elections and direct demands—are discussed, with occupation efforts in these areas noted. Steiner views the future of the *buraku* as having "considerable importance for the political development of Japan as a whole" and shows why the *buraku* is weakening. The article concludes with a look at the prospects for occupation reforms as Japan finds a new consensus along the lines of democracy or authoritarianism.

1328 ———. *Local Government in Japan.* Stanford, Calif.: Stanford Univ. Pr., 1965. ix, 564p.
The author's major concerns are to determine the degree of local autonomy in Japanese government and to examine

the relationship between local autonomy and democracy. He conducts a historical survey of local government from feudal times through prewar Japan, then discusses postwar changes and applies legal and sociological approaches to postwar developments in local government. In chapter 5 Steiner, a professor of comparative politics, discusses basic occupation objectives, SCAP's attitudes toward the prewar functions of the Home Ministry, and the role of the Government Section of SCAP in initiating the local government reforms of 1946 along with the drafting of the new constitution and the Local Autonomy Law. Chapter 6 covers SCAP's attempt to decentralize Japanese police and educational administration, the significance of the purge of local officials, the land reform, reform of the local finance system, and the Shoup Mission of September 1949.

1329 ———. "Local Government in Japan: Reform and Reaction." *Far Eastern Survey* 23:97–102 (July 1954)

Using the issue of "centralization versus local autonomy" as a touchstone, Steiner, a SCAP official in Japan from 1945 to 1951, discusses the reaction to and the proposed revision of the occupation's reforms in the field of local government.

Supreme Commander for the Allied Powers. Monograph 6. *Local Government Reform, 1945–December 1950.* 1952. See no.288.

———. Monograph 38. *Local Government Finance, 1945–March 1951.* 1952. See no.320.

———. Civil Affairs Div. *Monthly Activities Report.* 1946–51. See no.264.

1330 ———. Civil Information and Education Section. Public Opinion and Sociological Research Div. *A Preliminary Study of the Neighborhood Associations of Japan.* Mimeographed. Tokyo: SCAP, 23 Jan. 1948. 84p.

A mimeographed sociological research report on neighborhood associations (*tonarigumi*) based on a thorough analysis of historical materials and interviews with actual neighborhood association leaders. Of particular interest is the discussion of wartime governmental controls over the neighborhood associations and especially over the Tokyo city organizations, which had a somewhat different structure. The monograph begins with an analysis of the nationwide organizational structure, the role of the Home Affairs Ministry, and the government's subsidies to the associations. It then considers the development of the Tokyo city associations since 1887 and explains the reasons they cited to justify their formation. It also discusses the development of the federated associations (*chōkai rengōkai*) in Tokyo since 1922, and shows the allocation of wartime work requests made by various governmental agencies among the Tokyo associations. The contents of weekly notices circulated among Tokyo association members are also studied as a means of analyzing the concerns of the central government during the war years. The abolition of the wartime system of neighborhood associations, which was supposedly completed by June 1947, is briefly treated. The texts of major legal documents and government statements that affected the structure and functions of neighborhood associations are appended with a useful bibliography and a list of interviews with neighborhood association leaders.

Available on microfilm from the National Archives, Washington, D.C.

———. Government Section. *The Japanese Elections, April 1947.* 1947. See no.1409.

———. Finance Div. *Summary of Japanese Taxes in Effect 1 April 1952.* 1952. See no.1693.

1331 Sutton, Joseph Lee. "Rural Politics in Japan." In Univ. of Michigan. Center for Japanese Studies. *Occasional Papers,* v.4. Ann Arbor: Univ. of Michigan Pr., 1953. p.40–50.

This study analyzes the rural basis of Japanese politics and assesses the "forces of change operating within it." In discussing "the hamlet in postwar Japan," the author shows why "the SCAP order for the abolition of hamlet councils (*burakukai*) and their headman (*burakukaichō*) could not be followed in the settlement pattern of Japanese rural areas without destroying local government." He describes how a headman is selected, the duties and qualifications of a headman, and the *buraku* organization below a headman. Under the heading "Rural Voters and Mayoralty Elections" the professional background of mayors, attitudes of rural voters toward the office of mayor, campaign techniques in mayoralty elections, and bossism are examined. Rural left-wing movements, attitudes toward the United States and the occupation forces, and women in rural politics are also discussed. In the conclusion the author notes that "the SCAP effort toward reforming the structure of rural politics has not proved successful."

1332 Tilton, Cecil G. "Local Government in Japan." *Military Government Journal* 1:14-19, 25 (July 1948)

The greater part of this article concerns the history of the establishment and development of local political structures in Japan. It traces their beginnings during the centuries of *bakufu* rule and concentrates on relevant reforms in administrative units that took place after the Meiji Restoration. There is a brief section at the conclusion of the article regarding changes in administration made in the thirties and forties to facilitate national control, for example, the creation of the *tonarigumi* system in 1940. Finally, brief mention is made of the present law under the occupation, the Local Autonomy Law, which has retained desirable aspects of the former system and provides political responsibility for 3 echelons of government—prefectures, cities, and towns and villages.

1333 Ulmer, S. Sidney. "Local Autonomy in Japan since the Occupation." *Journal of Politics* 19:46-65 (Feb. 1957)

Worried about the trend of increased control and domination by the central government, Ulmer examines the system of local government to see if the original occupation goals are still being fulfilled. He examines the system of local government, the police, and local education and finance. He also examines the centralizing trends which have begun on these levels. Ulmer concludes that these trends towards further centralization will continue and that perhaps the occupation tried to change too much in too brief a period.

1334 U.S. Dept. of State. *Administrative Subdivisions of Japan, with Appendix of 47 Prefectural Maps*. Washington, D.C.: Government Printing Office, 1947. xv, 652p. (Dept. of State publication 2749; Far Eastern series 19)

A gazetteer listing all of Japan's prefectures, cities, counties, towns, and townships and providing for each one its area, its population in both 1940 and 1945, and its name in Japanese characters as well as in romanized form. The publication was prepared by the State Department's Division of Research for Far East and was undertaken with the cooperation of the Army Map Service and the Board on Geographical Names. The main listing is arranged according to prefectures starting in the north of Japan and proceeding southward. It is supplemented by an extensive alphabetical listing of place names. All code numbers within the volume are keyed to the 47 prefectural maps which accompany the volume in a separate binding.

————. *Tax Mission to Japan. Report on Japanese Taxation.* 1949. *See* no. 1696.

————. ————. *Second Report on Japanese Taxation.* 1950. *See* no.1697.

1334a Wales, Horace G. Q. "Hope for Democracy in Japan." *America* 74:484-86 (2 Feb. 1946)

Wales finds Japan's past experiences with liberals and with parliamentary government by no means reassuring. He believes that the best hope for democracy in Asia lies in "the strengthening and expansion of the frequently existing village self-government."

1335 Ward, Robert Edward. "Patterns of Stability and Change in Rural Japanese Politics." In Univ. of Michigan. Center for Japanese Studies. *Occasional Papers*, v.1. Ann Arbor: Univ. of Michigan Pr., 1951. p.1–6.

Conclusions in this article are based on studies conducted by members of the University of Michigan's Center for Japanese Studies in Okayama prefecture throughout 1950. Ward examines "the persistence of old attitudes and patterns of action in rural Japan" and contrasts them with "whatever signs of significant change" became apparent during the occupation years. He includes consideration of basic attitudes of most peasants towards government, the importance of the *buraku* and the family, and other attitudes and practices which show patterns of stability in rural Japanese politics. He also points out "evidence of a slow process of change."

———. "The Socio-political Role of the *Buraku* (Hamlet) in Japan." 1951. *See* no.1985.

1336 ———. "Some Observations on Local Autonomy at the Village Level in Present-day Japan." *Far Eastern Quarterly* 12:183–202 (Feb. 1953)

Ward begins by noting the importance attached by high occupation officials to the "new and drastically decentralized system of local government" which was brought to Japan by 4 laws of 20 September 1946 and revised and consolidated in the Local Autonomy Law of 17 April 1947. The claims of success by the occupation in the field of local government are evaluated in this article "by comparing them with actual practice as observed by the writer in several villages of southwestern Honshū." Section 1 presents a brief summary of the major provisions on village autonomy of the Local Autonomy Law. Section 2 describes the structure and actual operations of village government and examines factors underlying "the lack of meaningful autonomy at the local level." In section 3 the author maintains "the actual practice of government and politics in villages of the writer's acquaintance has not changed from prewar patterns to anywhere near the extent intended and frequently but erroneously claimed by leaders of the Occupation." He concludes by looking at the probable future of local autonomy in Japan in terms of the reasons for the persistence of these prewar patterns.

———. "Urban-Rural Differences and the Process of Political Modernization in Japan: A Case Study." 1960. *See* no.1427.

1337 Warp, George A. "'Americanization' in Japan." *National Municipal Review* 41:443–48 (Oct. 1952)

During a 6-month stay in Japan where he served as a consultant for the Public Administration Clearing House and as adviser to various Japanese associations of local government officials, Warp had the opportunity to study the impact and extent of American-inspired changes in local self-government institutions. In this article, written shortly after his return, he discusses some of these changes, notes how private citizens have established new civic associations, and examines the nature of the national associations organized by officials on the prefectural as well as city, town, and village levels. He points out that administrative reorganization continues to be a controversial subject in Japan and that many Japanese opposed SCAP's efforts to decentralize Japanese administration. He predicts that many modifications will be made once the occupation is terminated.

1338 ———. "In Our Image and Likeness." *National Municipal Review* 42, no.4:175–78, 188 (Apr. 1953)

Warp, associate director of the Public Administration Center at the University of Minnesota, discusses the efforts of the occupation authorities to superimpose such American democratic trappings as a system of local administrative boards and commissions, an enlarged local legislature, and an American system of civil service commissions upon Japan's local government. He points out many of the problems of organization, efficiency, finances, and intergovernmental relations that have resulted and notes the strong possibility that these reforms will prove impermanent.

Changes in the Police System

In consonance with the general movement toward local autonomy, the Japanese police system also underwent a drastic degree of decentralization at the hands of the occupation authorities. In practice this was moderated at a relatively early date. In 1950 with the establishment of the paramilitary National Police Reserve as a consequence of the outbreak of the war in Korea, the further development of the police force became entangled with the larger issues of rearmament and remilitarization. The following entries relate to these matters. Entries in the section on rearmament (p.781) are also relevant to this latter stage.

1339 Braibanti, Ralph J. D. "Japan's New Police Law." *Far Eastern Survey* 18:17–22 (24 Jan. 1949)

This comprehensive article on Japan's police system begins with a discussion of the prewar and wartime conditions wherein Japanese police "symbolized . . . the negation of personal liberty" and the police system was characterized by an extreme centralization of authority and a wide range of powers. There is a brief discussion of the reasons for the decline in the prestige of the Japanese police at the outset of the occupation, and a thorough description of the reforms initiated by SCAP authorities is provided. The report describes the activities and recommendations of the 2 American consulting teams, the Valentine Commission and the Rural Police Planning Commission headed by Oscar J. Olanders, including their suggestion that power be transferred from the police to other agencies of government through the abrogation of the Public Peace Preservation Act, and their recommendation that what remained the responsibility of the police "required extensive modification and had to be integrated with the new autonomy given to prefectural and local governments." An objective and comprehensive analysis of the new Police Law put into effect on 7 March 1948 is followed by a consideration of SCAP's considerable efforts in the reeducation of police personnel—which began as early as June 1946. In defining and discussing SCAP's reform of the structure of Japan's new police system, this article should be extremely useful to students of the occupation.

1339a Costello, William. "Cops and Robbers in Japan." *Nation* 168:96–97 (22 Jan. 1949)

Costello reports that the new SCAP-designed Japanese police force is weak and ineffective, paralyzed by lack of certainty about new civil rights laws and losing its best men on account of poor pay. Training is still "feudalistic and militaristic," and the police are poorly equipped. Costello concludes that ultimate responsibility lies with the Diet, which appears to have deliberately sabotaged the police reforms by refusing adequate appropriations.

1339b "Directive from General MacArthur to the Imperial Japanese Government." *Department of State Bulletin* 13: 730–32 (4 Nov. 1945)

This undated directive spells out in detail the actions to be taken by the Japanese government for the purpose of dismantling its secret police and thought control apparatus. The release of all political prisoners also is ordered.

1340 "Fear Spreads in Germany and Japan." *U.S. News and World Report* 29: 22–23 (4 Aug. 1950)

An article concerning the creation of a 75,000–man National Police Reserve force as a supplement to the existing 125,000–man local police force. This reserve is to be used in case of domestic strife and as a Japanese contribution to the defense of non-Communist Asia. The author suggests that the advent of the Korean War shifted priorities within MacArthur's headquarters and caused the acceptance of proposals by SCAP's intelligence chief, Major General Charles E. Willoughby, for a larger and more highly centralized police system. Statements by Yoshida that the revival of thought control and of a police state must not be allowed are included, as are tables presenting statistics on Japanese weapons production potential.

1341 Hays, Frank E. "The New Japanese Police Law." *Military Government Journal* 1, no.7:15–16, 27 (May 1948)

Within this brief but informative article, the special advisor to the chief of SCAP's Government Section discusses Japan's municipal and rural police forces, the public safety commissions in general, the Police Reorganization Act, and the National Public Safety Commission which has been empowered to act in the case of national emergencies.

1341a "In the Allied Council for Japan: Statement by Lt.-Gen. Derevyanko, Soviet Member of the Allied Council." *Current Digest of the Soviet Press* 1, no.2:26–29 (8 Feb. 1949)

This article, which first appeared in the 8 January issues of *Pravda* and *Izvestia*, reproduces the text of Derevyanko's statement on the Japanese police forces made at the 5 January 1949 regular meeting of the council. Derevyanko points out the serious danger inherent in increasing the numerical strength and arms of Japan's police force and cites figures to show that the size of the force has increased 2 and a half times since the end of the war. He notes that recent U.S. policy statements indicate that a further increase in the size of the force is imminent and claims that such an action would "represent a real threat of the re-establishment of the Japanese armed forces." He also cites statements by various Japanese officials to show that the present Japanese police force is regarded as the nucleus of a future army. Then, in a 3 point proposal, the Soviet representative calls upon the council to restrict the size of the police force in the future and to insure the dissolution of all secret police organizations in Japan. The article concludes with brief summaries of statements by the U.S. and British representatives to the council in which they expressed their reactions to the Soviet demands.

1342 "Japan Drills an 'Army of Sergeants'." *Life* 30:30–33 (5 Feb. 1951)

Life reports on the training and arming of a 75,000–man police reserve, manned and led by war veterans. This reserve is expected to be the core of a postpeace treaty army which could be increased to 500,000 men.

1342a "Japan Takes First Steps to Build U.S.-Style Army." *U.S. News and World Report* 31:20 (30 Nov. 1951)

Plans for expanding the 75,000-man National Police Reserve into an army of 200,000 to 300,000 men are outlined. Japanese leaders are reported to be counting upon U.S. aid to finance the training and arming of these soldiers inasmuch as Japan is said to be too weak to contribute anything more than men and uniforms at the present time.

1343 "Letter Sent by SCAP to Prime Minister Yoshida, Authorizing the Increase of the Police Reserve Force and the Expansion of the Maritime Safety Board, July 8, 1950." *Contemporary Japan* 19: 458–59 (July/Sept. 1950)

MacArthur points out in this letter that he is permitting an increase in Japan's internal police force in order that the peaceful situation now existing "will continue unchallenged by lawless minorities, here as elsewhere committed to the subversion of the due process of law and assaults of opportunity against the peace and public welfare." Accordingly, he authorizes the Japanese government to establish a National Police Reserve of 75,000 men and to expand the existing Maritime Safety Board by an additional 8,000 men.

1344 Nakahara, Hidenori. "The Japanese Police." *Journal of Criminal Law, Criminology, and Police Science* 46:583–94 (Nov./Dec. 1955)

This article is divided into 2 parts, the first a brief history of the Japanese police system from 1871 until 1954, and the second an outline of the police system after the reforms in 1954. Nakahara writes about the influence of the reforms proposed by SCAP and its goals of decentralizing and democratizing the police. The outline of the present system includes sections on the National Public Safety Commission, the National Police Agency, and the prefectural police. Also included in the article is a table describing the organization of the police system.

1344a Nakajima, Kenzō. "A Warning against Police Control." *Contemporary Japan* 19:423–25 (July/Sept. 1950)

After recounting the development of the modern Japanese police system and, in particular, the history of the so-called thought-control police, Nakajima offers suggestions about ways for combatting the revival of the old-style police force. First, the authority of the police must be strictly limited by law, and the police establishment should be kept rigidly separate from administrative authority; police activity should always be in harmony with human rights. Secondly, the Japanese people must observe the fundamental principles of democracy and not succumb to mob psychology. Finally, the people must give more sympathetic consideration to others than to themselves. Now that the National Police Reserve has been established, Nakajima cautions, particular care also should be taken to see that individual rights are safeguarded against police infringement.

1344b Nishi, Kantarō. "Democratization of the Metropolitan Police." *Contemporary Japan* 18:236–39 (Apr./June 1949)

This article by a well-known authority on the Japanese police system originally appeared in Japanese in the May 1949 issue of *Shakai*. Most of the postwar changes in the police system, according to Nishi, have been well received by the police themselves. The depoliticization of the police force is especially welcome; instead of serving the government by enforcing political ordinances, the police are now free to serve the people. The Metropolitan Police Board is now buttressed by numerous non-official auxiliary groups, but the author feels that democratization still has a long way to go. Bureaucratization and old elitist attitudes still prevail, and since the police are necessarily a tool wielded by those with political power, the full democratization of Japan's police force will come about only through the democratization of the country in general.

1345 Petty, Edward Avin. *Directed Change and Culture Adhesion: A Study of Functional Integration in the Police Administration of Japan.* Ph.D. dissertation, Univ. of Southern California, 1961. 386p. (Abstracted in *Dissertation Abstracts* 22: 1707 [1961]; University Microfilms order no.61–3823)

Through an examination of changes in the Japanese police system and administration initiated by SCAP reforms, Petty presents a case study in cultural adhesion. He defines the process of cultural adhesion as one which occurs after the introduction of a foreign cultural innovation into another nation. The extent to which the innovation remains intact or "adhesive" is indicative of the degree to which directed change across cultural barriers is successful. When a new technique is transferred, recipients either readjust their own heritage to it or mold the foreign cultural element into their traditional patterns. Petty regards the Japanese policeman as a preserver of traditional values and analyzes the process by which the occupation attempted to make the Japanese police system less authoritarian and more decentralized. He notes that in the post-occupation period, the Japanese synthesized their cultural values with the new police system, retaining an element of popular participation in police management, while recentralizing the system at the national and prefectural levels. He also notes that retention of the "obligation system of interpersonal relationships" characterized the selective process of cultural adhesion in Japanese police administration, and that cultural elements supporting a hierarchical pattern were readily accepted.

Röhl, Wilhelm. *Fremde Einflüsse im modernen japanischen Recht.* 1959. See no.1291.

1346 Roth, Andrew. "Japan's Police Terror." *Nation* 161:250–51 (15 Sept. 1945)
The history and present operations of the Japanese police system are briefly outlined in this article. The author emphasizes the repressive measures taken against groups and individuals desiring democratic reforms in the thirties and early forties and warns against any Allied leniency toward individuals formerly connected with the system. He also advises SCAP authorities not to encourage the development of a stronger police force for the so-called purpose of keeping order because he believes the latent strength of the police to be dangerous.

1347 Saitō, Noboru. "The New Police of Japan." *Military Government Journal* 1:18 (June 1948)
A brief description of the elimination of the old, oppressive Japanese police system and the inauguration of a new system which is characterized by decentralized control. The author considers the undesirable elements that were removed at the termination of the war, discussing such things as the elimination of the Special Higher Police force, the prohibition of acts infringing on the people's rights, and the improvement of treatment in jails. He then discusses the nature and function of the new system inaugurated on 7 March 1948, which is divided into 2 categories—the national rural police controlled by a National Public Safety Commission under the jurisdiction of the prime minister, and the municipal police who are controlled by local Municipal Public Safety Commissions. There is also mention of the provision made for emergency situations whereby the prime minister, upon the advice of the National Public Safety Commission, may temporarily unify the entire police force to deal with a crisis more effectively.

1348 Sugai, Shūichi. "The Japanese Police System." In *Five Studies in Japanese Politics*, ed. by Robert E. Ward. Ann Arbor: Univ. of Michigan Pr., 1957. p.1–14. (Univ. of Michigan, Center for Japaese Studies, occasional papers, no.7)
In this study of the postwar Japanese police system, Sugai Shūichi of Kyoto University's Law School assesses the impact and effectiveness of the reforms undertaken by the Allies in a move designed to democratize the system. Sugai opens with an outline of police organization and authority before the war. He then describes the enactment of the Police Law of December 1947 and the occupation's effort to decentralize the country's police agencies and to limit their powers, place the police under popular control, and neutralize them as a political force. Finally, he illustrates some of the subsequent reactions to these changes and discusses the government's decision in 1954 to recentralize the police system. This latter development, the author asserts, is a reaction that not only exemplifies the revisionist sentiment relating to Allied innovations in the field of government but that also may be indicative of the ultimate fate of many other occupation reforms.

Supreme Commander for the Allied Powers. Monograph 55. *Police and Public Safety, 1945–October 1951.* 1952. See no.337.

1348a "The Text of the Ordinance Governing the Functioning of the New National Police Reserve Promulgated and Enforced on August 10, 1950." *Contemporary Japan* 19:462–63 (July/Sept. 1950)
This document includes provisions

for (1) strict civilian control of the police reserve by placing it under the prime minister; (2) fixed limits on the size of the reserve; (3) regulations concerning personnel matters and labor disputes; and (4) funding.

"Washington Now Plans to Lighten the Japanese Occupation Load." 1948. *See* no.578.

1348b Worden, William L. "The Japs Are Marching Again." *Saturday Evening Post* 223, no.30:26–27, 60+ (20 Jan. 1951)

Worden chooses to emphasize the fact that despite its official name, the Japanese National Police Reserve is in a reality a full-fledged military organization. The 75,000-man reserve and an expansion of the Maritime Safety Board, he explains, were authorized by MacArthur when the outbreak of hostilities in Korea required the transfer of American military forces from Japan. Worden describes various training and drill techniques and interviews typical members of the force, many of whom are identified as former veterans of the wartime Japanese army.

POLITICAL PARTIES AND ELECTIONS

The following entries describe developments in the areas of political parties and elections during the occupation. Many of them also provide general assessments and commentaries on the contemporary political scene. They are, consequently, closely related to many of the entries in the section providing a calendar of general commentaries (p.152).

1349 Allen, Lafe Franklin. "Japanese Election." *Commonweal* 50:116–18 (13 May 1949)

Characterizing the January 1949 general election in Japan as "orderly and enthusiastic," the author provides a thoughtful analysis of the results. He examines the factors behind what he characterizes as "the pronounced trend to extremes of both right and left and the collapse of middle-of-the-road parties." He discusses the significant increases by the Communist party and the impressive triumph of the Democratic Liberal party as well as the fate of the middle-of-the-road parties. In conclusion, he voices concern for Japan's lack of capable and dynamic leadership as evidenced by the election results.

1350 ———. "Japan's New Diet." *Current History* 13:96–99 (Aug. 1947)

In his account of Japan's new Diet, Allen, a military officer in Japan during the occupation, notes that the Communists' poor showing in the general election was primarily due to the widespread resentment they promoted by stimulating strikes in key industries, their urging of the abolition of the emperor system, and a comparatively small turnout of urban voters. The Japanese indicated that they wanted a more liberal government but without equivocation, they flatly repudiated the excesses of communism.

1350a Arai, Tatsuo. "Watching the General Election." *Contemporary Japan* 15: 41–57 (Jan./Apr. 1946)

Arai comments on the unprecedented nature of the 1946 general election, which came after a long void in political activity. The purge, he notes, has created a good deal of commotion, and a large percentage of the new Diet's members have had no previous political experience. The campaign itself, however, did not excite any great interest among the voters, although the participation rate was not bad considering the fact that many newly-enfranchised women failed to vote. Arai follows a brief analysis of the personnel and platforms of the major parties with a discussion of certain unusual results of the election. These include the successful candidacy of a high percentage of the women who ran for office, and the large number of "substitute candidates" elected. The latter are relatives or other associates standing in for purged politicians; most of them are not really qualified for office.

1351 Avarin, V. "The Situation in Japan." *New Times* no.9:12–18 (1 May 1946)

Focusing on the results of the recent parliamentary elections in Japan, this article discusses occupation policies to date. The author alleges that the elections were held too soon after Japan's surrender, thus enabling "the imperialist reactionaries and the fascist residue" to regain control of the country. He discusses SCAP's land reform program which he terms inadequate and notes that Japan's finances and industry are in a state of prostration. In this dire situation, he maintains, "the Communist Party of Japan has become the natural rallying centre for the elements which are striving for the democratization of the country." He expresses confidence in that party's future growth and development.

Beloff, Max. *Soviet Far Eastern Policy since Yalta*. 1950. See no.775.

1352 Brumbaugh, Thoburn T. "Kagawa: Christian Socialist." *Christian Century* 63:1531–32 (18 Dec. 1946)

Brumbaugh explains Kagawa Toyohiko's role in maintaining a balanced, moderate coalition in the Social Democratic party. His close association with the postwar revival of consumers cooperatives, farm organizations, the seaman's union, and the fisherman's league is noted. The author stresses Kagawa's rejection of the material realism of America in favor of world reform and regeneration based on "one God, one human family, and world order."

1353 Bryn-Jones, David. "Japan's General Election 1952: An Interpretation." *Contemporary Japan* 21, no.7/9:371–89 (1952)

In this article the results of the first general election since the end of the occupation of Japan are examined in order to determine its significance in relation to such things as possible changes in alignment of political forces, trends in Japanese public opinion, political prospects in Japan, and the direction of future policies. The statistical data are studied and the continued decline of small minor parties noted. The possibility of a reversion to political patterns of the prewar years is considered. Results and implications of the fact that purged members of prewar parties were permitted to be active again are discussed. The decline in the Communist vote is also studied, as well as the stable position maintained by independent candidates in postwar Japan. A look at the question of the future of political democracy in Japan concludes the article.

1354 Byrne, P. J. "How MacArthur Thwarted a Red Japan." *Plain Talk* 2:23–31 (Feb. 1948)

A loosely structured, oversimplified account of the efforts of the Soviet Communists to gain control in occupied Japan. After illustrating the numerous advantages the Communists were given in Japan, the author describes how, in his opinion, they were thwarted through their own miscalculations and MacArthur's astuteness.

1355 Clubok, Alfred Bernard. "Japanese Conservative Politics, 1947–1955." In *Five Studies in Japanese Politics*, ed. by Robert E. Ward. Ann Arbor: Univ. of Michigan Pr., 1957. p.21–59. (Univ. of Michigan, Center for Japanese Studies, occasional papers, no.7)

Based upon a master's thesis completed at the University of Michigan, this study of postwar Japanese politics focuses upon the geographical distribution of support for the Liberal and Democratic parties and upon the urban-rural distribution of their strength. The author first discusses the 1945 and the 1947 House of Representatives Election Laws and their impact upon the Japanese election system, and then examines the results of the general elections for 1947, 1949, 1952, 1953, and 1955. He also assesses some of the strengths and weaknesses of the 2 parties and shows that the conservative tradition of prewar Japan has carried over into the postwar political scene.

1356 Colbert, Evelyn S. *The Left Wing in Japanese Politics*. New York: Institute of Pacific Relations, International Secretariat, 1952. xii, 353p.

Colbert provides an extensive scholarly examination of the prewar origins and postwar revival and activities of the left-wing movement in Japan. The book is divided into 5 major sections: section 1 deals with the Proletarian Movement, 1918–40; section 2 describes the revival of left-wing organizations after Japan's surrender to the Allies; section 3 details the major developments in left-wing politics, 1945–46; section 4 is a discussion of the Katayama cabinet and the Ashida cabinet; and section 5, the epilogue, is an examination of left-wing politics, 1949–50. The author is concerned with the effect of SCAP policies on the left-wing movement and does not attempt any general discussion of occupation programs and policies.

1357 Cole, Allan Burnett. *Political Tendencies of Japanese in Small Enterprises, with Special Reference to the Social Democratic Party*. New York: Institute of Pacific Relations, 1959. ii, 155p.

Part of a research project entitled "Studies on Japan's Social Democratic Parties," this volume seeks to interpret why and how a minority of the millions engaged in small and middle sized enterprises (*chūshō kigyō*) were willing to support the Social Democratic party. The author concludes that there has been a growth in postwar Japan in political consciousness and activity among many individuals engaged in small-scale sales and production and that petty mercantile interests tend to be more sympathetic toward left-wing parties, whom they feel will more actively promote their main economic interests.

1358 ———, George O. Totten, and Cecil H. Uyehara, with a contributed chap. by Ronald P. Dore. *Socialist Parties in Postwar Japan*. New Haven, Conn.: Yale Univ. Pr., 1966. xvii, 490p.

In this study of Japan's non-Communist Social Democratic parties from their revival in 1945 to 1960–61, "the authors have combined the historical method with political description and analysis." The book is divided into 4 major parts: postwar party history; theories, tactics, and policies; organization and leadership; and electoral and organized support. Because of the time span of the work, occupation reforms, policies, and activities are directly related to activities and policies of the Socialist parties. This relationship is studied in terms of the Social Democratic party and the Katayama coalition on the one hand and the occupation and its program for democratization on the other. The authors look at the reasons why between 1949 and 1951 Japanese Socialists' attitudes toward occupation policies "changed from oblique criticism to direct attack." The impetus given to the organization of labor by SCAP and its dealings with unions and Socialist labor leaders are examined. SCAP attitudes toward and legislation concerning strikes are considered along with Socialist reactions to these policies. Occupation and Socialist economic policies are studied in some detail. Socialist opposition to the expansion and strengthening of the Japanese police forces, especially when the Korean War brought SCAP encouragement of these measures, is also discussed. A number of tables, charts, and illustrations are included in the work.

1359 Colton, Kenneth E. "Conservative Leadership in Japan." *Far Eastern Survey* 24:90–96 (June 1955)

Colton explains that the conservative movement is still in transition after war, defeat, and occupation. He points out that its present course is largely determined by 2 factors: the results of the depurge program and the rise of the Socialist movement. Kenneth Colton formerly served with the Civil Historical Section of SCAP.

1360 ———. "The Conservative Political Movement." *Annals of the American Academy of Political and Social Science* 308:40–53 (Nov. 1956)

This article traces the development of the Japanese conservative political movement primarily after Japan became independent in 1952. First, however, the author examines various prewar and occupation influences on the movement such as the role of those who had been purged from office, SCAP influence, and the development of Yoshida Shigeru's power. Colton then moves to postoccupation developments including the struggle against Yoshida's rule, the position of the Progressive party, and the union of the conservatives. Party leaders and factionalism and the growth of party power are also discussed. The article ends with notice of the growing challenge presented to conservatism by the Social Democratic party.

1361 ———. "Pre-war Political Influences in Post-war Conservative Parties." *American Political Science Review* 42:940–57 (Oct. 1948)

This article is concerned with "the elements of pre-war political leadership present in the founding of the two major post-war conservative parties, the effect of the purge directive upon their leadership, their organizational and institutional character, the political influence of governmental bureaucracies, and the problem of party finance." The author believes that in general both of the postwar conservative parties, the Democratic Liberal party and the Democratic party, have followed prewar patterns regarding party structure, party action in the Diet, and the formation of nonparliamentary associations. According to him, a somewhat different situation has evolved concerning party financing.

1362 Costello, William. "Report from Tokyo." *New Republic* 116:7 (5 May 1947)

The outcomes of Japan's 3 April 1947 elections—for prefectural governors, the House of Councillors, and the House of Representatives—are briefly analyzed in this report. The author suggests that the victory of the conservative parties is not as sweeping as it might seem on the surface. Indeed, according to him, many Japanese interpret the vote as a loss of face for Premier Yoshida Shigeru and the Liberal party since they won fewer seats in the lower house than did the Social Democrats.

Council on Foreign Relations. "The World at the Crossroads: 3. East Asia on the Eve." 1951. *See* no.779.

1363 Cowley, George A. "B.C.'s Pacific Neighbour: Will Democracy Take Hold in Japan?" *Queen's Quarterly* (Kingston, Ontario) 65:222–33 (Summer 1958)

This article deals mostly with Japanese politics during the late 1950s, but it does discuss SCAP reforms as a background to the current political situation and analyzes the effect of the occupation's changes on the prospects for democracy in Japan. Cowley is optimistic, noting that democratic thinking seems to be well entrenched at least in the cities, but he also warns that old ways often persist for a long time.

Deverall, Richard L. G. *Red Star over Japan.* 1952. *See* no.782.

1364 "Dissolution of the Japanese Parliament." *Soviet Press Translations* 4:100–102 (15 Feb. 1949)

Originally written for *Izvestia* on 31 December 1948 during the interim between the dissolution of Parliament on 23 December and the holding of elections on 23 January, this article considers some of the reasons behind these recent moves. According to the author, the reactionary Liberal Democratic party under Yoshida is a pawn of the SCAP authorities and both organizations are intent upon destroying all democratic elements in Japan, particularly the Communist party. Therefore, they are mounting a terrorist campaign to subjugate the Communist party and to make Japan into "a military, industrial and strategic base for American imperialism."

1365 Dull, Paul Shirley. "The Japanese General Election of 1952." *American Political Science Review* 47:199–204 (Mar. 1953)

Dull points out that an analysis of the election is not easy, for despite the controversial questions, the Japanese voter was confused by both the complexities of intraparty quarrels and the ambiguities of many of the candidates' campaigns. The election results, although establishing a majority party, did not give any positive mandate regarding the major issues of the campaign.

1366 Ebata, Kiyoshi. "The Japan Communist Party: Its Development since the War." *Japan Quarterly* 5:426–34 (Oct./Dec. 1958)

This article deals with the post-World War II history of the Japan Communist party. The author follows in detail events surrounding the JCP since 1945. He analyzes the influences of foreign Communist party criticisms of the JCP, various national elections, and the break in 1955 with "ultra-leftist adventurism." He writes also of the public's attitude toward the JCP and the way this might change the JCP's ideas and methods in the future.

1367 "L'évolution électorale du Japon depuis la dernière guerre (1945–1959)." *Notes et études documentaires* no.2661: 1–46 (3 May 1960)

Farley, Miriam S. "Japanese Political Issues Present Dilemma for U.S." 1948. See no.1751.

1367a Fukui, Haruhiro. *Party in Power: The Japanese Liberal-Democrats and Policy-Making.* Berkeley: Univ. of California Pr., 1970. xi, 301p. (Publications of the Center for Japanese and Korean Studies)

Chapter 2 of this study, "Transmission of the Prewar Heritage to Postwar Parties," deals with the political upheavals and the multiparty system of the occupation period and with the ultimate emergence of the Liberal Democratic Party in 1955. The remainder of the work is an analysis of the policy-making process within the party, and 2 chapters —7 and 8—deal with the formation of LDP policy on 2 questions related to the occupation: the compensation of former landlords divested of their holdings by the land reform, and constitutional revision. Both chapters contain summaries and analyses of actions taken during the late 1940s, and provide considerable information as well on current Japanese attitudes toward the occupation and on the political consequences of the SCAP reforms. Fukui's book was submitted as a Ph.D. dissertation to the Australian National University in 1967 under the title *The Japanese Liberal-Democratic Party and Policy-Making.*

1367b Gauntlett, Hugh. "Cherry Blossom Election." *Spectator* 184:423 (31 Mar. 1950)

Gauntlett reminisces about his experiences as interpreter for a British team assigned to supervise the Japanese election of May 1947 in a remote rural area. After relating a few anecdotes about local personages, the author comments on the low voter turnout and the high number of invalid votes characterizing the election, and he concludes that "the enlargement of the democratic process was greeted with dutiful and unenthusiastic submission."

1368 "General MacArthur's Letter to Prime Minister Shigeru Yoshida, Directing the Suspension of *The Akahata* and Other Publications Employed in the Dissemination of Communist Propaganda in Japan, July 18, 1950." *Contemporary Japan* 19: 461–62 (July/Sept. 1950)

MacArthur explains in this letter why he has directed the Japanese government to maintain indefinitely the suspensions previously imposed upon publication of the *Akahata* and its successors and affiliates. Insisting that the majority of the Japanese people would not be unduly influenced by such Communist propaganda, he nevertheless voices his concern that Communist use of public information media will incite "the irresponsible and lawless minority elements of society to oppose law, disturb order and subvert the general welfare."

1369 "General MacArthur's Letter to Prime Minister Yoshida Directing the Japanese Government to Purge Twenty-Four Communist Leaders, June 6, 1950." *Contemporary Japan* 19:453–54 (July/Sept. 1950)

This letter discusses the general progress of the occupation before considering the reasons why the entire membership of the Central Committee of the Japan Communist party is a threat to the attainment of SCAP's goals. MacArthur names the 24 leaders and directs that they be removed from public service and subject to the prohibitions and liabilities of SCAP directives nos.548 and 550.

1370 "General MacArthur's Letter to Prime Minister Yoshida Ordering the Purge of the Editorial Staff of *The Akahata*, Organ of the Japanese Communist Party, June 7, 1950." *Contemporary Japan* 19:454 (July/Sept. 1950)

After briefly reviewing the development of the Japanese press from the beginning of the occupation and the lifting of SCAP censorship upon press activities, MacArthur points to what he terms a glaring exception to the responsible Japanese press—the Communist organ *Akahata*. After discussing various stern corrective actions that might be taken to remedy the situation, the supreme commander announces his resolve to add 17 of the newspaper's editorial staff to an earlier list of Communist party Central Committee members, all of whom are to be purged from their offices.

"General MacArthur's Statement on the Third Anniversary of Japan's New Constitution, May 3, 1950." 1950. *See* no.941.

1371 "General of the Army Douglas MacArthur's Letter to Prime Minister Shigeru Yoshida, Calling on the Japanese Government to Hold a New General Election after the Close of the 92nd Session of the Diet, February 7, 1947." *Contemporary Japan* 16:104 (Jan./Mar. 1947)

In this brief letter, the supreme commander outlines the reasons why he believes the time is ripe for holding general elections in Japan, and he urges the Japanese government to work out the details of such an election themselves.

"General of the Army Douglas MacArthur's Statement anent the House of Representatives Election of April 25th, April 27, 1947." *See* no.934a.

1372 Haring, Douglas Gilbert. "Speculations on Japanese Communism." *Far Eastern Survey* 22:10–12 (14 Jan. 1953)

Haring, author of several studies on Japan, notes that among the main obstacles to Communist control of Japan are former occupation policies of a decentralized police system and constitutional guarantees of individual rights, and of public trials for arrested persons.

1373 Ikematsu, Fumio. "Political Parties in Flux." *Contemporary Japan* 22, no.7/9: 416–26 (1953)

The subject of this article is the turmoil existing within and between political parties in Japan since the dissolution of the House of Representatives on 14 March 1953, which resulted from a nonconfidence bill at the fifteenth extraordinary session of the Diet. In the election subsequent to this dissolution the parties maintained the same platforms as announced at the twenty-fifth general election. The statistics for and features of this twenty-sixth general election are cited by Ikematsu. He then discusses the political activities between parties during the sixteenth extraordinary session of the Diet convened on 18 May 1953. Efforts of the Liberal party and the Yoshida cabinet to secure political stability following this session are reviewed, followed by an examination of various measures and objectives of the political parties during the seventeenth and eighteenth sessions of the Diet. Political stability having not yet been guaranteed, the article concludes by noting the desires of the Liberal party and the Yoshida cabinet for a coalition or coordination with the Progressive party and the negotiations being carried out between the right-wing and the left-wing of the Socialist party.

1374 ———. "Political Parties Today and Tomorrow." *Contemporay Japan* 21, no. 7/9:390–409 (1952)

The discussion of Japan's political parties in this article is based on the twenty-fifth general election for the House of Representatives on 1 October 1952, the first election since sovereignty was restored to Japan. The characteristics of the election are outlined and reasons for the victory of the Liberal party discussed, with the author naming the president of the party as the major cause of victory. Right-wing and left-wing Socialist Democratic parties are examined in terms of their support, and the effect of the rearmament issue on the election is considered. Chances for the emergence of 2 major parties in Japan are weighed, and the significance of the defeat of the Communists and the reelection of depurgees are discussed. Two features of the election funds looked at in the article are the contribution of funds by labor unions to parties and candidates they supported and the conditions imposed on the donations made by industrial and financial circles. The struggle between Yoshida and Hatoyama and the political unrest in Japan are also studied. In the conclusion a comparison is made between Japanese politics and the politics of the United States and Great Britain and future prospects for the Japanese political parties are noted.

1375 Ikeuchi, Hajime, et al. "The Japanese Communist Party as Seen by the Japanese Press during the Allied Occupation, 1945–1952." *Gazette* 6, no.1:79–93 (1960)

Ikeuchi Hajime, Okazaki Keiko, and Kubo Naoko attempt in this article to ascertain the amount and the type of attention that the Japan Communist party received from the press during the occupation period. They conclude that the 2 major dailies—*Yomiuri* and *Asahi*—at first were favorable in their attitudes towards the party but that in 1946 and 1948 respectively they became much more critical as well as hostile of Communist activities within the country.

1375a "Imposed Political Democracy." *Commonweal* 44:108 (17 May 1946)

Commenting on developments since the most recent Japanese parliamentary election, this editorial ponders the timing of SCAP's evidently sudden decision to prevent Hatoyama Ichirō from forming the coalition government he was in the process of putting together. The editors suggest 2 possible explanations: either MacArthur has special, as yet undisclosed, reasons for wanting to humiliate the Japanese or to remind them that he is in charge, or he has yielded to Chinese and Soviet pressures at the eleventh hour. The editorial concludes that regardless of the reasons behind this particular turn of events, it is another demonstration that political democracy in an occupied country "simply cannot be."

1375b Inahara, Katsuji. "Diet after Surrender." *Contemporary Japan* 14:171–81 (Apr./Dec. 1945)

The role of the "surrender" Diet under the Higashikuni Cabinet was primarily that of providing information to the public at large. The information it actually supplied, however, was too concise and failed to indicate the extent of Japan's defeat and overall war losses. Prince Higashikuni's address to the Diet on 5 September is cited to illustrate this point: he explained Japan's surrender largely in terms of production failures and the exhaustion of the people, and failed to mention either the army's blunders in strategy or larger ethical and legal questions. Inahara next summarizes Japan's war losses and concludes with a few comments on the remarkable progress that the Japanese have already made on the road to democracy and peaceful government.

1375c "Japanese Election System Described." *National Municipal Review* 40: 434, 454 (Sept. 1951)

This brief article is an abstract of *Elections in Japan* (Japanese National

Election Commission; Tokyo: August 1950. 18p.). It describes the current electoral system and how it differs from the old one but does not refer specifically to the occupation itself.

1376 "Japanese General Elections." *Department of State Bulletin* 14:639–41 (21 Apr. 1946)

This article consists of 2 items: a communication from the Far Eastern Commission (dated 21 March 1946) to MacArthur regarding the April 1946 general election, and MacArthur's reply of 29 March 1946. The chairman of the FEC indicates the commission's fear that the early date set for the election might give the reactionary political parties too great an advantage, since the liberal parties have not yet had sufficient time to organize their support. Furthermore, FEC members are concerned that the voters may not have enough time to examine the draft constitution and to consider the attitudes of the various parties toward it. MacArthur replies that postponement would merely keep the present wartime Diet in power; that the true reactionaries have already been discredited or removed by the purge; that postponement would be misunderstood by the Japanese people; and that the constitution is a separate issue, of no particular advantage to one party or another.

1376a "The Japanese General Elections." *Department of State Bulletin* 14:1067–73, 1090 (23 June 1946)

This article consists of excerpts from issue no.7 of SCAP's *Summation of Non-Military Activities in Japan and Korea* (no.262) dealing with the general election held in April 1946. Various aspects of the election are briefly treated, among them the parties and their respective platforms, SCAP supervision, statistics on candidates and voter turnout, and the election results. Also included is MacArthur's statement of 23 April in which he characterized the election as a "healthy forward advance for democracy in Japan."

Kamichika, Ichiko. "Japanese Women Enfranchised." 1956. *See* no.2253.

1376b Kennedy, Malcolm D. *A History of Communism in East Asia*. New York: Praeger, 1957. ix, 556p. English edition published under the title *A Short History of Communism in Asia* (London: Wiedenfeld and Nicolson, 1957. ix, 556p.)

Kennedy, a former employee of the British Foreign Office, traces the origins and the development of nationalism and communism in East Asia from the early 1920s through the mid-1950s. In the first part of chapter 34, he discusses communism in Japan during the occupation, focusing on the revival of the Japan Communist party, the Communist-instigated strikes of the period, MacArthur's suppression of major Communist leaders, and Communist policy in Japan.

1376c Kiyose, Ichirō. "The New Election Law." *Contemporary Japan* 15:1–23 (Jan./Apr. 1946)

The author of this article served as chairman of the Special Committee for Extending Suffrage—a committee whose recommendations led to the new election law promulgated on 18 December 1945. According to Kiyose, there are 5 major points to this new law: (1) the expansion of the franchise; (2) new regulations on the size of electoral districts; (3) restrictions on campaigning, and anti-corruption provisions; (4) the prevention of official interference in elections; and (5) the establishment of public facilities for campaigns. Kiyose next discusses the election reforms in their historical perspective, comparing them point by point with the older laws. The present law, he suspects, will prove to be only an interim measure because (1) Allied–Japanese relations are not yet in their final form and there are unresolved questions about the status of the Koreans, Formosans, and Ryukuans; (2) a new constitution is expected before long; (3) the position of the House of Peers will undoubtedly change; and (4) the reestablishment and reorganization of the political parties will probably necessitate changes within the law.

1377 Kudryavtsev, V. "The Shadow of General Tanaka over Japan." *Soviet Press Translations* 2:5–7 (1 July 1947)

The passage on 31 March of a government bill amending that part of the election law which deals with the system of electoral districts is the subject of this brief article translated from the 16 April 1947 issue of *Izvestia*. The author views this new law, which reverts to the former system of "medium-sized" election districts, as a "shameless violation of the Potsdam Declaration which will offer greater advantages to the old reactionary parties and the traditional Japanese ruling classes." He accuses the American occupation authorities of attempting to mislead world opinion by minimizing the importance of such a reversion.

1377a ———. "Club Law—Epitome of Gen. MacArthur's 'Democracy'." *Current Digest of the Soviet Press* 2, no.27:30–31 (19 Aug. 1950)

The United States, according to this article which first appeared in the 2 July issue of *Izvestia*, is intentionally reviving aggressive Japanese militarism and is suppressing democratic organizations throughout Japan. Examples of this are the 22 July 1948 directive forbidding government personnel from striking and the more recent directives against the Japan Communist Party and its organ *Akahata*. MacArthur is accused, moreover, of seeking to turn Japan into an "unprivileged American colony" and of trying to make the Japanese people an obedient tool of American imperialism. This "dictator's" actions are compared with General Tanaka's persecution of the Japan Communist Party in 1928, and according to Kudryavtsev, MacArthur is "turning Japan back to the club laws of the times of Tanaka and Tojo," when only groups sanctioned by the government were permitted freedom of political expression and activity.

1377b ———. "On the Results of the Japanese Parliamentary Elections." *Current Digest of the Soviet Press* 1, no. 4:19 (22 Feb. 1949)

In this summary of an article which appeared in the 26 January issue of *Izvestia*, Kudryavtsev discusses the measures which the American occupation authorities and the Japanese government have taken to restrict the freedom of various Japanese trade unions and to limit the activities of the Japan Communist Party. He attributes these restrictions in part to SCAP's desire for a strong conservative showing at the 23 January parliamentary elections. The author acknowledges the victory of the Liberal Democrats in that election but at the same time points out that the Japanese Communists made outstanding progress and can no longer be regarded by the Japanese ruling circles as an insignificant minority.

1378 Kurihara, Kenneth K. "Japan's New Diet." *Far Eastern Survey* 15:145–48 (22 May 1946)

An American economist describes the background, composition, and relative strengths of the political parties as they emerged in the April 1946 general election. Particular attention is given to the 36 female members elected and to individual, "colorful," male members. Kurihara concludes that the forces of reaction are still alive in Japan, and he worries about an early end to the occupation.

1378a Kuroki, Yukichi. "From War to Peace Cabinets." *Contemporary Japan* 14:182–92 (Apr./Dec. 1945)

After briefly describing the nature of the wartime cabinets and the circumstances surrounding their downfall, Kuroki writes that the Higashikuni Cabinet should be regarded as nothing more than a transitional, caretaker regime. Its own downfall was due in large measure to Higashikuni's lack of administrative ability, but the immediate cause was the government's hesitation at complying with those SCAP directives which ordered the release of all political prisoners and the abolition of restrictions on the freedom of speech, assembly, and the press. Kuroki views the Shidehara Cabinet as being ideologically sound, but he has doubts about its efficiency and aptitude. He urges that it begin taking the initiative, rather than merely waiting for orders from SCAP, for only in that way will the government be able to establish a sound working relationship with the occupation authorities.

1379 Kyōgoku, Jun'ichi, and Masumi Junnosuke. *Japanese Politics: Is It Democratized? A Psychological Approach.* Tokyo: Nihon Taiheiyō Mondai Chōsakai, 1954. 35p. (Japan paper, 10)

A preparatory paper for the twelfth conference of the Institute of Pacific Relations held in Kyoto in 1954.

1380 ———, and Ike Nobutaka. "Urban-Rural Differences in Voting Behavior in Post-war Japan." *Economic Development and Cultural Change* 9, pt.2:167–85 (Oct. 1960)

By applying statistical tests to official election returns, the authors analyze the voting behavior of urban and rural voters. The study, focusing attention on the electoral district, details participation in elections as well as party support.

Langer, Paul F., and Arthur Rodger Swearingen. *Japanese Communism: An Annotated Bibliography of Works in the Japanese Language, with a Chronology, 1921–1952.* 1953. See no.16.

1381 ———, and ———. "The Japanese Communist Party, the Soviet Union, and Korea." *Pacific Affairs* 23, no.4:339–55 (Dec. 1950)

This article traces the history of the Japan Communist party from its origins in the 1920s until 1950, emphasizing Russian influence on and even control over the Japanese party. Ties with Russia continued even after being repudiated in 1945. For example, Japanese prisoners held by the Russians were indoctrinated and the Japan Communist party cooperated with the Russians in repatriating them. Also, the Japanese were close to the Korean Communists, knowing in advance of the invasion of South Korea and aiding the Korean Communists by strikes and sabotage in Japan.

1381a "A Lesson in American 'Democracy' in Japan." *Current Digest of the Soviet Press* 1, no.4:18 (22 Feb. 1949)

Izvestia, in this summary of an article which it published on 22 January 1949, comments on the parliamentary elections which were to be held in Japan the following day. It accuses both SCAP and the Japanese government of taking steps directed against left-wing candidates and cites as examples restrictions on the distribution of campaign literature and on speech making. The article concludes by stating that "the present election campaign in Japan is a clear lesson revealing to all peoples the pattern of the compulsory export of American 'democracy'."

1381b "Letter of Soviet Representative in Allied Council for Japan to Gen. MacArthur." *Current Digest of the Soviet Press* 2, no.26:30 (12 Aug. 1950)

The text of General Derevyanko's letter of 24 June 1950, which first appeared in the 25 June issues of *Pravda* and *Izvestia*, is a protest of SCAP's actions against the Japanese trade unions, the Japan Communist Party, and other democratic Japanese organizations. MacArthur is strongly criticized for his directives of 6 and 7 June in which he deprived 24 Communist leaders and 17 senior employees of *Akahata* of the right to engage in political and social activities and to publish any of their writings. Derevyanko insists that the directives be annulled immediately since they violate the Potsdam Declaration and the FEC decision on the democratization of Japan. He also demands that the Japanese government be made to "cease police arbitrariness and not allow suppresion of the work of trade unions and other democratic organizations, cease the repressive actions regarding the leaders of trade unions and other democrats, and punish the culprits of the police violence and mass arrests."

1381c "MacArthur's Election." *New Statesman and Nation* 27:94 (29 Jan. 1949)

This critical commentary on Japan's most recent general elections interprets the landslide vote for the ultraconservative Democratic Liberal party as a strong endorsement of MacArthur's policies inasmuch as this party's political philosophy most closely resembles the one espoused by the General. While the catastrophic defeat of the Democrats and Socialists may have personally pleased MacArthur and will make it easier for him to convert Japan into a strong capitalist base close to the Soviet Union and Communist China, however, it is questionable whether this is the type of situation that the Allied powers originally had in mind.

1382 Maki, John McGilvrey. "Japan's New Cabinet." *Far Eastern Survey* 15:177–80 (19 June 1946)

This article was written while Maki was serving with SCAP at the time of the first Yoshida cabinet. The article's emphasis is on the new political leadership and its composition since the surrender, and the effects of a disrupted society on internal politics. Maki feels that internal politics will continue to center around the basic issues of survival, such as food and housing, for some time to come.

1383 Markov, M. "Parliamentary Elections in Japan." *Soviet Press Translations* 2:1–4 (14 June 1947)

Written immediately after the election of Japan's second postwar Parliament, this article translated from the 26 April 1947 issue of *Pravda* briefly discusses the new structure of the upper and lower houses and outlines the general political situation leading to SCAP's February announcement calling for general elections. The author describes the positions of the "reactionary" Liberal party and the recently established Democratic party and presents his analysis of their political maneuverings to slander the legitimate activities of the Japan Communist party. In spite of all the difficulties of the struggle, the Communist party and various liberal factions of the Socialists "blasted the hopes of the reactionaries for a complete victory" and gained added strength in Japanese politics.

1384 ———. "The Political Situation in Japan after the Elections." *New Times* no.28:13–17 (11 July 1947)

Contrary to the statements of high SCAP officials, the author charges that neither the political, military, nor economic aims of the occupation have been achieved. He confines his comments here to the political sphere, examining the election of a new Diet and the party machinations and alliances it produced. The author bitterly condemns the Socialist party claiming that its leader, Katayama, is "a faithful menial of the Japanese militarists." He concludes that the advent of the right-wing Socialists to power has changed nothing in what he conceives to be Japan's desperate economic and political situation.

1385 Matsumoto, Tsuyoshi. "Japan's Election." *New Republic* 114:46–47 (14 Jan. 1946)

A contention that the United States is losing the peace in Japan is the theme of this article. After outlining the character of the major political parties that were contending, the author discusses the probable outcome of the January elections as one manifestation of the failure of the occupation to achieve real reform. According to him, the election will bring back into power the Old Guard, namely, those who support the emperor system and token democracy in Japan.

1386 Matsuo, M. "Parties and Politics in Contemporary Japan." *Foreign Affairs Reports* 3:1–13 (Jan. 1954)

Matsuo views the basis of problems in contemporary Japanese politics as "the inherent difficulty of applying the pattern of the modern parliamentary political system ... to a still basically Asian society like Japan within a considerably short time." He discusses how the 2 distinctively characteristic features of Japanese politics, the trend to follow the pattern of parliamentary politics of Western countries and the existence of premodern factors in Japanese society which prevents exact reproduction of that pattern, "are at work in the prevailing line-up of Japanese political parties." He then briefly examines the nature of existing Japanese political parties, concentrating on the interplay of policy differences and historical and personal factors. The 2 salient characteristics of Japanese politics are also revealed in the author's study of the fifth election since the end of World War II held on 19 April 1953. Comparing the party composition in the lower house which emerged out of this election with that of the previous house, the author cites certain developing trends in Japanese politics, noting that the "political situation in Japan is very unstable and confusing." He concludes, however, that Japan is moving slowly towards a general opposition of 2 major political forces. Two appendixes are included at the end of the article, one containing extracts of the programs of the main political parties of Japan and the other extracts of the constitution of Japan.

1387 Mayevsky, V. "The Japanese Right-Wing Socialists in the Service of the Americans." *Soviet Press Translations* 3: 203–5 (1 Apr. 1948)

Katayama's Socialist party comes under severe criticism in this article, which appeared in *Pravda* on 9 February 1948. The right-wing Socialists are termed lackeys of American capital and judged to have repudiated everything socialist. They are condemned for their alliance with the reactionary parties in Japan, as well as for their catastrophic economic policy. The article provides an uncomplimentary analysis of the government's financial and labor policies, as well as its anti-Communist stance, all of which are considered to be in opposition to the will of the Japanese people.

1388 ———. "What the Parliamentary Elections in Japan Revealed." *Soviet Press Translations* 4:99–100 (15 Feb. 1949); abridged version published under the title "What the Parliamentary Elections in Japan Have Shown" in *Current Digest of the Soviet Press* 1, no.5:31 (1 Mar. 1949)

In a brief report reprinted from a *Pravda* article of 1 February 1949, the author comments upon the outcome of the recent parliamentary elections. The author maintains that in spite of their impressive gains, the elections were really a defeat for the Liberal Democratic and Socialist parties since they were achieved by bribery and repression. In contrast, the Communist party is viewed as having achieved success since it received 3 times as many votes as it had in the 1947 elections.

1389 Monahan, James. "Red Mirage in Japan." *Reader's Digest* 49:73–77 (Dec. 1946)

Monahan discusses the increased popularity of communism in Japan following the removal of political restrictions by occupation edict and the release of the Communist leadership from prison. The strength of left-wing groups through mid-1946 in the press and broadcasting industries is explained. Discounting the lack of Communist success in the 1946 election, the author maintains that their activities and popularity are growing. This article has been condensed from an article appearing in the 2 November 1946 issue of the *New Leader*.

1390 Napier, Jack P. *A Survey of the Japan Communist Party.* Tokyo: Nippon Times, 1952. 66p.

Napier indicates in his survey that because General MacArthur's insight and American economic aid forestalled chaotic postwar upheavel in Japan, the Communist party had no opportunity to seize control. The party is so discredited in the eyes of the public and so weakened by internal schism that it is unlikely to show any material increase in strength in the foreseeable future. A Japanese-language edition of Napier's book appeared under the title *Watashi no mita Kyōsantō* (Tokyo: Asahi Shimbunsha, 1951. 156p.).

1391 Niiseki, Kinya. "The Postwar Activities of the Japan Communist Party." In *Japan's Problems*, ed. by Japan. Ministry of Foreign Affairs. Bureau of Public Information and Cultural Affairs. Tokyo: The Ministry, 1954. p.58–78.

Niiseki explains that immediately after the war, the Japan Communist party masqueraded as a real proletarian party determined to evolve a socialist system by peaceful and democratic methods under the American occupation. In 1947, however, a new party line was adopted that was designed to initiate opposition to the occupation. In detailing this and later party policies, Niiseki explains that the persistent moves of the JCP to regain popular support require careful watching. Niiseki Kinya is a specialist of European and American affairs in the Ministry of Foreign Affairs.

1392 Pak, Kun. *Political Parties in Postwar Japan*. Ph.D. dissertation, Univ. of Pennsylvania, 1958. 441p. (Abstracted in *Dissertation Abstracts* 19:861–62 [1958]; University Microfilms order no.58–3366)

In an attempt to answer the question, Is Western democracy exportable to an Asian nation? the author focuses on the putative democratic nature of postwar parties and the extent to which they have become institutionalized within the Japanese political framework. The study, which is focused primarily on the Liberal Democratic and the Social Democratic parties, consists of 3 parts: (1) an historical analysis of the issues and factors that have shaped the parties under consideration; (2) an analysis of both the basic ideological trends in Japanese history and the ideology of these parties; and (3) a consideration of party organization on the national and local levels. Pak's analysis reveals what he believes to be basic sociopolitical characteristics of postwar Japanese political parties. He concludes that although major parties in postwar Japan are "democratic" functionally and ideologically, they have yet to be institutionalized. Hence, he terms postwar Japanese political parties "uninstitutionalized" democratic parties.

1392a "The Political Ferment in Japan." *Nation* 162:87 (26 Jan. 1946)

According to this brief editorial, many former members of nationalist and military-fascist groups continue to be active in the countryside. Accordingly, the chances of an antifascist victory in the coming elections and the possibility of real land reforms (which must be enacted with the support of an aroused and organized peasantry) have been imperiled. To counteract these developments, closer relations must be established between the occupying forces and the peasant unions, SCAP's administrative structure must be recentralized, and people capable of carrying out a democratic transformation of rural Japan must be enlisted.

"The Political Purge Demanded in the Two Directives to the Shidehara Government." 1946. *See* no.111b.

1393 "The Political Situation in Japan." *World Today* 7:36–46 (Jan. 1951)

In generally describing the political situation in Japan after 5 years of liberal occupation, the author believes that "the political consciousness of the people shows signs of steady awakening, but old traditions and practices handed down from feudal days die hard, often interfering seriously with the rapid and smooth adoption of the political pattern practiced in Western democracies." He considers that Japanese politics have been unstable in the 5 years since the occupation began, discusses reasons why he believes this to be true, and illustrates by using data from Japan's 3 general elections. He divides Japan's numerous political parties into 2 groups—right-wing conservatives and left-wing progressives—and discusses the recent activities and developments in all significant parties. The concluding paragraphs briefly touch upon reasons why the political parties are advocating that Japan's autonomy be restored in the near future and the implications of such autonomy for the political parties' development.

1394 "Post-war Election Trends." *Oriental Economist* 27:464–68 (Aug. 1959)

This brief review of Japanese elections since the war examines the voting rate and party orientation of voters in local as well as upper house and lower house elections.

1395 "The Road to the Liberation of the Japanese People." *Soviet Press Transla-*

tions 5:151–52 (1 Mar. 1950); also published under the title "The Path to Liberation of the Japanese People" in *Current Digest of the Soviet Press* 2, no.4:25–26 (13 Mar. 1950)

Originally appearing in the 17 January 1950 issue of the Chinese-language daily, *Jen-min Jih-pao*, and subsequently published in *Pravda* on 21 January 1950, this editorial criticized the Japan Communist party, and in particular Nosaka Sanzō. This criticism centered on remarks made by Nosaka which claimed that power could be won by utilizing peaceful, parliamentary means. The subsequent rebuttal of this position by the Cominform (Communist Information Bureau) is noted and Japanese Communists are urged to examine and correct their mistakes in accord with Cominform policy. They are further urged to avoid using parliamentary methods except as a purely auxiliary method of exposing the enemy and to engage in serious revolutionary struggle.

Rosinger, Lawrence K. "Hirohito's Denial of Divinity Reveals Ferment in Japan." 1946. *See* no.1252.

1396 ———. "Rightist Victory Must Not Act as Break on Japanese Democracy." *Foreign Policy Bulletin* 25:1–2 (19 Apr. 1946)

In the aftermath of Japan's first postwar elections, this article considers the still dominant trend toward conservatism which they illustrate. After considering some of the unique aspects of the election such as their unprecedented freedom, the wide range of views presented, reduced ages for voting, and woman suffrage, the author discusses the 2 main alternatives that are open to SCAP: "(1) to accept the vote as a healthy expression of the long-term desires of the Japanese people and to deal with the new cabinet as if it were virtually a genuine government, or (2) to regard the results largely as an early 'poll' of Japanese sentiment that imposes no obligation upon us." He favors the latter course of action to encourage further democratic reform in the country. Finally, one of the most important tasks of the Diet—the consideration of a draft constitution—is discussed in some detail and the writer argues against what he considers the premature adoption of a definitive government charter so soon after the surrender.

1397 ———. "Unrest in Japan Leads MacArthur to Order New Elections." *Foreign Policy Bulletin* 26:2–3 (14 Feb. 1946)

Popular dissatisfaction with the conservative Yoshida government is the topic of this article. The author interprets the attempt of the labor unions to call a general strike for 1 February as an illustration of mass unrest. He believes General MacArthur's 7 February directive calling for new national elections to be a result of this dissatisfaction and hopes that it will become an opportunity for SCAP to disassociate itself from Japan's ultraconservative political elements.

1398 ———, and O. K. D. Ringwood. "The Japanese Elections of April–May 1947." *Foreign Policy Reports* 23:60 (15 May 1947)

The results by party of the 4 elections preceding the "launching" of the new Japanese constitution on 3 May 1947 are presented in this article. The elections involved governors of prefectures, city and town mayors, village headmen, and members of local assemblies; members of the House of Councillors; members of the House of Representatives; and prefectural councils. The authors give 6 conclusions they have drawn from these election results.

1399 Roth, Andrew. "Japan's Political Ferment." *Nation* 161:731–33 (29 Dec. 1945)

The approaching national elections—the broadest and most nearly democratic in Japan's history—are the topic of this article. The author discusses the importance of the outcome in determining the character and rate of speed of political and social reform in Japan. He then discusses the party platforms, the important political leaders, and estimated strengths of what he terms the 4 major national parties—the Progressive party

(*Shimpotō*), the Liberal party (*Jiyūtō*), the Socialist party (*Shakaitō*), and the Communist party (*Kyōsantō*). He predicts that the Liberals and moderate Socialists will emerge as the 2 strongest parties but believes that there will be a gradual increase of radical strength in the next few years.

1400 Saffell, John. "Japan's Post-war Socialist Party." *American Political Science Review* 42:957–69 (Oct. 1948)

Saffel divides the development of Japan's postwar Socialist party into 3 periods. The first period, that of reorganization, began in August 1945 and continued until the first postwar election in April 1946. The second period comprised the months between April 1946 and June 1947 during which the Socialists were gathering strength as the chief opposition party. The third period, from May 1947 to February 1948, saw the revolutionary passage of Japan's government into the hands of a Socialist-led cabinet.

1401 Scalapino, Robert Anthony. "Japan and the General Elections." *Far Eastern Survey* 21:149–54 (29 Oct. 1952)

In discussing the victory of the Liberal party in the 1952 general election, Scalapino notes the tide of resurgent nationalism sweeping the country. He regards it as basically a reaction to 7 years of occupation but also the result of a swing away from the intense self-criticism characteristic of many immediately following the war.

1402 ———. *The Japanese Communist Movement, 1920–1966*. Berkeley: Univ. of California Pr., 1967. ix, 412p. (A Rand Corp. research study; Publications of the Center for Japanese and Korean Studies)

The greater portion of Scalapino's study is devoted to the period since 1945 when the Japan Communist party was permitted to become a legal part of Japanese political life. Attention is given to the ideological and programmatic evolution of the party; to its organizational structure, its elite, and its political strength, with special attention to their socioeconomic implications; to the functional operations of the party as they relate to other political forces in Japan; and to JCP foreign policy. This study was initially a Rand Corporation research report undertaken for the U.S. Air Force.

1402a ———. "Politics and Public Opinion in Japan." *Foreign Policy Reports* 27, no.1:2–11 (15 Mar. 1951)

Scalapino, assistant professor of political science at the University of California (Berkeley campus), prepared this report in response to a request for information about Japan's present political alignment, the principal objectives of her foreign policy, Japanese attitudes towards rearmament and the granting of military bases to the United States after the occupation, and Japanese views on the future role of their country. In his article, therefore, he provides considerable factual information on the activities of Japan's major political parties and on their programs and foreign policy positions. In addition, Scalapino points out how the party movement as a whole is still weak and woefully inadequate to meet the needs of a democratic society, and he indicates concern about the ability of Japanese democracy to overcome the many grave economic and political problems that will continue to confront it after the occupation is terminated.

Soukup, James R. *Labor and Politics in Postwar Japan: A Study of the Political Attitudes and Activities of Selected Labor Organizations*. 1957. See no.1779.

1403 Spinks, Charles Nelson. "Postwar Political Parties in Japan." *Pacific Affairs* 19:250–59 (Sept. 1946)

This article describes Japanese political parties as of the April 1946 election. Spinks feels that the conservative victory in that election primarily shows popular support of the emperor. Links between prewar and postwar parties are carefully explained. The author concludes that the victorious conservatives are generally reliable though the Japanese people are politically immature and need some degree of supervision.

1404 "Statement Issued at a Press Conference by Mr. Guy J. Swope, Chief of the Government Section, SCAP, on the Constitutionality of the Designation by the Diet of Mr. Hitoshi Ashida, President of the Democratic Party as the New Prime Minister, February 24, 1948." *Contemporary Japan* 17:108–9 (Jan./Mar. 1948)

Swope voices his approval of the recent political development in which Ashida was elected prime minister after the resignation of Prime Minister Katayama. Outlining the arguments of those who claim the transition to have been unconstitutional, the author claims they are completely inaccurate and more in keeping with the spirit of the old rather than the new constitution.

1405 Stewart, Kermit G. "Japanese Politics: 1947–1948." *Far Eastern Survey* 17:152–55 (7 July 1948)

Stewart, serving with the Historical Section of SCAP, details the events leading up to and following the general election of April 1947 which make the position of the coalition government of Prime Minister Ashida Hitoshi precarious.

Supreme Commander for the Allied Powers. Monograph 10. *Election Reform 1945–November 1951*. 1952. See no.292.

———. Monograph 11. *Development of Political Parties, 1947–November 1951*. 1952. See no.293.

1406 ———. Civil Information and Education Section. *Anti–Communist Report*. Tokyo: SCAP, Apr. 1949–Oct. 1951. irregular.

Issued irregularly every 2 or 3 weeks by the Press and Publications Branch of the Civil Information and Education Section, this report notes all anti–Communist material disseminated by the branch in the preceding period. In addition to noting the titles of the U.S. Information Service news releases, it also indicates anti–Communist magazine and newspaper articles citing the title of the article, the name of the publication, and its circulation.

Available at the Washington National Records Center, Suitland, Maryland.

1407 ———. Government Section. *Election Report*. Tokyo: SCAP, 22 Apr. 1946. 26p.

Prepared by Brigadier General Courtney Whitney, chief of the Government Section, this report was written shortly after the first general election in occupied Japan which was held on 10 April 1946. The author presents the text of SCAP's instructions to the Eighth Army regarding the election and describes the political background against which the elections were held. There is an evaluation of the attitude of the Japanese press as well as coverage by other media prior to 10 April, a description of the observing and reporting of the election itself, and a résumé of postelection comments. The final section of the report describes the political implications of the election and analyzes the results, including campaign expenditures, voting trends discerned, party changes and regrouping, the women's vote, and popular interest in the election.

Available at the Washington National Records Center, Suitland, Maryland.

1408 ———. ———. *General Elections of January 23, 1949*. Tokyo: 1949. 28p.

1409 ———. ———. *The Japanese Elections, April 1947*. Mimeographed. Tokyo: SCAP, 1947. 123p., illus.

Written shortly after the April 1947 elections, this mimeographed report provides a brief analysis of the historical background of elections in Japan before presenting a thorough discussion of their importance in the postsurrender period. The new organizational structure and responsibilities of the postwar houses of the Diet are outlined along with new procedures in the popular election of local assemblies and executives. There is a discussion of such related factors as timing, public interest, and the mechanics of the new electoral system. Treatment also includes a summary of new Diet legislation regarding elections, the effects of the purge on political candidates, and methods of electoral surveillance by the occupation forces. There is also a lengthy outline of measures used by SCAP and the Japanese government to publicize the 1947 general elections. A large portion of the report is devoted to campaign issues and party platforms in these elections and a chart sets forth the platforms of the 5 major parties. Another chapter considers the elections of prefectural and local officials. The role of women in the elections is also given considerable attention. Other topics discussed are: campaign financing, election law violations, invalid ballots, and analyses of election results. The report concludes with a statement by the supreme commander discussing the importance of fair and democratic elections and suggesting ways in which the electoral system might be improved. Charts and tables throughout the report provide statistics on many facets of elections in postwar Japan.

This report is available at the Library of Congress, Washington, D.C. and the Washington National Records Center, Suitland, Maryland.

1410 ———. ———. *Japanese Political Parties.* Mimeographed. 16 Sept. 1946. Record Group 5, Box 100. MacArthur Memorial, Bureau of Archives, Norfolk, Va.

The information in this mimeographed series of reports was gathered in the spring and midsummer of 1946 by the Political Parties Branch, Political Affairs Division, Government Section, under the direction of P. K. Roest, chief of the Political Affairs Division. The series comprises 8 reports, 5 of which are devoted to the major parties of Japan, i.e., the Liberal party, the Progressive party, the Co–Operative party, the Social Democratic party, and the Communist party. All of these plus another, entitled "Diet Groups and Independents," were written by Harry Emerson Wildes. The other reports on minor parties and women in the Diet were prepared by Beate Sirota. The discussion includes party origins, the effects of the purge on their development and efforts at reformation, present organization, internal crises, coalitions, present political platform, cliques and factions within the party, and descriptions of prominent party officials. The section on minor parties is based on data from a Japanese Home Ministry report and concerns the post-April 1946 election alignment of minor parties and the interests they represent. It is supplemented by an "Annex" which provides more specific data on the 23 minor parties then represented in the Diet. The section on the 39 women representatives in the ninetieth Diet discusses their party affiliations as well as their political activities in and outside of the Diet. The final chapter on Diet groups and independents considers representatives without strong partisan loyalties and various efforts that have been made within the Diet to organize them.

1411 ———. ———. *Laws Relating to House of Representatives' General Election.* Mimeographed. Tokyo: SCAP, Jan. 1948. 103p.

In anticipation of a coming general election of members of the House of Representatives, the Government Section of SCAP published this mimeographed report providing a general description of postwar elections as well as the texts of relevant laws. The introductory section describes who is eligible to vote, the qualifications necessary for political candidacy, election campaigns procedures, supervision of elections, violations of election laws, and the newly inaugurated program of popular review of Supreme Court judges. Following this section are 3 sections which present the texts of: (1) the Law for Election of Members to the House of Representatives, (2) the Law Concerning the Provisional Exceptions to Election Campaigns and Others, and (3) the Law Concerning the Regulation of Political Contributions and Expenditures. Along with each there is the text of the ordinance relating to its enforcement as well as indexes to both the law and the ordinance.

Available at the Washington National Records Center, Suitland, Maryland.

———. ———. *Review of Government and Politics in Japan.* 1948–51. See no.280.

1412 Swearingen, Arthur Rodger. "The Communist Line in Japan." *Far Eastern Survey* 23:56–61 (Apr. 1954)

Swearingen, author and professor of international relations, discusses Communist strategy in Japan since the war. He notes that while the postwar switch was a logical and effective means of enlisting support for the Communist cause, it must be evaluated carefully before concluding that the Nosaka theory was a major departure and not merely a tactical maneuver in tune with the times in Japan.

1413 ———. *Communist Strategy in Japan, 1945–1960.* Santa Monica, Calif.: Rand Corp., 1965. xii, 409p. (Rand Corp. Memorandum, RM–4348–PR)

The author, acting director of the School of International Relations and director of the Research Institute on Communist Strategy and Propaganda at the University of Southern California, provides a case study of the policies, platform, and techniques of a major Communist party. The first part of the book deals primarily with the occupation, and within this the following are the most relevant sections: Communist strategy for the periods 1945–1951 (p.13–31) and 1951–58 (p.31–53); JCP organization with special reference to the labor field (p.68–81); and the JCP and the labor movement in occupied Japan, 1945–51 (p.88–122).

1414 ———. "Japanese Communism and the Moscow–Peking Axis." *Annals of the American Academy of Political and Social Science* 308:63–75 (Nov. 1956)

In this article Swearingen discusses the changing nature of communism in Japan primarily since the signing of the Japanese peace treaty. He first examines Japanese Communist policy during the period of the occupation, terming it the time of "peaceful revolution" with "moderation" and "autonomy" as the 2 tactical considerations. He notes that during this period from 1945 through 1949 the new legal Communist party made substantial progress but was "intrinsically, neither peaceful nor independent." The author continues by describing the more militant, Cominform-inspired policy beginning in 1950 and a new policy, the "national-liberation democratic revolution," announced by the Japan Communist party shortly after the peace treaty was signed. Three implications of the posttreaty Communist strategy are studied along with the question of whether the orientation of the Japan Communist party would be toward Moscow or Peking. The last 2 major sections of the article deal with the post-Stalin period and the effects of the new line adopted by the Japan Communist party at its sixth national council meeting in July 1955.

1415 ———, and Paul Langer. *Red Flag in Japan: International Communism in Action, 1919–1951.* Cambridge, Mass.: Harvard Univ. Pr., 1952. xii, 276p.

Following an introduction by Edwin Reischauer (p.ix–xii), this book surveys the development of the Japan Communist party until 1951, pages 87–252 covering the postwar period. It describes the party's rebirth after the war, its organization, leadership, program, tactics, etc., with emphasis on internal problems rather than relations with the occupation, though the occupation itself is discussed in detail in such sections as "SCAP Intervention," pages 209–12, and chapter 21, "The Anti-Communist Act," pages 242–52. The tone of the book is distinctly anti-Communist. A Japanese version of this publication has appeared under the title *Nihon no akai hata* (Tokyo: Kosumoporitansha, 1953. 367p.).

1415a "Swing to the Right in Japan." *Economist* 156:186 (29 Jan. 1949)

SCAP's expressed preference for the Democratic Liberals is said to have had a definite influence upon many Japanese voters in the most recent elections, while American warnings against "improvident political conflict, unobjective labour strife and destructive ideological pressures" have certainly not helped the Socialists although they did play into the hands of the resurgent Communist party. The recently completed land reform also has had an impact upon the Japanese political spectrum, for the reform appears to have deprived the Communists of much of their potential support in the countryside and has limited them to being a party primarily of the industrial workers.

1416 Takahashi, Masao. "Contemporary Japanese Political Forces." *Pacific Affairs* 21:399–404 (Dec. 1948)

A description of postwar Japanese political parties from the point of view of the Socialist party's left-wing. The author criticizes the conservatives for being split into 2 bourgeois parties, the Communists for advocating violence, the small parties for containing fascist elements, and the right-wing of his own party for being right-wing. With economic recovery, he foresees political stabilization with one conservative party, a major opposition party of petty bourgeois and working class elements, and a small but crucial third party of intellectuals and advanced members of the working class based on scientific socialism.

Tiltman, Hessell. "Letter from Tokyo: What Is the Council?" 1946. *See* no.886.

1417 Tokuda, Kyūichi. "On the 30th Anniversary of the Communist Party of Japan." *Current Digest of the Soviet Press* 4, no.31:20–23 (13 Sept. 1952)

In reviewing the activities of the Japan Communist party, Tokuda Kyuichi, general secretary of the Central Committee, describes the party's stubborn resistance to American imperialism during the occupation years. He notes that one of the basic questions for the party was whether postwar Japan should be considered an imperialist nation or whether it had become a colonial, dependent country.

This article was originally published in the 2–3 August 1952 issue of *Pravda*.

1418 "Too Soon for Elections in Japan." *New Republic* 113:300 (10 Sept. 1945)

This brief editorial concerns reports that the Japanese government intends to hold democratic elections in January 1946. The author believes that there has not been sufficient time to develop political parties which really represent popular democratic opposition to the existing system. Thus, he concludes, early elections would strengthen rather than weaken the feudal and industrial powers and he urges that SCAP postpone them for the present.

1419 Topekha, Petr Pavlovich. "Ideological Camouflage of American Occupation in Japan." *Current Digest of the Soviet Press* 4, no.20:13–15 (28 June 1952)

In these excerpts from his article, "Ideologicheskaia maskirovka amerikanskoi okkupatsii v IAponii" published in the January/February 1952 issue of *Voprosy Filosofi*, Topekha notes how both the Americans and the Yoshida government have used right-wing Socialist leaders to implement various postwar changes. In sharp contrast, the Japan Communist party, which has seen through the camouflage that attempts to mask the true intentions of the nation's postwar leadership, has refused to cooperate with the "American occupiers and their Japanese network of agents" and will seek to rally together all of the country's progressive forces in order to create a truly democratic and peace-loving Japan.

"Le traité de paix avec le Japon." 1951. *See* no.2426a.

1420 Troitsky, S. "Japanese Workers in the Struggle Against the Enslaving Plans of Reaction." *Soviet Press Translations* 4: 205–6 (1 Apr. 1949)

In an article published in the 22 January *Trud*, the day before the general parliamentary elections in Japan, the author describes what he considers to be the 2-fold struggle in which the Japanese masses are engaged. The first, he believes, is the struggle against the forces of reaction which are attempting to destroy the vital rights of the working class and the second is the struggle against the American plan to enslave Japan and make it permanently an economic dependent of the United States. The writer predicts that these forces of reaction in Japan and the United States will meet resounding defeat from the workers and intelligentsia in the forthcoming elections.

1421 Tsukahira, Toshio George. *The Postwar Evolution of Communist Strategy in Japan.* Cambridge, Mass.: Massachusetts Institute of Technology. Center for International Studies, 1954. 89p. At head of title: Communist Bloc Program. China Project, B/54–9.

In his introduction the author states, "It is the purpose of this paper to examine the strategy of the Japan Communist Party in the period since the end of World War II and to show how Soviet foreign policy and the rise of Communist China have influenced the course of its development." Thus, emphasis is placed on the party's internal development and relations with other Communist countries. The role of the occupation itself is not stressed.

U.S. Army. Eighth Army. *Collection of Messages.* 1947–51. See no.339.

1422 ———. Dept. of State. Div. of Research for Far East. *Major Political Parties of Japan.* Washington, D.C.: The Dept., 1951. 5p. (DRF information paper no.402)

This brief account of Japan's 5 major political parties discusses their leadership, political outlook, and support.

1423 ———. ———. Office of Intelligence Research. *An Analysis of the 1947 Japanese House of Representatives Elections.* Washington, D.C.: The Dept., 1947. viii, 76, A–6, B–206p. (OIR report no.4310)

This analysis of the 1947 election indicates that progress has been made in constructing an electoral framework that will permit maximum freedom of political organization and expression based on a broad electorate. Considerable political instability still exists, however, and the conflict between old and new political forces continues to produce a situation of political fluidity with the result that the pattern of future Japanese political development cannot yet be ascertained.

1424 ———. ———. ———. *The 1947 Japanese House of Councillors Election.* Washington, D.C.: The Dept., 1948. xi, 85, A–2, B–119p. (OIR report no.4334)

This analysis of the conduct and results of the 1947 House of Councillors election includes a discussion of significant developments in the operation of the upper house in the postelection period.

1425 Van Kirk, Walter W. "Japan's New Political Outlook." *Christian Century* pt.1, 63:13–14 (2 Jan. 1946); pt.2, 63: 44–46 (9 Jan. 1946)

This 2–part series presents a review and analysis of the political climate in postwar Japan. In part 1, the author first notes the importance for Japanese politics of the liberalization of election laws and the encouragement of political discussion. He then reviews the status and activities of the existing conservative parties. The Progressives are seen as carryovers from the prewar Seiyūkai and Minseitō parties. Because of their financial support by landlord and *zaibatsu* groups, their skill in politics, and their prolonged public exposure, they are expected to run well in the immediate postwar elections. The Liberal party is examined as well. The style of its platform is compared with nineteenth century European rhetoric and its leadership is regarded as a holdover from the Shidehara cabinet. In part 2 Van Kirk focuses on the liberal political parties in postwar Japan. He maintains that the Social Democrats are a less potent force than either the Progressive or Liberal parties because they lack a nationally recognized leadership. Their platform, however, is praised as being straightforward and very much in the spirit of occupation directives. The Communists are regarded as the country's weakest party on account of their revolutionary attitude towards the imperial institution, their lack of leadership and inability to gain popular support outside of the cities, and their failure to display sufficient concern for such pressing matters as improving the supply of food and housing on a national basis. Van Kirk concludes the series by stating that for the time being, at least, permanent political alignments in Japan will be very heavily influenced by American policy.

1426 "Vital Vote for the Diet." *Newsweek* 35:42 (12 June 1950)

This article first describes the upper house elections of 4 June 1950 and explains that its results have been interpreted as an endorsement of the Yoshida government's pro-American policies. It then presents a personal account by Compton Pakenham of the electoral process in a rural district, where the constituents voted for both local and national candidates. Pakenham notes that the voters still do not understand the principles of a democratic election and that "most of those questioned considered that they had performed a required chore and [had] contributed toward the operation of an inexplicable lottery without prizes."

1427 Ward, Robert Edward. "Urban-Rural Differences and the Process of Political Modernization in Japan: A Case Study." *Economic Development and Cultural Change* 9, pt.2:135–65 (Oct. 1960)

Basing his analysis on research done in the prefecture of Okayama and the city of Osaka, Ward attempts to determine some of the characteristics of the traditional political base in Japan and what specific changes occur between it and the current terminus of the modernization process. Many of the modernizing changes described have their origins in the occupation period and the systematic attempts by SCAP to change traditional institutions and patterns of behavior in Japan.

Wheeler, Romney. "Stalin's Target for Tomorrow." 1951. *See* no.844.

1428 Wildes, Harry Emerson. "Democracy: By Divine Decree." *Asia and the Americas* 46:18–20 (Jan. 1946)

In his account of Japan's newborn political parties, Wildes points out that they are still to be considered opportunist bands following ambitious leaders. Few of them seem to have platforms; none seem to have principles. The occupation officers, he notes, eager to detect signs of Japanese regeneration, take them at face value and Japanese politicians would never upset these comfortable American delusions.

1429 ———. "Underground Politics in Post-War Japan." *American Political Science Review* 42:1149–62 (Dec. 1948)

A carefully documented discussion by a former SCAP official of the network of organizations underlying the postwar Japanese political system which extend from rural villages to the central government in Tokyo. The article includes a consideration of the nature of the 1,250 officially recognized political groups and the sources of their financial support. The powerful *oyabun-kobun* system and its wide ramifications in Japanese politics also receive attention. The author categorizes the following groups as the primary *oya-ko* organizations: (1) gamblers, (2) hoodlums, (3) street stall merchants, (4) blackmailers, and (5) political clubs, and then briefly discusses SCAP's attempts to cleanse Japan of these societies.

1430 Williams, Justin. "Party Politics in the New Japanese Diet." *American Political Science Review* 42:1163–80 (Dec. 1948)

A study of how the political parties have adjusted their postwar operations in the Diet which is, according to the new constitution, the highest organ of state power. The author shows how parties manage the Diet and discusses the structure and operations of such agencies as the Steering Committee, the other Diet standing committees, and the Interparty Negotiating Conference. He also provides a detailed description of the Diet's plenary sessions and the techniques of filibustering and lobbying that are employed by political parties during sessions. There is a brief discussion of party involvement in the process of designating a prime minister and of the new relationship between the parties and the executive branch of the government. The author concludes that political parties have demonstrated an ability to exercise the powers authorized in the new constitution and have cooperated with cabinet leaders on policy agreements. Nevertheless, he points out the dangers to successful party government of weak coalition governments, lobbying, and rowdyism and strongly urges that the parties make every effort to eliminate the last two.

1431 Yamamoto, George. "How Japan Votes." *New Statesman and Nation* 44: 469–70 (25 Oct. 1952)

In a somewhat perfunctory survey of the results of the first postoccupation general election, the author points to signs of Japanese repudiation of American guidance. The increase in Socialist seats from 46 to 111 is interpreted as an indication of general support for a policy of antirearmament and anti-Americanism. The split of the Liberal party into factions and the rise of Hatoyama Ichirō are interpreted as a preface to weak governmental leadership.

1432 Yanaga, Chitoshi. "Japanese Political Parties." *Parliamentary Affairs* 10:265–76 (Summer 1957)

After presenting a highly critical history of Japanese political parties and description of their status and organization as of the mid-1950s, this article devotes a few pages to the question of constitutional revision which the right supported and the left opposed. The author feels that some revision is inevitable for the sake of Japanese self-respect if nothing else.

1433 Yoshimura, Tadashi. "Conservative Parties during the First Ten Years of Post-war Japan." *Waseda Political Studies* 1:1–25 (1957)

Yoshimura finds the frequent changes in membership as well as in the formal names of Japan's political parties to be one of the most distinguishing characteristics of immediate postwar party politics. Between 1945 and 1955, 16 conservative parties appeared, of which 14 underwent major changes in name, membership, and structure. He attributes this phenomenon to the operation of 3 major factors: (1) the disruption of traditional ties within the prewar parties and the confusion resulting from the reentry of depurged politicians into political life; (2) changes in the methods of raising and distributing political funds; and (3) the lack of grass-roots political organizations. Yoshimura devotes a good deal of space to a detailed comparison between prewar fund-raising techniques and those prevailing in the 1950s.

Administrative Organization and the Bureaucracy

The numerous constitutional changes effected during the occupation entailed corresponding changes in administrative structure and practice. Attempts were also made to alter quite substantially recruitment, training, and personnel practices affecting in particular the classified and professional civil service that staffed the higher administrative posts of the Japanese government. Although both of these are subjects of great practical and scholarly interest, they have not yet been extensively studied. The relevant literature appears below. There are also incidental references to developments in these fields in a number of entries listed in the section containing general materials (p.113).

1434 Burch, Betty B., and Allan B. Cole, eds. *Asian Political Systems: Readings on China, Japan, India, Pakistan.* Princeton, N.J.: Van Nostrand, 1968. xiv, 446p. (Van Nostrand Political Science series)

A book of edited readings selected from the writings of Asian scholars and authorities. Two of the readings on Japanese political institutions, respectively by a professor at Tokyo University and an editorial writer for the *Asahi Shimbun*, focus on issues relating to the occupation: (1) "The Bureaucracy Preserved and Strengthened," by Tsuji Kiyoaki (no. 1447b)—a study of the Japanese bureaucracy during the occupation; (2) "The Peace Constitution Controversy," by Nishijima Yoshiji (no.1008)—an examination of conflicting views over Article 9 of the new constitution.

1435 Esman, Milton J. "Japanese Administration: A Comparative View." *Public Administration Review* 7:100–112 (Spring 1947)

This excellent analysis of the Japanese administrative structure defines that system as a formalistic and legalistic one, as contrasted with the American administrative system which is defined as pragmatic in approach. These terms are carefully defined and several illustrations are provided. The author then discusses the history of the development of the Japanese administrative system based on German models, its preservation by means of the rigid Tokyo University curriculum, and its dependence upon the national police prior to the occupation. The author affirms that any administrative system is not an independent entity but reflects the social values of the society in which it functions. Therefore, he concludes, "the current widespread Japanese acceptance of American administrative techniques and concepts will outlast the Allied Occupation only if social values similar to the American gain ascendency in the minds and in the behavior of the Japanese."

Fernbach, Alfred P. "Japanese Government under the 1946 Constitution." 1949. See no.1175a.

1436 "General MacArthur's Letter to Prime Minister Hitoshi Ashida Concerning the Revision of the National Public Service Law, July 24, 1948." *Contemporary Japan* 17:404–9 (July/Dec. 1948)

After reviewing the conclusions drawn from joint Japanese government–SCAP studies as to the adequacy of the National Public Service Law with respect to its provisions regulating public servants, MacArthur outlines his understanding of the nature of that law in this letter to the prime minister. Distinguishing between laborers in private enterprise and laborers in public service, he affirms the right of the former to strike but insists that "no person holding a position by appointment or employment in the public service of Japan or in any instrumentality thereof should resort to strike or engage in delaying or other dispute tactics which tend to impair the efficiency of governmental operations." In conclusion MacArthur strongly recommends that the National Public Service Law be comprehensively revised in accord with the above concepts and offers the assistance of personnel from SCAP's headquarters in this task.

1436a Higa, Mikio. *The Role of Bureaucracy in Contemporary Japanese Politics.* Ph.D. dissertation, Univ. of California at Berkeley, 1968. 398p. (Abstracted in *Dissertation Abstracts* 29:3194A [1969]; University Microfilms order no.69–3612)

In order to determine the degree of discrepancy between law and reality, Higa describes, analyzes, and compares the prewar and postwar constitutions and civil service laws as well as their actual operation. From an examination in this fashion of such variables as recruitment procedures, composition, functions, and career patterns, he concludes that there was little discrepancy in the case of Japan's bureaucracy before 1945. The reforms introduced by the occupation authorities, however, embodied concepts of popular sovereignty, legislative supremacy, and public service which were alien to the Japanese tradition. These reforms were resisted, and as a result, the formal and informal structures and the ideology of the postwar bureaucracy differ from the constitutional provisions and civil service regulations of the postwar period. In contrast, the civil service shows considerable continuity between the prewar and postwar eras in regard to its actual operations, for it has maintained both its independence of parliamentary control and its strong influence over the policy-making process.

1437 Japan. Allowance Bureau. *A Critical Survey of the Government Service Personnel and Their Salaries and Wages.* Tokyo: 1947. v, 79p.

A study that is divided into 4 sections: (1) general information about government service personnel; (2) an historical survey of salaries and wages; (3) present salary and wage structures; and (4) special payments under the present system (e.g., pensions).

1438 ———. Ministry of Foreign Affairs. *Organization Report of the Japanese Government.* particular dates not known. monthly.

Submitted each month to SCAP, this report lists the responsibilities of each office, agency, or section within the central Japanese government, notes any important structural changes that have taken place during the month, and lists the current officials in all ministries and offices.

Available at the Washington National Records Center, Suitland, Maryland.

1439 ———. National Personnel Authority. *Report on the Progress of Appointment of Personnel to Designated Government Positions under Article IX of the Supplementary Provisions of the National Public Service Law.* Tokyo: 1950. 1v.

1439a Kim, Paul Sunik. *The Higher Public Service in Japan: An Introductory Analysis of Japanese Administrative Behavior.* Ph.D. dissertation, New York Univ., 1964. 265p. (Abstracted in *Dissertation Abstracts* 26:1757–58 [1965]; University Microfilms order no.65–1641)

This dissertation examines the effect of the administrative system, recruitment policy, and education on the attitudes of Japan's higher civil servants toward their subordinates in particular and towards the citizenry in general. Kim first describes the prewar bureaucratic system, then proceeds to a description and a detailed analysis of the postwar civil service system as it emerged from the occupation reforms. He finds that despite great changes in the content of the civil service examination, the creation of a new system of job classification, and the establishment of a National Personnel Authority to administer the civil service system, the composition of the body of higher public servants in postwar Japan shows little change from the prewar period. Officials are still largely graduates of Tokyo University, for instance, and patterns of age distribution, length of administrative experience, and professional training are virtually the same. This lack of change, Kim concludes, has resulted in a continuation of the prevalent prewar attitudes of high-ranking bureaucrats.

1439b ———. "Japan's National Civil Service Commission: Its Origin and Structure." *Public Administration* 48: 405–21 (Winter 1970)

Kim's study analyzes the origins, organization, and activities of Japan's National Civil Service Commission, also known as the National Personnel Authority, in order to show how postwar Japan has attempted to democratize her civil service. After a brief introduction, Kim first explores the origins in 1946–47 of the National Public Service Law and the National Personnel Authority, then describes the structure and functions of this controversial public body as they subsequently evolved. The third part of his article considers the authority's most significant achievements—among them the enactment of an expanded and diversified entrance examination, the recruitment of new employees for the higher public service from a more varied background, and the creation of a vastly improved compensation scale—while the remaining sections review the sources and nature of bureaucratic opposition to the commission and the reorganization which it underwent in 1965. Kim points out that many Japanese bureaucrats have criticized the commission from the beginning not only on account of SCAP's involvement in its establishment and the commission's advocacy of American concepts and practices in public personnel administration, but also because it interfered with traditional forms of management and stressed the principal that bureaucrats were to view themselves as public servants. At the same time, Kim also states, in spite of the considerable opposition that the commission has encountered, many people feel that the commission has successfully carried out its original and primary objective: the democratization of the Japanese public service.

1440 Kubota, Akira. *Higher Civil Servants in Postwar Japan: Their Social Origins, Educational Backgrounds, and Career Patterns.* Princeton, N.J.: Princeton Univ. Pr., 1969. xv, 197p.

In an attempt to identify the major characteristics of higher civil service personnel in Japan during the period 1949–59, the author selected 1,353 incumbents in 1949, 1954, and 1959 and collected their relevant biographical data. These data were then tabulated in terms of (1) position level, (2) ministry, and (3) survey years, although longitudinal and regression analysis also were used. His findings indicate that, despite differences in social origins, the educational and career backgrounds of these individuals are relatively similar. Kubota demonstrates that in terms of origin, education, and career, the Japanese higher civil service displayed a high degree of stability during the period under consideration, despite the purge policies of the occupation. Kubota's publication is a revised version of the doctoral dissertation that he submitted to the University of Michigan in 1966 (Abstracted in *Dissertation Abstracts* 27:3505A [1967]; University Microfilms order no.67–1764). A Japanese translation of his book has appeared under the title *Kōkyū kanryō* (Tokyo: Fukumura Shuppansha, 1972. 211p.).

1440a MacDonald, Hugh H., and Milton J. Esman. "The Japanese Civil Service." *Public Personnel Review* 7, no.4:213–24 (Oct. 1946)

While this article describes the structure and practices of the prewar Japanese civil service, the authors make critical comments on various aspects of the system that provide insight into occupation views on the bureaucracy. Changes in the civil service system since the surrender—principally those connected with the dismantling of the national police system—also are briefly noted. MacDonald was chief legal advisor to SCAP's Public Health and Welfare Section at the time he coauthored this article, while Esman was attached to SCAP's Government Section.

1441 Maki, John McGilvrey. "The Role of the Bureaucracy in Japan." *Pacific Affairs* 20:391–406 (Dec. 1947)

An analysis of the Japanese bureaucracy, which the author describes as a "powerful though unspectacular force in Japanese politics." The article provides an account of the history of the bureaucracy since 1868 and then examines the changes in the bureaucratic system wrought by the occupation, particularly through the enactment of the new constitution. It includes a detailed description of the role of the Central Liaison Office, the bureaucratic channel through which business between SCAP and the Japanese government was conducted. The author argues for effective SCAP control of the bureaucracy if representative government is to succeed in Japan.

1442 Miyake, Tarō. "Central Theme of the Prewar and Postwar Personnel Administration in Government Offices." *Waseda Bulletin of Social Sciences* p.69–90 (1962)

This study compares the prewar *kanri* system of government officials with the postwar national civil service system. It includes a review of early postwar Japanese government reforms connected with the appointment and classification of government officials, and a discussion of the position-classification plan that the National Personnel Authority subsequently enacted with advice from Blaine Hoover and other members of the U.S. Personnel Advisory Mission to Japan.

1442a Nakamura, Tetsu. "Democratization of Bureaucratic State." *Contemporary Japan* 16:191–94 (Apr./June 1947)

This article by a professor of law at St. Paul's University (Tokyo) was translated from the May 1947 issue of *Kaizō*. Nakamura finds that the Japanese people are still apathetic about politics despite the promulgation of a new constitution. In at least one important respect, moreover, the postwar constitution itself is open to criticism, for it provides that the emperor may continue to confer ranks and honors on government officials. This seemingly innocuous clause undermines various democratic principles in that it will only reinforce the tendency of the bureaucrats to regard themselves as a privileged class. The bureaucracy and especially the police remain fundamentally unchanged, and while the constitution has eliminated political absolutism, Nakamura feels that the adoption of the American spoils system might be a successful counterbalance to the continuing absolutism among Japan's bureaucrats.

1443 Rice, Stuart A., and Calvert L. Dedrick. *Japanese Statistical Organization.* Washington, D.C.: July 1951. ii, 29p.

A report to SCAP prepared by the Second Statistical Mission to Japan in cooperation with the Programs and Statistics Division of the Economic and Scientific Section and the Statistics Commission of the Prime Minister's Office. The authors are members of a 3-man mission which stayed in Japan from 25 March to 20 April 1951 appraising the current statistical organization of Japan and making recommendations for further improvements. The first such mission presented its report in 1947. In the present report there are 50 specific recommendations including ones calculated to enhance the position of the chairman of the Statistics Commission and the heads of statistical units within the national government, to establish a more coherent system of compatible statistical data, to solicit advisory assistance from business organizations, to utilize private statistics, and to promote international statistical comparability.

1443a Roser, Foster B. "Establishing a Modern Merit System in Japan." *Public Personnel Review* 11, no.4:199–206 (Oct. 1950)

Roser was involved with the establishment of an examination section for the new Japanese civil service. He first briefly describes the presurrender bureaucracy, then proceeds to a discussion of the major SCAP reform measures affecting the civil service. The most important of these was the passage in 1947 of a new civil service law, which the author characterizes as "a thoroughly and completely emasculated instrument" compared with that recommended by SCAP advisors. The law nevertheless established the National Personnel Authority, whose fundamental purpose is to enforce merit-based recruitment and promotion practices. The article describes in some detail the activities of the Personnel Authority, including the administration of the new examination system, and the establishmet of job categories and pay scales. Roser concludes with some comments on how lasting the effects of the reforms will be.

1443b Shirven, Maynard N., and Joseph L. Speicher. "Examination of Japan's Upper Bureaucracy." *Personnel Administration* 14, no.4:48–57 (July 1951)

This article describes in detail the rationale and planning behind the civil service examination administered to higher-ranking Japanese bureaucrats on 15 January 1950. The primary purpose of the examination, according to the authors, was to establish the principle of appropriate qualifications for each position within the bureaucracy; the result was to remove from office somewhere between 30% and 40% of the incumbent officeholders. It was felt that the old examination and promotion system had overemphasized abstract legal knowledge, producing a bureaucracy with little practical training or administrative ability. The new system, in contrast, was designed to require of the candidates the administrative aptitude and technical knowledge necessary for the performance of their duties. The authors furthermore discuss the opposition encountered within the government to the examination itself as well as other efforts made in the direction of administrative reform. At the time they prepared this piece for publication, Shirven was chief of the Civil Service Division in SCAP's Government Section while Speicher served as chief of the Examination Branch of the same division.

1444 "Statement Issued by Mr. Blaine Hoover, Chief of the Civil Services Division, Government Section, GHQ, SCAP, Concerning the National Personnel Authority, August 24, 1948." *Contemporary Japan* 17:412–14 (July/Dec. 1948)

The chief of the Civil Services Division of SCAP's Government Section addresses himself to the question of how government employees can best be assured of receiving fair treatment in their offices of employment. He advocates that the National Personnel Authority be given full responsibility for the entire matter, and in explaining his reasons for his stand, asserts that the authority will be capable of guaranteeing the sovereignty of the Japanese people in addition to safeguarding the rights of all government personnel.

Supreme Commander for the Allied Powers. Monograph 9. *National Administrative Reorganization, 1945–1949.* 1952. See no.291.

———. Monograph 13. *Reorganization of Civil Service, 1945–1951.* 1952. See no.295.

1445 ———. Government Section. *Report of the United States Personnel Advisory Mission to Japan.* 24 Apr. 1947. Record Group 5, Box 80. MacArthur Memorial, Bureau of Archives, Norfolk, Va. 50p. 1 folder.

The first part of this report of the U.S. Personnel Advisory Mission to Japan presented to General MacArthur by Blaine Hoover, chairman of the mission, on 24 April 1947. It treats the entire personnel system of the Japanese government, its laws, policies, practices, and procedures. It also includes the group's recommendations for the improvement of the system. It is divided into 5 main divisions. The first 4 cover the general background and organization of the mission and the nature of the personnel problems encountered in Japan. Section 5 presents the text of a draft National Public Service Law which the mission recommends be enacted, outlining its purpose, providing for the creation of a National Personnel Authority, prescribing its organizational structure, and stating its duties and powers. Three appendixes provide additional comments on the nature of the National Personnel Authority Law, the mission's recommendations that a Civil Service Division be established in the Government Section of General Headquarters, and a summary of the aims of the current report. There is an additional section termed Supplement A, outlining the duties of the Office of Special Assistant to the Chief, General Headquarters of SCAP, which the mission recommends be created. Also included in the folder are a memorandum and letter from Hoover to General Courtney Whitney and General MacArthur respectively discussing the proposed National Public Service Law and various aspects of its application to the Japanese governmental system.

1446 ———. ———. *Report on the Organization of the Japanese Government.* Aug. 1946–Apr. 1950. Record Group 5, Boxes 94 and 95. MacArthur Memorial, Bureau of Archives, Norfolk, Va. 6 folders.

This extensive series of reports on the Japanese government was published monthly from information prepared by the Japanese government and submitted to SCAP in accordance with directives set forth in SCAPIN no.292. Reports note changes in the cabinet, in each of its bureaus and boards, and in the ministries and the Attorney General's Office with respect to personnel or methods of organization on operation. They also record the issuance of any new imperial ordinances. The Norfolk collection consists of reports as of August 1946 (111p.), September 1946 (35p.), November 1946 (22p.), December 1946 (77p.), February 1947 (126p.), March 1947 (20p.), April 1947 (28p.), May 1947 (44p.), June 1947 (88p.), July 1947 (33p.), August 1947 (19p.), September 1947 (23p.), October 1947 (160p.), November 1947 (28p.), December 1947 (15p.), January 1948 (24p.), February 1948 (23p.), March 1948 (19p.), April 1948 (36p.), May 1948 (31p.), June 1948 (36p.), and April 1950 (23p.). A less complete set may be found at the Army Library in the Pentagon.

1447 Tsuji, Kiyoaki. "The Cabinet, Administrative Organization, and the Bureaucracy." *Annals of the American Academy of Political and Social Science* 308: 10–17 (Nov. 1956)

A professor of political science and public administration at Tokyo University discusses changes in the executive branch of the Japanese government since the peace treaty came into effect in 1952. He first points out the constitutional status of the cabinet. In studying the Yoshida cabinet he examines the following 3 reasons why this cabinet began losing its control: the return of wartime leaders, unpopular policies, and corruption. After describing the appearance of the Hatoyama cabinet, the author points out characteristics of Japanese administrative organization, especially that of "departmentalism." The administrative organization at the time of writing is outlined and 4 postindependence changes in administrative organization are discussed. These are: the emergence of the Defense Board, the reduction of the staff of the National Personnel Authority, the reform of the police system, and the change in the design of local government. The article concludes with a look at the trends and characteristics of the Japanese bureaucracy.

1447a ———. "Bureaucracy and the National Public Service Law." *Contemporary Japan* 17:371–74 (July/Dec. 1948)

According to this article, which first appeared in the October 1948 issue of *Asahi Hyōron*, the National Public Service Law (enacted on 1 July 1948) attracted little attention until MacArthur "suggested" that a provision be added prohibiting strikes by public employees. In the ensuing furor, the basic objective of the law—the establishment of a responsible and efficient public service in Japan—tended to be overlooked. Focusing on various provisions of the new law, Tsuji points out that the new Government Personnel Committee has been given powers broad enough to raise a danger of dictatorial administration unless the committee remains under firm control. Moreover, the extension of the law's guarantees to almost every government official may lead to the preservation of privilege on an even wider scale. Accordingly, there should be an increase in the number of positions beyond the control of the law. Tsuji argues in conclusion that restrictions on the right of public servants to strike will encourage corruption if bureaucratic salaries are not raised.

1447b ———. "The Bureaucracy Preserved and Strengthened." *Journal of Social and Political Ideas in Japan* 2:88–92 (Dec. 1964); reprinted in Betty B. Burch and Allan B. Cole, eds. *Asian Political Systems: Readings on China, Japan, India, Pakistan*. Princeton, N.J.: Van Nostrand, 1968. p.136–41.

In this condensed translation of an article that appeared in *Gendai Nihon no seiji katei* (ed. by Oka Yoshitake. Tokyo: Iwanami Shoten, 1958. p.109–25), Tsuji contends that the Japanese bureaucracy demonstrated, both directly and indirectly, a tenacious ability to preserve itself from the very outset of the occupation period. To support this assertion, he notes the continuity of personnel as well as the sabotage of SCAP reforms which occurred, and cites examples drawn from the areas of local government, the police force, and the new National Personnel Authority. Three principal factors have enabled the bureaucracy to survive intact. First, SCAP's decision to rule indirectly placed the implementation of reforms, even those affecting the bureaucracy itself, in the hands of the bureaucrats. Second, the Japanese people have generally continued to maintain a "vague but obstinate notion" that the bureaucracy is neutral and impartial. Third, the political parties were weak and inexperienced during the early postwar years and accordingly incapable and unwilling to take over complex administrative duties. Tsuji also states that neither the parties nor the Diet have done anything effective since the war to check the expanding authority of the bureaucracy.

1448 U.S. Bureau of the Budget. Div. of Statistical Standards. *Statistical Mission to Japan. Preliminary Report on Japanese Statistical Organization.* Washington, D.C.? 1947.

1449 ———. Dept. of State. Office of Intelligence Research. *Political Rights in the Japanese National Public Service.* Washington, D.C.: 1950. ii, 11p. (OIR report no.5168)

1449a Varney, Richard M. "The Position of a Forester in Japan." *Journal of Forestry* 45:483–91 (July 1947)

The author, a former member of the Forestry Division in SCAP's Natural Resources Section, deals with the anachronistic system of Japanese public administration. He focuses in particular on the evils attendant upon appointing professional administrators (in certain cases, only graduates of Tokyo University's Faculty of Law) rather than technicians to all higher posts in the Bureau of Forestry. Varney describes the efforts of several SCAP officials in early 1946 to have the Ministry of Agriculture and Forestry select a technically trained forester as the bureau's new chief. While ultimately successful, these officials encountered considerable resistance from higher-level bureaucrats who defended the practice of appointing career and political officials to executive posts and of placing technical experts in subordinate positions. Varney vehemently criticizes such traditional practices and concludes that the existence of the higher civil service group remains the greatest single obstacle to the development of democratic government and efficient administration in Japan.

Economic Aspects

In the course of the occupation there occurred one major and several minor shifts of emphasis. The major shift concerned the economic aspects of SCAP's mission and activities. At the outset the basic policy in the economic field is well summed up in the words of the U.S. Initial Post-Surrender Policy for Japan: "The policies of Japan have brought down upon the people great economic destruction and confronted them with the prospect of economic difficulty and suffering. The plight of Japan is the direct outcome of its own behavior, and the Allies will not undertake the burden of repairing the damage." Starting in 1947, however, this "hands-off" policy began to shift, and in 1948 the United States openly signified its intention to assist actively in the economic recovery of Japan. This change in basic policy was linked with some deemphasizing of the democratization program where the major reforms had for the most part already been put into effect and a concomitant gradual shift from the initial policy of demilitarizing Japan to one of encouraging limited remilitarization by the time of the Korean War.

The post–1948 period of the occupation is consequently marked by a far greater degree of active intervention by SCAP in Japan's domestic economy than had been the case earlier. This change, incidentally, offers one means of periodizing the occupation into an earlier stage marked by primary emphasis on the adoption of a series of political reforms and a later stage marked by a comparable emphasis on economic reform programs calculated to restore stability and an increasing measure of productivity to the economy. This shift and the changing conditions of the economy are documented in the literature that follows.

The reader is reminded of the close relationship that exists between this literature on the economic aspects of the occupation and the more general developments described in the section including general materials (p.113) and the section on reparations payments (p.379).

Calendar of General Commentaries on the Economy and SCAP's Role Within It, 1946–72

There exists a sizable body of literature, for the most part in the form of press and periodical reports, on the state of the Japanese economy in general and the nature of occupation activities affecting the economy. Taken collectively, items of this sort constitute a sort of running account and interpretation of Japanese economic history for the years 1945–52. The most useful way of presenting this material would seem to be in chronological sequence according to the period under consideration, which has been done with the following entries. Where a particular item covers developments over a span of several years time, it has been classified under the last of the years involved.

During the early years of the occupation the literature tended to focus on the disastrous state of the economy and the many problems that flowed from it. Beginning in 1947 this emphasis started to shift first to plans and then to specific policies on the part of the United States to rehabilitate the Japanese economy and bring about a substantial degree of recovery. The Dodge Plan and many other policies and actions calculated to restore stability and productivity, revive foreign trade, and cope with problems in the fields of public finance, monetary, and price policy relate to this American endeavor and are treated in the entries that follow.

Developments in these fields are intimately linked with those of a more general nature described on pages 113 and 152 in particular. The interested reader is also referred to the section on reparations payments (p.379). Entries relating to Japan's taxation problems during the occupation have been classified separately and are presented in the section that immediately follows. Many entries in the present section, however, also treat the subject of taxation in some larger context. The reader also is advised to examine the issues of the *Far Eastern Economic Review* and of the *Oriental Economist* which appeared during the occupation period since articles within these journals by and large have not been included within this bibliography.

1946

1450 Bate, H. Maclean. "Japan Too Must Export or Starve." *Great Britain and the East* (Far East Issue) 62:F49–50F (Dec. 1946)

Although the Allies need not feel sorry for Japan's present economic plight, they cannot disregard the fact that many people, especially those living in the cities, are facing near starvation. Such living conditions will lead to strife unless Japan is to import adequate quantities of food from abroad. In order to pay for such imports, the Japanese must be allowed to resume their exports—especially cotton, woollen, and rayon textiles that are in demand in other Asian countries—even if this means a potential loss of markets for Great Britain.

1451 Bennett, Martin Toscan. "Japan's Capacity to Produce." *Far Eastern Survey* 15:129–33 (8 May 1946)

Bennett, a consulting engineer on SCAP's Reparations Committee, presents an optimistic picture of Japan's future capacity to produce based on the findings of the committee. Heavy industry, communications, shipping, and the textile industry were examined, and Bennett concludes that the decline in their productive capacities is due more to disorganization than to war damage. According to him, the major problems consist of the lack of incentive for making improvements in the factories because of cheap labor, and the stifling of small enterprises by monopolies.

1452 Crane, Esther M. "Japan: Economic Phases of Occupation Program." *Foreign Commerce Weekly* 23:3–5, 41–42 (13 Apr. 1946)

In an analysis of the overall Japanese economy, a serious food shortage is emphasized as an outstanding factor in the country's deteriorated economic condition. The author considers the broad policies undertaken by SCAP to alleviate the situation and describes the indigenous conditions responsible for the lack of food, i.e., a poor rice crop due to war destruction, typhoons, and soil depreciation. The author also describes the control associations' rationing of food, the government's difficulty in collecting food, and war damage to fisheries. In addition to discussing Japan's food shortage, she illustrates the nation's destitute economy by citing the number of other products rationed, such as clothing, fuel, and reading materials, as well as by noting the slow and unsatisfactory revival of industry.

Engineers Joint Council. National Engineers Committee. *Report on the Industrial Disarmament of Japan, Submitted to the Secretaries of State, War, and Navy.* 1946? See no.1000.

1453 Garbuny, Siegfried. "Japan: Regeneration." *Current History* 11:493–99 (Dec. 1946)

This article discusses some important economic consequences of the occupation, concentrating both on the effects wrought on the Japanese economy by territorial changes and on the programs of demilitarization, industrial demobilization, and reparations.

1453a "How U.S. Runs Defeated Japan." *United States News* 20:24–25 (25 Jan. 1946)

The first tasks of the occupation, according to this analysis, are feeding the people, providing them with work, and getting the economy moving once again. There still are severe shortages of food, housing, clothing and fuel which demand immediate attention, but MacArthur has already managed to institute many far-reaching reforms in politics, education, and economic organization.

1454 "Japan's Economy in Transition." *World Today* 2:452–61 (Oct. 1946)

A brief review of the Japanese economy after one year of occupation as compared to the period immediately after the surrender. There is also an attempt to predict some of the most important economic issues that will face Japan in the future. The author considers Japan's present economic policy as formed by 3 factors and briefly examines each. The factors are: (1) Japan's own efforts to mobilize her resources for the war, (2) the destruction of the sources of wealth that occurred during the war, and (3) present Allied economic policy in the country. The author agrees that SCAP's economic policy should be directed toward preventing future Japanese aggression but argues against destroying Japan

1454a "Japan's Road Back." *Fortune* 33: 124–31 (Mar. 1946)

This article has no formal byline, but a special note states that its author is John Kenneth Galbraith. He reports that Japan's physical desolation is far greater than that of Germany. Japan's government has survived, however, and she still has the basis for a viable economy. Recovery will be complicated by the fact that 8 years of war have pushed the economy too far in the direction of heavy industry. The problem of food shortages and of inflation also must be met. The dissolution of the *zaibatsu* is regarded as one of the most important and central tasks of the occupation, but Galbraith is pessimistic about SCAP's ability to conduct a successful trustbusting program. Finally the author focuses on the issue of reparations and notes that China automatically has become heir to a vast amount of permanent improvements left by Japan, particularly in Manchuria, because the industrially advanced nations among the Allies have little use for them. Indeed, the West has little need for the goods and services which Japan can provide at this point.

1455 Kurihara, Kenneth K. "Post-war Inflation and Fiscal–Monetary Policy in Japan." *American Economic Review* 36: 843–54 (Dec. 1946)

A systematic analysis of the economic measures adopted by Japan under SCAP guidance in order to overcome the post-war inflationary crisis. The author views this inflationary crisis as threatening the economic security of the country and also deterring Allied efforts to effect democratic reforms. He discusses in detail the 2 factors he believes responsible for the inflation—namely, deficit war financing and the general scarcity of goods; then he describes monetary and fiscal measures that have been taken by the government to remedy the situation. The author concludes that "on the whole, such methods are too indirect and too negative to be particularly effective in the immediate post-war period." Yet he believes that the degree of success Japan has achieved in combatting inflation is a favorable commentary on Allied economic policy thus far. Tables citing the circulation of bank notes in 1945 and the general price index from 1941 through 1945 are provided.

1456 Lockwood, William Wirt. "Economic Issues in the Occupation of Japan." *Yale Review* 36:46–65 (Autumn 1946)

A discussion of the important economic issues in occupied Japan, which the author groups into categories revolving around 3 basic Allied objectives: reparations and disarmament, reform, and recovery. He discusses in detail the policies for the elimination of the war industry and the formation of a reparations program, as well as the actual steps that have been taken in the implementation of those policies. He considers the last 2 Allied objectives at length, viewing them as long-term security measures for all of East Asia. Particular topics include the promotion of the trade union movement, the dissolution of the *zaibatsu* combines, the formulation of a new agricultural policy, the rehabilitation of civilian industry, and the regulation of government finance. Finally, the author expresses his belief that the success of the second year of the occupation will be based on 2 issues, the first being the coordination and harmonious cooperation of the various Allied governments involved in the occupation, and the second the development of a responsible democratic government within Japan itself.

1456a Minobe, Ryōkichi. "Japan's Economic Revolution." *Contemporary Japan* 15:202–16 (May/Aug. 1946)

Minobe was an editorial writer for the *Mainichi Shimbun* and the author of several works in the field of economics at the time he wrote this article. The rehabilitation policies of the Japanese government, he believes, have so far been confused, superficial, and overly optimistic. Despite SCAP encouragement to the contrary, government policy has been capitalistic in character and inflationary to the extreme. Measures to combat inflation have been either unproductive or counterproductive. Public trust in the government must be reestablished first of all by making the financiers and bankers share the burdens of rehabilitation with the wage- and salary-earners. Strong, forceful, and progressive government leadership is absolutely essential.

1457 Mukai, Shikamatsu. "The Structure of Japan's Post-war Economy." Tr. by A. J. Grajdanzev. *Public Affairs* 19:90–95 (Mar. 1946)

The author, a Japanese economist, argues that postwar Japan will have difficulty in maintaining its people's livelihood because of: (1) lost territory, (2) reduced production facilities, (3) greater need to import finished products, (4) overpopulation, and (5) high reparations payments. The production of consumer goods will have to remain at wartime levels. Mukai feels that the Japanese economy can survive only by rationalizing production, particularly in small and middle-sized enterprises. This article originally appeared in the October 1945 issue of *Shin Tōa Keizai*.

Pauley, Edwin W. *Report on Japanese Assets in Manchuria to the President of the United States, July 1946*. 1946. See no.1138.

———. *Report on Japanese Reparations to the President of the United States, November 1945 to April 1, 1946*. 1948. See no.1139.

1458 "Program for Japan's Industry." *United States News* 20:25–26 (8 Mar. 1946)

There are many obstacles to Japanese economic recovery, among them reparations, trade rivalries among the victorious nations, the loss of Japan's mainland sources of raw materials, and SCAP's prohibition against the construction of new ships. SCAP is committed, nevertheless, to reviving the Japanese economy and is making a number of efforts in that direction. These include the import of raw cotton for the textile industry and food to ease the current critical shortage as well as the establishment of new export-import machinery.

Supreme Commander for the Allied Powers. Economic and Scientific Section. *Progress Report*. 1946. See no.276.

1459 ———. ———. Research and Statistics Div. *The Cancellation of War Indemnities*. Tokyo: SCAP, 15 Dec. 1946.

1460 Tamagna, Frank M. *An Economic Reform for Japan*. Typescript. Washington, D.C.: Federal Reserve System, Board of Governors, Research Div., 3 May 1946. 111p.

1461 ———. "The Financial Position of China and Japan." *American Economic Review* 36:613–27 (May 1946)

This article is a discussion of the wartime and postwar economies of both China and Japan. The first part of the report is focused on the historical development of the 2 Asian economies and on a description of the losses they incurred during the war. Following this part, attention is focused on the effects of the war on the postsurrender financial and economic situations of both countries, and upon a comparative analysis of their finances, industrial resources, etc. There is also a detailed consideration of the Japanese inflationary situation and occupation policies regarding the establishment of the value of the Japanese yen.

1461a "Terms of Reference of the Inter-Allied Trade Board for Japan. *Department of State Bulletin* 15:753–54 (27 Oct. 1946)

This measure, unanimously approved by the Far Eastern Commission on 10 October 1946, establishes an Inter-Allied Trade Board for Japan to be made up of 1 representative for each member nation of the FEC. The Trade Board will seek to expedite consultation on all matters regarding trade to and from Japan, to advise the United States government on trade matters, and to facilitate Japanese exports and imports while keeping the objectives of the occupation in mind.

1462 Tiltman, Hessell. "Letter from Tokyo: Cooptimists Ride High." *New Republic* 115, no.23:763 (9 Dec. 1946)

Japan's political and economic leaders are reportedly preparing for a trade boom which will lead to rapidly improving economic conditions. They firmly believe that the conclusion of a peace treaty ending the stigma of "enemy nationals" will enable them to trade freely with other nations and to meet much of the global demand for consumer goods.

Tiltman points out, however, that Japan continues to face an acute shortage of basic raw materials, that much of her industry remains in ruins and that there is no immediate prospect of importing new machinery, that the country's communications facilities and harbors still need to be repaired, and that efforts at industrial recovery and expansion may well be hampered by the increasingly strong trade union movement which has been engaging in a series of strikes and other disruptions.

1463 U.S. Dept. of State. Office of Research and Intelligence. *The Place of Foreign Trade in the Japanese Economy*. Mimeographed. Washington, D.C.? 1946. 2v.

1947

"Allied Council for Japan." 1947. See no.849.

1464 "A Businessman's Impressions of Trading Conditions in Japan." *Board of Trade Journal* 153, no.2656:1968–69 (15 Nov. 1947)

The businessman concerned was impressed with the pace and effectiveness of Japan's reconstruction program, specifically with the effort to assist foreign buyers. However, he notes the difficulties of having to work only in Tokyo, lack of contact by SCAP officials with recent world trade trends, and the complicated price valuation procedure SCAP used.

1464a Butler, Sir Paul. "Satellite Japan." *Spectator* 179, no.6218:262–63 (29 Aug. 1947)

Butler focuses on the basic shift in American policy toward Japan that was taking place at the time his article appeared. After noting that it was quite natural for American views to prevail in the occupation on account of their prominent role against Japan during World War II and their willingness to bear most of the expenses of the occupation, he asks how this reorientation of policy would affect the interests of both Great Britain and the British Commonwealth. Ideally the British would want a demilitarized, adequately supervised, democratic Japan limited in the extent to which she could rebuild her industry and compete once again in various export markets. Since the United States is anxious to lessen Japan's need for outside aid, however, it is understandable that the Americans will want to increase Japan's industrial capacity and exports in order that she may come to have a favorable trade balance. With protection from the United States and backed by American resources and capital, Japan should be able to return to a state of relative prosperity and stability. While this may result in her being an American satellite for some time, under existing Far Eastern conditions such a solution is preferable to that of her entering the Soviet orbit.

1465 Crane, Burton. "Some Problems of Reconstruction." *Contemporary Japan* 16:437–45 (Oct./Dec. 1947)

American policy toward the economic reconstruction of Japan is the topic of this article. The author discusses such relevant aspects as the procurement of raw materials and the availability of world markets for finished goods, and also considers the effects on Japan's economy of the fact that social reforms were given a higher priority than industrial recovery. He speculates as to the possible effects of the economic decentralization law (which had not yet been passed) and considers both the advantages and disadvantages of breaking up the *zaibatsu* organizations. Finally, there is a discussion of European and Asian dependence on American aid which is viewed as an important factor in Japan's economic reconstruction.

1466 Far Eastern Commission. "Interim Import-Export Policies for Japan." *Department of State Bulletin* 17:368–69 (24 Aug. 1947)

The Far Eastern Commission approved this policy decision on 24 July 1947. The report has 5 sections. The first section outlines long-range policy objectives which aim for private participation in Japanese trade and the remaining 4 concern interim measures that will be adopted. Section 2 describes controls that will be imposed, and section 3, the development of an import-export program, whereas sections 4 and 5 present more detailed considerations relating to imports and exports respectively.

"Far Eastern Commission." 1948. *See* no.865.

1467 "General of the Army Douglas MacArthur's Letter to Prime Minister Shigeru Yoshida, Urging the Japanese Government to Take Definite Measures to Effect the Stabilization of the Economic Conditions of the Country, and Prime Minister Yoshida's Reply to the above, March 22, 1947." *Contemporary Japan* 16:113–16 (Jan./Mar. 1947)

Although concentrating on Japan's current food problem as a significant indication of the present economic plight of the nation, MacArthur nevertheless sees the food shortage as "only part of the overall problem of economic stabilization." He urges the Japanese government to formulate an integrated approach in order to meet this particular problem as well as the tasks of increasing the production of raw materials and industrial products, and of stabilizing wages and prices. He recommends they aim for greater exports and sound public finance.

Holman, D. S. "Japan's Position in the Economy of the Far East." 1947. *See* no.1127.

1468 Horner, Francis J. "Japan as a Trade Competitor." *Great Britain and the East* (Far East Issue) 63:F47–48F (Jan. 1947)

In this brief examination of Japan's postwar reentry into international trading markets, the author evaluates the potential of the Japanese for becoming a serious economic rival of Great Britain. After considering the effects of wartime destruction, the pervasiveness of small-scale industrial enterprises, reduced wage levels, and SCAP labor reforms, Horner concludes that Japan cannot produce items of first-class quality similar to those exported by Britain and that the British need not fear Japanese trade competition as a result.

1469 Horoth, V. L. "China and Japan." *Magazine of Wall Street* 80:699–701, 725 (27 Sept. 1947)

The author contrasts the postwar recoveries of Japan and China. The increasing self-sufficiency of Japan is discussed in terms of raw material imports from the United States and the gradual reopening of unrestricted international trade. Horoth suggests that a drastic reevaluation of the yen from 50 to 400 per U.S. dollar is necessary before Japanese goods can be marketed worldwide.

1470 Japan. *Economic Condition of Japan*. Official "white paper" submitted by the Japanese Government on 4 July 1947. Tokyo: 1947. 4p.; Also in special supplement *Nippon Times* (Tokyo) 16 July 1947.

1471 Japan. Board of Trade. *Who's Who of Industrial Japan*. Tokyo: 1947. 4v.

A directory of the leading industrial figures in Japan during the years immediately following World War II. The 4 volumes respectively cover machinery and metals, textile goods, general merchandise, and natural products and chemicals.

1471a "Japan's Foreign Trade in 1947." *Far Eastern Economic Review* 5:17–19 (7 July 1948)

This article summarizes Japan's foreign trade activities in the year 1947. Changes in the volume and nature of exports and imports are analyzed, and the following statistical tables are appended: (1) Index of Trade Volume; (2) Ratio of Actual Imports of Principal Goods to Required Volume; (3) Japan's Exports and Imports by Countries; and (4) Exports and Imports by Commodities. A list of commodies available for export from Japan is also included.

1471b "Japan in Race between Peace and Starvation." *Christian Century* 64:915 (30 July 1947)

In view of the critical food shortage facing Japan, this editorial urges that every effort be undertaken to arrange for a peace treaty as quickly as possible. A decision must be made soon on "the basis of which the Japanese economy can be reconstituted." The magazine recommends that the 11-nation conference proposed by the United States adopt a two-thirds rule in order to avoid the deadlocks which have resulted in the European negotiations on account of their acceptance of the one-nation veto rule.

1472 Kauffman, James Lee. "A Lawyer's Report on Japan Attacks Plan to Run Occupation Far to the Left of Anything Now Tolerated in America." *Newsweek* 30:36–38 (1 Dec. 1947)

In these excerpts from a report prepared for the American government, Kauffman discusses SCAP economic policy. He criticizes the quality of SCAP leadership, claiming financial adventurism and technical inexperience, and calls for an end to economic experimentation and for the replacement of SCAP theorists by experienced businessmen. A document prepared by the State Department in the spring of 1947, directive FEC–230, is selectively quoted. This document indicates that all big business in Japan is to be broken down and redistributed to small and medium-sized concerns. The Labor Standards Law and the Enterprise Reconstruction and Reorganization Law are cited as examples of the implementation of this plan for destroying and reconstituting the economy.

Kern, Harry F. "Trouble in Japan: How the Struggle to Win the Peace Now Threatens the Success of the American Occupation." 1947. *See* no.507.

1473 Kirby, E. Stuart. *Japan's Economic Future*. Mimeographed. London: Royal Institute of International Affairs, 1947. 50p. (Institute of Pacific Relations, 10th conference, United Kingdom paper no.1, 1947)

A comprehensive examination of Japanese economic conditions is undertaken, and a prediction regarding the future of the Japanese economy is made. Kirby is in favor of most of the agrarian reforms implemented by SCAP; however, he does not believe that these reforms will stimulate urbanization, which is necessary to increase the number of export-bound, capital-intensive, industrial products manufactured in urban areas. In the author's opinion, *zaibatsu* dissolution appears to have been carried out successfully. He believes that the implementation of the Pauley proposals concerning Japan's reparations would severely reduce the country's industrial potential and that internal conditions could deteriorate into revolution unless freedom of external trade is permitted. The condition of Japan's export trade is compared with that of 1936, with reference to cotton textiles, raw silk, rayon, machinery, foodstuffs, bicycles, cement, toys, vegetables, etc. The conclusion states that Japanese democracy will be guaranteed only under the "watching and guidance" of the Allies and that in view of Japan's political instability, the situation closely resembles that of 1868.

1473a Koenig, Nathan. "Postwar Japan: How Long Must We Help Her?" *Land* 6:351–60 (Autumn 1947)

Koenig, the head of a U.S. government mission which surveyed the food and fertilizer requirements of Japan and Korea, provides some general observations on the state of the Japanese economy at the time of his visit. He found that continued American aid would be necessary inasmuch as Japan would not be able to produce sufficient food for some time to come and lacked the funds with which to pay for imports. Furthermore, he determined from his discussions with General MacArthur and his staff that SCAP was aware of the need for exports if Japan were to pay her own way and thus relieve the American taxpayer of an unwanted burden. Japan must be permitted to export, Koenig concluded, so that her economy may be rehabilitated and democratic reforms can succeed. Changes in the reparations programs are required lest industry remain paralyzed by uncertainty over its future, and either a revolving fund or a loan controlled by American officials should be established to enable the Japanese to increase the import of raw materials and other commodities with which to rebuild the country.

1474 Kramer, R. C. "Japan Must Compete." *Fortune* 35:112–13, 176–79 (June 1947)

A brief article concerning Japanese trade relations. It was written by an American business leader and former MacArthur staff officer who believes that the ultimate success of the occupation will depend to a large degree on the fairness, intelligence, and farsightedness of U.S. economic policy toward Japan. He criticizes American business interests that would like to eliminate Japan from world trade competition and emphasizes the fact that Japan must export services and manufactured goods in order to survive. Finally, the author argues that the short-term risks involved in allowing Japanese competition will be rewarded by the achievement of the long-range goals of peace and prosperity and that substantial American financial investment in Japanese industry could have many advantages.

1475 Kudryavtsev, V. "The Japanese Problem in Sino–American Relations." *Soviet Press Translations* 2:226–29 (15 Nov. 1947)

This careful analysis of the effects of the American occupation of Japan upon U.S.–China relations originally appeared in the 2 September 1947 issue of *Izvestia*. Noting that U.S. policy vis-à-vis China and Japan has undergone marked modifications in recent months, the author characterizes America as becoming more interested in the resurgence of Japan and less interested in the internal problems of China. He cites the large number of loans and credits that are being proferred to Japan and the recent postponement of the $500,000,000 loan to China as convincing examples of such a policy change. The article accuses the United States of acting unilaterally in the occupation of Japan and disregarding the interests of its Allies, including China, which has a special interest in the disarmament and permanent demilitarization of Japan.

1476 Nehmer, Stanley. "The Occupation of Japan: The Third Phase." *Current History* 13:92–95 (Aug. 1947)

According to the author, the occupation may be divided into 4 phases signifying different SCAP objectives. The first phase is demilitarization and demobilization, the second the establishment of a peaceful democratic state, the third the economic reconstruction of the country, and the final phase, not yet reached, is the peace settlement. This article concentrates upon the third phase, discussing SCAP's programs of land reform and rehabilitation of the Japanese economy. The author stresses the seriousness of Japan's inflationary problem and describes the efforts of the Japanese government to control mounting inflation.

Ohkita, Saburō. "Japan Views Her Reparations." 1947. *See* no.1134.

1477 Oriental Economist. *Japan's Export Industries*. Tokyo: 1947. 150p.

1478 Ouchi, Hyōye. *Financial and Monetary Situation in Post-war Japan*. Mimeographed. New York: Institute of Pacific Relations, International Secretariat, 1947. 23p. (Institute of Pacific Relations, 10th conference, Japanese supplementary paper, 1947)

A Japanese economist briefly reviews the economic reforms implemented by SCAP and economic problems in Japan. He begins with a consideration of Japanese productivity at the time of surrender and the inflationary trends which prevailed thereafter and discusses SCAP directives regarding economic democratization and antiinflationary measures. They include the creation of a war profits tax and a property tax, the freezing of wartime compensation, land reform, *zaibatsu* dissolution, and the emergency antiinflationary measures announced in February 1947. He also examines the 1946–47 budget, which he contends will intensify inflation, and deplores the state of the nation's finances which are far from normal. However, he stresses that the occupation has given great hope to the Japanese and that the nation will eventually recover. This paper subsequently was published under the same title by the Japan Institute of Pacific Studies (no.1508).

"Peace with Japan." 1947. *See* no. 2325.

1479 Reubens, Edwin P. "Small-scale Industry in Japan." *Quarterly Journal of Economics* 61:577–604 (Aug. 1947)

This report discusses the ways in which the Allied occupation has influenced the character of small-scale industry in Japan. The first section of the article covers prewar and wartime trends of production, and the second and third sections deal with the situation during the occupation and analyze the effects on both large- and small-scale industry of the Allied program for the democratization of Japanese industry. The article discusses the possibility of small-scale industry contributing toward one of the chief objectives of SCAP—the development of a strong and stable middle class—and provides suggestions for measures that might be taken to enable small-scale enterprise to function more successfully. The author concludes that small-scale industry will contribute more toward the solution of immediate problems than toward the long-run economic and social objectives of the occupation. A number of statistical tables and charts are provided which indicate the percentage distribution of employment and the number of small-scale businesses in Japan. These statistics are drawn from Japanese sources and the findings of the U.S. Strategic Bombing Survey of which the author was a member.

1480 Rosinger, Lawrence K. "Should U.S. Rebuild Japan as the 'Workshop' of Asia?" *Foreign Policy Bulletin* 26:2–3 (16 May 1947)

The author discusses the pros and cons of an Allied policy which would assist the economic recovery of Japan. He believes that there is a real need to promote a higher level of Japanese foreign trade in view of Japan's economic plight, but at the same time he warns against too rapid a restoration of the economy that might promote a resurgent Japan. Finally, he alludes to the recent April elections and suggests some conclusions to be drawn from the results.

1481 ———. "U.S. Faces Difficult Economic Issues in Japan." *Foreign Policy Bulletin* 26:2–3 (25 Apr. 1947)

Japan's mounting economic crisis—its causes and possible remedies—are considered in this article. The author briefly touches upon SCAP's position as indicated by recent statements of General MacArthur and the suggestions of the Allied Council as stated by the British Commonwealth member, W. Macmahon Ball. In conclusion, the author urges the Japanese government to develop a more lively interest in economic reform rather than to rely on American programs of assistance.

1481a Roskolenko, Harry. "Letter from Japan." *Modern Review* 1:375–77 (July 1947)

In this brief report, Roskolenko discusses current economic conditions with particular focus on the bartering that has become widespread among the Japanese. He also gives concrete examples of exchange rates on the black market and examines the business arrangements that are overseen by SCAP.

1482 Stewart, John R. *Notes on the Economic Aspects of the Allied Occupation.* Mimeographed. New York: Institute of Pacific Relations, International Secretariat, 1947. 52p. (Institute of Pacific Relations, 10th conference, supplementary paper, 1947)

The author, who worked with SCAP in 1946, describes the major economic developments of the first year of the Allied occupation. He begins with a description of the economic objectives of the occupation, explaining economic democratization and economic disarmament and describing SCAP directive no.3 (22 Sept. 1945) which was the first important step taken by SCAP regarding economic matters. Stewart also describes the organizational structure of SCAP for the implementation of economic reforms, mentioning the Economic and Scientific Section, the Natural Resources Section, and the Statistical and Reports Section. Topics discussed include reparations, the *zaibatsu*, control associations, labor, land reform, industrial production, the food situation, the role of the Economic Stabilization Board, and foreign trade. The economic statistics included go up to October 1946.

——— Supreme Commander for the Allied Powers. *Summary of Data on Problems of Major Interest.* 1947. See no.261.

———. Civil Information and Education Section. *General Economic Press of Japan.* 1948. See no.2158.

1483 ———. Economic and Scientific Section. *Report on Japanese Trade for the Far Eastern Commission.* Tokyo: 5 Dec. 1947.

1484 "U.S. Trade Deals Abroad: Aid to Germany and Japan." *United States News* 22:16 (4 Apr. 1947)

This short piece on the functioning of the U.S. Commercial Co. (USCC) as salesman and financier for the U.S. occupation governments in both Germany and Japan describes the monopoly which that company holds in all U.S.–Japanese trade to the exclusion of private traders. The role of the USCC in reviving the textile industry by financing the shipment of raw cotton to Japan is presented as one example of this monopoly.

1485 Yarovoi, V. "The Post-war Economy of Japan and American Monopolies." *Soviet Press Translations* 2:4–7 (15 Jan. 1947)

This article, appearing in *Izvestia* on 14 November 1946, criticizes the role of American capital in Japan in 2 important areas. The first is its use of Japan as a market only for American goods and the second is the heavy investment of American capital in various branches of the postwar economy of Japan. The author maintains that such American involvement with the Japanese economy has given strength to the very forces MacArthur has decreed should be destroyed—i.e., the powerful financial and industrial magnates.

1486 "Yet Another Land of Crisis." *Newsweek* 30:31–32 (3 Nov. 1947)

Economic stagnation in Japan, particularly in the area of foreign trade, is the focal point of this article. The lack of cheap labor which had been plentiful in the prewar era, the breakup of corporations and the resulting technical deterioration, and the absence of a revival of shipping are cited as reasons for the failure of trade to develop. SCAP is criticized for adhering to "democratic principles" at the expense of economic rationalization.

1948

1487 "Ambassador Panyushkin's Statement of December 2, 1948." *USSR Information Bulletin* 8, no.23:728, 748 (8 Dec. 1948)

Panyushkin responds to the American representative to the Far Eastern Commission, General McCoy, who asserted on 11 November 1948 that Soviet proposals for the economic redevelopment of Japan would serve no useful purpose (no.1504a). The Soviet representative rejects this charge and accuses SCAP of unnecessarily delaying the implementation of various FEC decisions.

1487a Barnett, Robert W. "Occupied Japan: The Economic Aspect." In *Foreign Economic Policy for the United States*, ed. by Seymour Edwin Harris. Cambridge: Harvard Univ. Pr., 1948. p.104–33.

Barnett offers a detailed scholarly report on events affecting the Japanese economy since the surrender. After a brief discussion of the relative influence of the United States and the other Allies in the formation and execution of occupation policy, he proceeds to analyze what he regards as the 3 major elements in SCAP's economic policy: reparations, the goal of economic self-support for Japan, and institutional reform. Barnett analyzes each of these elements, assessing the political background of various policy decisions and the effects of these decisions on the overall objectives of the occupation.

1487b Baruch, Walter B. "Japanese Trade Prospects." *Military Government Journal* 1, no.10:1–3, 12 (Aug. 1948)

Baruch, vice-president of the Schenley International Corp., indicates in his discussion of trade prospects with Japan that it will be years before Japan will have the dollars to import anything except raw materials and capital goods. He points out some of the difficulties facing American investors such as the unfavorable laws and regulations of the occupation, the problem of converting currency, trademark protection, and unfair tax laws.

1488 Carus, Clayton D. "Japan as an Economic Problem." *Proceedings of the Institute of World Affairs* 24:111–13 (1948)

The postwar Japanese economy is briefly described in the light of prewar achievements. The author considers such elements as the land reform, the food supply programs, housing reconstruction, the development of the textile industry and heavy industry, the availability of sources of both hydroelectric power and coal, and the development of the chemical industry. He also briefly considers the financial activities of the country. Many useful statistics of Japan's prewar and postwar economy are included in the report.

1489 Cohen, Jerome Bernard. "Japan: Reform versus Recovery." *Far Eastern Survey* 17:137–42 (23 June 1948)

An article treating SCAP's economic policy and focusing on the complete reversal of its original position of non-responsibility in the economic sphere. The author explains the reasoning behind this turnabout of policy which involved fully reopening trade, decelerating the decartelization process, halting the purge of former business leaders, reopening the stock market, reducing corporate taxes, largely eliminating reparations payments, and rebuilding the Japanese merchant marine. He discusses the content and significance of the Pauley report, the Overseas Consultants' report, the findings of the Draper Mission, and the recommendations of the Johnston Committee. He also briefly discusses the reaction of other Far Eastern nations, i.e., the Philippines, China, and Australia to this reversal of policy, warns against further alienating Japan from these countries, and suggests a more integrated and cooperative Far Eastern economic recovery program.

1490 ———. "Japan's Economy on the Road Back." *Pacific Affairs* 21:264–79 (Sept. 1948)

A review of the major aspects of the course of the Japanese economy during the early occupation years in which the writer contrasts SCAP's inefficient policy of economic stabilization with its well-executed reforms in wage control. He discusses the inflation that is vitiating Japan's economic recovery. He attributes it primarily to a shortage of goods but also to large government deficits and unsound management of the money and banking structure. The report studies in detail the consequences of the inflationary spiral on various sectors of the economy —i.e., farmers, organized labor, industrial concerns, and business corporations—and also discusses efforts by SCAP and the Japanese government to induce recovery, particularly in the coal mining industry, and to reestablish Japan's foreign trade through the rebuilding of the textile trade. In concluding, the author argues that Japanese recovery cannot be achieved in a Far Eastern vacuum and suggests that a Far Eastern economic conference be called to arrange for reciprocal trade agreements between Japan and China, Indonesia, the Philippines, India, and Australia as a means of rehabilitating not only Japan but the rest of Asia as well and integrating Japan's economy with those of other Far Eastern countries.

1490a "Conduct of Trade with Japan." *Department of State Bulletin* 19:770–71 (19 Dec. 1948)

This article reprints the text of a policy decision approved by the Far Eastern Commission on 18 November and released to the press on 6 December 1948. The document indicates that trade with Japan will be oriented towards helping the Japanese economy become self-sustaining and democratic. Further provisions define the categories of traders to be admitted to Japan and establish rules about permissible port and service charges. All trade will be conducted in accordance with the overall objectives of the occupation as determined by SCAP.

1491 "The Cost of Victory." *Newsweek* 31:34–39 (15 Mar. 1948)

A report on the findings of the Overseas Consultants, Inc. regarding economic recovery is presented here. These findings indicate that the Japanese are confronted with huge obstacles in their attempt to support a vastly increased population at prewar living standards. The report recommends abandoning all plans for reparations payments in order to utilize all available resources for reconstruction purposes.

1492 Egekvist, W. Soren. "Postwar Economic Problems in Japan." *Education* 69:167–70 (Nov. 1948)

The author, a former chief of Price Control and Rationing for SCAP, emphasizes the need for economic recovery to ensure the durability of occupation social and political reforms. He suggests that economic integration into a Western-oriented trade system and a democratization of domestic economic relationships are necessary to prevent a rebirth of Japanese aggression. Egekvist discusses the need for rational economic planning, the natural market in Southeast Asia which Japan must promote for her own benefit as well as that of Asia, and the shift in American priorities which required the abandonment of reparations. In conclusion, the renunciation of both a *zaibatsu*-dominated and a Socialist economy in favor of "free enterprise" based on the American model is advocated.

1493 Farley, Miriam Southwell. "Pacific Powers Scrutinize Japan's Reconstruction." *Foreign Policy Bulletin* 28:2–3 (26 Nov. 1948)

The economic program of the occupation is described and then contrasted with the basic aims of the original postsurrender policy of the Allies. The author provides a brief but accurate description of the change of policy in the course of the occupation, and cites as well reasons for and effects of that change. She notes, in particular, that under the new policy, the program to dissolve the *zaibatsu* combines and encourage free enterprise has been seriously hindered and organized labor is now subject to considerably more restraint. In addition to the American outlook, the article describes the attitudes of other East Asian powers and Great Britain toward a Japan that is again the "workshop of Asia."

1494 "The Foreign Trade of Japan since the Surrender." *Current Notes on International Affairs* 19:485–91 (Aug. 1948)

Japan's postwar foreign trade situation is analyzed in comparison with that of the prewar period. Japan's trade with Far Eastern countries is described as having decreased markedly since the surrender. The role of the Inter-Allied Trade Board, established by the Far Eastern Commission, is referred to in the discussion of quotas of foreign businessmen who can enter Japan. The article reports that since mid-1947 Japan's trade has begun to increase as bilateral trade agreements have been signed, Asian countries such as India and Pakistan have begun to export cotton to Japan, and private businessmen have again been permitted to enter Japan.

1494a Frazer, D. J. M. "Japan in Defeat." *Australian Quarterly* 20:46–50 (Mar. 1948)

Frazer, an Australian banker, records the impressions he received of Japan during a short visit there. His comments deal primarily with economic matters, touching upon living conditions, the shortage of food, the low level of industrial production, and the deleterious effect of the purges on management efficiency —particularly in the areas of banking and finance. According to his analysis, one of the primary goals at present must be the recovery of Japan's foreign trade. Only after that has happened can many of her other problems be solved.

1495 "General MacArthur's Letter to Prime Minister Shigeru Yoshida Dated December 19, 1948, Regarding the Economic Stabilization Program for Japan, Released to the Press, December 20, 1948." *Contemporary Japan* 17:434–35 (July/Dec. 1948)

In this letter to Prime Minister Yoshida, MacArthur briefly outlines the philosophy behind the U.S. interim directive which is intended to achieve "fiscal, monetary, price and wage stability in Japan as rapidly as possible," and to maximize production for export. He strongly urges the Japanese government and people to comply with the spirit of the directive and make renewed efforts to implement it.

1496 Granada, Yole. "Should We Rebuild Japan?" *Nation* 167:180–82 (14 Aug. 1948); reply by Harold Strauss in *Nation* 167:214 (21 Aug. 1948); rejoinder by Yole Granada in *Nation* 167:411–12 (9 Oct. 1948)

The agrarian situation in occupied Japan is briefly outlined by a member of the Natural Resources Division of SCAP, who views the solution of Japan's agrarian problems as crucial for the nation's survival. After citing statistics indicating that increased crop yields and control of the birth rate, though necessary, will only be palliatives and not remedies, the author advocates a carefully controlled revival of Japanese industry to make Japan once again the workshop of Asia. In this way, she believes, American aid may gradually be decreased and Japan will be able to pay for both the food and industrial raw materials needed for domestic consumption.

Harold Strauss, a former member of SCAP's Civil Information and Education Section, expresses disagreement with Granada in a letter addressed to the editors of *The Nation* published one week later. In his opinion it would be morally reprehensible and detrimental to the interests of other Asian countries to rebuild Japan to the extent which Granada advocates. Instead, he recommends a policy of equal help to all Asian nations, a revocation of the law against the dissemination of birth-control information, and a revision of foreign immigration laws in order that more Japanese could easily emigrate overseas.

Granada apparently felt strongly about her views, for in a subsequent rejoinder she reiterated her belief that economic realities dictated that Japan be rebuilt. Unless the internal pressures of the Japanese economy are alleviated, she wrote, "we cannot hope to create conditions which would preclude the revival of militarism or the emergence of other extreme philosophies." Granada also indicated that Japan would be the most logical and the cheapest source of supply of industrial plant to other Asian countries and that various Southeast Asian trade delegations were already turning again to Japan for commodities which they needed.

1497 Horoth, V. L. "Rebuilding of Japanese Trade." *Magazine of Wall Street* 82:431–33, 454–55 (31 July 1948)

Horoth discusses the reasons for creating a self-supporting economy in Japan. He mentions the cost of supporting Japan as $400,000,000 per year and the need for a strong Japan to replace China as America's ally in East Asia. The Johnston Committee report is presented with the author's comments on the need to change certain occupation policies if Japan's economy is to be reconstituted. The revaluation of the yen from 50 to 270 per U.S. dollar is examined as the beginning of such a policy.

1498 Jain, L. C. "The Future Economy of Japan." *India Quarterly* 4:327–33 (Oct./Dec. 1948)

The major economic problems facing Japan after her defeat such as restricted productive capacity, runaway inflation, and shortages of food and housing and some attempted solutions are examined in this article. The author points out that the cooperation of other countries is needed for Japan's economic recovery, and the importance of Japan's economy to the rest of the world is noted. The diminished and unbalanced nature of Japan's postwar foreign trade is also discussed.

1499 "Japan as a U.S. Outpost: 4-Year Plan for Recovery." *United States News* 24:24 (20 Feb. 1948)

A skeletal presentation of the funding procedures which the United States envisions as necessary in order to rejuvenate Japanese industry. The author contends that America's primary goals are to have Japan "as a commercial outpost and a political friend close to Russia's sphere of influence."

The Japan Who's Who and Business Directory, 1948. 1948. See no.557a.

1500 Johnson, William R. "Banking Today in Japan." *Banking* pt.1, 40, no.8:54–55, 126 (Feb. 1948); pt.2, 40, no.9:49–50, 106 (Mar. 1948)

Johnson, a special consultant for SCAP on the rehabilitation of the Japanese banking system, spent part of 1947 in Japan studying Japanese banks and proposing certain reforms. In this 2-part article, Johnson focuses on the system's organization, Japanese banking procedures and services, and SCAP policy and regulations that affected the banking world. He also discusses in some detail the major readjustment that the system went through in order to comply with the Financial Emergencies Measures Ordinance of February 1946.

1501 K. B. "SCAPitalism in Japan." *Fortune* 38:6, 10 (Sept. 1948)

SCAP's "historical and theoretical misconceptions" are held responsible for what the author terms the failure of its economic program. Besides misunderstanding and misjudging the *zaibatsu*, he claims, occupation authorities are enacting a much stricter antitrust program than ever attempted in the United States. There is bitter criticism of SCAP's pattern of rigid foreign trade control which the author believes has entrenched monopoly more strongly than did the *zaibatsu*. The article concludes with the gloomy assertion that "free competitive enterprise languishes under the influence of those who promised to establish it."

1502 Kitasawa, Shinjirō. "The Birth of the New Japan." *Education* 69:171–75 (Nov. 1948)

In his review of the problem of Japanese economic rehabilitation. Kitasawa Shinjirō, professor of economics at Waseda University, seeks to demonstrate that the Japanese have learned that democracy can be a way of life rather than a technical political device for electing responsible government. He discusses various aspects of recovery such as the need for massive increases in production, for prompt and stringent action against inflation, and for peace in industry between business and the reborn labor movement. The author quotes extensively from both the *Industrial Reparations Survey of Japan* (1948) (no.1136) and the report of the Johnston Mission (1948) (no.1518) concerning the desirability of eliminating reparations payments. He concurs with the evaluation made by occupation personnel that the economic reconstruction of Japan will serve the well-being of all Asiatic peoples.

1503 Kudryavtsev, V. "The Fruits of MacArthur's Policy." *Soviet Press Translations* 3:134–37 (1 Mar. 1948)

An article which appeared originally in the 9 January 1948 issue of *Izvestia* sharply criticizes the occupation as an American-dominated endeavor which has refused to effect a democratic reorganization of the Japanese economy. The author accuses SCAP authorities of pursuing a policy aimed at deliberately thwarting economic recovery in Japan and thereby converting the country into an appendage of the American economic system. He also condemns the Japanese government as reactionary and lacking the support of the people.

1504 Lindstrom, Siegfried F. "The Problem of Japan's Rehabilitation." *Export Trade and Shipper* pt.1, 58:5–7, 31–32 (20 Sept. 1948); pt.2, 58:5–7, 28–31 (27 Sept. 1948)

This 2-part article by a former member of the Economic and Scientific Section of SCAP provides a discussion of postwar economic conditions in comparison to prewar industrial and trade patterns and resource availability. The author examines economic reorganization under the aegis of directive FEC-230 and questions the value of the total liquidation of *zaibatsu* holdings. The goal of Japanese self-support by 1953 is explained in terms of the need for guaranteed imports and minimal reparations. The function of the Far Eastern Commission is commented upon and SCAP policy concerning silk exports analyzed.

1504a McCoy, Frank R. "U.S. Interest in Revival of Japanese Economy on Peaceful Self-Supporting Basis." *Department of State Bulletin* 19:645–46 (21 Nov. 1948)

McCoy's statement before the Far Eastern Commission on 11 November 1948 asserts that the United States has repeatedly advocated measures designed to revive a peaceful Japanese economy. Accordingly, his government welcomes the recent Soviet statement which focuses attention on and supports the American efforts in this regard. In contrast, however, a second Soviet proposal —one calling for the establishment and exercise of international controls over Japanese war industries after the peace treaty becomes effective—would serve no useful purpose and, in any case, falls outside the jurisdiction of the FEC.

1505 Miyakawa, Saburō, ed. *Japan's Export Industries, 1949*. Tokyo: Oriental Economist, 1948. 168p.

This book describes the status and expectations of many Japanese export industries in 1948. Industries covered range from lily bulbs and Japanese umbrellas to shipbuilding and industrial chemicals, with about a page of comment devoted to each. There also are detailed tables on Japanese imports (1947) and exports (Jan.–Mar. 1948) by commodity and country. The occupation itself is not discussed directly, although its rules and regulations covering private trade are explained.

1505a "More American Help for Japan?" *Economist* 155:828 (20 Nov. 1948)

The prospect of a new and more benevolent Congress, which might be willing to provide Japan with increased aid for the reconstruction of her economy, has prompted U.S. Army Undersecretary William Draper to renew his efforts at getting the American government to provide Japan with assistance along the lines of the European Recovery Program, although on a less ambitious scale. European textile manufacturers, alarmed by the possibility of renewed Japanese competition, may well protest any efforts of the United States to rebuild Japanese industry. In the long run, however, such protests will probably fail to deter the Americans from attempting to strengthen the Japanese economy and thereby make Japan "pay its own way."

1506 Morgan, Alfred. "The Japanese Currency Reform." Oxford Univ., Institute of Statistics. *Bulletin* 10:424–37 (Dec. 1948)

Morgan illustrates the extent to which monetary reform has affected Japan's inflationary trend and outlines the chief reasons for the failure of the Japanese antiinflation program. The currency reform measure, he notes, could not have been expected to check the inflation in Japan unaided, but its value as a "breathing spell" measure might have been enhanced had it been fully implemented with the other facets of the antiinflation plan.

1507 Nishiyama, Haruji. "Some Problems of Japanese Business." *Military Government Journal* 1, no.8:21–22 (June 1948)

Nishiyama, councillor of the Reparations Board of the Japanese government, discusses some of the problems that discourage foreign investment, and the desirability of eliminating or modifying governmental regulations which control the prices and movements of commodities.

1508 Ōuchi, Hyōe. *Financial and Monetary Situation in Post-war Japan.* Tokyo: Japan Institute of Pacific Studies, 1948. i, 51p. (Pacific Studies series)

This pamphlet was first presented as a paper to a symposium on the democratization of Japan sponsored by the Institute of Pacific Relations (no.1478). Ōuchi, a former professor of economics at Tokyo University, characterizes the economic consequences of Japan's defeat in World War II as the defeat of one goal and the substitution of another. The goal of Japanese economic and financial domination over East Asia was replaced with the as-yet-unrealized goal of democratizing Japan's national economy. Following a brief sketch of Japan's economic position at the end of the war, the author reviews such occupation programs as *zaibatsu* dissolution, the land reform program, and the encouragement of labor unions. He also discusses inflation, the 1946–47 national budget, and property taxes. The author characterizes postwar Japanese economics and finance as "a vicious circle of unbalanced public finance, inflation, shrinking production, and unstable daily life." He offers no solutions but suggests that Allied assistance and occupation policy hold the key to Japan's economic future.

Overseas Consultants, Inc. *Report on Industrial Reparations Survey of Japan to the United States of America.* 1948. See no.1136.

1509 "Plans for a Stronger Japan." *United States News* 24:20–21 (12 Mar. 1948)

The tone of this article is set by the statement that "peace terms and reform programs are to wait while the United States gets recovery started." The basic assumption is that Japan is the key both to American economic recovery plans for Asia and to resistance against Russia in East Asia. As a result, the emphasis is on those occupation policies which promote optimal economic growth. It is reported that plant removals for reparations are to be scaled down by five-sixths and that the United States has intervened directly to enforce tax payments and crop collections. The economic steps outlined lead to the conclusion that there is in store for Japan both more U.S. aid and a longer occupation than previously anticipated.

1509a "Prime Minister Hitoshi Ashida's Administrative Speech before the Diet, March 20, 1948." *Contemporary Japan* 17:111–17 (Jan./Mar. 1948)

In his introductory remarks, Ashida defends his middle-of-the-road stance as necessary in a time of crisis if conflict and violence are to be avoided. The occupation he regards as "one of fairness and tolerance unparalleled in history" and one which has inspired the genuine cooperation of the Japanese people. Aside from a few general remarks evaluating the progress of various reform programs, Ashida devotes the remainder of his address to outlining the goals and programs he regards as vital for economic rehabilitation. These include (1) overcoming inflation through an increase in production and the absorption of floating purchasing power; (2) capital accumulation; (3) the rationalization of management and the improvement of production technology; (4) the development of industries suited to their location; (5) an expansion of hydroelectric power resources; and (6) increased food production. Japan is immensely grateful for the Allies' material assistance, Ashida concludes, but she must continue to deserve it by strictly adhering to the terms of the Potsdam Declaration and by continuing to democratize herself.

1509b "Prospects of Japanese Recovery." *Economist* 155:381–82 (4 Sept. 1948)

Most of the basic problems which faced the Japanese economy at the end of the war remain unsolved. Japanese industrial production is limited, inflation is rampant, and there is little foreign trade. SCAP has been seeking to increase domestic production in several ways and has tried to put Japan's domestic finances in order by means of sound budgeting and strict controls over wages, prices, and the allocation of scarce raw materials. Japanese officials, however, have been lax in carrying out appropriate directives. General MacArthur has also attempted to reduce the level of reparations, to modify plans for breaking up the *zaibatsu*, and to secure funds from Congress not only to cover relief expenditures but also to finance Japan's recovery. His efforts have been marked by some success. Nonetheless, it has become clear to SCAP that Japan must rely on private foreign investment to finance her industrial recovery and that the country's immediate economic prospects are not cheerful. Japan's political leaders will have to convince the population, therefore, of the necessity for tolerating a low standard of living for some time to come.

1510 "Reconstruction in Japan." *World Today* 4:288–96 (July 1948)

A brief survey of the internal and external problems besetting Japanese rehabilitation—particularly in the economic sphere. After discussing economic difficulties related to the procurement of raw materials, fuel and transportation facilities, the problem of controlling the economic system, the difficulties caused by mounting inflation, and the reparations question, the author discusses changes in SCAP's overall economic policy as a result of recommendations made by Overseas Consultants, Inc. and the Draper report. The effects of fluctuations in world market conditions upon Japan's economy are also briefly discussed. Statistics on import-export ratios and rates of industrial production during 1946 and 1947 are provided, and these figures are compared to prewar statistics.

1511 "Reconstruction of Japan under 'Informal Peace'." *United States News* 24:28 (23 Apr. 1948)

This brief article enumerates the extraordinary economic privileges accorded Japan, despite the fact that the country is legally a defeated enemy in a state of armistice. The author points out the changes in the original American policy that called for a rapid peace and the resumption of formal relations with Japan. It has changed, he believes, to the postponement of a formal peace and the utilization of direct military control of the country to gain economic and political advantages.

1512 "Report on the Economic Condition of Japan Issued by the Economic Stabilization Board, May 23, 1948." *Contemporary Japan* 17:214–22 (Apr./June 1948)

This report attempts to trace the progress of the Japanese economy in the period between July 1947 and May 1948 and to describe possible paths of future development. The report carefully and concisely discusses the fundamental conditions of the postwar Japanese economy, such as loss of property and reduction of trade as a result of war and the occupation and the rapid increase of population in the postwar period. There is a description of the present status of production, foreign trade, prices, money and finance, and wages, which is useful in assessing the condition of the Japanese economy mid-way in the occupation. In conclusion, the report briefly outlines the economic problems which Japan must face in the near future.

"The Report Prepared by the Johnston Committee and Submitted to United States Secretary of the Army Kenneth Royall (Released to the Press), May 19, 1948: The Text of the 'Summary of the Report'." 1948. *See* no.1142c.

Sansom, Sir George B. "Conflicting Purposes in Japan." 1948. *See* no.567.

1513 Supreme Commander for the Allied Powers. *Draper Mission Messages.* Mar.–Apr. 1948. Blue Binder series. MacArthur Memorial, Bureau of Archives, Norfolk, Va. 1 folder.

Two unclassified radio messages between the commander in chief for the Far East and the Department of the Army reporting the recommendations of the Draper Mission and urging the Senate Foreign Relations Committee and House Foreign Affairs Committee to appropriate funds for the economic rehabilitation of Japan, Korea, and the Ryukyus in order to secure a stable situation in East Asia.

1514 ———. Economic and Scientific Section. Research and Programs Div. *Japanese Housing Requirements.* Tokyo: The Division, 1948. 35p.

1515 Teters, Barbara Joan. "American Policy as Regards Japan." *Proceedings of the Institute of World Affairs* 24:56–59 (1948)

Occupation reform policies, particularly those specifically relating to the economic situation, are the topic for consideration at a round table discussion chaired by Jesse F. Steiner. In addition to discussing SCAP's dissolution of the *zaibatsu* and its encouragement of a vigorous labor union movement, the members comment on the peace treaty, discussing possibilities of postponement until an agreement is reached among the Allies, as well as the possibility of a series of separate treaties with Japan if agreement cannot be reached.

Thomas, Elbert D. "Leadership in Asia under a New Japan." 1948. *See* no.571.

1516 "Trends in United States Policy towards Japan." *Current Notes on International Affairs* 19:251–53 (May 1948)

Five statements made by American officials and businessmen in the first 3 months of 1948 are introduced here to document changes in U.S. occupation policy toward Japan. Those making the statements are K. C. Royall, secretary of the army; Major General F. R. McCoy, chairman of the Far Eastern Commission; Overseas Consultants, Inc., engaged by the Department of the Army to advise MacArthur on Japanese industry; Percy H. Johnston, member of an advisory group of businessmen which visited Japan under the leadership of William H. Draper, undersecretary of the Department of the Army; and General MacArthur. All statements point to the need for a relaxation of restrictions imposed on Japanese trade and commerce. They also warn that the removal of productive facilities and the deconcentration of the *zaibatsu* would hurt rapid industrial recovery, thus keeping the Japanese economy from becoming "self-supporting." The full text of each statement is appended on pages 284–97.

1517 Tsuru, Shigeto. "Japan's Five-Year Plan." *Christian Science Monitor* magazine section p.2 (14 Aug. 1948)

Tsuru analyzes the Japanese government's recently published "Five-Year Plan of Economic Rehabilitation." The goals of this plan include a 300 percent growth in industrial production, a doubling of labor productivity, and a 9-fold increase in export volume when compared with 1947 figures. While the Japanese objective is to become self-supporting, the success of this plan nevertheless will depend largely on the timing and amount of American aid. Furthermore, it will be necessary to limit domestic consumption since the Japanese national output at present is less than basic consumption needs and any kind of rehabilitation will require a sustained investment out of current output that is bound to leave little slack for increased consumption. In order to avoid wasting aid from abroad and postponing economic self-sufficiency, the government must decide quickly on appropriate economic control methods.

1518 U.S. Committee to Inquire into Economic Problems of Japan and Korea. *Report on the Economic Position and Prospects of Japan and Korea and the Measures Required to Improve Them.* Washington, D.C.: 1948. 22p.

The report of this committee under the chairmanship of Percy H. Johnston consists of a brief general analysis of the economic situation of Japan and Korea and recommendations for U.S. policy in light of the problems uncovered. Coverage of the Korean situation is cursory; all but 3 pages of the report are devoted to Japan. Among the issues addressed are raw materials and foreign trade, reparations, prospects for foreign investment, and budget and foreign trade policy. The committee found that relief costs of the occupation of Japan neared $400 million per year for the first 2 and one-half years and that now the United States must face the problem of assisting the Japanese people to become self-supporting. They agreed with General MacArthur and the Department of the Army that industrial recovery is necessary to a self-supporting economy in Japan and that this was properly a primary objective of the occupation.

"Unizonia in Japan." 1948. *See* no. 838.

1518a "Which Path for Japan?" *Statist* 147:688–90 (26 June 1948)

While it is still hard to predict the future status of her economy, Japan's natural role is for her to become the industrial workshop of East Asia. Industrial diversity will be the best guarantee against a flood of Japanese textiles into the world market, which is one of Great Britain's fears. In any case, the article concludes, the only way for Japan to survive in the postwar era is to increase her foreign trade.

1519 Whitman, Roswell H. "Economic Recovery in Japan." *Military Government Journal* 1:2–5, 15 (Jan. 1948)

The associate chief of the Division of Japanese and Korean Economic Affairs of the Department of State clearly and concisely discusses the postwar Japanese economy after 2 years of military occupation. He describes the nature of the Japanese economy—pointing up Japan's inherent dependence on economic conditions in other countries and its vulnerability to any impediments to the flow of trade. Then he describes the current economy—comparing it to the prewar and wartime situations and making suggestions as to possible remedies in the present economic crisis. He advocates that the Japanese government take 2 types of action: (1) control of the total money supply, and (2) direct controls over wages, prices, and the distribution of commodities. There is a discussion of the minimum economic measures taken by SCAP so as to "prevent disease and unrest," such as importing food and loaning vital commodities, but the author cites letters from General MacArthur to the Japanese indicating SCAP's position that recovery must rest with the Japanese. Finally, he considers the possibility of an eventual revival of trade between Japan and her former trading partners throughout the world.

1949

1520 "Ambassador Panyushkin Points out Violation of FEC Code." *USSR Information Bulletin* 9, no.4:114–15 (25 Feb. 1949)

The Soviet representative to the Far Eastern Commission takes the United States to task for its economic policies in occupied Japan. Quoting Japanese newspaper accounts of SCAP policies regarding such matters as the unhindered investment of foreign capital in Japan and Japanese government subsidies to export industries, he asserts that SCAP is "subjecting the Japanese economy to the interests of American monopolies at the expense of Japan's economic independence."

1520a "Announcement Issued by GHQ, SCAP Concerning Private Commercial Entrants, January 14, 1949." *Contemporary Japan* 18:128–39 (Jan./Mar. 1949)

The full text of General Headquarters circular no.1 has been included here. In 8 sections, the announcement includes a general description of the reasons for which an authorized person might enter Japan, provides details concerned with the application for entry, and describes the status of commercial entrants and their logistic support and the functions performed by the General Headquarters, SCAP, and the Eighth Army in this matter. The text is useful to determine SCAP's regulations for alien visitors to occupied Japan.

1521 "Announcement Issued by GHQ, SCAP Regarding Foreign Business and Investment Activities in Japan, January 14, 1949." *Contemporary Japan* 18:140–43 (Jan./Mar. 1949)

The full text of General Headquarters circular no.2 which concerns the operation of foreign business and investment in Japan. Following a definition of foreign firms and their business activity in Japan, the document discusses the matter of permission to do business with regard to specific individuals or groups—i.e., the military personnel, non-Japanese nationals, firms of Allied or neutral nations, etc., and also establishes terms for the acquisition of properties and rights in Japan.

1522 "Announcement Issued by the Supreme Commander for the Allied Powers on the Subject of Minimum Standards for Business and Investment Activities of Non-Japanese in Japan, January 15, 1949." *Contemporary Japan* 18:143–45 (Jan./Mar. 1949)

This SCAP document outlines the conditions under which non-Japanese nationals and foreign-controlled businesses may operate in Japan. Following 3 reasons why such conditions are considered essential, there are 10 detailed criteria of standards for investments that must be adhered to by any non-Japanese nationals or firms intending to do business in occupied Japan.

1523 Barnett, Robert W. "Problems in Japan's Economic Recovery." *Far Eastern Survey* 18:103–4 (4 May 1949)

The author, an adviser to the director of the Office of Financial and Development Policy of the Department of State and economic adviser to the chairman of the Far Eastern Commission, briefly discusses the U.S. directive issued to SCAP on 10 December 1948 regarding Japan's economic recovery. He perceives this directive, which sets forth 9 basic objectives, as "representing the most comprehensive effort yet made to deal with the problem" and a measure which will eventually lead to the establishment of a single general exchange rate for the yen. Japan's economic difficulties are considered as they concern 3 general areas: (1) the problem of administration which must be solved by the Japanese themselves; (2) the problem of policy whereby SCAP may intervene directly in the productive processes of Japan's economy to effect policy changes not inaugurated by the Japanese; and (3) the problem of bringing Japanese prices into some kind of harmony with world prices and procuring raw materials which are in short supply, a process that involves American financing of Japanese deficits. While acknowledging that the Japanese and Americans will encounter serious administrative, political, and economic problems in their search for economic stability, the author affirms that the U.S. directive to SCAP "represents an effort to deal, within the limits of practicality, with all three aspects of the problem."

1523a Britton, James Cleland. "Foreign Trade of Japan Is Being Restored to Private Channels." *Foreign Trade* 6: 937–39 (19 Nov. 1949)

The author, a commercial representative for Canada, reports on SCAP decisions to restore control of Japan's foreign trade to private channels as of 1 January 1950 and to stimulate foreign trade activities. Efforts are being made to rebuild the complex foreign trade machinery covering such matters as exchange controls, floor prices for exports, and regulations concerning unfair trade practices. Britton also briefly discusses the probably minimal impact of these proposed changes on Japanese–Canadian trade.

1524 Cohen, Jerome Bernard. *Japan's Economy in War and Reconstruction.* Minneapolis: Univ. of Minnesota Pr., 1949. xix, 545p. Issued also as Ph.D. dissertation submitted to Columbia Univ. under the title *The Japanese War Economy, 1937–1945.*

The first 6 of the 7 chapters of this book are a portrayal of the Japanese wartime economy from 1937 through 1945. Labeling the 1930s "a decade of preparation" for Japan's external aggression, Cohen provides a carefully documented account of Japan's economic development, covering topics such as government control of capital, credit, production, and distribution; the role of the Bank of Japan; the function of the Munitions Ministry; and the role of *zaibatsu* groups. The last chapter is a treatment of the economic problems which confronted a defeated Japan during the first 3 years of the occupation. Beginning with a description of the turnabout in early 1947 in SCAP's original position of nonresponsibility in economic matters, consideration is then given to SCAP's role in Japanese economic life including reparations, *zaibatsu* dissolution, labor reform, and land reform. Cohen notes that during the first 3 years of the occupation, no decision was made on the reparations problem, and that although the dissolution of the *zaibatsu* was ordered, little was done in actuality. He then suggests that hostilities between labor and management caused by SCAP's labor reform may be eased soon and that land reform will not result in a rapid increase in agricultural output. Each of the efforts by SCAP to initiate reform is well documented, using Japanese and English official sources. A prognosis for the economy is included. The author directs attention to the "hare-and-tortoise race" between inflation and the slow revival of industrial activity, regarding these events as 2 basic but divergent trends in the postwar economy. He is critical of SCAP's initial reluctance to intervene in economic matters since he believes this reluctance impaired subsequent recovery efforts by Japan and SCAP. This book has been translated into Japanese under the title *Senji sengo no Nihon keizai* (Tokyo: Iwanami Shoten, 1950–51. 2v.).

1524a ———. "Asia's Economic Problems." *Far Eastern Survey* 18:217–21 (21 Sept. 1949)

This article deals at a high level of generalization with Asian economic problems. One section, however, is devoted specifically to Japan. In it Cohen summarizes a talk given in Tokyo in June 1949 by P. S. Lokanathan, executive secretary of the United Nations Economic Commission for Asia and the Far East (ECAFE). By this time it was becoming clear that SCAP policy had shifted to a strong emphasis upon economic recovery, and Lokanathan's talk accordingly is a plea for consideration of the needs of Asian nations as the direction of Japan's recovery is considered. His specific recommendations center around ECAFE's belief that Japanese exports to Asia should consist of capital goods that will increase Asian development of food and mineral resources. Japan's economic problems, he argues, will remain insoluble unless they are viewed in a larger Asian context; tailoring Japan's exports to the true needs of Asian markets is the best way for reducing her dependence on trade with the United States.

1525 ———. "Japan's Economy under Occupation." *Foreign Policy Reports* 24, no.18:214–23 (1 Feb. 1949)

Cohen's review of the postwar Japanese economy focuses on the variety of economic problems that the country faced in 1947 and 1948 and on some of the measures that were being taken to resolve them. One by one the article covers the controversy over reparations, the Johnston Committee's report on the Japanese economy, SCAP's actions against the *zaibatsu*, labor reforms, land reform, basic economic trends during the first 3 years of the occupation, the revival of production, and the position of Japanese foreign trade. The author occasionally adds personal comments on the advisability of certain measures, but by and large his report simply presents the reader with an overall view of the current state of Japan's economy at that time.

Council on Foreign Relations. "American Policies in the Far East (II): Changes in Occupied Japan." 1949. *See* no.583.

———. "Search for a Far Eastern Policy: 3. Problems of Japan and Korea." 1950. *See* no.584.

Detroit, Mich. Detroit Public Library. Joseph M. Dodge papers. *See* no.45.

1526 "Economic Stabilization Programs to Be Carried out by Japanese Government." *Department of State Bulletin* 20:60 (9 Jan. 1949)

This joint press release, issued by the Department of State and Army leaders on 18 December 1948, is concerned with directives from SCAP to the Japanese government regarding the establishment of an economic stabilization program. This program would cover attempts to balance the budget, strengthen tax collecting, control credit extension, and deal with wage stability, price control, food collection and distribution, and foreign trade control.

1527 Far Eastern Commission. "Policy toward Patents, Utility Models, and Designs in Japan." *Documents and State Papers* 1, no.14:795–97 (May 1949)

Approved by the Far Eastern Commission on 17 March 1949, and published by the U.S. State Department's Office of Public Affairs in this documentary series, this policy decision outlines the newly expanded functions of the Japanese patent office.

"Far Eastern Commission." 1949. *See* no.868.

1528 Farley, Miriam Southwell. "What Role Does the U.S. Expect Japan to Play in Asia?" *Foreign Policy Bulletin* 28:3–4 (26 Aug. 1949)

Japan's position in the American attempt to formulate a new regional policy in the Far East is the topic of this article. Essential to the discussion is SCAP's attitude towards the economic rehabilitation of Japan, and in this respect the author discusses the SCAP sponsored 9-point "austerity" program of December 1948 which has apparently checked the accelerated pace of inflation and started Japan toward greater economic stability and independence. However, according to the author, "the basic problem for Japan's economic recovery is restoration of its overseas trade," particularly in Asia. She predicts that the Communist takeover in China will pose many complications for the United States as well as Japan since "a Japan economically severed from China is a liability not an asset."

1529 Feraru, Arthur N. "Japanese Trade with China." *Far Eastern Survey* 18:200–202 (24 Aug. 1949)

Feraru, a research assistant with the American Institute of Pacific Relations, discusses the difficult question of reviving Japanese trade with China. He points out that aside from the objections to Sino-Japanese trade raised by the United States, one must also take into account the animosity between SCAP-controlled Japan and Communist China, the reluctance of many European and American traders to see Japan competing once more in world trade, and the fear that an economically strong Japan might be able to reinstate her political power in the Orient.

1530 *Foreign Exchange and Foreign Trade Control Law.* Mimeographed. Law no. 228. 1 Dec. 1949. Tokyo: 1949? 16p.

1531 "Full Text of a Speech Made by Major General William Marquat, Chief of the Economic and Scientific Section, GHQ, SCAP at the Labor–Management Conference on Economic Stabilization, January 27, 1949." *Contemporary Japan* 18:145–50 (Jan./Mar. 1949)

Insisting that there can be no permanent political or social security without economic stability, the author maintains that at the present time and in the immediate future, Japan's economic development must receive prime emphasis. The author argues that the sole way to increase wages and standards of living in Japan is to increase production "by adopting and insisting upon high and sound working standards, development and recognition of specialist capacities, regulation and adjustment of working hours and development of a fair employer-employee relationship." In conclusion, Marquat is optimistic about Japan's prospects for a speedy economic recovery.

1532 "Getting Japan off U.S. Dole." *U.S. News and World Report* 26:24–25 (4 Mar. 1949)

The U.S. desire to put Japan on its feet, independent of massive American aid, is discussed briefly. To accomplish this feat and to prevent domestic Communist victories, it is claimed that earlier reforms, such as the abolition of a strong police force and the purge of wartime leadership, are to be abandoned. The author emphasizes the need for the development of new patterns of resource imports and manufacturing exports in the belief that a return to traditional Japanese–Chinese trade patterns would result in a Japanese economic—and eventually in a political—alliance with Communist Asia.

1533 Hoashi, Kei. "Japan's Economic Rehabilitation." *Contemporary Japan* 18: 448–63 (Oct./Dec. 1949)

In an article devoted to a general summation of the current economic situation in Japan, the author considers various problems hindering the economic recovery of the country and measures that have been adopted by the Japanese government and SCAP to remedy the situation. Primary emphasis is placed on the burden of the Japanese population of 80 million people and the need for population control programs and increased production. There is a discussion of the steps that have been taken thus far by way of aid from the United States through the GARIOA (Government and Relief in Occupied Areas) and EROA (Economic Rehabilitation of Occupied Areas) funds and the U.S. Aid Counterpart Fund, SCAP's 9-point Economic Stabilization Program, the Five-Year Industrial Plan prepared by the Economic Stabilization Board, and the Dodge Plan. In conclusion, the author discusses the necessity for renewed trade with China and other Asian nations and notes that "the most serious dilemma and difficulty facing the economic reconstruction of Japan is the fact that Japan is endeavoring to follow politically the way of American democracy while economically she belongs to the Asiatic zone." In reconciling this dilemma, he recommends: (1) that Japan follow a path of peace and neutrality; (2) that it remain a democracy; and (3) that Japan endeavor to establish favorable relations with the Asian countries on whom her economy is vitally dependent while remaining on amicable terms with the United States.

1534 Horoth, V. L. "Problems of Japan's Recovery." *Magazine of Wall Street* 84: 67–69 (23 Apr. 1949)

Changes in the philosophy of SCAP's economic program from one of reform-punishment to self-sufficiency and finally to independent strength are stressed. The need to ally Japan with the United States as a partner rather than as a dependent in the fight against communism is emphasized. Horoth examines the slow recovery of the steel industry and general inflationary trends. He also discusses the need to integrate Japan into the Asian community to facilitate the development of new markets to replace those controlled by the Communists.

1534a Hsieh, Nan-kuang. "Occupation Policy in Japan Viewed from Japanese Budget." *China Economist* 5, no.6:94–95 (9 May 1949)

Originally appearing in the 17 April 1949 issue of *Ta Kung Pao*, this article analyzes some of the changes that SCAP has made in the most recent Japanese budget. Hsieh explains that Joseph M. Dodge, Financial Adviser to SCAP, had thoroughly revised the draft budget prepared by the Yoshida cabinet and was advocating increases in taxation and in most—but not all—areas of government expenditures. Considerable sums were to be allocated for the construction of military bases in Japan and Korea from which to attack the USSR, far less money than in the past was to be made available for covering the expenses involved in dismantling, packing, and shipping earmarked reparations materials to other countries, and the Japanese people were to bear an increasingly heavy tax burden on account of Dodge's recommendations that the overall increase in government expenditures be made good largely through higher rates of taxation. Hsieh concludes that the budget provides a good indication of the changing nature of Allied occupation policy, and he charges the United States with seeking to place all important Japanese industries under the control of American capitalists in time of peace while trying to turn Japan into America's military supply base in the Far East in time of war.

1535 Institute of World Economy (Tokyo). *Economic Condition of Present Day Japan.* Tokyo: 1949. vi, 81p.

This publication contains 2 articles: "Analysis of Current Economic Situation of Japan," by the Economic Stabilization Board of the Japanese government, and "Japanese Resources and United States Policy," by Edward Ackerman.

1536 International Labor Office. "A Survey of Economic and Social Conditions in Japan." *International Labour Review* 60: 1–27 (July 1949)

This article deals with a trip to Japan made in 1949 by officials of the International Labor Office for the purpose of examining the country's postwar economic and social conditions and, in particular, the status of Japanese labor. The authors discuss prewar economic conditions, the growth of industry, wartime labor policy, and postwar economic development. They conclude with a statement calling for the reintegration of the Japanese economy into the world economy.

1537 Ivtsev, I. "The Colonization of Japan by American Monopolies." *Soviet Press Translations* 5:8–10 (1 Jan. 1950)

Ivtsev maintains that the United States has actively prevented the rapid postwar recovery of the Japanese economy by dispersing existing stocks of raw materials, by preventing most imports until 1947, and by being primarily concerned with optimal American profit rather than basic Japanese reconstruction. He discusses as part of a program to convert Japan into an economic colony and military springboard, the revitalization of *zaibatsu* cartels, the liquidation of 4,000 small and medium-sized enterprises, and the disproportionate tax burden placed on workers and peasants. The close tie between American capitalism and the *zaibatsu* is stressed. The author closes by noting the increase in organized strikes and the 1949 electoral gain by the Communists which he regards as evidence that American imperialism will fail.

This article was originally published in the 7 October 1949 issue of *Trud*.

†1538 "Japan: Gratitude to Grumbling."

U.S. News and World Report 27:22–23 (29 July 1949)

While recognizing the imminent success of America's policy for Japanese economic recovery, the author emphasizes the hardships this policy entails, particularly reduction in the workers' right to strike and increased unemployment. The author also reports dissipation of Japanese gratitude to the United States for a lenient peace and extensive postwar aid and discusses increased Japanese demands for political independence as well as a rebirth of Japanese self-confidence.

1539 Japan. Ministry of Finance. *The Import Tariff of Japan, with Customs Regulations.* Tokyo: Maruzen, 1949. ii, 300p. In English and Japanese.

1540 "Japan: Off U.S. Dole by 1953?" *U.S. News and World Report* 27:26–27 (12 Aug. 1949)

This article describes the MacArthur plan for a self-sufficient Japan by 1953. There is a discussion of the levels of aid required, of the various industries which must be developed, and of Japan's projected future trade pattern which is envisioned as closely linked to Communist China and Manchuria and only secondarily linked to the United States. The major concern of the author is how to eliminate American aid as rapidly as possible.

1540a "Japan Tariffs and Trade Controls." *Foreign Commerce Weekly* p.20–21 (19 Sept. 1949)

This brief report on the activities of SCAP's recent trade and financial mission to Central and South America discusses and summarizes the provisions of the interim arrangements concluded on behalf of Japan with Argentina, Brazil, Chile, Colombia, Mexico, Peru, Uruguay, and Venezuela. These arrangements are said to be merely exploratory steps in Japan's efforts to resume its trading relations with Latin America.

1541 Jessup, Alpheus W. "Japan's Economic Outlook." *China Economist* 5, no.4:62–64 (24 Apr. 1949)

The writer rejoices at the "long overdue awakening" of the occupation to the fact that Japan's economic recovery to the point of self-sufficiency is of prime importance for the Far East. In great statistical detail the goal of self-support by 1953 is outlined, along with full realization of impediments, which center in Japan's current lack of export-import facilities and industrial plant. The article decries Japanese and SCAP attempts at a "cover-up" and pleads for the necessary austerity to achieve the goal. A 5–point plan for the attainment of self-support is given.

1542 Johnston, Bruce Foster. "Japan: Problems of Deferred Peace." *Far Eastern Survey* 18:221–25 (21 Sept. 1949)

A valuable discussion of SCAP's role in the reform of the Japanese economy from the first year of the occupation to the latter part of 1949. Rather than discussing the issue of economic reform itself, the author of this article seeks "to examine the framework in which the economic recovery effort is to be carried out, and particularly the division of responsibility between the United States and the Japanese government." Johnston, previously the chief of the Food Branch, Price Control, and Rationing Division, Economic and Scientific Section, General Headquarters, SCAP, discusses initial occupation involvement, noting that in the first year and a half there was little direct SCAP action in economic operations except for its control of foreign trade. He subsequently describes growing SCAP participation in 1947 and 1948 in such areas as the collection of taxes and food and emphasizes the consequences of the State Department directive issued to General MacArthur in December 1948 calling upon him to intervene more directly in economic affairs. Following a discussion of the reasons why such participation seemed necessary, the author presents several cogent objections to continued U.S. involvement in Japan's economic affairs and suggests that the recent elimination of the Military Government Section of the Eighth Army and the 45 prefectural military government teams "appears to indicate a trend toward decreasing participation by the Occupation forces in operational problems of the Japanese economy."

In the concluding section of the report there is a consideration of America's future role in the Japanese economy in the light of the probable deferment of a peace treaty. In the author's opinion, this probability makes it difficult to justify continuation of the current restrictions on Japan's international economic relations. He urges SCAP to make every effort to normalize commercial relations with other nations and to encourage Japanese participation in such agencies as the Economic Commission for Asia and the Far East (ECAFE) and the Food and Agricultural Organization (FAO).

1543 Kawata, Fukuo. "Trade Controls in Occupied Japan (1945–1949)." *Kobe Economic and Business Review* 13:9–22 (1966)

Kawata details the principal measures taken by the occupation authorities to control and reorganize the foreign trade of Japan.

MacArthur, Douglas. "General MacArthur Replies." 1949. *See* no.944.

1543a McCoy, Frank R. "Economic Stabilization for Japan Supports FEC Objectives." *Department of State Bulletin* 20:271 (27 Feb. 1949)

This article reprints a press release of 17 February containing a statement made at the 3 February meeting of the Far Eastern Commission by McCoy, the United States representative. His statement is a reply to the Soviet member's criticism (no.1560a) at the 27 January meeting of the interim directive issued by the United States government regarding the economic stabilization of Japan. McCoy categorically denies the Soviet member's allegations that the United States unilaterally modified the regime of control in Japan by issuing the directive and that the United States has ceased being concerned with the objective of democratizing Japan.

1544 McDiarmid, Orville J. "The Japanese Exchange Rate." *Far Eastern Survey* 18: 133–35 (15 June 1949)

The 25 April 1949 SCAP directive to the Japanese government to establish a single commercial exchange rate of 360 yen to the U.S. dollar is the topic of this article. The author, the acting associate chief of the Department of State's Division of Financial Affairs and a member of the Dodge Mission to Japan, considers this directive which was established only 4 months after the initiation of the economic stabilization program as a positive indication of economic recovery. The benefits and deficiencies of economic measures adopted earlier in the occupation are described and a longer analysis is provided of the many economic aspects that had to be considered before adopting a fixed rate of currency. McDiarmid also describes the effects of the new measure on Japan's import-export activities. In the concluding section, there is a brief consideration of the future of the Japanese economy. This report is a very useful analysis of an important SCAP measure.

1544a Mayevsky, V. "Attack of Reaction on Rights of Japanese Workers." *Current Digest of the Soviet Press* 1, no. 3:35–36 (15 Feb. 1949)

The United States government, according to Mayevsky, has adopted a so-called program for the "restoration and the stabilization" of the Japanese economy which in fact aims at restoring the potential of Japan's military armaments industry, at establishing the *zaibatsu* as junior partners of U.S. monopoly capital, at strengthening the country's reactionary elements, and at suppressing the democratic movement of the Japanese masses. He points out how the United States has been dominating Japan's foreign trade, and how serious the impact of inflation has been. He also comments on the continuing opposition of many Japanese to American policies. Mayevsky concludes by stating that "the attack of reaction on the rights of the Japanese workers is meeting a decisive rebuff from progressive forces" and notes that the rapid growth of the Japan Communist Party is "clear evidence of the solidarity of the forces of true democracy" in Japan. This article first appeared in the 20 January issue of *Pravda*.

1545 Metzger, Laure. "Export Competition: German and Japanese Postwar Trade." *American Perspective* 3:217–32 (Sept. 1949)

Pointing to the lack of worldwide coordination which has characterized America's international trade policy since the end of the war, Laure Metzger explains that incentives and organizations in Japan comparable to those which led to export planning in Europe do not exist. The abrupt termination of reparations deliveries and the complete turnabout in the occupation's economic policy, with the introduction of the severe deflationary policy recommended by the Dodge Mission, add to the confusion.

1546 Minobe, Ryōkichi. "The Economic Stabilization Program for Japan." *Contemporary Japan* 18:20–33 (Jan./Mar. 1949)

An explanation of Joseph Dodge's 9 economic objectives for Japan communicated to Premier Yoshida Shigeru on 19 December 1948 is the starting point for an analysis of Japan's current economic status. Affirming that the Japanese economy has not yet approached the stage of ultimate stability and discussing the causes for the continuing inflationary spiral, the author marshalls an impressive array of statistics to underscore his thesis that economic recovery is not taking place at a sufficiently rapid rate. Tables cite the foreign trade returns of postwar Japan, those returns compared to the foreign trade of other Asian nations, the postwar annual treasury expenditures, and the deficits of various enterprises for 1945–46. The author supports the 9-point program of Dodge and General MacArthur. His criticism is directed primarily at those postwar Japanese officials who are overly optimistic and unrealistic and who are pursuing temporizing policies instead of addressing themselves to real reform measures.

1547 Nakayama, Ichirō. "Facts about Japan's Unemployment." *Contemporary Japan* 18:292–308 (July/Sept. 1949)

The introduction of this article quotes the preamble of the first recommendation of the Unemployment Counter-Measure Council, set up in the Prime Minister's Office in July 1949. In order to shed light on how the unemployment situation in Japan was affected by the Japanese government's economic stabilization policy, the author examines: (1) the figures for the number of unemployed; (2) the causes of this unemployment; (3) the nature of the unemployment; and (4) the formulation of unemployment countermeasures. He explains the reasons for the unexpectedly low unemployment figure revealed by the national census of 1947. An increase in these figures is seen as inevitable following the economic stabilization program. Additional causes of unemployment that are discussed include the efforts to check inflation and to balance employment and productivity, the shifting of population between various branches of industry (particularly to agriculture), and the increase in Japan's population. The author describes the salient feature of Japanese unemployment as "so-called dormant unemployment," linking it to the unstable employment in the country. He concludes the article by showing why countermeasures must cover the whole economic structure and include "big circumstantial measures." Numerous tables are provided to aid in studying the unemployment problem.

"New Year's Message Issued by General Douglas MacArthur, Supreme Commander for the Allied Powers on January 1, 1949." 1949. See no.937.

1547a Ōuchi, Hyōe. "Dodge Plan and the Japanese Economy." *Contemporary Japan* 18:233–36 (Apr./June 1949)

In this article, translated from the June 1949 issue of *Hyōron*, Ōuchi briefly analyzes and comments upon the Dodge Plan. The primary objective of the plan, he writes, are a reduction of the Japanese economy's dependence on government subsidies and American aid. Balancing the budget and enforcing austerities in accordance with the plan, however, will produce continuing difficulties for many Japanese.

1547b Penworth, D. Wilfred. "Japan's Millions Must Export or Perish." *Great Britain and the East* 65:43 (June 1949)

Overpopulated Japan must export. She can supply neighboring lands with inexpensive commodities which others cannot competitively produce, and it is proper for her to maintain trading relations with those East Asian nations to whom her economy was closely linked in the past. Indeed, Penworth asserts, Japan's postwar reconstruction is inseparably bound up with that of Asia as a whole.

1548 "Private Commercial Entrants to Japan." *Documents and State Papers* 1, no.11:666–72 (Feb. 1949)

Prepared by Major General Paul J. Mueller as SCAP circular no.1, 14 January 1949, and published in this series of documents by the U.S. State Department's Office of Public Affairs, this text regulates the visits of foreign businessmen to Japan.

1549 "Razor Edge in Japan." *Economist* 157:60–61 (9 July 1949)

The consequences of the closing of the markets of Communist Manchuria, North Korea, and China to Japan are treated in this article. There is a discussion of the nation's economic instability prior to the Dodge Mission along with a description of that mission's recommendations and their results. The bulk of the article discusses the country's current economic plight which, the author warns, plays directly into the Communist hands. He considers the possibility of Japan's turning to the Communist Chinese market but concludes that "the United States is still the country's fundamental source of livelihood."

1549a Satō, Kiichirō, et al. "How Can Japan Become a Self-Supporting Nation?" *Town Meeting* 15, no.22:1–21 (27 Sept. 1949)

This transcript of a radio discussion presents the views of 4 prominent individuals on Japan's immediate and long-range needs for economic recovery. Dr. Sherwood Fine, director of economic and finance in SCAP's Economic and Scientific Section, list 7 requisites, among them the necessity of increasing the production of food and minerals through the adoption of more efficient practices, the termination of foreign restrictions upon Japanese exports, and the need for Japan to develop a new set of international trading partners. Kodaki Akira, administrator general for international trade in the Japanese Ministry of Trade and Industry, emphasizes the fact that Japan must utilize her vast resources of manpower to produce more industrial goods for export and expresses himself as being in favor of Japanese trade with the Communist countries of Asia and of Japan's assumption of greater responsibility for domestic economic matters. Satō Kiichirō, the president of the Teikoku Bank, in turn suggests that Japan must limit the growth of her population, rebuild her merchant marine, and diversify her trade agreements. He also notes that the efficiency of Japanese labor has declined during the postwar era. Finally, Brooks Emeny, president of the Foreign Policy Association of the United States, recommends that Japan's mountainsides and upland areas be cultivated, that adequate transportation facilities be built within the country, and that those people who can contribute to Japan's economic growth should be depurged. Many of the views expressed by the 4 men are clarified as well as criticized during the course of the radio program.

1550 "SCAPitalism Marches on." *Fortune* 40:76–77 (Oct. 1949)

In analyzing the present Japanese economy, the writers commend the Dodge Plan for disinflation but indicate that the Americans "appear unable or unwilling to implement the whole Dodge Plan." Just when there should be a revival of trade, the authors insist, SCAP authorities are attempting to thwart such a development by creating irksome and unnecessary red tape for any business transaction. The authors also criticize SCAP's insistence that Japan remain in the "dollar bloc" and not utilize sterling currency. The writers claim that most businessmen who have been in Japan favor the immediate withdrawal of SCAP and the restoration of economic autonomy to Japan.

1550a "Seizure of Japanese Economy by American Capital." *Current Digest of the Soviet Press* 1, no.12:38–39 (19 Apr. 1949)

The author characterizes the U.S. program for promoting Japan's economic recovery as a plan for the "complete subordination of the Japanese economy to American monopoly capital." He points out how the United States wishes to remilitarize the country as well as to convert it "into a factory subordinate to the U.S.A. for the production of textiles and other commodities for sale to the colonial peoples." This plan is to be carried out by concentrating Japanese production in the hands of monopoly capital, and various examples are cited to support this fact. The author concludes that as a result of Japanese government measures connected with the implementation of the plan, as many as 3,000,000 people are expected to lose their jobs. This article first appeared in the 23 March issues of both *Pravda* and *Izvestia*.

1551 "Shift in Japan Means Tougher Trading." *Business Week* p.81–82, 84 (13 Aug. 1949)

This article predicts that the end of direct occupation controls over internal Japanese affairs will result in a return to the old economic order. As the occupation's reforms are progressively scrapped, low-priced Japanese goods will once again flood world markets on account of (1) a conscious depression of domestic consumption and a complete suppression of trade union activity (both allowing for low wage scales) and (2) a reestablishment of monopolistic control over raw materials. These changes are seen as inevitable, however, given both SCAP's desire to cut its costs by promoting rapid economic recovery and the military establishment's fear of communism, compared with which even a reestablishment of the *zaibatsu* is preferable. The article concludes with a series of examples of SCAP reforms already abandoned or sidestepped.

1552 "Statement Issued by Joseph M. Dodge, Economic Adviser to SCAP at a Press Conference Held on March 7, 1949." *Contemporary Japan* 18:150–54 (Jan./Mar. 1949)

At the outset of his visit to Japan, Dodge makes some general remarks on the current conditions of the Japanese economy and some measures which in his opinion will help or hinder a healthy economic growth. Believing that a currency devaluation such as occurred in occupied Germany should be avoided, he maintains that a single rate of exchange should be established as soon as possible. Moreover, he insists that "there must be less of thinking solely in terms of how much U.S. aid will be forthcoming and more thinking of increased production, decreased costs and greater exports." In order to increase exports, he urges continued limitation on domestic consumption and an emphasis on the needs of the export consumer rather than that of the domestic consumer. In conclusion, he affirms that each individual Japanese has to make this a personal as well as national goal and must produce and save more in order to insure a sounder Japanese economy.

1553 "Statement Issued on the Japanese Budget for 1949–50 by Joseph M. Dodge, Financial Adviser to SCAP, April 15, 1949." *Contemporary Japan* 18:269–74 (Apr./June 1949)

In a well-documented analysis of the current Japanese budget, Dodge comments on the most important aspects of an extremely complex system. After defining the primary objective of the 9-point stabilization program as the creation and implementation of a balanced budget, he attempts to describe why such a budget has not been established to date. He argues that the Japanese government's budgetary system is inadequate "both in its mechanism and the time elements allowed for preparing a budget" and claims it has been completely ineffective as an instrument of administrative control. The report includes numerous statistics supporting the author's statements. He recommends that the Japanese cease relying on the cushion of American aid to boost their economy and regain their independence by their own efforts. In addition, he suggests that the undesirable practice of subsidies be eliminated entirely from the system. The concluding section of the brief report discusses the structure and function of the recently established Counterpart Fund, a powerful fiscal instrument under the control of SCAP.

1554 Supreme Commander for the Allied Powers. *Guide for Commercial Entrants to Japan.* Tokyo: SCAP, Jan. 1949. 1v. (various paginations)

A booklet designed to assist foreign private businessmen in undertaking business activities in Japan. It describes the restrictions and controls set by SCAP with respect to entry into Japan, extension of stay, finances, communications, housing, medical care, and trading. Appendixes cover 3 circulars issued by SCAP and the international postal service regulations.

1555 ———. *Program for Visit of Secretary of the Army Kenneth C. Royall to the Far East Command.* Jan.–Feb. 1949. Record Group 5, Box 77. MacArthur Memorial, Bureau of Archives, Norfolk, Va. 1 folder.

The material in this folder describes SCAP arrangements for ceremonies in honor of the secretary of the army and a tentative schedule of his itinerary while in Japan. The schedule includes review of the First Cavalry Division, a visit to Eighth Army installations, press conferences, and intelligence briefings on the strategic situation in the Far East Command and the economic situation of Japan. There are brief biographies of Royall and members of his entourage. Of particular interest are those on the members who eventually formed the Dodge Mission, e.g., Joseph M. Dodge and Paul M. O'Leary.

The folder also contains a speech by Secretary Royall to the Chamber of Commerce of Tokyo on 7 February 1949 which discusses his favorable reaction to the occupation and what he perceives to be its beneficial effects on Japan.

———. Economic and Scientific Section. *Mission and Accomplishments of the Occupation in the Economic and Scientific Fields.* 1949. See no.273.

1556 ———. Office of the Financial Adviser (Joseph M. Dodge). *Reports on Taxation and Budget Plans.* 4–15 Nov. 1949. Record Group 5, Box 79. MacArthur Memorial, Bureau of Archives, Norfolk, Va. 1 folder.

This collection concerns SCAP activities in the budget reform program of the Japanese government. It includes the minutes of a 7 November 1949 meeting of Dodge and the highest officials of the Ministry of Finance during which Dodge presented his view of the circumstances of Japan's economy and possible solutions for the problem. Another meeting between Dodge and Finance Minister Ikeda regarding tax reform is also described as is the draft of a letter from the prime minister committing the Japanese government to a program of tax reform and enforcement. Of prime importance is the text of the report submitted to General MacArthur by Joseph Dodge concerning the fiscal year 1949 supplemental budget and the fiscal year 1950 regular budget. This report concerns expenditures in the supplemental budget's general accounts, basic assumptions and commitments, the Japanese cabinet's commitments, and general revenues and expenditures in the fiscal year 1950–51 budget. There is also a memorandum to General MacArthur from W. F. Marquat, chief of the Economic and Scientific Section of SCAP, analyzing the current financial situation and the tax reduction program proposed by the Japanese Diet.

1557 "A Survey of Economic and Social Conditions in Japan." *International Labour Review* 60:1–26 (July 1949)

Officials of the International Labor Organization prepared this detailed report of economic conditions in Japan during and after the war. A brief survey of the organization and activities of the ILO mission is followed by an historical report on prewar and wartime economic developments in Japan in which agricultural and industrial conditions, Japanese economic manpower organization, and wartime labor policy are discussed. The report notes that by the end of the war real wages were below 1930–34 levels, the employment market was controlled by the government, protective labor legislation was suspended, and the trade union movement was nonexistent. Postwar land reform, food rationing, monopoly liquidation, working conditions, welfare legislation, and union reorganization are examined. The authors conclude with an evaluation of the effectiveness of industrial and labor reform in terms of traditional patterns of industrial relations.

1558 "Time Extended for Patent Applications in Japan." *Department of State Bulletin* 20:502 (17 Apr. 1949)

This State Department press release gives the text of an interim directive issued to SCAP concerning the filing of Japanese patent applications by foreigners. In the commentary on the directive is a discussion concerning the right of the U.S. government to issue unilateral directives in the event of inaction by the Far Eastern Commission.

1559 Tsuru, Shigeto. "Toward Economic Stability in Japan." *Pacific Affairs* 22, no.4:357–66 (Dec. 1949)

This article emphasizes the American role in stabilizing the economy of postwar Japan. Using U.S. aid as an inflationary control, Japan's economy began to stabilize in 1948. A 9-point program was initiated late that year. Based on the principle that supply and demand were decisive factors, it aimed at reconstituting and stabilizing the economy. Tsuru concludes, however, that economic goals can only be achieved through enlightened Japanese political leadership.

1560 "Two–Billion Dollar Failure in Japan." *Fortune* 39:67–72, 204+ (Apr. 1949)

U.S. businessmen involved with Japan, one of whom was in charge of the industrial division of the Economic and Scientific Section of SCAP, analyze current Japanese business and industry. While congratulating SCAP on the success of its political and social reforms, the authors term the economic reforms "massive failures." After a brief summation of the demilitarization and democratization programs and reforms in labor and education, they criticize SCAP for failing to channel Japanese obedience and skill into productive works. Furthermore, they contend that bureaucracy—American and Japanese, military and civilian—has hampered real economic reform and recovery. An 8-point summary outlines problems relating to: (1) inflation, (2) industrial stagnation, (3) taxes, (4) foreign trade, (5) the climate of uncertainty, (6) the cost of the occupation, (7) the inefficient bureaucracy, and (8) dependence on the United States. General MacArthur is described as having become "the strong right arm of the leftists," and the writers conclude that there is no inducement for foreign capital to enter Japan under present circumstances. For General MacArthur's reply to this article, see the June 1949 issue of *Fortune* (no.944). The article was also translated into Japanese and published in the August 1949 issue of *Chūō Kōron*.

1560a "Unilateral Moves in Japan Held Evading FEC Policy." *USSR Information Bulletin* 9, no.3:88, 102 (11 Feb. 1949); also published under the title "In the Far Eastern Commission" in *Current Digest of the Soviet Press* 1, no.5:29–30 (1 Mar. 1949)

In this statement before the Far Eastern Commission on 27 January 1949, Alexander Panyushkin accuses the United States of overstepping its authority in its interim directive of 10 December 1948 whereby MacArthur was ordered to work for the economic stabilization of Japan. The Soviet representative to the FEC points to SCAP's failures in controlling foreign trade and inflation, stating that they constitute a major reason for the commission's present concern with SCAP's plans. He also asserts that any decisions regarding Japan's economic recovery are the FEC's exclusive prerogative.

1561 "The U.S.A. Violates the System of Control over Japan." *Soviet Press Translations* 4:233–35 (15 Apr. 1949); abridged version published under the title "The U.S.A. Is Violating the Control Regime over Japan" in *Current Digest of the Soviet Press* 1, no.7:27–28 (15 Mar. 1949)

Reprinted from the 20 February 1949 issue of *Izvestia*, this article severely criticizes American attempts to bypass the Far Eastern Commission and unilaterally undertake the stabilization of the Japanese economy. The author reiterates the claims of Soviet Ambassador Panyushkin that it is a matter which should be determined by the FEC and that the United States should furnish the FEC exhaustive information as to SCAP's economic activity. The author concludes that the U.S. action can be explained only in terms of its desire to infringe upon the economic independence of Japan.

1562 Vladimirova, V. "The Program of the American Monopolies for Japan." *Soviet Press Translations* 4:325–28 (1 June 1949)

This translation of an 18 February 1949 *Trud* article is severely critical of several aspects of SCAP's economic policy for Japan. It condemns the American aid program as being an instrument of enslavement, it characterizes the *zaibatsu* dissolution program as ineffectual and a ruse to rebuild the monopolies, it criticizes the government's tax program as disproportionately heavy for the working population, and it views the economic stabilization program as one aimed at reducing the workers' standard of living to an even lower level.

1563 "What's Wrong in Japan? Plenty, Blasts Survey Expert." *Newsweek* 33:45 (18 Apr. 1949)

In an attempt to uncover reasons for Japan's postwar industrial lag, *Newsweek* reports on a survey of the Japanese chemical industry by Frederick Pope, former president of the Chemical Construction Co. of New York. Extensive quotations from Pope make the following points: (1) the purge removed all business leadership from industry; (2) reconstruction funds are not available and should be provided through Japanese banks from American sources; (3) reparations should be avoided in all cases; and (4) occupation personnel making economic decisions were inexperienced and irresponsible.

1563a Wigglesworth, Edwin French. *An Appraisal of Allied Foreign Trade Policy for Japan*. Ph.D. dissertation, New York Univ., 1949. 408p.

This dissertation is divided into 4 major sections. Part 1 examines the basic factors involved in reestablishing Japan's foreign trade and covers the prewar pattern of her trade, significant changes in the Asiatic markets, and postwar economic conditions. Part 2 studies the Allied war aims and trade policy, with particular focus on the evolution and implementation of an appropriate trade policy for postsurrender Japan. Part 3, in turn, presents the factual results of important Allied foreign trade policies. Finally, part 4 appraises the results of Allied war aims and foreign trade policies and provides a number of the author's personal recommendations.

1563b Wolpert, V. "Japan's Foreign Trade." *Eastern World* 3:30–32 (Sept. 1949)

In reviewing the development of Japan's postwar foreign trade, Wolpert points out how fundamental the change has been in the nature and direction of this trade and how the country's economic collapse in 1945 and the slow nature of its recovery under the occupation have affected Japan's overseas commerce. The adverse trade balance, Wolpert notes, is being financed by United States appropriation funds. Indeed, as American authorities are in effect directing Japan's economic activities, Japan has virtually become a part of the dollar area. There are several obstacles to trade recovery, among them the dollar shortage in most countries that are interested in purchasing goods from Japan, the continued animosity in many Asian countries, and the fear of many people that revived Japanese trade may lead to renewed Japanese expansion. The concluding portion of the article summarizes the trends in Japan's postwar trade with the United States, Great Britain, and Asia as well as general developments regarding imports and exports. It also briefly discusses some of the economic plans that may affect trade in the immediate future.

1950

1564 Bouchier, C. A. "American Help Has Transformed Japan's Economy." *Great Britain and the East* 66:40–42 (June 1950)

In an article which formed the basis of an address delivered at a press conference at the Federation of British Industries, Bouchier calls the occupation the most beneficent one ever in world history. He first traces the progress of Japan's economic recovery to date, pointing out how overpopulation and the loss of a vast colonial empire (the source of food and vital raw materials) have made postwar reconstruction even more difficult. He then discusses in some detail American efforts to prevent starvation, disease and social unrest by rehabilitating Japan and the positive impact which Dodge's austerity program has already had upon the country. The generosity of the American government and the work of SCAP officials in implementing United States policy, Bouchier concludes, together with the advice rendered by American economic and technical experts have led to Japan's being firmly established on the road to economic recovery.

1564a Britton, James Cleland. "Import Trade of Japan Restored to Regular Private Channels." *Foreign Trade* 7:138–40 (28 Jan. 1950)

This article reports on the official restoration of the Japanese import trade to private hands. Britton discusses the various institutions and mechanisms which have been set up to support the new system, including the Foreign Exchange Control Board, the governmental Foreign Exchange Budget, and official listings of import items. He predicts that there will be considerable confusion until the new regulations are thoroughly understood.

1564b ———. "Japan Accorded Wider Control of Its Economy and Foreign Trade." *Foreign Trade* 7: 286–90 (18 Feb. 1950)

Britton provides a general analysis of Japanese economic conditions. Improvement, he notes, will be dependent on the success of the country's export drive, but exports are still below prewar levels. Now that China and Manchuria are closed to Japanese products, new markets must be found. In addition, it is essential that Japan's old markets in Southeast Asia be recovered. Full economic recovery will demand that Japan diversify her exports as well. This will take considerable time and careful cooperative planning among private concerns and government agencies. Britton concludes with a brief discussion of the increases in industrial production and such new economic rehabilitation programs as price stabilization, labor rationalization, and the establishment of a single exchange rate for the yen.

1565 Bronfenbrenner, Martin. "Four Positions on Japanese Finance." *Journal of Political Economy* 58:281–88 (Aug. 1950)

The author discusses 4 viewpoints concerning Japanese financial and economic reconstruction with respect to 2 problems, namely, the question of a desirable level of stabilization and recovery, and the extent of government control and regimentation. The "Dodge line," i.e., SCAP's official policy, favors self-support at below prewar levels and the continuation of temporary governmental controls to avoid inflation. The "Ishibashi line," influential in Japanese government circles, advocates promoting business recovery without limitation while permitting inflation if it is accompanied by production and employment increases. The policy of the Economic Stabilization Board, supported by Socialists and a minority of SCAP personnel, favors achieving consumption recovery at prewar levels before attempting inflation stabilization. The Communist line is characterized by support for simultaneous recovery and price stabilization based on extensive government-sponsored public works and income redistribution.

1566 Browne, Martha S. "The Japanese Economy: 1949–50." *United Asia* 3, no. 2:107–11 (1950)

Browne, a Brooklyn College economist, writes a moderately optimistic account of the Japanese economy in 1949–50. She begins by describing the destruction of the economy during the war and by considering the early postwar "goat pasture" policies that were aimed at reducing Japan's industrial potential. These were soon replaced by programs to democratize—but not rebuild—the economy. From late 1948, stability, tax reform, and increasing exports were made Japan's economic objectives. It was hoped that Japanese exports of machinery could be used in the development of other Asian countries, though the prospects for the textile industry appeared mixed.

1567 Cohen, Jerome Bernard. "Economic Recovery in Japan." *Current History* 19:217–22 (Oct. 1950)

In the introductory section of this examination of Japan's current economy, the author juxtaposes various statements from responsible individuals and organizations concerning that economy. He mentions the conflicting views of General MacArthur, the *Asahi Shimbun*, the *Oriental Economist*, Finance Minister Ikeda, etc., before presenting his own careful analysis of the situation. He demonstrates that production has increased considerably since the inception of the occupation but, on the other hand, he maintains that output has clearly not regained prewar levels. The author provides a concise analysis of Japan's current fiscal situation and an assessment of the work of the Dodge Mission wherein he discusses and evaluates 7 concrete accomplishments wrought by the mission. In the final paragraphs the author speculates as to Japan's future economic situation and envisages "a long, hard road ahead, particularly as growing chaos in Asia further limits Japanese markets." At the same time, he insists that Japan's best future trade prospects lie in Asia and that this fact should not be ignored.

1568 ———. "Fiscal Policy in Japan." *Journal of Finance* 5, no.1:110–25 (Mar. 1950)

This study of postwar fiscal policy in Japan focuses on the recommendations of the Dodge Mission and the Shoup Tax Mission. Cohen first discusses many of the activities and achievements of the Dodge Mission and praises it for its success in producing a financial about-face. He notes among their achievements the elimination or reduction of subsidies, the ending of deficit financing, the establishment of a set exchange rate, the ending of the Reconstruction Finance Bank's deficit loans and enormous credit expansion activities, and the reopening of stock markets in the principal cities of the country. Cohen then turns his attention to the Shoup Tax Group, which advocated the adoption of a tax structure that could be fully enforced without undue hardship and that would not upset the Dodge stabilization program. He discusses the various Shoup recommendations under 5 headings—(1) personal income tax, (2) taxation of corporations, (3) local government finance, (4) indirect taxes, and (5) administration and enforcement—and in his conclusion points out that these fiscal policies seem to be working well even though it is still too early to judge fully the effectiveness of the programs that developed in the wake of the activities of these 2 missions.

1569 Coughran, Tom B. "California Banker Discusses Financing Trade with Japan." *Export Trade and Shipper* 61:5–6, 20–24 (5 June 1950)

A vice-president of the Bank of America discusses Japanese foreign trade, noting Japan's need for raw materials, ocean shipping, and postwar Asian trade partners. Methods for financing a trade revival are suggested, including establishing a Counterpart Fund, requiring a yen deposit for industrial development, and supplying letters of credit for import trade by private entrepreneurs. Restrictions concerning the operation of foreign banks in Japan are delineated. The author attempts to explain the advantages and disadvantages of conducting American business activity directly with Japan.

1570 Horoth, V. L. "The Growing Economic Crisis in Japan." *Magazine of Wall Street* 86:199–201, 231–32 (20 May 1950)

Horoth discusses SCAP antiinflationary policies in terms of Japanese dissatisfaction with a continued occupation. The Dodge reforms are analyzed in terms of their success in arresting inflation and their failure to stimulate production, and the difficulties arising out of a return to unrestricted international trade are examined. The importance of the South and Southeast Asian markets to Japanese economic revival is noted.

1571 Iwasa, Yoshizane. *Present Conditions and Financial Problems of Japan's Economy.* Tokyo: Fuji Bank, 1950. 25p.

1572 "Japan–Burma Trade Agreement." *Department of State Bulletin* 22:525 (3 Apr. 1950)

This press release reports on the trade agreement signed 21 March 1950 between Japan and Burma, providing for the exchange of $49,000,000 of goods in calendar 1950. The kinds of articles to be included in Japanese–Burmese trade are listed as are the financial terms of the agreement.

1573 Japan. Economic Stabilization Board. *Recent Trend of Japan's Economy.* Tokyo: 1950. 62p.

This report covers the period between May and October 1950. While reporting a general leveling of prices and declining black market activities, it stresses that there are new demands on the economy as a result of the Korean War. Other subjects treated are: public finance and banking; mining and manufacturing production; foreign trade; prices, wages, and living costs; food and agriculture; and employment.

1574 ———. ———. *Report on Current Economy: Japan's Economy under Stabilization Program.* Tokyo: 1950. 88p.

The first volume in a series of annual reports that subsequently appeared under the title *Economic Survey of Japan*, this report reviews economic conditions in Japan during 1949–50.

1575 ———. ———. Research Section. *Analysis of the Post-war Japanese Economy.* Tokyo: 1950. 84p.

1576 ———. Ministry of Finance. *Guide to Economic Laws of Japan.* Tokyo: Kōbunsha, 1950. xxix, 876p.

1577 ———. ———. Finance Commissioner's Office. *Guide to Economic Laws of Japan.* Tokyo: Kōbunsha, 1950. 10p.

1578 ———. ———. Research Section. *A Guide to Investment in Japan.* Tokyo: Federation of Economic Organizations, 1950. 97p.

This book is divided into 3 main sections: the condition of the postwar economy, the procedure for foreign nationals entering Japan, and investment procedures for foreign nationals. There is also an appendix which includes selected graphs of foreign trade, production, and other topics; the government's general budgets (1948–50); and foreign trade by country and commodity.

1579 "Japan Will Be Factory for Free Asia." *Business Week* no.1106:133–34 (11 Nov. 1950)

Business Week reports on the efforts of John Foster Dulles to negotiate a peace treaty with Japan which would provide for a total economic and trade revival based on the elimination of continued massive American aid and the transformation of Japan into the largest industrial supplier and an important financier of economic programs in Southeast Asia. Mention is made of the decision to concentrate on heavy rather than light industry and of the British aversion to Japanese economic expansion.

"Japanese to Open Agencies in the United States." 1950. *See* no.2522.

1580 Mears, Helen. "Japan: Challenge to Our Prestige." *Harper's Magazine* 201: 73–78 (July 1950)

The author presents her analysis of SCAP's complex economic policies since the initiation of the occupation. Divided into 4 general sections, the article first emphasizes the fact that the occupation is a testing ground of American ability and sincerity, particularly since its policy in China has failed. The author stresses the fact that the economic situation in present-day Japan is crucial. A second section discusses the collapse of the Japanese economy at the end of the war. This surprised the Allied nations, who had overestimated Japan's industrial strength. There also is a convincing explanation of the initially harsh American economic policy and the gradual realization that such a policy would not work. Section 3 focuses upon the operation of the economy throughout the occupation with the support of American aid, and the author stresses the gradual decontrol of commodities and the mounting threat of inflation. The concluding section discusses the increasing tensions of the cold war and their effect upon trade between Communist China and Japan. The author presents the dilemma of the American position with regard to such trade. Without suggesting any definite course, she indicates that our task must be to restore Japan's economic well-being—or all other occupation reforms will fail.

1581 Natori, Jonosuke. "Survey on Securities Market." *Contemporary Japan* 19: 19–29 (Jan./Mar. 1950)

The author begins this article by discussing the slump in the stock market in Japan since the fall of 1949, the main cause of which he sees as the "movement for the so-called democratization of securities; in other words, to a policy to effect a fairer distribution of securities among the people." After showing why this policy led to a result contrary to the original aim, he outlines countermeasures which, in his opinion, would restore equilibrium in securities transactions. Since the general public was chiefly responsible for the slump, he maintains that "any policy regarding securities should primarily begin with the training of the public to become reliable investors." Measures are suggested to provide the public with the power of accumulating capital, to avoid drastic changes in the prices of shares, to maintain the flexible nature of shares, and to raise a large amount of long-term industrial funds.

Obama, Toshie. "A Warning to Financial Leaders." 1950. *See* no.1111a.

1582 Okamoto, Tadashi. "Economic Independence and the Future of Foreign Trade." *Contemporary Japan* 19:530–36 (Oct./Dec. 1950)

An examination of Japan's economic dependence on foreign trade, postwar trends in this trade, and prospects for the future. Noting the recent improvement in foreign trade, the author points out that it does not insure permanent security and shows the handicap Japan suffers due to a lack of funds. In this connection he argues for the establishment of "an adequate financial organ to administer financial facilities exclusively, to meet the requirements of foreign trade." He comments on difficulties resulting from wartime controls and the dissolution of the *zaibatsu*. In order to attain economic independence for Japan, he concludes, the entire nation will be called on to make contributions.

1583 Pevsner, Ya. "The Japanese Working Class in the Struggle against American Imperialism." *Soviet Press Translations* 5:431–44 (1 July 1950)

In his study, Pevsner devotes considerable attention to the implementation of American plans announced on 17 December 1948 to create a program of economic stabilization in Japan. He discusses the Soviet claim that the United States wilfully sacrificed rapid economic revival in order to dominate the later years of reconstruction by tight financial control. Economic statistics for 1948 are presented as evidence of the failure of stabilization policies and mention is made of the failure of the American silk market and of deterioration in employment and wage rates. Pevsner also analyzes in depth the history of the postwar labor union movement. The establishment of Sanbetsu, Sodomei, and Zenrōren are explained as are the various federations created and dissolved during 1949. He is particularly critical of attempts by right-wing elements to take the leadership of the union movement away from "progressives." Economic stabilization practices are discussed as means of dismissing activist workers and progressive leaders from their jobs and thus from union positions.

This article was originally published in the March 1950 issue of *Professionalniye Soyuzy*.

1584 Popov, Konstantin. "The American Colonization of Japan." *Soviet Press Translations* 5:403–9 (1 July 1950); abridged version published under the same title in *Current Digest of the Soviet Press* 2, no.22:33–34 (15 July 1950)

In a 4–part article, which was originally published in the 26 and 30 May 1950 issues of *Izvestia*, the author surveys the American exploitation of Japan. Part 1 looks at the cooperation between the *zaibatsu* and American big business and at the overall failure of the occupation to liquidate the *zaibatsu*. Part 2 concerns American policy with regard to Japanese reparations and reports on the Pauley, Strike, and Draper missions. Part 3 deals with the infiltration of American capital into Japan and the subsequent dependence of Japanese monopolies on American financing. In particular, the activities of the Dodge Mission in drafting Japanese government budgets, raising taxes, and revaluing the yen are considered. Part 4 is a review of the Japanese economy in late 1949. Emphasis is placed on the recovery of certain industries with military potential—such as coal, pig iron, electric power, and shipbuilding—to prewar levels of production and this recovery is contrasted with the plight of most light industries and agriculture. The author points out the control of Japanese trade by the United States which resulted in above average profits for American companies. He also highlights massive unemployment, the low level of real wages, and the chaos in housing reconstruction.

The Reminiscences of Harlan Youel. 1961. See no.44k.

Supreme Commander for the Allied Powers. Economic and Scientific Section. *Mission and Accomplishments of the Supreme Commander for the Allied Powers in the Economic and Scientific Fields.* 1950. See no.274.

1585 Tsuru, Shigeto. *Japan's Economy: Present and Future*. Mimeographed. Tokyo: Japan Institute of Pacific Relations, 1950. 18p. (Institute of Pacific Relations. 11th conference. Japanese paper no.1, 1950)

In this general survey of the Japanese economy a professor at the Tokyo University of Commerce reviews the extent of the damage to the economy caused by Japan's participation in the war and various postwar changes. He discusses the state of Japan's economy in 1950, noting the standard of living, the scale of foreign trade, and the composition of exports and imports by commodity groups and trading areas. Tsuru outlines several major problems facing the Japanese economy, including the need for increased foreign trade, the danger of excessive dependence on foreign trade, the importance of developing indigenous resources, and the shortage of capital accumulation.

Uyehara, Shigeru. "Population Problem of Japan." 1950. *See* no.2011a.

1585a Volle, Hermann, and Herbert Rehbein. "Die wirtschaftliche Lage Japans nach dem Zweiten Weltkrieg: Probleme des Wiederaufbaus und des Aussenhandels." *Europa-Archiv* 5, no.5:2865–78 (5 Mar. 1950)

This article is essentially a detailed study of the postwar economic problems of Japan with particular focus on her reconstruction and foreign trade. After presenting a general overview of the economy and, in particular, of Japanese industrial development between 1937 and 1949, the authors discuss the measures which SCAP undertook to stabilize the economy: the economic stabilization program, and the establishment of a fixed exchange rate for the yen. They then consider Japan's postwar trade, including the commodities which were involved, her geographical trading partners, the extensive financial assistance extended by the United States government, SCAP controls over trade, trade agreements, and some of the difficulties of Japan's trading position as of 1949. They conclude with an analysis of the prospects for Japanese trade in the immediate future.

1586 Yamada, Yūsō. "The National Income and Industrial Structure in Japan." *Annals of the Hitotsubashi Academy* 1: 15–33 (Oct. 1950)

Yamada Yūzō, professor of economics at Hitotsubashi University, investigates both statistically and analytically the national income "produced," or the net products in various branches of economic activity after deducting all expenses for producers goods consumed from the gross value of the products.

1587 Yershov, N. "The Japanese Working Class Will Repulse the Attacks of Reaction." *Soviet Press Translations* 5:628–30 (15 Nov. 1950)

Yershov reviews the conflict between democracy and reaction in occupied Japan, touching on matters such as unemployment, "economic stabilization," and trade union activity. Documentation of the arrest and persecution of Communist party leaders after June 1950 is included as is data concerning the discrepancies between the initial 1950–51 budget prepared by the Yoshida cabinet and the final budget approved by SCAP. Such items as the tripling of industrial subsidies, the cut in unemployment compensation by 7.5 times, and the cut in public education expenditure by 17 times are noted. Data dealing with the proportion of national revenues derived from direct and from consumption taxes are also provided.

The article originally appeared in the July 1950 issue of *Professionalniye Soyuzy*.

1951

1588 Bee, John M. "Japan's Testing Time Is Near." *Great Britain and the East* 67:32 (Mar. 1951)

With American aid scheduled to terminate in 1952 and the occupation itself likely to end around the same time, Bee wonders whether an independent Japan will be able to find sufficient export markets that will enable her to import essential foodstuffs and raw materials. He points out that a growing population in Japan will necessitate a steady increase of imports and concludes with a brief discussion of export possibilities and of opportunities for foreign investment in Japan.

1588a Bronfenbrenner, Martin. "Economic Policy under MacArthur." *United Asia* 3, no.4:249–55 (1951)

The author, a SCAP economist in 1949–50, divides occupation economic policies into 3 periods. During the "military period," 1945–46, soldiers with no formal economic training were in control. They left economic problems to civilians, usually Japanese, and favored maximum comfort at minimum cost for the occupation itself. The "reform period," 1947–48, saw leadership move into the hands of New Deal civil servants whose goal was to democratize the economy at the cost of financial stability. The final "financial period," 1949 to the writing of the article, began when missions of American businessmen visited Japan and recommended programs of price stabilization, budget balancing, and progressive decontrol.

1589 "Can Japan Pay Her Own Way?" *Fortune* 43:72–74 (May 1951)

The question of whether America can end all subsidies to the Japanese economy given Japan's present healthy economic state is taken up in this article. The authors believe that subsidies will have to continue but in small amounts. There is consideration of 2 short-term hazards to Japan's current prosperity—(1) the ending of the Korean War, and (2) the terms of the forthcoming peace treaty—as well as a discussion of long-range uncertainties involving monetary stabilization, foreign investment capital, the quality of manufactured goods, price competition with the West, trade with China, and the increasing birth rate.

1590 Cohen, Jerome Bernard. "Japan's Fight against Inflation: How the 'Dodge Plan' Has Worked." *Banking* p.42–43, 150–51 (May 1951)

According to Cohen, a member of the U.S. Tax Mission to Japan, the goals of the Dodge Plan were first, to restore the Japanese economy to private operation and control, and second, to make the Japanese economy self-supporting. The most significant measure taken under the plan was the balancing of the national budget in an effort to halt the inflationary spiral which had come with the collapse of wartime controls. Critics of the plan argued that the severity of this action led to a halt in the postwar recovery of Japanese business and industry. Proponents, however, argued that the reforms successfully stopped inflation, rationalized business practices, and put industry and the economy in general back on to its feet. Cohen feels that the plan was clearly successful in the short run, although he notes that painful readjustments were necessary. While the Korean War subsequently brought new inflationary measures, Japan was in a better position to resist them.

1591 Fain, Irving Jay. "A Practical Exporter Describes Current Problems in Japanese Trade." *Export Trade and Shipper* 63:1–2 (26 Mar. 1951)

The importance of the Japanese business boom created by increased demand during the Korean War is analyzed, as is the lack of price controls on exporters. Fain notes the continuation of a *zaibatsu* spirit and the strength of the prewar trading firms. Various other business considerations, such as the enforcement of import controls, the overextension of credit in Japan, and the popularity of American technical methods and manufactured goods, are mentioned.

1592 Fiske, Redington. "Long Range Impact on U.S. World Trade of Japan's Economic Struggle." *Export Trade and Shipper* 64:3–4 (24 Sept. 1951)

Fiske focuses on Japan's dependence on imported raw materials and foodstuffs which must be paid for by manufactured exports. The communist control of Japan's prewar mainland markets and the need to shift trade patterns toward America and develop international markets are examined. The author warns against the possibility of a return to prewar cutthroat competition techniques by the Japanese to facilitate market penetration.

Gane, William J. *Foreign Affairs of South Korea, August, 1945, to August, 1950.* 1951. See entry no.1155b.

1593 Hollerman, Leon. "Japan and Far Eastern Development." *Pacific Affairs* 24, no.4:372–97 (Dec. 1951)

Hollerman states that Japan's postwar recovery is tied to underdeveloped Asia, not to the West. The revival of trade with Asian nations will require Japanese participation in efforts to develop those countries' economies but, because of slow progress in such programs, Japan's trade remains at a low level. As of 1949, Japanese industry was operating below 50 percent of capacity and could well have produced more machinery for export to less developed countries in Asia. Foreign investment is important to Asian economic development but America must coordinate its investment policy if it is to achieve maximum efficiency.

1594 Japan. Board of Audit. *Fiscal Statutes.* Tokyo: 1951? 1v. (loose-leaf)

1595 ———. Economic Stabilization Board. *Economic Stabilization Board Reports.* Mimeographed. Tokyo: 1946–51. nos.1–35. irregular.

This mimeographed series, issued sporadically throughout the occupation period, presents the Economic Stabilization Board's analysis of the current situation, its description of measures that are being taken to remedy pressing problems, and the progress of the economic reform programs. Most reports include a general survey of the Japanese economy as well as the findings of detailed examinations of prices, wages, the current cost of living, food, clothing, housing facilities, industrial and agricultural production, transportation, communication, public finance and banking, labor and employment, and foreign trade.

Available at the Washington National Records Center, Suitland, Maryland.

1596 ———. Ministry of Finance. *The Import Tariff of Japan, with Customs Regulations.* Tokyo: Maruzen, 1951. ii, 268p. In English and Japanese.

1597 ———. Prime Minister's Office. Bureau of Statistics. *Establishment Census of 1951.* v.3–6. Tokyo: 1952–53. 4v.

1598 ———. Self-Supporting Economy Council. *Report on Economic Self-supporting Program. Submitted to the President of the Economic Stabilization Board.* Tokyo: 1951. 35p.

1598a "Japan's Industrial Resurgence" [and] "The Future of Japan." *Great Britain and the East* pt.1, 67:31 (June 1951); pt.2, 67:29 (July 1951)

This 2-part article summarizes the conclusions presented by Daniel Duxbury in a recent series of articles appearing in the *Financial Times* wherein he examined the progress of Japan's recovery under the occupation and the present conditions of the country. His major points are as follows: (1) Japan has again become a formidable rival and the Japanese are producing high-quality textiles, iron and steel, machinery, and ships; (2) Japan's large population is at one and the same time her greatest asset and her greatest liability; (3) Japan should be guaranteed access to 1 or 2 great markets for her textile exports or else be free to trade in all markets; (4) restricted openings for exports are a major problem for Japanese heavy industry; (5) the trade unions have greatly increased their strength during the postwar period; (6) the lack of adequate capital for development is a major economic problem; (7) the *zaibatsu* may again become important economic organizations, but they will not have sufficient capital to meet all of Japan's development needs; (8) there are immense opportunities for foreign investment in Japan; and (9) the serious political clash between the right and the left in Japan still has to come.

1599 Ohkawa, Kazushi. "Measurements of Standards of Living of the Working Classes in Japan." *Annals of the Hitotsubashi Academy* 1:120–37 (Apr. 1951)

Ōkawa, a member of Hitotsubashi University's Institute of Economic Research, compares the prewar and postwar living standards of urban and rural laborers and provides interregional comparisons of the cities and countryside. In addition, he measures the rate at which Japanese living standards have improved since the end of World War II.

1600 Ōkita, Saburō. "Japan and Asia's Economic Development." *India Quarterly* 7:336–50 (Oct./Dec. 1951)

In this article Japan's economic development is compared to that of Western countries and other Asian countries, and a combination of the features of both is pointed out. Explanations for the technically and economically advanced position of Japanese agriculture relative to other Asian countries are discussed including the farmland reform effected during the occupation. Japan's history of industrialization is also briefly characterized with suggestions given for what other Asian countries might learn from this development. An analysis of Japan's dependence upon foreign trade points to the importance of trade with the United States and the rest of Asia.

1601 ———. "Japan's Economy and the Korean War." *Far Eastern Survey* 20: 141–44 (25 July 1951)

Ōkita of the Economic Stabilization Board in Japan discusses the effects of the Korean War on the revival of an economy which hinges on foreign trade. Two outstanding factors were the new demands created by the "direct procurement" program of the United Nations forces for the Korean War, and the increase in exports and slackening of imports which remarkably improved Japan's international balance of payment.

1602 Philippines. Office of Economic Coordination, ed. *Reports of the First Industrial Survey Group to Japan*. Manila: Bureau of Printing, 1951. 83p.

The first Philippine Industrial Survey Group to Japan, formed on 2 January 1951 under the Quirino administration and composed of 6 government officials and 16 private industrialists, visited Japan from 6 February through 16 March 1951. The group had extensive contacts with SCAP and Japanese government officials and traveled to Nagasaki, Hiroshima, Kobe, Osaka, Kyoto, and Nagoya, inspecting industries of varying kinds and sizes. The publication consists of 10 reports, the first of which is a summary of the group's findings in Japan and its recommendations. The remaining 9 reports concern different specialized industries studied. The reports recommend that the Philippine government assist more strongly the development of its own industries, especially home and small industries, that the Department of Education play a greater role in the educational phase of the home industry development program, and that the Philippines develop insofar as is possible basic metal, power, fuel, and chemical industries. The report is useful in describing the state of the economy in occupied Japan in 1951.

1603 "Procedure for Filing Claims against Closed Institutions in Japan." *Department of State Bulletin* 24:580–81 (9 Apr. 1951)

The Closed Institutions Liquidation Commission (CILC) of the Japanese government invites the filing of claims arising outside Japan against 800 closed financial institutions being liquidated by CILC. Information concerning eligibility for filing claims, the institutions covered, and the procedures for filing are included.

1604 Shimizu, Kō. "A Survey of the Securities Market." *Contemporary Japan* 20: 46–59 (Jan./Mar. 1951)

The director of the Tokyo Securities Exchange first describes the securities market as it existed during World War II. He then discusses the development of the securities market following SCAP notification on 25 September 1945 that its approval was necessary for opening exchanges and following the abolition of the Japan Securities Exchange Law on 27 March 1947. Development of the market progressed with the new Securities Exchange Act promulgated in April 1948, and the author examines this process and the principles governing exchanges and transactions.

The second section of the article discusses the economic democratization campaign designed by the occupation authorities and points out the basic change which occurred in the securities market when the 9–point economic program or the "Dodge Line" was adopted in December 1948. The postwar method

1605 "Statement Issued by Ambassador Joseph M. Dodge on the Occasion of His Departure from Japan, November 20, 1951." *Contemporary Japan* 20:581–83 (Oct./Dec. 1951)

In his brief address, Dodge defines Japan's most fundamental problems as "too many people, too high a birth rate, too little land, too few natural resources." He also indicates that the key to the nation's survival is not its productive capacity but "the supply of materials out of which the goods and products essential to the life and future development of the economy are created." He sets forth 3 points which he considers to be essential in maintaining the present standards of living and production and in improving them. He then enumerates 15 delusions from which Japan is suffering and which will have to be eliminated immediately in order for the country to make sound economic progress.

1606 "Statement Issued by Major General William F. Marquat, Chief of Economic and Scientific Section, GHQ, SCAP on the U.S.–Japan Economic Cooperation Program, May 16, 1951." *Contemporary Japan* 20:273–76 (Apr./June 1951)

The author summarizes his 3-week trip to Washington to confer with various government officials regarding future U.S.–Japanese economic relations. He is optimistic about such relations, and he emphasizes American concern that Japan be accorded world markets and sources of raw materials on a nondiscriminatory basis in order to ensure her continued economic recovery. He then elaborates upon what he believes to be the prerequisites for membership in international bodies. Voicing his hope that Japan will soon regain full political and economic autonomy, he urges that as soon as possible Japan announce to the world the long-term economic policies which the country has determined to follow.

1607 Supreme Commander for the Allied Powers. Economic and Scientific Section. *Japanese Economic Statistics*. Tokyo: SCAP, Sept. 1946–Nov. 1951. nos.1–63. monthly.

One of the most authoritative of SCAP's statistical reports on the Japanese economy prepared monthly from September 1946 through the end of 1951. Reports range from 40 to 300 pages and are based primarily on data of Japanese origin. There is comprehensive coverage of conditions in industrial production, transportation, foreign trade, food distribution, prices and family expenditures, population, wages, and finance. Later reports contain improved and more carefully classified subject heads and include brief discussions of each subject. Bulletins subsequent to no.34 (June 1949) are divided into 3 sections: (1) industrial production; (2) foreign and domestic commerce; (3) population, labor, food supply, and prices. Bulletins nos.38–40 (Oct.–Dec. 1949) have an additional fourth section which discusses general economic trends during the curent month. From no.64 on, this bulletin was prepared by the Economic Stabilization Board of the Japanese government.

1608 Takahashi, Kamekichi. "Problems of Post-treaty Economy." *Contemporary Japan* 20:309–16 (July/Sept. 1951)

The author begins this article by considering both the unfavorable and the favorable aspects of Japan's posttreaty economy. He shows why he sees no reason to fear another inflation caused by the posttreaty expansion of national expenditures. In section 2 the problem of the exhaustion of accumulated capital is discussed. The author outlines 3 drawbacks which have delayed general economic recovery. In section 3 the significance of the shortage of floating capital is shown. Section 4 points to the overestimation of capital accumulation as another vital problem. Due to the loss of capital, the author sees "no alternative but a major operation to give a transfusion of foreign capital investments."

1609 Tanaka, Seiji. "The 1950 Amendment Act of the Business Corporation Law." *Annals of the Hitotsubashi Academy* 1:163–80 (Apr. 1951)

Tanaka details the major reasons for adopting this amendment; first, it helps corporations in obtaining funds by issuing stock; second, it assists in the introduction of foreign capital; and third, it promotes the democratization of stockholding.

"Le traité de paix avec le Japon." 1951. See no.2426a.

1952

1610 Bisson, Thomas Arthur. "Japan: Recovery and Reaction." *Nation* 174:101–3 (2 Feb. 1952)

The Japanese economy of 1951 is reviewed and an attempt is made to explain the revision of SCAP economic directives and the financing of rearmament. The dissatisfaction expressed over limiting economic recovery to prewar levels is examined. Bisson questions the assumption that democracy will be the natural result of economic revitalization. Rather, he suggests that recovery is increasingly being entrusted to authoritarian officials who are jettisoning rather than strengthening social and political reforms.

1611 Cohen, Jerome Bernard. *Economic Problems of Free Japan.* Princeton, N.J.: Princeton Univ., Center of International Studies, 1952. 96p. (Princeton Univ., Center of International Studies, memorandum no.2)

This comprehensive analysis of the Japanese economy represents an attempt to provide some assessment of the potential for economic growth and development in a post-peace treaty Japan. Cohen examines industrial activity and strength, capital formation, foreign investment and trade, and balance of payments problems. He asserts that a distinct potential for economic revival exists despite numerous difficulties. Thirty-three tables of economic data are included.

1612 ———. "Japan's Foreign Trade Problems." *Far Eastern Survey* 21:167–70 (19 Nov. 1952)

Cohen, author of several studies on Japan, sees few prospects for Japanese trade with China but many with underdeveloped countries. He points out that a viable economy by trade expansion will depend not only on Japanese resourcefulness and ingenuity, but perhaps even more on the trade and aid policies of the United States and the United Kingdom.

1613 Eidus, Khaim. "In American Bondage." *Soviet Press Translations* 7:176–78 (15 Mar. 1952)

The deterioration of Japanese living standards resulting from excessive military expenditure and production is the focal point of this article which was originally published in the 25 January 1952 issue of *Trud*. Eidus notes the weakness of peacetime industry accompanied by inflation, rampant unemployment, heavy taxation on workers and peasants, and attempts to revise labor laws and civil rights legislation. He concludes with Stalin's New Year's message to the Japanese people in which the freedom of the workers, the peasants, and the intelligentsia from economic and cultural burdens is stressed.

1614 Number not used.

1615 Fine, Sherwood Monroe. *Japan's Post-war Industrial Recovery.* Tokyo: Foreign Affairs Assn. of Japan, 1953. 52p. Also as *Eastern Economist Pamphlets*, no.13. New Delhi: 1952. 58p; reprinted from *Contemporary Japan* 21, no.4/6:165–216 (1952)

This concise and perceptive study analyzes the joint effort by SCAP and the Japanese government to rehabilitate Japanese industry, giving brief attention to other aspects of Japan's economic recovery. The author was chief of the Government Division of the Civil Affairs Section (G-5), Headquarters, U.S. Far East Command at the time this study was written. He also served throughout the Allied occupation as director of Economics and Planning in the Economic and Scientific Section of SCAP. Along with an evaluation of the problems confronted and the policies pursued, the course of Japanese industrial recovery in the postwar period is charted through the termination of the occupation in April 1952. The author measures the successes and failures experienced and provides a brief appraisal of the outlook for Japanese industry. An introduction to postwar developments is provided by a brief sketch of the rise of Japanese industry and of some of its major characteristics. Policy development is briefly described and evaluated in such areas as reparations, democratization of the monopolistic business structure, and purges of business leaders. The occupation is divided into 3 phases. The first phase, September 1945 to December 1947, is described as one of arrested chaos, adjustment, and reform resulting in only a modest beginning on the problem of economic recovery. The second phase, from 1948 to the outbreak of the Korean War, was a period of economic recovery and stabilization marked by a continuous rise in industrial activity. The third period, from June 1950 to the end of the occupation in April 1952, is characterized as one of war-stimulated recovery and reinflation. Fine is generally optimistic about Japan's economic future. He correctly forecasts impressive advances in production techniques in Japan given the industry and skill of her labor force.

1616 Fujii, Shigeru. "The Foreign Trade and Industrial Structure of Post-war Japan, with Reference to Her Trade with South and South-East Asian Countries." *Economia Internazionale* 5, no.3:640–52 (Aug. 1952)

In his article, Fujii Shigeru of Kobe University seeks to clarify the correlation between postwar Japan's industrial structure and her foreign trade, and to forecast the nature of Japan's trading relationship with South and Southeast Asia after the occupation is over. He briefly describes how Japan revived her industrial production and her foreign commerce and how the promotion of Japanese ties with other Asian countries stimulated the domestic economy. He points out that there still is a structural weakness within the Japanese economy because foreign trade has recovered more slowly than industrial production, and argues that Japan must increase her exports—particularly those directed towards Asian countries—in order to overcome this economic problem.

1617 Golay, Frank H. "Economic Problems Facing Post-treaty Japan." *Federal Reserve Bulletin* 38, no.1:11–21 (Jan. 1952)

This article provides both a summary review of Japan's economic recovery during the occupation period and an analysis of posttreaty prospects with particular focus on foreign trade, the balance of payments situation, financial claims settlements, fiscal and banking problems, and the problems of Japan's industrial production and her formation of capital. Golay's study was prepared under the supervision of Arthur C. Bunce, chief of the Far Eastern Section of the Federal Reserve Board's Division of International Finance.

1618 Inagaki, Riichi. "America's Japanese Dilemma." *New Statesman and Nation* 44:258 (6 Sept. 1952)

In this treatment of the relationship between foreign trade and the cold war, Inagaki emphasizes the elimination of the Chinese market for Japan and increasing Japanese dependence on the United States. In his opinion, this necessitates procuring both new markets for industrial products and new sources of raw materials. In the domestic realm, he suggests that the maintenance of the current abnormally low standard of living would cause intense dissatisfaction among the populace and provide an opening for Communist gains.

1619 Irvine, Reed J. "Japan's Balance of Payments Prospects." *Far Eastern Survey* 21:196–203 (31 Dec. 1952)

Irvine points out that problems of trade raise serious questions for Japan's future and for American policy. In suggesting possible solutions, he indicates that hopes for the continued viability of the Japanese economy rest upon a combination of uncertainties, one of the most important of which is the volume of U.S. military spending in Japan and the immediate vicinity. Reed J. Irvine is an economist with the Division of International Finance, Board of Governors of the Federal Reserve System.

1620 Japan. Economic Stabilization Board. *Economic Survey of Japan (1951/1952)*. Tokyo: 1952. 318p.

Part 1 of this annual survey evaluates Japan's current economic potential for achieving self-sufficiency as defined in terms of the country's balance of international payments and the maintenance of an economic structure under which a high living standard can be permanently secured. It also provides a summary of Japan's economic recovery since 1945 and considers some of the future problems that will have to be met. Furthermore, it includes a study of the economic structure of post-peace Japan with regard to national income and expenditure, living standards, the problems of capital accumulation, present industrial development, and trade structure. Part 2 in turn covers economic developments during the 1951 fiscal year in some detail with focus on prices, foreign trade, industrial production, transportation, business, public finance and banking, food and agriculture, labor, and the country's living standards. This volume is one of the first in a very useful series of annual surveys which since 1953 has been issued by the Economic Planning Agency.

1621 ———. Ministry of Finance. *The Import Tariff of Japan, with Customs Regulations*. Tokyo: Maruzen, 1952. ii, 322p. In English and Japanese.

1622 ———. ———. Financial Bureau. *Laws, Ordinances, and Other Regulations Concerning Foreign Exchange and Foreign Trade (March 1, 1952)*. Tokyo: 1952. viii, 495p.

Contains the texts of laws and regulations pertaining to foreign exchange banks, export and import controls, the control of foreign exchange, foreign investment, and the acquisition of properties and rights by foreign nationals and by foreign governments.

1623 ———. ———. Research Section. *A Guide to Investment in Japan, 1951–52*. Tokyo: Federation of Economic Organizations, 1952. iii, 37p.

1624 "Japan's Economic Recovery." *World Today* 8:392–404 (Sept. 1952)

Following a description of Japan's economic situation immediately after the war, this article attempts to indicate the main trends in Japan's economic recovery. It describes the Allied attitude toward Japan's economic plight at the outset of the occupation, and the changes which took place in SCAP's economic policy in 1947 and again in 1949 when Dodge's recommendations caused a considerable increase in American financial aid to the Japanese economy. There are clear and detailed accounts of occupation measures in food and agriculture, the textile industry, iron, steel and coal, and shipbuilding, and a summation of Japan's present position in foreign trade. Within the article is a table charting key production trends for various commodities such as electricity, coal, iron, and raw silk. Also given are the statistics for each year of the occupation through 1951.

1625 Kubota, T. "Private Foreign Investment in Japan." *Far Eastern Survey* 21:71–72 (7 May 1952)

This article, condensed from Kubota's "Induction of Private Foreign Capital in Japan after the War" (in the monthly circular of the Mitsubishi Economic Research Bureau, Tokyo, November 1951), describes foreign investment as well as technological aid in Japan since 1949,

1626 Nakayama, Ichirō. "Some Characteristics of the Japanese Economy." *Economia Internazionale* 5:152–67 (Feb. 1952)

Nakayama attempts to explain the contradiction between the sharp rise in production during 1950 and 1951 and the continued low level of Japan's standard of living. Mining and manufacturing, he explains, have greatly increased due to the Korean War and the procurement demand of UN forces, the expansion of general exports, and enhanced domestic consumer demand, while living standards have remained below prewar levels on account of population pressures, the small-scale nature of Japanese agricultural holdings and industries, and the nature of Japanese industrialization since the Meiji era. Nakayama calls for efforts to elevate the living standard and asserts that this can be done by expanding foreign trade since that sector has traditionally supported a large share of Japan's real national income.

Supreme Commander for the Allied Powers. Monograph 23. *Japanese Property Administration.* 1952. See no.305.

―――. Monograph 26. *Promotion of Fair Trade Practices, 1945–October 1951.* 1952. See no.308.

―――. Monograph 34. *Price and Distribution Stabilization: Non-Food Program.* 1952. See no.316.

―――. Monograph 37. *National Government Finance, 1945–March 1951.* 1952. See no.319.

―――. Monograph 39. *Money and Banking, 1945–June 1951.* 1952. See no.321.

―――. Monograph 40. *Financial Reorganization of Corporate Enterprises.* 1952. See no.322.

―――. Monograph 50. *Foreign Trade.* 1952. See no.332.

―――. Monograph 51. *Land and Air Transportation.* 1952. See no.333.

―――. Monograph 52. *Water Transportation, 1945–1951.* 1952. See no.334.

―――. Monograph 53. *Communications, 1945–December 1950.* 1952. See no.335.

―――. Economic and Scientific Section. *Mission and Accomplishments of the Supreme Commander for the Allied Powers in the Economic, Scientific, and Natural Resources Fields.* 1952. See no. 275.

1627 ―――. ―――. Programs and Statistics Div. *Japanese Trade Patterns.* Tokyo: SCAP, 24 Apr. 1952. i, 162p.

This document presents detailed statistics of Japan's foreign trade for 1930–34. It is classified according to country and commodity. The import and export of 9,940 commodities involving Japan and some 180 areas in the world are covered. Both commodities and areas are coded, and the net quantity and its dollar value are given for each trade item. The data are based on: Japanese Government, Ministry of Finance, *Annual Return of Foreign Trade of Japan, 1930–1939*: Government of Taiwan, Customs, *The Annual Return of the Trade of Taiwan (Formosa), 1930–1939;* and Government General of Chōsen (Korea), *Table of Trade and Shipping, 1930–1939.* Adjustments are made so as to treat the movement of goods between Japan and Korea and between Japan and Taiwan as foreign trade although at the time trade with these areas was treated as domestic trade.

1628 ―――. ―――. ―――. *Problems and Prospects of Accelerated Economic Development in the ECAFE Region through Increased Trade with Japan.* Tokyo: n.d.

1629 Takahashi, Ryūtarō. "Trade Policies of the New Japan." *Foreign Affairs* 30: 289–97 (Jan. 1952)

By detailing economic conditions and

describing trade policies now being followed by the Japanese government, Takahashi attempts to clear up certain misgivings about the quality of Japanese exported goods, the concern that Japan will revert to dumping practices, or that Japan may be creating undue complications by exercising export and import controls not called for by the realities of current commercial transactions.

1630 Thompson, Elizabeth M. "Trade with Japan." *Editorial Research Reports* v.1 1952:21–39 (9 Jan. 1952)

This report discusses Japanese foreign trade under restored Japanese sovereignty with the conclusion of the peace treaty, Japan's international trade position at the end of the occupation period, and the future outlook for Japanese trade with the United States, Southeast Asia, and Mainland China.

1953–72

1631 Adams, Thomas F. M. *Japanese Securities Market: A Historical Survey.* Tokyo: Seihei Okuyama, 1953. 142p.

During the years (1946–50) that Adams served in SCAP's Economic and Scientific Section, he played a leading role in the reopening of the Japanese stock exchanges. Accordingly, while this book surveys the entire historical development of securities trading in Japan, several substantial sections deal with the overall structure and functioning of the securities market in the late occupation period. In addition, one chapter deals specifically with the Securities and Exchange Law of 1948, which the author helped to draft. This particular chapter provides detailed descriptions and explanations of the provisions of the law as well as information on the theory, philosophy, and compromises with established Japanese practice upon which they were based. Adams also briefly treats the regulations affecting foreign investment in Japan at the time his book was written.

1632 ———, and Hoshii Iwao. *A Financial History of Modern Japan.* Tokyo: Research, 1964. xii, 328p.

Part 1 of this book begins with the Meiji Restoration and traces the background and development of the capitalistic economy in Japan up through World War II. Part 2 deals with postwar developments in the Japanese economy. The general economic condition of Japan at the end of the war and what was to be the position held by the Allied occupation are noted. The major occupation goals of demilitarization and democratization are outlined with the chief measures for democratization of the economic sphere said to be the dissolution of the *zaibatsu* and democratization of agriculture and labor. A discussion of the initial occupation policies and the inflation in the Japanese economy and a picture of the postwar securities markets illustrate the period of postwar confusion in the financial development of Japan. The change in occupation policies and the end of the inflation are then treated. The "positive" economic policy occasioned by the Korean War, particularly because of Japan's geographical proximity to the war area, is examined. The last sections of the book concern economic normalization after the Korean War, the securities business, and the developments in all phases of finance up to the time of writing. The book closes with a look at problems for further Japanese economic growth. A liberal supply of tables throughout the book aids the reader in understanding the financial descriptions presented.

1633 Allen, George Cyril. *Japan's Economic Expansion.* London: Oxford Univ. Pr., 1965. xi, 296p. (Royal Institute of International Affairs publication)

This book, by a professor of political economy at the University of London, is a rewritten and much enlarged treatment of his *Japan's Economic Recovery* (1958) (no.1634). In the present work, the author does not focus on the occupation period, but in examining the factors responsible for Japan's rapid postwar development in agriculture, industry, finance, and trade, he does refer constantly to the occupation reforms and activities that in part accounted for the nature of Japan's growth during the 1950s and early 1960s.

1634 ———. *Japan's Economic Recovery*. London: Oxford Univ. Pr., 1958. xiii, 215p.

A survey of Japan's postwar resurgence in the areas of agriculture, finance and banking, light and heavy industry, and trade. The author, professor of political economy at the University of London, is particularly concerned with identifying the similarities and the differences in the organization and functioning of the Japanese economy during the mid-1930s and the mid-1950s. His description of actual economic conditions does not focus on the years 1945–52. Nevertheless, this book will be useful to the specialist on the occupation in light of Allen's attempt to evaluate the immediate and the enduring consequences of occupation reforms, particularly with regard to the dissolution and reconstruction of the *zaibatsu*, the postwar land reform program, and SCAP-sponsored changes in trade union organization and industrial relations.

Bennett, John W., and Ishino Iwao. "Futomi: A Case Study of the Socioeconomic Adjustments of a Marginal Community in Japan." 1955. *See* no.693.

1635 Brochier, Hubert. "Les groupes financiers dans le capitalisme japonais d'après guerre." *Tiers-Monde* 3, no.12:599–623 (Oct./Dec. 1962); reprinted in *Asie nouvelle* 13:110–25 (June/July 1963)

Brochier, the former director of the Maison franco-japonaise in Tokyo and at present a member of the faculty of Grenoble University, focuses his attention on *zaibatsu* activity in postwar Japan. His study is concerned particularly with the organization and power of the principal *zaibatsu* (notably Mitsui, Mitsubishi, and Sumitomo), their ties with the banking world, and their expansion and diversification as well as their rationalization and consolidation.

1635a Bronfenbrenner, Martin. "The American Occupation of Japan: Economic Retrospect." In *The American Occupation of Japan: A Retrospective View*, comp. by Grant K. Goodman. Lawrence: Univ. of Kansas, Center for East Asian Studies, 1968. p.11–25.

Pointing out that the occupation became a venture in economic reconstruction within a few months of the Japanese surrender, Bronfenbrenner focuses his attention on describing and analyzing the important successes and failures that marked the occupation's economic record. First, however, he indicates what he considers to be 6 major handicaps of the occupation itself that considerably influenced SCAP's ability to carry out its programs. They are: (1) the impermanence of the occupation, which frequently led to passive resistance on the Japanese side and to excessive zeal and haste on the U.S. side; (2) the inadequacies of most SCAP personnel; (3) the overwhelming influence which changes in America's overall East Asian policy had upon the course of the entire occupation; (4) the continuous harassment of the occupation by suspicious American businessmen who feared the revival of Japanese economic competition on the world markets and who were concerned that some of SCAP's policies for the control of a country's economy might eventually be applied within the United States itself; (5) the suspicions that conservative Japanese had of specific occupation policies; and (6) the poor coordination among the several sections and bureaus of SCAP. Turning then to the occupation's actual record, Bronfenbrenner argues that the success of certain economic programs was not dependent upon the cooperation of many Japanese other than the programs' immediate beneficiaries. To support this thesis, he cites the accomplishments of the relief and rehabilitation program which provided Japan with billions of dollars worth of economic aid, the agricultural land reform, and SCAP efforts to control American "carpetbaggers" (i.e., to insure that no significant fraction of Japanese landed property or capital wealth would find its way into U.S. hands). By way of contrast, Bronfenbrenner contends, some of the ultimate failures of the occupation in the economic sphere occurred largely because those Japanese interests which were adversely affected could either outsmart SCAP personnel or wait out the occupation period. The examples he points to in this regard are (1) the inflation of 1945–1948, which benefitted great business and banking groups, (2) the failure of the occupation's efforts to break up the *zaibatsu* and rebuild Japanese capitalism along more competitive lines, and (3) SCAP's trade-union policy, which resulted in the creation of a strong anti-capitalist, anti-American union movement.

1636 Chenery, Hollis B., Shishido Shuntarō, and Watanabe Tsunehiko. "The Pattern of Japanese Growth, 1914–1954." *Econometrica* 30, no.1:98–139 (Jan. 1962)

This study presents a comprehensive method for analyzing structural change in a developing economy. The authors develop an interindustry model for measuring changes in (1) the composition of domestic demand; (2) the volume of exports; (3) the volume of imports; and (4) technology and organization. They then apply this model to explain the process of industrialization in Japan between 1914 and 1954. Their results show that most of Japan's industrial growth during those years was due not to increases in exports and changes in domestic demand but to changes in supply conditions, including the substitution of domestic manufactures for both imported manufactures and primary products. Changes that occurred during the occupation period are treated within the context of the entire analysis.

1637 Cohen, Jerome Bernard. *Japan's Postwar Economy*. Bloomington: Indiana Univ. Pr., 1958. xvii, 262p.

A general survey of Japan's economic recovery in the postwar period is undertaken here. The analysis which is presented is primarily concerned with the years from 1945 to 1956; however, statistical data on the postwar economy are often compared with those of the 1930s. In the examination of the nature of Japan's economic growth and economic problems, aspects such as food, income, production output, employment, changing industrial structure, trade, and balance of payments are considered. Cohen states that the occupation's economic measures were one of the factors in promoting Japan's economic rehabilitation. While most of the book deals with economic matters, chapter 11 discusses attempts by the occupation authorities to nurture forces which could counteract prewar social forces, particularly the military, the bureaucracy, and the *zaibatsu*. He concludes that although efforts by SCAP to destroy Japanese military strength and to encourage the labor movement as a "democratizing element" were successful, the attempts to weaken the power of the *zaibatsu* and the bureaucracy failed.

1637a Collier, David Swanson. *The Politico-Economic Position of Japan*. Ph.D. dissertation, Northwestern Univ., 1953. 360p. (Abstracted in Northwestern Univ. *Summaries of Doctoral Dissertations* 20: 364–68 [1952])

This study of postwar politics and economics in Japan contains considerable information on SCAP's labor policies and on the promotion of foreign trade through such measures as the Dodge Stabilization Program, which gave Japan an international competition price position.

1638 Ehrlich, E. E. "Note on Postwar Credit Policies in Japan." *Review of Economics and Statistics* 39:469–71 (Nov. 1957)

In certain months during the occupation years the 11 largest banks were in debt to the Bank of Japan in an amount exceeding one-third of their outstanding loans. Ehrlich notes that although there is a general tendency for Japanese banks to operate with low reserves and to overextend their lending, the overextensions of these years were brought under control only after the Bank of Japan adopted aggressive measures to counter the credit expansion in the fall of 1953. In discussing these steps, she examines the special circumstances responsible for this situation as well as the control techniques that were employed.

1639 Emi, Kōichi. *Government Fiscal Activity and Economic Growth in Japan, 1868–1960*. Tokyo: Kinokuniya Bookstore, 1963. v, 186p.

The author, a lecturer associated with the Institute of Economic Research at Hitotsubashi University in Japan, presents his ideas concerning the role of government in the economic development of Japan. Primary emphasis is given to statistical comparisons which indicate the dynamic relationship between government fiscal activity and the growth of the whole economy. Little attempt is made to provide a theoretical analysis of these relations. Emi's focus is on the analysis of government expenditure. Although the entire period from 1868 to 1960 is treated generally, the main emphasis is on economic development before the end of World War II. The author demonstrates that in the postwar years in Japan "the functions of government activity have been increasing in importance relative to the whole economy." The role of the occupation is specifically discussed in a section on the reform of local administration in the postwar period. The reform of local government directed by the occupation authorities and the expansion of local financing activities prompted by the Shoup Mission are briefly discussed. Much use is made of tables and charts throughout this work and it also contains 2 appendixes, one providing estimates of total government expenditures and the other 39 pages of tables, to aid in the analysis of the 1868–1960 period.

1639a Fujita, Masahiro. "The Exchange Control Policy in Post-war Japan." *Kobe Economic and Business Review* 1:65–91 (1953)

This detailed scholarly study analyzes the rationale behind and the effects of the establishment of a fixed yen-dollar exchange rate on 25 April 1949. It also examines the inflationary surge which subsequently followed with the outbreak of the Korean War.

1640 Hayakawa, Miyoji. "Distribution of Income in Japan, 1905–1956." *Waseda Economic Papers* no.4:19–35 (1959)

Using Pareto's law of distribution of income, the author divides the article for the sake of analysis by periods since the Meiji Restoration. The occupation years are covered in the fifth section—1946 to 1956. From his analysis he concludes that during the 11 years since the war there was a slight decrease in the inequality of income, while in the 41 years before the war there was a slight increase.

1640a Honjō, Eijirō. "The Post-war National Life of Japan." *Kyoto University Economic Review* 27, no.2:1–18 (Oct. 1957)

Honjō presents an overall picture of living conditions in Japan between 1945 and 1955 that focuses on the immediate postwar economic chaos, the destitute conditions which characterized the country through 1948, the gradual amelioration of conditions during the ensuing few years, and the dramatic rise in living standards after 1950. Of particular interest is his description of the manner in which life was disrupted between 1945 and 1948, when there were very bad housing conditions, an acute shortage of food, an increase in violent crimes, a succession of labor disputes and strikes, and a flourishing black market. Honjō points out how the limited availability of money and the difficulties in acquiring food compelled many people to sell their personal possessions simply in order to survive. Indeed, throughout this period, the cost of food accounted for well over half the total income of the ordinary Japanese citizen.

1641 Huh, Kyung-mo. *Japan's Trade in Asia: Developments since 1926, Prospects for 1970*. New York: Praeger, 1966. xx, 283p. (Praeger Special Studies in International Economics and Development)

Huh undertook research for this study while preparing his dissertation for the

Ph.D. degree, which he received from the University of Michigan in 1965. His work examines the development of Japan's trade with 10 major Asian countries, referred to in the book as the "ECAFE region." Japan's postwar recovery and the Korean War period receive some coverage in the study, the recovery period (1945–55) being discussed briefly on pages 24–25. The major economic policies of SCAP and their effects are noted and "the uncertainty and lack of consistency in the economic policy of the Occupation Authorities" are commented on. The occupation is again briefly mentioned in the section dealing with factors responsible for Japan's postwar economic growth. A general survey of the nature of Japan's trade, 1945–55, on pages 57–59, describes the control exercised by the General Headquarters of SCAP through the Trade Board and outlines the development of trade during this period. Considerable use is made of tables and charts, and pages 212–67 consist of a statistical appendix.

1642 Hutchinson, Edmond Carlton. *Inflation and Stabilization in Post-war Japan.* Ph.D. dissertation, Univ. of Virginia, 1954. 412p. (Abstracted in *Dissertation Abstracts* 14:2217–18 [1954]; University Microfilms order no.9649)

This historical account of efforts by the Japanese government and the occupation authorities to combat postwar inflation includes an analysis of the results of the differing approaches adopted before and after December 1948. The policy pursued prior to December 1948 attempted to increase supplies, hold down prices through price controls supplemented by extensive subsidies, and limit demand through rationing. It resulted in new inflationary pressures and generated large government deficits and wage increases. The policy adopted after December 1948 was an attempt to generate a large budgetary surplus, progressively eliminate subsidies, adjust prices upward, reduce capital programs, and adopt a unitary exchange rate. According to Hutchinson, it worked and inflation came "almost to an abrupt halt." He concludes that stabilization of an economy can be achieved through a severely restrictive fiscal policy without necessarily causing deflation.

1643 Igarashi, Torao. "Japan's Foreign Exchange Policies, Past and Present." *Oriental Economist* 27:26–30 (Jan. 1959)

Igarashi, former director of the Bank of Japan, describes the features of Japan's postwar exchange system and its trend toward normalization. He notes that while the system had of necessity to be determined and directed in accordance with Japan's own needs, it had to be such that it fell in line with the new concepts of international finance.

1644 Industrial Bank of Japan (Tokyo). *Semi-annual Industrial and Financial Statistics* nos.6–8 (June 1952–June 1953)

1645 Japan. Economic Counsel Board. *The Trend of Japanese Economy in the Past Ten Years.* Tokyo: 1955. 83p.

1646 Khonsary, Reza. *The Role of Commercial Banks in Financing Economic Growth of Japan, 1951–1963.* Ph.D. dissertation, New York Univ., 1966. 192p. (Abstracted in *Dissertation Abstracts* 28:2419A–20A [1968]; University Microfilms order no.66–10,577)

Although concerned primarily with the postwar structure, development, and methods of operation of commercial banks in Japan, Khonsary also comments upon the contribution made by these banks to the financing of economic growth in postwar Japan. In his study he includes an examination of general economic conditions in postwar Japan, the contemporary structure of commercial banks, and the sources and uses of bank funds, as well as comments on the role of the banks in economic growth. He notes that commercial banks played a vital role as a source of capital funds, which were made available as a result of the banks' promotion, collection, and distribution of national savings. According to Khonsary, these activities were possible because: (1) the banks were relatively unhampered by government restrictions; (2) their relationship with the central banking institution, the Bank of Japan, was well defined; and (3) Japanese households exhibited a high propensity to save.

1647 Klein, Lawrence R., and Y. Shinkai. "An Econometric Model of Japan, 1930–1959." *International Economic Review* (Osaka) 4:1–28 (Jan. 1963)

The authors write of their creation of an annual economic aggregates model covering the 1930–58 period in Japan. Using this model they are able to calculate prospects for Japanese economic development. Their predictions for the 1960–61 period include a steady growth in "population, world trade, fertilizer import, the price level, and government spending."

1648 Kodera, Takeshirō. "Post-war Inflation in Japan." In Kansei Gakuin Daigaku (Nishinomiya) *Annual Studies* 1: 17–56 (1953)

Based on the author's master's essay submitted to the faculty of political science at Columbia University in 1952, this study is a detailed analysis of the origins of Japan's postwar inflation, the measures that were taken to curb it, and its effects on Japan's postwar recovery and development. Considerable attention is paid to the monetary aspects of this inflation throughout the article.

1649 Komiya, Ryūtaro, ed. *Postwar Economic Growth in Japan.* Tr. by Robert S. Ozaki. Berkeley: Univ. of California Pr., 1966. xviii, 260p. (Publications of the Center for Japanese and Korean Studies)

This publication consists of selected papers presented by Japanese scholars at the first conference of the Tokyo Economic Research Center (Tōkyō Keizai Kenkyū Sentā), translated and with an introduction by Robert S. Ozaki. Tachi Ryūichiro's "Fiscal and Monetary Policy" (p.11–31) examines the monetary policies of the Bank of Japan and the Ministry of Finance and shows how they have helped to intensify and accelerate investment in the private sector. "Tax Policy" (p.32–59), by Fujita Sei, discusses the evolution of tax policies since the Shoup reforms showing how some of the government's special measures were tantamount to outright subsidies to large firms. "Price Problems," by Niida Hiroshi, analyzes inflation in postwar Japan. Kanamori Hisao maintains in "Economic Growth and the Balance of Payments" that the growth of Japanese exports is a result rather than a cause of Japanese internal economic development. Fukuoka Masao's "The Balance of Payments and a Model of Cyclical Growth" is a mathematical analysis of the relation between trade cycles in postwar Japan and the balance of payments. "The Employment Structure and Labor Shares," by Tsujimura Kōtaro, argues that one factor in Japan's growth has been optimal labor shares, large enough to sustain consumer demand yet small enough to maintain a high rate of capital formation. Baba Masao, in "Economic Growth, Labor Unions, and Income Distribution," maintains that the impact of labor unions is not as great as is commonly believed. Komiya Ryūtaro's "The Supply of Personal Savings" argues that Japan's high rate of savings is to be attributed to bonuses and the underdevelopment of consumer credit. "Stabilization Effects of Fiscal Policy," by Kaizuka Keimei, examines the government's fiscal policy, concluding that it has been either fairly stabilizing or neutral vis-à-vis the private sector. Finally, "Postwar Japanese Executives," by Noda Kazuo, evaluates the role of entrepreneurs in Japan's postwar economic growth, emphasizing the role of the occupation in creating a competitive environment.

1650 Levine, Solomon Bernard. "Management and Industrial Relations in Postwar Japan." *Far Eastern Quarterly* 15:57–75 (Nov. 1955)

This article focuses on the efforts to restructure the Japanese management system in the 10 years since the end of World War II. In characterizing industrial management with respect to labor-management relations "only those sectors of the Japanese economy which may be termed 'modern' in the sense of Western industrialization" are included. As a background, the traditional internal organization and approaches of Japanese management are examined. A study of postwar change in the field of Japanese management follows, and the article is concluded with a discussion of the implications of these changes for industrial relations and productivity in Japan.

1651 Lockwood, William Wirt, ed. *The State and Economic Enterprise in Japan: Essays in the Political Economy of Growth.* Princeton, N.J.: Princeton Univ. Pr., 1965. x, 753p. (Studies in the Modernization of Japan, 2)

This analysis by 16 noted scholars of Japan's rapid economic modernization, describes the historical opportunities and human responses that have molded her development. The second half of the volume concentrates on Japan since World War II, when the forces of growth reappeared with such strength to suggest a second industrial revolution.

1652 Matsumura, Yutaka. *Japan's Economic Growth, 1945–1960.* Tokyo: Tokyo News Service, 1961. 654p.

This detailed study of the postwar Japanese economy is divided into the following 12 chapters: (1) General Observations; (2) The Four Basic Industries; (3) Petroleum, Gas, Non-ferrous Metals; (4) Manufacturing Industries; (5) Construction Activities; (6) Transportation, Communications, Tourism; (7) Foreign Trade; (8) Domestic Commerce; (9) Prices, Living Conditions, Wages, Labor; (10) Agriculture, Fisheries, Forestry; (11) Public Finance; and (12) Economic Planning [and] Other Topics. While the focus is on Japan's economic recovery and related developments during the 1950s, the volume has considerable information on economic matters during the occupation period. Appendix no.2 (p.640–49) provides a chronological listing of some important dates affecting the Japanese economy between 1945 and 1960.

1653 Misawa, Mitsuru. *The Historical and Comparative Study of the Postwar Japanese Securities Markets in the Light of Law and Business Practices.* Ph.D. dissertation, Univ. of Michigan, 1967. 212p. (Abstracted in *Dissertation Abstracts* 28: 4764A–65A [1968]; University Microfilms order no.68–7675)

Misawa analyzes the effects of governmental controls and American business practices on the Japanese securities market and attempts to ascertain the extent to which the controls, regulations, and financial practices imposed on Japan by occupation authorities interfered with the efficient operation of the originally German-influenced Japanese market. He expresses the belief that the lethargy of the Japanese securities market in 1961 was a result of structural considerations, primarily a lack of harmony between practices of varying origin. After a historical survey of the development of the securities market in the postwar period, he compares the business practices and regulatory laws of Japan, Germany, and the United States, and evaluates these practices and controls in terms of their adaptability or nonadaptability. He concludes that market practices of German and American origin must be changed if the market is to function efficiently.

1653a Miyata, Kiyozō. "Development of Devaluation-Problem in Post-war Japan." *Kobe Economic and Business Review* 1: 17–36 (1953)

Miyata describes and analyzes in some detail the causes of Japan's dramatic postwar inflation and the currency-related measures which both SCAP and the Japanese government took to combat it. He divides the postwar period into 4 parts: (1) a period of "chaotic inflation" (from the surrender to the end of 1946), during which time the Emergency Financial Measures Ordinance of 16 February 1946 was the primary currency measure employed; (2) a period of economic rehabilitation and inflation caused by loans from the Reconstruction Finance Bank (1947–48); (3) the period of currency stabilization (January 1949–June 1950), during which time the yen's official exchange rate was established; and (4) the Korean War period, which witnessed a new inflationary drive. The author considers the Dodge Plan in particular to have been an influential factor in Japan's postwar economic development.

1654 Noda, Kazuo. "Postwar Japanese Executives." In *Postwar Economic Growth in Japan*, ed. by Komiya Ryūtaro. Berkeley: Univ. of California Pr., 1966. p.229–49.

In this article, Noda evaluates the role which entrepreneurs have played in Japan's postwar economic development. He shows how a more competitive environment and a new social climate conducive to entrepreneurial activities have come about through the dissolution of the *zaibatsu*, the abolition of prewar economic controls, and the implementation of various SCAP reforms. He also contends that Japan's successful recovery from wartime destruction and the country's subsequently rapid growth are a direct consequence of the energy and enthusiasm with which Japan's corporate executives have tackled their work.

1654a Ōhira, Zengo. "Settlement of the U.S.A.'s Postwar Assistance to Japan." *Japan Annual of International Affairs* no.2:128–48 (1962)

This study applies legal analysis in its consideration of the question of Japan's obligation to repay the aid given her by the United States from its Government and Relief in Occupied Areas (GARIOA) fund. Some have argued, Ōhira points out, that the aid can be regarded as an outright voluntary gift and therefore not as a debt to be repaid. After a complicated academic discussion of the legal principles involved, however, the author concludes that Japan does have an obligation to repay a part of the total amount of aid received in cash and materials. He asserts that Japan's indebtedness should be balanced against the direct and indirect benefits received by the United States as a consequence of its extension of aid. These include the profits earned on Japanese–American trade during the late 1940s and early 1950s and the American use of the occupation as part of an overall defense strategy, which went beyond SCAP's original mission of merely implementing the Potsdam Declaration. The article closes with the texts of the "Agreement between Japan and the United States of America Regarding the Settlement of Postwar Economic Assistance to Japan," dated 9 January 1962, and related Japanese legislation.

1655 Ōkita, Saburō. "Post-war Structure of Japan's Foreign Trade." *Economia Internazionale* 13, no.1:83–102 (Feb. 1960)

The author, a leading Japanese economist, first seeks to interpret the nature and extent of Japan's actual foreign trade recovery as it relates to the country's postwar economic development and the overall level of world trade. He then discusses the size of Japan's overseas commerce and studies its recent trends. This discussion is followed by an examination of various changes in the postwar commodity structure and marketing patterns of Japanese imports and exports. Finally, Ōkita outlines the major developments that have characterized world commerce since 1945 and shows how they have affected Japan in both a direct and indirect fashion.

1656 Ott, D. J. "The Financial Development of Japan, 1878–1958." *Journal of Political Economy* 69:122–41 (Apr. 1961)

Ott in this article analyzes Japanese fiscal development from 1878 to 1958 in the context of real economic development in Japan. He first describes the framework from which his data are taken. Ott then traces the growth of primary securities and the role of financial intermediaries during these 8 decades. He concludes with a comparison of financial growth in Japan and the United States.

1657 Ozaki, Robert Shigeo. *Japan's Postwar Resurgence in International Trade*. Ph.D. dissertation, Harvard Univ., 1960. ix, 313p.

Ozaki examines the revival of Japanese foreign trade in the postwar period up to the late 1950s and discusses the effects of the international economic situation at the end of the war on Japan. A review of SCAP's policies concerning Japan's future role in world trade is included. Chapter 3 is primarily a discussion of the occupation period.

Available at the Harvard University Archives, Widener Library, Cambridge, Massachusetts.

1658 ———. "Postwar Expansion of Japanese Exports." *Western Economic Journal* 1, no.2:140–55 (Spring 1963)

The author, Robert Ozaki then of Alameda State College, analyzes the expansion of Japanese exports from 1950 to 1957. He presents a simple model "to illustrate the significance of external trade for a country like Japan." Ozaki goes on to analyze the particular products which are being exported and the way they compare with the export index of other industrial countries. He manages to show the way shifting external demands for certain commodities are influencing Japanese exports. He concludes by pointing out how the "absence of excessive inflation combined with high productivity gains has sustained the high level of Japan's exports."

1659 Patrick, Hugh Talbot. "The Phoenix Risen from the Ashes: Postwar Japan." In *Modern East Asia: Essays in Interpretation*, ed. by James B. Crowley. New York: Harcourt, Brace and World, 1970. p.298–336.

In his account of Japan's economic resurgence since World War II, Patrick notes that the Japanese accepted the striking changes of the occupation such as income distribution, ownership of assets, and political power because most of the adjustments represented transfers from a small minority to a large majority of the Japanese; because the previous holders of power and wealth were under attack politically, economically, and socially and were not able to sustain their vested interests; and because Japan was so utterly defeated that tremendous sacrifices could be demanded of everyone simply to get the country back on its feet. Hugh Patrick is professor of Far Eastern economics at Yale University.

1660 "Quarter Century of Japan's Economy: War, Defeat, Reconstruction, Growth." *Oriental Economist* 27:249–64 (May 1959)

In reviewing the course of Japan's postwar reconstruction, the article discusses the Dodge Plan, the Korean War, and the effects of the Japanese peace treaty.

1661 Ramaswamy, T. N. *Outlines of the Economic History of Japan (1853–1953)*. Banaras, India: Banaras Hindu Univ. Pr., 1955. iii, 137p.

1662 Rosen, George. "Japanese Industry since the War." *Quarterly Journal of Economics* 67:445–63 (Aug. 1953)

Changes in Japanese industry since the war are discussed first, in terms of the factors of production—capital in its various aspects, labor, and raw materials; and second, in terms of the demand for Japanese goods.

1663 Sakurai, Kinichirō. *Financial Aspects of Economic Development of Japan 1868–1958*. Tokyo: 1964. 155p. (Science Council of Japan, Div. of Economics, Commerce, and Business Administration, Economic series no.34)

A history of banks and banking in Japan and their relationship to Japanese economic development, which focuses on such financial intermediaries as postal savings accounts, *zaibatsu* banks, and the Bank of Japan. The publication is based on the author's Ph.D. dissertation, entitled "Financial Aspects of Economic Development of Japan from 1868 to Present," which he submitted to Syracuse University in 1961.

Salwin, Lester N. "The New Commercial Code of Japan: Symbol of Gradual Progress toward Democratic Goals." 1962. See no.1291a.

1664 Schiffer, Hubert F. *The Modern Japanese Banking System*. New York: University Publishers, 1962. 240p.

1664a The Occupation

This book is a survey of the history of Japanese banking from Meiji times until the late 1950s with emphasis on the later period. Though occupation fiscal and banking reforms are described, there is no really systematic treatment of occupation activities in these areas.

1664a Shinjō, Hiroshi. *History of the Yen: 100 Years of Japanese Money-Economy.* Kobe: Research Institute for Economics and Business Administration, Kobe Univ., 1962. iii, 205p. (Kobe Economic and Business Research series, 1)

Chapter 9 of this study of modern Japan's monetary history focuses on the postwar inflation. Shinjō, a specialist in the field of money and banking at Kobe University, evaluates SCAP's economic policies and states that the occupation's initial emphasis on reform measures rather than on the reconstruction of the Japanese economy was a major catalyst for Japan's inflationary spiral. Inflation tapered off in 1947–48, however, at the time SCAP initiated its policy of strengthening the Japanese economy and turning the country into the industrial workshop for Asia. SCAP's emphasis on stabilization culminated in the Dodge Plan, which Shinjō describes and analyzes in some detail and which ultimately brought prosperity and growth to postwar Japan.

1665 Shinohara, Miyohei. "Structure of Saving and the Consumption Function in Postwar Japan." *Journal of Political Economy* 67:589–603 (Dec. 1959)

Shinohara, then of Hitotsubashi University, writes about the saving-consumption relation in postwar Japan. He is especially interested in its impact upon the rapid recovery rate of the Japanese economy. In this article he describes the saving-ratio discrepancies between macro- and microdata, farmers' consumption-savings pattern, urban workers' consumption-saving patterns, and the role consumption functions play in economic planning.

1666 Shiotani, Tadao. "Postwar Progress in Public Finance." *Contemporary Japan* 24, no. 1/3: 33–46 (1956)

In one of several articles written by Japanese authorities for the series "Ten Years of Reconstruction and Development" that appeared in *Contemporary Japan*, the chief of the Research Section of Japan's Ministry of Finance traces the development of public finance in Japan during the decade following defeat in World War II. He classifies this development into 4 periods and then studies each in turn. The periods cover: (1) the postwar inflation, 1945–48; (2) the enforcement of the Dodge Plan, 1949–50; (3) the economic expansion during the Korean War, 1951–53; and (4) the retrenchment policy, 1954–55. In the first section, after describing the inflationary trend, the author looks at the problems of the disposition of war indemnities and the confiscation of wartime profits, the annual increases in government expenditures, the acute shortage of fiscal revenue, and the supply of industrial funds. In the section on the Dodge Plan the author also mentions the Shoup Tax Mission and reform of the Japanese taxation system. In conclusion Shiotani cites economic problems yet to be solved in Japan.

1667 Tokoyama, Tsunesaburō. "Economic Recovery and Public Finance in Post-war Japan." *Public Finance* 8, no.3:283–316 (1953)

Tokoyama, professor of public finance at Waseda University, divides the postwar Japanese economy into 5 periods. The first period, August 1945–December 1946, was one of confusion and frustration. The second, January 1947–December 1948, was one of "recovery first" when economic recovery through inflation was attempted. The third period, January 1949–September 1951, one of "stability first," began with the adoption of an overbalanced budget and a single rate of exchange. Efforts were made to stop inflation. The fourth period, October 1951–May 1953, of transfer to economic independence, saw Japan's political and economic independence recovered. Finally, the "new era," June 1953 to the time of writing, found Japan forced to consolidate its independence following the Korean War. The author concludes it can only be achieved through "cooperativism," a new economic system based on a "happy coordination of capital, labor and management."

1668 Tsuru, Shigeto. "Post-war Democratization in Japan: Economics." *International Social Science Journal* 13, no.1: 35–43 (1961)

This article presents an historical approach to the controversy over postwar economic democratic reforms in Japan. Tsuru gives 2 major reasons for the occupation's failure to democratize the economy: first, the recentralization of the former *zaibatsu* and, second, the problems of a dual wage structure and an antiquated market economy. A short bibliography of English-language books on the postwar economy is included.

1669 Uchida, Katsutoshi. "Japan's Foreign Trade after the War: With Special Emphasis on the Structure of Foreign Markets." *University of Osaka Prefecture Bulletin* s.D, v.1:117–32 (1957)

Uchida discusses Japan's prewar and postwar trade structure, pointing out the important differences between them and analyzing the country's postwar export markets as well as her sources of imports. In his conclusion he notes that the composition of Japan's foreign trade has undergone remarkable changes since the war. The severance of relations with China has been particularly felt. In addition, many underdeveloped countries have initiated significant programs of industrialization while Japan has become heavily dependent on the United States in the area of foreign trade.

1670 Uchiyama, Isamu. "Construction Works in Past Decade." *Contemporary Japan* 24, no.4/6:244–54 (1956)

A technical officer in the Ministry of Construction's Research and Statistics Bureau reports on the construction that has occurred during the occupation period and the years immediately following it. He focuses on the work undertaken by individual contractors as well as on river improvement, road construction, the building of additional housing, and city planning. Uchiyama's report is a straightforward, factual account which shows both the progress and some of the problems of the postwar Japanese construction industry.

1671 Ueno, Hiroya. "A Long-term Model of the Japanese Economy, 1920–1958." *International Economic Review* (Osaka) 4:171–93 (May 1963)

This paper presents an annual econometric model of the Japanese economy, 1920–58. The author's purpose is to explain the economic development of the prewar and postwar periods as well as to forecast levels of economic activity in the future. Using his model he computes econometric forecasts for 1962 and then compares them with actual results.

1672 Watanabe, Susumu. "Revaluation in Japan." *Kobe Economic and Business Review* 1:157–69 (1953)

This study first analyzes the difficulties which many Japanese businesses experienced on account of the rapid postwar inflation. It then describes the stabilizing nature of the measures ultimately taken to allow for the revaluation of assets. In the course of his article, Watanabe discusses in detail both the Shoup Mission's recommendations on revaluation and the Assets Revaluation Law of 1950.

1673 Winiata, Whatarangi. *United States Managerial Investment in Japan, 1950–1964: An Interview Study.* Ph.D. dissertation, Univ. of Michigan, 1966. 170p. (Abstracted in *Dissertation Abstracts* 28: 9A [1967]; University Microfilms order no.67–8368)

Winiata investigates the factors which motivated managerial investment by American companies from 1950 to 1964, as well as the decision-making units responsible for determining investment commitments, and the considerations on which these decisions were based. During his study he interviewed 47 American corporations with investments in Japan. These companies held 88 percent of the investment validations granted to American corporations. He concludes that the initiative for investment during these years came primarily from Japanese corporations, that the Japanese government and Japanese and American corporations had the greatest decision-making powers, and that criteria for investment decisions varied according to objectives.

1674 Yamamura, Kōzō. *Economic Policy in Postwar Japan: Growth versus Economic Democracy.* Berkeley: Univ. of California Pr., 1967. xvii, 226p. (Publications of the Center for Japanese and Korean Studies)

The economic democratization policy of SCAP from 1945 to 1950 and the subsequent revisions of this policy by the Japanese government after 1950 are carefully analyzed. The author examines SCAP's measures dealing with *zaibatsu* dissolution, land distribution, and labor and tax reform. He also probes the consequences of these measures following SCAP's shift in emphasis from economic reform to recovery. Japanese policy formulated in 1950 is discussed vis-à-vis the impact of the Korean War, tax laws, and the revision of the Shoup taxation approach. The abandonment of the antimonopoly policy in the period from 1953 to 1957 and the process by which the government indicated support for monopolies after 1958 are examined. There is also a comparative study of prewar and postwar *zaibatsu* control and of changes in labor and wages in the postwar period. Yamamura's book is a revision of the Ph.D. dissertation he submitted to Northwestern University in 1964 under the title *Competition and Monopoly in Japan, 1945–1961.* (Abstracted in *Dissertation Abstracts* 25:3878–79 [1965]; University Microfilms order no.64–12,356)

1675 Yamane, Tarō. *Postwar Inflation in Japan.* Ph.D. dissertation, Univ. of Wisconsin, 1955. 319p. (Abstracted in Univ. of Wisconsin. *Summaries of Doctoral Dissertations, 1954–1955* 16:255–56 [1955])

Two major inflationary periods—the first from August 1945 through December 1945, and the second from June 1950 to December 1952—are examined in terms of a theoretical model in which the Japanese economy is presented as a circular flow. This flow is dissected at 3 points—expenditures, production, and distribution. The first inflation is attributed mainly to extensive deficit spending by the government and to the lax lending policies of government and financial institutions. The second is regarded as a result of procurement orders from the United States during the Korean War and the attendant large increases in domestic consumption and investment.

1676 Yoshino, Toshihiko. "Economic Recovery and Banking System." *Contemporary Japan* 24:570–95 (Apr. 1957)

Yoshino of the Economic Research Department in the Bank of Japan presents a general survey of the role of the banking system in the reconstruction of Japan's postwar economic recovery (1945–55).

TAXATION

In general the occupation, while not ignoring the problem of adapting the Japanese tax system to the new conditions and needs of postwar Japan, did not seriously come to grips with it until the appointment of the U.S. Tax Mission to Japan (the Shoup Mission) in 1949. As a result of this mission's findings, very extensive and basic changes were recommended to the Japanese government. In practice, many of these recommendations were not given effect.

Many entries in the preceding section (p.481) also devote some attention to the field of taxation.

1677 Bronfenbrenner, Martin. "The Japanese Value-added Sales Tax." *National Tax Journal* 3:298–313 (Dec. 1950)

The institution of the value-added sales tax, based on proposals of the Shoup Mission, as the principal independent revenue source for prefectural government is discussed as are the theoretical advantages of this type of tax over other sales taxes. A variety of problems concerning the determination of "value-added" and their tentative solution by SCAP and government officials are mentioned. These problems cover such areas as the significance of interfirm rent, interest, and dividend payments, and of investment expenditure and expense accounts in ascertaining tax coverage. Administrative concern with the rate of taxation and the allocation of revenue between prefectures are considered. The author concludes with a discussion of the political and theoretical disadvantages of the value-added tax.

1678 ——, and Kogiku Kiichirō. "The Aftermath of the Shoup Tax Reforms." *National Tax Journal* pt.1, 10:236–54 (Sept. 1957); pt.2, 10:345–60 (Dec. 1957)

Part 1 of this study describes the recommendations of the Shoup Mission concerning national and local tax systems and their subsequent legislative history. The author utilizes the mission as a case study in planned economic reform and closely reviews pre-Shoup occupation tax reform from 1946 to 1949. Six main aims of the Shoup Mission are explained and the Japanese implementation of each delineated. These aims are: (1) to provide immediate, direct tax relief for every Japanese; (2) to retain progressive and broad-based personal income taxes as the mainstay of the national tax structure; (3) to revaluate land and fixed capital for taxation in the light of wartime and postwar inflation; (4) to minimize indirect and consumption taxes; (5) to establish a substantial tax base for prefectural and local governments that would ensure their fiscal autonomy; and (6) to introduce fiscal innovation with a net worth tax, an accessions tax, and a value-added sales tax. Seven appendixes list and explain all the recommendations of the Shoup Mission and the extent of Japanese legislation from 1949 to 1956 concerning each. These appendixes cover personal and corporate income taxes, other national direct and indirect taxes, intergovernmental fiscal relations, and local taxation.

Part 2 of this study is a discussion of factors explaining Japanese modifications of the Shoup tax system. The continued political opposition of the Japanese government is noted as is the alienation of specific interest groups representing privately owned utilities, banking and security interests, and the foreign community. The economic factors mentioned are the inability of the mission to convince the Japanese of the necessity of substantial taxation to finance government services, to inculcate tax consciousness among prefectural and municipal authorities, and to reconcile optimal resource allocation with problems concerning the distribution of economic power and economic growth. The social causes discussed include the inability to improve taxpayer morale in a self-assessed progressive income tax system; the social habit of preferring indirect taxation; and the handicaps on American suggestions for reform during this late stage of the occupation. In conclusion, the authors suggest methods by which the Shoup Mission might have overcome this opposition.

Cohen, Jerome Bernard. "Fiscal Policy in Japan." 1950. *See* no.1568.

1679 ——. "Tax Reform in Japan." *Far Eastern Survey* 18:307–11 (28 Dec. 1949)

One of the members of the 7–man Shoup Mission to Japan presents a lucid account of their 4–month survey undertaken in the early part of 1949. According to the author, the mission was not primarily concerned with immediate questions of Japanese tax policy but rather attempted "to effect permanent reforms which will provide Japan with a more efficient, a more scientific, and above all a more equitable system of taxation than she has hitherto possessed." The article concisely summarizes the recommendations of the mission under 5 general headings: the personal income tax, corporation taxes, indirect taxes, intergovernmental fiscal relations between national and local government, and administration and enforcement. There is a brief discussion of the estimated effects of the new tax system upon various segments of the Japanese nation—i.e., wage workers, those in the top income brackets, and corporations—and in his concluding paragraphs the author considers SCAP's role in implementing the reform of the tax structure and observes that one of the best qualified divisions of SCAP's Economic and Scientific Section is on hand in Tokyo to insure that the mission's recommendations are followed and that a proper administrative system is established by the Japanese government. This report is an excellent analysis of the program of one of the more ambitious U.S. missions sent to Japan during the occupation.

1680 ———. "Tax Revision in Japan." *Taxes* 28, no.6:526–33 (June 1950)

Cohen, an economist who participated in Shoup's tax mission, summarizes the mission's findings and recommendations. First, he notes that Japan's high corporate tax rate produces little revenue because of numerous loopholes. A simplification of the tax structure and a reduction in the rate, it was thought, would result in a higher tax return. The personal income tax was found to be basically sound, though the rate at the highest brackets and exemptions for dependents needed to be increased. A low, net-worth tax on wealthy individuals and the reform of gift, estate, and property taxes also were proposed. Finally, it was noted that under the occupation foreigners were not taxed at all, but according to Cohen this situation was scheduled to be changed shortly.

1681 Hicks, Ursula K. "The Reform of Japanese Taxation." *Public Finance* pt.1, 6, no.3:199–220 (1951); pt.2, 6, no.4: 338–41 (1951)

In this article Hicks, an English economist, describes in some detail and criticizes the "Report on Japanese Taxation" (no.1696), by the Shoup Mission of 1949. The main article is followed by a résumé in French, pages 218–20, and a brief "Further Report," pages 338–41, on how the Shoup report was being put into effect and the problems that arose. The author is generally impressed with the Shoup report, but objects to its emphasis on direct taxes and the idea that to reject one part would ruin the whole plan. The article is divided into sections analyzing the report's recommendations on assessment and administration, on local and regional finance, and on direct tax proposals for the central government.

1682 Itō, Hanya. "Direct Taxes in Japan and the Shoup Report." *Public Finance* 8, no.3:357–83 (1953)

Itō of Hitotsubashi University describes the history of the Japanese tax system, the reforms introduced as a result of the Shoup Report, and the modifications of these reforms in actual practice. There is a French résumé on pages 384–87. The personal income tax, corporate income tax, inheritance tax, and revaluation tax are described in detail along with the problems they have presented. The author concludes, first, that the occupation's tax reforms are being revised into something closer to the prewar tax system and, second, that there is a tendency to reduce taxes on big business in the name of economic recovery at the expense of other social classes.

1683 ———. "The Value-added Tax in Japan." *Annals of the Hitotsubashi Academy* 1:43–59 (Oct. 1950)

Itō Hanya, professor of public finance at Hitotsubashi University, discusses the controversial value-added tax proposed by the Shoup Mission as a part of the tax reform program. The subject is dealt with in 4 parts: the first being the character and advantages of the tax; the second, the disadvantages; the third, suggestions for amendment; and the fourth gives an outline of the system to be followed in Japan.

Japan. Ministry of Finance. Bureau of Taxation. *Internal Revenue Code of Japan.* 1951. See no.1280.

1684 *Local Tax Law and the Local Finance Commission Establishment Law; the Local Finance Equalization Grant Law; Law for the Temporary Measurement Concerning the Partial Allocation of the Local Finance Equalization Grant in a Rough Estimate; Law Concerning Exceptions to the Charge on the Treasury for Disasters, Rehabilitation Works for the Fiscal Year 1950–51.* Tokyo? Local Autonomy Agency, 1950. 411p.

1685 Natori, Jonosuke. "Commentary on the Shoup Taxation Reform." *Contemporary Japan* 18:309–14 (July/Sept. 1949)

This brief analysis of the Shoup Mission's tax reform program provides some insight into the reaction of the Japanese population to the new tax proposals. Rather than summarizing all of the Shoup recommendations, the author concentrates on several features he believes are of significance. Noting that Shoup, the head of the mission, encouraged intelligent discussion of the program by Japanese representing all facets of the population, the author contrasts it with their unquestioning acceptance of prewar legislation. Other features informally discussed are the establishment of a local autonomy structure in relation to the taxation system, the encouragement of the accumulation of capital at all levels of taxation, and the introduction of some aspects of the circulation tax into the business tax program. The author is somewhat skeptical about certain aspects of the income tax system and the effects of indirect taxes on consumer goods; however, he generally supports the new program as an effective measure to improve the Japanese economy.

1685a Nose, Nobuko. "A Research of Wage Income in Post-war Japan." *Kobe Economic and Business Review* 1:139–56 (1953)

The objective of this scholarly study is to analyze the changes in real wage income of Japanese workers since the surrender, and their relationship to consumer price changes and direct as well as indirect taxation. The author's argument and conclusions unfortunately are obscured by a poor translation, but the article includes a good deal of potentially useful statistical material and will be of considerable interest to those interested in postwar Japan's tax structure.

1686 Pierson, Harry E. "Taxes in Japan." *Taxes* 25:733–38 (Aug. 1947)

Changes in the taxation system in postwar Japan are discussed in the light of the overall economic situation. Japan's financial history is reviewed from 1932 to the present with particular emphasis on the postwar period. Topics considered include the financing of the annual budget, the distribution of the tax burden, local government finance, and taxes on individuals and business. There are useful charts which cite the purpose and effects of the income tax bills of 1946–47 and 1947–48, as well as a table which sets forth Japanese government revenues and expenditures in millions of yen from 1932 to the present.

1687 Ramineni, Ayyanna. *A Comparative Analysis of the Kaldor Indian Tax Reforms and the Shoup Mission Japanese Tax Reforms.* Ph.D. dissertation, Univ. of Minnesota, 1966. 87p. (Abstracted in *Dissertation Abstracts* 27:587A [1966]; University Microfilms order no.66–9038)

The *Indian Tax Reform, Report of a Survey* prepared by Nicholas Kaldor (New Delhi: Ministry of Finance, Dept. of Economic Affairs, 1956. 139p.), and the *Report on Japanese Taxation* by the Shoup Mission (no.1696), submitted in 1949 by a committee headed by Professor Carl S. Shoup, are compared here. Ramineni notes the defects which existed in the 2 systems prior to their reform and observes that both reports, with some minor differences, urged the implementation of a comprehensive personal tax system. He suggests that although the tax reforms as projected were similar, their results were dissimilar. The post-reform Japanese tax system operated more efficiently and had fewer adverse effects on the economy than did the Indian system. These results are attributed to the fact that the goals of the Japanese were capitalistic while those of the Indians were socialistic and egalitarian. The Indian reform was also hamstrung by constitutional difficulties.

1688 "SCAP Memorandum to the Japanese Government Concerning the Reorganization of the National Tax Administration Issued on May 6, 1949." *Contemporary Japan* 18:276 (Apr./June 1949)

A brief but important memorandum outlining SCAP's directive to the Japanese government to remodel the structure of the national tax administrative system. The memorandum orders that 6 particular measures be adopted by the Japanese government that relate to the creation within the Ministry of Finance of a Tax Administration Bureau which would be constituted as an external bureau for the administration of national taxation. The memo also authorizes direct communications between the Ministry of Finance and the Education and Scientific Section of SCAP regarding matters of tax administration.

1689 Shavell, Henry. "Postwar Taxation in Japan." *Journal of Political Economy* 56: 124–37 (Apr. 1948)

Prior to a consideration of Japan's tax reform during the occupation, the author discusses the historical development of the Japanese tax system, the reforms undertaken during the early 1940s, and the inadequacies and inequities of that system. Following this are an account of the "extraordinary tax program," which was enacted in 1946 and provided for the capital levy and war indemnity taxes, and of the general tax reforms of 1947, which radically altered such taxes as the personal income tax, the estate and gift taxes, and the corporation tax. The attempts of the postwar Finance Ministry to overhaul its administrative machinery are also briefly discussed. The article includes a number of charts relating to various fiscal issues during the 1940s.

1690 ———. "Taxation Reform in Occupied Japan." *National Tax Journal* 1:127–43 (June 1948)

The taxation adviser of the Finance Division, Economic and Scientific Section, SCAP, discusses the social and economic objectives of occupation tax reform. He regards taxation as a tool which can promote economic and price stabilization and insure the growth of democratic institutions by encouraging a wide distribution of income and property. Following a short explanation of Japan's immediate postwar fiscal situation, the "extraordinary tax program" of 1946 is explained. The general taxation and fiscal administration reforms of 1947–48 are discussed and attention is given to the initiation and enforcement of personal income taxation on a withholding basis.

1691 Shiomi, Saburō. *Japan's Finance and Taxation, 1940–1956*. Tr. by Hasegawa Shōtarō. New York: Columbia Univ. Pr., 1957. xi, 190p.

The development of the Japanese national and local tax systems from 1940 to 1956 are treated along with the author's assessment of occupation tax policies. While critical of the occupation's initial policies, the author supports its later policies such as Joseph Dodge's financial stabilization plan and Carl S. Shoup's taxation reform plan. The book also includes Shiomi's research on the effects of taxation on disparities between the rich and poor and a financial survey of Osaka and surrounding municipalities.

1692 Sundelson, J. Wilner. "Report on Japanese Taxation by the Shoup Mission." *National Tax Journal* 3:104–20 (June 1950)

The author examines Japan's postwar economy and summarizes the Dodge report concerning a fiscal formula for arresting inflation. The Shoup Mission report is regarded as a corollary to Dodge's concern for the collection of increased revenue by the Japanese government. The main recommendations of the Shoup Mission are discussed and primary emphasis is given to the sections dealing with personal income taxation, corporate income, and national-local fiscal relations. The author includes a brief discussion concerning SCAP's success in implementing these recommendations.

Supreme Commander for the Allied Powers. Monograph 37. *National Government Finance, 1945–March 1951.* 1952. See no.319.

———. Monograph 38. *Local Government Finance, 1945–March 1951.* 1952. See no.320.

1693 ———. Finance Div. *Summary of Japanese Taxes in Effect 1 April 1952.* Tokyo: SCAP, 1952. 13p.

The Japanese tax system as of 1 April 1952 is described in this report. Various kinds of national taxes, such as the personal income tax, corporation taxes, accessions taxes, revaluation taxes, and liquor and stamp taxes are described in the first section of the report. Average rates or percentages are cited for each particular tax. The second section on local taxes is divided into 2 parts—prefectural taxes and municipal taxes. Under prefectural taxes are included enterprise and special net income taxes, amusement taxes, automobile taxes, mine lot taxes, extralegal taxes, etc., whereas under municipal taxes fall inhabitants' taxes, property taxes, electricity taxes, and extralegal taxes. The report provides a very brief outline of the tax structure in Japan at the conclusion of the occupation.

Available at the Army Library, the Pentagon, Washington, D.C.

———. Office of the Financial Adviser (Joseph M. Dodge). *Reports on Taxation and Budget Plans.* 1949. See no.1556.

1694 Takahashi, Chōtarō. "The Income Tax Burden: A Japanese Experiment." *Annals of the Hitotsubashi Academy* 1:60–79 (Oct. 1950)

Takahashi of the Institute of Economic Research analyzes the transition and present position of the tax burden in Japan, with emphasis on income tax. In order to show the position which income tax occupies in the total tax system, he considers it first from the standpoint of national finance and then from the standpoint of national life.

1694a "Tax Turnabout." *Business Week* p.128–29 (19 Nov. 1949)

This article reports on the changes in the Japanese tax system recommended by a group of American tax experts headed by Carl Shoup. While these changes appear to favor the higher income classes, their real intention is to make tax evasion less necessary by lowering the country's tax rates applying directly to those income groups. The success of the new measures will depend upon the willingness of the government to enforce the law, even against the kinds of influential people who have traditionally avoided paying full taxes.

1695 Uematsu, Morio. "Computation of Income in Japanese Income Taxation: A Study in the Adjustments of Theory to Reality." In *Law of Japan: The Legal Order in a Changing Society*, ed. by Arthur Taylor von Mehren. Cambridge, Mass.: Harvard Univ. Pr., 1963. p.567–621.

The Shoup recommendations concerning the computation of income for taxation purposes, which have decisively influenced the postwar Japanese income tax system, are evaluated here by a senior official in the Tax Bureau of the Ministry of Finance. The author feels that, although the American taxation missions headed by Columbia University Professor Carl S. Shoup in 1949 and 1950 were of outstanding service in modernizing the Japanese tax structure and administration, the proposals, which were theoretically logical, were nevertheless often divorced from the concrete needs and practices of Japanese society. Noting that the struggle between theory and reality has characterized the postoccupation Japanese efforts to revise the taxation system and modify the Shoup approaches, Uematsu carefully documents the process by which the taxation system has been revised in such respects as definition of income.

1696 U.S. Tax Mission to Japan. *Report on Japanese Taxation.* Tokyo: SCAP, 1949. 4v. In English and Japanese.

This report is the outcome of the work of the U.S. Tax Mission sent to Japan in 1949 at the request of SCAP with an assignment to recommend a new permanent tax system for Japan. The mission is better known as the Shoup Mission, named after its director, Professor Carl S. Shoup of Columbia University. The report consists of 4 volumes, each providing an English text on the left-hand page and a Japanese text on the right. The first 2 volumes contain recommendations for a revised taxation system, while the last 2 are appendixes providing supporting material. Following a review of the Japanese tax system, volume 1 presents the mission's recommendations in such areas as intergovernmental fiscal relations, government expenditures and corresponding tax reforms, and personal and corporation income taxes. Volume 2 discusses income taxes, gift and bequest taxes, taxes on tobacco and liquor, other indirect taxes, the inhabitants tax, and the real estate tax. This volume also considers problems related to the enforcement of the tax laws, compliance, and the right of appeal. Volumes 3 and 4 present discussions of more specific subjects under the following 4 headings: finance of local governments, treatment of irregular income under the personal income tax, evaluation of assets, and administration of the individual and corporate income taxes.

Excerpts from this report may be found in the periodical, *Contemporary Japan* 18:386–98, 412–37 (July/Sept. 1949)

1697 ———. ———. *Second Report on Japanese Taxation.* Tokyo: Japan Tax Assn., 1950. 186p. In English and Japanese.

In this report, prepared after a return visit to Japan, the Shoup Mission assesses problems of tax administration. Measures to combat tax evasion in liquor and gasoline tax collections, continuing procedures to maintain property listings, and predictions of local budgetary needs for the coming fiscal year are given. Confidence is expressed in the acceptance and potential for more efficient administration of the national income tax and suggestions in this area are made.

1698 ———. ———. *Tax Survey Conclusions and Recommendations, Memorandum for the Supreme Commander.* Tokyo: SCAP, General Hdqters., The Mission, 1950. 1v.

LAND REFORM

One of the most basic changes attempted by the occupation lay in the field of land reform. As a result of two major laws enacted in 1945 and 1946, the system of agrarian land tenure was fundamentally revised, the tenancy rate drastically lowered, and the terms of the economic relationships between landlords and the remaining tenants carefully regulated. The relevant literature is set forth below.

1699 "Agrarian Reform in Japan." *Depart- of State Bulletin* 20:670–71 (22 May 1949)

This article reprints 2 press releases of 6 May 1949. The first is the text of a policy decision approved by the Far Eastern Commission on 28 April regarding agrarian reform, and the second summarizes and interprets that particular decision. The policy decision itself appears to be nothing more than an endorsement of the principles underlying the reform program then being carried out under SCAP's guidance.

Andō, Nisuke. *Surrender, Occupation, and Private Property in International Law: An Evaluation of Some United States Practices during the Occupation of Surrendered Japan.* 1971. See no.2236.

1699a Berrigan, Darrell, and Wolf Isaac Ladejinsky. "Japan's Communists Lose a Battle." *Saturday Evening Post* 221:28, 101 (8 Jan. 1949)

Berrigan and Ladejinsky first describe the old system of land tenure in Japan, providing statistics on farm size, tenancy rates, etc. The inherent injustices of the system and the fact that the peasantry gave stronger support to the reactionaries than to any other social group made land reform one of the occupation's highest priorities. From very early on, the Russians began agitating for drastic land reform measures; their propaganda backfired, however, when SCAP pushed through its own radical program. The Soviet government then attacked those reforms because of their emphasis upon private rather than collective land ownership, but the peasants were too happy with the windfall just provided them to pay any further attention to Communist appeals. The authors conclude that although the reforms have been a boon in general to Japanese farmers, no amount of reform can resolve Japan's basic problem—overpopulation.

Bisson, Thomas A. "Making Japan over." 1945. See no.65.

1699b Blumenthal, Tuvia. "Agricultural Development in Postwar Japan." *Asian and African Studies* (Jerusalem) 6:113-25 (1970)

This study assesses the extent to which agriculture has stimulated or hindered economic growth in postwar Japan. Blumenthal finds that the occupation's land reform determined the basic postwar structure of agriculture and that its impact is still visible. The reforms, he points out, have had certain adverse effects on economic development. The trend toward small farm units was not reversed but rather reinforced, and as a consequence, productivity increases have been limited. Furthermore, the new regulations made renting one's land unprofitable and accordingly have kept an undetermined number of people on the farm and out of the fulltime industrial labor market. An examination of recent agricultural trends leads Blumenthal to conclude that modifications of the agricultural system established under the occupation are necessary if output is to continue rising and if agriculture is to make its proper contribution to Japan's overall economic growth.

1699c Campbell, Colin D. "Weak Points in the Japanese Land Reform Program." *Journal of Farm Economics* 34:361-68 (Aug. 1952)

The author raises questions about the aims and implementation of the land reform program during the occupation. He questions whether the redistribution of income has been equitable and whether this program has led to greater productivity in the agricultural sphere. He also questions SCAP's attempt to control land prices by placing price ceilings on land. In his conclusion Campbell discusses the occupation's goals and whether they will be achieved under this program. He feels the weaknesses of this program will not only diminish Japan's agricultural output but could also effect the political stability of the country.

1700 Chia, Franklin. "Mr. Hewes, Jr. on Land Tenure in Japan: A Reply." *Land Economics* 25:433-34 (Nov. 1949)

A short critique of Lawrence Hewes' article on land tenure in *Land Economics*, August 1949 (no.1710), concentrating on Hewes' alleged lack of appraisal of the effects of land reform on the life of Japanese farmers. Chia presents evidence which suggests that the increase in real income in the near future for new farmer-owners will not be greater than under the previous tenant system. He points out that all the impetus for land reform came from SCAP and discredits Hewes' assertion that "the emphatic response of the entire farm population to the opportunity of sharing in the operation of the program speaks well for the inherent capacity of Japanese farmers to govern themselves and to participate in national affairs." Such a claim, he charges, is based on unfounded conjecture.

1701 Dore, Ronald P. "The Administration of the Japanese Land Reform." *Journal of Local Administration Overseas* 1, no.4: 231–38 (Oct. 1962)

A brief review of the administrative side of the postwar land reform program. Dore first discusses the main provisions of the October 1946 reform legislation, then focuses on the special advantages with which Japan embarked upon this reform. These included a well-established land-registry system, the long tradition of modern bureaucratic administration which reached down to the village level, and the relatively high educational level of the Japanese farmers. The author then points out some of the ways in which the landlords were prevented from evading various reform laws and concludes with some brief comments on the successful features of the reform itself.

1702 ———. "The Japanese Land Reform in Retrospect." *Far Eastern Survey* 27: 183–88 (Dec. 1958)

Dore, author of a study on the Japanese land reform published in 1959 (no. 1703), notes that the land reform can be regarded as the most successful of occupation reforms because, first, the paper plans were carried through to full execution, and second, the reform has every chance of being permanent.

1703 ———. *Land Reform in Japan.* London: Oxford Univ. Pr., 1959. xix, 510p.

Perhaps the best appraisal that has so far appeared of the social, economic, and political consequences of the land reform program undertaken in postwar Japan. The author, a British sociologist, stayed in Japan from February 1955 to August 1956, lived in villages in Yamagata, Yamanashi, and Shimane prefectures, and collected survey data from 6 prefectures. He interviewed a total of 628 male heads (or their eldest sons) of all the households in 1 or 2 hamlets selected from within the villages surveyed. In part 1, the author discusses the Japanese tenancy system prior to World War II and relates prewar agrarian unrest to Japan's external aggression since the 1930s. Of particular interest to students of the Allied occupation is the second part, which discusses how the Land Reform Law was enacted and executed through compromise made by the various groups concerned, including the U.S. State Department, the Japanese cabinet, the Ministry of Agriculture, SCAP's Natural Resources Section, and the Allied Council for Japan. In the next 3 parts, Dore attempts to characterize the impact of the land reform on standards of living in villages, help and mutual help arrangements, feelings of solidarity in hamlets, and the hereditary status held by new and old owners. He also identifies some of the factors that account for the support that the Liberal Democratic party draws from the farmer, for the agricultural policies pursued by different political parties including the Socialist and Communist parties, and for the political roles of various farmers' unions and agricultural cooperative organizations. Some 35 tables are included in the appendix.

1704 Eyre, John D. "Elements of Instability in the Current Japanese Land Tenure System." *Land Economics* 28, no.3:193–202 (Aug. 1952)

Even though postwar reforms have modified them, the forces which gave rise to the prereform land tenure system and all of its shortcomings remain firmly entrenched in rural Japan. Not only has the landlord class survived, but the traditional landlord-tenant relationship also continues to be strong. These conclusions are based on observations which Eyre made during his stay in the Inland Sea region in 1950 and 1951, and they point out some of the elements of instability which he regards as potentially dangerous to the current land tenure system.

1704a ———. "The Changing Role of the Former Japanese Landlord." *Land Economics* 31:35–46 (Feb. 1955)

This study sought to determine whether the influence and power of the landlords who had been deprived of their holdings under the land reform were being reasserted only a few years after the end of the occupation. On the basis of interviews conducted in 1953–54 with farmers and former landowners in Yamagata prefecture, Eyre concluded that rural conservative interests in the person of former landlords had already made decided progress in reestablishing their local influence. He illustrates this development through a case study of the Homma family. Despite the resurgence of such families, Eyre found that many former tenants were more prosperous than ever before as a result of the land reforms. He concluded that as long as the government maintained the economic controls and the protection of the rights and interests of individual farmers which had been instituted by SCAP, the gains of the reforms would be preserved. At the same time, he warned that the former landlords were waiting in the wings to profit, either as landowners once again or as merchants and politicians, from a monopoly on important segments of village life.

Fukui, Haruhiro. *Party in Power: The Japanese Liberal-Democrats and Policy-Making.* 1970. See no.1367a.

1705 "General Douglas MacArthur's Letter to Prime Minister Shigeru Yoshida on the Progress of Land Reform, October 21, 1949." *Contemporary Japan* 18:564–65 (Oct./Dec. 1949)

Written on the third anniversary of the initiation of the land reform program, this letter describes that program as possibly the most successful in history and "one of the most important single demonstrations of her [Japan's] approaching maturity as a democratic nation." The supreme commander states that the benefits brought about by the land reform program must become a permanent part of the texture of Japanese rural society. Under no circumstances should there be a reversion to the land tenure system which existed prior to the occupation.

1706 Gilmartin, William M., and Wolf Isaac Ladejinsky. "The Promise of Agrarian Reform in Japan." *Foreign Affairs* 26:312–24 (Jan. 1948)

Following a description of conditions of land tenure in Japan prior to the occupation, the authors discuss in detail the provisions of the new land reform legislation under the occupation. In their opinion "the most formidable part of the task is to put them [the new programs] into effect" and the latter half of the article describes the arguments and objections of those who oppose the reform, i.e., landlords, politicians, and even intellectuals. After discussing some delaying tactics that have been used to slow reform, the authors express their optimism regarding the success of the venture. They conclude that "the real measure of progress will be the amount of land which is actually purchased by tenants and registered under new titles."

1707 Gontcharov, V. "The Hard Life of the Japanese Peasantry." *Soviet Press Translations* 4:559–61 (15 Oct. 1949)

This report of Japanese peasants first appeared in *Sotsialisticheskoye Zemledelie* on 9 August 1949. It focuses on conditions of Japanese peasant life and on SCAP efforts at agrarian reform. The author describes the conditions of the peasant class as deplorable and blames them on the occupation authorities. He characterizes the agrarian reform as an undemocratic program "designed to preserve and defend the interests of the Japanese landowners." The last part of the article is a description of the organization and activities of the National Peasant Union, which the author believes will be an effective force in improving the situation of the farmers.

Grad, Andrew Jonah. *Land and Peasant in Japan: An Introductory Survey.* 1952. See no.1839.

1708 ———. "Land Reform in Japan." *Pacific Affairs* 21:115–35 (June 1948)

This report proposes: "(1) to indicate the significance of the land problem in the democratization of Japan, (2) to demonstrate the attitude toward land reform of the Japanese ruling groups, (3) to analyze the Land Reform Law from which the reform stems, and (4) to examine the present stage of reform." The first section of the article discusses provisions of early drafts of the land reform programs that were drawn up by the Japanese at SCAP's suggestion—the first Land Reform Law and the second land reform program, both of which were considered unsatisfactory by SCAP. They are then compared with the provisions of the final SCAP-approved bill, the October Land Reform Law which was enacted on 21 October 1946. The operation of the land commissions and the provisions of the Agricultural Land Adjustment Law are considered, and the author evaluates the progress of the land reform program as of March 1948 in the light of the 31 December 1948 deadline imposed by the present law. He concludes with suggestions for minor revisions of the Land Reform Law and argues for a speedy conclusion of the reform program. There are useful tables charting the extent of land tenancy for 1946–47.

Greene, Marc T. "Danger-Point in Japan." 1950. *See* no.1840.

1709 Hewes, Laurence Ilsley, Jr. *Japan: Land and Man, an Account of the Japanese Land Reform Program, 1945–1951.* Ames: Iowa State College Pr., 1955. viii, 154p.

A full and favorable account of the land reform program of 1945–51 given by a SCAP agricultural economist who was responsible for executing the program. Providing historical background on the Japanese farming system from the seventh century through World War II, the author stresses tenancy as characteristic of Japanese agriculture and describes occupation policy toward the tenancy problem. His discussion covers the government's initial resistance to Allied policy, the process through which land reform proposals became law under SCAP direction, SCAP maneuverings with the Allied Council for Japan, the American and Japanese personnel involved in planning the program, and how the program was implemented. This last subject takes up the second half of the book. The author explains the aims of the reform, the training of prefectural administrators, election of land commission members at different administrative levels, the time schedule of the reform, landlord opposition, judicial hindrances, Russian "obstructionist" tactics, problems of land transfer, taxation, former military lands, and finally, successes and shortcomings of the reform. A useful bibliographical list is appended.

1710 ———. "On the Current Readjustment of Land Tenure in Japan." *Land Economics* 25:246–59 (Aug. 1949)

Hewes begins with a historical sketch of the Japanese system of land tenure, concentrating on the increase of tenancy since the Meiji period and the inability of the government of Taishō Japan to alleviate or improve the situation. The author contends, first, that the military-agrarian coalition of the 1930s arose out of the "dynamics of widespread rural discontent caused chiefly by inequities of tenancy," and, second, that at the end of the war 68 percent of agricultural households were full- or part-time tenants and that the landlords were still in control. These are the reasons given for the priority accorded land reform by SCAP, which hoped to retain agrarian social stability and productivity while drastically reducing the amount of tenancy and controlling and remaining tenant-landlord relations. The article describes in detail the Owner-Farmer Establishment and Special Measures Law and the Agricultural Land Adjustment Law—the legal foundations for SCAP's land reform program. The administration of these laws is traced and statistics on the acquisition and sale of land through 31 December 1948 as well as procedures for financing such operations are presented. Land reform and tenant reduction are also viewed in the broader context of agricultural reform. The author concludes that this reform has given Japanese farmers a voice in national affairs.

1711 Japan. Ministry of Agriculture and Forestry. Agricultural Land Bureau. *Agricutural Land Reform Legislation.* Tokyo: The Ministry, 1949. 295p.

The agricultural land reform measures sponsored by SCAP consisted of 2 major laws: the Owner-Farmer Establishment Special Measures Law (law no.43 of 21 Oct. 1946) and the Agricultural Land Adjustment Law (law no.64 of 28 Dec. 1945). These laws provided the basis for a series of related ordinances and regulations. This publication lists the full English text of these laws, ordinances, and regulations, revised as of September 1949, and the legislation in effect prior to this land reform, namely, the Farm Tenancy Arbitration Law (law no.18 of 22 July 1924) and the Agricultural Land Adjustment Law (law no.67 of 2 Apr. 1938), plus 8 related ordinances and regulations. The SCAP memorandum on land reform issued 9 December 1945 is included. There is also a brief historical account in Japanese of the evolution of land reform legislation, particularly the First Agricultural Land Reform Law of December 1945, and the second reform of October 1946.

1712 ———. ———. ———. *Supplement to Agricultural Land Reform Legislation.* Tokyo: The Ministry, 1951. ii, 72p.

This supplement sets forth the revisions as of February 1951 of agricultural land reform legislation. Major amendments made between September 1949 and January 1951 include primarily the election of members to the agricultural land commission and the increased power of the cabinet to govern the transfer of lands. The supplement contains the full text of General MacArthur's letter of 21 October 1949 to Prime Minister Yoshida (no.1705) in which he stresses the need for continued efforts by the government to counteract any tendency to revert to the prewar tenancy system, and also the full texts of 14 cabinet orders, ministerial ordinances, ministerial notifications, and bills for partial amendments to the Owner-Farmer Establishment Special Measures Law and the Agricultural Land Adjustment Law.

1713 Kajita, Masaru. *Land Reform in Japan.* Tokyo: Agriculture, Forestry, and Fisheries Productivity Conference, 1959. 50p. (Agriculture, Forestry, and Fisheries Productivity Conference, Agricultural Development series, 2)

1714 Katō, Masao. "On the Post-war Land Laws in Japan: Their Development and Criticism." *Doshisha Law Review* international ed. no.3:30–50 (1958)

Katō Masao, professor of civil law at Doshisha University, describes the development and transformation of Japanese land laws during the postwar era. Drawing extensively from a Japanese-language report on farm reform edited by the Recording Committee of Land Reform of Japan, he discusses how each of the 2 land reform measures were drawn up, points out what their contents were, and reviews the enactment and ramifications of the Land Act of 15 July 1952.

1715 Klein, Sidney. *The Pattern of Land Tenure Reform in East Asia after World War II.* New York: Bookman, 1958. 260p. (Bookman monograph series)

In this review of postwar land tenure reforms in Communist China, Japan, Taiwan, and North and South Korea, Klein notes that although numerous abuses of the prereform systems disappeared, new ones such as higher taxes appeared. In Japan, where tenancy was reduced from 50 percent to 10 percent of all cultivated land, reforms were implemented with only minor disruption of existing farm management patterns and operations. The reforms included subjecting landlord-tenant relations to the scrutiny of local land commissioners, requiring that lease contracts be written, and reducing rent payments. The author reports that similar changes occurred in Taiwan. Tenancy was reduced to 16 percent of cultivated land with little disruption of the farm economy. In South

Korea, the number of half-tenants and full-tenants was cut by 77 percent, but partial tenancy increased by 171 percent. Partial tenancy (owning more than 50 percent of the land) increased together with land ownership. In addition to this increase in partial tenancy, other deficiencies such as the retention of oral leases for indefinite periods of time and over-renting persisted. In North Korea, land which formerly belonged to absentee landlords and the Japanese government was distributed to the landless. Although parcels averaged 3 and one-quarter acres per family, it was rarely enough land to support a family. Furthermore, "use-rights" were often withdrawn if the owner incurred the wrath of the ruling Communists. Many North Koreans, oppressed by high taxes, longed for the days of Japanese rule. The situation in Communist China was very similar to that in North Korea.

This study was submitted to Columbia University in 1957 as the author's doctoral dissertation. (Abstracted in *Dissertation Abstracts* 17:1006 [1957]; University microfilms order no.20,584).

1715a Kobayashi, Tatsuo. *The Land Reform in Japan*. Ph.D. dissertation, Univ. of California at Berkeley, 1970. 221p. (Abstracted in *Dissertation Abstracts International* 32:631A–32A [1971]; University Microfilms order no.71–20,836)

This dissertation analyzes the effects of the land reform on Japan's agricultural productivity. Kobayashi first critically reexamines the supposition that the prewar land tenure system obstructed the growth of productivity and output within Japan. He finds a positive correlation between increases in the rate of tenancy and the rapid growth of agricultural production, and demonstrates the significance of the contributions which Japanese landlords could make through the promotion of improved production techniques and the input of capital. Kobayashi then critically evaluates developments during the postwar period and shows that the land reform not only failed to contribute to the growth of agricultural production (in large part because farms are too small to permit the economic use of farm machinery) but also hindered general economic growth. He concludes that in the case of postwar Japan at the very least, a land reform was unnecessary when considered in purely economic terms.

1716 Kondō, Yasuo. *The Land Reform in Japan*. Tokyo: National Research Institute of Agriculture, Ministry of Agriculture and Forestry, 1952. 36p.

Kondō of Tokyo University examines both the background and results of the land reform program. He points out that because the ownership of land was transfered without any change in methods of cultivation, the effect of the reform upon the productivity of agriculture was a psychological rather than a technical one.

1717 Kudryavtsev, V. "Sabotage of Agrarian Reform in Japan." *Soviet Press Translations* 2:197–99 (1 Nov. 1947)

This article, translated from the 20 July 1947 issue of *Izvestia*, is an examination of the agrarian reform program of SCAP. Viewing the subject as "a striking example of the discrepancy between word and deed" of the occupation authorities, the author cites various weak or ineffectual aspects of the bill for agrarian reform, for example, the excessively high repurchase price for land and the subsidization of farmer-landowners at the expense of the government. Moreover, he sharply criticizes the half-hearted implementation of the weakened program by Japanese and American officials who, he claims, are intent upon the sabotage of any effective agrarian reform program that will take power from the landowners.

1718 Ladejinsky, Wolf Isaac. "Agrarian Revolution in Japan." *Foreign Affairs* 38:95–109 (Oct. 1959)

Ladejinsky, former consultant on the staff of SCAP, discusses the effectiveness of the land reform directive. Present-day, rural Japan, he notes, demonstrates that only free people and widely distributed private ownership of land can make the best use of the productive forces of the village. Moreover, it demonstrates that the land problem can be dealt with free of the upheavals unleashed by the Soviet and Chinese agrarian revolutions.

1719 ———. "Japan's Land Reform." *Foreign Agriculture* 15:187–89 (Sept. 1951)

Ladejinsky, agricultural attaché at the American embassy in Tokyo in 1951, writes of the farming conditions in Japan prior to the land reform and of the changes which the reform brought. He states that General MacArthur wanted his land reform directive of 15 December 1945 to accomplish 2 things: "multiply the number of freeholders and prevent the Communists from making political capital by posing as advocates of peasant interests." The article describes the forming of the land reform policies and discusses the principal provisions of the reform. The author comments on opposition to the reform but shows how this opposition dwindled. Although he maintains it is too early to assess the consequences of the land reform, he does cite some apparent results, such as the general acceptance of the program by tenants, the critical attitude of former landlords, and the fact that "widespread land ownership makes the Japanese countryside almost impervious to communism." The article concludes with mention of the lesson the reform in Japan holds for the rest of Asia.

1720 ———. "Land Reform Progress in Japan." *Foreign Agriculture* 13:38–41 (Feb. 1949)

With SCAP's extensive land reform program nearing completion, one of its authors provides a general analysis of its effectiveness throughout Japan. He discusses the work of the local land commissions which allocate land for purchase by the tenants, new methods of water utilization, landowners' reactions to the new program, and efforts to thwart its implementation. The speed of the American military government teams in affecting necessary changes is commended, and the author closes with a description of the reasons behind the Communist disapproval of the program. He concludes that "the agrarian reform now in progress has cut the political ground from under the feet of the Communists in the Japanese countryside, thereby strengthening the forces that make for a middle-of-the-road, stable, *petit bourgeois*, rural society."

1721 ———. "Landlord vs. Tenant in Japan." *Foreign Agriculture* pt.1, 11, no. 6:83–88 (June 1947); pt.2, 11, no.8/9: 121–28 (Aug./Sept. 1947)

The author was on duty with the Agricultural Division, Natural Resources Section, SCAP in Tokyo from January 1946 through January 1947 and assisted in formulating SCAP's land reform program. In this 2-part article, drawn from his field trip notes, he contrasts the attitudes of the landowners toward the land reform program then under consideration with those of the tenants. Part 1 describes a landowning clan in Yamagata prefecture and the attitudes of a typical family on such topics as land reform, absentee landlordism, the proposed official price of land, and the Agricultural Associations. An account of the tenants in another village in the same area and their attitudes toward landownership and land taxes follows this. Within part 2, in turn, Ladejinsky shifts his area of focus to the island of Hokkaido and to Fukuoka prefecture, both of which differ from other parts of Japan. He discusses the impact which the SCAP land reform program then under consideration would have in 1 Fukuoka and 4 Hokkaido villages. He also compares prewar and wartime agricultural conditions with present conditions under the occupation and contrasts the attitudes of land-owners toward the provisions of the reforms with the views held by tenants. In his conclusion, Ladejinsky contends that the land reform program will be of benefit to both areas.

1722 Lindstrom, David E. "Outlook for the Land Reform in Japan." *Contemporary Japan* 24, no.1/3:88–100 (1956)

The author, a former professor of rural sociology at International Christian

University, assesses the implementation of the SCAP land reform through the end of the occupation period. On the basis of data from surveys carried out by I.C.U.'s Rural Welfare Institute, he reports that a high percentage of the farmers queried felt that the reforms were either beneficial or of little consequence; only 6.4% voiced strong objections to them. These results are confirmed by other surveys. The problems which the land reform has created, Lindstrom concludes, are not the fault of the law itself but rather of its implementation or of conflicts with other postwar legislation such as the provision of the new civil code for equal inheritance instead of primogeniture.

1723 McDonald, Angus. "Japanese Land Reforms." *New Republic* 117:31–32 (1 Sept. 1947)

SCAP's land reform program in Japan which is just beginning to be implemented is briefly described in this article. The author treats the injustices of large-scale and absentee landownership, which the program attempts to eliminate, and cites the reactions of the landlords who are in vehement opposition to the reforms.

1724 Mannin, Ethel. "Japanese Agriculture and the Land Reform Act." *Eastern World* pt.1, 14, no.2:15–16 (Feb. 1960); pt.2, 14, no.3:20 (Mar. 1960)

After briefly describing the land reform, Mannin asserts in part 1 that the problem of too many people cultivating too little land persists in Japan. Poor tenant farmers have been liberated from landlordism but not from poverty, for the reform could not resolve the age-old problem of how to extract a decent living by small-scale farming as it is carried on within Japan. Moreover, the reform created certain new problems: (1) farmers have been denied the use of forest lands for the collection of fuel and building materials and for gathering fallen leaves with which to make fertilizer since the forests were not covered by the Land Reform Act; (2) even though tenant rents are now nominal, a considerable number of farmers are still working land owned by others and in this manner are perpetuating landlordism; (3) individual plots of land are generally too small to support their cultivators and many farmers are being forced to seek additional sources of income outside of the villages; and (4) with such minute holdings, most families are unable to leave their land to more than one of their sons. Part 2 of this article contrasts the small farmer and his subsistence farming in central and southern Japan with farming in northern Honshu and Hokkaido, where there is still much uncultivated land available. Mannin describes the organization and resources of a huge dairy farm near Morioka in Iwate Prefecture, the relatively minor impact which land reform had upon this farm, and some of its successes as well as its modern, up-to-date nature. She points out that the reform did not go far enough in this particular case, for it failed to turn this vast estate into a peasants' cooperative and instead allowed it to continue as a big business enterprise. Likewise, the occupation authorities failed to persuade Japanese farmers elsewhere in the country to establish cooperative farming in order to minimize the negative impact of their fragmented farm holdings. Mannin concludes that "the land reform scheme which did so much could nevertheless with a little more boldness of enterprise and vision have done so very much more."

1725 Mizutani, Chōsaburō. "Readjusting Our Farmland Reform." *Contemporary Japan* 16:1–10 (Jan./Mar. 1947)

The changes sought by the Social Democratic party to the Agricultural Land Adjustment Law passed in the eighty-ninth Diet are outlined. A detailed outline and analysis of the amendments to the law are given, focusing on the democratizing effects of reducing compensation to landowners, setting a low maximum rental charge, and broadening tenant representation on the land commissions.

1726 ———. "Reforming Our Farmland." *Contemporary Japan* 15:87–89 (Jan./Apr. 1946)

The author cites as factors for land reform pressures the need to foster rural social-political democracy and greater productivity. His critique of the reform bill emphasizes the conservative membership of the land commissions and the unduly large land allotments permitted to single owners.

Nehmer, Stanley. "The Occupation of Japan: The Third Phase." 1947. *See* no.1476.

1726a Oh, Ki Song. *Land Reform in Communist China and Postwar Japan.* Ph.D. dissertation, Univ. of Pennsylvania, 1966. 448p. (Abstracted in *Dissertation Abstracts* 28:743A–44A [1967]; University Microfilms order no.67–7868)

Oh compares the 2 fundamental patterns for land reform which emerged in East Asia after World War II in order to answer such key questions as: How was the Japanese land reform program accomplished without violent opposition? To what extent were the aims and consequences of the 2 programs different? and, What differences are evident in the structure and political impact of the respective programs? Some of his conclusions are as follows: (1) While the redistribution of land had a significant socio-political impact, the immediate economic impact was much less. Within Japan, the land reform destroyed a fertile field for Communism and created many individual owner-cultivators. (2) An element of compulsion was necessary in order for land reform to be effective. Also, it was interesting that in both cases the reforms were motivated and enforced by new powers which dominated the political scene. (3) Although a sweeping land reform was demanded in Japan, it was carried out without an emphasis on class war and occurred at a time when the country's political climate was stabilized under the authority and power of SCAP. (4) The fundamental problem of "too many people for too little land" was not resolved by the redistribution of land.

1727 Ōuchi, Tsutomu. "The Japanese Land Reform: Its Efficacy and Limitations." *Developing Economies* 4:129–50 (June 1966)

While Ōuchi's primary focus is upon the longrange effects of the occupation's land reforms, he necessarily deals at length with the reforms themselves. His major argument is that the combined effect of the occupation's land policy and postwar inflation was (1) to expropriate land from landlords virtually without compensation, making it available in turn to cultivators at nominal prices, and (2) to make the role of the landlord economically unattractive by not allowing legal rents to rise with the inflation. The end result was the reduction of tenancy to virtual insignificance. Ōuchi also notes a marked decrease in political activity on the part of the farmers—a phenomenon that led to the collapse of Socialist influence within the countryside—and he points out that land ownership promoted an increase in the investment that farmers made in land improvement and mechanization. In short, the occupation's land reforms were in large part responsible for the dramatic changes in Japanese farming and village life after the war. At the same time, however, Ōuchi feels that by the early 1960s the reforms may have begun to outlive their usefulness, for the rigid laws governing rent and the alienation of land increasingly inhibited further rationalization and consolidation in Japanese agriculture.

1727a Ōwada, Keiki. "Land Reform in Japan." In *Land Tenure: Proceedings of the International Conference on Land Tenure and Related Problems in World Agriculture Held at Madison, Wisconsin, 1951,* ed. by Kenneth H. Parsons, Raymond J. Penn, and Philip M. Raup. Madison: Univ. of Wisconsin Pr., 1956. p.219–24. Together with "Land Reform in Japan: A Comment," by Wolf I. Ladejinsky. p.224–29.

A short sketch of Japanese agriculture is followed by a survey of prewar agricultural conditions and a discussion of the basic cause for land reform after the Japanese surrender. Ōwada then describes the main provisions of the land reform legislation drafted by the Ministry of Agriculture and Forestry in consultation with SCAP officials and outlines the difficulties encountered in carrying out this reform, the accomplishments of the reform program, and the major agricultural problems which Japan faced in the early 1950s. The author, a member of the Ministry of Agriculture and Forestry, asserts that the reform was successfully enacted not only on account of the support of SCAP which helped overcome opposition among the landlords but also because of the "fact that the farmers wanted the reform, that the land commissions worked with great devotion, and that the government, through the Ministry of Agriculture, did its part." He concludes by pointing out the need for increasing farm income through higher productivity, for providing the farmers with a good credit system, and for taking certain other urgent measures to insure the viability of farming in postwar Japan.

Ladejinsky's comments on Ōwada's paper focus on the factors which enabled the Japanese to carry out the land reform so peacefully in spite of the staunch opposition of most landlords to a program that compelled them to sell their land at very low prices. Among the factors he cites are (1) the traditional acceptance by the landlords of the doctrine of absolute obedience to authority which led them to accept the land reform on account of the support which SCAP—the main source of authority during the occupation—extended to it; (2) the fact that the land reform idea was originally a Japanese idea rather than one imposed by the conqueror upon the conquered; (3) the realization by many landlords who carefully followed the deliberations of the Allied Council in Japan that the American-supported program was much more moderate than the agrarian reform demanded by the council's Soviet representatives; and (4) the high literacy rate among the tenant farmers, who consequently could grasp the main provisions of the reform legislation. Ladejinsky also discusses some of the economic, social, and political benefits derived from the reform and expresses his agreement with Ōwada's assertion that the Japanese land commissions were instrumental in carrying out the reform.

Price, Willard. *The Japanese Miracle and Peril*. 1971. See no.2154a.

1728 "Problem of Land Reform." *Amerasia* 10:53–55 (Feb. 1946)

The author explains that the principal point to be noted about the 10 December directive is that even if it should be fully implemented, it would not in itself solve the basic land problem of Japan. Some means must be found to increase the size of Japanese farms to a point that will permit mechanization and profitable operation. For if the agricultural population of Japan remains impoverished, Japan cannot attain the prosperous internal market and economic stability that is essential for her to remain a democratic and peaceful nation.

1728a "Procedure for Claiming Land in Japan." *Department of State Bulletin* 20:571 (1 May 1949)

This article reprints a press release of 18 April 1949 announcing the receipt of a communication from SCAP stating that the Japanese government is seeking information from former Japanese nationals who own land in Japan and who are exempt from the provisions of the land reform laws.

1729 Raper, Arthur F. "Some Effects of Land Reform in Thirteen Japanese Villages." *Journal of Farm Economics* 33: 177–82 (May 1951); reprinted in *Seven Articles on Land Reform*, comp. by the Asian Studies Center, Michigan State Univ. East Lansing: The Center, 1965. p.15–20.

Writing during the occupation when the land reform program was being carried out, the author, then a member of the Bureau of Agricultural Economics, writes about the effect of this program upon 13 selected Japanese villages. Raper analyzes the farm tenure classification system and the changes in landownership by tenure groups brought about by the land reform program. He goes on to discuss the role played by the village land commissions and the attitude of villagers to land reform. He finds that through the program ownership units were assimilated to operating units. Raper concludes that this program is also leading to the growing democratization of the Japanese village.

1729a ———. "Attitudes of Farm People to Land Reform in Japan and Taiwan." In *Seven Articles on Land Reform*, comp. by the Asian Studies Center, Michigan State Univ. East Lansing: The Center, 1965. p.21–28.

Basing his observations on the results of field surveys made in Taiwan in 1952 and 1954 and in Japan in 1947–48, the author finds that the majority of farmers in both countries were responding favorably to the land reforms then being implemented. The Japanese survey addressed itself to such questions as the farmers' judgments of the benefits of the reform for their villages and families, and the degree to which the cultivators themselves participated in the reform process. Raper arrives at several general conclusions applicable to both Japan and Taiwan. These include the following: (1) the farmers themselves overwhelmingly prefer ownership to tenancy; (2) the farmers generally agree on the need for the greater availability of technical assistance and other services; (3) the new farm owners, especially in Japan, began to take added interest in public affairs as a consequence of the land reform; and (4) former landlords, while pointing out their personal losses, tended to feel that the local community as a whole would benefit from the reforms. Raper's article was originally presented as a paper in December 1955 at the United Nations Land Tenure Conference in Baghdad, Iraq.

1729b ———, et al. *The Japanese Village in Transition*. Tokyo: SCAP, Natural Resources Section, Nov. 1950. 242p., app. (SCAP. Natural Resources Section. Report no.136)

Prepared by Arthur F. Raper, Tamie Tsuchiyama, Herbert Passin, and David L. Sills in cooperation with several Japanese social scientists, this report sought to evaluate the progress of SCAP's basic rural reforms—particularly the land reform—over a 2-year period. The authors conducted intensive field work in 13 "typical" Japanese villages scattered throughout the country. A summary of their findings was published by Raper in his article "Some Effects of Land Reform in Thirteen Japanese Villages" (no. 1729).

1730 "Retrospect on and Documents of Land Reform in Japan." *Developing Economies* 4:195–219 (June 1966)

A survey of the history of the land reform movement before, during, and immediately after the war is followed by a set of documents relating to the postwar land reforms. The effects of wartime mobilization on the agricultural system are discussed in some detail, and the authors suggest that by the end of the war the dual price system for rice had already undermined the position of the rural landlords. The abortive efforts of the Japanese government to institute land reform in the autumn of 1945 are then analyzed. These efforts, based on the results of extensive research and experience within the government, were negated by SCAP's insistence upon a more drastic reform law—the last subject to be dealt with in the introductory portion of this article. The documents which follow consist of (1) a memorandum of the Ministry of Agriculture dated 16 November 1945 and entitled "Matters Relating to the Reform of the Land System;" (2) a Cabinet memorandum of 22 November 1945 entitled "General Provisions for the Reform of the Land System;" (3) a memorandum of 9 December 1945 from the SCAP Central Liaison Office to the Japanese government on the subject of land reform; and (4) a confidential memorandum dated 26 October 1945 from George Atcheson, Jr., United States political adviser, to General MacArthur which includes a paper by Atcheson's assistant, Robert T. Fearey, entitled "Japan: Agrarian Reform." This particular paper appears to have been one of the major sources for subsequent SCAP land reform proposals as outlined in the 9 December memorandum listed above.

1730a Sakamoto, Kusuhito. "Marxian Studies of Agricultural Problems of Post-war Japan." *Japan Science Review: Economic Sciences* 2:71–83 (1955)

This bibliographical essay prepared by a member of the faculty of agriculture at Tokyo University focuses on the differing evaluations and criticisms of the land reform program of the 2 main schools of Japanese Marxian agricultural theorists: the Kōzaha and the Rōnōha. Sakamoto discusses the major writings of a variety of academicians within these 2 schools and points out that many of these men differed particularly over the economic significance and the effectiveness of SCAP's landholding reforms.

1731 Shimazaki, Minoru. "Some Comments on R. P. Dore's *Land Reform in Japan*." *Developing Economies* 4:256–63 (June 1966)

The major deficiency of Dore's work on land reform (no.1703), according to Shimazaki, is his failure to evaluate "the results of land reform in the historical context of the Japanese economy." Shimazaki's critique focuses on Dore's treatment of 3 major problems: landownership after the land reforms, the strengthening of village discipline under the new system, and local government and social control. Shimazaki faults Dore generally for underemphasizing the tensions and contradictions within rural society which still remain after the full implementation of land reforms. In addition, he finds that Dore's work suffers for having been based too heavily on data obtained during one period of field research conducted in the mid-1950s.

The occupation itself is treated only obliquely within the article.

1731a Spillers, A. R. "A Forest Goes Back to the People." *American Forests and Forest Life* 53:70–71 (Feb. 1947)

This account of the disposition of crown forests under MacArthur's plan for agrarian reform describes the efforts of people in Kanazawa-mura, Nagano prefecture to reacquire control over a forest which had belonged to the Japanese royal family.

1732 Strauss, Harold. "MacArthur in the Paddy Fields." *Nation* 163:521–23 (9 Nov. 1946)

The belief that SCAP's land reform program has backfired is the central theme of this article. A discussion of the formation of the program and its provisions is followed by an account of the various liberal Japanese leaders who first approved of the land reform provisions but later became disillusioned and denounced them. There is brief mention of the ambivalent position of some leftist groups who supported the basic principles of the act while condemning particular aspects. The author concludes that the standard of living of the Japanese farmer cannot be raised until farming has been mechanized. Such mechanization is prevented by the small holdings encouraged by SCAP's program and, in the author's opinion, can only be accomplished by the establishment of collective farms.

Supreme Commander for the Allied Powers. *Japanese Agriculture Programs under the Occupation*. 1949. See no.1865.

———. Monograph 27. *The Rural Land Reform, 1945–June 1951*. 1952. See no.309.

"Swing to the Right in Japan." 1949. See no.1415a.

1733 Takeuchi, K. "Agricultural Problems of Japan in the Postwar Period." *Il Politico* 26:790–806 (Dec. 1961)

This article by a Tokyo University geographer criticizes the occupation land reform program because the many small, owner-cultivated farms it created are basically inefficient and retard the development of modern agriculture in Japan. The reform is seen as almost inevitable in light of prewar Japan's anachronistic land system, but by strengthening the individual farmer's commitment to his small, labor-intensive farm, the reform also retarded the growth of large-scale, more efficient farming. This argument is supported with a fairly detailed statistical description of postwar Japanese agriculture.

1734 Tōhata, Shiro. "Land Reform: Results and Problems." *Contemporary Japan* pt.1, 27, no.4:673–84 (Oct. 1963); pt.2, 28, no.1:83–97 (Sept. 1964)

An overall appraisal of the significance of the land reform for the postwar recovery of the Japanese economy. In part 1—"Results of the Land Reform"—Tōhata points out that although agricultural production regained its prewar level following the land reform, it surpassed it only after 1951, when the mining and manufacturing industries attained their prewar production level and showed signs of further development. In part 2—"Economic Growth and Agriculture"—he describes the effects which the land reform had on the income of farm households and on agricultural production in general. He also notes that land reform should be regarded as the first step, or as an intermediary aim, in the course of achieving the ultimate goal of modernizing Japanese agriculture. Tōhata Shiro was chairman of the Agriculture, Forestry, and Fisheries Productivity Conference.

1735 Trewartha, Glenn T. "Land Reform and Land Reclamation in Japan." *Geographical Review* 40:376–96 (July 1950)

The land reform program is seen here as primarily aimed at the stabilization of agriculture and as a method by which one of the specific underlying causes of war could be removed, while the land reclamation program is viewed as inspired largely by economic considerations. The author briefly relates the historical background of the land tenure system, the reform of which was one of the primary objectives of the occupation. A number of maps are included to show the distribution of farm tenancy. The land reform program, the Land Reform Law, and accomplishments of the program are discussed, although the author says it is too early to make any comprehensive appraisal of the effects of the land reform program on agricultural productivity in general. It is noted that Japan's cultivated area has increased very little since 1934, but the augmented postwar population has made it necessary for the Japanese government under Allied pressure to look at possibilities for increasing the area of agricultural land. In evaluating the reclamation programs and estimates of reclaimable land, the author agrees with the SCAP belief that the Japanese government's proposals and estimates are highly ambitious and unrealistic. Results of several SCAP surveys are indicated. A brief look at possible modifications or improvements in Japanese agriculture and in the utilization of upland sites concludes the article.

1736 Tuma, Elias Hanna. *Twenty-six Centuries of Agrarian Reform: A Comparative Analysis.* Berkeley: Univ. of California Pr., 1965. xi, 309p.

This book develops a theory or set of generalizations about land reform with which to guide and evaluate specific reforms. The study is based on a comparative analysis of 8 reform movements including the postwar Japanese case, which is treated in chapter 9 (p.129–46). Tuma begins with an historical analysis of land tenure prior to the reforms. He then traces the political and legal maneuvering that resulted in the Land Reform Law of 21 October 1946, which he analyzes in some detail. Tuma next discusses the effects of the reform, which included an increase in owner-cultivated land, a reduction in the average size of Japanese farms, a rise in farm income, and a presumed increase in equality of ownership. The sociopolitical effects in turn included a weakening of the rigid village social structure and of the influence wielded by the former landlord class. In conclusion, the author speculates on the future prospects of the reforms and indicates that the continuing resentment of former landlords, the inefficient size of the average new holding, and low farm incomes make the new rural economic and social structure inherently unstable. Tuma's book is based on an earlier study entitled *Economics, Politics, and Land Tenure Reform: A Comparative Study* (542p.), which he submitted as a doctoral dissertation to the University of California at Berkeley in 1962. (Abstracted in *Dissertation Abstracts* 24:1007–8 [1963]; University Microfilms order no.63–6048).

1737 Wagatsuma, Sakae, and Katō Ichirō. "Post-war Agricultural Land Reform in Japan." In *Atti del Primo Convegno Internazionale di Diritto Agrario.* Milan: Giuffrè, 1954. vol.1, p.713–68.

Presented at the first International Congress of Agrarian Law held in Florence during the spring of 1954, this account reviews the background and enactment of Japan's postwar land reform and assesses some of its results. The authors first describe the conditions of Japanese tenants before the reform, emphasizing the personal relations that existed between the landowners and their tenants as well as the inability of most farmers to improve their lot. Wagatsuma and Katō then turn their attention to the legislation enacted by the Diet in October 1945 and explain why the occupation authorities found it inadequate. Subsequent SCAP directives, Japanese government legislation during 1946, the implementation of the agricultural land reform program, and the steps which were taken to insure the enforcement of the agricultural land laws are also discussed in considerable detail, and in their conclusion the authors seek to evaluate the success of the reforms themselves. From a legal standpoint, the reforms fostered owner-farming to such an extent that the large majority of Japanese farmers presently own the land which they cultivate. Economically speaking, however, the program did not radically alter the amount of land available to a single farming family. Finally, while the reforms did not immediately produce a modern social structure within Japan's farming villages, they did eliminate many of the obstacles to democratization and modernization. The privileges of the landowning class greatly decreased, and those of the farmers themselves increased considerably. Generally speaking, therefore, the land reform as a political reform has succeeded.

Waln, Nora. "The Grass Roots Revolution in Japan." 1949. *See* no.616.

1738 Williamson, Mark B. "Land Reform in Japan." *Journal of Farm Economics* 33:169–76 (May 1951)

This article is an evaluation of the land reform program carried out by SCAP. The author outlines the background of the program, the steps initiated by SCAP, and the accomplishments. Williamson concludes with an evaluation of the entire program and mentions that land reform was not meant to be the panacea for all the problems of agriculture in Japan. He then outlines various SCAP programs which he felt would have brought about the long-range stabilization of Japan's agricultural sector.

1739 Wolpert, V. "Land Reform in Japan." *Eastern World* 3:36–37 (Dec. 1949)

Wolpert asserts that "the land reform carried out in Japan during the last 3 years may become a vital factor in influencing the entire social structure of the country, provided that the benefits of the reform outlast the Occupation, and provided that the reform will be followed by further measures for the progressive development of rural Japan." He describes the prewar conditions of tenancy and overcrowding that led to the passage of the Land Reform Law, and points out its major features. He indicates that the law dealt a severe blow to "reactionary forces in Japan's agricultural life," as did the Agricultural Co-operative Association Law which the Diet subsequently passed in November 1947. The latter sought to assist farmers in borrowing money and in acquiring new farming techniques; without it, the land reform would have remained only a half measure. Through these two laws, Wolpert concludes, the occupation authorities hope to have established "a basis for democracy in Japan's villages, and at the same time, by turning tenant farmers into owner-farmers, to make them immune against Communist doctrine."

LABOR UNIONS AND LABOR CONDITIONS

Another series of basic changes attempted by SCAP lay in the field of labor union organization. While unions had existed in prewar Japan, their numbers and impact were small and their legal status dubious. During the war such unions either dissolved or were merged with the National Labor Front. It was the policy of the occupation, however, to encourage the development of labor unions and, as a consequence, they sprang up on all sides soon after the end of the war. From the beginning most of them had political as well as economic objectives which constantly involved them in the larger political arena. Their evolution is best understood, consequently, in terms of the parallel and related activities of political parties (p.452) and of developments on the political front in general (p.152).

1740 Amis, Robert T. "Japanese Labor in 1950." *Monthly Labor Review* 71:445–49 (Oct. 1950)

A condensation of a report to the thirty-third session of the International Labor Organization presented in June 1950 by the author, who was the director of the Labor Division of the Economic and Scientific Section of SCAP. The report summarizes general labor conditions for the year, particularly developments in the trade union movement whereby the anti-Communist forces regained control of the labor movement and whereby a complete reorganization of trade union federations "strengthening labor's position through a united front, more concrete organizational structure, and more responsible leadership" was brought about. There is a brief discussion of labor relations and the right of most workers (except government employees) to negotiate collective bargaining contracts. Finally, the author discusses amendments and revision of the present labor laws since no new basic legislation was enacted during 1950.

1741 Ayusawa, Iwao Frederick. *A History of Labor in Modern Japan*. Honolulu: East-West Center Pr., 1966. xvi, 406p.

Written by an internationally renowned authority, this publication is a historical account of organized labor in Japan from the Meiji Restoration through 1962. Chapter 5 (p.232–301), entitled "From Surrender (1945) to the Outbreak of the Korean War (1950)," examines in some depth significant developments in the labor movement and related occupation policies during the early postwar years. Ayusawa begins this portion of his account with a description of early SCAP and Far Eastern Commission principles regarding trade union activity and with a discussion of MacArthur's policies implementing the Potsdam Declaration. He reviews the establishment of the Rōmu Hōsei Shingi Kai (Labor Legislation Council) in late 1945, the drafting of major labor laws, the rapid development of trade unions, and the spread of labor unrest and disputes in 1946. Viewing the ill-fated, Communist-led plan for staging a spectacular general strike on 1 February 1947 as a turning point in SCAP policy towards labor, he devotes several pages to the development of this labor offensive, MacArthur's move to ban the strike, and the subsequent rise of the Mindō and Zenrōren movements. The author then focuses on MacArthur's letter of 22 July 1948, addressed to Premier Ashida, which prohibited strikes by government and municipal employees and which signaled the beginning of an increasingly strong control by occupation authorities of organized union activities. Ayusawa concludes chapter 5 with a study of subsequent changes in the Japanese government's own labor policy, of continuing frictions in the labor movement, and of Sōhyō's formation in 1950.

1742 ——. "Organized Labor in Present-day Japan." *Contemporary Japan* pt.1, 25, no.4:564–82 (Mar. 1959); pt.2, 26, no.1:66–81 (Aug. 1959); pt.3, 26, no.2:267–82 (Dec. 1959); pt.4, 26, no.3:482–501 (May 1960); pt.5, 26, no. 4:710–29 (Nov. 1960); pt.6, 27, no. 1:83–114 (May 1961). Subsequently published under the title *Organized Labor in Japan*. Tokyo: Foreign Affairs Association of Japan, 1962. 2v.

Ayusawa traces in more or less chronological fashion the development of organized labor in Japan through 1960. He begins by covering in parts 1 and 2 labor's general strike plot of February 1947 which ended in fiasco because of MacArthur's intervention, labor developments during the ensuing 3 years, the Korean War and its impact on labor, and the strong opposition of labor together with various leftist groups within Japan to the terms of the peace treaty. The remainder of the article does not deal specifically with the occupation but does shed light on the economic consequences of peace for Japan and the continuing role of organized labor in the country's politics.

1743 ——. *Post-war Developments in Organized Labor*. Tokyo: Foreign Affairs Assn. of Japan, 1953. 110p.

In the first half of the book, the author covers the origins and development of postwar unions under SCAP's protection and encouragement. He explains the growth of enterprise unions and the rise of politically oriented labor federations, and he accounts for changes in civil service workers' status. The remaining portion contains the transcripts of the Trade Union Law, Labor Relations Adjustment Law, and Labor Standards Law.

1744 Azuma, Mitsutoshi. "Labor Legislation in Japan." *Annals of the Hitotsubashi Academy* 1:181–95 (Apr. 1951)

Azuma Mitsutoshi, professor of civil and labor law, reviews postwar labor legislation in relation to labor legislation prior to the war, particularly noting the constitutional guarantee of fundamental rights of labor.

1745 Camacho, Martin Thomas. *The Administration of the SCAP Labor Policy in Occupied Japan*. Ph.D. dissertation, Harvard Univ., 1954. v, 783p.

Camacho describes, analyzes, and criticizes the structure, policy aims, administrative procedures, and political environment of the SCAP agencies concerned with labor problems. From December 1948 to May 1951 he was director of labor and labor relations in the Kantō Military Government and Civil Affairs Region. His data were derived from official SCAP documents, materials issued by Japanese authorities, and his own interviews, notes, and observations.

Available at the Harvard University Archives, Widener Library, Cambridge, Massachusetts.

Collier, David S. *The Politico-Economic Position of Japan*. 1953. See no. 1637a.

Costello, William. *Democracy vs. Feudalism in Post-war Japan*. 1948. See no.546.

1746 Daily Labor Press, Inc., ed. *The Labor Union Movement in Postwar Japan*. Tokyo: Daily Labor Pr., 1954. 97p.

This publication first presents an overview of general trends in the postwar Japanese labor economy beginning with a picture of the losses caused by the war and demonstrating with the aid of numerous tables what has happened in the areas of economic recovery, population and employment, standard of living, and the development of labor unions and labor disputes since the end of the war. The authors then discuss the postwar Japanese labor union movement in detail, dividing its history into 3 periods with emphasis placed on occupation labor policy and SCAP directives and the evolution of this policy. Chapter 3 examines the major national labor organizations in Japan in terms of the circumstances leading to the establishment, activities and main principles and views of each organization. The authors acknowledge that the labor policy of the occupation was primarily responsible for the present stage of development of the Japanese labor movement. In addition to describing the progress made under SCAP's protection and patronage, the authors point out how the occupation's labor policy was inappropriate in a number of cases.

1746a Deverall, Richard L. G. "MacArthur and the Japanese Unions." *America* 80: 509–11 (12 Feb. 1949)

Deverall, the chief of labor education in occupied Japan for a period of 2 years, tells how MacArthur blocked a Soviet attempt to seize Japan through the labor unions.

1747 Duke, Benjamin C. *Japan's Militant Teachers: A History of the Left-wing Teachers' Movement*. Honolulu: Univ. Pr. of Hawaii, 1973. xvi, 236p. (An East-West Center Book)

Part 1 of this study (p.3–72) traces the origins and growth of the left-wing teachers movement from its prewar beginnings through its postwar rebirth under SCAP's aegis. The early occupation period witnessed a good deal of competition among newly-formed leftist, moderate, and conservative teachers' groups for influence within the teaching profession. At this time, the overwhelming concern of the teachers was simply the matter of their survival as inflation eroded their already minimal fixed salaries. From 1947 onwards, however, political issues began to dominate the educational world as teachers took stands on the reforms being carried out by SCAP. The left-wing teachers, through the Japan Teachers Union (Nikkyōso), at first allied themselves with SCAP. According to Duke, however, as economic conditions deteriorated and the cold war began to affect SCAP policy, Nikkyōso became increasingly militant and SCAP became more nervous about the union's heavy Communist membership. As a result, the final years of the occupation, which Duke discusses in his fourth chapter (p.75–99), were marked by growing tension between SCAP and the union—a relationship that has carried over into the postoccupation period (to which the remainder of the book is devoted) in the form of periodic confrontations between the militant teachers and the Japanese government over both economic and ideological issues. A selection of documents, many of them related to SCAP directives and occupation period reforms, supplement this work. The book itself represents a revised and expanded version of the author's Ph.D. dissertation entitled *The Japan Teachers Union: Twenty Years of Militancy 1947–1967* (Univ. of London, 1969; 328p.).

1748 Eby, Kermit. "The Labor Movement in Japan." *Asia and the Americas* 46: 399–401 (Sept. 1946)

The author studied and observed the labor unions when he visited occupied Japan as a member of the U.S. Education Mission. The introductory section of his article discusses the development of the labor union movement in the 1920s and 1930s and labor's situation at the end of the war. He outlines MacArthur's labor policy and the terms of the new trade union bill which encourages the labor union movement; he describes meetings with numerous labor leaders of all political persuasions and discusses their attitudes and preoccupations. The last section defines the uniquely Japanese labor technique of production control and the isolation which the Japanese unions feel from the international labor union movement. The author lists 3 general recommendations with regard to labor: (1) the postwar economy must give the laborers a stake in a democratic order; (2) the Japanese labor movement must feel that it has friends in the overseas democracies; and (3) Japanese labor must be given the tools to do the job, i.e., they must be taught the most modern labor union practices and techniques.

1749 Edwards, Marie Alice. *Political Activities of Japanese Postwar Labor Unions.* Ph.D. dissertation, Northwestern Univ., 1956. 470p. (Abstracted in *Dissertation Abstracts* 17:393-94 [1957]; University Microfilms order no.18,981)

In this description of postwar Japanese labor unions, the author first examines the factors inhibiting the development of a democratic labor movement. They include the absence of a union tradition among working people, their lack of experience with union functions, the slow recovery of the postwar Japanese economy, and the persistence of feudal relationships between employer and employee. As a result of these factors, the labor union movement sought to achieve political rather than social objectives. Most unions supported the Socialist party. A lengthy discussion of the 2 major union federations, the General Council of Japanese Trade Unions (Sōhyō), and the Japanese Trade Union Congress (Zenrō), is included.

Eidus, Khaim. "General MacArthur's Campaign against the Japanese Working Class." 1950. *See* no.588.

1750 Farley, Miriam Southwell. *Aspects of Japan's Labor Problems.* With a supplement by William T. Moran. New York: Day, 1950. x, 283p.

A balanced, introductory survey of the Japanese labor movement from the beginning of the occupation through 1950. Farley was a former researcher for the American Institute of Pacific Relations and worked in SCAP on labor and related problems. She treats the major developments of Japanese labor through 1948. Developments in 1949 and 1950 are covered by another occupationnaire, William T. Moran. Farley begins with a brief sketch of prewar labor organization and the postwar economic and political background and then discusses occupation policy toward labor in 1945-47, the growth of labor organization in 1945-46, the nature of labor disputes, the "labor offensive" of 1946-47, and SCAP's encouragement of the formation of different kinds of labor unions such as the All Japan Newspaper and Radio Workers' Union, the All Japan Electric Industry Workers' Union, the Federation of Government Railway Workers' Unions, and the All Japan Seamen's Union. Also dealt with are labor unrest within the government and SCAP's ban of a general strike planned for 1 February 1947, the Katayama cabinet's handling of organized labor, and SCAP's stricter policy on union rights for government employees after 1948. The authors base their presentation primarily on SCAP publications such as *Summation of Non-Military Activities in Japan, Japanese Economic Statistics,* and *Labor Division Activities and Labor Department in Japan* published by SCAP's Economic and Scientific Section, and on Japanese and American press reports in the *Asahi Shimbun,* the *Nippon Times,* the *New York Herald Tribune,* and the *New York Times.* Appendixes include the full texts of the Far Eastern Commission's policy statement on principles for Japanese trade unions adopted in December 1946, MacArthur's statement of 31 January 1947 banning a general strike, MacArthur's letter to Prime Minister Ashida of 22 July 1948 urging the revision of the National Public Service Law, and the text of the Trade Union Law as revised in 1949.

1751 ———. "Japanese Political Issues Present Dilemma for U.S." *Foreign Policy Bulletin* 28:1-2 (10 Dec. 1948)

The recent and gradually increasing conflict between the Japanese government and organized labor is the topic of this article. After a discussion of the most important political parties and their platforms and of the most powerful labor unions, the author discusses the reasons for the frequent clashes between the unions and the conservative Yoshida government. In addition, the author, a former member of the SCAP staff, attempts to define SCAP's stance on these economic and political issues. She believes that MacArthur has not backed reactionary elements in Japanese politics deliberately, but rather "in the interests of stability has tended to support whatever government was in power" with sometimes unfortunate results.

1752 ———. "Labor Policy in Occupied Japan." *Pacific Affairs* 20:131–40 (June 1947)

This article concerns SCAP efforts to develop among the working classes both the desire and the ability to effectively support a democratic philosophy and democratic institutions. The author discusses SCAP's 2-fold policy involving: (1) the removal of old restrictions against organized labor through such directives as the Removal of Restrictions on Political, Civil, and Religious Liberties of 4 October 1945, and (2) the positive encouragement of labor organization through such measures as the Trade Union Law of October 1945 or the Labor Relations Adjustment Law of September 1946. Also discussed are the recommendations of the Advisory Committee of American Labor Experts, which urged revision of factory legislation to raise minimum standards, the development of a constructive wage policy, and the development of efficient, modern machinery of labor administration, centering on the establishment of a Ministry of Labor. After outlining SCAP's aims, the author examines and contrasts SCAP's performance with those aims, concluding that its labor policy is, in general, a successful one. The article includes useful statistics on prewar and postwar union membership and a discussion of the development of the 2 major Japanese labor federations.

"General MacArthur's Letter to Prime Minister Hitoshi Ashida Concerning the Revision of the National Public Service Law, July 24, 1948." 1948. *See* no.1436.

1753 Gribov, B. "The Japanese Trade Unions." *New Times* no.16:12–14 (18 Apr. 1947)

Charging that "the American Occupation authorities are doing their best to prevent any real democratic reconstruction of the civic and political life of the country," this article concentrates upon the labor union movement in Japan. Three topics are discussed: (1) the origin of Japanese trade unions and their revival after the war, (2) the current 2–directional trends in the movement signified by what is termed the "progressive democratic" National Congress of Industrial Organizations and the "conservative reformers" of the Japan Federation of Labor Unions, and (3) the development of the strike movement culminating in MacArthur's 31 January 1947 order forbidding a general strike. In spite of what he terms SCAP efforts to subvert the laborers of Japan, the author insists that they will succeed.

1753a Harari, Ehud. *The Politics of Labor Legislation in Japan: National-International Interaction.* Berkeley: Univ. of California Pr., 1973. xiv, 221p. (Publications of the Center for Japanese and Korean Studies)

This study of Japanese labor policy investigates the interrelationship of politics at the local-provincial, national, and international levels as witnessed in the case of Japan's ratification of the International Labor Organization's Convention no.87 ("Freedom of Association and Protection of the Right to Organize") and the concomitant revision of several Japanese labor laws. In chapter 4—"The Allied Occupation"—Harari examines the occupation's labor policies and how they were affected by Japanese domestic politics, the international labor movement, and the advent of the cold war. At first, he writes, SCAP vigorously encouraged the growth of a strong, unified, and independent labor movement. As the unions became increasingly militant and as the international situation deteriorated from the American point of view, however, SCAP began to curb labor's influence by having the Japanese government enact a series of retrogressive laws which restricted certain kinds of union activities as well as strikes, and by encouraging the strengthening of various employers' organizations. One consequence of SCAP's action was the transplantation of American labor law into Japan. This, together with the subsequent efforts to assimilate it, "fostered the growth of a fragmented, highly complex, and often very confusing system of labor legislation" in postwar Japan. Harari's book is a revised and updated version of the doctoral dissertation he submitted to the University of California at Berkeley in 1968 under the title "The Politics of Labor Legislation in Japan" (Abstracted in *Dissertation Abstracts International* 30:1212A–13A [1969]; University Microfilms order no.69–14,902).

1754 Hepler, Chester W. "The Labor Boss System in Japan." *Monthly Labor Review* 68:47–49 (Jan. 1949)

SCAP efforts to eliminate the labor-boss system in Japan are discussed in this article written by the chief of the Labor Division, Economic and Scientific Section of the occupation. By the author's definition, a labor boss is "a contractor who in essence supplies nothing other than a work force which remains completely under his control." Involving unskilled workers at the lowest rung of the employment scale, it is an extension of the ancient social patterns of rural feudalism and the *oyabun-kobun* concept and is a system which SCAP intends to eliminate. The report discusses several measures enacted by the Japanese government in the constitution and the Employment Security Law of 1 March 1948 designed to abolish the labor-boss system. However, the author affirms that at present not more than 30 percent of all workers under the system have been freed and even these suffer discrimination from the regular skilled work force.

Hsieh, Chiang. "Post-war Developments in the Japanese Textile Industry." 1950. *See* no.1879.

International Labor Office. "A Survey of Economic and Social Conditions in Japan." 1949. *See* no.1536.

1754a Ishino, Iwao. "Motivational Factors in a Japanese Labor Supply Organization." *Human Organization* 15:12–17 (Summer 1956)

Ishino finds a change in the motivations of boss-controlled workers during the occupation toward an incentive system that approximates "rationality" and approaches the classical "wage theory" of motivation. The decline in the power of labor gang bosses, in his view, is attributable not only to direct occupation reforms but also indirectly to a broader movement under occupation stimuli towards a more flexible institutional structure surrounding all workers.

1754b ———, and John W. Bennett. *The Japanese Labor Boss System: A Description and a Preliminary Sociological Analysis.* Columbus: Ohio State Univ., Dept. of Sociology, 1952. iv, 67p. (Ohio State Univ. Research Foundation project 483, report no.3; Office of Naval Research project NR 176–110, interim technical report no.3)

This report consists of a generalized description, some typical case studies, and a preliminary theoretical interpretation of the Japanese "labor boss" system. Considerable attention is focused upon the *kumi* (the association of a labor supplier and a group of workers who are formally related through *oyabun-kobun* ties)—the primary organization of the labor-boss system—and upon related secondary organizations. The materials covered in this report were collected by staff members of SCAP's Public Opinion and Sociological Research Division in 1950–51 and subsequently were incorporated in the authors' publication *Paternalism in the Japanese Economy: Anthropological Studies of Oyabun-Kobun Patterns* (1963) (no. 1912).

1755 "Japan: Labor Aspects of the Economic Emergency Program." *Monthly Labor Review* 65:337–40 (Sept. 1947)

A detailed description of the 8-point program devised by the coalition cabinet headed by the Social Democrat Katayama Tetsu for the purpose of dealing with the mounting economic crisis in Japan. Although the program covers a wide range of economic and social measures, only those aspects directly related to Japanese labor are handled in this report, i.e., provisions of section 3 for revision of the price and wage structure, provisions of section 5 for the increase of production and productivity, and provisions of section 6 for the security of working people. Also considered are the contents of the government's "white paper" of 4 July 1947 informing the Japanese people of their critical economic situation.

1756 Japan. Ministry of Labor. Liaison Affairs Section. *The Japan Labor Legislation* [sic]. 1st ed. Tokyo: Takehiko, 1950. 673p. In English and Japanese.

The texts of the most important postwar legislation on Japanese labor may be found in the present volume. The 1950 edition was unavailable for examination, but subsequent editions which sought to bring that one up to date included the following laws and ordinances passed between 1945 and 1949 and presumably incorporated in this publication from the beginning: (1) the constitution of Japan; (2) Ministry of Labor Establishment Law (Law no.162 of 31 May 1949); (3) Trade Union Law (Law no. 174 of 1 June 1949) together with its enforcement order (Cabinet Order no. 231 of 29 June 1949); (4) Labor Relations Adjustment Law (Law no.25 of 27 Sept. 1946) and its enforcement order (Imperial Ordinance no.478 of 11 Oct. 1946); (5) Public Corporation and National Enterprise Labor Relations Law (Law no.257 of 20 Dec. 1948); (6) Labor Standards Law (Law no.49 of 7 Apr. 1947) and its enforcement ordinance (Ministry of Welfare Ordinance no.23 of 30 Aug. 1947); (7) Ordinance on Industrial Safety and Hygiene (Ministry of Labor Ordinance no.9 of 31 Oct. 1947); (8) Ordinance on Dormitory Attached to Enterprise (Ministry of Labor Ordinance no.7 of 31 Oct. 1947); (9) Workmen's Accident Compensation Insurance Law (Law no.50 of 7 Apr. 1947); (10) Employment Security Law (Law no.141 of 30 Nov. 1947); (11) Unemployment Insurance Law (Law no.146 of 1 Dec. 1947) and its enforcement ordinance of 1 June 1949; and (12) Emergency Unemployment Countermeasures Law (Law no.89 of 20 May 1949).

1757 "Japanese Teachers Study AFT Organization." *American Teacher* 31:18–19 (Mar. 1947)

This brief editorial describes some of the recent efforts on the part of Japanese teachers to develop teachers' unions in order to deal more effectively with "the problems of reorganizing Japanese education along democratic lines, reconstructing school buildings, obtaining educational supplies . . . and improving their own economic status." The writer discusses some of the demands upon the government by the 2 most important teachers' unions and cites the encouragement of such unions given by the members of the U.S. Education Mission to Japan.

1758 "Japan's Postwar Labor Movement." *Amerasia* 10:179–85 (Dec. 1946)

This report is written to refute English-language press reports and SCAP releases which the author believes give "a highly distorted version of the aims and activities of the Japanese trade unions" and picture them as trying to seize political power. The article considers initial SCAP policy toward the formation of labor unions, provides statistics showing the growth in labor union membership, and discusses such topics as the labor technique of "production control" and the development of national labor organizations. The organizational structure and development of the 3 most important labor organizations, the Congress of Industrial Unions, the National Federation of Labor, and the Japan Congress of Labor, are given particular attention. Finally, the author attempts to answer the charge that Japanese labor activity is political and, therefore, dangerous, by citing examples showing that Japanese labor was forced to take political action because political action had been taken against it by the Japanese government and SCAP authorities.

1758a Katayama, Tetsu. "Dawn for Our Labour Movement." *Contemporary Japan* 15:58–73 (Jan./Apr. 1946)

Katayama, a lawyer and the secretary-general of the Japan Socialist Party, first summarizes the history of the Japanese labor movement, then offers some comments on the December 1945 labor law. According to Katayama, the Shidehara government is performing well from labor's point of view, for the new labor law contains several progressive amendments which were initiated by the government itself. Their provisions include (1) guarantees of the right to organize unions and to bargain collectively; (2) the placing of union activities under the general criminal code (rather than the enactment of separate standards for labor); (3) the right of government officials (excluding police, fire, and prison officials) to organize unions; and (4) the elimination of portions of the draft that would have made unions and their members liable to the payment of indemnities when strikes were conducted while arbitration was in progress. The new law comes 20 years later than it should have, but labor has few complaints about it and management has no defensible objections.

1759 Kennard, A. "Strikes and the Japanese Labour Movement." *Nineteenth Century* 140:147–51 (Sept. 1946)

Some significant characteristics of prewar labor unions in Japan are discussed so as to provide an understanding of the nature and history of the organizations that SCAP was trying to revitalize. The author describes the formation of the first union in 1897 and the subsequent development of important labor organizations such as the Yūaikai, the Federation of Labor (Sōdō Sōdōmei), and the Government Labor Front (Sangyō Hōkokukai). He concludes that the flaw throughout the history of the labor movement was that "it has lacked leadership both in the industrial and the political fields" and believes that it will be an extremely difficult task for the occupation authorities to make the labor unions operate in a democratic fashion.

1760 Kennedy, John. "Labour Crisis in Japan." *Eastern World* 3:4–6 (Sept. 1949)

This article chronicles the swift growth of Japan's trade unionism under the occupation. Statistics extend to March 1949. The recovery from wartime repression began with the 4 October 1945 SCAP directive to remove restrictions on personal liberties. SCAP policy, abetted by MacArthur's personal influence, led to Diet passage of the Trade Union Law in December 1945. In September 1946, a somewhat retrogressive Labor Relations Adjustment Law was passed. A Ministry of Labor was created in 1947. The general picture is one of SCAP pressure to overcome Japanese reluctance to accept or to enforce trade unionism. The writer, who sees the working class as the "buttress of democracy," looks forward to the end of the occupation with misgivings.

1761 Kitamura, Fusako. *A Study of the Japan Teachers Union and Recommendations for Improvement*. Ed.D. dissertation, Columbia Univ. Teachers College, 1962. 605p. (Abstracted in *Dissertation Abstracts* 23:4189 [1963]; University Microfilms order no.63–2264)

Kitamura analyzes the organization and policies of the Japan Teachers Union and suggests ways in which the union might be strengthened and improved. She submitted a series of recommendations on this subject to a group of 18 prominent Japanese and Americans who synthesized them into a new set of proposals. They include: (1) the decentralization of the power structure of the union; (2) a change in membership units from prefectural unions to either local unions or mixed membership unions similar to the National Education Association in the United States; (3) limitation of elected officials' terms in office; (4) a requirement that elected union officials take leaves of absence from teaching; (5) separation of the union from politics; (6) reevaluation of the code of ethics in accord with public opinion; (7) acceptance of national trends in educational philosophy as a guiding force in public education; (8) termination of peace education; and (9) open channels of communication between the union and the Ministry of Education. Although these proposals involve administrative and policy changes, Kitamura recognizes that the union must deal with cultural problems as well.

1762 Kudryavtsev, V. "The Struggle for Democracy in Japan." *Soviet Press Translations* 2:1–4 (15 May 1947)

Although critical of reactionary Japanese circles and the occupation authorities, the author is quite optimistic about the democratic movement which has developed in the year and a half since the capitulation of Japan. In an article which originally appeared in *Izvestia* on 5 March 1947, he discusses the growth of mass movements of workers and of employees' organizations, notes various demonstrations and strikes, and suggests that the coalition of the Yoshida government and SCAP authorities will soon lose power to parties more representative of the Japanese people.

1763 "Labor Conditions in Japan." *Monthly Labor Review* 61:651–68 (Oct. 1945)

A summation of the Japanese labor movement up to the end of the war, this study is both detailed and comprehensive. Three characteristics are cited as influential in Japanese labor: the newness of Japanese industrialization, a deeply rooted paternalism, and the domination of Japanese finance and industry by a few closely knit groups. Topics discussed include employment conditions; the labor force; occupational distribution of the peacetime population; employment in industry from 1931–42; employment exchanges; wages, hours and working conditions over the years; labor administration and legislation; labor and employer organizations; industrial relations; the cooperative associations; and social insurance. Statements are supported by much data and 7 tables chart such information as the population employed in 1930, the number of workers in specific industries 1931–41, the operation of public employment exchanges 1933–45, average daily wages and working hours by occupation, and conditions in Tokyo in 1940.

1764 "Labour Conditions in Japan in 1950." *International Labour Review* 62:31–43 (July 1950)

This report reviews information provided by Robert T. Amis, director of the Labor Section of SCAP, for the International Labor Organization. A short summary of trade union reorganization and unification around such organizations as Sōhyōgikai and Zenrōren is followed by a discussion of union education policies and of the implementation and expansion of collective bargaining techniques. Enforcement of labor legislation and trends in wages and workmen's compensation are dealt with. Employment practices, including the elimination of labor bosses, the creation of employment offices, and measures to combat unemployment, are presented. The final section examines vocational training and female labor.

"Letter of Soviet Representative in Allied Council for Japan to Gen. MacArthur." 1950. *See* no.1381b.

1765 Levine, Solomon Bernard. *Industrial Relations in Postwar Japan*. Urbana: Univ. of Illinois Pr., 1958. xiii, 200p.

The author presents a succinct picture of the postwar Japanese system of industrial relations, examining its origins and process of development. He treats such subjects as the institutions of management and organized labor, the interrelationships between employers and trade unions, the significance of collective bargaining, and the role of government. The first chapter, which describes the historical and environmental context of contemporary industrial relations, is of special interest to the study of occupied Japan. The author analyzes the reforms undertaken by SCAP in this field. SCAP's early guidance of postwar labor legislation is favorably described, while changes in SCAP's labor policies and attitudes are somewhat critically noted.

1766 ———. "Labor Patterns and Trends." *Annals of the American Academy of Political and Social Science* 308:102–12 (Nov. 1956)

Reasons for the Japanese worker's insecure position in spite of the occupation's policy which "called for deliberate efforts to strengthen the economic status and political effectiveness of the wage earner" are studied in this article. Japan's economic structure is briefly described and the labor market characterized with consideration given to wage and nonwage employment and their wage and benefit differentials. The role of SCAP in trade union membership is discussed along with the problem of the rapid growth of unionism during the early postwar years. In considering the problem of unity in the labor movement, the author notes that "enterprise" unionism is the principal feature of the Japanese labor movement. He discusses the major national developments in brief sketches of the national federations: Sanbetsu, Sōdōmei, Sōhyō, and Zenrō. Levine compares the political and economic aspects of Japanese labor activity, commenting particularly on collective bargaining. He concludes with a look at prospects for the future of the Japanese labor movement.

1767 ———. "Postwar Trade Unionism, Collective Bargaining, and Japanese Social Structure." In *Aspects of Social Change in Modern Japan*, ed. by Ronald P. Dore. Princeton, N.J.: Princeton Univ. Pr., 1967. p.245–85.

Levine indicates that no reform was more pathbreaking than the occupation's guarantee for all industrial workers of the right to organize autonomous unions, to conduct collective bargaining with employers, and to engage in disputes and strikes if union and management failed to agree. He reviews the results of these changes in terms of the extent to which the collective bargaining institution has grown, the structure the institution has taken, the process it represents, and the scope of the matter it deals with, and then with respect to their implications for Japanese social structure in industry.

1767a "MacArthur Quotes Roosevelt." *Economist* 155:330–31 (28 Aug. 1948)

While one of the occupation's principal objectives has been the development of a strong trade union movement, SCAP has been compelled to limit increases in the salaries and wages paid to State employees in order to balance the fiscal budget and to check inflation. Private Japanese concerns, however, have not only granted their employees substantial pay increases in order to avoid possible labor unrest but have also been providing full-time union officials with unprecedented privileges. These developments understandably have angered many State employees, some of whom undertook a go-slow movement on the state-owned railways which began to impede the country's industrial recovery. SCAP's reaction—a letter from General MacArthur to Prime Minister Ashida declaring that public servants were forbidden to strike or in any other way disrupt essential services—shocked many Japanese but has been accepted with far less opposition than had at first been expected.

1767b "MacArthur's Strike Ban Criticized by Ambassador Panyushkin." *USSR Information Bulletin* 9, no.5:161–62, 170 (11 Mar. 1949)

Ambassador Panyushkin, the Soviet representative to the Far Eastern Commission, elaborates in detail why the SCAP directive and subsequent Japanese laws restricting the participation of public employees in labor union activity are in violation of the 6 December 1946 FEC decision on "Principles for Japanese Trade Unions." He cites examples of the abuse of workers' rights that extend beyond the public service sector to back up his charges.

1767c "MacArthur's Strike Ban Rapped by Ambassador Panyushkin." *USSR Information Bulletin* 9, no.1:3 (14 Jan. 1949)

The Soviet representative criticizes his colleagues on the Far Eastern Commission for their support of the 22 July 1948 directive in which MacArthur ordered the Japanese government to ban strikes and collective bargaining by employees of the government and public enterprises.

1768 McCoy, Frank R. "Labor Policy in Japan." *Department of State Bulletin* 21: 107–8 (25 July 1949)

The statement reprinted here was made on 13 July 1949 in response to a speech in which the Soviet member of the Far Eastern Commission attacked the American and Japanese handling of labor unrest in Japan. The Soviet criticism had been provoked by incidents in Tokyo and Hiroshima in which force was employed to quell labor demonstrations. McCoy justifies the use of force by arguing that the incidents were caused by "lawless elements" engaged in "a centrally directed campaign to create fear, social unrest, confusion, and disorder."

1768a McPherson, William H. "Industrial Relations in Occupied Japan." In *Labor in Postwar America*, ed. by Colston Estey Warne. Brooklyn: Remsen Pr., 1949. p.623–39.

After describing the severe restrictions placed on Japanese labor activity during the prewar and wartime years, McPherson proceeds to a detailed discussion of labor during the first part of the occupation period. It has been necessary to build the labor movement virtually up from scratch, he writes, and progress has been slow and difficult. Nevertheless, SCAP took appropriate steps from a very early point on to stimulate its growth. Not only did it remove the legal barriers to union growth, but SCAP also enacted a trade union law in December 1945. McPherson explains the major provisions of this law and reviews their effects to date. He points out that the law has been subject to considerable criticism on account of its emphasis on restrictive and regulatory mechanisms, but that it has still proved successful in many respects. McPherson also pays some attention to the Japanese wage structure and SCAP activities in the area of standard and minimum wages during the course of his discussion.

1768b Markov, M. "The Japanese Labour Movement." *New Times* no.31:3–8 (28 July 1948)

The essay is divided into 4 general sections—all describing an aspect of the labor movement in postwar Japan. The first describes SCAP labor reforms which are regarded as minimal and token. The author discusses the inflation and the resulting conditions of poverty throughout Japan which he claims are ignored by the occupation authorities. The second section describes the development of the labor union movement from the inception of the occupation to the present. Although acknowledging that MacArthur's "dictatorial interference" in forbidding the general strike temporarily set back the union movement, the author insists that current unions are stronger than ever. Section 3 accuses SCAP of savagely persecuting trade union leaders, particularly Communist trade unionists, while the final section describes the actions of the Japanese government which the author regards as complete submission to the dictates of Washington.

1769 Moran, William T. "Labor Unions in Postwar Japan." *Far Eastern Survey* 18: 241–48 (19 Oct. 1949)

The writer, who served in SCAP's Labor Division in various capacities for 3 years, presents a progress report on the postwar labor movement in Japan. There is comprehensive coverage of SCAP's initial directives concerning labor and the formation and political orientation of national unions and federations, particular attention being paid to the 2 largest federations—the Japanese Federation of Labor and the National Congress of Industrial Unions. The author analyzes threats to union growth in Japan such as weak participation of the rank and file and company domination of the unions. There is also consideration of favorable signs such as increased internal democracy and improvement in the nature of agreements between labor unions and management. Following a discussion of the kinds of organizations and industries where unionization has been most successful, the author provides a useful summary of the development of labor union tactics such as collective bargaining and production control. The controversial order of General MacArthur which resulted in the Japanese cabinet order no. 201 outlawing acts of dispute by all government workers is objectively treated, and the criticism of this order by Japanese and American labor groups as well as by some SCAP officials is included in the account. The concluding paragraphs provide a valuable summary of labor's present situation and a discussion of possible future directions. The author believes that Japanese unions have remarkable resilience and ingenuity in coping with both internal and external problems and predicts that they will increase their political role in the future.

1770 Naoi, Takeo. "Unions and Democracy." *New Leader* 31, no.47:7 (20 Nov. 1948)

Naoi Takeo, the *New Leader* correspondent in Japan, provides an up-to-date account of the activities and objectives of the emerging trade union movement in Japan. He describes the major characteristics of the 3 leading groups—Sanbetsu, Zenkankō, and Sōdōmei—and seeks to explain the reasons for their respective positions. He criticizes many of the union leaders for encouraging the rank-and-file members to engage in political strife and notes that responsible trade unionists were beginning to question such political tactics. Naoi also points out that General MacArthur's 22 July decision to prohibit a general strike planned by the Communist party and Zenkankō had had a major impact upon the labor movement. As the author put it, MacArthur's action had helped the unions move "from political strife to sound trade unionism, from a policy of destructive unionism to one of constructive rebuilding, [and] from the dictatorship of the Communist Party to the democratic management of the trade unions."

1771 Ōkōchi, Kazuo. *Labor in Modern Japan*. Tokyo: Third Div. of the Science Council of Japan, 1958. 126p. (Science Council of Japan, Div. of Economics, Commerce, and Business Administration, Economics series no.18)

A historical survey by a professor at Tokyo University of Japanese labor conditions and the labor movement in Japan from the early Meiji period through 1949. It is supplemented by a chapter on labor developments between 1950 and 1955 written by Professor Solomon Levine of the University of Illinois' Institute of Industrial and Labor Relations. In this work, Ōkōchi argues that the nature of Japan's labor problems and the character of its labor movement have been the inevitable product of the special institutional forces which accompanied the process of Japan's rapid industrialization since early Meiji. They also have shaped the course of Japan's postwar industrial relations despite the deliberate efforts of the Allies to restructure her society. Chapter 3—"Labor Problems during and after World War II" (especially p.73–82) —deals with the occupation period itself and focuses on the development of trade unions, various disputes, and the problem of unemployment. The supplementary chapter, entitled "Japan's Labor Problems and Labor Movement, 1950–1955," carries Ōkōchi's analysis forward and deals in particular with the organizational characteristics and activities of Japanese trade unions before and after the conclusion of the peace treaty, the internal problems of Japanese unionism, and the economic status of Japan's industrial wage earners after 1950.

1771a "Panyushkin Cites Police Terror under MacArthur Policy." *USSR Information Bulletin* 9, no.14:429, 437 (29 July 1949); abridged version published under the title "In the Far Eastern Commission: Statement of A. S. Panyushkin" in *Current Digest of the Soviet Press* 1, no.29:32 (16 Aug. 1949)

Ambassador Panyushkin cites a number of examples of Japanese police brutality in suppressing "peaceful" union strikes and demonstrations. He attributes these excesses to the recently-passed Trade-union Law and the Labor Relations Adjustment Law. Panyushkin urges the Far Eastern Commission to consider these revised labor laws in terms of their negative impact on Japanese society.

Pevsner, Ya. "The Japanese Working Class in the Struggle against American Imperialism." 1950. See no.1583.

1771b "Principles for Japanese Trade Unions." *Department of State Bulletin* 15:1177–78 (29 Dec. 1946)

This article reprints the text of a policy paper adopted by the Far Eastern Commission on 6 December 1946 and released to the press a few days later. The policy recommendations urge strong efforts to encourage the formation of labor unions, to guarantee various labor rights, and to foster union activity in such fields as adult education and the dissemination of information about democratic processes. The FEC also recommends that employers be prohibited from playing a role in union organization and administration, and that no one subject to the purge directive be permitted to hold union office.

The Reminiscences of Jake R. Harold. 1962. See no.44m.

1772 Reubens, Beatrice G. " 'Production Control' in Japan." *Far Eastern Survey* 15:344–47 (6 Nov. 1946)

This article is a discussion of the Japanese labor tactic of "production control" whereby the workers, instead of striking and holding up production, lock out their employers and take over the operation of the company. When a settlement is reached, they turn it back to the owners. The author considers reasons for its increased use in postwar Japan, the areas in Japan where such methods are employed, the kinds of industries affected, as well as the attitudes of SCAP and the Japanese government towards this tactic of organized labor. The Takahagi coal mine dispute in March 1946 is cited as an illustration of the characteristics and complications of production control. Finally, the author attempts to forecast the future role of production control in the Japanese labor movement.

1773 ———. "Social Legislation in Japan." *Far Eastern Survey* 18:269–75 (16 Nov. 1949)

The author brings her experiences as an economist in the State Department's Division of Research, Far East, and as economic secretary to the Far Eastern Commission to bear on this account of postwar social reform in Japan. Her report includes a discussion of such factors as the occupation's time schedule, its general aims, and divergences of opinion among Americans within SCAP concerning the social reforms inaugurated after 1945. The greatest portion of the article concerns labor legislation—prewar conditions, as well as SCAP innovations—and there is a clear and concise summation of such important legislation as the Trade Union Law of 1945, the Labor Relations Adjustment Law of 1946, and the Labor Standards Act of 1947. The remainder of the article is devoted to a description of social insurance measures and compulsory insurance. The prewar situation is contrasted to the current one, and the author discusses the passage and implementation of such laws as the Daily Life Security Act of 1946 and the Employment Security Law of 1947. In looking forward to the future of such SCAP-inspired reforms, the author believes that further development will be a slow, evolutionary process and, of course, will depend on the economic recovery of the nation.

1774 Schwartz, Robert. "Some Aspects of Japanese Unionism during the Occupation." *Industrial Labor Relations Forum* 2:161–74 (Nov. 1965)

1775 "The Shape of Things." *Nation* 167: 197–98 (21 Aug. 1948)

This brief editorial criticizes the Japanese government's recent attitude toward unions among government workers. Acknowledging the fact that strikes against the government are banned even in the Soviet Union, the author nevertheless protests against the Japanese government's prohibition of all collective bargaining rights for government and municipal workers and the abolition of previously existing arbitration and mediation machinery. He considers such action at variance with the labor policies of the occupation authorities.

1776 Shiota, Shōbē. *Some Aspects of the History of the Labour Movement in Japan*. Tokyo: 1961. 40p. (Science Council of Japan, Div. of Economics, Commerce, and Business Administration, Economic series no.25)

This publication focuses on the history of trade unions, and strikes and lockouts in Japan.

1777 Shurcliff, Alice W. "Wage Developments in Japan during the Occupation." *Monthly Labor Review* 75:395–99 (Oct. 1952)

Alice W. Shurcliff of the U.S. Labor Department's Division of Foreign Labor Conditions, points out that trade union pressure and the rise in production and worker productivity contributed to the rapid increase in earnings during the occupation. The bargaining power of workers is much greater than it was in the prewar period as a result of trade union legislation and the labor education programs of the occupation.

1778 Smethurst, Richard Jacob. "The Origins and Policies of the Japan Teachers' Union 1945–56." In *Studies in Japanese History and Politics*, ed. by Richard K. Beardsley. Ann Arbor: Univ. of Michigan Pr., 1967. p.115–60. (Univ. of Michigan, Center for Japanese Studies, occasional papers, no.10)

Rampant inflation and poverty-level salaries played as large a part as SCAP's permissive attitude toward unionization in the launching of Japan's first teachers' unions. Discovering through experience that disruptive demonstrations were the most effective way to secure concessions from the government, the most militant of the unions—the Japan Teachers' Union (Nikkyōso)—grew to become the largest of all of Japan's labor unions. Both SCAP and the Japanese cabinet feared this union, as Smethurst shows in his study of the controversial evolution of Japan's postwar school boards.

1779 Soukup, James Rudolph. *Labor and Politics in Postwar Japan: A Study of the Political Attitudes and Activities of Selected Labor Organizations*. Ph.D. dissertation, Univ. of Michigan, 1957. 336p. (Abstracted in *Dissertation Abstracts* 18: 1479–80 [1958]; University Microfilms order no.58–1464)

This analysis of Japanese trade unions is divided into 4 parts: part 1 is an examination of postwar labor developments in general; part 2 deals with the political attitudes of major labor organizations and their leaders, particularly vis-à-vis issues of domestic economic policy, foreign policy, and the means for attaining political goals; part 3 is an analysis of union election activities, relations with political parties, etc.; and part 4 presents Soukup's conclusion that the activities of a majority of Japanese labor unions were hindering the development of democracy at that time, and that these unions were likely to become more moderate in the future.

The author has published the following articles based on the thesis: "Reflections on Japanese Labor." *Today's Japan* 5:59–66 (Jan./Feb. 1960); "Labor and Politics in Japan: A Study of Interest-group Attitudes and Activities." *Journal of Politics* 22:314–37 (May 1960).

1780 Starr, Mark. "Japanese Trade Unions Today." *American Teacher* 31:16–18 (Mar. 1947)

The author, the education director of a large American labor union and labor education consultant to SCAP in Tokyo, provides a brief summation of the development and growth of the trade union movement in Japan. He describes the political affiliation of the 2 leading union federations in Japan, Sōdōmei and Sanbetsu, and points out some of the drawbacks that are the result of the rapid growth of Japanese unions. On the whole, however, he is optimistic about the future of Japan's trade union movement whose members will be "the base of a rehabilitated Japan." The latter part of the article discusses the teachers' unions and describes some of the difficulties they encounter. There is a description of the achievements of such groups in terms of the political, social, and economic changes they have effected.

1781 ———. "Japan's Labor Unions." *Forum* 107:116–21 (Feb. 1947)

This informative study of the labor union movement in Japan includes a description of the development of the early labor unions in the twenties and thirties, their repression during the war years, and finally their reemergence in postwar Japan. The author provides useful labor statistics regarding wage rates as well as a table citing the number of unions in specific industries and their membership as of August 1946. He discusses the general aims of the unions (in terms of wages, hours, and other benefits) and then considers patterns of organization and operation that are unique to Japan such as the production control strike. Lastly, the author attempts to summarize the various attitudes of labor unions towards SCAP, pointing up both favorable and unfavorable views of its labor policy.

1782 ———. "Leaders of Labor in New Japan." *Labor and Nation* pt.1, 3:51–53 (Jan./Feb. 1947); pt.2, 3:14–15 (Mar./Apr. 1947)

The personalities and careers of 4 important Japanese labor leaders are the focus of this article. The 4 Japanese are Kikunami Katsumi, chairman of the Sanbetsu (National Congress of Industrial Unions) and president of the Newspaper and Radio Workers Union; Dobashi Kazuyoshi, president of the National Union of Government Communications Workers; Matsuoka Komakichi, president of Sōdōmei (National Federation of Labor); and Katō Kanju, an influential leader of the Social Democratic party. The author, an American labor leader, discusses these leaders' prewar activities as well as their present roles in the occupation endeavor to develop a strong Japanese labor movement. In addition, he considers their attitudes toward SCAP's labor policy. Finally, there is a brief discussion of General MacArthur's recent ban against the proposed general strike of government workers in which the author defends MacArthur's position.

1783 "The Statement Issued by General of the Army Douglas MacArthur in Connection with the February 1 General Strike of the Government and Public Office Workers Union, January 30, 1947." *Contemporary Japan* 16:103 (Jan./Mar. 1947)

In his explanation of why he prohibited a general strike of government workers, MacArthur asserts that if the strike had been allowed to take place, it "would produce dreadful consequences upon every Japanese home regardless of social strata or direct interest in the basic issue." Moreover, he claims the persons involved in the threatened strike are but a small minority and do not represent the Japanese people.

"Statement Issued by Mr. Blaine Hoover, Chief of the Civil Services Division, Government Section, GHQ, SCAP, Concerning the National Personnel Authority, August 24, 1948." 1948. See no.1444.

Supreme Commander for the Allied Powers. Monograph 28. *Development of the Trade Union Movement, 1945–June 1951*. 1952. See no.310.

———. Monograph 29. *Working Conditions, 1945–September 1950*. 1952. See no.311.

1784 ———. Advisory Committee on Labor. *Final Report: Labor Policies and Programs in Japan*. Tokyo: 1946. viii, 130p., app.

The Labor Advisory Committee recruited by SCAP early in 1946 to advise on labor policies in Japan and Korea presents a summary of its principal findings and recommendations regarding labor programs in occupied Japan. The report discusses the organization of the committee and the qualifications of its personnel in an introductory section. The body of the report presents the committee's observations on the overall progress of the SCAP labor program, its relationship to other occupation programs, and methods advocated by committee members to achieve proposed objectives and develop a more democratic labor movement. Considerable attention is paid to past progress, current problems, and future needs in such fields as labor relations, general employment policies, wage and salary policies, labor legislation, the Japanese labor exchange system, and government labor administration. Two appendixes present the texts of the first interim report on the treatment of workers' organizations since the surrender by the Economic and Scientific Section of SCAP on 30 June 1946, and the first interim report of the Advisory Committee on Labor of 5 April 1946.

Available at the Library of Congress, Washington, D.C.

1785 ———. Civil Information and Education Section. *A History of Teachers' Unions in Japan.* Mimeographed. Tokyo: 1948. v, 104p.

The Education Research Division of the Civil Information and Education Section of SCAP undertook this study in order "to record factually and concisely the development in Japan of teachers' unions." Apart from describing the origins, activities, and programs of the national unions, the mimeographed report describes in detail developments which have taken place between December 1945 and June 1947. It treats SCAP directives regarding teachers' unions, the structural organization and political orientation of important unions, the unions' relationship with the Ministry of Education, union demonstrations, and attempts at the unification and amalgamation of various unions. Fifteen appendixes provide information on such topics as the salaries of teachers by rank, the Tokyo consumer price index, and statistics on membership in the 2 national teachers' unions (Nippon Kyōiku Rōdō Kumiai and Kyōin Kumiai Zenkoku Remmei). The report also contains a bibliography which notes English-language publications on the subject and a list of union conferences held during the period 1946–47.

Available at the Library of Congress, Washington, D.C.

1786 ———. Economic and Scientific Section. *Japanese Labor Postwar Policies, Programs, and Developments.* Tokyo: SCAP, Aug. 1949. 1v.

This collection of materials relating to SCAP's labor program is divided into 5 general sections. Section A, entitled "Current Labor and Economic Conditions," presents selected data on wages, family income and expenditures, consumer prices, and production indices from 1937 through 1949. Also included in the section are several semimonthly reports of the Economic and Scientific Section's Labor Division in 1949, and a brief report on the Labor Division's activities to implement the economic stabilization program. Section B outlines SCAP's basic labor policies and includes statements by General MacArthur as well as extracts from relevant SCAP correspondence and Far Eastern Commission policy decisions. Section C discusses the responsibilities of the Economic and Scientific Section and the particular responsibilities of the Labor Division within that section. Section D provides an historical outline of the development of the Japanese labor movement and includes the texts of the Labor Division's reports of August 1946, August 1947, and August 1948. Finally, Section E presents a digest of the postwar labor legislation of the Japanese government including the Trade Union Law, the National Public Service Law, the Labor Standards Law, and the Japanese Unemployment Compensation Laws.

Available at the Library of Congress, Washington, D.C.

1787 ——. ——. *Labor Division Manual.* pt.1. Tokyo: 1949. 184p.

This manual is designed to give SCAP sections and the Eighth Army military government an integral picture of the development of the SCAP labor programs and policies. It is divided into 2 parts: part 1 deals with occupation policies and procedures on labor matters, while part 2 (which was unavailable for examination) covers relevant Japanese laws and regulations and other basic documents. Subjects covered in part 1 include SCAP's basic directives, the labor decisions of the Far Eastern Commission, the organization and operation of the Labor Division of SCAP's Economic and Scientific Section, the structure and functions of Japanese labor unions, labor relations, employment practices, and unemployment problems as well as wages and working conditions. This manual also discusses labor research, labor statistics, and SCAP efforts to promote an understanding of its labor programs and Japanese labor laws by both labor and management.

1788 ——. ——. *Statistical Survey of Labor Unions and Federations in Japan, 31 December 1947.* Tokyo: SCAP, The Section, Labor Div., 1948. 47p.

1789 ——. ——. Labor Div. *Labor Developments in Japan.* Tokyo: 1946– . annual.

1790 ——. ——. ——. *List of National Labor Unions and Federations in Japan.* Mimeographed. 31 December 1948. Record Group 5, Box 107. MacArthur Memorial, Bureau of Archives, Norfolk, Va. 17p.

All of Japan's national labor unions and federations are listed in this mimeographed report according to affiliation with the General Federation of Japanese Trade Unions, the National Congress of Industrial Unions, the Japan Congress of Trade Unions, or national industrial organizations not affiliated with any of the major federations. In addition, separate lists show nationwide unions organized on an enterprise basis and unions of national, quasi-governmental agencies (*Kodan*) which are not affiliated with national industrial organizations. The listings indicate English and Japanese names and cite local union affiliates and membership. There is also a general description of the organization of postwar labor unions, the development of industrial unions and major federations, attempts to unify the labor front in 1947 and 1948, and the democratization of the labor movement in late 1947 and 1948. The report contains 8 charts of labor unions by industry and by prefecture as of 31 December 1948.

1790a "Text of Soviet Statement on Violations of Decisions Concerning Japan." *USSR Information Bulletin* 8, no.18: 555, 562 (22 Sept. 1948)

Alexander Panyushkin, the Soviet representative to the Far Eastern Commission, calls upon the commission to request that MacArthur rescind his directive to the Japanese government of 22 July 1948 forbidding government employees to strike or to bargain collectively. According to the Soviet government, government personnel had these particular rights as a consequence of various measures adopted by the FEC to encourage trade unionism in Japan.

Uhlan, Edward, and Dana L. Thomas. *Shoriki, Miracle Man of Japan: A Biography.* 1957. See no.2163a.

U.S. Army. Eighth Army. *Collection of Messages.* 1947–51. See no.339.

1791 "United States Analysis of Soviet Statement, 158th FEC Meeting." *Department of State Bulletin* 21:108–13 (25 July 1949)

An exceptionally detailed, point-by-point rebuttal of Soviet criticism of the Revised Labor Relations Adjustment Law and the Revised Trade Union Law enacted by the Japanese government. American spokesmen reply to each point made by the Soviet government and quote the relevant sections of the law in question. The 9 areas of contention are: (1) the extent of the government's ability to declare an industry "public" and thus prevent strikes; (2) the power of employers to dismiss workers for their participation in labor conflicts; (3) the prohibition of labor disputes during periods of compulsory negotiation with employers; (4) the application of a fine up to 100,000 yen for failure to abide by the above prohibition; (5) the merging of labor relations committees into the Labor Ministry; (6) the power of government labor committees to intervene in trade union affairs; (7) the power of the Central Labor Relations Committee over all local committees; (8) the prohibition of 30,000 supervisory employees from labor union membership; and (9) punishment for the violation of the above prohibition by fines and imprisonment.

1792 Weigert, Oscar. "Labor Policies and Programs in Japan under the Occupation." *Monthly Labor Review* 64:239–54 (Feb. 1947)

Prepared by a member of the Bureau of Labor's foreign labor conditions staff, this article is a comprehensive account of SCAP's labor program to date. Following a description of the activities of the Advisory Committee on Labor in Japan from February through July 1946, there is detailed and comprehensive coverage of the SCAP program for labor-management relations, the Trade Union Act of 1945 and Labor Relations Adjustment Act of 1946, unionism in Japan, collective agreements, the settlement of labor disputes, and the inauguration of a new wage policy for Japan. The author discusses the future of protective labor legislation, employment policies, and the public employment service. He insists that SCAP's labor policies will succeed only if labor and management develop indispensable initiative and if the government is qualified and willing to support and control this initiative within the framework of broader national policies.

THE *Zaibatsu* DECONCENTRATION PROGRAM

The occupation authorities were at the outset convinced that political democracy could not be successfully introduced into Japan if it were not reinforced by what was frequently referred to as economic democracy. This meant primarily the establishment of strong labor unions on the one hand, and the dissolution of the great combines, commonly known as *zaibatsu*, on the other. SCAP accordingly launched a series of efforts from 1945 to 1948 to bring about the breaking of the ties that linked the component firms of these *zaibatsu* organizations. Beginning in 1947, however, strong opposition began to develop in the United States against this policy and, after the decision was taken to assist Japan's economic recovery, the deconcentration program was greatly deemphasized and in the end largely abandoned.

The interested reader will find related entries in the sections on reparations payments (p.379) and the state of the economy (p.481).

Andō, Nisuke. *Surrender, Occupation, and Private Property in International Law: An Evaluation of Some United States Practices during the Occupation of Surrendered Japan.* 1971. See no.2236.

1793 "Antitrust Fizzles in Japan." *Business Week* p.116–18 (29 Apr. 1950)

After briefly describing the prewar *zaibatsu*, this article assesses the outcome of SCAP's antitrust activities. While there appears to have been some progress, pressure from American businessmen and other factors have led to a softening of the antitrust measures. Many major industries remain untouched, and nothing effective has been done to undermine the central role of the old *zaibatsu* banks. The article concludes that the United States will have to maintain control for a long time in order "to keep Japanese business from reverting to some of its old bad habits."

1793a Ballantine, Joseph William. "Japan: Nationalization vs. Free Enterprise?" *Far Eastern Survey* 19:30 (8 Feb. 1950)

In response to Eleanor Hadley's article in the 14 December 1949 issue of *Far Eastern Survey* (no.1799), Ballantine makes the following major points: (1) No comprehensive changes in Japanese society can be brought about by forceful imposition from the outside; changes must be freely accepted by the Japanese leaders if they are to outlast the occupation. (2) The first priority of the occupation must be economic recovery, for unless the Japanese are assured of a "decent livelihood" the future of democracy and peace will remain in doubt. (3) Antitrust activities in Japan have gone far beyond what would be tolerated by public opinion if they were to be undertaken in the United States. (4) The program advocated by Hadley would more likely promote state socialism than free enterprise because the elimination of the entrepreneurial and capital resources of the *zaibatsu* would cripple development. The choice to be made, Ballantine concludes, is not between Hadley's "competition and private collectivism," but rather between the nationalization of industry and free enterprise. Finally he argues that nationalization would in the long run be more conducive to a resurgence of militarism than the *zaibatsu* ever were.

1793b Bisson, Thomas Arthur. *Zaibatsu Dissolution in Japan.* Berkeley: Univ. of California Pr., 1954. xi, 314p.

Perhaps the first serious study of the occupation's attempts to dissolve *zaibatsu* combines and their consequences. A former official of the Government Section of SCAP and a former research associate of the Institute of Pacific Relations, Bisson presents a careful analysis of SCAP's economic democratization program. He reviews the characteristics of Japanese financial combines since the Meiji Restoration and then describes the methods by which SCAP undertook their dissolution. Discussed are the hasty sweeping program of dissolution in October 1945, the shortcomings of the Yasuda plan approved by SCAP in November 1945, the quick dispatch in January 1946 of the Edwards Mission to recommend more effective dissolution programs, subsequent cautious steps taken during 1946, renewed emphasis on the program in 1947-48, and partial reversal in 1949-50. As he observes the trend toward financial regrouping in 1952-53, the author is pessimistic about the consequences of the SCAP program. The subjects dealt with include political relationships between Washington and SCAP and between *zaibatsu* and SCAP, *zaibatsu* family assets and their freezing, the functions of the Holding Company Liquidation Commission, the role of the Diet Supervisory Committee, disposal of securities, the Deconcentration Law of December 1947, purging of combine personnel, the Antimonopoly Law of April 1947, and the role of the Fair Trade Commission. Appendixes contain the text of major occupation policy statements on *zaibatsu* dissolution, the substance of the Yasuda plan and SCAPIN no.244, the statement on the Holding Company Liquidation Commission (HCLC), relevant Japanese laws, a list of actions taken by HCLC on 83 designated holding companies, a list of companies reorganized under the Deconcentration Law, etc. The end pocket contains charts illustrating the extensive ramifications of the Sumitomo, Mitsui Mitsubishi and Yasuda interests.

———. "Making Japan over." 1945. See no.65.

1794 "Breaking the Zaibatsu Monopoly." *Amerasia* 10:51-53 (Feb. 1946)

In his description of the directive intended to break the *zaibatsu* stranglehold over Japan's economic and financial life, the author notes that the occupation authorities apparently believe that they can deal with these great combines on the basis of American antitrust laws. He explains that it will be almost impossible to prevent the repurchase of securities by the *zaibatsu* through dummy purchasers, assuming that the government remains in the hands of men who have a stake in the preservation of these giant trusts.

Brochier, Hubert. "Les groupes financiers dans le capitalisme japonais d'après guerre." 1962. *See* no.1635.

Costello, William. "Japanese 'Plunderbund'." 1948. *See* no.547.

1795 Edwards, Corwin D. "The Dissolution of the Japanese Combines." *Pacific Affairs* 19:227–40 (Sept. 1946)

A discussion of SCAP's reasons for the dissolution program as outlined in the U.S. Initial Post-Surrender Policy for Japan and an analysis of the American policy toward the *zaibatsu*. The author speaks of the institutional rather than personal *zaibatsu* responsibility for the war in so far as the combines provided a setting favorable to military aggression. Three kinds of *zaibatsu* are distinguished. The first group are the 4 great enterprises of Mitsui, Sumitomo, Mitsubishi, and Yasuda; their history and areas of industrial development are briefly outlined. The second group consists of more recently developed commercial combines of smaller size such as Nomura, Riken, Okura, Nippon Nitrogenous Fertilizer, and Oji Paper. The third group consists of those combines that became important during the war or immediately preceding it, such as the Nakajima Aircraft Co. and Nissan enterprises. The author analyzes the complex corporate structure of these groups and the extent to which they controlled economic life in presurrender Japan through size, diversification, and their special relation to banks and to the government. Statistics of their degree of control of various industries are also provided. The article then discusses the SCAP actions which attempted to reduce *zaibatsu* power, i.e., the seizure of overseas assets, seizure of property for reparations, and the levying of special taxes. It analyzes the Yasuda plan for the voluntary dissolution of 4 large combines as well as the stopgap measures that were enacted before the dissolution program could be implemented. Finally, the author points up the difficulties in effecting permanent changes in the system and sets forth 3 indispensable factors if the SCAP program is to be successful: (1) the reorganization of the *zaibatsu* combines must take place rapidly; (2) innovations must assume the protective coloration of Japanese law and custom; and (3) the destruction of the *zaibatsu* must be part of an international attack of supranational cartels and combines.

1796 Far Eastern Commission. *Major Post-surrender Legislation Affecting the Zaibatsu* (MI–064/1). Washington, D.C.: 19 Jan. 1948.

Gayn, Mark. "Japan: Full Speed Astern." 1948. *See* no.1126.

1797 Hadley, Eleanor Martha. *Antitrust in Japan.* Princeton, N.J.: Princeton Univ. Pr., 1970. 528p.

An economist who worked in the Government Section of SCAP from April 1946 to September 1947 carefully traces the American reasons for the experiment described as the "most ambitious antitrust action in history." The author also analyzes the revival of the *zaibatsu* after the end of the reforming phase of the occupation in 1947. Among the topics treated are the historical development of Japanese combines and their social roles, Allied positions with regard to business concentrations in Japan, the work of the Holding Company Liquidation Commission, the dissolution of interlocking ownership and directorates, the work of the U.S. Mission on Japanese Combines in early 1946 and its contributions to the Deconcentration and Antimonopoly Laws of 1947, the Far Eastern Commission's 1947 policy decision on the subject (directive FEC–230), the Draper–Johnston

Mission, subsequent American withdrawal of support for directive FEC–230 on 12 March 1948, and the work of the Deconcentration Review Board. Having outlined the measures taken by SCAP to create a more competitive industrial structure and widen the distribution of income and ownership of the means of production, the author concludes that MacArthur had both successes and failures. Holding companies were dissolved and ownership in the modern sector was broadened, but the critical banking-industrial ties were not broken. Evaluating the continuing growth of monopolistic structures in Japan in the mid-1930s, the author notes that the Japanese government views the advantages of industrial concentration as very substantial and has adopted a policy of promoting mergers and cartelization. But at the same time Hadley feels that the Antimonopoly Law has helped the Japanese economy achieve remarkable growth and has been instrumental in opening the Japanese market to international competition. Appended are documents and statistical data relating to *zaibatsu* dissolution released by the U.S. and Japanese governments, the Far Eastern Commission, and the Holding Company Liquidation Commission.

1798 ———. *Concentrated Business Power in Japan.* Ph.D. dissertation, Radcliffe College, 1949. iii, 432p.

The author analyzes the Japanese combine and its management structure through case studies (with particular emphasis on Mitsui). The work is based on interviews with *zaibatsu* officials and SCAP personnel conducted while she was a member of the SCAP staff in 1946 and 1947. Hadley is concerned primarily with the nature of the *zaibatsu* before and during the war; however, because she was directly involved with the formulation and execution of SCAP antimonopoly and economic purge policies, her analysis gives insight into SCAP's perceptions concerning the role of the *zaibatsu* in Japanese society and in the war machine.

This dissertation is available at the Harvard University Archives, Widener Library, Cambridge, Massachusetts.

1799 ———. "Japan: Competition or Private Collectivism?" *Far Eastern Survey* 18:289–94 (14 Dec. 1949)

This article addresses itself to the question of whether the occupation has succeeded in destroying the Japanese combines or whether SCAP has largely abandoned this policy, as many critics charge. There is a discussion of the various steps that were taken by SCAP with emphasis on the program established by the Deconcentration Review Board which was organized after the Draper Mission's visit in May 1948. The author, formerly an economist on the staff of General Headquarters, SCAP in 1946 and 1947, defines 6 major objectives as of primary concern in SCAP's deconcentration program: (1) the dissolution of the top holding companies; (2) the elimination of intercorporate stock ownership and interlocking directorates below the top level; (3) elimination of *zaibatsu* family control; (4) reshuffling the executive personnel in combine enterprises; (5) breaking up the giant operating companies; and (6) the enactment of permanent antitrust laws. In her concluding remarks, she characterizes the deconcentration program that was originally conceived as "fairly adequate to accomplish its declared purpose." However, she maintains that in recent months it has been extensively modified and "even in its modified form it is still far from completion." To support such statements she cites comparative statistics indicating the deconcentration goal and the actual accomplishments, concluding that Japan's combines have been seriously affected "but have not been weakened to the point where restoration of the old pattern is impossible or even improbable." Finally, she reasserts the need for continuing the deconcentration program in order to achieve the major objectives of American policy. Two tables in the article present statistics of the Holding Company Liquidation Commission's report on the status of securities subject to liquidation as of April 1949 and a list of companies affected by the Excessive Concentrations of Economic Power Law as of August 1949.

For a response to Hadley's arguments, see Joseph W. Ballantine's article "Japan: Nationalization vs. Free Enterprise?" in the 8 February 1950 issue of *Far Eastern Survey* (no.1793a).

1800 ———. "Trust Busting in Japan." *Harvard Business Review* 26:425–40 (July 1948)

This article represents the author's effort to refute the opposition of some American political and business figures who protest that the SCAP-inspired legislation of December 1947, entitled the Elimination of Excessive Concentrations of Economic Power, is socialistic and even "un-American." She discusses the origins of the bill derived from the findings of the U.S. Mission on Japanese Combines which operated from January to March of 1946. The author then moves to a comprehensive analysis of (1) why SCAP is concerned with reforming the *zaibatsu*—one of the 4 chief power groups in presurrender Japan; (2) what steps it has taken to attack these cartels and eliminate intercorporate stock ownership and excessive corporate size; and (3) what problems remain to be solved including the problems of management control, capital formation, and the discovery of new and suitable Japanese investors. The author strongly supports MacArthur's efforts thus far and advocates continued SCAP support for competitive free enterprise as the only possible way to make democracy in Japan truly feasible.

1801 Hall, Peirson M. "The Japanese Zaibatsu." *Vital Speeches* 12:394–400 (15 Apr. 1946)

A speech delivered to the Los Angeles Bar Association on 28 March 1946 by a U.S. district judge who was a member of the 21-man reparations mission to Japan headed by Ambassador Pauley. In addition to providing relevant data on prewar and postwar industrial conditions in Japan, the speaker successfully evokes a picture of everyday life in Japan in the initial stages of the occupation. There is a general summation of the entire reparations issue involving such matters as the property which may be considered reparable and what nations are entitled to such reparations. In the opinion of Hall, "Japan, now at the close of the war, has by far more industrial capacity than she needs or has ever used for the civilian economy of the Japanese Home Islands. That excess capacity is reparable." Since it was one of the special functions of the judge to make a study of the control of Japanese industrial, economic, and political life by the *zaibatsu* families, the latter half of his speech concentrates on this particular area. He discusses the structure of the largest organizations, citing as illustration the Articles of Association of the Yasuda Hozensha, a top holding company, and also considers their involvement in prewar and wartime Japanese aggression. In conclusion he recommends that: (1) SCAP take absolute legal title to all stocks, bonds, and other securities owned or held by the *zaibatsu* companies; (2) all reparations claims, insofar as possible, be taken from *zaibatsu* companies; (3) after reparations, SCAP liquidate or sell all securities, properties, and enterprises other than government bonds of the *zaibatsu*; and (4) SCAP forbid indemnification by the Japanese government or the Bank of Japan to any of the *zaibatsu* for war damages, cancelled war contracts, confiscated properties, or government bonds. The speech offers valuable insight into the predominant mood of the Pauley Mission with regard to the reparations issue.

1802 Japan. Holding Company Liquidation Commission. *Final Report on Zaibatsu Dissolution*. Tokyo: 11 July 1951.

1803 ———. ———. *Rules and Regulations Concerning the Holding Company Liquidation Commission*. Tokyo: 1947. 86p.

1804 ———. ———, ed. *Laws, Rules [and] Regulations Concerning the Reconstruction and Democratization of Japanese Economy*. Tokyo: Kaiguchi Pub. Co., 1949. xxiii, 426p.

A collection of the English versions of some 40 major laws, ordinances, and regulations relating to the democratization and reconstruction of the Japanese economy which were issued between August 1945 and 20 December 1948. Introductory notes to the English edition are provided by the Holding Company Liquidation Commission. The compilation consists of 6 parts: (1) imperial ordinances based on the Potsdam Declaration; (2) dissolution of the *zaibatsu* combines; (3) democratization of securities; (4) prevention of monopolies and the promotion of fair trade; (5) postwar rearrangements of corporate enterprises; and (6) related prewar legislation. The English translations are taken from several sources, including the English edition of the *Official Gazette*, unpublished government translations, the Codes Translation Committee's work, and work done by the Holding Company Liquidation Commission's staff.

The Japan Who's Who and Business Directory, 1948. 1948. See no.557a.

1804a "Japanese Industrial Trusts." *Nation* 167:683 (18 Dec. 1948)

This editorial voices doubt over the optimism shown by SCAP about the progress of antitrust efforts in Japan. The abandonment of direct SCAP involvement in antitrust activities, which will hereafter be controlled by new Japanese laws and agencies, is seen as an effort to disguise a SCAP failure.

1804b "Japan's Zaibatsu." *Life* 19:51–54 (29 Oct. 1945)

This brief article reports on interviews conducted with selected moderate *zaibatsu* leaders who claim that the militarists forced the war upon them and that *zaibatsu* holdings should be retained to help Japanese economic revival.

1804c "MacArthur the Trust Buster." *Business Week* p.113–14, 116 (1 Dec. 1945)

This article begins with a summary of current SCAP antitrust activities. It then points out that these policies had been strongly opposed by Undersecretary of State Joseph Grew, who argued that the defeat and demobilization of the Japanese army and the destruction of Japanese war industries were sufficient. Grew's departure from the State Department, however, cleared the way for the adoption of the anti-*zaibatsu* policies. The article concludes with a series of questions about the contemplated program: Will *zaibatsu* families be compensated to such an extent that they will be able to recapture control after the occupation ends? What effect will inflation have on the bonds used to compensate them? How effective will the prohibition in fact be against stock ownership and management by members of *zaibatsu* families? To what extent will the impoverished Japanese public be able to absorb the confiscated shares offered for sale by the government?

1805 McCoy, Frank R. "U.S. Suspends Consideration of Proposal for Japanese Deconcentration of Finances and Industry." *Department of State Bulletin* 19: 768–69 (19 Dec. 1948)

McCoy's statement of 9 December 1948 to members of the Far Eastern Commission seeks to explain the action of the United States in suspending consideration of FEC–230. He reviews the significant progress attained by SCAP in breaking up the major *zaibatsu* and in securing passage of related Japanese economic legislation designed to insure that the deconcentration measures will not be reversed. He argues that the economic situation in Japan is changing and that the continuation of the deconcentration program in its present form would do more harm than good. He stresses that the American action should not be interpreted to mean that the program will be terminated in its entirety. Some firms still need to be reorganized, and some legislation must still be undertaken. Nevertheless, there will be no development of policy calling for further *major* steps in *zaibatsu* deconcentration.

1805a "Monopolies in Japan's Economic Structure." *Great Britain and the East* (Far East Issue) 62:46F–F47, 50F (Feb. 1946)

This article provides a review of the prewar structure and scope of the *zaibatsu* and a brief commentary concerning the activities of these monopolistic enterprises during the war. A few concluding remarks deal with postwar attempts to dissolve the *zaibatsu*.

1805b Neel, Samuel E. "Zaibatsu Control in Japan." *Journal of the Missouri Bar* 3:11–12 (Jan. 1947)

This article, written by a member of the special group of lawyers and economists who were sent to Japan to study the *zaibatsu* and recommend a program for their dissolution, is a summary of part of the report which the group prepared for publication as a State Department document (no.1809). It is devoted almost entirely to a discussion of the prewar legislation which not only permitted but even compelled many Japanese firms to participate in the formation of monopolies and trusts. Without these laws, the author explains, the *zaibatsu* would have been unable to achieve their phenomenal growth and their control of the major portions of Japanese industry and commerce deemed necessary for Japan's rapid industrialization. Neel classifies the existing laws into 4 broad categories and briefly examines their nature and intent. They are: (1) laws authorizing or creating outright government monopolies in various industries; (2) laws requiring government approval before a person or company can enter into or expand a business within a given industry; (3) national policy on special company laws (i.e., the formation of companies for specific purposes such as colonial development, banking, and communications); and (4) laws creating or giving broad grants of authority to control organizations, with power to make rules and regulations for the control of various industries or types of commercial enterprises. Almost every conceivable type of monopolistic practice and procedure frowned upon in the United States and specifically prohibited by American anti-trust laws, Neel notes, were found on the books by the time the occupation period began.

The Reminiscences of Joseph Ballantine. 1961. See no.44n.

1805c "Report on the Mission on Japanese Combines." *Department of State Bulletin* 15:823 (3 Nov. 1946)

This article summarizes and comments on the report presented to SCAP by the U.S. Mission on Japanese Combines (no.1809).

Salisbury, Laurence E. "The Zaibatsu as War-Makers." 1945. See no.120.

1806 Salwin, Lester N. "Japanese Anti-Trust Legislation." *Minnesota Law Review* 32:588–605 (May 1948)

Part 1 of this article briefly reviews the important events directly leading to the formulation and passage by the Diet on 31 March 1947 of the Act Relating to Prohibition of Private Monopoly and Methods of Preserving Fair Trade (Law no.54). This is followed by excerpts of editorial comments on the law which appeared in the English-language press of Japan during that winter and spring. The remainder of the article is devoted to a paraphrase of this act of Japanese anti-trust legislation. Salwin served during the occupation as an attorney on the staff of the General Counsel, Office of the Alien Property Custodian, and as Chief, Antitrust Legislation Branch, of SCAP's Antitrust and Cartels Division.

1806a Samain, Bryan. "Japan's Zaibatsu Are Still Thriving." *Great Britain and the East* 65:48 (July 1948)

American policies for breaking up the *zaibatsu* have failed. Both SCAP and the American public are becoming conscious of the indispensability of these trusts for Japan's economic rehabilitation. Nonetheless, in order to keep the *zaibatsu* from achieving too great a hold on the economy, SCAP should increase its supervision of the ex-*zaibatsu* employees who are working for various Allied control units and should insure that the occupation's economic policies are coordinated by implementing closer liaison between the military and civilian elements of the Allied forces.

1807 Strauss, Harold. "Big Business in Japan." *Nation* 163:470–72 (26 Oct. 1946)

The author, formerly a staff member of the Civil Information and Education Section of SCAP, discusses the recent trends in the attitudes of big business leaders in Japan toward socialization of the country's industry. He considers several reasons—both economic and political—why these capitalists were in favor of socialization or nationalization prior to June of 1946 and then briefly notes their change of attitude. The author attributes their recent opposition to nationalization programs to their realization that the whole nature of the occupation was changing and henceforth SCAP would be more lenient toward private business interests. This change, in the author's opinion, was due to "the pressure of international events, notably U.S.–USSR tension," with a consequent softening of SCAP's attitude toward the Japanese economy.

1808 Supreme Commander for the Allied Powers. *Deconcentration Review Board Messages.* Jan. 1948–June 1949. Blue Binder series. MacArthur Memorial, Bureau of Archives, Norfolk, Va. 1 folder.

This folder contains 3 unclassified radio messages sent by SCAP and the commander in chief for the Far East to the Department of the Army outlining detailed policies for the Deconcentration Review Board and the Japan Holding Company Liquidation Commission (26 Jan. 1948), discussing the first meeting between these 2 groups, and reporting the termination of the Deconcentration Review Board as of 30 June 1949 (30 May 1949).

———. Monograph 24. *Elimination of Zaibatsu Control, 1945–June 1950.* 1952. See no.306.

———. Monograph 25. *Deconcentration of Economic Power, 1945–December 1950.* 1952. See no.307.

———. Monograph 40. *Financial Reorganization of Corporate Enterprises.* 1952. See no.322.

Tiltman, Hessell. "Letter from Tokyo: What Is the Council?" 1946. See no.886.

1809 U.S. Mission on Japanese Combines. *Report of the Mission on Japanese Combines.* Pt.1, *Analytical and Technical Data.* Washington, D.C.: Government Printing Office, 1946. x, 230p. (Dept. of State publication 2628; Far Eastern series 14)

Known informally as the Edwards Mission or the Zaibatsu Mission, this group was sent to Japan by the State and War Departments from 6 January to 15 March 1946. The mission's primary purpose was to examine and evaluate the so-called Yasuda plan for voluntary reorganization, submitted in 1945 by the Yasuda combine, and to make recommendations regarding the scope of the whole *zaibatsu* deconcentration program, the manner of dissolution, future ownership and management, compensation for former owners, safeguards against revival of *zaibatsu* power, and means of encouraging the development of more democratic policies. The report sketches the structure of *zaibatsu* power, referring to relationships among *zaibatsu* groups and between them and the Japanese government. It describes financial institutions in Japan and their relationships with *zaibatsu* groups, and also discusses control laws. The report then suggests several potential groups which could take over part of the *zaibatsu* holdings, such as cooperative associations and small and medium-sized enterprises.

1810 Vernon, Raymond, and Carolene Wachenheimer. "Dissolution of Japan's Feudal Combines." *Department of State Bulletin* 17:55–60, 64 (13 July 1947); reprinted in U.S. Dept. of State. *Cartels and Combines in the Occupied Areas.* Washington, D.C.: Dept. of State, 1947. p.7–13 (Dept. of State publication 2889)

This study of the *zaibatsu* combines discusses the issue under 3 heads. The first presents an account of the early history and development of the *zaibatsu*. The second section considers the organizational structure of these companies, differentiating between the original *zaibatsu* and the newer ones resulting from the expansion of the Japanese empire in the 1930s. The final and longest section of the report considers SCAP efforts to dissolve the *zaibatsu*. The authors discuss the terms of the Yasuda plan as well as its weaknesses, the findings and recommendations of the U.S. State and War Departments' Mission on Japanese Combines which studied the situation early in 1946, and the work of the Holding Company Liquidation Commission. Although the authors believe that a basically effective policy has been formulated and much already accomplished, they nevertheless recommend the adoption of additional steps including the sale of the stock of *zaibatsu* companies, the expansion of sources of credit, an overhauling of the tax structure, and the reorientation of Japanese public opinion toward a *zaibatsu*-free economy.

1810a Vith, Fritz. *Zaibatsu: Die Auflösung der Familienkombinate in Japan.* Inaugural-Dissertation, Philipps-Universität Marburg/Lahn, 1957. ii, 136p.

This doctoral study of the *zaibatsu* problem from a constitutional and administrative standpoint focuses on the *zaibatsu* system, its development, and its structure; the American policy and program for breaking up these family financial combines; and the outcome of the programs which SCAP sought to implement. The appendixes of the dissertation contain a collection of documents, materials on the history of the Mitsui, Mitsubishi, and Sumitomo families, and a tabular summary of their spheres of interest.

Available at Marburg/Lahn, Universitätsbibliothek, no. 4° Z 58/12.

1810b "Who's Paying for Japan's Economic Democracy?" *Saturday Evening Post* 221:116 (14 Aug. 1948)

This editorial attacks many of the occupation's policies for their tendency to prolong the expensive dependence of a defeated enemy upon the United States. SCAP's purges, anti-*zaibatsu* measures, and reparations policies all tend to impede the economic recovery that is essential for an early end of the occupation. *Zaibatsu*-busting is particularly subject to criticism, the editors feel, for as one of our lessons in democracy we are teaching the Japanese "confiscation as national policy."

1811 Yamamura, Kōzō. "Concentration in the Postwar Japanese Economy: Comment." *Journal of Political Economy* 73: 523–25 (Oct. 1965)

This short article is a comment by Yamamura on an article by Eugene Rotwein, entitled "Economic Concentration and Monopoly in Japan" (*Journal of Political Economy* 72:262–77 [June 1964]). Yamamura feels that Rotwein's conclusions that further economic growth in Japan would continue to deconcentrate the Japanese market structure must be qualified. He points out weaknesses in Rotwein's methods and concludes that Rotwein has overstated the case for the continuing trend of deconcentration.

———. *Economic Policy in Postwar Japan: Growth versus Economic Democracy.* 1967. *See* no.1674.

1812 ———. "Growth vs. Economic Democracy in Japan: 1945–1965." *Journal of Asian Studies* 25:713–28 (Aug. 1966)

The author is concerned about the Japanese government's attempt to place highest priority upon rapid economic growth while neglecting economic democracy. Yamamura maintains that the occupation had set down certain guidelines in order to prevent the growth of prewar types of *zaibatsu*, but that the Japanese government had ignored them in order to maintain Japan's rapid economic growth. He specifically points out the lack of enforcement of antimonopoly legislation and the current tax policy which aids capital accumulation rather than ensuring "equality and justice."

1813 ———. "Market Concentration and Growth in Postwar Japan." *Southern Economic Journal 32:451–64 (Apr. 1966).

Yamamura of San Diego State College shows in technical economic language how the postwar Japanese economy returned to a market structure resembling that of prewar Japan despite the occupation's anti-zaibatsu program. It happened in 2 phases. Between 1950 and 1958 large firms sought to "rationalize" their structure, reducing the concentration ratios of the 10 largest firms at the cost of small-medium firms. After 1958, the balance of power began to shift in favor of the largest firms. This return to prewar patterns, the author adds, was officially sanctioned.

1814 ———. "An Observation on the Post-war Japanese Anti-monopoly Policy." *Indian Journal of Economics* 45: 31–68 (July 1964)

This article, part of the author's research project on postwar Japanese economic policy and growth, traces the gradual weakening of Japan's anti-monopoly policy in general and the relaxation of the 1947 Anti-Monopoly provisions in particular. An explanation for these developments is given which links the fate of anti-*zaibatsu* legislation with the country's rapidly changing economic situation. An attempt also is made to evaluate both SCAP's original policy and the policy which the Japanese government itself followed after the end of the occupation.

1815 ———. "Zaibatsu Prewar and Zaibatsu Postwar." *Journal of Asian Studies* 23:539–54 (Aug. 1964)

The author writes about the *zaibatsu* controversy in the Japanese postwar economy. He disagrees with those who claim there is a revival of the kind of *zaibatsu* that existed in the prewar period. Yamamura maintains that "The Zaibatsu . . . have been dissolved and have not revived." The author describes the extent of *zaibatsu* control in the economy and the extent to which he believes patterns of mutual stockholding and interlocking directorships still exist. Finally, he argues that the economy is no longer as concentrated as before and that the large companies have no monopoly on market power.

1815a Yanaga, Chitoshi. *Big Business in Japanese Politics.* New Haven, Conn.: Yale Univ. Pr., 1968. xi, 371p.

This study of the close relationship between business and government that enabled Japan to reemerge after World War II as a leading industrial and commercial power describes in detail the many ways in which organized business participates in the Japanese government and outlines the supporting role played by the Japanese bureaucracy. Yanaga's focus is on the 1950s, but his work is of considerable value to the student of the occupation on account of the information it offers on the fate of SCAP's *zaibatsu* dissolution policy (see chapter 6—"Anti-Monopoly Policy and Government-Business Collaboration"), on the role played by business groups in concluding reparations agreements with Burma, the Philippines, Indonesia, and South Vietnam that were more generous than the original government plans and that proved to be mutually beneficial (see chapter 8—"Southeast Asia Reparations Settlement"), and on the involvement of big business in the shaping of a peace treaty which would contribute directly to Japan's economic recovery and would insure the nation's future (see the first part of chapter 9—"United States–Japan Partnership").

1816 "Zaibatsu Revival?" *Oriental Economist* pt.1, 26, no.578:633–37 (Dec. 1958); pt.2, 27, no.579:10–12 (Jan. 1959); pt.3, 27, no.580:65–68 (Feb. 1959); pt.4, 27, no.581:122–24 (Mar. 1959); pt.5, 27, no.582:178–80 (Apr. 1959)

This 5-part series of articles describes developments in the mid- and late 1950s that were indicative of a rapid regrouping of the *zaibatsu*-affiliated companies. The biggest motivation for this group formation is said to be competition among big business. Particular attention is paid to the Mitsui, Mitsubishi, and Sumitomo group-affiliations.

1817 Zhukov, E. "American Aggression and the Remilitarization of Japan." *New Times* no.51:10–13 (20 Dec. 1950)

The economic policies of SCAP come under fire in this brief article. The author accuses American and Japanese monopolists of an open alliance. As proof of such a conspiracy, he cites the recommendations of U.S. Secretary of the Army Royall concerning the *zaibatsu* and MacArthur's termination of what the author believes to be a token organization—the Economic Deconcentration Board.

NATURAL RESOURCES IN GENERAL

In its concern first for sustaining the Japanese economy at viable performance rates and later for assisting its recovery, SCAP undertook a number of wide-ranging surveys of the country's natural resource endowments and circumstances. They were carried out with exemplary skill by the Natural Resources Section. The results are noted below. These entries frequently overlap in coverage with those in the two following sections as well as the section on land reform (p.544). The reader should take note that a complete list of the *Reports* (no.1829) and *Preliminary Studies* (no.1828) series published by the Natural Resources Section of SCAP is set forth in an appendix to the Ackerman entry (no.1818) below, in the SCAP publication *Japanese Natural Resources: A Comprehensive Survey* (no.1822), and in v.4, p.284–88, of the *Cumulative Bibliography of Asian Studies, 1941–1965: Author Bibliography* (no.2).

1818 Ackerman, Edward Augustus. *Japan's Natural Resources and Their Relation to Japan's Economic Future*. Chicago: Univ. of Chicago Pr., 1953. xxv, 655p.

An expanded revision of *Japanese Natural Resources: A Comprehensive Survey* (no.1822) published by the Natural Resources Section of SCAP in 1949. The author served in the section between 1946 and 1948 and participated in the research for the original volume. He claims the present volume to be "the first undertaken for a detailed analysis of the total resource position of any nation and the possibilities of integrated resource management for the nation." The present version covers the period through 1951. Part 1 deals with Japan's resources such as food, energy, fibers, nonmineral construction materials, minerals for construction, and industrial raw materials whereas part 2 discusses the production and exploitation of resources such as lumber, fibers, fuel and power, food, and water as well as Japanese progress in the field of conservation and scientific research. The last section, part 3, compares Japan's position to that of the Western world, examining Japan's basic deficiencies and Japanese policy toward resource management. There are useful appendixes on sources of data, glossary of terms, and bibliographies, The bibliographies include a complete list of the titles of the *Reports* series (155 plus 3 unnumbered reports) (1945–51) (no.1829) and *Preliminary Studies* series (73 items) (1946–52) (no.1828) published by the Natural Resources Section of SCAP during the occupation years.

1818a Baldwin, Roger Nash. "Where Trees Are Venerated." *Audubon Magazine* 51: 84–89 (Mar. 1949)

In the course of a visit to Japan, Baldwin found that the principles of conservation—vital to Japan's economic recovery—have long been understood there. The role of SCAP conservationists, therefore, has been primarily that of providing the Japanese with the latest technical advice, rather than that of convincing them of the need for good resource management. American experts, moreover, have been able to help in one important way—by encouraging the Japanese to establish longterm conservation policies on a national scale, thus enabling them to coordinate more efficiently the conservation practices which have been followed for years on a local scale.

1818b Grant, Robert Y. "Japanese Mining and Petroleum Industries: Programs under the Occupation." *Science* 112:577–88 (17 Nov. 1950)

The author, a member of the Mining and Geology Division of SCAP's Natural Resources Section, describes the activities of his division during the occupation period. The division, he explains, sought to provide Japanese groups engaged in the mining and petroleum industries with useful technical advice and assistance. Accordingly, it emphasized instruction in up-to-date techniques and methods in the areas of exploration, mining, and refining with particular regard to coal, oil and various metals. In addition, the division tried to get Japanese government agencies to undertake constructive action where mine safety and mining laws were involved, while simultaneously seeking to reorient these same agencies toward a policy of responsibility rather than of control. The division's ultimate goals, Grant states, included a reduction in Japan's dependence on foreign sources of mineral products. A useful list of all Natural Resources Section reports prepared by the Mining and Geology Division completes the article.

1819 Schenck, Hubert G. "Conservation for Peace." *Contemporary Japan* 20:301–8 (July/Sept. 1951)

Schenck, who was chief of the Natural Resources Section, General Headquarters of SCAP, writes of the problem of conservation as it relates to Japan and shows the difficulty of explaining this concept to the Japanese, partly due to a language problem. He uses several examples to demonstrate the nature of this problem. In addition to showing the importance of conserving natural resources, the author uses analogies to demonstrate the importance of conserving fundamental human rights and privileges. He maintains that "conservation for peace depends upon a balance between nature on the one hand and economic and social values on the other."

1820 ———. "Natural Resources Problems in Japan." *Science* 108:367–72 (8 Oct. 1948)

Prepared for presentation at the International Geological Congress, this article is a detailed and technical outline of present problems concerning the natural resources of Japan. The author, chief of SCAP's Natural Resources Section, begins with an outline of the organizational structure and operations of the section, as well as the qualifications and activities of its members. He describes the problems SCAP officials encountered immediately after the war and contrasts them with later challenges. Topics discussed include food production, erosion control, land use programs, fisheries, forestry, and the quality and location of Japan's mineral resources. The article is a concise summation of the published SCAP *Reports* on Japan's natural resources (1945–51) (no.1829).

1821 Solomon, Albert H. "Revision of the Japanese Mining Law under the Occupation." *Washington Law Review* 26, no.3:232–46 (Aug. 1951). Reprinted from Supreme Commander for the Allied Powers. Natural Resources Section. *Weekly Summary* no.286.

The revised Mining Law (Law no. 289, 1950) promulgated by the Japanese government on 20 December 1950 is discussed here in some detail by the deputy chief of the Mining and Geology Division in SCAP's Natural Resources Section. Solomon first reviews the history of mining in Japan and notes the essential features of the Mining Industry Law of 1905 and of the mining legislation drawn up between 1937 and 1943 as part of Japan's overall war effort. He next studies the major problems of the immediate postwar mining industry insofar as they dictated changes in existing laws. Finally, he describes the basic features of the new law, focusing on its enhanced protection of such nonmetallic minerals of economic value as dolomite, feldspar, silica sand, and limestone whose mining had not been covered in previous legislation; its curbs on the virtual monopoly of mining which certain companies had previously had as well as its provision of greater opportunity to individual citizens to explore and mine; its insistence on the diligent prosecution of the search for minerals by those filing prospectus permits in order to correct a widespread prewar abuse of mining claims; and its constitutional protection of the individual citizen against arbitrary bureaucratic action directed either against the mining applicant or against the owner of the surface land in question. Solomon praises the law not only for its comprehensiveness and scope but also for the fact that it represented the "free and voluntary act" of concerned Japanese lawmakers.

Supreme Commander for the Allied Powers. Monograph 41. *The Petroleum Industry, 1945–June 1951.* 1952. See no. 323.

———. Monograph 45. *Coal.* 1952. See no.327.

1822 ———. *Japanese Natural Resources: A Comprehensive Survey.* Tokyo: SCAP, 1949. xxii, 559p.

A comprehensive and analytical work undertaken by SCAP "to answer the need for an over-all investigation of Japanese resource management problems, and their bearing on the creation of an economically self-supporting Japan." It outlines the general nature of the basic resources available in Japan, namely, food, power and fuel, fibers, and minerals. It also discusses Japan's resource requirements and possible improvements in resource utilization and the development of scientific research potentialities. This analysis of Japan's short-term and long-term capacity for the production of food, fuel, and raw materials is accompanied by a discussion of the outlook for a self-supporting economy with a 1930–34 standard of living or better. The book includes numerous and excellent photographs, statistical tables, charts, and maps. Statistical information and interpretations are based on field surveys made by members of SCAP's Natural Resources Section and on data presented by Japanese government sources. Appendixes include a list of titles of all issues of serials entitled *Report* (1945–51) (no. 1829) and *Preliminary Study* (1946–52) (no.1828) published by the Natural Resources Section and an index by author and subject. Nine maps are enclosed indicating surface features, land use, geology and soil types, electric power generating plants (1949), forest types (1947), irrigation types (1943), and population in 1947.

———. Economic and Scientific Section. *Mission and Accomplishments of the Supreme Commander for the Allied Powers in the Economic, Scientific, and Natural Resources Fields.* 1952. See no. 275.

1823 ———. Natural Resources Section. *Japan's Recovery through Her Natural Resources.* Tokyo: SCAP, 1950. 6p., illus.

The author attempts to summarize occupation reforms dealing with Japan's natural resources. Defining the primary purposes of the Natural Resources Section to be to "(1) maximize immediate production and promote efficient utilization of the materials produced in order to minimize import requirements, and (2) maximize long-range production in order to reduce Japan's future dependence on foreign sources for its supplies," the author outlines some of the more important activities of the Natural Resources Section in various fields, such as agriculture, fishing, forestry, mining, and geology. He concludes that SCAP's advice, guidance, and material assistance will help Japan become a self-sustaining nation in the future.

Available at the Army Library, the Pentagon, Washington, D.C.

1824 ———. ———. *Mission and Accomplishments of the Occupation in the Natural Resources Field.* Tokyo: 1949. 23p.

A brief report prepared by the SCAP Natural Resources Section regarding its efforts to improve conditions in the area of natural resources. It covers agriculture, the fishing industry, and mining as well as measures that were taken to preserve the wildlife and forests of Japan.

1825 ———. ———. *Mission and Accomplishments of the Occupation in the Natural Resources Field.* Tokyo: SCAP, 1950. 43p., maps, diagrams.

The entire scope of the responsibilities of SCAP's Natural Resources Section is summarized in this pamphlet which supplements a briefer report with the same title issued the previous year (no. 1824). Defining the section's mission as: "(1) to produce in order to minimize import requirements, and (2) to maximize long-range production in order to reduce Japan's future dependence on foreign sources for its supplies," the report discusses the organizational structure of the section and the activities of its 4 technical divisions—agriculture, fisheries, forestry, and mining and geology. In describing each of these divisions, the report outlines the postwar situation, emphasizes important postwar problems and discusses measures adopted by SCAP to solve these problems. Sixteen charts provide data in such areas as food crop production, fertilizer consumption, land reform, aquatic production, pulp production, petroleum production and consumption, and mine safety measures.

More detailed accounts of the activities of the Natural Resources Section may be found in its 125 technical reports and 35 preliminary studies as well as in the *Weekly Summary* (1945–51) (no. 1830) of the section.

Available at the Library of Congress, Washington, D.C.

1826 ———. ———. *Mission and Organization of the Natural Resources Section.* Tokyo: SCAP, 1947. 38p., charts.

The primary purposes of this report are to state the mission of the Natural Resources Section and its relationship to the overall occupation and to delineate the responsibilities and duties of the section's personnel. Arranged in outline form, it provides a systematic description of the structure and operations of the Natural Resources Section. There is also an account of the particular responsibilities and duties of its executive personnel, i.e., the section chief and the heads of such various service divisions as the Personnel Branch, the Library Branch, and the Supply and Transportation Branch. The final section of the report discusses the particular responsibilities of the chief of the technical divisions which includes the Agriculture, Fisheries, Forestry and Mining, and Geology Divisions. It also describes the duties of the heads of such branches as the Economics Branch, the Soils and Fertilizers Branch, the Pulp and Paper Branch, and the Mineral Branch.

Available at the Army Library, the Pentagon, Washington, D.C.

1827 ———. ———. *Natural Resources of Japan.* rev. ed. Tokyo: SCAP, 15 Apr. 1947. 64p.

A very general summary of the natural resources of Japan. It treats Japan's natural geographic environment and resources in agriculture, fisheries, forestry, minerals, and wildlife. It also discusses the interrelationships between the natural environment and its occupants. The discussion includes an analysis of Japan's raw materials and prospects for her economic rehabilitation. The last 6 pages provide selected references regarding Japanese natural resources.

1828 ———. ———. *Preliminary Studies.* Mimeographed. Tokyo: SCAP, 29 Oct. 1946–May 1952. nos.1–73.

This mimeographed monograph series represents a series of studies undertaken by SCAP staff specialists in the field of Japan's natural resources. Of a total of 73 studies published, nos.1 (29 Oct. 1946) through 69 (Dec. 1951) were prepared by the Natural Resources Section, and the last 4 studies, nos. 70 (Jan. 1952) through 73 (May 1952) were by the Natural Resources Division of the

Economic and Scientific Section. Subjects covered relate to food supply, power and fuel, fibers, industrial raw materials, construction minerals, scientific research, and natural resources conditions in areas outside Japan. Each number deals with a specific topic. Included among such topics are: the supply of coke in Japan, experimental smelting and refining of iron-chromium-nickel ore in Japan, the condition of the coated paper industry, the position of the rice crop and other foodstuffs, and the operations of large fishing companies. Treatments vary in length, ranging from 10 to 50 pages. In general, the first 30 studies (1946–48) are of a more preliminary nature than are subsequent ones which provide more detailed statistical data and analytical discussion. The last 2 numbers represent particularly detailed and substantial work. No.72 (Mar. 1952) is 73 pages long and gives a statistical description of Japan's agricultural insurance system, discussing the effectiveness of the crop and livestock insurance programs. It includes some 10 tables and figures. No.73 (May 1952) is a 212-page work in 2 volumes. It was prepared by Fujioka Yasuo and concerns crop diseases in Japan. There are 1,974 entries listed, each of which has a Japanese, an English, and a scientific name. There is also a list of the English names of the hosts of these diseases.

1829 ———. ———. *Reports.* Tokyo: SCAP, 31 Oct. 1945–Apr. 1952. nos. 1–158.

A series of 158 SCAP reports on various problems associated with Japanese natural resources. The series was published between 1945 and early 1952. While *Preliminary Studies* (1946–52) (no.1828), another of the Natural Resources Section's serial publications, presents essays on various subjects, these reports contain statistical information on natural resources collected primarily from Japanese sources. The publications make use of statistical data from as far back as 1925. The length of the reports varies. Early reports are 15 to 30 pages but later ones tend to be longer, ranging from 20 to 270 pages. Subjects covered concern the food supply, whaling expeditions, power and fuel resources, fiber production, minerals and nonmineral construction materials, and industrial raw materials. Also included are reports on recent scientific research done by the Japanese and analyses of their technical competence. There are a few reports on areas outside Japan. Some reports deal exclusively with administrative conditions. Sample reports would be: no.1, *Possibility of Reparations from Japan's Natural Resources* (31 Oct. 1945); no.2, *Food Position of Japan Proper for 1945 and 1946* (13 Nov. 1945); no.3, *Basic Problems of the Coal Mining Industry in Japan* (14 Nov. 1945); no.43, *Hydrology of Japan* (1 July 1946); no.58, *The Forestry Situation in Northern Honshu* (10 Oct. 1946); no.122, *Pearl Culture in Japan* (31 Oct. 1949); no.136, *The Japanese Village in Transition* (Nov. 1950). At the end of each report, there is a complete list of the reports published prior to it.

1830 ———. ———. *Weekly Summary.* Mimeographed. Tokyo: SCAP, 13–30 Oct. 1945—21–31 Oct. 1951. nos. 1–307. weekly.

A mimeographed weekly report on the activities of the Natural Resources Section and developments in Japan in this field. Ranging between 25 and 70 pages, each of the 307 issues published between October 1945 and October 1951 regularly reports on the following subjects: agriculture, fisheries, forestry, mining and geology, and matters relating to the section's Library and Production Division. The reports contain useful statistical information on Japanese mineral, forestry, whaling and fishery conditions as well as on land reclamation, the food situation, agrarian reform, and pulp and paper production.

AGRICULTURE, FISHERIES, AND FORESTRY

An extremely urgent and difficult problem confronting SCAP immediately after the surrender was how to insure the maintenance of at least the minimal requisite food supply for the Japanese people. As a consequence, both the Natural Resources Section and the Economic and Scientific Section found themselves continuously and heavily involved with the organization and operations of Japanese agriculture, fisheries, and forestry as well. This continued to be the case throughout most of the occupation period, although the urgency diminished as the acute food crisis of the early years gradually eased. The relevant literature is set forth below. The interested reader is also referred to the sections on land reform (p.544) and natural resources (p.586).

Bennett, John W. *Social Aspects of Japanese Forestry Economy: Two Case Studies.* 1953. See no.1910.

1831 Bishop, William W., Jr. "The Need for a Japanese Fisheries Agreement." *American Journal of International Law* 45:712–19 (Oct. 1951)

Noting the extent to which fisheries problems complicated U.S.–Japanese relations prior to the war, Bishop suggests immediate steps to be taken to prevent the reoccurence of potential friction between the 2 countries. He proposes a mutual agreement between the United States and Japan under which the fishing vessels of each country would be required to refrain from carrying on fishing activities in areas close to the other country.

1832 Brown, Lindsey A. "Agricultural Development in Japan and the Ryukyus." *Foreign Agriculture* 15:177–78 (Aug. 1951)

Brown was chief, Research Branch, Agriculture Division, Natural Resources Section, SCAP in 1948 and 1949 and director, Food and Natural Resources Department, Military Government of the Ryukyu Islands during 1950. He argues in this article that, contrary to popular belief, Japan and the Ryukyu Islands have not yet reached maximum efficiency in food production. He explains opportunities he sees "to increase the area's output through improved farming practices, further coordination of research and extension, and opening of the large areas of tillable but relatively inaccessible land now lying idle and needing improvement." The article concludes with a 4-point summary of agricultural development in these islands.

Churchill, Arthur C. "Cooperatives in Japan." 1945. See no.67.

Crane, Esther M. "Japan: Economic Phases of Occupation Program." 1946. See no.1452.

1832a Dunbabin, Thomas. "Australia and Antarctic Whaling: Claims on Japan and the Canberra Conference." *Eastern World* 1:25, 29 (Aug. 1947)

Dunbabin discusses the Australian plans that are to be put forth when the British Commonwealth Conference on peace terms for Japan meets in Canberra on 26 August 1947. Australia, he notes, has already claimed as reparations from Japan the floating factory ship *Ishili maru* and 12 whale-chasers and has protested against SCAP's decision not only to permit the Japanese to whale in the Antarctic during the southern summer of 1946/47 but also to allow them to mount an ever larger expedition in the coming year. The Australians are particularly incensed by the reckless slaughtering carried out by the Japanese and fear that this will lead to the depletion of the whaling grounds near Australia. Great Britain and Norway have also sent protests to SCAP, and the Commonwealth nations in general are strongly opposed to letting the Japanese rebuild their long-range whaling fleets in the near future.

1833 Espenshade, Ada. "A Program for Japanese Fisheries." *Geographical Review* 39:76–85 (Jan. 1949)

Espenshade, who served with the Fisheries Division of the Natural Resources Section of SCAP, discusses the major problems of the Japanese fishing industry by contrasting the future of the industry with developments before World War II and during the occupation. Japan's basic philosophy before the war was the exploitation and continuous expansion that led to a serious reduction of resources in Japan's coastal and near offshore waters. The excellent recovery of the industry since September 1945 was achieved, the author states, through the efforts of Japanese fishermen and as a result of SCAP aid and encouragement. Ways in which the rehabilitation of the fishing industry was promoted by the occupation are noted. The author outlines a 7–point program for improving long-range and short-term production in Japanese fishing, focusing on the problem of providing as much protein food as possible for Japan. The reorientation and improvement of fishery research is indicated as the greatest contribution the occupation could make in this field. The author concludes that unless the Allied nations strongly support a farsighted policy in fishing and other fields of basic production, "Japan will become less nearly self-sustaining rather than more so."

1834 Esterly, Henry Hermon. *Japanese High Seas Fisheries and the International Politics of the Occupation, 1945–1951.* Ph.D. dissertation, Columbia Univ., 1965. 408p. (Abstracted in *Dissertation Abstracts* 29:305A–6A [1968]; University Microfilms order no.68–5646)

The rivalry between Washington and SCAP on the one hand and other member nations of the Far Eastern Commission and the Allied Council for Japan on the other regarding the formation of occupation policy for Japanese high seas fisheries is recounted. Esterly notes that one of the first indications of rivalry among the Allies for a dominant role in the occupation occurred in early 1946 when SCAP recommended the expansion of Japanese fishing areas. SCAP's authorization of Japanese Antarctic whaling operations increased this conflict. The study includes a description of the tactics employed by the Allies to further their positions: the Russian and Chinese harrassed Japanese fisherman on the high seas, and the United States resorted to parliamentary tactics of delay and vetoing at FEC sessions. The development of cold war tensions is described; this development prompted many FEC members to approve American policies designed to promote Japanese economic recovery. Pursuit of these policies led to a Japanese decision to cooperate with international controls and conserve the natural resources of the high seas.

1834a ———. "Japan's Reentry into Pelagic Fisheries: From Surrender to the North Pacific Fisheries Convention, 1945–1952." In *The Law of the Sea: The Future of the Sea's Resources. Proceedings of the Second Annual Conference of the Law of the Sea Institute June 26–June 29, 1967, The University of Rhode Island, Kingston, Rhode Island,* ed. by Lewis M. Alexander. Kingston: Univ. of Rhode Island, 1968. p.151–53.

Esterly's article focuses on SCAP's control of Japanese high seas activities during the 7-year long occupation period. The author first describes the regulations which delimited the so-called authorized fishing areas, then explains how SCAP sought to teach the Japanese to respect and observe national and international conservation practices in order to overcome the worldwide resentment which Japanese fishermen had previously brought upon themselves on account of their ruthless exploitation of the seas. The concluding paragraphs discuss the steps which led to the signing on 9 May 1952 of the North Pacific Fisheries Convention with the United States and Canada. This agreement, Esterly points out, marked the culmination of the program SCAP designed to achieve for Japan reentry into international fisheries on the basis of equality. A map illustrating the progressive enlargement of SCAP's authorized fishing areas accompanies the text of this article.

1835 "Ex-president Hoover's Statement (Excerpts) at Press Conference, Tokyo, May 6, 1946, Released by SCAP Headquarters May 9, 1946." *Contemporary Japan* 15:309–12 (May/Aug. 1946)

The present food crisis in the world due to the degeneration of agriculture and the effects of the war are described by Hoover. He discusses measures being taken in the United States to alleviate the shortage and concentrates his remarks on the situation in Japan. Commending the SCAP food staff as a very able group, he describes their work and discusses the operation of the black market in Japan. He concludes his brief statement by insisting that Japan must have some food imports and that these imports will not prejudice the supplies given to other Allied nations in need.

1836 "Food and Politics in Japan." *Economist* 154:85–86 (17 Jan. 1948)

Citing statistics from the October 1947 census, the author notes that Japan's present population of 78 million cannot be supported exclusively on food produced within Japan. However, he maintains, maximum indigenous food production must be encouraged, in spite of the reluctance of farmers to increase production according to the government's wishes. There follow a description of the basic political conflict between the interest of the peasants in free market prices for food and the interest of the urban workers in rationing at low prices and a description of the stands taken by the Social Democrats and the Communist parties. In his concluding remarks, the author states that "until there is enough food in the town for the workers to eat and enough goods in the villages to make it worthwhile for the peasant to produce to feed the towns, there can be no firm foundation for the new regime in Japan."

1836a "Food Supplies for Japan." *Department of State Bulletin* 14:756–57 (5 May 1946)

This article consists of 3 related items. The first is a FEC policy statement of 25 April 1946 approving surplus food shipments to Japan on the condition that they not be of sufficient quantity to have the effect of giving Japan priority over Allied nations or liberated areas. The second item reports a news conference of 26 April in which Acting Secretary of State Acheson urges speedy United States action to meet its goals in supplying food to the rest of the world. While there is a real danger of food riots in Japan, he notes, American policy has always been to give priority in relief shipments to Allied countries and liberated areas. The third item consists of a statement released on 25 April in which Assistant Secretary of State Hilldring expresses his pleasure at seeing that the Far Eastern Commission has approved American policy regarding relief food shipments. He regrets that it is not possible to meet the goals previously set due to the worldwide food shortage.

1837 Ginsburgs, George, and Scott Shrewsbury. "The Postwar Soviet–Japanese Fisheries Dispute." *Orbis* 7, no.3:596–16 (Fall 1963)

This study of the perennial dispute over the fishing resources of the northwest Pacific discusses the origins of the conflict during the decade immediately following World War II, and the Japanese–Soviet negotiations of 1956 which somewhat ameliorated the situation. The authors maintain that the fisheries issue continues to be an expedient form of leverage to which Moscow periodically resorts when seeking to pry some fresh political advantage from Japan and that Soviet economic plans for the region have successfully limited Japanese activities there. As they point out, however, the Soviet government still has to secure Japan's formal acceptance of the postwar territorial status quo.

1838 ———, and ———. "The Soviet–Japanese Fisheries Problem in the Northwest Pacific, 1945–1956." *International Studies* 5:259–80 (Jan. 1964)

A history of the Soviet position in the Soviet–Japanese fisheries problem. The article begins at the end of World War II, when the present problem emerged, and ends in 1956, when the USSR consolidated her postwar gains on the issue. Much of the research is from Soviet sources.

1838a Godwin, George. "Whale-hunting Folly." *Spectator* 179, no.6223:423 (3 Oct. 1947)

Arguing that it is necessary to restrict whaling in the Antarctic in order to preserve the whale from extinction and condemning the Japanese for their past indiscriminate hunting, Godwin deplores the fact that SCAP has granted Japanese whalers permission to hunt again. Reaction to his article—in the form of readers' letters published in the 17 October (p.495) and 31 October (p.560) issues of *Spectator*—was mixed. One reader advocated that SCAP should seize the opportunity to undertake reforms and should caution the Japanese against indiscriminate hunting but that it should not forbid the Japanese from sending a whaling expedition to the Antarctic in view of the importance of whale meat to the Japanese diet.

1839 Grad, Andrew Jonah. *Land and Peasant in Japan: An Introductory Survey.* New York: Institute of Pacific Relations, International Secretariat, 1952. xii, 262p.

A comprehensive survey of Japanese agriculture outlining some of the basic factors concerned, examining how some of these factors were changed because of World War II and the occupation, and suggesting some of the problems that will remain or emerge after the termination of the occupation. A research staff member of the Institute of Pacific Relations, the author worked with the occupation in Japan between 1946 and 1947 as chief of the Prefectural Branch of the Government Section of SCAP and also served as liaison officer with the Natural Resources Section in the implementation of the land reform program. After discussing the natural conditions and historical background of Japanese agriculture, Grad discusses the wartime situation and the postwar land reform program. He also presents a fairly detailed treatment of agricultural techniques employed for the production of rice, wheat, beans, and vegetables as well as changes in methods of irrigation and the use of fertilizers. There are chapters on farm family structure, village organization, peasant unions, and agricultural cooperatives. Also discussed are related subjects such as the mechanization of agriculture, land development, population growth, and subsidiary peasant organizations. The author is pessimistic regarding the prospect of an improvement in the peasants' standard of living, despite efforts for agrarian reform, technical innovation, and organization of peasant interests. A Japanese version of this book was published as *Nihon no tochi to nōmin* (Tokyo: Kōdosha 1954. 300p.).

Grajdanzev, Andrew J. *Japan's Postwar Agriculture.* 1945. *See* no.79.

Granada, Yole. "Should We Rebuild Japan?" 1948. *See* no.1496.

1840 Greene, Marc T. "Danger-Point in Japan." *Fortnightly* 174:162–69 (Sept. 1950)

Occupation reforms in Japanese agriculture, fisheries, and forestry are considered in this report. The author, a special correspondent covering both the military and civilian branches of the occupation, briefly discusses the prewar and wartime conditions to be found in each sector and compares them with the present situation. He analyzes SCAP's land reform program as well as the new insurance programs for farmers, reforestation, and the flood control programs that were inaugurated by the Natural Resources Section of the occupation. Finally, he relates all of these particular reforms to what he considers the more general American goal of rebuilding the Japanese economy so that the nation will become a strong partner in the cold war confrontation.

1841 Huberman, Morris Abraham. "Backwoods Japan during American Occupation." *National Geographic Magazine* 91: 491–518 (Apr. 1947)

The work of SCAP's Forestry Division in determining the location, quantity, and quality of Japanese timber resources is outlined here. SCAP's survey and interview techniques are described and there is elucidation of the rural bureaucratic setup wherein power is divided between prefectural governors, local headmen, and police officials. A general survey of the Japanese lumber industry is provided and the author comments on the unchanged quality of life in rural areas. Emphasis is placed on the fraternal aspect of the occupation and on SCAP's encouragement of the development of a strong tourist trade in rural Japan that would stimulate industry and expose the Japanese to foreign ideas.

1841a Japan. Fisheries Agency. *The Fisheries Law. The Enforcement Law Concerning the Fisheries Law*. Tokyo? Fisheries Agency, 1949. 107p.

This publication provides a translation of the Fisheries Law and related legislation. The law itself deals with such matters as the specific areas of the ocean that are open to Japanese fishermen; the size of boats and the kinds of nets and equipment permitted; licensing fees; and the organs established to administer the law.

———. Ministry of Agriculture and Forestry. Economic Research Div. *List of Papers and Materials upon Agricultural Economy, January 1938–December 1948*. 1949. See no.14.

1842 ———. ———. National Research Institute of Agriculture. *Summary Report of Researches, 1946–1948*. Tokyo: The Institute, 1951. xii, 164p.

1843 "Japanese Request for Post-treaty Fisheries Negotiation." *Department of State Bulletin* 24:351 (26 Feb. 1951)

An exchange of letters between Prime Minister Yoshida and Ambassador Dulles. Yoshida's letter—dated 7 February 1951—stresses the need for comprehensive fishing negotiations on both an international and bilateral level and explains the unilateral decision of his government to prohibit Japanese fishing in all areas currently under agreement to prevent overharvesting. Dulles' reply, also dated 7 February, expresses gratification at the Japanese position and recognizes the importance of fishing negotiations.

1844 "Japanese Whaling: Press Statements in Canberra by the Minister for External Affairs, Rt. Hon. H. V. Evatt, 23rd June, 1947." *Current Notes on International Affairs* 18:409–11 (June/July 1947)

The Australian foreign minister here issues 2 statements on 23 and 27 June 1947 strongly opposing the unilateral action of the United States in authorizing a Japanese whaling expedition in Antarctic waters for the 1947–48 season without the prior consultation and approval of the Far Eastern Commission.

1845 Johnston, Bruce Foster. *Food and Agriculture in Japan, 1880–1950*. Ph.D. dissertation, Stanford Univ., 1953. 495p. (Abstracted in *Dissertation Abstracts* 13: 691 [1953]; University Microfilms order no.5799)

This thesis traces the major elements in Japan's agricultural economy—domestic production, imports, and population—over a 70 year period and examines in detail the improvements made in Japanese agricultural productivity and the country's critical food problems during World War II. A final chapter—on the immediate postwar period—describes the severe shortage of food during the first 3 years of the occupation, when the level of imports was restricted by a worldwide grain shortage which made it impossible for food-deficit countries to satisfy their import needs in full. The chapter also considers postwar programs for enlarging Japanese agricultural production and for insuring a continuing supply of food adequate to meet the needs of a rapidly growing population.

1846 ———, with Hosoda Mosaburō, and Kusumi Yoshio. *Japanese Food Management in World War II*. Stanford, Calif.: Stanford Univ. Pr., 1953. xii, 283p. (Food, Agriculture and World War II)

Written while the author was preparing his Ph.D. dissertation at Stanford University, this work deals primarily with Japanese governmental controls over food production and consumption during World War II. However, it also treats the period prior to the war in order to clarify the effects of the war on food production and consumption. Wartime food control, especially control over the distribution of staple foods, is described in detail. The last chapter treats the postwar shortage in Japan up to 1948 and SCAP's efforts to increase food production. The author was chief of the Food Branch of the Price Control and Rationing Division in the Economic and Scientific Section of SCAP from 1946 to 1948. Hosoda was chief of the Overseas Section of the Staple Food Management Bureau during the war and after the war served as chief of the Documents and Archives Section in the Minister's Secretariat of the Ministry of Agriculture and Forestry. Kusumi was also a specialist in this field, serving in the early postwar period as chairman of the Agriculture and Forestry Committee of the House of Councillors.

1847 Kawano, Shigetō. "Features of Agricultural Policy in the Postwar Economic Rehabilitation of Japan." *Asian Affairs* 1, no.2:149–63 (June 1956)

Pointing out that SCAP officials (after 1947) and various national leaders were committed to rebuilding the country's industrial base, Kawano of Tokyo University studies some of the measures they undertook in order to prevent war-devasted Japan from reverting to an agrarian economy. He explains how postwar agricultural policy was geared to rehabilitating the economy and, among other things, notes that food prices were lowered through an increase in the output and supply of farm products, that the level of farm income was suppressed through the importation of large quantities of food, and that a new class of farmers was created through an extensive reform of the landowning system.

1848 Ladejinsky, Wolf Isaac, Warren H. Leonard, and Mark B. Williamson. "Prospects for Japanese Agriculture." *Foreign Agriculture* 12:240–45 (Nov. 1948)

All 3 authors were associated with the Agricultural Division of SCAP's Natural Resources Section. Divided into 4 sections, the study deals with: (1) the food problem, (2) industrial (nonfood) crops, (3) other agricultural problems, and (4) the immediate general outlook. There is a consideration of Japan's general food requirements, the amount of labor needed to harvest that food, the redevelopment of sericulture and introduction of new crops, the fertilizer problem, changes in the livestock industry, and shortages of farm equipment. One remedy to what the authors view as a dire situation is the transfer of surplus workers in agriculture to other occupations, primarily those of an industrial nature.

1849 Namiki, Masayoshi. "The Farm Population in the National Economy before and after the Second World War." *Economic Development and Cultural Change* 9, no.1, pt.2:29–42 (Oct. 1960)

In his summary of the farm population in postwar Japan, Namiki of the Institute of Agricultural Research in Tokyo notes that an explanation of the postwar acceleration in out-migration should be sought not only in terms of labor supply but also in the increase in nonagricultural employment opportunities in rural districts.

1849a "Occupation Orders for Japanese Fishing and Aquatic Industries." *Department of State Bulletin* 14:346–47 (3 Mar. 1946)

This article summarizes SCAP policy conclusions regarding the Japanese fishing and aquatic industries. SCAP's present policy is to insure that domestic consumption needs are met by aiding the industry through the provision of adequate fuel supplies and assistance in rehabilitating production and processing facilities. The emphasis will be on coastal fisheries and pisciculture; no permission has yet been granted for the resumption of deep-sea fishing.

1850 Ohkawa, Kazushi. "Significant Changes in Japanese Agriculture since 1945." *Journal of Farm Economics* 43: 1103–11 (Dec. 1961)

This analysis of major trends and changes in postwar agriculture focuses on the land reform, the worsened man-land ratio, technical progress and mechanization on Japanese farms, rapid increases in output and productivity, and the problem of the unbalanced position of agriculture in Japan's national economy. Ohkawa's paper is followed by several brief comments offered by Bruce F. Johnston of Stanford University.

1851 Price, Willard. "Desperate Peasants." *Asia and the Americas* 46:14–17 (Jan. 1946)

In an excerpt from his book *Key to Japan* (no.455b), Price explains that the most important task of the occupation authorities will be the improvement of the living and working conditions of the Japanese peasantry. He points out that if their desperate circumstances continue unaltered, the peasants will provide "ready fuel" for Japan's war leaders after the occupation is over.

1852 "Problems Affecting North Pacific Fisheries." *Department of State Bulletin* 26:340–46 (3 Mar. 1952)

Part 1 of this article is a report by William Herrington, special assistant to the U.S. undersecretary of state and conference chairman, concerning the Tripartite Fisheries Conference at Tokyo, 4 November–14 December 1951. Herrington reviews American concerns and interests in North Pacific fishing over the past 30 years, concentrating on the concern for conservation of fish stocks off the North American coast. The Tripartite Fisheries Conference with Canada and Japan represented an attempt to ensure conservation without recourse to measures restricting foreign fishing operations. Conference negotiations are carefully explained in terms of the compromises accepted by all parties.

Part 2 of the article sets forth the texts of documents prepared by the conference. They include a general protocol, entitled "Resolutions and Request of the Tripartite Fisheries Conference;" a substantive agreement, "Proposed International Convention for the High Seas Fisheries of the North Pacific Ocean," which consists of fishing agreements among the 3 nations and discusses the establishment of a permanent commission to oversee future North Pacific fishing; and an additional protocol pertaining to the functioning of this permanent commission. These documents provide protection for fisheries already fully utilized by forbidding their exploitation by countries not previously involved.

1853 "Progress of Japanese Fishing Industry Conservation Program." *Department of State Bulletin* 20:833 (26 June 1949)

This article reprints a press release of 10 June 1949 issued jointly by the Departments of State, Interior, and the Army. The release announces that progress has been made in implementing a SCAP-developed conservation program for the Japanese fishing industry. The program calls for the Japanese to terminate the excessive exploitation of various resources, to collect and analyze statistics relating to aquatic life, and to cooperate with other nations in the use of common fishing grounds.

1854 Roelofs, Garritt E. "Japan's Extension Service: Some Problems and Progress." *Foreign Agriculture* 15:243–45 (Nov. 1951)

Roelofs was agricultural information and extension specialist, Agricultural Division, Natural Resources Section of SCAP from 1947 to 1950. An early problem of the extension service was "the suspicion with which farmers first viewed the program." Other problems which plagued the new extension service were terminology and the lack of leaders. The author discusses these problems and the efforts made to solve them. He also notes the response to the clubs for farm boys and girls organized by the extension service. Rural home improvement is cited as one of the most challenging problems for Japan's extension workers, and the author explains why it is so. The article concludes with a comment on prospects for the agrarian reforms in the future.

1855 Seibert, Howard W. "Rebuilding the Japanese Fishing Industry." *Military Government Journal* 1:5–8 (Apr. 1948)

After a detailed description of the nature and history of the fishing industry in Japan, the author discusses problems more recently associated with fishing as well as efforts on the part of SCAP officials and the Japanese Agriculture and Forestry Ministry to overcome them and modernize the industry. There is a clear explanation of the traditional unit of organization in fishing communities known as the *funanaka* as well as various useful statistics on personnel engaged in fishing and the percentage of fish in the Japanese diet. SCAP efforts to improve the industry through the inauguration of boat construction programs, the improvement of transportation facilities, and the enactment of legislation aimed at democratizing the present feudalistic system of vested fishing right controls are all briefly discussed.

1856 Seidensticker, Edward G. "Japanese Fisheries Reform: A Case Study." *Far Eastern Survey* 20:185–88 (24 Oct. 1951)

Investigating the Japanese fisheries program as it operated in a single village, Seidensticker attempts to draw limited conclusions about the fisheries reform as a whole. The heart of the matter, he explains, seems to be that a very important part of the Japanese fishing industry, unlike Japanese farming, has entered the industrial age. Accordingly, it would be more to the point to further healthy relations between the laborer-fisherman and the capitalist-owner than to try by half-measures to redistribute ownership.

1857 Smith, Howard F. "Food Controls in Occupied Japan." *Agricultural History* 23:220–23 (July 1949)

The author, who is chief of the Food Branch, Price and Distribution Division of the Economic and Scientific Section of SCAP, provides a detailed, technical account of the promulgation of the Emergency Imperial Food Ordinance of 17 February 1946. He places it in the larger context of SCAP's overall program of surveillance and direction of food control programs in postwar Japan. He notes that the occupation has marked no significant departure in policy from prewar and wartime Japanese food control programs and describes 12 pieces of Japanese legislation in this area enacted between April 1939 and February 1942. Smith then explains the breakdown of these policies following the war and the resulting food crisis brought on by the decline in effectiveness of the administrative control machinery, the lack of patriotic or economic incentives to facilitate the collection of crop quotas, and such physical factors as a bad harvest and abnormal typhoons in September 1945. Finally, the article discusses direct SCAP involvement after February 1946 in the following areas: production estimates, quota assignments, quota collections, price determination, black market control, rationing organization and technique, and ration levels. The increasing difficulty of implementing policies in these areas is discussed. The article closes on the pessimistic note that, while austerity and foreign aid may enable Japan to achieve self-support by 1953, tensions will arise because of the dilemma posed by maintaining strict, government-ordered food controls within the framework of an open, democratic society.

1857a Sogawa, Masao. "Fishing Grounds and Marine Product Industry of Japan." *Contemporary Japan* 18:315–21 (July/Sept. 1949)

The original SCAP limitations on Japanese fishing areas, according to Sogawa, were too drastic and threw many fishermen out of work. Furthermore, various SCAP measures led to considerable competition between the highly capitalized, commercial deepsea fishermen and the primitive, smallscale coastal fishermen—a development which resulted in a depletion of marine resources which has made Japan's food shortage even worse. SCAP is presently cooperating by enlarging the area within which the Japanese may legally fish and by supplying such necessary commodities as fuel oil. The marine products industry, Sogawa concludes, is making a fast recovery, but Japan must learn to observe international regulations and to conserve aquatic resources.

Spillers, A. R. "A Forest Goes Back to the People." 1947. See no.1731a.

1857b ———. "U.S. Foresters in Japan." *Journal of Forestry* 44:1047–52 (Dec. 1946)

The first chief of the Forestry Division in SCAP's Natural Resources Section presents a detailed account of the division's initial activities and responsibilities. After outlining in administrative terms how forestry work in general was organized in postwar Japan, he discusses the division's set-up and indicates the names and background of its personnel. Spillers' account of the work carried out by the division describes how it sought to provide lumber and other forest products for the occupation forces, to undertake studies that would provide the data necessary for properly advising and assisting the higher echelons of SCAP, to meet the minimum civilian needs of the Japanese population for charcoal and lumber, and to get the Japanese government to appoint a technically trained individual as chief of its Bureau of Forestry for the first time in history. Spillers concludes with an assessment of the division's working conditions, in particular its relations with Japanese officials throughout the country.

1858 Spinks, Charles Nelson. "Japan's Not-so-desperate Peasants." *Asia and the Americas* 46:173–76 (Apr. 1946)

Spinks, chief of the Manpower, Food, and Civilian Supplies Division of the U.S. Bombing Survey, states that the directive issued on agrarian reform seems to be primarily based on a prewar conception of the position of the Japanese farmer. The salvation of the Japanese farmer, he explains, lies in making him less dependent upon agriculture for a living so that his microscopic farm is not his sole source of income.

1859 Sugiyama, Shigeo. "Postwar Japan and High Seas Fishery." *Japan Annual of International Affairs* no.1:59–90 (1961)

The author traces the developments in high seas fishery in postwar Japan. He covers the period from the end of the occupation to 1957. Sugiyama is concerned with the legal aspects of high seas fishing and the diplomatic history of negotiations between Japan and other nations. He writes about the negotiations with the occupation forces, South Korea, the United States, Canada, and the Soviet Union. He ends by covering the *Fukuryū maru* incident in the Marshall (Bikini Atoll) Islands in 1954.

Supreme Commander for the Allied Powers. Monograph 30. *Agricultural Cooperatives, 1945–December 1950.* 1952. See no.312.

———. Monograph 35. *Price and Distribution Stabilization: Food Program.* 1952. See no.317.

———. Monograph 36. *Agriculture, September 1945–December 1950.* 1952. See no.318.

———. Monograph 42. *Fisheries, 1945–1950.* 1952. See no.324.

———. Monograph 43. *Forestry, September 1945–January 1951.* 1952. See no.325.

1860 ———. Civil Information and Education Section. Public Opinion and Sociological Research Div. *Some Aspects of the Fishery Right System in Selected Japanese Fishing Communities.* Tokyo: SCAP, Nov. 1948. iii, 139p.

A study of the operation of the fishery right system in Japan based on a field survey. A description of the historical and sociocultural background of the Japanese fishery right system is followed by a discussion of recent technological impacts on fishing operations and the pattern of fishermen's lives. The monograph presents the major findings of a survey prepared by the Fisheries Division of the Natural Resources Section of SCAP and conducted at 9 fishing communities representative of particular regional characteristics. Findings relate to the membership of fishery associations, the attitudes of ordinary fishermen toward the fishery right system, participation in the allocation of rights, and the leasing of fishery rights owned by fishery associations. The first 20 pages present general findings, and they are followed by a description of more detailed findings on each community. Attached to the report are maps showing respective fishery right areas. In the appendixes are tables on the ownership status of fishery rights, fixed net rights, and demarcated rights according to prefecture as of 1946–47, plus a list of basic laws and ordinances concerning fishing and the texts of questionnaires prepared by the National Resources Section.

Available on microfilm from the National Archives, Washington, D.C.

1861 ———. Economic and Scientific Section. *Food Situation during the First Year of Occupation.* Tokyo: SCAP, 1947. 36p., illus.

Prepared by the Price Control and Rationing Division of the Economic and Scientific Section, this report is one of two which discuss the food situation in Japan in the early years of the occupation. The other is entitled *Food Situation during the Second Year of Occupation* (1948) (no.1862). This report considers Japan's historical food position before discussing the food deficit in 1946 and the effects of the staple food rationing system inaugurated in the early months of the occupation. There is an analysis of the administrative and psychological factors responsible for the development of the 1946 food crisis, an account of the effects of this food shortage, and a description of measures taken by SCAP and the Japanese government to cope with it. The final portions discuss factors which serve to alleviate the food crisis and give a summary of the causes and consequences of the food shortage in 1946. Five tables and 7 charts provide statistics on Japanese food imports, rice production, the use of land in Japan, food consumption levels, and nutritional levels of the rural and urban population.

Available at the Army Library, the Pentagon, Washington, D.C.

1862 ———. ———. *Food Situation during the Second Year of Occupation.* Tokyo: SCAP, 1948. iii, 77p., diagrams, tables.

This report was prepared jointly by the Economic and Scientific Section, the Natural Resources Section, and the Public Health and Welfare Sections of SCAP. It is considerably more detailed than the earlier report of the Economic and Scientific Section, entitled *Food Situation during the First Year of Occupation* (1948) (no.1861), and studies the wider implications of the food situation. It begins with a general statement describing the past history of the food supply in Japan but concentrates on the wartime and postsurrender periods. The next major section is a description of food production, collection quotas, and food collections as well as food distribution during the 1947 rice year, which extended from 1 November 1946 through 31 October 1947. Considerable attention is paid to public health aspects of the food shortage, and the study concludes with an estimate of Japan's long-term food prospects. More than half of the report consists of tables and charts offering data on land use, population rates, industrial production, food imports, and symptoms associated with nutritional deficiencies.

Available at the Army Library, the Pentagon, Washington, D.C.

1863 ———. ———. Research and Programs Div. *Staple Food Prices in Japan, 1930–1948.* Tokyo: SCAP, Apr. 1949. ii, 26p.

This brief report contains 3 charts and 26 tables showing monthly and annual price data for the principal staple food crops of Japan for the period 1930–

48. Relative movements at the producer, wholesale, and retail levels are presented, and relationships between the agricultural parity index and the price of rice and between the price of rice and the prices of other staples are reflected. Among these other staples are wheat, barley, naked barley, white potatoes, and sweet potatoes.

1864 ———. Natural Resources Section. *Agricultural Technical Assistance Programs in Japan, 1945–1950.* Tokyo: SCAP, 1951. 112p.

Mark B. Williamson, chief of the Agricultural Division of the Natural Resources Section, prepared this report with the assistance of various staff members of the division. It is an attempt to summarize the activities of the Agriculture Division from the beginning of the occupation to its near-conclusion. The introductory section provides a synopsis of the division's work in areas which include agricultural production statistics, the occupation's fertilizer program, insect and disease control, the livestock program, land reclamation and improvement programs, soil survey, the land reform program, the agricultural insurance program, and agricultural credit and tax programs. These synopses usually provide a comprehensive description of the present situation as contrasted with past and possible future developments in the particular field. There is considerable emphasis on the effects of particular SCAP programs and policies. More detailed and documented accounts of the same topics follow the summation, a chapter being devoted to each area of major importance. Appendixes include a list of reports prepared by the Agricultural Division for the Natural Resources Section's series (1945–51) (no.1829), a list of U.S. personnel who have worked in the Agricultural Division, and organization charts of the division.

Available at the Army Library, the Pentagon, Washington, D.C.

1865 ———. ———. *Japanese Agriculture Programs under the Occupation.* Tokyo: SCAP, 1949. 1v.

The nature and scope of the agricultural programs instituted by SCAP during the occupation are outlined in some detail. The report defines the 2 major objectives in the field of agriculture to be: (1) maximum food production, and (2) the achievement of social and economic stability for the farm population. There is a summary of problems encountered and progress made in 8 major areas: food production, food collection, crop reporting, agricultural research, agricultural extension, land reform, agricultural cooperatives, and crop and livestock insurance. Following this summary are discussions of each program which include an historical sketch of previous conditions, comparative production figures, and an outline of SCAP aims and programs. The report is a valuable summation of SCAP's aims and their implementation.

Available at the Army Library, the Pentagon, Washington, D.C.

1866 ———. ———. *1948 Annual Report for Japan to the Food and Agriculture Organization.* Tokyo: SCAP, June 1948.

1867 Swanson, C. L. W. "Land Use and Soil Conservation in Japan." *Journal of Soil and Water Conservation* 3:159–64 (Oct. 1948)

1868 ———. "Reconnaissance Soil Survey Work in Japan." *Science* 106:256–58 (19 Sept. 1947)

A former head of the Soils and Fertilizer Branch, Agriculture Division of the Natural Resources Section of SCAP describes the section's project of classifying and mapping Japanese soils in terms of their morphological features. The project is described as of particular importance due to the current food shortage in postwar Japan. After describing earlier, less scientific soil surveys undertaken in Japan, the author discusses the findings of the present survey. A table charts surveys that have been completed in the Kanto Plain and Kyushu. Soil and crop maps of Japan are provided.

1869 Taguchi, Shinji. "Japanese–Korean Fishery Dispute." *Contemporary Japan* 22, no.7/9:392–415 (1953)

This article traces the historical background of the Japanese–Korean fishery dispute, examines the issues involved, and notes the importance of and possibilities for a settlement. Section 1 of the article discusses the MacArthur Line in relation to the Rhee Line, blaming the former for being the source of the beginning of the current dispute. Section 2 traces the development of the dispute, beginning from Japan's surrender on 15 August 1945, and also notes the various efforts to reach a negotiated settlement. Section 3 in turn "answer[s] the question why Japanese fishermen are so eager to operate in those dangerous fishing grounds within the Rhee Line" by summarizing the current development of Japanese fishery. Trawling and otter trawling and other types of fishery operations are specifically examined. Section 4 considers the possibilities of coordination between Japanese and Korean fisheries. A number of tables throughout the article are of value in studying the dispute.

1870 Tahara, Otoyori. "Class Differentiation of Farmers and Social Structure of Farming Communities in Postwar Japan." In *Japanese Sociological Studies*, ed. by Paul Halmos. Keele, Staffordshire: Univ. of Keele, 1966. p.45–67.

Tahara Otoyori, professor of sociology at Tohoku University, explores the changes that have taken place in the social structure of agricultural communities in Japan against the background of the economic structure which has developed since the postwar land reform. Centering his discussion on class differentiation in the farming community, he illustrates to what extent the characteristic features of the social structure have affected the growth of a new economic structure.

1871 Tamura, Kōsaku. "The Rhee Line and International Law." *Contemporary Japan* 22, no.7/9:379–91 (1953)

The purpose of this article is to show that the proclamation issued by President Rhee of Korea on 18 January 1952 which claimed Korean sovereignty over a vast expanse of the high seas is not valid under international law. The author attacks the preamble and 3 paragraphs of the proclamation, each in turn, and attempts to demonstrate that 2 proclamations issued in 1945 by President Truman of the United States are not "well-established international precedents." Tamura discusses the reference in the preamble to the "national defense" as a ground for issuing the proclamation. He then turns to the first paragraph, viewing it as "a distorted adoption of the theory of continental shelf," a theory still "under the deliberations of the International Law Commission of the United Nations." The second paragraph concerns the establishment of a "conservation zone," and the question of the legality of such zones is studied in the article. The third paragraph involves such an area on the high seas that it "touches the Japanese territory known as Takeshima." The author describes why it is not a valid claim. The proclamation itself and the Japanese government's note of protest are quoted at the conclusion of the article.

1871a Tohbata, Shiro. "Future of Japan's Agricultural Industry." *Contemporary Japan* 16:453–58 (Oct./Dec. 1947)

In this article, the vice-director of the Economic Stabilization Board's Production Section welcomes the land reform law as marking the end of a period of neglect for Japanese agriculture. Economic rehabilitation, he notes, will depend upon the solution of basic agricultural problems and the recognition of agriculture as the nucleus of the nation's future industrial structure. The problems demanding solution include the overpopulation of the countryside, the low level of agricultural profits, inefficient land use, and too narrow a range of agricultural products. Generally speaking, Tohbata continues, agriculture is in good shape since it escaped the wartime destruction which the industrial sector experienced and is currently benefitting from high prices for its products. These gains are being solidified by the land reform, but care must be taken that there be no backsliding.

1872 U.S. Dept. of State. Office of Intelligence Research. *The Japanese Fishing Industry, 1928–1939 and Prospects for 1953.* Washington, D.C.: 1948. vi, 38p. (OIR report no.4627)

In projecting the state of the Japanese fishing industry in a normal postwar year, this article indicates that the main problem of the industry will be to increase production in order to meet domestic requirements of animal protein and contribute to the restoration of Japan's balance of payments by maximizing exports of canned fish. A solution to this problem depends chiefly on the possibility of raising the fish catch through expansion of coastal and offshore fishing.

Varney, Richard M. "The Position of a Forester in Japan." 1947. *See* no. 1449a.

1873 Wakukawa, Seiyei. "Japanese Tenant Movements." *Far Eastern Survey* 15:40–44 (13 Feb. 1946)

This article is an excerpt from a symposium, entitled *Japan's Prospect*, edited by Douglas G. Haring (Cambridge, Mass.: Harvard Univ. Pr., 1946. xiv, 474p.). Its emphasis is on the history of tenant movements and their relationship with the government to 1946. Wakukawa sees no panacea for the problem in the postwar period, but calls for a redivision of the land to increase acreage, and a radical reduction of rents for the tenants.

1874 Ward, Gordon H. "Japan's Agricultural Cooperative Program." *Foreign Agriculture* 16:115–19 (June 1952)

Ward was in charge of the agricultural cooperative program in Japan from September 1949 through June 1951. He writes of the development and functions of agricultural cooperatives in Japan which "are the primary credit, marketing, purchasing, and processing agencies in almost every village." He puts the development of cooperatives since the Agricultural Cooperative Association Law was enacted in December 1947 into historical perspective by first describing the previous half century of cooperative development. He then discusses the agrarian reforms fostered by the occupation officials as a step toward developing democracy in the farm villages. The establishment of independent member-controlled cooperatives made possible by twin laws on 15 December 1947 and their subsequent development are described by the author. He continues by discussing the functions of cooperatives and federations. A description of measures taken to strengthen farmer cooperatives, such as continuing education and information programs, efforts to improve business management and operating practices, and solutions for the lack of adequate member investment, concludes the article.

1875 Yamaguchi, Shinrokurō. *Some Aspects of Agrarian Reform in Japan.* Tokyo: Japan Institute of Pacific Studies, 1948. 36p. (Pacific Studies series)

Yamaguchi traces the enactment of the Rural Land Adjustment Act and the developments which followed its enactment. He includes a discussion of the views of the Allied Council of Japan insofar as the agrarian reform program was concerned, information on the demands of various landowners up to June 1946 for the return of their land, and details about the land commissions after December 1946. Translations of materials from the publications of various Japanese agricultural organizations also may be found within this volume.

TEXTILES, POWER, AND OTHER INDUSTRIES

The extent of SCAP's involvement with the Japanese economy was so great as to bring it into contact with practically all major Japanese industries in one context or another. The literature resulting from such contacts is ephemeral and elusive, however. The available items are noted below. The reader is also referred to the section on natural resources (p.586).

1876 Arita, Takeshi. "Postwar Development of Transportation." *Contemporary Japan* 24, no.4/6:233–43 (1956)

Arita Takeshi of the Ministry of Transportation presents a brief survey of the development of transportation during the postwar 10 years. He notes that in the early years after the war the industry was subjected to furnishing transportation to Japanese repatriates as well as to the Allied occupation forces, and, at the same time, suffered from unfavorable financial conditions caused by the postwar inflation.

1877 Echigo, Kazunori. "Development of Postwar Japanese Shipbuilding Industry and Revival of Monopoly: Particularly, Problems of Rationalization and Grouping in the Industry." *Kyoto University Economic Review* 28:35–58 (Oct. 1958)

While the Japanese shipbuilding industry has recovered to such an extent that Japan surpassed Great Britain in 1956 to become the world's leading shipbuilding country, this phenomenon should not be understood to mean that the industry has returned to a situation similar to that of prewar days. There have been many changes, among them the decrease in the construction of warships, the "completely weakened and narrowed domestic market for shipbuilding," and the increased building capacity of Japanese yards as well as the growth in the number of companies. Keen competition among the companies has necessitated the rationalization of facilities and the formation of combinations between big shipping and banking concerns, and these factors in turn have been extremely important for the revival and growth of shipbuilding in Japan. This development, however, has been accompanied by the revival of monopolistic companies of the type that SCAP had sought to eliminate through its economic deconcentration policies immediately after the war.

1878 "Heavy Industry for Japan." *Business Week* p.121–22 (26 Mar. 1949)

Reporting on recent developments in American plans for Japan, this article indicates that the United States government intends to shift the emphasis in Japanese industrial production from the manufacture of textiles to the manufacture of machinery and other finished products in the course of helping the country rebuild her war-damaged industry. Great increases in the production and export of steel, pig iron, cotton yarn, and ships will be necessary if Japan is to be in a position by 1953 to pay for most of her imports and thereby end her dependence on American economic aid.

1879 Hsieh, Chiang. "Post-war Developments in the Japanese Textile Industry." *International Labour Review* 62:364–88 (Nov. 1950)

In this survey of the Japanese textile industry, the effects of the war, the textile policy of the occupation, the extent of the postwar recovery, and changes in textile labor conditions are discussed briefly. The importance of the textile industry as a nonstrategic industry and its position in Allied plans for economic recovery is underscored. Government control of the procurement and allocation of material, production planning, and exports is noted as is the SCAP decision to allocate a maximum proportion of textile output for export at the expense of the domestic consumer. The author analyzes postwar production in relation to deficiencies in foreign demand and the shortage of raw material imports. In conclusion, he comments on labor conditions, the common practice of using young women as workers and the methods of recruitment, payment of wages, and unionization which result from this practice.

1880 Jessup, Alpheus W. "Japanese Textile Industry Equipment, Technology Range from Good to Ancient." *Textile World* 98, no.1:104–7 (Jan. 1948)

Jessup, the Far Eastern correspondent of McGraw-Hill World News, discusses the state of postwar Japanese textile equipment and technology. He indicates that Japanese rayon equipment is "ancient," that the country's cotton spinning equipment is not in good condition, and that the plant layout of most manufacturers of woolen textiles is inadequate even though their equipment is relatively up-to-date. This article is a companion piece to Jessup's study on the revival of the Japanese textile industry (no.1881).

1881 ———. "Japanese Textiles Will Be Slow in Revival." *Textile World* 98, no. 1:101–3, 182–86 (Jan. 1948)

On the basis of personal observations, talks with Japanese textile manufacturers, and information received from the Textile Division of SCAP's Economic and Scientific Section, Jessup concludes that the Japanese textile industry will require another 10 years to recover fully from the war and for Japanese production levels to reach those of the mid-1930s. He indicates that over two-thirds of the 12 million cotton spindles which Japan possessed in 1937 had still not been replaced. He notes as well that postwar Japan's supplies of coal and hydroelectric power were insufficient to meet the needs of a revived textile industry and that the wartime destruction of Japan's foreign trade organization could make it difficult for the country to acquire all of the necessary raw materials and to find overseas markets for her anticipated textile exports. Finally, Jessup points out that such occupation-inspired labor reforms as restrictions on child labor and a limitation on the maximum number of hours which employees could work had nullified the competitive advantage which Japanese labor had previously enjoyed.

1882 Katsube, Toshio. "The Steel Industry Today." *Contemporary Japan* 19:520–29 (Oct./Dec. 1950)

Here the director and chief of the External Affairs Department, Fuji Iron and Steel Co., discusses the conditions and prospects of the Japanese steel industry. To become established as a peaceful nation, he states, Japan must become the "workshop of Asia." Katsube shows what part Japan's scarcity of iron and coking coal will play in this development. He comments on the effect of the Deconcentration Law and describes how developments in the Far East have aided the progress of the steel industry. The Japanese steel industry, he maintains, is eager to take part in plans to promote higher living standards for Asiatic nations. Katsube discusses the controls on the industry following the war and shows how the abolition of government subsidies and the decrease in U.S. aid as recommended by Joseph Dodge will stimulate the steel industry. While noting drawbacks the industry faces, he predicts a steady expansion for it. Several tables are included in the article.

1883 Kroese, Willem Titus. *The Japanese Cotton Industry: Report of a Journey to Japan in the Autumn of 1949*. Leiden: Stenfert Kroese, 1950. 158p. At head of title: Vereniging Katoen-, Rayon- en Linnenindustrie (Association of the Netherlands Cotton-, Rayon and Linenindustry)

1884 Marx, Daniel, Jr. "The Future of Japanese Shipping." *Far Eastern Survey* 18:9–11 (12 Jan. 1949)

A brief but authoritative discussion of shifting American policy toward the curtailment of Japanese shipping. The author discusses the history of the shipping industry since the surrender of Japan, including the recommendations made by the Pauley Mission of April 1946, the markedly different appraisal given in February 1948 by Overseas Consultants, Inc., and the conclusions of the April 1948 Draper Mission which agreed with the Overseas Consultants' report and recommended that Japan be allowed to build up her merchant fleet. In addition to citing the specific terms of the various groups' recommendations, the author attempts to explain the reasons behind their analyses. The concluding section of the article discusses the importance of shipping in the economic recovery of Japan and also considers the problem as American policy-makers view it, i.e., in terms of American self-interest as well as Japanese recovery. In the author's opinion, it will be more in the American taxpayers' interest as well as the interest of Japan if "the future should see a greater Japanese tonnage than was contemplated immediately after the war."

1885 Matano, Kensuke. "Shipping Industry in Postwar Japan." *Contemporary Japan* 19:30–34 (Jan./Mar. 1950)

Here the president of the Iino Shipping Co., Ltd. briefly outlines the condition of Japanese shipping during the war, immediately following the war, and as it is developing at the time of writing. At the end of the war all vessels of above 100 tons were placed under the control of the occupation, and the author examines the implications of this control by the Civilian Merchant Marine Committee. He discusses why he sees as urgent the establishment of a new financial organ to supply long-term loans to shipping companies. Matano concludes that freedom to navigate in foreign waters is more important than government and U.S. aid for the Japanese shipping industry.

1886 Nehmer, Stanley. "The Future of Japanese Textiles." *Far Eastern Survey* 15: 261–64 (28 Aug. 1946)

In this article, Nehmer, executive secretary of the International Textile Mission to Japan, discusses the key role of the textile industry in the rejuvenation of the Japanese economy because of textiles' foreign exchange potential. Some of the problems which must first be overcome, such as a shortage of fuel and labor, are listed. Nehmer concludes that he does not foresee competition with U.S. and British industries as long as the Allies continue to control the necessary raw materials.

1887 ———, and Marguerite C. Crimmins. *Significance of Textiles in the Japanese Economy.* Washington, D.C.: Government Printing Office, 1948. 8p. (Dept. of State publication 3199; Far Eastern series 26); reprinted from *Department of State Bulletin* 18, no.460:527–33 (25 Apr. 1948)

The authors, both research analysts in the Division of Research for the Far East, Office of Intelligence and Research, Department of State, point up the significance of the textile industry in Japan's domestic economy and in its foreign trade. Reviewing the industry's prewar contribution to production and employment, this short article discusses SCAP policies for rehabilitating the Japanese textile industry in the postwar period. The authors refer to the American Textile Mission to Japan in January 1946 which recommended in its *Report* (1946) (no.1901) that the cotton-textile industry could be easily rehabilitated. There is a discussion of SCAP's encouragement in 1946–47 of the redevelopment of raw silk, woolen, and cotton-textile production, and a consideration of the Far Eastern Commission's policy discussions which established the maximum level of textile production permitted Japanese companies. Finally, the authors analyze the position of textile exports in postwar Japanese trade and the future of the industry under the occupation. They note that the rehabilitation of the Japanese textile industry, dependent as it may be upon world trade conditions as well as Allied and American policies, will nevertheless be a significant factor in determining the postoccupation status of the Japanese economy.

1888 Oku, Shōsuke. "A Statistical Survey of the Textile Industry." *Contemporary Japan* 19:358–66 (July/Sept. 1950)

In this article the author summarizes the conditions of various sectors of the textile industry, pointing specifically to postwar difficulties and showing the progress made since the end of the war. He comments on postwar problems such as shortages of raw materials, labor troubles, and inefficient transportation facilities. Controls placed on the industry following the war, as under the Pauley plan which set the number of spindles allowed the cotton spinning industry, and SCAP's elimination of these controls are discussed. The article is divided into sections dealing with the cotton spinning industry, chemical fiber industry, raw silk industry, spun silk spinning industry, wool spinning industry, hard and bast fiber spinning industry, and waste fiber spinning industry.

1889 Pope, Frederick. "Report on the Japanese Chemical Industry." *Far Eastern Survey* 18:295–98 (14 Dec. 1949)

In his report and recommendations presented to General MacArthur on the state of the Japanese chemical industry, Pope reviews plant and labor conditions as well as the question of reparations.

1889a Pyatnitsky, N. "The Japanese Textile Industry in 1948." *Current Digest of the Soviet Press* 1, no.22:44–46 (28 June 1949)

Pyatnitsky describes the impact of World War II and the American occupation upon Japan's once thriving textile industry and shows how SCAP curtailed Japanese production because American textile monopolies feared the expansion of Japan's cotton industry and its possible competition in various international textile markets. Recently, however, American exporters have changed their attitudes and have shown increasing interest in producing textile goods in Japan inexpensively for export to foreign markets. The article concludes with a description of some of the agreements and arrangements that have been conducted with this aim in mind. Pyanitsky's article first appeared in the April 1949 issue of *Vneshyaya torgovlya* (p.38–40) and is reproduced here in a condensed version.

1889b "Report of Textile Mission to Japan." *Department of State Bulletin* 14: 1009–10 (9 June 1946)

This press release of 29 May 1946 is a digest of the report of the Textile Mission to Japan (no.1901), which analyzed the current state of Japan's textile industry, its productive capacity, its need for raw materials, and some of the industry's future prospects.

1890 Rinoiye, Takashi. "Japan's Ship-building Industry." *Contemporary Japan* 19: 151–61 (Apr./June 1950)

Section 1 of this article surveys the condition of Japan's shipbuilding industry at the end of World War II and comments on its present state. Mention is made of the Pauley plan for Japanese reparations and the Strike plan. Section 2 discusses postwar shipbuilding activities, outlining the reconstruction measures for the shipping industry undertaken by the government. Section 3 examines the characteristics of Japan's shipbuilding industry and points out that this industry combines various other industries and, therefore, occupies a predominant position in the national economy. It is noted that Japan's shipbuilding industry has contributed to the promotion of foreign trade, partly as an exporter of superior vessels. The importance of developing shipping is studied. Part 4 discusses some problems regarding the industry and outlines 6 suggestions the author feels represent "the minimum requirements to enable the industry to cope with the current situation."

1891 Stewart, John R. *Japan's Textile Industry: A Report Prepared for the UN Economic Commission for Asia and the Far East.* New York: Institute of Pacific Relations, International Secretariat, 1949. iv, 82p.

One of a series of studies on the reconstruction and reform of postwar Japan prepared as part of the international research program of the Institute of Pacific Relations, this book points out that the textile industry was the most important component of Japan's prewar economy and that SCAP consequently placed great emphasis on its rehabilitation. Stewart examines overall conditions within the industry and concludes that recovery was still in its initial stages and would proceed slowly until adequate raw materials and power were available and until the industry's management and worldwide organization, as well as its machinery and equipment, could be rebuilt and expanded. The bulk of the report consists of detailed analyses of the cotton, silk, rayon and woollen industries, for which the author provides abundant statistical data. In appendix 2, Stewart also presents a similar and complementary study of the textile industry in Asian nations other than Japan.

1892 ———. "The Position of Silk in Japanese Exports." *Pacific Affairs* 21:46–51 (Mar. 1948)

After nylon and war had drastically reduced Japanese silk output, SCAP ordered the rehabilitation of the silk industry hoping to create exports, but found no market for raw silk. From 1947 emphasis was placed on exporting woven silk and exports improved, but the author argues that the Japanese would be better off producing food. When conditions return to normal, silk will again become an important export.

1893 Stone, K. "British–Japanese Textile Rivalry." *China Weekly Review* 109: 405–6 (29 May 1948)

Stone claims that General MacArthur and the United States were building up the Japanese textile industry beyond the 1930–34 level specified by the Potsdam Declaration. He advocates restricting the number of spindles to 3,500,000. The Japanese claimed that this number was not sufficient for home consumption and pressed SCAP to allow their textile industry to return to the 1937 level, the prewar peak of the industry. MacArthur's plans at the time of the article called for at least 4,000,000 spindles.

Supreme Commander for the Allied Powers. Monograph 41. *The Petroleum Industry, 1945–June 1951.* 1952. See no. 323.

———. Monograph 44. *Rehabilitation of the Non-Fuel Mining Industries.* 1952. See no.326.

———. Monograph 45. *Coal.* 1952. See no.327.

———. Monograph 46. *Expansion and Reorganization of the Electric Power and Gas Industries, 1945–March 1950.* 1952. See no.328.

———. Monograph 47. *The Heavy Industries, 1945–1950.* 1952. See no.329.

———. Monograph 48. *Textile Industries, September 1945–December 1950.* 1952. See no.330.

———. Monograph 49. *The Light Industries, 1945–March 1951.* 1952. See no.331.

———. Monograph 51. *Land and Air Transportation.* 1952. See no.333.

———. Monograph 52. *Water Transportation, 1945–1951.* 1952. See no.334.

———. Monograph 53. *Communications, 1945–December 1950.* 1952. See no.335.

1894 ———. *A Program for the Japanese Woolen Industry.* Tokyo: 25 Aug. 1947.

1895 ———. Economic and Scientific Section. *Copper Metallurgy in Japan.* Tokyo: SCAP, General Hdqters., Economic and Scientific Section, Natural Resources Div., 1952. 108p. (SCAP, Natural Resources Section, report no.155)

This report describes the history, organization, and types of copper smelting in Japan. The major portion of the work consists of figures and tables for each of the significant smelting operations.

1896 ———. ———. *Japanese Coal Mine Housing.* Tokyo: SCAP, Apr. 1948. 17p.

A concise report on a SCAP program of financial assistance to the Japanese government to build improved housing for coal miners. The program was in effect during the fiscal year 1 April 1947 through 31 March 1948. Five charts indicate that there is no appreciable relationship between coal production and housing for the laborers. The charts are followed by detailed tables on coal-mining companies in all regions of Japan,

1897 ——. ——. *Japan's Power Plants and Their Equipment, Special Report No.6.* Tokyo: SCAP, Feb. 1946. 1v.

This volume provides the text of a special report by the Statistics and Research Division of the Economic and Scientific Section. It is supplemented by another volume entitled *Special Report: Appendices* (1946) (no.1900) and may be viewed as an introduction to the much more extensive *Appendices*. It outlines the general operating conditions and sizes of thermal plants and indicates the quality and quantity of fuel utilized by them. Several tables classify power plants according to size, capacity, and fuel consumption.

Available at the Army Library, the Pentagon, Washington, D.C.

1898 ——. ——. *Outlook for the Japanese Cotton Industry, 1948–1949.* Tokyo? 1948. 37p.

1899 ——. ——. *The Petroleum Refineries of Japan.* Tokyo: SCAP, 1949. 1v., diagrams, maps.

This survey of the condition of Japanese petroleum refineries in early 1949 is intended "to amplify, clarify, and reappraise the information contained in previous reports and to form the basis for a decision as to the relaxation of restrictions now limiting refinery operation." The body of the report contains brief descriptions of the 18 oil refineries in Japan together with drawings of significant items of repairable or intact equipment. Appendixes chart the main items of equipment in Japanese refineries, provide various maps of refinery locations, cite petroleum consumption in Japan, show the financial status of oil companies, and provide drawings of the refineries.

Available at the Army Library, the Pentagon, Washington, D.C.

1900 ——. ——. *Special Report: Appendices.* Mimeographed. Tokyo: SCAP, 1946. 4 app. in 1v.

Data from the Economic and Scientific Section's inventory entitled *Japan's Power Plants and Their Equipment* (1946) (no.1897) are presented in this mimeographed volume. The appendixes cover some 1,840 power stations. Appendix 1 is limited to plants of 2,000 kilowatts or over, whereas the other appendixes include those of 2,000 kilowatts and under. Appendix 2 contains data sheets on thermal power plants owned by private companies, distribution companies, or by the Japanese government in the districts of Hokkaido, Tōhoku, and the Kanto. Appendix 3 provides information about thermal plants owned by private companies, distribution companies, or the government in Chūbu, Hokuriku, Kansai and Chūgoku, and appendix 4 concerns the same kinds of plants in Shikoku and Kyushu. Information includes the plants' location, the raw materials they use, their capacity, war damage sustained, and the years of manufacture of their machinery.

Available at the Library of Congress, Washington, D.C.

1901 Textile Mission to Japan. *The Textile Mission to Japan: Report to the War Department and to the Department of State, January–March 1946.* Washington, D.C.: Government Printing Office, 1946. x, 39p. (Dept. of State publication 2619; Far Eastern series 13)

The Textile Mission to Japan, organized in December 1945 by a directive of the U.S. secretary of state, submitted its report to SCAP on 31 March 1946. The report was then presented to the State and War Departments. The mission was to study Japan's capacity for cotton-textile export to meet the existing short-term world shortage of textiles. It was also to recommend measures to assist Japan in maximizing her textile exports. The report covers Japan's production capacity for various kinds of textiles including cotton, rayon, woolens, worsteds, and silk. For each textile industry, data are collected to indicate Japan's mid-1930 production capacity, the effects of the war on this capacity, registered capacity for January 1946, and the actual productive and reserve capacity for that year. The report also discusses in its latter half some operational problems of Japan's textile industry such as machinery conditions, the labor shortage, and insufficient electric power and transportation. The mission was composed of 5 representatives of the U.S. government and 4 observers, 2 from the United Kingdom and one each from China and India. It was headed by Fred Taylor, agricultural commissioner, Department of State.

1902 Torrens, James G. "Japan's Textile Industry." *Far Eastern Survey* 16:124–27 (4 June 1947)

The chief of the Textile Branch, Foreign Trade Division, Economic and Scientific Section, SCAP reviews the rehabilitation of Japan's textile industry. Cotton, silk, and wool production are examined and future prospects delineated. SCAP's reluctance to drastically restructure ownership and production units is discussed and raw material shortages and patterns of textile exports are noted.

1903 U.S. Dept. of State. Div. of Research for the Far East. *Current Status of the Japanese Textile Industry*. Washington, D.C.: The Dept., 1949. 5p. (Information note 176A)

1904 ———. ———. Office of Economic Security Policy. *Administration of Coal Production in Japan*. Washington, D.C.: The Dept., 1946. 99p. (Interim Research and Planning Div.)

1905 Van Zandt, Howard F. "The Japanese Telephone-System." *Contemporary Japan* 19:494–512 (Oct./Dec. 1950)

Van Zandt was traffic operations adviser in the Telephone and Telegraph Division of the Civil Communications Section, General Headquarters, SCAP beginning in 1946. In this article he examines the problems associated with the rehabilitation of the telephone system following World War II and makes suggestions for steps needed to further improve it. After considering the destruction of the system caused by the war, he comments on factors which impeded rehabilitation such as the cultural traits of the Japanese, inflation, and the fact that the long-distance system was copied largely after a European model. The improvement in the public telephone service using the honor system is treated. The author outlines a number of projects underway to improve the telephone system and discusses long-term planning as a necessary means of providing satisfactory telephone service.

1905a Weinstein, Wilmer. "Japan's Postwar Wool Industry under Military Authority." *Foreign Commerce Weekly* 29, no.5:6–7, 32–33 (1 Nov. 1947)

SCAP's desire to increase the production of Japan's textile industry to meet domestic needs and to earn foreign exchange is examined in this article. The author, a member of the Office of International Trade's Textile and Leather Division, concludes that the capacity and markets are assured but that it is doubtful whether Japan will have adequate supplies of coal (for power), dyes, and raw wool. He is therefore pessimistic about SCAP's plans for revitalizing the industry.

1905b Yamamoto, Hiromasa. "The Recovery Method of the Japanese Shipping Industry in Post-war Period." *Kobe Economic and Business Review* 2:89–106 (1954)

This study of the postwar rehabilitation of the Japanese merchant marine focuses primarily on the difficulties faced by shipbuilders because of SCAP's decision to leave the financing up to the companies themselvs. Yamamoto argues that the decision both retarded the industry's recovery and helped the old *zaibatsu*-connected shipbuilding firms reestablish their supremacy within the industry.

Other Areas of Occupation Participation

SCAP undertook a variety of other activities that do not readily lend themselves to categorization under a single descriptive head. It was concerned, for example, at the most general level with problems relating to the nature, characteristics, and amenability to change of Japanese society as a whole and, at lower levels, with a broad range of problems and programs in such fields as population control, education, public health and welfare, religion, and the mass media. For convenience of reference, the relevant literature on such subjects has been assembled below. Related materials will be found in the section devoted to general materials (p.113).

JAPANESE SOCIAL ORGANIZATION AND NATIONAL CHARACTER

In a long-term sense the success or failure of the occupation in achieving its goals depended upon the amenability of Japanese social organization, attitudes, and behavior patterns to the types of change proposed. It is an elusive subject, characterized more by imaginative speculations than by solidly based findings and, in practice, SCAP did not devote a great deal of time or attention to struggling with it. Its operational style was more pragmatic than theoretical in this respect. A number of individuals, in some cases associated with SCAP, were interested, however—especially anthropologists and psychologists—and they have made the following contributions to the literature.

1906 Abegg, Lily. "Japan Reconsiders." *Foreign Affairs* 33:402–15 (Apr. 1955)

A discussion of the political and social attitudes and actions of conservatives and radicals in postoccupation Japan is viewed in the context of the occupation reforms themselves. On the one hand, the author discusses such recent conservative tendencies as the mass pilgrimages to shrines and temples and the reappearance of ultranationalistic and reactionary elements in Japanese political and social life. On the other, she considers the activities of those leftists who are seeking a Communist order. The reasons for which there are so few exponents of true democratic government in postoccupation Japan, she claims, are inherent in Japanese society and in the manner in which democracy was brought to Japan, i.e., a military occupation introducing democracy by foreign fiat. Several examples of the undemocratic nature of the occupation are provided by way of illustration. According to the author, both of the above factors account for the present "conflict between faith in individualism and a form of society that is organic and collectivist." Although conceding that present-day Japan must be considered a democracy because the people have a vote which has real effect, nevertheless, she concludes that the Japanese people seem likely at present not to take the road to the left but the one to the right in their search for independence.

1907 Ariga, Kizaemon. "Research on Social Stratification and Social Mobility in the Japanese Rural Community." *Explorations in Entrepreneurial History* supplement 8:61–62 (Winter 1956)

This paper by Ariga of Tokyo University was one of several presented to the Third Working Conference on Social Mobility and Social Stratification held in Amsterdam in December 1954. It presents an outline of the plans, working procedure, and theoretical as well as methodological problems of a long-term study that he was conducting in 3 rural communities in order to determine the

Beardsley, Richard K., John W. Hall, and Robert E. Ward. *Village Japan*. 1959. See no.691.

1908 Benedict, Ruth Fulton. *The Chrysanthemum and the Sword*. Cambridge, Mass.: Houghton Mifflin, 1946. 324p.

In 1944 Ruth Benedict, a cultural anthropologist, began a study of Japanese society based on interviews with Japanese then present in the United States, studies done in prewar Japan, and written documents. Beginning with the observation that Japan appears to be a land of contradictions—chrysanthemums and swords—Benedict attempted to interpret these contradictions as rational parts of a complex and, to Americans, alien culture. Benedict found that a strong consciousness of social hierarchy and equally strong concepts of reciprocal obligation in social relationships were among the most distinctive traits of the Japanese culture. The traditional Japanese accordingly lived in a highly structured social environment where it was always clear who one's superiors and inferiors were and what sort of behavior was expected of each person in any given situation. This system was reinforced by habits consciously and strictly inculcated in childhood and by a strong sense of shame which was felt when one's behavior violated the accepted norms. The universalistic ethical systems of the West based on concepts of sin were thus replaced in Japan by a particularistic and conditional code of behavior. Benedict systematically outlines these Japanese concepts in the first part of her book. She then explores in successive chapters how conflicting imperatives of the system were resolved and how these concepts related to Japanese childrearing practices and to attitudes toward one's emotions, sensual pleasure, and self-discipline. Benedict's conclusions were provocative and had a great influence on American thinking in regard to Japan, though they also were somewhat outdated even when her book was being written since many of her sources described a Japan of 50 years earlier.

Benedict's book was translated into Japanese by Hasegawa Matsuji and appeared under the title *Kiku to katana* (Tokyo: Shakai Shisō Kenkyūkai Shuppanbu, 1948. 454p.).

1908a ———. "'The Japanese Are So Simple'." *Asia and the Americas* 46: 500–3 (Nov. 1946)

This article is a condensation of chapter 12 ("The Child Learns") of the author's forthcoming book *The Chrysanthemum and the Sword* (no.1908). It deals with many aspects of preschool training and with the learning process in primary and secondary school.

1909 ———. *Japanese Behavior Patterns*. Washington, D.C.: 1945. (Office of War Information, Area III, Overseas Branch, Foreign Morale Analysis Div., report no. 25)

Bennett, John W. "Community Research in the Japan Occupation." 1951. *See* no.890.

———. *Social and Attitudinal Research in Japan: The Work of SCAP's Public Opinion and Sociological Research (PO and SR) Division*. 1952. See no. 891.

1910 ———. *Social Aspects of Japanese Forestry Economy: Two Case Studies*. Columbus: Ohio State Univ., Dept. of Sociology, 1953. 55p. (Ohio State Univ. Research Foundation project 483, report no.5; Office of Naval Research project NR 176–110, interim technical report no.5)

The 2 cases presented here are part of a larger study examining the effects of social customs and institutions upon a rational and effective exploitation of forestry resources in Japanese rural communities. The first case study touches upon some of the factors leading to the overcutting of forests and includes an analysis of the economic role of the "skid trail" and its control by the timber dealer. The second, and longer, study describes the economic power and social influence of a village "boss" who has come to monopolize the entire forest industry of his community. The activities of this boss illustrate the tendency of certain individuals to manipulate the local forestry economy in the search for personal gain and power, thus demonstrating that economic factors in the pure sense are not wholly responsible for the overexploitation of Japanese forests. The data for both of these studies were gathered in a community in central Japan.

1911 ———, and Ishino Iwao. *Japanese Social Relations.* Columbus: Ohio State Univ., Dept. of Sociology, 1953. 74p. (Ohio State Univ. Research Foundation project 483, report no.2; Office of Naval Research project NR 176–110, interim technical report no.2)

This report, the second in a series of interim technical reports dealing with research in Japanese social relations (see nos.891, 1754b, and 1910), presents the broad theoretical point of view from which project personnel were conducting research, and compares their basic research policy and orientation with those found in the standard works of other scholars engaged in research on East Asian societies. The authors are critical of many of the publications that had served as a basis for the study of Japan up to that time, asserting that these works tended to ignore many vital and significant variables, utilized principles of explanation which were relatively unsystematic and random, and showed a preoccupation with certain problems which were no longer particularly relevant in light of the changing nature of East-West relations. The authors argue for the need of a more interdisciplinary, systematic approach in all future social science-type research on Japan.

1912 ———, and ———. *Paternalism in the Japanese Economy: Anthropological Studies of Oyabun-Kobun Patterns.* Minneapolis: Univ. of Minnesota Pr., 1963. x, 307p.

A study based on research conducted during the occupation of *oyabun-kobun* (boss-henchman) patterns in labor relations and other segments of Japanese society. Though much of the data is drawn from the occupation period, the emphasis is usually not on the occupation itself. Exceptions are the first 2 chapters, "Social Research in a Military Occupation" and "Views of Japanese Society," which describe the nature and impact of the research done by the Public Opinion and Sociological Research Division of SCAP and how Japanese society was viewed by different groups within the occupation forces. Finally, chapter 5, "Social Change and Motivation in the Boss System," gives some attention to changes in the labor-boss system under the influence of occupation reforms.

1913 ———, and Nagai Michio. "A Summary and Analysis of 'The Familial Structure of Japanese Society,' by Takeyoshi Kawashima." *Southwestern Journal of Anthropology* 9:239–50 (Summer 1953)

This summary of *Nippon shakai to kazokuteki kōsei* (Tokyo: Nippon Hyōronsha, 1948) was prepared by the staff of the research project in Japanese social relations at Ohio State University as part of their analysis of data on Japanese society and culture collected during the occupation. Professor Kawashima's book, the authors explain, contains a "pioneering and valuable interpretation of the historical and typological aspects of Japanese kinship institutions." It also demonstrates the importance of such concepts as "rights" and "duty" and shows the way in which traditional family patterns impede or even hinder the full democratization of Japanese society.

1913a ———, and ———. "The Japanese Critique of the Methodology of Benedict's 'Chrysanthemum and the Sword'." *American Anthropologist* 55:404–11 (Aug. 1953)

Ruth Benedict's *The Chrysanthemum and the Sword* (no.1908) appeared in Japanese translation in 1948 under the title *Kiku to katana*. The work immediately became the focus of journalistic and scholarly activity. Bennett and Nagai briefly outline the principal points made by Japanese scholars with regard to Benedict's methodology. In the eyes of these Japanese, the work's desirable methodological features include (1) the abundance and depth of Benedict's data, (2) evidence of productivity and efficiency in the utilization of the data, and (3) the strength and uniqueness of Benedict's conceptual approach and her attempt to portray the whole of Japanese culture. In short, the Japanese "see in Benedict's work all the most desirable features of American social science." The negative criticisms of these same scholars are as follows: (1) It is not clear what Benedict means by the term "Japanese." Does she have an ideal type in mind, or is she speaking of an actual subgroup, such as the military? (2) It is unclear whether Benedict has demonstrated that the concept of culture patterns is real. (3) Benedict tends to generalize too freely from data originating at different points in time and from military propaganda. (4) Benedict should have tried to define the differences in behavior according to social strata, region, occupation, age, etc. (5) Benedict's tendency to overstress the "feudal" aspects of Japanese society leads to a failure to understand the dynamic aspect of contemporary Japan. (6) The study of an entire national culture such as Japan's requires a great number of small-scale research undertakings on different dimensions of social behavior rather than an intense effort like Benedict's.

1914 Bush, Henry C. "Impact of American Culture." *Contemporary Japan* 20:331–40 (July/Sept. 1951)

Bush states that "the purpose of this article is to consider the probable effects of Japan's return to sovereign status upon Japanese scholars and intellectuals, and, conversely the effects Japanese scholars and intellectuals can have upon Japan's status." He considers it likely that Japan and the United States will continue to have a close relationship. Great Britain is used to illustrate numerous examples of the cultural impact of America. The author suggests that an economically powerful country creates culture which is exported abroad and that "American culture has become the scapegoat for resentment of America's economic and political predominance." He continues by pointing out that since Japan will probably continue to receive American aid, Japan will also feel, increasingly, the impact of American culture. As this happens, criticism of American culture will likely follow. He shows how this criticism could produce a harmful effect on future Japanese–American relations. The article concludes by suggesting what Japanese scholars and intellectuals could do in light of the facts presented.

1915 Cole, Allan Burnett. "Social Stratification and Mobility: Some Political Implications." *Annals of the American Academy of Political and Social Science* 308:121–29 (Nov. 1956)

The means by which occupation policies redistributed economic and political power among various social classes after World War II in Japan, thus encouraging social mobility, are summarized by Cole. Characteristics of the Japanese bureaucracy are outlined, followed by a discussion of the urban middle strata of Japanese society. The author notes research findings that show how social attitudes of various occupational groups in Japan have significance for political behavior. The article also examines features of the urban working class and of stratification and mobility in the Japanese countryside. It concludes with a summary of the political tendencies of the various strata in Japan.

Coleman, Rex. "Japanese Family Law." 1956. *See* no.1271.

1916 Cornell, John Bilheimer. "Matsunagi: The Life and Social Organization of a Japanese Mountain Community." In University of Michigan. Center for Japanese Studies. *Occasional Papers*, v.5. Ann Arbor: Univ. of Michigan Pr., 1956. p.xvii–xxiv, 113–232.

Social organization and kinship aspects of *buraku* life are the primary focus of this study. Cornell was in Matsunagi from October 1950 through August 1951. His structural analysis "reveals that Matsunagi people not only are organized as a community but also form smaller, less generalized aggregates, varying in relative importance." The paper includes chapters on native resources and material culture; household organization, housing and domestic life; *buraku* social organization and community life; and external relations in the cultural milieu. Numerous maps, charts, and tables are included in the work.

1917 Deverall, Richard L. G. "Democratizing Japan?" *Commonweal* 69:318–21 (7 Jan. 1949)

A general discussion of the task of democratizing postwar Japan emphasizes that Japan is a nation whose society is "utterly alien in its basic thought patterns to the thought patterns of the West." The author discusses various uniquely Japanese concepts such as *giri* and *ninjō* and insists that such concepts must be understood before real democratization can be achieved.

1918 De Vos, George Alphonse. "Social Values and Personal Attitudes in Primary Human Relations in Niiike." In *Studies in Japanese Culture: 1*, ed. by Richard K. Beardsley. Ann Arbor: Univ. of Michigan Pr., 1965. p.53–91. (Univ. of Michigan. Center for Japanese Studies, occasional papers, no.9)

"This paper presents a non-technical summary of results obtained from three of the psychological tests given to inhabitants of Niiike village in Okayama prefecture, Japan, in 1954." Social values related to specific social role relationships are examined and "the derivation of social values from a traditional premodern social code" and undercurrents of change in Niiike are discussed. The major areas studied in the piece include the expression of primary emotions in Niiike; attitudes regarding (1) achievement and success, (2) work and leisure, and (3) marriage relationships; attitudes toward authority; and general sources of worry. A "Summary Description of Psychological Tests" is appended to the article.

1919 Dore, Ronald Philip. *City Life in Japan: A Study of a Tokyo Ward*. Berkeley: Univ. of California Pr., 1958. 472p.

In his description of social changes in a Tokyo ward since the beginning of the occupation, Ronald Dore examines the family structure as well as political attitudes, education, and religion. His study is based on direct observations and the formal interview.

1920 ———, ed. *Aspects of Social Change in Modern Japan*. Princeton, N.J.: Princeton Univ. Pr., 1967. xi, 474p. (Studies in the Modernization of Japan, 3)

This study of changing interpersonal relations in Japan since 1870 includes the following papers from the fields of sociology, anthropology, psychology, and social relations: Reinhard Bendix, "Preconditions of Development: A Comparison of Japan and Germany"; Thomas C. Smith, " 'Merit' as Ideology in the Tokugawa Period"; Ezra F. Vogel, "Kinship Structure, Migration to the City, and Modernization"; R. P. Dore, "Mobility, Equality, and Individuation in Modern Japan"; Erwin H. Johnson, "Status Changes in Hamlet Structure Accompanying Modernization"; Edward Norbeck, "Associations and Democracy in Japan"; George O. Totten, "Collective Bargaining and Works Councils as Innovations in Industrial Relations in Japan during the 1920's"; Solomon B. Levine, "Postwar Trade Unionism, Collective Bargaining, and Japanese Social Structure"; George A. DeVos, and Mizushima Keiichi, "Organization and Social Function of Japanese Gangs: Historical Development and Modern Parallels"; L. Takeo Doi, "Giri-Ninjō: An Interpretation"; John B. Cornell, "Individual Mobility and Group Membership: The Case of the *Burakumin*"; Wagatsuma Hiroshi and George A. DeVos, "The Outcast Tradition in Modern Japan: A Problem in Social Self-identity"; John W. Bennett, "Japanese Economic Growth: Background for Social Change."

1921 Embree, John Fee. "Standardized Error and Japanese Character: A Note on Political Interpretation," *World Politics* 2, no.3:439–43 (Apr. 1950)

Embree, author of a number of studies of Japanese character, sharply criticizes the interpretations of Japanese "national character" which became popular in the United States during World War II. He points out that many of the generalizations which were designed to explain the international and domestic behavior of Japan—including ones advanced by Geoffrey Gorer, Margaret Mead, and Ruth Benedict—are based on insufficient information or are demonstrably false.

1921a Fisher, Charles. "The Japanese as Problem Children." *Political Quarterly* 17, no.3:201–13 (July/Sept. 1946)

On the basis of his own experiences and those of other Allied prisoners of war in Malaya, Fisher tries to characterize and explain the mentality and behavior of the Japanese people. He argues that their arrogance, pride, and extreme suspiciousness mask a pronounced inferiority complex and that their consciousness of being little men in a physical sense underlies everything that they think or say whenever they come into contact with Westerners. He calls their sudden enthusiasms and wild tempers an indication of childishness but feels that it would be misleading to compare them with normal youngsters. Instead they should be regarded as "a nation of problem children, irritable, unstable, and repressed." Despite his harsh criticisms, however, Fisher does praise them as frequently being exceptionally gifted and capable of great achievements. In his conclusion, therefore, he recommends that the Allies refrain from treating the Japanese too sternly during the occupation period and notes that what ultimately happens to Japan will depend in large measure on the attitude and actions of the outside world.

1922 Fujiwara, Hirotatsu. "Nationalism and the Ultraright Wing." *Annals of the American Academy of Political and Social Science* 308:76–84 (Nov. 1956)

This article looks at the future of the right wing in Japan against the background of the impact made by military defeat and alien occupation on the movement and the relationship between ultranationalism and the political mood of present-day Japan. The anti-Communist attitude of occupation authorities revealed in 1947 when General MacArthur banned a projected general strike gave the ultrarightists "a permissible sphere for action" for the first time since the end of the war, and the author examines this trend on into the period following the outbreak of the Korean War. The rest of the article concerns the activities of the ultrarightists after the enforcement of the peace treaty in 1952 including the appearance of organized former soldiers' or veterans' groups. Fujiwara examines the state of nationalism in Japan and the future prospects for ultrarightism, noting a lack of "nationalism" and viewing as "not favorable" the prospects for a recovery of the prewar influence of the ultraright.

1923 Fukutake, Tadashi. "The Communal Character and Democratic Development of Farming Villages." *Journal of Social and Political Ideas in Japan* 2, no.3:83–87 (Dec. 1964)

In an article translated from the November 1960 issue of *Shisō* Fukutake writes about the *buraku* (hamlet) and the problems that democratic development faces in these communal villages. He contends that the usefulness of the *buraku* is gone and that functional diversification must take place if democracy is to grow on both the local and national levels. He feels that interest groups which would cut across *buraku* lines would liberate the villages from their traditional ties.

1924 ———. "Democracy and the Japanese Background." *Orient/West* 7, no.3:33–42 (Mar. 1962)

Fukutake's article is in large measure a discussion of the nature of prewar and postwar Japanese society. His focus is on (1) the forces that shape Japanese character; (2) Japanese attitudes toward life; (3) the new aspects and old vestiges of Japanese class structure in postwar Japan; (4) the recent development of a mass society within the country; and (5) the direction of change within Japanese society.

1925 ———. *Japanese Rural Society*. Tr. by Ronald P. Dore. London: Oxford Univ. Pr., 1967. xiv, 230p.

Although this book is primarily a description of the contemporary village in Japan, it presents a picture of the development and changing patterns of Japanese rural society as well. Part 1 in particular, on Japanese agriculture and Japanese villages, traces the development of agriculture and discusses structural changes in rural society, specifically noting the "first land reform" of December 1945 and the "second land reform" which began in 1946. Results of this reform are also mentioned. Though not dealing specifically with the occupation, other sections of the book, such as those on the political structure of Japanese villages and on village culture and the farmer's mentality, do point out postwar developments occasioned by conditions resulting from defeat in World War II and postwar reform policies. This book is a translation by Ronald P. Dore from the Japanese of Fukutake's *Nihon nōson shakairon* (Tokyo: Tōkyō Daigaku Shuppankai, 1964. 256p.).

1926 ———. "Post-war Democratization in Japan: Rural Society." *International Social Science Journal* 13, no.1:65–77 (1961)

A general account of the conditions of prewar and postwar Japanese rural society. Fukutake believes that democratization of rural society is particularly important because "the undemocratic structure of Japanese society stems from the persistent rural character of the people." He concludes that democratization in the countryside will remain incomplete as long as the people must struggle against poverty. A short bibliography of books in English is included.

1927 ———. "Village Community (*Buraku*) in Japan and Its Democratization." In *Japanese Culture: Its Development and Characteristics*, ed. by Robert J. Smith and Richard K. Beardsley. Chicago: Aldine, 1962. p.86–90.

Fukutake argues that the typical *buraku* is still not a democratic local community formed by voluntary relationships among free inhabitants. The interest of the *buraku* as an undifferentiated entity continues to be placed above the interests of its members, whose rights accordingly are not satisfactorily protected and whose opinions are not fully respected. If the *buraku* is to be democratized, it will be necessary to transform it from a traditional folk community into a functional local unit and to differentiate the *buraku*'s accumulated functions, assigning them to such functionally specific groups as the agricultural cooperative, the irrigation cooperative, the fire brigade, the women's association, and the youth association. Villagers will then be much freer to assert and realize their interests independently through these new groups and will no longer be forced to regard *buraku* solidarity as a paramount principle.

1928 Gibney, Frank. *Five Gentlemen of Japan: The Portrait of a Nation's Character*. New York: Farrar, Straus and Young, 1953. 373p.

Gibney describes his book as a character study of a people. This study wrestles in elaborately worded phrases with the oft-discussed dichotomy of the Japanese character between sensitive artist and power-seeking demon. The author focuses on the lives and characters of 5 men—Hirohito, 124th emperor of Japan; Sanada Sakaji, a farmer; Shimizu Fumio, an engineer and former vice admiral in the Japanese navy; Yamazaki Tadao, a newspaperman; and Kisei Hideya, foreman in a steel mill—and attempts to portray their diversities as minor deviations from a central tendency of national homogeneity. He includes scattered, peripheral, journalistic remarks about the postwar occupation of Japan. Gibney's book has appeared in Japanese under the title *Nihon no gonin no shinshi* (Tokyo: Mainichi Shimbunsha, 1953. 317p.).

Gorer, Geoffrey. "The Special Case of Japan." 1943. See no.78.

1929 Gulick, Addison. "The Problem of Right and Wrong in Japan and Some of Its Political Consequences." *Journal of Social Psychology* 26:3–20 (Aug. 1947)

Contending that the history of ethical thinking among the Japanese has been basically different from that in the Occident, the author of this article attempts "to highlight a few crucial aspects of Japan's ethical evolution." Beginning from primitive times, he traces the development of basic Japanese social and ethical concepts and in the final section of the report, which deals with the future, he discusses the manner in which the occupation has effected changes in these concepts. According to the author, "imposing democracy upon [the Japanese] by military compulsion is sheer nonsense for the simple reason that democracy is par excellence the unimposable form of government." However, he is in favor of SCAP's development of free educational and political institutions as well as broad-minded news media that might have a powerful influence upon the thinking of the nation. While he believes that actual democracy is a distant goal to be attained in the future, he is optimistic about the process of progressive liberalization "if our representatives are skillful in handling our relations with Japan."

Hani, Setsuko. *The Japanese Family System*. 1948. See no.2245a.

1929a Haring, Douglas Gilbert. "Aspects of Personal Character in Japan." *Far Eastern Quarterly* 6:12–22 (Nov. 1946)

In this article on contemporary Japanese personality, Haring works on the premise that there is a pressing need for studies of this subject if the occupation's reeducation programs are to succeed. After summarizing the theoretical bases of the scientific study of character structure, he proceeds with a synthesis of the findings contained in a number of wartime investigations of Japanese personality and social behavior. The effects of childrearing practices and of the Japanese family system receive the most attention. The studies indicate in general a high degree of personal repression leading to the subsequent outburst of antisocial or self-destructive behavior. Those writers who have sought to provide psychoanalytical interpretations, Haring finds, agree that the approved pattern of masculine behavior tends to be narcissistic and autoerotic; to judge from the published studies, "genuine neurosis . . . occurs far more frequently in Japanese society than in many other societies," he concludes. Haring cautions that these findings are at best inadequate and spotty, and that they are probably contaminated by wartime bias. He recommends that longterm, cooperative field research projects be instituted; otherwise, the occupation's attempts at reeducation and democratization will be "blind and foolish."

1930 Hidaka, Rokurō. "Impact of the Occupation on Japanese Life." *United Asia* 8:235–38 (Sept. 1956)

Hidaka of Tokyo University analyzes the impact and influence of Western ideas brought into Japan during the occupation period. He mentions the "philosophy of efficiency" of the occupation forces and the demand for consumer goods which many Japanese now feel essential. Hidaka points out how the occupation with its new concepts and new ideas brought about changes in Japan in terms of people's daily behavior. He also shows how democracy has found a place in Japan.

1931 Hulse, Frederick S. "Convention and Reality in Japanese Culture." *Southwestern Journal of Anthropology* 4:345–55 (Winter 1948)

A scholarly critique of Ruth Benedict's views of the nature of Japanese social structure and practice as set forth in *The Crysanthemum and the Sword* (1946) (no.1908).

1931a ———. "A Sketch of Japanese Society." *Journal of the American Oriental Society* 66:219–29 (July 1946)

The most outstanding trait in Japanese behavior, according to this article, is its highly planned quality. Responses tend to be determined by rules learned within the family, which Hulse characterizes as primarily a social rather than a genetic unit. Concepts developed in the course of the article include a highly visible rural-urban contrast, the importance of the status hierarchy, and the dominance of group-oriented behavior. A marked reluctance to assume individual responsibility for important decisions is viewed as one important consequence of this group orientation. Generally speaking, Hulse concentrates on Japan's highly developed social control mechanisms and the various ways in which the Japanese circumvent them or make them more tolerable.

1932 ———. "Some Effects of the War upon Japanese Society." *Far Eastern Quarterly* 7:22–42 (Nov. 1947)

The author brings to this account his experience as a member of the Civilian Morale Division of the U.S. Strategic Bombing Survey from October 1945 through June 1946, during which time he collected and analyzed information on civilian morale and attitudes during and after the war. Before discussing the results of his polling random samples of Japanese, he provides a concise description of the prewar social structure of Japan and also describes in detail the wartime adjustments made in that structure. In the final section of the report, the author discusses the postwar situation in Japan by attempting to relate current Japanese behavior to earlier patterns and also to indicate new elements wrought by the Allied occupation. He discusses the role of General MacArthur, the results of the first postwar elections, and the changes that he has observed in various groups of Japanese—i.e., farmers, craftsmen, women, returned soldiers, etc. The report concludes with the affirmation that just as the Japanese assimilated foreign techniques into their culture "so now they are, making a supreme and by no means wholly unconscious effort to fit into the same pattern the new ideas which defeat and Occupation have brought."

1933 ———. "Status and Function as Factors in the Structure of Organizations among the Japanese." *American Anthropologist* 49:154–57 (Jan./Mar. 1947)

To the extent that understanding the social realities of Japanese society is a prerequisite to the administration of a successful occupation, this article is relevant to a study of the occupation. The author has utilized data from a study of Japanese civilian morale under the stress of war and bombing which was conducted by the U.S. Strategic Bombing Survey in 1945. He discusses the establishment and structure of cooperative associations to aid the war effort, contrasts them with American associations for the same purpose, and relates the wartime associative patterns to more basic patterns of the Japanese social structure which remain in effect.

1934 ———. "Technological Development and Personal Incentive in Japan." *Southwestern Journal of Anthropology* 3:124–29 (Summer 1947)

The author treats the interrelationship between basic Japanese personality types and economic activity, contrasting the Western work ethic of industriousness with a Japanese one in which skill is valued but work, of itself, is neither a virtue nor a pleasure. This distinction is viewed as affecting craftsmen and industrial workers differently. Wartime and postwar information is utilized to ascertain the frequency of absenteeism and of flight from the cities in the face of imperial calls for maximum economic production. The author concludes that the introduction of occidental industrial technology and methods has not created work incentives such as exist in Western society but instead may have depressed existing incentives. The article raises questions as to the feasibility of any attempts to impose Western economic and political institutions and practices on Japan.

1935 Ijichi, Junsei. *When Two Cultures Meet: Sketches of Postwar Japan 1945–*

1955, by Junesay Iddittie. Tokyo: Kenkyūsha, 1955. xiv, 209p.

The sketches in this book originally appeared in the *Nippon Times* and *Waseda Guardian* and are journalistic accounts of Iddittie's (Ijichi) impressions of the influences of American culture on Japanese culture during the 10 years following the end of World War II. The first articles present a picture of Japanese life and its hardships during the early stages of rehabilitation. One section in particular describes the image of the GIs in Japan. A chapter on food shortages is entitled "MacArthur Bread." The remaining half of the articles concentrate on describing some of the imprints of American culture which have shown up in Japanese style of living, dress, and behavior.

1936 Ike, Nobutaka. " 'National Socialism' in Japan." *Pacific Affairs* 23, no.3:311-14 (Sept. 1950)

Ike notes that prewar style Japanese ultranationalism was bound to reappear and describes briefly the program of one postwar right-wing group, the Japan Revolutionary Chrysanthemum Flag Association which advocated "national socialism." Its program closely resembles that of the prewar Japanese ultranationalists and German National Socialists, but Ike points out certain modifications that have been made in response to postwar conditions, i.e., its renunciation of force, its use of democratic symbols, and its appeal for mass support.

1937 Inouye, Kichijirō. "Whither Our Family System?" *Contemporary Japan* 15: 346-58 (Sept./Dec. 1946)

After a discussion of the earliest origins of the family system in clan (*uji*) society and its development throughout Japanese history, the author discusses the social benefits of family solidarity and questions the wisdom of those who advocate total destruction of the traditional family system in the postwar period.

1938 Jansen, Marius Berthus. "Ultranationalism in Post-war Japan." *Political Quarterly* 27, no.2:141-51 (Apr./June 1956)

This article describes the revival of Japanese ultranationalist groups following initial SCAP efforts to discredit them. This revival reached its peak in 1954 after the end of the occupation and the subsequent election of the conservative Hatoyama government. These rightist groups were critical of old-style militarism, showed only moderate interest in rearmament, supported both democracy and the imperial system, and were strongly anticommunist. Despite these common ideals, they were held back by organizational disunity, a lack of new ideas, and weak popular support. Nevertheless, Jansen suggests that internal political or economic problems could still lead to a rightist takeover.

1939 Japan. Cultural Science Society. *Brief Report of Research on Social Tensions in 1951*. Tokyo? Japanese National Commission for UNESCO, 1953. 26p.

This report is a summary of research done by the Japan Cultural Science Society (Nihon Jimbun Kagakkai) on the various kinds of tensional relations in Japanese society. "The research was carried out by experts in various branches of science organized into ten sections according to the kinds of tensions which they treated." After an introduction to what is meant by "social tension," this summary is divided into the following sections: (1) tensions in family life, (2) tensions in communities, (3) factional tensions, (4) tensions of the *Eta*—outcasts in Japan, (5) racial tensions, (6) tensions in religious life, (7) tensions in economic life, (8) ideological tensions, and (9) tensions of youth. The research on family life attempts to explain causes of tensions after World War II within various families. The section on factions investigated "so-called anti-social groups which caused many of the social problems in Japan after 1945." The summary of ideological tensions centers around the problem of nationalism and the investigation of the Nippon Kakumei Kikuhata Dōshikai (Japan Revolutionary Chrysanthemum Flag Organization). The section on youth mainly considers the postwar student movement. The written reports of the research in Japanese were published under the title *Shakaiteki kinchō no kenkyū* (A Research in Social Tensions) (Tokyo: Yūhikaku, 1953. 490p.).

1940 ———. ———. *Brief Report of Research on Social Tensions in 1952*. Tokyo? Japanese National Commission for UNESCO, 1955. 73p.

This report is considered a sequel to the *Brief Report of Research on Social Tensions in 1951* (no.1939), published in 1953. The survey for this present report was intended as an expanded and developed continuation of the previous one. The main divisions or sections in this brief report are: (1) family tension, (2) social tension in farm villages, (3) bureaucratic tension caused by the legislative process, (4) studies on *buraku* people, or the outcasts in former days, (5) religious section, (6) industrial labor section, and (7) rightist nationalism or thought section. The booklet contains only fundamental, abbreviated results of the survey, and plans were underway at the time of writing for publication of the full report of the results in Japanese in book form.

1941 Kalmer, Joseph. "The 'Etas' of Japan: The End of a Caste." *Eastern World* 4:13–14 (Feb. 1950)

This overview of the vicissitudes of the *Eta* class ends with a brief recognition of the role played by the occupation in affording increased opportunities for the *Eta*.

1942 Kerlinger, Frederick Nichols. "Behavior and Personality in Japan: A Critique of Three Studies of Japanese Personality." *Social Forces* 31, no.3:250–58 (Mar. 1953)

Kerlinger strongly criticizes the view of Japanese character presented in studies made during the war by Geoffrey Gorer ("Themes in Japanese Culture." *Transactions of the New York Academy of Sciences*, s.2, v.5, no.5:106–24 [1943]), Weston LaBarre ("Some Observations on Character Structure in the Orient: The Japanese." *Psychiatry* 8:319–42 [1945]) and Arnold Meadow (*An Analysis of Japanese Character Structure*. New York: Institute for International Studies, 1944. Mimeographed.). Basically these men all argue that the Japanese are a neurotic, compulsive people who have a store of repressed and hostile aggressions. On the basis of his experience at the University of Michigan's Okayama field station, Kerlinger points out that these men reached their conclusions using inadequate and often inaccurate information in addition to having strong ethnocentric cultural biases.

1943 ———. "Decision-Making in Japan." *Social Forces* 30:36–41 (Oct. 1951)

This study is based on Kerlinger's experiences as education officer for the Shikoku district. A general discussion of Japanese decision-making practices in an historical perspective is followed by a section on the effect of the occupation upon traditional decision-making patterns. Kerlinger suggests that SCAP personnel may well have failed to realize that the Japanese generally lack a full understanding of what "democratic" procedures entail. As a consequence, while democratic forms may be followed, traditional decision-making based on consensus still prevails and continues to be dominated by old style considerations of social status and authority.

1944 ———. "Local Associations of Shikoku." In University of Michigan. Center for Japanese Studies. *Occasional Papers*, v.2. Ann Arbor: Univ. of Michigan Pr., 1952. p.59–72.

This article is a product of Kerlinger's experience in the Shikoku area as a civil education officer from September 1947 to December 1949, working with the Allied occupation civil affairs region to develop democratic local associations. The author attempts to assess the effectiveness of the occupation authorities' efforts to bring democratic institutions to Japan in part through the development of these local associations. A brief summary of local associations in prewar Japan is presented first. Then the creation of a new legal framework for the social education system and local associations under the occupation is outlined. The 3 stages in which reform progressed are noted. Against this background the postwar local associations in Shikoku are studied in some detail. In conclusion, Kerlinger looks at the probable future for the trends begun under the occupation.

1944a ———. *Techniques of Democracy: A Guide to Procedure for Japanese Organizations.* Takamatsu, Japan: 1948. 66p.

"The single greatest obstacle in the way of achieving true democracy in Japan," Kerlinger writes, "is not only the general lack of understanding of the basic principles of democracy, but also an almost complete lack of knowledge of how to conduct organization meetings in a democratic manner." Accordingly, within this publication which also was published in Japanese, he provides considerable information on the following 6 topics: (1) how to start an organization; (2) order of business; (3) rules of order; (4) duties and responsibilities of officers; (5) responsibilities and rights of members; and (6) the Japanese system of making decisions. Illustrations accompany the text.

Kerr, William C. *Japan Begins Again.* 1949. See no.594.

1945 Kinoshita, Hanji. "Echoes of Militarism in Japan." *Pacific Affairs* 26, no.3: 244–51 (Sept. 1953)

This article describes the postwar activities of various groups of Japanese military men. After the signing of the peace treaty, many former officers were depurged in 1952. Army officers were divided on political issues into 4 main groups which eventually came together to form the nonpolitical Kaikokai. Navy officers organized the nonpolitical Suikokai. Smaller groups like the Hattori Organization and the Institute on Continental Affairs are also mentioned along with the activities of a few individuals such as Tsuji Masanobu.

1945a Klinger, Wallace R. "The Character of the Japanese." *Social Studies* 38:258–66 (Oct. 1947)

This essay on Japanese national character is based largely on examples drawn from Japanese history. Klinger finds that vertical loyalty and group ideology have been and are the most pronounced tendencies in the Japanese character. Until the mid-1930s, however, individualism also was making some headway, and the occupation's reforms are now providing fresh impetus for it. The wisdom of the Allied governments and of Japan's leaders, Klinger concludes, will be the determining factor in what emerges from the chaotic conditions of present-day Japan.

1946 Lifton, Robert Jay. "On Death and Death Symbolism: The Hiroshima Disaster." *Psychiatry* 27:191–210 (1964); also in *American Scholar* 34:257–72 (Spring 1965), and in *History and Human Survival*, comp. by Robert Jay Lifton. New York: Random, 1970. p.156–86.

Examining the Hiroshima experience with an emphasis upon various kinds of death imagery and symbolism, Lifton explores the psychological elements of what he refers to as the "permanent encounter with death" which the atomic bomb created within those exposed to it. He first discusses 4 different stages of this encounter—(1) immersion in death, (2) invisible contamination, (3) "A-bomb disease," and (4) identification with the dead—and then suggests a few general principles in the area of the psychology of death and dying that are essentially derived from this investigation but are by no means limited to the Hiroshima experience.

1947 ———. "Psychological Effects of the Atomic Bomb in Hiroshima: The Theme of Death." *Daedalus* 92, no.3:462–97 (Summer 1963); reprinted under the title, "The Hiroshima Bomb." In *History and Human Survival*, comp. by Robert Jay Lifton. New York: Random, 1970. p.114–55.

On the basis of lengthy interviews conducted with 2 groups of survivors of the Hiroshima holocaust (one group of 33 was randomly selected from a list of over 90,000 survivors; the other group of 42 was more highly educated and members were selected because of their ability to articulate their experiences), Lifton probes the psychological effects of this event. His study is divided into 3 parts: the first part deals with the recollection of the experience itself and its meaning 17 years later; the second part deals with residual concerns and fears, particularly relating to delayed radiation effects; the third part deals with the survivors' sense of self and society, or of special group identity. Lifton concludes that: (1) the survivors experience a continuous daily psychological encounter with death; (2) the broad society in which the survivors exist tends to regard them with both sympathy and suspicion; (3) the survivors were forced by the magnitude of the disaster into a state of "psychological closure," a state in which normal emotional feelings and responses were stifled or completely absent; and (4) the state of "psychological closure" was followed by intense feelings of guilt and shame for personal inability to cope effectively with the tragedy and to mitigate the enormous suffering of family, friends, and fellow citizens.

1948 ———. "Youth and History: Individual Change in Post War Japan." *Asian Cultural Studies* 3:115–36 (1962); also in *Daedalus* 172–97 (Winter 1962), and in *History and Human Survival*, comp. by Robert Jay Lifton. New York: Random, 1970. p.24–57.

Blending psychological theory and historical perspective, Lifton engages in a detailed discussion of the psychological perceptions of Japan's postwar youth. Noting at the outset the counter pressures of inertia (maintained by traditional psychological patterns) and flux (stimulated by pressures toward change), Lifton proceeds with an analysis of psychological dissonance created by historical dislocation and examines the concepts of selfhood, logic and beauty, and direction and principles within the postwar setting. He concludes with several brief generalizations concerning youth experiences and historical change.

Loduchowski, Heinz. "Amerikanische Demokratie als Lebensform im japanischen Schul- und Familiensystem. Ein pädagogisches Experiment in einem moralischen Vakuum." 1962. See no.2083.

1949 Maki, John McGilvrey. *Japanese Nationalism in Transition*. Mimeographed. New York: Institute of Pacific Relations, International Secretariat, 1947. 18p. (Institute of Pacific Relations, 10th conference, supplementary paper, 1947)

The author, a former member of the Government Section of SCAP and a political scientist, gives a cautious view of the future of Japanese nationalism. While agreeing that aggressive militant Japanese nationalism has been crushed by the American forces and contained by SCAP's policy of social and political reforms, particularly by the new constitution which denounces war and replaces monarchical by popular sovereignty, the author contends that an actual change in the content of Japanese nationalism will not occur unless there is a change in Japanese attitudes. Maki observes that pressure by the Japanese themselves for positive and democratic changes has not been strong. To demonstrate this point, he cites the lack of new effective leadership and the continued presence of the emperor system, and states that Japan's cabinet ministers, bureaucrats, and educators still share the attitudes of prewar and wartime ruling groups. He warns that it would be "a great mistake" to assess the progress of the occupation simply in terms of the number and nature of directives issued, the pro-American attitudes of Japanese officials and people, the writing of new laws, and the expulsion of prominent figures from public life. Nevertheless, he feels that there is a possibility that Japanese nationalism can become a healthy social factor, primarily because Japan emerged from the war in a better position economically than any other area in Asia.

1950 Maruyama, Masao. *Nationalism in Post-war Japan*. Mimeographed. Tokyo: Japan Institute of Pacific Relations, 1950.

25p. (Institute of Pacific Relations, 11th conference, Japanese paper no.3, 1950)

A political scientist from Tokyo University discusses the nature of Japanese nationalism and its future form. After reviewing its historical development, Maruyama observes that after the Meiji Restoration Japanese nationalism developed in support of the imperial system and the ruling regime's expansionist policies, becoming rich in emotional and patriotic expression but failing to inculcate a mature sense of responsibility in the modern citizen. The author contends that the defeat of Japan destroyed ultranationalism and the "charismatic authority" that the emperor had enjoyed and dispersed nationalistic sentiments into nonpolitical dimensions of life. To support this contention, he cites the collapse of the political symbols of the old nationalism, the loss of the idea of national mission, and the success of the early occupation policy which encouraged various democratic elements. Yet at the same time, because former, aggressive, nationalistic sentiments have been dispersed into sports and other activities of a nonpolitical nature, and because the Japanese bureaucracy, strengthened by the occupation authorities, as well as the rural communities which were not seriously harmed by the national catastrophe, hold conservative views, he feels that Japanese nationalism may reemerge in a new form. He concludes that the occupation authorities are in a difficult position, since if the occupation continues, the Japanese may revive their nationalistic sentiments and become critical of the occupation but, if it ceases to enforce democratization, prewar ultranationalistic leadership may revive.

1951 Matsumiya, Kazuya. "Family Organization in Present-day Japan." *American Journal of Sociology* 53, no.2:105–10 (Sept. 1947)

Through an analysis of such characteristics of the Japanese family unit as the hierarchy of positions, the cohabitation of different generations, and the relationship of relatives, the author seeks to determine the extent to which the patriarchal family organization exists in postwar Japan. He discovers that the large family household is disappearing as Japan becomes an industrialized and urbanized country and that this trend is most apparent in the cities, where married sons are increasingly establishing homes of their own. Nonetheless, because of the presence of consanguinates of several generations and of boarders, the average Japanese urban household remains larger than many of its European counterparts.

1952 Meadow, Arnold. *An Analysis of Japanese Character Structure*. Mimeographed. New York: Institute for International Studies, 1944.

1953 Minami, Hiroshi. "The Post-war Social Psychology of the Japanese People." *Annals of the Hitotsubashi Academy* 1:104–10 (Apr. 1951). Reprinted in *Japan Christian Quarterly* 20:106–12 (Apr. 1954).

Minami surveys some of the most outstanding features of the changing Japanese mentality as part of his initial effort to study postwar Japanese social psychology in a systematic fashion. He notes that Japanese psychology is very complicated and burdensome for the individual and that individuals often undergo tremendous mental strain.

1954 Moloney, James Clark. *Understanding the Japanese Mind*. New York: Philosophical Library, 1954. xvix, 252p.

Moloney examines the thesis that systems of psychotherapy are involved with implicitly assumed goals which differ from society to society. Noting that Japanese psychoanalysis aims at reinforcing pressures toward categorical and arbitrary conformity, he indicates the changes it has undergone in being imported to Japan and syncretized with Japanese culture.

1955 Moos, Felix. *Inertia and Change: Elements of the Japanese Family and Kinship Organization since 1945*. Ph.D. dissertation, Univ. of Washington, 1963. 297p. (Abstracted in *Dissertation Abstracts* 24:2650 [1964]; University Microfilms order no.64–422)

The effects of the occupation on the organization of Japanese society, particularly vis-à-vis kinship relations and family structure, are outlined here. Moos notes that during the occupation period alternatives representing modifications of intra- and interfamily relationships were presented to the Japanese. He concludes that the traditional family pattern, which was primarily hierarchical, has shifted to a more egalitarian basis. However, the themes of inertia and change which are responsible for the contradictions of contemporary Japan are still conspicuous. According to Moos, change is occurring on a microlevel rather than on an overall basis. The conclusions of this study were used by the author in his article entitled, "Japan: Culture Change and Acculturation: Some Considerations," in *Transactions of the International Conference of Orientalists in Japan* 5:104–9 (1960).

1956 Morris, Ivan Ira. *Nationalism and the Right Wing in Japan: A Study of Postwar Trends.* London: Oxford Univ. Pr., 1960. xiii, 476p.

Morris discusses the form that nationalism has taken in the postwar period, noting its development in a direction very different from that which led Japan to defeat in 1945. He points out that Western concern with the extreme left may at times lead us to concentrate our concern overwhelmingly on Communist movements and, consequently, to underrate the potential threat that may come from the opposite extreme. One aim of his study is to correct this inbalance. Ivan Morris served with the occupation in Japan. Most of the material for this book was derived from primary Japanese sources, interviews, and direct observation.

1957 Muramatsu, Tsuneo. *Japan: Some Psychological Perspectives.* Tokyo: SCAP, Civil Information and Education Section, 12 Oct. 1949. 25p.; reprinted in George W. Kisker, ed. *World Tensions: The Psychopathology of International Relations.* New York: Prentice-Hall, 1951. p.191–206.

The monograph represents one of the first professional comments on Japanese national behavior by a Japanese psychiatrist to appear in English. Beginning with an explanation of traditional interpersonal relations, attitudes toward authority, and the customs and emotions implicit in such terms as *giri* and *on*, the author relates them to the development of such cultural activities as flower arrangement and the composition of the 17 syllable *haiku* as outlets for suppressed energies. The author further relates traditional cultural values to the authoritarian style of Japanese politics in post-Meiji times. The defeat in World War II led the Japanese, especially Japanese youth, to distrust authority in any form and to be aggressive in their attitudes as a reversed expression of their actual submissiveness. In light of his conclusions, the author cautions against verbal imitations of democracy and notes that the generally passive tendency still persistent among the majority of the Japanese people is a likely invitation to a resurgence of authoritarianism.

This monograph is available on microfilm from the National Archives, Washington, D.C.

1958 Nakano, Takashi. "Recent Studies of Change in the Japanese Family." *International Social Science Journal* 14, no.3: 527–38 (1962)

A survey of trends in the study of change within the Japanese family by Japanese sociologists. The works of Kawashima Takeyoshi, Ariga Kizaemon, Kitano Seiichi, Koyama Takashi, Fuse Tetsuji, Morioka Kiyomi, and Kakizaki Kyōichi are discussed. The article focuses on the household or *ie* and postwar family changes.

1959 Namba, Monkichi. "Some Problems of Social Change in Japan." *Sociologia Internationalis* 1:219–26 (1963)

Namba discusses some of the distinctive phenomena of social change in Japan after the war and points out that various reforms undertaken by the occupation served as major catalysts for changes in both urban and rural society.

1960 Nambara, Shigeru. "Creation of New

Japanese Civilization." *Ethics* 56:291–96 (July 1946)

In an address delivered to Japanese students, the president of Tokyo University proposes "the transformation of Japan's first military defeat into a spiritual victory." In a brief analysis of the main characteristics of the Japanese tradition, he notes that although the Japanese people have a strong national consciousness, "there was little evidence of any awakening of the individual human consciousness as an independent personality or of development of the capacities of human nature among the people." He notes that, through the emperor's renunciation of divinity, he has achieved the independence of his own human nature and insists that all Japanese must achieve a similar independence. According to the author, the character of the people must be changed and not merely the social and political systems within which they operate. The revolution must be a "subjective spiritual revolution, intellectual, and religious in nature."

1961 Norbeck, Edward. "Postwar Cultural Change and Continuity in Northeastern Japan." *American Anthropologist* 63: 297–321 (Apr. 1961)

Norbeck provides a detailed discussion of postwar economic and social changes in 5 communities of Miyagi prefecture in the Tōhoku region of Japan. His basic concern is to trace patterns of change in the agricultural sphere and in community structure. He includes sections dealing with standards of living, local finance and social welfare, kinship ties, exchange and wage labor, and non-kin associations. He concludes that change has been a function of both indigenous development and occupation reforms, and that a trend toward the strengthening of cooperative associations is discernable.

1962 ———. *Takashima: A Japanese Fishing Community.* Salt Lake City: Univ. of Utah Pr., 1954. xii, 232p.

In discussing some of the major changes observable in the *buraku* since the occupation, Norbeck notes that the institutions of American-sponsored ideas such as education, the public welfare system, the Community Chest, government, and law appear to be meekly accepted and, as a whole, approved. They are, however, still new and their effects are as yet hardly discernible. This study of Takashima is based on Edward Norbeck's field work conducted in Japan during 1950–51 and submitted to the University of Michigan in 1952 as a Ph.D. dissertation entitled *Takashima: A Fishing Community of Japan.* (Abstracted in *Dissertation Abstracts* 12:124–25 [1952]; University Microfilms order no. 3541.)

1963 Pinkerton, Florence Stebe. *The Concept of National Character: Its Historical Development, Its Study, and Its Relevance to International Relations.* Ph.D. dissertation, New York Univ., 1960. 498p. (Abstracted in *Dissertation Abstracts* 27: 1891A–92A [1966]; University Microfilms order no.66–9741)

The author's discussion of research dealing with the Japanese and German national characters is used to support her thesis that national character as a concept is valid. She points out that research on the Japanese national character done by psychiatrists and anthropologists during World War II was of use at the end of the war in that it revealed that Japan was ready to seek peace in May 1945 and that the Allied occupation of Japan could be accomplished through Japanese political machinery. The thesis includes also a discussion of the divisions of opinions in the psychocultural disciplines with respect to the delineation of national character.

Raper, Arthur F. "Some Effects of Land Reform in Thirteen Japanese Villages." 1951. *See* no.1729.

1964 ———. "Some Recent Changes in Japanese Village Life." *Rural Sociology* 16:3–16 (Mar. 1951)

Arthur Raper of the U.S. Department of Agriculture notes that changes at the village level toward more democratic ways of life are of special significance since the village is the all-important locality and functioning group in Japan. Among the numerous reforms initiated by the occupation, he considers the land reform program and the establishment of farmers' cooperatives to have had the greatest effect on peoples' lives.

1965 Scott, William A. "The Information Meeting as an Instrument of Social Change in Occupied Japan." *Public Opinion Quarterly* 16, no.2:160–78 (Summer 1952)

In this article, the author draws upon his experiences as a civil information officer in occupied Japan to formulate a systematic program of information meetings as an important part of the reorientation of the Japanese people towards democratic values and procedures. Audience-centered meetings and the use of behavioral criteria in their evaluation are recommended. This article gives a useful picture of democratization—its content and techniques—at the grass-roots level.

1966 Seshaiah, S. "Post-war Reforms and Changes in the Leadership Structure of Village Japan: A Case Study." *Eastern Anthropologist* 19, no.1:1–28 (Jan./Apr. 1966)

Seshaiah, a member of the Department of East Asian Studies at the Indian School of International Studies in New Delhi, focuses his attention on changes in the structure and formation of village leadership in Japan as a consequence of SCAP's land and local autonomy reforms. On the basis of the case study he conducted between July 1961 and July 1962 in Kannari village, Miyagi prefecture, he concludes that the basic structure of village leadership has undergone only limited change since prereform leaders still have control over many spheres of local affairs. This is partly because the traditional methods of choosing leaders—by consensus and by compromise—remain strong. Nevertheless, leadership is no longer the monopoly of a few privileged persons, who in prewar days had acquired their positions largely on account of their wealth or traditional prestige. Individuals now must compete for those positions by means of building up local support groups through *oyabun-kobun* relationships and other means and by campaigning for elections.

1967 Smith, Robert John. "Cooperative Forms in a Japanese Agricultural Community." In University of Michigan. Center for Japanese Studies. *Occasional Papers*, v.3. Ann Arbor: Univ. of Michigan Pr., 1952. p.59–70.

The *buraku* of Kurusu, in Yasuhara-mura, Kagawa prefecture, is examined in order to describe the variety of cooperative groupings which still exist in postwar Japan in a rural community. The author divides the cooperative groups to which Kurusu residents belong into 4 categories and then proceeds to a discussion of the various groups. Cooperative groups in the study include the *dōgyō* to which every household belongs and which acts on 7 specified occasions, the *Kurusu Yōsui Kumiai* (Kurusu Irrigation Union), the *Keikōtō Kumiai* (Insect Lamp Union), and *tema-gae* groups (exchange labor). In addition to these more formalized aspects of cooperation, the author also notes other ways in which Kurusu considers itself a distinct social unit, and he points out how the *buraku* acts as a unit in local politics.

1968 ———. "Kurusu: A Japanese Agricultural Community." In University of Michigan. Center for Japanese Studies. *Occasional Papers*, v.5. Ann Arbor: University of Michigan Pr., 1956. p.ix–xvi, 1–112.

This study, written originally as a doctoral dissertation submitted to Cornell University in 1953, presents a general picture of life in a *buraku*. Smith was in Kurusu from September 1951 through August 1952. He discusses various aspects of village life such as neighborly cooperation, day-to-day life, agricultural methods and practices, family and household, the life cycle, and religious and ceremonial life. He also includes an examination of the nature and effects on Kurusu of the land reform begun in 1946. The last chapter which is entitled "Aspects of Change" notes that

Kurusu "has seen vast changes within the past fifty years, changes merely accelerated by World War II and the Occupation."

1969 ———, and Richard King Beardsley, eds. *Japanese Culture: Its Development and Characteristics.* Chicago: Aldine, 1963. ix, 193p. (Viking Fund publications in Anthropology, no.34)

A collection of anthropological studies on Japan. Only the article by Y. Scott Matsumoto, "Notes on Primogeniture in Postwar Japan" (p.55–69), deals with the occupation. It demonstrates that among older, less educated, and rural Japanese traditional views on primogeniture tend to persist, but that in other sectors of the population, reforms begun by the occupation are gaining acceptance.

1970 Smythe, Hugh H. "The Eta: A Marginal Japanese Caste." *American Journal of Sociology* 58, no.2:194–96 (Sept. 1952)

This brief article on the *Eta*, a racially and ethnically Japanese group which had been prevented by the stigma of caste from fully participating in Japanese society, deals in part with their position after World War II. The author notes that their lot has improved somewhat as a consequence of SCAP prohibitions on all forms of social, religious, racial, and political discrimination. Nevertheless, the *Eta* continue to follow their traditional occupations and remain largely a segregated, poor, and socially ostracized segment of the society.

1971 ———. "Nationalism in Japan." *Fortnightly* 178:147–54 (Sept. 1952)

The reemergence of nationalistic, militaristic, and extreme right-wing groups is examined in this article, and Smythe warns that the West should be careful when encouraging Japan to become a military ally in fighting communism. He cites the poverty existing in cities and rural areas, the dispirited nature of the intelligentsia, the corruption in government, and the weakness of political parties as factors aiding the growth of the rightist movement. The groundwork for this comeback of nationalist groups was laid, he writes, in 1951 when more than 2,500 right-wing leaders were depurged, former field officers from the old Imperial Army began to be incorporated into the new Japanese army, and the way for actual rearmament was opened with the signing of the peace treaty and security pact with the United States. Eight influential rightist groups plus minor ones and the exmilitary officers' groups are discussed. The emperor is looked at as another force providing Japan historically with the background for the reemergence of nationalism and militarism.

1972 ———. "Note on Racial Ideas of the Japanese." *Social Forces* 31, no.3:258–60 (Mar. 1953)

The author, a faculty member at Yamaguchi National University in Japan, briefly describes the origins and nature of the racial ideas that the Japanese presently have and strongly urges that an analysis be made without delay of race consciousness among the Japanese.

1973 ———. "A Note on Racialism in Japan." *American Sociological Review* 16, no.6:823–24 (Dec. 1951)

This brief article not only notes the Japanese dislike of the *Eta* and the Korean residents of Japan but also points out that racialism as understood in the United States is still unknown in Japan despite Japanese experiences and contacts with foreigners during the occupation period.

1974 ———, and Mabel M. Smythe. "The Impact of the American Occupation." *Commonweal* 55:633–35 (4 Apr. 1952)

In the final stages of the occupation 2 American members of the faculty of Yamaguchi University discuss some of the changes that have been wrought in contemporary Japanese culture. They describe the Westernization of clothing and hair styles, the popularity of foreign movies, books and food, and other innovations in the culture, all of which reflect occupation influence. At the same time, however, they note a reawakening of interest in traditional Japanese art and culture that has come about in recent months.

1975 ———, and ———. "Race, Culture, and Politics in Japan." *Phylon* 13, no.3: 192–98 (Sept. 1952)

An impressionistic analysis of Japanese culture based on the authors' experiences teaching at Japanese universities during the occupation. Although defeat is seen as having done much to change traditional Japanese "feudal" culture, still "the old racial-cultural ideas persist." Thus, Japanese are concerned about American anti-Japanese racism which may well drive Japan to prefer alliances with other Asian nations.

1976 ———, and Naitoh Yoshimasa. "The *Eta* Caste in Japan." *Phylon* pt.1, 14, no.1:19–27 (Mar. 1953); pt.2, 14, no.2: 157–62 (June 1953)

After the first part of this article (p.19–27) describes the history of the outcaste *Eta*, the second part (p.157–62) goes into their status under the occupation. Although the occupation attempted to wipe out all forms of discrimination and segregation between groups and sexes, in the case of the *Eta* the attempt seems to have been unsuccessful. The *Eta* continued to be discriminated against in housing, work, education, marriage, etc. Various organizations working to end this discrimination are described.

1977 Steiner, Jesse Frederick. "Social Change in Japan." *Sociology and Social Research* 31:3–11 (Sept./Oct. 1946)

Japan's historical adjustment to foreign cultures is described in an effort to predict her reaction to their reforms initiated during the occupation. The author describes in detail what he considers to be the 2 main foreign incursions on Japan—that of the Chinese in the sixth century and of the Western powers at the time of the Restoration—emphasizing the extent to which the government controlled all social change. He then relates these experiences to the various reactions of the Japanese to the occupation, i.e., to their willingness to adapt to radical reforms in the social and political structure of the nation and their docility toward the occupation authorities. At the same time he warns that the experience of the Japanese in adapting and integrating foreign cultures in the past suggests that they will ultimately treat the occupation's reforms in the same manner. In conclusion, he advises that "the role of the Allied powers should be limited to insistence upon a demilitarized, popular form of government with freedom to put into effect economic policies that will make possible a fully self-supporting nation." The detailed steps whereby these policies would be implemented and the ultimate forms of the social and political structures should be left to the Japanese themselves.

Steiner, Kurt. "The Revision of the Civil Code of Japan: Provisions Affecting the Family." 1950. *See* no.1292.

1978 Stoetzel, Jean. *Without the Chrysanthemum and the Sword: A Study of the Attitudes of Youth in Post-war Japan.* New York: Columbia Univ. Pr., 1955. 334p. (A UNESCO publication)

A sociological study of youth in postwar Japan. It was conducted in late 1951 and early 1952 by the French sociologist Jean Stoetzel and the Dutch Japanologist Fritz Vos who were working for UNESCO. Through sociological techniques (surveys, interviews, etc.) it investigates many of the ideas first presented by Ruth Benedict in *The Chrysanthemum and the Sword* (1946) (no.1908), with particular attention to Japanese attitudes towards occupation reforms of the status of the emperor and other authority figures, the new role of women in society, pacificism, etc. Pages 239–311 reproduce the data collected.

1979 Taeuber, Irene Barnes. "Family, Migration, and Industrialization in Japan." *American Sociological Review* 16, no.2: 149–57 (Apr. 1951)

This article by a member of the Princeton University faculty focuses on industrialization, urbanization, the role of the family, and migration between 1920 and 1940. It also includes, however, a brief discussion of the postwar period in which the author notes the rapid growth of Japan's population as well as significant changes in the composition and nature of the work force under the occupation.

1980 Takahashi, Akira. "Post-war Democratization in Japan: Development of Democratic Consciousness among the Japanese People." *International Social Science Journal* 13, no.1:78–91 (1961)

This article is based on the findings of opinion polls and social research studies carried out by Japanese sources. An explanation of the ideology of familism is given, and 3 stages in the development of democratic consciousness among the Japanese people are discussed. The stages are: (1) 1945–50 when democracy was adopted as a form but not as an ideology under the occupation; (2) 1950–55 when the Japanese people began themselves to defend democratic rights; and (3) 1955–60 when the movement toward a classless society was intensified and public support for the peace movement grew.

1981 Takashima, Zenya. "The Social Consciousness of the People in Post-war Japan." *Annals of the Hitotsubashi Academy* 1:91–103 (Apr. 1951)

Takashima Zenya, professor of sociology at Hitotsubashi University, describes the factors that are making the substance of Japan's democratization so complicated and obscure. He discusses how 5 ideological types—liberalism, modified capitalism, cooperative-ism, socialism, and communism—have been handled in the consciousness of the postwar Japanese.

1982 Tanimo, Setsu. "Post-war Democratization in Japan: Family Life." *International Social Science Journal* 13, no.1: 57–64 (1961)

The author discusses the democratization of family life in Japan under the new constitution. Four major trends emerge: (1) a trend toward smaller families; (2) changes in marital relations providing for greater individual choice of spouse; (3) slow changes in customs concerning succession; and (4) a rising social status for women.

1983 Titiev, Mischa. "Changing Patterns of *Kumiai* Structure in Rural Okayama." In University of Michigan. Center for Japanese Studies. *Occasional Papers*, v.4. Ann Arbor: Univ. of Michigan Pr., 1953. p.1–28.

The introduction of this article defines the concept of *kumiai* or "neighborhood associations comprising a small number of households" as they exist in Japanese rural social organization. In this study the author analyzes 10 *kumiai* which are distributed among 4 villages and are all farming communities situated in Okayama prefecture, Japan. After detailed examination of each of the 10, Titiev notes 6 contrasts between "mature" and "recent" *kumiai* and then points out the underlying "trend in modern Japan away from reliance on and cooperation with relatives and toward greater ties with non-kin." In the closing section, social structures in Okayama City are discussed briefly and it is noted that "the close bonds typical of rural *kumiai* have not been duplicated in the structures of any of the formal social units set up at Okayama City." Pages 13–28 consist of tables, maps, and pictures.

1984 Tsurumi, Kazuko. *Social Change and the Individual: Japan before and after Defeat in World War II*. Princeton, N.J.: Princeton Univ. Pr., 1970. xiv, 441p.

This study is a test of the hypothesis that socialization occurs throughout an individual's life and that personality changes resulting from socialization can occur throughout adulthood and old age. Tsurumi discusses the interrelationship of value orientations and adult socialization, adult socialization and subsequent adult-personality changes, and effects of societal change on adult socialization. She then compares adult socialization in Japan before and after the nation's defeat in 1945. In her conclusions she states that adult socialization prior to defeat was primarily of a negative-affect type, oriented toward the glorification of death in war, while postwar socialization appears to be more positive. Prewar adult socialization tended to produce ever-committed and reversely-committed as well as many-layered and conflicting-self types of personality, while postwar socialization has produced what she terms reverse-committed, many-layered, conflicting-self, and innovator personalities. The author relied heavily on personal documents, such as letters, diaries, and life records in her study.

This book represents a revised version of the author's Ph.D. dissertation, entitled *Adult Socialization and Social Change: Japan before and after Defeat in World War II*, submitted to Princeton University in 1967. (Abstracted in *Dissertation Abstracts* 28:1913A–14A [1967]; University Microfilms order no. 67-13,512.)

Wagatsuma, Sakae. "Democratization of the Family Relation in Japan." 1950. *See* no.1296a.

1984a ———. "The Family System under the New Civil Code." *Contemporary Japan* 16:482–83 (Oct./Dec. 1947)

In this article, translated from the October 1947 issue of *Shakai Shisō*, the dean of the Law College at Tokyo University first takes note of the criticisms being leveled at the new family code. Most of these are laments over the passing of the "beautiful customs" of the traditional home and the order that was maintained by the old family head. Wagatsuma asserts, however, that the critics err in assuming that the old customs had some connection with the legal position of the family head, and that the democratization of the family will automatically lead to the collapse of domestic harmony. Order maintained by power, he declares, is not the ideal sort of order. Democracy is essential not only in Japanese politics and the economy but also in "the basic principles of plebian life."

1985 Ward, Robert Edward. "The Sociopolitical Role of the *Buraku* (Hamlet) in Japan." *American Political Science Review* 45:1025–40 (Dec. 1951)

This article, based primarily on research carried on by Ward throughout the year 1950 in Okayama prefecture, Japan, examines the internal organization, functions, external relations, and political importance of the *buraku* in Japanese society. The writer describes the important role of the *buraku* in Japnese culture and politics as the preserver of the traditional culture with its family and collective bases, its intricate status relationships, and the personal attitudes and behavior patterns derived from them.

1985a Williamson, Maude. "Changing Social Patterns in Japan." *Journal of Home Economics* 42:789–91 (Dec. 1950)

The author, a homemaking consultant to SCAP's Civil Information and Education Section, advised the Ministry of Education on homemaking programs for the public schools. Her remarks center on the nature of Japanese family life and the effects of various educational reforms and new women's rights legislation upon it. She predicts, for instance, that the establishment of coeducation will have a great impact on marital customs, boy-girl and man-wife relations, and the family in general. She also comments on the present situation of preschool education and on the position of Japanese women, particularly housewives.

1986 Yanaga, Chitoshi. "Japan: Nationalism Succeeds and Fails." *Current History* 19:67–72 (Aug. 1950)

In tracing modern Japanese nationalism, Yanaga notes that postwar nationalism finds itself in a state of confusion. He explains that while it is doubtful that Japan, with her population pressure and economic needs, could become like Switzerland, no intelligent Japanese would think it possible or probable for the nation to again follow a course of nationalism as it did prior to the war. Yanaga Chitoshi, author and professor of political science, served as a research analyst in the Department of State during the war.

1987 ———. "Japan: Tradition and Democracy." *Far Eastern Survey* 17:68–71 (24 Mar. 1948)

In an article considering the democratization of Japan in the postwar era, the nation's tradition of authoritarianism is described at length since the author believes that an understanding of this tradition is a prerequisite to effective democratization of the nation. In his opinion "although the mechanics of Japanese government and politics have shown a considerable degree of Westernization, the dynamics have remained quite unchanged and are as Japanese as they ever were." In developing a new political philosophy which would replace the old one, the author advocates education in the broadest sense of the term for the general population, making use of the new mass communication media as well as the reformed, formal educational system. In considering the latter, he particularly stresses the need for a change in the traditional Confucian-inspired student-teacher relationship which hampers the "give and take" so essential to education on the higher levels. In conclusion, the author recommends that effective programs of international cultural and information exchange be established that would benefit both the Japanese and the peoples whom they contact.

1988 Yoshino, Roger. *Selected Social Changes in a Japanese Village, 1935–1953*. Ph.D. dissertation, Univ. of Southern California, 1954. 188p. (Abstracted in Univ. of Southern California. *Abstracts of Dissertations* 218–19 [1955]); also in State College of Washington, *Research Studies* 24:1–182 (June 1956) under the title, "A Re-study of Suye-mura: An Investigation of Social Change."

This study, an investigation of what the author terms "selected social changes," was conducted in Suye Mura in south central Kyūshū. This village was the subject of a well-known earlier study by Professor John Embree in 1935, and Yoshino illuminates the changes that have transpired since then. He concludes that substantial change has occurred—particularly with respect to family structure, landholding, educational and political practices, and rural attitudes towards the emperor—as a result of various policies instituted during the occupation.

POPULATION PROBLEMS

The abrupt increase in the rate of population growth that characterized the immediate postwar years in Japan constituted one of the occupation's most difficult and delicate problems. The following items relate to the dimensions of that growth, the nature of the attendant problems, and the various attempts to deal with them.

1989 "Birth Rate Going Down." *Newsweek* 35:42 (8 May 1950)

A short résumé of the provisions and results of the Eugenics Protection Law of 1949 is presented. Three aspects of the law are discussed including the unrestricted sale of birth control devices and information concerning their use, the establishment of marriage consultation offices to explain the use of contraceptives, and the legalization of abortion for health and economic reasons. The conclusion states that these 3 approaches will not be sufficient to reduce the Japanese birth rate and must be supplemented by a vast increase in education and by industrialization of the economy.

1990 Cole, Allan. "Population Changes in Japan." *Far Eastern Survey* 15:149–50 (22 May 1946)

This article briefly discusses the results of a SCAP *Summation* which analyzed the quinquennial census of Japanese population that was taken on 1 November 1945. It presents total population figures, and suggests reasons for such totals and the trends in population growth they imply. The author draws attention to such factors as wartime dislocation, urban exodus, and repatriation to and from Japan as affecting the statistics, and concludes that Japan's rate of population increase, which has been declining since 1930, will be accelerated by the effects of the war and economic depression.

Granada, Yole. "Should We Rebuild Japan?" 1948. *See* no.1496.

1991 Ike, Nobutaka. "Birth Control in Japan." *Far Eastern Survey* 17:271–74 (8 Dec. 1948)

Ike, a lecturer at the Johns Hopkins University, traces the population problem which has reemerged as a topic of discussion since Japan's defeat. In discussing birth control, he notes its political implications as an increasingly important question in future years.

1992 Japan. Prime Minister's Office. Bureau of Statistics. *Population Census of Japan, 1 October 1947: Summary Report.* Tokyo: 1949. 253p.

1993 ———. ———. ———. *Population Census of 1950.* v.1, *Total Population.* Tokyo: 1951. iii, 249p.

This report, which is partly in English and partly in Japanese, presents the final count of the population by *to, do, fu, ken, shi, machi,* and *mura* according to the population census of 1 October 1950, the first regular census to be conducted after the war in accordance with the statistics law. Volume 1 is a general summary of the census. Detailed results were published in successive volumes based upon 1 percent and 10 percent sample tabulations and, finally, 100 percent tabulations.

1994 ———. ———. ———. *Reports of 1947 Population Census.* no.7, *Population by Age.* Tokyo: 1949. 301p.

English version of nos.1–6 in Japanese.

1995 Minoguchi, Tokijirō. "The Overpopulation Problem in Post-war Japan." *Annals of the Hitotsubashi Academy* 1: 111–19 (Apr. 1951)

Minoguchi points out that overpopulation in Japan must be measured by the real income per head of the population, and never from the volume of unemployment. He notes that the reason the number of unemployed in postwar Japan is abnormally small, in spite of the immense volume of overpopulation, is due to the fact that family enterprises still survive extensively in various industries.

1996 Morita, Yūzō. "Sampling Tabulation of the 1950 Population Census in Japan." *Bulletin of the International Statistical Institute* 33, pt.4:47–54 (1954)

Morita's paper, one of several presented by Japanese scholars and officials in December 1951 at the International Statistical Conferences held in India, explains the methods that were designed for tabulating the 1950 Japanese census. The tabulation, which was carried out in 3 stages, was based on 1 percent, 10 percent, and 100 percent respectively of the questionnaires. The planning and execution of this census was done by the Japanese government under the supervision and with the advice of experts in SCAP.

1997 Okazaki, Ayanori. "Le problème et la politique démographiques au Japon." *Population* 7, no.2:207–26 (Apr./June 1952)

Okasaki first discusses Japan's demographic situation prior to the end of World War II. He then examines the postwar increase in her population, Japan's demographic age structure, the relationship between the country's economic resources and her living standards, the distribution of the Japanese working population, the possibilities of Japanese emigration, and current efforts to popularize birth control. He concludes that the situation remains grave for Japan and notes that it is necessary for his nation to rebuild her economy as rapidly as possible if Japan's growing labor force is to be assured of full employment in coming years.

1997a Okazaki, Fumikata (Ayanori). "Population Problems of Japan." *Contemporary Japan* 17:248–54 (July/Dec. 1948)

The present food shortages, Okazaki argues, are part of the larger problem of overpopulation. Birth control has been widely publicized since the surrender, but it provides no immediate solution. The only possible approach is to increase Japan's ability to support her present population and thus eliminate the social unrest attendant upon overpopulation. One alternative is to increase agricultural production, but Okazaki points out that this will do little other than lead to a higher rural birth rate. He concludes, therefore, that the only practical solution is a rapid increase in industrial production destined for export markets.

1998 Pelzel, John Campbell. "Some Social Factors Bearing upon Japanese Population." *American Sociological Review* 15, no.1:20–25 (Feb. 1950)

In this paper, which the author originally presented at the 1949 annual meeting of the American Sociological Society, Pelzel focuses upon some of the changes in Japan that have resulted from urbanization and industrialization. He observes that the family has ceased to be an economic group and is losing many of its traditional functions. He also points out that the government, with its vast prestige and its traditional role as the arbiter of public morality, remains a powerful force for inducing changes in Japanese society and may be able to bring about a solution to Japan's population problem.

1999 Population Problems Research Council (Tokyo). *Population Problem Series.* Tokyo: Mainichi Newspapers, 1950–58. nos.1–15.

A series of publications dealing with various aspects of Japan's postwar population. The individual publications are as follows: no.1, *The Population of Japan* (1950) 25p.; no.2, *Various Forms of 'Invisible' Unemployment in Agricultural Districts* (1950) 22p.; no.3, *A Survey of Public Opinion in Japan on the Readjustment of Over-population* (1951) 31p.; no.4, *Problems of Population and Economy of Japan* (1951) 25p.; no.5, *Activities of the Population Problems Research Council* (1951) 19p.; no.6, *Family System and Population of Farming Communities in Japan* (1952); no.7, *Public Opinion Survey on Birth Control in Japan* (1952) 55p.; no.8, *Influence of Emigrants on Their Home Village: Report of a Survey of Amerika-Mura* (1953) 36p.; no.9, *Family Planning Movement in Japan* (1953) 46p.; no.10, *Japan's Economy and Problems of Employment* (1954) 34p.; no.11, *The Future of Japan: Her Population and Natural Resources* (1955) 29p.; no.12, *Some Facts about Family Planning in Japan* (1955) 120p.; no.13, *Third Public Opinion Survey on Birth Control in Japan* (1955) 38p.; no.14, *Facts about the Population of Japan—Shown in Figures and Charts* (1956) 55p.; no.15, *Fourth Public Opinion Survey on Birth Control in Japan* (1958) 59p.

2000 Price, Willard. "Do the Japanese Need More Room?" *Asia and the Americas* 46:84–87 (Feb. 1946)

In an excerpt from his book *Key to Japan* (no.455b), Price notes that Japanese claims of overpopulation must be examined not by the number of people to the square mile but by the productive facilities and power of the people in addition to their access to food supplies. He estimates that an industrialized Japan can support a population of from 80 million to 100 million on an unprecedented level of well-being without resorting to plots of territorial aggression.

2001 Satō, Naotake. "Population Problem." *Contemporary Japan* 21, no.1/3: 56–65 (1952)

After presenting the nature of the population problem in Japan and showing why it must be solved on an international level, the author proposes various steps which could be taken to alleviate the problem. Before Japan looks to emigration as a means of solving the problem, Satō believes it should have done everything possible by domestic policy to improve the situation. He considers the possibilities for the development of

Hokkaido in this regard. The problems of using emigration as a solution and of finding employment for farmers' sons are mentioned. The author then discusses his proposals for emigration in order to balance the population of the world in relation to land areas. He describes President Truman's Point Four proposal and the United Nations' cooperative plan and suggests that a plan is needed "to shift people from the countries suffering from over-population to those under-developed areas and utilize this man power for their development." This shift should be done, he maintains, within the framework of the United Nations. Such a plan would help solve Japan's population problem.

2002 Steiner, Jesse Frederick. "Dilemma: Twenty Million Surplus Japanese." *New York Times Magazine* p.9, 41 (7 Oct. 1945)

Steiner, a sociologist who taught in Japan before the war, sees overpopulation as the greatest postwar problem facing Japan. The repatriation of some 20 million overseas Japanese will further complicate the already severe economic conditions in the home islands. He suggests that the Japanese government and the giant corporations offer aid. If conditions become too desperate, he warns, the masses will revolt, overturning the autocratic political and economic regimes. As a long-range solution, the author proposes family planning and the rebuilding of industries to create urban employment.

2003 ———. "Japan's Post-war Population Problems." *Social Forces* 31, no.3: 245–49 (Mar. 1953)

Jesse Steiner of Tokyo's International Christian University gives a detailed account of Japan's population problem and efforts as of 1953 to solve it, concluding that "the present decline in birth rates will probably continue during the next few years but there is little reason to believe that there will be any drastic efforts to slow up population growth." Topics discussed include the composition of the postwar population increase, postwar birth and death rates, postwar restriction of births, changing attitudes towards family limitation, postwar conquest of disease and increased life expectancy, overpopulation of farms, and the postwar economic situation.

Supreme Commander for the Allied Powers. Monograph 4. *Population*. 1952. See no.286.

2004 ———. Economic and Scientific Section. *Census of Population: Japan, 1 October 1950*. Tokyo: SCAP, 1951. 1v.

Although issued by SCAP this report records the results of the population census of Japan, undertaken by the Bureau of Statistics, Office of the Prime Minister of Japan, on 1 October 1950. The tabulations cover the total population of Japan residing in each prefecture as well as in all cities (*shi*) and counties (*gun*) within each prefecture.

Available at the Army Library, the Pentagon, Washington, D.C.

2005 ———. ———. Research and Programs Div. *Annual Change in Population of Japan Proper, 1 October 1920–1 October 1947*. Tokyo: SCAP, July 1948. i, 33p.

This statistical survey of Japanese population aims "to provide reliable historical series on the major components of annual net change in Japan's population since the first census of 1920." It gives special attention to the relative importance of 4 components: births, deaths, in-migrations, and out-migrations. It includes a discussion of basic sources of information and deficiencies in data published thus far, specific procedures followed in constructing the annual series, particularly intercensal and annual adjustments, the repatriation program in 1945–47, and out-migrations 1920–45. Three of the 5 tables in the appendix show monthly changes in vital statistics in 1940–45 and provide estimates for 1946.

2006 Taeuber, Irene Barnes. "Demographic Transition in Japan: Omens for the Future of Asian Populations." In *The Interrelations of Demographic, Economic, and Social Problems in Selected Under-*

developed Areas: Proceedings of a Round Table at the 1953 Annual Conference of the Milbank Memorial Fund, comp. by Milbank Memorial Fund. New York: Milbank Memorial Fund, 1954. p.9–31.

This study of modern Japan's demographic transition from high levels of mortality and fertility to the low levels characteristic of Western cultures seeks to pinpoint some of the aspects of Japanese industrialization and urbanization which facilitated this shift. Most of the description and analysis pertains to the prewar period, but there are references as well to population changes during the occupation period.

2006a ———. "Demographic Imperatives for the Peace in the Former Japanese Empire." In *New Compass of the World: A Symposium on Political Geography*, ed. by Hans Werner Weigert, Vilhjalmur Stefansson, and Richard Edes Harrison. New York: Macmillan, 1949. p.338–53.

Taeuber opens her discussion with the statement that: "Nowhere was the relationship between population growth, industrialization, and the aggressiveness that leads to war more apparent than in prewar Japan, and in few regions of the world is population so preeminent a hazard to the maintenance of the peace in the coming decade." She then describes the urbanization process in the former Japanese empire, demographic developments during the course of World War II, and the impact of Japan's defeat on the country's population. Pointing out that between April 1946 and February 1948 alone, births exceeded deaths by 2,300,000, Taeuber concludes with the prediction that Japan's demographic future depends on economic developments. "Only an industrial development more substantial than that which existed before the war," she asserts, "can provide the physical basis of subsistence for these increasing numbers" in the postwar era.

2007 ———. "Japan's Increasing People: Facts, Problems, and Policies." *Pacific Affairs* 23:271–93 (Sept. 1950)

In a carefully documented study the author considers the problem of present and future increases in the Japanese population. She mentions several ineffectual solutions which have been advocated to alleviate the situation before presenting an historical outline of demographic conditions in Japan from 1850 to the present. There is a discussion of Japanese government and SCAP Economic and Scientific Section predictions of population growth in the future and an outline of critical problems that will arise in connection with this growth. Finally, Taeuber describes the establishment and activities of the Population Problem Council (Jinkō Mondai Shingikai) created by the cabinet in April 1949. She maintains that "the basic factor in the evolution of realistic and humanitarian population policies . . . is the maintenance of a political democracy" and warns that if economic development sufficient to maintain Japan's increasing numbers is not achieved, then the issue of population will become Japan's primary problem.

2008 ———. "Population Growth and Economic Development in Japan." *Journal of Economic History* 11:417–28 (Fall 1951)

The author traces population growth and economic development throughout Japanese history. In this outline she questions a number of "myths" surrounding these 2 processes such as the presumably unchanging agrarian economy and stable population of the late Tokugawa period. Throughout the article the author points out the close ties between economic development and population growth. She notes that population growth in the future could motivate Japan to undertake further expansion in the Pacific.

2009 ———. *The Population of Japan.* Princeton, N.J.: Princeton Univ. Pr., 1958. xv, 461p.

Taeuber of the Office of Population Research, Princeton University, indicates that the extent to which SCAP policies or their absence were responsible for the national resort to abortion is an unanswerable question but, on the whole, the indirect influence of SCAP and the occupation seems to have been a positive factor in the decline of fertility rates. SCAP policies barred American action in the population field, but the numerous controversies on the subject awakened Japanese to the inconsistencies between policies in Japan and the limitation practices of the American people.

2010 ———. "Recent Population Developments in Japan: Some Facts and Reflections." *Pacific Affairs* 29:21–36 (Mar. 1956)

Modern science has lowered death rates and increased birth rates in many Asian countries. Japan is one country which has been able to control its rapid birth rate. In 1948, revised laws permitting birth control and abortion were passed. The birth rate went down, largely through the use of abortion. The relative popularity of abortion is explained by the lack of religious prohibitions and low cost. Possible economic consequences of Japan's population control program are briefly discussed. The author concludes that other Asian countries, behind Japan educationally and economically, may have trouble following Japan's example.

2011 Thompson, Warren S. "The Need for a Population Policy in Japan." *American Sociological Review* 15:25–33 (Feb. 1950)

Thompson of the Scripps Foundation for Research in Population Problems focuses his attention on the urgent population problem in postwar Japan. He seeks to determine whether Japan can become self-supporting and can maintain a reasonably decent standard of living under present political, demographic, and economic conditions. In addition to describing Japan's present economic situation and estimating the probable growth of her population, therefore, he discusses the critical relationship between population and resources within the country. His conclusion is a very forthright one. The Japanese must adapt their numbers to their resources by taking immediate steps to limit population growth if they wish to enjoy substantial improvements in their living conditions.

2011a Uyehara, Shigeru. "Population Problem of Japan." *Democratic Japan* (Tokyo) no.9:2–3 (Nov./Dec. 1950)

Given Japan's loss of her empire and the destruction of her industries, Uyehara argues, only a reduction of the present restrictions on Japan's industrial production to the minimum deemed necessary by the Allies will allow her to become self-sufficient once again and capable of feeding her people.

2011b Vikentyev, A. "MacArthur and Malthus." *Soviet Press Translations* 4: 495 (15 Sept. 1949); abridged version published under the same title in *Current Digest of the Soviet Press* 1, no.22:46 (28 June 1949)

This *Izvestia* article of 1 June 1949 comments on SCAP's intensive campaign for the establishment of birth control in Japan. Vikentyev notes that the Japanese are being advised to curtail their birth rate and that various SCAP officials are stating that the Japanese should be permitted to emigrate to such sparsely populated regions as New Guinea. Such statements as these, the author points out, only reinforce past Japanese imperialist arguments for overseas expansion. He interprets them as an indication of the American desire to encourage Japanese reactionaries to rebuild a militarist Japan which would serve as "a bulwark of American imperialism in the Far East."

2012 Warner, Denis Ashton. "Japan's New Live Weapon." *United Nations World* 3: 13–16 (June 1949)

The problem of rapid population growth in postwar Japan is examined and 4 solutions to this problem are presented. Warner evaluates each vis-à-vis its feasibility and the probability of its gaining support among occupation and Japanese officials. They include: (1) domestic migration and subsequent land reclamation for agricultural purposes to provide a partial solution and a means of absorbing up to 7,000,000 people; (2) rapid industrialization to increase employment opportunities (Massive agricultural imports are discounted because they would necessitate economic development far beyond anything previously considered acceptable for postwar Japan.); (3) birth control, discounted because of the occupation's refusal to institute it and because the Japanese reaction to it is unknown; and (4) emigration, discussed at length, especially in reference to New Guinea, but discarded because of the difficulties it presents.

The Educational System

It was widely understood among the planners of the occupation that the long-term success of their endeavors to democratize Japan depended ultimately upon changes in the educational system. Accordingly, a great deal of time and attention was devoted to attempts to "reform" the structure and functioning of Japanese schools at all levels—from preschool through graduate and adult education. The models involved were typically American and they were often applied in what seemed to be an excessively literal and uncritical manner. Such efforts aroused extensive interest and concern both in Japan and abroad. This interest is reflected in the sizeable body of literature set forth below. It includes the reports of the several American advisory missions on education and the occupation-sponsored attempts at language reform, i.e., the substitution of a syllabic for an ideographic script. Items relating to teachers' unions, however, will be found in the section on labor unions (p.559). For even more extensive and detailed lists of references on this subject, readers are referred to Herbert Passin, *Japanese Education: A Bibliography of Materials in the English Language* (1970) (no.22) and to Walter Crosby Eells, *The Literature of Japanese Education, 1945–1954* (1955) (no.8).

2013 Abe, Yoshishige. "An Address to the U.S. Education Mission." *School and Society* 64:73–75 (3 Aug. 1946)

This article is the second half of an address by the Japanese Minister of Education to the U.S. Education Mission in Tokyo on 8 March 1946. Abe suggests that the occupation period involves the most comprehensive era of Japanese isolation since the period prior to the Meiji Restoration and he requests a rapid end to restricted access to foreign books and information. He also calls for a balance between enthusiasm for educational change and respect for cultural traditions, noting the American tendency to impose their own educational system and to experiment with as-yet-untried ideas. In conclusion, an emphasis on science in the new school curricula is requested and the mission is reminded that the educational community is the most liberal in Japan and the most willing to cooperate with occupation officials.

2013a Alden, Jane M. "Japanese Education in Review." *Department of State Bulletin* 27:654–58 (27 Oct. 1952)

Alden, a special assistant in the International Information Administration's Office of Field Programs, first discusses the development of Japan's educational system before World War II and then reviews the major changes which occurred during the occupation period. She points out that SCAP's educational reforms sought to eliminate the prewar militaristic and ultranationalistic ideology and its exponents from the schools and attempted to establish an educational system and ideology which would "further the development of a representative government and a society based on the freedom and dignity of the individual." In view of the importance which Japanese leaders attach to the future status of the country's educational system, Alden assumes that they will modify the reforms which SCAP has initiated. The key question, however, is "the extent and nature of these modifications and whether they will be confined to the organization of the school system or whether they will affect the basic philosophy which was the goal of the reforms." In any case, she does expect changes involving the local boards of education inasmuch as the decentralization of education has been controversial and their operation has been "the weakest link in the present decentralized system."

2014 Allen, Lafe Franklin. "Educational Reform in Japan." *Yale Review* 36:705–16 (Summer 1947)

SCAP's educational policy is the subject of this article. Some attention is given to early occupation directives which were aimed at the destruction of undesirable elements within the previous system. Under this category such things as the rooting out of ultranationalistic and militaristic teachers and books are treated. The greater part of the article is focused on the positive reforms that were initiated in an extensive and fundamental revision of the nation's educational system. It considers the inculcation of democratic concepts through revised textbooks as well as various audiovisual aids, the reeducation of teachers, and the reinstatement of educators silenced by the militarists. The efforts of the military government teams working at the prefectural level and the recommendations of the education mission headed by Stoddard are also covered. The author is optimistic regarding educational reform in Japan. However, at the conclusion of his article, he cites the various problems which must be met if the reforms are to take hold. Among these are low teachers' salaries, the shortage of buldings and textbooks, and the insufficient number of SCAP personnel working on educational reform.

2015 Anderson, Paul Seward. *The Reorientation Activities of the Civil Education Section of the Osaka Civil Affairs Team: A Case Study in Educational Change.* Ph.D. dissertation, Univ. of Wisconsin, 1954. 437p. (Abstracted in University of Wisconsin. *Summaries of Doctoral Dissertations, 1953–1954* 15:510–12 [1955])

In this dissertation the writer describes and analyzes the efforts of the Osaka Military Government team under the Eighth Army to guide the educational reform program in Osaka prefecture between October 1945 and November 1949. The activities of the team's Civil Education and Information Section and its relations with SCAP are emphasized. The study shows the way in which the role of civil educational personnel changed from that of supervision to that of instruction during the period from 1945 to 1949. The topics discussed include the removal of shrines from schools, the termination of emperor worship in the schools, the introduction of school lunch programs, school reorganization, curriculum revision, coeducation, teacher training, the introduction of elective school boards, teachers' unions, libraries, public halls, and the initiative of the military government team in organizing parent-teacher associations, women's civil groups, and youth associations. Cited as factors that hindered the progress of civil education are changes in personnel, inconsistencies in program emphasis, and limited liaison between SCAP staff sections in Tokyo and local teams in Osaka.

2016 Anderson, Ronald Stone. "An Adult-Education Project in Japan." *School and Society* 71:337–42 (3 June 1950)

Anderson, a former civil education officer for the Kinki Military Government Region, writes in detail about the adult education program established by his office for the inculcation of democracy in southern Japan. He begins with an outline of the content of the lesson plan utilized to explain occupation reforms dealing with such topics as labor, government, public health, and civil education. An explanation of the publication of these lessons and companion texts such as the *Primer of Democracy* (1948) (no. 2063) and the preparation of visual aids is linked to a discussion of the training of qualified discussion leaders. The author is candid about revealing various local officials' general lack of interest and their reluctance to open the program to everyone. He comments on the various techniques used in different parts of the country and discusses his personal experience in Osaka and rural Shiga prefectures. One goal of the program is to provide an alternative to Communist information, and the attempt is made to send only highly competent teams to areas of Communist strength. The results of this policy are noted. The author emphasizes the participation of women and gives figures on general participation through mid-1949. The abolition of military government teams in November 1949 is linked to the failure of programs in various areas and it is contrasted to the success and expansion of adult education in urban Hyōgo and Osaka.

2017 ———. *Japan, Three Epochs of Modern Education.* Washington, D.C.: Dept. of Health, Education, and Welfare, Office of Education, 1959. xii, 219p. (U.S. Office of Education. Bulletin 1959, no.11)

The 3 epochs referred to in the title of this work are: (1) initial modernization epoch (1872–1937) when modern education was introduced and developed in Japan, (2) wartime epoch (1937–45) when education was converted to the needs of a nation at war, and (3) democratization epoch (1945 to the time of writing) when a new democratized system of education was built. Each facet of education dealt with in this book—such as educational opportunity; curriculum, teaching methods, and textbooks; and teacher education—is generally divided into these 3 epochs for consideration. The democratization epoch is further divided into the early period (the years under the Allied occupation, 1945–52) and the present period (since the peace treaty went into effect, 1952 to the time of writing). Anderson cites 4 major goals during the first 2 years of the occupation: (1) the elimination of militarism and ultranationalism, (2) democratization, (3) modernization, and (4) decentralization of educational control. Measures used to accomplish these goals and other occupation and government reforms and policies are discussed in the sections on the early period of democratization. Appendixes, charts, and tables aid the student in studying this subject.

2018 Aoki, Hideo. *The Effect of American Ideas upon Japanese Higher Education.* Ph.D. dissertation, Stanford Univ., 1957. 363p. (Abstracted in *Dissertation Abstracts* 17:1506 [1957]; University Microfilms order no.21,563)

Three periods in modern Japanese history during which American ideas concerning higher education were introduced into Japan are compared and evaluated here in terms of the adaptive capacity of Japanese culture. These periods include the first decade of the Meiji era (1870–80), during which the American single-track system was adopted, the years during World War I when the University Act of 1918 which officially recognized private universities was adopted, and the occupation era. Aoki describes 7 major reforms of higher education which were recommended by the U.S. Education Mission and implemented during the occupation, including the 6–3–3–4 system, the introduction of general education programs at the university level, and decentralized control of higher education. He also reviews the effect of American–Japanese cultural exchange on Japanese higher education in the postwar period. Two problems created by the occupation are identified, namely, the conflict which developed between general education and special education, and the one that arose between functional and structural study at junior colleges. Aoki concludes that the American influences voluntarily introduced and adapted to Japanese culture in the 1870s and 1920s were able to survive 2 decades of ultranationalism, while occupation reforms "hastily imposed and transplanted uncritically from American culture, appear less likely to be permanently integrated into the Japanese education system."

2019 Ashmead, John, Jr. "A Modern Language for Japan." *Atlantic Monthly* 179: 68–72 (Jan. 1947)

Advocating speedy reform of the Japanese written language, Ashmead bases his argument upon his own knowledge of the language and statistics provided by Robert King Hall for SCAP's Civil Information and Education Section. After a description of the low literacy rate among the Japanese masses, the author attempts to demonstrate its effects upon the occupation. He maintains that by taking up excessive time in the school curricula, the teaching of ideographs adversely affects the promulgation of democratic principles. "Only with language reform will our plans for revising and democratizing Japanese education have any chance for success." The conservative militarists and nationalists as well as the older intellectuals present the most staunch opposition to language reform, but the author urges SCAP to disregard them and strongly promote effective language reform.

2020 Atkinson, Carroll. "Japanese Education Is Getting Revised—à la Americain!" *School and Society* 64:115–16 (17 Aug. 1946)

Atkinson, public relations counselor at the University of California, Berkeley, strongly criticizes the products of American education and calls on occupation leaders to avoid adopting the same educational system in Japan. He criticizes the U.S. Education Mission to Japan, stating that its members lack the necessary background for reforming Japanese traditions and claiming that a program of democratization can be undertaken only by educators who know and appreciate the Japanese. According to his proposal, the University of Hawaii, the only institution in America with the necessary knowledge and appreciation, should be allowed to apply its Nisei education program to enable trained Nisei to establish democratic idealism and practices in Japan.

For an immediate response to Atkinson's criticisms, see the reply of Isaac Leon Kandel which appeared in the succeeding issue of *School and Society* (no. 2074).

2021 ———. "Japanese Education is Getting an American Pattern." *Modern Language Journal* 30:268–69 (May 1946)

Atkinson briefly reports and comments on the introduction of radio broadcasting into Japanese schools as a partial substitute for the prewar and wartime textbooks which have been banned on account of their ideological content and have not yet been replaced. The author also notes the potential contribution which Japanese–Americans can make to the rebuilding of Japan's educational system.

2022 Bagley, William C. "The Report of the U.S. Education Mission to Japan." *School and Society* 63:388–89 (1 June 1946)

Bagley, editor of *School and Society*, comments on the report of the education mission concerning the decentralization of administrative control, the recreation of curriculum and teaching methods along democratic American lines, and the replacement of the ideographic script with one based on a phonetic script.

Ballantine, Joseph W. "The New Japan: An American View." 1948. *See* no. 537.

2022a Ballou, Richard Boyd. "American Education and the New Japan." *Journal of Higher Education* 23:229–36 (May 1952)

Ballou, a former consultant for the Institute for Educational Leadership, critically assesses the educational reforms which the occupation undertook in order "to deny any minority in the future a monopoly upon public opinion and understanding." He criticizes SCAP for carrying out too many changes in too short a time and for failing to take into account basic cultural differences between Japan and the West. "Patterns of education which had evolved in the United States over many decades," he writes, "were transplanted and expected to flourish in a cultural climate totally unused to such patterns and ideas." At the same time, Ballou continues, one must remember that the occupation authorities were required to deal with many problems; education was but one of the areas of immediate concern. The author calls upon American educators to continue assisting the Japanese even after the occupation ends and concludes his remarks by outlining 4 areas in which they could play an important role.

2023 Baltz, William Matthew. *The Role of American Educators in the Decentralization and Reorganization of Education in Postwar Japan (1945–1952)*. Ed.D. dissertation, State Univ. of New York at Buffalo, 1965. 212p. (Abstracted in *Dissertation Abstracts* 26:6495 [1966]; University Microfilms order no.65–8894)

Educational reform activities undertaken by SCAP are described and special emphasis is placed on the contribution of individuals in the Education Division of the Civil Information and Education Section who, according to the author, furnished "leadership in the formulation of policy and the even more difficult task of implementing these policies." The author stresses the importance of identifying the division staff members as well as their functions and accomplishments during the occupation. The study is based primarily on unpublished materials of the Education Division, official SCAP publications and records, and doctoral dissertations written by the personnel of the Civil Information and Education Section.

2023a Beard, Eva. "New Woman for a New Japan." *Independent Woman* 29: 330–32, 356 (Nov. 1950)

This article dealing with the changing status of women in Japan is based on an interview with Yuasa Hachirō, the president of International Christian University in Tokyo. Yuasa notes that the high proportion of women among the faculty and trustees of I.C.U. reflects the university's strong commitment to female education, and he asserts that the opening of the school marks a "new dawn" for Japanese women of all ages.

2024 Benjamin, Harold. "New Education for a New Japan." *School Life* 28:1, 3–4 (June 1946)

The author's experiences as a member of the first U.S. Education Mission to Japan make his personal observations on Japanese education particularly informative. He defines the educational needs of the Japanese for: (1) social-civic education, (2) scientific and technological education, and (3) education along artistic and individual lines. In discussing specific changes to be made, he urges that *romaji* or some other phonetic alphabet be adopted for Japanese and that secondary schools be expanded and improved if they are to be adequate to the needs of a new Japan.

2025 Benoit, Edward George. *A Study of Japanese Education as Influenced by the Occupation*. Ed.D. dissertation, Michigan State Univ., 1958. 303p. (Abstracted in *Dissertation Abstracts* 19:3168 [1959]; University Microfilms order no.59–1319)

Benoit discusses the changes in Japanese educational philosophies and administration brought about by the occupation. A review of ultranationalistic educational aims and organizations in prewar Japan is followed by an examination of the reforms directed by the Education Division, Civil Information and Education Section of SCAP, and the legislation subsequently adopted by the Japanese government. To determine Japanese attitudes toward the occupation's educational reforms, Benoit conducted interviews from 1952 to 1955 with people of various occupations, including school board members, administrative personnel, and university professors. He also administered questionnaires to teachers and pupils in the sixth, ninth, and twelfth grades in the schools of Gumma prefecture. The results indicated that the occupation had efficiently accomplished its mission and had laid the foundation for democratic education. The conclusion states that a system of democratic education had been adapted to the Japanese way of life and that reversion to ultranationalism was extremely unlikely.

2026 Blumhagen, Herman Herbert. *Nationalistic Policies and Japanese Public Education from 1928 to March 31, 1947*. Ed.D. dissertation, Rutgers Univ., 1957.

314p. (Abstracted in *Dissertation Abstracts* 18:1708–9 [1958]; University Microfilms order no.22,566)

Blumhagen evaluates both the effects of nationalistic educational policies upon Japanese external aggression and the effects of the occupation's educational reforms upon Japanese democracy. His discussion of the occupation includes a survey of the directives issued by SCAP and the function of these agencies in educating Japanese youth in accord with democratic concepts. The writer questions the wisdom of occupation authorities who endeavored to effect reforms, stating these authorities may have tried to Westernize Japan too quickly. He also questions the merit of abolishing state Shinto and the teaching of ethics courses, arguing that it might have been better to retain those aspects that encourage the improvement of the individual and national morality.

2027 Brinkman, Albert R. "Higher Education in Japan Today." *Harvard Educational Review* 16:167–72 (Summer 1946)

This article depicts the more formal side of educational reconstruction in Japan. Describing the unique mixture of indigenous and foreign elements in Japan's modern culture, the author attempts to point up some of the complex issues of content, organization, and methods of teaching which must be dealt with during the occupation. There is a valuable description of the contemporary structure of Japanese colleges and universities, an outline of the curricula of the various specialized schools, and a discussion of procedures for obtaining higher degrees in graduate schools.

2027a ———. "Social Studies in Japan." *Social Studies* 37:365–66 (Dec. 1946)

Brinkman devotes most of this article to a description of the Japanese education system on the eve of the occupation's reforms, paying special attention to the "core program" in Japanese ethics, history, and geography with its emphasis on state propaganda. There have been few changes since the surrender in classroom teaching, he finds, but many fundamental changes in subject matter. SCAP's attention has naturally focused on the area of social studies. While new curricula and texts are not yet widespread, the worst distortions in the old have been eliminated by fiat.

2028 Brown, Delmer Myers. "The Social Sciences in Japan." *Far Eastern Survey* 18:53–55 (9 Mar. 1949)

This article, based on research done in Japan by Brown as a consultant for the army, describes some of the problems encountered in the democratization of Japan's social sciences. He indicates, however, that it would appear that the full support of social scientists can be obtained if greater attention is given to improving their economic position and to increasing the opportunities of learning more about the philosophy and history of democratic nations.

2029 Caiger, John Godwin. "The First Post-war History Book in Japan: Japanese or American?" *Journal of the Oriental Society of Australia* 3, no.2:2–15 (Dec. 1965)

2029a ———. "Ienaga Saburō and the First Postwar Japanese History Textbook." *Modern Asian Studies* 3:1–16 (Jan. 1969)

This article describes the chain of events which led to the publication of Japan's first postwar history textbook, *Kuni no ayumi* (The Progress of the Country), in October 1946. Its appearance was the culmination of a process initiated by the Ministry of Education as early as 20 September 1945, when it ordered the deletion of objectionable nationalistic and militaristic passages from then existing textbooks. SCAP soon followed suit with directives of its own, and after several false starts, Ienaga Saburō and other progressive historians were delegated the task of producing a new history text which would conform with the objectives of the occupation. Caiger describes Ienaga's role in particular, and in addition the author compares several passages from the presurrender textbook with their equivalents in *Kuni no ayumi*

2030 ———. "A 'Reverse Course' in the Teaching of History in Postwar Japan?" *Journal of the Oriental Society of Australia* 5, no.1/2:4–16 (Dec. 1967).

Caiger outlines some of the recent discussions in Japan over the revision of the treatment of Japanese history and World War II in school textbooks. Although the Ministry of Education's statement of aims shows "no hint of retreat by the Ministry from the postwar values endorsed in 1946 and 1951," he writes, "there is evidence from the [1955] syllabus itself that it was used to check left-wing thought: it offered no encouragement to those who wanted to teach revolutionary social theory, or to those who slighted Japan's traditional culture and denounced her foreign wars as purely aggressive."

2031 Cassidy, Velma Hastings. "The Program for Reeducation in Japan: A Survey of Policy." *Documents and State Papers* 1, no.1:3–31 (Apr. 1948).

Prepared by a member of the Division of Historical Policy Research, this policy paper published by the Office of Public Affairs of the U.S. State Department discusses the basic reeducation program undertaken by SCAP. The author describes the activities of various advisory educational groups, surveys the reforms regarding ultranationalism and militarism and the reforms enacted within the Japanese school system between October 1945 and March 1947, and studies the new basic education laws and the revised administrative organization of Japanese education.

2031a "Changes in Japanese Textbooks." *School and Society* 68:7 (3 July 1948).

This brief notice of an exhibition at the Library of Congress of Japanese textbooks from the Meiji period to the present reprints a Library of Congress description of postwar textbooks. The description notes that by 1947 a large number of new textbooks were in the hands of Japanese students, but that most of the texts thus far printed under SCAP control were shabby in appearance due to paper shortages and printing difficulties.

2032 Chapman, John Griffin. *The Reeducation of the Japanese People*. Ph.D. dissertation, Univ. of Houston, 1954. 288p. (Abstracted in *Dissertation Abstracts* 14:1988–89 [1954]; University Microfilms order no.9847)

Chapman, a political and social adviser on MacArthur's staff for 5 years, examines the effects of occupation reforms concerning education in terms of the occupation's fundamental objectives of achieving cultural and social changes. He compares the educational experiences of the Japanese in the preoccupation and occupation periods and favorably evaluates occupation reforms. He maintains that the Japanese were receptive to democratic concepts of education and to the ideologies of Western civilization and that education is now "controlled by the people through democratic processes." He also maintains that the American occupation forces "redirected the thought and energy of all the people toward the building of a more democratic life than the Japanese had ever known in the past."

2033 Chee, Changboh. *Development of Sociology in Japan: A Study of Adaptation of Western Sociological Orientations into the Japanese Social Structure*. Ph.D. dissertation, Duke Univ., 1959. 289p. (Abstracted in *Dissertation Abstracts* 20: 3875–76 [1960]; University Microfilms order no.60–402)

In an attempt to show that the development of sociology in a given social context is determined by the structure of the sociocultural components of that society, Chee contends that the adaptation of Western sociology in Japan is functionally related to structural changes in the sociocultural structure of Japan. He discusses this adaptation in terms of the liberal philosophies popular during the Meiji period, the growth of encyclopedic and organic sociology, the influence of

German formal and cultural sociology, and the attempt to create a new Japanese sociology under the aegis of American sociology after World War II. According to Chee, Japanese sociology has become more empirical and has begun to associate more freely with the other social sciences as a result of American influence.

2033a Colwell, Ernest, Edward D'Arms, and George Stoddard. "Are We Re-educating the Germans and the Japanese?" *University of Chicago Round Table* no. 436:1–18 (28 July 1946)

Stoddard, the chairman of the United States Education Mission to Japan, provides interesting comments about American reeducation policies in this transcript of a radio broadcast sponsored by the University of Chicago. He points out that SCAP has already issued directives for the revision of various Japanese textbooks, discusses the size and scope of the reeducation program as a whole, comments on proposals for language reform, and indicates that the Japanese are supporting the occupation's activities with considerable enthusiasm. Stoddard feels that the most significant feature of the mission's report is its recommendation that the Japanese decentralize their educational system and indicates as well that the report places considerable emphasis on the need for teacher education in Japan.

2034 Counts, George S. "Can the Schools Build Democracy in Japan?" *American Teacher* 31:11–13 (Nov. 1946); reprinted from *World Outlook* (Sept. 1946)

Five major educational reforms in Japan are recommended by the author of this brief article. A former president of the American Federation of Teachers and a member of the U.S. Education Commission to Japan, Counts suggests that Allied priorities should center around: (1) development of democratic loyalties and powers, (2) abolition of authoritarian methods, (3) modification of the role of the teacher, (4) democratization of the educational administration, and (5) alteration of the Japanese system of writing. He insists educational reform will be truly successful only when the economic situation of the country is made stable.

Crane, Burton. "Educating a Prince." 1946. *See* no.1233.

2034a ———. "Making Japanese Easy: To Westernize the Language." *New York Times Magazine* p.27 (24 Mar. 1946)

Crane feels that an increasing number of Japanese educators and scholars now believe that the romanization of their writing system is no longer "just a dream." Previous efforts at reform have failed because of the force of tradition and the government's willingness to keep the populace fundamentally ignorant. This situation has changed, however. In addition, the Japanese undoubtedly will be borrowing many new words from European languages in the future, and the romanization of their language (as opposed to the use of native phonetic systems) will greatly facilitate that process.

2034b Cronbach, Lee J. "Educational Reform in Japan." *School Review* 56:188–91 (Apr. 1948)

This article describes the basic aims and programs of the occupation with respect to its educational reform efforts and concludes with Cronbach's observations on their effectiveness. Progress has been slow on all fronts, he notes, because it is difficult to change the teaching methods of teachers who have long been accustomed to a rigid, authoritarian system and who generally lack the ability to exercise initiative. Japan's present economic troubles also inhibit progress by limiting the money and materials available for new textbooks, equipment, and school construction. Nevertheless, the author concludes, the Japanese are committed to the goals of educational reform and are working hard to achieve them. Cronbach served as a consultant for 2 months in 1947, advising Japanese psychologists on problems of child development and testing.

2035 Crow, Lester D. "Problems in Educational Psychology in Japan." *School and Society* 75:87–89 (9 Feb. 1952)

Crow reports on the introduction of educational psychology into teacher training programs in Japan. Commenting specifically on teacher education programs sponsored by the Department of the Army in September 1950 and January 1951, he considers the increasing importance of theories concerning child development, individual aptitude, learning motivation, creative thinking, and child evaluation in Japanese education. The need to create social experiences for Japanese students which would promote student attitudinal development is stressed and the present lack of such social stimuli beyond the kindergarten level is noted.

2036 De Francis, John. "Japanese Language Reform: Politics and Phonetics." *Far Eastern Survey* 16:217–20 (5 Nov. 1947)

In this article a teacher of Chinese and Japanese language argues for the replacement of ideographs with *romaji*. De Francis traces the history of Japanese opposition to the *romaji* movement since the 1880s, and attempts to prove the democratic potential of *romaji* on the basis that ideographs hold back the semi-literate's ability to express himself.

2037 Deverall, Richard L. G. "Babel in Japan." *Forum* 111:193–99 (Apr. 1949)

The nature and history of the Japanese language are briefly outlined before the author describes the confusion caused by the spoken and written language even among the Japanese people themselves. As the former chief of labor education under General MacArthur, the author concentrates on the difficulties of the laboring classes in acquiring literacy. He attributes the delay in reform of the language to the intransigence of the conservative forces and intellectual elite who have a vested interest in the retention of ideographs. In conclusion, he discusses the U.S. Education Mission's recommendations related to language reform and strongly argues for radical change—either use of a romanized script or a syllabary—by SCAP authorities.

2037a Doi, James Isao. *Educational Reform in Occupied Japan, 1945–1950: A Study of Acceptance of and Resistance to Institutional Change.* Ph.D. dissertation, Univ. of Chicago, 1952. vii, 390p. Available from the Photoduplication Dept., Joseph Regenstein Library, Univ. of Chicago.

Doi studies the general social setting, the methods of educational reform, some of the more important changes attempted, and the reactions of the Japanese to the educational changes in order to "determine whether or not the perspectives and attitudes of the Japanese people concerning the schools and the education of their children underwent change" between 1945 and 1950.

2038 Donovan, Eileen. "Japan–United States Educational Exchange." *American Foreign Service Journal* 27:24–25 (Apr. 1950)

The author reports briefly on the work of the Educational Exchange Survey Mission to Japan in August 1949 concerning the establishment of a 2-way educational exchange program of students, teachers, and research workers between the United States and Japan.

2039 Dore, Ronald Philip. "The Ethics of the New Japan." *Pacific Affairs* 25, no.2: 147–59 (June 1952)

This article describes the end of the Imperial Rescript on Education and the search for a substitute when people protested the lack of morality and patriotism in postwar Japan. In 1951, the minister of education announced a teacher's guide to moral education which is translated and analyzed in the article. Strongly criticized in leading newspapers for being too conservative and undemocratic, the proposed guide was withdrawn. Although Dore, too, is critical of the proposal, he is optimistic that its withdrawal in the face of popular criticism is a step towards democracy.

2040 Duke, Benjamin C. "American Education Reforms in Japan Twelve Years Later." *Harvard Educational Review* 34: 525–36 (Fall 1964)

The author, then assistant professor of comparative education at the International Christian University in Tokyo, analyzes both the educational reforms brought about during the occupation and the trends since 1952 in Japanese education. While praising the freedom and progressive nature of the Japanese educational system, the author points out what he sees as reactionary trends since 1952. He is concerned primarily about how politics and the political parties are now playing a role in Japanese education. He blames the Liberal Democratic Party for undoing a number of occupation reforms especially in the fields of the school board system, curriculum study, the teachers unions, and university autonomy.

2041 ———. "The Irony of Japanese Postwar Education." *Comparative Education Review* 6, no.3:212–17 (Feb. 1963)

The author, assistant professor of education at the International Christian University in Tokyo, contends within this article that conservative forces in Japan, especially those aligned with the United States, are eroding the democratic educational reforms of the occupation. The curriculum reforms—especially in social studies—are being gradually replaced by a return to prewar curricula, e.g., in moral education. The occupation decentralized the control of education, but since 1952 the Ministry of Education has slowly regained its dominant position. A 1956 act ended the occupation-established (1948) elective local school boards and returned to a system of appointive boards. The ministry has also challenged the right of teachers to organize and act politically.

———. *Japan's Militant Teachers: A History of the Left-wing Teachers' Movement.* 1973. See no.1747.

2042 Eby, Kermit. "Japan Then and Now." *Christian Century* 63:750–52 (12 June 1946)

After reviewing his participation in the first U.S. Education Mission, Eby dwells on the need to eliminate educational regimentation in Japanese schools. He emphasizes the importance of goodwill and friendliness on the part of American occupation troops, and he states that Japan, as a spiritual and intellectual vacuum, will be receptive to democratic reform. Two actions deemed necessary to insure reform are economic revival in order to feed the people and eliminate unemployment and the establishment of a position of diplomatic and strategic neutrality for Japan, enabling her to avoid becoming an outpost of American imperialism.

2043 ———. "Re-education of Japan." *Far Eastern Survey* 15:203–5 (3 July 1946)

A member of the first U.S. Education Mission to Japan and director of the Department of Education Research of the Congress of Industrial Organizations, the author of this brief article presents an informal and well-organized account of the mission's findings. He enumerates and discusses what he considers to be the mission's chief recommendations regarding the reform of the Japanese educational system, summarizing them as follows: (1) improvement of the aims and content of the Japanese educational system must be along democratic lines; (2) some form of romanized script should be brought into common use; (3) educational administration must be removed from the tightly controlled Ministry of Education and be placed in the hands of local administrators elected by popular vote; (4) teaching and the education of teachers must conform to the principles outlined in the above proposals; (5) adult education is necessary in order to reconvert the nation from a warlike to a peaceful philosophy; and (6) institutions of higher learning must be increased and progressive doctrines encouraged.

2043a "Education Advisory Group to Japan." *Department of State Bulletin* 14:345–46 (3 Mar. 1946)

This press release dated 18 February 1946 summarizes the duties of the Education Mission to Japan. It names the members of this group and indicates how they were selected and which organizations they were representing.

2044 "Education in Japan." *Current Notes on International Affairs* 19:675–83, 734–42 (Nov./Dec. 1948)

The progress of educational reforms as implemented by the Civil Information and Education Section (CIE) of SCAP is described here. A brief account of Japanese education from 1868 to World War II is followed by a discussion of the functions of CIE, SCAP policy on education, the purge of educational leaders, the abolition of state Shinto, the U.S. Education Mission, and related decisions by the Far Eastern Commission. There are also discussions of economic problems which affect educational issues and of the role of the board of education type system newly introduced by the United States. The texts of SCAP and FEC decisions and directives on Japanese educational reforms are appended on p.734–42 and consist of the following: (1) "Functions of the Civil Information and Education Section" (General Order no. 27, GHQ, SCAP, of 3 June 1946); (2) "Administration of the Educational System of Japan" (SCAP memo to the Japanese government of 22 October 1945); (3) "Abolition of State Shinto" (SCAP memo to the Japanese government of 15 December 1945); (4) "Suspension of Courses in Morals, History, and Geography" (SCAP memo to the Japanese government of 31 December 1945); and (5) "Policy for the Revision of the Japanese Educational System" (FEC policy decision approved on 27 March 1947).

2045 Eells, Walter Crosby. "Coeducation in Japan." *School and Society* 74:183–85 (22 Sept. 1951)

Eells undertakes a statistical discussion of coeducation. The almost universal coeducation in elementary and lower secondary schools is noted as are new programs in homemaking and the participation of women as elected members of prefectural and local school boards. Half of the article is devoted to the paucity of coeducation in higher education. Certain innovations, such as the Japanese Association of University Women and home economics and nursing curricula, are also noted.

2046 ———. "Decentralization of Control of Education in Japan." *School and Society* 73:388–91 (23 June 1951)

The author analyzes the division of educational functions among the Ministry of Education, prefectural agencies, and local agencies based on the Board of Education Law of July 1948 and the Ministry of Education Establishment Law of May 1949. He explains in detail the organization and functions of prefectural and local boards of education and the results of the October 1948 election in relation to those boards. Eells mentions the lack of fiscal independence of these boards and the continuation of centralization in higher education, then devotes considerable attention to the need for psychological as well as legal reforms concerning educational decentralization. The reorganization of the Ministry of Education to incorporate the functions of advice and stimulation rather than control is considered in terms of the need to develop professional competence and inculcate a sense of responsibility on the part of ministry personnel.

2047 ———. "Language Reform in Japan." *Modern Language Journal* 36, no.5: 210–13 (May 1952)

Intended to update the 2-volume SCAP publication *Education in the New Japan* (1948) (no.2124), this article outlines some of the significant steps that the Japanese undertook during the latter half of the occupation period to simplify and otherwise reform their language. These measures include the restricted use of *kanji*, the teaching of *romaji* in both elementary and secondary schools, and the adoption of colloquial language in official documents. Eells notes, however, that there still are certain major obstacles hindering the progress of language reform within the country. These obstacles, he explains, are the Japanese failure to agree on 1 system of *romaji* for official use, the refusal of many writers and publishers to limit themselves to the officially sanctioned *kanji*, and the difficulty of altering set habits and patterns of speech.

――――, comp. *The Literature of Japanese Education, 1945–1954.* 1955. See no.8.

2048 Engineering Education Mission to Japan. *Report of the Engineering Education Mission to Japan, 5 July to 26 August, 1951.* Mimeographed. Tokyo: SCAP, 1951. iv, 79, 3, 127p.

The Engineering Education Mission to Japan, requested by SCAP's Economic and Scientific Section and organized by the American Society for Engineering Education, submitted this report to SCAP. It relates to long-range measures that might be taken to improve engineering education in Japan. The report, drawn up by a 15-member mission headed by Professor Harold I. Hazen of the Massachusetts Institute of Technology, offers 14 recommendations including a recommendation that greater freedom be given individual institutions to determine educational policies, that there be a closer coordination between research and teaching as functions of the university, that there be freer interchange between students and faculty members, and that there be closer communication between engineering educators and interested industrialists. It also criticizes the inadequacies of the new occupation-directed 4-year undergraduate engineering program. Appended are a list of members of the Japanese committee that received the American mission and a collection of conference papers, speeches, and data relevant to the mission's work in Japan.

2049 Finn, Dallas. "Reform and Japanese Higher Education." *Far Eastern Survey* 20:201–6 (21 Nov. 1951)

In discussing reforms within the Japanese university system, Finn notes that the occupation imposed the superficial form of American colleges and universities on a society and an economy unable to give it life. Following the American model too closely instead of making use of a system the Japanese respected may unnecessarily have stirred up national resentment which will endanger the contributions the occupation has made.

2050 ――――. "Reform and Japan's Lower Schools." *Far Eastern Survey* 20:193–99 (7 Nov. 1951)

Finn, a school teacher in Japan, describes the reformation of Japan's lower schools by the occupation and the Japanese reaction to it up to the signing of the peace treaty. She notes that the occupation viewed the "aristocratic" prewar system as a bar to democracy but points out that democracy is attainable only in so far as it meets the conditions of Japanese life.

2051 Givens, Willard E. "United States Education Mission to Japan." *Proceedings of the National Education Association* 83/84: 85–92, 228 (1945/46)

This address, given before the representative assembly of the National Education Association in July 1946, reports on the work of the U.S. Education Mission to Japan (USEM). It includes a short résumé of the history and organization of USEM as well as a list of the democratic principles on which USEM recommendations to SCAP were based. Givens explains these recommendations in detail in light of the Japanese prewar and wartime educational system. He discusses the need for decentralization and the need to use teachers and community personnel to staff popularly elected educational agencies at the local and prefectural levels. The proposal to extend free, compulsory education from 6 to 9 years is stressed as is the need to expand facilities for free higher education to offer opportunities for all, especially women. The reeducation of teachers to facilitate the adoption of democratically-oriented educational methods is also emphasized.

2051a ――――. "Mission Completed: Report of Second US Education Mission to Japan, September 1950." *Journal of the National Education Association* 39:649–51 (Dec. 1950)

Givens was chairman of the Second U.S. Education Mission to Japan, whose purpose was to assess the results of SCAP's educational reforms. The 5 members of this mission, all of whom had participated in the first mission in 1946, were in Japan again during the summer of 1950. After conferring with SCAP education officials and with those Japanese involved in the reforms, the group toured the Kansai area and spoke there with teachers, P.T.A. members and officials, and Board of Education members. The mission concluded that the reforms have generally gone well, although teachers have sometimes had difficulty adjusting to the changes—particularly the abolition of instruction in ethics and Shinto. Givens concludes with praise for SCAP's "brilliant record of achievement in democratizing Japan."

2051b ———. "U.S. Education Mission to Japan." *Journal of the National Education Association* 35:380–81 (Oct. 1946)

Givens, the executive secretary of the National Education Association, was a member of the U.S. Education Mission to Japan. This article is his informal report to the association about its work. The objective of the educational reforms which the mission proposed, he states, is to replace the old ideological underpinnings of Japanese education with the articles of democratic faith. The mission's recommendations included in particular the transfer of control over educational policy to local school districts and the abolition of the old morals courses and militaristic curricula. Givens also expresses personal satisfaction with the recommendations to institute vocational and technical education on a wide scale and to increase the number of years of free compulsory schooling.

2052 Griffith, Harry Elmer. *Japanese Normal School Education*. Ed.D. dissertation, Stanford Univ., 1950. 392p. (Abstracted in Stanford Univ., *Abstracts of Dissertations, 1949–1950* 25:364–69 [1950])

Parts 1 and 2 of this 4-part study are a review of the history of Japanese education and normal schools prior to 1945. The third part deals specifically with changes that occurred in normal school education from 1945 to 1950, and the fourth part is a proposed plan for introducing the democratic principles outlined in the Cairo and Potsdam Declarations into Japanese normal school education. The author presented this plan to various Japanese and American officials, including members of the U.S. Education Mission to Japan, the Education Division of the Civil Information and Education Section of SCAP, the Japanese Ministry of Education, and the Japanese Education Reconstruction Committee. Their responses reflect substantial agreement concerning the merit of his suggestions. They include proposals to establish a national standard for teacher training, local administrative autonomy over educational matters, and a placement service and more effective counseling services at all normal schools.

Gulick, Addison. "The Problem of Right and Wrong in Japan and Some of Its Political Consequences." 1947. *See* no.1929.

2053 Hall, Robert King. "The Battle of the Mind: American Educational Policy in Germany and Japan." *Columbia Journal of International Affairs* 2:59–70 (Winter 1948)

A critical evaluation of U.S. educational policy in occupied Japan two and one-half years after its inception. Throughout the article, the author emphasizes the fact that it is of utmost importance to study the interpretations of policy which are made in the field as well as the official SCAP policy documents. His analysis of U.S. educational policy includes a study of policy statements, discussion of the dual nature of SCAP personnel concerned with educational reform, and a consideration of the implementation of policy at local levels. He concludes that 2 lessons may be drawn from our experience in educational reform in both Japan and Germany: (1) even the best program will fail if it is administered by inadequately trained, unprofessional, indifferent personnel; and (2) "punitive action is relatively futile in a re-education program which has as its goal the development of democratic processes."

2054 ———. *Education for a New Japan.* New Haven, Conn.: Yale Univ. Pr., 1949. xiv, 503p.

A professor of comparative education, Robert K. Hall served as chief of the Education Section of the Planning Staff for the occupation of Japan and then as chief of the Education Subsection, educational reorganization officer, and language simplification officer for SCAP until the latter part of 1946. Hall's introductory chapter outlines the immediate postwar situation in Japan; he then considers the tasks involved in changing Japan's national philosophy through the educational system. The impact of defeat upon militarism, national Shinto, ultranationalism, and the imperial system is discussed in some detail. Hall suggests 2 basic educational reforms to serve as bulwarks against conservatism, traditionalism, and nationalism. They are the establishment of a decentralized administrative structure less susceptible to manipulation by a small group and the adoption of a phonetic writing system to facilitate communication and the development of an informed electorate. He makes detailed recommendations concerning the implementation of these reforms. Although sources are not footnoted and there is no bibliography, a detailed index is provided.

2054a ———. "Japan: American Policy and Influence." *Year Book of Education, 1949.* London: Evans, 1949. p.634–51.

After commenting upon conditions in Japan during the months immediately following the country's surrender, Hall reviews the general state of education and SCAP's educational policies to date. He then describes the 5 major programs of reform which have been undertaken: (1) the substitution of democratic laws for anachronistic, militarist and ultranationalistic regulations; (2) the enactment of a purge of teachers on all levels and the revision of many school textbooks; (3) the introduction of technical improvements in the instruments and organizations of education; (4) the decentralization of administrative control; and (5) the development of more ready access to knowledge, particularly through language reform. He stresses the problem of language reform, but otherwise does not attempt to assess SCAP's policies and the Japanese reactions to them in any great detail. Hall concludes by noting that while education can be an effective instrument of political action, democracy cannot be forced upon a people.

2055 ———. *Shūshin: The Ethics of a Defeated Nation.* New York: Columbia Univ. Teachers College, Bureau of Publications, 1949. xvi, 244p.

A specialist in the area of Japanese education, King provides the reader with a selection of translated materials from prewar school texts together with an historical introduction to the development of the ethics courses taught in Japan. His book is divided into 4 major parts. The first, a "prologue," examines the belief that a change in Japanese ethics and value judgments is basic to a fundamental educational reform in Japan and to the success of a lasting democratic political order. The second, entitled "*Kōdō*: The Imperial Way," traces the historical evolution of modern Japan's ethical teachings. The third and most important section—presented under the title "*Shūshinsho*: The Japanese Ethics Textbooks"—provides an annotated translation of the official textbooks used in elementary schools immediately prior to World War II. Finally, the "epilogue" notes the striking parallelism between the impact of Western culture on Japan at the beginning of the Meiji Restoration on the one hand and at the outset of the occupation period on the other.

2056 Harsaghy, Fred Joseph. *The Administration of American Cultural Projects Abroad: A Developmental Study with Case Histories of Community Relations in Administering Educational and Informational Projects in Japan and Saudi Arabia.* Ph.D. dissertation, New York Univ., 1965. 820p. (Abstracted in *Dissertation Abstracts* 27:1899A [1966]; University Microfilms order no.66-5730)

Part 2 of this dissertation is a historical case study of an American educational project in postwar Japan—the Hakodate Information Center. Prior to his discussion of the project, Harsaghy describes historical, geographical, and cultural aspects of Japanese life and customs. In regard to the center, he considers political and personnel problems, personnel selection, the training of Japanese personnel, budgetary and financial considerations, and other factors concerning its operation. The work is based on the author's experience as a regional director of information and education during the occupation and on observations made during a 1960 tour of American cultural centers in Japan.

2056a Hartford, Ellis Ford. "Problems of Education in Occupied Japan (as Seen by 69 Japanese Educators)." *Journal of Educational Sociology* 23:471–81 (Apr. 1950)

A professor of education at the University of Kentucky provides information on some of the critical problems facing Japanese educators as determined on the basis of a survey of 69 professors working in Japanese institutions of teacher education. The 3 most important problems are (1) a fear of Communist infiltration into the teachers' unions and of Communist use of classroom teaching situations to indoctrinate Japanese youth; (2) apprehension about the current shortage of teachers (particularly for the elementary schools) and concern about their inability to recruit capable young people as teachers; and (3) the perennial problem of adequate financial support for the schools—a problem aggravated by the fact that the budget enacted by the Diet on the basis of Dodge's austerity recommendations failed to allocate sufficient funds to pay adequate salaries, rebuild the schools, and provide equipment for new secondary school programs. Hartford also briefly discusses other problems indicated in the survey, among them the need for programs of in-service education for the large number of inadequately-qualified teachers, the need for more qualified school administrators, the lack of libraries within most Japanese schools, and the inadequacies of existing programs of vocational education and guidance.

2056b Hicks, Charles Roger. "Reorientation of Japanese Education." *School and Society* 62:433–34 (29 Dec. 1945)

Hicks argues that Japanese achievements and abilities have been overstressed. The school system in particular is little more than a cheap imitation of elements borrowed from foreign countries. Its highly organized and regimented nature, nonetheless, may greatly help the occupation authorities, for mass reeducation will be a simple matter once firm control has been established in Tokyo at the top.

Holmes, Lulu H. *Higher Education for Women in Japan, 1946–1948.* 1968. See no.45a.

2057 Holtom, Daniel Clarence. "Japanese Language Reform: Ideographs and Ideas." *Far Eastern Survey* 16:220–23 (5 Nov. 1947)

In this article a Shinto scholar, with 30 years experience in Japan, argues for the retention and simplification of Chinese characters in the Japanese language during the postwar period. Besides refuting the U.S. Education Mission's argument that ideographs are a drag on democracy, Holtom includes a well-balanced survey of both sides in this argument.

———. "The Japanese Mind." 1945. See no.82a.

2058 Itō, Ryoji. "Reforms in Education." *Contemporary Japan* 23, no.10/12:650–68 (1955)

The chief of the Ministry of Education's Research Section summarizes the educational reforms which have been carried out during the ten years since World War II. Most of these occurred under the occupation. His article also includes a statistical summary of the number of schools of all types, school enrollments, and the number of teachers at all levels from 1946 through 1954.

2059 Japan. Education Reform Council. *Education Reform in Japan: The Present Status and the Problems Involved.* Tokyo: The Council, 1950. 198p.

The Education Reform Council, a successor to the Education Reform Committee organized on 10 August 1946, played a principal part in formulating basic principles and policies for postwar Japanese educational reform. It acted on the basis of the recommendations of the first and second U.S. Education Missions to Japan. Policies and principles developed by the council were passed on to the Education Ministry, which carried out the actual reforms with the approval of the Diet and the consent of the Civil Information and Education Section of SCAP. This report represents this council's views of postwar educational changes and its evaluations of the recommendations of the American missions. It is comprehensive in scope, covering decisions which the council adopted between 1946 and 1949 and suggestions and appeals that the council made to SCAP. Subjects treated include the fundamental principles of education, educational administration and finance, reforms of the elementary and secondary education systems as well as the higher education system, teacher training, teachers' unions, living conditions of students, inadequacy of educational facilities, language simplification, social education, and education for the understanding of different cultures. The report concludes that financial support for new educational undertakings is the most difficult problem to solve. A list of council membership is appended.

2060 ———. Ministry of Education. *Bricks without Straw.* Tokyo: The Ministry, 1950. 69p.

This government report details Japan's school building needs as of May 1950. The authors point out how great the need continues to be for further educational funding, and they support their arguments with numerous tables and illustrative graphs.

2061 ———. ———. *Guide to New Education in Japan.* v.1, pt.a, *Fundamental Problems of the Establishment of New Japan.* Tokyo: The Ministry, 1946. 66p.

Dealing with the theory and aims of the new education in Japan, this publication is stated to be "the first concrete evidence of a studied effort to reeducate the teachers of Japan in compliance with orders contained in directives from the Supreme Commander for the Allied Powers to the Imperial Japanese Government." It is divided into the following 6 chapters—(1) The Present Condition of Japan and Self-Reflection by the People; (2) Elimination of Militarism and Ultra-Nationalism; (3) Respect of Human Nature, Personality, and Individuality; (4) Development of Scientific Standards and Philosophical and Religious Culture; (5) The Complete Accomplishment of Democracy; and (6) Conclusion: The Construction of a Peaceful, Cultural State and the Mission of Education—and each chapter is followed by a list of several problems for discussion that are intended to encourage Japanese teachers to familiarize themselves with different educational materials and teaching practices. This book originally appeared in Japanese and was to be followed by a second volume describing materials and teaching techniques which could be used in carrying out the new aims of Japanese education. Volume 2, however, apparently was never published.

2062 ———. ———. *Monthly Report.* Tokyo: SCAP, Dec. 1946–June 1947. monthly.

The purpose of the Ministry of Education's *Monthly Report* in English was to provide SCAP with an outline of projects that have been completed, those in progress, and projects planned for the future. Reports are generally about 75–80 pages in length and consist of a summation of the ministry's activity prepared by the vice minister and his secretariat. They also include descriptions of developments within each of the bureaus—the School Education Bureau, the Social Education Bureau, the Scientific Education Bureau, the Physical Education Bu-

2063 The Occupation

reau, the Textbook Bureau, and the Investigation Bureau.

The *Monthly Report* is available at the Washington National Records Center, Suitland, Maryland.

2063 ———. ———. *Primer of Democracy.* Tokyo: 1948–49. 2v.

The English translation of the text written by a committee of Japanese scholars under the supervision of the Ministry of Education which was intended for use by students in upper secondary schools and adult education groups initiated by SCAP. It is an attempt to provide an explanation of both the spiritual and institutional content of democratic thought. Its basic theme emphasizes the inherent worth of all individuals and the need to deal with all men as individuals. There are 11 chapters: chapters 1, 8, and 9 are explanations of the general philosophy of individualism and the way in which it relates to the social and economic aspects of life; chapter 2 is a historical treatment of democratic theory in England, France, and the United States; chapter 3 provides an analysis of the American, British, and Swiss governmental systems; chapters 4–7 present a discussion of suffrage and voting procedures, the theory of majority rule, and the need for an informed and enlightened electorate which will actively participate in politics; in chapter 10 the proper role of labor unions and union practices is treated; and in chapter 11 the contrast between democratic and Communist systems is discussed.

2064 ———. ———. *Progress Report of Educational Reform in Japan.* Tokyo: 1950. 194p.

An official report of the Japanese government concerning Japan's educational conditions during the first 5 years of the postwar period. Although the report makes little reference to SCAP's policies on educational reform, it is, in effect, an account of the impact of such occupation policies on Japanese education. In the introduction, the report expresses gratitude to the U.S. Education Mission to Japan for its "cordial encouragement and guidance." It takes the general line of praising Japan's new education and the "democratic education of a peace-loving nation." Subjects covered include the school system, teachers' problems, higher and social education, the promotion of scientific research, language reform, and the financing of education. There are also useful statistical data in the appendix. Of equal use is the table showing the degree to which the recommendations of the first U.S. Education Mission to Japan were implemented along with remarks on the difficulties in adapting those recommendations to the Japanese educational system.

2065 ———. ———. Bureau of Higher Education and Science. *A List of Scientific Periodicals from Japanese Learned Organizations.* 1949 ed. Tokyo: Ministry of Education, Higher Education and Science Bureau, Science Section, Literature Team, 1949. 58p.

2066 ———. ———. Bureau of Research and Publications. *Local Educational Expenditures in Japan, 1949–50: Report of a National Survey.* Tokyo: The Ministry, 1951. xxiv, 284p.

The first of a number of annual reports translated into English for distribution to interested governmental and educational agencies in foreign countries, this publication provides considerable information on expenditures for public education in Japan at the elementary and secondary school levels. In addition to the basic text and numerous tables, it contains a foreword by Walter E. Morgan of SCAP's Civil Information and Education Section—noteworthy because Morgan served as the American adviser for the national survey.

2067 ———. ———. Bureau of Scientific Education. *The List of Natural Science Research Organizations under the Jurisdiction of the Ministry of Education, as of July 1, 1948.* Mimeographed. Tokyo: The Ministry, 1948. 140p.

This classified listing of research organizations connected with various Japanese universities, other higher schools and colleges, and the Ministry of Education provides useful data on personnel, data, etc. An appendix lists the universities with the names of the deans of the various scientific faculties.

2068 ——. ——. ——. *List of the Learned Societies in Japan (Cultural Science).* Mimeographed. Tokyo: The Ministry, The Bureau, Scientific Data Section, 1949. 14p.

This publication provides the names, locations, year of establishment, and information about the publications of 184 societies in the fields of economics, history, law, literature, and philosophy.

2069 ——. ——. ——. *The List of the Learned Societies of Science and Technology.* Tokyo: The Ministry, The Bureau, Scientific Data Section, 1948. 78p. In English and romanized Japanese.

——. Ministry of Foreign Affairs. Public Information and Cultural Affairs Bureau. *Japan's Problems.* 1954. See no. 1186.

"Japanese Teachers Study AFT Organization." 1947. See no.1757.

2070 "Japan's Christian University." *Christian Century* 67:1191–93 (11 Oct. 1950)

This analysis of the disintegration of Japanese faith in America is undertaken within the context of a discussion of the founding of the International Christian University (ICU). The abandonment by the occupation forces of their role as champion of peace and disarmament is its focal point. The tendency for SCAP to consider peace organizations subversive, the increasing resemblance of police techniques to those used by prewar thought-control groups, and the reconstitution of the army has served to discredit the American claim that it represented a viable democracy and has given communism new validity. The establishment of ICU is seen to be a powerful deterrent to the return of authoritarianism and a necessary stimulus to the development of cooperative Protestantism in Japan.

2071 Kaigo, Tokiomi. "The American Influence on the [sic] Education in Japan." *Journal of Educational Sociology* 26:9–15 (Sept. 1952)

The author, then professor of education at Tokyo University, describes the establishment of the modern education system in Meiji Japan. He writes of the important influence of American educational concepts, American textbooks, and American educators upon the Japanese during this crucial period. He also writes of the changes which took place in the development of Japanese education, the influence of German education, and briefly of the post-1945 period.

2072 ——. "A Short History of Postwar Japanese Education." *Journal of Social and Political Ideas in Japan* 1, no.3:15–23 (Dec. 1963)

Translated from *Sengo Nihon shōshi*, edited by Yanaibara Tadao and published by the Tokyo University Press in 1960, this article by Kaigo traces the history of Japanese education beginning with the reform of the occupation. Kaigo reviews the early SCAP directives on education, the educational missions to Japan, and the educational system which resulted. He also describes actions taken by the central government to improve Japanese schools and education.

2073 Kandel, Isaac Leon. "Reorienting Japanese Education." *Educational Forum* 11:11–18 (Nov. 1946)

A review of the work of the U.S. Education Mission (USEM) vis-à-vis proposed reforms to promote a change in the orientation of Japanese society toward liberalism and democracy and away from aggressive nationalism is presented here. A brief summary of prewar educational practices is followed by an examination of the immediate, unilateral decrees issued by SCAP which dealt with matters such as government sponsorship of the dissemination of national Shinto through the morals, history, and geography curriculum and the reading of the Imperial Rescript. Kandel then discusses USEM proposals regarding decentralization of Education Ministry control, increased participation of teachers and community personnel in designing curricula, extension of compulsory education from 6 to 9 years, and the introduction of adult education. He also makes considerable mention of the difficulties of the written language and of proposals for its romanization. The concluding statement emphasizes the consistent cooperation between Japanese and Americans in the field of educational reform.

2074 ——————. "The Revision of Japanese Education." *School and Society* 64:134 (24 Aug. 1946)

As a member of the U.S. Education Mission to Japan, Kandel responds to criticism of the mission by Carroll Atkinson in *School and Society* of 17 August 1946 (no.2020). The author stresses the work done by the mission with a wide variety of Japanese educators and notes that the mission's aim is to guide the Japanese in the reconstruction of their own education system. Kandel quotes MacArthur's reaction to the mission's report as evidence of the mission's value and its sensitivity to Japanese educational concepts.

2075 Kao, Ming-huey. *An Analysis of Moral Education in Japanese Public Schools, 1945–1960*. Ph.D. dissertation, Univ. of Southern Illinois, 1964. 398p. (Abstracted in *Dissertation Abstracts* 26:5917 [1966]; University Microfilms order no.66-1077)

The development of pragmatic, conservative, and socialistic elements related to postwar moral education in Japan is traced here. Kao begins with a discussion of Confucian, Shinto, Buddhist, and entrepreneurial morals and of the moral concepts institutionalized in the Imperial Rescript on Education (1890), the Cardinal Principles of the National Policy (1932), and the Way of Subjects (1941). He then examines what he terms the pragmatic movement, which was characterized by SCAP directives emphasizing the cultivation of practical intelligence and a reflective morality. In contrast to SCAP's approach, he notes policy pursued by the conservative Ministry of Education and its attempts to reestablish courses dealing with morals and revive an emperor-centered moral theory. He also outlines a third movement in which collectivity and companionship were stressed. He concludes that a trend toward the cultivation of practical intelligence and the individual mind was apparent between 1945 and 1960, despite the crisis in moral education precipitated by ideological conflicts and the difficulties posed by the retention of traditional means of cultivating morality.

2076 Kerlinger, Frederick Nichols. *The Development of Democratic Control in Japanese Education: A Study of Attitude Change in Shikoku, 1948–1949*. Ph.D. dissertation, Univ. of Michigan, 1953. 254p. (Abstracted in *Dissertation Abstracts* 13:722–23 [1953]; University Microfilms order no.5686)

The depth and extent of occupation influence on Japanese education are examined here through an investigation of changes that took place in Shikoku from October 1948 to November 1949. Following a discussion of the preoccupation educational system and philosophy which reflected the concepts of hierarchy and authority inherent in Japanese society, Kerlinger, who had been a field observer in Shikoku, goes on to describe occupation objectives for educational reform, one of which was the establishment of elective local boards of education. The author observed the election of the 4 prefectural boards in Shikoku in October 1948 and the operations of these boards during their first year. According to several criteria which he defines, these boards functioned in a democratic way. In Kerlinger's opinion, the positive influence of the occupation on educational democracy in Shikoku outweighed the negative. He notes that the most important of these positive influences was the creation of an atmosphere of freedom, coupled with a marked acceptance of the new reforms in education.

2077 Kilpatrick, William H. "Education and Enduring Peace." In *Approaches to World Peace: Fourth Symposium*, ed. by

Lyman Bryson, Louis Finkelstein, and Robert M. MacIver. New York: Conference on Science, Philosophy and Religion in Their Relation to the Democratic Way of Life, 1944. p.352–72.

Professor Kilpatrick of Columbia University's Teachers College offers general remarks on the prerequisites for effective reeducation programs in postwar Germany and Japan. The most basic ones are overall economic prosperity, the retention of national self-respect, and the conquered nation's sincere acceptance of such programs. The actual reeducation programs, in the author's view, will fall into three phases. During the first one, the emergency period, the occupying forces must devote themselves to managing the inevitable social chaos immediately following defeat and to carrying out relief work which will foster a positive attitude toward the occupation among the citizens of the defeated nation. In the second phase, the transitional period, the educational establishment of the defeated nation must establish a school commission to recommend an acceptable school system. In this connection, Kilpatrick makes note of proposals to set up a temporary educational council of the United Nations to supervise and to make recommendations regarding the new educational system and the content of the new curricula. Finally, the third phase is to be one of international educational endeavors to offer guidance to educators around the world in a peacetime environment.

Kitamura, Fusako. *A Study of the Japan Teachers Union and Recommendations for Improvement.* 1962. See no. 1761.

2078 Kitasawa, Shinjirō. "The New Educational System of Japan." *Education* 70: 355–56 (Feb. 1950)

The author, an economics professor at Waseda University, reports on the reform of the educational system and the idea that educational reform should be designed to instill the meaning and spirit of democracy in the minds of the Japanese people. He maintains that contributions to social welfare and civic duty through education should be based on a responsible democratic value system rather than on one of paternalistic nationalism. A discussion of the initiation of the 6–3–3-system, of a national, federated parent-teacher association, of a 4-year university system free from government control, and of the activities of UNESCO in Japan is included.

2079 Klee, Loretta E. "Social Studies for the New Japan." *Social Education* 16, no.8:356–58, 360 (Dec. 1952)

Klee spent 8 months in 1951–52 in Japan as educational consultant in the social sciences for the Universities of Hiroshima and Tokyo, where she conducted a series of workshops on teaching social studies, a subject which the occupation introduced into the Japanese school curriculum. The author describes problems faced by teachers, some universal, others particular to Japan. The workshops experimented with writing curricula and conducting classroom research on the learning process. Japanese educators were found to be very interested in American democracy and in adapting its ideals to Japanese conditions.

2080 Kobayashi, Tetsuya. *General Education for Scientists and Engineers in the United States of America and Japan.* Ph.D. dissertation, Univ. of Michigan, 1965. 401p. (Abstracted in *Dissertation Abstracts* 26:2576 [1965]; University Microfilms order no.65–10,984)

Kobayashi analyzes educational trends in the United States and Japan from 1945 until 1962. He states that the general education movement which developed in America prior to World War II and in Japan during the occupation was the result of growing awareness among educators of shortcomings in specialized education. Despite widespread support of this movement in both the United States and Japan, international competition in the sciences during the mid-1950s brought renewed emphasis on science, particularly in Japan. As a result, Japanese support for general education decreased.

The author contends that it reflects the strength of the Japanese tradition of specialization, particularly evident in the scientific and engineering professions. He concludes that educators in both countries recommend general education as a basis for specialized study rather than as a basis for social democracy. His source materials include articles in English and Japanese that were published in professional and nonprofessional journals as well as government reports and documents. This study has been published in the University of Michigan Comparative Education Dissertation series (Ann Arbor: Malloy Lithoprinting, 1965. iv, 404p.) and is available for purchase from the University of Michigan's Comparative Education Dissertation Series Office, 4124 School of Education, University of Michigan, Ann Arbor, Michigan 48104.

The author has also written an article in German, "Die Reform des japanischen Bildungswesen seit 1945 und ihr Einfluss auf die Gesellschaft," *Internationales Jahrbuch für Geschichtsunterricht* 9:65–70 (1963/64).

2081 Kobayashi, Victor Nobuo. *John Dewey in Japanese Educational Thought*. Ph.D. dissertation, Univ. of Michigan, 1964. 203p. (Abstracted in *Dissertation Abstracts* 25:7060 [1965]; University Microfilms order no.65–5332)

Before discussing the occupation and the "Dewey Boom" of the 1950s, Kobayashi reviews the prewar period when Dewey's concepts were introduced into Japan and the progressive education movement at that time. The postwar "Dewey Boom" was the result of increased interest in his concepts among Japanese educators and the actions of a small group of Dewey scholars who renewed their prewar efforts to promote the publication of his works. Because occupation policies regarding education were similar to Dewey's ideas, promulgation of these policies also increased educators' interest in him. Kobayashi concludes that Dewey's educational philosophy, the study of which has become standard among Japanese educators, is being integrated into the Japanese educational tradition. The study is based on interviews with various Japanese educators, articles in Japanese about Dewey, government publications, materials issued by the U.S. occupation forces, and various secondary sources. It has been published as no.2 in the University of Michigan's Comparative Education Dissertation series (Ann Arbor: Malloy Lithoprinting, 1964. v, 198p; available for purchase from the University of Michigan's Comparative Education Dissertation Series Office, 4124 School of Education, University of Michigan, Ann Arbor, Michigan 48104) and has been used as the basis for 2 articles, "Nationalism and Educational Progressivism in Japan, 1900–1941," *Educational and Psychological Review* (Bombay) 6:88–92 (Apr. 1966) and "Japan's Progressive Movement and the Rise of National Schools," *Teachers College Record* 68:551–57 (Apr. 1967).

2081a Kozhin, Aleksei I. "Under Occupiers' Boots." *Current Digest of the Soviet Press* 4, no.18:17 (5 Apr. 1952)

In this condensed translation of an article which appeared in the 24 February issue of *Pravda*, Kozhin records the impressions he received when visiting Tokyo University and accuses the United States of trying to "train obedient slaves in the Japanese educational Institutions" and of seeking to impose American culture and values upon the Japanese. He criticizes many of the educational reforms and attributes to American rule the impoverished condition of most university students. Kozhin concludes by noting that many people are now demanding an end of the occupation and the withdrawal of American troops from Japan.

Lamott, Willis. *Nippon: The Crime and Punishment of Japan*. 1944. See no. 95.

2081b Lewis, Dora S. "Conference in Washington on Occupied Countries: The Case for Japan." *Journal of Home Economics* 42:295–97 (Apr. 1950)

Lewis reports on the proceedings of the National Conference on the Occupied Countries held in Washington, D.C. on 9–10 December 1949. The conference focused on educational activities in 3 countries, and the part of the article dealing with Japan summarizes addresses by Howard Bell, a member for Japan of the Commission on Occupied Countries and the author of *A Primer for Democracy* (a work which Lewis claims has become exceedingly popular in Japan), and Donald R. Nugent, chief of SCAP's Civil Information and Education Section. Bell advocated an increased emphasis on educational and cultural exchanges between Japan and the United States based on a greater involvement of private organizations. Nugent's report in turn was a very general and highly optimistic assessment of educational reform programs under SCAP.

2081c ———. "Education for Family Living in Japan." *Journal of Home Economics* 41:117–20 (Mar. 1949)

The author, a home economics consultant for SCAP's Civil Information and Education Section, reports that Japanese educators and students appear sincerely interested in learning "how to make homemaking education a greater factor in the preparation of young people for life in a democratic society." Lewis assisted in the establishment of homemaking education in the upper secondary schools, working in consultation with Japanese educators on the preparation of curricula. She recommends that home economics training, particularly in the colleges, be broadened to include areas such as general home management, child development and marriage as well as nutrition, food management, and related matters.

2082 Lloyd, Wesley Parkinson. *Student Counseling in Japan: A Two-Nation Project in Higher Education.* Minneapolis: Univ. of Minnesota Pr., 1953. xv, 204p. (Minnesota Library on Student Personnel Work)

In 1951 and 1952, a series of teaching institutes were held in various parts of Japan in order to introduce American concepts and techniques in the area of student services and guidance. This book is the final report on that program and has been written by its director. Each institute lasted approximately 3 months, during which time representatives of Japanese colleges and universities attended lectures and participated in group discussions on such topics as university admissions and recordkeeping; tests and measurements; education, vocational and personal counseling; student financial aid and housing; and the administrative organization of student services. The institutes were run by a group of American experts in student personnel work under the direction of a binational group of educators who worked closely with SCAP's Civil Information and Education section in planning the program.

2083 Loduchowski, Heinz. "Amerikanische Demokratie als Lebensform im japanischen Schul- und Familiensystem. Ein pädagogisches Experiment in einem moralischen Vakuum." *Monumenta Nipponica* 17:67–125 (1962)

Drawing upon data available through 1958–59, Loduchowski describes the serious social and pedagogical problems which have resulted from the transplantation of American democracy into the Japanese school system. Democracy, as the author points out, was meant not only to be a form of government but also to become an essential element in the life of both the individual and society. As such, democracy came to disrupt the Japanese family structure and the traditional system of child rearing and education. Far from bringing about the desired democratization of Japanese life, its promotion led to a growing religious and moral vacuum.

Loduchowski questions in particular whether the American educational system with its assumption of relativism, secularism, and individualism and with a neutral stand on values can be transferred to Japanese society with its basically differing assumptions. He points out, furthermore, the problems which result from the Japanese misunderstanding of the terms "democracy" and "democratic freedoms." On the one hand, there has been a dangerous rise in juvenile delinquency as well as an increase in deplorable birth control practices; on the other hand, the negation of certain moral obligations and an undermining and rejection of authority have occurred. While the equality of the sexes may be desirable, moral standards have been relaxed to such an extent that considerable sexual license now exists. The separation of church and state effectively ended State Shinto and brought about legislation providing for religious freedom, but it also increased the gap between religion and daily life and further contributed to the growth of a moral vacuum. To reinforce this latter point, Loduchowski characterizes the traditional education system as a basically unreligious system and as one that was non-supportive of values—hence as one in which the beginnings of an ethical vacuum could be found. Moreover, he argues that the major principle underlying traditional Japanese education is Confucian-based conformity while the dominant theme in American educational methods is individualistic conformity.

Aside from having serious repercussions upon the traditional Japanese family structure and from resulting in attendant moral and ethical problems, the introduction of various American educational methods has created a variety of financial and political difficulties. The decentralization of the school system placed heavy financial burdens upon local authorities and, coupled with the increase in the number of years of compulsory education, led to major problems particularly within the poorer parts of the country. Furthermore, the establishment of coeducational schools, the increase in the number of students, difficulties in teacher education, and the necessity of reeducation all resulted in a lowering of academic standards. Loduchowski views the political problem primarily in terms of the tendency of many students and teachers to espouse Communism as a consequence of their openness to new, and not only American, ideas and experiments.

In conclusion. Loduchowski considers progressive education as a relativistic and democratic system and American educational methods with their basic assumption of individual freedoms of development and expression as potentially untenable and dangerous to Japanese life.

2084 Luhmer, Nicholas. "Revision of the Postwar Educational Reform in Japan?" *School and Society* 75:337–40 (31 May 1952)

Luhmer summarizes the proposals of the "Report of the Reform of the Educational System" undertaken by the Government Investigation Committee and published in the *Japan Education Newspaper* on 22 November 1951. Seven items are presented: (1) the reinstitution of dual tracking in both vocational and general education schools at secondary and higher levels; (2) strengthening the authority of the Ministry of Education; (3) abolition of school districts; (4) restriction of school boards to the prefectural level and to cities with over 150,000 population; (5) appointment of school board members by prefectural governors rather than by popular election; (6) placement of private schools under the authority of public school boards; and (7) national standardization of textbooks.

2085 Maeda, Tamon. "The Direction of Postwar Education in Japan." *Japan Quarterly* 3:414–25 (Oct./Dec. 1956)

The author who served briefly as minister of education at the beginning of the occupation period writes about the reforms brought about under the Allied occupation. He discusses the role and power of the Civil Information and Education section of SCAP and the reforms carried out under their authority. Maeda praises a number of these reforms such as the advances made in terms of middle schools and the establishment of social science courses. However, he criticizes some of the reforms carried out in the universities, especially those changing the status of the specialized schools to that of universities. He feels this has led to an overemphasis upon attaining a university degree and is not in keeping with the democratic ideals set forth by the occupation.

2086 Makino, Tatsumi. "Educational Sociology in Japan." *Journal of Educational Sociology* 26:37–42 (Sept. 1952)

Makino examines the state of educational sociology in Japan. He begins by tracing its development and examining some of the important works which have influenced this development. He also examines a number of studies written by Japanese on educational sociology.

2087 ———. "Post-war Democratization in Japan: Japanese Education." *International Social Science Journal* 13, no.1: 44–56 (1961)

This article discusses the democratizing process of the Japanese educational system with particular reference to the school system, educational administration, and school curricula. Problems of educational method and teachers' unions are discussed incidentally as they affect these areas. Makino includes a bibliography of books, both in Japanese and in English, on the subject.

2087a Miwa, Keiko. *Analysis of the Effect of Major American Ideas upon the Organization of Japanese Higher Education from 1946 to 1967.* Ed.D. dissertation, Washington State Univ., 1969. 106p. (Abstracted in *Dissertation Abstracts International* 30:933A–34A [1969]; University Microfilms order no.69–14,460)

Miwa's dissertation analyzes the effect of major American ideas introduced into Japan during the occupation upon the organization of higher education from 1946 to 1967. The author first examines the recommendations of the U.S. Education Mission to Japan, explaining their rationale and noting some of the ways in which they were implemented. She then assesses their impact and durability. Many of the reforms created serious problems for the postwar educational system. The multiplication of junior colleges and universities, for instance, led to increased competition for limited financial resources and to the creation of an oversupply of college graduates, while it failed to reduce the fierce entrance competition to certain institutions of higher learning inasmuch as many Japanese still sought admission to a handful of prestigious universities. Eventually, Miwa notes, most Japanese came to the conclusion that neither traditional values nor Western models were suitable to meet the complex and unique needs of modern Japanese life.

2088 Mochida, Eiichi. "The Reform of Boards of Education and Its Aftermath." *Journal of Social and Political Ideas in Japan* 1, no.3:43–47 (Dec. 1963)

Translated from the September 1956 issue of *Kyōiku*, this article examines the reform of the local boards of education. Mochida points out the influence of this reform, its disadvantages for Japanese education, and the way teachers and educators should act towards this law. Mochida's main objection is that this new reform gives the Liberal Democratic party an opportunity to dominate the local boards and bring politics into education.

2089 Morito, Tatsuo. "Educational Reform and Its Problems in Postwar Japan." *Teachers College Record* 60, no.7:385–91 (Apr. 1959)

Morito, president of Hiroshima University and the first minister of education to administer the new school system, analyzes postwar educational reforms in terms of modern Japanese history. The author argues that the Meiji period saw a revolution while the occupation merely introduced reforms into an already existing system, reforms which succeeded only because of the positive cooperation of Japanese educators. The various reforms are summarized, only the abolition of the Imperial Rescript on Education being considered solely the work of the occupation. The new system is criticized for having inadequate financial support, no guiding moral principles, and being insufficiently unified. Finally, the author objects that left-wing teachers are returning education to the political arena where it had been before the war.

2090 Moriya, Fumio, and Nakamura Shūichirō. "Development of Marxian Economics in Postwar Japan." *Japan Science Review: Economic Series* no.2:41–69 (1955)

Written by 2 members of the Economic Division of the Association of Democratic Scientists, this article is a compilation of most of the important Japanese writing done on the development of Marxian economics. The works are grouped in 3 categories: "Study of Marxian Economic Theories," "History of Development of Capitalism," and "Analysis of the Present Conditions of Japanese Economy." The authors cover the important Marxist writing done in each field with their dates and in most cases some sort of description of the writing.

2091 Munakata, Seiya. "Education in Postwar Japan." *United Asia* 8, no.4:243–46 (Sept. 1956)

Munakata of Tokyo University's faculty of education criticizes the occupation's educational reforms as being in the spirit of "the out-dated liberalism of the 18th century." Moreover, the transformation of Japanese education was imposed, not voluntary. By the end of the occupation, education was becoming anti-Communist and with the signing of the peace treaty, Japanese conservative leaders continued this reverse trend. Munakata sees the social studies program as inadequate to explain the stages of history through which Japan passed. The new system is also considered an excessive economic burden. Local boards of education were part of a conservative plot to restrict progressive teachers. Finally, the author explains the constructive role of the Japan Teachers' Union.

2091a Munekata, Masaya. "Criticism on Education Reform." *Contemporary Japan* 16:194–99 (Apr./June 1947)

This critique of the occupation's educational reforms is an abstract of an article originally published in the May 1947 issue of *Asahi Hyōron*. Munekata's criticism centers on his belief that the reforms are being carried out with no realistic goals in mind and with scant attention being paid to the realities of the Japanese educational system. One announced goal, for instance, is to open secondary education up to the general public. Munekata asserts, however, that this will not happen until the closed nature of the Japanese academic elite, which is involved in the execution of the reforms, is exposed and changed. Other goals which he critically discusses include the efforts to teach children to think for themselves and to learn through discussions, and plans to decentralize the educational administration. These latter plans, Munekata believes, will run into great difficulties because of the lack of a tradition of decentralization. Furthermore, on account of their dictatorial methods, local school committees representing the local elites may be expected to force the teachers to organize unions and thereby will increase the possibility of conflict.

2092 Murakami, Shunsuke, and Iwahashi Bunkichi. "Post-war Reconstruction of Japanese Education and Its Social Aspects." *Journal of Educational Sociology* 29:309–16 (Mar. 1956)

In this article Murakami and Iwahashi describe the reforms of the Japanese educational system since the end of the war. They discuss the reorganization of the educational administration system and the changes in the structure and control of the schools. They also examine the extension of educational opportunity to working youth and the development of teaching materials.

2093 Murata, Suzuko. *A Study of the Impact of the American Educational System on Higher Education in Japan.* Ph.D. dissertation, Indiana Univ., 1969. 247p. (Abstracted in *Dissertation Abstracts International* 30:1838A [1969]; University Microfilms order no.69–17,755)

In this dissertation the writer assesses the impact of American ideas regarding education upon the Japanese educational system during the occupation years and discusses the problems involved in communicating between 2 vastly different cultures. After examining the pre-Meiji and pre-World War II educational systems, Murata describes the postwar "educational revolution imposed from without and supported by liberal educators and political leaders." She raises several questions concerning the future of university education, including the ways in which higher education can promote the education of women, the improvements that can be made in curricula, and the ways in which Japan might be able to help other Asian nations in this regard.

2094 Nishida, Kikuo. "Students' Movement." *Contemporary Japan* 21, no.10/12:555–72 (1953)

This article seeks to discover the causes of students' activities and suggests ways in which educators and the general public might deal with the problem of the students' movement. The author first examines the psychological background of modern students, maintaining that "the post-war social and economic anomalies were mainly responsible for the formation of peculiar characteristics commonly observed among the students of today." He then outlines the characteristics of the students' movement and presents a brief survey of the postwar development of the movement. The objectives of the students' movement as enumerated in the resolution adopted by the Zengakuren in April 1952 are also presented. Nishida points out some basic weaknesses of the students' activities and mentions the nature of the Zengakuren. He concludes with suggestions for possible educational measures to deal with the students' movement and shows how the public can cooperate with these efforts.

2095 Nishimoto, Mitoji. "Educational Change in Japan after the War." *Journal of Educational Sociology* 26:17–26 (Sept. 1952)

This article deals with the educational changes in Japan brought about by the occupation. The author groups these changes in 3 categories: the 6–3–3–4 plan, textbooks and teaching methods, and other problems affecting education. While Nishimoto writes of the problems and successes of each change, he focuses on the changes in the first category. He carefully diagrams the extent to which the new 6–3–3–4 system has changed both the concept of Japanese education and the number of students receiving a better education.

2095a Nishimoto, Yoichi. *Improving Moral Education in the Upper Elementary Grades in Japan*. Ed.D. dissertation, Columbia Univ. Teachers College, 1962. 422p. (Abstracted in *Dissertation Abstracts International* 23:1628 [1962]; University Microfilms order no.62–4909)

Nishimoto first reviews the history of moral education in Japanese elementary schools. Then, in chapter 3, he examines the ideas of democracy which were used as the foundation for the practice of moral education after 1945, and analyzes the 1947 constitution and the Fundamental Law of Education—both of which set the legal framework for the content of moral education during the postwar period. Chapter 4 in turn seeks to determine whether democratic ideals are compatible with the Japanese cultural and social tradition. The 2 final chapters describe the nature of moral education in a democracy and present the author's recommendations for ways of improving moral education in Japan's elementary schools.

2095b Noble, Harold J. "We're Teaching the Children to Lead Japan." *Saturday Evening Post* 219:9–11, 52–53+ (27 July 1946)

Basing his conclusions on visits he made to Japanese elementary schools, Noble finds that the schoolteachers are confused about their new mission under the occupation. When the entire future of Japan is in doubt, they complain, it is difficult to relate education to the real future needs of the students. These teachers have many questions about how to teach "democracy" and what the goals of practical education should now be. Noble notes that the future of language reform, a subject of considerable discussion, remains extremely uncertain.

2096 O'Connell, Alfred Christopher. *Junior College Education in Japan.* Ed.D. dissertation, Columbia Univ. Teachers College, 1965. 238p. (Abstracted in *Dissertation Abstracts* 26:851 [1965]; University Microfilms order no.65–8853)

The purpose of this study is 4-fold: (1) to examine the nature and development of Japanese education at the junior college level from an historical perspective; (2) to evaluate junior college education; (3) to determine the extent to which these colleges were influenced by American concepts, particularly after 1945; and (4) to compare and contrast junior colleges in the United States and Japan. The author provides a checklist of characteristics of contemporary Japanese junior colleges and concludes that although the term "junior college" was not formally adopted by the Japanese until 1949, this level of education existed in Japan, albeit in a different form, before the end of the nineteenth century.

2097 Ogawa, Tarō. "Reflections on Postwar Education." *Journal of Social and Political Ideas in Japan* 1, no.3:24–30 (Dec. 1963)

In an article translated from *Nihon kyōiku no kōzō* (Tokyo: Kokudosha, 1955. 261p.) Ogawa examines the postwar education system. He compares the teaching systems, the courses, and the discipline problems of the new system with the prewar system. He feels many of today's problems are caused by the attitudes of those teachers who have had difficulty in changing from the old teaching system. Ogawa feels they must understand more completely the meaning of educational democracy.

2098 Olds, C. Burnell. "The Language Problem." *Asia and the Americas* 46: 20–23 (Jan. 1946)

Arguing that the occupation reforms will not be complete until a language reform has been effected, the author presents a brief history of the Japanese language. He stresses the complexity of the characters and the inadequacy of the *kana* syllabary used alone. After a brief discussion of the motives of those who refuse to consider reform, the author suggests that SCAP persuade rather than coerce the Japanese to abandon their ideographic system in favor of a romanized system. He is confident that such a change can come about and that it would revolutionize the Japanese way of life.

2099 Orr, Mark Taylor. "Military Occupation of Japan (1945–1952)." *Year Book of Education, 1954.* London: Evans, 1954. p.413–24.

Orr, chief of the Education Division of the Civil Information and Education Section of SCAP from 1946 to 1949, gives a comprehensive picture of the occupation's efforts to institute educational reform. He outlines SCAP's objectives with regard to the decentralization of the educational system and the attempt to define the aims of education. Programs dealing with the reform of the educational system's organization, personnel, curriculum, youth organizations, and teaching methods are discussed. The author comments that, as the occupation progressed, the attitude of the Education Division "shifted from dictation to general supervision and finally to friendly counsel." He also comments favorably on the attempts to further democratic tendencies in education by groups such as the U.S. Education Mission, the Institute for Educational Leadership, and the U.S. Cultural Science Mission.

2099a ———. *Education Reform Policy in Occupied Japan.* Ph.D. dissertation, Univ. of North Carolina, 1954. 278p.

Orr is concerned with the reshaping of the Japanese educational system between 1945 and 1952. He examines Japanese educational policy and the governmental machinery for making reform policy, the reform policies themselves, and the ways in which policy was formulated and applied. Orr concludes that the joint efforts of the Japanese people and the occupation authorities resulted in the establishment of a democratic educational system, in the decentralization of prewar controls over education, and in a number of other fundamental reforms.

2100 Ōta, Takashi. "A Study of Educational Practices in the Postwar Period." *Journal of Social and Political Ideas in Japan* 1, no.3:116–21 (Dec. 1963)

Translated from the August and November issues of *Kyōiku* in 1956, this article by Ōta examines the new educational practices which recently have taken place in Japan. He describes methods used by some teachers to stimulate class discussion, make relevant courses like history and geography, and foster closer relationships between teacher and student. Ōta points out the importance of these new practices and the necessity of continuing them in the future.

2101 Parrott, Lindesay. "Educating Japan's Children for Democracy." *New York Times Magazine* p.10, 64–65 (10 Nov. 1946)

The author reports on the work of the U.S. Education Mission to Japan headed by George D. Stoddard. Although most of the reforms are long-range projects, certain immediate steps, such as the purge of teachers and the removal of military drill, have improved the quality of Japanese education. Preparing new texts and teaching the children how to think independently are also positive steps. Parrott sees the education of the children of Japan's middle class as the key to change in Japan.

2102 Passin, Herbert. *The Development of Public Opinion Research in Japan*. Typescript. n.p., n.d. 14p.

This typewritten speech regarding public opinion research outlines the factors which have retarded public opinion research in Japan and describes the postwar developments in this field. The author describes the occupation's role in creating interest in public opinion research and discusses the 2-fold role of the Public Opinion and Sociological Research Division of SCAP's Civil Information and Education Section, i.e., informing SCAP of Japanese reactions to programs of national importance and furnishing advice and guidance to Japanese research organizations. He also describes the establishment of new Japanese research institutions and the updating of old ones and evaluates the progress that has been made during the occupation as compared with future needs.

The speech is available at the Washington National Records Center, Suitland, Maryland.

———. *Japanese Education: A Bibliography of Materials in the English Language.* 1970. *See* no.22.

2103 ———. *Society and Education in Japan*. New York: Columbia Univ. Teachers College, Bureau of Publications, 1965. xvii, 347p. (Teachers College, Columbia Univ., Comparative Education series)

In the course of discussing the occupation's reorganization of Japan's educational system, Passin points out that SCAP's reforms have had profound implications for Japanese life and society. One obvious effect has been to keep young people out of the labor force for a prolonged period of time. As a result, not only must they be supported by their parents for several more years but they also are likely to entertain higher expectations than those who joined the country's work force before the war.

Penrose, William O. "Japanese Re-education: The Imperial Carp vs. Civil Rights." 1946. *See* no.453.

2104 "Persecution of Koreans in Japan." *Soviet Press Translations* 3:366–67 (15 June 1948)

This article which originally appeared in *Pravda* on 26 April 1948 relates specifically to a decree of the Japanese Ministry of Education ordering all Koreans in Japan to educate their children only in Japanese schools. In the author's opinion this constitutes persecution of a minority group. He attributes this action of the Ministry of Education to a SCAP directive of November 1946 ordering the Japanese government to take control of the educational system for the Korean population in Japan. The article cites various demonstrations that have been staged in protest but claims that no substantial measures have been taken by SCAP to correct the injustice.

2104a "Policy for the Revision of the Japanese Educational System." *Department of State Bulletin* 16:746–47 (27 Apr. 1947); also in *Current Notes on International Affairs* 19:740–42 (Nov./Dec. 1948)

This Far Eastern Commission policy decision of 27 March 1947 is divided into 3 sections. The first indicates that the guiding principle for the educational reforms is the concept of education as the pursuit of truth and the preparation of the individual for a life in a democratic society. The second section deals with such matters as the training and recruitment of teachers and prohibits the employment of ultranationalistic, totalitarian, or militaristic teachers. The third and final section discusses textbooks, curricula, and teaching methods, the overall goals of which will be to encourage independent thinking and to provide an understanding of progressive ideas.

2104b "Re-educating Japan." *Elementary School Journal* 47:8–10 (Sept. 1946)

This editorial comment on the report of the first U.S. Education Mission to Japan focuses on the reform of the Japanese written language—an item of particular concern to those interested in elementary school education. The editors implicitly support the report's recommendations for reforms in this area, pointing out that the need for language reform has long been recognized by the Japanese themselves.

2104c "Religion in Public Education." *Contemporary Religions in Japan* 8, no. 1:85–100 (Mar. 1967)

This collection of official documents on the relationship of religion to public education in Japan consists of 3 memorandums dated 9 September 1949 and addressed respectively to the chief of staff, the Japanese government, and the commanding general of the Eighth Army. The documents deal specifically with (1) the prohibition of religious instruction in public schools; (2) voluntary religious activities of students and teachers outside of school hours; (3) the status of religious leaders who are either invited to speak at various schools or who are employed as qualified teachers by various boards of education; (4) school-sponsored group visits to shrines and other religious institutions; and (5) the use of school buildings by nonschool community religious groups outside of school hours.

The Reminiscences of Dr. Lauren V. Ackerman. 1961. See no.44g.

The Reminiscences of Harold C. Henderson. 1962. See no.44l.

The Reminiscences of Jake R. Harold. 1962. See no.44m.

The Reminiscences of Josephine Colletti McKean. 1962. See no.44p.

2105 "Report of U.S. Education Mission to Japan." *Department of State Bulletin* 14:767–72 (5 May 1946)

This article consists of 4 items related to the Education Mission's report: (1) a transmittal letter dated 19 April 1946 from Assistant Secretary of State William Benson to the secretary of state, which includes a strong recommendation that a system of romanization replace the present Japanese writing system inasmuch as "the literacy of the Japanese people has been greatly overrated;" (2) a transmittal letter to General MacArthur dated 30 March; (3) a highly laudatory statement on the report by MacArthur, dated 6 April; and (4) a digest of the report itself (no.2129a), touching on such topics as the aims and content of Japanese education, language reform, educational administration, teaching and teacher training, adult education, and higher education.

2105a Rohrlich, George F. "Transformation of Culture: A Postscript from Japan." In *Perspectives on a Troubled Decade: Science, Philosophy, and Religion, 1939–1949*, ed. by Lyman Bryson, Louis Finkelstein, and Robert M. MacIver. New York: Conference on Science, Philosophy and Religion in Their Relation to the Democratic Way of Life, 1950. p.125–34.

Rohrlich examines the principles of adult education from perspectives gained as a social economist in SCAP's Public Health and Welfare Section. While the Japanese have been remarkably receptive to reeducation, he writes, it has become evident that there are many obstacles to their being fully reeducated—in large measure because of deep-seated conflicts between Japanese and American ways of thinking. To illustrate these differences, Rohrlich offers examples drawn from his own experiences in helping to set up new social security programs in Japan. In conclusion, he offers 3 hypotheses regarding adult education (or reeducation): (1) Before meaning can be imparted to specific reeducation programs, their aims as well as their techniques must be understood and agreed upon by all concerned; (2) Everyone involved in the teaching process must be able to make the knowledge or skills that are taught appear as a partial means to a specific goal; (3) Techniques and institutions transplanted from one culture to another but not absorbed into the recipient culture's "spirit" may survive even though they fail to become an integral part of the new culture.

2105b Sansom, Sir George B. "Education in Japan." *Pacific Affairs* 19:413–15 (Dec. 1946)

In response to postwar criticism of Japanese education, Sir George Sansom points out in this letter that: (1) Japanese official figures showing a high rate of school attendance are probably accurate, (2) the U.S. Education Mission's report that most Japanese are virtually illiterate is not true, and (3) the quality of Japanese education was mixed.

2106 Schwantes, Robert Sidney. "Educational Influence of the United States of America." *Contemporary Japan* 26:442–58 (May 1960)

In his discussion of the results of the occupation, Schwantes notes that the trend in education is toward greater uniformity under a Ministry of Education which again exercises authority rather than being merely advisory.

2107 Second U.S. Education Mission to Japan. *Report of the Second United States Education Mission to Japan.* Washington, D.C.: Government Printing Office, 1950. ii, 17p.

This report by a second mission of 5 American educators was submitted to SCAP on 22 September 1950. Chaired by Willard E. Givens, the mission was intended to evaluate the progress of SCAP educational reforms and the extent to which they had followed the recommendations given by the first mission. As such, the report supplements the earlier mission's *Report of the United States Education Mission to Japan* (1946) (no. 2129a). Consequently, it deals with essentially the same subjects that were discussed in the first report and points out those aspects of Japanese education that have yet to be improved, such as school facilities, teacher shortages, the lack of teachers' colleges, higher education, social education, language usage, vocational education programs, and private education. The report is highly favorable regarding the progress made in educational reform by SCAP. A Japanese version has appeared under the title of *Dai Niji Beikoku Kyōiku Shisetsudan hōkokusho* (Tokyo: Nippon Hōsō Shūppan Kyōkai, 1950. 106p.).

2108 Shiba, Giye. "University Students of Postwar Japan." *Contemporary Japan* 19:180–90 (Apr./June 1950)

The chief of the Students' Welfare Section of Tokyo University writes about the living conditions of postwar Japanese university students and their problems and needs. The effects of housing difficulties, food shortages, and lack of educational funds are discussed. The author suggests various measures to be taken by university authorities and the community in general to alleviate these conditions. In addition to measures to improve students' living conditions, he advocates appropriate guidance of students. The development of the National Federation of Students' Autonomies (Zengakuren) and its significance for the academic institution are discussed. In examining the "causes of the recent undisciplined actions taken by some university students" the author attributes part of the misuse of leadership by some students to the fact that democracy was "bestowed" on the Japanese after defeat in the war rather than won by them.

2109 Shimbori, Michiya. "The Fate of Postwar Educational Reform in Japan." *School Review* 68, no.2:228–41 (Summer 1960)

Shimbori, associate professor of educational sociology at Hiroshima University, describes some of the major characteristics of postwar Japan's educational system and points out how the occupation's reforms have had a tremendous impact upon the entire system. He considers certain reforms—e.g., greater education for women—to be beneficial, but he stresses that many other changes which were imposed "without due respect for Japanese culture and social structure" have created serious problems for Japan. The extension of compulsory education from 8 to 9 years, for example, has strained the country's financial resources. Educational standards as a whole also have declined. Furthermore, the shift from a dual system of education (whereby Japanese children after completing primary school either received university-oriented higher education or went on to a vocational school) to a unitary system has led to a weakening of vocational training in Japan as well as to greater and more intense competition for entrance into good universities.

Smethurst, Richard J. "The Origins and Policies of the Japan Teachers' Union 1945–56." 1967. *See* no.1778.

2110 Smith, Thomas Vernor. "Ethics in the Japanese Educational Curriculum." *Ethics* 56:297–302 (July 1946)

An editor of this periodical presents his views on the teaching of ethics in the postwar Japanese curriculum "for General MacArthur's guidance in the democratization of moral instruction in the Japanese schools." The article consists mainly of a summary of what the author believes should be the moral philosophy of a democratic society and an attempt to relate this concept of morality to several specific phenomena—manners, civics, workmanship, and religion. Insisting that the method of teaching morals be left to the Japanese themselves, the author concludes with several general recommendations in the event that ethics are to be taught as a single and separate course in Japan.

2111 ———. "The Re-education of Conquered Peoples." *Proceedings of the National Conference of Social Work* p.25–38 (1947)

The American occupation policy concerning education in Japan, Italy, and Germany is discussed here vis-à-vis 3 general problems: how to conduct schools without buildings, how to censor textbooks and yet have materials with which to teach, and how to purge teaching personnel yet keep the schools open and operating. Smith emphasizes the general American policy of legislating only what may not be taught, which permits each nation to reconstitute its own curricula. He comments on his own work which is an attempt to create a new ethics course for Japanese schools. This attempt is based on the strengthening of selected aspects of traditional ethics in order to provide a foundation for a democratic morality.

2111a ———. *The Re-education of Germany, Italy, and Japan.* Claremont, Calif.: Friends of the Colleges at Claremont, 1947. 22p.

The text of an address presented at a dinner meeting of the Friends held in Los Angeles on 19 February 1947, this publication compares and contrasts American efforts to reform the educational systems of the 3 defeated Axis countries. During the course of his presentation Smith stated, "I hazard the impressions (1) that in the three major countries conquered our problems are common and triune; (2) that the educational policy of American forces is fairly unitary and chiefly sound; and (3) that the results so far are tolerable and that the philosophy of the policy may be pointed to with pride, modest pride."

2112 Snyder, Harold E., and Margretta S. Austin, eds. *Educational Progress in Japan and the Ryukyus.* Washington, D.C.: American Council on Education, 1950. iv, 52p.

A report of a conference of major American nongovernmental agencies sponsored in Washington, D.C. on 25 May 1950 by the Commission on Occupied Areas of the American Council on Education. The report includes excerpts of speeches given by Lieutenant Colonel D. R. Nugent, chief of the Civil Information and Education Section of SCAP, and Lewis Q. Moss, head of the Vocational and Home Economics Section, Civil Information and Education Section of SCAP. It also contains a speech on educational leadership training in Japan by Paul E. Webb, director of the Institute for Educational Leadership, Japan. All of the speakers discuss current developments in Japan and problems involved in "reorienting" the Japanese people toward the new postwar goal of building a democratic nation.

Spinks, Charles N. "Indoctrination and Re-education of Japan's Youth." 1944. *See* no.122a.

2112a Stanley, Louise. "Report on the Conference on Occupied Areas." *Journal of Home Economics* 43:118–20 (Feb. 1951)

This article reports on the proceedings of the Second National Conference on Occupied Areas, held in Washington, D.C. on 30 November–1 December 1950. The conference dealt primarily with educational programs in Austria, Germany, Japan and the Ryukyus. The section of the article dealing specifically with Japan briefly summarizes SCAP measures to decentralize the educational system, extend the length of compulsory education, and institute new curricula in the areas of health, technical education, and vocational education. According to the author, an expansion of adult and women's education also is well under way.

Starr, Mark. "Japanese Trade Unions Today." 1947. *See* no.1780.

2113 Steig, Milan B. *Administration of Schools in Tokyo, Japan, 1945–1950.* Ph.D. dissertation, Nihon Univ., 1951. (Abstracted in Association of Literature, Philosophy, and History Depts. *Kenkyū ronbunshū* (Tokyo) 4:214–16 [1953])

A civil education officer in the occupation describes educational developments in Tokyo in the postwar years, stressing the recommendations of 2 U.S. Education Missions, the functions of the new boards of education and superintendents of schools, and the significance of the new education laws. An account is also given of student councils, parent-teacher associations, teachers' unions, school libraries, school principals' associations, etc. The author evaluates the program of school visitation by the military government civil education officers, the work of the teachers' screening committees, and school lunch programs. He is somewhat critical of the current situation, stating that student participation in classroom learning is lacking, that counseling and guidance are inadequate, and that teachers have organized to promote their own social standing as well as democratic principles of education.

2114 Stoddard, George D. "MacArthur and the U.S. Education Mission to Japan." *National Parent-Teacher* 41:22–24 (Sept. 1946)

The chairman of the U.S. Education

Mission to Japan provides a firsthand account of the mission's recent trip to Japan. He first discusses the mission's interview with MacArthur, pointing out the supreme commander's views on such subjects as the constitution, the proper role of women in Japan, and the Japanese character. He then notes the assistance rendered the mission by SCAP and various Japanese educators and reviews the substance of the mission's recommendations. The author concludes with a brief sampling of the Japanese reaction to the mission's accomplishments as reported in the Japanese press.

2115 Sullivan, Walter, Jr. "Enlightening the Japanese Mind." *Free World* pt.1, 11: 28–31 (Apr. 1946); pt.2, 11:49–54 (May 1946)

In the first of these 2 articles, the author (a staff member of the *New York Times*) states his contention that "reform of Japanese behavior must begin with a remolding of the Japanese mind." He discusses the history of the Japanese from the Meiji Restoration to the present, emphasizing the gradual advancement toward liberal government that was arrested by the militarists. Characterizing the Japanese as men who traditionally harken faithfully to the commands of their rulers, the author suggests that the conquerors of Japan should encourage independent thinking in every individual Japanese citizen. He concludes that "without a basic feeling of individualism, they will never absorb the political ideas that are being poured into the caldron every day." In his second article, Sullivan concentrates upon the need to reform Japan's educational system. He charges that the former system was a highly centralized one which stifled any individuality on the part of the student. After a brief account of the historical development of the Japanese educational system, he discusses reforms enacted by SCAP. Particular emphasis is placed upon textbook revision, the use of the radio to supplement textbooks, and a reform of Japanese teachers themselves. The author concludes his remarks by urging that the Allied nations commit themselves to a 20-year occupation in order to insure the implementation of all SCAP reform programs.

2116 "Summary of the Report of the United States Education Mission to Japan." *International Conciliation* no.427: 20–26 (Jan. 1947)

This document reprints the concluding portion of a Department of State publication (no.2129a) and provides a summation of the findings and recommendations of the U.S. Education Mission which was made up of 27 representatives of American education under the chairmanship of George D. Stoddard. The report discusses the mission's appraisal of the prewar educational system and its recommendations that explicit courses in morals be eliminated, vocational training be emphasized at all levels, *romaji* be brought into common use, the control of schools be as widely dispersed as possible, popular participation in educational administration at local and prefectural levels be encouraged, the years of compulsory education be increased, and libraries and research facilities be expanded. There also are sections devoted to a discussion of the education of teachers and the role of colleges and universities in the educational system.

Supreme Commander for the Allied Powers. Monograph 31. *Education, 1945–September 1949.* 1952. See no.313.

———. Monograph 54. *Reorganization of Science and Technology in Japan, 1945–September 1950.* 1952. See no.336.

———. Civil Information and Education Section. *C I and E Bulletin.* 1947–49. See no.266.

2117 ———. ———. *The Development and Present Status of Romaji in Japan.* Mimeographed. Tokyo: SCAP, 1950. 42p., app., diagrams.

Focusing on the issue of a possible change from Japanese ideographs to roman letters, this mimeographed report has 2 general purposes: "to outline the general features of the Japanese language structure with a view to throwing some light on the problems posed by Romanization," and "to treat in some detail the progress that has been made in the teaching and use of Roman letters for writing Japanese to date." Although some attention is given to the prewar period, the report emphasizes the postsurrender developments, describing SCAP's attitudes and the recommendations of the SCAP-sponsored first U.S. Education Mission to Japan. It discusses such issues as the establishment of the Research Organization on *Romaji*, the issuance of *romaji* textbooks, and the inauguration of *romaji* societies. The final 2 sections of the report provide a brief summation of progress achieved in the field of *romaji* education and discusses impediments to its further development. Seven appendixes describe the quantity and variety of newspapers and textbooks making use of *romaji* and provide statistics on the number of schools teaching some form of romanization in their curricula.

Available at the Library of Congress, Washington, D.C.

2118 ———. ———. *Developments in Japanese Education in Terms of the Report of the United States Education Mission to Japan.* Tokyo: SCAP, Aug. 1950. 488p.

Intended by the Education Division of the section as a working document not to be published, this extensive report provides a comprehensive picture of educational reform programs in Japan toward the close of the occupation. Supplementing it is another volume entitled *Legislation, Statistics, and Other Informational Materials Pertaining to Education in Japan* (1950). This report is written specifically in terms of the report submitted by the U.S. Education Mission to Japan in March 1946 (no.2129a) and in its organization follows the structure of the mission's report. Material gathered from the Civil Information and Education Section's unpublished daily conferences, weekly reports, and reports of field trips throughout Japan is arranged in the following 7 sections: (1) "The Aims and Content of Japanese Education," (2) "Language Reform," (3) "Administration of Education at the Elementary and Secondary School Levels," (4) "Teaching and the Education of Teachers," (5) "Adult Education," (6) "Higher Education and Research," and (7) "Additional Programs." Throughout the report, attempts are made to relate the U.S. mission's original recommendations, SCAP attempts at reform, and the actual situation at the time. The document is as comprehensive a statement of SCAP's educational policies during the occupation as can be found.

Available at the Washington National Records Center, Suitland, Maryland.

———. ———. *A History of Teachers' Unions in Japan.* 1948. See no.1785.

2119 ———. ———. *Japanese Educational Institutions with Religious Affiliations.* Tokyo: SCAP, 20 Feb. 1948. 88p.

Providing reliable statistical data for Japanese educational institutions with religious affiliations, this report covers 407 schools (232 Christian, 162 Buddhist, and 13 Shinto) ranging from kindergartens to universities. Information on the location, date of establishment, number of students and of teachers, and religious affiliation is provided.

2119a ———. ———. *Postwar Developments in Physical Education through the First Two Years of the Occupation.* Mimeographed. Tokyo: SCAP, 15 Mar. 1948. 43p.

Following a brief introductory history, this report describes important developments in the field of physical education between September 1945 and the fall of 1947. It includes sections on the abolition of militaristic practices, the establishment of a new physical education program, and 72 physical education conferences held during the period covered.

2120 ———. ———. *Roster and Statistics of Japanese Educational Institutions, April and November 1946.* Tokyo: SCAP, 1948–49. 46v.

Published between 30 January 1948

and 13 September 1949, this series of 46 reports (1 for each prefecture) provides statistical information for more than 40,000 educational institutions in Japan. Covered are the name of each school, its date of foundation, address, enrollment by sex and by totals, and the teaching force by sex, by full-time or part-time classification, and by totals. The publications themselves ran between 51 and 226 pages in length, and each one provided a statistical summary of the information contained within it.

2121 ———. ———. *Some Problems in Japanese Social Science Research*. Tokyo: SCAP, 1950. 15p.

A report presented to the chief of the Civil Information and Education Section of SCAP in an attempt to describe the current status of research in the social sciences in Japan toward the end of the occupation. After briefly discussing the historical background of the social sciences in Japan, the author undertakes a cursory inspection of the major kinds of social science research undertaken in Japan in recent years. He distinguishes between the anthropological, sociological, and psychological sciences and characterizes present research in Japan as tending to be too all-inclusive in scope. He suggests that it overemphasizes the gathering of general data instead of seeking solutions to specific problems. The report also considers problems associated with the financing of research programs and Japan's research needs as well as the unique opportunities the country provides for the social scientist. The author concludes by recommending collaborative work between Japanese and American social scientists and the exchange of textbooks which are critically needed in Japan.

Available at the Army Library, the Pentagon, Washington, D.C.

2122 ———. ———. Analysis and Research Div. *Journalism Education in Japan*. Tokyo: SCAP, 1948. iv, 33p.

This report gives a summary of a limited survey conducted in 1948 by SCAP on the extent of journalism education in Japanese institutions of higher learning and newspaper companies. The survey covers the historical background of each of the journalism programs, current and prospective courses, enrollments, instructors, and relations between universities and newspaper companies in training prospective journalists. The report also refers to the efforts of the Japan Newspaper Association to promote journalism education in universities.

2123 ———. ———. Education Div. *Education in Japan*. Mimeographed. Tokyo: SCAP, 15 Feb. 1946. vi, 132p.

A mimeographed handbook designed for use by members of the U.S. Education Mission during their stay in Japan in March 1946 and by SCAP education officers throughout Japan. The handbook is composed of 2 parts. The first gives a summary of the history of Japanese education before 1945, with particular emphasis on the national educational system of 1937 and wartime changes therein. The second part describes occupation policies on educational reform, referring to SCAP efforts to remove all elements of militarism and to encourage democratic reforms. This section also discusses the relevant functions and administrative responsibilities of both SCAP and the Japanese Education Ministry. Appended are texts of all major SCAP directives on educational reform issued as of January 1946, together with statistics and charts on Japanese education up to 1944. The appendix also includes a list of major Ministry of Education orders issued between the end of the war and January 1946. This publication has largely been superseded by the more carefully compiled and complete *Education in the New Japan* (no.2124).

2124 ———. ———. ———. *Education in the New Japan*. 1st ed. Tokyo: SCAP, May 1948. 2v. Reprint ed., with minor corrections: Washington, D.C.: Government Printing Office, 1948.

This represents an effort by the Civil Information and Education Section to outline SCAP's educational reform policy and objectives and discuss achievements in the 3 years since surrender. It consists of 4 parts in 2 volumes. The first volume, which has 3 parts, begins with a general description of the historical background of Japanese education from the fifth century through 1945. The second part discusses the prewar educational system, covering the general administration of the school system at elementary, secondary, and higher levels. This part also treats such special topics as education for the handicapped, religious education, and women's education. The third part, which constitutes the major portion of volume 1, introduces SCAP's education reform policies and the rationale behind them and discusses steps taken by the Japanese Ministry of Education to implement these policies. Subjects covered are elementary, secondary, and higher educational curricula, textbook problems, the education of teachers, women, and adults, vocational education, physical education, audiovisual education, school libraries, and language simplification. The fourth part, which comprises the whole of volume 2, presents 10 appendixes containing basic documents of SCAP and the Japanese government on relevant subjects, as well as statistical data on Japanese education and a bibliography.

2124a ———. ———. ———. *Educational Progress in Japan.* Mimeographed. Tokyo: SCAP, January 1951. 211p.

This publication was designed to provide information on developments in the field of education since 1948, when SCAP released its report *Education in the New Japan* (no.2124). Although its circulation was restricted, the *substance* of about half of the volume subsequently appeared in articles in various educational journals. These are as follows:

Chapter 1 ("Nondemocratic Ideologies") published in: Walter Crosby Eells. "Communist Influence on Education in Japan, the Philippines, and Southeast Asia." *Educational Record* 33:41–70 (Jan. 1952);

Chapter 4 ("Compulsory Education") and Chapter 5 ("Structural Reorganization") published in: Walter Crosby Eells. "Compulsory Education and School Reorganization in Japan." *School Executive* 71:69–70 (Nov. 1951);

Chapter 6 ("Secondary Education") published in: Walter Crosby Eells. "Secondary Education in Japan." *National Association of Secondary School Principals Bulletin* 35:21–24 (Oct. 1951);

Chapter 7 ("Coeducation") published in: Walter Crosby Eells. "Coeducation in Japan." *School and Society* 74:183–85 (22 Sept. 1951) (no.2045);

Chapter 8 ("Decentralization") and Chapter 9 ("Ministry of Education") published in: Walter Crosby Eells. "Decentralization of Control of Education in Japan." *School and Society* 73:388–91 (23 June 1951) (no.2046);

Chapter 12 ("Textbook Publication") published in: Walter Crosby Eells. "Textbook Publication in Japan." *School Executive* 72:76–78 (Sept. 1952);

Chapter 17 ("Curriculum Improvement") published in: Walter Crosby Eells. "Curriculum Improvement in Japan." *Educational Administration and Supervision* 37:423–30 (Nov. 1951);

Chapter 21 ("Higher Education") published in: Walter Crosby Eells. "Recent Higher Educational Developments in Japan." *Education Record* 32:380–92 (Oct. 1951);

Chapter 24 ("Adult Education") published in: Walter Crosby Eells. "Adult Education in Japan." *Adult Education* 2:3–8 (Oct. 1951);

Chapter 25 ("Extension Education") published in: Walter Crosby Eells. "Extension Education in Japanese Universities." *Association of American Colleges Bulletin* 37:383–84 (Oct. 1951);

Chapter 28 ("Language Reform") published in: Walter Crosby Eells. "Language Reform in Japan." *Modern Language Journal* 36:210–13 (May 1952) (no.2047);

Chapter 33 ("Recommendations for Improvement in Higher Education") published in: Walter Crosby Eells. "Improvement of Higher Education in Japan." *Higher Education* 8:127–30 (1 Feb. 1950).

2125 ———. ———. ———. *Post-war Developments in Japanese Education.* Tokyo: SCAP, Apr. 1952. 2v.

This 2-volume report on postwar Japanese developments in the field of education supplements the division's earlier 2-volume report, *Education in the New Japan* (1948) (no.2124). In this later report the description of developments in the Japanese educational reform program is updated to April 1952. Although the 2 reports focus on the same areas of Japanese education, they do not overlap. Volume 1 of this second report begins with a discussion of the basic objectives of postwar educational reforms and considers matters relating to school curriculum, teaching materials, and health and physical education as well as vocational education and language simplification. The volume also deals with such problems as the decentralization of school administration, the availability of school facilities, educational personnel training, higher education, and adult and youth education. It concludes with a description of cultural exchange programs developed on an international scale through SCAP's initiative. Volume 2 is an appendix containing basic laws and cabinet orders related to education issued from 1945 to 1952. Laws and orders listed in the first report are included here along with their subsequent amendments. This volume also provides useful statistical information on Japanese education from 1940 to 1952.

———. ———. ———. *Weekly Report.* 1945–51. See no.272.

———. Economic and Scientific Section. *Science and Technology in Japan: Reports.* 1947–50. See no.2273.

2126 Tanaka, Kōtarō. "The Present Crisis of Japanese Education." *Contemporary Japan* 20:5–14 (Jan./Mar. 1951)

In this article a professor at Tokyo University and former minister of education in Japan states that one factor leading Japan to war was the "grave defects in Japanese education." He presents the historical background of the present educational crisis, showing that foreign ideas were used for superficial and utilitarian motives. He demonstrates how education was conceived of as a means merely of achieving the aims of the state. He views the character of the teachers as being of prime importance in reforming education in the postwar days. The Fundamental Education Law, promulgated in March 1947, is discussed, and the author comments on problems which have come with the introduction of principles of democracy. Education, he says, "badly fails in the formation of the moral character of the students." Despite what he considers were positive steps taken by SCAP, education in Japan, he maintains, "is still in peril from the threat of Communism." He concludes by outlining measures necessary to overcome this crisis.

2126a ———. "Education and Democracy." *Contemporary Japan* 15:253–57 (May/Aug. 1946)

This article by Japan's minister of education was translated from the April 1946 issue of *Chūō Kōron*. According to Tanaka, all of Japan's "recent mistakes" can be traced to errors in education. The new democratic trends in politics will naturally be reflected in education, and Japan's new goal will be the training and the improvement of the personality of the individual as a member of society. The autonomy of the colleges and middle schools (both public and private) must be guaranteed, and the Ministry of Education should hereafter represent rather than control Japan's educational institutions. Tanaka's final recommendation is a constitutional provision insuring the independence of education.

2127 Tiltman, Hessell. "A Textbook Made in Japan." *New Republic* 116:20–21 (6 Jan. 1947)

The revision of Japanese textbooks as a part of SCAP's larger program of educational reform is the subject of this article. Focusing on the publication of *Kuni no ayumi* (Tokyo: 1946), an elementary school history issued with SCAP approval, the report points up several accounts in the text which would seem to reecho the former nationalistic biases. He is particularly critical of the account of Japan's international relations prior to the war and, in conclusion, judges the history to be a "quaint and dangerous" one.

2128 U.S. Cultural Science Mission to Japan. *Report.* Tokyo: SCAP, Civil Information and Education Section, 1949. 67p.

Prepared by George K. Brady, Charles E. Martin, Edwin O. Reischauer, Luther W. Stalnaker, and Glenn T. Trewartha (the 5 members of the mission), this report covers the role, nature and financing of postwar Japanese research in the humanities and the social sciences. It closes with 11 specific and several more general recommendations. The mission was known in Japan as the Amerika Gasshūkoku Jinbun Kagaku Komondan and a Japanese version of its report appeared under the title *Nihon jinbun kagaku no atarashii shinro* (Tokyo: Gakujutsu Shiryō Kankōkai, 1950. 110p.).

2129 ———. Educational Exchange Group to Japan. *Report of the Education Exchange Survey to the Supreme Commander for the Allied Powers.* Tokyo: 1949. iv, 59p.

In August 1949 a group of 5 American educators and government officials involved in education traveled to Japan under SCAP auspices in order to look into the possibilities of setting up a formal educational exchange program between the 2 countries. This report was prepared at the end of the group's 2-month stay. The survey group felt that "education in the principles and practices of democracy should gradually become the dominant objective" of the occupation and that educational exchange was one valuable means for promoting practical instruction in democratic ways. With this in mind, the group recommended that a number of different exchange programs be arranged. First of all, teachers from the United States— especially those specializing in fields such as sociology, political science, psychology, philosophy, literature, and the English language which would help Japan "most quickly to become an understanding, cooperative member of the family of nations"—would be encouraged to serve in Japan. The group next recommended that arrangements be worked out for bringing Japanese teachers and researchers to the United States. It was expected that the teachers of Japanese language, literature, art, foreign trade and the like would be in the greatest demand and that they would be most welcome at the college level and above. Japanese other than academics also would be invited to study and observe at American institutions. These people would include students, educators, government officials, and "molders of public opinion." A final category of persons included in the recommendations was American students and researchers who would be placed in Japanese universities and other institutions. It was suggested that care be taken to find serious students in order to avoid an excessive proportion of romantics, malcontents, and immature persons. The survey team also included detailed and specific recommendations relating to methods of funding (the respective governments would be expected to bear much of the burden), the selection of participants, placement, housing, and general logistical problems.

2129a ———. Education Mission to Japan. *Report of the United States Education Mission to Japan.* Tokyo: SCAP, 1946. v, 46p. Issued also in Washington, D.C.: Government Printing Office, 1946. vi, 62p. (Dept. of State publication 2579; Far Eastern series 11)

A report prepared for SCAP in March 1946 by the 27-member U.S. Education Mission headed by George D. Stoddard. Their report, submitted on 30 March 1946, discusses what should be the bases of a philosophy of education in a democratic society and suggests extensive reforms for Japan in language, the administration of education at the primary and secondary levels, the training of teaching personnel, and the structure of higher education and adult education. A summary of the report is given in the last portion. This report was probably the most important single basic document of the occupation in the field of education and helped determine the general policy for most of SCAP's subsequent educational reforms.

2129b Van Staaveren, Jacob. "The Educational Revolution in Japan." *Educational Forum* 16:229–40 (Jan. 1952)

Van Staaveren begins with a general discussion of the occupation's educational activities, paying particular attention to their legal aspects, and then discusses hopeful developments in several areas. Student government activities, he finds, are becoming increasingly popular due to SCAP encouragement, and a large number of students are experiencing democratic processes at first hand. Textbook reform, one of SCAP's first projects, is nearly complete, and the development of new social studies curricula is going well. The unionization of teachers is contributing to the goal of educational autonomy. Finally, the founding of International Christian University is a symbol of revolutionary changes within higher education in the direction of liberalism and international cooperation.

2130 Van Zandt, Howard F. "Japanese Try to Make Their Language Understandable." *Modern Language Journal* 33:541–43 (Nov. 1949)

Van Zandt, a SCAP officer, describes the chaotic nature of the Japanese writing system, especially insofar as proper nouns are concerned, and alludes to language reform efforts undertaken during the occupation period.

2130a Webb, Paul E. "Education for Democracy in Japan." *Educational Outlook* 26:43–52 (Jan. 1952)

Webb reviews the occupation's efforts to democratize Japanese education through a discussion of reforms in teacher education, the revision of prewar textbooks, the designing of new curricula, and the decentralization of education. He points out that there was initially considerable opposition among the Japanese to many of the changes, but "today's educational program in Japan," he concludes, "is largely the making of the Japanese themselves and has set the pattern for future growth and development."

2130b Weideman, Elizabeth. "House of Sand." *American Teacher* 36, no.3:6–9 (Dec. 1951)

The author, whose husband served as an officer in SCAP, offers her observations on various aspects of Japanese society based on her experiences living in Japan. First of all, she finds that many Japanese—not just the leftists—are uneasy about the proposed peace treaty because it will not be signed by all of the Allies and encourages Japanese rearmament as well. To assess the progress of democratization, Weideman then looks at the field of education. She notes that "only token reforms have been achieved." The schools, moreover, are in poor physical condition, are overcrowded, and are poorly lighted; nevertheless, in at least one instance, SCAP ordered the Japanese government to cut its education budget. The fundamental impediment to the progress of democratization, Weideman argues, is SCAP's own nature as a military organization that cannot admit its mistakes and that believes that circumstances never alter cases. She concludes with a plea that the American Federation of Teachers establish contact with the members of the Japanese Teachers' Union and aid them whenever and wherever possible.

2130c Werth, Richard. "The Development of Boards of Education in Japan." *American School Board Journal* 118:19–23 (Mar. 1949)

After describing the principles behind the occupation's control of the educational system, Werth illustrates the operation of that policy with concrete examples drawn from his experiences as an education officer in Yamanashi prefecture. He describes the local board of education elections of 1948 in detail, and analyzes the backgrounds and platforms of the candidates as well as the local power politics which were involved. It remains to be seen, Werth concludes, whether local control will be beneficial. There already are some indications, however, that little more than a new educational bureaucracy is being created and that the lack of fiscal autonomy is inhibiting the proper operations of local school boards.

2131 "The World to Japan." *New York Times Magazine* p.26 (10 Feb. 1946)

Brief quotations taken from recently banned school texts show how history was interpreted and presented to elementary and high school children. The texts were collected by the United Nations' International Educational Organization.

2132 Wunderlich, Herbert John. *The Japanese Textbook Problem and Solution, 1945–1946*. Ed.D. dissertation, Stanford Univ., 1952. 382p. (Abstracted in Stanford University. *Abstracts of Dissertations, 1951–1952* 27:726–27 [1953])

Wunderlich, textbook revision officer of the Civil Information and Education Section of SCAP from 1945 to 1946, reviews the efforts of occupation authorities to provide Japanese school children with acceptable texts for the 1946–47 school year. He also examines the significance of *Kokutai no Hongi* (Cardinal Principles of the National Polity) as a source of propaganda for the wartime indoctrination of Japanese children and shows that SCAP tried to replace it by democratic ideas when it issued its basic educational directive to the Japanese government on 22 October 1945.

Yanaga, Chitoshi. "Japan: Tradition and Democracy." 1948. *See* no.1987.

2132a Young, James Russell. "Education in Japan." *Journal of the National Education Association* 35:76–77 (Feb. 1946)

Young offers observations and recommendations on the goals of the occupation's educational reforms. The occupying forces' primary duty, he states, is to correct "the unfortunate doctrines of Japanese group thinking." Conformity, evidenced in the identical uniforms and haircuts of Japanese school children, must be eliminated. Now that the major obstacle to educational reform—the Imperial Rescript on Education—has been abolished, true progress towards individualism and democracy can be made.

2132b Yuasa, Hachirō. "Japanese Learn Democracy." *Rotarian* 78:12–14 (Mar. 1951)

Yuasa, president of the new International Christian University in Tokyo, reports considerable progress towards democracy in many areas of Japanese society and especially within the field of education. While much still remains to be done, Japanese educators are conscious of the central role of education in democratization. International Christian University is an example of the kind of progress that cooperation between Japanese and foreign groups can bring. Yuasa is particularly proud of I.C.U.'s efforts at sexual equality and of the opportunity it offers to spread the influence of Christian ethics, the foundation of democratic thinking.

2133 Zook, George F. "The Educational Missions to Japan and Germany." *International Conciliation* no.427:3–19 (Jan. 1947)

A discussion and comparative analysis of the United States' educational missions to Japan and Germany. The article discusses the backgrounds against which the missions were formed, the members' experiences with the country concerned, and the findings and recommendations of the missions. Topics included in the report are: grade structuring, the reorientation and training of teachers and administrative officials, changes in curricula and textbooks, and the provisions of adult education courses and language reform.

Mass Media and Censorship

An interesting and important aspect of the occupation was the rapid and vigorous revival of the mass media of communication in postwar Japan—the daily and periodical press, books, translations, films, and the theater. Given the circumstances of the times, all of them were subject to varying degrees of either direct or indirect censorship, the standards for which were ultimately set by SCAP. The following items describe or comment upon the state of the several mass media or their attendant problems of censorship. The reader is also referred to the earlier section on analyses and translations of the Japanese press (p.142).

2134 Allen, Lafe Franklin. "Effect of Allied Occupation on the Press of Japan." *Journalism Quarterly* 24:323–31 (Dec. 1947)

Allen, a military government officer during the early months of the occupation, reports that the Japanese press came under heavy attack by SCAP during the early months of the occupation. It was charged with obstructing and undermining the occupation through its failure to explain SCAP directives properly and its publication of distorted or false stories which conveyed a negative image of SCAP activities. The occupation authorities initiated many measures, however, which liberated the press from its former subservience to government control. While the press was slow to take advantage of its new freedom, by 1946 liberal tendencies became increasingly evident. Allen's article also discusses in some detail the labor movements at a number of major newspapers which led to the expulsion of wartime executives and to employee control of those publications.

2134a Anderson, Joseph L., and Donald Richie. *The Japanese Film: Art and Industry.* Tokyo: Tuttle, 1959. 456p.

Chapter 9 of this general survey of the history and techniques of Japanese filmmaking covers the period 1945–1949. The film industry, like other communications media, was under close SCAP control and supervision during the first few years of the occupation. By the end of 1945, SCAP had not only abolished the wartime censorship rules but had also replaced them with directives of its own banning the favorable treatment of such subjects as militarism, nationalism, and other undesirable social phenomena, and encouraging the incorporation of themes that would advance the goals of the occupation. The chapter describes SCAP's film-related censorship units and their procedures, the evasive tactics of the Japanese film industry, and the impact of SCAP censorship on film content. Chapter 10 treats the period 1949–1954.

2135 Berkov, Robert H. "The Press in Postwar Japan." *Far Eastern Survey* 16: 162–66 (23 July 1947)

Berkov discusses the postwar development of the Japanese press which, while free of constant control by the central government, was subject to sporadic censorship based on an elastic and imprecise 10-point "press code" promulgated on 19 September 1945. The importance of reorganizing *Yomiuri, Mainichi,* and *Asahi* to incorporate a certain degree of employee control of management and editorial content is stressed. The role of SCAP in permitting and promoting the establishment of new newspapers that represent political party and prefectural interests is examined.

2135a "British Secure License to Import Books into Japan." *Publishers' Weekly* 154:2352–53 (11 Dec. 1948)

This article first notes that SCAP has approved the import of British books and explains the legal and foreign exchange details involved. It also points out that SCAP is seeking to acquire large numbers of American books for its regional information centers and has been distributing surplus Armed Forces Institute textbooks to various Japanese schools. Finally, the article reports an announcement that bidding has begun again for the rights to translate American, British, and French titles into Japanese.

2136 Chapman, Ralph. "Japan: Propaganda to Pornography." *Saturday Review of Literature* 31:8–9, 34 (31 July 1948)

Midway through the occupation a former Tokyo correspondent for the *New York Herald Tribune* presents his observations of literary and publishing activities in occupied Japan. It is the author's opinion that "the stamp of defeat is nowhere more evident in Japan than in the field of literary endeavor." His article considers 2 aspects of the topic—first, the quality of publications and, second, the nature and extent of SCAP's censorship of these publications. He criticizes the few books that have been published as being either nostalgic or pornographic and attributes this dearth of quality and quantity to a variety of causes: "the activities of unscrupulous publishers, an acute paper shortage, Army censorship, the ineptness of those at MacArthur's headquarters charged with the 'reeducation' of the Japanese, and, to a lesser degree, the thorny and highly involved problem of language reform." There is a brief discussion of the situation in the magazine publishing industry which is issuing more but not better quality material than the book publishers.

2137 Coughlin, William James. *Conquered Press: The MacArthur Era in Japanese Journalism*. Palo Alto, Calif.: Pacific Books, 1952. 165p.

Coughlin's purpose is to illustrate and comment critically on SCAP's treatment of Japanese and Allied journalists and the press during the occupation period. He gives an informed and concise account of such topics as the wartime role of the Japanese press, Dōmei's "insolent" actions during late August and early September 1945, SCAP's policy for introducing and establishing freedom of the press in Japan, SCAP's censorship policy, censorship operations, relationships between the Civil Information and Education Section of SCAP and the Civil Censorship Detachment of the Civil Intelligence Section (G–2), various SCAP personalities involved, and measures taken to cope with the paper shortage. Coughlin also makes extensive reference to SCAP's involvement in the dissolution of Dōmei, the formation of the Japan Newspaper Publishers' and Editors' Association in July 1946, and the establishment of a press code of ethics. He discusses the impact of the purge program and reform movements within the press organizations and describes Communist attempts to control editorial policies, such as in the case of *Yomiuri-Hōchi* in May–July 1946. Finally, there is treatment of SCAP's stormy relations with foreign correspondents over such policies as the ban on certain correspondents' entry or reentry into Japan, the quota system, and restrictions on their living quarters. The author supplements each of these topics with factual accounts of numerous incidents.

2138 Eells, Walter Crosby. "Reading Gifts to Japan: New Policy on Books and Periodicals as Gifts to Japanese Institutions or Individuals." *Wilson Library Bulletin* 22:302–3 (Dec. 1947)

This article describes the details of a new SCAP policy on books and journals sent to Japan and explains the practical mechanics involved in this regard. Eells also provides a long list of the subjects concerning which there is the greatest need at present for gifts of books and periodical subscriptions.

2139 Furukaki, Tetsurō. "Broadcasting Enterprise in Japan." *Contemporary Japan* 20:177–83 (Apr./June 1951)

This article, written by the president of the Broadcasting Corporation of Japan (Nippon Hōsō Kyōkai—NHK), focuses on the development of NHK since its beginning in 1925. After tracing the history of the broadcasting industry prior to the conclusion of World War II, the author discusses changes which have taken place since the end of the war when the industry was no longer tightly controlled. The reorganization of the industry placed "a greater importance upon the local autonomous management rather than upon the centralized administration." Furukaki then emphasizes changes resulting from the Broadcast Law of June 1950. The 3 aims of a new project to keep the Japanese "correctly informed of developments both at home and abroad" are also discussed, and in conclusion the implications of international radio broadcasts are briefly mentioned.

"General MacArthur's Letter to Prime Minister Shigeru Yoshida, Directing the Suspension of *The Akahata* and Other Publications Employed in the Dissemination of Communist Propaganda in Japan, July 18, 1950." 1950. *See* no.1368.

"General MacArthur's Letter to Prime Minister Yoshida Ordering the Purge of the Editorial Staff of *The Akahata*, Organ of the Japanese Communist Party, June 7, 1950." 1950. *See* no.1370.

2140 Granada, Yole. "Glamour Replaces Banzai." *United Nations World* 2:28–31 (Feb. 1948)

Granada, a correspondent with the occupation forces in Japan, surveys the movie scene in early postwar Japan. In the cities, she writes, American movies and actors were very popular, but rural audiences preferred Japanese works. SCAP banned both wartime propaganda films and those on feudalistic themes but otherwise did not censor the movie industry. Japanese producers at first tended to make dull, moralizing films, but by 1947 their productions were more entertaining and popular. The article includes interviews with film stars and descriptions of major movie companies.

Ikeuchi, Hajime, et al. "The Japanese Communist Party as Seen by the Japanese Press during the Allied Occupation, 1945–1952." 1960. *See* no.1375.

2141 Imboden, Daniel C. "Censorship in Japan." *Commonweal* 46:213–15 (13 June 1947)

In reply to Paul V. Miller's earlier critical article on censorship in occupied Japan in the same periodical (no.2150) Imboden, a SCAP officer, defends his organization asserting that such action was imperative in order to achieve the Allied goals of demilitarization and democratization. After describing the press code for Japan issued by MacArthur in September 1945, Imboden discusses the manner in which the code has been implemented. He also discusses the activities of foreign correspondents in Japan and insists that "no one on General MacArthur's staff attempts to influence what the Allied correspondents send to their offices." Japan would not have progressed as far as it has, he concludes, without strict and responsible censorship.

2142 ———. "Free Press for a New Democracy." *Contemporary Japan* 20:169–76 (Apr./June 1951)

Imboden was officer in charge of the Press and Publication Branch, Information Division, Civil Information and Education Section of SCAP. In this article he praises the progress made by the Japanese press since August 1945. He notes the reorganization of the press under the MacArthur Press Code issued 19 September 1945, and quotes the definition of a free newspaper as set forth by the chief of the Civil Information and Education Section. He comments on some of the tests the press has encountered since the war and warns that "freedom of the press is always endangered by apathy and complacence of the people." The 10 requirements for a good newspaper as presented in a questionnaire by the Japan Newspaper Publishers' and Editors' Association are given. The author cites the scarcity of newsprint as a reason why no Japanese newspaper was then on parity with the major U.S. papers, but concludes that "the responsible, democratic press of Japan has a right to be proud of its contribution to democracy and peace and prosperity."

2143 Katō, Shūichi. "The Mass Media: Japan." In *Political Modernization in Japan and Turkey*, ed. by Robert E. Ward and Dankwart A. Rustow. Princeton, N.J.: Princeton Univ. Pr., 1964. p.236–54.

Katō briefly examines the role of the mass media in Japan during the occupation with particular reference to the interaction between the media and national political agencies. He notes that the occupation dissolved the tie between the press and the government and that the opposition was encouraged to express its opinions within the framework of the press code and the censorship imposed by the occupation forces.

2144 Kido, Mataichi. "Freedom of the Press in New Japan." *United Asia* 8: 239–42 (Sept. 1956)

The author, a professor at the Research Institute for Journalism at the University of Tokyo, writes about the concept of freedom of the press in Japan. He first traces the history of government censorship and press regulations since the Meiji Restoration. The latter half of the article deals with the occupation authorities and the Japanese press. Kido concludes that "the Occupation Forces were both its [i.e., the Japanese press'] liberators and its new dominators." He is concerned about the censorship authority of the occupation forces, their policy of purges, and the way he sees the present government continuing these policies. He concludes that the danger of censorship still threatens the press in Japan.

2145 Kim, R. "American 'Educators' in Japan, or the Kangaroo Prize." *Soviet Press Translations* 2:4–7 (31 May 1947)

The quality of American books, magazines, and movies that are being distributed in Japan for mass consumption by the Civil Information and Education Section of SCAP is the subject of this article, translated from the *Literaturnaya Gazeta* of 22 March 1947. Emphasizing the plethora of sensational American detective stories and SCAP's encouragement of militaristic Japanese *samurai* movies, the author contrasts them with the quality of Soviet-sponsored magazines which publish articles on the problems of democracy, unemployment, inflation, and the imperial system.

2146 Kuroda, Andrew Y. "Periodicals in Occupied Japan." *Pacific Affairs* 22:43–52 (Mar. 1949)

The enormous range of periodicals available in occupied Japan is discussed in some detail. Although the author notes the continuation of a paper shortage, he affirms that "a pent up demand plus relative freedom of expression have combined to create a booming market for periodicals." These he estimates to number 3,000 at present. He discusses the quality and frequency of publication of a number of individual postwar periodicals under the categories of: bibliography, history, government, social welfare and foreign relations, economy and finance, labor, and general.

2146a "MacArthur Says No: A Statement by the Editors." *Nation* 169:609–11 (24 Dec. 1949)

This editorial reviews the efforts of Andrew Roth, Far East correspondent for *The Nation*, to enter Japan. After nearly a year of negotiations, Roth and his editors were informed that SCAP had decided for unspecified reasons to refuse Roth entry. Roth, who had written a book entitled *Dilemma in Japan* (1945; no.117) attacking policies he correctly predicted the occupation would follow, claims in a letter reproduced within this article that he was illegally being denied entry for political reasons.

2147 Martin, Robert Pepper. "The MacArthur Censorship: Arbitrary Restrictions Deny to U.S. Its Best Base for Coverage in Asia." *Nieman Reports* 2, no.2:3–4 (Apr. 1948)

Martin, a veteran China correspondent for the *New York Post*, strongly criticizes General MacArthur for his efforts to restrict and regulate foreign press activities in Japan. Citing several cases of Allied correspondents who either were denied permission to enter Japan or were prevented from making Tokyo their working base for East and Southeast Asia, he asserts that SCAP has been waging a "campaign to reduce criticism and control correspondents" in Japan. Martin accepts the possibility that

MacArthur may be unaware of certain censorship cases, but he asserts that the general must still bear responsibility for all actions that his subordinates take against the press.

2148 Melcher, Frederic G. "A Report on the Japanese Book Market." *Publishers' Weekly* 151:2295–96 (3 May 1947)

After a 2-month stay in Japan studying the problems involved in supplying the Japanese with rights to American books, the author presents a favorable report on the activities of the Civil Information and Education Section of SCAP in this area. He attributes the scant supply of books not to any lack of interest on the part of the Japanese or neglect by SCAP but to the fact that "the mechanism for assignment of translation rights and completion of contracts between Japanese and American publishers and authors has only recently been completed." A book publisher and editor of *Publishers' Weekly*, the author describes in detail the various steps involved in an application for a license and the drawing up of contracts with Japanese firms. In discussing SCAP censorship, the author merely notes that "in general, books approved must further the objectives of the Occupation." He concludes his report with a brief discussion of the dissemination of other printed material and films from America throughout Japan and is optimistic regarding their success.

2149 ———. "Booksellers in Japan and Their Buying Public." *Publishers' Weekly* 151:2932–36 (14 June 1947)

An earlier issue of this periodical contains a formal report (no.2148) of the author's trip to Japan as consultant to army headquarters on copyright matters. This article is an informal description of the trip. The author concentrates on the condition of bookstores in occupied Japan, noting the renewed and vigorous operation of particular bookshops such as Maruzen and Sanseidō as well as the nature of the U.S. Post Exchange (PX) bookstore, which he believes to be inadequate and unsatisfactory. He stresses the insufficient supply of books in the stores and insists upon the importance of SCAP's encouraging the publication of "those books which can be most useful and most desirable to a country that is rebuilding itself."

2150 Miller, Paul V. "Censorship in Japan." *Commonweal* 46:35–38 (25 Apr. 1947)

In a discussion of SCAP's censorship policy in Japan, the author is highly critical of several aspects of that policy. Admitting that censorship is necessary after the defeat of an enemy nation, he nevertheless believes that there have been too many instances of "arbitrary and stupid" censorship which have created considerable bad feeling among the Japanese and unduly restricted the freedom of the Japanese information media. He cites several instances of inept or inappropriate censorship and criticizes the attempt of the SCAP censors "to cloak their operations in secrecy" and hide actions from the American people whom they represent. For SCAP's reply to this article see Daniel C. Imboden's "Censorship in Japan" in the 13 June 1947 issue of the same periodical (no.2141).

2151 Moran, R. "Movie Magnates on MacArthur's Staff." *Soviet Press Translations* 2:204–5 (1 Nov. 1947)

The author of this sharply critical article accuses the United States of playing Hollywood agent for American films in Japan. In a brief report translated from the 9 July 1947 issue of *Izvestia*, he claims that SCAP authorities are deliberately sabotaging the showing of Soviet films, even nonpolitical ones, in occupied Japan and condemns SCAP's circular no.12 which forbids showing any films in Japan without the permission of General MacArthur's staff. This circular, he claims, has virtually prevented the showing of any non-American films in Japan.

2152 Mott, Frank Luther. "A Survey of the Japanese Daily Press as of April 1947." *Journalism Quarterly* 24:332–38 (Dec. 1947)

On the basis of reports prepared by SCAP's Civil Information and Education Section, information supplied by Charles

E. Tuttle (chief of Information Media Research of the section), available documentary material, and interviews conducted early in the spring of 1947, Mott provides the reader with an overview of the Japanese daily press 18 months after the start of the occupation. His survey of the 139 dailies of general news coverage focuses on the 3 major city papers —*Asahi, Mainichi,* and *Yomiuri.* His account first outlines the history of their growth and the form and nature of their current circulation. It then comments on the amazingly large staffs that are characteristic of Japanese newspapers, attributing this to their particular form of organization, the paternalism of Japanese firms in general, and the strength of the postwar labor unions, which have prevented newspaper staffs from being drastically reduced in size. The article also discusses the 4 major handicaps which Japanese dailies must face: the unhealthy personnel situation, the acute shortage of paper, the nature of the written language with its typographical difficulties, and SCAP censorship, said to be concerned only with "misrepresentation, adverse comment, or improper news of the military and civil activities of the occupation." On the whole, Mott notes, Japanese newspapers have accepted the occupation and SCAP rule very well. Accordingly, he is optimistic about their ability to work themselves out of their various difficulties and to put the democratic ideas and practices advocated by the occupation authorities into permanent effect.

2153 Nihon Shimbun Kyōkai. *The Japanese Press, Past and Present.* Tokyo: Japan Newspaper Publishers' and Editors' Assn., 1949. 101p.

2154 Okonishnikov, A. "Zenshinza." *New Times* no.16:26–29 (18 Apr. 1951)

The history and present activities of what the author terms Japan's progressive theater (the company called Zenshinza) are briefly outlined in this letter from Tokyo. The leftist nature of the plays performed and the talent and dedication of the performers are discussed. Finally, there is mention of the adverse conditions under which the company works. Banned by SCAP from performing in Tokyo, the company is described as harassed by occupation officials and reactionary Japanese local officials. Nevertheless, the author notes that Zenshinza has enjoyed great success among the people.

2154a Price, Willard. *The Japanese Miracle and Peril.* New York: John Day, 1971. ix, 341p.

This book by an American journalist and author of several popular works on Japan contains 2 chapters focusing on the occupation. Chapter 15, "'Move over, God, It's Mac'," is largely devoted to an extensive catalogue of SCAP's efforts (usually successful) to guarantee by various means that the news reports of American and other Western journalists would contain little but positive assessments of occupation activities. SCAP censorship and the intimidation of Japanese journalism are also discussed in some detail. Chapter 16, "Desperation but not Despair," in turn deals mainly with the occupation's land reforms. Price clearly approves of the goals and philosophy of the reforms. He concludes, however, that they were bound to fail in their ultimate objective of improving the lot of the Japanese farmer because there are simply "too many people for too little land" in Japan. Because of the popular nature of this book, Price's descriptions and judgments are generally unsubstantiated; nonetheless, they are moderate and judicious in tone.

2155 Roth, Andrew. "Japan's Press Revolution." *Nation* 162:315 (16 Mar. 1946)

The author discusses the changes in the postwar press, beginning with an account of the recent history of the *Yomiuri-Hōchi* which was formerly a militaristic, sensational tabloid and which has become a liberal and responsible newspaper since the start of the occupation. He describes the manner in which such changes came about in Tokyo's major newspapers—partly through SCAP's encouragement and partly through independent efforts of the Japanese—and subsequently discusses the emergence of the new leftist publications such as the *Jiji* and *Minshu* of the Socialists and the *Minpo* and *Akahata* of the Communists. According to the author these significant changes in the press are having a deep and lasting effect on the thinking of the Japanese people.

Rudnev, A. "Occupied Japan." 1951. *See* no.661.

2156 Sasaki, Senichi. "Magazines in Postwar Japan." *Contemporary Japan* 19: 378–88 (July/Sept. 1950)

A general analysis of changes and developments in Japan's magazine industry during the occupation. In discussing the rapid growth of Japanese magazines in number and circulation, the author describes the different kinds of magazines and their varying qualities. Included is a useful table that charts the various kinds of magazines such as women's, children's, mass literature, and foreign affairs, and the amount of paper allocated to each in the course of 2 months in 1950. There is no reference in the article to any control of periodicals by SCAP aside from the remark that freedom of speech has been assured by the occupation. In conclusion, the author attempts to contrast the present situation with the preoccupation situation, affirming that "the Japanese magazine reader of today has a wider range of choice in both serious and light reading than he had during the war years."

2157 Siggins, Jack A. *Publishing and Censorship Policies of the Occupation Government in Japan: 1945–1952.* Ph.D. dissertation, Univ. of Chicago, School of Library Science. In progress.

This dissertation is a study of SCAP policies and administrative and decision-making processes in the censorship and control of Japanese media. It will include an examination of the necessity and effectiveness of these policies, as well as an analysis of their impact upon Japanese attitudes. The research for the thesis will be based in large part on a special collection of documents from SCAP's Civil Censorship Detachment located in the East Asia collection of the University of Maryland's McKeldin Library.

Supreme Commander for the Allied Powers. Monograph 15. *Freedom of the Press, 1945–January 1951.* 1952. *See* no. 297.

———. Monograph 16. *Theatre and Motion Pictures, 1945–December 1951.* 1952. *See* no.298.

———. Monograph 33. *Radio Broadcasting, 1945–1951.* 1952. *See* no.315.

———. Civil Information and Education Section. *Activities Report.* Nov. 1945–Dec. 1946, Jan. 1949, May 1951. *See* no.265.

2158 ———. ———. *General Economic Press of Japan: Special Report Prepared by the Information Media Branch, Research Unit.* Mimeographed. Tokyo: SCAP, 1948. 47p.

Ten leading magazines, 3 news services, and 3 newspapers in the field of Japanese economics are described in this booklet. In addition to providing a brief history and background of each, the report discusses its major personalities, editorial policies, and reputation as well as any other special characteristics of the publication. The appendix presents a listing of some 30 additional general economic periodicals along with their addresses, frequency of publication, and circulation. A brief bibliography is attached.

Available at the Library of Congress, Washington, D.C.

———. ———. *Information Programs.* 1948. *See* no.924.

2159 ———. ———. *Memos and Correspondence with Various Missions in Japan.* 1948–51. 7 folders.

Letters and memorandums concerning the publication activities of various foreign missions in occupied Japan are chronologically arranged in folders. They concern translations into Japanese for publication in Japan, the issuance of licenses for such publication, etc. The most voluminous file contains correspondence with the United Kingdom Liaison Mission while others concern the French Mission, the Italian Mission, the Netherlands Mission, the Swiss Mission, the Swedish Mission, the Danish Mission, and the Soviet Trade Representative.

Available at the Washington National Records Center, Suitland, Maryland.

2160 ———. ———. *Rural-Urban Circulation of Principal Dailies in Japan: Special Report Prepared by Information Media Branch, Research Unit.* Tokyo: SCAP, 1948. 28p.

2161 ———. ———. Analysis and Research Div. *Prefectural Survey of Printing Facilities of Members of the Japan Printers Union.* Tokyo: SCAP, 1948. 54p.

A statistical report on members of the Japan Printers' Union, which included nearly all printers in Japan. There are 47 tables of statistical data including the number of employees, their income levels, paper consumption by each firm between April 1946 and March 1947, and the amount and quality of their equipment as of 20 May 1947. Survey data are arranged by prefecture. The report also provides prefectural production capacity ratings for 3 periods: the prewar average, October 1945, and May 1947.

2162 Telberg, Ina. "The Japanese State of Mind." *Saturday Review of Literature* 34:25–26, 54–55 (18 Aug. 1951)

The author presents an analysis of the quality of postwar Japanese radio broadcasts, the Japanese press, books and magazines, as well as theater and movies. The introductory section concerns Japanese adjustment to defeat and acceptance of SCAP innovations whereas the body of the article draws upon literary works and information media to support the author's conclusions. The article treats individual books, films, and newspapers produced by left, right, and center groups, and provides a useful description of some important postwar Japanese books and films that reflect the contemporary attitudes of the citizenry.

2163 Tuttle, Charles E. "Japan Wants American Books." *Publishers' Weekly* 149:1518–20 (9 Mar. 1946)

A member of SCAP's Civil Information and Education Section explains what he terms a Japanese "craving" for American books. He believes that the Japanese desire to find out as much as possible about the conquerors and have a sincere wish "to absorb American liberalism and democracy through contact with our authors." He notes the number of Japanese able to read English, partially as a result of their education and partially from contact with occupation troops, and concludes that there is a tremendous potential market for American books in Japan both in English and in translation.

2163a Uhlan, Edward, and Dana L. Thomas. *Shoriki, Miracle Man of Japan: A Biography.* New York: Exposition Press, 1957. 202p.

This biographical account of the individual who built the *Yomiuri Shimbun* into one of Japan's 3 largest dailies contains considerable information of interest to the student of the occupation. Chapter 8, entitled "Strike at *Yomiuri* and Shoriki's Imprisonment," first discusses general conditions in Tokyo during the months immediately following Japan's surrender, then focuses on the labor strike at *Yomiuri* which resulted in part from SCAP's abolition of many prewar governmental restrictions on the Japanese labor movement. Shoriki Matsutarō's imprisonment as a major war-crimes suspect between December 1945 and September 1947 also is treated at length. The authors describe the manner in which he spent those 21 months largely engaged in religious meditation and point out that Shoriki—like many others at Sugamo—did not know the law under which they were being held nor what they had to defend themselves against. In the end, Shoriki was released without ever having been tried by a military court for his activities as publisher of an influential newspaper. Chapter 9, "Victory over Communism," focuses on the efforts of Japanese communists to take over control of the Japanese press through their "cynical manipulation of the Japanese labor movement." SCAP's involvement in the labor controversies which erupted at *Yomiuri* during the spring of 1946 also make this chapter one of immediate relevance to those interested in the Allied occupation.

2163b Uyemura, Takachiyo. "Democracy and Journalism." *Contemporary Japan* 15:74–86 (Jan./Apr. 1946)

This article by a journalist associated with the Kyōdō News Agency examines the liberation of the journalistic profession as a consequence of SCAP directives and activities. One of the most important developments in postwar journalism is a movement for greater staff autonomy within the major newspapers—a movement which has led to the formation of nationwide newspaper unions and the establishment of a liberal editorial line. Uyemura cites by way of illustration the dispute at the *Yomiuri Shimbun* which resulted in a staff takeover of the newspaper despite management opposition. The objective of the staff members was not only unionization but also a greater role for employees in editorial decisions together with the purge of management personnel with militaristic inclinations. Similar disputes occurred at the other major newspapers as well.

2164 Wildes, Harry Emerson. "Can Hollywood Win the Peace?" *Asia and the Americas* 46:81–83 (Feb. 1946)

As a member of a special committee investigating social and economic conditions in Japan, Wildes describes the Japanese government's skillful utilization of the motion picture industry for propaganda purposes. He points out that the usual Hollywood pattern cannot counteract the materialistic American image, but an almost entirely new technique must be developed—a method that will use Eastern types and oriental folkways.

———. "The Japanese Press." 1945. *See* no.131.

Worden, William L. "G.I. Is Civilizing the Jap." 1945. *See* no.931a.

2165 Yamagiwa, Joseph Koshimi. "Fiction in Post-war Japan." *Far Eastern Quarterly* 13:3–22 (Nov. 1953)

The quality and quantity of Japanese short stories, serial novels, and novels published since the beginning of the occupation are considered in this paper. Information was obtained from a study of books, newspapers, and magazines as well as from a questionnaire distributed in Japan and a number of conversations the author had with Japanese critics and writers. Although the author devotes attention to the writers' organizations and to translations of foreign works appearing in Japan, he concentrates upon Japanese writers and their works, noting a prevailing strain of pessimism and nihilism "resulting probably from defeat in war and prolonged suffering in its aftermath." The works of 41 of Japan's most talented or popular writers are briefly described and Yamagiwa notes similarities with past writers and schools of writing as well as new points of view and novel literary movements. He concludes that in contrast to the war years the total literary scene "is one of great activity and diversity."

2166 ———. "Reforms in the Language and Orthography of Newspapers in Japan." *Journal of the American Oriental Society* 68:45–52 (Jan./Mar. 1948)

In this article Yamagiwa discusses recent reforms of the Japanese language. He talks about (1) the colloquialization of the documentary style, (2) a reduction in the total number of different Chinese characters that may be used, and (3) greater approximation to phonetic norms of spelling in the syllabic characters.

Public Health, Welfare, and Social Security

The occupation undertook extensive programs of reform in the fields of public health, welfare, and social security including social insurance. The resulting literature, while not extensive, is of an unusually high quality insofar as the description of conditions in these fields and their changing circumstances both before and during the occupation is concerned.

2167 American Pharmaceutical Association. *Report of the Mission of the American Pharmaceutical Association.* Mimeographed. Tokyo? July 1949. 23p.

Led by the association's president Dr. Glenn L. Jenkins, a 5-member mission visited Japan at the invitation of SCAP in order to study the education and organization of pharmacists; the manufacture, control, and distribution of pharmaceuticals; and the practice of pharmacy in general within Japan. The report which this mission submitted to SCAP's Public Health and Welfare Section describes conditions within Japan and makes 45 recommendations in all for improvements within the industry and within the colleges of pharmacy. A summary of the report together with the personal comments of Crawford F. Sams, chief of the Public Health and Welfare Section, subsequently appeared under the title "Findings and Recommendations of the A.Ph.A.'s Mission to Japan" in the *Journal of the American Pharmaceutical Association* (10:619; Oct. 1949).

2167a Berlin, Richard B. "Impressions of Japanese Medicine at the End of World War II." *Scientific Monthly* 64:41–49 (Jan. 1947)

Berlin of the U.S. Navy medical corps gives his observations of medical practice in Nagasaki where he was stationed from September 1945 to January 1946. He begins with a description of the physical remains of Japanese medicine after the atomic bombing. Though impressed with the ruins of former hospitals, he is critical of postsurrender medical practice. Surviving equipment—X-ray machines, surgical tools, medicines, etc.—is described in some detail along with comments on the conditions for hospital patients, the status of doctors, the price of medical treatment, and other social factors. Care of atomic bomb victims is also mentioned.

2167b Holliday, Kate. "We're Cleaning up Japan." *New Leader* 34, no.8:12–14 (19 Feb. 1951)

Under the direction of Brigadier General Crawford Sams, SCAP has carried out a medical revolution in Japan, transforming the country into the healthiest nation in Asia. The occupation authorities first organized sanitation teams in a massive campaign against flies, lice and rats, then vaccinated millions against various diseases, undertook efforts to control venereal disease, and initiated programs of preventive therapy against tuberculosis. Holliday also points out SCAP's efforts to keep disease under control and discusses major steps that were made to raise the level of doctors, nurses, and hospitals within the country.

2168 Japan. Advisory Council on Social Security. *Recommendation for a Social Security Program.* Tokyo: 1950. 48p.

2169 ———. Ministry of Welfare. *A Brief Report on Public Health Administration in Japan.* Tokyo: 1951. 27p.

2170 ———. ———. Bureau of Social Affairs. *Daily Life Security Legislations.* Tokyo: The Ministry, The Bureau, 1950. 93p.

2171 ———. ———. Insurance Bureau. *The Health Insurance Law, with Enforcement Regulation and References.* Tokyo: The Ministry, The Bureau, 1951. 1v.

This booklet reproduces in translated

form the texts of the Health Insurance Law, the orders enforcing it, and subsidiary implementing legislation dealing with such new organs and offices as the Social Insurance Council, the Social Insurance Appeals Committee, and the Social Insurance Referee.

2172 ———. ———. ———. *National Health Insurance Law, with Regulations, Cabinet Order, and Others.* Tokyo: The Ministry, The Bureau, 1951. 53p.

2173 ———. ———. ———. *The Seamen's Insurance Law with Enforcement Regulation.* Tokyo: The Ministry, The Bureau, 1949. ii, 72p.

2174 ———. ———. ———. *The Welfare Pension Insurance Law, with the Enforcement Regulation of the Welfare Pension Insurance Law.* Tokyo: The Ministry, The Bureau, 1949. 135p.

2175 ———. ———. ———. *The Welfare Pension Insurance Law, with the Enforcement Regulation of the Welfare Pension Insurance Law and References.* Tokyo: The Ministry, The Bureau, 1951. 1v.

2176 ———. Prime Minister's Office. Bureau of Statistics. *Report of the Coalminer's Family Income Survey, December 1948–April 1950.* Tokyo: 1950. 89p. In English and Japanese.

The Reminiscences of Dr. Lauren V. Ackerman. 1961. See no.44g.

Reubens, Beatrice G. "Social Legislation in Japan." 1949. See no.1773.

2177 "Japanese National Health Insurance Act." *Industry and Labour* 1:408–10 (15 May 1949)

Reprinted from *Weekly Bulletin* no. 104 (20–26 Dec. 1948) of SCAP's Public Health and Welfare Section, this report describes the amended version of the Japanese National Health Insurance Act which makes provision for insurance against sickness, injury, maternity, and death. The act applies mainly to the self-employed, to persons employed in small establishments, to farmers and fishermen, and to their families. The report itself covers the benefits and contributions, administration, and various health insurance associations involved.

2178 Rohrlich, George F. "National Health Insurance in Japan." *International Labour Review* 61:337–66 (Apr. 1950)

Rohrlich, chief of the Economic Analysis Branch, Social Security Division, Public Health and Welfare Section, SCAP, analyzes in depth the National Insurance Act of 1938 and the amendments made to it in 1948. He begins with a discussion of trends in national health insurance prior to 1938 and then examines the organization, scope, and functioning of the system through the early postwar years. The triangular relationship among the insured and their associations, the insurance doctors, and the government is emphasized and the amendments of 1948 are analyzed with special mention of the methods for ensuring greater administrative and financial stability. The transfer of operational responsibility to local authorities, the contractual relationship between insured and medical personnel, and the advisory and coordinating function of the national government are stressed. The author notes that the initiative for the 1948 amendments came primarily from Japanese sources and that these amendments were very similar to legislation proposed in the 1930s. In conclusion, 2 needs not dealt with by the 1948 legislation, the extension of national subsidies and the widening of insurance coverage, are mentioned.

———. "Transformation of Culture: A Postscript from Japan." See no.2105a.

2179 Sams, Crawford F. "American Public Health Administration Meets the Problems of the Orient in Japan." *American Journal of Public Health and the Nation's Health* 42:557–65 (May 1952)

The chief of the Public Health and Welfare Section of SCAP discusses the postwar creation of a health and welfare organization in Japan incorporating functions concerning disease prevention, medical care, welfare, and social security. The organization and cooperative functioning of a national Ministry of Health and Welfare, prefectural health and welfare departments, and local health center districts are examined; the training and staffing of these local health centers are analyzed. The author also explains the creation of such subsidiary institutions as a school health program, the National Institute of Health, the National Hygenic Laboratory, and the collection and evaluation of health and vital statistics. In addition, Sams outlines the progress of disease prevention programs concerned with tuberculosis, enteric diseases, and smallpox, and explains the postwar changes in Japanese death rates and life expectancy.

2180 ———. "Japan's New Public Health Program." *Military Government Journal* pt.1, 1:9–10, 14 (Sept./Oct. 1948); pt.2, 2:7–9 (Jan./Feb. 1949); pt.3, 2:11–12 (Summer 1949)

The chief of the Public Health and Welfare Section of SCAP has written 3 comprehensive articles describing and analyzing the health and welfare programs in Japan and contrasting the situation as it existed at the beginning of the occupation with that following SCAP's implementation of a variety of reforms designed to remedy widespread disease. He also discusses the nature and function of the former Ministry of Health and Welfare, abolished in 1948; the operations of the new Ministry of Welfare and the prefectural Health Departments and Welfare Departments, established in 1946 and 1947; and SCAP's inauguration of new health center districts—one for each 100,000 people. The first article in this series concentrates on the efforts made to control communicable diseases, i.e., smallpox, typhus, diphtheria, cholera, dysentery, typhoid, and tuberculosis. The author cites various statistics in this regard to indicate the considerable success that the new programs have enjoyed.

The second article focuses on sanitation, and within it Sams describes the prewar and wartime waterworks and sewage systems and their repair and improvement during the occupation. Other aspects of sanitation covered include the reorganization of the Institute of Public Health in Tokyo, the establishment of training schools to instruct officials in better sanitary practices, the tightening of the Japanese quarantine system, and the introduction of a health education program for the general public. The author also discusses changes in the Japan Medical Association that were designed to make it a less political and more effective organization, as well as improvements made in the physical facilities of hospitals, leprosaria, and sanatoria.

The last of these 3 well-documented articles presents a brief summation of preoccupation conditions as well as a review of the changes effected by SCAP and the new Japanese government. Improvement in hospital administration is described first, then there is a consideration of the implications of the new Daily Life Security Law, which provided assistance to numerous destitute orphans and homeless persons. The author next describes the innovations in the Japanese Red Cross organization, the inauguration by SCAP of a school lunch program, and the inadequate social security conditions leading to the dispatch of the Social Security Mission from the United States in September 1947. The description of legislation regarding pharmaceuticals and narcotics completes this excellent series, and Sams concludes with the observation that 4 fundamental aspects of public health (preventive medicine, adequate overall medical care, an effective welfare program, and an adequate social security program) have been integrated in the SCAP program in order to prevent widespread disease and unrest in Japan.

2181 Sagrista Freixas, Antonio. *Social Security in Japan: Its Evolution, Present Status, and Economic Implications.* Ph.D. dissertation, Cornell Univ., 1963. 290p. (Abstracted in *Dissertation Abstracts* 24: 4850–51 [1964]; University Microfilms order no.64–3711)

The Japanese social security system is analyzed from historical and economic perspectives. After reviewing the system's main features, the author examines elements which he believes were influential in its formation. These include the family system, paternalistic tendencies in Japanese enterprises, the dual structure of the Japanese economy, the development of labor unions, military hegemony prior to World War II, the new Japanese constitution of 1947, and the influence of the occupation. He also attempts to assess the potential of increased income and expenditures as stabilizing factors in the economy. In his conclusion, he states that noneconomic factors have had a greater impact on the Japanese social security system than economic factors, that the system has not reached the level of welfare-statism found in European countries, that the full macroeconomic implications of the system are yet to be felt, that a change in the dual structure of the economy and the social security system is necessary before the system can reach the lower strata of society, and that the private sector of the economy must work with the government to attain economic security for the Japanese people.

2182 Shimizu, Yoshihiro. "The Problems of Juvenile Delinquency in Post-war Japan." *Journal of Educational Sociology* 26:32–36 (Sept. 1952)

The author examines the problem of juvenile delinquency in postwar Japan. The first part of the article deals with the rising number of crimes, the aggressive nature of the crimes, the propensity to group-forming, and the fact that many crimes are by children of "good" families. Shimizu then writes of the causes of this rise in delinquency. He lists his causes under: (1) postwar economic impoverishment in general, (2) psychological reaction to liberation, and (3) the distortion of the social structure.

2183 "Social Security in Japan: Report of United States Mission." *Industry and Labour* 1, no.5:204–9 (1 Mar. 1949)

This article presents a straightforward summary of the report concerning public health and welfare which was submitted to SCAP by a group of American experts and which was made public on 25 July 1948. The report describes existing social security programs as well as the medical and public health services and facilities associated with them, and it makes detailed recommendations which are accompanied by the analyses that led to them.

2184 Social Security Mission to Japan. *Report of the Social Security Mission to Japan*. Washington, D.C.: Dept. of the Army, 25 July 1948. 164p.

2184a Stuart, Gordon Hackworth. *Public Health in Occupied Japan*. Ph.D. dissertation, Univ. of London, 1950. iii, 93p.

This dissertation discusses the postwar reestablishment of Japanese health standards and the efforts to prevent the spread of disease and to maintain an adequate level of hygiene through the combined use of traditional practices and modern methods. A section on Japanese social habits is included. The author concludes that overpopulation is the major problem of the future.

Supreme Commander for the Allied Powers. Monograph 18. *Public Welfare, 1945–December 1949*. 1952. See no.300.

———. Monograph 19. *Public Health, September 1945–December 1950*. 1952. See no.301.

———. Monograph 20. *Social Security, 1945–March 1950*. 1952. See no. 302.

2185 ———. Medical Section. *Public Health and Welfare in Japan: Final Summary 1951–52*. Tokyo: SCAP, 1952. 136p.

The last of a series of annual summaries which describe the operations and responsibilities of the Public Health and Welfare Section in Japan from the outset of the occupation to its conclusion in April of 1952. During the period described in this final report, the Public Health and Welfare Section became the Public Health and Welfare Division of the Medical Section of SCAP (on 1 July 1951). The format in this report is basically the same as in the earlier summaries. A description of current activities of the Japanese Ministry of Welfare is followed by chapters describing the division's programs concerning preventive medicine, the compilation of health and welfare statistics, the improvement of medical and nursing care as well as veterinary medicine, the inauguration of welfare measures, nutrition and supply programs, and an improved narcotics program. Five charts and 10 tables provide relevant statistical information regarding birth and death rates and communicable diseases in Japan for the period.

2186 ———. Public Health and Welfare Section. *Bulletin.* Mimeographed. Tokyo: SCAP, weekly through 14 Aug. 1949; semimonthly from 15 Aug. 1949.

This mimeographed series describing the activities and responsibilities of the Public Health and Welfare Section was published weekly until mid-August 1949, and subsequently semimonthly. It provides brief descriptions of the most significant programs being implemented at the time in the fields of public health and welfare. The format varies slightly over the years, but material is generally organized under one of several headings, i.e., preventive medicine, hospital administration, veterinary affairs, nursing affairs, supplies, narcotic control, welfare, social security, and legal affairs. Bulletins often include charts and graphs providing statistics on such matters as birth and death rates, communicable diseases according to prefecture, social insurance statistics, etc. The Library of Congress has issues from 13 September 1948 through 31 March 1951, and the McKeldin Library of the University of Maryland, College Park, Maryland has several issues from 1946 and 1947 (22 June 1946, 29 June 1946, 6 July 1946, 30 July 1946, 13 Sept. 1947, and 25 Oct. 1947).

2187 ———. ———. *Mission and Accomplishments of the Occupation in the Public Health and Welfare Fields.* Mimeographed. Tokyo: SCAP, Oct. 1949. 40p.

The attempts of SCAP's Public Health and Welfare Section to prevent widespread disease and unrest in Japan are summarized in this brief mimeographed pamphlet. In addition to reviewing occupation policy and programs in the interrelated fields of health and welfare, the report describes health and welfare organization in Japan in the period immediately after the surrender. Specific topics are treated under 8 heads: preventive medicine, medical care, veterinary affairs, welfare, social security, nutrition, supply, and narcotics. There is a general description of the existing situation and problems encountered as well as a discussion of solutions proposed to alleviate poor health and welfare conditions in each area. The final section of the report presents some remarks summing up the accomplishments of the Public Health and Welfare Section and outlining future tasks. Statistical charts indicate the extent of smallpox in Japan for 1939–49, comparative tuberculosis death rates, civilian hospital patients in Japan from 1946–49, persons receiving public assistance, and social insurance and related programs.

Available at the Library of Congress, Washington, D.C.

2188 ———. ———. *Mission and Accomplishments of the Occupation in the Public Health and Welfare Fields.* Tokyo: SCAP, Dec. 1949. 40p., diagrams.

A later edition of an October 1949 report which bears the same title (no. 2187). Although essentially the same as the earlier report, this study provides 2 additional sections in its discussion of the activities of the Public Health and Welfare Section of SCAP, namely, a section on health and welfare statistics and one on nursing affairs. The report briefly discusses the situation prior to the occupation and contrasts this with the postwar period. As with most official occupation publications, the reports tend to emphasize what has already been accomplished rather than what has yet to be done. Charts included are the same as in the earlier report.

Available at the Library of Congress, Washington, D.C.

2189 ———. ———. *Public Health and Welfare in Japan.* Tokyo: SCAP, 1949. 220p.

An account of progress made by SCAP in the field of public health and welfare in Japan up to the end of 1948. The report also provides an historical background and survey of the presurrender conditions of public health services in Japan. A brief description of the reorganization of the Japanese Ministry of Welfare after 1945 is followed by a presentation of SCAP programs under the headings of preventive medicine, medical care, nursing activities, veterinary affairs, welfare, social security, nutrition, drug supply, and narcotics. For each subject there is provided a short analysis of the prewar situation as well as the results of a government survey conducted from 1945 to 1948 to assess postwar conditions in areas affected by SCAP programs. Containing some 60 charts, many of which refer to 1938–48 conditions, this report is comprehensive and useful.

2190 ———. ———. *Public Health and Welfare in Japan: Annex and Charts.* Tokyo: SCAP, 1949. 54p., 33 charts.

This report, together with *Public Health and Welfare in Japan: Tables* (no.2193), gives a provisional summary of health statistics for 1948 and a summary of historical health data from 1900 through 1948. As such, the report represents the first in a series of annual summaries regarding progress made by SCAP in this field. It was published as an annex to SCAP, *Public Health and Welfare in Japan* (no.2189) that appeared in the same year. This provisional annual report of health statistics for the calendar year 1948 is based on monthly statistical reports prepared by the Health Statistics Department of the Ministry of Welfare of the Japanese government and submitted to the Health and Welfare Statistics Division of SCAP's Public Health and Welfare Section. With few exceptions, data refer only to Japanese nationals and only to events which occurred within Japan proper. Subjects covered are population and its natural rate of increase, births, mortality, morbidity, deaths and selective death causes, infant mortality and its causes, still births, marriages and divorces, non-Japanese nationals, and vital statistics for Japanese nationals outside of Japan. This general, factual account is supplemented by 33 charts. Some statistics concerning birth and death rates and marriage and divorce rates cover periods since the 1880s. Most postwar data are broken down by month, while morbidity statistics are shown with an additional breakdown according to prefecture. Also included are the forms that citizens use to report vital statistics.

2191 ———. ———. *Public Health and Welfare in Japan: Annual Summary 1949.* Tokyo: SCAP, 1950. 51p., 112 tables, 28 charts.

A 2-part provisional summary of health and welfare statistical information for the calendar year 1949, this represents the second report in a series. It "supplements the tabulations published in the 1948 summary plus thirteen additional historical tabulations previously not available." The first 51 pages describe SCAP activities in 1949 in the area of public health. In addition to information on vital statistics, the report also refers to the enlarged and improved hospital facilities, the treatment of venereal disease, clinic activities, nutrition surveys, school lunch programs, and public assistance programs. The 28 charts and 112 tables are concerned, for the most part, with the years 1948 and 1949, but some treat the 1947–49 period as well as the 1920–49 period.

2192 ———. ———. *Public Health and Welfare in Japan: Annual Summary 1950.* Tokyo: SCAP, 1951. 432p.

The third in a series of annual summary reports on SCAP public health and welfare activities. "Many of the charts and tables appearing in the 1949 summary are not reproduced in the narrative portion of this summary." The topics covered herein are the same as those in the previous 2 publications. The first 98-page narrative account of SCAP activities is followed by an appendix composed of 4 parts: two 45-page statistical analyses and evaluations of public health conditions in Japan, 27 historical tables, 29 current tables, and 19 charts. There is a useful alphabetical subject index to the statistical tables.

2193 ———. ———. *Public Health and Welfare in Japan: Tables.* Tokyo: SCAP, 1949. 600p.

This voluminous collection of 86 tables represents an extensive historical health tabulation for Japan. It is coordinated with another publication of SCAP's *Public Health and Welfare in Japan: Annex and Charts* (no.2190) that appeared in the same year. The latter publication provides an index to the tables collected in this volume. These tables provide detailed information on vital statistics. A majority of them cover the period from 1920 through 1948, but data on communicable diseases extends from 1900 through 1948. Most of the tables are further broken down by month and arranged according to prefecture. Of a total of 86 tables, those subsequent to table no.48 are devoted to a report for the calendar year 1948. Most tables are more than 10 pages in length and some are even longer, for instance, "Case Rates for Selected Communicable Diseases by Month, 1900–1948" which is 26 pages and "Deaths from Selected Causes by Month and by Prefecture, 1948" which is 89 pages.

2194 ———. ———. *Public Health and Welfare in Japan.* Tokyo: 1948–52. 6v.

A series of summaries on the progress and future plans of the Public Health and Welfare Section of SCAP. As of 1 July 1951, this section became the Public Health and Welfare Division of the Medical Section of SCAP and the final volume is titled accordingly (no. 2185). In addition to providing a full and detailed account of solutions found and problems yet to be overcome, the summaries include numerous detailed charts and tables which provide valuable statistical information. The series consists of a summary of public health and welfare programs from the beginning of the occupation through 1948 (3v.), a summary for the calendar year 1949 (1v. in 2pts.), a summary for the calendar year 1950 (1v.), and a final summary which discusses the work of the section throughout the occupation period (1v.).

Available at the Library of Congress, Washington, D.C.

2195 ———. ———, and Economic and Scientific Section. *Japanese Social Insurance Systems through 30 June 1950.* Tokyo: SCAP, Apr. 1951. 43p.

A succinct report on Japan's social insurance system from 1926 through 30 June 1950. Jointly prepared by 2 SCAP sections, the report describes various insurance programs, including health insurance, national health insurance, welfare pension insurance, seamen's insurance, National Public Service Mutual Aid Associations, the government pension system, unemployment insurance, and workmen's accident compensation insurance. Each program for change in the system is explained with its legislative history, coverage provisions, taxable wages, contributions, benefit structure, and benefit provisions.

2196 Ushimaru, Yoshitome. "Progress in Social Security." *Contemporary Japan* 23, no.10/12:693–99 (1955)

This article by the chief of the Program Evaluation Office of the Ministry of Health and Welfare summarizes the development of social welfare programs in Japan since the war. Ushimaru finds that great progress has been made in carrying out the provisions of the constitution guaranteeing the right to certain minimum standards of "wholesome and cultured living," but the low level of national income is still hampering the full implementation of some programs. Included within the article are statistical summaries of social security expenditures by category between 1952 and 1954, and statistics on public assistance programs during the postwar period.

2197 Wildes, Harry Emerson. "Post-war Public Health Developments." *Contemporary Japan* 21, no.10/12:573–92 (1953)

Wildes served as chief of the Political and Social Affairs Division, Civil Information Section, General Headquarters, SCAP. In this article he describes public health conditions at the beginning of the occupation and traces activities of both SCAP and the Japanese government in this field. He states that the reform of public health conditions developed slowly during the occupation and attempts to point out why. Among the causes were the unavailability of relief supplies, inadequate understanding of the relief problem, indifference among both Allied and Japanese officials, and the bankruptcy and internal chaos which favored the spread of epidemics. The author depicts the lack of medical care available when Brigadier General Crawford F. Sams, then a colonel, undertook the task of correcting the deficiencies. The "sweeping reorganizations and improvements" discussed in the article include administrative and supervisory reforms, provision of better professional education, and hospital improvement. Progress made in the public health field during the occupation is described, with the introduction of new drugs and improved disinfectants and insecticides given much credit for the victories achieved. In spite of steps taken, however, dysentery, tuberculosis, and venereal disease remained as pressing problems when the occupation closed; efforts against these diseases are also examined in the article.

2197a Wilson, Donald V. "Social Work in the Japanese Occupation." *Social Work Journal* 31:80–83, 96 (Apr. 1950)

Wilson, a social welfare officer in SCAP's Public Health and Welfare Section, sees the introduction of social welfare programs as especially important in Japan, where the people have always had strong feelings of duty towards the state but where the state has had no tradition of responsibilities toward its citizens. The article catalogues the new programs introduced by the occupation and the kinds of problems that arose in their implementation. Wilson feels that one of the most important activities in the field was the establishment of training programs for public and private welfare workers, centering on schools of social work set up in Osaka and Tokyo. These programs have generally been crowned with success, but the basic principles of social work have sometimes had to take second place to the more immediate goals of the occupation.

RELIGION

SCAP, acting through directives and the new constitution, made a clear distinction between the state and all institutions of religion. Special pains were taken to bring about the disestablishment of state Shinto because of its alleged prewar status as an official religion. Every effort was also made to secularize the position and role of the emperor. Buddhism and Confucianism were less serious problems for the occupation. Many Christians, however, perceived the occupation as a unique opportunity to spread their faith in Japan. The literature relating to all these faiths and to SCAP's activities in the religious field is described below.

2198 "Abolish the Yasukuni Shrine." *Contemporary Japan* 14:237–39 (Apr./Dec. 1945)

Appearing first (in Japanese) in the 12 October 1945 issue of the *Tōyō Keizai Shimpō*, this editorial advocates the abolition of Japan's foremost shrine for the spirits of the country's war dead. The editors state that it would be awkward to carry out the proper rituals there even if SCAP were to allow their continuation. Furthermore, "common sense" would argue that since World War II proved to be a disaster, it might be inappropriate to enshrine its dead. Finally, the editors contend, the maintenance of the shrine could inspire in future generations the potentially dangerous feeling that Yasukuni *jinja* is a monument of shame and humiliation for Japan.

2198a Ashizu, Yoshihiko. "The Shinto Directive and the Constitution: From the Standpoint of a Shintoist." *Contemporary Religions in Japan* 1, no.2:16–34 (June 1960)

Critical of the Shinto directive that led to an overall separation of religion and the state in Japan, and insisting that this SCAP directive (whose principles were incorporated in the constitution) became null and void upon the end of the occupation, Ashizu advocates what he calls the "correct" interpretation of articles 20 and 89 of the postwar constitution. The author argues that these 2 constitutional provisions—on the freedom of religion and on the prohibition of state aid to religion—should be interpreted in accordance with the principle of separation of "church" (i.e., religious organizations) and state, not of religion and state. The provision forbidding compulsory participation in religious ceremonies is necessary in order to guarantee religious freedom, but it is unreasonable to maintain a prohibition on the performance of traditional, widely-accepted religious rites at state funerals, memorial services, and wedding ceremonies, etc. Ashizu compares the provisions on religion in the postwar Japanese constitution with comparable provisions in many other national constitutions and with actual practices within the United States in order to show that there are very few countries in which there is complete separation of state and religion. He concludes with a discussion of the controversy surrounding the establishment of a small shrine in the Self Defense Force's compound at Shibata (in Niigata prefecture) and the differing interpretations of article 89 regarding the use of state property for the sake of religion.

A translation of the Shinto Directive issued by SCAP on 15 December 1945 for the abolition of governmental sponsorship, support, perpetuation, control, and dissemination of state Shinto is published on p.85–89 of the same issue of *Contemporary Religions in Japan.*

Baker, Alonzo L. *The Influence of the Divine Emperor Doctrine upon Japan.* 1948. See no.1229.

Ballou, Robert O. *Shinto: The Unconquered Enemy.* 1945. See no.64a.

Blumhagen, Herman H. *Nationalistic Policies and Japanese Public Education from 1928 to March 21, 1947.* 1957. See no.2026.

2198b Braibanti, Ralph J. D. "Religious Freedom in Japan." *Christian Century* 64:850–52 (9 July 1947)

The breakup of state Shinto and the attempt by SCAP to maintain religious impartiality in Japan are discussed. Difficulties with the abandonment of state Shinto are attributed to the lack of a tradition of the separation of church and state and to the habit of the Japanese people to obey and follow directions without understanding their meaning or spirit. Braibanti notes that SCAP policy is unique in the history of occupations of conquered non-Christian territories in that the cross has not followed the flag. He suggests that this lack of favoritism for Japanese Christians is the result of the detachment of military government from matters of prefectural and local civil administration. The lack of special consideration for foreign missionaries is also discussed and deplored.

2199 ———. "State and Religion in Japan." *Far Eastern Survey* 16:185–87 (3 Sept. 1947)

This article discusses SCAP's policy toward religion, especially toward the Christian missionaries, and describes in detail the 6 major SCAP directives concerning religion, attempting to show the evolution of SCAP's policy, particularly towards state Shinto. It includes a discussion of violations and misunderstandings of the SCAP directives on the part of the Japanese. As an example Braibanti points to the utilization of chiefs of the neighborhood associations (*tonarigumi*) to collect money for the upkeep of Shinto shrines, even though a SCAP directive forbade public officials to sponsor or support Shinto in their official capacity.

Brumbaugh, Thoburn T. "Behind America's Shield of Steel." 1948. See no.542.

———. "Japan Believes in the Now." 1946. See no.2282.

———. "Perilous Opportunity in Japan." 1947. See no.482.

2200 ———. "The Protestant Handicap in Japan." *Christian Century* 64, no.23: 708-9 (4 June 1947)

An experienced Japan missionary, while engaged in raising the funds needed to found Tokyo's International Christian University, compares the size of Roman Catholic and Protestant missionary forces in both prewar and postwar Japan. At the time of writing the Catholics had the greater staff by about 7 to 1. The author, who approves of MacArthur's view that Japan's problems are basically theological, points out that the 1,000 missionaries requested by the general would merely restore the staff to its prewar numbers. The article concludes with a plea for a Protestant strategy comparable in effectiveness to that of the Roman Catholics.

2201 Bunce, William K. *Religions in Japan: Buddhism, Shinto, Christianity*. Tokyo: Tuttle, 1955. xi, 194p.

The revised edition of an earlier report prepared by SCAP, entitled *Religions in Japan* (1948) (no.2229). Except for minor editorial changes, the new edition basically retains all of the original chapters, but the last chapter of the original edition, "Evaluation of Religious Trends in Japan," has been deleted in the new edition. The author was chief of the Religious Division of the Civil Information and Education Section of SCAP and was responsible for the original report. He later became acting chief public affairs officer of the U.S. embassy in Tokyo in 1954. The revised edition also carries a foreword by William Woodard, director of the International Institute for the Study of Religions in Japan, which presents comments on developments in Japanese religions between 1948 and 1954.

2202 "Christ for Japan." *Christian Century* 63:135-37 (30 Jan. 1946)

In this discussion of the spiritual needs of the Japanese during reconstruction, both Catholic and Protestant prospects for winning converts are evaluated. A call is made for an unofficial American commission of Christians to go to Japan and actively seek to convert the entire nation, including the emperor.

2202a Christian Deputation to Japan, 1945. *The Return to Japan: Report of the Christian Deputation to Japan, October-November 1945*. New York: Friendship Pr., published for the Federal Council of the Churches of Christ in America and the Foreign Missions Conference of North America, 1946. 64p.

The deputation was led by Douglas Horton and included Bishop James C. Baker, Luman J. Shafer, and Walter W. Van Kirk.

2203 Constitution Investigation Council. "The Constitution and Religion." *Contemporary Religions in Japan* 8, no.2: 145-76 (June 1967)

A translation of part of the proceedings which the Commission on the Constitution conducted at its thirty-eighth general meeting on 2 December 1958. It consists primarily of the testimony offered by Dr. Kishimoto, a specialist in religious studies, on the religious problems created by the implementation of the postwar constitution. They include the inability of public schools to provide appropriate religious instruction and the uncertain relationship of shrine Shinto to the Japanese state.

2204 Creemers, Wilhelmus Helena Martinus. *Shrine Shinto after World War II.* Leiden: Brill, 1968. xviii, 261p.

Creemers examines shrine Shinto after the SCAP directive of 1945 which marked the end of government control and support of some 100,000 Shinto shrines. He discusses the separation of church and state achieved in February 1946, at which time a majority of shrines organized themselves as private religious institutions within the Association of Shinto Shrines. He also describes attempts to reestablish some of the prewar privileges enjoyed by shrine Shinto, particularly one involving financial support from the state, and notes the constitutional difficulties involved in such a change. Creemers' publication is a slightly revised version of the doctoral dissertation that he submitted to Columbia University in 1966. (Abstracted in *Dissertation Abstracts* 27:1101A [1966]; University Microfilms order no.66–9356)

2205 Dabney, Vaughn. "Thanks for the Bibles." *Christian Science Monitor* magazine section p.5 (27 Nov. 1948)

Dabney reports on a recent visit to Japan, where he met with Japanese Christian leaders, politicians and students and engaged in the distribution of Bibles to various organizations. He describes the warm reception given him in the cities and towns he visited, and records an interview with the emperor, who told him that if Bibles can check the disintegration and demoralization of the Japanese people and can teach them morals and good character, then their distribution is needed. Dabney feels that "the tested principles of the Word of God must be known and applied" if a democratic Japan is to be built."

2206 Durgin, Russell L. "Christianity in Postwar Japan." *Far Eastern Survey* 22: 13–18 (28 Jan. 1953)

In his discussion of Japanese churches since 1945, Durgin describes the affects of General MacArthur's directive concerning freedom of worship. He notes that among Christians in Japan there is a keen interest in ecumenicity and a desire to bear their share of responsibility in the world church. Russell L. Durgin represented the International Committee of the YMCA in Japan for over 25 years.

2207 Holtom, Daniel Clarence. *Modern Japan and Shinto Nationalism: A Study of Present-day Trends in Japanese Religions.* rev. ed. Chicago: Univ. of Chicago Pr., 1947. ix, 226p.; reprinted in New York: Paragon Book Reprint, 1963.

An analysis of the significance of Shinto in the development of modern Japan. The original edition of 6 chapters appeared in 1943; a revised edition was published in 1947 with 2 additional chapters. In these the author views favorably the new status of state Shinto in post-surrender Japan and its possible value as a cultural resource to Japan and the world. He discusses the directive issued by the occupation authorities on 15 December 1945 to abrogate Shinto as a state religion, the emperor's renunciation of divinity on 1 January 1946, the impact of the destruction of the central idea of Japanese state ideology that the imperial will is infallible, and the impact of these changes on SCAP's concurrent reforms of the Japanese educational system. Noting that Shinto has given "blessings to whatever was considered as vitally important in the general social and national experience" such as the imperial system and the racial superiority of the Japanese people, Holtom maintains that through scholarly studies and new orientations Shinto can be used to support such universal values as human equality and democracy.

2208 ———. "New Status of Shinto." *Far Eastern Survey* 15:17–20 (30 Jan. 1946)

This article discusses the implications of SCAP's directive involving the disestablishment of Shinto as the state religion of Japan. After an account of the historical development of Shinto and its more recent role in the Japanese educational system, the author examines 2 of the major results of the SCAP directive: (1) the severing of Shinto from the state, and (2) the elimination of Shinto teachings from the public schools. He also considers some specific matters in the implementation of the SCAP directive such as the screening of teachers and the banning of nationalistic books.

―――. "Shinto in the Postwar World." 1945. *See* no. 82.

2209 Horner, Francis J. "Japan and the Ideal." *Commonweal* 48:630–34 (16 Apr. 1948)

In the face of what he defines as the "psychological incompleteness" of the Japanese, the author suggests that such a lack may be filled by the importation of Christianity into occupied Japan. He asserts that "General MacArthur has made no secret of his hopes of seeing not only the democratization of Japan but also its Christianization." In the last section, the author attempts to demonstrate ways in which traditional concepts such as the Japanese *kami* could be incorporated into Christianity.

2210 Horton, Douglas. "The Church of Christ in Japan Today." *Christendom* 11:165–74 (Spring 1946)

Horton first describes some of the problems faced by the Japanese Christian church during the war and asserts that the Japanese Christian community remained generally loyal to the Gospel throughout the trying period. He then points out that Japanese Christians, who had been suspect on account of their ties with the West, have since become "a popular hope" and that many people have taken up the study of the Bible. Indeed, he reports, Christianity is said to offer Japan the best foundation for national democracy and a means for uniting the country "in sympathetic fashion to the ranking nations of the world." Horton concludes by calling upon the Christian churches of America to provide the Japanese with relief supplies and—eventually—with people prepared to take up missionary work there again.

2211 Hutchinson, Paul. "Japan: A Laboratory Test." *Christian Century* 64:39–41 (8 Jan. 1947)

The question of continuing the forced Christian ecumenism created by the wartime government-sponsored Kyōdan (Church of Christ in Japan) is discussed in this letter. The author predicts that Christian ideas will create a strong impression in postwar Japan because of the assumed link between liberalism and Christianity and its consequent popularity among young people. Hutchinson warns, however, against a mass conversion to "Americanism" as a consequence of the rise of Christianity.

2212 Iglehart, Charles. "The Christian Church in Japan." *International Review of Missions* 41:273–87 (July 1952)

Most of this article deals with the size and structure of the postwar Japanese Christian movement, the relationships among the various churches in Japan and between Japanese Christians and foreign missionaries, and the missionary obligations of the postwar Japanese churches. Direct reference occasionally is made to the occupation itself, with Iglehart noting in this regard the favorable impact of SCAP-dictated social changes upon the Christian movement, the value of the unofficial assistance of American chaplains and the semi-public encouragement extended by General MacArthur at the beginning of the occupation period, and the efforts of Japanese Christians from the outset to associate themselves in the public eye with their fellow-Christians from the West.

2212a "Japanese New Year." *Commonweal* 43:347–48 (18 Jan. 1946)

The editors of *Commonweal* view the rescript of 1 January 1946 in which the emperor formally renounced his divinity as an irreversible statement symbolic of the immense changes wrought by the Americans and of their amazing acceptance by the Japanese. The editors wonder, however, what the West will offer to fill the vacuum created by the collapse of traditional Japanese values. While there is no clear answer, they do suggest that Japan is ripe for Christianity now that Shinto has been uprooted.

2213 Jorgensen, Arthur. "Future of Missions in Japan." *Far Eastern Survey* 14: 317–20 (7 Nov. 1945)

Jorgenson, a former secretary of the YMCA, discusses the problems involved in reestablishing Christian missions in Japan after World War II. He emphasizes how important it is to work together with the Japanese Christian community and to keep evangelical activities politically independent of SCAP.

2214 Kan, W. E. "The Religious Situation in Japan Today." *Ecumenical Review* 2, no.3:254–58 (Spring 1950)

A brief discussion of the historical position of Shinto, Buddhism, and Christianity in Japan is followed by a few remarks concerning the changes brought about by the occupation and the present role of Christianity within the country.

Kao, Ming-huey. *An Analysis of Moral Education in Japanese Public Schools, 1945–1960.* 1964. See no.2075.

2215 Kitagawa, Joseph Mitsuo. *Religion in Japanese History.* New York: Columbia Univ. Pr., 1966. xi, 475p.

This study of the involvement of religion in Japanese history and in the social and political life of the country is in part a major contribution to the literature on the occupation period. In chapter 6—"Old Dreams or New Vision? Some Reflections on the Religious Situation in Postwar Japan"—Kitagawa discusses such SCAP policies towards Japanese religion as the disestablishment of state Shinto, the repudiation of the emperor's divinity, and the incorporation of the principle of religious liberty in the new constitution. In addition, he describes at length how the postwar guarantees of religious freedom permitted both the revival of Christianity and the emergence of numerous groups based to a greater or lesser extent on traditional beliefs.

2216 Lensen, George Alexander. "The Orthodox Church in Occupied Japan." *Florida State University Studies* no.8: 93–95 (1952)

This short survey of the history of the Russian Orthodox Church in Japan includes a brief description of its current (1952) state and its future prospects. The author notes in particular the increasing foreign support which the church is receiving and the occupation's efforts to guarantee religious freedom to all.

2217 McLaren, Charles I. "The Church and Reconciliation with Japan." *International Review of Missions* 35:293–302 (July 1946)

McLaren calls for the display of Christian tolerance, suffering, and understanding toward Japan, urging that relief be sent to avert mass starvation there and that Japan be treated as an equal by other nations. He also comments favorably on the Imperial Rescript of 1 January 1946 by which the emperor disavowed his divine status, and indicates his agreement with Australian, New Zealand, and Chinese moves for arraigning Hirohito as a war criminal provided that the emperor is held strictly accountable for only "that measure of responsibility which . . . [he] can himself accept."

2218 Mann, John C. "Christianity in Japan." *Eastern World* 3:11–12 (Mar. 1949)

This article by the Anglican Bishop of Osaka deals with the postwar recovery of the Japanese churches. No mention is made of the occupation except to commend it for its policy of neutrality in religious matters.

2219 Nugent, Donald R. "Disposition of State-Owned Land Currently Used by Religious Institutions." *Contemporary Religions in Japan* 7, no.3:209–16 (Sept. 1966)

Nugent, chief of SCAP's Religions and Cultural Resources Division, prepared this staff study in order "to determine what disposition should be made of State-owned precincts of religious institutions and of national forests in custody of Shinto shrines and Buddhist temples." He points out that the principle of separation of church and state rendered the Japanese government's continued possession of title to lands used for religious purposes undesirable and that religious freedom seemed to require that religious institutions be given control over areas necessary to their religious functions and in which they have more than just possessory interest. He notes, moreover, that the disposition of State-owned lands was a matter of vital concern to over 150,000 shrines and temples. Nugent then examines the historical background of this particular land problem and presents the proposed solution that has been put forth by the government. He concludes that the Japanese government's proposal to restore to religious institutions title to the precincts they occupy has considerable merit and recommends that the government be instructed to do so provided that the lands in question belonged to the shrines and temples before the Meiji Restoration and had subsequently been taken over by the State without any compensation or had been obtained by the religious organizations from non-governmental sources and without the expenditure of public funds. Interestingly enough, however, he argues against the transfer of land titles to the military shrines (Yasukuni Jinja, Gokoku Jinja, Shōkonsha) which had been created in order to glorify the military ideal through deification of the men who had died in battle.

Price, Willard. "Behind the Mask of Modern Japan." 1945. See no.1250.

2220 ———. "Shall Japan Be Allowed Freedom of Religion?" *Asia and the Americas* 45:413–16 (Sept. 1945); abridged and published under the title "Why Japs Are Crooked Thinkers" in *Science Digest* 18:35–37 (Dec. 1945)

In discussing this question, Price points out that a clear distinction must be made between sectarian Shinto and state Shinto. He suggests that the Japanese be permitted to continue the traditional religion but the occupation forces should not hesitate to interfere with state Shinto. Price's article is adapted and expanded from chapter 21 of his book *Japan and the Son of Heaven* (no.110a).

"Religion in Public Education." 1967. See no.2104c.

The Reminiscences of Harold C. Henderson. 1962. See no.441.

2221 Root, Robert. "Japanese Vacuum." *Christian Century* 65:1299–1301 (1 Dec. 1948)

Root briefly reviews the attempts of shrine Shinto, Buddhism, and communism to fill the postwar ideological vacuum in Japan. The financial poverty of the 2 religions and the link between Communist success and material destitution are noted. The bulk of the article is devoted to the work of Catholics and Protestants in Japan. The Kyōdan is discussed and its role in education and rural mission work is highlighted. SCAP's cooperation with missionaries is considered vital for Christian expansion.

2222 Sansbury, Cyril Kenneth. "Christianity in Japan, 1549–1949." *International Review of Missions* 38:432–42 (Oct. 1949)

While this survey focuses on Christianity in pre-Tokugawa Japan, the author does comment briefly on the post-World War II period, noting that the political scene at that time was favorable for preaching the Gospel and that MacArthur, "without in any way attempting to favour one religion at the expense of another, has taken care that the Japanese should have full opportunities of hearing the Gospel and deciding for themselves."

2223 Shafer, Luman J. "Christianity in Japan." *International Review of Missions* 35:121–30 (Apr. 1946)

Shafer describes the state of the Japanese church following several years of government repression and wartime destruction. He visited Japan in the fall of 1945 and at that time found the church "intact and vigorous in its faith," with local church organizations intact and functioning, their ministers able to carry on their regular work, and church attendance everywhere on the increase. He feels certain that the Christian community will not return to the denominational chaos of prewar years even though the church's present *kyōdan* form of organization will have to be changed. The occupation forces, he continues, have made a good impression on the Japanese, some of whom credit the kindliness of the American soldiers to their Christian background. Furthermore, as a result of directives from SCAP, the Japanese government is taking steps to remove various prewar and wartime restrictions on church activities: The Religious Bodies Law has been abrogated and state Shinto disestablished, Christian schools will not be severely regimented in regard to curriculum and general educational practices as they had been before the war, the chauvinistic nationalism based on Shinto which characterized elementary school education is being eliminated, and plans for the establishment of outstanding Christian universities in the Tokyo and Kansai areas are under way. Indeed, Shafer concludes, the opportunities for Christianity in the new Japan are almost unlimited.

2224 ———. "Freedom's New Frontier." *Missionary Herald at Home and Abroad* 144:52–56 (June 1948)

The secretary for the China, Japan and Africa committees of the Reformed Church in America's Board of Foreign Missions states that the Japanese people are eager to escape the poverty, disease, breakdown in moral standards, and confusion brought about by Japan's wartime defeat. Whether they will listen to those who advocate a revival of nationalism, the espousal of communism, or the acceptance of Christ will depend in part on the activities undertaken by Christians both in Japan and in North America. To assist its Japanese colleagues, the Japan committee of the Board has developed a five-year, $20,000,000 program calling for the dispatch of several hundred missionaries to Japan, extensive proselytization in the countryside, the establishment of 80 urban centers in connection with various city churches, aid to theological schools and to leaders in Christian home and family life, the establishment of a Japan Christian University near Tokyo, and the publication and distribution of Christian literature —in particular, copies of the Scriptures in Japanese.

2225 ———. "Missions and Union in Japan." *Christian Century* 64:332–33 (12 Mar. 1947)

Shafer, a missionary in Japan for many years, returned to Japan after the war to report on the state of the Protestant Church. He points out that 60 percent of the Protestant denominations have united their postwar missionary activities. The planning for this unified action took place before the end of the war. Hutchinson is the leader of the unified activities.

2226 ———. "Report on Japan." *Christian Century* 65, no.15:327–28 (14 Apr. 1948)

Shafer was for many years a missionary in Japan and returned immediately after the war for a visit. His article deals with the state of the Protestant Church in Japan. In passing he mentions foreign-financed relief work in the form of bibles, religious books in general, missionaries, and converts.

2227 Shorrock, Hallam C., Jr. "The Church of Christ in Japan (Nippon Kirisuto Kyodan)." *International Review of Missions* 41:193–201 (Apr. 1952)

Shorrock traces the historical concern of the Japanese church with problems of church unity, independence from foreign control, and the ability to be self-supporting. He also outlines the postwar nature and problems of the United Church of Christ in Japan, touching briefly on the reconstruction of the many damaged religious buildings and Christian schools and on the reestablishment of close ties between Japanese Christians and foreign missionary boards.

2227a Sinn, Ephraim Edward. "Ancestor Worship and the Peace." *Connecticut Bar Journal* 23:189–91 (June 1949)

Praising ancestor worship as a natural extension of filial piety and noting that the reverence of one's parents is a virtue which pervades the Japanese institutions of religion, the state, the family and property, Sinn asserts that the occupation authorities would do well to respect this practice. He agrees with Helen Mears, author of *Mirror for Americans: Japan* (1948; no.562), that state Shinto is merely a Japanese form of Western nationalism, and he notes that Americans err when they believe that the religious practices of the Japanese made them into a militaristic nation. "The era of enlightenment and peace," Sinn concludes, "will not come by persuading the Japanese to forsake their ancestral tablets on the Kamidana and to destroy their Shinto shrines."

Supreme Commander for the Allied Powers. Monograph 32. *Religion*. 1952. See no.314.

2227b ———. "The Shinto Directive." *Contemporary Religions in Japan* 1, no. 2:85–89 (June 1960)

The text of the memorandum popularly known as the Shinto Directive that called for the abolition of governmental sponsorship, support, perpetuation, control and dissemination of state Shinto (*kokka shintō, jinja shintō*). It was issued by SCAP on 15 December 1945 and in particular sought to "free the Japanese people from direct or indirect compulsion to believe or profess to believe in a religion or cult officially designated by the state" and "to separate religion from the state, to prevent misuse of religion for political ends, and to put all religions, faiths, and creeds upon exactly the same basis, entitled to precisely the same opportunities and protection."

2228 ———. Civil Information and Education Section. *Report on Postwar Religious Developments in Japan*. Tokyo: SCAP, 1950. 14p., app.

Three topics are treated in this brief discussion of religious developments in occupied Japan—(1) the impact of the occupation on religious groups in Japan, (2) present trends in religion in Japan, and (3) the role of voluntary efforts in American church relations with Japan. There is a brief historical outline of Japanese religions prior to the surrender but emphasis is placed on new trends and developments that have come about as a result of the defeat and subsequent occupation. Buddhism, Shinto, Christianity, and other religions are separately considered. The voluntary effort of American Christians in offering relief and rehabilitation as well as education to the Japanese is considered to be an important determining factor in the religious development of Japan. Appendixes compare the number of adherents claimed by religious organizations in Japan with the distribution of religious belief among the adult population as indicated by public opinion surveys. They also provide statistics on clearances of missionaries into Japan and data on the disposition of the state-owned precincts of shrines and temples.

Available at the Army Library, the Pentagon, Washington, D.C.

———. ———. *Japanese Educational Institutions with Religious Affiliations*. 1948. See no.2119.

2228a ———. ———. "National Holidays: Official Documents." *Contemporary Religions in Japan* 7, no.2:154–65 (June 1966)

This official SCAP memorandum prepared by William K. Bunce, chief of SCAP's Religions and Cultural Resources Division in the Civil Information and Education Section, and issued on 27 May 1948 sought to determine whether certain Japanese national holidays which had their origin and significance in state Shinto mythology, doctrines, rites, practices, ceremonies, and observances should be abolished or not. After defining the scope of the problem, the memorandum examines the historical background and nature of such holidays as *Genshi-sai* (the "Festival of Origin"), *Jimmu Tennō-sai* (the holiday commemorating the death of Emperor Jimmu), *Niiname-sai* (a harvest festival), *Kigen-setsu* (the holiday commemorating the enthronement of Emperor Jimmu, which was considered to have been the founding of the nation), and *Meiji-setsu* (the anniversary of Emperor Meiji's birth). The attitude of the Japanese government towards the retention of these holidays also is considered. SCAP concluded that the existing Japanese national holidays were generally ultranationalistic in nature and were perpetuating certain ideas and principles based on Shinto mythology which had been repudiated in the new constitution. It therefore recommended that they be abolished and replaced by "new national holidays more in keeping with democratic ideals."

2229 ―――. ―――. Religions and Cultural Resources Div. *Religions in Japan*. Tokyo: SCAP, Mar. 1948. ix, 204p.

This report was prepared as a handbook for the members of SCAP and military government teams to assist them in understanding Japanese religions and their historical and social significance as well as the objectives of occupation policy as they related to religion. It consists of 4 parts. Part 1 is a historical outline of Japanese religions which begins with legendary times; it discusses the role of government in religious life, particularly in post-1931 years. Part 2, discussing religious systems in present-day Japan, describes the doctrines of Buddhism, Shinto, Christianity, and a variety of new minor sects. Part 3 pertains to the impact of the occupation on Japanese religions, considering the constitutional establishment of religious freedom, the separation of state and religion, the elimination of ultranationalism, and the changed role of Christian groups. Finally, part 4 evaluates the religious situation in Japan, providing an analysis of present religious trends in Japan and future problems that religious institutions may face in the areas of finance, organizational unity, leadership, and doctrinal appeal. On the whole, institutional aspects of religion are given considerable attention, while special emphasis is placed upon the relationship between state and religion in Japan. Appended are statistics of religious sects on their installations, workers, and adherents as of 1946; SCAP directives on religion; a glossary of religious terms; and a selected bibliography of works written in English.

A revised version of this report was prepared by William K. Bunce and published in 1955 under the title *Religions in Japan: Buddhism, Shinto, Christianity* (no.2201).

Tolischus, Otto D. "The God-Emperor: Key to a Nation." 1945. *See* no. 1261.

2229a Union of the New Religious Organizations of Japan. Research Office, ed. "Reminiscences of Religion in Postwar Japan." *Contemporary Religions in Japan* pt.1, 6, no.2:111–203 (June 1965); pt.2, 6, no.3:295–314 (Sept. 1965); pt.3, 6, no.4:382–402 (Dec. 1965); pt.4, 7, no.1:51–79 (Mar. 1966); pt.5, 7, no.2:166–87 (June 1966); pt.6, 7, no.3:217–73 (Sept. 1966)

Compiled from materials collected by the Union of New Religious Organizations of Japan, this study of religious activity during the occupation years (an "epoch-making period," according to the authors) seeks to determine the background and purpose of reforming Japan's religious system, the attitude of the various religious groups in Japan at that time, and the nature of the activities in which those groups engaged. As a detailed record of postwar changes written from the Japanese point of view, this work is valuable for understanding such phenomena as the establishment of religious freedom, the abolition of state Shinto, and the rise of the new sects. Chapter 1, entitled "The Allied Forces Arrive; Freedom of Religion Established," and chapter 3, "Various Problems under the Occupation," are particularly relevant for the scholar interested in SCAP's involvement in religious change. The first of these comments on (1) the religious world at the end of

World War II, (2) the establishment of a Religions Division within the Civil Information and Education Section of SCAP in November 1945, (3) Dr. William K. Bunce, chief of the Religions Division, (4) the abolition of the Religious Organizations Law of 1939 and the enforcement of the Religious Corporations Ordinance of 28 December 1945, (5) the Shinto Directive of 15 December 1945, (6) the emperor's rejection of his divine status in his New Year's Day Imperial Rescript of 1946, and (7) the new constitution and its provisions for the freedom of religion. Chapter 3, in turn, covers a wide variety of problems involving religion under the occupation. In discussing the handling of various problems by the Religions Division, for example, the authors point out that the purge did not touch the religious world itself but that ultranationalistic views and attitudes within religious organizations were completely suppressed, restrictions were placed on the doctrine and faith of Shinto and various Japanese sects, and several organizations—among them the Yuishinremmei, Tenshin-kyō, and Higashikunikyō—were dissolved. Furthermore, in accordance with the Shinto Directive, public funerals were prohibited, strict restrictions were placed on monuments to fallen soldiers and other notables, and school children were not permitted to visit temples or shrines in formal groups. Chapter 3 also discusses some of the problems raised with regard to religion and education, the impact of inflation and the disposition of state-owned lands upon religious bodies, and the reform of the prison chaplain (*kyōkaishi*) system. The entire study concludes with an overview of religion in Japan towards the end of the occupation period and during the first few years following Japan's recovery of her national independence.

2230 Van Kirk, Walter W. "The Future of Christianity in Japan." *Christian Century* 63:169–71 (6 Feb. 1946)

The author discusses the potential development of Christianity in postwar Japan and regards the Christian community as a group capable of surviving the spiritual hardships of defeat. Van Kirk discusses the contemporary inadequacies of the traditional religions, pointing out the postwar rejection of state Shinto and the failure of Buddhism to incorporate the concept of the dignity of man which is of primary importance to the successful development of democracy. He feels that these inadequacies combined with the lack of legal restraints on Christianity will produce a climate favorable for its development.

2231 Wittner, Lawrence S. "MacArthur and the Missionaries: God and Man in Occupied Japan." *Pacific Historical Review* 40, no.1:77–98 (Feb. 1971)

Wittner points out that General MacArthur considered the religious aspect of his work to be of great significance. Despite his sponsorship of the new Japanese constitution which affirmed freedom of religion, MacArthur held that the occupation had every right to propagate Christianity—a different view of religious freedom than his superiors in Washington. The author is a member of the history department at Vassar College.

2232 Woodard, William P. *The Allied Occupation of Japan, 1945–1952, and Japanese Religions.* Leiden: Brill, 1972. xx, 393p.

Written by a head of SCAP's Religious Research Unit, this book deals primarily with the policies, the activities, and the decision-making of the Religions Division of the Civil Information and Education Section of SCAP during the occupation period. It also discusses briefly the specific work of the regional and prefectural military government teams, comments upon the activities of the Japanese Ministry of Education that were related to those of the Religions Division, and provides information on MacArthur's own attitude towards Japan's religions.

2233 Yanaibara, Tadao. *Religion and Democracy in Modern Japan.* Tokyo: Japan

Institute of Pacific Studies. 1948. 41p. (Pacific Studies series)

Yanaibara, a professor at Tokyo University and a scholar who had suffered for his liberal thought before World War II, describes the democratization of religion in Japan as a result of the Potsdam Declaration, various SCAP directives, and Article 20 of the new constitution. One section of his study details the growth of new sects and churches following the repeal of the Religious Organizations Law, but the author expresses personal criticism of some of them. Yanaibara concludes this work by asserting that "unless the belief in Christianity is implanted in the hearts of the Japanese people, Japan will not become a real and well-founded democratic country."

2234 Young, James R. "The Menace of Shintoism." *United States Naval Institute Proceedings* 74:463–65 (Apr. 1948)

Claiming that the occupation authorities are allowing the Japanese "to perpetuate the Emperor-Shinto shrine preservation theory," the author strongly warns against still-powerful Shinto traditions. He claims that emperor worship has not been abolished and will revive once the occupation has terminated. The final paragraph charges that the Allied forces should be shattering Japan's basic myths and inherited traditions but in fact are not doing so.

MISCELLANEOUS

There are assembled below a small number of entries that do not logically fit in any of the earlier categories. The principal subjects involved are: the status of women in postwar Japan, the revival of youth organizations, the reorganization and rehabilitation of the library system, the work of SCAP's Arts and Monuments Division, and reports on the postwar status of Japanese science and technology.

2235 "AEC Program on Isotope Distribution: Japan to Participate in Program." *Department of State Bulletin* 21:834 (28 Nov. 1949)

Atomic Energy Commission officials announce the participation of Japan in a program of foreign distribution of radio isotopes. It marks the first such participation by any occupied country and is the result of the desire of American leaders to enable the Japanese to use radio isotopes in medicine, biology, and research in the physical sciences.

2236 Andō, Nisuke. *Surrender, Occupation, and Private Property in International Law: An Evaluation of Some United States Practices during the Occupation of Surrendered Japan.* Ph.D. dissertation, Fletcher School of Law and Diplomacy, Tufts Univ., 1971. vii, 290p.

This thesis examines the legal basis within international law for the measures that SCAP adopted for purging the militarists and ultranationalists, for breaking up the *zaibatsu*, and for carrying out an extensive land reform. In this regard, Ando's primary concern is with the American treatment of the private Japanese property that was affected by each of these measures. He first investigates the applicability of the Hague Regulations of 1907 (which provide for the extensive protection of *private* enemy property during a period of military occupation) to the Japanese occupation in light of the unconditional nature of Japan's surrender. He then examines past theory, state practice, and judicial precedents relating to armistices, capitulations, and military occupations and compares Japan's postwar experience with that of the other Axis states and their satellites. Finally, the author turns to a discussion of the American actions themselves and points out how great an impact they had on millions of private Japanese citizens. In his evaluation of the measures in question, Ando notes that they were aimed at changing the political, economic, and social structure of Japan and thus contravened the Hague Regulations, which were based on the assumption that an occupying power should refrain from changing the fundamental institutions of an occupied territory. He argues, therefore, that these measures "were justifiable only as the implementation of the Potsdam Declaration," which was specifically incorporated into the Instrument of Japanese Surrender authorizing the Allied powers to take whatever measures were necessary to demilitarize and democratize Japan.

2237 Betz, Betty. "Jap Kids Are Our Job." *Collier's* 123:14–15, 52–53 (9 Apr. 1949)

The author of this article studied in Japan just prior to the war and returned to teach there during the occupation. After describing the amusing reactions of her young Japanese students to her lessons on democracy and the American way of life, she devotes a good deal of space to criticizing the arrogant and antidemocratic behavior of Americans in Japan and to lashing out at discriminatory occupation policies. Betz took it upon herself to find every opportunity to increase the amount of contact between American and Japanese youth in spite of strict SCAP regulations to the contrary.

2238 Clapp, Verner W. "The National Diet Library of Japan." *Science* 107:497–501 (14 May 1948)

In an article describing the establishment of the National Diet Library on 4 February 1948, the author also presents a survey of the development of libraries in Japan. Following a description of early libraries, he treats war damage to Japan's libraries and discusses the Allied occupation authorities' encouragement of the reconstitution and strengthening of the library system. He briefly relates the duties of the library officer of the Civil Information and Education Section of SCAP and discusses current and projected SCAP activities in this field. The author, the chief assistant librarian of the Library of Congress, is particularly qualified to describe the establishment of the National Diet Library since he was one of 3 men who were invited by SCAP to Japan to assist in its planning. He is very optimistic about the success of the endeavor and its value in "aiding good government and assisting research and the free flow of information."

2239 Cowley, G. A. "Post-war Changes in Status of Japanese Women." *Transactions of the International Conference of Orientalists in Japan* 7:27–34 (1962)

The author, second secretary of the Canadian embassy in Tokyo, focuses on the considerably improved postwar status of Japanese women. Comparing their situation with prewar society, when their influence was normally limited to the home, he discusses their increasing interest and influence in politics, their growing numbers in the universities as well as in the professions, and some of the changes in the patterns of family life that have affected their status in general.

2240 Dilts, Marion May. "New World for Japanese Women." *Christian Science Monitor* magazine section p.2 (23 Aug. 1947)

Dilts finds that the elevation of Japanese women to equal status not only offers them opportunities but also creates problems. She notes that an increasing number of women are now actively participating in all kinds of organizations and that 39 women were elected to the Diet in the first postwar general election. At the same time, however, the qualifications of these new Diet members have come under attack and the average Japanese woman's world remains far too restricted from the standpoint of SCAP officials and many others. Only if Japanese women enlarge their horizons from the family to the world at large will they be able to play an effective role in their country's postwar reconstruction.

2241 Downs, Robert B. "Japan's New National Library." *College and Research Libraries* 10:381–87, 416 (Oct. 1949)

Downs reports on his trip to Japan from June to September 1948 which was made to assess the progress of Japan's new National Diet Library. It was Japan's first national library and was patterned after the United States' Library of Congress. Established by an act of the Diet on 4 February 1948, it was at first housed in the Akasaka Palace. He concludes that Japan's national library has numerous obstacles to overcome not the least of which is the lack of professional librarians and widespread public support.

2242 ———. *National Diet Library: Report on Technical Processes, Bibliographical Services, and General Organization.* Tokyo: Kokuritsu Kokkai Tosyokan (National Diet Library), 1948. 31, 24p. In English and Japanese.

2243 Durgin, Russell L. "Japan Thumbs Freedom's Pages." *Christian Science Monitor* magazine section p.3 (3 July 1948); abridged and published under the title "What about Japan's Youth." *Reader's Digest* 53:127–30 (Aug. 1948)

The author examines the reestablishment of YMCA branches in postwar Japan and, in answer to questions about democracy and the future of Japan, discusses the new patterns of intellectual endeavor among youth.

2243a ———. "Japan's Youth Looks Ahead." *Contemporary Japan* 17:223–35 (July/Dec. 1948)

Durgin, a former officer in charge of youth organizations within the Educational Division of SCAP's Civil Information and Education Section, explains that the basic thrust of occupation policy has been to abolish the old, paramilitary youth organizations and to encourage self-governing youth societies. As many young people lack adequate experience in self-government, youth leaders have been invited to attend government-sponsored training conferences. Durgin provides examples of the kinds of activities pursued by rural and urban youth groups but notes that many of the latter still exist only on paper or serve merely as "fronts" for people with various "ulterior purposes." A good deal of progress, he reports, has been made by the YMCA in its youth activities. Indeed, the student Christian movement is now more effective than ever before. In addition, many people are looking to Christianity for a solution to youth's search for truth and reality since Christianity—as Durgin points out in his conclusion—provides the foundation and substance of democracy and freedom.

2243b Feely, Gertrude Marie. *A Program for Youth in Oita Japan.* Ed.D. dissertation, Columbia Univ. Teachers College, 1949. 142p.

Prepared by a missionary to Japan, this doctoral dissertation surveys Japan's cultural heritage and developments within the country since 1941 and formulates plans for the organization of a city-wide youth program in Ōita (a city in northeastern Kyushu) which will enable young people to acquire a better understanding of democratic principles and values.

2244 Fujita, Taki. *Japanese Women in the Postwar Years.* Tokyo: Nihon Taiheiyō Mondai Chōsakai, 1954. 13p. (Japan supplementary papers, 1)

This paper was prepared for presentation at the twelfth conference of the Institute of Pacific Relations held in Kyoto in 1954.

2245 ———. "The Progress of the Emancipation of Japanese Women." *Contemporary Japan* 16:274–84 (July/Sept. 1947)

This article describes the history of the women's movement to gain social, political, and legal equality since 1868 and considers the work of various early champions of women's rights. The author discusses the repression of such liberal movements prior to World War II and then analyzes the reforms effected by the occupation including the enfranchisement of women and the liberal provisions of the new constitution. A brief description of some contemporary exponents of women's rights is included. The article concludes with a discussion of the preparation of the new civil code, the implications for women's rights of the new Labor Standards Law, and the establishment of such women's organizations as the New Japan's Women's League, the Women's Democratic Club, and the Democratic Women's Association.

2245a Hani, Setsuko. *The Japanese Family System.* Tokyo: Japan Institute of Pacific Studies, 1948. 41p. (Pacific Studies series)

Hani studies the influence which the head of the family has had on the position of women in Japanese family life and asserts that economic inequality (e.g., the right of the head of the family to dispose of the family inheritance) has been a primary cause for the inequality of women in modern Japan. She hopes that women will achieve real equality in postwar society as a consequence of the new constitution and the new civil code.

2246 Hara, Kimi. "Women's Status in Modern Society." *Contemporary Japan* 20:496–508 (Oct./Dec. 1951)

This article by a teacher at Tsuda College for Women in Tokyo first discusses postwar changes in the Japanese family system and how they are likely to affect the younger generation, particularly young women. The changing position of women and their greater participation in politics and in society are a second major topic. She concludes that the roles of women as mothers, teachers, and community workers are central to the success of the democratization program.

2247 Hollis, Howard. "The Work of the Arts and Monuments Division in Tokyo." *Bulletin of the Cleveland Museum of Art* 34:239–41 (Nov. 1947)

In a description of the nature and function of the Arts and Monuments Division of SCAP's Civil Information and Education Section, the author contrasts the group in Japan with its counterpart in occupied Germany. In Japan, he notes, experts work through the Japanese government and have less concern with the discovery and return of looted cultural property than do Americans in Germany. He outlines the gradual transition in the division's restoration of Japanese cultural property. In concluding, he discusses the kinds of registered objects of art and notes the difficulties associated with finding or restoring them.

2248 Holmes, Lulu H. "Women in the New Japan." *Journal of the American Association of University Women* 91:137–41 (Spring 1948)

Changes in the way of life of Japanese women and the postwar adoption of coeducation despite prewar prejudices are examined here. After reviewing the structure of the new higher education system, Holmes concludes that the best alternative for providing new opportunities for women would be the establishment of new and independent women's universities. The creation and functioning of the Japanese College Alumnae Association (Daigaku Fujin Kyōkai) is discussed. It is regarded as the institution best able to popularize education and individuality among women in Japan.

2249 Ichikawa, Taijirō. "The National Diet Library in Japan." *Journal of Documentation* 7:113–18 (June 1951)

The author, then director for International Affairs at the National Diet Library, describes in detail the National Diet Library and its functions. He outlines the various facilities and some of the types of information available at this library.

2250 James, Weldon. "Japan's at Batto Again." *Collier's* 120:44–47 (2 Aug. 1947)

This popularly written article on the revived interest in baseball among the Japanese contains certain interesting comments on the effects of democratization within Japan. The deferential attitude of the players toward the umpire (known as *shinbankan*—"supreme authority"—in Japanese) has ended and batters are no longer doffing their caps to him upon entering the batter's box.

The players are being urged to act more like Americans and SCAP is actively propagandizing baseball everywhere. American officials do not expect that baseball in itself, James explains, will make the Japanese any more democratic than it did before the war. "But compared with the schools' old military drill, it's practically Jeffersonian."

Japan. Ministry of Education. Scientific Education Bureau. *The List of the Learned Societies of Science and Technology.* 1948. *See* no.2069.

2251 ———. Ministry of Labor. Women's and Minors' Bureau. *Advance of Japanese Women in the Post War Years.* Tokyo: The Ministry, 1952. 11p.
A general discussion of political, economic, legal and social developments affecting the status and activities of women in Japan since the end of World War II.

2252 ———. Postal Bureau. *Mail of Japan.* Published in commemoration of 80th anniversary of Japanese Postal Service, 1951. Tokyo? 1952? 46p.

2253 Kamichika, Ichiko. "Japanese Women Enfranchised." *Contemporary Japan* 24, no.1/3:101–11 (1956)
The author begins the article by pointing out the differences in the women's suffrage movement in Japan compared to similar movements in other countries. She shows why the Japanese movement has "never demonstrated the same zeal and persistence as characterized a similar movement" elsewhere. She then traces the history of the women's suffrage movement before the outbreak of World War II by dividing it into 2 major periods: 1868–1918 and 1919–40. Along with other democratization measures following the war came the enfranchisement of women. The author says that women's interest in suffrage "grew considerably following the first postwar general election in April 1946, in which they were permitted to vote for the first time in the history of Japanese politics." Tables are included to show the participation of women in postwar general elections and the number of women elected to office at various levels of government. In conclusion, the author notes the improved political consciousness among women and their abandonment of prewar influences.

2254 Kan, Shina. "Japanese Women Move Forward." *Far Eastern Survey* 19:122–24 (14 June 1950)
Kan discusses the gains made by Japanese women during the occupation, particularly noting their entry into political life, the establishment of a Women's Bureau and the improvement of working conditions for women. Kan Shina is dean of the Social Welfare Department at Japan Women's University.

2255 Kantor, Ken. "Japanese Libraries, American Style." *Wilson Library Bulletin* 24:54–55 (Sept. 1949)
A staff writer for the Public Information Office of the Far East Command describes some of the "reference libraries" (i.e., information centers) established by SCAP's Civil Information and Education Section in the major cities of Japan with the purpose of providing the Japanese with publications from the United States and Western Europe. The activities of the centers go beyond the mere provision of reading materials. Many have organized cultural programs, the author points out, and some even offer classes to the public in English conversation.

2256 Keeney, Philip O. "Reorganization of the Japanese Public Library System." *Far Eastern Survey* pt.1, 17:19–22 (28 Jan. 1948); pt.2, 17:32–35 (11 Feb. 1948)
This 2-part series of articles on the Japanese public library system was prepared by the officer in charge of libraries at SCAP's Civil Information and Education Section. Part 1 discusses the development of the library system in Japan from its beginnings in 1890 and the damages incurred during the war. It points out deficiencies in the prewar sys-

tem, such as limited numbers of books, restricted clientele, and inadequate training of librarians. Included are prewar statistics on the budget of the library system as compared to that of the United States. The author recommends increased financial support as a necessary step in improving the library system.

The second part discusses specific efforts of the Civil Information and Education Section of SCAP to reform the Japanese public library system. Recommendations include raising professional standards through in-service training of librarians, reconstitution of the Library Association of Japan as a democratic organization, the importation of occidental materials prohibited in the prewar and wartime periods, the creation of a more unified national library system based on the California library system, the appointment to library posts of qualified persons, and the establishment in local areas of community centers which would include a library and museum of local history. The author also discusses the new library law enacted in 1947 and several important conferences held by prefectural librarians concerning the condition of regional libraries.

2257 Kelly, Harry C. "Japanese Science and Technology." *Research* 3:341–44 (Aug. 1950)

This report on the postwar state of Japanese science and technology briefly describes SCAP's policy towards scientific research and technological activity, the handicaps (primarily economic) faced by Japanese scientists interested in engaging in serious research, and the reorganization of the country's 3 important prewar national scientific organizations.

2258 ———. "A Survey of Japanese Science." *Scientific Monthly* 68:42–51 (Jan. 1949)

Kelly, a Massachusetts Institute of Technology scientist and deputy chief of the occupation's Scientific and Technical Division, describes primarily the institutional aspects of Japanese science. The history, membership, activities, and organization of such bodies as the Japanese Imperial Academy, the Scientific Liaison Group, the Renewal Committee, the Science Council of Japan, and the Scientific and Technical Administrative Commission are described. The author found Japanese postwar research to be on a generally high level with an emphasis on the practical because of both economic necessity and occupation restrictions on certain areas of research (nuclear research, aeronautics, etc.).

2259 Kume, Ai. "Status of Women and the Family System." *United Asia* 8:247–51 (Sept. 1956)

The author, a professor at Meiji University and a lawyer, writes about the status of women in Japanese history and in Japanese society today. She maintains that the old "family system" and the Japanese concept of "house" not only kept women in an inferior position but also were working against democracy. She examines the Japanese concepts of filial piety, divorce, the relationship between husband and wife, and inheritance rights. She also writes about the effects of the Civil Code of 1898 and the new Civil Code of 1947. She concludes that Japanese women face a "bright future" if the democratic ideas established in the new constitution continue to grow.

2260 Mishima, Sumie Seo. *The Broader Way: A Woman's Life in the New Japan*. New York: Day, 1953. 247p.

Sumie Seo Mishima presents a Japanese view of the occupation, the war crime trials and the peace treaty, especially noting their affect on the Japanese woman. She states that although the old bureaucracy backed by strong police power seems to be reappearing, the most essential accomplishment of the occupation has been the right to fight and control the menace of the return to fascism.

2261 Mitchell, Richard Hanks. *The Korean Minority in Japan*. Berkeley: Univ. of California Pr., 1967. xii, 186p.

Chapter 8 in Mitchell's study of Japan's twentieth century Korean minority covers the occupation period and outlines some of the major differences which arose between the Koreans on the one hand and SCAP and the Japanese government on the other. The author first notes that SCAP's restrictions on the amount of currency and personal goods which Koreans desiring repatriation could take with them was in part responsible for the decision of approximately 600,000 Koreans to remain in Japan. He then points out that the postwar status of the Korean minority became a problematic issue for the officials in charge of the occupation. Those who refused repatriation demanded the same status granted other members of the United Nations in Japan or, at the very least, a preferential position in relation to the Japanese. SCAP, however, decreed that they would be treated as Japanese nationals for administrative purposes. Tensions between the Koreans and Japanese arose over this and over such other matters as registration and education—matters in which SCAP inevitably became involved. Furthermore, as the Koreans became increasingly active in both the Japanese and the international communist movements, SCAP came to regard them as subversive to its democratization program and took steps to dissolve Korean left-wing organizations and to suppress the left-wing Korean press in Japan. Mitchell acknowledges that many Americans were sympathetic towards the Korean minority during the months immediately following the Japanese surrender in 1945, but he concludes that SCAP's preoccupation with maintaining order and carrying out its various reform programs as well as the increasing tensions generated by the cold war quickly led to a dissipation of this sympathy and to the tendency of regarding the Koreans in Japan as a major security problem.

2262 National Academy of Sciences, Washington, D.C. Scientific Advisory Group. *Reorganization of Science and Technology in Japan: Report of the Scientific Advisory Group to the National Academy of Sciences, USA.* Mimeographed. Tokyo: 1947. xii, 44p.

The findings and recommendations of a 6-man scientific advisory group which spent 6 weeks in Japan are set forth in this mimeographed report. By way of background information the foreword presents details of the establishment of the group in mid-1947 and the texts of various letters confirming official appointments and defining the objectives of the mission. The report contains a concise description of the current status of science and technology in Japan and emphasizes the vital role of science and technology in the recovery and reconstruction of Japan. There is a brief discussion of the responsibilities of a Renewal Committee composed of Japanese scientists which worked to effect reforms in the administration of Japanese science and technology and an analysis of professional societies and the quality of university education in science and technology. Recommendations generally concern changes in the administrative structure of higher education and scientific research in Japan.

Available at the Washington National Records Center, Suitland, Maryland.

2262a Ogawa, Kiichi. " 'Women's Week' in Japan." *Democratic Japan* (Tokyo) no.11:3–4 (Mar./Apr. 1951)

Ogawa finds that while considerable effort has been expended on encouraging women to participate more fully in society as equal citizens, their level of civic consciousness remains low and their way of life is little different from what it was prior to the adoption of the new constitution with its equal-rights guarantees.

2262b Ohara, Fujiko. "Women of Japan." *Democratic Japan* (Tokyo) no.5:6, 16 (May/June 1950)

Ohara writes about the organization of a new women's movement sponsored by the Labor Ministry whose slogans are "eliminate feudalistic elements from families and workshops" and "be aware of our rights and obligations." She notes that Yamakawa Kikue, director of that ministry's Women's and Minors' Bureau, recently made a speech pointing out that despite the enactment of the Labor Standards Act, working women are still subject to unreasonable and discriminatory treatment, and rural women have not yet been emancipated from the feudal fetters of the old family system.

2263 Parrott, Lindesay. "Now a Japanese Woman Can Be a Cop." *New York Times Magazine* p.18, 56 (2 June 1946)

With postwar reforms, more opportunities are open to Japanese women. The author cites cases of women receiving equal pay with men in the police force, a woman union leader, and 39 women elected to the Diet in the first postwar election. He concludes that Japanese women are eagerly taking advantage of their new equality.

2264 ———. "Out of Feudalism: Japan's Women." *New York Times Magazine* p.10, 44 (28 Oct. 1945)

This article, partially based on an interview with Ishikawa Fusae, a leader of the feminist movement since the 1920s, describes changes in the status of Japanese women. The author characterizes the traditional role of the Japanese woman as that of an obedient, submissive wife who had no rights. This concept changed with the wartime demand for labor when women discovered that they could contribute to society outside the home. The major change, however, was psychological. Women now view themselves as full partners in marriage with equal rights. In spite of the immediate gains, the author concludes that the full realization of equal status for women will be a long process dependent on the changed attitudes of the younger generation.

2265 Penrose, Gertrude. "Reporting on Japan's Women." *Independent Woman* 27, no.11:322–24 (Nov. 1948)

The findings of a State Department liaison officer who was assigned to SCAP for 3 months' study of Japanese women's organizations are described by Gertrude Penrose in this article. Doris Cochrane, the officer, consulted with Japanese women and conducted leadership training institutes "whereby women's organizations might develop effective programs democratically drawn up by their own members." Several of Cochrane's anecdotes are related and the article concludes with an affirmation of her belief that women's organizations in Japan will be a strong factor in Japan's future democratic development.

The Reminiscences of Ai Kume. 1962. *See* no.44c.

2265a Roedel, M. A. "Arigato, Say Japanese." *Library Journal* 74:1792–95, 1806 (1 Dec. 1949)

Roedel first explains the mission and activities of the information centers maintained by SCAP's Civil Information and Education Section in Japan's 17 largest cities. These libraries proved extremely popular despite the fact that all of their holdings were in English. Roedel, who worked in the library serving the Sendai area, then devotes the remainder of his article largely to anecdotes describing the attitudes and behavior of the library's patrons—particularly their treatment of library materials, which was one of respect bordering on reverence.

2266 Sakanishi, Shio. "Women's Position and the Family System." *Annals of the American Academy of Political and Social Science* 308:130–39 (Nov. 1956)

This article begins with a brief outline of the changes in the position of women since the Meiji Restoration. The various reforms pertaining to the status of women initiated under the occupation are then summarized. The revision of the Civil Code is viewed here as "most important and far-reaching in its effects" concerning women's rights. Among its provisions those dealing with divorce are specifically noted. The author discusses the movement to revive the old system, noting particularly economic difficulties and common inheritance problems which she maintains are incorrectly attributed to the revised Civil Code. She notes the persistence and continuity of old patterns concerning marriage. The article contains a section demonstrating women's political interest and participation. Though the economic independence of women is growing, their wages are substantially lower than men's and they face many employment difficulties. Sections on family planning and on prostitution conclude the article.

2266a Salomon, Henry, Jr. "Assignment in Japan." *United States Naval Institute Proceedings* 74, no.8:973–77 (Aug. 1948)

Salomon, assistant to Professor Samuel Eliot Morison at the time that Morison was working on his multivolume *History of United States Naval Operations in World War II* (Boston: Little, Brown, 1947–62. 15v.), writes about his efforts to secure the information that would enable them to check the factual accuracy of existing accounts and to present the Japanese point of view. Throughout the article, Salomon discusses how he worked through SCAP and the Japanese Naval War Records Section and what problems he faced during his stay in Japan. In this fashion he provides interesting details as well as insights into the activities of those SCAP offices which prepared many of the historical reports on the occupation found scattered throughout this bibliography.

2266b "SCAP Favors Large Sum for Buying American Books." *Publishers' Weekly* 156:814–16 (27 Aug. 1949)

This article briefly summarizes the activities of SCAP's regional information centers and makes note of the efforts under way to increase the number of American books available to Japanese readers. SCAP reportedly plans to spend large sums to support its present library program.

2267 Shimbori, Michiya. "Comparison between Pre- and Postwar Student Movements in Japan." *Sociology of Education* 37, no.1:59–70 (Fall 1963)

Shimbori of Hiroshima University views the postwar history of the Japanese student movement in 3 stages. Intra-campus student movements, prevalent in 1945–47, concerned themselves with individual institutions, were run by local students, occurred spontaneously, and attracted the support of the majority of students on the campuses involved. Inter-campus movements, 1948–50, began when the problems were not resolved on the campuses themselves and when students from many schools began to form such cooperative groups as the Zengakuren. Finally, after 1951, extracampus activities predominated as students began to work with political parties and labor unions in various political disputes. The primary difference distinguishing the postwar students movements from their prewar predecessors, the author remarks, is the open and legal but uncohesive nature that characterized them.

2267a Smith, Jean Pauline. "Women in Japan." *Spectator* 186:807–8 (22 June 1951)

The author, a women's affairs officer in Tokyo from 1947 to 1949, finds that there has been a dramatic increase in the number of women participating in civic affairs. The inclusion of female suffrage in the new constitution, she feels, is one factor which accounts for the mushrooming growth of women's clubs and organizations nationwide. She sees this liberation of the Japanese woman as part of a larger picture of a genuine democratization process underway within Japan.

2268 Spence, Elizabeth. "What Place Women in Postwar Japan?" *Independent Woman* 35:4–5, 27 (Mar. 1956)

The author, a former civilian magazine officer for the Civil Information and Education Section of MacArthur's command, reviews the status of women in Japan. In Japan during the occupation when reform measures concerning women were introduced, the writer tells about the initial problems Japanese women faced in trying to achieve equality. She goes on to examine some of the problems Japanese women face today and the way in which they are trying to overcome them.

Supreme Commander for the Allied Powers. Monograph 54. *Reorganization of Science and Technology in Japan, 1945–September 1950.* 1952. *See* no.336.

2269 ———. Civil Information and Education Section. *Important Art Objects.* Tokyo: Religions and Cultural Resources Div., SCAP, 1948. 3v.

2270 ———. ———. *Libraries in Japan (Each Containing 3,000 Volumes or Over).* Mimeographed. rev. ed. Tokyo: SCAP, 1947. viii, 195p.

This special report, issued on 29 March 1947, provides basic data (location, year of establishment, number of volumes, visitors, and budget) on 848 public, school, and private libraries in Japan.

2271 ———. ———. *Libaries [sic] in the Kyoto–Nara–Osaka Area: Special Report Prepared by Cultural Resources Research.* Mimeographed. Tokyo: SCAP, 1947. ii, 37p.

Released on 7 August 1947, this report provides descriptive information for 54 libraries: 10 public, 4 private, and 40 operated by educational institutions.

2272 ———. ———. *Objects Designated as National Treasures: Special Report Prepared by Cultural Resources Unit, Research Branch.* Tokyo: 1948. 3v.

2273 ———. Economic and Scientific Section. *Science and Technology in Japan: Reports.* Tokyo: SCAP, Oct. 1947–Apr. 1950. 13v.

This series, numbered from 10 through 22, comprises all reports published by the Scientific and Technical Division of the Economic and Scientific Section of SCAP. It provides a wide variety of indexes, listings, and bibliographies concerning important institutions, organizations, and materials in the fields of science and technology in Japan. The complete list, which is available at the Army Library, the Pentagon, Washington, D.C., is as follows: no.10, *Scientific and Technological Societies of Japan.* pt.1 (Oct. 1947) 87p.; no.11, *Research Activities of Tokyo Shibaura Electric Company and Subsidiaries* (Nov. 1947) 47p.; no.12, *Index to Japanese Research and Development, during Period July–December 1946* (Apr. 1947); no.13, *Report on Natural Science Research under the Influence of the Japanese Ministry of Education* (Apr. 1947) 57p.; no.14, *Statistical Study of the Research Expenditures of the Ministry of Education* (Oct. 1947) 87p.; no.15, *Report on Foundational Juridical Persons: Zaidan Hojin* (June 1948) 176p.; no.16, *Natural Science Research in Leading Japanese Universities.* pt.1 (June 1949) 26p.; no.17, *Japanese Natural Science Awards* (June 1948) 32p.; no.18, *University Research Institutes* (Natural Science Research) (June 1948) 89p.; no.19, *Abstracting Program: Japanese Scientific Journals Covering the Period December 1941–1948* (Apr. 1949) 13p.; no.20, *Scientific and Technological Societies of Japan.* pt.2: *Natural Science Societies* (Dec. 1948) 185p.; no.21, *A Conspectus of Japanese Research in Environmental Psychology and Closely Related Fields* (June 1950) 180p.; no.22, *A List of Scientific and Technical Journals Currently Published in Japan* (Apr. 1950) 242p.

2274 Takeda, Kiyoko. "What Is the Mind of Japanese Youth To-day?" *Ecumenical Review* 3, no.4:393–404 (July 1951)

A discussion of the changes brought about by the occupation, the reintroduction of Western-style democracy and some of the ensuing disillusionments with it, and the role that Christianity can play in the spiritual reconstruction of Japan.

2275 Tuge, Hideomi. *Historical Development of Science and Technology in Japan.* Tokyo: Kokusai Bunka Shinkōkai (Japan Cultural Society), 1968. xv, 200p. (Japanese Life and Culture series)

Chapter 6 of this general survey—"Science under Occupation after World War II"—relates developments in the postwar Japanese scientific world to various shifts in occupation policy. Tuge points out that SCAP's initial priority was the demilitarization of Japan, and accordingly, science at first was redirected from service to the state to peaceful pursuits, with scientists being encouraged to participate in the democratization efforts. With the advent of the cold war, however, "measures were taken to suppress democratic movements in the field of science," Tuge maintains. Furthermore, "a policy was adopted of organizing scientific and technical researches in Japan . . . to render them serviceable in the global policy of the U.S.A." One consequence of this shift in policy was the deemphasis of basic and theoretical scientific work in favor of applied research. Tuge also describes in some detail the SCAP measures which affected the contributions science could make to the country's postwar economic rehabilitation.

2276 U.S. Dept. of Labor. Women's Bureau. *Advance of Women in Japan.* Washington, D.C.: 1952. 5p.

The address of Mrs. Sumiko Tanaka, chief of the Women's Section in the Japanese Labor Ministry's Women's and Minors' Bureau, dealing with the progress made by Japanese women since the end of the war. This address was delivered over N.H.K. on 5 September 1951.

2277 ———. Library Mission. *Report of the United States Library Mission to Advise on the Establishment of the National Diet Library of Japan.* Washington, D.C.: Government Printing Office, 1948. iii, 41p. (Dept. of State publication 3200; Far Eastern series 27)

The mission, organized by SCAP upon the request of the responsible committees of the National Diet, came to Tokyo on 14 December 1947 and made a series of recommendations regarding the functions and responsibilities of a National Diet Library. Their report, submitted to SCAP on 8 February 1948, includes a statement by the mission of the services which an adequate national library may be expected to render and a summary of the proposals submitted by the mission to the Diet committees as modified through discussions with the latter. The proposals pertain to the organization and administration of such a library, the scope of its collections, the principles of planning for library buildings, budgetary considerations, and the training of librarians. Appended are the National Diet Library Law and the National Diet Library Building Commission Law, both enacted on 4 February 1948, and the mission's recommendations regarding the organization of a National Diet Library given on 3 January 1948.

2277a Wagner, Edward Willett. *The Korean Minority in Japan, 1904–1950.* New York: International Secretariat, Institute of Pacific Relations, 1951. v, 108p.

This historical treatment of the Korean minority problems begins with a summary account of the early aspects of Korean migration to Japan. Wagner then studies in a detailed and comprehensive fashion the history of the Korean minority during the war years and during the first half of the occupation period, the efforts of the U.S. Military Government in Korea and of Korean government officials on behalf of the Koreans who were either seeking repatriation or were planning on remaining in Japan, and the major developments affecting Japan's Korean minority after 1948. Chapters 4–6 are of particular relevance to the scholar interested in the occupation. They touch upon such subjects as repatriation, the Korean League and other organizations, American occupation policy towards the Korean minority, the role of the Japanese vis-à-vis this minority, the deterioration of the Korean community's economic position, the suppression of various Korean organizations, and the controls imposed upon Japan's Korean community following the outbreak of the Korean War. Wagner's characterization of SCAP policy and his many comments on the impact of the occupation upon the Korean minority are both interesting and insightful. He points out, for example, that SCAP lacked a consistent, integrated policy towards the Korean community because Washington failed to provide it with any instructions in this regard other than that of permitting Koreans in Japan to return to Korea voluntarily, and because each separate occupation office took action on problems involving the Korean minority only as they came to its attention in the course of its daily work. Wagner also explains that as SCAP came to consider those Koreans who remained in Japan as Japanese nationals, the occupation authorities increasingly entrusted the Japanese government with the responsibility for the Korean community and ceased to take a direct hand in the Korean problem. The text of Wagner's study is supplemented by some very useful appendixes showing the distribution of Korean residents in Japan as well as by a bibliography which lists 68 SCAPINS issued between 10 September 1945 and 24 December 1947 applying specifically to the Korean minority in Japan.

2278 Yamakawa, Kikue. "Japanese Women under the New Constitution." *Contemporary Japan* 17:141–44 (Apr./June 1948).

A brief but useful article on the new position of women in postwar Japan. Cautiously optimistic concerning the benefits that have been bestowed upon Japanese women by the constitution, the author nonetheless points up existing factors that impede greater progress—particularly lack of political knowledge and practical experience in many fields. The article outlines the implications of such innovations as the establishment of the Women and Children's Bureau of the Ministry of Labor, the provisions of the new Labor Standards Law (Sept. 1947), improvements in the education of women, the growth of independent women's civil and social organizations throughout the country, and the effects of the revised Civil Code (Jan. 1948) and the Children's Welfare Law (May 1948).

Japanese Reactions

From the standpoint of the U.S. government one of the most unexpected aspects of the occupation was the Japanese reaction to the American presence. The overwhelming majority of the people were orderly, compliant, and, in a remarkable number of cases, positively cooperative and helpful. Against the immediate background of Japan's wartime and prewar national record this was, to say the least, surprising. It naturally gave rise to a great deal of speculation as to the genuineness and durability of such attitudes by both foreign and Japanse commentators. Studies focusing on this question have been assembled below. In addition to them many of the entries in the section containing general materials on the occupation (p.113)—especially the subsection on analyses and translations of the Japanese press (p.142)—and in the section on Japanese social organization and national character (p.611) deal in part with this problem. Also included below are a few items dealing with public opinion polls and their results.

Abegg, Lily. "Japan Reconsiders." 1955. *See* no.1906.

Allen, Lafe F. "Democracy in Japan." 1947. *See* no.477.

American Institute of Pacific Relations, ed. *Some Japanese Views on American–Japanese Relations.* 1953. *See* no. 2509.

2279 Asahina, Soh-ghen [Sōgen]. "Duty of Defeated Japan." *Contemporary Japan* 14:234–36 (Apr./Dec. 1945)

This article by the chief abbot of the Enkakuji temple in Kamakura is translated from the September 1945 issue of *Gendai.* In Asahina's opinion, the major reasons for Japan's defeat were the overwhelming power of the United States and Japan's inability to undertake a prolonged war. In addition, the Japanese authorities were overly optimistic and lacking in foresight. Their failure to involve the general public led to an overall feeling that the prosecution of the war was purely the government's responsibility. In the future, Asahina asserts, Japan should reject any notions of revenge and should encourage pacifist feelings. Furthermore, the country's educational system should be overhauled in order that it may produce a new generation of high quality statesmen who can serve Japan with foresight and vision.

Asahi Shimbun. Staff. *The Pacific Rivals: A Japanese View of Japanese–American Relations.* 1972. See no.688a.

Baba, Tsunego. "Japanese Response to Peace Treaty." 1951. See no.2364.

2280 "Banzai." *New Statesman and Nation* 43:426–27 (12 Apr. 1952)

The author reports a "brutal nip of ingratitude" in Japan on the eve of the country's return to sovereign status. He anticipates alterations in the style and content of some occupation legislation and discusses the possibility of Japan's assuming the role of manipulator of both East and West.

Benoit, Edward G. *A Study of Japanese Education as Influenced by the Occupation.* 1958. See no.2025.

2281 Bowles, Gordon T. "Postwar Trends in Japanese Attitudes toward America." *Japan Quarterly* 3:276–86 (July/Sept. 1956)

Bowles examines Japanese attitudes toward America and factors which influence the formulation of such an attitude. He discusses Japanese attitudes on the basis of 3 kinds of reactions: (1) reactions resulting from person-to-person contacts, especially with the occupation forces; (2) reactions to SCAP policies, the peace treaty, etc.; and (3) reactions to American foreign policy at the international level. Bowles lists specific incidents which caused anti-American feelings and the ways in which Japanese attitudes have changed since the end of the war.

2282 Brumbaugh, Thoburn T. "Japan Believes in Us Now." *Christian Century* 63:1434–35 (27 Nov. 1946)

The author lists 4 explanations of Japanese cooperation with occupation reform policies: (1) respect for American military power, (2) the friendliness of the American occupation troops, (3) the success of General MacArthur's leadership, and (4) a persistent fear of the Soviet Union. The new constitution and the democratization of the imperial institution are cautiously hailed as beginnings of vital change. The author concludes with a call for the Japanese Christian community to assume the leadership of a democratic Japan.

2283 Buck, Pearl. "The Good People of Japan." *United Nations World* 3:14–16 (Feb. 1949)

Buck is extremely critical of U.S. occupation policies. Her article is based on quotes from personal letters by Japanese which she feels are representative of a typical Japanese attitude of anxiety. She likens American control to prewar thought control, sees a complete reversal of democratic directives between 1945 and 1949, and anticipates the reemergence, with American aid and encouragement, of a military-controlled, war-oriented government.

2284 Busch, Noel Fairchild. "Occupation of Japan." *Horizon* 16:159–81 (Sept. 1947)

This article uses the character of the Japanese and the factors accounting for particular traits as the basis for explaining the Japanese response to the occupation and for projecting what will likely be their response after the occupation is terminated. The Japanese attitude toward defeat is examined in terms of the concepts of "face" and sincerity and their penchant for imitation. In accounting for Japanese character traits as the results of specific environmental factors, the author studies the matter of Japanese clothes and then concentrates on analyzing peculiarities of the childhood of a Japanese. He relates the Japanese adult's attitudes toward such things as food, education, and social relations to childhood conditioning. Japanese character and conduct are further examined in relation to religion, the emperor, and the *zaibatsu* —conduct which is also related to childhood conditioning. The author suggests that no true alteration of the Japanese can take place until the manner in which Japanese children are brought up is altered. Implications of this for the occupation are considered as well as ways in which the Japanese might react in a direction opposite to that intended by MacArthur. This article is an abstract from the book *Fallen Sun: A Report on Japan* (1948) (no.543).

"Can We Keep Japan's Friendship?" 1950. *See* no.619b.

2285 Cole, Allan Burnett. "Children of a Vacuum." *Pacific Spectator* 4, no.2: 153–59 (Spring 1950)

Cole gives his informal impressions gained from an international student conference held in Japan in the summer of 1949. Although Japanese students were highly critical of old ways, they also felt the loss of a psychic security which prewar ideology had supplied. The individualistic demands of democracy were too great for them and many were turning to communism. Women enjoyed their new status but could not yet feel secure in it. Japanese liberals are viewed as grateful for American reforms but critical of American materialism and anticommunism.

2286 ———, and Nakanishi Naomichi, comps. and eds. *Japanese Opinion Polls, with Socio-Political Significance, 1947–1957.* Published under the auspices of the Fletcher School of Law and Diplomacy, Tufts University, and the Roper Public Opinion Research Center, Williams College. n.p.: 1958? xv, 917p. (3v. in 1)

This collection of data was compiled from surveys made by the National Public Opinion Research Institute, the Association for the Science of Public Opinion, and major newspaper research offices. Put together initially to facilitate the analyses of studies on Japan's social democratic parties being undertaken by Cole in conjunction with George O. Totten and Cecil H. Uyehara, they obviously are also invaluable for anyone doing research on Japanese politics during the decade following the war. The collection is divided into 3 major parts. Volume 1 is devoted to questions of political support and preference, volume 2 focuses on political institutions, processes, and legislation, and volume 3 deals with military problems and Japan's foreign relations. All of the polls are presented in tabular form without any accompanying explanations except for the brief introductions to each of the volumes.

While the majority of the polls deal with the years following the termination of the occupation, there are several which are of particular interest and value to the specialist on the occupation. They include the following:

(1) polls inquiring whether people believe that the former militarists still have some power (Aug. 1946; p.282), and whether people have read the text of the new constitution (Aug. 1947; p.378) and a draft of the peace treaty (Aug. 1951; p.391);

(2) polls of public opinion concerning the constitutional provisions for the Diet, the renunciation of war (Article 9), and the retention of the emperor system; the revision of the Civil Code; and the desirability of the emperor system (all conducted in 1946–48 and found on p.427–42);

(3) the section entitled "The U.N. Occupation and Democratic Reforms" (p.480–88) containing polls on the awareness of the program to democratize the holding of securities (Apr. 1948), popular satisfaction with the land reform (July 1948), popular satisfaction with the manner in which elected governors and mayors were discharging their duties (July 1948), attitudes toward the overall value of the occupation for Japan (Apr. 1951 and May 1952), and atti-

tudes toward the recall of General MacArthur (Apr. 1951);

(4) polls determining the attitudes toward the general strike crisis of government employees and school teachers (Feb. 1947; p.498–501) and the activities of the labor unions (Mar. 1948; p.504);

(5) Japanese attitudes toward rearmament and related issues (p.560–646)—important in light of SCAP's policy of disarming Japan and of drafting a constitution that renounced war as a sovereign right;

(6) polls regarding the Russo–Japanese negotiations conducted in 1955–56 and dealing in large measure with the future status of Southern Sakhalin and the Kurile Islands (p.707–50).

The reader should note that while the Japanese conducted many polls between 1945 and 1952 that dealt with domestic issues not directly involving the occupation itself, there are relatively few polls dealing specifically with the public evaluation of SCAP policies inasmuch as this type of polling was discouraged by the occupation authorities.

2287 Coox, Alvin D. "Japanese Attitudes toward the Soviet Union." *World Affairs Quarterly* 26, no.4:338–57 (Jan. 1956)

A former visiting professor of history at Shiga National University discusses several of the factors that have shaped postwar Japanese attitudes toward the Soviet Union. They include the perennial conflict over the fisheries north of Hokkaido, the fear that American defensive measures in Japan (e.g., the maintenance of military bases on Japanese soil) may "needlessly irritate" the Russians, the continued resentment of Russia's sudden betrayal of Japan in August 1945, and the proliferation of cultural and educational contacts between the 2 countries. The author also reports on the June 1955 *Tōkyō Shimbun* poll which sought to determine Japanese sentiment over the advisability of restoring normal relations with the Soviet Union.

Cornwall, Peter G. "Japanese Political Reaction to Constitutional Revision 1945–46." 1967. *See* no. 1173.

Costello, William. *Democracy vs. Feudalism in Post-war Japan.* 1948. *See* no.546.

2288 Cousins, Norman. "They Love Us for the Wrong Reasons." *Saturday Review of Literature* 35:20–21 (19 Jan. 1952)

Some less attractive aspects of America's influence abroad are the general topic of this editorial. The author discusses the current adoption of what the young people of Japan consider to be American "social behavior." He describes the widening gulf between generations in occupied Japan whereby the older Japanese "have come to regard democracy not so much as a necessary revolution in thought and social and political conduct as a revolution in manners and morals, generally for the worse."

Crofts, Verna I. "Japan as I Saw It." 1948. *See* no.548a.

2288a Greenwood, Russell. "What Japan is Thinking." *Spectator* 179, no.6228: 585–86 (7 Nov. 1947)

As a result of observations made during his extensive travels in Japan between late 1946 and late 1947, Greenwood concludes that the ordinary Japanese citizen "seems fully determined first to accept the rule of the occupying Power and second to rebuild his country." There is a constant preoccupation with the material side of existence, but many people also are interested in the elections on both the national and local levels. How much the "newly-sown seeds of democracy" will flourish, though, depends significantly on the policies of the occupation and on the nature of the coming peace treaty. Everywhere, Greenwood notes, the Tōjō regime is thoroughly discredited, and for the moment there is very little interest in religion. The author concludes by pointing out the desire among the better-educated classes for closer relations with Great Britain, especially on a cultural level, and urges the British Council to provide appropriate educational support.

2289 Hayashi, Kentarō. "How to Approach Postwar Japanese History." *Journal of*

Social and Political Ideas in Japan 3, no. 2:67–71 (Aug. 1965); also published in German under the title "Wie ist die Nachkriegsgeschichte zu betrachten." *Kagami* 3, no.2:105–8 (1965)

In this article which was translated from the September 1964 issue of *Chūō Kōron*, Hayashi introduces a way to analyze postwar Japanese history. He feels one's understanding of history is gained through one's own experience and value consciousness. He criticizes writers like Maruyama Masao who, Hayashi feels, interprets the present world in terms of past value consciousness. Hayashi points out the different ideologies of the postwar period and the ways in which they failed to face the challenges of "reality."

2290 Henry, Jules. "Initial Reactions to the Americans in Japan." *Journal of Social Issues* 2:19–25 (Aug. 1946)

The writer describes and compares the attitudes of the Japanese people toward their American conquerors at the time of surrender and at the present time (July 1946). Discussing what he terms the "psychodynamic and politico-economic factors" which have affected such attitudes, he examines the nature of the "American monster" myth which was prevalent immediately after Japan's surrender and its disappearance during the initial stages of the occupation. According to the author, the Japanese people vented their hostility at this time not on the Americans but on their own war leaders. Finally, there is a consideration of the new image of Americans in the minds of the Japanese which the author maintains is based almost exclusively on their impressions of American troops stationed in Japan.

2291 Herzog, Peter, S.J. "Yanks in Japan: A Frontline View." *America* 74:121–22 (3 Nov. 1945)

A Catholic missionary writes of the surprise that the Japanese populace and the occupying forces both experienced upon encountering little hostility from each other.

2292 Hilgard, Ernest R. "The Enigma of Japanese Friendliness." *Public Opinion Quarterly* 10:343–48 (Fall 1946)

The author, head of the Department of Psychology at Stanford University and a member of the U.S. Education Mission to Japan, describes and attempts to explain the attitude of friendliness on the part of the Japanese people toward the occupying American troops and the Japanese lack of resentment of their former enemy. He believes this is psychologically understandable in view of the fact that the Japanese people have 2 other foci "for their aggressive and hostile feelings —turned outward upon the Japanese military and turned inward upon themselves." Moreover, in addition to this psychological explanation, he asserts that the liking for Americans is also due to the favorable impressions created by individual American servicemen upon the Japanese people.

"Interview with the First Japanese Editor to Visit U.S. since 1941." 1948. *See* no.556.

James, Weldon. "Democracy: So Sorry." 1947. *See* no.503.

2293 "Japan Adrift." *Fortnightly* 172:93–98 (Aug. 1949)

In this article, the author reviews the psychological and emotional adjustments that were demanded of young Japanese men who fought for their nation and who endured her defeat, and he underscores the sense of aimlessness and uprootedness that they experienced. To insure that the friends and associates from whom he derived his impressions and opinions remain anonymous, the author fictionalizes his narrative and remains anonymous himself.

2294 "Japan Blames U.S. for Troubles." *U.S. News and World Report* 28:23–24 (28 Apr. 1950)

An article emphasizing increasing Japanese dissatisfaction with U.S. policies in the following areas: the restriction of trade with Communist China, continued interference in domestic Japanese affairs by U.S. officials, and the increasing military entanglement of Japan with the United States.

2295 "Japan Looks Back on the Occupation: A Symposium of Japanese Views." Tr. by Victor (Masaru) Otake and ed. by Douglas G. Haring. *Far Eastern Survey* 22:26–32 (25 Feb. 1953)

Numerous educators, businessmen, and politicians reflect on Japan's gains and losses during the American occupation. This symposium on the occupation first appeared in a special issue of the Tokyo magazine *Bungei Shunjū* of 5 June 1952.

2295a "The Japanese Accepted Change Calmly." *Great Britain and the East* 65:41–42 (Nov. 1949)

A great transformation has taken place as a result of the war and the occupation. While there are still signs of destruction in the suburbs, downtown Tokyo has been completely cleaned up and rebuilt and is swarming with American officers and civilians. The Japanese have responded to the commercial opportunities posed by the needs of the large number of Americans within the Tokyo area and have been very friendly and cooperative with the occupation forces. Japan presents a "peaceful and orderly spectacle" to the casual observer and the people appear to be docile and disciplined. Much of this change, however, is superficial in nature. At heart the Japanese are still very nationalistic in spirit, and while there are few signs of want, the country is still beset by enormous economic problems and remains dependent on United States aid.

Kawai, Kazuo. *Japan's American Interlude*. 1960. See no.714.

2296 ———. "The New Anti-Americanism in Japan." *Far Eastern Survey* 22:153–57 (Nov. 1953)

Kawai, former editor of the *Nippon Times*, points out that anti-Americanism thus far is hardly more than a mild inclination, but under assiduous cultivation by the Communists it could grow into something dangerous. He noted that Japanese criticisms of America are directed at specific occupation reforms and policies and that the United States, in dealing with these complaints, will have to study the Japanese more carefully and win their cooperation.

2297 Kent, Beryl F. "Letters to General MacArthur." *Army Information Digest* 3:20–25 (Dec. 1948)

A staff officer in the News Division of the Far East Command's Public Information Office presents an informal summary of the letters received by General MacArthur from Japanese citizens since the beginning of the occupation. After presenting sections from several of the more colorful ones and indicating the usual kinds of requests made to SCAP, he concludes that "the vague, lengthy and highly imaginative letters of an earlier day are being supplanted, increasingly, by logical, succinct messages which stick to the point."

Kerlinger, Frederick N. *The Development of Democratic Control in Japanese Education: A study of Attitude Change in Shikoku, 1948–1949*. 1953. See no.2076.

2298 Kitani, Tadashi. "Attitudes towards America." *Japan Quarterly* 3:27–35 (Jan./Mar. 1956)

Writing about the attitudes of the Japanese people towards Americans, the author examines factors which he feels cause anti-American feelings in Japan. He writes about the trouble caused by the stationing of American troops in Japan, the problems of the expansion of military bases, American-caused deaths, and "fraternization." Kitani also discusses the role of the Japanese left-wing movement in fostering anti-American feeling and the effect of the war upon the Japanese psychology. He concludes that the so-called "anti-American feeling" is actually a feeling of insecurity and helplessness.

2299 Knutson, Andie L. "Japanese Opinion Surveys: The Special Need and the Special Difficulties." *Public Opinion Quarterly* 9:313–19 (Fall 1945)

Convinced that a real understanding of Japanese public opinion is a prerequisite for a successful occupation, the author of this article defines and discusses some of the difficulties associated with conducting opinion polls in Japan. He attributes the most formidable problems to the following facts: (1) there is a lack of background data and a dearth of meaningful popular surveys in the prewar and wartime periods, (2) there are enormous language difficulties to be overcome, (3) there are uniquely Japanese cultural and religious habits that the interviewer must be aware of to obtain valid information, and (4) there is the problem of selecting an interviewer who will be trusted by those interviewed. Although polling in Japan is fraught with difficulties, the author believes it will yield invaluable insights into the Japanese character and will help to make the occupation more successful.

May, Henry F., Jr. "MacArthur Era, Year One." 1946. See no.443.

Morley, James W. "The First Seven Weeks." 1970. See no.394.

2299a Murdock, John. "Black Curtain." *Eastern World* 2, no.1:18 (Jan. 1948)

SCAP's discovery of a "hidden government" working behind a *kuromaku* (black curtain) and said to be planning the overthrow of many occupation reforms and posttreaty stipulations has prompted D. B. Copeland, the Australian Minister in China, to express his hope that the conclusion of an early peace settlement with Japan would not result in a complete and immediate withdrawal of the occupation forces. According to Charles Kades, deputy chief of the Government Section of SCAP, these anti-democratic forces are being supported by people in all walks of life—farmers, admirals, generals, former millionaires and kamikaze troops, and even pickpockets and ordinary Japanese spies.

Naoi, Takeo. "Japan: 'Orphan in the Pacific'." 1951. See no.967a.

Natori, Jonosuke. "Commentary on the Shoup Taxation Reform." 1949. See no.1685.

2300 Ōi, Atsushi. "Anti-Americanism in Japan." *Reporter* 10:30–35 (16 Feb. 1954)

Ōi Atsushi, a former Japanese navy captain and the editor of a Tokyo magazine, explains that the first signs of anti-Americanism appeared as a result of developments outside rather than inside Japan. With the loss of China to communism, indications of American weakness in the face of aggressive Soviet moves, and the Korean War, American prestige declined and doubt gradually became dominant in Japanese thinking. A peace movement advocating a permanent pacifist reorientation of Japanese policy soon became the most effective agent in spreading anti-American ideas.

Parrott, Lindesay. "GI's Are Great Guys: Yanks Make a Hit with the Kids of Japan." 1946. See no.912.

"Party Comments on Soviet Peace Memorandum." 1951. See no.2411.

2301 Passin, Herbert. "The Development of Public Opinion Research in Japan." *International Journal of Opinion and Attitude Research* 5:20–30 (Spring 1951)

Passin examines the emergence of public opinion research in Japan, which was designed to record attitudinal changes among the Japanese people. The historic Japanese idea that public opinion was to be controlled rather than measured is examined within the context of an authoritarian, "thought controlled" society in which all nonauthorized expressions of opinion were suppressed. The author contends that "the democratic atmosphere created by the occupation has resulted in a widespread feeling among both government officials and the people at large that knowledge of public opinion is important for democratic government," and relates aspects of the revival of social science and public opinion research. Such things as the lack of methodological and technical sophistication and the contributions of government-sponsored agencies, private opinion institutes, and national and prefectural news agencies are covered. The article is a good, semi-technical treatment of postwar developments in public opinion research and in social science methodology in general and offers insights in the permanent psychological effects of occupation techniques of Westernization and the inculcation of "democratic" modes of thought.

"Re-examination of Post-war Legislations." 1952. See no.682a.

The Reminiscences of Ai Kume. 1962. See no.44c.

The Reminiscences of Douglas W. Overton. 1960. See no.44h.

Sayre, John N. "Miracle of Reconciliation." 1950. See no.682a.

Scalapino, Robert A. *What Trends Will Emerge in Post-MacArthur Japan?* 1951. See no.977.

2302 Seligmann, Albert L., and Gordon D. Clark. "Public Opinion in Japan." *Columbia Journal of International Affairs* 2:83–87 (Winter 1948)

A brief and informal discussion of what the authors consider to be popular Japanese attitudes toward the occupation forces and toward the social and political changes wrought in their country by the occupation. Particular issues considered include the emperor's position and the matter of reparations payments.

Shiba, Kimpei. *I Cover Japan.* 1952. See no.683.

Splane, Russell. "Our Far-Flung Correspondents: SPUSA." 1948. See no. 977b.

Supreme Commander for the Allied Powers. Civil Information and Education Section. *Special Reports.* 1946–1950. See no.270.

2303 ———. ———. Public Opinion and Sociological Research Div. *Current Japanese Public Opinion Surveys.* Tokyo: SCAP, 29 May 1948–19 Mar. 1949. nos. 1–19.

A publication of the Civil Information and Education Section of SCAP concerned with the analysis of surveys on Japanese attitudes toward 19 significant current issues in 1948–1949. The surveys analyzed were conducted by various Japanese public opinion polling agencies such as the Cabinet Inquiry Office (Naikaku Shingishitsu), the Association for Public Opinion Science (Yoron Kagaku Kyōkai), the Nagasue Public Opinion Research Institute (Nagasue Yoron Kenkyūjo), the Public Opinion Room of the *Asahi* newspaper, and other newspapers and news agencies. These surveys are critically evaluated primarily in terms of the general reliability of their interviewing techniques and findings. Analyses of the surveys vary in length, ranging from 4 to 25 pages. While the majority evaluate individual surveys, some few report on several surveys that concern the same topic. The analyses include the kind of survey undertaken, its dates, the survey agency (or agencies), and a summary of the findings of the survey, as well as a discussion of the reliability of the findings, the significance of the findings, and a critical evaluation of the survey. Survey findings are generally considered reliable. The surveys study the attitudes of Japanese toward such topics as: the Ashida cabinet, the emperor system, postwar educational reforms, urban consumer problems, labor union activities, land reclamation, and currency reform. These reports are continued in revised form in another publication of the Civil Information and Education Section, entitled *Survey Series* (no.2304).

Current Japanese Public Opinion Surveys are available on microfilm at the National Archives, Washington, D.C.

2304 ———. ———. ———. *Survey Series.* Tokyo: SCAP, 22 Jan. 1949–2 Feb. 1951.

This publication, which is available

on micofilm from the National Archives, Washington, D.C., was designed to provide information for the use of SCAP and the Civil Affairs Section of the Eighth Army military government teams. Two kinds of survey studies are analyzed. The first are surveys conducted by Japanese polling agencies; the second are surveys conducted by the Public Opinion and Sociological Research Division of SCAP either independently or in cooperation with other organizations. The latter are classified as "Divisional Public Opinion Surveys." The Civil Information and Education Section surveys were not intended to determine the reliability of the techniques and findings used, as was the case with the division's earlier publication, *Current Japanese Public Opinion Surveys* (no.2303). Rather, they provide new information and attempt to evaluate the social and political circumstances of Japan. The analyses of Japanese polls vary in length from 8 to 24 pages and cover the following 5 subjects: basic attitudes toward foreign countries, the population problem, the independent enterpriser and his income tax, reactions to postwar changes, and attitudes toward Japan's role in the cold war. The division's own surveys vary from 12 to 57 pages in length and treat Japanese attitudes toward traffic safety, the labor movement, the problems of working women, agricultural problems, and various international questions.

2305 ———. ———. ———. *Unpublished Reports*. Mimeographed. 1948–49.

These mimeographed reports were prepared by the Civil Information and Education Section and are either preliminary summaries of public opinion surveys that were later published or special reports that were never intended for publication but were restricted for use within the SCAP organization. Ranging from 5 to 15 pages in length, they provide background information and chart popular reaction to a wide variety of issues including the Densan strike of 1948, the efficiency of government services, the salaries of government workers, the content of particular films, the experiences of unemployed persons in the Tokyo area, and the forthcoming peace conference.

Available at the Washington National Records Center, Suitland, Maryland.

2306 Tatsuki, Yasuo. *General Trend of Japanese Opinion Following the End of the War: Based Especially on Public Opinion Surveys*. Tokyo: Japan Institute of Pacific Studies, 1948. 54p. (Pacific Studies series)

Tatsuki presents 7 surveys carried out by Japanese newspapers on matters of political, economic, and social significance. Two of these deal with the popularity of the Yoshida cabinet; the remainder survey popular opinion with regard to the Katayama cabinet, the new constitution, the adequacy of the government's steps to curb inflation, the SCAP prohibition of a general strike by government workers on 1 February 1947, and the abolition of the concept of "household" (*ie*) in the revised Civil Code. The survey covering the constitution, Tatsuki notes, showed overwhelming popular support for retaining the emperor, for the inclusion of Article 9 renouncing war, and for a bicameral legislature. In the other surveys, the majority of those queried expressed support for all the subjects in question.

2306a Taylor, George E. "The Japanese State of Mind." *Virginia Quarterly Review* 29, no.2:174–86 (Spring 1953)

Taylor's study of the views and concerns of Japanese intellectuals during the months immediately following the end of the occupation period opens with the author's assertion that the formation of close ties between Japan and the United States in political, economic, and military matters has not been accompanied by "a corresponding intellectual and emotional intimacy." Japan's intellectuals cooperated with the occupation during its initial stages when SCAP sought to rid the country of its militaristic heritage and when the prestige of democracy was high. The subsequent peace treaty, security pact, and drive for rearmament, however, have alienated many of the writers and thinkers who are now charging that the Japanese government and the American authorities have returned to their normal reactionary policies. These intellectuals, many of whom have considerable influence over public opinion, are strongly opposed to rearmament and the revision of Article 9 in the postwar constitution and hold the United States responsible for their fear that the militarists may be able to return to power. General MacArthur's statement that Japan was America's first line of defense in the Pacific has only served to encourage their general suspicion of the United States. In addition, Taylor explains, these same intellectuals tend to hold the occupation authorities responsible for the fact that their economic position in postwar Japan is relatively very much worse than before World War II. It is important, therefore, to reestablish the faith of the intellectuals in the future of democracy within Japan while time still permits and to convince them that "in supporting rearmament we are building an army to defend and not to destroy democratic institutions."

Telberg, Ina. "The Japanese State of Mind." 1951. *See* no.2162.

2306b Thayer, James T. "Japanese Opinion on the Far Eastern Conflict." *Public Opinion Quarterly* 15:76–88 (Spring 1951)

Thayer's article is a summary of some research undertaken by SCAP's Public Opinion and Sociological Research Division at the request of the U.S. Department of State and the Information Division of SCAP's Civil Information and Education Section. The study consisted of a series of surveys on the reactions of selected Japanese citizens to the changing international situation. While it was clear that most Japanese were friendly towards the United States, the surveys revealed the Japanese willingness to recognize the possible necessity of coming to terms with both the People's Republic of China and the Soviet Union. Attitudes toward such an issue as the maintenance of American military bases in Japan after the occupation indicated sharp differences of opinion among the general population. Most respondents also displayed a sober, self-interested, nationalist attitude particularly as the fortunes of the war changed in Korea.

2307 Tomikawa, Sōji. *Impact of Public Opinion on the Postwar Administration of Japan: Problems Connected with the Supplying of Facilities and Areas for Use by United States Forces.* Ph.D. dissertation, Syracuse Univ., 1966. 375p. (Abstracted in *Dissertation Abstracts* 27: 1418A [1966]; University Microfilms order no.66–9868)

Tomikawa is concerned primarily with the influence of public opinion upon the Japanese government during the period 1952–64, and concentrates particularly on public reactions to U.S. bases on Japanese soil. He examines the pre-World War II and occupation periods only as historical background for his analysis. He notes that in contrast to the prewar period, especially the late 1930s, when there was unquestioning popular compliance with government regulations and policy, the occupation period witnessed a great political awakening among Japanese citizens. Public opinion had considerable influence on the government.

U.S. Dept. of State. *Out Messages.* Jan. 1950–Apr. 1951. *See* no.672.

———. ———. Historical Div. *Foreign Relations of the United States, 1947.* v.6, *The Far East.* 1972. *See* no. 203b.

U.S. Strategic Bombing Survey. Morale Div. *The Effects of Strategic Bombing on Japanese Morale.* 1947. *See* no. 157.

Van Der Water, Marjorie. *Psychology in Japan.* 1945. *See* no.412.

"Views on Peace and Security: A Symposium." 1951. *See* no.2439b.

2307a Walker, Gordon W. "Japan: Introspection." *Christian Science Monitor* magazine section p.2 (1 May 1948)

Walker finds that while Japanese thought is undergoing considerable ferment and rapid change, Japanese intellectuals are tending to confine their efforts to self-criticism and are producing nothing by way of new constructive ideas or true ideological transformation. At the same time, however, he does note that they are demonstrating a healthy skepticism about traditional Japanese ideology and leadership as well as about SCAP's optimistic judgments on the progress being made in reeducation and democratization.

2308 Waln, Nora. "As Japanese See Themselves." *Saturday Evening Post* 220:15–17, 147–53 (20 Mar. 1948)

Nora Waln, a correspondent attached to General MacArthur's headquarters, gives a personal glimpse of a rural Japanese family and the impact of the occupation on their lives. She notes that while they were not ashamed that they had been loyal to their emperor and to the leaders of the army, they were ready to accept defeat and its consequences.

2308a ———. "What the Japanese Think of Us." *Saturday Evening Post* 221:26–27, 126–29 (30 Apr. 1949)

Waln bases her article on a series of conversations with Japanese women from all walks of life. Among her more interesting interviewees are a woman repatriated from Dairen (Manchuria), who offers a description of life under Soviet occupation; a woman of academic background whose husband was jailed on several occasions for violating presurrender thought-reform regulations; and the empress, who expresses gratitude for the protection and guidance given Japan by the occupation. Most of the women are positively inclined toward the occupation and toward Americans. They are also free with their criticisms, however, and often stress the contradiction between American statements about racial equality and the reality of American racism.

2309 Willoughby, Charles A. "Occupation of Japan and Japanese Reaction." *Military Review* 26:3–8 (June 1946)

This article by the assistant chief of staff of SCAP's government section first summarizes the early history of the occupation in general terms, emphasizing the smooth and rapid establishment of Allied control in Japan. This is followed by a discussion of the reactions to the occupation discernible in various quarters of Japanese society including the imperial household, the press, the government, the armed forces, industry, the police, educators, and religious leaders. Also included are a few comments on the occupation of Korea, which Willoughby says "has not been on the even keel as noted in Japan." His remarks on the occupation of Japan, by contrast, are uniformly positive and optimistic and conclude by asserting that "the principles of democracy are beginning to make themselves felt throughout the land." It should be noted, however, that one of Willoughby's introductory paragraphs strongly suggests that the article was at least partially a reaction to adverse foreign criticism of the occupation, which the author felt resulted from the failure of both the press and the general public to appreciate the range and character of the Allied efforts to reform Japan.

Yoshida, Shigeru. *Japan's Decisive Century, 1867–1967.* 1967. *See* no.768.

Termination of the Occupation

There were a number of conflicting viewpoints as to how long the occupation should last and the manner in which it should be terminated. Pressed by General MacArthur, the United States made a first endeavor to bring about a general treaty of peace with Japan and an end to the occupation as early as the spring of 1947. Others were of the opinion, however, that any occupation that lasted less than a generation at minimum would be useless. It was not until 1950–51 in the midst of the Korean and cold wars that it was possible to gain sufficient agreement among a majority of the former Allies to permit the negotiation of the actual peace treaty. It was finally signed by forty-nine of the fifty-two nations attending the San Francisco Conference on 8 September 1951. It took effect on 28 April 1952, thus bringing the occupation to a close some six years and eight months after the formal surrender of Japan on 2 September 1945.

The negotiation of the peace treaty in combination with the implications of the Korean and cold wars posed in acute fashion the question of how to assure the future security of a still-disarmed Japan against external—or even internal—aggression. In practice it was done through the simultaneous signing at San Francisco of a Mutual Security Treaty between Japan and the United States. Associated with this agreement was the entire question of the continued presence in Japan of American armed forces and the legitimacy, necessity, and utility of some degree of defensive rearmament on the part of Japan. Still another related problem centered about how Japan was to manage her reentry into a postwar international community that was still in many cases hostile or at least suspicious.

All of these developments began and gathered mass and form during the occupation period proper. But since they all focus on the general problem of terminating the occupation, it has seemed useful to classify them separately below. They are also treated with somewhat less specificity and detail in a number of the entries set forth in the 1945—1953–72 sections of the calendar of general commentaries (p.152).

2310   Termination of the Occupation

The Peace Treaty, 1947-72

The first authoritative suggestion that the time had come for the negotiation of a peace treaty with Japan and, consequently, for the end of the occupation originated with General MacArthur in March 1947. This initiative was pursued by the Department of State but quickly foundered for lack of even a modicum of agreement among the powers most immediately concerned. Discussions of the subject continued at a variety of levels, however, and became serious once more with the assignment in May 1950 of John Foster Dulles to handle the making of such a treaty on behalf of the United States. The ensuing negotiations consumed some fifteen months before the signature of the Treaty of San Francisco on 8 September 1951.

The literature relating to the entire peace treaty issue has been assembled below. It has been thought most useful to arrange it chronologically according to the period with which the item in question is primarily concerned. If the coverage extends to more than a single year, the item has been filed under the latest year concerned. This subject is also treated in a number of the entries in the section containing general materials (p.113), especially for 1947 (p.178), 1950 (p.215), 1951 (p.222), and 1952 (p.231), and the section on the international aspects of the occupation (p.260). Other related entries will be found in the two sections immediately succeeding this one.

1947

2310 "Australia and the Japanese Treaty." *Economist* 153:311–12 (23 Aug. 1947)

Australia's role during and particularly after the war is described in this brief article. The nation's attitudes toward the great powers are described with particular emphasis upon the USSR's and the United States' policies in Japan. There is an amusing but informative discussion of the occupation experience of the Australian member of the Allied Council for Japan as well as of the role of Australian Minister for External Affairs Herbert Evatt. The article concludes by outlining Australia's present policy towards Japan and discussing several important political and economic issues related to Japan that concern the Australians.

2311 Bohlen, Charles E. "Eleven-Power Conference on Japanese Peace Treaty Suggested." *Department of State Bulletin* 17:395 (24 Aug. 1947)

The text of an *aide-mémoire* presented by Bohlen, counselor of the State Department, to Semyon K. Tsarapkin, chargé d'affaires of the Soviet embassy in Washington, on 13 August 1947. It acknowledges the Soviet request that the question of a conference regarding a peace treaty with Japan be examined by the Council of Foreign Ministers composed of representatives from the USSR, China, Great Britain, and the United States. However, in the light of the discussion which took place at Potsdam regarding an eventual peace treaty, the United States feels such action by the council is not authorized or required. The United States recommends that a peace settlement be considered by a larger group than the council—one which would include the 11 members of the Far Eastern Commission.

2312 "British Commonwealth Conference on the Japanese Peace Settlement." *Current Notes in International Affairs* 18:433–52 (Aug. 1947)

An Australian report on the British Commonwealth Conference on the Japanese Peace Settlement held in Canberra from 26 August through 2 September 1947. It gives a full list of delegates, advisers, and staff members as well as the full texts of the opening and closing speeches made by participating delegations. The agenda is also provided. The conference was attended by Australia, Burma, Canada, India, New Zealand, Pakistan, South Africa, and the United Kingdom. The delegates exchanged views and reached broad agreement on the major policy issues presented by a future peace treaty with Japan. The nature of the proceedings and the machinery for a peace settlement, the enforcement of such a settlement, the territorial, political, and economic provisions of such a treaty, and the form of the peace settlement were discussed. No summary statement of the conference results is given in this report. However, the gist of the conference decisions is given in press releases issued daily during the conference period. These press releases are reprinted in the appendix of this issue on pages 483–87.

2313 "The British Commonwealth Conference on the Peace Settlement with Japan." *Current Notes on International Affairs* 18:376–77 (June/July 1947)

A short statement explaining the reasons for which Australia has proposed a preliminary conference of British Commonwealth nations to discuss problems related to the Japanese peace settlement. The Australian government here emphasizes the importance of meeting in Canberra because of the important position of Australia in Pacific affairs. The conference was called for 26 August 1947.

2314 "Chinese Views on Japanese Peace Treaty: Joint Memorandum of Control Yuan Members." *China Magazine* 17: 22–29 (Nov. 1947)

Sets forth 2 recommendations to the Chinese government by domestic groups concerning the proposed Japanese peace treaty. The first is a 15-point plan adopted by the Resident Committee of the People's Political Council on 23 September. The second is a joint memorandum prepared by the Control Yuan on 15 September. Both stress the need for a powerful Chinese role in treaty negotiations preferably involving a veto over all decisions. They stress that the imperial system lay at the heart of Japanese aggressions and insist on its total abolition. Both plans support the territorial restrictions outlined in the Cairo Declaration, insist on absolute Japanese disarmament and the removal of military potential by the restriction of Japanese industrial output to 1928 base levels, and emphasize the need for extensive reparations, particularly to China. The People's Political Council plan advocates an Allied occupation of Japan for at least 30 years.

2314a Costello, William. "Report from Tokyo." *New Republic* 116, no.13:28–29 (31 Mar. 1947)

MacArthur's completely unexpected announcement at a press-club luncheon that he believes the time has come to withdraw the Allied occupation force from Japan and to permit the Japanese to undertake their own economic recovery has led to immediate and major repercussions. Many people in SCAP's General Headquarters contend that the political, economic, and social reforms ordered by SCAP still exist principally on paper, that the cabinet, the bureaucracy, and big business are stalling and hope to avoid carrying out the various reforms, and that democracy has yet to take root in Japan. Costello, a CBS correspondent in Tokyo, attributes MacArthur's statements to the supreme commander's unwillingness to assume responsibility for Japan's economic woes or to take command of the country's economic recovery and his realization that an economic collapse—something which could occur at almost any moment—would tarnish his illustrious reputation.

Council on Foreign Relations. "American Responsibilities in the Far East: 1. The Occupation of Japan." 1947. *See* no.491.

2314b "Early Peace with Japan." *Collier's* 120:90 (4 Oct. 1947)

This editorial concurs with the opinion held by General MacArthur and others that a peace treaty with Japan should be concluded as quickly as possible. Now is the time to do so, it argues, for occupation and relief costs to the United States are mounting and it seems that the majority of the Japanese people have already come to trust and admire the Americans. A longer occupation could begin to use up that reservoir of good will.

2315 "International Affairs: Statement by the Minister for External Affairs, Rt. Hon. H. V. Evatt, to the House of Representatives, 6th June, 1947." *Current Notes on International Affairs* 18:378–405 (June/July 1947)

Evatt, the Australian foreign minister, reports to Parliament on developments in international affairs relating to the United Nations and its specialized agencies, conditions in Europe, a new U.S. policy called the "Truman Doctrine," the Antarctic, and the situation in the Pacific and the Far East. On the last point he calls for Australia's increasing its responsibilities in the region, stresses the importance of a coming British Commonwealth conference on the Japanese peace settlement, and reports that a preparatory working group for the Pacific settlement is making a close study of Australia's policies with respect to a Japanese peace treaty. He also lays out general principles for such a treaty. He rejects the Far Eastern Commission as a peace-making agency, claiming that it was set up to deal only with occupation policies. He also states Australian opposition to Japanese whaling in Antarctic waters but mentions that Australia does not press for reparations from Japan "which would cripple her economy."

2316 "International Affairs: Statement to the House of Representatives by the Minister for External Affairs, the Rt. Hon. H. V. Evatt, 26th February, 1947." *Current Notes on International Affairs* 18:109–30 (Feb. 1947)

In an address to Parliament Evatt covers a wide range of international problems. Subjects revelant to the occupation of Japan include Australia's support of the UN Security Council's decision regarding the future of the Japanese mandated islands in the Southwest Pacific, a proposed general outline for a peace settlement with Japan, an evaluation of occupation policy, and an assertion of Australia's right to participate fully in any decisions regarding a peace treaty with Japan. Evatt points out that Australia has contributed greatly to Allied war efforts and to the control of Japan and that Australia's basic principles for a peace settlement with Japan are security in the Pacific and a democratic form of government for Japan. He also argues for an early peace conference of Pacific nations to deal with the overall settlement with Japan that "could review and determine the time and extent of the necessary occupation" after a peace treaty has been signed.

2317 "International Affairs: The Minister of External Affairs, Rt. Hon. H. V. Evatt, in the House of Representatives, 6 March 1947, Concluding a Debate on International Affairs." *Current Notes on International Affairs* 18:184–94 (Mar. 1947)

Evatt here expresses the urgent necessity for an early and satisfactory peace settlement with Japan and for Australia to play a leading part in framing the peace treaty. In stressing Australian participation in the peace settlement, he criticized Big Power domination of the decisions regarding Japan but supported the United States' assumption of trusteeship over the former Japanese mandated territories. He also praised the achievements of General MacArthur in Japan although with some reservations on the Japanese relinquishment of militarism to the degree claimed by MacArthur.

2317a "Japan in the Far East." *New Statesman and Nation* 34:203 (13 Sept. 1947)

Focusing on the recently held Canberra conference and the coming Washington conference—both of which deal with the terms of a peace treaty designed to end the state of war with Japan—the author points out some of the differences in positions taken by the United States on the one hand and the various Allies on the other. He expresses concern for the American neglect of Allied interests and argues as well that the Washington conference proceedings would be unrealistic if they did not include as participants the governments of Indonesia, Vietnam, and the two Koreas and representatives of the Chinese Communist Party.

Kern, Harry F. "Trouble in Japan: How the Struggle to Win the Peace Now Threatens the Success of the American Occupation." 1947. See no.507.

2318 ———. "The U.S. Answer to Russia: A Revived Japan." *Newsweek* 30:38 (4 Aug. 1947)

According to the author of this article, the foreign editor of *Newsweek*, the presence of the Soviet Union in peace treaty negotiations with Japan is not a necessity. He believes that the response of the Soviet government to the continuation of these negotiations without a Soviet representative would only take the form of an increase in Communist-sponsored strikes within Japan. Kern discusses the possibility of Japan's becoming a buffer state in light of the growing Communist menace in China. He also notes the possibility of Japan's being rearmed with American help and how such an act could threaten Soviet security in Siberia east of Lake Baikal. He comments that the possibility of Japanese remilitarization is viewed with disfavor by other Pacific nations as well, particularly Australia.

2319 Levi, Werner. "Australia and the Peace with Japan." *Far Eastern Survey* 16:234–37 (26 Nov. 1947)

Australian interest in concluding a peace treaty with Japan is delineated, and the Australian aversion to permitting Japanese rearmament and to encouraging a strong, revitalized, Japanese economy are examined. Levi discusses Australia's attitude toward a treaty in the context of her maneuvering for a position of leadership in Pacific affairs within the Commonwealth.

2320 "MacArthur Proposal to Let UN Rule Japan: Reactions of Press." *United States News* 22:28 (28 Mar. 1947)

This collection of editorial comments concerns MacArthur's statement that the time has come to conclude a peace treaty with Japan and substitute UN control for military occupation. The papers represented range from the *Lancaster* (Penn.) *New Era* to the *Washington Post*. While all acknowledge MacArthur's expert knowledge of Japan, most question the rapidity with which he is willing to restore independence to an ex-enemy. Some newspapers also mention the danger of a Communist take-over if the United States leaves Japan.

2320a "MacArthur's Gadfly." *New Republic* 117:8–9 (28 July 1947)

This article briefly analyzes the reasons behind the U.S. State Department's effort to call an FEC conference on 19 August 1947 to discuss the Allied peace treaty with Japan. The effort failed because of a conflict with a British Commonwealth conference on the same subject already scheduled for 26 August. The article suggests that the United States had hoped that the Commonwealth conference might be postponed, for the United States wished to get discussions underway before Australian Foreign Minister Herbert Evatt had the opportunity to detail his objections to MacArthur's occupation policies in a well-publicized forum.

2321 Markov, M. "Drafting the Peace Treaty with Japan." *New Times* no.35:7–10 (27 Aug. 1947)

The Soviet view of American efforts to negotiate a peace treaty with Japan is outlined in this article. Affirming that all 4 great powers defeated imperialist Japan and have a vital interest in the Far Eastern peace settlement, the author bitterly criticizes the unilateral action of the United States as a move "to protect the narrow grasping interests of the

American monopolies in that part of the world." The American insistence that all 11 nations of the Far Eastern Commission participate in the negotiation of a treaty and that decisions be taken on the basis of a majority of votes are also reviled. The author concludes by stating that such an arrangement would be a gross violation of the Potsdam Agreement.

2322 Michael, Franz H. "Peace Arrangements for the Pacific Area." *Proceedings of the Institute of World Affairs* 21:149–55 (1946)

The actual policies of the occupation are discussed in the light of presurrender proposals and declarations concerning this matter. The problems regarding treatment of the Pacific area are considered as they fall into 2 categories: those problems related to the Japanese state itself and those dealing with the territories of the former Japanese empire. The author presents a concise description of the postwar treatment of Japan as elaborated in the Cairo Declaration of 1 December 1943, the United Nations charter of 22 June 1945, and the Potsdam Declaration of 26 July 1945, and also briefly discusses the implication of the Russo-Chinese treaty of 26 August 1945 with regard to Japan's postwar status.

2322a Morito, Tatsuo. "Establishment of a Peaceful State." *Contemporary Japan* 15:109–17 (Jan./Apr. 1946)

This article by a former professor of law at Tokyo University originally appeared in the January 1946 issue of *Kaizō*. The author first defines a "peaceful state" as one which either cannot or does not desire to wage war. Japan is certainly unable to undertake another war at the moment, but how can her pacifism be insured? According to Morito, she first must become economically independent. Secondly, the Japanese must believe that peace is the social idea and that it is definitely feasible at the present time. Furthermore, a genuine peace movement free of ideological bias must be promoted. Finally, the Japanese must establish democracy and a socialist economy and carry out a cultural revolution in order that Japan's international role will be that of leading the smaller, weaker nations toward peace and the renunciation of war.

Naoi, Takeo. "Japan Views the Peace." 1951. See no.2408a.

2323 New Zealand. Dept. of External Affairs. *Japanese Peace Settlement: Report on British Commonwealth Conference, Canberra, 26 August—2 September 1947, and Comments and Proposals Regarding New Zealand Policy towards Certain Issues of the Japanese Peace Settlement.* Wellington: Government Printer, 1947. 36p. (Dept. of External Affairs publication 38)

A Commonwealth conference was proposed by the Australian government and held in Canberra from 26 August to 2 September 1947 with 8 participating nations. It was intended to discuss on an informal basis the main points of a future peace treaty with Japan. This publication presents the report of the New Zealand delegation to the conference submitted to Parliament upon its return, together with comments and proposals regarding New Zealand's policy toward certain aspects of the Japanese peace settlement. The documents stress New Zealand's security interests in the settlement, the interconnection between welfare and security, the posttreaty supervision of Japan, and the relationship between the Japanese settlement and the United Nations.

2324 Parrott, Lindesay. "Japan Still Worships at Shinto Shrines." *New York Times Magazine* p.11, 20–21 (10 Aug. 1947)

With talk that a peace treaty will soon be forthcoming, the author questions whether Japan is ready for independence physically, economically, and psychologically. He answers a qualified yes to all 3. The treaty must be realistic and recognize Japan's need for help in keeping its economy and political system stable. Because of its strategic importance for the western Pacific, some provision must be made for Japan's posttreaty defense. He sees the 3 main dangers facing Japan as a powerful tendency to swing back to an old-style regime, the threat of communism, and the lack of competent leaders who really understand democracy.

2324a Patch, Buel W. "Peace with Japan." *Editorial Research Reports* v.2 1947: 683–705 (19 Sept. 1947)

Divided into 3 sections, this report is a straightforward, factual account designed primarily for journalists. Section 1, entitled "Coming Conference on Japanese Treaty," discusses American proposals for an 11-nation conference involving the states represented on the Far Eastern Commission, Soviet objections and the issue of voting procedure, questions raised by possible Soviet refusal to sign a peace treaty, and the advantages as well as disadvantages of separate action by the United States and certain other countries in drawing up permanent peace arrangements for Japan without Soviet participation. Section 2 in turn covers the principal changes that have occurred in Japan under the Allied occupation. It focuses on the contrasts between the occupation of Japan and that of Germany, the policy-making and control machinery for Japan (with special reference to the FEC, the Allied Council for Japan, and SCAP), the basic Allied policies for the occupation, various reforms, and the differences of opinion over the lasting nature of the changes effected in Japan to date. The third and final section—"Peace Terms and Future Position of Japan"—examines the territorial questions to be raised at the peace conference with particular reference to the disposition of Okinawa, the Bonins, and the Volcano Islands, problems of Japanese security after the end of the occupation, Japan's obligation to fulfill reparations requirements (which are to be restated in the proposed treaty), and related provisions such as restrictions on Japanese industrial activity.

2325 "Peace with Japan." *Economist* 153: 53–54 (12 July 1947)

In a discussion of problems associated with a peace conference for Japan, the author of this editorial comments that although Japan has avoided the political disintegration of Germany, "its economic plight is quite as serious and its position as an object of rivalry between Russia and the United States is very similar." The article then concentrates upon the economic system—as it was at the outset of the occupation and after 2 years of Allied control. He discusses the reasons behind the change in American policy from a laissez faire attitude to active aid to the economy and the effects of this change on other Allied powers. The final paragraphs consider the growing disagreement between the United States and the USSR regarding Japan's future role.

2325a Pearce, Ronald. "Not So Far East." *National Review* (London) 129:201–4 (Sept. 1947)

Written shortly after the conference of Commonwealth nations in Canberra, this article presents a number of general comments on Japan with particular focus on the projected peace settlement. Many of the author's statements are made with the Australian point of view in mind. Pearce points out, for example, that the United States wants a peace treaty with Japan rubber-stamped as soon as possible and that MacArthur has consistently refused to listen to suggestions and criticisms from the various Allies. He also notes Australian demands for a major role in any peace settlement, Australian resentment of the unilateral nature by which SCAP authorized the Japanese to send a second whaling expedition to the Antarctic, Canberra's belief that the gradual economic development of Japan should become part of a general plan for Asia as a whole, and Australia's call for the establishment of an Allied supervisory authority which would be stationed in Japan for up to ten years after the signing of the peace treaty in order to insure the observance of treaty provisions. Finally Pearce indicates that an American policy singling out Japan in Asia for favorable treatment and encouraging considerable U.S. capital investment within the country would be repugnant to the Australian government.

2326 "Report on Mission to Japan: The Minister for External Affairs, the Rt. Hon. H. V. Evatt, 17th August 1947." *Current Notes on International Affairs* 18:469–74 (Aug. 1947)

Evatt visited Japan in August 1947 to observe conditions and to discuss with General MacArthur the terms and machinery of peace-making with Japan. He indicates that his visit confirmed the position of the Australian government which favored an early peace for Japan. He suggested, however, that an Allied supervisory authority be established in Tokyo to prevent the reestablishment of Japanese war potential as well as to coordinate the Japanese economy with those of other Pacific and Asian nations. The report also refers to the low Japanese standard of living, the control of imports to prevent Japanese rearmament, the serious economic effects of Japan's loss of territories, and growing Japanese trade unionism.

2327 Rosinger, Lawrence K. "China Fears United States Policy Will Revive Japanese Power." *Foreign Policy Bulletin* 27:2–4 (12 Dec. 1947)

Various nations' attitudes toward the negotiation of a peace treaty are treated in this article. The author discusses proposed differences of procedure and policy between the United States on the one hand and the Soviet Union and China on the other. Moreover, he illustrates the widespread dissatisfaction on the part of Chinese moderates as well as conservatives with the U.S. policy in Japan. As indicated in statements cited from several Shanghai newspapers, the Chinese fear a resurgent Japan as a threat to their internal security. In the face of this distrust and Soviet recalcitrance, the author suggests that renewed efforts be made by all nations to produce a single peace conference for the formulation of a treaty with Japan.

2328 ———. "MacArthur Seeks Japan Peace Treaty." *Foreign Policy Bulletin* 26:3 (28 Mar. 1947)

A brief discussion of General MacArthur's surprise announcement of 17 March to the effect that there should be an early peace treaty and withdrawal of Allied occupation personnel. The author comments on the State Department reaction to this statement as well as the reaction of the Yoshida government.

2329 Shafer, Luman J. "Make Peace with Japan!" *Christian Century* 64:1519–20 (10 Dec. 1947)

The author believes a fundamental change of heart has taken place among the Japanese people which must be fostered and developed by constructive statesmanship. However, Shafer feels that the army of occupation and the Allied military government cannot provide this statesmanship and that their continued presence jeopardizes the possibility of a permanent settlement. A deterioration in army morale and morals is noted as is the stagnation of the economy resulting from undue market restrictions. The possibility of concluding a peace treaty without Soviet participation is considered.

2330 "Summary of Responses by Other Governments to U.S. Japanese Treaty Proposals." *Department of State Bulletin* 17:435–36 (31 Aug. 1947)

A brief summation of the formal responses of 9 of the members of the Far Eastern Commission (FEC) to the American proposal that a peace conference be arranged with all due haste and that the members of the FEC participate in such a conference. This procedure was preferred to the Soviet suggestion that the matter be considered only by the Council of Foreign Ministers—comprised of the USSR, China, Great Britain, and the United States. The nations, whose responses are all in agreement with the U.S. proposal, are: Australia, Canada, China, France, India, the Netherlands, New Zealand, the Philippines, and the United Kingdom. The Soviet response is not included. The Chinese government further suggests a compromise voting procedure whereby "decisions at the conference be made by a two-thirds majority of the members of the conference present and voting, including the affirmative votes of three of the representatives of China, the U.S., the U.K., and the Soviet Union."

Supreme Commander for the Allied Powers. Diplomatic Section. *Atcheson Correspondence.* 1945–47. See no.926.

2331 U.S. Dept. of State. Office of Public Affairs. *Aspects of Current American Foreign Policy, October 20, 1947.* Washington, D.C.: Government Printing Office, 1947. iii, 60p. (Dept. of State publication 2961)

A summary statement of American positions with respect to a variety of current international issues: the United Nations, free nations, European rehabilitation, the international economic system, dependent areas, armaments, atomic energy, and the inter-American system. There is a section entitled "Peacemaking and Occupation," which sets forth American reasoning on the peace settlements with occupied Japan and Germany. It briefly touches on the political, economic, and social reforms being implemented in Tokyo under the leadership of General MacArthur and notes the Soviet Union's opposition to an early peace conference for Japan.

2331a Walker, Alan. "Planning Peace in the Pacific." *Australian Quarterly* 18: 86–95 (June 1946)

When the time comes to conclude a treaty with Japan, Walker contends, it must be kept in mind that peace in the Pacific will rest on 4 basic principles: racial equality, the primacy of native welfare, economic freedom and independence, and collective security rather than individual national strength as a basis for defense. The article explains each of these basic principles and their implications by applying them to concrete situations in Asia and the Pacific.

2331b "Why General MacArthur Wishes to End Military Rule in Japan." *United States News* 22:62, 64 (9 May 1947)

This article discusses rumors that MacArthur has become convinced of the value of terminating the military occupation of Japan. He is said to feel that the original twin objectives of the occupation—demilitarization and democratization—have just about been accomplished and that the country's severe economic problems would best be solved by concluding a peace treaty, by turning further supervision of Japan over to the United Nations, and by doing everything possible to encourage the growth of a strong and independent Japanese economy.

1948

Borton, Hugh. "Occupation Policies in Japan and Korea." 1948. See no.539.

2332 Chang, Hsin-hai. "The Treaty with Japan: A Chinese View." *Foreign Affairs* 26:505–14 (Apr. 1948)

The author presents his analysis of various aspects of the coming negotiations for a Japanese peace treaty as seen from a Chinese point of view. After discussing the terms of China's compromise suggestion for participation in the negotiations, which seems to reconcile American and Soviet proposals, he outlines China's expectations with regard to 5 general areas: (1) demilitarization and disarmament, (2) posttreaty control, (3) the limits of Japan's new territorial sovereignty, (4) its economic and industrial level, and (5) reparations. The author stresses the fact that China is in a position to be vitally affected by any resurgence of militarism or expansionism in Japan.

2333 "Japanese Peace Conference." *Eastern World* 2, no.1:3 (Jan. 1948)

The Soviet Union is strongly urged to agree to the convening of a peace conference in which all 11 members of the Far Eastern Commission will be allowed to participate. At the same time, MacArthur's work in Japan, where the Diet has passed legislation designed to implement his plans for breaking up the *zaibatsu*, is highly praised. The author notes, however, that certain circles within the United States as well as in Japan are anxious to counteract a possible shift of industrial power to the leftwing trade unions. Unless a peace treaty is signed shortly, these circles may be able to exert sufficient pressure to organize Japan's production in such a fashion that those industries competing with American interests will be restricted while all others will be encouraged to rebuild and expand.

Keeton, George W. "Peace-Making with Japan." 1948. *See* no.799.

2333a Krainov, Pavel. "Peace Is Sole Objective in Policy of USSR in the Far East." *USSR Information Bulletin* 8, no. 22:700–1 (17 Nov. 1948)

This correspondent elaborates basic Soviet policy positions on the demilitarization and democratization of Japan. Of particular note is the Soviet government's insistence that a peace treaty with Japan be prepared by the Council of Foreign Ministers, composed of representatives of the United States, the USSR, China, and Great Britain.

Ladejinsky, Wolf I. "Trial Balance in Japan." 1948. *See* no.559.

2334 Latourette, Kenneth Scott. "Peace with Japan." *Annals of the American Academy of Political and Social Science* 257:142–50 (May 1948)

The problems of peacetime Japan are discussed under 2 general categories: (1) internal problems within Japan proper and (2) external problems involving the attitudes of and relations with foreign powers. Concerning internal problems, in a brief historical survey, the author emphasizes the persistence of traditional Japanese patterns of behavior in the face of foreign incursions. He suggests this may occur during the occupation as well, and that the Japanese, once left to themselves, will revert to their military traditions. There also will be a resurgence of the *zaibatsu* and the bureaucracy since the equivalent of their experience in business and government is not yet to be found elsewhere. Regarding external problems, he discusses the Far Eastern roles of China, the USSR, and the United States with particular reference to Japan, and also briefly considers the lesser roles of countries such as Australia and Great Britain. His final topic is the peace settlement with Japan, which he treats under 4 headings: (1) reparations, (2) territorial adjustments, (3) economic opportunity, and (4) safeguards against a renewal of Japanese imperialistic adventures. The author discusses the issue of reparations and favors the abolition of a reparations program except for such properties as remain in China and Korea. He also discusses the disposition of such former Japanese territories as Formosa, Sakhalin, the Kuriles, the Ryukyus, and other smaller islands such as the Bonin and Volcano Islands. The author advocates an early end to the occupation and withdrawal of the armed forces of the United States and other powers and their replacement by a supervisory civil commission whose authority would be enforced by the United Nations.

McEvoy, Dennis. "Let's Get out of Japan." 1948. *See* no.560.

2335 Mui, King-chau. "The Japanese Peace Treaty." *China Monthly* 9:51–53 (Feb. 1948)

In anticipation of the opening of negotiations leading to a treaty of peace with Japan, the Chinese minister to Cuba pleads for international recognition of "the legitimacy of China's demands." According to him, these demands include (1) the abolition of the imperial institution, which "in itself constitutes a dangerous breeding ground for war;" (2) a major share of the Japanese industrial equipment seized by the Allies for reparations purposes; (3) the return of all Chinese art works and treasures looted by the Japanese; and (4) an adequate standard of living for the Japanese people, based on "the general industrial coefficient of 1928."

2336 New Zealand. Dept. of External Affairs. *Annual Report of the Department of External Affairs, 1 April 1947 to 31 March 1948*. Wellington: Government Printer, 1948. 117p. (Dept. of External Affairs publication 65)

This annual report of the Department of External Affairs for the year 1947–48 contains a section entitled "The Far East and South-East Asia" (p.19–26), most of which is devoted to the question of a Japanese peace settlement and New Zealand–Japanese relations. The report refers to New Zealand's favorable response to an early conclusion of a peace treaty with Japan as advocated by General MacArthur and Australian Foreign Minister Evatt in early 1947. It describes the Commonwealth conference held in Canberra in late August 1947 to discuss the major aspects of a peace settlement with Japan. With respect to the Far Eastern Commission it states that emphasis has shifted during the year from political to economic matters although progress in this field has been slow. It calls the Allied Council for Japan "ineffectual in absence of any desire by SCAP to make real use of its advisory functions."

2337 Ray, Donald P. "Problems of a Japanese Peace Settlement." *World Affairs* 111:106–11 (Summer 1948)

A report devoted to some of the important objectives that will need to be considered at a peace conference with Japan, which the author believes will have significance not only for Japan but also for the whole of Asia. He points out 3 areas of major importance: (1) that the treaty insure against a recurrence of Japanese military aggression, (2) that it encourage Japan to embrace peaceful and progressive government, and (3) that it enable the Japanese to achieve a stable economic structure. In considering these 3 areas, the article touches on the possibility of Japan's retaining a standing army, on the matter of its eventually joining the United Nations, and on measures that must be taken to provide for stability in the Japanese balance of payments. The author advocates a reparations policy that would be confined to the removal of heavy equipment and the dissolution of Japan's foreign assets, and he proposes that a way be found to allow Japanese commercial intercourse with other Asian nations without this leading again to Japanese imperialism.

Sansom, Sir George B. "Conflicting Purposes in Japan." 1948. *See* no.567.

2337a Stewart, Neil. "Japan and the Peace Treaty." *Eastern World* 2, no.8–9:20–21 (Aug./Sept. 1948)

The author concludes from a study of American press opinion and visits by key U.S. business and government policy leaders that Japan's economy is to be reconstructed. Through a strong Japan, the United States will become dominant politically and economically in Asia and Commonwealth and European trade will suffer. The currently discussed peace conference is expected to be dictated by American policy needs.

Teters, Barbara. "American Policy as Regards Japan." 1948. *See* no.1515.

Vandenbosch, Amry. "The Flaming East." 1948. *See* no.574.

2337b Walker, Gordon W. "Peace: Japanese Style." *Christian Science Monitor* magazine section p.2 (24 Jan. 1948)

The Japanese Foreign Office, Walker reports, has set up a treaty bureau to prepare for peace negotiations by analyzing reports and rumors of Allied opinions about potential peace terms. Recently, he continues, a secret Foreign Office paper detailing Japanese hopes for possible treaty provisions was leaked to both foreign diplomats and the press. Among the Japanese desiderata are permission for Japan to appeal disputes over treaty implementation to the International Court; Japan's immediate entry into the United Nations as a security measure; minimal restrictions on Japanese industries; and guarantees that Okinawa and the Kuriles will be returned to Japanese jurisdiction. Walker speculates that this position paper was leaked as a "trial balloon" in order to test Allied reaction to its contents.

"Washington Now Plans to Lighten the Japanese Occupation Load." 1948. *See* no.578.

2338 World Affairs Council of Northern California. *Peace Making with Japan.* San Francisco: The Council, 1948. (Study Group report no.2)

1949

Council on Foreign Relations. "American Policies in the Far East (II): Changes in Occupied Japan." 1949. *See* no.583.

———. "Search for a Far Eastern Policy: 3. Problems of Japan and Korea." 1950. *See* no.584.

2339 Eidus, Kh. "The Fourth Anniversary of the Victory over Japan." *Soviet Press Translations* 4:654–56 (1 Dec. 1949)
This brief article is a translation of a report published in *Trud* on 3 September 1949. After a lengthy description of how the Soviet Union was the determining factor in Japan's decision to surrender, the author complains about the American imperialists who are attempting to prolong the occupation in order to maintain a secure foothold in Japan. He maintains that this is the reason why the Americans refuse to take up the issue of the conclusion of a peace treaty with Japan in spite of Soviet insistence that the matter be considered as soon as possible.

Green, Owen M. "De-mok-ra-sie." 1949. *See* no.589.

2340 Markov, M. "American–Japanese 'Peace Settlement' without a Treaty." *New Times* no.26:5–8 (22 June 1949)
Presenting the Soviet Union's position with regard to a peace treaty for Japan, this article discusses what the fundamental principles of the peace conference should be, the procedures which should be followed, and some essential terms of the treaty. There is an outline of the "quite different intentions of the American authorities towards Japan." The author claims that Washington seeks to prolong the occupation as much as possible. Soviet insistence on complete demilitarization and the exaction of reparations from Japan are contrasted with American desires to rearm Japan and develop it into an industrial subsidiary of the United States. In conclusion, the author claims that world opinion "is demanding a reversion to the principles of the Potsdam declaration and the speedy conclusion of a peace treaty with Japan."

2341 Mayevsky, V. "The USA Is Disrupting the Democratization of Japan." *Soviet Press Translations* 4:515–16 (1 Oct. 1949); abridged version published under the title "U.S. Undermines Democratization of Japan" in *Current Digest of the Soviet Press* 1, no.36:19–20 (4 Oct. 1949)
This article, which initially appeared in *Pravda* on 3 September 1949, first discusses the Soviet contributions in the war, based on the claim that the USSR "played the decisive role in liquidating the hives of aggression in the West and in the East." The author criticizes what he terms the American refusal to agree with the Soviet suggestion to conclude a peace treaty with Japan as quickly as possible. He believes this refusal is based on the American intent to establish Japan as a strategic military springboard aimed against the Soviet Union and the "national liberation movements" in neighboring Asian countries.

2341a ———. "The U.S.A. and the Peace Treaty with Japan." *Current Digest of the Soviet Press* 1, no.27:18 (2 Aug. 1949)
Unlike the USSR, the United States is not anxious for the rapid conclusion of a peace settlement in the Far East. As it is, the Americans already have renounced the policy of demilitarizing and democratizing Japan, as set forth in

the Potsdam Declaration, and have ceased reparations deliveries on the one hand while rebuilding the Japanese economy on the other. A treaty would mean the withdrawal of American troops from Japan and the end of American domination over the country. Accordingly, Mayevski concludes, the United States would prefer no treaty at all. This article first appeared in the 29 June issue of *Pravda* and is a condensation of the Russian-language text.

2342 New Zealand. Dept. of External Affairs. *Annual Report of the Department of External Affairs, 1 April 1948 to 31 March 1949.* Wellington: Government Printer, 1949. 110p. (Dept. of External Affairs publication 83)

The section on Japan takes the view that a peace conference for Japan is a remote possibility and notes that the Far Eastern Commission and the Allied Council for Japan have sharply decreased their activities due to mounting international tensions and that the U.S. government and SCAP have thereby gained greater freedom of action in the occupation of Japan. The same section also reports briefly the outcome of the International Military Tribunal for the Far East, which delivered its final judgment on 4–11 November 1948, and describes New Zealand's role in the proceedings. It also notes the activities of the New Zealand government's trade representative in Tokyo.

2342a Nomura, Kichisaburō. "A Peace Treaty and Japan." *Contemporary Japan* 18:525–28 (Oct./Dec. 1949)

This article by a former ambassador to the United States was originally published in Japanese in the November 1949 issue of *Chūō Kōron*. Nomura looks forward to the early conclusion of a peace treaty but wishes one signed by all parties concerned. True independence after the signing of the treaty, he says, will depend on the achievement of economic self-sufficiency, to which end a number of concrete suggestions are offered. Japan is eager for a peace treaty, he concludes, but he is concerned about her security and about the maintenance of domestic order after the occupation ends. He would prefer peace without a treaty if a treaty that fully guarantees Japanese security—i.e., one including all parties—is not to be forthcoming.

2343 "A Peace Treaty for Japan." *New Republic* 121:5–7 (31 Oct. 1949)

This editorial first summarizes the occupation's reforms, chiefly emphasizing political and economic programs. The editor then attempts to describe Japan's position in world power politics and to demonstrate the various options that are open in terms of siding with the East or the West in the cold war. Finally, he refers to the various dangers of a continuing occupation and suggests that these can be avoided only by a peace treaty. The editor urges that the United States negotiate such a treaty with the USSR and not insist that Japan become an American protectorate.

2344 "Peace with Tokyo?" *Economist* 157:1107–8 (19 Nov. 1949)

After enumerating the different reasons why the United States and Great Britain want a peace treaty with Japan in the near future, the author addresses himself to an explanation of the difficulties which prevent the conclusion of a treaty, i.e., the objections of the USSR. In the judgment of the author the most important ends to be obtained through a peace treaty are 3: (1) Japan should be prevented from rearming and again menacing its neighbors, (2) its newly established political democracy should be preserved from domestic violence either from the right or left, and (3) having been totally disarmed, it should be protected against external aggression. He believes it will be necessary to arrange that American troops remain somewhere in Japan for the purposes of protection for an indefinite period of time.

2344a Reischauer, Edwin Oldfather. "It's Time We Encouraged the Japanese to Build a Democracy of Their Own." *Saturday Evening Post* 221:12 (23 Apr. 1949)

Reischauer finds the growing Japanese interest in Communism well worth American notice, but cautions that Americans should not leap to the conclusion that the occupation is a failure. The rapid growth of Communist influence is not the result of any inherent strength of the movement in Japan, he feels. Rather, as a "forbidden fruit" some Japanese find it attractive; the slow economic recovery has led to some discontent; Japanese economic growth is suffering because it has so far been impossible to restore Japan's economic ties with the rest of Asia; and, most importantly, many of the better-educated Japanese are increasingly chafing at continued American control. This irritation results in their turning to communism, if only as a gesture of protest, and accordingly is an indication that the time has come to let Japan "go it alone."

"Time to Leave Japan." 1949. *See* no.612.

2344b Wood, Junius Boyd. "It's Our Move in the Far East." *Nation's Business* 37: 50, 52–55 (July 1949)

Wood argues that the future American role in Asia will be determined by how rapidly and successfully the occupation can be terminated. Leveling criticism at SCAP's reforms and reeducation efforts, he contends that occupation personnel know far too little about Japan, that democracy is being forced upon Japan, that the antitrust program has been a failure, and that the massive purges have resulted in only the "mediocre" being left to run things. It is time, therefore, for the United States to stop playing schoolteacher and instead to set Japan on her feet.

1950

2345 "Challenge of a Japanese Treaty." *New Republic* 123, no.16:5–6 (16 Oct. 1950)

This editorial sees a Japanese peace treaty as holding forth both a temptation and a challenge to American policymakers. The temptation is to see the treaty solely as a device for rearming Japan, and the challenge lies in the opportunity for the United States to demonstrate "constructive international leadership in the Far East." According to the editors, the United States is faced with the dilemma of having to provide for Japan's security against Communist aggression while simultaneously having to guarantee the continued existence of a genuinely free society within the country. The editors propose the continued exercise of Allied authority in Japan on a judicial basis in order to insure the continued enforcement of the Japanese constitution as the supreme law of the land, coupled with the gradual development of a Japanese self-defense force which would act only as a component of other Allied forces in northeastern Asia. These treaty controls should remain in effect until Japan is granted membership within the United Nations.

2345a Colton, Kenneth E. "How Will a Peace Treaty Affect Japanese Politics?" *Foreign Policy Bulletin* 29:3–4 (28 Apr. 1950)

Questions concerning what kind of peace treaty will be negotiated with Japan and what kind of a government Japan is likely to have after a peace treaty are the main considerations of this article. The author arranges the most important parties or coalitions in a spectrum and concentrates on the political character of the Democratic Liberal party since this is the party that will most likely be in power at that time. According to the author, the principle decision the Japanese will have to make regards U.S. military protection and the granting of military bases to the United States by the Japanese government. The author views the negotiations as offering the United States an opportunity "not only to help stabilize the Japanese government and party politics, but also to stabilize peace in Asia."

Green, Owen M. "Japan and Korea." 1950. See no.623.

2345b "Hanging on." *Commonweal* 52: 283–84 (30 June 1950)

The current situation in Japan, according to this editorial, illustrates how the cold war "throws things out of whack." Despite nearly universal agreement that the occupation should end and in spite of growing Japanese impatience, the United States has no alternative but to remain in Japan. Japan is still weak politically and economically. The occupation, therefore, must continue until the external threat of Communist aggression is tempered and until Japan gains more strength.

2346 Harper, Norman Denholm. *Australia and the Peace Settlement with Japan.* Mimeographed. Sydney: Australian Institute of International Affairs, 1950. 16p. (Institute of Pacific Relations, 11th conference, Australian paper no.3, 1950)

Harper discusses Australian policy regarding the Japanese peace settlement, reviewing international relations in the Far East from 1945 through early 1950. He shows that Australian policy favoring the rapid conclusion of a peace treaty with Japan continues unchanged, but that her policy supporting a militarily weak Japan has changed due to the emergence of Communist China and the cold war tensions. He agrees that Japan should develop a viable economy, that this development would serve the interests of Asia and America as well as Japan, and that Japan should be allowed to reduce her reparations and retain "primary war facilities." The differences in American and Australian estimates of the extent of social and political changes needed in Japan are noted; more extensive reforms are favored by Australians. Australian support for including in the peace treaty clauses guaranteeing essential postwar reforms and a clause establishing a civil commission to replace SCAP after the conclusion of the peace treaty and to oversee Japan's continuous execution of necessary reforms is discussed.

2346a Iwamura, Michio. "Separate Peace and Sino–Japanese Relations." *Contemporary Japan* 19:110–12 (Jan./Mar. 1950)

This article, translated from the February 1950 issue of *Sekai Hyōron*, is by the director of the Institute for the Study of China. It examines the potential impact of a peace treaty which excludes the Soviet Union and the People's Republic of China. Such a treaty, it is asserted, would inevitably lead to conflict or at least to strained relations between Japan and those 2 nations. A detrimental effect on Sino–Japanese trade may also result, though some people would argue that the 2 countries are so interdependent economically that the negative impact would be lessened by practical considerations. Iwamura recognizes other opinions as well: that, for instance, reduced trade with China will reduce the danger of Communist influence, and that trade with other East Asian countries will compensate for any losses in the China trade. He argues, however, that Japanese trade with other parts of Asia exclusive of China will continue to be limited to textiles and other light industrial products; only Chinese demand for the products of Japan's heavy industry will guarantee her economic recovery.

2346b "Japan Asks for a Peace Treaty." *Christian Century* 67:724 (14 June 1950)

According to this editorial, the Yoshida cabinet formally asked the United States for a peace treaty 3 days before the Japanese elections because it wished to show that the Liberals were not "American puppets." If it is to keep its friends in power, therefore, the United States will have "to come through with such a treaty." Before the treaty is signed, however, a decision regarding Japan's future defense arrangements must be reached, and such a decision seems not to be readily forthcoming. "Mr. Dulles, Secretary Johnson and General Bradley," the editorial concludes, "are not reaching Tokyo a minute too soon in their effort to find the puzzle's answer."

Leathem, Samuel. *New Zealand's Interests and Politics in the Far East.* 1950. See no.807.

Lippmann, Walter. *Commentaries on American Far Eastern Policy.* 1950. See no.811.

2347 Martin, Charles E. "Prospects for a Japanese Peace Treaty." *International Journal* 6:13–19 (Winter 1950/51)

Writing in 1950 the author reviews American attempts to formulate a peace treaty with Japan. Martin writes of the importance of a peace treaty for Japan and for the world community. He lists possible ways in which agreement over a treaty could be reached. He also goes over the reasons why certain countries have not begun negotiations with Japan.

2348 Mears, Helen. "Problems of a Japanese Peace." *American Perspective* 4:92–100 (Winter 1950)

Helen Mears explains that although there are many specific issues to be settled before a peace treaty can be signed, the major obstacle is the tension between Russian and Western interests.

2348a Naka, Masao. "Interest in Japan on the Peace Conference." *Democratic Japan* (Tokyo) no.1:7–8, 16 (Jan. 1950)

Naka reports that the Japanese are eager for the conclusion of a peace treaty, which has received a good deal of attention in the press and in the Diet. The issues most frequently discussed, he states, are whether the treaty will be signed by all of Japan's former enemies and what provisions will be made for Japan's future security.

2349 New Zealand. Dept. of External Affairs. *Annual Report of the Department of External Affairs, 1 April 1949 to 31 March 1950.* Wellington: Government Printer, 1950. 103p. (Dept. of External Affairs publication 91)

This *Annual Report* allots only 3 pages to Japan. It states that no progress has been made toward a Japanese peace settlement due to disagreements among the major powers over procedures for the peace treaty. However, it also notes that the meeting of Commonwealth Foreign Ministers held in Colombo, 9–14 January 1950, agreed to set up a working party which would study the details of a treaty under the direction of the Commonwealth High Commissioners in London. The Far Eastern Commission and the Allied Council for Japan, it indicates, deteriorated further in function and activity during the year owing to the Soviet Union's boycott. It also reports briefly on the role and activities of the New Zealand official trade representative in Tokyo, who, working on the Restitution Advisory Committee, assists SCAP in the disposition of unidentified looted properties.

2350 Nomura, Kichisaburō. "A Peace Treaty and Japan's Security." *Contemporary Japan* 19:350–57 (July/Sept. 1950)

Marking the Korean War as a significant turning point in international affairs, the author discusses how that confrontation affects Japan's position and how it affects the terms of the approaching peace treaty. He maintains that in the new situation, Japan cannot maintain a neutral position in world politics and favors continued American occupation even after the conclusion of a peace treaty "mainly for the maintenance of security." The concluding paragraphs concern the Russian-held Kurile Islands and the author questions the inclusion of several islands in the group which he believes are rightfully Japan's. There is no discussion of the American-held Ryukyu chain to the south.

2351 Parrott, Lindesay. "The Touchy Issue of Peace with Japan." *New York Times Magazine* p.10, 39 (26 Feb. 1950)

With the Communist victory in China and the conclusion of a Sino–Soviet agreement, the author reviews the pros and cons of an immediate peace treaty with Japan. Although he believes, as does MacArthur, that there is little likelihood of a Communist takeover in Japan, he lists some problems such as overpopulation and economic recovery which may be potential dangers. Another problem is Japan's defense; the author believes that Japan must remain closely tied to the West.

"Peace and Protection for Ex-enemy." 1950. See no.822.

2352 "Peace for Japan." *Economist* 158: 1315–17 (17 June 1950)

Speculating on Japan's future after the termination of the occupation, the author of this article considers 2 important aspects of this matter, first, the nature of the treaty ending the war and, second, the nature of British and Commonwealth interests. He explains the various conflicts between the U.S. Department of State and the Defense Department over the terms of the coming peace treaty which will end the occupation. He also discusses the external difficulties which must be anticipated from the USSR and Communist China. The latter half of the article primarily concerns economic matters relating to the policy which an independent Japan will follow. The author asserts the need for Anglo–American cooperation in order that the economies of Japan and the countries of Southeast Asia may be safeguarded against the threat of communism.

2353 "Peace Treaty with Japan?" *New Statesman and Nation* 39:476 (29 Apr. 1950)

Written shortly before the American and Commonwealth Foreign Ministers' Conference, this article deals with the conclusion of a Japanese peace treaty without the participation of either the USSR or the People's Republic of China. The idea of a separate treaty is deplored, as is the notion of a remilitarized Japan as a pawn in an East-West cold war. It is suggested that the only occupation policy which was carried out effectively was demilitarization. Any reversal of Japan's demilitarized status at the initiation of the United States would, the writers maintain, be against the directly expressed interest of both the Japanese and of all other peoples in the Pacific area.

2354 "Peace with Japan." *Eastern Economist* (New Delhi) 14, no.22:869–70 (9 June 1950)

The article first discusses the elections which had been held in Japan that week, then turns to the matter of a peace treaty with Japan and suggests that the opportunity to conclude peace be seized upon without further delay. At the same time, the unidentified author writes, "any course which would exclude India, as a member of the Far Eastern Commission, from participating in the discussion of appropriate treaty terms for Japan would naturally be strongly resented."

"Planning a Japan without MacArthur." 1950. See no.632.

2355 Riggs, Fred W. "Japan Peace Treaty Both Necessary and Hazardous." *Foreign Policy Bulletin* 29:3–4 (15 Sept. 1950)

The outbreak of the Korean War is seen as underlining the necessity to negotiate a peace settlement with Japan. The author discusses the American dilemma —to negotiate a treaty jointly with the Soviet Union as well as other Allied nations, or to attempt a separate settlement in view of the many complications attached to the first course of action. He discusses the possible consequences of either decision and mentions other solutions that have been suggested—such as submitting the issue to the United Nations or giving Japan autonomy without a formal treaty. Finally he warns that the United States must keep in mind "a long range of considerations affecting every facet of the Far Eastern situation" before it makes a final decision on this matter.

2356 ———. "Separate Peace for Japan?" *Nation* 171:307–9 (7 Oct. 1950)

The author considers the implications of the United States' proposal to sign a separate peace treaty with Japan in view of increasing disagreement between the U.S. and the Soviet Union. He considers the attitudes of the Japanese on this issue and speculates on the possible effects of such a program on other Asian nations such as Communist and Nationalist China, India, and Indonesia. Lastly, he considers the issue of Japan's security and suggests a pattern of defense that would be controlled by the United Nations rather than unilaterally by the United States.

2357 *Sekai.* Editorial Staff, comp. *Three Statements for World Peace.* Tokyo: Yoshino Genzaburō, n.d. 39p. of English text, 27p. of Japanese text.

This compilation consists of 3 statements on world peace printed both in English and Japanese. They are: "A Statement by Eight Distinguished Social Scientists on the Cause of Tensions which Make for War," emerging from a UNESCO project entitled: "Tensions Affecting International Understanding" in July 1948; "A Statement by Scientists in Japan on the Problem of Peace," by the Peace Study Group, made up of 59 leading Japanese scholars, in December 1948; and "A Statement by the Peace Study Group on the Problem of the Peace Settlement for Japan," in January 1950. The latter statement by the Peace Study Group is supplemented by summaries of their reasoning on issues such as an overall versus partial peace treaty, the relationship of a peace settlement to the cold war, and Japan's economic position and posttreaty security in relation to a peace settlement. The first of the 2 statements by the Japanese Peace Study Group is essentially an endorsement of the UNESCO statement, which emphasizes the preventability of war and the responsibility of scholars to cooperate across national boundaries to promote international understanding and freedom. The 1950 statement of the Peace Study Group deals more specifically with the problem of a Japanese peace settlement. The group endorses an "overall peace," i.e., one agreed upon by all of the Allied nations. They acknowledge the problems raised by the cold war, but they believe that Japan cannot achieve economic self-support through a peace settlement that is agreed to by only some of the Allies. They believe that Japan's posttreaty status should be that of "inviolable neutrality" guaranteed by the United Nations. They stand unalterably opposed to foreign military bases on Japanese soil, which they perceive as tantamount to involvement in the cold war or even incitement to war.

2357a "Statement by the Minister for External Affairs, the Hon. P. C. Spender, K.C., M.P., in the House of Representatives, 28th November, 1950." *Current Notes on International Affairs* 21:796–807 (Nov. 1950); extracted in *Contemporary Japan* 19:620–22 (Oct./Dec. 1950)

Spender's statement covers the entire range of Australia's relations with her Pacific neighbors, but a subsection entitled "Japanese Peace Treaty" (p.803–4) contains his views on the discussions currently under way among the Allies regarding a peace settlement with Japan. In commenting upon John Foster Dulles' views on a peace treaty, Spender reiterates the usual Australian concern about the possible resurgence of Japanese militarism. Nevertheless, he does acknowledge both the advisability of concluding an agreement without further delay and the need to provide for the security of Japan. The early normalization of Japanese–Australian relations is greatly desired, he concludes, but Australia must be certain that Japan will not opt again for the militarist route.

2357b Suzuki, Ichirō. "A Japanese Peace Treaty." *Democratic Japan* (Tokyo) no. 8:3–5 (Sept./Oct. 1950)

This article summarizes in outline form the conflicting positions taken on a potential peace settlement by the Liberal, Social Democratic, and People's Democratic parties.

2358 "A Treaty with Japan." *Christian Century* 67:1040–41 (6 Sept. 1950)

The sudden determination of the U.S. government to conclude a peace treaty with Japan is criticized here. Quotations from General MacArthur are utilized to show the U.S. abandonment of a progressive, peaceful Japan in favor of a rearmed military ally. The willingness of the Japanese cabinet to support rearmament is made clear. A question is raised concerning the attitudes of the Japanese public, particularly the youth who are faced with this ambivalent and 2-faced American policy.

2358a Union of Democratic Control. *Crisis in Japan.* London: The Union, 1950. 24p.

The authors of this publication are extremely critical of American policy in Japan and remind the British government that it can still bring its influence to bear against present American aims. The idea of a separate peace treaty which would not be signed by the Soviet Union and the People's Republic of China also is rejected.

2359 "U.S. Sets Forth Principles for Japanese Peace Treaty." *Department of State Bulletin* 23:881–82 (4 Dec. 1950); reprinted in *Current History* 20:43–44 (Jan. 1951) and in *International Organization* 5:242–44 (Feb. 1951); also published under the title "On Question of Peace Treaty with Japan" in *Current Digest of the Soviet Press* 2, no.47:9–10 (6 Jan. 1951)

A memorandum from the U.S. government to the governments represented in the Far Eastern Commission concerning suggested principles for a Japanese peace treaty and a responding *aide-mémoire* from the Soviet government. The American memorandum, dated 26 October 1950, includes the following main points: only nations willing to conclude a treaty on American terms will participate in negotiations; Korean independence and American trusteeship of the Ryukyu and Bonin Islands will be recognized; the future status of Formosa, Sakhalin, and the Kuriles should be decided by the United States, the USSR, Britain, and China within a year or thereafter by the United Nations General Assembly; after the treaty there would continue to be cooperative responsibility on the part of the United States and Japan for the maintenance of Japanese peace and security. The Soviet *aide-mémoire*, dated 20 November 1950, requests clarification of certain aspects of the American memorandum. Six questions are raised: (1) Is a separate peace treaty with Japan contemplated by the United States? (2) Are previous agreements concerning the return of Taiwan to China and Sakhalin and the Kuriles to Russia to be ignored by the United States? (3) Is there to be a unilateral decision, without precedent in either the Cairo or Potsdam agreements, to withdraw the Ryukyu and Bonin Islands from Japanese sovereignty? (4) Are occupation troops to be withdrawn from Japan? (5) Does "joint responsibility" for Japanese security mean Japanese rearmament or the maintenance of military force in Japan? (6) Is the peace treaty directed toward peaceful economic independence and revival?

2359a Uyehara, Shigeru. "About the Peace Conference." *Democratic Japan* (Tokyo) no.3:8 (Mar. 1950)

Uyehara first notes that the stubborn attitude of the Soviet Union has diminished hopes for a satisfactory peace settlement. He then summarizes Prime Minister Yoshida's opinions, expressed on various occasions, that the opposition's demand for an overall peace treaty is both unrealistic and contrary to the wishes of the Japanese people, and that he shares the concern of the people over territorial questions and disputes the Allied claims to the Ryukyus, Bonins, and Kuriles.

2359b ———. "Opinions on the Peace Conference." *Democratic Japan* (Tokyo) no.2:4–5 (Feb. 1950)

This article reports that the questions of Japan's self-defense and whether all of Japan's former enemies will participate in the peace conference are being hotly debated in the Diet. The liberal and leftist elements are attacking Prime Minister Yoshida for "trying to transform Japan into a military base for other countries," while the Yoshida forces criticize the leftists as obstructionists for insisting on an overall peace treaty without trying to persuade the Soviet Union to change its position on certain issues.

―――. "The Peace Conference and the Residents of Southern Kurile." 1950. See no.998a.

2360 Woodman, Dorothy. "Japanese Question Mark." *New Statesman and Nation* 39:703–4 (24 June 1950)

In an article opposing the forcing of a separate peace treaty on the Yoshida government, the author contends that the Japanese people no longer view the American occupation authorities as operating in their best interests and are not willing to continue as junior partners of the United States. She believes that the remilitarization of Japan will come about only as a result of American insistence and that Japan would do best to break its satellite relationship with the United States and reestablish strong economic and cultural ties with China.

1951

2361 Acheson, Dean Gooderham. *Our Far Eastern Policy: Debate, Decision, and Action*. Washington, D.C.: Dept. of State, 1951. 11p. (Dept. of State publication 4201; Far Eastern series 41); also in *Department of State Bulletin* 24:683–87 (30 Apr. 1951)

An address delivered by the then secretary of state before the Women's National Press Club in Washington on 18 April 1951. The speech is primarily concerned with American policy on security arrangements in the Pacific with special reference to the Korean conflict, but it briefly refers to the peace treaty negotiations with Japan as a "constructive" task for peace in the Far East. Acheson affirms that with the coming peace treaty Japan can contribute greatly to the security of the area.

2361a ―――. "An Act of Spirit: 'That This Treaty Yields Its True Fruits'." *Vital Speeches* 17, no.23:711–12 (15 Sept. 1951)

In an emotional address delivered before the San Francisco Peace Treaty Conference on 8 September 1951, the U.S. secretary of state terms the treaty "an act of greatness of spirit" and "a true act of reconciliation" and calls upon all of its signatories to implement the various treaty terms. He also expresses regret over the unwillingness of certain countries to sign the treaty in its present form.

2362 "Address Delivered by Ambassador John Foster Dulles at the Luncheon Jointly Given by the American Chamber of Commerce in Japan and the Japan Chamber of Commerce and Industry, December 14, 1951." *Contemporary Japan* 20:584–89 (Oct./Dec. 1951)

Dulles looks back upon the previous year and discusses the problems which arose in connection with the negotiation of a peace treaty and the ways in which those problems were overcome. The latter half of his speech concerns future U.S.–Japanese relations, particularly in the strategic and economic spheres. He affirms the necessity of a close relationship between the 2 countries "to demonstrate the possibility of cooperation between the Free East and the Free West as equals."

2362a "Address Delivered by Prime Minister Shigeru Yoshida at the Twelfth Session of the Diet, October 12, 1951." *Contemporary Japan* 20:423–29 (July/Sept. 1951)

Yoshida presents the San Francisco peace treaty to the Diet and recommends its speedy approval. After explaining the treaty's various provisions, he evaluates the conference proceedings themselves. The overall atmosphere in San Francisco was one of understanding, sympathy, and friendliness. Some signatories expressed concern about Japan's ability to fulfill her reparations commitments, but Yoshida was pleased with the Allies' trust in Japan as a new member of the international community. The fears of certain countries about Japanese economic competition are unjustified, Yoshida asserts, since it will be a long time before the economy has fully recovered.

Likewise, the Soviet Union's complaint that the treaty fails to prevent a resurgence of militarism is "a piece of absurd and groundless propaganda." He feels too that the U.S.–Japan Security Treaty is the only possible way to guarantee Japan at present from foreign aggression. After urging prompt Diet approval of the treaty, Yoshida devotes the remainder of his address to remarks on the budget and on various governmental economic programs.

2362b "Address Delivered by Prime Minister Shigeru Yoshida, Head of the Japanese Delegation, at the Japanese Peace Conference, San Francisco, September 7, 1951." *Contemporary Japan* 20:409–12 (July/Sept. 1951)

Yoshida first notes that the Japanese delegation was satisfied with the draft of the treaty from the very beginning of the conference, for it is a "fair and generous treaty" which can be supported by the vast majority of the Japanese people. Regarding the criticisms and complaints which have been made about the treaty, Yoshida replies that in respect to territorial questions, Japan is satisfied to be granted residual sovereignty over the Ryukyus and the Bonins, and disturbed by the Soviet implication that Japan unlawfully seized the Kuriles and Southern Sakhalin. As for the fears of some countries that Japan will not be able to meet her reparations commitments, Yoshida reiterates Japan's determination to meet her obligations but asks that his country's present economic difficulties be taken into account. Yoshida also notes his concern about the 300,000 Japanese nationals who have yet to be repatriated from the Soviet Union, and regrets the absence of China from the conference and of India and Burma from among the signatories. It is unfortunate, he concludes, that a separate treaty has had to be signed, but Japanese security demands it.

2362c "After the San Francisco Conference: Indonesia's 'Great Debate'." *Report on Indonesia* p.1–5 (30 Sept. 1951)

A review of Indonesian policy with regard to the signing of the Japanese peace treaty that appeared in a publication of the Indonesian Republic's New York information office.

2363 "Answer to Soviet Questions on Principles of Japanese Treaty." *Department of State Bulletin* 24:65–66 (8 Jan. 1951); reprinted under the title "United States Note to Soviet" in *Current History* 20: 111–12 (Feb. 1951)

State Department officials here reply to questions concerning the proposed peace treaty asked in a Soviet government *aide-mémoire* dated 20 November 1950 (no.2359). This reply states that although the United States will not allow any country to veto its peace proposals, its government hopes that all countries concerned will participate in the peace treaty; that all territorial agreements made during the war are subject to approval or change in the final peace settlement; that both the Potsdam Declaration and the United Nations trusteeship procedures allow American supervision of the Ryukyu and Bonin Islands; that the United States considers the occupation legally over when peace is concluded; that the treaty will not limit in any way Japanese peacetime economic development; and that the United States refuses to deal with the government of the People's Republic of China.

2364 Baba, Tsunego. "Japanese Response to Peace Treaty." *Contemporary Japan* 20:293–300 (July/Sept. 1951)

Affirming that the predominant feeling of the Japanese toward the Allied powers during the occupation was one of gratitude and goodwill, the author briefly describes the benefits wrought by the new constitution before discussing some significant aspects of the peace treaty—particularly the matter of Japan's security. He supports the concept of foreign military protection for Japan, claims that it has popular approval, and disparages those Japanese who criticize any of the provisions of the peace treaty.

2365 Ball, William Macmahon. "The Peace Treaty with Japan." *Australian Outlook* 5:129–39 (Sept. 1951)

A former British Commonwealth member of the Allied Council for Japan takes the position that the peace treaty with Japan is less a settlement of Pacific affairs than a legitimization of a most unsatisfactory situation. The author suggests that Japan has not been fundamentally democratized and that her present utilization of wartime leadership and future economic reconstruction may produce a rearmed and dangerous neighbor. Ball claims that significant reversals of American policy may be found in the treaty, particularly in the lack of any limitation on Japanese rearmament or restriction on the reconstitution of war-support industries and in the acceptance of the notion that an independent Japan may change any or all of the occupation reforms. The author contends that the economic, demographic, and political motivations for Japanese expansion still exist and that the power to expand once again could be readily acquired through an alliance with the Union of Soviet Socialist Republics.

2366 Beal, John Robinson. "Bull's Eye for Dulles." *Harper's Magazine* 203:88–94 (Nov. 1951)

A detailed account of John Foster Dulles' role in the formulation of the peace treaty with Japan. Following a general description of the provisions of the treaty and the reactions of various nations (including the Soviet Union) to it, there is a report of the manner in which the treaty originated. Dulles' 3 trips to Japan are described—the first to confer with SCAP officials and formulate the principles which should guide such a document; the second to attend to the security problem that would emerge with a withdrawal of occupation troops; and the third after MacArthur's recall simply "to assure the Japanese that General MacArthur's departure did not mean the end of the world." The author contrasts Russian efforts to subvert the treaty with the calm determination of Dulles to negotiate the treaty, and he concludes that the Japanese peace treaty may be fairly described as "the first approach to achievement of Woodrow Wilson's ideal of 'open covenants, openly arrived at'."

2367 Bolles, Blair. "Asian Tensions to Tax San Francisco Conference." *Foreign Policy Bulletin* 30:1–2 (31 Aug. 1951)

The decision of the Soviet Union to participate in the peace treaty conference is analyzed in terms of weaknesses in American Far Eastern policy. The author believes that at San Francisco the Soviets will attempt to capitalize on the fact that "the State Department—for various reasons—has been unsuccessful in efforts to gain widespread Asian support for this treaty with a leading Asian state." After a general discussion of the reasons why China, Burma, Korea, and India refuse to participate, the author describes the attitudes of the Japanese themselves, affirming that this is more important than the attitude of the Soviet Union.

2368 ———. "U.S. Makes Headway on Japanese Peace Treaty." *Foreign Policy Bulletin* 30:1–2 (22 June 1951)

A clear and concise analysis of the background and recent developments in the peace treaty negotiations between the Allied powers and Japan. After explaining the reasons behind the Soviet–American dispute regarding the negotiations, the author outlines what he believes to be an important aspect of American Far Eastern policy, namely, maintaining Japan as the "Asian bastion of the New World." There is considerable emphasis on the effect of recent developments in China and Korea on Washington's aims and attitudes regarding the peace conference. Finally, the author discusses the attitudes of several significant Japanese groups regarding peace negotiations.

2369 ———. "U.S. Strives for Flexibility in Accord with Japan." *Foreign Policy Bulletin* 30:1–2 (20 July 1951)

This report constitutes a general analysis of the terms of the proposed peace treaty for Japan as well as the tripartite security treaty between the

United States, Australia, and New Zealand. According to the author, the drafters of these treaties have departed from American precedent and formulated documents which have "addressed themselves simply to a few principles and have given the prospective signers of the treaties a limited set of obligations" which will allow for greater flexibility in the future. After discussing some important political and economic provisions of the peace treaty, the author explains why the security treaty is necessary and points out its potential impact on U.S. foreign policy.

2370 Buss, Claude A. "U.S. Policy on the Japan Treaty." *Far Eastern Survey* 20: 113–19 (13 June 1951)

Buss, a former U.S. government official in Japan, discusses the approaches to peace-making with Japan by the nations concerned, particularly noting the American proposal.

2371 "Conference for Conclusion and Signature of Japanese Peace Treaty." *Department of State Bulletin* 25:383–89 (3 Sept. 1951)

Included under this general title are several important documents and statements related to the negotiation of the Japanese peace treaty. Following a list of the countries which have accepted the invitation to attend the peace conference, there are the texts of letters between Matthew Ridgway, the supreme commander for the Allied powers, and Prime Minister Yoshida, regarding the conclusion of the treaty, and a complete listing of the personnel of the U.S. delegation to the peace conference. Included also are the texts of the Indian note of 23 August to John Foster Dulles explaining why India refuses to be a party to the treaty and of the U.S. reply of 25 August attempting to clarify the American position. Finally, there is a statement by John M. Allison, deputy to Dulles, providing a general discussion of the treaty and terming it "a treaty of reconciliation, a treaty of opportunity" which is based on reality and on trust. He urges all nations which really desire peace to join with the United States in signing the treaty.

2372 Council on Foreign Relations. "Toward a Pacific Security System." In *The United States in World Affairs 1951*. New York: Harper, published for the Council, 1952. p.169–208.

The conclusion of a peace treaty with Japan and its significance for the future of democracy in Japan and the maintenance of Pacific security are examined in this 4-part chapter. In part 1, the results of occupation policies concerned with economic revival and political reconstruction are analyzed. Japanese opinions regarding the consultations held by Dulles are stressed. Part 2 presents a discussion of the procedures used by the Allies in negotiation. Controversial aspects of the treaty, including economic leniency and the ratification of the American policy line in Asia, are examined, as are the methods utilized to circumvent disagreement. Part 3 is concerned with the San Francisco Conference and the reasons for which the Soviets, Chinese, and Indians disassociated themselves from the resultant treaty. The willingness of the Japanese to accept the treaty and their reservations to it are noted. In Part 4, the bilateral security treaty is regarded as one link in an Asian collective security network. Mention is made of Japan's future relations with China.

2373 De Silva, Colvin R. "Against the Japanese 'Peace' Treaty (Speech Delivered during Debate on the Draft of the Treaty in the Ceylon Parliament, on August 23, 1951)." *Fourth International* 12:132–38 (Sept. 1951)

An editorial note indicates that this speech represents the attitude of the Lanka Samasamaja Party toward the peace treaty. De Silva strongly denounces the treaty on several counts. First, the territories stripped from Japan were merely turned over to her imperialist enemies, either directly or by means of U.N. trusteeship. Second, the reparations clauses of the treaty represent an attempt to perpetuate an Allied stranglehold on the Japanese economy. De Silva also regards as hypocritical the explanation that China was absent from the conference because her government is unrepresentative; as a puppet of the occupation, he points out, Japan's government can hardly be called representative either. One of the treaty's major effects, he believes, will be to facilitate close cooperation between American and Japanese capital. The true historical significance of the peace settlement is to be found, however, in its contribution to the continuing solidification of the opposing Anglo-American and Soviet power blocs.

2374 "Draft Treaty of Peace with Japan." *Current Notes on International Affairs* 22:380-98 (July 1951)

The text of the draft treaty of peace with Japan was formulated on 3 July 1951 and released to the public by the United Kingdom and the United States on 12 July 1951. This issue of *Current Notes* gives background notes to the text, showing how the Australian position has been reflected in the draft treaty through lengthy consultations with the 2 sponsoring governments and other Allied nations. Included are the texts of Australian Foreign Minister R. G. Casey's statements in Parliament on 12 and 13 July, the text of the draft treaty of 3 July plus the declaration to be made by Japan, the protocol to be attached to the draft treaty, and amendments as of 20 July 1951 to the text of the draft treaty of 3 July. The text of the draft treaty and the declaration which Japan was to make also appear in *Contemporary Japan* 20:281-91 (Apr./June 1951); while the text of the draft treaty together with a statement by John Foster Dulles which was released to the press on 11 July appear in the *Department of State Bulletin* 25:132-38 (23 July 1951).

2375 Dulles, John Foster. *Essentials of a Peace with Japan*. Washington: Government Printing Office, 1951. 11p. (Dept. of State publication 4171; Far Eastern series 40); reprinted in *Department of State Bulletin* 24, no.614:576-80 (9 Apr. 1951) and *Contemporary Japan* 20:127-33 (Jan./Mar. 1951)

An address which Dulles delivered on 31 March 1951 at Whittier College in Los Angeles. In it he presents a progress report on his negotiations with Japan and the Allies regarding a peace treaty. Briefly discussing the topics involved in the negotiations, he touches upon such items as the future territorial boundaries of Japan, her participation in United Nations activities, trade and transportation agreements, fishing rights, and reparations. Dulles emphasizes that the peace with Japan is to be a peace of reconciliation and that the "major objective of any Japanese peace treaty is to bring the Japanese people hereafter to live with others as good neighbors." Throughout the address he points out that the United States is unwilling to continue providing Japan with financial support and that the American government is concerned with working out security arrangements that could involve an American military commitment in place of Japanese rearmament. Finally, Dulles criticizes the Soviet Union for her failure to join in the negotiations.

———. "Japan and the Philippines." 1951. See no.784.

2376 ———. *Laying Foundations for Peace in the Pacific*. Washington, D.C.: Government Printing Office, 1951. 12p. (Dept. of State publication 4148; Far Eastern series 39); reprinted in *Department of State Bulletin* 24:403-7 (12 Mar. 1951)

In this March first address over the Columbia Broadcasting network, Dulles discusses the American desire to bring about a formal end of the war with Japan and to build that country into a bulwark against Communist aggression. He points out that the occupation has already succeeded in creating a democratic society in Japan, and he presents 4 ideals for peace which he considers basic elements of any future Japanese peace treaty. They are: (1) the restoration of Japan as an equal nation without any restrictions upon her sovereignty;

(2) the creation of a self-sustaining economy; (3) the encouragement of close cultural contacts with the West; and (4) a guarantee for Japan of her internal and external security. In this latter regard, Dulles states that the Japanese are prepared to accept a post-treaty, temporary military alliance with the United States in which Japan will assume increasing responsibility for her own defense.

2377 ———. "U.S. Solicits Opinions of American Republics on Japanese Settlement." *Department of State Bulletin* 24:617–18 (16 Apr. 1951)

This article summarizes remarks which Dulles made in Washington on 3 April 1951 before a meeting of the foreign ministers and ambassadors of the Latin American republics. He begins with general comments on the gravity of the confrontation between communism and the free world in Asia, then narrows his discussion to Japan and the peace negotiations. The views of other Western hemisphere nations on the Japanese settlement will be received and carefully considered, Dulles says, since there is an obvious community of interest and outlook between the United States and her sister republics.

2378 ———. *A Peace Treaty in the Making.* Washington, D.C.: Government Printing Office, 1951. 55p.

An account of the Japanese peace conference held at San Francisco on 4–8 September 1951.

2379 ———. "Peace with Justice and Freedom." *Contemporary Japan* 20:431–34 (Oct./Dec. 1951)

Discussing the peace treaty recently negotiated between Japan and 48 Allied nations, Dulles commends that treaty as being "as nearly perfect as consultation and compromise could make it." He outlines some of the concrete proposals made by the Soviet Union at the San Francisco Conference and sharply criticizes them—particularly those concerning reparations and Japan's military security.

In concluding, the author reaffirms his faith in the future of a democratic Japan.

2380 ———. "Peace without Fear." *Department of State Bulletin* 24:726–31 (7 May 1951)

The continuity of the American desire for a prompt and just peace insured by collective power, despite the changes in Japan occasioned by the removal of General MacArthur, is emphasized by Dulles. He stresses the consistently firm position of the United States in regard to its policy in the Pacific and American willingness to provide comprehensive aid to Japan to prevent both direct aggression and indirect, domestic subversion by communism. The author defends the need for collective security rather than neutrality and closes with a call for Japanese economic well-being and support for human rights.

2381 ———. "The San Francisco Conference on Proposed Japanese Peace Treaty." *Department of State Bulletin* 25:346–48 (27 Aug. 1951)

Expressing his pleasure that a final text of the peace treaty has been drawn up, Dulles notes the fact that the Soviet government will send a delegation to San Francisco and warns the USSR against any attempts "to demolish a structure of Japanese peace which has been built carefully and soundly." He further describes the origins of the treaty and emphasizes the fact that the treaty is not an American-dictated document, as the Communists have suggested, but rather a treaty which has been drawn up by all of the Allied powers. He briefly discusses the issue of reparations particularly involving the Philippines, Indonesia, and Burma and reaffirms his faith that the treaty will insure lasting peace for Japan.

2382 ———. "Strategy for the Pacific." *Department of State Bulletin* 24:483–85 (26 Mar. 1951)

Dulles relates the faithfulness with which the United States has undertaken to inform the Soviet Union of all discussions concerning the peace treaty with

Japan. He accuses the Soviets of unilaterally breaking off negotiations and attempting to "murder peace."

2383 Eichler, David K. "The Treaty and the Future of Japan." *New Republic* 125:5–7 (17 Sept. 1951)

A former deputy secretary general of the Far Eastern Commission analyzes the peace treaty in the context of the possibility of a Japanese reversion to authoritarian social and political patterns. The necessity of a future bond between the United States and Japan and the need for American leadership and goodwill to ensure the maintenance of a democratic society in Japan is emphasized.

2383a "Exchange of Memoranda with U.S.S.R." *Department of State Bulletin* 25:138–45 (23 July 1951)

The first of 2 items within this article is a lengthy Soviet memorandum dated 10 June 1951 responding to earlier American comments on a previous Soviet statement dealing with the American draft of a Japanese peace treaty (no. 2437). The major Soviet complaint is that the draft does not contain adequate guarantees against the resurgence of Japanese militarism; in fact, the United States is alleged to be carrying out a calculated policy of reviving militarism in Japan. Furthermore, the draft fails to establish any timetable for the withdrawal of occupation forces from Japan. In addition, this particular memorandum contains an indirect attack on American plans for including Japan in a collective security system in the Pacific. The second of the 2 items is the United States government's memorandum of 9 July attacking the propagandistic nature of the Soviet complaints and refuting their contentions point by point.

2384 Farley, Miriam Southwell. "San Francisco and after." *Far Eastern Survey* 20:162–64 (26 Sept. 1951)

Miriam Farley, editor of the *Far Eastern Survey*, details the objections and reservations raised by various nations to the peace treaty signed in San Francisco.

2384a Field, F. V. "Japan: Peace Treaty or Aggressive Alliance." *New World Review* p.5–10 (May 1951)

Field summarizes the various wartime and postwar agreements that relate to Japan and criticizes the actions and policy of the United States government with regard in particular to treaty negotiations designed to bring about a formal end to the state of war between the two countries.

2384b Filippov, I. "Schemes of Enemies of Peace Exposed." *Current Digest of the Soviet Press* 3, no.36:12–14 (20 Oct. 1951)

In his article of 8 September 1951, the staff correspondent for *Pravda* who was assigned to cover the San Francisco Peace Treaty Conference provides an exposé of American activities connected with the signing of the treaty. He first characterizes the conference as one which "was convened for purposes which have nothing in common with the interests of the preservation of peace" and asserts that its participants were there merely to rubber-stamp the draft treaty prepared by the United States and Great Britain. As proof he then cites several facts, among them: (1) the composition of the participants (the chief Asian countries were unrepresented, while the majority of participants were Latin American and European nations that had hardly participated in the Pacific War); (2) American pressure before and during the conference on the participating delegations to sign the treaty as is; and (3) the American use of procedural rules which were intended to impede the work of the Soviet delegation by restricting the number of speeches and the time allotted for a speech. Filippov also discusses the main points of the speech delivered by A. A. Gromyko, the leader of the Soviet delegation, and points out the "immense impression [it] produced in the conference circles and among world public opinion."

2384c Fitzgerald, Charles Patrick. "Peace with Japan?" *Spectator* 186:777–78 (15 June 1951). Reply by W. H. Murray

Walton: *Spectator* 186:816 (22 June 1951)

Fitzgerald examines the prospects for a peace treaty with Japan and finds them poor in large measure because of major disagreements among the potential signatories. The chief obstacle to a joint-treaty is the hostility between the United States and the two Communist powers involved—the Soviet Union and the People's Republic of China. Other problems such as Australian uneasiness over Japanese rearmament and Chinese demands for recognition as the chief victim of Japanese aggression, however, are nearly as grave. The proposed treaty, in Fitzgerald's view, will solve none of the fundamental problems in Asia which arose from World War II, and it will be "a very doubtful contribution to peace."

In reply, Walton argues that the treatment that Western nations accorded Japan after World War I was largely responsible for the resurgence of Japanese militarism during the 1930s. A generous Allied policy toward Japan will prevent an accumulation of Japanese grievances and thereby will undermine future support for militarism within the country.

2385 Frankel, J. "The Pacific Pact." *World Affairs* (London) 5:490–501 (Oct. 1951)

According to Frankel, the peace treaty is best understood as a product of the cold war. The defeat of Japan brought the United States and the Soviet Union face to face in Asia. Conflicts arose over the American refusal to grant Moscow an occupation zone in Japan and over the Soviet pillage of Manchuria, but at first the goals of both sides remained basically defensive. The concerted Communist drive marked by the fall of China, however, changed the nature of the confrontation and ultimately made an overall peace treaty impossible. The agreement reached among the signatories of the San Francisco Peace Treaty, Frankel concludes, is still not fully acceptable to all parties and leaves the Pacific security pattern incomplete.

2386 Great Britain. Foreign Office. *Amendments to Draft Treaty of Peace with Japan.* London: HMSO, 1951. 3p. (Gt. Brit. Foreign Office. Japan, 1951, no.2; Gt. Brit. Parliament. Papers by Command, Cmd.8316)

Revisions of the draft peace treaty with Japan of 3 July 1951, agreed upon by Great Britain and the United States as of 13 July 1951, are presented here. The revisions are primarily changes in phrasing, such as a change in the title of the treaty from "Peace Treaty with Japan" to "Treaty of Peace with Japan" and the substitution of "continue" for "keep."

2387 ———. ———. *Draft Peace Treaty with Japan.* London: HMSO, 1951. 16p. (Gt. Brit. Foreign Office. Japan, 1951, no.1; Gt. Brit. Parliament. Papers by Command, Cmd.8300)

The texts of the draft peace treaty with Japan, 2 declarations to be issued by Japan, and the protocol are set forth here. These drafts represent the agreement reached by Great Britain and the United States on 3 July 1951 concerning a peace settlement with Japan.

2388 ———. ———. *Draft Treaty of Peace with Japan as Amended 13th August, 1951.* London: HMSO, 1951. 17p. (Gt. Brit. Foreign Office. Japan, 1951, no.3; Gt. Brit. Parliament. Papers by Command, Cmd.8341)

The full texts of the draft treaty of peace with Japan, the 2 declarations and the protocol revised as of 13 August 1951 are set forth here.

2389 ———. ———. *Treaty of Peace with Japan, San Francisco, 8th September, 1951 (with Declarations and Protocol).* London: HMSO, 1951. 24p. (Gt. Brit. Foreign Office. Japan, 1951, no.5; Gt. Brit. Parliament. Papers by Command, Cmd.8392)

The full text of the final draft of the Treaty of Peace with Japan is presented here, as are 2 declarations issued by Japan and a protocol which was also signed on the same day.

2390 Gromyko, Andrei A. "A Separate Peace: Soviet Refusal to Sign Treaty."

Vital Speeches 17:718–21 (15 Sept. 1951); also published in a slightly different translation under the title "Statement to the Press by A. A. Gromyko" in *New Times* supplement to no.37:15–20 (12 Sept. 1951)

The reasons behind the Soviet refusal to sign the peace treaty with Japan are the focus of this speech delivered by the deputy foreign minister of the USSR at a press conference held in San Francisco on 8 September 1951. Contending that the draft treaty cannot serve as a basis for a genuine peace settlement in the Far East, he particularly emphasizes its omission of any guarantee against the revival of Japanese militarism. He also claims that the draft treaty provides for the conversion of Japan into an American military base. The latter half of the statement concerns Chinese participation in the treaty and Gromyko castigates the United States for refusing the People's Republic of China its rightful role in the peace negotiations and for violating China's right to Taiwan, the Pescadores, the Paracels, and other islands. He describes 6 amendments relating to the above issues which the Soviet delegation submitted to the conference and asserts that only with these amendments would the treaty be a just and honorable one.

2391 Horoth, V. L. "Making Peace with Japan." *Magazine of Wall Street* 88: 603–4, 640–42 (8 Sept. 1951)

Economic considerations on the part of various nations are cited as a deterrent to those nations signing the peace treaty with Japan. The importance of the Korean War to Japanese economic revival is mentioned as is the tendency for Japan to reexamine and discard certain occupation reforms following independence. Horoth notes the need for future stable Chinese–Japanese relations.

2391a "Hsinhua on American Draft of Peace Treaty with Japan." *Current Digest of the Soviet Press* 3, no.29:7, 25 (1 Sept. 1951)

This *Pravda* article of 22 July 1951 presents (in translation) the 20 July article of Hsinhua (the Chinese news agency) on the steps taken by the Western powers to conclude a separate peace treaty with Japan. The Anglo–American draft of 12 July is criticized as contradicting international agreements on the question of Japan; as violating the sovereignty and interests of the People's Republic of China, the USSR, and other countries which fought during the Pacific War; and as aimed at turning Japan into a colony and military base for American aggression in East Asia. The article then analyses various clauses of the draft treaty—in particular those relating to China and to Japanese militarism—and concludes by noting that the treaty basically rejects the right of other countries to submit reparations claims to Japan and illegally grants both the United States and Japan the right to release Japanese war criminals.

Hsu, Immanuel C. Y. "Japan: A Progress Report." 1951. *See* no.648.

2392 Iizawa, Shōji. "A Peace Treaty and Political Parties." *Contemporary Japan* 20:36–45 (Jan./Mar. 1951)

Written before the adoption of the peace treaty ending the occupation of Japan, this article is a thorough examination of the various attitudes expressed toward a treaty by Japan's major political parties. The author first considers the 3-point resolution for a peace treaty set forth by the Social Democratic party before discussing the considerably different proposals suggested by the Liberal party and the Democratic party. There is a provocative discussion of the effect of the Korean War and the Dulles Mission to Japan on the parties' attitudes. The article provides some insight into Japanese aspirations for a peace treaty.

2393 Japan. Ministry of Foreign Affairs. Public Information Div., comp. *Collection of Official Foreign Statements on Japanese Peace Treaty*. Tokyo: n.p., n.d. 3v.

A compilation of official statements and documents prepared by foreign governments with regard to the Japanese peace treaty and issued by the Japanese

Ministry of Foreign Affairs. Volume 1 treats the period before September 1950. Volume 2 covers the period from 14 September 1950 through 25 May 1951, and volume 3 that from 28 May 1951 through 22 August 1951. The statements and notes, press conference speeches, and other documents collected here originate in Australia, France, Indonesia, Nationalist China, the Netherlands, the Philippines, the People's Republic of China, the Soviet Union, the United Kingdom, the United States, SCAP's General Headquarters, and elsewhere.

2394 "Japan Gets New Kind of Peace." *Life* 31:28–37 (17 Sept. 1951)

Life reports on the San Francisco Conference and the inability of the Soviet Union to disrupt the proceedings. Included is the text of the speech made by John Foster Dulles before the conference, in which he stresses the initiative taken by the United States in drafting a peace treaty designed to restore total sovereignty to Japan. Dulles also discusses the voluntary nature of any future security negotiations to be conducted by Japan. He concludes with an explanation of the United States' position on the participation of China in treaty negotiations with Japan.

2394a "Japanese Peace Treaty." *World Today* 7:273–75 (July 1951)

This article summarizes the developments to date in the Allied discussions of a Japanese peace settlement. In sharp contrast to continuing Soviet obstructionism, both the British and American governments feel a sense of urgency about concluding an acceptable treaty. Certain other allies are balking at suggestions that Japan be permitted to rearm, but the writer suspects that Japanese economic self-interest will keep Japan from rearming to any significant degree.

2394b "Japanese Peace Treaty." *External Affairs* 3:330–32 (Oct. 1951)

This article reprints a brief statement made by Canadian Secretary of State for External Affairs Lester B. Pearson at the San Francisco Peace Treaty Conference on 7 September 1951. Pearson attacks the destructive and delaying tactics of the Soviet and Czech governments and urges that the treaty be accepted despite its inevitable imperfections. The treaty, he says, is "just, even generous, and without rancor or revenge." He notes in passing that Canada will begin negotiations on a fisheries agreement with Japan as soon as the treaty is signed. In concluding, Pearson voices regrets over the absence of a Chinese delegation and claims that the government in Peking must bear the blame.

2394c "Japanese Peace Treaty." *International Organization* 5:834–35 (Nov. 1951)

This article is a brief outline summary of the proceedings of the San Francisco Peace Treaty Conference. It is based largely on press reports.

2395 "The Japanese Treaty." *Christian Century* 68:982–84 (29 Aug. 1951)

This article makes predictions concerning the objections to the American draft peace treaty with Japan which may be raised by nations participating in the San Francisco Conference. The Soviet Union's potentially disruptive role and the possibility of a breakup of the conference is foreseen. The work done by John Foster Dulles to create a "Christian" treaty based on forgiveness and helpfulness is emphasized as is the responsibility of the American public to urge the adoption of this treaty.

2396 "Japanese Peace Treaty Deadlock." *Newsweek* 37:30–31 (18 June 1951)

Intricacies of diplomacy between the United States and Great Britain concerning the drafting of a peace treaty with Japan are dealt with in this article. Meetings between Presidential Representative Dulles and British Foreign Secretary Morrison are highlighted, as is the reluctance of the British government to accept Nationalist Chinese participation in peace treaty negotiations to the exclusion of Communist China. The conclusion states that it is in the best interests of the United States rapidly to conclude a peace treaty, even a bilateral treaty if necessary, in order to halt the drain on American funds caused by the occupation, to prevent Japanese disillusionment, and to support the Yoshida cabinet.

2397 "The Japanese Treaty: Will It Stick?" *Nation* 173:82–83 (4 Aug. 1951)

This editorial is a discussion of the leniency of the Japanese peace treaty. Mention is made of Japan's ability to develop a viable, stable polity in contrast to the turbulent situation in Asia and of the necessity for the United States to counteract Soviet influence in East Asia. Three doubts are expressed concerning the Dulles treaty: (1) if approved, its signatories would unrealistically ignore Chinese and Russian opinions; (2) the treaty permits continuation of the U.S.–Japanese alliance which is unpopular among Asian nations; and (3) it does not guarantee Japanese access to continental Asian markets without which Japanese economic revival is uncertain.

2397a Jerome, V. J. "Wall Street Orders a 'Peace' Treaty." *Political Affairs* 30, no.9:1–14 (Sept. 1951)

The chairman of the American Communist Party's Cultural Commission charges that the peace treaty conference is a "fitting climax to a unilateral occupation policy which has from the start trampled upon the interests of the other Allies and the Japanese people." He calls the treaty which is being concluded with Japan's "monopolist-militarist Zaibatsu-Samurai ruling clique" a "Wall Street *diktat* which other countries are ordered to rubber stamp." Jerome backs up his assertations by pointing to the exclusion of the People's Republic of China from the conference, to the fact that the countries participating in the San Francisco Conference were there to sign the treaty rather than to amend or debate it, and to various treaty clauses that will enable the United States to keep its armed forces in Japan and to retain control over the Japanese economy. Jerome also notes that there is condemnation and criticism of the treaty everywhere—even in such countries as Australia, New Zealand, the Philippines, and South Korea.

2398 Kano, Kizō. "Japan as Judas." *Nation* 173:213 (15 Sept. 1951)

The editor of the *Nishi Nippon Press* discusses Dulles' recent meetings with purged Japanese leaders Hatoyama Ichirō and Ishibashi Tanzan. Kano contends that the support extended by Japanese leaders to American policies is strictly tactical and intended to hasten the restoration of Japan's independence and sovereignty.

2399 Kirchwey, Freda. "A Treaty with the Past." *Nation* 173:164–65 (1 Sept. 1951)

American consternation resulting from the Soviet decision to participate in the San Francisco Conference is discussed. The possibility that the conference could be disrupted by dissatisfaction concerning the nonparticipation of Mainland China and the rearmament and economic revitalization of Japan is noted. Kirchwey suggests that the treaty is unpopular among Asian nations not because it deals generously with Japan but rather because it embodies relationships based on foreign interference and entanglement which are increasingly antithetical to Asian aspirations.

2400 Koever, J. F. "Le traité de paix avec le Japon, source de querelles et d'une évolution du droit international." *Revue politique et parlementaire* 204:166–70 (May 1951)

This article deals essentially with Soviet–American relations insofar as they have centered around the proposed peace treaty with Japan. According to Koever, the Soviet government has expressed its opposition to present American moves for restoring Japan to her normal, international position. Moscow's negative attitude, however, appears to be backfiring on this particular occasion. Koever predicts that the Soviet Union will fail to stop the normalization of the political situation within the Far East and that her obstructionist tactics will simply reinforce the United Nations in its efforts to secure worldwide respect for international law and for collective action against aggression of any kind.

2400a Koizumi, Shinzō. "Security for Tomorrow's Japan." *Contemporary Japan* 20:435–43 (Oct./Dec. 1951)

Koizumi, an educator, suspects that many proponents of an overall peace treaty are less interested in peace than they are in promoting a pro-Soviet atmosphere in Japan. There is, he argues, no practical alternative to the present treaty. The neutrality which an overall peace settlement would necessitate probably could not be maintained, and if the present treaty is rejected, the consequence would be a continued Allied occupation—something which would be unsatisfactory to everyone.

Kudryavtsev, V., and M. Mikhailov. "Dulles Prepares Alliance of U.S.A. with Japanese Revanchists." 1951. *See* no. 2483a.

2401 Kuh, Frederick. "After Japan: Germany." *Nation* 173:225–28 (22 Sept. 1951)

Kuh's analysis of the San Francisco Peace Treaty Conference is based on the contention that the presence of Soviet and East European delegations stifled criticism by other participants who feared they would be regarded as pro-Soviet. The serious dissent expressed by India, the Philippines, Australia, and various Arab and Scandinavian countries regarding the treaty is noted, as is the concern of Asian countries.

2402 Lattimore, Owen. "What Kind of Peace for Japan?" *New Republic* 124:13–14 (11 June 1951)

Lattimore anticipates the failure of an American "Japan policy" based strictly on bilateral relations between 2 countries. He advocates an alliance of non-Communist Asian nations based on independent self-interest rather than American dominance to counterbalance Russian and Chinese power. He suggests that Japan will not tolerate permanent American dominance but rather will be motivated by national desires for independence and neutrality to assume a leadership role among Asian nations.

2403 Lawrence, David. "Peace without Revenge." *U.S. News and World Report* 31:88 (14 Sept. 1951)

This editorial praises the United States for being the first humane conqueror in history. The peace treaty is deemed a treaty "of reconciliation which looks to the future." The author notes, however, that the treaty is also an American expiation for its refusal in the 1920s to recognize Japan's "legitimate expansion of business and trade on the continent."

2404 "A Letter from *Ta Kung Pao* to the Japanese People." *Soviet Press Translations* 6:556–58 (15 Oct. 1951)

This open letter to Japan, which originally appeared in the 15 August 1951 issue of *Ta Kung Pao* (Shanghai), is a call for Chinese–Japanese friendship and cooperation. Emphasis is placed on the subjugation of Japan by foreigners and American imperialism is linked with a rebirth of Japanese militarism. Japan is warned that a unilateral peace with the United States would amount to a Japanese declaration of war on China and the Soviet Union. Japanese leaders are urged to repudiate a separate peace and an economic-military alliance with America in favor of independence and Asian solidarity.

2405 "MacArthur Never Dies." *New Statesman and Nation* 42:60 (21 July 1951)

This editorial strongly criticizes the peace treaty proposed by the United States. The author views the U.S.-Japanese bilateral defense agreement as the confirmation of absolute American control over Japan and defines Japanese democratic institutions as mere trappings. He states that the supremacy of the *zaibatsu* and the "most rigid, oppressive, and undemocratic social system known in any Twentieth Century indusdustrial power" have scarcely been challenged. The commercial articles of the treaty are condemned as fostering resurgent commercial imperialism. The article reflects injured British pride, bruised politically by the United States and threatened economically by the recent enemy, Japan.

2405a Maki, John McGilvrey. "Japan: Problems of Peace." *New Leader* 34, no.50:6–7 (10 Dec. 1951)

Maki calls the San Francisco Peace Treaty Conference an "unqualified diplomatic success for the United States" and the treaty itself a document that is far more generous and lenient to the Japanese than they could have hoped for at the time of their defeat. Nonetheless, while the formal conclusion of peace represents a major step in the direction of Japan's regaining her full sovereignty, peace will either create or intensify a whole range of strategic, economic, and diplomatic problems. The withdrawal of the occupation army which guaranteed Japan's security may leave Japan partially exposed to foreign aggression—especially if the United States has to concentrate its armed forces elsewhere in the world in the event of another war. The Japanese economy will no longer be supported by American aid and the Japanese will have to decide whether to establish economic relations with the People's Republic of China in spite of the American disapproval that such an action would bring. Finally, it should be remembered that the treaty does not bring with it complete peace. China, India, and the Soviet Union are still technically at war with Japan and the latter may be expected to bloc Japan's entry into the United Nations.

2406 Markov, M. "The Separate Treaty with Japan: A Weapon of American Aggression." *Soviet Press Translations* 6:452–55 (1 Sept. 1951); abridged version published under the title "Separate Treaty with Japan Is Instrument of American Aggression" in *Current Digest of the Soviet Press* 3, no.29:6–7 (1 Sept. 1951)

Markov discusses the American separate peace treaty as a means of converting Japan into an accomplice of American aggression in an article which appeared originally in the 16 July 1951 issue of *Pravda*. He notes an absence of clauses in the treaty regarding the status of American occupation forces, the limitation of the size of Japanese military forces, and the prohibition of war industry. The separate treaty is analyzed in terms of domestic Japanese suppression of democracy and a reversal of earlier occupation reforms. Also mentioned is the finality of the American draft of the treaty and the rubberstamp quality of the proposed San Francisco Conference.

2407 Mayevsky, V. "England and the Separate Treaty with Japan." *Soviet Press Translations* 6:455–57 (1 Sept. 1951); abridged version published under the title "Britain and Separate Treaty with Japan" in *Current Digest of the Soviet Press* 3, no.30:12–13 (8 Sept. 1951)

Mayevsky regards British acquiescence to the revival of Japanese militarism as indicative of the British desire for a bulwark against national liberation movements in the Far East even at the expense of the loss of British power and economic strength in the Pacific. He highlights the American refusal to allow participation of the Chinese People's Republic in treaty negotiations. A variety of British publications are quoted indicating that the treaty is not in the interests of an Asian settlement, and Indian, Australian and Malayan dissatisfaction is noted. This article appeared originally in the 27 July 1951 issue of *Pravda*.

2407a Morrison, Herbert. "A Deliberate Moral Decision: 'Let Peace, Progress and Security March on'." *Vital Speeches* 17, no.23:712–13 (15 Sept. 1951)

In an address to the Japanese Peace Treaty Conference on 8 September 1951, the foreign secretary of Great Britain expresses British pleasure at the formal restoration of Anglo–Japanese ties. He calls the Allied decision to draft a liberal and non-restrictive treaty not an act of charity or condescension but rather "a deliberate moral decision" taken in order to improve chances for an enduring peace in the Pacific. The treaty is also an act of faith in Japan's willingness to work for the welfare of mankind. Morrison deplores the refusal of certain countries, especially China, to sign the treaty but states that it would not have been right to delay the restoration of Japan's freedom and independence until friendly and normal relations between China and the rest of the world are restored.

2407b "Mr. Gromyko at San Francisco." *Economist* 161, no.5637:541 (8 Sept. 1951)

Few people are greatly impressed by the threats contained in the speech on the Japanese peace treaty which Andrei Gromyko delivered at the San Francisco Conference. Most governments have already made up their mind to sign the treaty in spite of reservations which they might have, and "nothing could possibly be sillier than, having decided to do what it was known the Russians did not like, to hesitate now merely because Mr. Gromyko's presence at San Francisco underlines the Kremlin's threats."

2408 Naoi, Takeo. "Japan Discusses the Peace Treaty." *New Leader* 34, no.30: 6–7 (23 July 1951)

Naoi reviews the activities of Japan's political parties, labor unions, and businessmen as they prepare to adjust to the new state of affairs that will follow the occupation. He focuses in particular upon the political situation, pointing out the confidence with which the Liberals face the future, the inability of the Democrats to find a competent leader who can take charge of the political battles that lie ahead, and the confusion predominant within the ranks of the Socialists on account of their overemphasis on ideology. The leaders of Japan's labor unions, Naoi continues, also are too absorbed in abstract ideological issues and are incapable of handling day-to-day issues. Despite the rapid expansion of labor under the occupation, he notes, the daily work of the unions has been generally neglected and as a consequence there is considerable apathy among the workers towards the unions as a whole.

2408a ———. "Japan Views the Peace." *New Leader* 34, no.41:11–12 (8 Oct. 1951)

The Tokyo correspondent of the *New Leader* writes that while the great majority of the Japanese people welcomed the signing of the peace treaty, many members of the Japan Socialist Party, a large majority of the intellectuals, and a major section of organized labor were unhappy both with it and with the accompanying U.S.–Japan Security Treaty. The Socialists were adamantly opposed from the beginning to a peace treaty that did not include the Soviet Union and the People's Republic of China, holding that trade with mainland China was indispensable and that the security treaty would expose Japan to attack from her Communist neighbors. The intellectuals generally shared the Socialist position and were vociferous in their criticism. Many labor leaders also actively opposed the treaties. Nonetheless, Naoi points out, a movement has been developing within the ranks of the Japan Socialist Party and of labor which opposes the policies of their leaders and supports the treaties.

2408b New Zealand. Dept. of External Affairs. *Annual Report of the Department of External Affairs, 1 April 1950 to 31 March 1951.* Wellington: Government Printer, 1951. 87p. (Dept. of External Affairs publication 103)

A report focusing on activities undertaken by the United States and Commonwealth nations with respect to the negotiations of a peace treaty with Japan. It stresses New Zealand's concern with Pacific security and the control of any resurgence of Japanese militarism.

2409 ———. ———. *Japanese Peace Settlement.* Wellington: Government Printer, 1951. 57p. (Dept. of External Affairs publication 106)

This publication gives a brief but comprehensive picture of the events that led to the conclusion of a peace treaty with Japan. It provides background information about the Japanese peace treaty negotiations which originated in 1947. It explains New Zealand's primary concern with its own security and with preventing any resurgence of Japanese militarism. It then comments on such major provisions of the treaty signed on 8 September 1951 as the territorial, security and economic provisions as well as the disposition of Allied property in Japan. It also refers to the 1947 Canberra conference where 8 Commonwealth nations met for a preliminary discussion of the main issues likely to arise in drawing up the treaty. Among the appendixes are the texts of the Treaty of Peace, protocol, and 2 declarations made by Japan, a report regarding the conference prepared by New Zealand's delegation for its Parliament, and the text of the statement by New Zealand's minister of external affairs made in the House of Representatives on 13 July 1951 in introducing the draft treaty to the House, as well as the security treaties among the United States, Australia, and New Zealand, between the United States and the Philippines, and between the United States and Japan.

2409a "No Asiatic Versailles." *Christian Century* 68:1070–71 (19 Sept. 1951)

The propaganda utilized by both the United States and the Soviet Union is highlighted in this analysis of the San Francisco Conference. Hope is expressed that the responsibility for treaty adjudication and for the future of Japan will be turned over to the United Nations and that the United Nations will provide a means for reconciling Japan to the world community.

2410 Opie, Redvers, et al. *The Search for Peace Settlements.* Washington, D.C.: Brookings Institution, 1951. xvii, 366p.

This volume recounts the efforts made through early 1951 to bring World War II formally to an end by the conclusion of peace treaties between the victors and the vanquished. Most of the book deals with Europe, but in addition to being mentioned in chapter 4's discussion of the Yalta Conference, Japan is studied at some length in chapter 12. Joseph W. Ballantine, the author of this particular section, first discusses the major issues to be considered in a coming peace settlement: disarmament, democratization, territorial dispositions, and economic rehabilitation and reparations. He points out that neither the procedure for initiating peace negotiations nor even the official body that is to negotiate the terms of peace for Japan has yet been determined, and that the entire matter has been complicated by recent events in China. At the same time, he continues, the outbreak of war in Korea has spurred the United States to make a renewed effort to conclude some settlement with Japan and to enter into some sort of military alliance with that country. "While the outlook is now favorable to some kind of a peace settlement," Ballantine concludes, "the latter may have to take the form of a series of bilateral treaties between Japan and powers that have views and interests similar to or identical with those of the United States."

2410a Orekhov, F. "Treaty for the Preparation of War." *Soviet Press Translations* 6:554–55 (15 Oct. 1951); abridged version published under the title "Treaty Preparing for War" in *Current Digest of the Soviet Press* 3, no.37:22 (27 Oct. 1951)

In an article which appeared originally in the 11 September 1951 issue of *Pravda*, Orekhov reports the results of the San Francisco Conference as being indicative of a deal between "American Imperialism and Japanese Irredentism." He discusses the failings of the treaty including its failure to prevent the rebirth of militarism, to provide for Asian security, to satisfy the victims of Japanese aggression, and to insure a peace-loving, independent, and democratic Japan. He asks how any document pertaining to basic Asian problems can have validity without the support of India, China, and the Soviet Union.

2410b "Our Inmost Feelings." *Nation* 173: 108–10 (11 Aug. 1951)

A Japanese economist observes that Japanese public opinion does not approve of the Dulles draft treaty and maintains that Japanese opinion is constrained by oppressive SCAP activities and cannot be expressed democratically under the Yoshida government. The plan to retain American troops in Japan after the end of the occupation is criticized, as are all attempts to link the Japanese economy to the American war economy. The author does not trust American aspirations in Asia and he asserts that dissatisfaction with the United States is increasing, especially among Japanese young people.

2410c "Pacific *Pax Americana.*" *Economist* 161, no.5630:156–57 (21 July 1951)

This article first discusses the American plans for a peace treaty with Japan and for security treaties with Japan and with Australia and New Zealand respectively. It then comments briefly on the coming San Francisco Conference, Dulles' role in drafting the peace treaty, and the misgivings which various Allies have expressed. The interlocked questions of the future of Taiwan and Chinese participation in the settlement came closer than is generally realized to provoking a major split in Anglo–American policy, the article continues, but a compromise solution has been reached: the Allies will allow Japan to decide whether to seek a similar peace treaty with Taipei or Peking. The United States is confident that Japan will not seek a settlement with Peking, yet—the *Economist* concludes—it is questionable how long Japan will toe the American line in regard to its policy vis-à-vis the 2 Chinas.

2411 "Party Comments on Soviet Peace Memorandum." *Contemporary Japan* 20: 238–41 (Apr./June 1951)

This article presents comments by leading political party figures on the Soviet response to the American draft of a peace treaty with Japan as recorded in the 23 May 1951 issue of *Pravda*. The leaders whose opinions appear are: Katsumata Seiichi, chairman of the Social Democratic Party's Political Affairs Investigation Board; Kitamura Tokutarō, a member of the National Democratic Party's Supreme Committee; Kuroda Hisao, leader of the Labor-Farmer Party; and Masuda Kaneshichi, secretary-general of the Liberal Party. A number of different points are made, but all men except for Kuroda share a strong negative reaction to the Soviet statement, which they tend to find hypocritical and untrustworthy.

2411a Patch, Buel W. "Japan and Pacific Security." *Editorial Research Reports* v.1 1951:139–57 (28 Feb. 1951)

Divided into 3 sections, this report is a straightforward, factual account designed for journalists who are expected to be writing on the subject. Part 1 reviews past efforts to make peace with Japan and the developments which have made the conclusion of a treaty with Japan—even without Soviet and Chinese participation—increasingly urgent. Part 2—on the terms of the settlement—covers the Allied wartime agreements on territorial changes, conflicting American and Soviet views on the disposition of the Ryukyus and Bonins, the question of war reparations and Philippine claims, and the reaction of various Pacific nations (especially Australia, New Zealand, and the Philippines) to the proposed rearmament of Japan. Part 3, entitled "Defense of Japan and Pacific Security," in turn examines the various offers of American aid to Japan on the basis of self-help, a proposed Pacific collective security treaty, Japan's relations with various Western powers before World War II, and Japan's key role in the balance of power within East Asia.

2411b "Peace with Japan." *Economist* 160, no.5625:1416–18 (16 June 1951)

Dulles' recent visit to London was only moderately successful. There still are a number of differences between the American and British governments which must be resolved, and the signing of the Japanese peace treaty accordingly will be delayed. The delay—like earlier ones—is regrettable, but the Allies do deserve credit for choosing to be liberal and magnanimous in their dealings with Japan. It is already clear that the treaty will be based on 4 principal ideas: (1) territorial dismemberment, (2) no war guilt clause, (3) certain economic provisions which will enable Japan to earn her own living, and (4) the importance of providing Japan with a sense of national security. Even while these broad outlines have been agreed upon, the article concludes, there is still some disagreement over the economic provisions and certain other serious points of difference remain to be settled. These include the advisability of concluding a separate peace with Japan, the nature of rearmament that Japan will be able to undertake, and the question of which government—Peking or Taipei—will be invited to the peace treaty conference to sign on China's behalf.

2411c Polyzoides, A. Th. "The Japanese Peace Treaty and after." *World Affairs Interpreter* 22:296–310 (Oct. 1951)

Polyzoides characterizes the peace treaty as a "unique success in treaty making." He first reviews the history of the negotiations among the Allies, giving particular emphasis to the disagreements over the rearming of Japan and to the conflicts between the United States and the Soviet Union on numerous issues, including that of Chinese participation. A detailed account of the proceedings at San Francisco follows, with Soviet tactics again receiving considerable attention. The treaty itself is described and analyzed section by section. Polyzoides concludes by speculating on the potentially disruptive effect that future Japanese economic expansion will have on the nations of Latin America, Southeast Asia, and Africa.

2412 "Proposed Japanese Peace Treaty." *External Affairs* 3:257–58 (July 1951)

This partial text of a speech by the Canadian secretary of state for external affairs, Lester B. Pearson, concerns his country's participation in the treaty negotiations. He favors the American plan of private diplomatic talks rather than a general peace treaty conference. Although Canada has not played a substantive role in the drafting of a treaty, Pearson indicates that he is satisfied with the proceedings thus far and that Canada's main concern is the rapid negotiation of a fishing treaty with Japan.

2413 Rawlings, E. H. "The Japanese Peace Treaty." *Contemporary Review* 180: 202–5 (Oct. 1951)

A useful article organized in 2 parts: the first considers the historical development of peace treaty negotiations among the Allies and stresses postponements and disagreements; the second part describes a variety of Allied complaints about the actual treaty, particularly the objections of India concerning American pressure to insure ratification by all governments, the American–Japanese military alliance, and the continuation of the American occupation of the Ryukyu and Bonin Islands on a semipermanent basis. The author concludes that Japan has changed her political and foreign policy goals and will play a new role as the economic and political right arm of the United States in East Asia.

2414 "Red Defeat at San Francisco: Is It Too Good to Be True?" *Newsweek* 38: 28–31 (17 Sept. 1951)

Newsweek presents a cursory review of the San Francisco Conference, emphasizing the failure of Soviet obstructionist tactics.

2415 Roach, James R. "Australia and the Japanese Treaty." *Far Eastern Survey* 20:206–8 (21 Nov. 1951)

Roach points out that Australia accepted the Japanese peace treaty reluctantly and that latent hostility to Japan remains, with trade issues a potential focus. Informed Australians, he states, doubt that the occupation made any major changes in the Japanese social and policital structure. Furthermore, as there are no treaty limitations or provisions for inspection, they feel that it will be quite easy for Japan to rearm and for her industrial combines to reappear.

2416 "Russian Rout." *Time* 58:30 (17 Sept. 1951)

This article reviews the failure of Soviet efforts to revise the peace treaty or to cause the dissolution of the San Francisco Conference. Excerpts from a speech by John Foster Dulles are quoted which rebut Soviet charges concerning Japanese reparations to the rest of Asia and the future role of the United States in Japanese affairs.

2417 Ryū, Shintarō. "The Timing of Japan's Peace Treaty." *Far Eastern Survey* 20:165–68 (26 Sept. 1951)

Examining possible Communist reactions, the editor of the *Asahi Shimbun* cautions that ratification of the treaty may deepen the crisis in the Far East. In concluding the peace treaty, he points out that it is essential to give due consideration to 2 points: first, that the disturbance in Korea has not yet been brought under control, and, second, the existence of the Sino–Soviet treaty.

2418 "San Francisco Conference on Japanese Peace Treaty." *Department of State Bulletin* 25:447–62 (17 Sept. 1951)

A major portion of this issue of the *Bulletin* is devoted to the Japanese peace treaty and the U.S.–Japan Security Treaty. Materials include the opening address at the conference by President Truman (no.2431), statements by Secretary Acheson (no.2361a) and John Foster Dulles, the complete text of the rules of procedure to be followed at the conference, and the United States' answers to 9 Soviet charges against the Japanese treaty. Texts of some of these speeches have been noted elsewhere, but this issue provides a convenient collection of important documents.

2419 Satō, Naotake. "Peace Treaty and Japan's Future." *Contemporary Japan* 20:135–44 (Apr./June 1951)

An excerpt from a speech delivered at the American–Japan Society by the president of the House of Councillors. It begins by noting the progress which has been made toward a peace settlement. Instead of discussing the coming treaty of peace, however, the article concentrates on presenting the writer's view of Japanese–American relations. Satō emphasizes the significance of the fact that Japan is to be a sovereign nation again with the signing of the peace treaty. He demonstrates at considerable length the efforts of the Japanese "to establish a peaceful democratic nation" under the conditions prescribed by the Potsdam Declaration, making clear that this was not done as a result of obligation due to defeat but because the Japanese "realized the value and significance of the spirit of democracy." He outlines the history of the Japanese–American relationship to show that historically friendly relations have existed and to point out that, in spite of defeat, no feeling of hatred toward Americans has existed since the surrender. He concludes by expressing the desire of the Japanese to be permitted to join the United Nations.

2420 Scalapino, Robert Anthony. "San Francisco: Content of Ideas." *Foreign Policy Bulletin* 31:1–2 (1 Oct. 1951)

An incisive analysis of the peace treaty conference in San Francisco. After mentioning those aspects which represent a victory for the Western powers, the author also cites unfavorable aspects, particularly the refusal of India, Burma, and China to attend the conference. The bulk of the article discusses the continuing ideological debates between the United States and the USSR, and the various charges and countercharges of their delegates are briefly described. The author concludes that "the conference was symbolic of the new role which the U.S. now assumes in the world" and advises caution in the future exercise of power.

2421 Seidensticker, Edward G. "Japanese Views on Peace." *Far Eastern Survey* 20:119–24 (13 June 1951)

Seidensticker reviews Japanese public opinion with regard to the proposed peace treaty and the nature of Japan's future relations with the United States. He points out that American policies do not have a firm and tested following in Japan because the views and attitudes of many Japanese individuals are surprisingly changeable and capricious. Furthermore, the prevailing mood of resignation towards the treaty terms and the growing Japanese resentment of continued American control over the Ryukyus and the stationing of American military personnel in Japan after the occupation ends, Seidensticker concludes, could lead to open hostility towards the United States.

2421a Shmelyov, N. "The Foreign Press on the Drafting of the Peace Treaty with Japan." *New Times* no.25:14–16 (20 June 1951)

This article surveys the reactions of a number of Western newspapers and journals to the Soviet proposal that a peace conference be convened in July or August to examine the various drafts of the peace treaty with Japan. Shmelyov contends that the United States is anxious to deprive the Soviet Union and China of any role in the framing and concluding of a treaty and that any conference called by Washington would be merely for the purpose of having the American treaty formally signed by its allies. He cites appropriate passages from the press, moreover, to demonstrate that the United States is seeking to convert Japan into a base of aggression against Asia and that American proposals to rearm Japan are causing alarm in several countries.

2422 "Smash America's Plot to Rearm Japan and Fight for a General and Just Peace with Japan." *Soviet Press Translations* 6:207–10 (15 Apr. 1951)

This translation from the Chinese by C. T. Hu of an editorial appearing in the 28 January 1951 issue of the Peking *People's Daily* is a condemnation of American efforts to negotiate a separate peace with Japan. These efforts are regarded as an attempt by the United States to revive Japanese militarism, rearm Japan, and make her a new instrument for imperialist aggression in Asia. The implacable opposition on the part of the Soviet Union and the People's Republic of China to a separate peace is noted and a number of agreements which were signed and broken by the United States concerning the conclusion of a separate peace are discussed.

2422a Smith, Denys. "An American–Japanese Peace Treaty." *National and English Review* 136:220–25 (Apr. 1951)

Smith begins with a general discussion of the prospects for a United States–Japanese peace treaty in the near future. He believes that peace has come relatively quickly because Japan is neither divided by a Soviet occupation nor ruled by an Allied Control Council, because her surrender was not unconditional in the sense that Germany's was (since she retained her emperor and civil government), and because she has no land frontiers with Communist countries. Smith then recounts some of the obstacles to a treaty and American efforts to surmount them and concludes with a prediction of the treaty's various provisions.

2422b Smith, Jessica. "A Treaty for War, Not Peace." *New World Review* p.53–57 (Oct. 1951)

A summary of the Soviet attitude towards the peace treaty as expressed by Deputy Foreign Minister Andrei Gromyko in various statements he made at the time of the San Francisco Peace Conference.

2423 "Speech of A. A. Gromyko at San Francisco Conference on September 5, 1951." *USSR Information Bulletin* 11, no.18:548–56 (21 Sept. 1951); also in the supplement to *New Times* no.37: 1–14 (12 Sept. 1951)

Ambassador Andrei Gromyko, Soviet minister of foreign affairs, delineates his delegation's views of the peace treaty with Japan that is being signed in San Francisco. He considers the draft of the treaty prepared by the United States and Great Britain completely unacceptable, for among other things, it fails to place any limitations on the size of future Japanese military forces, does not provide for the immediate withdrawal of all Allied occupation troops, and neglects to acknowledge the rights of the Soviet Union to Southern Sakhalin and the Kurile Islands. Furthermore, the treaty is calculated to empower once again the "militarists and reactionaries" of Japan. Gromyko then stresses the point that no real peace treaty can emerge which does not have the approval of the Soviet Union and the People's Republic of China, and he notes the refusal of India and Burma even to attend the San Francisco conference. Finally, the ambassador cites a long list of modifications to the draft of the treaty which would make that treaty acceptable in Soviet eyes.

2423a "Start at San Francisco." *Spectator* 187:285 (7 Sept. 1951)

This brief editorial commentary on the opening of the San Francisco conference for the conclusion of a peace treaty with Japan concedes that the treaty represents "the best compromise practicable" despite its indulgent, liberal attitude towards Japan. The Soviet Union is said to have little right to criticize and obstruct the treaty in its present form, for it had its chance to participate in the treaty negotiations earlier and failed to do so.

2423b "Statement by Chou En-Lai on the Question of a Japanese Peace Treaty." *Soviet Press Translations* 6:48-50 (1 Feb. 1951); also published under the title "Chou En-lai's Statement on Question of Peace Treaty with Japan" in *Current Digest of the Soviet Press* 2, no.47:10-11 (6 Jan. 1951)

This statement by Chou En-lai, made on 4 December 1950 and originally appearing in the 6 December 1950 issue of *Pravda*, includes the following points: (1) the People's Republic of China (PRC) is the only rightful representative of China and without her participation in Japanese peace treaty negotiations any treaty is illegal and invalid; (2) the PRC and the Soviet Union have consistently attempted to conclude a peace treaty while the United States has pursued delaying and obstructionist tactics; (3) the Cairo, Yalta, and Potsdam Declarations and Far Eastern Commission resolutions are the proper basis for a peace treaty; (4) territorial decisions concerning Taiwan, Sakhalin, and the Kuriles have been made at Cairo and Yalta and are not negotiable; (5) American occupation troops must be withdrawn from Japan; (6) Japan must remain totally demilitarized; (7) Japanese economic reconstruction must be undertaken without the enhancement of military potential; (8) the American memorandum of 26 October 1950 concerning a peace treaty is designed to promote the economic and military colonization of Japan and is utterly unacceptable.

2423c "Statement by Mongolian People's Republic Minister of Foreign Affairs." *Current Digest of the Soviet Press* 3, no.39:20-21 (10 Nov. 1951)

This translation of an article published in *Pravda* on 27 September 1951 presents Foreign Minister Lkhamsurun's statement in regard to the conclusion of a separate peace treaty with Japan at the San Francisco Peace Treaty Conference. Three major points are made: (1) The treaty is not a multilateral peace treaty but a separate treaty fabricated by the U.S. government. The Mongolian People's Republic was illegally excluded from participating in its preparation and in the ceremonies for signing the document, and accordingly regards the treaty as null and void. (2) The treaty is a gross violation of international agreements on a peace settlement with Japan. Only by adopting the USSR's just proposals for a peace treaty can there be a basis for a genuine settlement in the Far East. (3) The treaty aims at restoring Japanese imperialism in Asia. The Mongolian people, who have been victims of recent Japanese aggression, are fully determined "to frustrate the threat of the extension of the war in the Far East created by the separate peace treaty with Japan."

2424 "Statement by the Minister for External Affairs, the Hon. P. C. Spender, K.C., M.P., in the House of Representatives, 14th March 1951." *Current Notes on International Affairs* 21:157–66 (Mar. 1951)

In an address to the lower house of Parliament, the Australian foreign minister discusses the Korean situation, the Japanese peace settlement, and proposals for security arrangements in the Pacific. He stresses that the Japanese peace treaty must provide "effective and reasonable limitations" on Japanese rearmament. He also calls for effective regional security in the Pacific.

2424a "Statement Issued by Mr. John Foster Dulles, Presidential Envoy of the United States on His Departure from Japan, February 10, 1951." *Contemporary Japan* 20:126–27 (Jan./Mar. 1951)

After a 2-week stay in Japan, Dulles briefly summarizes the matters considered by his mission—particularly those in connection with the impending peace settlement. He discusses the principles which might be embodied in a peace treaty, the matter of Japan's future security, the economic problems which the nation will encounter in the future, and the development of cultural ties between the United States and Japan. He expresses gratitude to SCAP and Japanese officials for their assistance and concludes that the visit was a valuable one.

2424b Terentyev, F. "Dulles in Tokyo." *Soviet Press Translations* 6:107–8 (1 Mar. 1951); also published under the same title in *Current Digest of the Soviet Press* 3, no.4:27 (10 Mar. 1951)

While the American press is characterizing Dulles' mission to Tokyo as an effort to speed up the conclusion of a peace treaty with Japan, the mission in fact is designed to step up Japanese rearmament activities. "The American imperialists," according to Terentyev, "look upon the 'Zaibatsu' and the Japanese militarists as their main bulwark of support and as their allies in perpetrating their adventurous and aggressive schemes against the people of Asia." Furthermore, Wall Street is opposed to a genuine peace treaty with Japan, for it would call for the demilitarization and democratization of that country, would not allow the United States to retain some sort of control over Japan, and would not permit the U.S. to maintain a preferential position in Japan compared to other members of the Anglo–American bloc. Terentyev's article first appeared in the 26 January issue of *Pravda* and is reproduced here in an abridged translation.

2425 Tiltman, Hessell. "Japan's Peace Treaty." *Nation* 172:509–12 (2 June 1951)

Tiltman discusses the significance of the occupation in shaping Japan's postwar destiny. The establishment of close economic and military ties between Japan and the United States, which was the goal of the Dulles treaty mission, is regarded as the logical final step to ensure a conservative, stable Japanese society. The combination of SCAP power, American insistence on dictating peace treaty terms, and Japanese impatience to regain domestic sovereignty is expected to be sufficient to overcome any opposition to a treaty by Russia, China, or the Commonwealth countries. Tiltman anticipates that Japan will again become the "workshop of Asia" and that there will be Japanese revision of significant portions of SCAP-inspired "democratic" legislation.

2425a "Time to Say No." *New Statesman and Nation* 42:219 (1 Sept. 1951)

This editorial urges that Great Britain oppose the United States position on the San Francisco peace treaty and insist that the signing of the treaty be postponed until both the U.S.S.R. and the People's Republic of China can be included among the signatories. To fail to do so, the editors argue, would be to alienate Britain's Asian allies and to increase the overall chances for a new outbreak of war in Asia. One strong objection to the American proposal is that by refusing even to discuss the participation of China in the peace treaty and, at the same time, by rearming Japan, the United States is saying in effect that it regards war with China as inevitable.

2426 "Towards a Japanese Peace Treaty." *Economist* 160:410–11 (24 Feb. 1951)

Commenting on the difficulties and problems involved in a peace settlement, the author points out that important questions concerning the nature of the final peace treaty and of Japanese rearmament remain unanswered. He concludes that it would be dangerous to delay the conclusion of a treaty any further on account of Soviet and Chinese unwillingness to agree to the proposed terms, that it is important that Japan rearm to a certain extent in order that the Japanese can bear some of the costs involved in defending their country, and that the United States must provide Australia and New Zealand with some form of definite security guarantee in order to secure the support and cooperation of these countries for the peace treaty negotiations.

2426a "Le traité de paix avec le Japon." *Chronique de politique étrangère* 4, no. 6:731–61 (Nov. 1951)

Appearing within a publication of the Bruxelles (Belgium)-based Institute for International Relations, this article provides a review of developments leading up to the conclusion of peace with Japan as well as information on the San Francisco Peace Treaty Conference itself. Part 1 discusses political events during the latter half of the occupation period and shows how Japanese politics after 1947 were characterized by the growing strength of the conservative parties and by the progressive reduction of SCAP involvement and intervention in domestic political affairs. The following section —on economic life—focuses on Japan's population problem, the postwar development of agriculture, increases in industrial production, and Japanese foreign trade. The authors then turn their attention to the Anglo–American project for drafting a peace treaty with Japan and after commenting on the clauses of the treaty itself indicate the reactions of Belgium, the Netherlands, France, India, Burma, Indonesia, the Philippines, China, the Soviet Union and Japan to the project. The concluding section of this article consists of a summary of the conference proceedings at San Francisco. The English-language text of the peace treaty may be found on p.795–804 of the same issue of *Chronique de politique étrangère*.

2427 "Treaties of Peace: Japan—Allied Powers." *Journal du droit international* 80:182–207 (1953)

Article by article, the complete text of the Treaty of Peace signed between Japan and the Allied powers in San Francisco on 8 September 1951 is presented in both French and English.

2428 "A Treaty for Japan." *Eastern Economist* (New Delhi) 17, no.17:683 (27 Apr. 1951)

This brief, unsigned article favors the conclusion of a peace treaty and indicates that it would be "regrettable if the restoration of Japan's status should be delayed further beyond these nearly six years by fresh hesitations caused by preoccupation with a more desirable state of things."

2429 "Treaty of Peace with Japan." *Current Notes on International Affairs* 22: 480–98 (Sept. 1951)

The complete texts of the Treaty of Peace with Japan signed at San Francisco, 2 declarations made by Japan, and the protocol issued on 8 September 1951 are reprinted here. There is also the text of the Allied Powers Property Compensation Law, which was to ensure compensation for damaged and injured Allied property that existed in Japan on 7 December 1941.

2430 Trigorin, Z. "The U.S. Draft Peace Treaty with Japan." *New Times* no.30: 4–9 (25 July 1951)

In a general description of the background and principal features of the U.S. draft treaty with Japan, the author considers the treaty to be in direct violation of the Cairo and Potsdam Declarations and the Yalta Agreement which directed that all participating countries sign the treaty. He strongly criticizes the draft which would exclude Communist China and overrule Soviet objections and views the treaty as one which will enable American capital to seize control of Japan's vital industries.

2431 Truman, Harry S. "Equals in the Partnership of Peace." *Vital Speeches* 17:706–8 (15 Sept. 1951); also in *Contemporary Japan* 20:405–9 (July/Sept. 1951); *Department of State Bulletin* 25: 447–50 (17 Sept. 1951); *U.S. News and World Report* 31:85–87 (14 Sept. 1951)

Harry S. Truman delivered this speech at the opening of the Japanese Peace Treaty Conference in San Francisco on 4 September 1951. He discusses the remarkable and unprecedented progress Japan has made during the occupation period, then briefly describes the cooperative efforts made during the past year to draw up a peace treaty with Japan. Although he mentions "differences of opinion among the nations concerned as to many of the matters covered by this treaty," he concludes that it is a good treaty which "takes account of the principal desires and ultimate interests of all the participants." After noting the probability of Japan's eventual entry into the United Nations Organization, the president emphasizes the necessity that "Japan be included as soon as possible in appropriate security arrangements for keeping the peace in the Pacific" and outlines the terms of the bilateral U.S.–Japan Security Treaty that will soon be negotiated.

2432 U.S. Dept. of State. *Draft Treaty of Peace with Japan, with Declarations by the Government of Japan.* Washington, D.C.: Government Printing Office, 1951. 32p. (Dept. of State publication 4330; Far Eastern series 49)

Four documents are included: (1) the text of the final draft of a peace treaty with Japan prepared primarily by the governments of the United States and the United Kingdom to be presented to the San Francisco Peace Conference; (2) the text of a draft declaration by the Japanese government pledging to observe the international laws and agreements to which Japan is a party; (3) the text of a draft declaration by the Japanese government recognizing Allied rights to examine their war graves in Japanese territory; and (4) the text of a radio speech given by John Foster Dulles on 15 August 1951. The first 3 documents were adopted without revision at the conference on 8 September 1951. For the official final texts of these documents, see U.S. Department of State publication 4561, Far Eastern series 54, released in May 1952 (no.2456).

2433 ———. ———. Office of Public Affairs. *Japanese Peace Conference, San Francisco, September 1951: Background.* Washington, D.C.: Government Printing Office, 1951. 12p. (Dept. of State publication 4335; International Organization and Conference series 2, Far Eastern 1)

Important events and issues related to the San Francisco Peace Conference are summarized here. Briefly discussed are the participating and the nonattending nations, the process of negotiations that originated in 1947, the successful work of the peace mission led by John Foster Dulles, the lack of Soviet cooperation, the nature of the treaty terms, the procedures for ratification, etc. Emphasis is placed on the treaty as a gesture toward "a peace of reconciliation."

2434 ———. ———. ———. *Japanese Peace Conference, September 4–8, 1951.* Washington, D.C.: Government Printing Office, 1951. 21p. (Dept. of State publication 4371; International Organization and Conference series 2, Far Eastern 2)

The Japanese peace conference was attended by 51 nations plus Japan and 48 of these signed the peace treaty with Japan. Czechoslovakia, Poland, and the Soviet Union participated in the conference but did not sign the treaty. The material in this publication contains the opening address by President Truman on 4 September 1951; the opening and closing statements by the conference president, Secretary of State Acheson; the text of the Rules of Procedure; the statement made by Ambassador John Foster Dulles on behalf of the U.S. delegation at the Second Plenary Session, 5 September; and Dulles' replies to the Soviet Union's charges against the treaty.

2435 ———. ———. ———. *Record of Proceedings of the Conference for the Conclusion and Signature of the Treaty of Peace with Japan.* Washington, D.C.: Government Printing Office, 1951. v, 468p. (Dept. of State publication 4392; International Organization and Conference series 2, Far Eastern 3)

An official record of the proceedings of the San Francisco Peace Conference containing a variety of official documents. There is a list of participants (officers of the conference, members of the 52 delegations, including the Japanese, and of the international secretariat). The text of the letter of invitation issued to 55 governments is included, along with the agenda of the conference as stipulated in Article 17 of the Rules of Procedure and the text of the Rules of Procedure. The verbatim minutes of the entire conference, namely, the welcoming ceremony, the 8 plenary sessions, and the signature ceremony, are provided in English. The complete texts of the Treaty of Peace with Japan, 2 declarations, and a protocol, each set forth in English, French, Spanish, and Japanese are provided and photostatic copies of the signatures are included as well. There are also an index and a list of documents issued at the conference.

2436 ———. ———. ———. *Supplement to the Record of Proceedings of the Conference for the Conclusion and Signature of the Treaty of Peace with Japan.* Washington, D.C.: Government Printing Office, 1952. v, 161p. (Dept. of State publication 4392A; International Organization and Conference series 2, Far Eastern 3)

The Japanese peace conference in San Francisco in 1951 was attended by 52 nations including Japan. All but Panama expressed their attitudes toward the draft peace treaty in the second through the eighth plenary sessions. Of those 51 formal statements, 29 were given in languages other than English, namely, French, Spanish, Russian, and Japanese. This supplement contains these 29 statements in their original languages. English versions may be found in the section of *Record of Proceedings* (no.2435) that records the verbatim minutes of the conference.

2437 "U.S. Analyzes Comments by USSR for Effecting Japanese Peace Treaty." *Department of State Bulletin* 24:852–58 (28 May 1951); "Remarks by the USSR" (p.856–58) also published under the title "Soviet Remarks on Peace Treaty with Japan in the U.S.S.R. Ministry of Foreign Affairs" in *Current Digest of the Soviet Press* 3, no.18:3–4 (16 June 1951)

This 2-part article consists of a note by the Soviet Union presented on 7 May 1951 commenting on the receipt of an American draft of the peace treaty with Japan and a reply to that note by the United States presented on 19 May. The Soviet text criticizes the unilateral method by which the draft was prepared, stating that the United States should have engaged in joint negotiations as provided by international agreement. The content of the treaty is criticized—particularly those sections dealing with the disposition of territory, the lack of guarantees against militarism, and the removal of occupation forces. The note closes with a call for a June or July meeting of the Council of Foreign Ministers with advisory participation by all combatants in the Pacific area. This meeting would draft a peace treaty containing limitations on Japanese military strength and would provide for the exclusion of all foreign military forces from Japan.

The State Department reply suggests that the American draft differs only with respect to Soviet demands that Formosa and the Pescadores be given to the People's Republic of China. The American memorandum points to Soviet policy ambiguities over time and asks for Soviet participation in the treaty.

2438 "U.S. Invites Fifty Nations to Sign Peace Treaty with Japan." *Department of State Bulletin* 25:186–87 (30 July 1951)

The nations which were extended an invitation to the San Francisco Peace Conference are listed along with the text of the invitation itself. The invitation, which was accompanied by the draft peace treaty, 2 declarations by Japan, and a protocol, presents the details of time and place. The governments of the United States and the United Kingdom state in this invitation that they "will be happy to receive comments on the enclosed draft," and after receipt of these comments they propose "to circulate a final text of the Peace Treaty on August 13, 1951." The invitation makes fleeting and veiled reference to the omission of China in the statement: "Concurrent and identical invitations are being sent to the other Allied Powers at war with Japan, except where special circumstances exist."

2439 "U.S. to Steamroller Gromyko if He Stalls at Japanese Pact." *Newsweek* 38: 37–38 (27 Aug. 1951)

Russian and American plans for a peace treaty with Japan are discussed on the eve of the San Francisco Conference. Strongly emphasized is the American determination not to permit negotiation or amendment of the final draft of the treaty. Russian attempts to use the Korean settlement as a lever for obtaining concessions on the Japanese treaty are mentioned.

2439a "U.S.S.R. Intimates Noncooperation on Japanese Treaty." *Department of State Bulletin* 24:453 (19 Mar. 1951)

This press release of 5 March 1951 comments on a statement made by Yakov Malik, the Soviet ambassador to the United Nations, which implies that the Soviet Union will not resume negotiations on a Japanese peace treaty. The release summarizes the history of previous discussions between Malik and John Foster Dulles and contrasts them with the present Soviet position.

2439b "Views on Peace and Security: A Symposium." *Contemporary Japan* 20: 372–78 (July/Sept. 1951)

This article consists of summaries of selections from the October 1951 issue of *Sekai*—an issue which was devoted to airing the views and opinions of prominent Japanese on the peace treaty and the future of Japan. The opinions presented here are those of Tsuru Shigeto, a former staff member of the Economic Stabilization Board; Watsuji Tetsurō, philosopher and professor emeritus of Tokyo University; Yamakawa Hitoshi, socialist leader and writer; Hasegawa Nyozekan, political critic; Yokota Kisaburō, professor of law at Tokyo University; and Rōyama Masamichi, political scientist. The commentators most frequently evince a concern about Japan's being placed in between 2 great powers locked in conflict. The signing of a "separate" peace made a security treaty inevitable, they believe, but the treaty will be a cause for continuing disturbances in Asia. All share a general feeling that Japan's renunciation of neutrality is a mistake. While the possibility of an armed invasion of Japan is remote, the country's security remains a matter of concern. Rearmament is generally frowned upon by all of the commentators, but opinion is divided on the advisability of stationing United States troops in Japan on an indefinite basis.

2439c Waithman, Robert. "Our Friends the Japanese." *Spectator* 187:321 (14 Sept. 1951)

This commentary on the closing of the San Francisco Peace Conference first emphasizes the generous nature of the settlement with Japan and points out the Japanese delegation's public stance of "penitence and humility." Aside from the refusal of a small number of combatants to sign the accord, the meetings and the actual signing went smoothly. The Allied treatment of Japan in the treaty, however, is said to be largely due to the anxiety of the signers over the power vacuum which the war has left in East Asia rather than to their innate generosity. Waithman concludes by remarking that "most of the delegates have left San Francisco without any profound belief that all their problems have been solved; and some of them have taken back home apprehensions which were only temporarily suppressed in the interest of unity."

Weideman, Elizabeth. "House of Sand." 1951. *See* no.2130b.

2440 "What the San Francisco Conference Showed." *New Times* no.37:1–4 (12 Sept. 1951)

This brief résumé of the San Francisco Peace Conference discusses the reasons for the absence of Burma, China, and India from the conference, outlines the proceedings, and analyzes the provisions of the peace treaty and the bilateral American–Japanese Security Treaty. The author charges that the peace treaty was drawn up exclusively by the United States, that it contains no guarantees against a repetition of Japanese aggression, and that it is unacceptable to all peace-loving nations. He then briefly describes the 6 basic issues concerning an independent Japan brought up by the Soviet delegation at the conference.

2441 "What Will Happen Now in Japan." *U.S. News and World Report* 30:30–34 (27 Apr. 1951)

An interview with John Foster Dulles, the chief U.S. negotiator in Japanese peace treaty discussions, sets forth Dulles' responses to a number of questions. He maintains that the Korean War presents no reason to postpone the signing of a peace treaty. A continued military alliance between the United States and Japan is envisioned which would closely tie in with a U.S. defense line running through the Aleutians, Ryukyus, Philippines, and Australia. It is anticipated that an independent Japan would contribute to its own defense to the extent of establishing land forces which would pose no offensive threat because their air and sea components would be provided by the United States. Soviet participation in a peace treaty is seen as improbable because of the USSR's interest in a vulnerable Japan open to Russian take-over. The United States in the near future will cut off direct aid to Japan. Finally, Dulles asserts that it is possible for Japan to become self-supporting without Chinese trade if the trade patterns in effect prior to 1930 are adhered to and if Japan cooperates economically with "free" Asia and the United States.

2441a *The Women of Japan Speak.* New York: Fellowship of Reconciliation, 1951. 16p.

The translation of a statement presented to John Foster Dulles in Tokyo on 6 February 1951 by the women members of the Diet expressing their opposition to Japanese rearmament and to a peace treaty which would provide for a military establishment in Japan.

2442 Yoshida, Shigeru. "Japan and the Crisis in Asia." *Foreign Affairs* 29:171–81 (Jan. 1951)

Prime Minister Yoshida views the cold war as the primary cause for the difficulties encountered in negotiating the peace treaty and as a factor that vitally affects Japan's security. He expresses his desire that a peace treaty be signed even if it does not include all nations with whom Japan was at war. He affirms his country's interest in aligning with the West in the ideological struggle and cites the Korean confrontation as proof that America will stand by Japan in times of military crisis. He follows this with an account of the Japan Communist party's efforts to subvert the nation from within. The final section of the report is devoted to a discussion of Japan's economic situation since the close of the war. The author cites SCAP efforts to boost the economy and lists related production figures indicating that the condition of the economy is continually improving. Finally, he expresses his hope that with the conclusion of a treaty, Japan may be privileged to become a member of the United Nations.

2443 Termination of the Occupation

1952

2443 Allison, John M. "The Japanese Peace Settlement." *Department of State Bulletin* 26:212–15 (11 Feb. 1952).

Allison, assistant secretary of state for Far Eastern affairs, reviews the occupation and the peace treaty settlement. He claims that it has been the American desire since 1943 to see a revived and vital Japanese society following the war and that the dual occupation goals of permanent demilitarization and peaceful, democratic reconstruction were intended to achieve this end. The author regards the American decision to abandon the conference method and engage in diplomatic consultations to negotiate the peace treaty as the result of Soviet insistence on operating through the Council of Foreign Ministers. He deals with current problems such as the necessity to strengthen the Japanese economy through increased foreign trade, the need for rearmament for defensive purposes, and the continuation of the healing process in Japan's relations with her neighbors.

2444 ———. "A New Approach to Treaty Making." *Department of State Bulletin* 26:689–93 (5 May 1952).

As assistant secretary of state for Far Eastern affairs, Allison discusses the peace treaty negotiations in terms of their significance to international law. He praises the cooperation between the executive and legislative branches of the U.S. government in concluding the treaty and explains the procedure for negotiating treaty terms among the Allied powers. He also states that the reason for abandoning the conference plan providing for the participation of Far Eastern Commission members was the division of the commission (by 1950) into 6 members supporting Nationalist China and 6 supporting Communist China (with Nationalist China as the thirteenth member). The consultation method utilized is carefully described up to the signing of the treaty at San Francisco.

———. "Our Far Eastern Policy." 1952. *See* no.2468a.

2445 Ball, William Macmahon. *Nationalism and Communism in East Asia*. Carlton, Victoria: Melbourne Univ. Pr., 1952. viii, 210p.

Chapter 2 (p.18–32) of this examination of Asian developments during the decade of the 1940s is devoted to a critical study of the peace treaty with Japan. The author notes the reservations that America's wartime allies have of the treaty and points out some of the ways in which the treaty marks a complete reversal of the main policy decisions reached by the Allies before and after Japan's surrender. He also focuses attention on the failure of the treaty to set limitations on Japanese rearmament—a major concern of the Australian government, which he has represented on various occasions—and speculates whether Japan might again become a threat to her neighbors.

2446 Bundy, McGeorge. *The Pattern of Responsibility*. Boston: Houghton, Mifflin, 1952. 309p.

Bundy discusses the public record of Dean Acheson as secretary of state from January 1949 to August 1951, utilizing statements by Acheson to help explain policy decisions. Japan is mentioned occasionally in regard to an American defense perimeter off the coast of East Asia. Pages 259–62 deal specifically with the conclusion of a peace treaty with Japan. Acheson's role as chairman of the San Francisco Conference and his views concerning the content of the peace treaty, particularly with respect to collective Asian security, are examined.

2446a Dulles, John Foster. "Japanese Peace Treaty Viewed as Positive Step in Free World's March toward Peace." *Department of State Bulletin* 25:616–20 (15 Oct. 1951); also published under the title "A Treaty of Reconciliation and Liberation" in *State Government* 24: 269–72, 285 (Nov. 1951)

This speech was made by Dulles before the Governors Conference in Gatlinburg, Tennessee, on 1 October

1951. The fall of China and the outbreak of the Korean War, says Dulles, drove home the need for actively pursuing a peace agreement. With bipartisan domestic support, the United States drafted a document free of discriminatory provisions, and after protracted negotiations secured the approval and unified support of the free Allies. Dulles notes that the treaty was agreed upon despite the threats and disruptive tactics of the Soviet Union and the People's Republic of China. The peace treaty with Japan, he concludes, was brought about by American action in conformity with the best American traditions of liberation, reconciliation, and generosity.

——. "Security in the Pacific." 1952. See no.2471a.

2447 Farley, Miriam Southwell. "Japan and U.S.: Post-treaty Problems." *Far Eastern Survey* 21:33–38 (27 Feb. 1952)

Miriam Farley, editor of the *Far Eastern Survey*, divides the posttreaty problems into 3 categories: first is unfinished business in the matter of liquidating the war; second is the problem of relations with third powers; and the third and most difficult problem is the reconciliation of Japanese and American national interests.

2447a Green, Leslie C. "Making Peace with Japan." *Year Book of World Affairs* 6:1–35 (1952)

Reflecting the fact that the conclusion of a peace treaty with Japan was one of the most significant events of 1951, Green, a lecturer in international law and relations at University College in London, presents an extended essay describing the steps that led to the signing of a formal peace with Japan. In chronological sequence he discusses the terms of Japan's surrender, the attempts to frame a peace treaty in 1946–47, the drafting of a peace treaty in 1950–51, the San Francisco conference, and the terms of the actual treaty of peace. Throughout he provides considerable information on the conflicting views and concerns that the various Allied powers had about Japanese rearmament, reparations, and Japan's economic activities, etc. Green concludes that "the significant feature of the history of the Japanese Peace Treaty [was] the method of drafting and the magnanimous attitude of the victorious Powers, albeit under the obstinate insistence of their leading member who had rendered great financial assistance to the defeated aggressor."

2447b "Japanese Peace and Security Treaties Enter into Force." *Department of State Bulletin* 26:687–89 (5 May 1952)

This article includes 5 items connected with the ceremonies marking the occasion on which the peace and security treaties officially came into effect: (1) a press release announcing that the treaties are in effect and describing the attendant ceremonies; (2) a statement by President Truman, read on his behalf by Secretary of State Acheson; (3) a presidential proclamation (no.2974, 17 Fed. Reg. 3813) terminating the state of war with Japan; (4) a statement by John Foster Dulles; and (5) a statement by Prime Minister Yoshida.

2448 "Japanese Peace Treaty." *External Affairs* 4:176–77 (May 1952)

An exchange of letters between the Canadian prime minister, L. S. St. Laurent, and Japanese Prime Minister Yoshida concerning the effectuation of the Japanese peace treaty and the establishment of full diplomatic relations between the 2 countries on 28 April 1952. Prime Minister St. Laurent calls for peace and freedom in East Asia and for mutual understanding and cooperation among nations. Yoshida also urges international cooperation and envisions a common destiny for free nations tied to the struggle against communism. In conclusion, he rejoices in the reentry of Japan as an independent power into the family of free nations.

2449 "Japanese Peace Treaty." *External Affairs* 4:193–94 (May 1952)

The partial text of a speech by the

Canadian secretary of state for external affairs, Lester B. Pearson, suggests that the peace treaty with Japan was a necessary and calculated risk which, on the whole, is not punitive but aimed at future peace. In response to criticism from nongovernment sources, Pearson concedes that Japan will now conduct her own affairs as she sees fit. However, he anticipates that Japan's political independence and economic strength will be used for the purpose of international cooperation and will result in peace and increased prosperity for all countries.

2450 Kern, Harry F. "Behind Russia's Maneuver to Win over the Japanese." *Newsweek* 39:39–40 (14 Jan. 1952)

Kern, international affairs editor, analyzes the 4 ways—diplomatic, psychological, economic, and military—by which the Russians sought to undermine the peace treaty. Particular emphasis is placed on Communist plans for internal guerrilla-type activity, on corresponding Japanese attempts to unify the police systems, and on an active campaign to undersell American business in raw material markets.

2451 Krylov, V. "Under American Occupation." *New Times* no.2:4–7 (9 Jan. 1952)

Terming the peace treaty "a betrayal of Japan's national interests," the author claims that it signifies the perpetuation of the American occupation. He notes the protest against such an enslaving agreement voiced by various sectors of Japanese society and insists that the Japanese people will not allow Japan to be rearmed and turned into a "permanent American base of aggression in Asia."

2451a Menzel, Eberhard. "Der Friedensvertrag mit Japan." *Europa-Archiv* pt.1, 7, no.21:5261–76 (5 Nov. 1952); pt.2, 7, no.24:5355–68 (20 Dec. 1952)

In part 1 of his detailed study of the Japanese peace treaty, Professor Menzel of the University of Hamburg reviews the events and negotiations that led up to the San Francisco Peace Treaty Conference in September 1951. He also provides the text of the peace treaty and certain other documents relating to the conference in German translation. Part 2 in turn examines the contents of the treaty. Considerable attention is paid to (1) territorial changes; (2) the formal end of a state of war between Japan and the Allies as well as of the Allied occupation; (3) reparations and the restitution of foreign property; (4) the settlement of debts and the waivering of claims; (5) the clauses referring to German property in Japan and Japanese property in Germany; (6) political and economic provisions; (7) the punishment of war criminals; and (8) the settlement of disputes. Menzel also speculates on the type of treaty which the Allies may be willing to sign with Germany in light of their recently concluded treaty with Japan.

2452 Metzger, Stanley D. "The Liberal Japanese Peace Treaty." *Cornell Law Quarterly* 37:382–402 (Spring 1952)

Metzger regards the treaty with Japan as a treaty of reconciliation. He compares clauses in the Italian Peace Treaty of 1947 with clauses in the Japanese treaty. Provisions concerning territorial revision, dispensation of financial and property claims, reparations payments, and future economic and commercial practices are examined. In the conclusion he notes that although the treaty restrictions and regulations are substantial, they do not constitute more than a fraction of the punitive measures which could have been instituted by the Allies.

2453 New Zealand. Dept. of External Affairs. *Annual Report of the Department of External Affairs, 1 April 1951 to 31 March 1952.* Wellington: Government Printer, 1952. 78p. (Dept. of External Affairs publication 117)

The portion on Japan reports the conclusion of the peace treaty in San Francisco and contains favorable comments on Pacific defense agreements with the United States. It views the peace treaty as "conciliatory and non-restrictive." It also states that a working party of Commonwealth officials in London studied the question of United Nations bases in Japan after the treaty and supported the continued presence there of UN forces engaged in the Far East.

2454 ———. ———. *Treaty of Peace with Japan and Related Documents.* Wellington: Government Printer, 1952. 22p. (Dept. of External Affairs publication 121; Treaty series 8)

This work presents the full texts of the Treaty of Peace with Japan, of the protocol signed in San Francisco on 8 September 1951, and of the two declarations issued by the Japanese government on the same day. New Zealand's ratification of the treaty was deposited in Washington on 10 April 1952. No commentary is provided.

2454a ———. Institute of International Affairs. *Must We Trust Japan? Eight Views on the Japanese Peace Treaty.* Wellington? 1952. 24p.

"Statement Issued by the Supreme Commander for the Allied Powers General Matthew B. Ridgway Concerning the Ratification of the Japanese Peace Treaty, April 27, 1952." 1952. See no. 985a.

2454b "Text of the Japanese–Indian Peace Treaty Signed in Tokyo and the Notes Exchanged Thereof, June 9, 1952." *Contemporary Japan* 21, no.4/6:325–28 (1952)

The text of a separate peace treaty between the 2 countries is divided into 11 articles including a provision for the Indian waiver of all reparations claims against Japan. The accompanying notes were exchanged on 9 June 1952 between Okazaki Katsuo, Japanese Minister for Foreign Affairs, and K. K. Chettur, the Ambassador Extraordinary and Plenipotentiary of India to Japan.

2455 "Treaties with Japan, Australia, New Zealand, and the Philippines Presented to the Senate." *Department of State Bulletin* 26:185–90 (4 Feb. 1952)

These remarks made by Dean Acheson and John Foster Dulles before the Senate Foreign Relations Committee on 21 January 1952 concern the presentation of 4 treaties for ratification. Acheson stresses the spirit of reconciliation and mutual confidence and trust upon which the treaty with Japan is based. He also comments on the role Japan can play in providing mutual security in the Pacific. Dulles mentions 5 principles basically related to Japan's postwar role: (1) the alliance with Japan is crucial for the future of American success against communism in Asia; (2) a disarmed Japan needs the alliance to ensure security against Russia; (3) the mutual goals of Japan and the Western world can be realized only if the occupation is ended and independence guaranteed; (4) the occupation has been totally successful in both the social and economic realms and Japan can be regarded as a dependable ally; and (5) American policy for combating despotism should emphasize faith in freedom. The Japanese peace treaty is a vote of confidence in such freedom.

2456 *Treaty of Peace with Japan, Signed at San Francisco, September 8, 1951, with Related Documents.* Washington, D.C.: Government Printing Office, 1952. 25p. (Dept. of State publication 4561; Far Eastern series 54)

This pamphlet contains 3 documents: (1) the English text of the Treaty of Peace with Japan signed by 48 nations plus Japan at a conference of 51 nations which had been at war with Japan; (2) 2 declarations issued by the Japanese government on the same date: one recognizing the full force of all presently effective multilateral international instruments to which Japan was a party on 1 September 1939, and the other recognizing any Allied group authorized to examine and maintain foreign war graves and cemeteries in Japanese territories: and (3) a protocol on contracts, periods of prescription, and negotiable instruments and on contracts of insurance signed by 26 nations plus Japan on the same date.

2457 Ulanovsky, Yu. B. "Territorial Issues in the Japanese Peace Settlement." *Soviet*

Press Translations 7:329–32 (1 Sept. 1952)

In a complex and heavily documented article, which appeared originally in the no.5 1952 issue of *Sovietskaye Gosudarstvo i Pravo*, the author seeks to establish the illegality of the American–Japanese peace treaty. Utilizing a variety of international agreements, particularly the Potsdam Declaration, Ulanovsky points to a variety of internationally accepted procedures which were abandoned by the United States, including the refusal to operate through the Council of Foreign Ministers and the avoidance of limitations on Japanese rearmament. The bulk of the article is concerned with alleged violations in territorial delineation. American actions such as the assumption of a United Nations trusteeship over the Pacific islands and direct "colonization" of the Ryukyu and Bonin Islands are criticized. A primary concern is to establish securely the Soviet claim to Southern Sakhalin and the Kurile Islands, and historical evidence supporting the Soviet claim is presented together with the demand that Japan renounce all claim to these territories.

2458 U.S. Congress. Senate. "Treaty of Peace with Japan." *Congressional Record* 82d Cong., 2d Sess. (1952) 98, pt.2: 2551–94.

The Senate debate conducted on 20 March 1952 concerning the ratification of the Treaty of Peace and the Mutual Security Treaty with Japan is recorded here. After lengthy discussion of reservations to be attached to the treaty, the Senate resolved to ratify it without change. The resolution passed with 66 votes in favor, 10 against, and 20 abstentions.

2459 ———. ———. ———. Committee on Foreign Relations. *Japanese Peace Treaty and Other Treaties Relating to Security in the Pacific. Hearings before the Committee on Foreign Relations, United States Senate, Eighty-second Congress, Section Session . . . January 21, 22, 23, and 25, 1952.* Washington, D.C.: Government Printing Office, 1952. iii, 182p.

The hearings conducted by the U.S. Senate Committee on Foreign Relations concerning the Japanese peace treaty and related security treaties are recorded here. The hearings took place on 21, 22, 23, and 25 January 1952; 17 persons testified and 12 written statements and letters were inserted in the record. The verbatim minutes of the hearings and written materials pertaining to them are included. Among those who testified were Dean Acheson (secretary of state), General Omar N. Bradley (chairman, Joint Chiefs of Staff), Ambassador John F. Dulles, A. J. Muste (member of the Fellowship of Reconciliation), and Rev. Willard Uphaus (American Peace Crusade). Written statements include a letter from Prime Minister Yoshida to Dulles, a statement by the foreign minister of Nationalist China regarding Yoshida's letter to Dulles, Dean Acheson's letter to Senator Wiley concerning the belligerent rights of the Soviet Union and China in Japan, Dulles' memorandum dealing with Japanese reparations, and a letter from the Women's International League for Peace and Freedom.

2460 ———. Dept. of State. *Treaty of Peace with Japan.* Washington, D.C.: Government Printing Office, 1952. iii, 173p. (Dept. of State publicattion 4613; Treaties and Other International Acts series 2490)

The official documents of the Treaty of Peace with Japan concluded at San Francisco on 8 September 1951 are collected in this volume. Signed by 48 Allied nations and Japan, the treaty was written in 4 languages: English, French, Spanish, and Japanese. All 4 texts are provided. Also given are the texts of President Truman's proclamation of 28 April 1952 effectuating the treaty, a list of countries that ratified the treaty, the text of Japan's declaration regarding the applicability of certain multilateral international instruments to Japan, and Japan's declaration with regard to Allied powers' war graves, cemeteries, and memorials in Japanese territory. These appear in all 4 languages. Finally, there are reprinted the texts of notes exchanged between American Secretary of State Dean Acheson and Japanese Prime Minister Yoshida Shigeru on 8 September 1951 regarding Japan's agreement to assist United Nations forces stationed in Japan in connection with the Korean War.

2460a Wint, Guy. *The Future of Japan.* London: Batchworth Press, 1952. 31p. (Background books)

On the background and provisions of the peace treaty and its effect on the future of Japan.

2460b Zanard, Richard J. "An Introduction to the Japanese Peace Treaty and Allied Documents." *Georgetown Law Journal* 40:91–109 (1951/52)

Zanard praises the peace treaty for replacing the spirit of revenge with one of conciliation and hope. It is "unique in the realm of multilateral treaties," he writes, because it evolved through diplomatic discussions rather than in a general conference. Zanard's article explores the historical background of the treaty and points out the Soviet Union's unwillingness to cooperate in order to explain the unusual way in which it was written. The provisions of the treaty also are discussed, with the most extensive treatment being given to the clauses that deal with territorial arrangements and with such items affecting the Japanese economy as reparations and foreign trade. He concludes with a brief summary of the U.S.-Japan Security Treaty.

1953–72

Amravati, Mallappa. *Relations between Japan and the United States since 1945 with Special Reference to the Peace Treaty and the Security Pact.* 1969. See no.688.

2461 Beal, John Robinson. *John Foster Dulles: A Biography.* New York: Harper, 1957. xvi, 331p.

Chapter 12 deals with Dulles' involvement in the Japanese peace treaty negotiations. The alleged inertia which characterized the definition of treaty terms by the State Department and the rivalry between the State and Defense Departments which resulted from the Defense Department's unwillingness to give up its military advantages in Japan are explained. The importance of the Korean War vis-à-vis the decision to proceed with the conclusion of the treaty is noted. Dulles' special position as presidential adviser and his negotiating style are discussed. Various British and Soviet objections to the treaty provisions are noted and the San Francisco Conference is examined.

2462 Cohen, Bernard Cecil. "Political Communication on the Japanese Peace Settlement." *Public Opinion Quarterly* 20:27–38 (Spring 1956)

A rather abstract study of how different interest groups communicate with and influence government. Public opinion on the signing of the Japanese peace treaty is taken as a case to be investigated. As the author concludes, "The case of the Japanese peace settlement suggests that different types of interest groups approach the political arena in varying ways, and that the pattern of their political communication on any issue reflects these different orientations toward key elements in the political process. . . . In this case, however, the consequences were not especially serious."

2463 ———. *The Political Process and Foreign Policy: The Making of the Japanese Peace Settlement.* Princeton, N.J.: Princeton Univ. Pr., 1957. x, 293p.

This penetrating and well-organized study by a professional scholar of international affairs examines the domestic political processes in the United States which were involved in the formulation and approval of the peace settlement with Japan. It was written as part of an evaluation of the Japanese peace settlement undertaken by the Princeton Center of International Studies. The settlement was viewed as a case study in the problems of foreign policy planning, the processes of international diplomacy, and the political processes of foreign policy-making. Scholars dealing with each of these aspects worked in close association but formulated and pursued their research projects individually. At the time this book was written Cohen was a research associate at the Center of International Studies, lectured in public and international affairs at Princeton, and was managing editor of *World Politics*. Following a brief introduction to the history of the peace settlement, the author examines separately the major elements in the American political system concerned with foreign policy-making to determine their interests and activities with respect to the peace settlement. Elements discussed include public opinion, interest groups, communications media, the executive branch, and the Congress. Cohen then analyzes their interrelationships and the patterns of influence exhibited. His conclusions are summarized in the final chapter. Among other things, he finds that the nature of the policy issue itself has an important effect on the character of the political processes attending it and that the climate of public opinion fundamentally affects the process by which foreign policy decisions are formulated. In the case of the Japanese peace settlement, lack of public interest enhanced the influence of the executive in the policy-making process, while in the case of the fishery treaty, public factors exercised influence on their own behalf. The volume includes numerous tables, footnotes, and a detailed index. Chapter 5 appeared in slightly different form in the Spring 1956 issue of the *Public Opinion Quarterly* (no.2462).

2463a Curtis, Gerald Leon. "The Dulles-Yoshida Negotiations on the San Francisco Peace Treaty." In *Columbia Essays in International Affairs. v.2: The Dean's Papers, 1966.* New York: Columbia Univ. Pr., 1967. p.37–61.

This scholarly study explains how Japan exerted "considerable influence" on those responsible for drafting the peace treaty despite the fact that her government could not, in strictly legal terms, engage in international negotiations because Japan was still under foreign occupation at that time. Curtis discusses the conversations which Dulles and Yoshida had in both June 1950 and January 1951, examining them in relation to the cold war and to the shifting interests of the various Allied nations. His analysis sheds light on the development of the treaty itself as well as on Japanese domestic politics during a crucial period. He concludes that while the treaty conformed in the short run to both Yoshida's and Dulles' ideological and political requirements, neither it nor the Security Treaty provided a viable long term solution to Japan's security needs.

2464 Dunn, Frederick Sherwood. *Peace-Making and the Settlement with Japan.* Princeton, N.J.: Princeton Univ. Pr., 1963. xviii, 210p.

A professor of international politics at Princeton University analyzes American decision-making leading to the peace treaty with Japan. In conducting research for this study, the last before his death in 1962, the author had unusual access to State Department papers, many of which were classified and could not be cited. Dunn was a legal officer in the State Department in the 1920s, became a teacher of international affairs in the 1930s, and founded the quarterly *World Politics* in 1948. Approached as a case study in American decision-making, the evolution of American policies regarding the Japanese peace settlement is divided into 4 periods. The first extends from the outbreak of the war to Japan's defeat in 1945 followed by the dissolution of the wartime coalition into Communist and non-Communist camps. The second period deals with the years 1945 to 1950 when the cold war formed the core of American foreign policy considerations. The third period, from 1950 to 1951, receives the most comprehensive coverage in this account. Discussed in some detail are the negotiations conducted by John Foster Dulles which culminated in the contrary, the treaty was not signed by all of Japan's enemies and has created or perpetuated a deep division among the Allies. The treaty, like the occupation, was primarily the work of the United States; not all of the complaints voiced by the Soviet Union in its exchange of notes with the U.S., therefore, can be easily dismissed. Generally speaking, Tixier argues, separate treaties are symptoms of international illness and are contrary to the principles of international organization. Still, he concludes, while the present treaty is an inadequate palliative measure, it does settle some important questions—chief among them the territorial issues.

2467a "Treaty of Peace between Japan and the Union of Burma, Signed at Rangoon, November 5, 1954." *Contemporary Japan* 23, no.4/6:424–27 (1955)

Signed for Japan and Burma respectively by Okazaki Katsuo and Kyaw Nyein, this is the complete text of the treaty concluding a state of war between the 2 countries. It contains 10 articles, in 1 of which Japan promises to reimburse Burma for war damages.

2467b "Treaty of Peace Signed by Japan and the Republic of Indonesia at Djakarta, January 20, 1958." *Contemporary Japan* 25, no.2:304–6 (Apr. 1958)

The text, without any accompanying commentary, of the treaty formally concluding a state of war between the 2 countries. The treaty contains 7 articles, 1 of which expresses Japan's willingness to pay Indonesia reparations for damages and other losses incurred during the course of World War II.

U.S. Dept. of State. *American Foreign Policy 1950–1955: Basic Documents.* 1957. See no.371.

Vinacke, Harold M. *Far Eastern Politics in the Postwar Period.* 1956. See no.757.

Yanaga, Chitoshi. *Big Business in Japanese Politics.* 1968. See no.1815a.

Yoshida, Shigeru. *The Yoshida Memoirs: The Story of Japan in Crisis.* 1962. See no.769.

The Security Treaty, Administrative Agreement, and Japanese Rearmament

Closely linked with the Treaty of San Francisco was the Mutual Security Treaty between the United States and Japan that was signed the same day. It provided for the national security of a still largely disarmed Japan through the continued presence of American forces after the end of the occupation. The Administrative Agreement of 28 February 1952 supplemented and spelled out in detail the arrangements under which these "garrison forces" would be maintained on Japanese soil. Associated with both of these developments was the entire issue of Japanese rearmament and the American and other foreign reactions to this prospect. They are the issues treated by the following entries. The entries in the section on termination (p.727) as well as those in the sections on international aspects (p.260) and on the demilitarization program (p.335) are also relevant.

2468 Allison, John M. "The Japanese Peace Treaty and Related Security Pacts." *Proceedings of the American Society of International Law* 46:35–43 (24–26 Apr. 1952)

Focusing on the negotiation and

conclusion of both the Japanese Peace Treaty and the related Mutual Defense and Security Treaties with the Philippines, Australia, and New Zealand, Allison first singles them out as significant examples of effective cooperation between the executive and legislative branches of the U.S. government. He lauds Ambassador John Foster Dulles, whom he credits with the achievement of a peace treaty, for his efforts to keep members of Congress fully informed of what the negotiators were doing and the way in which they were doing it. This procedure, he explains, proved its value when the Senate subsequently agreed to a prompt ratification of the treaty. Allison then turns his attention to the manner in which the treaty was negotiated with America's allies, terming the procedure "unique in the modern history of diplomacy." Instead of convening a large international conference of nations to draft mutually acceptable treaty terms, the United States consulted its allies and representatives of the Japanese government on an individual basis and then circulated a first draft for their critical reactions. Changes were suggested, a revised joint United States–United Kingdom draft was prepared, and a conference was held in San Francisco simply for the purpose of signing the peace treaty. Had this procedure not been followed, peace with Japan might not have been concluded for a much longer time.

2468a ———. "Our Far Eastern Policy." *Department of State Bulletin* 26:652–57 (28 Apr. 1952)

This article consists of excerpts from an address delivered at the 14th Annual Public Affairs Conference in Elsah, Illinois on 16 April 1952. In the course of describing the current situation in East Asia, Allison comments on SCAP's various endeavors in Japan, discusses the new security system in the Pacific (with particular reference to the U.S.–Japan Security Treaty), and makes a number of observations about the recently concluded peace treaty with Japan. He points out that the treaty was especially noteworthy inasmuch as Japan was treated as an equal during the related negotiations, at the San Francisco Peace Treaty Conference, and in the treaty itself.

American Institute of Pacific Relations, ed. *Some Japanese Views on American–Japanese Relations.* 1953. *See* no. 2509.

2468b "American-Japanese Defense Pact." *Current History* 21:240–41 (Oct. 1951)

The complete text of the security treaty negotiated immediately after the signing of the Treaty of Peace with Japan on 8 September 1951. The document consists of an introductory section explaining why the 2 countries deem such a treaty necessary, followed by 5 articles outlining the specific terms of the agreement. Also reprinted are an exchange of notes regarding the peace treaty by Japanese Prime Minister Yoshida and U.S. Secretary of State Dean Acheson.

Amravati, Mallappa. *Relations between Japan and the United States since 1945 with Special Reference to the Peace Treaty and the Security Pact.* 1969. *See* no.688.

2468c Arnot, R. Page. "Re-militarising West Germany and Japan." *Labour Monthly* 33:65–71 (Feb. 1951)

While focusing on the rearming of West Germany, a development which has shocked many people in Great Britain, Arnot also comments on MacArthur's 1951 New Year's message announcing that it was time to rearm Japan and predicts that the "Japanese militarists will be back in the saddle" when rearmament plans are carried out. He bitterly criticizes American actions in this regard and calls upon the British people to disassociate themselves from these militaristic American activities.

Ashida, Hitoshi. "Japan: Communists' Temptation." 1951. *See* no.770.

2469 Baba, Tsunego. "An Open Letter to Those Who Oppose Rearmament." *Con-*

temporary Japan 20:554–55 (Oct./Dec. 1951)

This article by the former president of the *Yomiuri Shimbun* first appeared in Japanese in the December 1951 issue of *Kaizō*. It is basically a plea to the anti-rearmament forces in Japan that they be realistic and understand that a defenseless nation is an irresistible temptation to the Communist military forces. By not signing the peace treaty, he states, the USSR, Czechoslovakia, and Poland have indicated that they prefer in effect to remain enemies of Japan—a fact which places Japan in a perilous position. Rearmament, he concludes, must be considered in light of changes within the international system; no nation can survive alone and unarmed in the modern world.

Bolles, Blair. "U.S. Strives for Flexibility in Accord with Japan." 1951. See no.2369.

2469a Brown, Cecil, and Ellis M. Zacharias. "Should We Rearm Germany and Japan?" *Town Meeting* 16, no.17:1–16 (22 Aug. 1950)

As the transcript of this radio discussion points out, there is a dilemma occasioned on the one hand by American fears that rearming Germany and Japan could lead to the growth of strong, uncontrollable military forces and, on the other hand, by the American desire to enlist these two countries in the world struggle against communism. With regard to Japan, Zacharias advocates that Japan be rearmed in order that she may be adequately defended against Soviet aggression. While he believes that precautions should be taken to insure that the Japanese do not use their forces some day against the United States, he feels that Japan could hardly become a menace again to the United States in view of her lack of a vast colonial empire. Brown, however, asserts that it would be morally and ethically wrong to rearm Japan and that the United States lacks the capacity to build up the military forces of both Germany and Japan. He also disputes the contention that the two countries can be trusted to support the United States in a military sense.

Cho, Sung-Yoon. *Jurisdiction over Foreign Forces in Japan, 1945–1960.* 1963. See no.1297a.

Council on Foreign Relations. "Toward a Pacific Security System." 1952. See no.2372.

2469b Davidson, Basil. *Japanese Ally? The Façade—and the Facts*. London: Union of Democratic Control, 1951. 11p. Also published in a "Peace News" edition under the title *Japan: For Peace or War? The Case against Remilitarising Japan*.

Davidson deals with the question of Japanese rearmament and the peace treaty and presents a number of proposals for a British policy that would condemn American actions in the Far East. In his conclusion he asserts (1) that the Americans—and not only General MacArthur—have decided to turn the clock back in Japan, (2) that Japan's former leaders are regaining their positions of power and pay only lip-service to the cause of peace and disarmament, and (3) that the combination of supporters of John Foster Dulles, the American government, and reactionary Japan can only result in the defeat of all major Allied objectives for the demilitarization and democratization of Japan.

2469c Denson, John. "Must We Rearm Japan?" *Collier's* 126:18–19, 69–70 (9 Sept. 1950)

Denson reports on the development of a 75,000-man National Police Reserve and on further plans to rearm Japan for defensive purposes. He notes the threat of Communist aggression as well as the success of SCAP's democratization program and asserts that the development of defensive forces in Japan does not indicate a revival of militarism. The recreation of a Japanese army is regarded as the final link in an American-Japanese alliance against Russia.

2470 Deverall, Richard L. G. "Are We Rebuilding Tojo's 'Red' Army?" *New Leader* 34, no.3:2–5 (15 Jan. 1951)

A former chief of labor education within SCAP asserts that many Japanese have remained interested in military affairs and that there is a danger of Japan's new self-defense force being dominated by "the political offspring of Tōjō and the Communist Party." He describes the feeling of superiority vis-à-vis the Americans that many ex-sailors and ex-soldiers felt and the considerable support that Tōjō received within Japan during the course of the war crimes trials. He also points out that many purged officers became members of the Communist Party and its labor front (the National Congress of Industrial Unions), while others entered the universities and became organizers of Communist activities on campus. The subsequent purging of Communists from both government and industry, he continues, has benefited the Communist Party in that many of these men are now preparing to infiltrate any new Japanese army that the United States seeks to form. Accordingly, occupation officials would do best to exercise utmost caution in selecting recruits for the self-defense force lest the end result be a revival of Tōjō's "red" army.

2470a Dewey, Thomas Edmund. "Mutual Defense of Pacific Nations: Neutralism an Illusion." *Vital Speeches* 17, no.20: 615–17 (1 Aug. 1951); also in *Contemporary Japan* 20:277–81 (Apr./June 1951)

In an address delivered on 6 July 1951 before the America–Japan Society in Tokyo, the governor of New York reviews postwar Japan's social and economic progress (which he called impressive) and points out the importance of insuring the security of the country once independence has been regained. He refers to the peace treaty negotiations and the arrangements that are being made for mutual defense in order "to assure the liberty and progress of the free peoples of the Pacific." He also expresses his confidence that Communist efforts to subvert other countries will fail and that when peace is consummated, the conduct of the Japanese people will justify past American efforts to help Japan rebuild.

2470b "Dilemma in Japan." *Economist* 156:357–58 (26 Feb. 1949)

Observing that external security is a matter of primary concern to the Japanese, the author calls upon the United States to decide whether it will provide Japan with a guarantee of future protection against foreign aggression. He points out that the success of the occupation to date has been due in large measure to the submissiveness and docility of the Japanese whose feeling that "American control and American bounty and protection have come to stay for a long time" has prompted them to cooperate with SCAP despite their preference not to be ruled by any alien power. As the results of the recent general elections demonstrate, however, there is a growing Communist minority within Japan that is hostile to the United States and is turning to Communist China and the Soviet Union for support. Unless the Americans are prepared either to defend Japan themselves or to permit the Japanese to rearm, many Japanese may feel it necessary to come to terms with "the prospective Russian conqueror" by climbing aboard the Communist bandwagon and by ceasing to comply and cooperate with the occupation authorities. Understandably, any proposal for creating a Japanese self defense army will arouse controversy within the United States and anger among many Australians. As long as Japan is forbidden to possess naval and air power, however, the creation of a land force sufficient for home defense will not threaten any of her neighbors while it certainly will allay present Japanese fears and will help deprive the Communists of additional support.

Dionisopoulos, P. Allan. "The No-War Clause in the Japanese Constitution." 1956. *See* no.999b.

2470c Dower, John. "The Eye of the Beholder: Background Notes on the U.S.–Japan Military Relationship." *Bulletin of*

Concerned Asian Scholars 2, no.1:15–31 (Oct. 1969)

This reinterpretation of postwar Japanese–American military relations begins by pointing out that the origins of the 1951 Security Pact go back as early as the initial months of the occupation period. Dower notes how members of the occupation forces—among them Major General Charles Willoughby—took steps to prepare Japan for a possible future military role vs. the Soviet Union. He also explains how the United States shifted its policy from one of demilitarization to one of gradual Japanese rearmament, and indicates that the American military was strongly opposed to any peace settlement with Japan which would deprive the United States of a secure base within the country. The author then traces the establishment of the 75,000-man National Police Reserve. In discussing the peace treaty and the bilateral security pact, Dower stresses the fact that their terms were not as magnanimous as they seemed inasmuch as the form which they took reflected a very definite American self-interest. Indeed, the conclusion of the peace treaty itself was contingent not only upon Japan's agreeing to a military alliance with the United States but also upon her willingness to rearm and to forego relations with the People's Republic of China. The author concludes that the military alliance distorted a more natural role for Japan in Asia and forced her into a rigid anti-Communist position. Furthermore, it endangered, rather than enhanced, Japan's national security by making her a possible pawn in any future war in Asia between the United States and the Soviet Union.

Dulles, John F. "Laying Foundations for a Pacific Peace." 1951. *See* no.2376.

2471 ———. "Peace May Be Won." *Department of State Bulletin* 24:252–55 (12 Feb. 1951)

This article reprints the text of an address made by Dulles, then a consultant to the secretary of state, before the America–Japan Society in Tokyo on 2 February 1951. Dulles asserts that the Japanese government and people have the primary responsibility for avoiding the risks to national security that fall short of direct aggression—i.e., subversion. Direct aggression will be deterred by regional and collective security arrangements until an effective United Nations-directed international security force comes into existence at some later date. Dulles also suggests that the best course for Japan would be to rely upon the United States for its security against largescale direct aggression without relinquishing its independence and ambitions as a member of the community of free nations.

2471a ———. "Security in the Pacific." *Foreign Affairs* 30, no.2:175–87 (Jan. 1952)

Dulles discusses one by one the major treaties that have recently been concluded with various Pacific nations: (1) the Peace Treaty with Japan, (2) the United States–Japan Security Treaty, (3) an American security treaty with the Philippines, and (4) American security treaties with Australia and New Zealand. He describes the Peace Treaty as a document which promotes reconciliation among former enemies and which will encourage Japan to contribute to collective security in the Pacific as a member of the free world. He points out, moreover, that the security treaty enables Japan to exercise her right of collective self-defense and that by being interlocked with the other security arrangements negotiated by the United States, Japan will be in a better position to resist foreign aggression. All in all the arrangements for the common defense of the offshore island chain which swings south from Japan to New Zealand will serve as "a formidable deterrent to the domination of the Pacific by Communist imperialism." Dulles concludes with a discussion of the future development of Pacific security and states that cooperation between Japan and her neighbors along the lines of the United States–Japan Security Treaty offers them the best insurance against renewed Japanese aggression in the future.

2471b "Eichelberger Sees Japan as Military Ally." *Christian Century* 66:1348 (16 Nov. 1949)

While praising Lt. General Robert Eichelberger for the quality of his service during the war and in the administration of the occupation, this editorial criticizes his recent comments hailing Japan as a prospective military ally against the Soviet Union and characterizing Japanese soldiers as "a commander's dream." Such remarks do "the cause of world understanding and peace no good, and may have done considerable harm," the editors write, for they "will be seized on by Communist propagandists in Japan" as proof that the anti-war clause of the Japanese constitution "is only a piece of pious fakery." The magazine warns that this sort of statement will also confirm the Soviet Union in its belief that the United States is preparing for war against it.

2471c Eidus, Khaim. "The American Policy for a Militarized Fascist Japan." *Soviet Press Translations* 6:35–45 (1 Feb. 1951); abridged version published under the title "American Policy of Militarization and Fascistization of Japan" in *Current Digest of the Soviet Press* 2, no.47:11–12 (6 Jan. 1951)

Eidus presents a comprehensive and detailed study of American occupation policies which he believes are based on the desire to transform Japan into an outpost in America's Pacific defense line. He provides information concerning the reorganization of a national police and naval police force and notes the use of former military personnel in various administrative positions. His review of Japan's industrial recovery includes statistics regarding the revival of heavy industry and military potential and the stagnation of light and consumer industry and he cites the examples of Japanese military production to fill American orders. Eidus reviews the economic stabilization program, Japan's stressing considerable dependence on U.S. markets, the vastly increased tax load on workers and peasants, and the increasing strength of *zaibatsu* monopolies in industry. Massive unemployment and real wage levels half those of 1939 are mentioned as are inadequacies of the land reform program which permitted substantial control by landlords and left peasants impoverished by heavy purchase payments. Labor legislation prohibiting both political activity by unions and collective bargaining and striking by state employees is discussed and persecution of the Korean minority and the Communist party is noted. In conclusion, the democratic potential of the Japanese people and the desire of the Soviet Union to negotiate a peace treaty on the basis of the Potsdam Declaration and the withdrawal of occupation troops from Japan are emphasized.

This article originally appeared in the no.8 1950 issue of *Voprosy Ekonomiki*.

"Fear Spreads in Germany and Japan." 1950. See no.1340.

2472 Guérin, Paul. "Le traité avec le Japon et les pactes de sécurité du Pacifique." *Revue des deux mondes* 1:416–24 (Dec. 1951)

Guérin analyzes the global significance of the signing of a peace treaty with Japan, which he regards as "the first major diplomatic act since 1945 to consecrate formally a profound division among the great allied powers of World War II." In his opinion, the two primary goals of the treaty are to regularize and liquidate the effects of Japan's wartime defeat and to prepare for the integration of Japan into the Western community. Another effect of the treaty is to provide for Japan's security by balancing her vulnerability as an unarmed state near an area of active hostilities (Korea) against the fears which the Pacific nations have of a resurgent Japanese military machine. The Soviet Union's refusal to go along with such goals, Guérin notes, is a natural continuation of her policy toward American occupation policy in general. He cites, for example, the strong and consistent Soviet opposition to American decisions regarding the emperor, the new constitution, electoral reforms, reparations, and Japan's economic recovery. The treaty signed in San Francisco thus formalizes and deepens a preexisting division between the United States and the Soviet Union and their respective camps. The article concludes with a few speculations about Japan's future in the world community, which Guérin feels will be determined by 3 factors: the continuing American military domination of the Pacific, Japan's traditional desire for guaranteed access to the resources of mainland Asia, and the fact that Japan must sooner or later recognize that her economic future depends on trade with Asia rather than with the West. These factors, however, will eventually become secondary to the power of a resurgent Japanese nationalism, which will demand that Japan find her rightful place in the world as an independent state.

2473 Guillain, Robert. "The Resurgence of Military Elements in Japan." *Pacific Affairs* 25, no.3:211–25 (Sept. 1952)

The members of Japan's military establishment lost their public appeal in 1945 but they reappeared with the beginning of the Korean War and Japanese rearmament. This article describes 2 groups of former officers. One was led by Colonel Hattori Takushirō who cooperated with the occupation and secretly formed a group of former officers—some rightwing—who hoped to lead Japan's new army. Colonel Tsuji Masanobu, in turn, refused to cooperate with them and instead publicized his ideas of rebuilding a strong but neutral Japanese army and formed a sizeable political organization.

2473a Harper, Norman Delholm. "Australia, Japan, and Korea: Australia's Shift to Qualified Approval of Japan's Rearmament." *Far Eastern Survey* 20:69–74 (18 Apr. 1951)

This article provides a digest of current Australian press and political opinion on occupation policies regarding Japanese economic recovery and rearmament. According to Harper, Australians tend to be markedly less optimistic than MacArthur about the success of the various occupation reforms, and they generally feel that "the ambitious program of reform has been drastically watered down." Other complaints about SCAP policy center on what one commentator described as "the tendency towards a piecemeal disposal of matters that should be dealt with in a peace treaty with Japan." Harper suggests that while economic competition from a resurgent Japan is a widespread fear among Australians, it is the actual or potential military danger posed by a strong, independent Japan that is most worrisome. Nevertheless, Australians have come to realize that changing political realities in Asia make Japanese economic recovery and rearmament unavoidable.

2473b Holbrook, Martin E. "Our Dilemma in Japan." *United States Naval Institute Proceedings* 76, no.1:23–25 (Jan. 1950)

The United States is faced with an increasingly serious dilemma. If Japan is to remain secure and the United States is to retain her bases both there and elsewhere in East Asia, the American government must either accept the complete burden of Japan's defense or must permit the Japanese to rearm and to assume part of the burden. The first course, if taken, would prove extremely expensive and could involve a drain on America's military and economic resources. The alternative could prove to be the "resurrection of a monster, now dead." The author is uncertain what final decisions will be made in this regard, but he does point out that the establishment of an armed constabulary of 10,000 men in 1947 and the creation of a coast guard force in 1948 could portend the resurrection, even if only partially, of Japan's military and naval strength.

"In the Allied Council for Japan: Statement by Lt.-Gen. Derevyanko, Soviet Member of the Allied Council." 1949. *See* no.1341a.

2473c "Is a Rearmed Japan Our Goal?" *Christian Century* 67:356 (22 Mar. 1950)

This article continues the magazine's

editorial campaign against Japanese rearmament with an attack upon General Eichelberger's comments in New York to the effect that "any peace treaty with Japan must provide for the raising of a Japanese army."

2474 "Its Future Lies with the West." *Newsweek* 37:32–34 (22 Jan. 1951)

The creation of an American–Japanese alliance against communism in East Asia is examined and much emphasis is given to the importance of the Korean War with respect to Japanese military and economic revival. The United States is regarded as irrevocably committed to providing military protection to Japan. The stabilization of trade relations with Southeast Asia is considered to be a means of insuring Japanese economic vitality. Dissent among allied nations in Asia concerning Japanese rearmament is noted but rearmament is accepted as a necessity.

"Japan Could Arm Millions, but Is Her Price Too High?" 1950. *See* no.796.

"Japan Drills an 'Army of Sergeants'." 1951. *See* no.1342.

"Japan Takes First Steps to Build U.S.-Style Army." 1951. *See* no.1342a.

2475 Kawai, Kazuo. "Japanese Views on National Security." *Pacific Affairs* 23:115–27 (June 1950)

It is the author's contention that the disarmament of Japan and the nation's constitutional renunciation of war pose a serious international problem. He maintains that the Japanese view of the situation should be taken into consideration but claims that it has been neglected by the Allied powers. He believes that increased Communist activity in East Asia contributes to a sense of uneasiness among Japanese concerning national security and stresses that the imminence of a peace treaty makes the problem immediate. He then describes the attitudes of various Japanese politicians toward such alternative solutions as rearmament, Japanese participation in a regional defense pact, protection by the United States, and perpetual neutrality. In summing up current Japanese attitudes, the author claims that the people favor either protection by the United States or perpetual neutrality guaranteed by the powers and that at present opinion is swinging toward the second alternative.

2476 Kawakami, Kiyoshi. "America and Japan's Permanent Neutrality." *World Affairs* 112:35–37 (Summer 1949)

The author of this report focuses upon the question of neutrality for a nation that has renounced war and the right to bear arms. Such neutrality, he maintains, is necessary but it may be achieved only through an international compact whereby all powers pledge to hold Japan inviolable. The author expresses grave concern over MacArthur's recent statements affirming American defense of Japan if the country were attacked. Such a statement, he believes, binds Japan to a U.S. alliance which must be avoided at all costs. The author insists that, since America was responsible for Japan's no-war clause, it is also responsible not for defending Japan from attack but for securing Japan's permanent neutrality. He considers the implications of such neutrality for Japanese membership in the United Nations Organization and notes that "if armament be a part of the price of membership in the United Nations, Japan should keep out of it." Lastly, he supports Japan's right to preserve internal order through a police force of 150,000 men.

2477 Kennan, George Frost. "Japanese Security and American Policy." *Foreign Affairs* 43:14–28 (Oct. 1964)

Kennan reconstructs the American assumptions that led to the signing of the security treaty and examines the extent to which these assumptions have been affected by subsequent developments. George F. Kennan of the Institute for Advanced Study, Princeton, is the author of several books on American foreign policy.

2478 Kern, Harry F. "What the New Sovereign Japan Will be Like and How It Will Get Along with the U.S." *Newsweek* 38:30–31 (24 Dec. 1951)

Newsweek's senior editor for international affairs reports on the likelihood of a symbolic removal of the U.S. military to the countryside and on the training and organization of its replacement, the National Police Reserve. He mentions the skepticism of most Japanese towards rearmament and the opinion of certain observers that most of the occupation reforms will vanish with the return of Japanese sovereignty. The introduction of women's rights is the one reform predicted to have a lasting effect.

2478a Kimura, Kihachirō. "Effects of the Administrative Agreement." *Contemporary Japan* 21, no.1/3:113–17 (1952)

This article is a translation of one that originally appeared in the May 1952 issue of *New Age*. Kimura, a member of the House of Councillors, begins by attacking the common assumption that the San Francisco Peace Treaty is based on the U.S.–Japan Security Treaty, which in turn is based on the Administrative Agreement between the 2 countries dealing with the disposition of American armed forces in Japan. The fact that the Security Treaty specifies in Article 3 that such an administrative agreement be concluded means, according to Kimura, that Diet approval of the Security Treaty automatically makes a Diet vote on the Administrative Agreement unnecessary. The remainder of Kimura's discussion centers on Article 12 of the Administrative Agreement, which spells out procurement procedures for the American forces staying on in Japan. He hopes that efforts will be made to encourage a fair distribution of procurement contracts in order not to affect small and medium-size Japanese firms adversely. Bills that are currently before the Diet relating to procurement arrangements under the agreement should be carefully examined and debated lest they harm the Japanese economy.

2478b Kobayashi, A. Hiroaki. *Der amerikanisch-japanische Sicherheitspakt*. Inaugural-Dissertation, Julius-Maximilians-Universität Würzburg, 1964. ix, 412p.

This doctoral dissertation presents a very detailed study of the historical background, origins, and development of the 2 security treaties which have been concluded between Japan and the United States since World War II. It concludes with an examination of the relationship between Japan's postwar constitution and the security pact.

2479 Krylov, V. "Rearming Japan." *New Times* no.10:11–15 (7 Mar. 1951)

The opening lines of this letter from a Tokyo correspondent describe Japan as resembling an armed camp. The writer charges that despite the objections of the Japanese people Japan's industries have been almost entirely geared to serve the war in Korea, although Japan has not yet directly participated in the war. The rearmament of Japan is also discussed from what the author conceives to be the American point of view and he charges that "American strategists are planning to make it [Japan] a component part of an aggressive Pacific bloc."

2480 ———. "What Is Going on in Japan?" *New Times* no.50:5–9 (12 Dec. 1951)

The resurgence of Japanese war industry is discussed in this letter from a Tokyo correspondent. Now that the peace treaty and the U.S.–Japan Security Treaty have been signed, the author claims that Japanese industry is being converted in order to assist in the Korean War and "other American ventures" in Asia. According to the author, the widespread poverty and want in present-day Japan are the natural outcome of SCAP's militaristic and imperialistic priorities. In the concluding portion of the letter, he expresses confidence that the suffering people of Japan will eventually mount a successful attack against these forces of fascism.

2481 Kudryavtsev, V. "The American Imperialists Are Reviving Japanese Militarism." *Soviet Press Translations* 6:143–45 (15 Mar. 1951)

American and Japanese government attempts to rearm Japan are presented as a contradiction of the desire of the Japanese people, including some businessmen, to avoid rearmament and alliance with American aggression. Japanese contributions to American military activities in Korea are discussed, as are free world pressures to expand the core of 75,000 police reservists into a new Japanese army.

This article was originally published in the 24 January 1951 issue of *Izvestia*.

2482 ———. "In the Wake of San Francisco." *Soviet Press Translations* 6:653–55 (1 Dec. 1951)

Kudryavtsev reviews events in Japan during the 6 weeks following the signing of a separate peace treaty in San Francisco in an article originally published in the 18 October 1951 issue of *Izvestia*. He quotes both Inada Hidezo in the Japanese *Economist* and a report by the private Research Institute for Defense concerning plans to expand Japan's army, navy, and air force units. He also reports on a law concerning national security proposed by the Procurator General's Office which allegedly involves the dissolution of democratic institutions, suppression of the press, and legal intervention of the government in meetings and strikes. To counter the measures in this law and the plans by the United States to increase military personnel and spending in Japan, mass public movements are suggested to protest remilitarization and promote peace.

2483 ———. "The USA Is Enslaving Japan." *Soviet Press Translations* 7:251–52 (15 May 1952)

Kudryavtsev regards the U.S.–Japan Security Treaty, which was signed on 28 February 1952, as a blatant continuation of the American military occupation. He lists extensively the location of bases, airfields, and arsenals. Secondary aspects of the treaty such as extraterritoriality and the waving of import-export and entrance-exit legislation for servicemen and their families are regarded as implying more than the analogous provisions written into the American–Philippine agreement. A variety of Japanese official and press opinions are quoted which indicate that the agreement makes Japan a strategic American satellite.

This article was originally published in the 7 March 1952 issue of *Izvestia*.

2483a ———, and M. Mikhailov. "Dulles Prepares Alliance of U.S.A. with Japanese Revanchists." *Current Digest of the Soviet Press* 3, no.6:17 (24 Mar. 1951)

During his visit to Japan, according to this *Izvestia* article of 11 February 1951, John Foster Dulles delivered a speech before the members of the America–Japan Society in Tokyo in which he gave a "frank description" of the purposes of his mission to Japan. At that time, Dulles in effect proposed a military alliance between Japan and the United States which would permit the rebirth of Japanese militarism and enable Japan to play a dominant role in Asia while simultaneously enabling the United States to keep its troops in Japan and utilize both Japanese industry and manpower. The authors conclude that "the American aggressors are interested not in a just multilateral peace treaty with Japan, the prompt conclusion of which is insisted upon by the Soviet Union, but in a separate deal with Japanese revanchist circles. They do not need a peaceful democratic Japan, but the Japanese war machine, this time, however, directed by the American imperialists."

"Letter Sent by SCAP to Prime Minister Yoshida, Authorizing the Increase of the Police Reserve Force and the Expansion of the Maritime Safety Board, July 8, 1950." 1950. See no.1343.

"MacArthur Upholds Disarmament and Right of Self-Defense." 1950. See no.966b.

2483b McBride, James H. *Japan's Self-Defense Forces: Background and Evolution.* Maxwell Air Force Base, Ala.: Documentary Research Division, Aerospace Studies Institute, Air University, 1971. viii, 153p. (Air University Documentary Research Study, AU–203–70–ASI)

Chapter 5 of this study—"From Occupation to Sovereign Protectorate" (p.33–44)—briefly surveys the changes in organization and status of Japanese security forces under the occupation. The first measures taken by SCAP in this regard, McBride relates, were of course the demobilization of the Japanese armed forces and the abolition of paramilitary police organizations. The advent of the cold war, coupled with the adoption of the "peace constitution," insured both that remilitarization would be inevitable and that it would be the cause of considerably political controversy. The chapter includes an extended discussion of the negotiations which resulted in the U.S.-Japan Security Treaty and of the arguments raised against it by various Japanese groups.

2483c Marinin, M. "The Remilitarization of Japan." *Soviet Press Translations* 6: 23–24 (1 Jan. 1951); also published under the same title in *Current Digest of the Soviet Press* 2, no.48:26 (13 Jan. 1951)

The American authorities are openly pushing remilitarization at a rapid pace and on a very wide scale. Japan's heavy industry is being reconstructed, the beginnings of a new army may be seen in the recently established National Police Reserve, and the Japanese naval fleet is being rebuilt. At the same time, SCAP has been pursuing a policy of persecuting various democratic groups within Japan. All of this activity, however, is taking place in 1950—not in 1936. The Japanese people are fighting for a new, peace-loving, democratic Japan and will demand a peace treaty that provides for the country's demilitarization as well as for the withdrawal of all occupation forces. Marinin's article originally appeared in the 26 November 1950 issue of *Pravda* and is reproduced here in full.

Markov, M. "The Separate Treaty with Japan: A Weapon of American Aggression." 1951. *See* no.2406.

2484 Martin, Robert Pepper. "Japan Rearmed." *Nation* 172:224–26 (10 Mar. 1951)

The rearmament of Japan is discussed and Martin indicates that the Japanese people and government will accept the rebirth of a military establishment. He examines the availability of raw materials and money and stresses the need for substantial American contributions to promote this rebirth. He also discusses the creation of a National Police Reserve and notes that wartime officers and enlisted men are available for this service. In contrast, the advocates of neutrality and the opponents of rearmament are relatively few.

2485 Mears, Helen. "The Japanese 'Insecurity' Treaty." *Nation* 174, no.12:277–78 (22 Mar. 1952)

Mears criticizes the American–Japanese Security Treaty as an example of an American preference for illusory strategic superiority over ideological commitment. The possibility that Japan would have voluntarily approved the treaty is derided, and the increased Japanese military budgets and financial support for American garrisons that resulted are deplored.

2486 Menzies, Robert Gordon. "The Pacific Settlement Seen from Australia." *Foreign Affairs* 30, no.2:188–96 (Jan. 1952)

Observing that Japan is destined to become a great industrial power once again and will need to be defended if she is not to become an easy prey to Communist expansion, Prime Minister Menzies admits that Australia's initial insistence upon a complete prohibition of Japanese rearmament was unrealistic. The only alternative to Japanese rearmament would have been the assumption of responsibility for Japan's defense on a long-term basis by the various Allied powers at their own expense—something that the Australians, at least, were not anxious to do. Nevertheless, Menzies questions whether it is necessary for Japan to acquire naval units of a long-range nature (e.g., submarines, ships of war) and to prepare herself in other ways for offensive military action. He acknowledges that the danger of renewed Japanese aggression against such countries as Australia will continue to exist but asserts that it would have been unwise to force a hard and bitter peace upon Japan because of such fears when there is a real and present danger of Communism overrunning the entire region. Finally, Menzies expresses his hope that the conclusion of security treaties by the United States with Japan, Australia, and other Pacific nations will lead to greater unity among those countries and to more overall strength to resist Communist aggression.

2487 Morris, Ivan Ira. "Significance of the Military in Postwar Japan." *Pacific Affairs* 31, no.1:3–21 (Mar. 1958)

After 1952, former military men became more political and more unified. They agreed on the military danger from communism and the need to create an independent army under the control of professional military men. They have also worked to encourage more popular enthusiasm for Japan's new military and to revive traditional morality and the martial spirit. These goals have been thwarted by both the postwar constitution and antimilitary sentiment. Still, the author points out that Japan does have an army and, particularly if there is some internal crisis, the possibility exists of a right-wing militaristic revival.

Murphy, Robert D. *Diplomat among Warriors.* 1964. See no.733.

Naoi, Takeo. "Japan Discusses the Peace Treaty." 1951. See no.2408.

New Zealand. Dept. of External Affairs. *Annual Report of the Department of External Affairs, 1 April 1950 to 31 March 1951.* 1951. See no.2408b.

2488 Nixon, Richard M. "To the Japanese People." *Contemporary Japan* 22, no. 7/9:363–78 (1953)

An excerpt from an address given by U.S. Vice-President Nixon at a luncheon jointly sponsored by the America–Japan Society and the American Chamber of Commerce in Japan on 19 November 1953. Nixon begins by noting similarities between Japan and the United States and commenting on the problem of misconceptions between nations. He discusses America's policy regarding war and peace and declares that the only threat to the peace of the world today "is the one presented by the international Communist movement with its power center in the Soviet Union." After mentioning the necessity of maintaining U.S. military and economic strength, he turns to the importance of Asia, noting that "if Japan falls under Communist domination, all of Asia falls." He then discusses the issue of Japanese rearmament, maintaining that "the primary responsibility for Japan's defense must rest upon Japan and the Japanese people." Other subjects covered by the vice-president include Japan's relations with Korea, the matter of trade, United States' negotiations with the Communists, anti-Americanism in Japan and the problem of Japan's admission to the United Nations.

Okajima, Eiichi. *The Japanese Peace Treaty and Its Implications for Japan's Post-war Foreign Policy.* 1956. See no. 2467.

Ozaki, Yukio. "Reminiscences." 1951. See no.657.

Patch, Buel W. "Japan and Pacific Security." 1951. See no.2411a.

"Peace with Tokyo?" 1949. See no. 2344.

Price, Willard. *Journey by Junk: Japan after MacArthur.* 1953. See no.682.

Reischauer, Edwin O., et al. *Japan and America Today.* 1953. See no.2532.

2489 Rōyama, Masamichi. "Japan's Neutrality and Rearmament." *Democratic*

Japan (Tokyo) no.8:3–5 (Sept./Oct. 1950)

Rōyama considers a suggestion by Walter Lippmann that Japan be given a neutral position in international relations at the same time that she is allowed to rearm for the purpose of self-defense. The author offers qualified approval of such a scheme but points out a number of potential problems. In any case, he argues, neither Japanese interests nor those of other Pacific nations including the United States will be served unless such problems are carried out under strict United Nations supervision.

2490 Rusk, Dean. "Administrative Agreement Negotiations with Japan." *Department of State Bulletin* 26:215–17 (11 Feb. 1952)

These remarks, made at the opening of the negotiations in Tokyo on 29 January 1952, deal with the disposition of American forces in and around Japan and with the understanding that financial responsibilities under the Administrative Agreement will be shared by Japan and the United States.

2491 Saheki, Kiichi. "The Rebuilding of Japan's Self-defense Force." *Japan Quarterly* 4:101–10 (Jan./Mar. 1957)

This article analyzes the history of the Self-Defense Forces since their establishment in 1950. The author traces the different stages through which the Self-Defense Forces increased in size and strength. In his charts Saheki also gives the present strength (1957) of the various branches of the forces and Japan's total defense expenditures from 1950 to 1956. Finally, the author writes of the present and future problems facing the defense forces including various international, domestic, and internal problems.

2492 Smith, Thomas Carlyle. "Japan Won't Take Sides." *Nation* 171:142–44 (12 Aug. 1950)

The issue of Japan's security in the postoccupation period is considered in this article. According to the author, the overwhelming majority of the Japanese people are opposed to U.S. military protection because they fear involvement in a possible Soviet–American war. He maintains that they would prefer a neutral position in world politics for Japan. The United States, he insists, "must decide whether strategic or political considerations are to prevail in deciding Japan's future status, for we cannot have both military bases and reliable support from the Japanese people." He argues that the political and social reforms of the occupation, not American military strength, have combated communism and strengthened democratic tendencies and urges a rapid end to the occupation and a withdrawal of American troops from Japanese soil.

"Statement by the Minister of External Affairs, the Hon. P. C. Spender, K.C., M.P., in the House of Representatives, 14th March 1951." *See* no.2424.

2493 Stuber, Stanley I. "Japan's Problem of Self Defense." *Christian Century* 68:1009–11 (5 Sept. 1951)

The way in which Japan can renounce war and, at the same time, maintain adequate defense forces without permanently relying on American support is discussed here. Stuber examines the renunciation of war article in the constitution and subsequent occupation and government clarifications of this item. He claims that the conservative parties and the Japanese public both foresee the need for a Japanese military defense force. In order to avoid a constitutional crisis Stuber feels that all Japanese forces could be placed under the direct command of the United Nations. He encourages the American Christian community to urge the United States not to sacrifice democracy and reconciliation with Japan in favor of an East Asian military strategy.

2494 Takagi, Sōkichi. "Rearmament and Strategy." *Contemporary Japan* 20:92–95 (Jan./Mar. 1951)

This article by a former member of the Japanese navy's general staff is translated from the March 1951 issue of

Nippon Hyōron. In the author's opinion, the first decision which Japan must make is whether her projected defense force should be a cog in a collective defense machine or should be limited to the defense of the home islands only. The nature of this defense force, he continues, would be dependent in any case upon that of the prospective invasion force and should be capable of holding off an invading enemy long enough to summon reinforcements. Takagi warns, however, that the security of Europe will always be the primary concern of the United States, and he recommends the establishment of Japanese air and naval forces if world and domestic opinion and the economy can tolerate such a move. Finally, Takagi provides specific recommendations about the numerical strengths of the country's air, sea and land forces and their training and recruitment programs.

2495 Takizawa, Makoto. *Japanese Rearmament: A Dilemma in the Search for Peace and Security.* Ph.D. dissertation, Florida State Univ., 1967. 229p. (Abstracted in *Dissertation Abstracts* 28: 279A–80A [1967]; University Microfilms order no.67–8474)

The impact of Japanese rearmament after World War II on domestic and foreign affairs is examined here. After a review of initial Allied occupation policy concerning rearmament, Takizawa records the policy changes brought about by the Korean crisis, emphasizing the reversal of the Allied demilitarization policy. He considers the implications of this reversal in terms of its effects on public opinion, its impact on administrative and judicial attitudes and the issue of militarism, and its effects on the nature of Japan's relationships with the United States, the USSR and Communist China. He also reviews the Japanese–U.S. Security Treaty issue. In his conclusion he states that Japan should not make any excessive military commitment; rather, she should concentrate on maintaining her economic and psychological stability and work to relax tensions in Asia.

Taylor, George E. "The Japanese State of Mind." 1953. *See* no.2306a.

Terentyev, F. "Dulles in Tokyo." 1951. *See* no.2424b.

"Towards a Japanese Peace Treaty." 1951. *See* no.2426.

2496 Tsuda, Minoru. "Jurisdiction over Foreign Military Personnel." *Oriental Economist* 25:413–15 (Aug. 1957)

Tsuda of the Office of the Minister of Justice reviews the U.S.–Japan Administrative Agreement, noting that its reasonable nature is typical of the understandings that now exist among modern states.

2497 U.S. Army. Far East Command. *Japan: Friend and Ally.* rev. ed. Tokyo? 1952. 43p.

This introduction to Japanese culture and laws for American military personnel summarizes the key points of the U.S.–Japan Administrative Agreement. A serious attempt is made to point out the sound reasons for Japanese cultural behavior, and appropriate conduct is suggested.

2498 ———. Congress. Senate. "Security Treaty between the United States of America and Japan." *Congressional Record* 82nd Cong., 2d Sess. (1952) 98, pt. 2:2596–2606.

The record of the Senate debate concerning the ratification of the Security Treaty between the United States and Japan, signed on 8 September 1951, is set forth here.

———. ———. ———. "Treaty of Peace with Japan." 1952. *See* no.2458.

———. ———. ———. Committee on Foreign Relations. *Japanese Peace Treaty and Other Treaties Relating to Security in the Pacific.* 1952. *See* no. 2459.

2499 ———. ———. ———. ———. *Treaty of Mutual Cooperation and Security with Japan. Hearing before the*

Committee on Foreign Relations, United States Senate, Eighty-sixth Congress, Second Session, on Ex. E, 86th Congress, 2nd Session, June 7, 1960. Washington, D.C.: Government Printing Office, 1960. iii, 101p.

2500 ———. Dept. of State. *Administrative Agreement under Article III of the Security Treaty between the United States of America and Japan.* Washington, D.C.: Government Printing Office, 1953. 80p. (Dept. of State publication 4823; Treaties and International Acts series 2492)

The official text in English and Japanese of the Administrative Agreement signed in Tokyo on 28 February 1952 and effective as of 28 April. The agreement consists of a preamble and 29 articles which stipulate administrative arrangements with respect to the legal status of property of members of the American armed forces and the jurisdiction of the Japanese judicial system over cases involving American servicemen. There is also the text of an exchange of notes signed by the U.S. representative, Dean Rusk, and Japanese State Minister Okazaki Katsuo in Tokyo, on 28 February 1952.

2501 ———. ———. *Administrative Agreement with Japan.* Washington, D.C.: Government Printing Office, 1952. 9p. (Dept. of State publication 4570; Far Eastern series 55); also in *Contemporary Japan* 21, no.1/3:144–58 (1952)

The full text of the Administrative Agreement signed by Japan and the United States in Tokyo on 28 February 1952 is provided here. The agreement implements the Security Treaty between Japan and the United States which was concluded on 8 September 1951, the date when the peace treaty with Japan was also signed. Notes exchanged in Tokyo between the representatives of the 2 governments, Dean Rusk and Okazaki Katsuo, are also included.

———. ———. *American Foreign Policy 1950–1955: Basic Documents.* 1957. See no.371.

———. ———. *In-Messages.* 1950–51. See no.671.

2502 ———. ———. *Security Treaty between the United States of America and Japan.* Washington, D.C.: Government Printing Office, 1952. 14p. (Dept. of State publication 4607; Treaties and Other International Acts series 2491)

The official English and Japanese language texts of the Security Treaty between the United States and Japan, signed at San Francisco on 8 September 1951 and effective on 28 April 1952. The treaty consists of a preamble and 5 articles, under which Japan granted the United States the right to station armed forces in and about Japan. The text of the treaty may also be found in *Current Notes on International Affairs* 22:503 (Sept. 1951), in *Contemporary Japan* 20:422–23 (July/Sept. 1951), and in the October 1951 issue of *Current History* (no.2468b).

———. ———. *Treaty of Peace with Japan.* 1952. See no.2460.

2503 "United States and Japan Sign Security Treaty." *Department of State Bulletin* 25:463–65 (17 Sept. 1951)

Materials relating to the bilateral security treaty signed on 8 September 1951 by Japan and the United States are presented in this issue. They include statements of the chief signatories—Secretary of State Dean Acheson of the United States and Prime Minister Yoshida Shigeru of Japan, the text of the treaty consisting of a preface and 5 articles, and notes exchanged by Acheson and Yoshida on 8 September concerning the responsibilities imposed upon both countries by the treaty.

2504 "United States–Japan Security Treaty and Administrative Agreement." *Current Notes on International Affairs* 23:127–30 (Mar. 1952)

This short article explains the political and military background of the U.S.–Japan Security Treaty and Administrative Agreement, negotiations for which began in Feburary 1951. It refers also to Dean Rusk's visit to Japan in January 1952 when the Administrative Agreement was negotiated. There is a short discussion of the concern in Japanese circles with respect to Article 17 of the agreement which stipulates United States' jurisdiction over criminal cases involving American forces in Japan.

2505 "U.S., Japan Sign Administrative Agreement." *Department of State Bulletin* 26:382–90 (10 Mar. 1952)

The full text of the Administrative Agreement concluded on 28 February 1952 concerning the implementation of the Security Treaty between the United States and Japan is provided. Commentary on the text emphasizes the executive nature of the agreement concerning the use of facilities and areas, the sharing of costs, jurisdiction over personnel and their privileges and exemptions, and methods of continuous mutual consultation. Included is an exchange of notes between Dean Rusk, American presidential representative, and Okazaki Katsuo, Japanese minister of state, also dated 28 February. These notes concern the continued use of facilities and areas by American military personnel for 90 days after the effective date of the peace treaty, pending a final settlement concerning these areas.

2505a Uyehara, Shigeru. "Japan's Security." *Democratic Japan* (Tokyo) no.6: 1–3, 15 (July 1950)

This editorial considers any suggestion that Japan rearm to be suicidal, since rearmament would merely invite an attack which could not be adequately countered in this nuclear age. Uyehara feels, however, that Japan's internal security forces must be strengthened in anticipation of the withdrawal of occupation troops. Japan's external security, he concludes, will best be handled by international guarantees once Japan enters the United Nations, and Japan should be willing to offer military bases to UN forces if requested to do so.

2505b ———. "Peace Treaty and Security." *Democratic Japan* (Tokyo) no.11: 1–2 (Mar./Apr. 1951)

This editorial notes with pleasure that the draft treaty is "founded on the highest level of fairness and justice." It is now necessary, Uyehara contends, for the Japanese people to renew their efforts to achieve economic independence and to strengthen the foundations of democracy in Japan. The offer of the United States to maintain Japanese security after the peace settlement should be accepted, even if it means the stationing of American troops in Japan. Ultimately, however, Japan will have to undertake limited rearmament in order to participate in a Pacific collective security arrangement.

2505c ———. "Permanent Neutrality." *Democratic Japan* (Tokyo) no.5:1–2 (May/June 1950)

This editorial agrees with MacArthur's belief that a peace treaty is now overdue, but argues that Japan nevertheless should oppose any settlement in which some of her former enemies refuse to participate. Rearmament should also be vehemently opposed, and a permanent unarmed neutrality recognized by the Allied powers including the USSR and the People's Republic of China must be sought.

Vaughn, Miles W. "American Policy and Future Security of Japan." 1949. *See* no.614.

"Views on Peace and Security: A Symposium." 1951. *See* no.2439b.

2506 Weinstein, Martin E. *Japan's Postwar Defense Policy 1947–1968.* New York: Columbia Univ. Pr., 1971. xii, 160p. (Studies of the East Asian Institute, Columbia Univ.)

By tracing Japanese defense policy from its origins during the early months of the occupation, Weinstein describes how Japan's leaders have gone about achieving security. He analyzes the role of the Self-Defense Forces and points to the line of conservative prime ministers since Yoshida Shigeru, all of whom have wanted to cooperate with the United States in defending Japan, but have had their own ideas on the form of Japanese-American cooperation. Weinstein, who served with the air force for 3 years in Japan, returned to Tokyo for a year's research culminating in this book.

Willoughby, Charles. "Tribute to Japan." 1952. See no.687.

2506a Woddis, H. C. "The Re-arming of Japan." *Eastern World* 5:9–11 (July 1951)

Woddis describes the measures being taken with SCAP's approval to rebuild Japan's army, navy, and air force as well as to revive the production of military armaments. He calls this policy of rearming Japan a terrible gamble, predicting that "the Japanese rulers will be able to 'play from strength' and pursue their own ambitions" once their armed forces are reestablished. He notes, however, that there are certain groups in Japan presently opposing this new policy and urges that they be supported for the sake of averting the outbreak of another war in East Asia.

Worden, William L. "The Japs Are Marching Again." 1951. See no.1348b.

2507 Zhukov, E. "The American Imperialists Are Arming Japan." *Soviet Press Translations* 6:203–6 (15 Apr. 1951); abridged version published under the title "American Imperialists Rearm Japan" in *Current Digest of the Soviet Press* 3, no.13:14 (12 May 1951)

Zhukov alleges that the Japanese government is willing to rearm in return for the conclusion of a separate peace treaty with the United States. This action, according to Zhukov, would deprive Japan of a real peace with the People's Republic of China and the Soviet Union. He states that, although Premier Yoshida is the author of calculated denials of demilitarization, he is inducing the American rearmament of Japan. American contracts totaling $228,000,000 for material and repairs relating to the Korean War are reported as evidence of American revival of Japan's armaments industry. The ways the Japanese people are combating this policy of aggression are summarized in conclusion.

This article was originally published in the 29 March 1951 issue of *Pravda*.

Japan's Reentry into the Postwar World

The effectuation of the treaty of San Francisco on 28 April 1952 restored Japan to the status of a sovereign and independent state responsible for planning and conducting its own foreign relations. Opinions differed widely as to the nature of the foreign policies that should be adopted. The following items relate to that problem in general and, in particular, to the posture that Japan should adopt with respect to the cold war. These entries are closely related to many of those in the section on foreign policies of the United States and other nations (p.260) as well as to a smaller number in the calendar of general commentaries (p.152, especially for 1951 [p.222], 1952 [p.231], and 1953–72 [p.235]). Relevant also are the entries in the two immediately preceding sections (p.728 and p.781).

2508 Allison, John M. "The Year Ahead in Japan." *Department of State Bulletin* 25:724–28 (5 Nov. 1951)

A discussion of Japan's future, the author insists, must be predicated upon its past. Consequently, the article concerns the occupation period as well as the future of the country. After a brief analysis of the negotiation of the peace treaty granting Japan autonomy and ending the occupation, the author considers the possibility of a Japanese revision of occupation measures motivated by 3 factors: (1) a doubt by many Japanese leaders of the practicability of certain occupation-sponsored measures; (2) a belief that certain of the punitive measures, notably the purge, have been enforced too long; and (3) a belief that certain of the occupation-sponsored measures would inhibit Japan's early economic and industrial recovery. There is considerable attention paid to the nation's economic situation—during the occupation, at the present time, and in the future—and the essay concludes with some comments on Japan's problem of self-defense. The author views the U.S.-Japan Security Treaty as a necessary and beneficial arrangement and expresses cautious optimism regarding Japan's future.

2509 American Institute of Pacific Relations, ed. *Some Japanese Views on American–Japanese Relations*. New York: American Institute of Pacific Relations, 1953. 25p.

Statements and papers by 4 Japanese who participated in the Conference on Japanese–American Relations held in Honolulu, 17–20 January 1953, are compiled here. They are: "Japan in the Changing World," by Nasu Shiroshi (emeritus professor, Tokyo Univ.); "Post-treaty Aspects of the Japanese Economy," by Kiuchi Nobutane (former chairman, Foreign Exchange Administration Board); "The Political Climate in Post-treaty Japan," by Ryū Shintarō (chief editor, *Asahi Shimbun*); and "Economic Difficulties Facing Japan," by Yamaguchi Shōgo (editorial board member, *Yomiuri Shimbun*). Nasu and Ryū comment on the occupation of Japan. Nasu notes that the Japanese understand why SCAP had to change from its policy of developing a militarily "weak Japan" to its policy of promoting a "strong Japan" during the occupation period, but he stresses that the "pacifist mentality" of the Japanese is genuine in spite of the possibility that they may be criticized for an unrealistic evaluation of the world situation. The editor of the *Asahi Shimbun* states that the occupation's initial measures to guarantee Japan's military disarmament were responsible for the subsequent Japanese hesitancy regarding disarmament. He further remarks that economic recovery should precede military revival and that America's posttreaty policy of noninterference in Japanese affairs is a welcome sign of continued improvement in Japanese–American relations.

2510 Ballantine, Joseph W. "The Future of the Ryukyus." *Foreign Affairs* 31: 663–74 (July 1953)

The past history, the present period of Allied control, and the future of the strategically situated Ryukyu Islands are considered in this thoughtful article. The author discusses the prewar affinities of the Ryukyuan people to China and Japan before discussing briefly the Allied economic, political, and educational reform programs of the postwar period. As the title implies, the main part of the article is a discussion of the future course of the islands and an explanation of the attitudes of its people toward Japan and toward the United States. The author explains the legal basis for the U.S. presence but affirms that there is strong sentiment in the Ryukyus that the islands be restored to Japan. After a clear explanation of the strategic implications of U.S. control of the islands, he suggests that there are 3 choices open to the United States: (1) to continue to administer the islands as at present; (2) to hold only the southern islands for strategic purposes and return the northern islands to Japan; and (3) to recognize Japan's sovereignty over all the Ryukyus and arrange for the continuation of military bases with Japan. He concludes that the third choice would be most advantageous from the American, Japanese, and Ryukyuan points of view.

2511 Chamberlin, William Henry. "Bases of American–Japanese Cooperation." *Far Eastern Survey* 21:193–96 (21 Dec. 1952)

Chamberlin, correspondent and author of several books on Japan, points out that the Communist threat precludes any ideas of neutralism and emphasizes the need for cooperation in all policies of mutual interest.

2512 Chambon, Paul. "Le Japon rentre en scène." *Temps modernes* 7:331–54 (Aug. 1951)

In a review of developments in Japan during the occupation period that led to Japan's reentry into the postwar world, Chambon speaks of the considerable progress made in the country's reconstruction and of the series of initiatives undertaken by the Americans since 1949 in rebuilding the Japanese economy. While generally praising SCAP, however, he is critical of the superficial manner in which the Japanese have adopted democracy and also points out that the economic chaos characterizing the first few years of the occupation was due in part to a number of decisions made by SCAP.

Cohen, Jerome B. *Economic Problems of Free Japan*. 1952. See no.1611.

2513 Dewey, Thomas E. "Can Japan Stay on Our Side?" *Collier's* 128:26–27, 63–68 (8 Dec. 1951)

Dewey discusses the Japanese fear of Russia evident prior to the restoration of Japanese independence. Party alignments, the decline in Communist popularity, the land reform program, and the current status of agriculture are examined. Japanese apprehension of economic isolation after the ratification of the peace treaty and the weaknesses in industrial recovery are noted. American–Japanese cooperation is urged in order to strengthen democracy and prevent a Communist take-over of the rest of Asia.

2514 Dunning, Alice L. "Japan in Transition." *American Foreign Service Journal* 29:15–18, 54–55 (Mar. 1952)

Dunning discusses the reemergence of Japan as a sovereign member of the free world in the manner provided in the peace treaty. She explains the importance of raw material imports to the Japanese economy and the superficial advantages of trade with Communist Asia. The responsibility of the United States and other free-world nations to ensure Japanese strength by financial and technical aid is underscored. The likelihood of a partial revision of occupation reforms in such areas as the ban on military forces, the decentralization of political and educational authority, and the restrictions on economic monopoly is examined. Dunning questions the permanence of the inculcation of democratic patterns of thought and action among the Japanese people.

2515 Greene, Marc T. "Japan: Asset or Liability." *Fortnightly* 177:20–25 (Jan. 1952)

An Englishman who was a correspondent assigned to both the military and civilian branches of the occupation discusses the future of Japan in light of its past experience during the occupation. In this brief report the author comments favorably on the U.S. rehabilitation of the Japanese economy but also describes what he terms American "reorganization and rehabilitation of the Japanese military," which he maintains is being financed by resurgent *zaibatsu* organizations. Japan's rigid economic growth is viewed with some alarm and it is noted that the peace treaty contains no preventive and few restrictive provisions with respect to Japan's expansion. The author predicts that the future will bring a more self-confident nation whose citizens will eventually insist upon the withdrawal of all military contingents. He concludes with the contention that Japan "holds every potentiality for becoming a valuable—perhaps an invaluable—asset to the West in the endeavor to contain Soviet Russia in the Orient" but warns against the possibility of a restoration which will imbue the Japanese "with something of the old dangerous arrogance."

2516 Hatano, Ken-ichi. "Japan's Choice: Taipei or Peking." *Contemporary Japan* 20:323–30 (July/Sept. 1951)

An examination of the factors to be considered by Japan when forming her posttreaty policies toward the governments of Nationalist China and Communist China. Nationalist China is depicted as anxious "to have Japan as her 'ally' in Asia's anti-Communist front." Plans of the Nationalist government for adjusting posttreaty relations with Japan are reviewed. Two major conditions stated as controlling Communist China's posttreaty actions in her relations with Japan are studied. They are: (1) Communist China is a Soviet satellite and her post-treaty attitude toward Japan will be decided by the Kremlin; and (2) developments in problems relating to Korea and Formosa will control Communist China's movements. Three possibilities which Communist China may choose in forming a relationship with Japan are suggested. The author maintains that Japan is in a position to make her own decision in this matter, but he concludes with the statement that Japan must realize "that there is only one way open to her to contribute to the establishment of peace in Asia, and that way is the conclusion of a treaty with the Nationalist Government of China."

2517 Holland, William L. "Japan and the New Balance of Power in the Far East." *International Affairs* 28:292–97 (July 1952)

Formerly editor of *Pacific Affairs*, secretary general of the Institute of Pacific Relations, and director of the U.S. Office of War Information in China, Holland outlines the position of Japan in the Far East and the kind of role she could play in the future. He writes about both the political and economic problems still facing Japan after the occupation. He is also concerned with Japan's role in international politics, specifically her relationship with the Soviet Union and China.

2518 Hsu, Immanuel C. Y. "Japan Re-enters International Society." *Far Eastern Survey* 17:227–28 (6 Oct. 1948)

Hsu, a member of the Political Section of the Chinese Mission in Japan, discusses the decision by the Far Eastern Commission to lift restrictions on foreign travel by Japanese.

2519 Japan. Ministry of Foreign Affairs. Bureau of Public Information and Cultural Affairs. *Japan, Her Security and Mission*. Tokyo: The Ministry, The Bureau, 1952. 15p.

2520 "Japan to Participate in Technical Agreements." *Department of State Bulletin* 22:414 (13 Mar. 1950)

This press release provides the text of a directive issued to MacArthur on 21 February 1950 authorizing him to permit Japan's participation with other nations or groups of nations in international agreements, conventions, and conferences of a technical nature.

2521 "Japanese Participation in International Relations Encouraged." *Department of State Bulletin* 21:307 (29 Aug. 1949)

In this statement issued on 18 August 1949, State Department officials declare their intention to allow Japanese government participation in international conventions, meetings, and consular arrangements, if an invitation is issued by a host country and approval is granted by SCAP regardless of Far Eastern Commission action on this matter.

2522 "Japanese to Open Agencies in the United States." *Department of State Bulletin* 22:819–20 (22 May 1950)

The opening of Japanese trade agencies in New York, San Francisco, Los Angeles, Seattle, and Honolulu is reported here. These agencies will provide information for American businessmen concerning Japanese trade opportunities and import-export laws and will permit Japanese research on market conditions and trade opportunities in the United States. They will also provide personal and property protection for Japanese nationals in the United States.

2523 "Japan's Future: Interview with John Foster Dulles." *Newsweek* 38:31–35 (10 Sept. 1951)

In this interview with Dulles, the following points are covered: (1) the contention that the peace treaty with Japan is one of reconciliation and can be accepted by other Asian countries; (2) the reasons for maintaining the emperor system and the prospects for developing sound Japanese leadership; (3) the importance of South Korea to the defense of Japan; (4) the relationship of Japan to U.S.–USSR cold war relations; (5) the potentiality of Japanese economic survival given the switch from Chinese to Southeast Asian markets; (6) the place of Japan in American policy toward Asia.

"Japan's Uncertain Future." 1951. See no.651.

2524 "Japan's Worry about Security." *U.S. News and World Report* 28:36–38 (7 Apr. 1950)

This interview with Ōno Katsumi, an official of the Japanese Foreign Office, focused upon Japan's concern for her future economic and political security. Two general points emerge: (1) Japan is chaffing under strict American control and would like to achieve her political independence, and (2) although the resources of Manchuria are still believed vital to a revived Japanese economy, her primary economic and political ties in the future will probably be with the United States.

Ketzel, Clifford. "The Occupation of Japan." 1949. See no.595.

2525 Kirchwey, Freda. "Beyond San Francisco." *Nation* 173:203–4 (15 Sept. 1951)

Kirchwey contends that the conclusion of the San Francisco Peace Treaty will not mitigate East Asian tensions and that there is no assurance that a rearmed Japan will use its power only against Communist nations after the withdrawal of American troops. She concludes that a viable future balance of power in Pacific Asia depends on the establishment of peaceful relations between Japan and China.

Lattimore, Owen. "Japan is Nobody's Ally." 1949. See no.805.

2526 ———. "When Japan Has a Treaty." *Nation* 173:88–89 (4 Aug. 1951)

The way in which Japan will conduct her international relations following the conclusion of a peace treaty is discussed. Lattimore contends that the Japanese must adopt a neutral policy to balance their position between the Soviet Union and the United States. The idea of a solid Japanese–American alliance is rejected as unrealistic. Japan's relations with Asian and Pacific countries are regarded as the principle determinants of future Japanese diplomacy.

2527 Nakano, Teru M. "A Future for Japan." *Current History* 20:272–77 (May 1951)

Teru Nakano, a student of American–Japanese relations, explains that the Korean situation has clearly shown that if the United States is to continue to wield influence in the Far East, it needs an economically stable, industrially sound Japan. She describes the dilemma this economic reconstruction poses for the United States: open the traditional trade areas of China and Manchuria to Japan and contribute to the war potential of a Communist government or restrict Japan's trade to other areas, thereby limiting levels of trade.

2528 Ono, Isamu. *The New International Position of Japan.* Tokyo: Japan Institute of Foreign Affairs, 1954. 18p.

2529 Parrott, Lindesay. "Challenges of Peace That Japan Faces." *New York Times Magazine* p.5, 27–29 (2 Sept. 1951)

With the signing of the peace treaty imminent, Japan prepares to face the problems of peace. The author believes that Japan will have a difficult course to steer in a troubled world. Dependent on trade, she must get raw materials and foreign markets and deal with the problem of overpopulation. Moreover, Japan must use the still unfamiliar institutions of democracy to handle the complex and pressing problems ahead.

———. "Japan's Mood as a New Chapter Opens." 1952. *See* no.680.

2530 Pfaff, William. "The Third Revolution." *Commonweal* 57:394 (23 Jan. 1953)

After indicating that the occupation has provided a "respectable foundation" for democracy in Japan, the author looks forward to the role America will play in Japan's future. He discusses the implications of the situation wherein American "security forces" will replace the occupation forces due to Japan's constitutional disarmament provision. In the author's opinion, such a military presence may threaten the growth of democracy in Japan, and he urges that America effect the protection of Japan not by itself but "within the framework of an Asiatic alliance."

2531 "A Reconditioned Japan: Her Place in the Post-war World." *Round Table* 42:126–33 (Mar. 1952)

In attempting to determine Japan's economic and political potential after war, defeat, and occupation, the author draws a comparison between the early 1940s and the final days of the occupation. By briefly examining the implications of the changes, he illustrates how they might affect Commonwealth interests.

2532 Reischauer, Edwin Oldfather, et al. *Japan and America Today.* Stanford, Calif.: Stanford Univ. Pr., 1953. ix, 166p.

Compiled and edited by Melvin A. Conant and Miriam S. Farley, this volume is a selection of the data papers that were presented and a summary of the discussion that ensued at the Conference on Japanese–American Relations held in Honolulu on 17–20 January 1953, under the auspices of the Institute of Pacific Relations of Hawaii and the Japan Institute of Pacific Relations. The papers focus on the attitudes and issues which were most likely at that time to determine the course of relations between Japan and the United States. They are: (1) "Potential Sources of Japanese–American Friction," by Edwin O. Reischauer (Harvard Univ.); (2) "Bases of American–Japanese Cooperation," by William Henry Chamberlin (editorial contributor to the *Wall Street Journal* and author of *Japan over Asia, Modern Japan,* etc.); (3) "United States Relations with Japan, 1945–1952," by members of the State Department's Office of Northeast Asian Affairs (no.837); (4) "Japan and America: Some Economic Problems," by J. Morden Murphy (chairman of the American Institute of Pacific Relations); (5) "Economic Difficulties Facing Japan," by Yamaguchi Shōgo (member of the editorial board of the *Yomiuri Shimbun*); and (6) "Japan's Foreign Trade Problems," by Jerome B. Cohen (associate professor of economics, City College of New York) (no.1612).

While all of the papers deal in part with the termination of the immediate aftermath of the occupation, none of them examine the American occupation of Japan in any detail. "United States Relations with Japan, 1945–1952," by far the longest paper within the volume, does include considerable information on the Treaty of Peace, the Security Treaty, and Administrative Agreement, and various related conventions and obligations. Like the accompanying papers, however, it is directed primarily towards an analysis of current Japanese–American relations and of some of their problems and prospects.

The Reminiscences of Douglas W. Overton. 1960. *See* no.44h.

2533 Ridgway, Matthew Bunker. "Korea and Japan: Military Operations, Armistice Negotiations, Relations with People." *Vital Speeches* 18:540–42 (15 June 1952); also in *Department of State Bulletin* 26:924–27 (9 June 1952)

This speech by the second supreme commander for the Allied powers concerns the conduct of the Korean War and relations with the Japanese government and people immediately after the termination of the occupation. In the section relating to Japan, Ridgway indicates that the continuation of mutual understanding, respect, and cooperation between Japan and the United States is of "vital importance to the national welfare of both nations and to the peace of the world." In his concluding remarks, Ridgway refers to the disorders which occurred in Tokyo on 1 May 1952, which he characterizes as "revealing to the Japanese people the character and objective of Communist designs." The disorders, he maintains were not anti-American and in any case were repudiated by the overwhelming majority of responsible Japanese.

2534 "The Rising Sun." *Twentieth Century* 150:388–94 (Nov. 1951)

Japan's soon-to-be terminated occupation is discussed as a backdrop for a consideration of the nation's future economic and political role in world affairs. The author considers the Japanese reaction to what ultimately became the chief American objective during the occupation, i.e., the establishment of a completely rehabilitated nation, and describes the Japanese aversion to the possibility of their becoming a pawn in the power struggle between the United States and the Soviet Union. He speculates about Japan's future economic and political role in the Far East vis-à-vis Communist China and the nations of Southeast Asia. Finally, he warns against 2 threats to the democratic government that are now emerging: reactionaries embodying the spirit of Old Japan on the right and members of the Communist party on the left.

2535 Sebald, William J. "Japan: Asset of the Free World." *Department of State Bulletin* 26:490–94 (31 Mar. 1952)

Sebald, political adviser to SCAP, reviews the occupation and the peace settlement. His emphasis is on the need for a policy of collective security in Asia directed against Soviet communism and on the role Japan should play in this policy. The vital part played by Japan during the Korean War is underscored as is the current exposure of Japan to Soviet harassment, aggression, and encouragement of internal disorder. The desire for cooperation with America on the part of the Japanese government and the vast majority of the people is represented as evidence of a genuine community of national interests.

———, and Russell Brines. *With MacArthur in Japan: A Personal History of the Occupation.* 1965. See no.748.

Supreme Commander for the Allied Powers. Diplomatic Section. *Correspondence of Political Adviser to SCAP.* 1947–51. See no.669.

2536 Takeuchi, Tatsuji. "Basic Issues in Japan's Foreign Policy." *Far Eastern Survey* 21:161–66 (19 Nov. 1952)

Takeuchi, author of several works on Japan, analyzes the foreign policy of Japan, pointing out that the need for security necessitates collaboration with the West despite neutralist sentiment and concern for the economic future.

U.S. Dept. of State. *In-Messages.* 1950–51. See no.671.

———. ———. Office of Northeast Asian Affairs. *United States Relations with Japan, 1945–1952.* 1953. See no. 837.

2537 "U.S. Views on Japan's Resumption of International Responsibilities." *Department of State Bulletin* 20:635 (15 May 1949)

In this response to press criticism, State Department officials clarify their position concerning the desirability of the gradual resumption by Japan of international responsibilities in accordance with the Potsdam Declaration and Far Eastern Commission directives. Activities in fields such as trade promotion, citizenship and property problems, cultural relations, and technical exchange would, in their opinion, contribute to rapid economic recovery.

Willoughby, Charles. "Tribute to Japan." 1952. See no.687.

Yoshida, Shigeru. *The Yoshida Memoirs: The Story of Japan in Crisis.* 1962. See no.769.

Author Index

References to authors who are cited within the annotations of specific entries are included within this index. All numbers refer to entry numbers.

Abe, Haruo, 1266
Abe, Yoshishige, 2013
Abegg, Lily, 1906
Acheson, Dean Gooderham, 54, 999, 2361, 2361a, 2455
Ackerman, Edward Augustus, 81, 1535, 1818
Ackerman, Lauren V., 44g
Adams, John Clarke, 633
Adams, Thomas F. M., 1631, 1632
Aduard, Evert Joost Lewe van, *see* Lewe van Aduard, Evert Joost
Advisory Committee on Labor, *see* Supreme Commander for the Allied Powers. Advisory Committee on Labor
Agatsuma, Sakae, *see* Wagatsuma, Sakae
Airey, Willis, 817
Aiso, John F., 63
Ajia Kyōkai, 1116a
Akademiia nauk SSSR. Institut narodov Azii, 1, 30
Alden, Jane M., 619, 2013a
Allen, George Cyril, 1633, 1634
Allen, Lafe Franklin, 477, 1045a, 1046, 1228, 1349, 1350, 2014, 2134
Allied Council for Japan, *see* Supreme Commander for the Allied Powers. Allied Council for Japan

Allied Translator and Interpreter Section, *see* Supreme Commander for the Allied Powers. Allied Translator and Interpreter Section
Allison, John M., 642, 2443, 2444, 2468, 2468a, 2508
Almond, Gabriel A., 1184
Alperovitz, Gar, 238
American Institute of Pacific Relations, 2509
American Pharmaceutical Association, 2167
Amidon, William C., 761, 986a
Amis, Robert T., 1740
Amravati, Mallappa, 688
Anderson, Joseph L., 2134a
Anderson, Paul Seward, 2015
Anderson, Ronald Stone, 2016, 2017
Andō, Nisuke, 2236
Angelino, Arnold D. A. de Kat, *see* Kat Angelino, Arnold D. A. de
Angus, H. F., 415a
Aoki, Hideo, 2018
Appleman, John A., 1047
Appleton, Richard B., 1267
Arai, Tatsuo, 1350a
Ariga, Kizaemon, 1907
Arita, Takeshi, 1876
Armstrong, Anne, 182
Army Library. Pentagon, 42
Arnold, David, 477a
Arnold, Henry Harley, 205

Arnot, R. Page, 2468c
Asahi Shimbun. Staff, 688a
Asahina, Sōgen, 2279
Ashida, Hitoshi, 770, 1509a
Ashizu, Yoshihiko, 2198a
Ashmead, John, Jr., 416, 2019
Association for Asian Studies, 2
Atcheson, George, Jr., 770a, 825, 876b, 945
Atkinson, Carroll, 2020, 2021
Attlee, Clement, 945
Austin, Margretta S., **2112**
Austin, Warren, 987
Australia. Dept. of External Affairs, 162, 163, 1012
Australian Institute of International Affairs, **164, 772**
Ausubel, Nathan, 249
Avarin, V., 1351
Ayusawa, Iwao Frederick, 1741, 1742, 1743
Azuma, Mitsutoshi, 1744

B., K., 1501
Baba, Masao, 1649
Baba, Tsunego, 417, 2364, 2469
Babcock, C. Stanton, 48a
Baerwald, Hans Herman, 1105, 1114
Bagley, William C., 2022
Bailey, Charles Waldo (II), 246
Bailey, Kenneth Hamilton, 164

Author Index

Baker, Alonzo Lafayette, 1229
Baker, Frayne, 532
Bakke, Edward Wight, 689
Baldwin, Hanson Weightman, 70, 239, 245
Baldwin, Roger Nash, 44a, 44b, 478, 533, 534, 1818a
Ball, William Macmahon, 535, 536, 667a, 690, 773, 793, 1230, 2365, 2445
Ballantine, Joseph W., 44n, 537, 580, 774, 1793a, 2410, 2510
Ballou, Richard Boyd, 2022a
Ballou, Robert Oleson, 64a
Baltz, William Matthew, 2023
Barnett, Robert W., 1487a, 1523
Baruch, Walter B., 1487b
Batchelder, Robert C., 239a
Bate, H. Maclean, 1450
Bates, M. Searle, 76c
Battaglini, Mario, 1184
Bayles, William, 1231
Beal, John Robinson, 2366, 2461
Beard, Eva, 2023a
Beardsley, Richard King, 691, 711
Beasley, William Gerald, 692
Bee, John M., 1588
Behrstock, Arthur, 479
Beitzell, Robert Egner, 183
Bell, A. T. J., 851a
Beloff, Max, 775, 776
Benedict, Ruth Fulton, 1908, 1908a, 1909
Benjamin, Harold, 2024
Bennett, John W., 693, 890, 891, 1754b, 1910, 1911, 1912, 1913, 1913a
Bennett, Martin Toscan, 1118, 1119, 1451
Benoit, Edward George, 2025
Berezhkov, V., 1048
Bergamini, David, 1048a
Berkov, Robert H., 2135
Berlin, Richard B., 2167a
Bernard, Henri, 1013
Berrigan, Darrell, 892, 987a, 1699a
Berton, Peter, *see* Burton, Peter
Betz, Betty, 2237
Beuschlein, Alice, 480
Bezrodnov, I., 952a
Bickerton, Max, 418
Bishop, William W., Jr., 1831
Bisson, Thomas Arthur, 65, 65a, 66, 133, 538, 581, 618, 667a, 1107, 1120, 1610, 1793b
Blackett, Patrick Maynard Stuart, 245
Blakemore, Thomas L. (Jr.), 1154b, 1268, 1269, 1293
Blakeney, Ben Bruce, 150, 1049, 1270
Blakeslee, George Hubbard, 203a, 852, 853
Blanchod, Frédéric Georges, 694
Blewett, George F., 1050
Bloch, Henry Simon, 229a
Blumenthal, Tuvia, 1699b
Blumhagen, Herman Herbert, 2026
Blunden, Edmund, 618a
Bogdanov, Nikolai, 374a
Bohlen, Charles E., 2311
Bolles, Blair, 375, 582, 2367, 2368, 2369
Borton, Hugh, 3, 50, 51, 52, 481, 505, 539, 619, 695, 696, 715
Bouchier, C. A., 1564
Bouterse, Arthur D., 900
Bowden, John, 43
Bowen, Helene, 48
Bowers, Faubion, 44j, 697
Bowles, Gordon T., 2281
Braibanti, Ralph J. D., 28, 893, 894, 895, 896, 1316, 1317, 1339, 2198b, 2199
Brenn, Bruce M., 1121
Bresler, Robert Joel, 240
Brett, Cecil Carter, 1318, 1319
Brewer, F. M., 1231a
Briggs, Everett F., 540
Brines, Russell, 541, 748
Brinkman, Albert R., 2027, 2027a
Britton, James Cleland, 1523a, 1564a, 1564b
Brochier, Hubert, 1635
Bronfenbrenner, Martin, 698, 698a, 709, 1565, 1588a, 1635a, 1677, 1678
Brooks, Lester, 134
Brown, Allan Robert, 1231b
Brown, Brendan Francis, 1072
Brown, Cecil, 2469a
Brown, Delmer Myers, 4, 2028
Brown, Lindsey A., 1832
Brown, Margery Finn, 643
Brown, Richard Gerard, 1168
Browne, Courtney, 1052
Browne, Martha S., 1566
Brumbaugh, Thoburn T., 482, 542, 1352, 2200, 2282
Bryn-Jones, David, 1353
Buck, Pearl, 2283
Buck, Philip Wallenstein, 619a
Bunce, William K., 2201, 2228a
Bundy, McGeorge, 216, 245, 2446
Bungei Shunjū Senshi Kenkyūkai, *see* Pacific War Research Society
Burch, Betty B., 1434
Burg, Moses, 586
Burks, Ardath Walter, 135, 699, 724
Burns, James MacGregor, 184
Burton, Peter, 5
Busch, Noel Fairchild, 419, 543, 2284
Bush, Henry C., 1914
Buss, Claude A., 483, 945, 2370
Butler, Sir Paul, 1464a
Butow, Robert Joseph Charles, 136, 1053
Butterworth, W. Walton, 48a
Byas, Hugh, 66a
Byrne, P. J., 1354
Byrnes, James Francis, 206, 207, 245, 855

Caiger, George, 420
Caiger, John Godwin, 2029, 2029a, 2030
Camacho, Martin Thomas, 1745
Cameron, Meribeth E., 700
Campbell, Colin D., 1699c
Campbell, Roy S., 945
Canham, Erwin D., 484
Capper, D. P., 855b
Carey, Jane Perry Clark, 1154c
Carus, Clayton D., 1488
Casey, R. G., 2374
Cassidy, Velma Hastings, 421, 2031
Caulfield, Genevieve, 953
Chamberlain, John, 983
Chamberlin, William Henry, 81, 376, 2511, 2532
Chambon, Paul, 2512
Chang, Hsin-hai, 2332
Chapman, John Griffin, 2032
Chapman, Ralph, 2136
Chatterjee, B. R., 701

Author Index

Chaze, Elliott, 485
Chazelle, Jacques, *see* Chéroy, Jacques, *pseud.*
Chee, Changboh, 2033
Chenery, Hollis B., 1636
Chenery, William Ludlow, 582a
Cheng, Peter Ping-chii, 777
Chéroy, Jacques, *pseud.*, 702, 702a
Chia, Franklin, 1700
Chiang, Wen-hsien, 1054
Chifley, J. B., 162
Cho, Sung-Yoon, 6, 1169, 1297a
Chou, En-lai, 2423b
Chou, Kêng-shêng, *see* Chow, S. R.
Chow, S. R., 165, 166, 166a
Christian Deputation to Japan, 2202a
Christian Science Monitor, 33
Chu, Djang, 724
Churchill, Arthur C., 67
Churchill, Winston L. S., 208
Civil Affairs Div., *see* Supreme Commander for the Allied Powers. Civil Affairs Div.
Civil Affairs Training School, *see* U.S. Civil Affairs Training School. University of Michigan
Civil Historical Section, *see* Supreme Commander for the Allied Powers. Civil Historical Section
Civil Information and Education Section, *see* Supreme Commander for the Allied Powers. Civil Information and Education Section
Clapp, Verner W., 2238
Clark, Blake, 544
Clark, Gordon D., 2302
Clifton, Allan Stephen, 422
Cline, Ray Steiner, 53
Close, Upton, 486
Clubok, Alfred Bernard, 761, 1355
Clune, Frank, 545
Clyde, Paul Hibbert, 488, 703
Coblenz, Constance G., 824
Cochrane, Robert B., 487
Cohen, Bernard Cecil, 2462, 2463
Cohen, Jerome Bernard, 644, 1489, 1490, 1524, 1524a, 1525, 1567, 1568, 1590, 1611, 1612, 1637, 1679, 1680, 2532
Colbert, Evelyn S., 1356
Cole, Allan Burnett, 704, 1357, 1358, 1434, 1915, 1990, 2285, 2286
Cole, Taylor, 488
Colegrove, Kenneth W., 68
Coleman, Rex, 1271
Collier, David Swanson, 1637a
Colton, Hattie Kawahara, 705, 1170, 1171
Colton, Kenneth E., 489, 705, 1359, 1360, 1361, 2345a
Columbia Univ. Oral History Research Office. Oral History Project, 44
Colwell, Ernest, 2033a
Commission on the Constitution, *see* Japan. Commission on the Constitution
Committee to Inquire into Economic Problems of Japan and Korea, *see* U.S. Committee to Inquire into Economic Problems of Japan and Korea
Committee on Foreign Relations, *see* U.S. Committee on Foreign Relations
Compton, Arthur Holly, 241, 245
Compton, Karl T., 242
Comyns-Carr, A. S., 1055, 1056
Conant, James B., 69
Constitution Investigation Council, *see* Japan. Commission on the Constitution
Contemporary Japan, 34
Coox, Alvin D., 2287
Corey, Herbert, 379
Cornell, John Bilheimer, 1916
Cornwall, Peter George, 1173
Costello, William, 490, 546, 547, 1339a, 1362, 2314a
Coughlin, William James, 2137
Coughran, Tom B., 1569
Council on Foreign Relations, 70, 491, 548, 583, 584, 779, 2372
Counts, George S., 2034
Cousins, Norman, 645, 2288
Cowley, George A., 1363, 2239
Craemer, Alice R., 1232
Craig, William, 137, 138
Craigie, Sir Robert Leslie, 167
Crane, Burton, 44e, 1233, 1465, 2034a
Crane, Esther M., 44i, 1452
Crawford, Robert H., 897
Creel, George, 954
Creemers, Wilhelmus Helena Martinus, 2204
Crimmins, Marguerite C., 1887
Crockett, Lucy Herndon, 585
Crofts, Alfred, 492
Crofts, Verna I., 548a
Cronbach, Lee J., 2034b
Crow, Lester D., 2035
Crowley, James B., 1659
Cultural Science Mission to Japan, *see* U.S. Cultural Science Mission to Japan
Current Digest of the Soviet Press, 34a
Curtis, Gerald Leon, 2463a

Dabney, Vaughn, 2205
Dai, Poeliu, 856a
Daily Labor Press, Inc., 1746
Dallek, Robert, 20
Dallin, David J., 780
Dangerfield, Royden, 706
Daoust, George Arlington, Jr., 781
Davidson, Basil, 2469b
Deane, John Russell, 209
De Becker, E. V. A., 1273, 1274
Dedman, J. J., 877
Dedrick, Calvert L., 1443
De Francis, John, 2036
de Jasay, A. E., *see* Jasay, A. E. de
Dempsey, David, 423
Dennett, Raymond, 853
Dening, Sir Esler, 707
Dennison, R. L., 397
Denson, John, 2469c
Derevyanko, Kuzma N., 1341a, 1381b
De Silva, Colvin R., 2373
Deverall, Richard L. G., 586a, 782, 1155, 1155a, 1746a, 1917, 2037, 2470
De Vos, George Alphonse, 1918
Dewey, Thomas Edmund, 673, 2470a, 2513
Dickinson, George, 1058
Dilley, Opal Lawrence, 673a
Dilts, Marion May, 2240
Dionisopoulos, P. Allan, 999b, 1174, 1298
Diplomatic Section, *see*

Author Index

Supreme Commander for the Allied Powers. Diplomatic Section
Dodge, Joseph M., 45, 674, 1552, 1553, 1556, 1605
Doi, James Isao, 2037a
Donovan, Eileen, 2038
Dooman, Eugene H., 783
Dore, Ronald Philip, 1358, 1701, 1702, 1703, 1919, 1920, 2039
Dorget, Guy, 423a
Dower, John, 707a, 707b, 2470c
Downs, Robert B., 2241, 2242
Dozier, Edwin Burk, 587
Duboscq, André, 493a
Duffield, E. S., 210
Duke, Benjamin C., 1747, 2040, 2041
Dull, Paul Shirley, 7, 761, 1320, 1321, 1322, 1365
Dulles, Allen, 48a
Dulles, John Foster, 48a, 784, 2362, 2375, 2376, 2377, 2378, 2379, 2380, 2381, 2382, 2424a, 2441, 2446a, 2455, 2471, 2471a, 2523
Dunbabin, Thomas, 1832a
Duncan, Walter George Keith, 164
Dunn, Frederick Sherwood, 2464
Dunning, Alice L., 2514
Dupays, Paul, 494
Durgin, Russell L., 2206, 2243, 2243a
Dutt, Vidya Prakash, 365, 785
Duverger, Maurice, 1184
Duxbury, Daniel, 1598a
Dyer, Armel, 955

Early, Stephen, 949
Ebata, Kiyoshi, 1366
Eby, Kermit, 1748, 2042, 2043
Echigo, Kazunori, 1877
Economic and Scientific Section, *see* Supreme Commander for the Allied Powers. Economic and Scientific Section
Education Mission to Japan, *see* U.S. Education Mission to Japan
Educational Exchange Group to Japan, *see* U.S. Educational Exchange Group to Japan
Edwards, Corwin D., 1795

Edwards, Marie Alice, 1749
Edwards Mission, *see* U.S. Mission on Japanese Combines
Eells, Hastings, 65a
Eells, Walter Crosby, 8, 2045, 2046, 2047, 2124a, 2138
Egekvist, W. Soren, 1492
Ehrlich, E. E., 1638
Ehrman, John, 168
Eichelberger, Robert L., 549
Eichler, David K., 646, 1122, 2383
Eidus, Khaim T., 588, 888a, 1613, 2339, 2471c
Eighth Army, *see* U.S. Army. Eighth Army
Eisenhower, Dwight David, 945
Eisenmann, C., 1185
Eliot, George Fielding, 70
Elisséeff, Serge, 3
Embree, John Fee, 71, 71a, 72, 381, 1921
Emeny, Brooks, 1549a
Emi, Kōichi, 1639
Engineering Education Mission to Japan, 2048
Engineers Joint Council. National Engineers Committee, 1000
England, H. G., 424
Epstein, Isidore, 73
Eskelund, Karl, 708
Esman, Milton J., 1435, 1440a
Espenshade, Ada, 1833
Esterly, Henry Hermon, 1834, 1834a
Eunson, Roby, 708a
Evatt, Herbert Vere, 786, 787, 1844, 2315, 2316, 2317, 2326
Eyre, John Douglas, 1704, 1704a

Fain, Irving Jay, 1591
Fainsod, Merle, 81
Fairbank, John King, 788
Falco, Tom, 1123
Falk, Ray, 898
Far East Command, *see* U.S. Army. Far East Command
Far Eastern Commission, 857, 858, 859, 860, 899, 1001, 1002, 1124, 1175, 1466, 1527, 1796
Far Eastern Economic Review, 35b
Farley, Miriam Southwell, 1493, 1528, 1750, 1751, 1752, 2384, 2447
Fearey, Robert T., 621, 1730
Feely, Gertrude Marie, 2243b
Feis, Herbert, 185, 243, 244, 789
Feldhaus, J. Gordon, 1059
Fellers, Bonner Frank, 549a
Feraru, Arthur N., 790, 1529
Fernbach, Alfred P., 1175a
Fertig, Norman, 495
Field, F. V., 2384a
Fifield, Russell Hunt, 988
Filippov, I., 2384b
Finance Div., *see* Supreme Commander for the Allied Powers. Finance Div.
Fine, Sherwood Monroe, 1549a, 1615
Finn, Dallas, 2049, 2050
First U. S. Education Mission to Japan, *see* U. S. Education Mission to Japan
Fishel, Wesley R., 9, 139
Fisher, Charles, 1921a
Fisher, Galen M., 75
Fisher, Harold H., 667a
Fiske, Redington, 1592
Fistie, Pierre, 17a
Fitzgerald, Charles Patrick, 2384c
Fleisher, Wilfrid, 76, 76a
Fogelman, Edwin, 245
Foreign Affairs Assn. of Japan, 550, 674
Forrestal, James, 210
Forsyth, W. D., 164
Frank, Benis M., 338
Frankel, J., 2385
Frazer, D. J. M., 1494a
Frederick, James O., 497, 1125
Freixas, Antonio Sagrista, *see* Sagrista Freixas, Antonio
Friedrich, Carl Joachim, 81, 230, 231, 900
Fromm, Joseph, 140, 651
Fuetō, Toshio, 1275
Fujii, Shigeru, 1616
Fujioka, Yasuo, 1828
Fujita, Masahiro, 1639a
Fujita, Sei, 1649
Fujita, Taki, 2244, 2245
Fujiwara, Hirotatsu, 1922
Fujiyama, Aiichirō, 2465
Fukase, Tadakazu, 1003
Fukuda, Sumio, 1288
Fukui, Haruhiro, 1175b, 1367a

Fukuoka, Masao, 1649
Fukutake, Tadashi, 738, 1923, 1924, 1925, 1926, 1927
Fuqua, Ellis E., 1059a
Furukaki, Tetsurō, 2139

Gaddis, John Wilson, 622a
Gaimushō, *see* Japan. Ministry of Foreign Affairs
Galbraith, John Kenneth, 1454a
Galbraith, T. D., 498
Galloway, George Barnes, 54a
Gane, William Joseph, 1155b
Garbuny, Siegfried, 1453
Gardner, D. H., 792
Gauntlett, Hugh, 1367b
Gayn, Mark J., 426, 427, 428, 429, 1126
George, Beauford James, Jr., 711, 1178, 1184
Gibney, Frank, 647, 1928
Gibson, James B., 708b
Gibson, Tony, 792a
Gilbert, Scott, 551
Gilchrist, Huntington, 988a
Gilmartin, William M., 1706
Gilmore, Robert John, 552
Ginsburgh, Robert Neville, 902
Ginsburgs, George, 1837, 1838
Givens, Willard Earl, 2051, 2051a, 2051b
Godshall, Wilson Leon, 77
Godwin, George, 1838a
Goette, John, 1251
Gokijo, Kakiwa, 1299
Golay, Frank H., 1617
Golunsky, S., 1060
Gontcharov, V., 1707
Goodman, Grant Kohn, 709
Gorbatov, Boris, 429b
Gordon, Joseph, 44o
Gorer, Geoffrey, 78
Government Section, *see* Supreme Commander for the Allied Powers. Government Section
Grad, Andrew Jonah, 79, 1708, 1839
Grajdanzev, Andrew Jonah, *see* Grad, Andrew Jonah
Granada, Yole, 1496, 2140
Grant, Robert H., 631b
Grant, Robert Y., 1818b
Grassmuck, George, 1176
Grattan, C. Hartley, 80
Grauer, Alvin, 902a

Graves, Alvin, 44d
Gray, Gordon, 902b
Great Britain. Foreign Office, 2386, 2387, 2388, 2389
Green, Leslie C., 552a, 2447a
Green, Owen Mortimer, 430, 499, 499a, 553, 589, 590, 623
Greene, Marc T., 624, 1840, 2515
Greene, William, 945
Greenwood, Gordon, 793
Greenwood, Russell, 2288a
Gresham, Alan, 554
Grew, Joseph Clark, 211
Gribachev, P., 955a
Gribov, B., 1753
Griffith, Harry Elmer, 2052
Griggs, Thurston, 1234
Grilli, Marcel, 555
Gromyko, Andrei A., 2390, 2423
Grover, Verinder, 1177
Guérin, Paul, 2472
Guillain, Robert, 36, 555a, 625, 2473
Gulick, Addison, 1929
Gunther, John, 956
Gustafson, Philip H., 141

Hadley, Eleanor Martha, 1797, 1798, 1799, 1800
Hall, John Whitney, 691, 710, 711
Hall, Peirson M., 1801
Hall, Robert King, 2053, 2054, 2054a, 2055
Hallett, Robert M., 902c
Halliwell, Martin, 431
Hallowell, John H., 488
Hamilton, Mary Glenn B., 591
Hanayama, Shinshō, 1061
Hani, Setsuko, 2245a
Hankey, M., 1062
Hara, Kimi, 2246
Harari, Ehud, 1753a
Haring, Douglas Gilbert, 81, 231, 667a, 1372, 1929a
Harold, Jake R., 44m
Harper, Norman Delholm, 772, 793, 794, 2346, 2473a
Harsaghy, Fred Joseph, 2056
Hart, Richard Harry, 432
Hartford, Ellis Ford, 2056a
Hashiguchi, Makoto, 1323
Hatano, Ken-ichi, 2516
Hayakawa, Miyoji, 1640
Hayashi, Kentarō, 2289
Hays, Frank E., 1341

Heinrichs, Waldo H., Jr., 81a
Heller, Maxine Jacobson, 1064
Hellmann, Donald Charles, 2465a
Henderson, Dan Fenno, 761, 762, 1178, 1276
Henderson, Harold C., 441
Henry, Jules, 2290
Henschel, Richard, 965
Hepler, Chester W., 1754
Herrington, William, 1852
Herzog, Peter, S. J., 1179, 2291
Hesse, Konrad, 1184
Hessel, Eugene A., 1064a
Hewes, Laurence Ilsley, Jr., 1709, 1710
Hicks, Charles Roger, 2056b
Hicks, Ursula K., 1681
Hidaka, Daishirō, 1186
Hidaka, Rokurō, 1930
Higa, Mikio, 1436a
Higashiuchi, Yoshio, 10
Hilgard, Ernest R., 2292
Hill, Walter, 164
Hilldring, John H., 397, 903, 1836a
Hille, Henry L., Jr., 904
Hoashi, Kei, 1533
Hogan, Willard N., 1064b
Holborn, Hajo, 232
Holbrook, Martin E., 2473b
Holding Company Liquidation Commission, *see* Japan. Holding Company Liquidation Commission
Holland, Charles D., 626
Holland, William L., 2517
Hollerman, Leon, 1593
Holliday, Kate, 2167b
Hollis, Howard, 2247
Holman, D. S., 1127
Holmes, Lulu H., 45a, 2248
Holtom, Daniel Clarence, 82, 82a, 1236, 2057, 2207, 2208
Honjō, Eijirō, 1640a
Hoover, Blaine, 1444, 1445
Hoover, Herbert, 945, 1835
Horner, Francis J., 433, 500, 501, 1468, 2209
Horoth, V. L., 1469, 1497, 1534, 1570, 2391
Horton, Douglas, 434, 2202a, 2210
Horwitz, Solis, 1065
Hoselitz, Bert F., 229a
Hoshii, Iwao, 1180, 1632
Hoska, Lukas Ernest, Jr., 186
Hosoda, Mosaburō, 1846

Author Index

Howard, Harry Paxton, 83
Hseih, Chiang, 1879
Hsieh, Nan-kuang, 1534a
Hsinhua, 2391a
Hsu, Immanuel C. Y., 648, 872, 2518
Huberman, Morris Abraham, 1841
Hudson, Geoffrey, 649
Huh, Kyung-mo, 1641
Hull, Cordell, 212
Hulse, Frederick S., 1931, 1931a, 1932, 1933, 1934
Hunt, Frazier, 957
Hussey, Alfred Rodman, 43
Hutchinson, Edmond Carlton, 1642
Hutchinson, Paul, 502, 2211

I., V., 1156
"I" Corps, see U.S. Army. Eighth Army. "I" Corps
Ichikawa, Taijirō, 2249
Iddittie, Junesay, see Ijichi, Junsei
Igarashi, Torao, 1643
Iglehart, Charles, 2212
Iino, David N., 711a
Iizawa, Shōji, 2392
Ijichi, Junsei, 1935
Ike, Nobutaka, 11, 712, 1380, 1936, 1991
Ikematsu, Fumio, 1373, 1374, 2465b
Ikeuchi, Hajime, 1375
Imboden, Daniel C., 2141, 2142
Inaba, Shūzō, 1127a
Inagaki, Riichi, 1618
Inahara, Katsuji, 186a, 1375b
Industrial Bank of Japan, 1644
Inomata, Kōzō, 1180a
Inouye, Kichijirō, 1937
Institut narodov Azii, see Akademiia nauk SSSR.
Institut narodov Azii
Institute of Pacific Relations, 84
———. International Secretariat, 12
Institute of World Economy (Tokyo), 1535
International Labor Office, 1536
International Military Tribunal for the Far East, 1016, 1017, 1018, 1019
Ireland, Gordon, 1068a

Irvine, Reed J., 1619
Ishida, Gladys, 1157
Ishida, Takeshi, 1237
Ishino, Iwao, 693, 1754a, 1754b, 1911, 1912
Isozaki, Tatsugorō, 1181
Itagaki, Yoichi, 1128
Itō, Hanya, 1682, 1683
Itō, Hiroshi, see Itoh, Hiroshi
Itō, Nobutaka (Nobufumi), 675
Itō, Ryoji, 2058
Itoh, Hiroshi, 1300
Ivtsev, I., 1537
Iwahashi, Bunkichi, 2092
Iwamura, Michio, 2346a
Iwasa, Yoshizane, 1571

Jaffe, Philip J., 85
Jain, L. C., 1498
James, D. Clayton, 958
James, David H., 142
James, Weldon, 503, 504, 905, 2250
Janeway, Eliot, 384a
Jansen, Marius Berthus, 1938
Japan. Advisory Council on Social Security, 2168
———. Allowance Bureau, 1437
———. Attorney General's Office, 1114, 1277, 1278, 1278a, 1278b, 1278c
———. ———. Bureau of Civil Affairs, 1279
———. Board of Audit, 1594
———. Board of Trade, 1471
———. Commission on the Constitution, 1182, 1183, 1184, 1185, 2203
———. Cultural Science Society, 1939, 1940
———. Dept. of Education, see Japan. Ministry of Education
———. Diet. Library, 13
———. Economic Counsel Board, 1645
———. Economic Stabilization Board, 1535, 1573, 1574, 1575, 1595, 1620
———. Education Reform Council, 2059
———. Fisheries Agency, 1841a
———. Gaimushō, see Japan. Ministry of Foreign Affairs
———. ———. Jōhō Bunka-kyoku, see Japan. Ministry

of Foreign Affairs. Public Information and Cultural Affairs Bureau
———. ———. Jōhōbu, see Japan. Ministry of Foreign Affairs. Public Information Div.
———. Holding Company Liquidation Commission, 1802, 1803, 1804
———. Keizai Antei Hombu, see Japan. Economic Stabilization Board
———. Keizai Kikakuchō, see Japan. Economic Counsel Board
———. Kōseishō, see Japan. Ministry of Welfare
———. Ministry of Agriculture and Forestry. Agricultural Land Bureau, 1711, 1712
———. ———. Economic Research Div., 14
———. ———. National Research Institute of Agriculture, 1842
———. Ministry of Education, 2060, 2061, 2062, 2063, 2064
———. ———. Bureau of Higher Education and Science, 2065
———. ———. Bureau of Research and Pub., 2066
———. ———. Bureau of Scientific Education, 2067, 2068, 2069
———. Ministry of Finance, 1539, 1576, 1596, 1621
———. ———. Bureau of Taxation, 1280
———. ———. Finance Commissioner's Office, 1577
———. ———. Financial Bureau, 1622
———. ———. Minister's Secretariat. Research Section, see Japan. Ministry of Finance. Research Section
———. ———. Research Section, 1578, 1623
———. Ministry of Foreign Affairs, 1129, 1438
———. ———. Bureau of Public Information and Cultural Affairs, 1186, 1391, 2519

———. ———. Public Information Div., 989, 1158, 2393
———. ———. Special Records Div., 366
———. Ministry of Justice. Immigration Bureau, 1281
———. Ministry of Labor. Liaisons Affairs Section, 1756
———. ———. Women's and Minors' Bureau, 2251
———. Ministry of Welfare, 2169
———. ———. Bureau of Social Affairs, 2170
———. ———. Insurance Bureau, 2171, 2172, 2173, 2174, 2175
———. Mombushō, see Japan. Ministry of Education
———. ———. Chōsakyoku, see Japan. Ministry of Education. Bureau of Research and Publications
———. ———. Daigaku Gakujutsukyoku, see Japan. Ministry of Education. Bureau of Higher Education and Science
———. ———. Kagaku Kyōikukyoku, see Japan. Ministry of Education. Bureau of Scientific Education
———. National Diet. Library, see Japan. Diet. Library
———. National Personnel Authority, 1439
———. Newspaper Assn., see Nihon Shimbun Kyōkai
———. Newspaper Publishers' and Editors' Assn., see Nihon Shimbun Kyōkai
———. Nōrinshō. Nōgyō Sōgō Kenkyūjo, see Japan. Ministry of Agriculture and Forestry. National Research Institute of Agriculture
———. Ōkurashō, see Japan. Ministry of Finance
———. ———. Chōsabu, see Japan. Ministry of Finance. Research Section
———. ———. Daijin Kambo. Chōsabu, see Japan. Ministry of Finance. Research Section
———. Postal Bureau, 2252

———. Prime Minister's Office. Bureau of Statistics, 367, 1597, 1992, 1993, 1994, 2176
———. ———. Pension Bureau, 1282
———. ———. Secretariat. Local Autonomy Section, 1324
———. Rōdōshō, see Japan. Ministry of Labor
———. Saikō Saibansho, see Japan. Supreme Court
———. ———. Jimusōkyoku. Keijikyoku, see Japan. Supreme Court. Bureau of Criminal Affairs
———. Scientific Education Bureau, see Japan. Ministry of Education. Bureau of Scientific Education
———. Self-Supporting Economy Council, 1598
———. Sōrifu, see Japan. Prime Minister's Office
———. ———. Tōkeikyoku, see Japan. Prime Minister's Office. Bureau of Statistics
———. Supreme Court, 1283, 1283a, 1301, 1302, 1303, 1303a, 1304
———. ———. Bureau of Criminal Affairs, 1305
Japan Times, 38
Jaranilla, Delfin, 1020
Jasay, A. E. de, 713
Jerome, V. J., 2397a
Jessup, Alpheus W., 1541, 1880, 1881
John, Arthur, 677
Johnson, Chalmers Ashby, 1305a
Johnson, Joseph Esrey, 853
Johnson, Nelson Trusler, 857, 873
Johnson, U. Alexis, 435
Johnson, Walter, 211
Johnson, William R., 1500
Johnston, Bruce Foster, 1542, 1845, 1846, 1850
Johnston, Percy H., 1516
Johnston Committee, 1142c
Johnstone, Anne, 436
Johnstone, William Crane, 90, 91, 436, 989a
Jones, E. Stanley, 652
Jones, Francis Clifford, 505
Jones, George E., 385, 1238
Jorgensen, Arthur, 2213

Journal of Finance and Commerce, 35c

Kagawa, Toyohiko, 505a, 592, 629
Kaigo, Tokiomi, 2071, 2072
Kaizuka, Keimei, 1649
Kajima, Morinosuke, 1070
Kajita, Masaru, 1713
Kakudo, Toyoji, 1306
Kalijarvi, Thorsten V., 373
Kalmer, Joseph, 1941
Kamichika, Ichiko, 2253
Kan, Shina, 2254
Kan, W. E., 2214
Kanamori, Hisao, 1649
Kanayama, Masanobu, 1284
Kandel, Isaac Leon, 2073, 2074
Kaneko, Eiichi, 1187
Kano, Kizō, 2398
Kantor, Ken, 593, 2255
Kao, Ming-huey, 2075
Kaplan, Benz, 386
Kaplan, Morton A., 824
Kase, Toshikazu, 143, 245
Kasteleiner, Rolf H., 1188
Kat Angelino, Arnold D. A. de, 429a
Katayama, Koshi, 92
Katayama, Tetsu, 1758a
Katō, Ichirō, 1737
Katō, Masao, 1285, 1714
Katō, Masuo, 144
Katō, Shūichi, 2143
Katona, Paul, 1071
Katsube, Toshio, 1882
Kauffman, James Lee, 1472
Kawai, Kazuo, 145, 146, 653, 714, 798, 1189, 1238a, 2296, 2475
Kawakami, Kiyoshi, 2476
Kawano, Shigetō, 1847
Kawashima, Takeyoshi, 738, 1286
Kawata, Fukuo, 1543
Keck, David Newton, 187
Keckskemeti, Paul, 188
Keenan, Joseph Berry, 945, 1040a, 1069, 1072
Keene, Donald Lawrence, 715
Keeney, Philip O., 2256
Keesing, Felix M., 990
Keeton, George W., 169b, 505b, 799
Kelley, Frank Raymond, 506, 960
Kelly, Harry C., 2257, 2258
Kempō, Chōsakai, see Japan.

Author Index

Commission on the Constitution
Kennan, George Frost, 48a, 800, 2477
Kennard, A., 1759
Kennedy, John, 1760
Kennedy, Malcolm D., 716, 1376b
Kenney, George Churchill, 961
Kent, Beryl F., 2297
Kerlinger, Frederick Nichols, 1942, 1943, 1944, 1944a, 2076
Kern, Harry F., 507, 2318, 2450, 2478
Kerr, George H., 93
Kerr, William Campbell, 594
Ketzel, Clifford, 595
Khonsary, Reza, 1646
Kido, Mataichi, 2144
Kikuchi, Akira, 505a
Kilpatrick, William H., 2077
Kim, Han-Kyo, 907
Kim, Paul Sunik, 1439a, 1439b
Kim, R., 2145
Kimura, Kihachirō, 2478a
King, John K., 630
King, Norman D., 15
Kinoshita, Hanji, 1109, 1190, 1945
Kirby, E. Stuart, 1473
Kirchman, Charles V., 1020a
Kirchwey, Freda, 94, 2399, 2525
Kirk, Grayson Louis, 70
Kislenko, A., 620
Kitagawa, Joseph M., 2215
Kitamura, Fusako, 1761
Kitasawa, Shinjirō, 1502, 2078
Kitani, Tadashi, 2298
Kiyose, Ichirō, 1376c
Klee, Loretta E., 2079
Klein, Lawrence R., 1647
Klein, Sidney, 1715
Klinger, Wallace R., 1945a
Kluckhorn, Frank L., 387, 388, 389, 1004
Knebel, Fletcher, 246
Knight, F. J., 169c
Knutson, Andie L., 2299
Kobayashi, A. Hiroaki, 2478b
Kobayashi, Naoki, 1191
Kobayashi, Shyōzō, 1239
Kobayashi, Tatsuo, 1715a
Kobayashi, Tetsuya, 2080
Kobayashi, Victor Nobuo, 2081
Kodaki, Akira, 1549a
Kodama, Yoshio, 1073, 1074
Kodera, Takeshirō, 1648
Koenig, Nathan, 1473a
Koever, J. F., 2400
Kogiku, Kiichirō, 1678
Koizumi, Shinzō, 2400a
Kokuritsu Kokkai Toshokan, see Japan. Diet. Library
Kolko, Gabriel, 246a, 716a
Kolko, Joyce, 716a
Komiya, Ryūtaro, 1649
Kondō, Yasuo, 1716
Kornhauser, Arthur William, 389a
Kōseishō, see Japan. Ministry of Welfare
Kozhin, Aleksei I., 2081a
Krainov, Pavel, 2333a
Kramer, R. C., 1474
Krane, Jay B., 801
Kreps, Leslie Roy, 55
Kroese, Willem Titus, 1883
Krueger, Walter, 346, 906
Kruse, Arthur, 407a
Krylov, V., 596, 2451, 2479, 2480
Kublin, Hyman, 717
Kubo, Naoko, 1375
Kubota, Akira, 1440
Kubota, T., 1625
Kudryavtsev, V., 508, 597, 598, 599, 962, 1075, 1192, 1377, 1377a, 1377b, 1475, 1503, 1717, 1762, 2481, 2842, 2483, 2483a
Kuh, Frederick, 2401
Kuhn, Arthur H., 1076
Kume, Ai, 44c, 2259
Kurata, Seiji, 802
Kurihara, Kenneth K., 1378, 1455
Kuroda, Andrew Y., 2146
Kuroki, Yukichi, 1378a
Kusumi, Yoshio, 1846
Kuwabara, Takeo, 718
Kyōgoku, Jun'ichi, 1379, 1380

La Cerda, John, 437
Ladejinsky, Wolf Isaac, 559, 1699a, 1706, 1718, 1719, 1720, 1721, 1727a, 1848
Lamott, Willis Church, 95, 95a, 95b, 438
Langdon, Frank, 719
Langen, Benita, 990a
Langer, Paul Fritz, 5, 16, 678, 720, 803, 1381, 1415
Latourette, Kenneth Scott, 76c, 721, 804, 2334
Lattimore, Eleanor, 991
Lattimore, Owen, 96, 97, 432, 670, 805, 806, 2402, 2526
Lauterbach, Richard Edward, 509, 963, 1240
Lawrence, David, 2403
Leahy, William D., 213
Leary, William M., Jr., 2466
Leathem, Samuel, 807
Lee, Clark Gould, 509a, 964, 965
Lee, Jin Won, 808
Leng, Shao-chuan, 809
Lens, Sidney, 722
Lensen, George Alexander, 195, 2216
Leonard, Warren H., 1848
Lequiller, Jean, 17, 17a, 722a
Lerrigo, Marion Olive, 441
Levi, Werner, 810, 874, 2319
Levine, Solomon Bernard, 1650, 1765, 1766, 1767
Lewe van Aduard, Evert Joost, 723
Lewis, Dora S., 2081b, 2081c
Lhamsurun, see Lkhamsurun
Library Mission to Japan, see U.S. Library Mission to Japan
Li-em, Channing, 390
Lifton, Robert Jay, 1946, 1947, 1948
Lin, Hu, 439
Lindstrom, David E., 1722
Lindstrom, Siegfried F., 1504
Linebarger, Paul Myron Anthony, 724
Lipp, Frederick J., 440
Lippmann, Walter, 811
Liu, James Tzu-chien, 18, 510, 812, 1077, 1078
Lkhamsurun, 2423c
Lloyd, Wesley Parkinson, 2082
Lockwood, William Wirt, 3, 1456, 1651
Loduchowski, Heinz, 2083
Loewenstein, Karl, 1184
Ludmer, Henry, 601
Luhmer, Nicholas, 2084
Luk'ianova, M. I., 1, 654
Lukyanov, M., see Luk'ianova, M. I.
Lyell, Thomas Reginald Guise, 392

Maack, Dorothy Howerton,

Author Index

630a
Maass, Arthur A., 900
MacArthur, Douglas, 437, 603a, 875, 901, 932, 933, 934, 934a, 935, 936, 937, 938, 939, 940, 941, 942, 942a, 943, 944, 945, 947, 949, 951, 1005, 1014, 1040b, 1339b, 1343, 1368, 1369, 1370, 1371, 1376, 1436, 1467, 1495, 1516, 1705, 1712, 1783
MacArthur Memorial. Bureau of Archives, 46
McBride, James H., 2483b
McCarthy, Charles W., 58
McClurkin, Robert J. G., 813
McCoy, Frank R., 875b, 1117, 1130c, 1504a, 1516, 1543a, 1768, 1805
McDiarmid, Orville J., 1544
McDonald, Angus, 1723
MacDonald, Hugh H., 1440a
McDonald, William J., 814
McEvoy, Dennis, 560
McEvoy, J. P., 967
Mackaye, Milton, 549
McKean, Josephine Colletti, 44p
McKeldin Library. Univ. of Maryland, 47
McLaren, Charles I., 2217
McNeill, William H., 189
McNelly, Theodore Hart, 368, 725, 1006, 1007, 1193, 1194, 1195
McPherson, William H., 1768a
McReynolds, George E., 700
Maeda, Tamon, 2085
Mahoney, Thomas H. D., 700
Maki, John McGilvrey, 19, 147, 251, 511, 709, 726, 727, 907, 1178, 1184, 1196, 1287, 1307, 1382, 1441, 1949, 2405a
Makino, Tatsumi, 738, 2086, 2087
Manchester Guardian, 36
Mann, John C., 2218
Mannin, Ethel, 1724
Marinin, M., 2483c
Markov, M., 1080, 1081, 1081a, 1131, 1383, 1384, 1768b, 2321, 2340, 2406
Marlio, Louis, 101
Marquat, William F., 1531, 1606
Martin, Charles E., 602,

2347
Martin, Edwin M., 512, 561
Martin, Howard H., 679
Martin, Kingsley, 728
Martin, Robert Pepper, 2147, 2484
Maruyama, Masao, 1950
Marx, Daniel, Jr., 1884
Masland, John Wesley, Jr., 513, 619a, 1325
Mason, John Brown, 233
Masumi, Junnosuke, 1379
Matano, Kensuke, 1885
Mateveev, Illarion, 170
Matsumiya, Kazuya, 1951
Matsumoto, Kaoru, 1197
Matsumoto, Toru, 441
Matsumoto, Tsuyoshi, 393, 442, 1241, 1385
Matsumura, Yutaka, 1652
Matsuo, M., 1386
Matsuoka, Yōko, 603
Maurer, Herrymon, 514
May, Ernest Richard, 20, 190
May, Henry F., Jr., 443
Mayevsky, V., 1081c, 1387, 1388, 1544a, 2341, 2341a, 2407
Meadow, Arnold, 1952
Mears, Helen, 99, 100, 444, 445, 562, 603a, 631, 1132, 1580, 2348, 2485
Medical Section, *see* Supreme Commander for the Allied Powers. Public Health and Welfare Section
Melcher, Frederic G., 2148, 2149
Mendel, Douglas Heusted, 729
Menken, Jules, 563
Menzel, Eberhard, 2451a
Menzies, Robert Gordon, 2486
Metzger, Laure, 1545
Metzger, Stanley D., 2452
Meyers, Howard, 1287a, 1308
Michael, Franz H., 2322
Mignone, Frederick, 564
Mikhailov, M., 2483a
Military Intelligence Section, *see* Supreme Commander for the Allied Powers. Military Intelligence Section
Miller, Frank Owen, 1198
Miller, Paul V., 2150
Miller, Perry, 730
Millis, Walter, 210
Millot, Bernard, 191
Minami, Hiroshi, 1953

Minear, Richard Hoffman, 1082
Minobe, Ryōkichi, 1456a, 1546
Minoguchi, Tokijirō, 1995
Misawa, Mitsuru, 1653
Mishima, Sumie Seo, 2260
Mission on Japanese Combines, *see* U.S. Mission on Japanese Combines
Mitchell, Richard Hanks, 2261
Miwa, Keiko, 2087a
Miyakawa, Saburō, 1505
Miyake, Tarō, 1442
Miyasawa, Toshiyoshi, 1186
Miyata, Kiyozō, 1653a
Mizutani, Chōsaburō, 1725, 1726
Mochida, Eiichi, 2088
Moloney, James Clark, 1954
Mombushō, *see* Japan. Ministry of Education
Monahan, James, 1389
Monnier, Claude, 1242
Montgomery, John Dickey, 908, 1110, 1111
Moos, Felix, 1955
Moran, R., 2151
Moran, William T., 1750, 1769
Morgan, Alfred, 1506
Morita, Yūzō, 1996
Morito, Tatsuo, 2089, 2322a
Moriya, Fumio, 2090
Morley, James William, 21, 394, 815, 1184
Morris, Frank D., 395
Morris, Ivan Ira, 731, 1956, 2487
Morris, J. Malcolm, 909
Morris, John, 395a, 446, 447
Morrison, Herbert, 2407a
Morton, Lewis, 57
Moseley, Harold W., 58
Mosley, Leonard Oswald, 1243
Mott, Frank Luther, 2152
Moulton, Harold Glenn, 101
Mountain, Roland, 164
Mueller, Gerhard, 1184
Mui, King-chau, 2335
Mukai, Hiroo, 656
Mukai, Shikamatsu, 1457
Mukherjee, Asoke Kumas, 732
Munakata, Seiya, 2091
Munekata, Masaya, 2091a
Murakami, Shunsuke, 2092
Muramatsu, Tsuneo, 1957
Murata, Suzuko, 2093
Murdock, John, 2299a

Author Index

Murphy, J. Morden, 2532
Murphy, Robert Daniel, 733
Mydans, Carl, 733a
Mydans, Shelley, 396, 515

Nagai, Michio, 1913, 1913a
Nagato, Masaji, 656a
Naitoh, Yoshimasa, 1976
Naka, Masao, 2348a
Nakahara, Hidenori, 1344
Nakajima, Kenzō, 1344a
Nakamura, Shūichirō, 2090
Nakamura, Tetsu, 1442a
Nakanishi, Naomichi, 2286
Nakano, Takashi, 1958
Nakano, Teru M., 2527
Nakasone, Yasuhirō, 1199
Nakayama, Ichirō, 1547, 1626
Namba, Monkichi, 1959
Nambara, Shigeru, 1960
Namiki, Masayoshi, 1849
Naoi, Takeo, 967a, 1770, 2408, 2408a
Napier, Jack P., 1390
Nasu, Shiroshi, 2509
Natarajan, L., 816
National Academy of Sciences, Washington, D.C. Scientific Advisory Group, 2262
National Archives and Records Service. Modern Military Records Div., 48
National Diet Library, *see* Japan. Diet. Library
National Engineers Committee, *see* Engineers Joint Council. National Engineers Committee
National Research Institute of Agriculture, *see* Japan. Ministry of Agriculture and Forestry. National Research Institute of Agriculture
Natori, Jonosuke, 1581, 1685
Natural Resources Section, *see* Supreme Commander for the Allied Powers. Natural Resources Section
Naval Technical Mission to Japan, *see* U.S. Naval Technical Mission to Japan
Neel, Samuel E., 1805b
Nehmer, Stanley, 448, 604, 1476, 1886, 1887
Neumann, William L., 192, 193
New York Times, 37
New Zealand. Dept. of External Affairs, 253, 369, 2323, 2336, 2342, 2349, 2408b, 2409, 2453, 2454
———. Institute of International Affairs, 817, 2454a
Newsweek, 37a
Nihon Jimbun Kagakkai, *see* Japan. Cultural Science Society
Nihon Shimbun Kyōkai, 2153
Niida, Hiroshi, 1649
Niiseki, Kinya, 1391
Nippon Times, 38
Nish, Ian Hill, 734
Nishi Kantarō, 1344b
Nishida, Kikuo, 2094
Nishijima, Yoshiji, 1008, 1434
Nishikawa, Kiyoharu, 1326
Nishimoto, Mitoji, 2095
Nishimoto, Yoichi, 2095a
Nishiyama, Haruji, 1507
Nixon, Richard Milhous, 2488
Noble, Harold J., 449, 818, 1159, 1243a, 2095b
Noda, Kazuo, 1649, 1654
Nōgyō Sōgō Kenkyūjo, *see* Japan. Ministry of Agriculture and Forestry. National Research Institute of Agriculture
Nomura, Kichisaburō, 2342a, 2350
Norbeck, Edward, 709, 734a, 1160, 1961, 1962
Nōrinshō, *see* Japan. Ministry of Agriculture and Forestry
Norman, E. Herbert, 586
Northcote, K. H., 164
Nose, Nobuko, 1685a
Notter, Harley A., 61
Nugent, Donald R., 2219

Obama, Toshie, 1111a
O'Connell, Alfred Christopher, 2096
Oda, James S., 1244
Ōe Seizō, *see* Ohe Seizō
Office of the Chief of Military History, *see* U.S. Dept. of the Army. Office of the Chief of Military History
Office of the Financial Adviser, *see* Supreme Commander for the Allied Powers. Office of the Financial Adviser
Ogawa, Kiichi, 2262a
Ogawa, Tarō, 2097
Oh, Ki Song, 1726a
Ohara, Fujiko, 2262b
Ohe, Seizō, 735
Ōhira, Zengo, 992, 1654a
Ohkawa, Kazushi, 1599, 1850
Ohkita, Saburō, *see* Ōkita, Saburō
Ōi, Atsushi, 2300
Okajima, Eiichi, 2466a
Okamoto, Tadashi, 1582
Okasaki, Ayanori (Fumikata), 1997, 1997a
Ōkawa, Kazushi, *see* Ohkawa, Kazushi
Okazaki, Fumikata, *see* Okasaki, Ayanori
Okazaki, Katsuo, 968
Okazaki, Keiko, 1375
Ōkita, Saburō, 1134, 1600, 1601, 1655
Ōkōchi, Kazuo, 1771
Okonishnikov, A., 2154
Oku, Shōsuke, 1888
Ōkubo, Genji, 1245
Ōkurashō, *see* Japan. Ministry of Finance
Olds, C. Burnell, 107, 2098
Olver, A. S. B., 819
Ono, Isamu, 2528
Ōno, Katsumi, 2524
Onoe, Masao, 820
Opie, Redvers, 2410
Oppenheimer, J. Robert, 245
Oppler, Alfred C., 1289, 1290, 1309
Orekhov, F., 2410a
Oriental Economist, 39, 1477
Orr, Mark Taylor, 2099, 2099a
Osborne, John, 969, **970**
Ostwald, Paul, 735a
Ōta, Takashi, 2100
Ott, D. J., 1656
Ōuchi, Hyō(y)e, 1478, 1508, 1547a
Ōuchi, Tsutomu, 1727
Overseas Consultants, Inc., 1135, 1136, 1516
Overton, Douglas W., 44h, 736
Ōwada, Keiki, 1727a
Ozaki, Robert Shigeo, 1657, 1658
Ozaki, Yukio, 657
Ozawa, Takeo, 1137

Pacific Air Command, *see* U.S. Army. Pacific Air Command
Pacific Stars and Stripes, 40
Pacific War Research Society, 148
Pacificus, *pseud.*, 108, 108a
Packenham, Compton, 1246

Pak, Kun, 1392
Pal, Radhabinod B., 1021
Panyushkin, Alexander S., 999a, 1008a, 1010a, 1487, 1520, 1560a, 1767b, 1767c, 1771a, 1790a
Park, Richard, 606
Parker, James Perkins, 1310
Parrott, Lindesay, 398, 451, 452, 516, 658, 659, 680, 912, 1247, 1248, 2101, 2263, 2264, 2324, 2351, 2529
Parsons, Talcott, 81
Passin, Herbert, 22, 23, 737, 758, 1729b, 2102, 2103, 2301
Patch, Buel W., 2324a, 2411a
Patrick, Hugh Talbot, 1659
Patten, Louise M. van, see Van Patten, Louise M.
Pauley, Edwin W., 945, 1138, 1139, 1140a, 1142b
Peake, Cyrus H., 44f
Pearce, Ronald, 2325a
Pearl, Jack, 971
Pearn, Bertie Reginald, 505
Pearson, Lester B., 2394b, 2412, 2449
Peffer, Nathaniel, 109, 109a, 109b
Pelzel, John Campbell, 3, 1998
Penrose, Gertrude, 2265
Penrose, William O., 453
Penworth, D. Wilfred, 1547b
Percival, Jack, 552
Petrie, W. F., 1140
Petrov, D., 399
Petty, Edward Avin, 1345
Pevsner, J. (Ya.), 454, 1583
Pfaff, William, 2530
Philippines. Office of Economic Coordination, 1602
Philips, O. Hood, 1182
Phillips, Philip David, 164, 170a
Pierson, Harry E., 1686
Piggott, F. J. C., 876a
Piggott, Francis Steward Gilderoy, 149, 1084
Pinkerton, Florence Stebe, 1963
Pogue, Forrest C., 194
Polyzoides, A. Th., 2411c
Pope, Frederick, 1889
Popov, Konstantin, 1584
Population Problems Research Council (Tokyo), 1999
Potter, John Deane, 1085

Prasad, Bisheshwar, 881
Pratt, John M., 972
Pratt, Julius William, 70, 633
Price, Willard, 110a, 455b, 681, 682, 1250, 1251, 1851, 2000, 2154a, 2220
Prime Minister's Office, see Japan. Prime Minister's Office
Profumo, J. D., 456
Public Health and Welfare Section, see Supreme Commander for the Allied Powers. Public Health and Welfare Section
Public Information Office, see Supreme Commander for the Allied Powers. Public Information Office
Pyatnitsky, N., 1889a

Quentin-Baxter, R. Q., 1085a
Quigley, Harold S., 518, 634, 660, 739, 1113, 1184, 1202, 1203, 1204
Quo, Fang-quei, 740

Rabinowitz, Richard William, 24, 1311, 1312
Raginsky, M., 1086, 1087
Rama Rao, T. S., 1088
Ramaswamy, T. N., 1661
Ramineni, Ayyanna, 1687
Rao, T. S. Rama, see Rama Rao, T. S.
Raper, Arthur F., 1729, 1729a, 1729b, 1964
Rawlings, E. E., 2413
Ray, Donald P., 519, 2337
Reday, Joseph Z., 1141
Redman, H. Vere, 171, 401, 456a
Reed, John Jay, 172
Reel, Adolf Frank, 1089, 1090
Reel, Frank A., see Reel, Adolf Frank
Rehbein, Herbert, 1585a
Reid, Ralph Waldo Emerson, 1205
Reischauer, Edwin Oldfather, 741, 742, 743, 788, 2344a, 2532
Reitzel, William, 824
Reparations Mission to Japan, see Pauley, Edwin W.
Reubens, Beatrice G., 1772, 1773
Reubens, Edwin B., 1479
Reynolds, Thomas F., 402
Rice, Stuart A., 1443

Richardson, Alvin F., 58
Richie, Donald, 913, 2134a
Ridgway, Matthew Bunker, 984, 985, 985a, 2533
Riggs, Fred W., 2355, 2356
Riley, Walter Lee, 1091
Ringwood, O. K. D., 1398
Rinoiye, Takashi, 1890
Roach, James R., 2415
Robb, Stephen, 973
Robbins, Robert R., 992b
Robinson, Laura, 744
Rōdōsho, see Japan. Ministry of Labor
Roedel, M. A., 2265a
Roelofs, Garritt E., 1854
Rogers, Charles A., 338a
Röhl, Wilhelm, 1206, 1291
Rohrlich, George F., 2105a, 2178
Röling, Bernard V. A., 1022, 1091a
Romulo, Carlos P., 826, 945
Root, Robert, 2221
Rosecrance, Richard Newton, 827, 828
Rosen, George, 1662
Roser, Foster B., 1443a
Rosinger, Lawrence K., 111, 112, 113, 114, 115, 116, 403, 404, 457, 458, 520, 878, 879, 880, 1252, 1396, 1397, 1398, 1480, 1481, 2327, 2328
Roskolenko, Harry, 1481a
Roth, Andrew, 117, 405, 459, 1346, 1399, 2155
Roucek, Joseph S., 993
Rovere, Richard H., 974, 975
Rowe, David Nelson, 118, 119, 143, 607b, 1207
Roxas, Manuel, 945
Royal Institute of International Affairs, 173
Royall, Kenneth C., 945, 1516
Rōyama, Masamichi, 745, 2489
Rozenblit, S., 1087
Rudnev, A., 661
Rusk, Dean, 2490
Russell, Edward Frederick Langley, 1092
Rustow, Dankwart A., 763
Ryan, Cornelius, 506, 960, 976
Ryan, Garry D., 1020a
Ryan, R. S., 829
Ryū, Shintarō, 2417, 2509

Saffell, John, 1400

Author Index

Sagrista Freixas, Antonio, 2181
Saheki, Kiichi, 2491
Saikō Saibansho, *see* Japan. Supreme Court
———. Jimusōkyoku Keijikyoku, *see* Japan. Supreme Court. Bureau of Criminal Affairs
Saitō, Noboru, 1347
Sakamoto, Kusuhito, 1730a
Sakanishi, Shio, 2266
Sakurai, Kinichirō, 1663
Salisbury, Laurence E., 120, 406
Salomon, Henry, Jr., 2266a
Salwin, Lester N., 1291a, 1806
Samain, Bryan, 1806a
Sams, Crawford F., 2167, 2179, 2180
Samuels, Veronica, 1253
Sands, William Franklin, 120a
Sano, Manabu, 460, 566
Sansbury, Cyril Kenneth, 2222
Sansom, Sir George B., 44q, 174, 174a, 567, 608, 662, 663, 664, 2105b
Sasaki, Senichi, 2156
Satō, Isao, 1178, 1208
Satō, Kiichirō, 1549a
Satō, Naotake, 2001, 2419
Satō, Tatsuo, 1209
Sayre, John Nevin, 634a
Scalapino, Robert Anthony, 664a, 746, 977, 1184, 1210, 1401, 1402, 1402a, 2420
Scarangello, Anthony, 747
Schenck, Hubert G., 1819, 1820
Scheuer, Stewart, 831
Schiffer, Hubert F., 1664
Schlesinger, Arthur M., Jr., 974, 975
Schmid, Peter, 665
Schoenberger, Walter Smith, 246b
Schroeder, Paul W., 1092a
Schwantes, Robert Sidney, 832, 2106
Schwartz, Charles, 568
Schwartz, Doris, 461
Schwartz, Robert, 1774
Scientific Advisory Group, *see* National Academy of Sciences, Washington, D.C. Scientific Advisory Group

Scientific Education Bureau, *see* Japan. Ministry of Education. Bureau of Scientific Education
Scott, Frank, 1184
Scott, J. W. Robertson, 175
Scott, John Richard, 833
Scott, William A., 1965
Sebald, William Joseph, 48a, 669, 748, 1162, 1162a, 1162b, 1163, 2535
Second Statistical Mission to Japan, *see* U.S. Second Statistical Mission to Japan
Second U.S. Education Mission to Japan, 2107
Seibert, Howard W., 1855
Seidensticker, Edward G., 1856, 2421
Seifert, Karl-Heinz, 1184
Sekai. Editorial Staff, 2357
Seligmann, Albert L., 2302
Seshaiah, S., 1966
Shafer, Luman J., 2223, 2224, 2225, 2226, 2329
Shalett, Sidney M., 406a
Shavell, Henry, 1689, 1690
Shaw, Henry I., Jr., 338, 338b
Shearer, J. O., 176
Sheean, Vincent, 609
Sheerin, John B., 634b
Sheldon, Walter J., 749
Shepard, Whitfield P., 914
Sherwood, Robert E., 214
Shiba, Giye, 2108
Shiba, Kimpei, 683
Shigemitsu, Mamoru, 149
Shimazaki, Minoru, 1731
Shimbori, Michiya, 2109, 2267
Shimizu, Kō, 1604
Shimizu, Nozomu, 1211
Shimizu, Yoshihiro, 2182
Shinjō, Hiroshi, 1664a
Shinkai, Y., 1647
Shinohara, Miyohei, 1665
Shiomi, Saburō, 1691
Shiota, Shōbē, 1776
Shiotani, Tadao, 1666
Shirven, Maynard N., 1443b
Shishido, Shuntarō, 1636
Shmelyov, N., 2421a
Shorrock, Hallam C., Jr., 2227
Shoup Mission, *see* U.S. Tax Mission to Japan
Shrewsbury, Scott, 1837, 1838
Shulman, Frank Joseph, 25
Shurcliff, Alice W., 1777

Sibiryakov, A., 521
Siggins, Jack, 2157
Silberman, Bernard Samuel, 26
Silkin, S. C., 1093a
Sills, David L., 1729b
Singh, Rajendra, 881, 881a, 881b
Sinn, Ephraim Edward, 2227a
Sirota, Beate, 1410
Sissons, David C. S., 635, 749a, 1009
Sixth Army, *see* U.S. Army. Sixth Army
Sleeman, Colin, 1093, 1093a
Slocum, Winthrop, 610
Smethurst, Richard Jacob, 1778
Smith, Daniel M., 194
Smith, Denys, 2422a
Smith, Howard F., 1857
Smith, Jean Pauline, 2267a
Smith, Jessica, 2422b
Smith, Kingsbury, 120b
Smith, Robert John, 1967, 1968, 1969
Smith, Roy, 407a
Smith, Thomas Carlyle, 2492
Smith, Thomas Vernor, 522, 914a, 2110, 2111, 2111a
Smythe, Hugh H., 666, 684, 684a, 764, 1254, 1255, 1970, 1971, 1972, 1973, 1974, 1975, 1976
Smythe, Mabel M., 1974, 1975
Sneider, Richard L., 569
Snell, John L., 195
Snow, Edgar, 462, 463, 1147
Snyder, Harold E., 2112
Social Security Mission to Japan, 2184
Sogawa, Masao, 1857a
Solomon, Albert H., 1821
Solow, Herbert, 1093b
Somerville, John C., 177
Sommers, Martin, 977a
Soong, Norman, 1256
Sōrifu, *see* Japan. Prime Minister's Office
Sosinskii, Sergei B., 888a
Soukup, James Rudolph, 1779
Sparkman, John J., 2466b
Speicher, Joseph L., 1443b
Spence, Elizabeth, 2268
Spencer, Joseph E., 464
Spender, Percy Claude, 2357a, 2424
Spillers, A. R., 1731a, 1857b

Spinks, Charles Nelson, 122, 122a, 1403, 1858
Splane, Russell, 977b
Sprout, Harold, 667a
Sprout, Margaret, 667a
Spurlock, Paul E., 1094
Stahmer, Hans Georg, 684b
Stanley, Louise, 2112a
Starr, Mark, 1780, 1781, 1782
Statistical Mission to Japan, see U.S. Bureau of the Budget. Div. of Statistical Standards. Statistical Mission to Japan
Statistics and Reports Section, see Supreme Commander for the Allied Powers. Statistics and Reports Section
Stead, Ronald Maillard, 1009a
Steele, Archibald T., 523
Steig, Milan B., 2113
Steiger, George Nye, 81
Steiner, Jesse Frederick, 123, 668, 1977, 2002, 2003
Steiner, Kurt, 1292, 1292a, 1327, 1328, 1329
Stephan, John Jason, 993a
Stettinius, Edward R., Jr., 215
Stewart, John R., 1482, 1891, 1892
Stewart, Kermit G., 1405
Stewart, Maxwell S., 524
Stewart, Neil, 578a, 2337a
Stimson, Henry Lewis, 216, 245, 247
Stoddard, George D., 2033a, 2114
Stoetzel, Jean, 1978
Stone, Isidor F., 408
Stone, Julius, 164
Stone, K., 1893
Storry, Richard, 750, 1184
Strategic Bombing Survey, see U.S. Strategic Bombing Survey
Stratton, Samuel S., 882, 882a
Strauss, Harold, 465, 751, 1496, 1732, 1807
Strauss, Lewis L., 248
Strike, Clifford S., 1148
Strong, Mary Katherine, 1257
Stuart, Gordon Hackworth, 2184a
Stuart, J. Leighton, 834
Stuber, Stanley I., 2493
Suda, Ryūsuke, 1258
Sugai, Shūichi, 761, 1348
Sugihara, Yasuo, 1212
Sugiyama, Shigeo, 993b, 1859

Sullivan, Sister Maria Regina, S.J., 752
Sullivan, Walter, Jr., 2115
Sun, Fo, 178
Sun, K'o, see Sun, Fo
Sundelson, J. Wilner, 1692
Sung, Cho Yoon, see Cho, Sung-Yoon
Supreme Commander for the Allied Powers, 221, 222, 223, 224, 225, 226, 259, 260, 261, 262, 263, 282, 354, 355, 356, 357, 358, 359, 360, 361, 362, 363, 364, 466, 883, 916, 917, 918, 919, 920, 921, 948, 1023, 1114, 1149, 1150, 1293, 1343, 1513, 1520a, 1521, 1522, 1554, 1555, 1688, 1808, 1822, 1894, 2227b
———. Advisory Committee on Labor, 1784
———. Allied Council for Japan, 884
———. Allied Translator and Interpreter Section, 349, 350, 351, 922
———. Civil Affairs Div., 264, 923
———. Civil Historical Section, see Supreme Commander for the Allied Powers. Statistics and Reports Section
———. Civil Information and Education Section, 27, 265, 266, 267, 268, 269, 270, 271, 347, 352, 353, 924, 1406, 1785, 2117, 2118, 2119, 2119a, 2120, 2121, 2158, 2159, 2160, 2228, 2228a, 2269, 2270, 2271, 2272
———. ———. Analysis and Research Div., 2122, 2161
———. ———. Education Div., 272, 2123, 2124, 2124a, 2125
———. ———. Public Opinion and Sociological Research Div., 1330, 1860, 2303, 2304, 2305
———. ———. Religions and Cultural Resources Div., 2229
———. Commander in Chief, see MacArthur, Douglas; Ridgway, Matthew Bunker

———. ———. Aide-de-Camp, 925
———. Diplomatic Section, 669, 885, 926
———. Economic and Scientific Section, 273, 274, 275, 276, 1483, 1607, 1786, 1787, 1788, 1861, 1862, 1895, 1896, 1897, 1898, 1899, 1900, 2004, 2195, 2273
———. ———. Labor Div., 1789, 1790
———. ———. Programs and Statistics Div., 1627, 1628
———. ———. Research and Programs Div., 1514, 1863, 2005
———. ———. Statistics and Research Div., 1459
———. Finance Div., 1693
———. Government Section, 277, 278, 279, 280, 636, 1024, 1115, 1294, 1407, 1408, 1409, 1410, 1411, 1445, 1446
———. International Prosecution Section, 1025, 1026, 1027, 1028, 1029, 1030, 1031, 1032, 1033, 1034, 1035, 1036, 1037, 1038, 1039
———. Medical Section. Public Health and Welfare Div., see Supreme Commander for the Allied Powers. Public Health and Welfare Section
———. Military Intelligence Section, 1010
———. Military Section, 950
———. Natural Resources Section, 1823, 1824, 1825, 1826, 1827, 1828, 1829, 1830, 1864, 1865, 1866
———. Office of the Financial Adviser, 1556
———. Public Health and Welfare Section, 2185, 2186, 2187, 2188, 2189, 2190, 2191, 2192, 2193, 2194, 2195
———. Public Information Office, 281, 348
———. Statistics and Reports Section, 283 through 337
Sutton, David Nelson, 1095
Sutton, Joseph Lee, 994, 1331

Author Index

Suzuki, Bunshirō, 556
Suzuki, Hisakazu, 1313
Suzuki, Ichirō, 2357b
Svensson, Eric H. F., 59, 60
Sveshnikov, I., 1096
Swanson, C. L. W., 1867, 1868
Swearingen, Arthur Rodger, 16, 1412, 1413, 1414, 1415
Swope, Guy J., 1404

Tabata, Shigejirō, 994a
Tabata, Shinobu, 1213, 1214
Tachi, Ryūichiro, 1649
Taeuber, Irene Barnes, 1979, 2006, 2006a, 2007, 2008, 2009, 2010
Tagami, Jōji, 1215
Taguchi, Shinji, 1869
Tahara, Otoyori, 1870
Takagi, Sōkichi, 2494
Takagi, Yasaka, 570
Takahashi, Akira, 738, 1980
Takahashi, Chōtarō, 1694
Takahashi, Kamekichi, 1608
Takahashi, Masao, 1416
Takahashi, Ryūtarō, 1629
Takano, Yūichi, 995
Takashima, Zenya, 1981
Takayanagi, Kenzō, 738, 1039a, 1178, 1216, 1259, 1294, 1313a
Takeda, Kiyoko, 2274
Takeshita, K. Lillian, 1217
Takeuchi, K., 1733
Takeuchi, Tatsuji, 2536
Takizawa, Makoto, 2495
Tallow, Adamin A., 1097
Tamagna, Frank M., 1460, 1461
Tamura, Kōsaku, 995a, 1871
Tanaka, Kōichi, 1163a
Tanaka, Kōtarō, 1186, 1314, 1315, 2126, 2126a
Tanaka, Seiji, 1609
Tanaka, Sumiko, 2276
Tanimo, Setsu, 738, 1982
Tatsuki, Yasuo, 2306
Tax Mission to Japan, *see* U.S. Tax Mission to Japan
Taylor, George E., 2306a
Taylor, Philip H., 28, 525, 900, 927
Telberg, Ina, 2162
Tench, C. T., 410
Terasaki, Gwen, 753
Terentyev, F., 2424b
Teters, Barbara Joan, 1515
Textile Mission to Japan, *see* U.S. Textile Mission to Japan
Textor, Robert B., 670
Thayer, James T., 2306b
Thomas, Dana L., 2163a
Thomas, Elbert D., 571
Thompson, Elizabeth M., 1630
Thompson, Warren S., 2011
Thomson, James C., Jr., 20
Tibesar, L. H., 1260
Tiedemann, Arthur Everett, 754
Tiltman, Hessell, 467, 526, 670a, 886, 1462, 2127, 2425
Tilton, Cecil G., 1332
Times (of London), 41
Timperley, Harold John, 178a, 178b
Titiev, Mischa, 1983
Titus, David Anson, 1260a
Tixier, Gilbert, 2467
Tōgō, Fumihiko, 150
Tōgō, Shigenori, 150, 245
Tōhata, Shiro, 1734, 1871a
Tohbata, Shiro, *see* Tōhata, Shiro
Tōjō Hideki, 1040
Tokoyama, Tsunesaburō, 1667
Tokuda, Kyūichi, 1417
Tokumaro, N., 685
Tolischus, Otto D., 1261
Tomikawa, Sōji, 2307
Tompkins, Pauline, 835
Topekha, Petr Pavlovich, 1419
Tormey, Gertrude, 637
Torrens, James G., 1901
Totten, George O., 705, 1358
Tracy, Honor Lilbush Wingfield, 638
Trainin, A., 1098
Tregaskis, Richard, 927a
Trewartha, Glenn T., 1735
Trigorin, Z., 2430
Troitsky, S., 1420
Truman, Harry S., 217, 245, 674, 2431
Tsai, Paul Chung-tseng, 1099b
Tsang, Chih, 178c
Tsuchiyama, Tamie, 1729b
Tsuda, Minoru, 2496
Tsuge, Hideomi, *see* Tuge, Hideomi
Tsuji, Kiyoaki, 755, 1434, 1447, 1447a, 1447b
Tsuji, Kiyoakira, *see* Tsuji, Kiyoaki
Tsujimura, Kōtarō, 1649
Tsukahira, Toshio George, 1421
Tsuneishi, Warren Michio, 1262
Tsuru, Shigeto, 738, 756, 1517, 1559, 1585, 1668
Tsurumi, Kazuko, 1984
Tsūshō Sangyōshō, *see* Japan. Ministry of International Trade and Industry
Tuge, Hideomi, 2275
Tuma, Elias Hanna, 1736
Turner, John E., 739
Tuttle, Charles E., 2163

Uchida, Katsutoshi, 1669
Uchiyama, Isamu, 1670
Uehara, Shigeru, *see* Uyehara, Shigeru
Uematsu, Morio, 1695
Ueno, Hiroya, 1671
Uhlan, Edward, 2163a
Ukai, Nobushige, 1178, 1218, 1219
Ulanovsky, Yu. B., 2457
Ulmer, S. Sidney, 1333
Ulyanov, A., 836
Umemura, Michael Takaaki, 7
Union of Democratic Control. Research Office, 2358a
Union of the New Religious Organizations of Japan, 2229a
United Nations, 254
———. Security Council, 996
U.S. Army. Air Force, 151
———. ———. Eighth Army, 339
———. ———. ———. Headquarters, 928, 929
———. ———. ———. Military Government Section, 340
———. ———. ———. ———. Historical Section, 341
———. ———. ———. ———. "I" Corps, 342
———. ———. ———. ———. 93d Military Government Co., 343
———. ———. Far East Command, 282, 2497
———. ———. ———. Military History Officer, 344
———. ———. ———. Military Intelligence Section, Historical Section, 930
———. ———. 93d Military Government Company, *see*

818

Author Index

U.S. Army. Eighth Army. "I" Corps. 93d Military Government Company
———. ———. Pacific Air Command, 931
———. ———. Service Forces, 235
———. ———. Sixth Army, 345
———. ———. ———. Headquarters. Sixth Information and Historical Service, 346
———. ———. Southwest Pacific Area. G-2 Section, 227, 228
———. Army Forces in the Pacific, 1041
———. Bureau of the Budget. Div. of Statistical Standards. Statistical Mission to Japan, 1448
———. Civil Affairs Training School. University of Michigan, 236
———. Committee to Inquire into Economic Problems of Japan and Korea, 1518
———. Congress. Senate, 255, 2458, 2498
———. ———. Committee on Foreign Relations, 370, 2459, 2499
———. Cultural Science Mission to Japan, 2128
———. Dept. of Defense, 179
———. Dept. of Labor. Women's Bureau, 2276
———. Dept. of State, 196, 256, 257, 371, 468, 469, 470, 613, 671, 672, 997, 1042, 1334, 2432, 2460, 2500, 2501, 2502
———. ———. Bureau of Public Affairs. Historical Office, 197, 198, 200, 201, 202, 203, 203a, 203b, 887, 998
———. ———. Div. of Research for the Far East, 527, 1422, 1902
———. ———. Historical Div., 199
———. ———. Office of Economic Security Policy, 1903
———. ———. Office of Intelligence Research, 1423, 1424, 1449, 1463, 1872
———. ———. Office of Northeast Asian Affairs, 837, 2532
———. ———. Office of Public Affairs, 61, 258, 372, 2331, 2433, 2434, 2435, 2436
———. ———. Office of Research and Intelligence, see U.S. Dept. of State. Office of Intelligence Research
———. Dept. of the Army. Civil Affairs Div., 573, 639
———. ———. Office of the Chief of Military History, 49
———. Education Exchange Group to Japan, 2129
———. Education Mission to Japan, 2129a; see also Second U.S. Education Mission to Japan
———. Far East Command, see U.S. Army. Far East Command
———. Library Mission to Japan, 2277
———. Mission on Japanese Combines, 1809
———. Naval Technical Mission to Japan, 613a
———. Second Statistical Mission to Japan, see Rice, Stuart A.
———. Strategic Bombing Survey, 29, 152
———. ———. Chairman's Office, 153, 154
———. ———. Civilian Defense Div., 155
———. ———. Manpower, Food, and Civilian Supplies Div., 156
———. ———. Morale Div., 157
———. ———. Naval Analysis Div., 158
———. ———. Over-All Economic Effects Div., 159
———. ———. Physical Damage Div., 160
———. Supreme Court, 1043
———. Tax Mission to Japan, 1696, 1697, 1698
———. Textile Mission to Japan, 1904
———. War Dept., 234, 237
USSR. Academy of Sciences. Institute of the Peoples of Asia, see Akademiia nauk SSSR. Institut narodov Azii
———. Ministry of Foreign Affairs. Commission for the Publication of Diplomatic Documents, 218
Ushimaru, Yoshitome, 2196
Uyehara, Cecil H., 31, 1358
Uyehara, Shigeru, 998a, 2011a, 2359a, 2359b, 2505a, 2505b, 2505c
Uyemura, Takachiyo, 2163b

van Aduard, Evert Joost Lewe, see Lewe van Aduard, Evert Joost
Van Benschoten, Arnold, 528
Vandenbosch, Amry, 574
Van Der Water, Margorie, 412
Van Kirk, Walter W., 472, 1425, 2230
Van Patten, Louise M., 126
Van Staaveren, Jacob, 2129b
Van Zandt, Howard F., 1905, 2130
Varney, Richard M., 1449a
Varshavsky, A., 575
Vasilyev, A. N., 1101, 1101a, 1101b
Vaughn, Miles W., 614, 1152
Vernon, Raymond, 1810
Vikentyev, A., 2011b
Viktorov, Ya, 1165a
Vinacke, Harold M., 686, 757, 839, 840
Vincent, John Carter, 62a, 397
Vining, Elizabeth Gray, 529, 1264, 1264a
Vith, Fritz, 1810a
Vladimirova, V., 1562
Vlasov, V. A., 1
Volle, Hermann, 1585a
von Mehren, Arthur Taylor, 1295, 1695
Voorhees, Tracy, 611
Vos, Fritz, 1978
Vosburgh, Frederick G., 640

Wachenheimer, Carolene, 1810
Wadham, Samuel MacMahon, 164
Wadsworth, Lawrence W., Jr., 1103
Wagatsuma, Sakae, 1219a, 1296, 1296a, 1737, 1984a
Wagner, Edward Willett, 2277a
Waithman, Robert, 2439c

Author Index

Wakefield, Harold, 576
Wakukawa, Seiyei, 81, 1873
Wales, Horace G. Q., 1334a
Walker, Alan, 2331a
Walker, Gordon W., 1010b, 2307a, 2337b
Walkinshaw, Robert B., 1104
Walliser, Blair, A., 615
Waln, Nora, 616, 1166, 2308, 2308a
Walser, T. D., 473
Walsh, J. M., 887a
Walter, Austin Frederic, 841
Walton, W. H. Murray, 2384c
Wang, Shih-chieh, 791
Wang, Yun-sheng, 530, 842, 843
Ward, Gordon H., 1874
Ward, J. M., 1220
Ward, Robert Edward, 32, 127, 691, 709, 758, 759, 760, 761, 762, 763, 1184, 1221, 1222, 1223, 1335, 1336, 1427, 1985
Ward, Robert Spencer, 128
Warner, Dave, 577
Warner, Denis Ashton, 552, 2012
Warner, W. F., 1167
Warp, George A., 1337, 1338
Watanabe, Hajime, 32
Watanabe, Masaharu, 764, 1255
Watanabe, Susumu, 1672
Watanabe, Tsunehiko, 1636
Watkins, Frederick Mundell, 81
Webb, Paul E., 2130a
Webb, Sir William F., 1044, 1048a
Weideman, Elizabeth, 2130b
Weigert, Oscar, 1792
Weinstein, Martin E., 2506
Weinstein, Wilmer, 1905a
Weldon, James, 978
Welles, Sumner, 843a
Wells, Roger H., 888
Werth, Richard, 2130c
Westerfield, Hargis, 474
Whan, Vorin E., Jr., 951

Wheeler, Herbert B., 925
Wheeler, Post, 475
Wheeler, Romney, 641, 844
Wherry, Kenneth, 54
Whitman, Roswell H., 1519
Whitney, Courtney, 466, 980 981, 982, 1024, 1407
Whyte, Alexander Frederick, *see* Whyte, Sir Frederick
Whyte, Sir Frederick, 181, 413
Widgery, Alban G., 130
Wigglesworth, Edwin French, 1563a
Wilcox, Francis O., 373
Wildes, Harry Emerson, 131, 132, 709, 765, 766, 1410, 1428, 1429, 2164, 2197
Wilhelm, Maria, 219
Wilkinson, Harry Richard, 888a
Williams, Justin, 1224, 1225, 1430
Williamson, Mark B., 1738, 1848, 1864
Williamson, Maude, 1985a
Willoughby, Charles A., 687, 983, 2309
Wilmot, Chester, 194
Wilson, Donald V., 2197a
Wincelberg, Simon, 476
Winiata, Whatarangi, 1673
Winnacker, Rudolph A., 203c
Wint, Guy, 2460a
Wittner, Lawrence S., 2231
Woddis, H. C., 2506a
Woddis, Jack, 578a
Wolfe, Henry Cutler, 132a
Wolfsohn, H. A., 793
Wolpert, V., 1563b, 1739
Wood, Frederick Lloyd Whitfield, 176
Wood, Gordon Leslie, 164
Wood, Junius Boyd, 2344b
Woodard, William P., 2232
Woodman, Dorothy, 2360
Woodward, Sir Llwellyn, 204
Wollacott, Derrick, 531
Worden, William L., 931a, 1348b

World Affairs Council of Northern California, 2338
Wu, To, 1145
Wunderlich, Herbert John, 2132
Wysor, R. J., 945

Yamada, Y., 1226
Yamada, Yūsō (Yūzō), 1586
Yamaguchi, Shinrokurō, 1875
Yamaguchi, Shōgo, 2532
Yamagiwa, Joseph Koshimi, 711, 2165, 2166
Yamakawa, Kikue, 2278
Yamamoto, George, 1431
Yamamoto, Hiromasa, 1905b
Yamamoto, Noboru, 1153a
Yamamura, Kōzō, 1674, 1811, 1812, 1813, 1814, 1815
Yamane, Tarō, 1675
Yamazaki, Kazuyoshi, 925
Yanaga, Chitoshi, 617, 767, 1432, 1815a, 1986, 1987
Yanaibara Tadao, 2233
Yarovoi, V., 845, 1485
Yazawa, Makoto, 1269
Yershov, N., 1587
Yokota, Kisaburō, 1178, 1227
Yoshida, Shigeru, 455a, 607a, 674, 717, 768, 769, 945, 1467, 1843, 2362a, 2362b, 2442
Yoshimura Tadashi, 1433
Yoshino, Roger, 1988
Yoshino, Toshihiko, 1676
Youel, Harlan, 44k
Young, James Russell, 2132a, 2234
Yuasa, Hachirō, 2132b

Zacharias, Ellis M., 161, 161a, 220, 2469a
Zaibatsu Mission, *see* U.S. Mission on Japanese Combines
Zanard, Richard J., 2460b
Zhukov, E., 846, 1817, 2507
Zook George F., 2133

Periodical Index

Periodicals are arranged alphabetically by title. Articles within are identified by author, if there is one named, but arranged chronologically. References are to entry numbers.

Academy of Political Science *Proceedings*, see *Proceedings of the Academy of Political Science*
Agricultural History: Smith, 7/49—1857
Amerasia: Colegrove, 10/25/42—68; 11/43—106; 1/21/44—164a; 3/3/44—104; 1/7 & 3/3/44—1249; 6/9/44—102; 8/44—66b; 12/1/44—125; 6/1/45—89; 9/45—409; 9/45—414; 2/46—415b; 2/46—1728; 2/46—1794; 10/46—425; 12/46—1758
America: Herzog, 11/3/45—2291; Wales, 2/2/46—1334a; Deverall, 2/12/49—1746a; Deverall, 3/12/49—586a
American Academy of Political and Social Science *Annals*, see *Annals of the American Academy of Political and Social Science*
American Anthropologist: Hulse, 1/3/47—1933; Bennett & Nagai, 8/53—1913a; Norbeck, 4/61—1961
American Association of University Women *Journal*, see *Journal of the American Association of University Women*
American Bar Association Journal: Blakeney, 8/46—1049; Walkinshaw, 4/49—1104; Sutton, 2/50—1095; Spurlock, 5/50—1094; Parker, 11/50—1310; Abe, 6/61—1266
American Economic Review: Tamagna, 5/46—1461; Kurihara, 12/46—1455
American Foreign Service Journal: Johnson, 7/46—435; Allen, 8/47—1045a; Johnson, 12/47—873; Ballantine, 10/49—580; Donovan, 4/50—2038; Dunning, 3/52—2514

American Forests and Forest Life: Spillers, 2/47—1731a
American Journal of Comparative Law: Blakemore & Yazawa, Winter 53—1269; Rabinowitz, Winter 55—24; Takayangi, Winter 55—1294a; Fueto, Autumn 57—1275
American Journal of International Law: U. S. Supreme Court, 4/46—1043; Dai, 1/48—856a; Blakemore, 7/49—1154b; Kuhn, 7/50—1076; Bishop, 10/51—1831
American Journal of Public Health and the Nation's Health: Sams, 5/52—2179
American Journal of Sociology: Embree, 11/44—71; Matsumiya, 9/47—1957; Smythe, 9/52—1970
American Magazine: Kornhauser, 10/45—389a; Behrstock, 5/47—479; Strike, 9/47—1148
American Mercury: Smith, 1/44—120b; Bayles, 9/46—1231; Keenan, 4/50—1069; Ryan, 10/50—976; Wheeler, 12/50—641; Wincelberg, 7/52—476
American Oriental Society *Journal*, see *Journal of the American Oriental Society*
American Perspective: Griggs, 4/49—1234; Metzger, 9/49—1545; Mears, winter 50—2348; Blewett, summer 50—1050
American Pharmaceutical Association *Journal*, see *Journal of the American Pharmaceutical Association*
American Political Science Review: Quigley, 10/47—1203; Colton, 10/48—1361; Saffell, 10/48—1400; Williams, 10/48—1224; Wildes, 12/48—1429; Williams, 12/48—

Periodical Index

1430; Braibanti, 4/49—893; Brown, 10/49—4; Ward, 12/51—1985; Dull, 3/53—1365; Mendel, 9/54—729; Kawai, 9/55—1189; Ward, 12/56—1223; Williams, 9/65—1225

American Scholar: Lifton, Spring 65—1946

American School Board Journal: Werth, 3/49—2130c

American Society of International Law *Proceedings*, see *Proceedings of the American Society of International Law*

American Sociological Review: Steiner, 4/45—123; Pelzel, 2/50—1998; Thompson, 2/50—2011; Taeuber, 4/51—1979; Smythe, 12/51—1973

American Teacher: Counts, 11/46—2034; 3/47—1757; Starr, 3/47—1790; Weideman, 12/51—2130b

Annals of Iowa: Colton, 10/47—489

Annals of the American Academy of Political and Social Science: Bennett, 7/46—1119; Borton, 1/48—539; Thomas, 1/48—571; Latourette, 5/48—2334; Vandenbosch, 5/48—574; Wells, 5/48—888; Braibanti, 1/50—896; Mason, 1/50—233; Taylor, 1/50—927; Kawai, 11/51—653; McClurkin, 7/54—813; Wildes, 7/54—766; Cole, 11/56—1915; Colton, 11/56—1170; Colton, 11/56—1360; Fujiwara, 11/56—1922; Gokijo, 11/56—1299; Levine, 11/56—1766; Sakanishi, 11/56—2266; Swearingen, 11/56—1414; Tsuji, 11/56—1447; Ukai, 11/56—1218

Annals of the Hitotsubashi Academy: Itō, 10/50—1683; Takahashi, 10/50—1694; Yamada, 10/50—1586; Azuma, 4/51—1744; Minami, 4/51—1953; Minoguchi, 4/51—1995; Ohkawa, 4/51—1599; Tagami, 4/51—1215; Takashima, 4/51—1981; Tanaka, 4/51—1609

Antioch Review: Dempsey, Spring 46—423

Armed Forces Talk: 47—517

Army Information Digest: Baker, 1/48—532; Kent, 12/48—2297

Army Quarterly: Piggott, 4/47—876a; Walsh, 10/48—887a

Asia: Timperley, 7/42—178b; Lamott, 10/42—95b

Asia and the Americas: Tsang, 7/44—178c; Ward, 5/45—128; Matsumoto, 9/45—1241; Price, 9/45—2220; Wildes, 9/45—132; Janeway, 10/45—384a; Olds, 1/46—2098; Price, 1/46—1851; Wildes, 1/46—1428; Price, 2/46—2000; Wildes, 2/46—2164; Matsumoto, 4/46—442; Spinks, 4/46—1858; Eby, 9/46—1748; Benedict, 11/46—1908a

Asian Affairs: Kawano, 6/56—1847; Miyata, 9/56—1133; Ozawa, 9/56—1137; Yamamoto, 9/56—1153a; Ajia Kyōkai, 3/60—1116a

Asian and African Studies (Jerusalem): Blumenthal, 70—1699b

Asian Cultural Studies: Lifton, 62—1948

Asian Survey: Ishida, 4/62—1237

Asiatic Review: Chow, 7/45—166; Lyell, 10/45—392; Redman, 10/45—401; Horner, 7/46—433; Horner, 1/47—500; Horner, 4/47—501

Asiatic Society of Japan *Transactions*, see *Transactions of the Asiatic Society of Japan*

Asie nouvelle: Brochier, 6-7/63—1635

Atlantic Monthly: Mears, 9/43—100; Lattimore, 1/45—96; Ashmead, 4/46—416; Compton, 12/46—242; Ashmead, 1/47—2019; Lattimore, 4/49—805; Waln, 11/49—1166; Waln, 12/49—616; Strauss, 8/53—751; Tsuru, 1/55—756

Audubon Magazine: Baldwin, 3/49—1818a

Austral-Asiatic Bulletin: Phillips, 3/45—170a; Caiger, 4/46—420

Australian Outlook: Ward, 9/47—1220; Harper, 12/47—794; Ball, 6/48—1230; Ryan, 3/49—829; Petrie, 3/50—1140; Sissons, 3/50—635; Ball, 9/51—2365

Australian Quarterly: Walker, 6/46—2331a; Frazer, 3/48—1494a; John, 3/52—677; Dickinson, 6/52—1058; Jasay, 12/53—713

Banking: Johnson, 3/48—1500; Cohen, 5/15—1590

Board of Trade Journal: 11/15/47—1464

Britannica Book of the Year: Yoshida, 67—768

British Survey: Sissons, 4/62—749a

Bulletin of Concerned Asian Scholars: Dower, 10/69—2470c

Bulletin of the Cleveland Museum of Art: Hollis, 11/47—2247

Business Week: 12/1/45—1804c; 8/9/47—1130a; 3/26/49—1878; 8/13/49—1551; 11/19/49—1694a; 4/29/50—1793; 11/11/50—1579; 4/21/51—959

Canadian Forum: 10/45—381a; Kaneko, 12/56—1187

Catholic World: Sheerin, 8/50—634b; Caulfield, 7/51—953

Chicago Schools Journal: Crofts, 10/48—548a

China Economist: 6/21/48—1145; Jessup, 4/25/49—1541; Hsieh, 5/9/49—1534a

China Magazine: 9/47—821; Wang, 9/47—530; Wang, 10/47—843; 11/47—2314; 7/48—791; Soong, 7/48—1256

China Monthly: Crofts, 3/47—492; Liu, 5/47—510; Liu, 7/47—1077; Liu, 8/47—1078; Mui, 2/48—2335

China Weekly Review: Stone, 5/29/48—1893

Christendom: Horton, Spring 46—2210
Christian Century: 1/10/45—76b; 9/19/45—966a; 10/3/45—383; 10/10/45—1261a; 11/7/45—375a; 12/26/45—384b; Van Kirk, 1/2/46—1425; Van Kirk, 1/9/46—1425; Van Kirk, 1/23/46—472; 1/30/46—2202; Van Kirk, 2/6/46—2230; 3/6/46—1297; 3/20/46—1172a; Eby, 6/12/46—2042; 8/7/46—889; 8/28/46—432a; Walser, 10/2/46—473; Brumbaugh, 11/27/46—2282; 12/11/46—1146; Brumbaugh, 12/18/46—1352; Hutchinson, 1/8/47—2211; Hutchinson, 1/15/47—502; 1/29/47—1115a; Brumbaugh, 2/5/47—487; Shafer, 3/12/47—2225; Brumbaugh, 6/4/47—2200; Braibanti, 7/9/47—2198b; 7/30/47—1471b; Kagawa, 12/3/47—505a; Shafer, 12/10/47—2329; Kikuchi, 12/31/47—505a; Shafer, 4/14/48—2226; Brumbaugh, 6/30/48—542; 11/24/48—1092b; Root, 12/1/48—2221; Kagawa, 1/26/49—592; 7/13/49—1063; Hessel, 8/24/49—1064a; 11/16/49—2471b; 1/18/50—966b; 3/22/50—2473c; 6/7/50—619b; 6/14/50—2346b; 8/23/50—631b; 9/6/50—2358; Grant, 10/4/50—631b; 10/11/50—2070; Jones, 6/31/51—652; 8/29/51—2395; Stuber, 9/5/51—2493; 9/19/51—2409a
Christian Science Monitor magazine section: Hallett, 6/15/46—902c; Taylor, 1/25/47—525; Walker, 4/5/47—1010b; Canham, 4/26/47—484; Dilts, 8/23/47—2240; Stead, 9/27/47—1009a; Walker, 1/24/48—2337b; Walker, 5/1/48—2307a; Durgin, 7/3/48—2243; Tsuru, 8/14/48—1517; Dabney, 11/27/48—2205
Chronique de politique étrangère: 9/48—568a; 11/51—2426a
City Club Bulletin: Smith & Kruse, 10/29/45—407a
Clearinghouse Bulletin of Research in Human Organization: Bennett, Winter 51—890
Cleveland Museum of Art Bulletin, see *Bulletin of the Cleveland Museum of Art*
College and Research Libraries: Downs, 10/49—2241
Collier's: Morris, 12/1/45—395; Gayn, 3/23/46—429; James, 1/25/47—503; James, 6/14/47—905; James, 6/28/47—504; James, 8/2/47—2250; Chenery, 9/13/47—582a; 10/4/47—2314b; Creel, 5/15/48—954; Betz, 4/9/49—2237; Denson, 9/9/50—2469c; Dewey, 12/8/51—2513
Columbia Journal of International Affairs: Hall, Winter 48—2053; Krane, Winter 48—801; Seligmann & Clark, Winter 48—2302; Sneider, Winter 48—569; Scheuer, Winter 51—831

Common Ground: Baldwin, Summer 48—534
Common Sense: Chamberlin, 12/45—376
Commonweal: Howard, 10/9/42—83; Sands, 6/29/45—120a; 1/18/46—2212a; 5/17/46 1375a; 7/26/46—915a; 12/13/46—972a; Miller, 4/25/47—2150; Imboden, 6/13/47 2141; Allen, 9/19/47—477; Frederick, 11/14/47—497; Frederick, 3/12/48—1125; Horner, 4/16/48—2209; 11/26/48—1065c; Deverall, 1/7/49—1917; Allen, 5/13/49—1349; 6/23/50—631a; 6/30/50—2345b; Smythe, 4/4/52—1974; Pfaff, 1/23/53—2530
Comparative Education Review: Duke, 2/63—2041; Passin, 2/65—23
Concerned Asian Scholars Bulletin, see *Bulletin of Concerned Asian Scholars*
Congregational Quarterly: Horton, 4/46—434
Congressional Record: U.S. Senate, 1952—2458; U.S. Senate, 1952—2498
Connecticut Bar Journal: Sinn, 6/49—2227a
Contemporary China: Chow, 4/30/45—166; 10/29/45—378
Contemporary Japan: Inahara, 1-3/45—186a; 4-12/45—2198; Asahina, 4-12/45—2279; Inahara, 4-12/45—1375b; Kuroki, 4-12/45—1378a; Arai, 1-4/46—1350a; Katayama, 1-4/46—1758a; Kiyose, 1-4/46—1376c; Mizutani, 1-4/46—1726; Morito, 1-4/46—2322a; SCAP, 1-4/46—856; Uyemura, 1-4/46—2163b; Hoover, 5-8/46—1835; Minobe, 5-8/46—1456a; Sano, 5-8/46—460; Tanaka, 5-8/46—2126a; 9-12/46—1172; Hashiguchi, 9-12/46—1323; Inouye, 9-12/46—1937; MacArthur, 9-12/46—932; Yoshida, 9-12/46—455a; Atcheson, 1-3/47—825; MacArthur, 1-3/47—933; MacArthur, 1-3/47—934; MacArthur, 1-3/47—1371; MacArthur, 1-3/47—1467; MacArthur, 1-3/47—1783; Mizutani, 1-3/47—1725; Ohkita, 1-3/47—1134; MacArthur, 4-6/47—934a; Munekata, 4-6/47—2091a; Nakamura, 4-6/47—1442a; Yokota, 4-6/47—1227; Fujita, 7-9/47—2245; SCAP, 7-9 & 10-12/47—281; Takayanagi, 7-9/47—1313a; Crane, 10-12/47—1465; Tohbata, 10-12/47—1871a; Wagatsuma, 10-12/47—1984a;
Ashida, 1-3/48—1509a; MacArthur, 1-3/48—935; Swope, 1-3/48—1404; Economic Stabilization Board, 4-6/48—1512; Johnston Committee, 4-6/48—1142c; MacArthur, 4-6/48—936; Vaughn, 4-6/48—1152; Yamakawa, 4-6/48—2278; 7-12/48—1102; Durgin, 7-12/48—2243a; Hoover, 7-12/48—1444; MacArthur, 7-12/48—1014; MacArthur, 7-12/48—1436; MacArthur, 7-12/48—1495; Okazaki, 7-12/48—1997a; Tsuji, 7-12/48—1447a;

Contemporary Japan (continued)
Dodge, 1–3/49—1552; MacArthur, 1–3/49—937; Marquat, 1–3/49—1531; Minobe, 1–3/49—1546; SCAP, 1–3/49—1520a; SCAP, 1–3/49—1521; SCAP, 1–3/49—1522; Dodge, 4–6/49—1553; MacArthur, 4–6/49—938; McCoy, 4–6/49—1117; Nishi, 4–6/49—1344b; Ouchi, 4–6/49—1547a; SCAP, 4–6/49—1688; Vaughn, 4–6/49—614; MacArthur, 7–9/49—901; MacArthur, 7–9/49—939; Nakayama, 7–9/49—1547; Natori, 7–9/49—1685; Sogawa, 7–9/49—1857a; U.S. Tax Mission to Japan, 7–9/49—1696; Voorhees, 7–9/49—611; Hoashi, 10–12/49—1533; MacArthur, 10–12/49—1705; Nomura, 10–12/49—2342a; Yoshida, 10–12/49—607a;

Dooman, 1–3/50—783; Iwamura, 1–3/50—2346a; MacArthur, 1–3/50—940; Matano, 1–3/50—1885; Natori, 1–3/50—1581; SCAP, 1–3/50—1161; MacArthur, 4–6/50—941; Rinoiye, 4–6/50—1890; Sebald, 4–6/50—1163; Shiba, 4–6/50—2108; 7–9/50—1348a; MacArthur, 7–9/50—1343; MacArthur, 7–9/50—1368; MacArthur, 7–9/50—1369; MacArthur, 7–9/50—1370; Nakajima, 7–9/50—1344a; Nomura, 7–9/50—2350; Oku, 7–9/50—1888; Sasaki, 7–9/50—2156; Katsube, 10–12/50—1882; Obama, 10–12/50—1111a; Okamoto, 10–12/50—1582; Spender, 10–12/50—2357a; Van Zandt, 10–12/50—1905; Ashida, 1–3/51—770; Dulles, 1–3/51—2375; Dulles, 1–3/51—2424a; Iizawa, 1–3/51—2392; MacArthur, 1–3/51—942; Sansom, 1–3/51—663; Shimizu, 1–3/51—1604; Takagi, 1–3/51—2494; Tanaka, 1–3/51—2126; 4–6/51—2374; 4–6/51—2411; Dewey, 4–6/51—2470a; Furukaki, 4–6/51—2139; Imboden, 4–6/51—2142; Marquat, 4–6/51—1606; Ozaki, 4–6/51—657; Satō, 4–6/51—2419; Steiner, 4–6/51—668; 7–9/51—2439b; 7–9/51—2502; Baba, 7–9/51—2364; Bush, 7–9/51—1914; Hatano, 7–9/51—2516; Schenck, 7–9/51—1819; Takahashi, 7–9/51—1608; Truman, 7–9/51—2431; Yoshida, 7–9/51—2362a; Yoshida, 7–9/51—2362b; Baba, 10–12/51—2469; Dodge, 10–12/51—1605; Dulles, 10–12/51—2362; Dulles, 10–12/51—2379; Hara, 10–12/51—2246; Koizumi, 10–12/51—2400a; Nagato, 10–12/51—656a; 1–3/52—2466c;

Inaba, 1–3/52—1127a; Kimura, 1–3/52—2478a; Oppler, 1–3/52—1309; Ridgway, 1–3/52—985a; Satō, 1–3/52—2001; 4–6/52—2454b; Fine, 4–6/52—1615; Bryn-Jones, 7–9/52—1353; Ikematsu, 7–9/52—1374; 10–12/52—682a; 7–9/53—1165b; Ikematsu, 7–9/53—1373; Nixon, 7–9/53—2488; Taguchi, 7–9/53—1869; Tamura, 7–9/53—1871; Nishida, 10–12/53—2094; Wildes, 10–12/53—2197; 4–6/55—1116; 4–6/55—2467a; Tabata, 7–9/55—994a; Itō, 10–12/55—2058; Suzuki, 10–12/55—1313; Ushimaru, 10–12/55—2196; Kamichika, 1–3/56—2253; Lindstrom, 1–3/56—1722; Shiotani, 1–3/56—1666; 4–6/56—1141c; Arita, 4–6/56—1876; Inomata, 4–6/56—1180a; Satō, 4–6 & 7–9/56—1209; Uchiyama, 4–6/56—1670; Nakasone, 7–9/56—1199; Ikematsu, 4/57—2465b; Yoshino, 4/57—1676; 4/58—1141b; 4/58—2467b; Ayusawa, 3/59–5/61—1742; Fujiyama, 8/59—2465; Schwantes, 5/60—2106; Tōhata, 10/63 & 9/64—1734; Okazaki, 9/64—968. *See also* no.34.

Contemporary Religions in Japan: Ashizu, 6/60—2198a; SCAP, 6/60—2227b; Union of the New Religious Organizations of Japan, 6/65–9/66—2229a; SCAP, 6/66—2228a; Nugent, 9/66—2219; 3/67—2104c; Constitution Investigation Council, 6/67—2203

Contemporary Review: Keeton, 7/43—169b; Whyte, 10/45—413; Gresham, 10/48—554; Green, 9/49—590; Fifield, 3/50—988; Rawlings, 10/51—2413

Cornell Law Quarterly: Metzger, Spring 52—2452

Cosmopolitan: Lee, 4/46—964

Current Digest of the Soviet Press: Derevyanko, 2/8/49—1341a; Mayevsky, 2/15/49—1544a; 2/22/49—1381a; Kudryavtsev, 2/22/49—1377b; Mayevsky, 3/1/49—1388; Panyushkin, 3/1/49—1560a; 3/15/49—1561; Kudryavtsev, 4/5/49—962; 4/19/49—1550a; Kudryavtsev, 6/14/49—1192; Pyatnitsky, 6/28/49—1889a; Vikentyev, 6/28/49—2011b; Vasilyev, 7/19/49—1101b; Kudryavtsev, 7/26/49—597; Mayevsky, 8/2/49—2341a; Panyushkin, 8/16/49—1771a; Mayevsky, 10/4/49—2341; Kudryavtsev, 1/17/50—599; 1/24/50—1065b; 2/18/50—1098a; 3/13/50—1395; 4/1/50—1154a; 4/15/50—1045; 4/29/50—1065a; Vasilyev, 6/24/50—1101a; 7/1/50—1082a; Popov, 7/15/50—1584; Derevyanko, 8/12/50—1381b; Gribachev, 8/19/50—955a; Kudryavtsev, 8/19/50—1377a; Viktorov, 10/7/50—1165a; 10/14/50—1093c; 1/6/51—2359; Chou, 1/6/51—2423b; Eidus, 1/6/51—2471c; Marinin, 1/13/51—2483c; Terentyev, 3/10/51—2424b; Kudryavtsev & Mikhailov, 3/24/51—2483a; Zhukov, 5/12/51—2507; 6/16/51—2437; Markov, 7/28/51—1081a; Hsinhua, 9/1/51—2391a; Markov, 9/1/51—2406; Mayevsky, 9/8/51—2407; Filippov, 10/20/51—2384b; Orekhov, 10/27/51—

2410a; Lkhamsurun, 11/10/51—2423c; Kozhin, 4/5/52—2081a; Topekha, 6/28/52—1419; Tokuda, 9/13/52—1417. *See also* no.34a.

Current History: 9/45—250b; 10/45—250a; 5/46—1200; Nehmer, 8/46—448; Garbuny, 12/46—1453; Allen, 8/47—1350; Nehmer, 8/47—1476; Baldwin, 2/48—533; 7/49—1117; Nehmer, 11/49—604; Yanaga, 8/50—1986; Cohen, 10/50—1567; 1/51—2359; 2/51—2363; Nakano, 5/51—2527; Hsu, 9/51—648; 10/51—2468b; Watanabe & Smythe, 1/53—764

Current Legal Thought: Feldhaus, 8/47—1059

Current Notes on International Affairs: Australia. Dept. of External Affairs, 1/45—163; Chifley, 8–9/45—162; Australia. Dept. of External Affairs, 10–11/45—1012; 1/46—854; 1/46—870; 10/46—871; Evatt, 2/47—2316; Evatt, 3/47—2317; 6–7/47—899; 6–7/47—2313; Evatt, 6–7/47—1844; Evatt, 6–7/47—2315; 8/47—2312; Evatt, 8/47—2326; 4/48—558; 4/48—1001; 5/48—1066; 5/48—1516; 6/48—1108; 8/48—877; 8/48—1494; 11–12/48—2044; 11–12/48—2104a; 3/49—1079; 4/50—861; 7/50—848; Spender, 11/50—2357a; Spender, 3/51—2424; 7/51—2374; 9/51—2429; 9/51—2502; 3/52—2504; 10/52—676. *See also* no.35.

Daedelus: Lifton, Winter 62—1948; Lifton, Summer 63—1947

Democratic Japan (Tokyo): Naka, 1/50—2348a; Uyehara, 1/50—998a; Uyehara, 2/50—2359b; Uyehara, 3/50—2359a; Ohara, 5–6/50—2262b; Uyehara, 5–6/50—2505c; Uyehara, 7/50—2505a; Rōyama, 9–10/50—2489; Suzuki, 9–10/50—2357b; Uyehara, 11–12/50—2011a; Tanaka, 1–2/51—1163a; Ogawa, 3–4/51—2262a; Uyehara, 3–4/51—2505b

Department of State Bulletin: 9/23/45—62; 9/30/45—54; 9/30/45—952; 10/7/45—397; Carey, 10/7/45—1154c; 10/14/45—856b; Vincent, 10/21/45—62a; 11/4/45—1339b; Moseley, McCarthy, & Richardson, 11/11/45—58; 2/10/46—854a; 2/10/46—986; 3/3/46—1849a; 3/3/46—2043a; 3/10/46—871a; 3/10/46—1040b; 4/21/46—1376; 5/5 & 5/12/46—449a; 5/5/46—1836a; 5/5/46—2105; 5/19/46—1040a; 6/9/46—1889b; 6/23/46—1376a; 6/30/46—999c; Hilldring, 7/14/46—903; 7/21/46—465a; 7/28/46—874a; 7/28/46—1143; Cassidy, 8/18/46—421; 8/25/46—876b; 9/8/46—425a; 10/27/46—1461a; 11/3/46—1805c; U.S. Dept. of State, 11/17/46—997; 11/24/46—1140a; 12/22/46—1142b; 12/29/46—1771b; 3/9/47—987; 3/9/47—1130b;
Atcheson, 3/30/47—770a; McCoy, 4/13/47—1130c; Acheson, 4/20/47—999; 4/20/47—1127b; 4/27/47—2104a; 5/4/47—995b; 5/4/47—1011a; 5/4/47—1201; Far Eastern Commission, 5/4/47—1175; Robbins, 5/4/47—992b; 6/22/47—1145a; Vernon & Wachenheimer, 7/13/47—1810; Far Eastern Commission, 8/3/47—899; MacArthur, 8/3/47—875; Bohlen, 8/24/47—2311; Far Eastern Commission, 8/24/47—1466; 8/31/47—2330; Far Eastern Commission, 9/14/47—1002; Borton, 11/23/47—481; 4/11/48—1143b; Nehmer & Crimmins, 4/25/48—1887; Stuart, 6/20/48—834; McCoy, 11/21/48—1504a; 12/19/48—1490a; McCoy, 12/19/48—1805; McCoy, 12/26/48—875b; 1/9/49—1526; McCoy, 2/27/49—1543a; 4/17/49—1558; 5/1/49—1099; 5/1/49—1728a; 5/15/49—1162; 5/15/49—2537; 5/22/49—1117; 5/22/49—1699; 6/26/49—1151; 6/26/49—1853; 7/25/49—1791; McCoy, 7/25/49—1768; 8/29/49—1143c; 8/29/49—2521; 10/24/49—1141a; 11/21/49—1143a; 11/28/49—2235; Sebald, 1/2/50—1162b; 1/16/50—1165; 2/13/50—1263; 3/13/50—2520; 4/3/50—1572; 5/22/50—2522; 7/10/50—1011; Sebald, 8/14/50—1162a; 8/21/50—860; 9/11/50—1164; 10/23/50—1298a; 12/4/50—2359; 1/8/51—2363;
Dulles, 2/12/51—2471; 2/26/51—1843; Dulles, 3/12/51—2376; 3/19/51—2439a; Dulles, 3/26/51—2382; 4/9/51—1603; Dulles, 4/9/51—2375; Dulles, 4/16/51—2377; Acheson, 4/30/51—2361; Dulles, 5/7/51—2380; 5/28/51—2437; 7/23/51—2374; 7/23/51—2383a; 7/30/51—2438; Dulles, 8/27/51—2381; 9/3/51—2371; 9/10/51—1129a; 9/17/51—2418; 9/17/51—2503; Truman, 9/17/51—2431; Dulles, 10/15/51—2446a; Allison, 11/5/51—2508; 2/4/52—2455; Allison, 2/11/52—2443; Rusk, 2/11/52—2490; 3/3/52—1852; 3/10/52—2505; Sebald, 3/31/52—2535; Allison, 4/28/52—2468a; 5/5/52—2447b; Allison, 5/5/52—2444; Ridgway, 6/9/52—2533; Alden, 10/27/52—2013a. *See also* no.35a.

Developing Economies: 6/66—1730; Ōuchi, 6/66—1727; Shimazaki, 6/66—1731

Diogenes (Montreal): Kuwabara, Winter 62—718

Documents and State Papers: Cassidy, 4/48—2031; Far Eastern Commission, 5/48—1001; Far Eastern Commission, 9/48—1124; 2/49—1548; Far Eastern Commission, 5/49—1527

Periodical Index

Doshisha Law Review: Kanayama, 56—1284; Katō, 56—1285; Tabata, 56—1214; Katō, 58—1714; Tabata, 58—1213
Dublin Review: 7/44—179b

Eastern Anthropologist: Seshaiah, 1–4/66—1966
Eastern Economist (New Delhi): 6/9/50—2354; 4/27/51—2428
Eastern World: Green, 5/47—499; Dunbabin, 8/47—1832a; Green, 9/47—499a; 1/48—2333; Murdock, 1/48—2299a; Gibson, 8–9/48—792a; Stewart, 8–9/48—2337a; Mann, 3/49—2218; Kennedy, 9/49—1760; Wolpert, 9/49—1563b; Wolpert, 12/49—1739; Kalmer, 2/50—1941; Greene, 7/50—624; 12/50—627; Woddis, 7/51—2506a; Mannin, 2 & 3/60—1724
Econometrica: Chenery, et al., 1/62—1636
Economia Internazionale: Nakayama, 2/52—1626; Fujii, 8/52—1616; Ōkita, 2/60—1655
Economic Development and Cultural Change: Kyōgoku, 10/60—1380; Namiki, 10/60—1849; Ward, 10/60—1427
Economist: 8/18/45—179a; 8/25/45—169a; 11/10/45—871b; 12/1/45—1142; 1/19/46—449b; 8/10/46—434a; 7/12/47—2325; 8/23/47—2310; 10/25/47—493; 11/1/47—496; 1/17/48—1836; 4/24/48—1144; 5/8/48—838; 8/28/48—1767a; 9/4/48—1509b; 11/20/48—1505a; 1/29/49—1415a; 2/26/49—586b; 2/26/49—2470b; 7/9/49—1549; 8/27/49—778; 9/17/49—797; 11/19/49—2344; 2/11/50—871c; 6/17/50—2352; 2/24/51—2426; 5/26/51—649a; 6/16/51—2411b; 7/21/51—2410c; 9/8/51—2407b; 10/20/51—1142a
Ecumenical Review: Kan, Spring 50—2214; Takeda, 7/51—2274
Editorial Research Reports: Brewer, 8/14/45—1231a; Patch, 9/19/47—2324a; Patch, 2/28/51—2411a; Thompson, 1/9/52—1630
Education: Egekvist, 11/48—1492; Kitasawa, 11/48—1502; Kitasawa, 2/50—2078; Tormey, 9/50—637; Martin, 2/52—679
Educational Forum: Kandel, 11/46—2073; Van Staaveren, 1/52—2129b
Educational Outlook: Webb, 1/52—2130a
Elementary School Journal: 9/46—2104b
Ethics: Nambara, 7/46—1960; Smith, 7/46—2110; Ohe, 7/56—735
Europa-Archiv: 2–3/47—504a; Volle & Rehbein, 3/5/50—1585a; Menzel, 11/5 & 12/20/52—2451a
Explorations in Entrepreneurial History: Ariga, Winter 56—1907
Export Trade and Shipper: Lindstrom, 9/20 & 9/27/48—1504; Coughran, 6/5/50—1569; Fain, 3/26/51—1591; Fiske, 9/24/51—1592

External Affairs: 12/48—855a; 2/49—1083; 11/49—586; 7/51—2412; 9/51—667; 10/51—2394b; 5/52—2448; 5/52—2449

Far Eastern Economic Review: 7/7/48—1471a; Ōhira, 7/3/58—992. See also no.35b.
Far Eastern Quarterly: Haring, 11/46—1929a; Hulse, 11/47—1932; Braibanti, 2/48—1317; Fishel, 8/49—139; Steiner, 2/50—1292; Braibanti, 5/50—1316; Morley, 5/50—21; Hsu, 2/51—872; Ward, 2/53—1336; Bisson, 5/53—1107; Yamagiwa, 11/53—2165; Dull, 2/54—1321; Burton & Langer, 2/55; Levine, 11/55—1650; Steiner, 2/56—1327
Far Eastern Survey: Embree, 9/20/44—72; Mateveev, 11/29/44—170; Johnstone, 1/31/45—91; Friedrich & Haring, 2/14/45—231; Holtom, 2/14/45—82; Kerr, 4/25/45—93; Van Patten, 5/9/45—126; Churchill, 8/1/45—67; Rowe, 8/15/45—119; Salisbury, 9/12/45—406; Keesing, 9/26/45—990; Jorgensen, 11/7/45—2213; Lattimore, 11/7/45—991; Holtom, 11/30/45—2208; Wakukawa, 2/13/46—1873; Holtom, 3/13/46—1236; Bennett, 5/8/46—1451; Cole, 5/22/46—1990; Kurihara, 5/22/46—1378; Maki, 6/19/46—1382; Eby, 7/3/46—2043; Burks, 8/14/46—135; Nehmer, 8/28/46—1886; Levi, 9/25/46—874; Reubens, 11/6/46—1772; Masland, 11/20/46—1325; Rowe, 1/29/47—1207; Rowe, 2/12/47—1207; Maki, 4/9/47—511; Torrens, 6/4/47—1901; Berkov, 7/23/47—2135; Braibanti, 9/3/47—2199; De Francis, 11/5/47—2036; Holtom, 11/5/47—2057; Levi, 11/26/47—2319; Bisson, 12/17/47—1120; Keeney, 1/28 & 2/11/48—2256; Yanaga, 3/24/48—1987; Mears, 5/5/48—1132; Cohen, 6/23/48—1489; Stewart, 7/7/48—1405; Liu, 7/28/48—18; Stratton, 8/25/48—882; Braibanti, 9/22/48—894; Hsu, 10/6/48—2518; Ike, 12/8/48—1991; Liu, 12/8/48—812; Ballantine, 12/22/48—537; Marx, 1/12/49—1884; Braibanti, 1/24/49—1339; Brown, 3/9/49—2028; Barnett, 5/4/49—1523; Comyns-Carr, 5/18/49—1056; McDiarmid, 6/15/49—544; Reday, 6/29/49—1141; Feraru, 8/24/49—1529; Cohen, 9/21/49—1524a; Johnston, 9/21/49—1542; Park, 9/21/49—606; Moran, 10/19/49—1769; Sansom, 11/2/49—608; Reubens, 11/16/49—1773; Hadley, 12/14/49—1799; Pope, 12/14/49—1889; Cohen, 12/28/49—1679; Ballantine, 2/8/50—1793a; Feraru, 5/17/50—790; Kan, 6/14/50—2254; McNelly, 9/13/50—1195; Scalapino, 3/21/51—

664a; Harper, 4/18/51—2473a; Buss, 6/13/51—2370; Dulles, 6/13/51—784; Seidensticker, 6/13/51—2421; Ōkita, 7/25/51—1601; Farley, 9/26/51—2384; Ryū, 9/26/51—2417; Quigley, 10/10/51—660; Seidensticker, 10/24/51—1856; Allison, 11/7/51—642; Finn, 11/7/51—2050; Finn, 11/21/51—2049; Roach, 11/21/51—2415; Farley, 2/27/52—2447; Kubota, 5/7/52—1625; Scalapino, 10/29/52—1401; Cohen, 11/19/52—1612; Takeuchi, 11/19/52—2536; Chamberlin, 12/21/52—2511; Irvine, 12/31/52—1619; Haring, 1/14/53—1372; Durgin 1/28/53—2206; 2/25/53—2295; Kawai, 11/53—2296; Swearingen, 4/54—1412; Steiner, 7/54—1329; Maki, 5/55—1196; Colton, 6/55—1359; Ward, 4/56—1222; Dore, 12/58—1702

Federal Reserve Bulletin: Golay, 1/52—1617

Florida State University Studies: Lensen, 52—2216

Foreign Affairs: Chow, 10/42—166a; Old, 4/44—107; Gilchrist, 7/44—988a; Sun, 10/44—178; Lin, 1/46—439; Gilmartin & Ladejinsky, 1/48—1706; Sansom, 1/48—567; Chang, 4/48—2332; Takagi, 7/48—570; Ladejinsky, 10/48—559; Yoshida, 1/51—2442; Dulles, 1/52—2471a; Menzies, 1/52—2486; Takahashi, 1/52—1629; Ballantine, 7/53—2510; Abegg, 4/55—1906; Ladejinsky, 10/59—1718; Quigley, 10/59—1204; Morton, 7/62—57; Kennan, 10/64—2477

Foreign Affairs Reports: Matsuo, 1/54—1386

Foreign Agriculture: Ladejinsky, 6/47 & 8-9/47—1721; Ladejinsky, 11/48—1848; Ladejinsky, 2/49—1720; Brown, 8/51—1832; Ladejinsky, 9/51—1719; Roelofs, 11/51—1854; Ward, 6/52—1874

Foreign Commerce Weekly: Crane, 4/13/46—1452; Weinstein, 11/1/47—1905a; 9/19/49—1540a

Foreign Policy Bulletin: Rosinger, 1/7/44—112; Rosinger, 8/18/44—114; Rosinger, 7/13/45—113; Rosinger, 8/17/45—115; Rosinger, 9/7/45—404; Bolles, 9/14/45—375; Rosinger, 9/21/45—403; Rosinger, 10/19/45—880; Rosinger, 1/4/46—878; Rosinger, 1/11/46—1252; Rosinger, 2/14/46—1397; Rosinger, 4/19/46—1396; Rosinger, 10/18/46—458; Rosinger, 10/25/46—879; Rosinger, 11/1/46—457; Rosinger, 3/28/47—2328; Rosinger, 4/25/47—1481; Rosinger, 5/16/47—1480; Rosinger, 12/12/47—2327; Farley, 11/26/48—1493; Farley, 12/10/48—1751; Bolles, 6/3/49—582; Farley, 8/26/49—1528; Colton, 4/28/50—2345a; Riggs, 9/15/50—2355; Scalapino, 5/18/51—977; Bolles, 6/22/51—2368; Bolles, 7/20/51—2369; Bolles, 8/31/51—2367; Scalapino, 10/1/51—2420

Foreign Policy Reports: Rosinger, 9/1/43—116; Rosinger, 6/1/44—111; Johnstone, 9/15/45—989a; Rosinger & Ringwood, 5/15/47—1398; Rosinger, 5/15/47—520; Cohen, 2/1/49—1525; Scalapino, 3/15/51—1402a

Foreign Trade: Britton, 11/19/49—1523a; Britton, 1/28/50—1564a; Britton, 2/18/50—1564b

Fortnightly: Green, 7/46—430; Morris, 11/46—446; Green, 6/48—553; 8/49—2293; Green, 8/50—623; Greene, 9/50—1840; Greene, 1/52—2515; Smythe, 9/52—1971

Fortune: 2/42—87; 4/44—129; 11/45—384c; 12/45—791a; 3/46—1454a; Maurer, 3/47—514; Kramer, 6/47—1474; K., B., 9/48—1501; 4/49—1560; Solow, 4/49—1093b; MacArthur, 6/49—944; 10/49—1550; 5/51—1589

Forum: Craemer, 10/45—1232; Shalett, 10/45—406a; Strong, 10/45—1257; 11/45—377; Li-em, 11/45—390; Gayn, 3/46—428; Gayn, 10/46—426; Starr, 2/47—1781; Clark, 7/48—544; Allen, 9/48—1228; McEvoy, 9/48—560; Deverall, 4/49—2037

Free World: Katayama, 3/42—92; Wildes, 8/45—131; Corey, 9/45—379; Price & Goette, 9/45—1251; Kaplan, 12/45—386; Baba, 2/46—417; Sullivan, 4 & 5/46—2115; Westerfield, 4/46—474; Katona, 11/46—1071; Lipp, 12/46—440

Fourth International: De Silva, 9/51—2373

Gazette: Ikeuchi, 60—1375

Geographical Review: Woollacott, 10/47—531; Espenshade, 1/49—1833; Trewartha, 7/50—1735

Georgetown Law Journal: Zanard, 51/52—2460b; Salwin, Spring 62—1291a

Georgia Review: Robinson, Summer 53—744

Great Britain and the East: 2/46—1805a; Bate, 12/46—1450; Galbraith, 1/47—498; Horner, 1/47—1468; Keeton, 6/47—505b; Rosinger, 8/47—520; Samain, 7/48—1806a; Penworth, 6/49—1547b; 11/49—2295a; Holland, 4/50—626; Bouchier, 6/50—1564; Bee, 3/51—1588; 6 & 7/51—1598a

Grotius Society *Transactions*, see *Transactions of the Grotius Society*

Harper's Magazine: Grattan, 1/44—80; Peffer, 4/44—109b; Lamott, 6/45—95a; May, 3/46—443; Stimson, 2/47—247; Cochrane, 9/47—487; Mears, 7/50—1580; Wheeler, 1/51—844; Rovere & Schlesinger, 7/51—975; Beal, 11/51—2366

Periodical Index

Harvard Business Review: Hadley, 7/48—1800
Harvard Educational Review: Brinkman, Summer 46—2027; Penrose, Summer 46—453; Duke, Fall 64—2040
Harvard Law Review: Meyers, 12/50—1308; Rabinowitz, 11/56—1311
Hibbert Journal: Scott, 4/45—175; England, 1/46—424
Historama: Samuels, 10/67—1253
Hitotsubashi Academy *Annals*, see *Annals of the Hitotsubashi Academy*
Hitotsubashi Journal of Law and Politics: Sugihara, 4/63—1212
Holiday: Sheean, 12/49—609
Horizon: Busch, 9/47—2284
Human Organization: Montgomery, Summer 49—908; Ishino, Summer 56—1754a

Illinois Law Review: Fuqua, 3–4/46—1059a
Independent Woman: Penrose, 11/48—2265; Beard, 11/50—2023a; Spence, 3/56—2268
India Quarterly: Grassmuck, 10–12/47—1176; Jain, 10–12/48—1498; Ōkita, 10–12/51—1600
Indian Journal of Economics: Yamamura, 7/64—1814
Indian Year Book of International Affairs: Rama Rao, 53—1088
Indiana Law Journal: Dionisopoulos, Summer 56—999b
Industrial Labor Relations Forum: Schwartz, 11/65—1774
Industry and Labor: 3/1/49—2183; 5/15/49—2177
Infantry Journal: Tench, 8/46—410; Compton, 2/47—242
Institute of World Affairs *Proceedings*, see *Proceedings of the Institute of World Affairs*
International Affairs: Redman, 1/44—171; 10/46—1172; Guillain, 7/50—625; Holland, 7/52—2517; Sissons, 1/61—1009
International and Comparative Law Quarterly: Yamada, 4/55—1226
International Commission of Jurists Journal: Tanaka, Winter 59/Summer 60—1314
International Conciliation: 4/45—110; 1/47—2116; Zook, 1/47—2133; Horwitz, 11/50—1065
International Conference of Orientalists in Japan *Transactions*, see *Transactions of the International Conference of Orientalists in Japan*
International Economic Review: Klein & Shinkai, 1/63—1647; Ueno, 5/63—1671
International Journal: Martin, Winter 50/51—2347
International Journal of Opinion and Attitude Research: Passin, Spring 51—2301
International Labour Review: 7/49—1557; International Labor Office, 7/49—1536; Rohrlich, 4/50—2178; 7/50—1764; Hsieh, 11/50—1879
International Organization: 2/47—847; 2/47—862; 2/47—1067; 6/47—863; 9/47—849; 9/47—864; 2/48—850; 2/48—865; 2/48—899; Stratton, 2/48—882a; 6/48—866; 6/48—995b; 6/48—997; 2/49—867; 2/49—1068; 5/49—868; 8/49—869; 5/50—1154; 2/51—2359; Blakeslee, 8/51—853; 11/51—2394c
International Review of Missions: Shafer, 4/46—2223; McLaren, 7/46—2217; Sansbury, 10/49—2222; Shorrock, 4/52—2227; Iglehart, 7/52—2212
International Social Science Journal: 61—738; Fukutake, 61—1926; Kawashima, 61—1286; Makino, 61—2087; Takahashi, 61—1980; Takayanagi, 61—1216; Tanimo, 61—1982; Tsuru, 61—1668; Nakano, 62—1958
International Statistical Bulletin: Morita, 54—1996
International Studies: Ginsburgs & Shrewsbury, 1/64—1838

Japan Annual of International Affairs: Sugiyama, 61—1859; Ōhira, 62—1654a; Tamura, 62—995a
Japan Christian Quarterly: Minami, 4/54—1953
Japan Interpreter: Morley, Summer 70—394; Titus, Summer 70—1260a
Japan Quarterly: Rōyama, 10–12/54—745; Kitani, 1–3/56—2298; Bowles, 7–9/56—2281; Maeda, 10–12/56—2085; Saheki, 1–3/57—2491; Ebata, 10–12/58—1366; Itagaki, 10–12/59—1128; Blakeney, 10–12/60—1270; Takayanagi, 7–9/62—1259; Nishijima, 1–3/63—1008
Japan Science Review: Economic Sciences: Moriya & Nakamura, 55—2090; Sakamoto, 55—1730a
Japanese Annual of International Law: Takano, 59—995
Journal du droit international: 53—2427
Journal of Asian Studies: Yamamura, 8/64—1815; Maki, 5/65—19; Ward, 5/65—1221; Borton, 2/66—51; Yamamura, 8/66—1812
Journal of Criminal Law, Criminology, and Political Science: Nakahara, 11–12/55—1344
Journal of Criminal Law and Criminology: Fuqua, 5/46—1059a
Journal of Documentation: Ichikawa, 6/51—2249
Journal of East Asiatic Studies (Manila): Bennett, 10/52—891
Journal of Economic History: Taeuber, Fall 51—2008
Journal of Educational Sociology: Hartford, 4/50—2056a; Kaigo, 9/52—2071; Makino,

9/52—2086; Nishimoto, 9/52—2095; Shimizu, 9/52—2182; Murakami & Iwahashi, 3/56—2092
Journal of Farm Economics: Raper, 5/51—1729; Williamson, 5/51—1738; Campbell, 8/52—1699c; Ohkawa, 12/61—1850
Journal of Finance: Cohen, 3/50—1568
Journal of Forestry: Spillers, 12/46—1857b; Varney, 7/47—1449a
Journal of Geography: Roucek, 10/52—993
Journal of Higher Education: Ballou, 5/52—2022a
Journal of Home Economics: Lewis, 3/49—2081c; Lewis, 4/50—2081b; Maack, 12/50—630a; Williamson, 12/50—1985a; Stanley, 2/51—2112a
Journal of International Affairs: Langer, Spring 52—678; Langer, 54—803
Journal of Local Administration Overseas: Dore, 62—1701
Journal of Political Economy: Shavell, 4/48—1689; Bronfenbrenner, 8/50—1565; Shinohara, 12/59—1665; Ott, 4/61—1656; Bronfenbrenner, 6/63—698a; Yamamura, 10/65—1811
Journal of Politics: Masland, 11/47—513; Ulmer, 2/57—1333
Journal of Public Law: Sparkman, 52—2466b
Journal of Social and Political Ideas in Japan: Kobayashi, 8/63—1191; Satō, 8/63—1208; Kaigo, 12/63—2072; Mochida, 12/63—2088; Ogawa, 12/63—2097; Ōta, 12/63—2100; Fukutake, 12/64—1923; Tsuji, 12/64—1447b; Hayashi, 8/65—2289
Journal of Social Issues: Henry, 8/46—2290
Journal of Social Psychology: Gulick, 8/47—1929
Journal of Soil and Water Conservation: Swanson, 10/48—1867
Journal of the American Association of University Women: Holmes, Spring 48—2248
Journal of the American Oriental Society: Hulse, 7/46—1931a; Yamagiwa, 1-3/48—2166
Journal of the American Pharmaceutical Association: Sams, 10/49—2167
Journal of the Missouri Bar: Neel, 1/47—1805b
Journal of the National Education Association: Young, 2/46—2132a; Givens, 10/46—2051b; Givens, 12/50—2051a
Journal of the Oriental Society of Australia: Caiger, 12/65—2029; Caiger, 12/67—2030
Journal of the Royal Central Asian Society: Profumo, 4/47—456; Kagawa, 4/50—629; Sansom, 10/51—664
Journal of the Royal United Service Institution: Redman, 2/46—456a; Slocum, 5/49—610
Journal of the United Service Institution of India: Singh, 7/49—881a; Singh, 7-10/51—881b
Journalism Quarterly: Allen, 12/47—2134; Mott, 12/47—2152

Kagami: Hayashi, 65—2289
Knickerbocker Weekly: 4/1/46—429a
Kobe Economic and Business Review: Fujita, 53—1639a; Miyata, 53—1653a; Nose, 53—1685a; Watanabe, 53—1672; Yamamoto, 54—1905b; Kawata, 66—1543
Koreana Quarterly: Lee, 59—808
Kyoto University Economic Review: Honjō, 10/57—1640a; Echigo, 10/58—1877

Labor and Nation: Starr, 1-2 & 3-4/47—1782
Labour Research: 11/46—415
Labour Monthly: Woddis & Stewart, 11/48—578a; Arnot, 2/51—2468c
Land: Koenig, Autumn 47—1473a
Land Economics: Hewes, 8/49—1710; Chia, 11/49—1700; Eyre, 8/52—1704; Eyre, 2/55—1704a
Library Journal: Roedel, 12/1/49—2265a
Library of Congress *Quarterly Journal*, see *Quarterly Journal of the Library of Congress*
Life: Fleisher, 4/16/45—76a; 7/16/45—86; 8/27/45—98; Mydans, 9/3/45—396; 9/10/45—411a; 10/29/45—1804b; 11/12/45—1068b; 12/3/45—391; Lauterbach, 1/14/46—963; 2/11/46—1158a; 2/18/46—471; 12/2/46—419; Mydans, 5/5/47—515; 1/26/48—1057; Osborne, 9/25/50—969; Osborne, 11/27/50—970; 2/5/51—1342; Gibney, 9/10/51—647; 9/17/51—2394

Magazine of Wall Street: Horoth, 9/27/47—1469; Horoth, 7/31/48—1497; Horoth, 4/23/49—1534; Horoth, 5/20/50—1570; Horoth, 9/8/51—2391
Military Government Journal: Gray, 1/48—902b; Whitman, 1/48—1519; Seibert, 4/48—1855; Hays, 5/48—1341; Oppler, 5/48—1289; Overseas Consultants, Inc., 5/48—1135; Warner, 5/48—577; Grilli, 6/48—555; Nishiyama, 6/48—1507; Saitō, 6/48—1347; Falco, 7/48—1123; Tilton, 7/48—1332; Baruch, 8/48—1487b; Schwartz, 8/48—568; Eichler, 9-10/48—1122; Sams, 9-10/48 & 1-2/49 & Summer 49—2180; Hamilton, 1-2/49—591; Shepard, Winter 49—914; Allen, Fall 49—1046; Crawford, Fall 49—897
Military Review: Willoughby, 6/46—2309; Hille, 2/48—904
Minnesota Law Review: Salwin, 5/48—1806
Missionary Herald at Home and Abroad: Shafer, 6/48—2224

Periodical Index

Missouri Bar *Journal*, see *Journal of the Missouri Bar*

Modern Asian Studies: Caiger, 1/69—2029a

Modern Language Journal: Atkinson, 5/46—2021; Van Zandt, 11/49—2130; Eells, 5/52—2047

Modern Review: Roskolenko, 7/47—1481a

Monthly Labor Review: 10/45—1763; Weigert, 2/47—1792; 9/47—1755; Hepler, 1/49—1754; Amis, 10/50—1740; Shurcliff, 10/52—1777

Monumenta Nipponica: Herzog, 51—1179; Wagatsuma, 56—1296; Loduchowski, 62—2083

Nation: Pacificus, 10/14/44—108a; Pacificus, 2/3/45—108; 6/16/45—229; 6/23/45—121; Bisson, 7/14/45—66; Salisbury, 7/14/45—120; 8/4/45—88; 8/25/45—105; Kirchway, 8/25/45—94; 9/1/45—103; 9/8/45—407; 9/15/45—380; Roth, 9/15/45—1346; 9/22/45—411; Matsumoto, 9/29/45—393; Roth, 9/29/45—405; Stone, 9/29/45—408; 12/22/45—374; Roth, 12/29/45—1399; 1/19/46—1111b; 1/26/46—1392a; Roth, 3/16/46—2155; Strauss, 10/26/46—1807; Strauss, 11/9/46—1732; Strauss, 11/30/46—465; Stewart, 7/26/47—524; Granada, 8/14/48—1496; 8/21/48—1775; Strauss, 8/21/48—1496; Granada, 10/9/48—1496; 12/18/48—1804a; Costello, 1/22/49—1339a; 12/24/49—2146a; Smith, 8/12/50—2492; Riggs, 10/7/50—2356; Martin, 3/10/51—2484; Tiltman, 6/2/51—2425; 8/4/51—2397; Lattimore, 8/4/51—2526; 8/11/51—2410b; Kirchwey, 9/1/51—2399; Smythe, 9/1/51—666; Kano, 9/15/51—2398; Kirchwey, 9/15/51—2525; Kuh, 9/22/51—2401; Bisson, 2/2/52—1610; Mears, 3/22/52—2485; Ball, 3/27/54—690

National and English Review: Smith, 4/51—2422a; see also *National Review* (London)

National Conference of Social Work *Proceedings*, see *Proceedings of the National Conference of Social Work*

National Education Association *Journal*, see *Journal of the National Education Association*

National Education Association *Proceedings*, see *Proceedings of the National Education Association*

National Geographic Magazine: Price, 11/45—1250; Huberman, 4/47—1841; Wallisen, 6/49—615; Vosburgh, 5/50—640; Price, 11/53—681

National Municipal Review: 9/51—1375c; Warp, 10/52—1337; Warp, 4/53—1338

National Parent-Teacher: Stoddard, 9/46—2114

National Review (London): Somerville, 7/45—177; Pearce, 9/47—2325a; Menken, 6/48—563; Capper, 4/49—855b

National Tax Journal: Shavell, 6/48—1690; Sundelson, 6/50—1692; Bronfenbrenner, 12/50—1677; Bronfenbrenner & Kogiku, 9/57 & 12/57—1678

Nation's Business: Fellers, 2/48—549a; Wood, 7/49—2344b

New American Mercury, see *American Mercury*

New Leader: Monahan, 11/2/46—1389; Sano, 4/10/48—566; Naoi, 11/20/48—1770; Deverall, 1/15/51—2470; Holliday, 2/19/51—2167b; Naoi, 5/7/51—967a; Naoi, 7/23/51—2408; Naoi, 10/8/51—2408a; Maki, 12/10/51—2405a

New Republic: Bisson, 5/28/45—65; Holtom, 5/28/45—82a; 7/30/45—124; 8/27/45—64; 8/27/45—73; 8/27/45—74; Bisson, 8/27/45—133; 9/3/45—1265; 9/10/45—1418; Reynolds, 9/10/45—402; Epstein, 9/17/45—73; Oda, 9/17/45—1244; 9/24/45—382; 10/1/45—400; 12/3/45—384; 1/14/46—1112; Matsumoto, 1/14/46—1385; 2/25/46—1100; Tiltman, 8/26/46—467; Tiltman, 9/30/46—886; Tiltman, 12/9/46—1462; 12/30/46—1090a; Tiltman, 1/6/47—2127; Costello, 2/10/47—490; Tiltman, 2/10/47—526; Lauterbach, 3/3/47—1240; Costello, 3/31/47—2314a; Costello, 5/5/47—1362; 7/28/47—2320a; McDonald, 9/1/47—1723; Costello, 1/5/48—547; Gayn, 8/9/48—1126; 5/30/49—612; 10/31/49—2343; 10/16/50—2345; Lattimore, 6/11/51—2402; Eichler, 9/17/51—2383; Smythe, 1/28/52—684a

New Statesman and Nation: 9/1/45—180; Roth, 4/6/46—459; 9/7/46—910; Bickerton, 9/28 & 10/5/46—418; 10/26/46—876; 11/23/46—851; 9/13/47—2317a; 12/11/48—771; 1/29/49—1381c; 11/26/49—608a; 4/29/50—2353; Woodman, 6/24/50—2360; 4/21/51—655; 7/21/51—2405; 9/1/51—2425a; 4/12/52—2280; Inagaki, 9/6/52—1618; Yamamoto, 10/25/52—1431; Martin, 9/24/55—728

New Times: Petrov, 10/1/45—399; Zhukov, 11/15/45—846; Markov, 4/15/46—1080; Avarin, 5/1/46—1351; Gribov, 4/18/47—1753; Golunsky, 5/1/47—1060; Markov, 7/11/47—1384; Markov, 8/27/47—2321; Markov, 9/10/47—1131; Bezrodnov, 12/10/47—952a; Berezhkov, 1/28/48—1048; Trainin, 3/17/48—1098; Markov, 4/21/48—1081; Markov, 7/28/48—1768b; 9/8/48—572; Varshavsky, 9/8/48—575; Sveshnikov, 11/10/48—1096; Krylov, 6/1/49—596; Markov, 6/22/49—2340;

Raginsky, 1/8/50—1086; 2/8/50—1051; I., V., 5/1/50—1156; 8/30/50—622; Zhukov, 12/20/50—1817; Krylov, 3/7/51—2479; Okonishnikov, 4/18/51—2154; Shmelyov, 6/20/51—2421a; Rudnev, 7/18/51—661; Trigorin, 7/25/51—2430; 9/12/51—2440; Gromyko, 9/12/51—2390 & 2423; Krylov, 12/12/51—2480; Krylov, 1/9/52—2451; Tokumaro, 6/11/52—685

New World Review: Field, 5/51—2384a; Smith, 10/51—2422b

New York Times Magazine: Tolischus, 8/19/45—1261; Wolfe, 8/26/45—132a; Kluckhorn, 9/2/45—1004; Peffer, 9/2/45—109a; Embree, 9/9/45—381; Kluckhorn, 9/9/45—388; Kluckhorn, 9/16/45—389; Jones, 9/23/45—1238; Kluckhorn, 9/30/45—387; Steiner, 10/7/45—2002; Parrott, 10/14/45—398; Romulo, 10/21/45—826; Parrott, 10/28/45—2264; Jones, 11/4/45—385; Evatt, 2/3/46—787; 2/10/46—2131; Parrott, 3/10/46—451; Parrott, 3/17/46—912; Crane, 3/24/46—2034a; Schwartz, 4/14/46—461; Parrott, 5/12/46—1247; Parrott, 6/2/46—2263; Parrott, 8/25/46—452; Parrott, 11/10/46—2101; Crane, 12/1/46—1233; Parrott, 1/5/47—516; Parrott, 8/10/47—2324; Parrott, 5/22/49—1248; Falk, 6/12/49—898; Kantor, 9/25/49—593; Parrott, 2/26/50—2351; Parrott, 4/15/51—658; Parrott, 9/2/51—2529; Parrott, 11/25/51—659; Parrott, 4/27/52—680; Bowers, 8/30/70—697

New Yorker: Mears, 10/19/46—444; Mears, 11/23/46—445; Splane, 4/10/48—977b

New Zealand Law Journal: Quentin-Baxter, 6/7/49—1085a

Newsweek: 1/27 & 2/10/47—1106; Kern, 6/23/47—507; Kern, 8/4/47—2318; 11/3/47—1486; Kauffman, 12/1/47—1472; 3/15/48—1491; Packenham, 6/7/48—1246; 10/25/48—578; Pope, 4/18/49—1563; 9/12/49—600; 2/20/50—822; 5/8/50—1989; 6/12/50—1426; 1/22/51—2474; 6/18/51—2396; 8/27/51—2439; 9/10/51—2523; 9/17/51—2414; Kern, 12/24/51—2478; Kern, 1/14/52—2450. See also no.37a.

Nieman Reports: Martin, 4/48—2147

Nineteenth Century: Kennard, 9/46—1759

Nineteenth Century and After: Green, 3/49—589

Northwestern University Law Review: Ukai, 1–2/57—1219

Notes et études documentaires: 5/3/60—1367

Öffentliche Verwaltung: Shimizu, 6/62—1211

Ohio Bar Association Report: Reel, 6/3/46—1090

Ohio Journal of Science: Ludmer, 11/49—601

Orbis: Ginsburgs & Shrewsbury, 63—1837

Orient/West: Hoshii, 5/62—1180; Fukutake, 3/62—1924

Oriental Economist: Tsuda, 8/57—2496; 12/58–4/59—1816; Igarashi, 1/59—1643; 4/59—1153; 5/59—1660; 8/59—1394. See also no.39.

Oriental Society of Australia *Journal*, see *Journal of the Oriental Society of Australia*

Osaka University Law Review: Kakudo, 53—1306; Isozaki, 55—1181

Osteuropa: Kurata, 10/55—802

Oxford Univ. Institute of Statistics *Bulletin*: Morgan, 12/48—1506

Pacific Affairs: Spinks, 12/42—122; Bisson, 3/44—65a; Spinks, 3/44—122a; 6/44—76c; 3/45—169; Rowe, 3/45—118; Mukai, 3/46—1457; Edwards, 9/46—1795; Spinks, 9/46—1403; Sansom, 12/46—2105b; Farley, 6/47—1752; Quigley, 9/47—1113; Holman, 12/47—1127; Maki, 12/47—1441; Ball, 3/48—536; Stewart, 3/48—1892; Bennett, 6/48—1118; Grad, 6/48—1708; Wang, 6/48—842; Cohen, 9/48—1490; Takahashi, 12/48—1416; Kuroda, 3/49—2146; Warner, 9/49—1167; Tsuru, 12/49—1559; Kawai, 6/50—2475; Ike, 9/50—1936; Taeuber, 9/50—2007; Langer & Swearingen, 12/50—1381; Sansom, 9/51—622; Hollerman, 12/51—1593; Dore, 6/52—2039; Guillain, 9/52—2473; Kinoshita, 9/53—1945; Smythe & Watanabe, 12/53—1255; Colton, 12/55—1171; Taeuber, 3/56—2010; Morris, 3/58—2487

Pacific Historical Review: Kawai, 11/50—146; Kawai, 11/53—145; May, 5/55—190; Wittner, 2/71—2231

Pacific Spectator: Smith, Summer 47—522; Bisson, Winter 50—618; Cole, Spring 50—2285; Mukai, Autumn 51—656

Parliamentary Affairs: Scalapino, Summer 52—1210; Yanaga, Summer 57—1432; Brett, Winter 57/58—1319

Personnel Administration: Shirven & Speicher, 7/51—1443b

Phylon: Smythe, 9/52—1975; Smythe & Naitoh, 3 & 6/53—1976

Plain Talk: Byrne, 2/48—1354; 11/49—875a

Politeia: McDonald, 52—814

Political Affairs: Jerome, 9/51—2397a

Political Quarterly: Fisher, 7–9/46—1921a; Quigley, 1–3/50—634; Jansen, 4–6/56—1938

Political Science (Wellington, N.Z.): Kawai, 9/58—1238a

Political Science Quarterly: Borton, 6/47—52; McNelly, 12/52—1006; Borton, 9/55—696; McNelly, 6/59—1194; McNelly, 9/62—1007

Periodical Index

Il Politico: Takeuchi, 12/61—1733
Politique étrangère: Dorget, 7/46—423a; Guillain, 2/48—555a; Morris, 5–6/56—731
Population: Okasaki, 4–6/52—1997
Proceedings of the Academy of Political Science: Overton, 1/55—736
Proceedings of the American Society of International Law: Allison, 4/24–26/52—2468
Proceedings of the Institute of World Affairs: Fisher, 43—75; Michael, 46—2322; Spencer, 46—464; Beuschlein, 47—480; Buss, 47—483; Fertig, 47—495; Carus, 48—1488; Teters, 48—1515; Ketzel, 49—595; King, 50—630; Martin, 50—602
Proceedings of the National Conference of Social Work: Smith, 47—2111
Proceedings of the National Education Association: Givens, 45–46—2051
Progressive: Lens, 12/53—722
Psychiatry: Lifton, 64—1946
Public Administration: Kim, Winter 70—1439b
Public Administration Review: Esman, Spring 47—1435
Public Finance: Hicks, 51—1681; Itō, 53—1682; Tokoyama, 53—1667; Nishikawa, 63—1326
Public Opinion Quarterly: Friedrich, Winter 43—230; Gorer, Winter 43—78; Knutson, Fall 45—2299; Hilgard, Fall 46—2292; Thayer, Spring 51—2306b; Scott, Summer 52—1965; Cohen, Spring 56—2462
Public Personnel Review: MacDonald & Esman, 10/46—1440a; Roser, 10/50—1443a
Publishers' Weekly: Tuttle, 3/9/46—2163; Melcher, 5/3/47—2148; Melcher, 6/14/47—2149; 12/11/48—2135a; 8/27/49—2266b

Quarterly Journal of Economics: Reubens, 8/47—1479; Rosen, 8/53—1662
Quarterly Journal of the Library of Congress: Takeshita, 5/53—1217; Cho, 10/66—1169; Cho, 10/67—6
Queen's Quarterly (Kingston, Ontario): Cowley, Summer 58—1363

Reader's Digest: Lamott, 8/45—95a; Zacharias, 12/45—161a; May, 6/46—443; Monahan, 12/46—1389; Baldwin, 3/48—532; Durgin, 8/48—2243; Clark, 9/48—544; McEvoy, 10/48—560; McEvoy, 5/50—967; Wheeler, 3/51—844; Willoughby, 2/52—687; Vining, 10/52—1264; Whitney, 2/56—982
Reconciliation: Sayre, 1/50—634a
Report on Indonesia: 9/30/51—2362c
Reporter: Tiltman, 3/20/51—670a; Ōi, 2/16/54—2300
Research: Kelly, 8/50—2257
Review: (Tokyo) Onoe, 5/65—820
Review of Economics and Statistics: Ehrlich, 11/57—1638
Review of Politics: Tibesar, 10/45—1260
Revue de Paris: Chéroy, 1/54—702
Revue des deux mondes: Guérin, 12/51—2472
Revue du droit public et de la science politique en France et à l'étrangère: Fukase, 11–12/63—1003
Revue française de science politique: Lequiller & Fistie, 10–12/57—17a
Revue générale de droit international public: Tixier, 54—2467
Revue politique et parlementaire: Koever, 5/51—2400
Rice University Studies: Norbeck, Winter 71—1160
Rotarian: Yuasa, 3/51—2132b
Round Table: 12/45—992a; 3/52—2531
Royal Central Asian Society *Journal*, see *Journal of the Royal Central Asian Society*
Royal Engineers Journal: Bell, 51—851a
Royal United Service Institution *Journal*, see *Journal of the Royal United Service Institution*
Rural Sociology: Raper, 3/51—1964; Bennett & Ishino, 3/55—693

Saturday Evening Post: Noble, 9/29/45—449; Tregaskis, 9/29–10/27/45—927a; 10/27/45—983a; Zacharias, 11/17/45—161a; Worden, 12/15/45—931a; Gustafson, 1/5/46—141; Snow, 5/11/46—463; Sommers, 5/25/46—977a; Snow, 6/15/46—1147; Snow, 6/22/46—462; Noble, 7/27/46—2095b; Noble, 8/10/46—1243a; Noble, 11/23/46—818; Berrigan, 11/8/47—987a; Waln, 3/20/48—2308; Berrigan, 6/19/48—892; 8/14/48—1810b; Berrigan & Ladejinsky, 1/8/49—1699a; Reischauer, 4/23/49—2344a; Waln, 4/30/49—2308a; Mears, 6/18/49—603a; MacArthur, 7/30/49—603a; Noble, 10/12/49—1159; Mears, 4/29/50—631; Worden, 1/20/51—1348b; Craig, 8/26/67—138
Saturday Review of Literature: Chapman, 7/31/48—2136; Cousins, 3/3/51—645; Cohen, 8/14/51—644; Telberg, 8/18/51—2162; Cousins, 1/19/52—2288
School and Society: Hicks, 12/29/45—2056b; Bagley, 6/1/46—2022; Abe, 8/3/46—2013; Atkinson, 8/17/46—2020; Kandel, 8/24/46—2074; 7/3/48—2031a; Anderson, 6/3/50—2016; Eells, 6/23/51—2046; Eells, 9/22/51—2045; Crow, 2/9/52—2035; Luhmer, 5/31/52—2084
School Life: Benjamin, 6/46—2024
School Review: Cronbach, 4/48—2034b; Shimbori, Summer 60—2109

Science: Swanson, 9/19/47—1868; Clapp, 5/14/48—2238; Schenck, 10/8/48—1820; Grant, 11/17/50—1818b
Science Digest: Price, 12/45—2220
Science News Letter: Van Der Water, 10/45—412
Scientific Monthly: Berlin, 1/47—2167a; Kelly, 1/49—2258
Social Education: Klee, 12/52—2079
Social Forces: Kerlinger, 10/51—1943; Kerlinger, 3/53—1942; Smythe, 3/53—1972; Steiner, 3/53—2003
Social Research: Smythe, 12/52—1254
Social Science: Godshall, 7/43—77
Social Studies: Brinkman, 12/46—2027a; Klinger, 10/47—1945a
Social Work Journal: Wilson, 4/50—2197a
Sociologia Internationalis: Namba, 63—1959
Sociology and Social Research: Steiner, 9–10/46—1977
Sociology of Education: Shimbori, Fall 63—2267
South Atlantic Quarterly: Widgery, 10/43—130; Hogan, 10/46—1064b; Mignone, 7/48—564
Southern Economic Journal: Yamamura, 4/66—1813
Southwestern Journal of Anthropology: Hulse, Summer 47—1934; Hulse, Winter 48—1931; Bennett & Nagai, Summer 53—1913
Soviet Press Translations: Pevsner, 11/30/46—454; Yarovoi, 1/15/47—1485; Yarovoi, 3/15/47—845; Sibiryakov, 4/15/47—521; Kudryavtsev, 5/15/47—1762; Kim, 5/31/47—2145; Markov, 6/14/47—1383; Kudryavtsev, 7/1/47—1377; Kudryavtsev, 9/15/47—508; Kudryavtsev, 11/1/47—1717; Moran, 11/1/47—2151; Kudryavtsev, 11/15/47—1475; Ulyanov, 12/1/47—836; Kudryavtsev, 3/1/48—1503; Mayevsky, 4/1/48—1387; Vasilyev, 4/1/48—1101; 6/15/48—565; 6/15/48—2104; 7/15/48—823; Raginsky & Rozenblit, 7/15/48—1087; Kudryavtsev, 2/1/49—1075; 2/15/49—1364; Mayevsky, 2/15/49—1388; Troitsky, 4/1/49—1420; 4/15/49—1561; Kudryavtsev, 5/1/49—962; Vladimirova, 6/1/49—1562; Kudryavtsev, 7/1/49—1192; Kudryavtsev, 9/1/49—597; Vikentyev, 9/15/49—2011b; Mayevsky, 10/1/49—2341; Gontcharov, 10/15/49—1707; Eidus, 12/1/49—2339; Ivtsev, 1/1/50—1537; Kudryavtsev, 1/1/50—598; Eidus, 2/1/50—588; 3/1/50—1395; Kudryavtsev, 4/15/50—599; Pevsner, 7/1/50—1583; Popov, 7/1/50—1584; Vasilyev, 7/1/50—1101a; Viktorov, 10/7/50—1165a; Yershov, 11/15/50—1587; Marinin, 1/1/51—2483c; Chou, 2/1/51—2423b; Eidus, 2/1/51—2471c; Kislenko, 2/1/51—620; Terentyev, 3/10/51—2424b; Kudryavtsev, 3/15/51—2481; 4/15/51—2422; Zhukov, 4/15/51—2507; Markov, 9/1/51—2406; Mayevsky, 9/1/51—2407; Lukyanov, 10/1/51—654; 10/15/51—2404; Orekhov, 10/15/51—2410a; Kudryavtsev, 12/1/51—2482; Eidus, 3/15/52—1613; Kudryavtsev, 5/15/52—2483; Ulanovsky, 9/1/52—2457
Soviet Russia Today: Arnold, 12/47—477a
Spectator: Halliwell, 5/24/46—431; Butler, 8/29/47—1464a; Godwin, 10/3/47—1838a; Greenwood, 11/7/47—2288a; Gauntlett, 3/31/50—1367b; Fitzgerald, 6/15/51—2384c; Smith, 6/22/51—2267a; Walton, 6/22/51—2384c; 9/7/51—2423a; Waithman, 9/14/51—2439c
Stanford Law Review: Coleman, 12/56—1271
State Government: Dulles, 11/51—2446a
Statist: 6/26/48—1518a; 12/18/48—565a
Survey Graphic: Baldwin, 8/47—478

Taxes: Pierson, 8/47—1686; Cohen, 6/50—1680
Teachers College Record: Morito, 4/59—2089
Tempes modernes: Chambon, 8/51—2512
Textile World: Jessup, 1/48—1880; 1/48—1881
Tiers-Monde: Brochier, 10–12/62—1635
Time: 1/14/46—455; 5/31/48—557; 5/9/49—605; 9/17/51—2416
Town Meeting: Satō, 9/27/49—1549a; Brown & Zacharias, 8/22/50—2469a
Transactions of the Asiatic Society of Japan: De Becker, 12/54—1274
Transactions of the Grotius Society: Comyns-Carr, 48—1055
Transactions of the International Conference of Orientalists in Japan: Cowley, 62—2239
Twentieth Century: Hudson, 8/51—649; 11/51—2534

United Asia: Browne, 50—1566; Bronfenbrenner, 51—1588a; Maki, 12/55—726; Hidaka, 9/56—1930; Kido, 9/56—2144; Kume, 9/56—2259; Munakata, 9/56—2091; Tsuji, 9/56—755
United Empire: Morris, 11/45—395a; Galbraith, 1–2/47—498; Blunden, 9–10/50—618a
United Nations World: Granada, 2/48—2140; Gilbert, 4/48—551; Buck, 2/49—2283; Warner, 6/49—2012; Zacharias, 8/49—161; Smythe, 6/52—684
United Service Institution of India *Journal*, see *Journal of the United Service Institution of India*
United States Department of State Bulletin, see *Department of State Bulletin*
United States Naval Institute Proceedings:

Periodical Index

Von Benschoten, 5/47—528; Young, 4/48—2234; Salomon, 8/48—2266a; Slocum, 1/49—610; Holbrook, 1/50—2473b

United States News: 1/25/46—1453a; 3/8/46—1458; 3/28/47—2320; 4/4/47—1484; 5/9/47—2331b; 2/20/48—1499; 3/12/48—1509; 3/19/48—959a; 4/16/48—966; 4/23/48—1511; 9/17/48—556

U.S. News and World Report: 3/4/49—915; 3/4/49—1532; 6/17/49—979; 7/29/49—1538; 8/12/49—1540; 8/26/49—911; 9/9/49—939; 2/17/50—795; 3/17/50—1235; 4/7/50—2524; 4/28/50—2294; 6/16/50—632; 8/4/50—1340; 12/15/50—796; 4/20/51—650; 4/27/51—2441; 9/7/51—651; Lawrence, 9/14/51—2403; Truman, 9/14/51—2431; 11/30/51—1342a

U.S. Office of Education *Bulletin*: Sansom, 45—174a

University of Chicago Round Table: Colwell, D'Arms & Stoddard, 7/28/46—2033a

University of Osaka Prefecture Bulletin: Uchida, 57—1699

USSR Information Bulletin: Bogdanov, 10/27 & 10/30 & 11/1/45—374a; Gorbatov, 4/23/46—429b; Markov, 5/18/46—1080; 9/11/46—1099a; Panyushkin, 2/28/48—1008a; Panyushkin, 9/22/48—1790a; Panyushkin, 10/6/48—999a; Krainov, 11/17/48—2333a; Panyushkin, 11/17/48—1010a; Panyushkin, 12/8/48—1487; Panyushkin, 1/14/49—1767c; Panyushkin, 2/11/49—1560a; Panyushkin, 2/25/49—1520; Panyushkin, 3/11/49—1767b; Panyushkin, 7/29/49—1771a; Mayevsky, 2/10/50—1081c; 2/24/50—1069a; 3/8/51—1082b; Gromyko, 9/21/51—2423

Virginia Quarterly Review: Lamott, Summer 46—438; Quigley, Autumn 47—518; Winnacker, Autumn 48—203c; Rowe, Autumn 49—607b; Taylor, Spring 53—2306a; Quigley, Winter 57—1202

Vital Speeches: Aiso, 12/15/43—63; Conant, 11/15/44—69; Hall, 4/15/46—1801; MacArthur, 4/15/46—1005; Close, 11/4/47—486; MacArthur, 5/15/50—941; Dewey, 8/1/51—2470a; Acheson, 9/15/51—2361a; Gromyko, 9/15/51—2390; MacArthur, 9/15/51—942a; Morrison, 9/15/51—2407a; Truman, 9/15/51—2431; Ridgway, 6/15/52—2533

Waseda Bulletin of Social Sciences: Miyake, 62—1442

Waseda Economic Papers: Hayakawa, 59—1640

Waseda Political Studies: Yoshimura, 57—1433; Matsumoto, 62—1197; Kobayashi, 68—1239

Washington Law Review: Oppler, 8/49—1290; Appleton, 11/49—1267; Meyers, 2/50—1287a; Steiner, 8/50—1292a; Wagatsuma, 11/50—1296a; Wagatsuma, 5/51—1219a; Solomon, 8/51—1821

Western Economic Journal: Ozaki, Spring 63—1658

Western Political Quarterly: Fishel, 6/51—9; Maki, 9/53—1287; Dionisopoulos, 12/57—1174; Dionisopoulos, 6/60—1298

Wilson Library Bulletin: Eells, 12/47—2138; Kantor, 9/49—2255

Wisconsin Law Review: Blakemore, 7/47—1268

Woman's Home Companion: Vining, 5/47—529

World Affairs: Ray, Summer 47—519; Ray, Summer 48—2337; Kawakami, Summer 49—2476; Gibson, Winter 55—708b

World Affairs (London): Keeton, 10/48—799; Frankel, 10/51—2385

World Affairs Interpreter: Kawai, 10/50—798; Polyzoides, 10/51—2411c

World Affairs Quarterly: Coox, 1/56—2287

World Outlook: Counts—2034

World Politics: Embree, 4/50—1921

World Report: 1/6/48—140

World Review (London): Knight, 11/44—169c

World Today: 10/46—1454; 11/46—450; 7/48—1510; 5/49—579; 1/51—579; 1/51—1393; 7/51—2394a; 9/52—1624

Yale Review: Mears, Winter 44—99; Lockwood, Autumn 46—1456; Allen, Summer 47—2014; Eichler, Winter 52—646

Year Book of Education: Hall, 49—2054a; Orr, 54—2099

Year Book of World Affairs: Ireland, 50—1068a; Green, 52—2447a

Appendix: List of High-Ranking Occupation Personnel

INTRODUCTION

It had been our original intention in compiling and annotating this bibliography of materials relating to the Allied occupation of Japan to include a reasonably definitive list of all individuals holding high office in SCAP together with current addresses for those still living. The hope, of course, was to facilitate scholarly access to such persons for interview purposes. A serious and time-consuming effort was made to carry out this design involving approaches through the Department of Defense, the Department of State, the Veterans Administration, the National Archives, the Army Library, the Office of the Chief of Military History, the MacArthur Memorial Library, the U.S. embassy in Tokyo, the major relevant research libraries of this country, and a number of former members of the SCAP staff. The result was an almost total failure insofar as the attempt to link current addresses to the names of former SCAP personnel was concerned. No public or private agency that we were able to discover maintains such records in a form that would yield the information required on the basis of the identifications we were able to supply.

It has been necessary, therefore, to restrict this part of the project to two sorts of information about high-ranking occupation personnel: (1) a classified list arranged in accordance with SCAP's Table of Organization limited for the most part to the seventy-two month period from May 1946 through April 1952, and (2) an alphabetic list of names occurring on the preceding list. Our primary source for this information was a set of the SCAP Telephone Directories for Tokyo and Vicinity. Again strenuous efforts were made both in this country and Japan to acquire a complete set. The result was the following run of eighteen editions:

Appendix

1946:	May	1951:	January
	September		April
	November		July
	December		October
1947:	February	1952:	January
	March–April		April
	May–June		
1949:	July		
1950:	January		
	April		
	July		
	October		

It will be noted that there are major gaps in this series for September 1945–April 1946, June 1946–August 1946, July 1947–June 1949, and August 1949–December 1949. For these periods only scattered information has been available, largely for the Government Section.

On the basis of the available telephone directories and a few miscellaneous sources of information it has been possible to compile the classified list that follows. These further points should be noted with respect to this list:

1. It is restricted to higher-ranking personnel. In general this has been interpreted to mean chiefs, deputy chiefs, assistant chiefs, directors, executive officers, and officers in charge of sections, divisions, or branches within SCAP; principal advisers, special assistants, coordinators, and counsellors; occasionally some of the more notable staff members of lower rank where identifiable; and major staff officers on the military side. A certain amount of inconsistency has been unavoidable due to variant practices followed in different editions of the telephone directories. For example, from July 1951 they list only the names of the highest ranking officials in each section. With these exceptions, however, the list is as complete as the available data permit.

2. The dates following names indicate the first and last occasions on which the name of the individual concerned appears in the available series of telephone directories. Consequently, they should not be taken as reliable indicators of actual terms of service. These may be longer than indicated.

3. The order in which sections and other organizational units of SCAP are presented is that used in the telephone directories. It begins with the commander in chief and the standard military staff sections and continues with other—largely the so-called "specialist"—sections arranged in alphabetical order. When known, reorganizations, changes in names, and the relevant dates are noted in connection with the units concerned.

4. The holders of particular offices are listed chronologically under the office concerned. If there were several individuals with the same title at the same time, their names are listed alphabetically.

ABBREVIATIONS OF RANK DESIGNATIONS

Brig. Gen.   Brigadier General, U.S. Army

List of Occupation Personnel

Capt.	Captain, U.S. Army
Capt. (USN)	Captain, U.S. Navy
Col.	Colonel, U.S. Army
Comdr.	Commander, U.S. Navy
Gen.	General, U.S. Army
Lt.	Lieutenant, U.S. Army (not differentiated by 1st or 2d Lieutenant)
Lt. Col.	Lieutenant Colonel, U.S. Army
Lt. Col. (USMC)	Lieutenant Colonel, U.S. Marine Corps
Lt. Comdr.	Lieutenant Commander, U.S. Navy
Lt. Gen.	Lieutenant General, U.S. Army
Maj.	Major, U.S. Army
Maj. Gen.	Major General, U.S. Army

CLASSIFIED LIST

COMMANDER IN CHIEF

Commander in Chief
  Gen. Douglas MacArthur, 9/45–4/51
  Gen. Matthew B. Ridgway, 4/51–4/52
Aides-de-Camp
  Col. Herbert B. Wheeler, 5/46–5/47
  Lt. W. P. Hogan, 5/46–5/47
  Col. L. E. Bunker, 9/46–4/51
  Col. S. L. Huff, 7/49–4/51
  Lt. Col. A. F. Story, 10/50–4/51
  Lt. Col. Emory S. Adams, Jr., 7/51–1/52
  Lt. Arnold A. Galiffa, 7/51–4/52
  Lt. Col. Walker F. Winton, Jr., 7/51–10/51
  Maj. Richard H. Maeder, 1/52–4/52
Office of the Commander in Chief
  Col. L. E. Bunker, 5/46
  Lt. K. Kitagawa, 5/46
  Col. Douglas B. Kendrick, Jr., 5/46–5/47
  Maj. A. F. Story, 5/46–7/50
  Lt. Col. Charles C. Canada, 7/49–4/51
  Lt. Kan Tagami, 7/49–4/51
Public Relations Adviser to the Commander in Chief
  Col. James T. Quirk, 7/51
Military Secretary to the Commander in Chief
  Col. Bonner F. Fellers, 9/46

OFFICE OF THE CHIEF OF STAFF

Chief of Staff
  Lt. Gen. Richard K. Sutherland, 9/45–12/45
  Maj. Gen. Richard J. Marshall, 12/45–5/46
  Maj. Gen. Paul J. Mueller, 5/46–2/49
  Maj. Gen. (from 4/51 Lt. Gen.) Edward M. Almond, 2/49–4/51
  Maj. Gen. (from 7/51 Lt. Gen.) Doyle O. Hickey, 10/50(?)–4/52
Aides-de-Camp, Chief of Staff
  Capt. K. R. Bull, 5/46–9/46
  Capt. Wilford L. Harrelson, Jr., 11/46–5/47
  Capt. P. A. Lamoure, 7/49–4/50
  Lt. Alexander M. Haig, Jr., 1/50–4/50
Deputy Chiefs of Staff (through 11/46 single office, then differentiation between AFPAC and SCAP 12/46, FEC and SCAP thereafter, see below)
  Maj. Gen. Percy W. Clarkson, 5/46–9/46
  Brig. Gen. Lester J. Whitlock, 5/46–11/46
Office of Deputy Chief of Staff (through 11/46, then Office of Deputy Chief of Staff, SCAP, see below)
  Brig. Gen. William A. Beiderlinden, 9/46–11/46
  Brig. Gen. Alonzo P. Fox, 9/46–11/46
Deputy Chief of Staff, FEC (in 12/46 called Deputy Chief of Staff, AFPAC; 10/50–7/51 called Deputy Chief of Staff FEC and Chief of Staff ROK Operations)
  Maj. Gen. Edward M. Almond, 12/46–5/47

837

Appendix

Maj. Gen. Doyle O. Hickey, 7/49–7/50
Maj. Gen. Roderick R. Allen, 10/50–1/51
Maj. Gen. Alonzo P. Fox, 4/51–7/51
Maj. Gen. Whitfield P. Shepard, 10/51–1/52
Maj. Gen. Blackshear M. Bryan, 4/52

Deputy Chief of Staff, SCAP (none 4/51)
Brig. Gen. Lester J. Whitlock, 12/46–5/47
Brig. Gen. (from 1/50 Maj. Gen.) Alonzo P. Fox, 7/49–1/51
Maj. Gen. Whitfield P. Shepard, 7/51
Brig. Gen. George V. Keyser, 10/51–4/52

Office of Deputy Chief of Staff, SCAP (12/46–7/51; from 1/50 named Executive for Administrative Affairs)
Brig. Gen. Alonzo P. Fox, 12/46–5/47
Brig. Gen. William K. Harrison, Jr., 12/46–5/47
Brig. Gen. George V. Keyser, 7/49–7/51

Secretary, General Staff
Col. Ferdinand M. Humphries, 5/46
Col. David Larr, 5/46
Lt. Col. M. H. Halff, 5/46
Lt. Col. Benjamin T. Harris, 5/46
Lt. Col. Samuel E. Otto, 5/46
Col. Legrande A. Diller, 5/46–5/47
Col. Samuel M. Lansing, 5/46–5/47
Lt. Col. John H. Chiles, 7/49–7/50
Lt. Col. John M. Hightower, 10/50–4/51
Lt. Col. (from 10/51 Col.) Frank W. Moorman, 7/51–4/52

GARIOA (Government and Relief in Occupied Areas)
Mr. Arthur M. McGlauflin, 10/50–10/51

G–1 Section

Assistant Chief of Staff, G–1
Brig. Gen. Matthew J. Gunner, 5/46
Maj. Gen. Edward M. Almond, 9/46–12/46
Brig. Gen. (from 10/50 Maj. Gen.) William A. Beiderlinden, 2/47–4/51
Brig. Gen. Bryan L. Milburn, 7/51–4/52

Deputy, G–1 (none 5/46, 9/46, or 7/49)
Col. Richard R. Coursey, 11/46–5/47
Col. Charles H. Owens, 1/50; 10/50–1/51
Col. Kenneth C. Strother, 4/50
Col. Esther C. Burkart, 7/50
Col. Richard G. McKee, 4/51–1/52

Executive Officer
Col. Robert Hackett, 5/46–9/46
Col. Richard R. Coursey, 11/46–5/47
Col. Charles H. Owens, 7/49; 4/50
Col. William E. Watters, 1/50
Lt. Col. (from 1/51 Col.) Alexander Graham, 7/50–4/51

G–2 Section

Assistant Chief of Staff, G–2
Maj. Gen. Charles A. Willoughby, 5/46–4/51
Brig. Gen. Riley F. Ennis, 7/51–4/52

Deputy, G–2 (from 11/46 Deputy and Executive Officer same man, same office)
Col. Collin S. Myers, 5/46; 11/46–1/50
Col. Rufus S. Bratton, 9/46; 4/50–1/52

Japanese Liaison (from 1/51 called Foreign and Japanese Liaison)
Col. M. A. Snyder, 5/46
Capt. G. G. Dubinets, 5/46
Maj. J. W. Schneider, 9/46–7/49
Lt. C. L. Stephen, 9/46
Lt. Francis T. Motofuji, 12/46–3/47
Mr. J. Tsuchiya, 5/47–4/51
Lt. Kiyoshi Kitagawa, 1/50–1/52
Lt. Col. David S. Tait, 1/50–10/50
Maj. Rosa E. Ennis, 1/51
Capt. Enrique J. Hubert, 1/51
Capt. (USN) E. S. Pearce, 1/51
Lt. Col. James D. Wilmeth, 4/51

Coordinator, Theater Intelligence (11/46 called Chief, Theater Intelligence; from 12/46 called Director, Theater Intelligence Division; from 1/52 called Chief, Intelligence Division)
Col. Rufus S. Bratton, 5/46–9/46
Col. Frank D. Sharp, 11/46; 2/47–3/47 (in 12/46 Sharp as Operations Head, Theater Intelligence)
Col. Ronald L. Ring, 12/46; 5/47 (in 2/47–3/47 Ring as Executive, Theater Intelligence)
Col. Louis J. Fortier, 7/49–7/50

Col. Earl C. Ewert, 10/50–1/51
Col. Horton V. White, 4/51–1/52

Chief Civil Intelligence Officer (none 5/46 or 11/46, only Deputy Chief; from 12/46 called Director, Civil Intelligence Division; from 1/52 called Chief, Security Division)
Col. Walter S. Wood, 9/46
Col. Rufus S. Bratton, 12/46–1/50 (11/46 Deputy Chief, Civil Intelligence)
Col. Arthur T. Lacey, 4/50–1/51 (also 7/49–1/50 head of Executive Group, Miscellaneous Division)
Col. Earl C. Ewert, 4/51–7/51

Commanding Officer, 441st Counterintelligence Corps (none 5/46)
Col. Archibald W. Stuart, 9/46
Lt. Col. W. E. Homan, 11/46–5/47
Col. R. G. Duff, 7/49
Col. Lawrence G. Smith, 1/50–1/52

Chief, Public Safety Division (none 5/46; from 12/46 Chief, Public Safety Branch, Civil Intelligence Division; from 7/49 Director, Public Safety Division; from 10/51 Chief, Public Safety Branch, Civil Intelligence Division; from 1/52 Chief, Public Safety Branch, Security Division)
Col. Howard E. Pulliam, 9/46–1/51
Mr. Harold F. Mulbar, 4/51–1/52

Commanding Officer, Allied Translator and Interpreter Service (ATIS)
Col. Isaac G. Walker, 5/46
Lt. Col. Thomas F. Wall, 9/46
Col. Eric H. F. Svensson, 11/46–12/46; 4/51–7/51 (also 12/46–3/47 Chief, War Department Intelligence Division; also 1/52 Chief, Military Intelligence Service Group, Far East)
Col. Archibald W. Stuart, 2/47–3/47
Lt. Col. Charles F. McNair, 5/47
Lt. Col. Harry L. Kinne, Jr., 7/49
Col. William R. Grove, 1/50
Col. Thomas N. Stark, 4/50–1/51

Chief, Historical Section (none 5/46; from 2/47 called Chief, Historical Branch; from 7/49 called Director, Military Historical Section)
Capt. W. M. Terry, 9/46
Col. Henry O. Swindler, 11/46–5/47
Dr. Gordon William Prange, 7/49–7/51
Col. Allison R. Hartman, 4/52

G–3 SECTION

Assistant Chief of Staff, G–3
Col. Carl A. Russell, 5/46–5/47
Brig. Gen. Ward H. Maris, 7/49
Brig. Gen. Edwin K. Wright, 1/50–4/52 (also 10/51 Chief, Joint Operations and Strategic Plans Group)

Deputy Assistant Chief of Staff, G–3 (11/46–12/46 no Deputy; Executive Officer as Second-in-Command at that time—see below)
Col. Walter A. Dumas, 5/46–9/46; 2/47–5/47
Col. William L. Mitchell, 7/49
Col. John A. Dabney, 1/50–7/50
Col. Carl H. Jark, 10/50–1/52

Executive Officer
Col. Frank S. Henry, 5/46–11/46
Col. Walter A. Dumas, 12/46

G–4 SECTION

Assistant Chief of Staff, G–4
Brig. Gen. Roy C. L. Graham, 5/46
Col. Harold E. Eastwood, 9/46–5/47
Maj. Gen. George L. Eberle, 7/49–4/52

Deputy Assistant Chief of Staff, G–4 (none 9/46)
Brig. Gen. Harold E. Eastwood, 5/46
Col. Maurice V. Patton, 11/46–5/47
Col. Andrew E. Forsyth, 7/49–7/52
Col. Maylon E. Scott, 7/49

G–5 SECTION

Assistant Chief of Staff, G–5
Col. Walter R. Hensey, Jr., 4/52

ADJUTANT GENERAL'S SECTION

Adjutant General
Brig. Gen. Burdette M. Fitch, 5/46
Col. John B. Cooley, 9/46–3/47
Col. Richard M. Levy, 5/47–7/49
Brig. Gen. Kenneth B. Bush, 1/50–7/51
Col. Cranford C. B. Warden, 10/51–4/52

CIVIL AFFAIRS SECTION (originated 4/50)
Chief
Maj. Gen. Whitfield P. Shepard, 4/50–7/51
Brig. Gen. Leroy H. Watson, 10/51–4/52

Appendix

Deputy Chief (4/50–10/50 only)
    Brig. Gen. E. C. B. Danforth, 4/50–10/50
Executive Officer
    Col. Harry L. Watts, 4/50
    Col. Frank Kowalski, Jr., 7/50–4/51
    Col. Bernard R. Papen, 10/50
Assistant Executive Officer
    Lt. Col. W. Glover, 10/50–4/51
Chief, Social Affairs Division (only 4/50–7/50)
    Lt. Col. V. C. Searle, 4/50
Chief, Public Welfare Division (4/50–7/50 a branch of Social Affairs Division)
    Mr. Philip Borish, 4/50–4/51
Chief, Public Health Division (4/50–7/50 a branch of Social Affairs Division)
    Lt. Col. (from 10/50 Col.) Lewis C. Shellenberger, 4/50–4/51
Chief, Civil Education Division (4/50–7/50 a branch of Social Affairs Division)
    Lt. Col. William M. Albergotti, 4/50–7/50
    Dr. R. B. Bowers, 10/50–4/51 (also 4/50–7/50 member, Civil Education)
Chief, Civil Information Division (4/50–7/50 a branch of Social Affairs Division)
    Mr. F. T. Yates, 4/50–4/51
Chief, Economics Division
    Lt. Col. (from 10/50 Col.) Bernard R. Papen, 4/50–7/50; 1/51–4/51
    Mr. Rue Link, 10/50
Chief, Legal and Government Division
    Mr. Howard D. Porter, 4/50–4/51

CIVIL COMMUNICATIONS SECTION
(terminated 10/51)

Chief of Section
    Brig. Gen. Spencer B. Akin, 5/46–2/47
    Brig. Gen. George I. Back, 3/47–4/51
    Col. Eldon F. Hammond, 7/51–10/51
Assistant Chief (none 5/46 or 9/46)
    Col. Gilbert Hayden, 11/46–12/46
    Col. Jay D. B. Lattin, 2/47–5/47
    Col. Maurice P. Chadwick, 7/49
    Col. Robert N. Kunz, 1/50–7/51
Deputy Chief (through 5/47 distinct from Assistant Chief)
    Mr. J. D. Whittemore, 5/46
    Mr. T. E. Nivison, 9/46–5/47

CIVIL HISTORICAL SECTION
(See Statistics and Reports Section)

CIVIL INFORMATION AND
EDUCATION SECTION

Chief
    Brig. Gen. Kermit R. Dyke, 5/46
    Lt. Col. (USMC) Donald R. Nugent, 5/46–4/52
Executive Assistant
    Lt. (from 7/49 Capt.) Glenna K. Crew, 9/46–1/52
Executive Officer
    Maj. E. D. Dodd, 5/46
    Lt. Col. Thomas B. Summers, 9/46–12/46
    Lt. Col. Theodore S. Hatzfeld, Jr., 2/47–5/47
    Lt. Col. Frederick C. Dahlquist, 7/49–7/50
Special Projects Officer
    Maj. Camille B. Swigert, 1/51–4/51
Education Division Chief
    Lt. Col. Donald R. Nugent, 5/46
    Lt. Col. (from 12/46 Mr.) Mark Taylor Orr, 9/46–5/47
    Dr. Arthur K. Loomis, 7/49–1/52
Education Division Deputy Chief (only from 7/49)
    Dr. Joseph C. Trainor, 7/49–1/52
Education Division Members (5/46–5/47 undifferentiated by office)
    Lt. Col. E. H. Farr, 5/46
    Lt. Col. B. A. Schmitz, 5/46
    Lt. Comdr. A. E. Crofts, 5/46
    Lt. Comdr. Robert King Hall, 5/46
    Maj. R. C. McAllen, 5/46
    Maj. J. W. Norviel, 5/46
    Maj. Mark Taylor Orr, 5/46
    Capt. Harry Elmer Griffith, 5/46
    Capt. R. S. McDowell, 5/46
    Capt. Eileen R. Donovan, 5/46
    Mr. H. I. Prien, 5/46–11/46
    Dr. (in 5/46 Lt. Comdr.) Joseph C. Trainor, 5/46–5/47
    Maj. R. W. Arrowood, 5/46; 12/46–5/47
    Capt. E. Cross, 11/46
    Dr. H. Bell, 12/46–5/47
    Miss L. Bowles, 12/46–5/47
    Mr. Arundel Del Re, 12/46–5/47
Education Division Adviser (from 7/49)
    Mr. Arundel Del Re, 7/49–4/51

Education Division, School Education Branch (from 7/49)
    Dr. W. W. Carpenter, 7/49–7/50
    Dr. Walter E. Morgan, 7/49–1/52
    (1/52 Education Reorganization, School Education Branch)
    Maj. Hazel B. Bundy, 1/51–1/52
    (7/51 Secondary Teachers Education; 1/52 Secondary Education, School Education Branch)

Education Division, Higher Education Branch (from 7/49)
    Dr. Verna A. Carley, 7/49–1/52
    (7/51–1/52 IFEL Director, Higher Education Branch)
    Dr. Walter Crosby Eells, 7/49–10/50
    Dr. Thomas H. McGrail, 1/51–1/52
    (from 4/51 University Education, Higher Education Branch)

Education Division, Adult Education Branch (from 7/49)
    Dr. L. Q. Moss, 7/49–7/50
    Mr. Raymond E. Culbertson, 10/50–7/51

Education Division, Education Specialist Branch (from 7/49)
    Dr. H. Bell, 7/49
    Mr. K. M. Harkness, 1/50–4/51

Education Division, Education Research Branch (from 7/49; from 7/51 called Special Projects Branch)
    Mr. John Mitchell, 7/49–1/52

Information Division Chief
    Mr. Don Brown, 9/46–1/52

Information Division, Policy and Programs Branch OIC (called Planning, 5/46; called Policy and Planing, 9/46)
    Mr. Arthur Behrstock, 5/46
    Mr. Don Brown, 9/46
    Lt. Col. John W. Gaddis, 11/46–5/47
    Mr. John F. Sullivan, 7/49–1/52

Information Division, Press and Publications Branch OIC
    Mr. Don Brown, 5/46
    Maj. (from 7/51 Lt. Col.) Daniel C. Imboden, 9/46–1/52

Information Division, Radio Branch OIC
    Maj. M. Harlan, 5/46–9/46
    Mr. Frank B. Huggins, 11/46–3/47
    Mr. A. R. Crews, 5/47
    Mr. D. B. Herrick, 7/49–7/51

Information Division, Motion Picture and Theatrical Branch OIC (called Motion Pictures and Drama Branch, 5/46)
    Mr. D. W. Conde, 5/46
    Maj. H. L. Roberts, 9/46
    Mr. George J. Gercke, 11/46–1/52

Information Division, SCAP–CIE Information Centers Branch OIC (from 7/49)
    Mr. Roland A. Mulhauser, 7/49–7/51

Analysis and Research Division Chief (from 7/49 called Public Opinion and Sociological Research Division)
    Mr. J. Woodall Greene, 5/46–5/47
    Dr. John William Bennett, 7/49–10/50

Analysis and Research Division Executive (9/46–5/47)
    Maj. C. G. Harris, 9/46–5/47 (also 9/46–3/47 OIC, Research Unit, Analysis and Research Division)

Analysis and Research Division Deputy Chief (from 7/49)
    Lt. Herbert Passin, 7/49–4/51 (also 9/46–5/47 member, Research Unit, Analysis and Research Division)

Religions Division Chief (from 7/49 called Religions and Cultural Resources Division)
    Dr. (in 5/46 Lt. Comdr.) William K. Bunce, 5/46–1/52

Religions Division Members
    Lt. J. H. Stob, 5/46
    Dr. Charles Wheeler Iglehart, 5/46
    Mr. William C. Kerr, 5/46
    Mr. (in 5/46 Lt.) George Albro Warp, 5/46–5/47

Religions Division Deputy Chief (from 7/49)
    Dr. J. F. Leach, 7/49
    Mr. Walter Nichols, 1/50–1/52 (also 7/49 Religious Adviser, Religions and Cultural Resources Division)

Religions Division, Protestant Religious Adviser (from 7/49)
    Mr. William C. Kerr, 7/49–7/51

Religions Division, Catholic Religious Adviser (from 7/49)
    Mr. John O'Donovan, 7/49–7/51

Religions Division, Buddhism–Shinto Religious Adviser (from 7/49)
    Mr. Francis T. Motofuji, 1/50–7/51

Religions Division, Fine Arts Adviser (7/49–7/50)
    Mr. G. N. Kates, 4/50–7/50

Religions Division, Special Projects and

Appendix

Research (from 7/49)
    Mr. William P. Woodard, 7/49–7/51

Civilian Property Custodian
(5/46 called Office of
Civil Property Custodian)

Custodian
    Brig. Gen. Patrick H. Tansey, 5/46–5/47
    Brig. Gen. John F. Conklin, 7/49–1/51
    Col. Francis E. Gillette, 4/51–1/52

Deputy Custodian (in 5/46 called Executive Director)
    Lt. Col. Franklin R. Sibert, 5/46–5/47
    Col. Edward C. Miller, Jr., 7/49–1/51
    Lt. Col. Edward H. Oswald, 4/51–7/51

Civilian Personnel Section
(in 5/46 and 9/46 Office of
Civilian Personnel)

Chief (in 5/46 and 9/46 called Director)
    Lt. Col. Lawrence G. Alexander, 5/46–9/46 (also 11/46–12/46 Assistant Chief)
    Col. Emmett M. Connor, 11/46–4/50
    Col. Robert H. Chard, 7/50–4/52

Civil Transportation Section

Chief
    Brig. Gen. Frank S. Besson, 9/46–5/47
    Col. Harold T. Miller, 7/49–1/52

Deputy Military Transportation (11/46–5/47)
    Col. Alexander B. MacNabb, 11/46–5/47

Deputy Civil Transportation (11/46 only)
    Lt. Col. D. R. Changnon, 11/46

Deputy Chief (from 7/49)
    Lt. Col. Lawrence D. Lally, Jr., 7/49–4/50
    Mr. Charles S. Woods, 10/50–7/51

Executive (from 12/46)
    Lt. Col. D. R. Changnon
    Mr. Charles S. Woods, 7/49–7/50

Operations Division Chief (9/46–11/46; 11/46 called Military Operations Division)
    Lt. Col. Henry D. Lind, 9/46–11/46

Rail Transportation (9/46–5/47)
    Lt. Col. D. R. Changnon, 11/46
    Capt. M. A. Fuegy, 9/46–3/47
    Mr. G. E. Degroat, 5/47

Water Transportation Chief (none 12/46)
    Maj. Louis M. Vierhus, 9/46
    Lt. Col. Henry D. Lind, 11/46
    Mr. R. C. Duane, 2/47–5/47
    Lt. Col. Kenneth W. Gillespie, 7/49–7/50
    Mr. Paul E. Richers, 10/50–7/51 (also 5/47–7/50 Deputy)

Motor Transportation (11/46–5/47)
    Mr. J. Reifsnider, 11/46–3/47
    Mr. Charles S. Woods, 5/47

Land Transportation Division Director (from 7/49)
    Mr. D. R. Changnon, 7/49–4/51

Ministry of Transportation Liaison (from 7/49)
    Mr. Y. Tasaka, 7/49
    Mr. A. Doi, 1/50–7/50
    Mr. T. Uejima, 1/50
    Mr. Y. Koseki, 10/50–4/51

Comptroller, Office Of (from 7/49)

Comptroller
    Brig. Gen. Laurn L. Williams, 7/49–4/52

Deputy Comptroller (end 1/51)
    Col. R. H. Bradshaw, 7/49–1/51

Executive (from 4/51)
    Col. Fielder P. Greer, 4/51–1/52

Diplomatic Section

Chief
    Ambassador George Atcheson, Jr., 5/46–5/47
    The Honorable William J. Sebald, 7/49–4/52

Deputy Chief
    Mr. Max W. Bishop, 9/46–3/47
    Mr. William J. Sebald, 5/47
    Mr. Cloyce K. Huston, 7/49–10/50
    Mr. Niles W. Bond, 1/51–1/52

Executive Officer
    Mr. Max W. Bishop, 5/46
    Mr. U. Alexis Johnson, 9/46–11/46

Mr. William J. Sebald, 12/46–3/47
(also 9/46–11/46 Diplomatic
Liaison Officer)
Mr. S. H. Browne, 5/47
Liaison Officer
Mr. J. D. Edwards, 5/46
*Division of Economic Liaison, Chief
Economic Counselor* (from 7/49)
Mr. Carl H. Boehringer, 1/50–4/50;
1/51–4/51

ECONOMIC AND SCIENTIFIC SECTION

Chief of Section
Maj. Gen. William F. Marquat,
5/46–4/52
Deputy Chief for Administration
(7/49 only)
Col. Earle A. Johnson, 7/49
Deputy Chief for Operations (7/49 only)
Lt. Col. William T. Ryder, 7/49
Deputy Chief (single office from 1/50)
Lt. Col. William T. Ryder, 1/50–7/51
Col. William I. Brady, 1/51
Economic Adviser (9/46–5/47)
Dr. Sherwood Monroe Fine, 9/46–5/47
Director, Economics and Finance (7/49
only, then split into Economics and
Planning, and Finance, see below)
Dr. Sherwood Monroe Fine, 7/49
Director, Economics and Planning (from
1/50)
Dr. Sherwood Monroe Fine, 1/50–1/52
Director, Finance (from 1/50)
Mr. J. R. Allison, 1/50–4/51
Director, Diplomatic Liaison (State
Department) (from 7/49)
Mr. D. R. Maynard, 7/49
Mr. Carl H. Boehringer, 1/50–7/50;
4/51
Mr. Edward Anderberg, 10/50–1/51
Director, Trade and Services (from 7/49;
in 7/49 called Trade and Commerce)
Mr. Peter A. McDermott, 7/49–7/51
Mr. Russel W. Hale, 1/52
Director, Labor (from 1/50)
Mr. Robert T. Amis, 1/50–1/52
Director, Production and Utilities (from
7/49)
Mr. Calvin Verity, 7/49
Mr. T. O. Kennedy, 1/50–4/51

Mr. W. S. Vaughn, 1/50–4/51
Mr. Maurice M. Class, 1/52
Trade Area Coordinator (from 1/50; from
10/50 called Financial Coordinator for
Trade)
Mr. James G. Torrens, 1/50–4/50
Mr. S. T. Baron, 7/50–4/51
Financial Cotton Adviser (4/50–7/50
only)
Mr. W. S. Carter, 4/50–7/50
Special Assistants (from 7/49)
Mr. Theodore Cohen, 7/49–10/50
Mr. L. A. Jones, 1/50
Dr. Harry C. Kelly, 1/50
Lt. Col. Paul A. Feyereisen, 4/50
Mr. Kenneth D. Morrow, 1/51
Investment Board Chairman (7/49–7/51;
in 7/49 called Foreign Investment
Board)
Mr. Frayne Baker, 7/49–7/51 (also
7/49 Director, Business and Investment;
also 1/52 Special Assistant,
Business Activities)
Investment Board Executive Secretary
(7/49–7/51)
Mr. Clark S. Gregory, 7/49–7/51
Deconcentration Review Board (7/49
only)
Mr. J. Robinson, 7/49
PIO Representative (from 7/49)
Mr. Stuart Griffith, 7/49–1/50;
10/50–1/51
Capt. Mary O. Kennedy, 4/50–7/50
Capt. J. R. Dickson, 4/51
Anti-Trust and Cartels Division Chief
(from 1/50 called Fair Trade Practices
Division, end 4/51)
Mr. J. McI. Henderson, 5/46–12/46
Lt. Col. V. H. Kupfever, 2/47–3/47
Mr. E. C. Welsch, 5/47–4/50
Mr. Roderick M. Gillies, 7/49–4/50
*Anti-Trust and Cartels Division Deputy
Chief* (from 7/49 called Assistant to
Chief)
Lt. Col. V. H. Kupfever, 5/46–12/46
Mr. I. T. Bush, 2/47–5/47
Mr. Roderick M. Gillies, 7/49–4/50
Mr. J. Rand, 7/50
Mr. H. Wohl, 10/50–4/51
*Anti-Trust Cartels Division, Liquidation
Branch Chief* (end 5/47)
Mr. P. E. Siff, 5/46
Maj. R. M. Cooper, 9/46–12/46

Appendix

    Mr. B. W. Henderson, 2/47–5/47
Anti-Trust and Cartels Division, Anti-Trust Legislation Branch Chief (none 11/46; in 7/49 called Trade Laws Branch; 1/50 merged with Controls into Anti-Trust and Controls Branch, see below)
    Mr. P. T. Kime, 5/46–9/46
    Mr. Lester N. Salwin, 2/47–7/49
Anti-Trust and Cartels Division, Control–Cartels Branch Chief (in 7/49 called Controls; 1/50 merged with Trade Laws Branch into Anti-Trust and Controls Branch, see below)
    Mr. J. G. Liebert, 5/46
    Mr. G. F. Sieker, 9/46
    Mr. T. K. Wright, 11/46–5/47
    Mr. M. J. Rose, 7/49
Anti-Trust and Cartels Division, Anti-Trust and Controls Branch Chief (from 1/50)
    Mr. Lester N. Salwin, 1/50–4/51
Anti-Trust and Cartels Division, Zaibatsu Branch Chief (ended 5/47)
    Mr. G. R. Lunn, Jr., 5/46–12/46; 5/47
    Mr. P. W. Byall, 2/47–3/47
Anti-Trust and Cartels Division, Liaison Branch Chief (ended 5/47)
    Capt. R. M. Cooper, 5/46
    Maj. S. G. Zybura, 9/46–5/47
Anti-Trust and Cartels Division, Reorganization Branch Chief (7/49 only; 1/50 merged with Securities into Securities and Reorganization Branch, see below)
    Mr. H. H. Sheier, 7/49
Anti-Trust and Cartels Division, Securities Branch Chief (7/49 only; 1/50 merged with Reorganization into Securities and Reorganization Branch, see below)
    Mr. Leland A. Randall, 7/49
Anti-Trust and Cartels Division, Securities and Reorganization Branch Chief (from 1/50)
    Mr. Leland A. Randall, 1/50–4/51
Finance Division Chief (5/46–7/49; 1/50 called Japanese Finance Division; dissolved 4/50, Public Finance Branch becomes separate division, see below)
    Lt. Col. D. H. Jennings (Acting Chairman), 5/46
    Mr. W. K. Lecount, 9/46–1/50
Finance Division Deputy Chief (from 7/49)
    Mr. J. R. Allison, 7/49–1/50
Finance Division Executive Officer (5/46–5/47)
    Lt. Col. D. H. Jennings, 5/46–5/47
Finance Division, Liquidation Branch Chief
    Maj. E. J. Burns, 5/46; 11/46–5/47
    Mr. William N. Rogers, 9/46
    Mr. W. S. Brower, 7/49–1/50
Finance Division, Public Finance Branch Chief
    Capt. S. S. Hertzmark, 5/46
    Lt. Comdr. P. C. Akin, 9/46
    Mr. Eugene M. Reed, 12/46–1/50 (also 9/46–11/46 Chief, Budget–National Branch, Finance Division)
Finance Division, Money and Banking Branch Chief
    Lt. Col. Orville J. McDiarmid, 5/46
    Mr. T. E. BoPlat, 9/46–5/47
    Mr. J. C. Smith, 7/49–1/50 (also 4/50–10/50 Chief, Domestic Financial Institutions Branch, Banking and Foreign Exchange Division)
Public Finance Division Chief (4/50–4/51; 7/51 called Finance Division because of merger with Banking and Foreign Exchange and Internal Revenue Divisions, see below)
    Mr. Eugene M. Reed, 4/50–1/52
Public Finance Division Deputy Chief
    Mr. Edmond Carlton Hutchinson, 4/50–1/51
    Mr. Ralph E. Phillips, 4/51–1/52
Public Finance Division, Fiscal Policy Branch Chief (from 7/51 called Monetary and Credit Branch)
    Mr. Ralph E. Phillips, 4/50–4/51
Public Finance Division, Budget Management Branch Chief
    Mr. Arthur M. McGlauflin, 4/50–7/50
Public Finance Division, Financial Administration Branch Chief (through 4/51)
    Mr. J. W. Harrison, 4/50–1/51
Internal Revenue Division (7/49–4/51; 7/51 merged into Public Finance Division [renamed Finance Division] as Taxation Branch)
    Mr. Lon. H. Moss, 7/49–4/51 (also 7/51 Chief, Taxation Branch, Finance Division)
Internal Revenue Division Deputy Chief
    Mr. Henry Shavell, 7/49–1/51

Internal Revenue Division Executive Officer
　Lt. Col. C. C. Gedulding, 1/50–7/50
　Mr. Robert A. Bieber, 10/50

Internal Revenue Division, Monopoly Branch Chief
　Mr. William H. Bass, 1/50–4/51
　　(also 7/51 Chief, Monopoly, Taxation Branch, Finance Division)

Internal Revenue Division, National Tax Administration Branch Chief (in 1/50 called Tax Administration)
　Mr. R. V. Lash, 1/50
　Mr. J. E. Monroe, 4/50–1/51 (also 1/50 Chief, Publicity and Education Branch; also 4/51 Chief, Local Government and Field Operations Branch, Internal Revenue Division)

Banking and Foreign Exchange Division Chief (7/49–4/51; 7/49 called Funds Control Division; 1/50 called Foreign Exchange Funds Division; 7/51 merged into Public Finance Division [renamed Finance Division] as International Finance Branch)
　Mr. Paul Cleveland, 7/49
　Mr. F. R. Gerard, 1/50–1/51
　Mr. V. L. Rich, 4/51

Banking and Foreign Exchange Division Deputy Chief
　Mr. F. R. Gerard, 7/49
　Mr. Reginald H. Marlow, 1/50–7/50 (also Chief, Bank Operations Branch, 7/49)
　Mr. V. L. Rich, 10/50–1/51 (also Executive, Funds Control Division, 7/49)

Foreign Trade Division Chief (in 5/46 called Import–Export Division; from 7/49 called Foreign Trade and Commerce Division)
　Mr. R. A. May, 5/46
　Mr. F. E. Pickelle, 9/46; 7/49–4/50
　Mr. Peter A. McDermott, 11/46–5/47
　Mr. Russel W. Hale, 7/50–7/51
　Mr. Carl C. Campbell, 1/52

Foreign Trade Division Deputy Chief (11/46–5/47 called Assistant Chief)
　Mr. (in 5/46 Maj.) F. E. Pickelle, 5/46; 11/46–5/47
　Mr. Russel W. Hale, 7/49–4/50
　Mr. Carl C. Campbell, 7/50–7/51
　Mr. W. J. Krossner, 1/52

Foreign Trade Division, Foreign Trade Adviser (9/46–3/47)
　Mr. S. H. Wright, 9/46–3/47

Foreign Trade Division, Special Adviser (7/49 only)
　Mr. A. B. Kram, 7/49
　Col. Ralph J. Mitchell, 7/49

Foreign Trade Division, Plans and Programs Branch Chief (9/46–7/49; from 12/46 called Programs Branch)
　Mr. James G. Torrens, 9/46–11/46
　Mr. G. R. Fleming, 12/46–5/47
　　(also 9/46–11/46 Assistant Chief)

Foreign Trade Division, Chemicals and Minerals Branch Chief (9/46–7/49)
　Mr. A. J. Greco, 9/46–7/49

Foreign Trade Division, Food Branch Chief (9/46–7/49)
　Mr. H. J. Zimmerman, 9/46–7/49

Foreign Trade Division, Machinery and Consumer Durable Goods Branch Chief (9/46–7/49)
　Mr. A. M. Lury, 9/46–12/47
　Mr. W. R. Mayers, 2/47–3/47
　Mr. S. H. Wright, 5/47
　Mr. A. B. Snell, 7/49

Foreign Trade Division, Textile Branch Chief (9/46–5/47)
　Mr. James G. Torrens, 9/46–12/46 (also Chief, Trade Areas Branch, Funds Control Division, 7/49)
　Maj. Edwin L. Atkins, 2/47–5/47

Foreign Trade Division, Services Branch Chief (12/46–5/47)
　Mr. E. J. Gaumond, 12/46
　Mr. J. E. Hitchcock, 2/47–5/47 (also 12/46 Chief, Records and Report Unit, Services Branch)

Foreign Trade Division, Pricing and Statistics Branch Chief (12/46–5/47)
　Mr. H. G. W. Sundelof, 12/46–5/47

Foreign Trade Division, Transportation Branch Chief (2/47–7/49; from 7/49 called Shipping Branch)
　Mr. H. Colton, 2/47–7/49

Foreign Trade Division, Trade Arrangement Branch Chief (from 1/50)
　Mr. W. J. Krossner, 1/50–7/51

Foreign Trade Division, Trade Arrangement Branch Deputy Chief
　Miss T. M. Tonole, 4/50

Foreign Trade Division, Trade Procedures Branch Chief (from 1/50)
　Mr. B. W. Adams, 1/50–4/50

Appendix

Mr. R. M. Catlin, 7/50
Mr. L. C. Barnes, 10/50–4/51
Foreign Trade Division, Trade Coordination Branch Chief (1/50–4/50 only)
Mr. W. N. Robins, 1/50–4/50
Foreign Trade Division, Trade Control Branch Chief (from 1/50)
Col. Ralph J. Mitchell, 1/50–7/50
Mr. A. B. Kram, 10/50–4/51 (also 7/50 Deputy Chief, Trade Control Branch)
Foreign Trade Division, Trade Control Branch, Textile Unit Chief
Mr. S. W. Hays, 1/50–10/50
Foreign Trade Division, GARIOA Office Chief (from 7/49; from 7/50 called GARIOA Import Unit)
Mr. G. R. Fleming, 7/49–7/50
Mr. E. J. Gaumond, 7/49
Mr. William B. Mathews, 10/50–7/51 (also 1/50–4/50 Chief, Cotton Import Unit, Trade Coordination Branch, Foreign Trade Division)
Textile Division Chief (5/46–1/50; in 5/46 Branch of Industrial Division)
Maj H. S. Tate, 5/46–5/47
Mr. R. D. Cleaves, 7/49
Industry Division Chief (in 5/46 called Industrial Division Chief; none 5/47)
Mr. G. T. Walker, 5/46
Mr. Joseph Z. Reday, 9/46–3/47
Mr. W. S. Vaughn, 7/49
Mr. Maurice M. Class, 1/50–7/51 (also Deputy Chief, Operations, Industry Division, 7/49)
Mr. Paul S. Fujii, 1/52
Industry Division, Reparations Branch Chief (5/46–3/47)
Capt. H. Palmer, 5/46
Mr. Norman J. Meiklejohn, 9/46–3/47 (also 5/47 Executive for Reparations, Deputy Chief of Staff, SCAP)
Industry Division, Machinery Branch Chief (5/46–5/47)
Mr. (in 5/46 Capt.) Carl D. Ross, 5/46–5/47
Industry Division, Manufacturing Branch Chief (5/46–5/47)
Maj. William L. Bunting, 5/46–11/46
Mr. Campbell Osborn, 12/46–5/47
Industry Division, Raw Material Branch Chief (5/46–7/49; 7/49 merged with Requirements Committee to become Raw Materials and Requirements Branch)
Maj. A. A. Rasmussen, 5/46
Mr. Ormond Freile, 9/46
Maj. Harry B. Overton, 11/46–12/46; 5/47–7/49
Capt. T. L. Nash, 2/47–3/47
Industry Division, Requirements Committee Chief (2/47–5/47 only)
Mr. Ormond Freile, 3/47 (also 11/46–2/47 Industry Economist, Industry Division)
Industry Division, Chemicals Branch (5/46–5/47)
Maj. R. C. A. Purl, 5/46–5/47
Industry Division, Shipbuilding Branch Chief (5/46–7/49; 7/49 merged with Construction and Gas and Electric into Construction, Shipbuilding and Utilities Branch)
Mr. George E. Meyers, 5/46–7/49
Industry Division, Construction Branch Chief (5/46–12/46; 5/47 only)
Maj. W. H. Daub, 5/46
Lt. E. T. Stanek, 9/46–12/46; 5/47
Industry Division, Gas and Electric Branch Chief (5/46–5/47)
Lt. Comdr. R. L. Wilson, 5/46
Mr. Vaughn A. Pierce, 9/46–5/47
Industry Division, Transportation and Communications Branch Chief (in 5/46 called Transportation Branch)
Mr. (in 5/46 Capt.) E. F. Powell, 5/46–9/46
Industry Division, Special Projects Branch Chief (11/46–12/46 only)
Lt. Col. V. Kolnitz, 11/46–12/46
Industry Division, Commodities Production Branch Chief (from 7/49)
Mr. A. B. Otis, 7/49–7/50
Mr. M. W. Hollingsworth, 10/50–1/52
Industry Division, Industrial Production and Construction Branch Chief (from 1/50)
Maj. (from 4/51 Mr.) Harry B. Overton, 1/50–7/51
Labor Division Chief
Mr. Theodore Cohen, 5/46–5/47
Mr. Chester W. Hepler, 7/49
Mr. Robert T. Amis, 1/50–1/52
Labor Division Deputy Chief (11/46–5/47)

Mr. P. L. Stanchfield, 11/46–5/47 (also 5/46–9/46 Labor Advisory Committee, Labor Division)

Labor Division Executive Officer
Lt. Col. H. M. Colbert, 11/46–12/46 (also 2/47–5/47 Compliance Officer, Labor Division)
Maj. (from 7/49 Lt. Col.) Samuel W. Thompson, 2/47–4/51

Labor Division, Labor Relations Branch Chief (5/46–5/47; 7/49 merged with Labor Information and Education into Labor Relations and Education Branch)
Mr. A. Constantino, 5/46–5/47

Labor Division, Employer Education Branch Chief (9/46 only; 11/46 merged with Trade Union Education into Labor Information and Education)
Mr. S. Korb, 9/46 (also 11/46–12/46 Assistant Chief, Labor Information and Education Branch)

Labor Division, Trade Union Education Branch Chief (9/46 only; 11/46 merged with Employer Education into Labor Information and Education)
Lt. Richard L. G. Deverall, 9/46

Labor Division, Labor Information and Education Branch Chief (11/46–5/47; 7/49 merged with Labor Relations and Education Branch)
Lt. Richard L. G. Deverall, 11/46–5/47

Labor Division, Labor Relations and Education Branch Chief (from 7/49)
Mr. Robert T. Amis, 7/49
Mr. V. Burati, 1/50–4/50; 10/50–4/51
Mr. M. B. Laupheimer, 7/50

Labor Division, Manpower Branch Chief (5/46 called Employment and Procurement Branch)
Mr. S. D. Collett, 5/46–4/50
Mr. Edgar C. McVoy, 7/50–7/51

Labor Division, Wages and Working Conditions Branch Chief (5/46 called Wages, Hours, and Working Conditions Branch)
Capt. E. A. Salk, 5/46–9/46
Miss Golda G. Stander, 11/46–7/51

Price and Distribution Division Chief (5/46 called Price Control and Rationing; 9/46 called Rationing and Price Control; 11/46–5/47 called Price Control and Rationing; ended 7/51)

Mr. (in 5/46 Capt.) W. Soren Egekvist, 5/46–5/47
Mr. F. L. Whittington, 7/49–10/50
Mr. Edmond Carlton Hutchinson, 4/51–7/51

Price and Distribution Division, Textiles Branch Chief (5/46)
Capt. F. E. Zelaney, 5/46

Price and Distribution Division, Rents and Housing Branch Chief (5/46)
Mr. J. W. Kirshenbaum, 5/46

Price and Distribution Division, Food Branch Chief (none in 5/46)
Mr. Bruce Foster Johnston, 9/46–5/47 (5/46 Perishable Foods Branch Chief)
Mr. Howard F. Smith, 7/49–10/50 (5/46 Staple Foods Branch Chief)
Mr. N. A. Stitt, 1/51
Mr. George Dolgin, 4/51–7/51

Price and Distribution Division, Enforcement Branch Chief
Mr. M. S. Diamond, 5/46–5/47
Mr. R. Goodman, 7/49–4/50
Mr. J. B. Harman, 7/50–4/51

Price and Distribution Division, Producer Goods Branch Chief (5/46–5/47)
Mr. J. I. Miller, 5/46
Mr. H. F. Alber, 9/46–5/47

Price and Distribution Division, Consumer Goods Branch Chief (5/46–5/47)
Miss M. T. Zahn, 5/46
Mr. Henry Harrison Bakken, 9/46–12/46
Mr. W. A. Ross, 2/47–3/47
Mr. Russel W. Hale, 5/47

Price and Distribution Division, Accounting Branch Chief (5/46–5/47)
Mr. (in 5/46 Capt.) V. R. McLeod, 5/46–5/47

Price and Distribution Division, Price Branch Chief (from 7/49)
Mr. V. L. Bankson, 7/49–7/50
Mr. Frank E. Kito, 10/50–7/51

Price and Distribution Division, Distribution Branch Chief (from 7/49; 10/50 renamed Special Projects Branch)
Mr. J. R. Boner, 7/49–1/51
Mr. Laurence Everett Potter, 4/51–7/51

Programs and Statistics Division Chief (5/46 called Statistics and Research; 9/46–5/47 called Research and Statistics; 7/49 called Research and Programs

Appendix

Division)
    Mr. E. Ross, 5/46–5/47
    Mr. Kenneth D. Morrow, 7/49–7/51
Programs and Statistics Division Deputy Chief (none 7/49)
    Mr. F. A. March, 5/46–5/47
    Mr. M. J. Rose, 1/50–4/50
Programs and Statistics Division Deputy Chief for Plans and Programs (from 7/49)
    Mr. M. Spair, 7/49–1/50
    Mr. M. W. Blanton, 4/50–4/51
Programs and Statistics Division Administrative Assistant
    Mr. J. J. Yoshiwara, 5/46
    Miss Ferne Gooch, 9/46–4/51
Scientific and Technical Division Chief (from 5/46)
    Brig. J. W. O'Brien, 5/46–5/47; 1/50–1/51
    Dr. Harry C. Kelly, 7/49
    Dr. B. C. Dees, 4/51
Scientific and Technical Division Deputy Chief (from 5/46)
    Lt. Col. H. Von Kolnitz, 5/46
    Dr. Harry C. Kelly, 12/46–1/50 (also 11/46 Chief, Fundamental Research Branch, Scientific and Technical Division)
    Dr. B. C. Dees, 4/50–1/51
Tourists and Service Division Chief (from 7/49; in 7/49 called Trade Service Division)
    Col. C. A. Mahoney, 7/49
    Mr. W. E. Bradford, 1/50–1/51 (also 7/49 Deputy Chief)
    Mr. David A. Stevens, 4/51 (also 1/50–1/51 Deputy Chief)
Utilities and Fuels Division Chief (1/50–1/51)
    Mr. G. R. Roames, 1/50–1/51
Legal Division Chief (5/46–5/47)
    Lt. Col. E. R. Minnich, 5/46
    Col. C. P. Muldoon, 9/46–5/47
Legal Division Deputy Chief
    Mr. H. T. Straitiff, 5/46–5/47

FINANCE OFFICE

Finance Officer
    Lt. L. P. Smith, 5/46
    Lt. Col. David A. Stevens, 9/46–5/47
    Lt. Col. J. M. Barrette, 7/49–7/51
    Col. E. E. Enger, 10/51–4/52

GENERAL ACCOUNTING SECTION (5/46–5/47)

Chief
    Lt. Col. W. F. Coudray, 5/46
    Col. H. Y. Brown, 9/46–5/47
Deputy Chief (in 5/46 called Executive Officer)
    Lt. Col. Emmanuel Franklin, 5/46–5/47

GOVERNMENT SECTION

Chief
    Maj. Gen. William E. Crist, 10/45–12/45
    Brig. Gen. Courtney Whitney, 12/45–4/51
    Mr. Frank Rizzo, 7/51–4/52
Deputy Chief
    Col. B. E. Clarke, 2/46
    Col. Charles D. Kades, 9/46–12/47
    Mr. Frank Rizzo, 7/49–4/51
    Lt. Col. Jack P. Napier, 7/51
    Capt. William E. Curtis, Jr., 1/52
Chief Plans and Operations Officer (9/46–5/47)
    Lt. Col. Frank E. Hays, 9/46–5/47
Special Assistant (ended 7/50)
    Lt. Col. Milo Rowell, 10/45
    Mr. Thomas Arthur Bisson, 9/46–3/47
    Mr. Frank Rizzo, 9/46–12/47
    Mr. Alfred R. Hussey, Jr., 2/47–5/47
    Col. Herbert B. Wheeler, 7/49–7/50
Special Assistant in Charge of Civil Service (7/49–10/50)
    Mr. Blaine Hoover, 7/49–10/50
Special Assistant for Local Affairs (1/52 only)
    Mr. Raymond Y. Aka, 1/52
Executive Officer
    Lt. Col. H. E. Robison, 2/46–5/46
    Lt. Col. Carl Darnell, 9/46–12/47
    Maj. (from 4/51 Lt. Col.) Jack P. Napier, 7/49–4/51
Administrative Division Chief (9/46–5/47 called Administrative Officer)
    Capt. Jack P. Napier, 9/46
    Lt. Col. Frank R. Harrison, 11/46–12/47
    Capt. R. E. Melvin, 7/49
    Capt. William E. Curtis, Jr., 1/50–7/51

Governmental Powers Division Chief (2/46–12/47; 2/46–8/46 branch of Public Administration Division)
    Mr. Alfred R. Hussey, Jr., 2/46–12/46; 12/47
    Mr. Cyrus Henderson Peake, 2/47–5/47

Governmental Powers Division Members
    Miss Ruth A. Ellerman, 5/46–3/47
    Dr. John McGilvrey Maki, 5/46
    Capt. G. A. Nelson, Jr., 5/46
    Mr. Alfred C. Oppler, 5/46
    Dr. Cyrus Henderson Peake, 5/46–12/46
    Miss Eleanor Martha Hadley, 9/46–5/47
    Maj. Robert A. Bieber, 11/46
    Miss Margaret M. Haverty, 5/47

Legal Division Chief (9/46–5/47; 9/46–11/46 called Legal Office, Governmental Powers Division; 5/47 called Courts and Law Division)
    Mr. Alfred C. Oppler, 9/46–5/47

Legal Division Member
    Mr. Thomas L. Blakemore, 9/46–5/47

Local Government Division Chief (2/46–12/47; 2/46–8/46 branch of Public Administration Division)
    Maj. (from 5/47 Lt. Col.) Cecil G. Tilton, 2/46–12/47

Local Government Division Member (5/46 branch of Public Administration Division)
    Dr. Andrew Jonah Grajdanzev, 5/46–5/47
    Dr. John Wesley Masland, Jr., 5/46
    Mr. Ralph Waldo Emerson Reid, 9/46–5/47
    Maj. Robert A. Bieber, 2/47–12/47

Public Administration Division Chief
    Col. Charles D. Kades, 2/46–8/46
    Mr. Carlos P. Marcum, 9/46–5/47
    Maj. (from 4/51 Lt. Col.) Jack P. Napier, 7/49–4/51
    Mr. Sakaye Hayashi, 1/52

Public Administration Division Members
    Mr. Thomas Arthur Bisson, 5/46–8/46
    Dr. Kenneth W. Colegrove, 5/46
    Lt. Col. Frank E. Hays, 5/46
    Dr. Cyrus Henderson Peake, 8/46
    Mr. Frank Rizzo, 8/46
    Lt. Joseph Gordon, 9/46
    Miss Gertrude Norman, 9/46–12/46
    Lt. Hans Herman Baerwald, 12/46
    Maj. Robert A. Bieber, 12/46
    Maj. R. W. Snow, Jr., 12/46
    Maj. Jack P. Napier, 2/47–3/47 (also 11/46–12/46 member, Korean Division)
    Capt. R. Borman, 7/49
    Mr. Makoto Matsukata, 7/49–10/50
    Capt. J. D. McWherter, 7/49–7/51
    Capt. A. A. Joseph, 1/50–4/51

Public Administration Division, Public Opinion Branch Chief (2/46–8/46; in 5/46 called Opinions Branch)
    Mr. Frank Rizzo, 2/46–5/46
    Mr. Carlos P. Marcum, 8/46

Public Administration Division, Review and Reports Branch Chief
    Lt. Osborne I. Hauge, 5/46

Parliamentary and Political Division Chief (2/46–8/46 called Political Parties Branch, Public Administration Division; 9/46–5/47 called Political Affairs Division)
    Dr. (in 5/46 Lt. Col.) Pieter K. Roest, 2/46–5/47
    Dr. Justin Williams, 7/49–1/52

Parliamentary and Political Division Members
    Miss Beate Sirota, 5/46–11/46
    Dr. Harry Emerson Wildes, 5/46–11/46 (also Historian, Government Section, 12/46–5/47)
    Miss M. Kuwaye, 12/46–5/47
    Capt. Thomas Diamantes, 2/47–5/47
    Capt. Crescenzo Guida, 7/49–4/51
    Maj. Roy Harris, 7/49
    Miss Helen Loeb, 7/49–4/51
    Miss V. Sheridan, 7/49
    Capt. Ch. Norris, 1/50–4/51
    Miss Virginia Sunderland, 1/50–7/50
    Miss Ruth Grahamslaw, 1/51–4/51

Legislative Division Chief (5/46–12/47; in 5/46 called Legislative and Liaison Branch, Public Administration Division; 8/46 called Legislative Branch, Public Administration Division; 9/46–3/47 called Legislative Office)
    Comdr. Guy J. Swope, 5/46
    Dr. Justin Williams, 8/46–12/47

Legislative Division Members
    Lt. Milton J. Esman, 5/46–9/46
    Miss Gertrude Norman, 5/46
    Capt. Justin Williams, 5/46
    Capt. Richard G. Brown, 11/46–5/47

Appendix

Public Affairs Division Chief (9/46–3/47 called Chief Information Officer; 5/47 called Special Projects Division Chief)
    Mr. Osborne I. Hauge, 9/46–4/51
Public Affairs Division Members
    Mr. Moses Burg, 12/46–5/47
    Miss Edna Ferguson, 5/47–4/51
    Mr. Nicholas Cottrell, 7/49–4/51
    Mr. Marcel Grilli, 7/49–4/51
    Lt. C. E. Skoglund, 7/49–4/51
    Mrs. Helen Demetros, 10/50–4/51
    Mr. Makoto Matsukata, 10/50–4/51
National Government Division Chief (5/47 only)
    Mr. Guy J. Swope, 5/47
National Government Division Member
    Mr. J. McLean, 5/47
    Mr. S. Tucker, 5/47
Civil Service Division Chief (from 12/47)
    Mr. Blaine Hoover, 12/47–10/50
    Mr. Maynard N. Shirven, 1/51–4/51
Civil Service Division Deputy Chief
    Mr. W. Pierce MacCoy, 12/47–7/50
    Mr. Maynard N. Shirven, 10/50
    Mr. Thomas K. Tindale, 1/51–4/51
Civil Service Division Members
    Mr. Robert S. Hare, 12/47
    Mr. Harry W. Marsh, 12/47
    Mr. Thomas K. Tindale, 12/47–10/50
    Miss Helen Machin, 7/49–7/50
    Mr. G. W. Peterson, 7/49–7/50
    Mr. McDonald Salter, 7/49–1/51
    Mr. Maynard N. Shirven, 7/49–7/50
    Mr. Foster B. Roser, 1/50
    Mr. Joseph Lewis Speicher, 10/50–4/51
    Mr. J. Sato, 4/51
    Mr. John R. Shively, 4/51

INSPECTOR GENERAL SECTION

Inspector General
    Col. Edward J. Dwan, 5/46–2/47
    Brig. Gen. Richard G. Tindall, 3/47–7/49
    Brig. Gen. Edwin A. Zundel, 1/50–4–52
Deputy Inspector General (5/46–7/49 called Assistant Inspector General)
    Col. Homer P. Dittemore, 5/46–5/47
    Col. James H. Hagan, 7/49
    Col. Darwin D. Martin, 1/50–7/51

JUDGE ADVOCATE SECTION

Judge Advocate
    Col. Clifford M. Ollivetti, 5/46
    Lt. Col. Samuel F. Cohn, 9/46–12/46
    Col. Franklin P. Shaw, 2/47–5/47
    Col. George W. Hickman, Jr., 7/49–4/52
General Counsel (from 7/49)
    Mr. Stephen H. Simes, 7/49–1/52
    (also 9/46–12/46 Executive Assistant; and 2/47–5/47 Counsel, Legal Affairs Division)
Legal Affairs Division Chief (2/47–5/47)
    Lt. Col. T. B. Beck, 2/47–5/47

LEGAL SECTION

Chief
    Mr. (in 5/46 Col.) Alva C. Carpenter, 5/46–4/52
Deputy Chief (from 7/49)
    Mr. C. R. Liggit, 7/49–1/51
Special Assistant to the Chief of the Section (from 7/49)
    Mr. George T. Hagen, 7/49–1/52
Executives (5/46–5/47)
    Maj. W. Holsinger, 5/46
    Lt. Col. F. E. Meek, 5/46
    Lt. E. M. Sweeney, 5/46
    Maj. T. R. C. King, 9/46–5/47
    Capt. J. R. Pritchard, 9/46–5/47
Administration Division Chief (5/46)
    Lt. Col. T. R. C. King, 5/46
Criminal Registry Chief (5/46–5/47)
    Maj. (in 5/46 Lt. Col.) C. A. Reinhard, 5/46–3/47
Liaison Division Chief (5/46–5/47)
    Maj. (in 5/46 Lt. Col.) C. A. Reinhard, 5/46–5/47
Law Division Chief
    Capt. H. P. Andrae, 5/46
    Mr. Julius Bassin, 9/46–7/51
Law Division Deputy Chief (from 7/49)
    Mr. H. T. Straitiff, 7/49–4/51
    Mr. John W. Canney, 9/46–5/47
Law Division Executive
    Capt. Julius Bassin, 5/46
    Mr. John W. Canney, 9/46–5/47
Prosecution Division Chief (5/46–5/47)
    Mr. L. G. Blackstock, 5/46–5/47
Investigation Division Chief (5/46–5/47)
    Lt. Col. R. E. Rudisill, 5/46–5/47

Legislation and Justice Division Chief
(from 7/49)
    Mr. Alfred C. Oppler, 7/49–1/52
Legislation and Justice Division Assistants
    Mr. Thomas L. Blakemore, 7/49
    Mr. Arthur J. McCormick, 7/49–1/52
    Mr. Kurt Steiner, 1/50–4/51

MEDICAL SECTION (See also Public Health and Welfare Section)

Chief Surgeon
    Maj. Gen. James A. Bethea, 7/49
    Maj. Gen. Edgar E. Hume, 7/49–10/51
    Maj. Gen. William E. Shambora, 1/52–4/52

MILITARY GOVERNMENT, HQ EIGHTH ARMY (2/47–5/47)

Chief
    Col. Rex W. Beasley, 3/47–5/47
Executive
    Col. Rochester F. McEldowney, 3/47–5/47
Internal Affairs Officer in Charge
    Lt. Col. Amel T. Leonard, 3/47–5/47
Legal Chief
    Mr. J. W. Renchard, 3/47–5/47
Economics Officer in Charge
    Col. Harry L. Watts, 3/47–5/47

NATURAL RESOURCES SECTION (from 1/52 a division of Economic and Scientific Section)

Chief of Section
    Lt. Col. (in 5/46 Col.) Hubert G. Schenck, 5/46–10/51
Deputy Chief (from 10/50)
    Mr. Marion N. Hardesty, 10/50–7/51
    Lt. Col. Harold B. Donaldson, 1/52
Executive Officer
    Lt. Col. Heinz Weisemann, 5/46–5/47
    Mr. H. F. Clippinger, Jr., 7/49–7/50
    Maj. James C. Walker, 10/50
Administration Division Chief (5/46)
    Maj. L. C. Barnes, 5/46
Agriculture Division Chief (5/46–4/51; from 7/51 merged with Forestry into Agriculture and Forestry Division)
    Mr. Warren H. Leonard, 5/46; 7/49
    Mr. (in 5/46 Maj.) Mark B. Williamson, 9/46–12/46; 1/50–4/51
    Mr. R. H. Davis, 2/47–5/47
Agriculture Division Deputy Chief (5/46 called Assistant Chief)
    Mr. (in 5/46 Maj.) Mark B. Williamson, 5/46; 2/47–7/49
    Mr. T. E. Richie, 9/46–12/46; 1/50–4/51
Fisheries Division Chief
    Lt. Col. R. H. Fiedler, 5/46–9/46
    Maj. J. F. Janssen, Jr., 11/46–12/46
    Mr. Claude M. Adams, 2/47–3/47
    Mr. William C. Herrington, 5/47–1/51
    Mr. William C. Neville, 4/51–1/52
Fisheries Division Deputy Chief (5/46–12/46 called Assistant Chief; 2/47–5/47 called Administrative Officer)
    Maj. J. F. Janssen, Jr., 5/46–9/46
    Capt. J. L. Kask, 11/46–12/46
    Lt. D. K. Polifka, 2/47–5/47
    Mr. William C. Neville, 7/49–1/51
Forestry Division Chief (5/46–4/51; from 7/51 merged with Agriculture into Agriculture and Forestry Division)
    Mr. W. S. Swingler, 5/46
    Mr. P. Hickie, 9/46–5/47
    Lt. Col. Harold B. Donaldson, 7/49–4/51 (also 7/51 Chief, Agriculture and Forestry Division)
Forestry Division Deputy Chief (5/46 called Assistant Chief)
    Capt. S. Grober, 5/46
    Lt. Col. Harold B. Donaldson, 9/46–5/47
    Mr. Laurence J. Cummings, 7/49–4/51 (also 7/51 Chief, Forestry Branch, Agriculture and Forestry Division; also 1/52 Chief, Forestry Branch, Natural Resource Division, Economic and Scientific Branch)
Mining and Geology Division Chief
    Mr. T. A. Hendricks, 5/46
    Mr. Q. D. Singewald, 9/46–12/46
    Mr. Robert Y. Grant, 2/47–7/51
Mining and Geology Division Deputy Chief (5/46–12/46 called Assistant Chief; 2/47–5/47 called Administrative Officer)
    Maj. J. C. Hogle, 5/46
    Mr. G. I. Purdy, 9/46–12/46

Appendix

    Lt. J. B. Gregg, 2/47–5/47
    Mr. J. S. Dodge, Jr., 7/49
    Mr. Albert H. Solomon, 1/50–4/51
Plans and Policies Division Chief (7/49–7/50)
    Mr. M. W. Roche, 7/49–4/50
    Mr. Marion N. Hardesty, 7/50
Plans and Policies Division Deputy Chief (1/50–7/50)
    Lt. Col. W. Glover, 1/50–4/50
    Lt. Col. W. Jackson, 7/50

PUBLIC HEALTH AND WELFARE SECTION
(from 7/51 a division in Medical Section)

Chief
    Col. (from 7/49 Brig. Gen.) Crawford Fountain Sams, 5/46–4/51
    Col. Cecil S. Mollohan, 7/51–1/52
Deputy Chief
    Col. Joseph U. Weaver, 5/46–12/46
    Col. Cecil S. Mollohan, 7/49–4/51
Executive
    Capt. George F. Pollock, 5/46–11/46
    Mr. Gordon E. Deville, 2/47–4/51
Dental Affairs Division Chief
    Lt. Col. Dale B. Ridgely, 5/46
Health and Welfare Statistics Division Chief (5/46–3/47 called Vital Statistics)
    Comdr. F. E. Linder, 5/46
    Mr. Leonard V. Phelps, 9/46–3/47; 7/49–4/51 (also 7/51 Secretary, Medical Section)
    Col. Oness H. Dixon, Jr., 5/47
Medical Services Division Chief (5/46 called Hospital Administration)
    Lt. Col. Dale B. Ridgely, 5/46
    Col. Harry G. Johnson, 9/46–4/51
Narcotics Control Division Chief (9/46–5/47 as Narcotics Control Branch, Supply Division; also 7/51–1/52 as Narcotics Control Branch, Public Health and Welfare Division, Medical Section)
    Mr. Wayland L. Speer, 9/46–1/52
Nursing Affairs Division Chief
    Maj. G. E. Alt, 5/46
Preventive Medicine Division Chief
    Maj. P. E. M. Bourland, 5/46–9/46
    Lt. Col. Lucius G. Thomas, 11/46–4/50
    Dr. I. D. Hirschy, 7/50–4/51
Social Security Division Chief (from 12/46)
    Mr. George F. Pollock, 12/46–3/47

    (also 5/47–4/51 Assistant Chief)
    Mr. William Hamlin Wandel, 5/47
    Mr. L. R. Anton, 7/49–4/51
Supply Division Chief
    Lt. Col. B. N. Riordan, 5/46–5/47
    Dr. Charles V. Band, 7/49–4/51
Veterinary Affairs Division Chief
    Col. Oness H. Dixon, Jr., 5/46–5/47
    Lt. Col. Marion W. Scothorn, 7/49–4/50
    Dr. C. T. Beechwood, 7/50–4/51
Welfare Division Chief
    Maj. G. K. Wyman, 5/46
    Col. (from 3/47 Mr.) N. B. Neff, 9/46–4/50
    Mr. Irving H. Markuson, 7/50–4/51 (also 7/51–1/52 Chief, Welfare Branch, Public Health and Welfare Division, Medical Section)

PUBLIC INFORMATION SECTION
(5/46–5/47 called Public Relations Section)

Public Information Officer (5/46–5/47 called Public Relations Officer)
    Brig. Gen. Frayne Baker, 5/46–5/47
    Col. Marion P. Echols, 7/49–4/51 (also 9/46–5/47 Executive Officer)
    Col. George P. Welch, 7/51–4/52

STATISTICS AND REPORTS SECTION
(Known as Statistical and Reports Section before 1947; renamed Civil Historical Section after 7/49)

Chief
    Maj. Stephen Silvasy, 9/46 (5/46 Acting Chief)
    Col. Charles H. Unger, 11/46–7/49
    Col. William L. Mitchell, 1/50–7/50
    Col. Daniel H. Hundley, 10/50–1/51
    Col. Norman C. Caum, 4/51–1/52
Deputy Chief
    Maj. M. M. Daugherty, 9/46
    Mr. William E. Hutchinson, 1/50–4/50
Special Assistant
    Mr. William E. Hutchinson, 7/50–1/52
Administrative Division
    Maj. L. S. Adamski, 5/46
Executive
    Maj. L. H. Pray, 5/46
    Maj. Stephen Silvasy, 11/46–5/47

Historical Division (5/46–7/49)
  Capt. J. F. Putnam, 5/46
  Mr. E. H. Loucks, 9/46–3/47
  Mr. K. P. McDonald, 9/46–5/47
Statistical Division (5/46–5/47)
  Mr. D. B. Carpenter, 5/46–5/47
Editorial Division (5/46–5/47)
  Lt. Col. P. C. Bouck, 5/46
  Mr. William E. Hutchinson, 5/46–5/47

Economic Affairs Division Chief (from 1/50)
  Dr. Lawrence Henry Battistini, 1/50–1/52
Social and Political Affairs Division Chief (from 1/50)
  Dr. Harry Emerson Wildes, 1/50–7/51
Social Projects Division Chief (from 1/50)
  Mr. Marvin E. Habel, 1/50–1/52

ORGANIZATIONAL CHARTS OF SCAP HEADQUARTERS

The following series of eight charts outlining the administrative organization of the Military Government Section during the fall of 1945 and the General Headquarters of SCAP between 1945 and 1951 is designed to complement our classified listing of high-ranking occupation personnel. The first six charts originally appeared in modified form within Monograph 2, *Administration of the Occupation*, of SCAP's *History of the Non-military Activities of the Occupation of Japan* (Tokyo: SCAP, 1952) (no.284 in this bibliography). Subsequently they were published with the names of SCAP personnel added to them in the Japanese companion volume to our bibliography, *Nihon senryō bunken mokuroku* (Tokyo: Nihon Gakujutsu Shinkōkai, 1972). We, in turn, have edited and corrected them for inclusion within this publication. To the best of our knowledge, the last two charts in the series (covering the years 1950 and 1951) first appeared in *Nihon senryō bunken mokuroku*. They have been included in our publication in a slightly revised fashion.

The reader who carefully compares this series of charts with our classified listing of SCAP personnel will note that there are certain discrepancies and inconsistencies between the two. On the one hand, for example, he will find that the Office of Civilian Personnel, the Inspector General Section, and the Judge Advocate Section which are included in the listing of SCAP personnel do not appear on any of the organization charts. On the other hand, he will discover that the charts name certain prominent men who never appear within the listing itself and that the listing lacks information about the individuals in charge of such offices as the Reparations Section, the Restitution Advisory Committee, the Office of General Procurement Agent, and the International Prosecution Section. Furthermore, the reader may initially be confused by the fact that in several cases a particular officer is given a high rank in one item and a lower rank in the other.

All of these discrepancies are a consequence of the peculiar nature of the source materials that were at our disposal. First, the original versions of the charts were abbreviated. They were designed primarily to explain the nonmilitary aspects of SCAP and, unlike the personnel listing, did not attempt to provide information for the military side of the occupation as well. Second, as we have explained in the introduction to the appendix, many of the telephone directories which served as the basis for the classified listing were not available to us. Ac-

Appendix

cordingly we were unable to provide complete and accurate information for high-ranking personnel during certain periods of the occupation and, in particular, during the eight months immediately following the surrender of Japan and during most of the months between July 1947 and December 1949—periods covered by four of the eight charts in question. Finally, many of the occupation personnel had different ranks at varying times, and it was not possible to check them in any systematic fashion. We are regretfully aware of these discrepancies and inconsistencies, but hope that the reader will still find the data useful.

List of Occupation Personnel

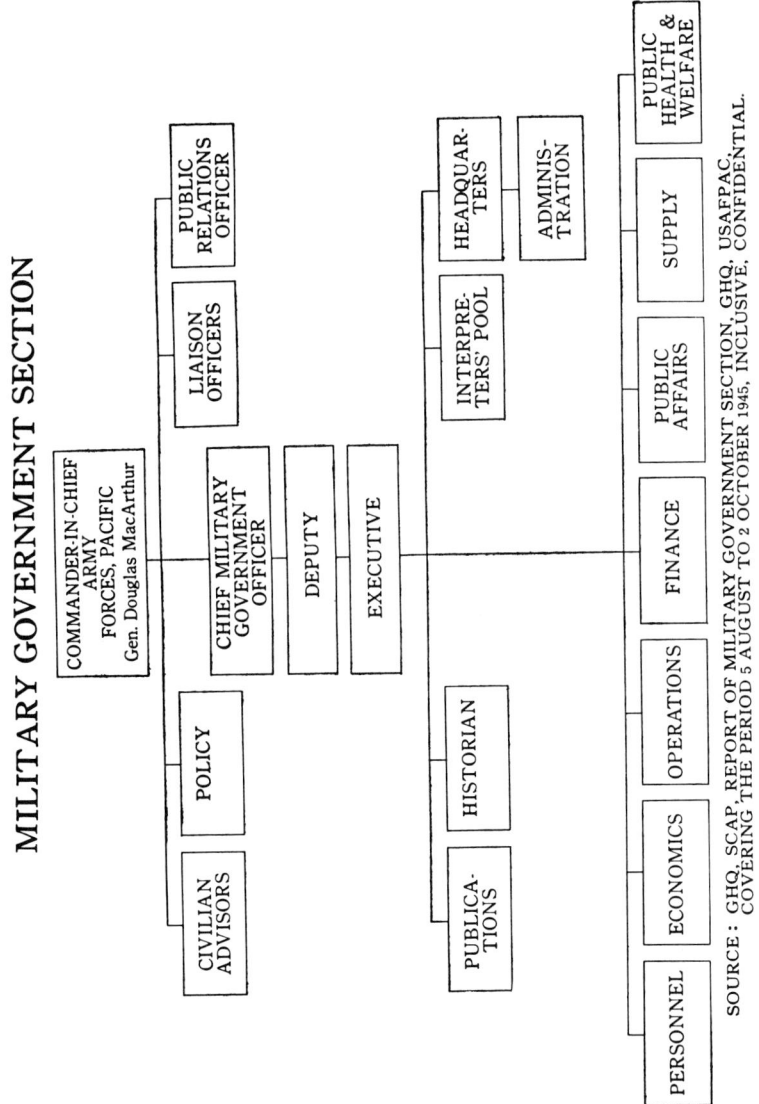

Appendix

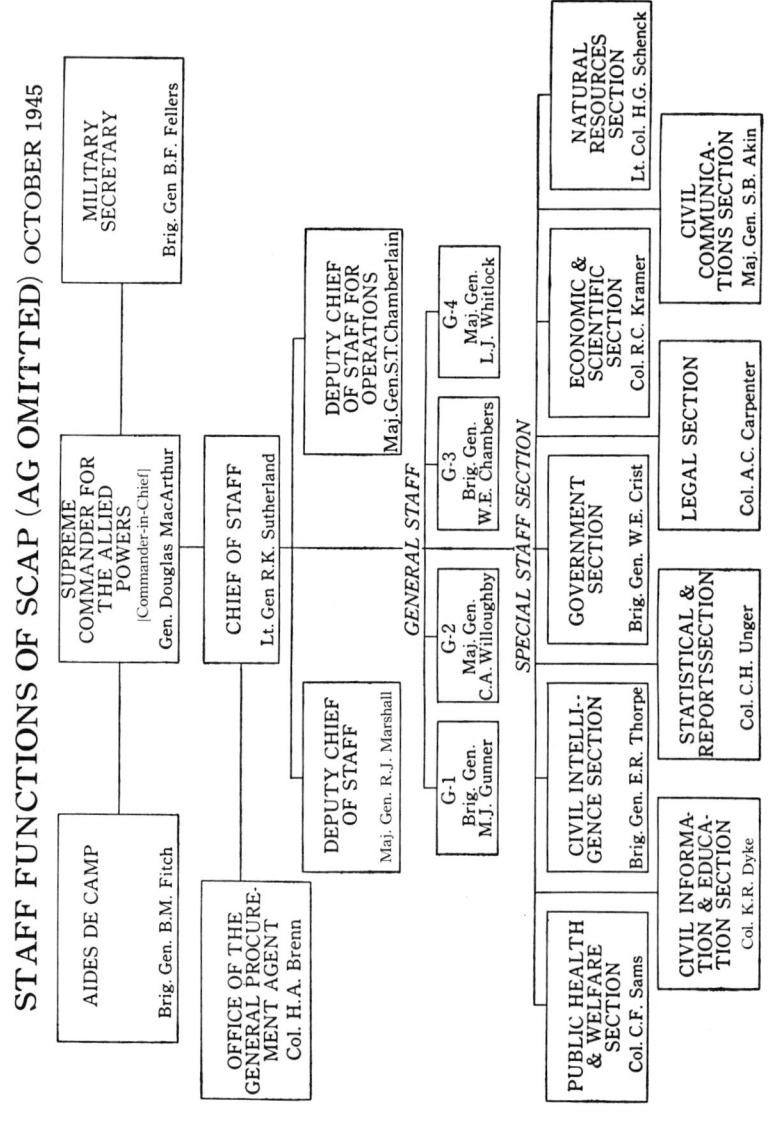

List of Occupation Personnel

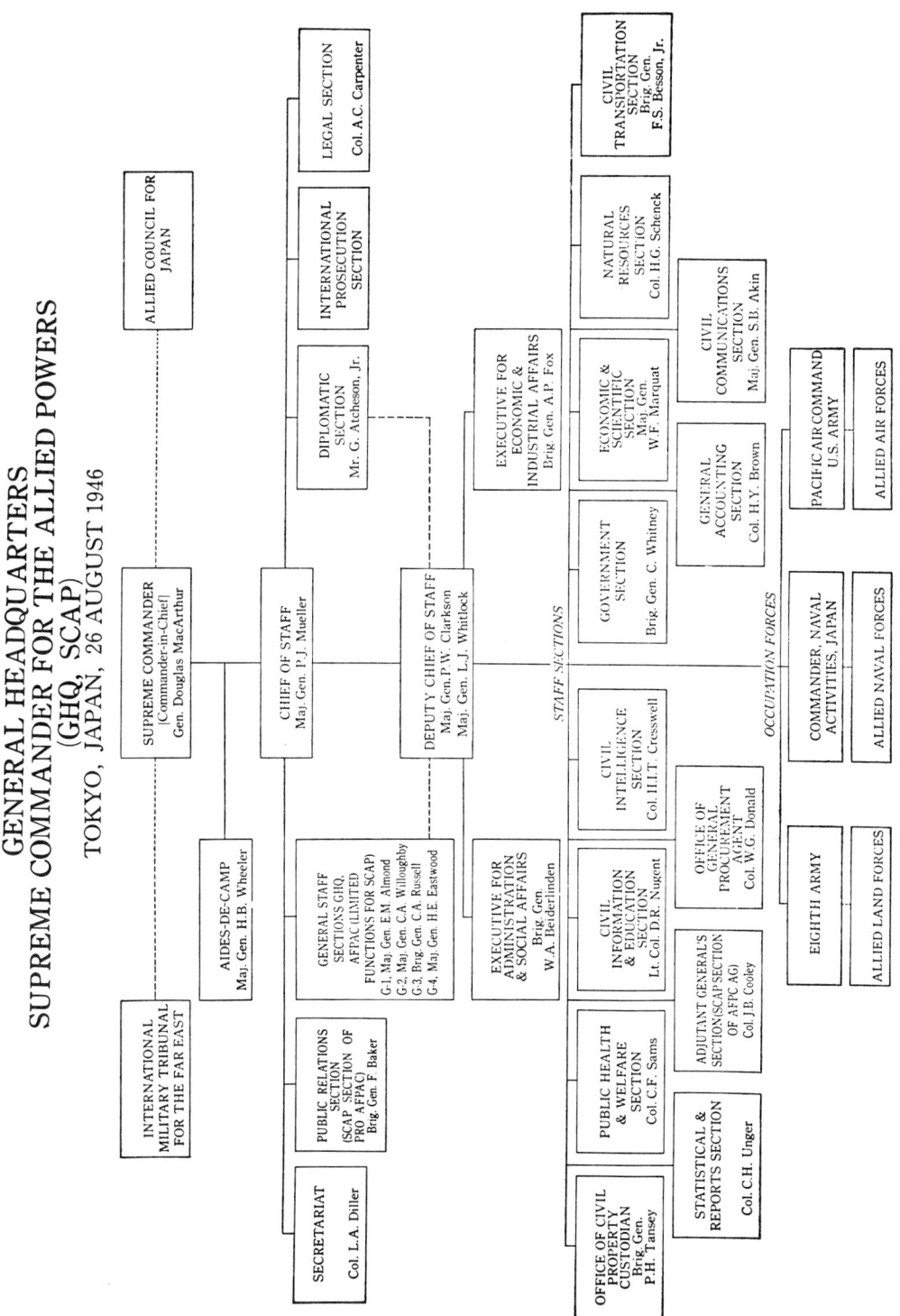

Appendix

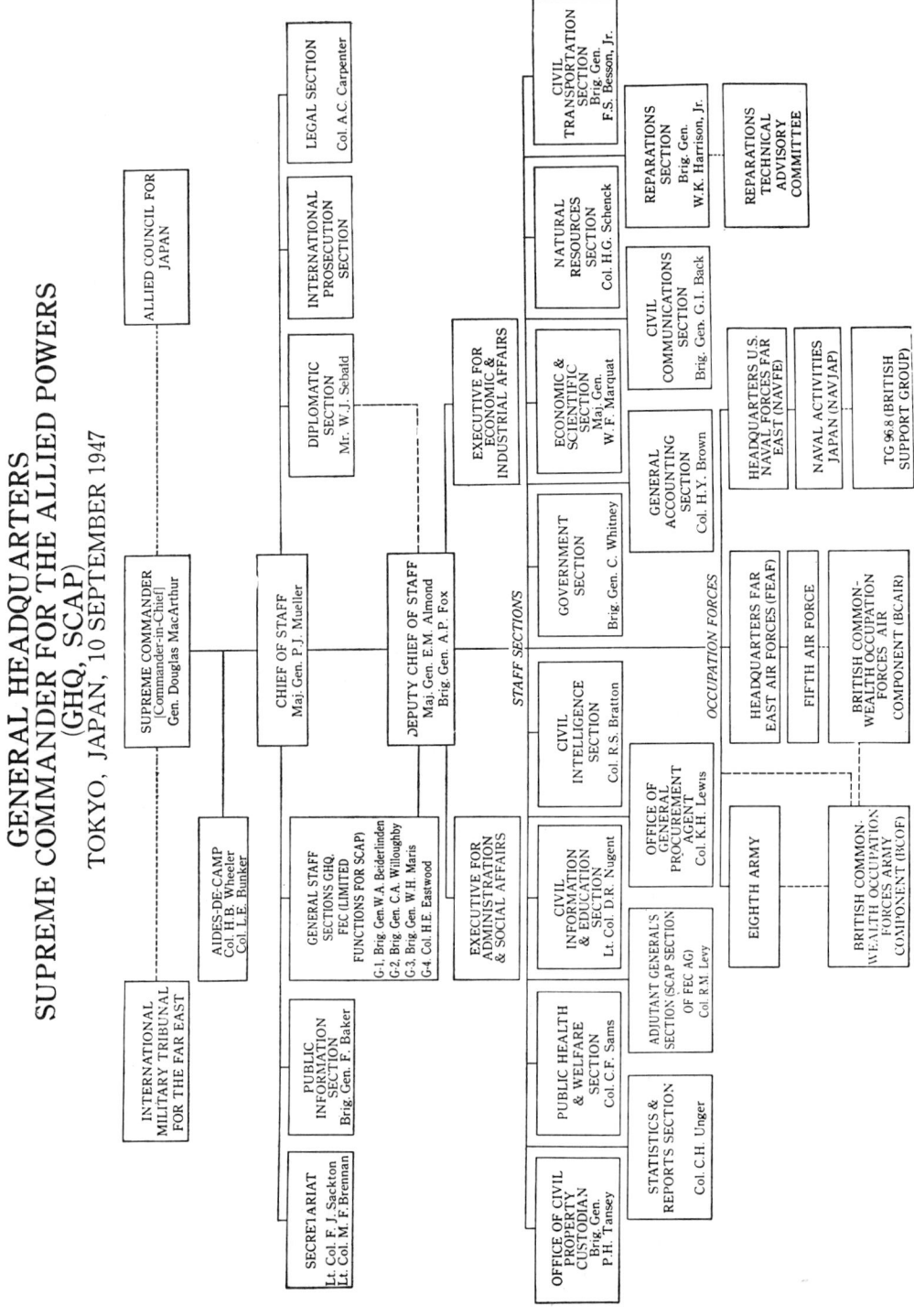

List of Occupation Personnel

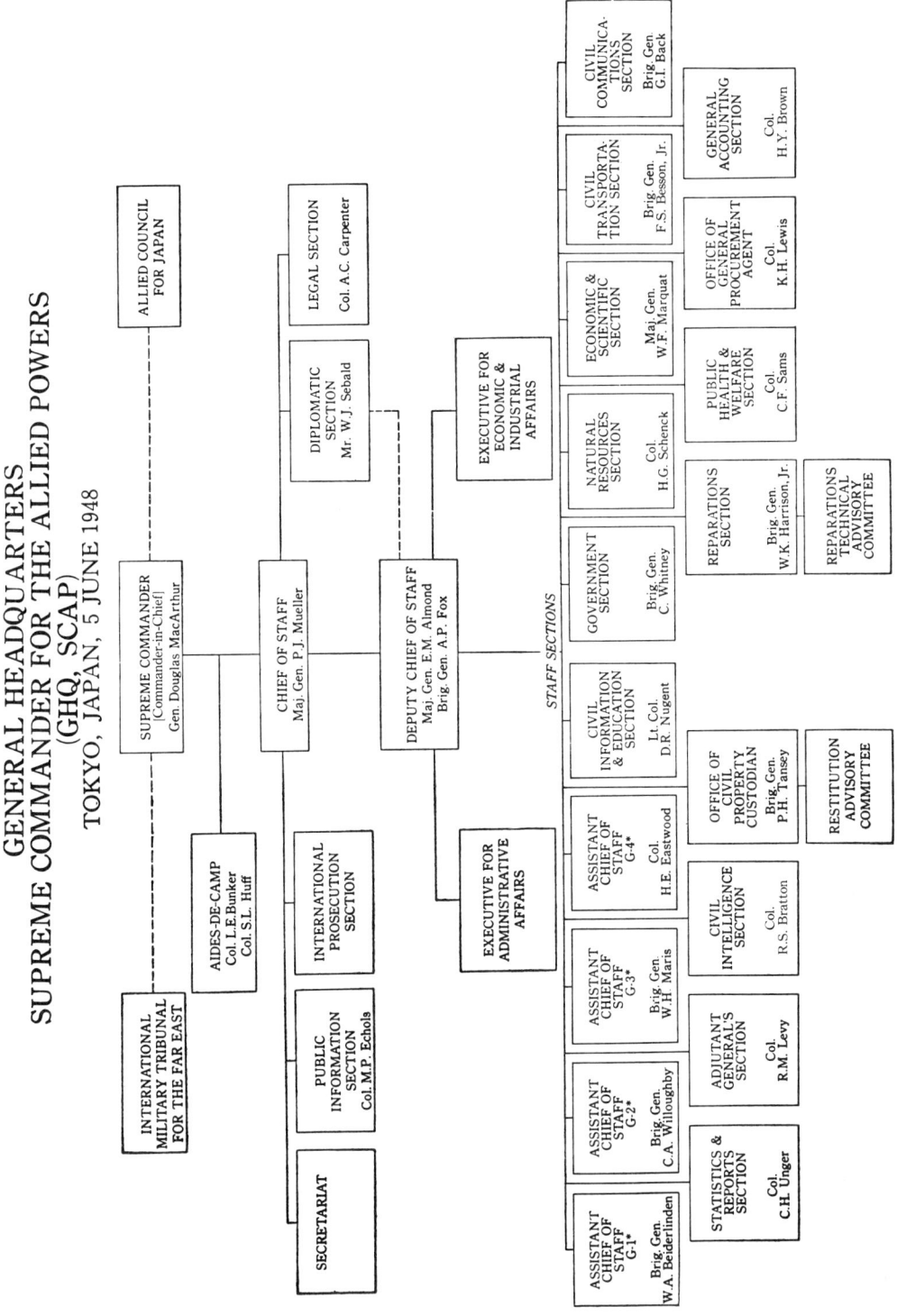

Appendix

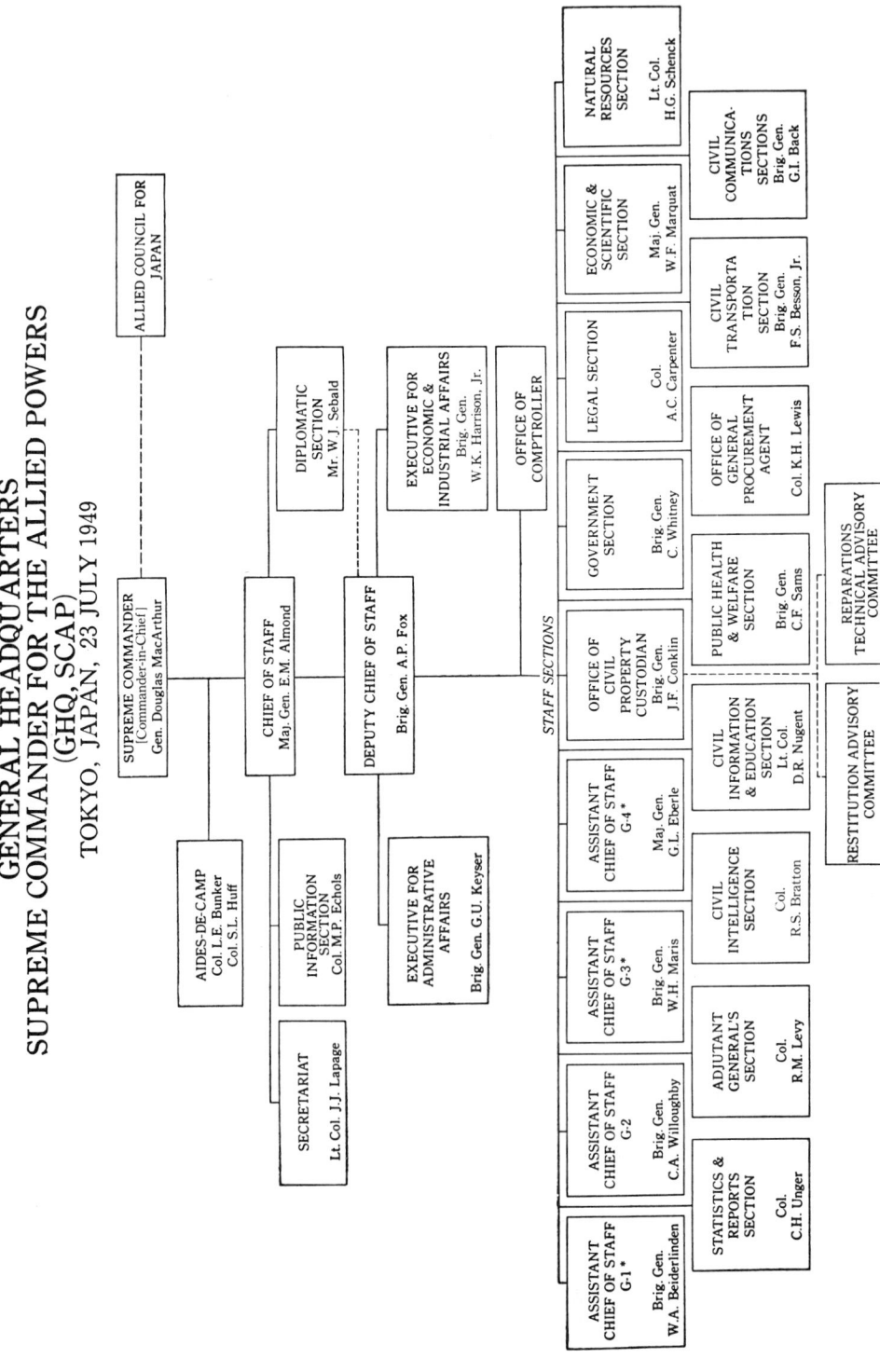

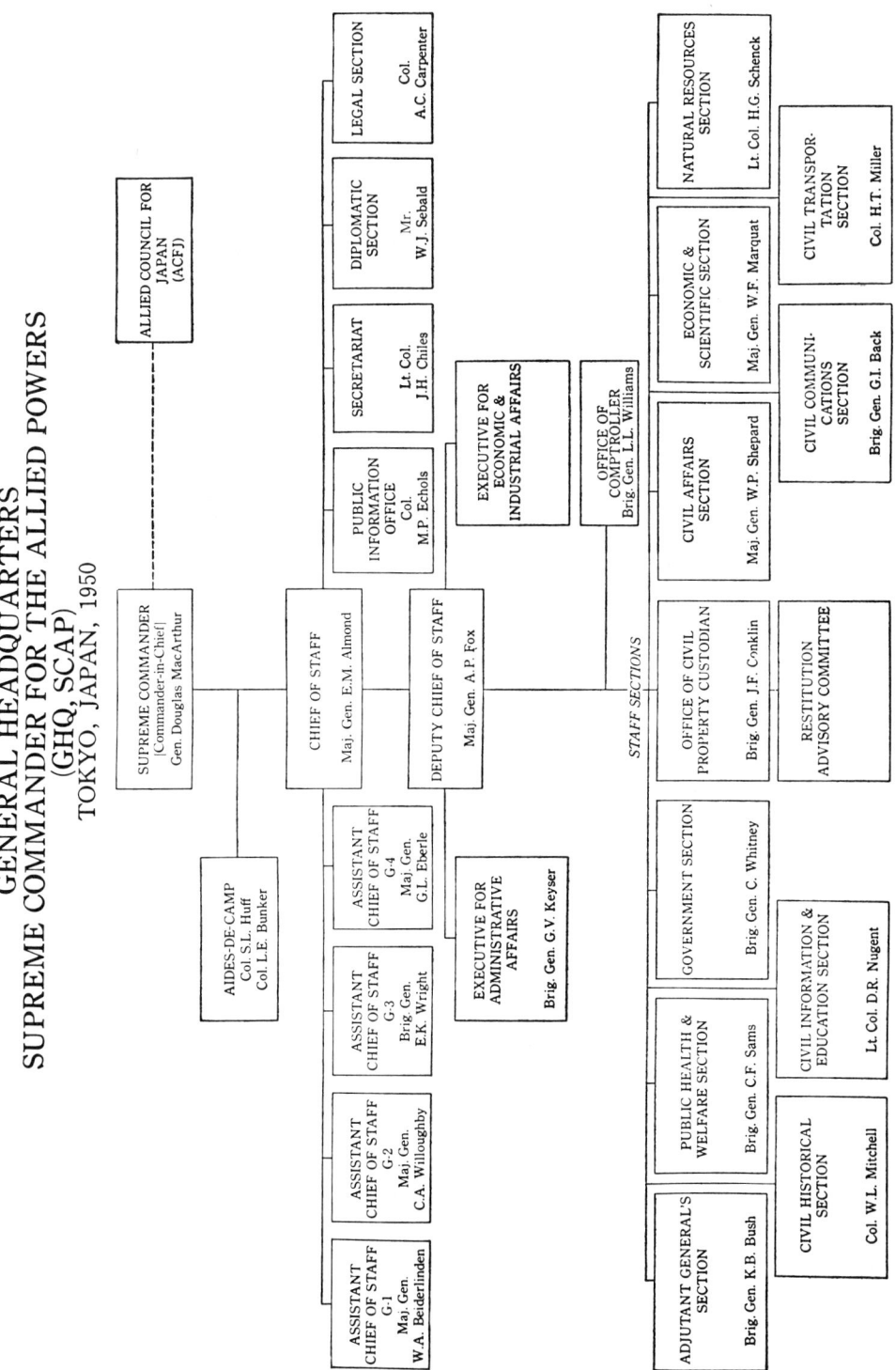

List of Occupation Personnel

Appendix

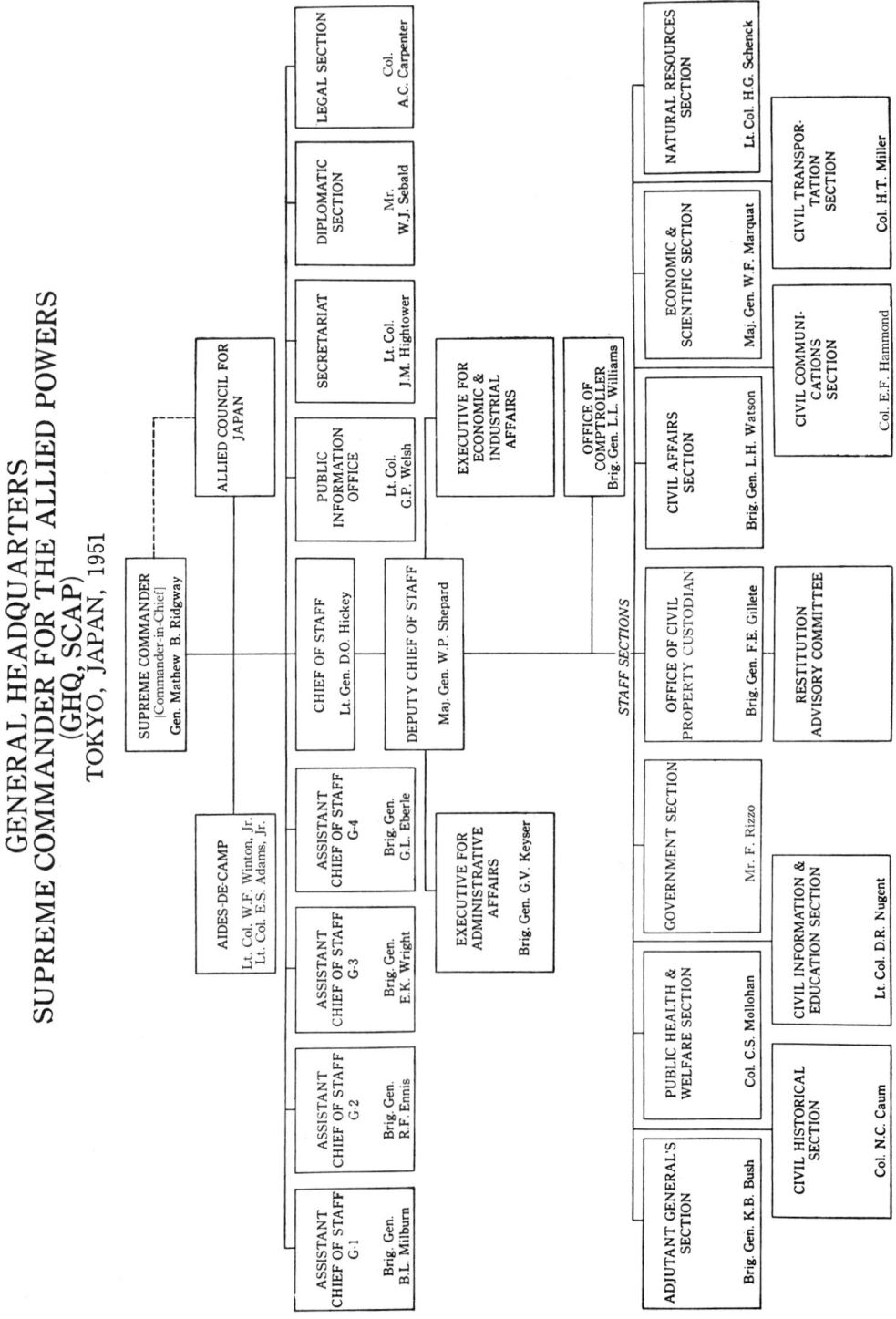

Personnel Name Index

All numbers refer to the page(s) of the appendix on which an individual's name appears. An asterisk preceding a page number indicates that the name in question appears two or more times on that particular page.

Adams, B. W., 845
Adams, Claude M., 851
Adams, Emory S., Jr., 837
Adamski, L. S., 852
Aka, Raymond Y., 848
Akin, P. C., 844
Akin, Spencer B., 840
Alber, H. F., 847
Albergotti, William M., 840
Alexander, Lawrence G., 842
Allen, Roderick R., 838
Allison, J. R., 843, 844
Almond, Edward M., *837, 838
Alt, G. E., 852
Amis, Robert T., 843, 846, 847
Anderberg, Edward, 843
Andrae, H. P., 850
Anton, L. R., 852
Arrowood, R. W., 840
Atcheson, George, Jr., 842
Atkins, Edwin L., 845

Back, George I., 840
Baerwald, Hans Herman, 849
Baker, Frayne, 843, 852
Bakken, Henry Harrison, 847
Band, Charles V., 852
Bankson, V. L., 847
Barnes, L. C., 846, 851
Baron, S. T., 843
Barrette, J. M., 848
Bass, William H., 845
Bassin, Julius, *850

Battistini, Lawrence Henry, 853
Beasley, Rex W., 851
Beck, T. B., 850
Beechwood, C. T., 852
Behrstock, Arthur, 841
Beiderlinden, William A., 837, 838
Bell, H., 840, 841
Bennett, John William, 841
Besson, Frank S., 842
Bethea, James A., 851
Bieber, Robert A., 845, *849
Bishop, Max W., 842
Bisson, Thomas Arthur, 848, 849
Blackstock, L. G., 850
Blakemore, Thomas L., 849, 851
Blanton, M. W., 848
Boehringer, Carl H., *843
Bond, Niles W., 842
Boner, J. R., 847
BoPlat, T. E., 844
Borish, Philip, 840
Borman, R., 849
Bouck, P. C., 852
Bourland, P. E. M., 852
Bowers, R. B., 840
Bowles, L., 840
Bradford, W. E., 848
Bradshaw, R. H., 842
Brady, William I., 843
Bratton, Rufus S., *838, 839
Brower, W. S., 844
Brown, Don, *841

Brown, H. Y., 848
Brown, Richard G., 849
Browne, S. H., 843
Bryan, Blackshear M., 838
Bull, K. R., 837
Bunce, William K., 841
Bundy, Hazel B., 841
Bunker, L. E., *837
Bunting, William L., 846
Burati, V., 847
Burg, Moses, 850
Burkart, Esther C., 838
Burns, E. J., 844
Bush, I. T., 843
Bush, Kenneth B., 839
Byall, P. W., 844

Campbell, Carl C., *845
Canada, Charles C., 837
Canney, John W., *850
Carley, Verna A., 841
Carpenter, Alva C., 850
Carpenter, D. B., 853
Carpenter, W. W., 841
Carter, W. S., 843
Catlin, R. M., 846
Caum, Norman C., 852
Chadwick, Maurice P., 840
Changnon, D. R., *842
Chard, Robert H., 842
Chiles, John H., 838
Clarke, B. E., 848
Clarkson, Percy W., 837
Class, Maurice M., 843, 846
Cleaves, R. D., 846
Cleveland, Paul, 845

Appendix

Clippinger, H. F., Jr., 851
Cohen, Theodore, 843, 846
Cohn, Samuel F., 850
Colbert, H. M., 847
Colegrove, Kenneth W., 849
Collett, S. D., 847
Colton, H., 845
Conde, D. W., 841
Conklin, John F., 842
Connor, Emmett M., 842
Constantino, A., 847
Cooley, John B., 839
Cooper, R. M., 843, 844
Cottrell, Nicholas, 850
Coudray, W. F., 848
Coursey, Richard R., *838
Crew, Glenna K., 840
Crews, A. R., 841
Crist, William E., 848
Crofts, A. E., 840
Cross, E., 840
Culbertson, Raymond E., 841
Cummings, Laurence J., 851
Curtis, William E., Jr., *848

Dabney, John A., 839
Dahlquist, Frederick C., 840
Danforth, E. C. B., 840
Darnell, Carl, 848
Daub, W. H., 846
Daugherty, M. M., 852
Davis, R. H., 851
Dees, B. C., *848
Degroat, G. E., 842
Del Re, Arundel, *840
Demetros, Helen, 850
Deverall, Richard L. G., *847
Deville, Gordon E., 852
Diamantes, Thomas, 849
Diamond, M. S., 847
Dickson, J. R., 843
Diller, Legrande A., 838
Dittemore, Homer P., 850
Dixon, Oness H., Jr., *852
Dodd, E. D., 840
Dodge, J. S., Jr., 852
Doi, A., 842
Dolgin, George, 847
Donaldson, Harold B., *851
Donovan, Eileen R., 840
Duane, R. C., 842
Dubinets, G. G., 838
Duff, R. G., 839
Dumas, Walter A., *839
Dwan, Edward J., 850
Dyke, Kermit R., 840

Eastwood, Harold E., *839
Eberle, George L., 839
Echols, Marion P., 852
Edwards, J. D., 843
Eells, Walter Crosby, 841
Egekvist, W. Soren, 847
Ellerman, Ruth A., 849
Enger, E. E., 848
Ennis, Riley F., 838
Ennis, Rosa E., 838
Esman, Milton J., 849
Ewert, Earl C., *839

Farr, E. H., 840
Fellers, Bonner F., 837
Ferguson, Edna, 850
Feyereisen, Paul A., 843
Fiedler, R. H., 851
Fine, Sherwood Monroe, *843
Fitch, Burdette M., 839
Fleming, G. R., 845, 846
Forsyth, Andrew E., 839
Fortier, Louis J., 838
Fox, Alonzo P., 837, *838
Franklin, Emmanuel, 848
Freile, Ormond, *846
Fuegy, M. A., 842
Fujii, Paul S., 846

Gaddis, John W., 841
Galiffa, Arnold A., 837
Gaumond, E. J., 845, 846
Gedulding, C. C., 845
Gerard, F. R., *845
Gercke, George J., 841
Gillespie, Kenneth W., 842
Gillette, Francis E., 842
Gillies, Roderick M., *843
Glover, W., 840, 852
Gooch, Ferne, 848
Goodman, R., 847
Gordon, Joseph, 849
Graham, Alexander, 838
Graham, Roy C. L., 839
Grahamslaw, Ruth, 849
Grajdanzev, Andrew Jonah, 849
Grant, Robert Y., 851
Greco, A. J., 845
Greene, J. Woodall, 841
Greer, Fielder P., 842
Gregg, J. B., 852
Gregory, Clark S., 843
Griffith, Harry Elmer, 840
Griffith, Stuart, 843
Grilli, Marcel, 850
Grober, S., 851
Grove, William R., 839
Guida, Crescenzo, 849
Gunner, Matthew J., 838

Habel, Marvin E., 853
Hackett, Robert, 838
Hadley, Eleanor Martha, 849
Hagan, James H., 850
Hagen, George T., 850
Haig, Alexander M., Jr., 837
Hale, Russel W., 843, *845, 847
Halff, M. H., 838
Hall, Robert King, 840
Hammond, Eldon F., 840
Hardesty, Marion N., 851, 852
Hare, Robert S., 850
Harkness, K. M., 841
Harlan, M., 841
Harman, J. B., 847
Harrelson, Wilford L., Jr., 837
Harris, Benjamin T., 838
Harris, C. G., 841
Harris, Roy, 849
Harrison, Frank R., 848
Harrison, J. W., 844
Harrison, William K., Jr., 838
Hartman, Allison R., 839
Hatzfeld, Theodore S., Jr., 840
Hauge, Osborne I., 849, 850
Haverty, Margaret M., 849
Hayashi, Sakaye, 849
Hayden, Gilbert, 840
Hays, Frank E., 848, 849
Hays, S. W., 846
Henderson, B. W., 844
Henderson, J. McI., 843
Hendricks, T. A., 851
Henry, Frank S., 839
Hensey, Walter R., Jr., 839
Hepler, Chester W., 846
Herrick, D. B., 841
Herrington, William C., 851
Hertzmark, S. S., 844
Hickey, Doyle O., 837, 838
Hickie, P., 851
Hickman, George W., Jr., 850
Hightower, John M., 838
Hirschy, I. D., 852
Hitchcock, J. E., 845
Hogan, W. P., 837
Hogle, J. C., 851
Hollingsworth, M. W., 846
Holsinger, W., 850
Homan, W. E., 839
Hoover, Blaine, 848, 850
Hubert, Enrique J., 838
Huff, S. L., 837
Huggins, Frank B., 841
Hume, Edgar E., 851
Humphries, Ferdinand M., 838

Personnel Index

Hundley, Daniel H., 852
Hussey, Alfred R., Jr., 848, 849
Huston, Cloyce K., 842
Hutchinson, Edmond Carlton, 844, 847
Hutchinson, William E., *852, 853

Iglehart, Charles Wheeler, 841
Imboden, Daniel C., 841

Jackson, W., 852
Janssen, J. F., Jr., *851
Jark, Carl H., 839
Jennings, D. H., *844
Johnson, Earle A., 843
Johnson, Harry G., 852
Johnson, U. Alexis, 842
Johnston, Bruce Foster, 847
Jones, L. A., 843
Joseph, A. A., 849

Kades, Charles D., 848, 849
Kask, J. L., 851
Kates, G. N., 841
Kelly, Harry C., 843, *848
Kendrick, Douglas, Jr., 837
Kennedy, Mary O., 843
Kennedy, T. O., 843
Kerr, William C., *841
Keyser, George V., *838
Kime, P. T., 844
King, T. R. C., *850
Kinne, Harry L., Jr., 839
Kirshenbaum, J. W., 847
Kitagawa, K., 837
Kitagawa, Kiyoshi, 838
Kito, Frank E., 847
Kolnitz, V., 846
Korb, S., 847
Koseki, Y., 842
Kowalski, Frank, Jr., 840
Kram, A. B., 845, 846
Krossner, W. J., *845
Kunz, Robert N., 840
Kupfever, V. H., *843
Kuwaye, M., 849

Lacey, Arthur T., 839
Lally, Lawrence D., Jr., 842
Lamoure, P. A., 837
Lansing, Samuel M., 838
Larr, David, 838
Lash, R. V., 845
Lattin, Jay D. B., 840
Laupheimer, M. B., 847
Leach, J. F., 841
Lecount, W. K., 844
Leonard, Amel T., 851

Leonard, Warren H., 851
Levy, Richard M., 839
Liebert, J. G., 844
Liggit, C. R., 850
Lind, Henry D., *842
Linder, F. E., 852
Link, Rue, 840
Loeb, Helen, 849
Loomis, Arthur K., 840
Loucks, E. H., 853
Lunn, G. R., Jr., 844
Lury, A. M., 845

McAllen, R. C., 840
MacArthur, Douglas, 837
McCormick, Arthur J., 851
MacCoy, W. Pierce, 850
McDermott, Peter A., 843, 845
McDiarmid, Orville J., 844
McDonald, K. P., 853
McDowell, R. S., 840
McEldowney, Rochester F., 851
McGlauflin, Arthur M., 838, 844
McGrail, Thomas H., 841
Machin, Helen, 850
McKee, Richard G., 838
McLean, J., 850
McLeod, V. R., 847
MacNabb, Alexander B., 842
McNair, Charles F., 839
McVoy, Edgar C., 847
McWherter, J. D., 849
Maeder, Richard H., 837
Mahoney, C. A., 848
Maki, John McGilvrey, 849
March, F. A., 848
Marcum, Carlos P., *849
Maris, Ward H., 839
Markuson, Irving H., 852
Marlow, Reginald H., 845
Marquat, William F., 843
Marsh, Harry W., 850
Marshall, Richard J., 837
Martin, Darwin D., 850
Masland, John Wesley, Jr., 849
Mathews, William B., 846
Matsukata, Makoto, 849, 850
May, R. A., 845
Mayers, W. R., 845
Maynard, D. R., 843
Meek, F. E., 850
Meiklejohn, Norman J., 846
Melvin, R. E., 848
Meyers, George E., 846
Milburn, Bryan L., 838
Miller, Edward C., Jr., 842
Miller, Harold T., 842

Miller, J. I., 847
Minnich, E. R., 848
Mitchell, John, 841
Mitchell, Ralph J., 845, 846
Mitchell, William L., 839, 852
Mollohan, Cecil S., *852
Monroe, J. E., 845
Moorman, Frank W., 838
Morgan, Walter E., 841
Morrow, Kenneth D., 843, 848
Moss, L. Q., 841
Moss, Lon H., 844
Motofuji, Francis T., 838, 841
Mueller, Paul J., 837
Mulbar, Harold F., 839
Muldoon, C. P., 848
Mulhauser, Roland A., 841
Myers, Collin S., 838

Napier, Jack P., *848, *849
Nash, T. L., 846
Neff, N. B., 852
Nelson, G. A., Jr., 849
Neville, William C., *851
Nichols, Walter, 841
Nivison, T. E., 840
Norman, Gertrude, *849
Norris, Ch., 849
Norviel, J. W., 840
Nugent, Donald R., *840

O'Brien, J. W., 848
O'Donovan, John, 841
Ollivetti, Clifford M., 850
Oppler, Alfred C., *849, 851
Orr, Mark Taylor, *840
Osborn, Campbell, 846
Oswald, Edward H., 842
Otis, A. B., 846
Otto, Samuel E., 838
Overton, Harry B., *846
Owens, Charles H., *838

Palmer, H., 846
Papen, Bernard R., *840
Passin, Herbert, 841
Patton, Maurice V., 839
Peake, Cyrus Henderson, *849
Pearce, E. S., 838
Peterson, G. W., 850
Phelps, Leonard V., 852
Phillips, Ralph E., *844
Pickelle, F. E., *845
Pierce, Vaughn A., 846
Polifka, D. K., 851
Pollock, George F., *852
Porter, Howard D., 840

Appendix

Potter, Laurence Everett, 847
Powell, E. F., 846
Prange, Gordon William, 839
Pray, L. H., 852
Prien, H. I., 840
Pritchard, J. R., 850
Pulliam, Howard E., 839
Purdy, G. I., 851
Purl, R. C. A., 846
Putnam, J. F., 853

Quirk, James T., 837

Rand, J., 843
Randall, Leland A., *844
Rasmussen, A. A., 846
Reday, Joseph Z., 846
Reed, Eugene M., *844
Reid, Ralph Waldo Emerson, 849
Reifsnider, J., 842
Reinhard, C. A., *850
Renchard, J. W., 851
Rich, V. L., *845
Richers, Paul E., 842
Richie, T. E., 851
Ridgely, Dale B., *852
Ridgway, Matthew B., 837
Ring, Ronald L., 838
Riordan, B. N., 852
Rizzo, Frank, *848, *849
Roames, G. R., 848
Roberts, H. L., 841
Robins, W. N., 846
Robinson, J., 843
Robison, H. E., 848
Roche, M. W., 852
Roest, Pieter K., 849
Rogers, William N., 844
Rose, M. J., 844, 848
Roser, Foster B., 850
Ross, Carl D., 846
Ross, E., 848
Ross, W. A., 847
Rowell, Milo, 848
Rudisill, R. E., 850
Russell, Carl A., 839
Ryder, William T., *843

Salk, E. A., 847
Salter, McDonald, 850
Salwin, Lester N., *844
Sams, Crawford Fountain, 852
Sato, J., 850
Schenck, Hubert G., 851
Schmitz, B. A., 840
Schneider, J. W., 838
Scothorn, Marion W., 852
Scott, Maylon E., 839

Searle, V. C., 840
Sebald, William J., *842, 843
Shambora, William E., 851
Sharp, Frank D., 838
Shavell, Henry, 844
Shaw, Franklin P., 850
Sheier, H. H., 844
Shellenberger, Lewis C., 840
Shepard, Whitfield P., *838, 839
Sheridan, V., 849
Shirven, Maynard N., *850
Shively, John R., 850
Sibert, Franklin R., 842
Sieker, G. F., 844
Siff, P. E., 843
Silvasy, Stephen, *852
Simes, Stephen H., 850
Singewald, Q. D., 851
Sirota, Beate, 849
Skoglund, C. E., 850
Smith, Howard F., 847
Smith, J. C., 844
Smith, L. P., 848
Smith, Lawrence G., 839
Snell, A. B., 845
Snow, R. W., Jr., 849
Snyder, M. A., 838
Solomon, Albert H., 852
Spair, M., 848
Speer, Wayland L., 852
Speicher, Joseph Lewis, 850
Stanchfield, P. L., 847
Stander, Golda G., 847
Stanek, E. T., 846
Stark, Thomas N., 839
Steiner, Kurt, 851
Stephen, C. L., 838
Stevens, David A., *848
Stitt, N. A., 847
Stob, J. H., 841
Story, A. F., *837
Straitiff, H. T., 848, 850
Strother, Kenneth C., 838
Stuart, Archibald W., *839
Sullivan, John F., 841
Summers, Thomas B., 840
Sundelof, H. G. W., 845
Sunderland, Virginia, 849
Sutherland, Richard K., 837
Svensson, Eric H. F., 839
Sweeney, E. M., 850
Swigert, Camille B., 840
Swindler, Henry O., 839
Swingler, W. S., 851
Swope, Guy J., 849, 850

Tagami, Kan, 837
Tait, David S., 838
Tansey, Patrick H., 842

Tasaka, Y., 842
Tate, H. S., 846
Terry, W. M., 839
Thomas, Lucius G., 852
Thompson, Samuel W., 847
Tilton, Cecil G., 849
Tindale, Thomas K., *850
Tindall, Richard G., 850
Tonole, T. M., 845
Torrens, James G., 843, *845
Trainor, Joseph C., *840
Tsuchiya, J., 838
Tucker, S., 850

Uejima, T., 842
Unger, Charles H., 852

Vaughn, W. S., 843, 846
Verity, Calvin, 843
Vierhus, Louis M., 842
Von Kolnitz, H., 848

Walker, G. T., 846
Walker, Isaac G., 839
Walker, James C., 851
Wall, Thomas F., 839
Wandel, William Hamlin, 852
Warden, Cranford C. B., 839
Warp, George Albro, 841
Watson, Leroy H., 839
Watters, William E., 838
Watts, Harry L., 840, 851
Weaver, Joseph U., 852
Weisemann, Heinz, 851
Welch, George P., 852
Welsch, E. C., 843
Wheeler, Herbert B., 837, 848
White, Horton V., 839
Whitlock, Lester J., 837, 838
Whitney, Courtney, 848
Whittemore, J. D., 840
Whittington, F. L., 847
Wildes, Harry Emerson, 849, 853
Williams, Justin, *849
Williams, Laurn L., 842
Williamson, Mark B., *851
Willoughby, Charles A., 838
Wilmeth, James D., 838
Wilson, R. L., 846
Winton, Walker F., Jr., 837
Wohl, H., 843
Wood, Walter S., 839
Woodard, William P., 842
Woods, Charles S., *842
Wright, Edwin K., 839
Wright, S. H., *845

Wright, T. K., 844
Wyman, G. K., 852

Yates, F. T., 840

Yoshiwara, J. J., 848

Zahn, M. T., 847
Zelaney, F. E., 847

Zimmerman, H. J., 845
Zundel, Edwin A., 850
Zybura, S. G., 844